Voter Registration Ap

Before completing this form, review the General, Applicati

MW01181303

Are you a citizen of the United States of America?	☐ Yes	☐ No
Will you be 18 years old on or before election day?	☐ Yes	☐ No

If you checked "No" in response to either of these questions, do not complete form.
(Please see state-specific instructions for rules regarding eligibility to register prior to age 18.)

1	(Circle one) Mr. Mrs. Miss Ms.	Last Name	First Name	Middle Name(s)	(Circle one) Jr Sr II III IV
2	Home Address	Apt. or Lot #	City/Town	State	Zip Code
3	Address Where You Get Your Mail If Different From Above		City/Town	State	Zip Code

4	Date of Birth / / Month Day Year	5	Telephone Number (optional)	6	ID Number - (See Item 6 in the instructions for your state)
7	Choice of Party (see item 7 in the instructions for your State)	8	Race or Ethnic Group (see item 8 in the instructions for your State)		

9 I have reviewed my state's instructions and I swear/affirm that:
- I am a United States citizen
- I meet the eligibility requirements of my state and subscribe to any oath required.
- The information I have provided is true to the best of my knowledge under penalty of perjury. If I have provided false information, I may be fined, imprisoned, or (if not a U.S. citizen) deported from or refused entry to the United States.

Please sign full name (or put mark)

Date: / / Month Day Year

If you are registering to vote for the first time: please refer to the application instructions for information on submitting copies of valid identification documents with this form.

Please fill out the sections below if they apply to you.

If this application is for a **change of name,** what was your name before you changed it?

A	Mr. Mrs. Miss Ms.	Last Name	First Name	Middle Name(s)	(Circle one) Jr Sr II III IV

If you were **registered before but this is the first time you are registering from the address in Box 2,** what was your address where you were registered before?

B	Street (or route and box number)	Apt. or Lot #	City/Town/County	State	Zip Code

If you live in a rural area but do not have a street number, or if you have no address, please show on the map where you live.

C
- Write in the names of the crossroads (or streets) nearest to where you live.
- Draw an **X** to show where you live.
- Use a dot to show any schools, churches, stores, or other landmarks near where you live, and write the name of the landmark.

Example

Route #2

Grocery Store

Woodchuck Road

Public School

X

NORTH

If the applicant is unable to sign, who helped the applicant fill out this application? Give name, address and phone number (phone number optional).

D

Mail this application to the address provided for your State.

Revised 10/29/2003

PEARSON ALWAYS LEARNING

Karen O'Connor • Larry J. Sabato • Alixandra B. Yanus

American Government

GOVT 2305

Custom Edition for Collin College

Taken from:
American Government: Roots and Reform, 2012 Election Edition
by Karen O'Connor, Larry J. Sabato, Alixandra B. Yanus

The 2012 Election
by L. Tucker Gibson, Jr. and Clay Robison

Cover Art: Courtesy of Photodisc/Getty Images.

Taken from:

American Government: Roots and Reform, 2012 Election Edition
by Karen O'Connor, Larry J. Sabato, Alixandra B. Yanus
Copyright © 2014, 2011, 2009 by Pearson Education, Inc.
Published by Pearson
Upper Saddle River, New Jersey 07458

The 2012 Texas Election
by L. Tucker Gibson, Jr. and Clay Robison
Copyright © 2014, by Pearson Education, Inc.
Published by Pearson
Upper Saddle River, New Jersey 07458

This special edition published in cooperation with Pearson Learning Solutions.

Pearson Learning Solutions, 501 Boylston Street, Suite 900, Boston, MA 02116
A Pearson Education Company
www.pearsoned.com

Printed in the United States of America

2 3 4 5 6 7 8 9 10 V0CR 18 17 16 15 14 13

000200010271773739

MT

ISBN 10: 1-269-35628-3
ISBN 13: 978-1-269-35628-2

BRIEF CONTENTS

On MyPoliSciLab

Note: The icons listed here and throughout this book lead to learning resources on MyPoliSciLab.

CONTENTS

Note: The icons listed here and throughout this book lead to learning resources on MyPoliSciLab.

PART IV PUBLIC POLICY

16 Domestic Policy 480

17 Economic Policy 516

On MyPoliSciLab

The Declaration of Independence

The Constitution of the United States

Federalist No. 10

Federalist No. 15

Federalist No. 51

Federalist No. 78

Anti-Federalist No. 17

Marbury v. *Madison* (1803)

McCulloch v. *Maryland* (1819)

Brown v. *Board of Education* (1954)

The Gettysburg Address

Washington's Farewell Address

TO THE STUDENT

As you open this book you may be asking

yourself, "what possible impact could the Framers of the Constitution—long gone—have on my life in the twenty-first century?" Why is learning about history important to the study of politics today? And how are the ideas of the Framers relevant for understanding modern political issues such as healthcare, immigration, and abortion rights? We believe that without knowing the history—the roots—of our government, we won't understand how movements for political change—or reform—came to pass.

As students of the American political process, it can be challenging to identify what is really important and how government truly affects your lives. It is tempting to get caught up in key terms and definitions and miss the major themes that prevail—not only in the American political system, but also around the world.

People like you are still the cornerstone of the political process, something we may forget from time to time. But your vote counts, and executing your rights as a citizen of the United States by taking the time to vote is an important facet of American life that has changed over time to include nearly all citizens, regardless of gender or race.

We hope that you will challenge prevailing notions about politics, ideas that suggest that government is bloated, inefficient, wasteful, and only for old people. We hope that you will come to see that politics can be a good thing, and that government is only able to represent the interests of those who actively pursue their own voice. To this end, we challenge you to identify the issues that affect your everyday lives—education, health care, the economy, just to name a few—and take every opportunity to make your voices heard. Just as the Framers' decisions in crafting a constitution live on in American political institutions, every decision made by policymakers today will have a lasting impact on your lives tomorrow.

Meet Your Authors

Watch on MyPoliSciLab

KAREN O'CONNOR is the Jonathan N. Helfat Distinguished Professor of Political Science and the Founder and Director Emerita of the Women & Politics Institute at American University. Before coming to American University, Karen taught political science for seventeen years at Emory University in Atlanta, GA, where she was the first woman to receive the university's highest teaching award. She has been recognized by several associations as the most outstanding woman in political science and public administration as well as by the Southern Political Science Association for her contributions to the discipline. From 2010-2012, she has been selected by *The Irish Times* as one of the top 100 Irish American lawyers in the United States.

LARRY J. SABATO Dubbed "the most quoted college professor in the land" by the *Wall Street Journal*, Larry J. Sabato bridges the gap between the ivory tower and the real world of politics. A Rhodes Scholar, Larry has taught more than 15,000 students in his career at Oxford University, Cambridge University, and the University of Virginia. He has received every major teaching award at the University of Virginia, and in 2001, he was named the Thomas Jefferson Award winner. Larry is the University Professor of Politics and director of the University of Virginia's Center for Politics, founded in 1998 to improve civic education and the political process. Follow Larry's Crystal Ball at www.centerforpolitics.org/crystalball.

ALIXANDRA B. YANUS is Assistant Professor of Political Science at High Point University, where she teaches courses in Enduring Questions in Political Science, American Government, and Research Methods. She holds a B.A. in Political Science from American University and a M.A. and Ph.D. in Political Science from the University of North Carolina at Chapel Hill. Her scholarly research has appeared in peer-reviewed venues including *Justice System Journal* and *Politics and Gender* and in book chapters published by Oxford University Press, CQ Press, and Sage.

TO THE INSTRUCTOR

- This country was founded with the express purpose of welcoming immigrants with open arms, providing safe haven from persecution in native lands. Could the Framers have foreseen tough immigration laws like those considered by the Court in *Arizona* v. *United States* (2012)?
- The Framers saw Congress as a body with limited powers. But modern members of Congress balance the roles of lawmaker, budgeter, and policy maker while also acting as representatives of their district, state, party, and sometimes their race, ethnicity or gender. How does this affect their behavior?
- The Twenty-Sixth Amendment lowered the voting age to 18. Today, young people are becoming increasingly civically aware and engaged. Could the Framers ever have anticipated how demographic changes would affect public policy?

American Government: Roots and Reform provides students with a historical context for understanding modern-day events and legislation. By drawing on more than 250 years of the American political experience, the text aids instructors and students in making comparisons between past and present. In so doing, it helps students realize that some of the challenges we face in American politics today are not new—they are simply new to us. Further, it emphasizes that by learning from the experiences of our predecessors, we may be more able to address these problems efficiently and effectively.

As instructors of American government and politics, we are faced with an increasingly challenging dilemma—persuading students to invest in the American political system at a time when trust in government is at all-time lows, and disillusionment is the norm. But as we well know, this task is perhaps more important than ever. Our students live in a rapidly changing political landscape, where the identity of America, as well as the role of the United States in the world, are being dramatically challenged and altered. We explore issues that the Framers could never have envisioned and how the basic institutions of governments have changed in responding to these new demands.

Our philosophy remains the same as always—roots and reform. By providing students with information about the roots of government and by explaining why it is important, they come to understand how their participation influences policy reforms today. And we hope that students will come to see that politics can be, and most often is, a good thing.

New to This Edition

While the content and pedagogy of this text stays true to its roots by continuing to provide clear, concise prose that receives high marks from students on readability and ease of comprehension, we strive to present a currency unparalleled by any other book on the market. *American Government* has been reformed to include **fully updated examples, figures, and text** that draw on experiences in American government that are relevant to students' lives.

- Complete coverage of the **2012 congressional elections** and the makeup of the 112th Congress and the incoming 113th Congress are included, as well as a discussion of major recent shifts in congressional rules and roles in budgeting, lawmaking, and oversight.

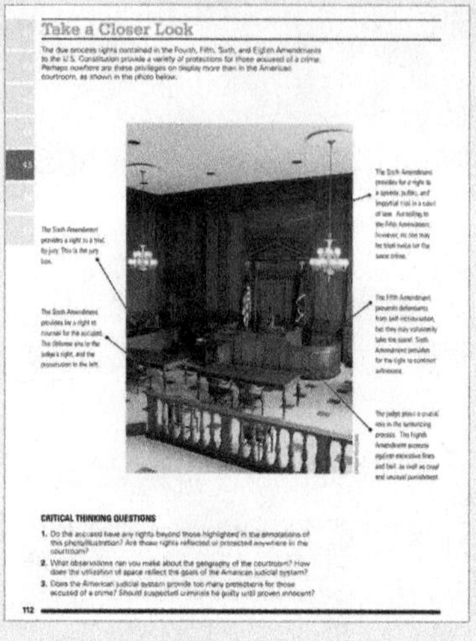

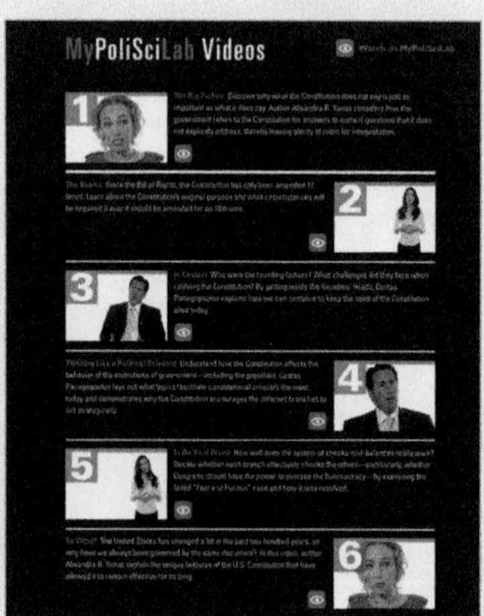

- Complete coverage of **the 2012 presidential election** contest, including the Republican primaries and the general election between Governor Mitt Romney and President Barack Obama. Coverage of election night results and analysis of the implications of the election for American politics are also included.
- Complete coverage of **the 2010-11 and 2011-12 terms of the U.S. Supreme Court** on important issues such as health care, immigration, and criminal procedure.
- **Policy chapters** have been dramatically revised with the latest information on healthcare, education, and energy and the environment in domestic policy today; new coverage of the 2012 fiscal cliff, how the government responded to the recession, and the debt ceiling crises of 2011 and 2012; and updated coverage of Obama's recent foreign policy engagement as well as the latest challenges the United States faces in the world today.
- **New opening vignettes for eleven chapters** deliver up-to-the moment coverage that address issues at the forefront of political debates. These openers were written to engage students in the conversations that take place in today's world.
- **Take a Closer Look** is a new visual feature that includes targeted critical thinking questions that encourage readers to progressively engage in deeper understanding and analysis. These features take students beyond answering solely the "what" of the visual and help them to better focus on the "why."
- **Explore Your World** is a new feature that includes a more comparative visual study of politics around the world, including up-to-date images and critical thinking questions that ask readers to examine some of the most commonly held assumptions about how American government does or should function in an increasingly globalized world.
- **Photos**—over 30% of which are new to this edition—capture major events from the last few years, of course, but to illustrate politics' relevancy, they show political actors and processes as well as people affected by politics, creating a visual narrative that enhances rather than repeats the text. Also, qualitative literacy—the ability to analyze, interpret, synthesize, and apply visual information—is essential to today's world, so all of the **figures and tables** included in this edition reflect the latest available data, facilitating quantitative analysis.

Finally, to create a tighter pedagogical connection between this book and **MyPoliSciLab**, we integrated several new features that move students from the book to online active learning opportunities. The icons listed throughout the book lead to learning resources on MyPoliSciLab.

- A new design simplifies the presentation of content to facilitate print and digital reading experiences. It also focuses reading by turning our book's **learning objectives** into a clear learning path backed by personalized study plans on MyPoliSciLab.
- **Videos** now support the narrative in each chapter. We—the authors—frame each chapter topic, and interviews with political scientists and everyday citizens look at interesting aspects of each topic. The videos are listed at each chapter's start and can be watched on MyPoliSciLab.

- **Infographics** demonstrate how political scientists use data to answer questions like "How Long Did it Take to Ratify the Constitution?" or "What Influences a President's Public Approval?" On MyPoliSciLab, students can use interactive data to further investigate the same question.
- In every chapter, **On MyPoliSciLab** helps students review what they just read. In addition to a chapter summary, key term list, short quiz, and further reading list, there are reminders to use the chapter audio, practice tests, and flashcards on MyPoliSciLab.

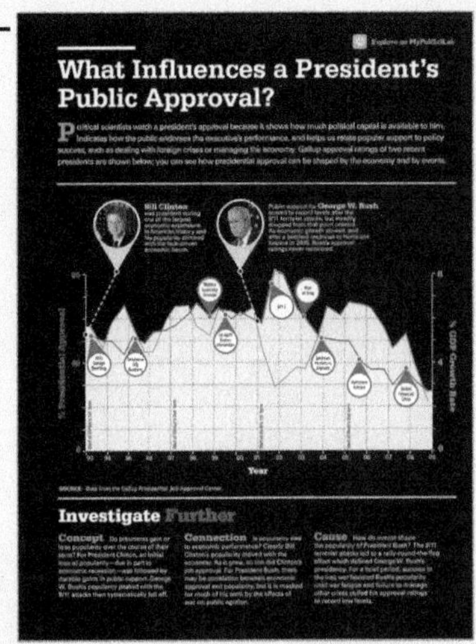

Features

Every chapter in this text uses history to serve three purposes: first, to show how institutions and processes have evolved to their present states; second, to provide some of the color that makes information memorable; and, third, to provide students with a more thorough appreciation of the fact that our government was born amid burning issues of representation and power, issues that continue to smolder today. A richer historical texture helps to explain the present.

With roots and reform providing the foundation from which all topics and concepts in this book are discussed, the text is divided into four parts. Part I, Foundations of Government, covers the American Government's Roots, Context, and Culture. Through a discussion of the Constitution, it considers those broad concepts associated with government in the United States: The Federal System, Civil Liberties, and Civil Rights. Part I sets the stage for the coverage in Part II, which introduces students to the institutions of government through its discussion of Congress, The Presidency, The Executive Branch and the Federal Bureaucracy, and The Judiciary. Political Behavior, Part III, delves into the ideas and processes that make democracy what it is: Public Opinion and Political Socialization, Political Parties, Elections and Voting, The Campaign Process, The News Media, and Interest Groups. Part IV rounds out the coverage with detailed discussions of Domestic Policy, Economic Policy, and Foreign and Defense Policy. Coverage in these chapters makes use of the most current data and debates to frame discussions of health care, energy and the environment, education, and the United States' role on the global political stage.

Each chapter also includes the following pedagogical features:

- **Roots of and Toward Reform** sections highlight the text's emphasis on the importance of the history of American government, as well as the dynamic cycle of reassessment and reform that allows the United States to continue to evolve. Every chapter begins with a "Roots of" section that gives a historical overview of the topic at hand, and ends with a "Toward Reform" section devoted to a particularly contentious aspect of the topic being discussed.
- **The Living Constitution** reflects the authors' emphasis on the origins of America's democratic system and expertise in constitutional law. To further support the text's emphasis on the constitutional underpinnings of government and politics, this boxed feature appears in every chapter. Each feature examines the chapter's topic in light of what the Constitution says or does not say about it.
- A running **marginal glossary** facilitates students' understanding of key terms related to the chapter content. A list of key terms also appears at the end of the chapter for easy reference; these key terms are also defined in a glossary at the end of the book.

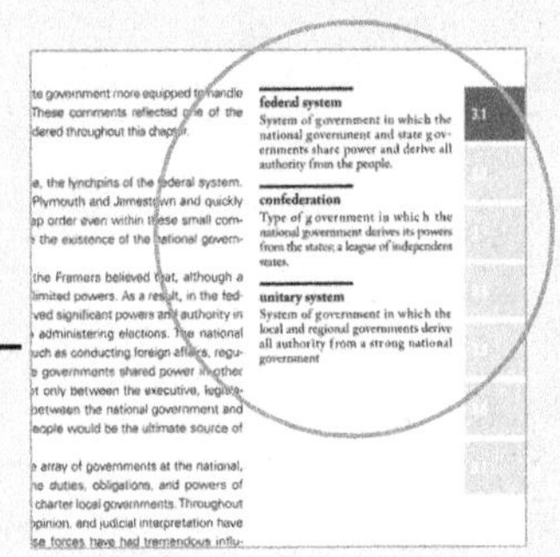

TABLE 7.1 WHO WERE THE U.S. PRESIDENTS?

- A focus on **qualitative literacy** helps students analyze, interpret, synthesize, and apply visual information—skills that are essential in today's world. We receive information from the written and spoken word, but knowledge also comes in visual forms. We are used to thinking about reading text critically, but we do not always think about "reading" visuals in this way. A focus on qualitative literacy encourages students to think about the images and informational graphics they will encounter throughout this text, as well as those they see every day in the newspaper, in magazines, on the Web, on television, and in books. Critical thinking questions assist students in learning how to analyze visuals.
  - **Tables** consist of textual information and/or numerical data arranged in tabular form in columns and rows. Tables are frequently used when exact information is required and when orderly arrangement is necessary to locate and, in many cases, to compare the information. All tables in this edition include questions and encourage critical thinking.
  - **Charts and Graphs** depict numerical data in visual forms. Examples that students will encounter throughout this text are line graphs, pie charts, and bar graphs. Line graphs show a progression, usually over time (as in how the U.S. population has grown over time). Pie charts (such as ones showing population demographics) demonstrate how a whole (total American population) is divided into its parts (different racial and ethnic groups). Bar graphs compare values across categories, showing how proportions are related to each other (as in how much money each party raised in presidential election years). Bar graphs can present data either horizontally or vertically. All charts and graphs in this edition are based on questions that encourage critical thinking.
  - Some of the most interesting commentary on American politics takes place in the form of **political cartoons**. The cartoonist's goal is to comment on and/or criticize political figures, policies, or events. The cartoonist uses several techniques to accomplish this goal, including exaggeration, irony, and juxtaposition. For example, the cartoonist may point out how the results of governmental policies are the opposite of their intended effects (irony). In other cartoons, two people, ideas, or events that don't belong together may be joined to make a point (juxtaposition). Knowledge of current events is helpful in interpreting political cartoons.

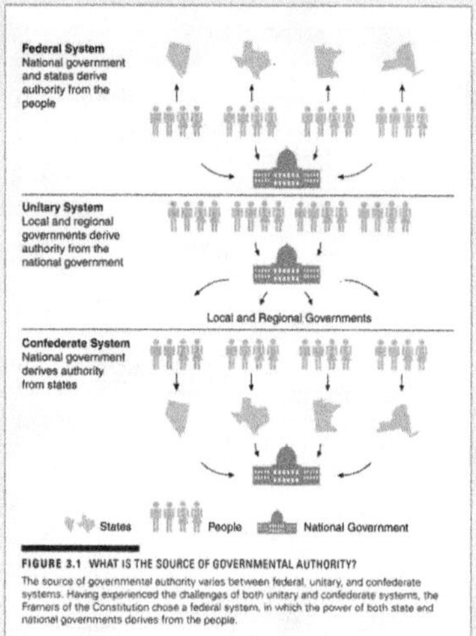
Federal System
National government and states derive authority from the people
Unitary System
Local and regional governments derive authority from the national government
Local and Regional Governments
Confederate System
National government derives authority from states
States
People
National Government

FIGURE 3.1 WHAT IS THE SOURCE OF GOVERNMENTAL AUTHORITY?

The source of governmental authority varies between federal, unitary, and confederate systems. Having experienced the challenges of both unitary and confederate systems, the Framers of the Constitution chose a federal system, in which the power of both state and national governments derives from the people.

GENDER GAP IN WAGES
'Three-fourths of a penny for your thoughts..'

WHAT ARE THE PRACTICAL CONSEQUENCES OF PAY EQUITY?

This cartoon pokes fun at a serious issue in gender equality: pay equity. In 2012, women earned between 75 and 80 cents for every $1.00 earned by their male counterparts.

MyPoliSciLab

MYPOLISCILAB is an online homework, tutorial, and assessment product that improves results by helping students better master concepts and by providing educators a dynamic set of tools for gauging individual and class performance. Its immersive experiences truly engage students in learning, helping them to understand course material and improve their performance. And MyPoliSciLab comes from Pearson—your partner in providing the best digital learning experiences.

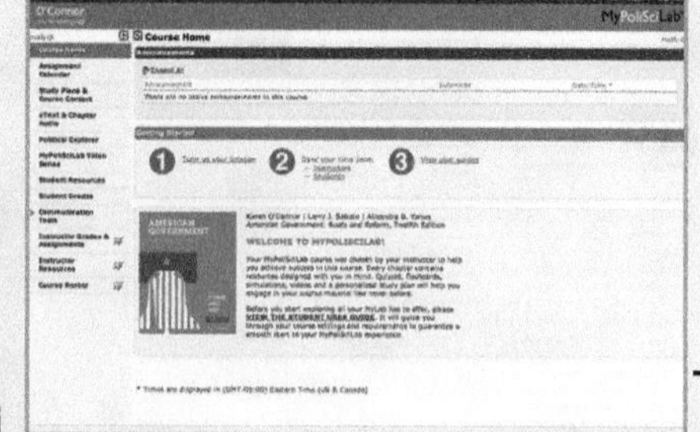
Course Home
MyPoliSciLab

PERSONALIZE LEARNING. Reach every student at each stage of learning, engage them in active rather than passive learning, and measure that learning. Refined after a decade of real-world use, **MyPoliSciLab** is compatible with major learning management systems like Blackboard and can be customized to support each individual student's and educator's success. You can fully control what your students' course looks like; homework, applications, and more can easily be turned on or off. You can also add your own original material.

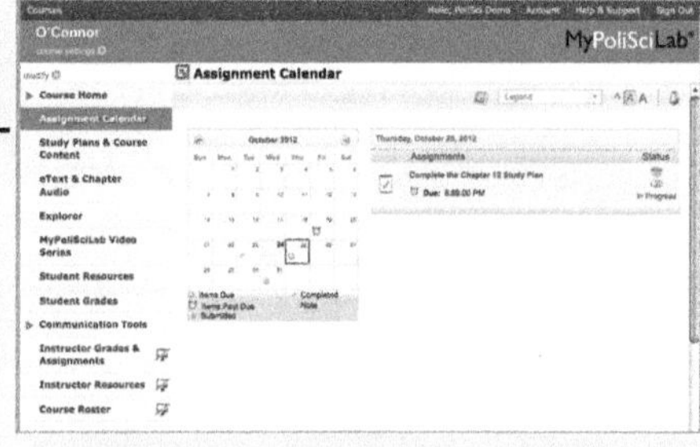

The intuitive assignment **calendar** lets instructors drag and drop assignments to the desired date and gives students a useful course organizer.

- Automatically graded assessment flows into the **gradebook**, which can be used in MyPoliSciLab or exported.

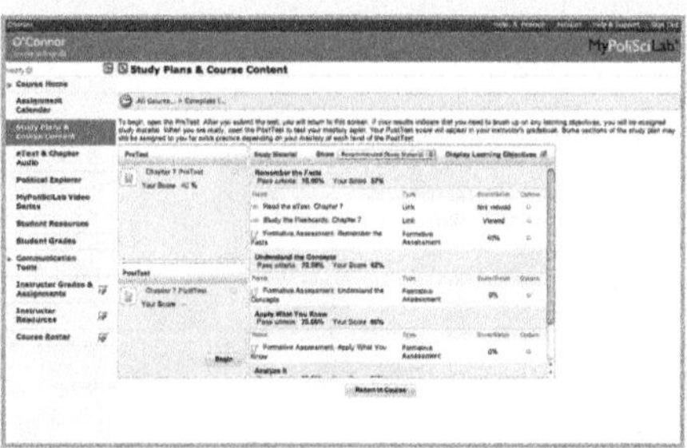

EMPHASIZE OUTCOMES. Keep students focused on what they need to master course concepts.

- **Practice tests** help students achieve this book's learning objectives by creating personalized study plans Based on a pre-test diagnostic, the study plan suggests reading and multimedia for practice and moves students from comprehension to critical thinking.
- Students can study key terms and concepts with their own personal set of **flashcards**.

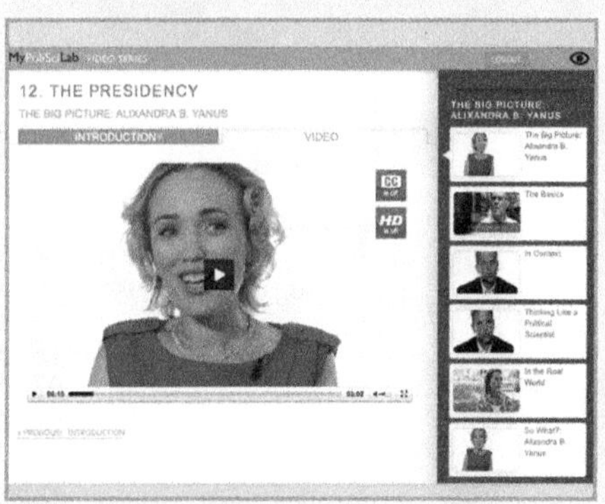

ENGAGE STUDENTS. Students—each one is different. Reach *all* of them with the new **MyPoliSciLab Video Series**, which features this book's authors and top scholars discussing the big ideas in each chapter and applying them to enduring political issues. Each chapter is supported by six videos that help students work through the material and retain its key lessons.

- ***The Big Picture.*** Understand how the topic fits into the American political system.
- ***The Basics.*** Review the topic's core learning objectives.
- ***In Context.*** Examine the historical background of the topic.
- ***Thinking Like a Political Scientist.*** Solve a political puzzle related to the topic.
- ***In the Real World.*** Consider different perspectives on a key issue in American politics.
- ***So What?*** Connect the topic to what is at stake for American democracy.

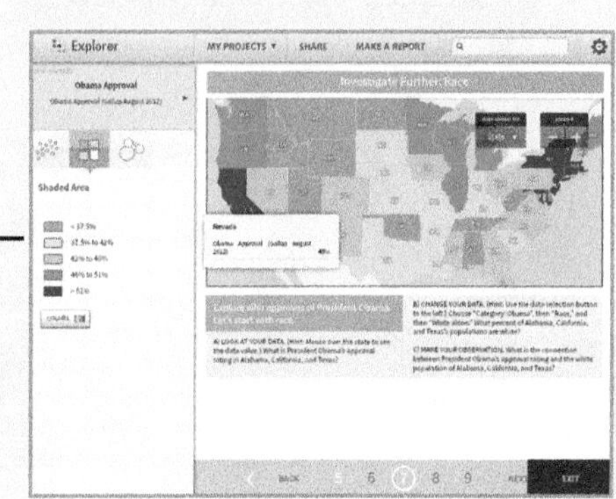

IMPROVE CRITICAL THINKING. Students get a lot of information about politics; your challenge as an instructor is to turn them into critical consumers of that information. **Explorer** is a hands-on way to develop quantitative literacy and to move students beyond punditry and opinion. In the book, infographics introduce key questions about politics. On MyPoliSciLab, guided exercises ask students to read the data related to the questions and then find connections among the data to answer the questions. Explorer includes data from the United States Census, General Social Survey, Statistical Abstract of the United States, Gallup, American National Election Studies, and Election Data Services with more data being regularly added.

ANALYZE CURRENT EVENTS. Prepare students for a lifetime of following political news. Coverage of the 2012 elections and more keeps politics relevant and models how to analyze developments in the American political system.

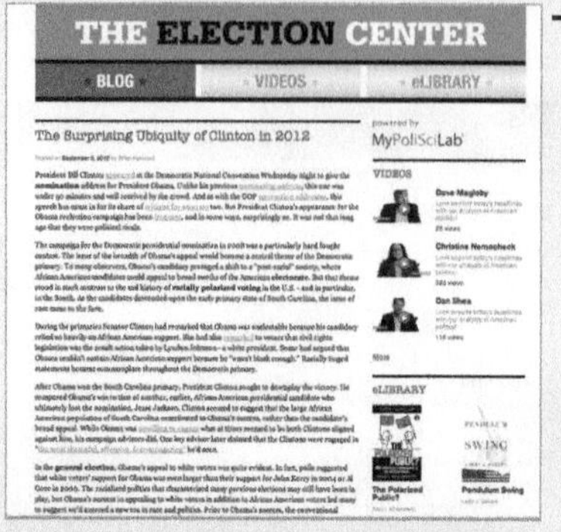

- Get up-to-the-minute analysis by top scholars on MyPoliSciLab's **blogs**, take the weekly quiz, and register to vote.
- Or reflect on a theoretical case with the **simulations** in MyPoliSciLab. Easy to assign and complete in a week, each simulation is a game-like opportunity to play the role of a political actor and apply course concepts to make realistic political decisions.

THE PEARSON ETEXT offers a full digital version of the print book and is readable on Apple iPad and Android tablets with the Pearson eText app. Like the printed text, students can highlight relevant passages and add notes. The Pearson eText also includes primary sources like the Declaration of Independence, Constitution of the United States, selected *Federalist Papers,* key Supreme Court decisions, Lincoln's Gettysburg Address, and Washington's Farewell Address.

CHAPTER AUDIO lets students listen to the full text of this book.

Visit **WWW.MYPOLISCILAB.COM** to test drive MyPoliSciLab, set up a class test of MyPoliSciLab, and read about the efficacy of Pearson's MyLabs. You can also learn more from your local Pearson representative; find them at **www.pearsonhighered.com/replocator.**

Supplements

Make more time for your students with instructor resources that offer effective learning assessments and classroom engagement. Pearson's partnership with educators does not end with the delivery of course materials; Pearson is there with you on the first day of class and beyond. A dedicated team of local Pearson representatives will work with you to not only choose course materials but also integrate them into your class and assess their effectiveness. Our goal is your goal—to improve instruction with each semester.

Pearson is pleased to offer the following resources to qualified adopters of *American Government: Roots and Reform.* Several of these supplements are available to instantly download on the Instructor Resource Center (IRC); please visit the IRC at **www.pearsonhighered.com/irc** to register for access.

TEST BANK. Evaluate learning at every level. Reviewed for clarity and accuracy, the Test Bank measures this book's learning objectives with multiple-choice, true/false, fill-in-the-blank, short answer, and essay questions. You can easily customize the assessment to work in any major learning management system and to match what is covered in your course. Word, BlackBoard, and WebCT versions available on the IRC and Respondus versions available upon request from **www.respondus.com.**

PEARSON MYTEST. This powerful assessment generation program includes all of the questions in the Test Bank. Quizzes and exams can be easily authored and saved online and then printed for classroom use, giving you ultimate flexibility to manage assessments anytime and anywhere. To learn more, visit **www.pearsonhighered.com/mytest.**

INSTRUCTOR'S MANUAL. Create a comprehensive roadmap for teaching classroom, online, or hybrid courses. Designed for new and experienced instructors, the Instructor's Manual includes a sample syllabus, lecture and discussion suggestions, activities for in or out of class, essays on teaching American Government, and suggestions for using MyPoliSciLab. Available on the IRC.

INSTRUCTOR'S ETEXT. The instructor's eText offers links to relevant instructor's resources and student activities in MyPoliSciLab. You can access these resources by simply clicking on an icon at the start of each chapter. Available on MyPoliSciLab.

POWERPOINT PRESENTATION WITH CLASSROOM RESPONSE SYSTEM (CRS). Make lectures more enriching for students. The PowerPoint Presentation includes a full lecture script, discussion questions, photos and figures from the book, and links to MyPoliSciLab multimedia. With integrated clicker questions, get immediate feedback on what your students are learning during a lecture. Available on the IRC.

CLASS PREPARATION. Add multimedia, figures, photos, and lots more from any of our political science books to your lectures. Available on MyPoliSciLab.

ALTERNATE EDITIONS. Don't teach policy? Removing this book's policy chapters is easy with Pearson Custom Library. To learn more, visit **www.pearsoncustomlibrary.com.**

TEXAS, CALIFORNIA, AND GEORGIA GOVERNMENT. Need coverage of your state's government? Add chapters from our bestselling Texas, California, and Georgia government books with Pearson Custom Library. To learn more, visit **www.pearsoncustomlibrary.com.**

Acknowledgments

Karen O'Connor thanks the thousands of students in her American Government courses at Emory and American Universities who, over the years, have pushed her to learn more about American government and to have fun in the process. She especially thanks Jonathan and Robin Helfat for their generous support. Her former students, too, have contributed in various ways to this project, especially John R. Hermann at Trinity University, Sue Davis at Denison University, and Laura van Assendelft at Mary Baldwin College. Laura has returned to the book this edition, taking on an important role in revising the domestic and economic policy chapters. She also thanks Professor Kent Miller for his ongoing review of the text.

For the past six editions, Alixandra B. Yanus of High Point University has offered invaluable assistance, unflagging support, and friendship. First, as a student at American University and the University of North Carolina at Chapel Hill, her fresh perspectives on politics and ideas about things of interest to students, as well as her keen eye for the typo, her research abilities, and her unbelievably hard work, made this a much better book. As a co-author on the last two editions, she has stepped up to be an invaluable contributor, bringing enthusiasm and the viewpoint of a new, outstanding, and devoted classroom teacher.

For this edition of the book, American University students Melissa Wiak, Tsion Hiltework, and especially Felicia Fognani, provided valuable research assistance. The help and humor of Felicia, now a graduate student at the University of Colorado at Boulder, are especially missed.

Last, but certainly not least, Karen further acknowledges the help and encouragement of Christina Stayeas and Armistead Williams, III. She also is appreciative of the constant companionship of Penny Louise, who asks for nothing more than any dog would, and keeps Karen (and often "Aunt Ali") from going crazy as she works to keep this book current and student-friendly.

Larry J. Sabato would like to acknowledge the 15,000 students from his University of Virginia Introduction to American Politics classes over 34 years and the many student interns at the UVA Center for Politics who have offered valuable suggestions and an abundance of thoughtful feedback. A massive textbook project like this one needs the very best assistance an author can find, and this author was lucky enough to find some marvelously talented people. Alixandra B. Yanus, assistant professor of political science at High Point University, worked endless hours researching the new edition and weaving together beautifully constructed sections on recent American politics. Her attention to detail and editor's eye have refined the behavior chapters and improved the overall text. As always, the staff of the University of Virginia Center for Politics and a team of extraordinary interns contributed in many important ways toward the successful completion of this volume, especially his chief of staff Ken Stroupe, and communications director Kyle Kondik. Their commitment to excellence is also obvious in their work for the Center's Crystal Ball website (www.centerforpolitics.org/crystalball)—a very useful resource in completing this volume.

Alixandra B. Yanus thanks Karen O'Connor and Larry Sabato for the opportunity to work on this textbook. Karen, especially, has been both mentor and "mom." She also thanks her colleagues at High Point University, especially Mark Setzler, Martin Kifer, and Ellen Gutman, who have supported her work, both on the book and in the classroom. Adam Chamberlain at Coastal Carolina University and Nicholas Pyeatt at Penn State—Altoona have also provided important advice on matters small (political science) and large (life).

She further acknowledges the contributions of her Honors American Government students at High Point University, who helped conceptualize new features and provided valuable student insight on the redesign and development of the e-Text. She also thanks her undergraduate research assistants, Kirsten Hunter and Melinda Poteet. Not only have they been a pleasure to work with, but they have also played an important role in bringing this book to life, responding with enthusiasm to odd research requests, keying endless Word documents, and even sharing their waffle fries and munchkins when the going got tough.

Most especially, she is grateful, as always, to her parents, Karen and Mark Yanus, for the assistance, encouragement, and guidance they have provided throughout her life. She also appreciates the patience and devotion of Daniel P. Tappen, who watches the Mets when she has to work, and takes her to Phillies games when she doesn't.

Particular thanks go to Laura van Assendelft at Mary Baldwin College, who contributed to the revisions of the chapters on Domestic Policy and Economic Policy; and David Bernell at Oregon State University, who provided great assistance in tackling the rapidly shifting landscape of Foreign and Defense Policy for this edition. Our continued thanks go to Christopher Simon at the University of Utah, Glenn Hastedt of James Madison University, Steven Koven at the University of Louisville, Daniel S. Papp of Kennesaw State University, and Kiki Caruson of the University of South Florida whose earlier work on policy content continue to serve as a strong foundation.

In the now many years we have been writing and rewriting this book, we have been blessed to have been helped by many people at Pearson Education. For this edition, our new editor, Vikram Mukhija, has responded to our fiery personalities and endless ideas with a few tricks—and a whole lot of enthusiasm—of his own. Our project manager, Maggie Barbieri, has invested her time, energy, and perhaps even sanity, into our project. She has become a valuable resource, sharing laughs, obtaining answers to our (many) questions, and using the most powerful means of coercion—Catholic guilt—to assure that we meet our deadlines. Our development editor, Angela Kao, has brought a quiet efficiency to the process; she has demonstrated great flexibility, advising us on content, developing infographics, assisting in photo research, and doing all the behind-the-scenes work that too often goes underappreciated. The production team, particularly Deb Wechsler at Pearson and Lois Lombardo at Cenveo, have provided valuable expertise and demonstrated remarkable patience and dedication. Our marketing manager, Wendy Gordon, has also done a terrific job. And, we would be remiss not to thank our former editor, Eric Stano, who guided this book for more than ten years. We would also like to acknowledge the tireless efforts of the Pearson Education sales force. In the end, we hope that all of these talented people see how much their work and support have helped us to write a better book.

The following text is taken from: *The 2012 Texas Election*
by L. Tucker Gibson, Jr. and Clay Robison

I. THE CONTEXT OF THE 2012 ELECTION IN TEXAS

Texas's 38 electoral votes were never really in question during the 2012 presidential election. Republicans, Democrats, and political analysts expected GOP nominee Mitt Romney to win the state, and he did with a significant majority. But although the presidential election was recognized as a foregone conclusion, Texas voters maintained a high interest in the national election as well as the various state and local elections that were on the ballot—they had critical decisions to make in numerous federal, state, and local races.

FEDERAL, STATE, AND LOCAL ELECTIONS IN 2012: THE LONG BALLOT

Besides the presidential campaign, the ballot item attracting the most attention was the race to succeed the longtime, moderate Republican U.S. Senator Kay Bailey Hutchison, who was retiring after 20 years in that office. Long regarded as influential among Senate Republicans, Hutchison had been instrumental in providing leadership to the Texas delegation to bring a great deal of federal dollars to Texas. Regardless of who won the presidential race, this post had the potential to significantly impact the face of Texas politics on the national stage. Would Texans elect a new U.S. senator who would help break the partisan impasse in Washington over immigration reform, tax policy, deficit reduction, and other critical issues? Or, would the new U.S. senator from Texas stake out a more ideological position that would contribute to the gridlock?

The same questions were hanging over the elections of 36 members of the U.S. House from throughout Texas. Four of these would be from new districts, which Texas had gained from population growth counted in the 2010 Census. Republicans were expected to retain a strong majority of the House delegation, following a redistricting process driven by the Texas Legislature's Republican majority. But a handful of the districts were competitive between the major parties.

The governor and most other state executive officeholders weren't on the ballot in 2012—they wouldn't be up for election until 2014. But every member of the Texas Legislature—31 members of the state Senate and 150 members of the Texas House—faced the voters in 2012 from districts redrawn in the 2011 redistricting process. The winners would make critical policy decisions that could potentially affect every Texan's life—from the quality of public schools to the adequacy of water supplies to the size of tax bills, to name but a few.

Most of the legislative races would be decided in the Republican primary, where some incumbents would lose because their new, redrawn districts favored challengers, and other incumbents would become embroiled in ideological battles. Only one of the 31 state Senate districts and fewer than a dozen of the 150 House seats would be competitive in the general election, but the outcomes of those races could have a significant impact on education and health care funding and other critical issues during the 2013 legislative session. In the Senate, Democrats were fighting to hold the Republican majority at 19-12, short of a critical two-thirds majority, a procedural barrier that would make it extremely difficult for the minority party to exercise much influence over legislation. In the House, Democrats were fighting to reduce a 102-48 Republican super-majority and regain some influence they had lost in the 2011 session.

Also on the 2012 ballot were two seats on the three-member Texas Railroad Commission, one-third of the seats on the Texas Supreme Court, one-third of the seats on the Texas Court of Criminal Appeals, and all 15 positions on the State Board of Education. Although most voters know little about these offices, they are also extremely important.

The Texas Railroad Commission regulates oil and gas production in Texas, including environmental issues related to energy production. Those issues have a strong impact on the quality of life in Texas, particularly with the increased oil and gas activity in the state and the potential environmental consequences of hydraulic fracturing—or fracking—a drilling technique now in widespread use. The Texas Supreme Court and the Texas Court of Criminal Appeals are the final arbiters of justice at the state level. The State Board of Education plays an important role in selected education issues, including textbook selection and curriculum development, and in recent years has gained national attention for ideological disputes over evolution and other issues.

After making their way through the federal and state contests on the ballot, voters also decided some county and special district elections, and ballots in urban areas were quite long. In Harris County alone, the state's most populous county, voters elected three county commissioners, 10 appellate judges, and 23 state district judges, as well as numerous justices of the peace and constables.

FACTORS IN THE 2012 TEXAS ELECTIONS

Three major factors would affect the outcomes of most of these races, as well as the presidential race in Texas. The first was Texas's conservative tradition and recent Republican domination. The second was heavy straight-ticket, partisan voting, which boosted Republican candidates in statewide races. And the third was Republican-dominated redistricting, which helped Republican candidates win most races in congressional and state legislative districts.

IDEOLOGY AND REPUBLICAN DOMINATION OF THE TEXAS PARTY SYSTEM

Even when Texas was a one-party Democratic state, conservative candidates usually won the Democratic nomination. Now, many of the children and grandchildren of Texas' old Democratic majority are Republicans. A Democratic presidential nominee hasn't carried Texas since Jimmy Carter in 1976. A Democrat hasn't won a U.S. Senate race in Texas since 1988 or any other statewide office since 1994. Republicans have held a majority of the state Senate since 1997 and a majority of the Texas House since 2003. Republicans have had the majority of Texas' seats in the U.S. House since 2005. Democrats have started to reclaim some county offices in urban counties, but Republicans have a lock on county governments in most suburban and rural counties. (City and other local races in Texas are nonpartisan, and few cities held elections in 2012.)

Ideology and intensely held political beliefs were prominent in the 2012 elections in Texas, and pragmatic policy solutions were frequently obscured by charges and counter-charges of conservatism or liberalism. The "conservative-liberal" divide that was prevalent nationally in the presidential race extended to Texans' views of the White House contenders and figured prominently in races for many other offices in Texas as well.

Many Republican candidates for federal, state, and county offices in Texas engaged in extensive ideological debates within their primaries, usually trying to "out-conservative" each other. Adding fuel to the ideological fire were the Tea Party movement—which was influential in a number of Republican primary races—and Republicans' strong animosity toward Obama over the Affordable Health Care Act and other policies they considered intrusive. Conservative Republicans concluded that they had nothing to lose by trying to push the politics of the state farther to the right. And, in general, that strategy worked.

By contrast, most Texas Democrats spent less time fighting amongst themselves and focused on trying to keep the legislative and congressional seats they held and to make whatever headway they could in the small number of competitive districts. Essentially, Democrats could not afford intense intra-party battles if they hoped to score any victories in the general election.

STRAIGHT TICKET VOTING

Most Texas voters in 2012 were faced with long ballots that included offices and candidates about which many voters had little or no knowledge. One reason was the redistricting process. Voters suddenly found themselves represented by new—at least to them—officeholders. Additionally, many voters don't know the differences between candidates in down-ballot races—such as those for the Texas Railroad Commission, court seats, or a constable's office—because those races receive relatively little media coverage and candidates can afford little, if any, advertising.

So, many voters in the general election simplify their choices by voting a straight party ticket. That means they mark either the Republican or Democrat box at the top of the ballot to vote for the respective partisan candidates for every office.

This practice was significant in the 2012 Texas elections, by both Democrats and Republicans. In the large metropolitan counties—Harris, Bexar, and Dallas, which were carried by Obama—more than 60% of the voters cast a straight party vote.[1] Republicans carried most of the other major counties, and there was a pattern of straight party voting in these counties.[2] Data collected by the state and county election offices showed that, statewide, more Republicans voted a straight

---

[1] http://www.harrisvotes.com/History/20121106/cumulative/cumulative.pdf; http://assets01.aws.connect.clarityelections.com/assets/connect/RootPublish/dallas-tx.connectclarityelections.com/ElectionDocuments/2012/GeneralElection-November062012/Updated_Final_Rsults/pdf; and http://elections.bexar.org/reports/PDF/20121106_ElectionTotals.HTM.

[2] Counties report election results, and several calculate straight party voting.

ticket than Democrats. This pattern greatly contributes to the Republican dominance of Texas elections.

REDISTRICTING SHAPED THE POLITICAL LANDSCAPE

As required by law, following population growth reported in the 2010 federal census, the Texas Legislature in 2011 redrew political boundaries for Texas House, state Senate, and U.S. House seats from Texas. The number of U.S. House seats from Texas increased by four, to 36. County governments also redistricted precincts from which county commissioners, justices of the peace, and constables are elected.

The new maps for the Legislature and U.S. House were quickly challenged in court by Democratic and minority plaintiffs as well as the U.S. Department of Justice, which contended that they were drawn unfairly and unconstitutionally to favor an undue number of Republican officeholders and candidates. While the plaintiffs' lawsuits slowly worked their way through the federal courts, the 2012 elections were held under interim redistricting maps drawn by a federal court. The party primaries and runoffs were also delayed because of the litigation. The March primaries were delayed until May 29 and the May runoffs until July 31.

Texas asked a three-judge federal panel in Washington to assess its redistricting plans' compliance with the Voting Rights Act—which prohibits legislative efforts to reduce or eliminate opportunities for minority voters to elect candidates of their choosing (the federal law applies to Texas and other states with histories of racial discrimination). The court rejected all three plans in August 2012, ruling that all three maps were discriminatory against minority voters.[3]

The judges held that the Republican legislative majority had ignored the strong growth of the minority population in drawing new districts. Some 89% of the population growth in Texas during the previous decade had been minorities, mainly Hispanics. Yet, the Legislature drew 150 districts for the Texas House without adding a single "Hispanic opportunity district," one in which Hispanic voters would constitute a majority of voters and therefore have an opportunity to elect their preferred candidate. The U.S. House map drawn by the Legislature kept 10 existing minority districts. But Texas gained four congressional districts because of the primarily minority population growth, and the court said that one additional minority congressional district was enough to meet the requirements of the Act.

The extended political and legal maneuvering over redistricting—and over a new state law to require voters to produce a government-issued photo ID before casting ballots—injected additional polarizing issues into the 2012 elections. Republicans said that the voter ID law was necessary to guard against voter fraud, but Democrats contended that it was designed to discourage Hispanics, who usually back Democrats, from voting. The Obama administration, through the U.S. Department of Justice, refused to approve the redistricting bills or the voter ID law under the Voting Rights Act. This reinforced Republican views of excessive federal intervention in the state's political system, but Democrats applauded the decisions.

---

[3] *State of Texas* v. *U.S.A and Eric Holder*, Civil Action No. 11-303 (2012)

THE ECONOMIC CONTEXT OF THE 2012 ELECTIONS

The economy was a major issue in the presidential race in many states, and Texas wasn't spared a share of misery from the Great Recession. But Texas' economy never sank as low as the national economy, and it was recovering strongly long before Election Day, even though many Texans criticized President Obama's economic policies. Whatever impact the economy had on election results in the Lone Star State served to benefit Republican candidates.

Texas began experiencing an economic downturn in 2008, and some problems persisted into 2011. But the recession in Texas was short-lived, and the state was a leader in the nation's comparatively slow economic recovery, a fact that Gov. Rick Perry and other Republican leaders frequently attributed to the state's low-tax, low-regulatory business climate. Many successful, incumbent Republican legislators campaigned on "business friendly" issues and Texas' economic advantages. Texans were feeling good about the state's economy and felt far less threatened by the economic uncertainties facing voters in other states.

Impact of Recession on State Revenues and Public Policy Sales tax collections, the main revenue source for state government, dropped 2.9% between the 2008 and 2009 fiscal years and continued to deteriorate for several more months. The governor and the Legislature averted a financial crisis during the 2009 biennial legislative session by spending several billion dollars of federal stimulus funds to balance the state budget without a tax increase. But by the time legislators convened to write the next state budget in 2011, the federal stimulus money was gone and lawmakers were confronted with a $27 billion revenue shortfall.

Gov. Rick Perry, who had courted the Tea Party movement during his 2010 reelection campaign and perhaps already was contemplating his race for the 2012 Republican presidential nomination, demanded from the outset that, even with the huge shortfall, the new budget would be balanced by cutting deeply into spending, not by raising taxes. He was backed by a large Republican majority in the Legislature, many of whose members also had been elected with Tea Party support and had come into office vowing to shrink the size of government. Lawmakers approved a new, two-year state budget that was about $14 billion leaner than the previous budget, with some of the deepest cuts inflicted on education and health care programs. Some $5.4 billion was slashed from the public schools alone, leading to a loss of 25,000 school jobs—including 11,000 teaching positions—in the 2011-12 school year. Legislators also deferred some spending and used accounting maneuvers to cover the remaining shortfall without raising taxes.

Road to Economic Recovery Even as the Legislature was cutting the state budget in 2011, sales tax collections were beginning to recover. By October 2012, the month before the election, sales tax receipts had increased for 31 consecutive months and were expected to continue. State Comptroller Susan Combs reported that sales tax revenue for fiscal 2012 was $24.1 billion, a 12.6% increase over the previous year.[4]

Candidates running for office in Texas did not have to face the economic issues confronting politicians in other states. As will be discussed in more detail later, Democrats tried to make an issue of the 2011 budget cuts in some legislative races in 2012, but with limited success. There was a perception that the economy was on a trajectory to improve and more revenues would be available to the Legislature in 2012 to restore some of the funding. Moreover, some of the low-income Texans who were most adversely impacted by the budget cuts were difficult to mobilize or simply were not part of the Republican base.

II. THE PRESIDENTIAL RACE IN TEXAS

Since the election of Richard M. Nixon in 1968, the Republican Party's successful southern strategy has focused on the states that were part of the Confederacy and extended through the plains and Rocky Mountain states. With its 38 electoral votes, Texas has long been a linchpin in this strategy. Of the Republican—or, red—states, Texas was regarded to be safely in the Republican column long before the 2012 presidential primaries and party conventions. For a number of years, in fact, Texas has been considered one of the most Republican states in the country.

Although Texas was not in play in the 2012 presidential race, both state parties had reasons to mobilize their activists and encourage Texas voters to the polls. The Republicans wanted to demonstrate their dominance and discourage Democrats from challenging them in future elections. Republicans also wanted to discourage future fundraising for Democrats. More immediately, though, Republicans recognized that a large number of straight ticket Republican voters would help the GOP win down-ballot races.

Democrats were unable to recruit strong candidates for the statewide races, but they hoped that interest in the presidential election would help them expand their voter base and create opportunities for future elections. Democrats believe that their future in Texas is primarily dependent on Hispanic and African American voters, and Democratic candidates who won legislative races included a number of Hispanics and African Americans who benefitted from high turnout in Democratic districts as well as a handful of swing districts.

THE REPUBLICAN PRIMARY

By the time Texas Republicans held their party primary in late May—after more than two months of delays—Mitt Romney already had secured the Republican presidential nomination over more conservative candidates who may have done well in Texas if the nomination had still been undecided. Texas Gov. Rick Perry's late entrance into the Republican presidential race in 2011 had generated some initial excitement from Republicans who believed he was the one candidate who could

[4] http://www.window.state.tx.us/news2013/130107-BRE.html

overtake Romney. But Perry's campaign quickly faltered, and he was long gone from the race before his constituents had a chance to vote for him.

THE GENERAL ELECTION CAMPAIGN

With both sides already counting Texas in the Republican column, the general election presidential campaign in the Lone Star State lacked the intensity of the campaigning in the highly competitive swing states, where voters were bombarded by television advertising, phone calls, door to door canvassing, and frequent candidate visits. Neither President Obama nor Romney campaigned in Texas during the months leading up to the general election, except for occasional fundraising trips. Despite its strong Republican majority, Texas remained an important source of campaign cash for both campaigns.

Campaign Operations and Fundraising By Election Day, the Obama campaign had established more than 800 field offices across the country, to the Romney campaign's 300. These offices, staffed by paid campaign workers and volunteers, were designed to carry out grassroots activities, including the tasks of identifying, registering, and targeting likely voters and conducting get-out-the-vote efforts. Each campaign put most of these offices in states that were heavily contested—such as Ohio, Florida, Virginia, and Wisconsin.

MOBILIZATION OF PARTY ACTIVISTS IN TEXAS

The Romney campaign had no field office in Texas, and the Obama campaign had only five—in Austin, Dallas, El Paso, Houston, and San Antonio.[5] Both campaigns relied heavily on state and local party organizations and other candidates to conduct basic campaign activities in Texas. The Texas Republican Party created a Victory Committee that channeled state assistance to county party organizations and local campaign efforts. The state party also paid for phone banks and contributed campaign money to approximately 100 Republican candidates across the state.[6] Republican volunteers in Texas also worked on phone banks in some of the battleground states, and some were recruited to travel to other states.[7]

Some volunteers in Obama's Texas field offices were focused on Texas voters, but most of them were asked to contact voters in states that actually were in play, such as Florida.[8] Volunteers were also recruited at their own expense to work for the Obama campaign in other states as well.

---

[5] Phone call with staff member of the Republican Party of Texas, 2-19-2013; phone call with staff member of the Dallas County Democratic Party, 2-19-2013.

[6] Republican Party of Texas, "Election Recap: Texas Holds the Line," November 15, 2012. http://www.texasgop.org/posts/303-election-recap-texas-holds-the-line.

[7] Phone call with staff member of the Tarrant Republican Party, 2-26-2012; phone call with staff member of the Bexar County Republican Party; phone call with staff member of the Dallas County Republican Party.

[8] Glen Maxey, Special Assistant to Chairman Hinojosa, Texas Democratic Party, e-mail, 2-19-2013.

Although there was little traditional campaigning by the presidential candidates in Texas, the national campaign organizations for both Obama and Romney used sophisticated computer technology to communicate with voters across the nation. These "virtual campaigns" used the Internet to bombard many Texas voters with emails of the candidates' positions and solicitations for donations. In effect, Texas party activists and others who supported the national candidates were incorporated effectively into the dynamics of the national campaigns.

As noted earlier, both Obama and Romney occasionally visited Texas to raise money to spend on advertising and other campaign activities in contested states where the spending could make a difference. According to reports filed with the Federal Election Commission, Texas ranked second in total direct contributions—following California— with $82 million raised. That amount included $57.9 million to all Republican candidates, including unsuccessful primary candidates such as Texans Rick Perry and Ron Paul. Romney received $39.7 million of the Republican donations from Texas. Obama raised $24.2 million in the state in direct contributions.[9] Texans also made significant additional contributions through various political action committees, Super PACs, and the national parties. The lion's share went to Republicans.

Even though their state had been written off, many Texans watched the presidential and vice-presidential debates and kept up with news of the presidential race. As the intensity of the campaigning increased and many polls pointed to a close election nationally, the party preferences of most Texas voters were reinforced. Evidence indicates that few Texas voters were converted by either the national or state campaigns. The national campaign drama also prompted many Texans who otherwise may have stayed home on Election Day to vote.

National Issues and Texas Voters On a national scale, taxes, the federal debt, health care, immigration, the economy, and unemployment were major issues in the presidential race. Not all of these issues had the same importance for Texas voters. As noted earlier, for example, the nation's economy was less of an issue in Texas than in much of the country. Yet, there continued to be concerns about the deep-rooted problems of budget deficits, the national debt, budget reductions, and entitlements. Many Texans in both parties were deeply concerned about immigration, border security, and the Affordable Care Act ("Obamacare").

IMMIGRATION AND BORDER CONCERNS

Opposition to "Amnesty" Gov. Rick Perry continued to support the state law, which he had signed and which had become an issue in his own unsuccessful presidential race, encouraging young illegal immigrants to go to college by making them eligible for in-state tuition at state universities.

---

[9] Federal Election Commission, "2012 Presidential Campaign Finances: Texas Contributions to All Candidates by 3 Digit Zip Code," http://fec/gov/disclosurep/PState.do.

But when President Obama used his executive authority in June 2012 to do the same, Perry pushed back. Obama also offered work permits to thousands of illegal immigrants younger than 30 who had come to the U.S. before they were 16. The policy didn't grant them legal status but allowed them to avoid deportation. Perry called Obama's action an "election year tactic to bypass Congress and arbitrarily grant amnesty to potentially millions of illegal immigrants." The governor said the decision was an example of the administration's "blatant disregard for our Constitution, our rule of law and our democratic process."[10]

Amnesty also was a term that many Texas Republicans—like conservative Republicans in other states—applied to the concept of giving undocumented immigrants a "pathway to citizenship." Such a provision, they said, would only encourage other foreigners to break American immigration laws. This issue continued to be a central point of contention when Congress began its immigration reform debate in early spring of 2013. Texas's two Republican U.S. senators and most of its Republican congressional delegation initially took a hard line in opposition to such a provision.

Border Security As the political debate over immigration raged on and drug violence in Mexico continued, concern over border security was not limited to one party, but the Texas Republican Party was outspoken. "Secure Our Borders!" was the first immigration plank in the state GOP's 2012 platform. Among other things, they called upon the federal government to "clarify" the 14th Amendment to the U.S. Constitution to limit citizenship by birth to individuals born to U.S. citizens, not to offspring of illegal immigrants who were in the U.S. when they gave birth.

The GOP also called for a temporary worker program, with several requirements for foreign applicants. Among other conditions, applicants would have to pass criminal background checks, demonstrate a proficiency in English, complete an American civics class, and waive all rights for financial assistance from public entitlement programs. Applicants and/or their employers would also have to prove that they could afford and obtain private health insurance.[11]

Ironically, the Obama administration through 2012 had deported approximately 1.5 million illegal immigrants and had endorsed enhanced border security. Moreover, Texans have been hiring illegal immigrants, almost openly, for years. Some sectors of the state's economy have been developed using immigrant labor. The Republican stance on this issue hurt Romney among Hispanic voters nationally. And, it has made it more difficult for Texas Republicans to make significant inroads into Texas' growing Hispanic population.

---

[10]Office of the Governor, Press Release, June 15, 2012, http://governor.state.tx.us/news/press-release/17344/.

[11] Republican Party of Texas, "Report of Platform Committee, 2012," http://www.texasgop.org/about-the-party.

HEALTH CARE AND UNINSURED TEXANS

Despite being a national leader in job creation and having an economy that many other states may envy, Texas is not without its problems. One nagging concern is a lack of access to health care for large numbers of (primary low income) residents. As the political debate over the Affordable Care Act was raging in the months leading up to the 2012 election, Texas had the largest percentage of citizens—25% (6.2 million people)—in the nation without health care.[12]

Another 4 million Texans were receiving health coverage under Medicaid or the Children's Health Insurance Program, although the state's health and human services budget had suffered cuts to help bridge a deep revenue shortfall during the 2011 legislative session.[13] But health care ranked very low on the list of most Texans' concerns and appears to have had little impact on the decisions of a large number of voters.

Nevertheless, opposition to the Affordable Care Act—or at least selected provisions of it—was strong in Texas. A provision allowing young adults to remain on their parents' insurance policies until age 26 and a provision to prohibit insurance companies from denying coverage for pre-existing medical conditions enjoyed some popularity. But many employers opposed the requirement for employee insurance coverage, and many individuals—particularly young people—resented the requirement that they obtain health insurance or pay a government penalty. Gov. Rick Perry was outspoken in his opposition to the law, which he considered an overreach of federal authority and another potential financial burden on state government. Texas joined a number of other states challenging the law in federal court.

The U.S. Supreme Court upheld most of the Affordable Care Act, including the key individual coverage mandate, in June 2012. But the court struck down another provision of the law, which would have imposed a severe penalty—loss of Medicaid funding—on states that did not expand Medicaid coverage to residents with incomes up to 133% of the poverty line.

Gov. Rick Perry announced that Texas would not expand its Medicaid coverage or establish an exchange to help people purchase health insurance. That meant Texas' exchange—an online marketplace for consumer insurance purchases—would be established by the federal government. The exchanges were to begin operating in October 2013. "I will not be party to socializing health care and bankrupting my state in direct contradiction to our Constitution and our founding principles of limited government," Perry said.[14]

---

[12] Texas Health and Human Services Commission, *Texas Medicaid and Chip in Perspective*, 9th Edition, January 2013. See also U.S. Census Bureau, Health Insurance Historical Tables, "Table HIB-4: Health Insurance Coverage Status and Type of Coverage by State--All Persons: 1999 to 2010," http://www.census.gov/hhes/www/hlthins/data/historical/HIB_tables.html (August 2012).

[13] Ibid.

[14] Office of the Governor, Press Release, July 9, 2012, http://governor.state.tx.us/news/press-release/17408.

Health care advocates and many Democratic legislators, nevertheless, tried to keep public attention focused on the issues, particularly the Medicaid expansion, for which the federal government would pay most of the cost.

HOW TEXANS VOTED

Republican nominee Mitt Romney carried 228 of Texas' 254 counties enroute to his victory margin of 57.2% to 41.4%. Most of Romney's strength came from heavily Republican and heavily conservative, rural and suburban Texas. He carried seventy-five counties—mostly rural—with more than 80% of the vote.[15] President Obama was strongest in heavily Hispanic south Texas, along and near the Mexican border, and in Texas' most populous urban counties with large concentrations of minority voters. Obama carried every major metropolitan county, except Tarrant County (Fort Worth) but lost the suburban counties around them.[16]

Voting by Race and Ethnicity No exit polling was done in Texas, but polling in other states indicated that Romney received 59% of the white vote. Most suburban counties in Texas are heavily Anglo. The metropolitan urban counties, which Obama carried in Texas, have large numbers of Hispanic and African American voters. Polling from other states indicated that Obama received 93% of the African American vote and 71% of the Hispanic vote.

Although Anglos comprise some 45% of Texans, they accounted for 58% of the state's eligible voters and approximately 60% of the state's likely voters. More than 75% of Anglos favored Romney over Obama.

According to the 2010 census, Hispanics made up 37.6% of Texas' population. But the Hispanic population is younger than the Anglo and African American populations, and Hispanics accounted for only 33.6% of Texans who were old enough to vote. The Hispanic voting pool is reduced even further (to 26.2%) by the fact that many Hispanics are not citizens and are ineligible to vote.

Votes by Texas Latinos comprised approximately 1/4 of all votes cast in the 2012 election, and based on a number of polls, evidence indicates that 70% voted for Obama, with the remainder cast for Romney. Latinos were much more concerned than Anglos with economic issues, jobs, and immigration.

African Americans comprised 13% of the state's voting population, and evidence indicates that they turned out at high rates in many areas of the state. They cast more than 90% of their votes for Obama.

Turnout and Straight Party Voting Despite robust population growth in Texas, the number of general election voters in 2012 (7,993,851) was lower than the

---

[15] Texas Secretary of State, Elections Division, "1992-Current Election History," http://elections.sos.state.tx.us/elchist.exe.

[16] Ibid.

number who voted in the 2008 presidential election (8,077,795). Turnout of registered voters in 2012 was 58.9% (45.6% of the voting age population).[17]

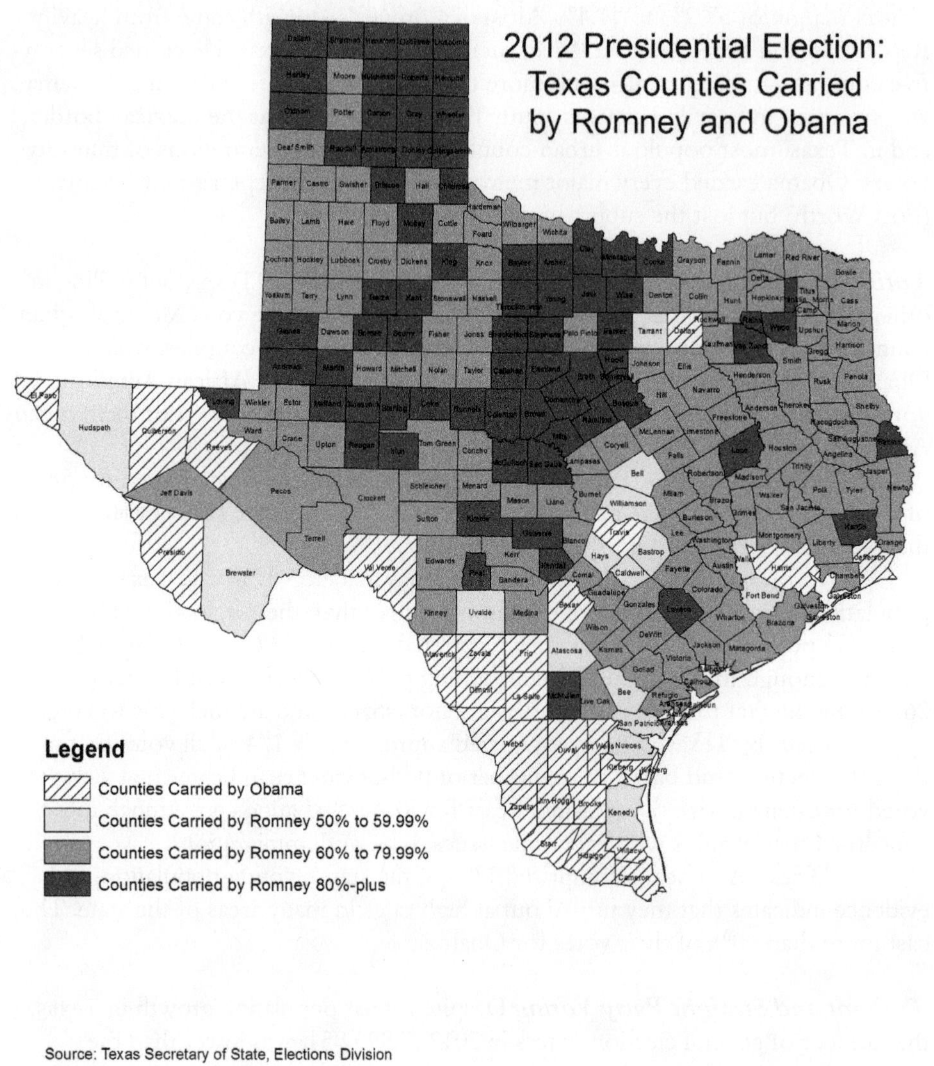

[17] Texas Secretary of State, Elections Division, "1992 – Current Election History," http://elections.sos.state.tx.us/elchist.exe.

Many Texans who voted in the general election did so to cast a ballot in the presidential race, even though the contest in their state wasn't considered close. National issues were debated within the context of their implications for Texas. Neither party stayed out of the presidential fray in Texas, anticipating the election's impact on down-ballot races and future elections. With Obama's victory, Republicans were likely to play a minimal role in the president's administration, but they would play a significant role in the House of Representatives. Despite losing the state, Texas Democrats could anticipate some influence and access to the Obama White House.

III. RACES FOR THE U.S. SENATE AND THE U.S. HOUSE IN TEXAS

Republican Sen. Kay Bailey Hutchison's decision not to seek reelection in 2012, after 20 years in the office, was seen as a potential loss for the state. She was a moderate, an influential insider in the Republican Senate leadership, and had successfully brought federal projects, jobs, and funds to Texas. But her announcement set off a scramble among Republicans and Democrats eager to climb the political ladder to one of the most prestigious offices in American politics.

THE REPUBLICAN RACE FOR AN OPEN SENATE SEAT

Nine candidates filed for the U.S. Senate seat in the Republican primary, but only three were perceived to be viable candidates—David Dewhurst, the state's lieutenant governor; Ted Cruz, a former state solicitor general who had never run for elective office; and Tom Leppert, a former mayor of Dallas. The race ultimately was reduced to a contest between Dewhurst and Cruz.

Dewhurst, 66, a multi-millionaire businessman, had served as the state's lieutenant governor since 2003 and before that had been state land commissioner for four years. As lieutenant governor, he had helped push conservative Republican priorities through the Legislature, including a voter identification law, restrictions on abortion, and deep budget cuts.

Cruz, 42, a Harvard-trained attorney and son of a Cuban immigrant, had been a law clerk for U.S. Supreme Court Chief Justice William Rehnquist and had served at the Department of Justice and the Federal Trade Commission during President George W. Bush's administration. Texas Attorney General Greg Abbott appointed Cruz as the state's Solicitor General in 2003. In that position, he represented Texas before the U.S. Supreme Court and other federal courts. He defended, among other issues, the public display of a Ten Commandments monument on government property and the state's 2011 redistricting plans.[18]

---

[18] For an extended biography of Ted Cruz, see his U.S. Senate Homepage. http://www/senate.gov/senators/113th Congress/Cruz_Ted.htm.

Ideology in the Republican Primary Both candidates were recognized as strong conservatives on fiscal and social issues, an essential qualification in a Republican primary dominated by conservative voters. But Cruz, despite his government experience, was able to appeal to members of the Tea Party movement and other grassroots groups as an "outsider" who would shake up a government that they disliked. Cruz painted Dewhurst as an "establishment" and "moderate" candidate who couldn't be trusted not to readily cave in and compromise with Democrats, if he got to Washington.

Campaign Styles and Personalities At the outset, Cruz was not nearly as well-known as Dewhurst among Republican voters and had much less money with which to campaign. This forced Cruz to pursue a substantively different strategy than Dewhurst. While Dewhurst relied extensively on a media campaign—with advertising financed by his substantial wealth and fundraising ability—Cruz waged a grassroots campaign. Cruz was a fiery speaker and was much more comfortable than Dewhurst meeting with neighborhood groups, participating in candidate forums and building relationships among conservative activists. And, he did so tirelessly, earning support, building name identification, and mobilizing an effective ground campaign among conservative voters. Cruz also relied heavily on social media, organizing a "virtual campaign" through the Internet.

Cruz was also eager to take combative stances, and his rhetoric often implied a conservative populism as he attacked Obama and the national government over health care, immigration, and other issues important to Texas Republicans.

Dewhurst was more reserved, deliberative, and less combative than Cruz. But he entered the Senate race with access to more money and endorsements from many "establishment" Republicans. Dewhurst's campaign organization seemed to anticipate that his name identification, public record, and media campaign would be enough to win the Republican nomination and, effectively, the Senate seat.

Approximately 11% of the state's 13 million-plus voters participated in the May 29 Republican primary, prompted, in part, by interest in the selection of delegates to the Republican National Convention as well as the heated Senate race.[19] State law requires a majority of votes to win a party's nomination, and nine candidates were competing. Dewhurst led with 44.6% of the votes, and Cruz came in second, with 34.2%, forcing a runoff.

THE REPUBLICAN RUNOFF

Cruz, in some respects, had an advantage at the beginning of the runoff campaign because he had a grassroots organization in place that could be mobilized a second time. His supporters were personally committed to him, shared his strong conservative views, and were activists who were likely to stay engaged. Dewhurst, by contrast, would continue to rely on a media campaign.

---

[19] Texas Office of Secretary of State, Elections Division, http://elections.sos.state.tx.us/elchist.exe

The runoff race became something of a shouting match over which candidate could claim the loudest and the most often to be the most conservative. Moderate was a dirty word. Cruz reminded audiences that, as solicitor general of Texas, he had gone to court to defend states' rights against the federal government, fight for religious freedom, and fight against gun control. He repeatedly vowed to continue defending free market principles, individual liberty, and the Constitution as a U.S. senator. He also attacked the health care reform law and other Obama policies, and promised to aggressively take on Washington insiders.

Dewhurst claimed to be just as conservative and reminded voters that as lieutenant governor, he had helped push conservative Republican priorities through the Legislature, including a voter identification law, restrictions on abortion, and deep budget cuts. But Cruz's aggressive style was more convincing to Republican voters who wanted a senator to "stand up" for Texas and take on the Washington elite. Moreover, Cruz, through his long ground campaign, had secured a lock on most grassroots volunteers who would likely vote and help bring other like-minded voters to the polls.

According to the Federal Election Commission, the race for the Republican nomination for the Senate seat from Texas—including spending by outside, independent groups—cost more than $60 million, making it the most expensive nonpresidential race in the country.[20] The Cruz and Dewhurst campaigns combined spent more than $32 million, with more than $24 million of that coming from Dewhurst, who dug deeply into his own personal wealth.[21]

With voter turnout in the Republican runoff dropping to 8.5%, Cruz beat Dewhurst, 56.8% to 43.2%.[22] Dewhurst remained lieutenant governor—he was in the middle of a four-year term—and, as the state Senate's presiding officer, soon began to prepare for the 2013 legislative session. He said he planned to seek another term as lieutenant governor in 2014, but would-be Republican challengers, sensing he was politically wounded, were already lining up against him.

Four Democrats also filed for the Senate seat in the Democratic primary, but only one, former state Rep. Paul Sadler, had ever held elective office. Few Democrats gave any of their candidates a chance of defeating the eventual Republican nominee. Turnout was very low, with only 590,000 Democrats—4.5% of registered voters—going to the polls. No candidate came out of the primary with a majority of the vote, forcing the top two into a runoff.

Paul Sadler, an attorney and former state representative (1991-2003) from Henderson in east Texas, beat retired educator Grady Yarbrough in a Democratic runoff that attracted little media attention or broad-based party support. Only 236,000—1.8% of the state's 13 million registered voters—cast a vote.[23]

---

[20] Federal Election Commission, 2012 House and Senate Campaign Finance for Texas, http://www.fec.gov/disclosurehs/HSState.do.

[21] Federal Election Commission, 2012 House and Senate Campaign Finance for Texas, http://www.fec.gov/disclosurehs/HSCandlist.do.

[22] http://elections.sos.state.tx.us/elchist.exe.

[23] Ibid.

GENERAL ELECTION

Against Cruz, Sadler was campaigning uphill in a state that had not elected a Democratic candidate to statewide office in almost 20 years, and he wasn't able to raise enough money for a statewide advertising campaign or grassroots campaign. For both the primary and general elections, Sadler raised approximately $703,000, a pittance compared to the money raised and spent by Republicans.[24] None of the other Democrats running for down-ballot statewide offices could help his campaign, and most of the party activists and volunteers mobilized by the Democrats were focused on the presidential race or county races. Cruz won the Senate seat with 56.4% of the vote to Sadler's 40.6.[25]

Cruz's election was historic because he was the first Hispanic elected to the U.S. Senate from Texas. But ironically, he lost most of the Hispanic vote. No exit polls were conducted in Texas, but election returns from heavily Hispanic counties indicated that most Hispanics voted for Sadler, while Cruz cruised to victory on a strong Republican, largely Anglo vote. Cruz won more of the Hispanic vote than Mitt Romney, the Republican presidential nominee. But Sadler handily carried heavily Hispanic counties along the Mexican border, some with 70% or more of the vote. Cruz's conservative message did not resonate with most Hispanic voters. If various polls are correct, they were concerned with economic issues, immigration reform, and improved educational and health care opportunities, not with the Washington-bashing that characterized much of Cruz's campaign.

ELECTION POST-MORTEM: THE GRASSROOTS IS NOT DEAD

Primary voters, whether Democratic or Republican, tend to be more ideological than voters who simply support the parties' nominees in the general election. They also tend to be more interested in politics and attentive to policy issues. As such, they can be easily mobilized to participate in campaigns. Largely out of necessity, Ted Cruz recognized this and effectively tapped into it. He also put his outspoken conservative views to great advantage among members of the Tea Party movement and other conservatives who dominate Texas' Republican primary.

For years, media-oriented campaigns had appeared to be the key to electoral success in Texas—particularly in major statewide races—and in many cases they still are. But Cruz's successful campaign is a strong example of how a well-organized grassroots effort can lead the way to victory.

TEXAS CONGRESSIONAL ELECTIONS

As discussed earlier, redistricting as a result of the 2010 census awarded Texas four additional seats in the U.S. House, increasing the state's total from 32 to 36. Texas

---

[24] http://www.fec.gov/fecviewer/CandidateCommitteeDetail.do

[25] http://elections.sos.state.tx.us/elchist.exe.

now holds 8% of the 435 seats in the U.S. House, second only to California, which has 53 seats (12% of the total membership).

Since lawsuits over this redistricting would not be resolved until months after the 2012 election, a federal court drew interim district maps from which officeholders and candidates ran in 2012. The interim congressional plan was more favorable toward minority candidates, but still strongly favored Republicans.

Democratic Gains Under the interim map, the two major parties split Texas' four new congressional seats, and a Democratic challenger unseated a Republican incumbent in another district. That left Republicans with a 24-12 edge in the Texas delegation, a smaller edge proportionately than the 23-9 GOP margin before the census and redistricting. The two Democrats who won seats from new districts were Marc Veasey, an African American state representative from Fort Worth (District 33 in north Texas), and Filemon Vela, a Hispanic attorney from Brownsville (District 34 in south Texas).

New Republicans Going to Congress The two Republicans elected to new districts were former Texas Secretary of State Roger Williams(District 25—stretching from Tarrant County south to Austin) and Steve Stockman, a former congressman (District 36 in southeast Texas). In another race of note, Republican state Rep. Randy Weber defeated former Democratic congressman Nick Lampson of Beaumont in District 14, also in southeast Texas, to succeed the retiring Ron Paul, former longtime Republican congressman and presidential candidate.

Swing District Swings Back to Democrats One traditionally Hispanic district—District 23 in southwest Texas—switched partisan columns when Democratic state Rep. Pete Gallego of Alpine unseated Republican incumbent Francisco "Quico" Canseco of San Antonio in a close, expensive race that received national attention. Of all the funds spent by independent groups in the Texas congressional races, more than two-thirds was spent in this contest.[26]

District 23 is the largest congressional district in Texas and one of the largest in the country. It stretches several hundred miles from San Antonio to El Paso and includes dozens of counties—many sparsely populated—in far west Texas and along the Mexican border. A rarity in Texas, the swing district almost evenly split its votes between Democrat Barack Obama and Republican John McCain in the 2008 presidential election. Canseco benefitted from the strong Republican wave in 2010, defeating then-Democratic incumbent Ciro Rodriguez.

In 2012, the battle for the seat was Texas' closest and most expensive congressional race, attracting the interest of both national parties and outside political groups, which spent more than $7 million on the race, according to the Federal Election Commission.[27] With two Hispanics squaring off against each other

[26] http://www.fec.gov/data/IndependentExpenditure.do?format=html&id=ieNational &election_yr=2012&candidateOfficeState=Tx&candOffice=H.

[27] http://www.fec.gov/data/IndependentExpenditure.do?format=html&id=ieNational

in a district where two-thirds of the residents are Hispanic, it was also an important race for Republicans trying to woo traditionally Democratic voters. Former President Bill Clinton campaigned for Gallego in San Antonio, another indication of how important the race was for Democrats. Immigration was a major issue in the race, with Gallego attacking Canseco for opposing the Dream Act, which would give young illegal immigrants a way to become U.S. citizens. Gallego defeated Canseco 50.3% to 45.6%, a margin of 9,129 votes out of 192,169 cast.[28]

Money in Congressional Race All congressional candidates in Texas combined raised close to $70 million for their 2012 campaigns. Republican candidates raised approximately 63% of these funds, which included direct contributions to campaigns from PACs. Additionally, independent organizations reported spending $9.6 million to influence congressional races in the Lone Star State.

Except for the Gallego-Canseco race, the candidate—Democrat or Republican—who raised the most money won the election. Twenty-four of the winning candidates raised $1 million or more. One Democratic incumbent won by spending only $351,000, but the average raised by the 12 Democrats who won exceeded $1 million. One winning Republican raised $3.3 million, while the average for winning Republicans was $1.3 million.

2012 Congressional Elections in Texas: Party Successes and Fundraising

	Republicans	Democrats
Seats Won	24	12
Districts with No Major Party Opposition	4	1
Winner Received 60% or More of the Vote	18	11
Money Raised by Party Nominees	$35,853,285	$15,046,233
Avg. Money Raised by Party Nominees	$1,024,380	$470,194
Money Raised by Winning Candidates	$32,479,556	$12,853,725
Avg. Money Raised by Winning Candidates	$1,353,315	$1,071,144

Source: Texas Secretary of State, Elections Division, "1992 - Current Election History," elections.sos.state.tx.us/elchist.exe; Federal Election Commission, "2012 House and Senate Campaign Finance," http://www.fec.gov/disclosurehs/hsnational.do?cf=hs_elec.

CONGRESSIONAL ELECTION POST MORTEM

Texas now has the largest Republican delegation in the U.S. House of Representatives. At the beginning of the 113th Congress, Republicans held 234 seats, Democrats 201. Ten percent of the Republican Conference is comprised of Texans. By contrast, California, which elects 53 members of the House, has only 12 Republicans.

&election_yr=2012&candidateOfficeState=Tx&candOffice=H.

[28] http://elections.sos.state.tx.us/elchist.exe.

The size of the Republican delegation increases its influence in the party's leadership and committee structure. Four Republicans from Texas serve as chairs of standing committees and others serve as subcommittee chairs.

The Republicans from Texas range from conservative to very conservative and, consequently, hold similar ideological and policy views. Their bloc of 24 votes provides them a great deal of influence in the decisions of the House.

Most of the Republican members ran on an anti-Obama theme, and they likely will take positions over the next four years in opposition to Obama's initiatives on the budget, taxes, and immigration reform. If House Republicans opt for an obstructionist strategy, Texas Republicans will provide the House leadership with a sizable number of votes.

The 12 congressional districts won by Democrats are in south Texas, along the Mexican border, and in urban areas—Houston, Dallas, San Antonio, Austin, and El Paso—and these areas were carried by President Obama in the election.

IV. RACES FOR STATE OFFICES

Races for the Texas House of Representatives and the state Senate dominated state elections in 2012. This was the first election after redistricting by the Legislature in 2011. All 31 state Senate seats, as well as the 150 seats in the Texas House, were on the ballot. The legislative elections—plus retirements—produced a large turnover in both chambers. However, Republicans remained in firm control of both chambers.

Besides the U.S. Senate campaign discussed earlier, the only statewide races in 2012 were for two seats on the Texas Railroad Commission, three seats on the Texas Supreme Court and three seats on the Texas Court of Criminal Appeals. All were won by Republicans.

All 15 positions on the State Board of Education, which were elected by newly redrawn districts, were also on the 2012 ballot. Republicans won 10 of those district races, and Democrats won five.

Overall, the state elections made it a good year for the Republican Party, extending the GOP's domination of the state's political system and the three branches of government. The legislative races, in particular, demonstrate the effectiveness of gerrymandering in the creation of safe seats and the elimination of real party competition. Democratic gains in the House were minimal, there were no Democratic gains in the Senate, and the consensus after the election was that the ideological tenor of both chambers would continue to be conservative. The Railroad Commission and the appellate courts were not expected to change their legal and political philosophies, but there was some speculation that changes on the State Board of Education could moderate its conservative orientation.

REDISTRICTING WAS CENTRAL TO MANY TEXAS HOUSE RACES

The interim redistricting maps were only slightly less friendly to Republican candidates in the general election than the plans drafted by Republican legislators in 2011. But the new districts prompted much of the turnover in the Texas House.

Some state representatives, both Republicans and Democrats, viewed redrawn districts and the two new congressional districts as opportunities to advance up the political ladder. Other lawmakers found themselves in realigned districts with large numbers of new constituents, making them vulnerable to reelection challenges, especially in the Republican primary. Some sought election to other offices or simply retired from the Legislature.

Most of the legislative races were decided in party primaries—mainly the Republican primary. Only one state Senate seat and fewer than a dozen House races were truly competitive in the general election.

Republican Primary Casualties House Speaker Joe Straus easily survived a Republican primary challenge from a Tea Party-backed candidate in San Antonio, his home district. And, Straus dipped into his own political funds to make campaign contributions to members of his leadership team and some other GOP incumbents who faced primary challenges of their own. But 10 Republican incumbents, including five of the speaker's committee chairs, were unseated in primary races.

Some of the losing incumbents were overcome by opposition from the right, comprised of groups and individuals stirred by lingering opposition to Speaker Straus, who was still considered too "moderate" by some conservative standards. But other casualties included some of the House's most conservative members. Factors in primary races also included the candidates' own campaign abilities, local issues and, in several cases, simple geography. As noted earlier, redistricting had produced some significantly redrawn districts that proved unfriendly to incumbents.

Committee chairs Rob Eissler and Vicki Truitt, each of whom received strong support from Austin-based trade associations, suffered two of the higher profile primary losses. Ultra-conservative groups—such as the Tea Party and Texans for Fiscal Responsibility, which had tried to unseat Speaker Straus at the beginning of the 2011 legislative session—supported Eissler's successful opponent, businessman Steve Toth of The Woodlands. Eissler was attacked over his ties to the speaker and for being too "moderate." His support of standardized testing of public school students, which was becoming very unpopular throughout Texas and which the Tea Party viewed as an unnecessary taxpayer expense, also became an issue. Texans for Fiscal Responsibility and other Tea Party-type groups were also instrumental in Truitt's loss to Giovanni Capriglione in a Tarrant County race. A major issue against Truitt was her previous support of a local option gasoline tax increase to raise money for highway improvements in traffic-clogged North Texas.

Another redistricting victim was Chuck Hopson of Jacksonville, a committee chairman who had represented a conservative, east Texas district for six terms. The first five were as a Democrat before he switched parties to run and win in 2010 as a Republican. In 2012, Hopson was supported by influential business and professional groups, the National Rifle Association, a major anti-abortion group, and Gov. Perry. He had joined other Republicans in voting for deep budget cuts in 2011 and was outspoken in opposition to "Obamacare." But Tea Party followers and other anti-establishment voters weren't comfortable with him, and his opponent, Travis Clardy, used Hopson's former Democratic label against him. The deciding factor, however, was the addition, through redistricting, of Nacogdoches County to the district. Hopson had never represented Nacogdoches County before, and Clardy, an attorney and small business owner, was a prominent resident of Nacogdoches County. Hopson lost a primary runoff by 361 votes out of more than 16,000 votes cast. Hopson easily carried the two counties that he had previously represented. The difference in the three-county district was Nacogdoches County, where Clardy won 83% of the votes.[29]

Democrats Regain Some House Seats Ninety-eight nominees for the 150-member Texas House didn't have major party opponents in November. Redistricting so effectively determined the House's partisan makeup that only 52 races in the general election had both Republican and Democratic candidates. Only a small number of those were actually competitive.[30]

The final result on Election Day would be a net gain of seven Democratic seats, slightly eroding the Republican edge to 95-55. Four Democrats—including former state Rep. Chris Turner of Arlington, who had been unseated only two years earlier—won in open seats, districts that had been so altered by redistricting that the previous Republican incumbent chose not to run for reelection. Three Democratic challengers unseated Republican legislators. And in each case, the winning Democrats—Joe Moody of El Paso, Abel Herrero of Robstown, and Philip Cortez of San Antonio—hammered the GOP incumbents for voting to slash $5.4 billion from public schools and make additional cuts in funding for higher education, health care, and other services. Election Day was particularly sweet for Moody and Herrero. Each had been unseated from the House by Republican challengers during the 2010 GOP surge, and each came back in 2012 to return the favor.

Taking advantage of higher Democratic voter turnout in a presidential election year, Moody unseated Republican Rep. Dee Margo in the third straight election year matchup between the two. Moody said the budget cuts that Margo supported had cost hundreds of El Paso County school teachers their jobs and harmed the University of Texas at El Paso. Two Democratic legislators from El Paso—Reps. Marisa Marquez and Naomi Gonzalez—took the unusual step of supporting Margo in the interest, they said, of maintaining a bipartisan delegation in Austin. But Moody noted that he had worked successfully with Republicans during his previous term in the House.

Running in his former south Texas district, which through redistricting had become more favorable to a Democratic candidate, Herrero unseated one-term Rep. Connie Scott of Robstown. Herrero said Scott's vote for budget cuts had cost about 200 teacher jobs in the legislative district and reduced Medicaid reimbursements to doctors and other health care providers. Scott defended her fiscal conservatism but fell short.

---

[29] http://elections.sos.state.tx.us/elechist.exe.

[30] Ibid.

Education, Budget Cuts as Issues The budget cuts imposed on education and other public services by the Legislature in 2011 clearly had an impact in the handful of swing districts won by Democratic challengers in the general election, as outlined above. The cuts were primarily a partisan issue since all but a small number of Republican legislators in either the House or the Senate had voted for them, and all but a small number of Democratic lawmakers had voted against them.

The cuts, particularly the $5.4 billion slashed from public schools, also may have been a factor in a handful of races in the Republican primary. They probably contributed to the unseating of Rep. Sid Miller of Stephenville, and of Reps. Jim Landtroop of Plainview and Marva Beck of Centerville. All had voted for the spending reductions, and their successful primary opponents were endorsed by public education advocates. Most of the legislators who voted for the cuts, however, were reelected, although education advocacy groups actively supported opponents against many, either in the Republican primary or the general election.

Even if Republican legislators were to refuse during the 2013 session to restore all the funding cut from education, a pending lawsuit brought by several hundred school districts against the state could eventually force the Legislature to increase school funding. The Texas Supreme Court wasn't expected to issue a final decision in that lawsuit until 2014. Speaker Joe Straus, who is among the more moderate Republicans in the House, listed education as well as water development, transportation, and other infrastructure needs among his priorities, and with the state's improved budgetary outlook, some progress was likely to be made in addressing those issues.

CONSERVATIVES INCREASE THEIR PRESENCE IN STATE SENATE

Five new state senators, all Republicans, emerged from the 2012 election cycle, but only one newcomer had unseated an incumbent. A sixth new senator, a Democrat, was elected after the 2013 legislative session was underway to replace a Democratic senator who had died. The Senate's partisan lineup remained unchanged with Republicans holding a 19-12 majority, but the new Republican faces signaled a more conservative body.

Republican Retirements Three veteran Republican senators—Steve Ogden of Bryan, Florence Shapiro of Plano, and Chris Harris of Arlington—chose to leave elected office in 2012, and a fourth—Mike Jackson of La Porte—ran unsuccessfully for Congress. All had been committee chairs. The four departing senators were conservatives, but each was replaced by a Republican House member who generally was considered more conservative.

Veteran Wentworth Unseated by GOP Voters Republican Jeff Wentworth, a 20-year Senate veteran from San Antonio, was unseated in a Republican runoff for District 25 by Donna Campbell, a Tea Party favorite who owed her election not only to conservative, anti-establishment voters but also to Texans for Lawsuit Reform (TLR), one of the state's most successful single-issue business groups. In 2011 Wentworth had voted against the final version of a TLR priority, a bill to reduce the amount of money that homeowners along the coast could recover in lawsuits after hurricanes.

So, when the 2012 election season came along, TLR went gunning for him. TLR's favored candidate in the Republican primary for the central Texas district was Elizabeth Ames Jones, a former member of the Texas Railroad Commission. TLR spent several hundred thousand dollars supporting Jones and unleashed attack ads against Wentworth, but Wentworth led the May 29 primary voting, although without a majority. Campbell, a physician from New Braunfels, finished second, and Jones, despite TLR's efforts, finished third and out of the running. TLR then got behind Campbell, who defeated a crippled Wentworth in a July 31 runoff by a 2-1 margin.[31] Wentworth and the other four senators who left office after 2012 had a combined 92 years of experience in the Senate.

Democrat Wendy Davis Survives Republican Challenge Sen. Wendy Davis of Fort Worth, a strong advocate for education and women's health care, was a rising Democratic star. Some in the party even considered her a potential candidate for statewide office for a party that hasn't won a statewide race since 1994. But first she would have to win reelection from Senate District 10 in Tarrant County, and Republicans in the legislature were working hard to keep that from happening. First, they redrew her district to make it extremely difficult for a Democrat to win. Then, when a federal judge replaced that district with an interim district that gave her a fighting chance, Republicans launched an aggressive campaign against her.

Even with the court-ordered changes, the new District 10 still leaned Republican. Davis' Republican opponent, state Rep. Mark Shelton, a physician, was aggressive. He accused Davis of using her position as a state senator to benefit clients of her private legal practice, a charge Davis denied. Davis campaigned against Shelton's votes to cut state funding for public schools and health care and his participation in Republican attacks on Planned Parenthood, an important health care provider for low-income women. Davis called for expansion of Medicaid to more low-income Texans, and Shelton opposed it. Davis defeated Shelton, 51% to 49%.[32] Her victory preserved—perhaps strengthened—her own political future. And, it kept Republicans from coming within one vote of the two-thirds majority they needed to make Democrats virtually powerless in the Senate.

Electing a Dead Senator Preserves a Democratic Seat State Sen. Mario Gallegos of Houston died in October—before the general election but too late to replace him on the ballot. Democrats urged votes for Gallegos over a Republican opponent in the heavily Democratic District 6, and Gallegos, although deceased, won the election. Gov. Rick Perry called a special election in February to fill his seat. No candidate won a majority, so the top two finishers—former Harris County Commissioner Sylvia Garcia and state Rep. Carol Alvarado, both Democrats—met again in a March 2 runoff. Garcia won the runoff, 53% to 47%, and took office to

---

[31] http://elections.sos.state.tx.us/elechist.exe.

[32] Ibid.

fill the vacant Senate seat about two months after the 2013 legislative session had convened.[33]

REPUBLICANS KEEP GRIP ON STATEWIDE OFFICES

Second Generation Craddick Wins Railroad Commission Seat Christi Craddick, an Austin attorney, political consultant, and daughter of former Texas House Speaker Tom Craddick, won an open seat on the Texas Railroad Commission, and Barry Smitherman, a Houston attorney, was elected to a seat to which he had been appointed by Gov. Rick Perry to fill a mid-term vacancy.

Craddick and Smitherman are both Republicans, and the only real competition either faced during the election cycle was Craddick's race for the Republican nomination against former state Rep. Warren Chisum of Pampa, a former House ally of her father's. This time, though, the former speaker supported his daughter, giving her more than $341,000 for her nomination campaign. Craddick defeated Democrat Dale Henry—a retired petroleum engineer from Lampasas—in the general election, and Smitherman faced no major party opponent.

Historically, the Railroad Commission has had a pro-industry orientation, and there was every reason to anticipate that its policies of supporting oil and gas production would continue. It remained to be seen how the commission would deal with increasing environmental concerns over fracking.

"Ten Commandments Judge" Elected to Texas Supreme Court Republican Justices Nathan Hecht and Don Willett were reelected to the Texas Supreme Court, the state's highest civil appellate court. Hecht defeated Democrat Michele Petty, a lawyer from San Antonio, and Willett had only minor party opposition in the general election. But a third justice on the all-Republican court, David Medina, was derailed in a Republican primary runoff by John Devine, a Tea Party-backed candidate who campaigned for the Ten Commandments and against abortion.

Two Houston attorneys contended that Devine had told them he was running against Medina because he thought he could beat someone with a Hispanic name, although Devine denied the allegation. And even as Medina was losing his runoff race, another Hispanic, Ted Cruz, was winning his runoff race for the U.S. Senate at the top of the Republican ballot.

Ever since Republicans gained a majority on the Texas Supreme Court more than 20 years ago, its decisions have predominantly favored business interests, doctors, and insurance companies over labor, environmental concerns, and consumers, and the 2012 election results are not likely to change that pattern. Unlike the U.S. Supreme Court, which deals with major constitutional issues, much of the Texas Supreme Court's activity involves contractual disputes and civil lawsuits pitting consumers against business, insurance, and medical defendants.

Controversial Criminal Appeals Judge Reelected A few years before her 2012 reelection campaign, Sharon Keller, presiding judge of the Texas Court of Criminal

---

[33] http://elections.sos.state.tx.us/elechist.exe.

Appeals, had sparked a legal and political firestorm by arbitrarily cutting off a condemned inmate's opportunity to file a late, but legitimate plea for a stay of execution only an hour before he was put to death. Even though the inmate's lawyers had notified the court's clerk that an appeal was being prepared, Keller ordered the office closed at 5 p.m.—the end of the normal workday—before the lawyers could file. And, she did so without consulting any other judges on the court. The State Commission on Judicial Conduct investigated and issued a "public warning" against Keller. Although the warning was later overturned, Keller had received enough negative publicity to sink most officeholders seeking reelection.

But Keller wasn't most officeholders. Keller was a Republican in a heavily Republican state. She ran unopposed in the Republican primary, and she defeated a Democratic challenger, Keith Hampton, a well-respected criminal defense lawyer, by 14% in the general election. Two other Court of Criminal Appeals judges, Barbara Parker Hervey and Elsa Alcala, both Republicans, had no Democratic opposition and easily defeated Libertarian challengers.[34]

This court is Texas' court of last resort in criminal cases, and the election results all but guarantee that the court will continue to decide most cases—including death penalty cases—in favor of prosecutors over criminal defendants.

STATE BOARD OF EDUCATION RACES

As noted earlier, Republicans won 10 of the 15 seats on the State Board of Education. But the key question for many board watchers was the size of the remaining bloc of ideological conservatives who in recent years have sought to impose their political and religious views on science and social studies curricula.

The Texas Freedom Network, a progressive organization that has battled social and religious conservatives on the State Board of Education for years, said the conservative bloc had been significantly reduced, perhaps to as few as four members. One member of the bloc, Carlos "Charlie" Garza, a Republican from El Paso, was unseated by Democrat Martha Dominguez of El Paso. Another, Gail Lowe of Lampasas, lost in the Republican primary to Sue Melton, a retired teacher from Waco. And, a third member, Republican Terri Leo of Spring, chose not to seek reelection. But the Texas Freedom Network believed the conservative group may have picked up a replacement in Marty Rowley, a Republican from Amarillo, who was elected to succeed moderate Republican Bob Craig of Lubbock, who didn't seek reelection.

LOCAL PARTISAN RACES

The vast majority of elected officials are elected in non-partisan elections. These positions include members of city councils, school boards, boards of junior colleges, and the governing bodies of special districts, and most of those were not up for election in 2012. County officials in Texas' 254 counties are elected in partisan elections, and several thousand of these officials were on election ballots in 2012.

---

[34] http://elections.sos.state.tx.us/elechist.exe.

One clear indication of party change and realignment in Texas is the number of county offices now controlled by the Republican Party. In 1974, Republicans held 75 offices in Texas, including 53 county offices. As the Republican Party developed and increased its appeal to Texans, it was able to capture an ever-increasing number of these county offices. By 2008, Republicans held 2,385 offices across the state, including 1,862 county offices and some 379 district offices. These totals continued to increase, and after the 2012 elections, Texas Republican Chairman Steve Munisteri announced that 3,191 Republicans now held offices across the state, including a large number of county and district officials.[35]

POST MORTEMS ON THE 2012 STATE ELECTIONS

Although there is still uncertainty over how redistricting lawsuits will affect the final Texas House and state Senate districts for the rest of the decade, the final districts likely will continue to give Republicans significant majorities in both legislative bodies. Few expect a radical departure from recent legislative sessions in terms of social or welfare policies.

Redistricting—not an insurgence led by any organized group—was largely responsible for the legislative turnover in 2012. And, most of that turnover occurred in the Republican primary—both because of geographical changes in districts as well as ideological differences.

Republicans will continue to control the policy agenda in both the House and the Senate, although Democrats may begin to see a restoration of some of their influence in the House, after their success in reducing the Republican super-majority in 2012. The election results probably made the state Senate more conservative. But, thanks to Democratic Sen. Wendy Davis' reelection, Democrats retained their 12-member bloc in the chamber, enough to block or, at least, slow down legislation and be involved in meaningful negotiations with their Republican colleagues.

Republicans maintained their monopoly on statewide offices, and none of the winning candidates for the Railroad Commission or the highest appellate courts is likely to veer from the conservative course. The election hinted at some moderate changes in the ideological orientation of the State Board of Education, but it is not clear how this might play out.

Republicans continued to make gains in county and district offices, indicating that many local GOP candidates benefited from the Republican turnout and straight ticket voting. The impact of Republican gains in local offices is likely to be minimal since most policy decisions are made at the state or national level.

V. LOOKING FORWARD

Comparatively speaking, Texas is one of the most Republican states. Every poll conducted in Texas prior to the election placed it clearly in the Romney column. In the short term, Texas is likely to remain this way.

---

[35] http://www.texasgop.org/posts/306-it-s-official-texas-gop-sets-a-new-record.

The fault line between the two major parties appears to center on race and ethnicity, but one should anticipate—as did the late V.O. Key, a mid-twentieth scholar of American political parties—a tension between race and ethnicity and economics. As the minority populations—primarily Hispanics—continue to grow in Texas and produce a larger share of the electorate, Republicans face the potential of slowly losing their majority. But as minorities move up the economic ladder, they may be attracted to the Republican Party on the basis of their economic interests.

The electoral divide also centers, in part, over ideology and the role of government in providing social and economic services. Polls show drastic differences between the beliefs and attitudes of Republicans and Democrats on many issues, including health care reform, Medicaid, and funding of public education.

For the near future, Republicans will continue to win most, if not all, statewide elections in Texas, as well as a majority of congressional, legislative, and county offices. And, conservative voters will continue to dominate the Republican primary and, hence, the selection of most officeholders and the development of public policy at the state level. But change may be on the way. The question of when that change will arrive will depend on several factors, including rebuilding efforts in the Texas Democratic Party, the political awakening of Hispanics, and whether moderate Republicans will fight for the "soul" of their party.

PROSPECTS FOR THE TEXAS DEMOCRATIC PARTY

Despite the current Republican lock on the state, Texas' growth and demographic changes—particularly the continued growth of the Hispanic population—have attracted the attention of Democrats well beyond Texas' borders. Even before Election Day 2012, there was anticipation of the time that the largest red (Republican) state in the country would become purple (a swing state) on its transformation to blue (Democratic). But, recognizing current political realities, the Obama campaign and national Democratic leaders mostly ignored Texas during the 2012 campaign, except to raise money there to spend in Ohio, Florida, and other competitive states. It was an all-too-familiar pattern to Texas Democrats. They continued to watch from the sidelines as Democratic candidates from other states swooped in to collect campaign cash from a dwindling number of Democratic donors as the Texas Democratic Party continued to founder. After losing every statewide election since 1996 and most legislative and congressional races over the past dozen years, Texas Democrats had seen their own party's morale, organizational infrastructure, and candidate recruitment ability deteriorate and, with them, their ability to regroup.

So, some veteran Texas Democratic operatives were skeptical when in early 2013 a former national field director for the Obama campaign, Jeremy Bird, announced a new Democratic initiative to identify and organize progressive voters in Texas with the goal of turning the Lone Star State purple.

Other state Democratic leaders, however, were excited at what the effort—dubbed Battleground Texas—potentially offered. All agreed, however, that this would require a substantial financial investment from national Democratic donors, and would take time—more than one or two election cycles—to make a significant comeback in one of the country's most conservative states. Another key would be the state's growing number of Hispanics and their future political participation.

The Democratic Party runs the risk of becoming a party of race and ethnicity. During the transition period when the state shifted from a one-party Democratic state to a one-party Republican state, Anglos moved dramatically into the Republican Party. At the same time, there was a tendency on the part of the Democratic Party in many counties to write off the Anglo vote. Many campaigns simply made no effort to target Anglo voters who were potentially aligned with the views and policies of the Democratic Party.

THE LOOMING HISPANIC VOTE

Texas is a majority minority state. Non-Hispanic whites make up only 45% of the population, according to the 2010 census. Hispanics are 38% of the population, African Americans are 12% and the remainder are Asian Americans and other racial or ethnic groups. Except for Asian Americans, Hispanics are the fastest growing group and are projected to become a majority of the state's population by 2040.[36]

Traditionally, Hispanics in Texas have voted heavily Democratic, leading to prolonged anticipation that Hispanic voters will turn the partisan tide and restore Democrats to political control in Texas. But that hasn't happened, at least not yet. Exit polls in other states indicated that President Obama won more than 70% of the Hispanic vote nationally in his 2012 reelection. But, although Texas has the second largest Hispanic population in the country, the state went strongly for Republican nominee Mitt Romney, and Republicans remain firmly in control of state government and the congressional delegation from the Lone Star State.

No statewide exit polls were conducted in Texas, but election results from heavily Hispanic counties in South Texas and along the Mexican border indicate that most Texas Hispanic voters cast their ballots for Obama and Democratic nominee Paul Sadler in the U.S. Senate race won by Hispanic Republican Ted Cruz.

Cruz won a higher percentage of the vote than Romney in those counties—Cameron, El Paso, Hidalgo, Maverick, Starr, Val Verde, Webb and Zapata—but with the exception of Val Verde County where the results were close, Obama and Sadler carried these counties with significant majorities.[37]

Although Hispanics in Texas usually vote for Democrats, they don't vote in proportion to their share of the state's population. Many of them are non-citizens or undocumented immigrants and ineligible to vote. Others are too young. The Hispanic population is disproportionately younger than the Texas population as a whole. Hispanics comprised 37.6% of the state's population in 2010, but the population of voting age was 33.6%. When the non-citizen population is taken into account, Hispanics comprised 26.2% of the citizens who were eligible to vote.[38]

---

[36] Texas State Data Center, http://txsdc.utsa.edu/Data/TPEPP/Projections/Index.aspx.
[37] http://elections.sos.state.tx.us/elechist.exe.
[38] U.S. Census Bureau, http://www.census.gov/2010census/data/.

But the Hispanic population is aging, as well as growing, and this is where the battle for Texas' political future will increasingly be fought. Republicans already have made some inroads and suffered some setbacks. Three Hispanic members of the Texas House are Republicans. Gov. Rick Perry has appointed several Republican Hispanics to vacancies on state courts and the Texas Railroad Commission. Some later have won election—including Texas Supreme Court Justice Eva Guzman and Texas Court of Criminal Appeals Judge Elsa Alcala—while others have lost challenges from Anglo candidates in the Republican primary.

Strong Republican support for voter identification and tough laws cracking down on illegal immigrants have hurt the party's cause with many Hispanics and may have contributed to President Obama's strong showing among Hispanics in the 2012 election. But, despite his strong conservatism and support of the voter ID law, Gov. Perry is among a growing number of Republicans who are trying to increase the party's appeal to Hispanics. As noted above, he has appointed several Hispanics to vacancies in statewide offices and signed a law giving the children of undocumented Hispanic immigrants a break on lower tuition at state universities. Conservative Republicans also believe that many Hispanics share their anti-abortion viewpoint and concerns on other social issues. But Democrats counter that Perry and the Republican majority in the Texas Legislature are alienating most Hispanics with their recent cuts in funding for education, health care, and other public programs important to low- and middle-income Hispanics.

Texas Republicans are encouraged by the 2012 election of Hispanic Ted Cruz—a Tea Party conservative Republican—to the U.S. Senate, despite his loss of most of the Hispanic vote, as well as George P. Bush's announcement that he would run for state land commissioner as a Republican in 2014. Bush is Hispanic—his mother is a native of Mexico—and he has a strong Republican pedigree. His father is former Florida Gov. Jeb Bush. His grandfather is former President George H.W. Bush, and his uncle is former President George W. Bush. The Democrats' list of candidates with the ability to wage an effective statewide campaign is short, but two Hispanics—the twin Castro brothers from San Antonio—have growing star power. San Antonio Mayor Julian Castro was chosen by President Obama to deliver the keynote address at the 2012 Democratic National Convention. And, the same year, voters promoted Joaquin Castro from state representative to a seat in Congress.

WILL MODERATES TRY TO REGAIN CONTROL OF THE TEXAS REPUBLICAN PARTY?

As noted in our introduction, the Texas economy fared much better than the national economy during the Great Recession, and Texas remains a national leader in job creation, a fact that Gov. Rick Perry and other Texas Republican leaders attribute to the state's low-tax, low-regulatory policies. Texas is one of the few states without a state personal income tax, and, during Perry's tenure, state and local governments have given private companies billions of dollars in grants, tax breaks, and other incentives to relocate to or expand in Texas.

But many Texas jobs pay low wages, and Texas ranks near the bottom among the states in funds spent on education, health care, and other social services that are important to low- and middle-income people. But these low rankings are not major issues for the relatively small number of overwhelmingly conservative voters who decide most races in the Republican primary and, consequently, most races in the general election. Many of them are social conservatives who are more concerned about abortion and prayer in schools than they are about the state of the Texas budget. Others, including many in the Tea Party movement, are distrustful of government, suspect waste in every public program, and want to shrink the size of government. This is why the Republican majority in the Texas Legislature was able to cut $5.4 billion from local schools in 2011, while leaving about $6 billion unspent in the state's Rainy Day Fund, without suffering many losses in the 2012 elections

But cuts in state education funding can result in higher local school property taxes, and reductions in health care spending at the state level mean more low-income people can be treated in county hospital emergency rooms, which helps raise local property taxes. A state district judge, in lawsuits brought against the state by several hundred school districts, ruled in early 2013 that the state's funding of public schools was woefully inadequate. The state appealed to the Texas Supreme Court, which may disagree with the ruling. But inadequate school funding may have potentially drastic consequences in the not-too-distant future for the state's economy and for businesses who need well-educated, well-trained employees.

Many roads and highways in metropolitan areas are insufficient, in need of repair, and clogged with traffic. This not only adds to travel times and increased gasoline consumption by commuters, but it also increases transportation costs for businesses. Texas' growth and recent drought have also increased pressure on state government to find ways to pay for a long-range water development and conservation plan.

But will these issues matter enough to moderate Republicans—and even conservatives—so that Republican candidates and officeholders may address some of these needs without fear of voter retribution in their own primary?

AN ALTERNATIVE SCENARIO

The transformation of the Texas political system from Democratic to Republican dominance occurred over many years during the latter part of the 20th century. Scholars refer to this process as "party realignment." The seeds for this change were planted in the 1950s and 1960s. Richard Nixon's presidential victory in 1968 might be considered the tipping point, and there were incremental gains over the next two decades, with Republicans first capturing all statewide offices, then the Texas Senate and Texas House, and then a majority of congressional seats.

Transformation or realignment back to Democratic dominance—or a competitive two-party system—is projected by some observers of Texas politics to occur, but not overnight. Each of the factors discussed previously—growing Hispanic population, ideological differences in the Republican Party, and the Democratic efforts to regroup—will play a role in this transformation.

AMERICAN GOVERNMENT

Listen to Chapter 1 on MyPoliSciLab

1

American Government: Roots, Context, and Culture

In December 1606, three ships—the *Susan Constant*, the *Godspeed*, and the *Discovery*—set sail from Blackwall, England, to America. These ships held 104 men and boys seeking their fortunes, for the New World was reputed to offer tremendous riches. However, this sorry mix lacked the skills necessary to sustain a colony in the harsh terrain and conditions they were to encounter.

The London Company, a joint stock company that was created to attract much-needed capital to aid British colonization of the New World, financed the colonists. Joint stock companies allowed potential investors to purchase shares of stock in companies anticipating large payoffs for their investments several years down the road. Enthusiasm for this new business model led thousands of English citizens to invest in the London Company. The company was issued the first Virginia Charter in April 1606, legally allowing it to settle a region extending from present-day Cape Fear, North Carolina, to the Long Island Sound. The settlers were under the direction of Sir Thomas Smith, reputed to be one of London's wealthiest financiers, lending further credibility to the venture.

Although Smith directed the expedition, he chose to remain in England when the ships set sail

1.1 Trace the origins of American government, p. 5.

1.2 Evaluate the different types of governments countries may employ, p. 7.

1.3 Explain the functions of American government, p. 9.

1.4 Describe American political culture, and identify the basic tenets of American democracy, p. 10.

1.5 Analyze the changing characteristics of the American public, p. 13.

1.6 Assess the role of political ideology in shaping American politics, p. 18.

1.7 Characterize changes in Americans' attitudes toward and expectations of government, p. 21.

THE U.S. POPULATION IS CHANGING Above, an artist's rendition of the first English settlement, Jamestown, in what is today Virginia. Below, Manhattan Island, New York City.

In Context Discuss the importance of American exceptionalism in American political culture. In this video, University of Oklahoma political scientist Allyson Shortle examines the core values that make up American political culture. She also discusses how these values gave rise to the American Dream.

Think Like a Political Scientist Find out how and why research on American politics has shifted. Boston University political scientist Neta C. Crawford discusses how scholars who once focused on voters and institutions are now looking at deliberation as the primary indicator of the health of a democratic system.

In the Real World What is the government s function in everyday life? Real people share their opinions on how involved the federal government should be in education by evaluating the effectiveness of the No Child Left Behind Act, which encourages standardized testing.

So What? What is your government doing for you? Author Karen O'Connor lays out the most pressing issues that America faces today—including student loans and Social Security—and argues that students must understand how the government works in order to be taken care of later on.

for the New World. The colonists settled in a swampy area 30 miles from the mouth of the James River, creating Jamestown, Virginia—the first permanent settlement in America—in 1607. Immediately, dismal conditions prevailed. Insufficient numbers of settlers opted to pursue agricultural ventures, and people began to starve. Settlers died of hunger, Indian attacks, lack of proper supplies, and disease.

One major problem with the settlement was a lack of strong leadership. This situation improved with the election of Captain John Smith as the colony's third president. Smith instituted improvements, forcing all colonists to work and attempting to negotiate food trade with local Indians. These efforts succeeded for a short time, but eventually failed, and the harsh winter of 1609–1610 was deemed "The Starving Time." The conditions reached such dire proportions that a few settlers resorted to cannibalism.

The introduction of tobacco as a cash crop in 1612 improved the economic status of the settlement, but living conditions remained grim. One resident called the area "an unhealthy place, a nest of Rogues, whores, desolute, and rooking persons; a place of intolerable labour, bad usage, and a hard Diet."[1] While eventually life in the settlement improved, it is important to remember the sacrifices of early colonists and the trials other waves of immigrants faced to be part of the American dream.

•••

In this text, we explore the American political system through a historical lens. This perspective allows us to analyze the ways that ideas and actions of a host of different Americans—from Indians, to colonists, to the Framers of the Constitution and beyond—have affected how our **government**—the formal vehicle through which policies are made and affairs of state are conducted—works. Much has changed since the days of the Jamestown Colony, and the people who live in America today differ greatly from those early settlers. The experiences and values of those settlers, however, continue to influence politics. This chapter explores the political process, placing people at its center.

government
The formal vehicle through which policies are made and affairs of state are conducted.

Roots of American Government: We the People

1.1 Trace the origins of American government.

The Preamble to the U.S. Constitution begins with the phrase "We the People." But, who are "the People"? In this section, we explore that question by looking at the earliest inhabitants of the Americas, their initial and ongoing interactions with European colonists, and how Americans continually built on the experiences of the past to create a new future.

The Earliest Inhabitants of the Americas

By the time the first colonists arrived in what is now known as the United States, indigenous peoples had been living in the area for more than 30,000 years. Most historians and archaeologists believe that these peoples migrated from present-day Russia through the Bering Strait into North America and then dispersed throughout the American continents. Some debate continues, however, about where they first appeared and whether they crossed an ice bridge from Siberia or arrived on boats from across the Pacific.

The indigenous peoples were not a homogeneous group; their cultures, customs, and values varied widely, as did their political systems. The number of these indigenous peoples, who lived in all parts of what is now the United States, is impossible to know for certain. Estimates, however, have ranged as high as 100 million people, a number that quickly diminished as colonists brought with them to the New World a range of diseases to which the indigenous peoples had not been exposed. In addition, warfare with the European settlers as well as within tribes not only killed many American

> *We the People of the United States, in Order to form a more perfect Union, establish Justice, insure domestic Tranquility, provide for the common defence, promote the general Welfare, and secure the Blessings of Liberty to ourselves and our Posterity, do ordain and establish this Constitution for the United States of America.* —PREAMBLE

The Preamble to the United States Constitution is little more than a declaration of intent; it carries no legal weight. But, its language has steered the American government, politics, institutions, and people for over 200 years. While the language of the Preamble has not changed since the Constitution was written, its meaning in practice has evolved significantly; this is what we mean by a living constitution. For example, the phrases "We the People" and "ourselves" included a much smaller group of citizens in 1787 than they do today. Voting was largely limited to property-owning white males. Indians, slaves, and women could not vote. Today, through the expansion of the right to vote, the phrase "the People" encompasses men and women of all races, ethnic origins, and social and economic statuses. This has changed the demands that Americans place on government, as well as expectations about the role of government in people's lives.

Many citizens today question how well the U.S. government can deliver on the goals set out in the Preamble. Few Americans classify the union as "perfect," and many feel excluded from "Justice" and the "Blessings of Liberty." Even our leaders do not believe that our domestic situation is particularly tranquil, as evidenced by the continuing debates about the best means to protect America. Still, in appraising how well government functions, it is imperative to look at not only the roots of the political system, but also how it has been reformed over time through amendment, legislation, common usage, and changing social mores.

CRITICAL THINKING QUESTIONS

1. **How do you think the Framers would respond to the broad interpretation of the Preamble's intent embraced by many modern political leaders?**
2. **How have ideas such as promoting "the general Welfare" evolved over time? How has this affected the role and power of American government?**

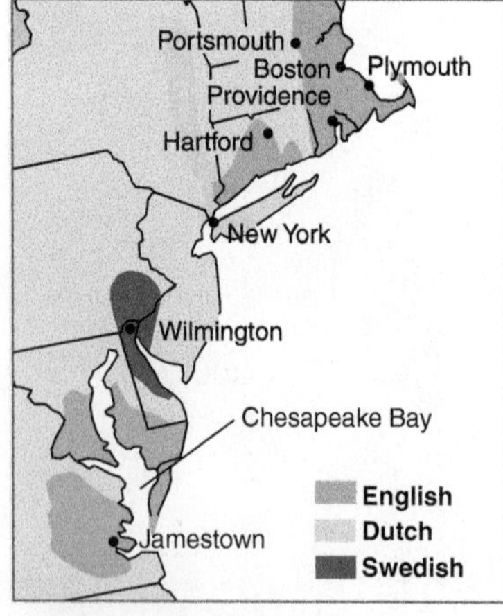

FIGURE 1.1 WHAT DID COLONIAL SETTLEMENT LOOK LIKE BEFORE 1700?

Prior to 1700, pockets of colonial settlement existed along the East Coast of what became the United States, from present-day Virginia to what is now Maine. These settlements were divided among a number of colonial powers, including the English in the Northeast and around the Chesapeake Bay, the Dutch in what is present-day New York, and the Swedes, largely in present-day Delaware.

Indians but also disrupted previously established ways of life. Furthermore, the European settlers displaced Indians, repeatedly pushing them westward as they created settlements and, later, colonies.

☐ The First Colonists

Colonists journeyed to North America for a variety of reasons. Many wealthy Englishmen and other Europeans left home seeking to enhance their fortunes. With them came a host of laborers who hoped to find their own opportunities for riches. In fact, commerce was the most common initial reason for settlement in North America.

In addition to the English commercial settlements in Virginia, in 1609 the Dutch New Netherlands Company settled along the Hudson and lower Delaware Rivers, calling the area New Netherlands. Later, the Dutch West India Company established trading posts on the Hudson River. Both Fort Orange, in what is now Albany, New York, and New Amsterdam, New York City's Manhattan Island, were populated not by colonists but by salaried employees. Among those who flocked to New Amsterdam (renamed New York in 1664) were settlers from Finland, Germany, and Sweden. The varied immigrants also included free blacks. This ethnic and racial mix created its own system of cultural inclusiveness that continues to make New York City and its citizenry unique today (see Figure 1.1).

A RELIGIOUS TRADITION TAKES ROOT In 1620, a group of Protestants known as Puritans left Europe aboard the *Mayflower.* Destined for Virginia, they found themselves off course and landed instead in Plymouth, in what is now Massachusetts. These new settlers differed from those in Virginia and New York, who saw their settlements as commercial ventures. Adhering to Calvinistic beliefs, the Puritans came instead as families bound together by a common belief in the powerful role of religion in their lives. They believed the Old Testament charged them to create "a city on a hill" that would shine as an example of righteousness. To help achieve this goal, they enforced a strict code of authority and obedience, while simultaneously stressing the importance of individualism.

Soon, the ideas at the core of these strict puritanical values faced challenges. In 1631, Roger Williams arrived in Boston, Massachusetts. He preached extreme separation from the Church of England and even questioned the right of Europeans to settle on Indian lands. He believed that the Puritans went too far when they punished settlers who deviated from their strict code of morality, arguing that it was God, not people, who should punish individuals for their moral shortcomings. These "heretical views" prompted local magistrates to banish him from the colony. Williams then helped to establish Providence, a village in present-day Rhode Island that he named for "God's merciful Providence," which he believed had allowed his followers a place to settle.

A later challenge to the Puritans' religious beliefs came from midwife Anne Hutchinson. She began to share her view that the churches established in Massachusetts had lost touch with the Holy Spirit. Many of her followers were women who were attracted to her progressive ideas on the importance of religious tolerance, as well as on the equality and rights of women. Authorities in Massachusetts tried Hutchinson for blasphemy for her views and banished her from the colony. She and her followers eventually settled in Portsmouth, Rhode Island, which became a beacon for those seeking religious toleration and popular—as opposed to religious—sovereignty.

Thomas Hooker, too, soon found himself at odds with the Calvinist Puritans in the Massachusetts Bay Colony. Hooker believed they were too narrow-minded; in his view all men should have the right to vote regardless of religious views or property qualifications. He and his supporters thus relocated to Connecticut, where they developed a settlement at Hartford.

Later colonies in the New World were established with religious tolerance in mind. In 1632, King Charles I granted a well-known English Catholic, George Calvert, the first Lord Baltimore, a charter to establish a Catholic colony in the New World. This area eventually became known as Maryland after Mary, the mother of Jesus.

In 1681, King Charles II bestowed upon William Penn a charter giving him sole ownership of a vast area of land just north of Maryland. The king called the land Pennsylvania, or Penn's Woods. Penn, a Quaker, eventually also purchased the land that is present-day Delaware. In this area, Penn launched what he called "the holy experiment," attracting other persecuted Europeans, including German Mennonites and Lutherans and French Huguenots. The survival of Penn's colony is largely attributable to its ethnic and religious diversity.

monarchy
A form of government in which power is vested in hereditary kings and queens who govern in the interest of all.

totalitarianism
A form of government in which power resides in a leader who rules according to self-interest and without regard for individual rights and liberties.

Types of Government

1.2 Evaluate the different types of governments countries may employ.

Early Greek theorists such as Plato and Aristotle tried to categorize governments by who participates, who governs, and how much authority those who govern enjoy. As Table 1.1 shows, a **monarchy,** the form of government in England from which the colonists fled, is defined by the rule of one hereditary king or queen in the interest of all of his or her subjects. Another form, an aristocracy, is government by the few in the service of the many.

Totalitarianism is a type of government that Aristotle considered rule by "tyranny." Tyrants rule their countries to benefit themselves. This is the case in North Korea under Kim Jong-Un. In tyrannical or totalitarian systems, the leader exercises unlimited power, and individuals have no personal rights or liberties. Generally, the

WHO WAS ANNE HUTCHINSON?

Anne Hutchinson was a midwife and minister who challenged the prevailing thinking of the Massachusetts Bay Colony. She was expelled from the colony and went on to found a new settlement at Portsmouth, Rhode Island.

oligarchy
A form of government in which the right to participate depends on the possession of wealth, social status, military position, or achievement.

democracy
A system of government that gives power to the people, whether directly or through elected representatives.

direct democracy
A system of government in which members of the polity meet to discuss all policy decisions and then agree to abide by majority rule.

TABLE 1.1 HOW DID ARISTOTLE CLASSIFY THE TYPES OF GOVERNMENTS?

	In Whose Interest	
Rule by	**Public**	**Self**
One	Monarchy	Tyranny
The Few	Aristocracy	Oligarchy
The Many	Polity	Democracy

SOURCE: Aristotle, *Politics* 3, 7.

rule of these systems tends to be based on a particular religion or orthodoxy, an ideology, or a personality cult organized around a supreme leader.

An **oligarchy** occurs when a few people rule in their own interest. In an oligarchy, wealth, social status, military position, or achievement dictates participation in government. China and Russia are countries that have governments with oligarchic tendencies.

Aristotle called rule of the many for the benefit of all citizens a "polity" and rule of the many to benefit themselves a "democracy." The term **democracy** derives from the Greek words *demos* ("the people") and *kratia* ("power" or "authority") and may apply to any system of government that gives power to the people, either directly, or indirectly through elected representatives. Most governments worldwide are democracies.

☐ Devising a National Government in the American Colonies

American colonists rejected a system with a strong ruler, such as the British monarchy, when they declared their independence. The colonists also feared replicating the landed and titled system of the British aristocracy. They viewed the formation of a republican form of government as far more in keeping with their values.

The Framers wanted to create a political system with the people at the center of power. Due to the vast size of the new nation, **direct democracy** was unworkable. As

WHAT DOES A MODERN MONARCHY LOOK LIKE?

Here, Queen Elizabeth II of Great Britain celebrates her Diamond Jubilee, or sixty years on the throne of Great Britain. She is followed by her presumptive heir, Prince Charles, and his wife, Camilla, Duchess of Cornwall. Behind them are Charles' sons, Prince William, accompanied by his wife, Catherine, Duchess of Cambridge, and Prince Harry. The British monarch's powers are largely ceremonial.

more and more settlers came to the New World, many town meetings were replaced by a system of **indirect democracy,** in which people vote for representatives who work on their behalf. The ancient Greeks considered representative government undemocratic; they believed that all citizens must have a direct say in their governance. And, in the 1760s, French political philosopher Jean-Jacques Rousseau argued that true democracy is impossible unless all citizens participate in governmental decision making. Nevertheless, most of the colonies operated according to the principles of indirect democracy.

Many citizens were uncomfortable with the term democracy because it conjured up fears of the people and mob rule. Instead, they preferred the term **republic,** which implied a system of government in which the interests of the people were represented by more educated or wealthier citizens who were responsible to those who elected them. Today, representative democracies are more commonly called republics, and the words democracy and republic often are used interchangeably. Yet, in the United States, we still pledge allegiance to our "republic," not our democracy.

indirect democracy
A system of government that gives citizens the opportunity to vote for representatives who work on their behalf.

republic
A government rooted in the consent of the governed; a representative or indirect democracy.

Functions of American Government

1.3 Explain the functions of American government.

In attempting "to form a more perfect Union," the Framers, through the Constitution, set forth several key functions of American government, as well as governmental guarantees to the people, which have continuing relevance today. These principal functions of government and the guarantees they provide to citizens permeate our lives. Whether it is your ability to obtain a low-interest student loan, buy a formerly prescription-only drug such as Claritin or Plan B over the counter, or be licensed to drive a car at a particular age, government plays a major role. And, without government-sponsored research, we would not have cell phones, the Internet, four-wheel-drive vehicles, or even Velcro.

Establishing Justice

One of the first tasks expected of any government is the creation of a system of laws allowing individuals to abide by a common set of principles. Societies adhering to the rule of law allow for the rational dispensing of justice by acknowledged legal authorities. Thus, the Constitution authorized Congress to create a federal judicial system to dispense justice. The Bill of Rights also entitles people to a trial by jury, to be informed of the charges against them, and to be tried in a courtroom presided over by an impartial judge.

Ensuring Domestic Tranquility

As we discuss throughout this text, the role of governments in ensuring domestic tranquility is a subject of much debate and has been since the period of the 1600s and 1700s known as the Enlightenment. In crises, such as the terrorist attacks of September 11, 2001, the federal government, as well as state and local governments, can take extraordinary measures to contain the threat of terrorism from abroad as well as within the United States. The creation of the Department of Homeland Security and the passage of legislation giving the national government nearly unprecedented ability to ferret out potential threats show the degree to which the government takes seriously its charge to preserve domestic tranquility. On a more practical front, local governments have police forces, states have national guards, and the federal government has both the armed services and the ability to call up state militias to quell any threats to order.

political culture
Commonly shared attitudes, beliefs, and core values about how government should operate.

personal liberty
A key characteristic of U.S. democracy. Initially meaning freedom *from* governmental interference, today it includes demands for freedom *to* engage in a variety of practices without governmental interference or discrimination.

1.1 1.2 1.3 1.4 1.5 1.6 1.7

☐ Providing for the Common Defense

The Framers recognized that a major purpose of government is to provide defense for its citizens against threats of foreign aggression. In fact, in the early years of the republic, many believed that the major function of government was to protect the nation from foreign threats, such as the British invasion of the United States in the War of 1812 and the continued problem of piracy on the high seas. Thus, the Constitution calls for the president to be commander in chief of the armed forces, and Congress has the authority to raise an army. The defense budget continues to be a considerable and often controversial proportion of all federal outlays.

☐ Promoting the General Welfare

When the Framers added "promoting the general Welfare" to their list of key governmental functions, they never envisioned how governmental involvement at all levels would expand so tremendously. In fact, promoting the general welfare was more of an ideal than a mandate for the new national government. Over time, though, our notions of what governments should do have expanded along with governmental size. As we discuss throughout this text, however, universal agreement on the scope of what governments should do is absent. For example, part of the debate over health care reform in 2010 centered on whether health care should be a fundamental right guaranteed by the federal government.

☐ Securing the Blessings of Liberty

Americans enjoy a wide range of liberties and opportunities to prosper. They are able to criticize the government and to petition it when they disagree with its policies or have a grievance. This freedom to criticize and to petition is perhaps the best way to "secure the Blessings of Liberty." Though they are on opposite sides of the political spectrum, the Tea Party and Occupy movements both demonstrate citizens' right to protest actions of the government.

American Political Culture and the Basic Tenets of American Democracy

1.4 Describe American political culture, and identify the basic tenets of American democracy.

We can define **political culture** as commonly shared attitudes, beliefs, and core values about how government should operate. American political culture emphasizes the values of liberty and equality; popular consent, majority rule, and popular sovereignty; individualism; and religious faith and freedom.

☐ Liberty and Equality

Liberty and equality are the most important characteristics of the American republican form of government. The Framers wrote the Constitution itself to ensure life and liberty. Over the years, however, our concepts of **personal liberty** have changed and evolved from freedom *from* to freedom *to*. The Framers intended Americans to be free from governmental infringements on freedom of religion and speech, from unreasonable searches and seizures, and so on. The addition of the Fourteenth Amendment to the Constitution and its emphasis on due process and on equal protection of the laws, as well as the subsequent passage of laws guaranteeing civil rights and liberties, however, expanded Americans' concept of liberty to include demands for freedom to work or go to school free from

Explore on MyPoliSciLab

How Do You Measure Freedom?

Two indicators are used to measure freedom in any given country: the right to free speech and the right to privacy. History has shown us that defense of these rights becomes even more important in the face of a foreign threat. Examine the data below, which shows how committed Americans are to these two ideals of freedom.

Free Speech Strengthens in the United States

Between 1980 and 2010, more Americans support free speech for more groups. The exceptions are racists and radical Muslims.

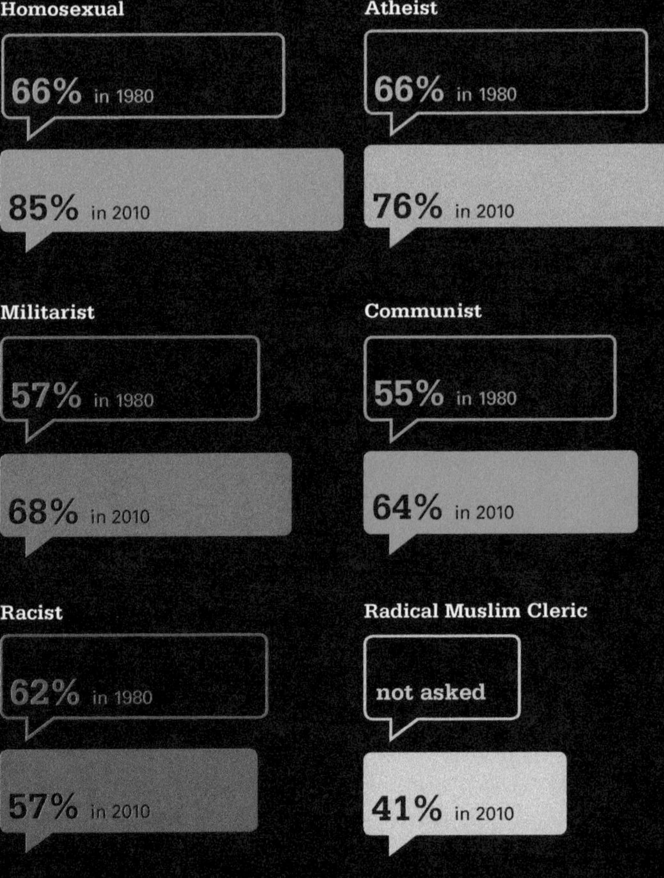

SOURCE: Data from General Social Survey, 1980, 2006, and 2010

Right to Privacy Weakens in the United States

If the government suspects that a terrorist act is about to happen, do you think the authorities should have the right to ...

Investigate Further

Concept How does support for free speech and individual privacy measure freedom? Protecting free speech ensures that all ideas can be expressed and debated, even if they are unpopular. Likewise, protecting the privacy rights of everyone, even those who appear to be threatening, ensures equal treatment for all.

Connection How has Americans' support for free speech changed between 1980 and 2010? Overall, Americans are more tolerant of speech from "controversial" groups. More Americans support free speech for people who were previously marginalized, particularly atheists and homosexuals. Fewer Americans are willing to tolerate racist speech.

Cause How did the threat of terrorism change freedom in America? Most Americans will still not tolerate random searches. But after 9/11, Americans don't support speech by radical Muslim clerics and they are willing to detain potential terrorists indefinitely and wiretap suspects' phones.

political equality
The principle that all citizens are the same in the eyes of the law.

popular consent
The principle that governments must draw their powers from the consent of the governed.

majority rule
The central premise of direct democracy in which only policies that collectively garner the support of a majority of voters will be made into law.

popular sovereignty
The notion that the ultimate authority in society rests with the people.

natural law
A doctrine that society should be governed by certain ethical principles that are part of nature and, as such, can be understood by reason.

discrimination. Debates over how much the government should do to guarantee these rights and liberties illustrate the ongoing conflicts in our democratic system.

Another key feature of our democracy is **political equality,** the principle that all citizens are the same in the eyes of the law. Notions of political equality have changed dramatically from the founding era. The U.S. Constitution once regarded a slave as equal to only three-fifths of a white person for purposes of assessing state population. No one then could have imagined that in 2008 and 2012, Barack Obama would be elected president. In both elections, President Obama even won Virginia, which is home to Richmond, the former capital of the Confederate States of America.

☐ Popular Consent, Majority Rule, and Popular Sovereignty

Popular consent, the principle that governments must draw their powers from the consent of the governed, is another distinguishing trait of American democracy. Derived from English political philosopher John Locke's social contract theory, the notion of popular consent was central to the Declaration of Independence. Today, a citizen's willingness to vote represents his or her consent to be governed and is thus an essential premise of democracy. Large numbers of nonvoters can threaten the operation and legitimacy of a truly democratic system.

Majority rule, another core political value, means that election of officials and transformation of policies into law will take place only if the majority (normally 50 percent of the total votes cast plus one) of citizens in any political unit support such changes. This principle holds for both voters and their elected representatives. Yet, the American system also stresses preservation of minority rights, as evidenced by myriad protections of individual rights and liberties found in the Bill of Rights.

Popular sovereignty, or the notion that the ultimate authority in society rests with the people, has its basis in **natural law,** a doctrine that certain ethical principles are part of nature and, as such, can be understood by reason. Ultimately, political authority rests with the people, who can create, abolish, or alter their governments. The idea that all governments derive their power from the people is found in the Declaration of Independence and the U.S. Constitution, but the term popular sovereignty did not come into wide use until pre–Civil War debates over slavery. At that time, supporters of popular sovereignty argued that citizens of new states seeking admission to the union should be able to decide whether or not their states would allow slavery within their borders.

☐ Individualism

Although many core political tenets focus on protecting the rights of all people, American democracy places heavy importance on the individual, an idea that may be traced back to the Puritans. This emphasis on individualism makes Americans quite different from citizens of other democracies such as Canada, which practices a group approach to governance. Group-focused societies reject the American emphasis on individuals and try to improve the lives of their citizens by making services and rights available on a group or universal basis. In contrast, in the U.S. system, all individuals are deemed rational and fair and endowed, as proclaimed in the Declaration of Independence, "with certain unalienable rights."

☐ Religious Faith and Religious Freedom

Religious conflicts in Europe brought many settlers to the New World. Seeking an opportunity to practice their religious faith, men, women, and their families initially settled large sections of the East Coast. However, that faith did not always imply religious tolerance. The clashes that occurred within settlements, as well as colonies, led the Framers to agree universally that notions of religious freedom must form the foundation of the new nation. Religious tolerance, however, has often proved to be more of

WHY IS RELIGIOUS FREEDOM A TENET OF AMERICAN DEMOCRACY?

Many of the first settlers came to the United States to escape religious persecution. While most of these people were Protestants, Catholicism has had a strong tradition in the United States, especially in the Northeast and Mid-Atlantic. Here, American Catholics greet Pope Benedict XVI during his visit to the United States.

an ideal than a reality. For example, as the nation waged war in Iraq and Afghanistan and attempted to export democracy, large numbers of Americans considered Islam "a religion that encourages violence" and did not view Islam as having much in common with their own religion.[2]

The Changing American Public

1.5 Analyze the changing characteristics of the American public.

One year after ratification of the U.S. Constitution, fewer than 4 million people lived in the thirteen states. Most of those people shared a single language and a Protestant-Christian heritage, and those who voted were white male property owners. The Constitution mandated that the number of members of the House of Representatives should not exceed one for every 30,000 people and set the size of the first House at sixty-five members

 **Explore** on **MyPoliSciLab** **Simulation:** You Are a City Council Member

As the nation grew westward, hundreds of thousands of new immigrants came to America, often in waves, fleeing war or famine or simply in search of a better life. Although the geographic size of the United States has remained stable since the addition of Alaska and Hawaii as states in 1959, in 2013 more than 314 million Americans populated the country. As a result of this population growth, most citizens today feel far removed from the national government and their elected representatives (see Figure 1.2).

Racial and Ethnic Composition

The American population has changed constantly by the arrival of immigrants from various regions—Western Europeans fleeing religious persecution in the 1600s to early 1700s; slaves brought in chains from Africa in the late 1700s; Chinese laborers arriving to work on the railroads following the Gold Rush in 1848; Irish Catholics escaping the

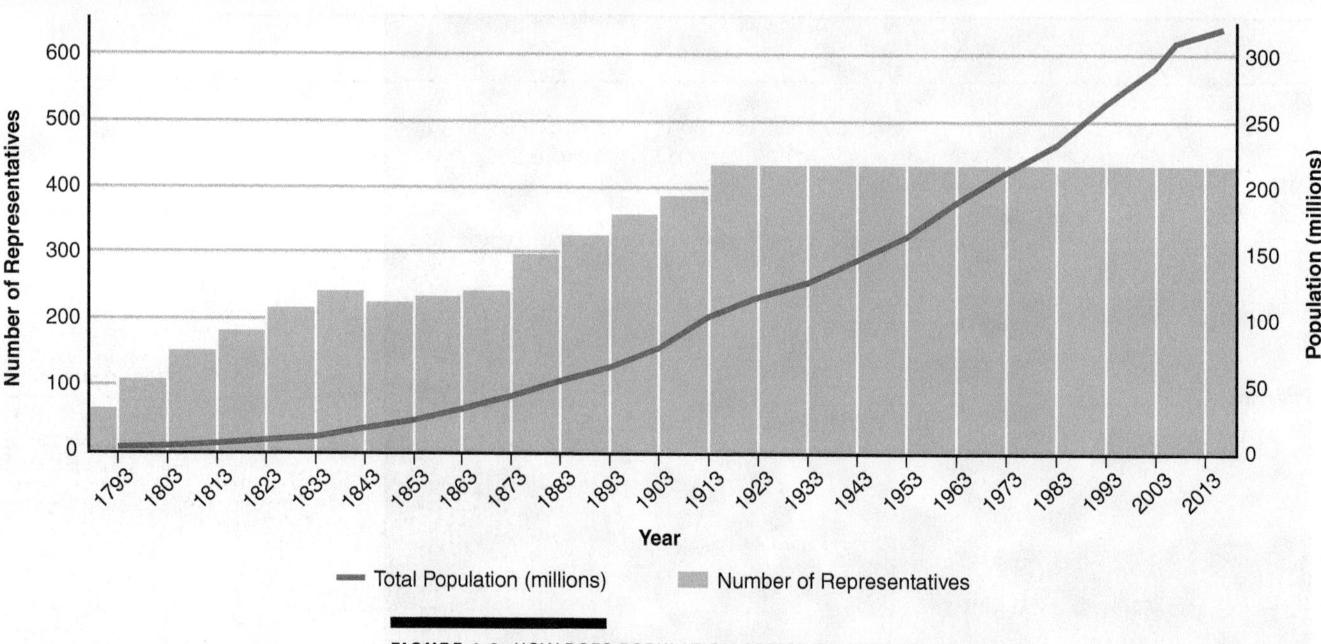

FIGURE 1.2 HOW DOES POPULATION AFFECT REPRESENTATION?

The population of the United States has grown dramatically since the nation's founding. Larger geographic area, immigration, and living longer have contributed to this trend. The size of the House of Representatives, however, has not kept pace with this expansion.

SOURCE: U.S. Census Bureau Population Projections, www.census.gov.

potato famine in the 1850s; Northern and Eastern Europeans from the 1880s to 1910s; and, most recently, South and Southeast Asians, Cubans, and Mexicans, among others.

Immigration to the United States peaked in the first decade of the 1900s, when nearly 9 million people, many from Eastern Europe, entered the country. The United States did not see another major wave of immigration until the late 1980s, when nearly 2 million immigrants were admitted in one year. Today, nearly 40 million people in the United States can be classified as immigrants, and most of them are Hispanic.* Unlike other groups that have come before, many Hispanics have resisted American cultural assimilation. Language appears to be a particularly difficult and sometimes controversial policy issue. In some sections of the country, Spanish-speaking citizens have necessitated changes in the way governments do business. Many government agencies print official documents in both English and Spanish. This action has raised a debate over whether all Americans should speak English or if the nation should move toward a more bilingual society such as Canada, where English and French are the official languages.

Immigration has led to significant alterations in American racial and ethnic composition. The balance in America has changed dramatically over the past fifty years, with the proportion of Hispanics overtaking African Americans as the second most common racial or ethnic group. The Asian American population, moreover, is now the fastest growing minority group in the United States. This means that the majority of babies born in the United States are now members of a minority group, a fact that will have a significant impact not only on the demographics of the American polity but also on how America "looks." In a generation, minorities may be the majority in America, as they are in nine states in 2013.

☐ Aging

Just as the racial and ethnic composition of the American population is shifting, so, too, is the average age. "For decades, the U.S. was described as a nation of the young because

*In this text, we have made the decision to refer to those of Spanish, Latin American, Mexican, Cuban, and Puerto Rican descent as Hispanic instead of Latino/a. Although this label is not accepted universally by the community it describes, Hispanic is the term used by the U.S. government when reporting federal data. In addition, a 2008 survey sponsored by the Pew Charitable Trusts found that 36 percent of those who responded preferred the term Hispanic, 21 percent preferred the term Latino, and the remainder had no preference. See www.pewhispanic.org.

Explore Your World

Immigration is a contentious issue in many countries around the world. States struggle to create immigration policies that balance having an open door with protecting their security and political culture. Many states screen their immigrants before allowing them to enter the country, placing them in detention facilities such as those seen below and requiring them to undergo mandatory health and background checks.

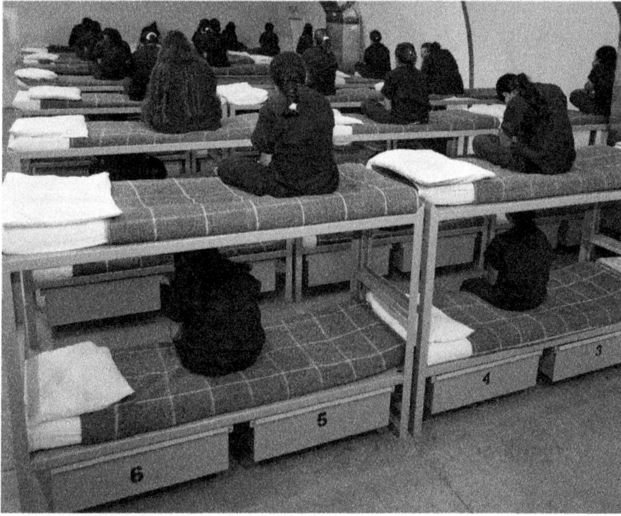

Female detainees are held in the Willacy Detention Center in Raymondville, Texas, United States. The facility, which was constructed in 2006 by the Department of Homeland Security, can house up to 2,000 suspected illegal immigrants in ten giant tents.

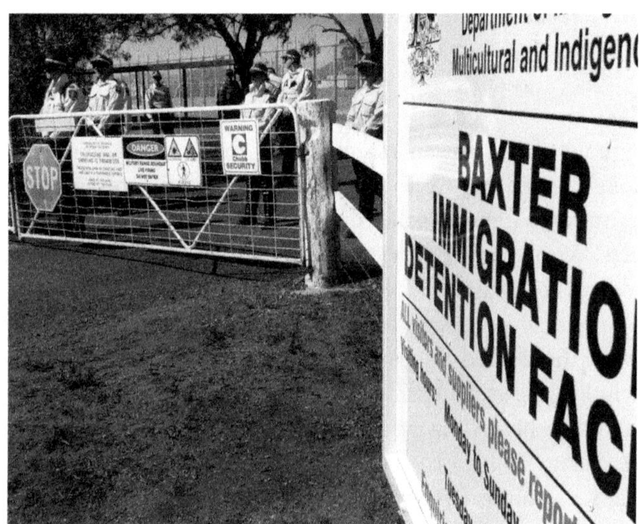

Multiple fences and guards limit exit and entry at the Baxter Detention Facility in Port Augusta, Australia. Note, especially, the height of the second fence and the barren terrain.

Migrants seeking refuge in Europe are held at this detention center on the island of Lampedusa, located in the Mediterranean Sea between Tunisia and Italy. The center can only be used during the winter months, as warmer weather and calm waters encourages many detainees to attempt to escape and make the trip to the nearby island of Sicily.

CRITICAL THINKING QUESTIONS

1. What role does national identity play in the creation of these policies? Do countries have an interest in screening immigrants before they are allowed to enter or remain in a country?
2. How do policies around the world compare to the immigration and detention policies used in the United States, both historically and in modern times?
3. Are the screening and detention practices depicted here acceptable in the name of national security? Do they violate basic human rights?

the number of persons under the age of twenty greatly outnumber[ed] those sixty-five and older," but this is no longer the case.[3] Because of changes in patterns of fertility, life expectancy, and immigration, the nation's age profile has altered drastically. At the founding of the United States, the average life expectancy was thirty-five years; by 2010, it was more than seventy-eight years.

An aging population places a host of costly demands on the government. In 2008, the first of the Baby Boomers (the 76.8 million people who were born between 1946 and 1964) reached age sixty-two and qualified for Social Security benefits; in 2011, they reached sixty-five and qualified for Medicare.[4] An aging America also imposes a great financial burden on working Americans, whose proportion in the population is rapidly declining.

These dramatic changes could potentially pit younger people against older people and result in dramatic cuts in benefits to the elderly and increased taxes for younger workers. Moreover, the elderly often vote against programs favored by younger voters, such as money for new schools and other expenditures they no longer view as significant. At the same time, younger voters are less likely to support issues important to seniors, such as Medicare, Social Security, and prescription drug reform.

☐ Religious Beliefs

As we have discussed throughout this chapter, many of the first settlers came to America to pursue their religious beliefs free from governmental intervention. Although these early immigrants were members of a number of different churches, all identified with Christian sects. Moreover, they viewed the Indians' belief systems, which included multiple gods, to be savage and unholy. Their Christian values still permeate American social and political systems.

While many people still view the United States as a Christian nation, a great number of religious groups—including Jews, Buddhists, Hindus, and Muslims—have established roots in the country. With this growth have come different political and social demands. For example, evangelical Christians regularly request school boards adopt textbooks with particular viewpoints. Likewise, American Jews continually work to ensure that America's policies in the Middle East favor Israel, while Muslims demand more support for a Palestinian state.

☐ Regional Growth and Expansion

Regional sectionalism emerged almost immediately in the United States. Settlers from the Virginia colony southward largely focused on commerce. Those seeking various forms of religious freedom populated many of the settlements to the North. That search for religious freedom also came with puritanical values, so that New England evolved differently from the South in many aspects of culture.

Sectional differences continued to emerge as the United States developed into a major industrial nation and waves of immigrants with various religious traditions and customs entered the country, often settling in areas where other immigrants from their homeland already lived. For example, thousands of Scandinavians flocked to Minnesota, and many Irish settled in the urban centers of the Northeast, as did many Italians and Jews. All brought with them unique views about numerous issues and varying demands on government, as well as different ideas about the role of government. Subsequent generations have often handed down these political views, and many regional differences continue to affect public opinion today.

One of the most long-standing and dramatic regional differences in the United States is that between the South and the North. During the Constitutional Convention, most Southerners staunchly advocated a weak national government. The Civil War was later fought in part because of basic philosophical differences about government as well as slavery, which many Northerners opposed. As we know from modern political polling, the South continues to lag behind the rest of the nation in supporting civil rights, while still favoring return of power to the states and downsizing the national government.

The West, too, has always appeared unique compared with the rest of the United States. Populated first by those seeking free land and then by many chasing dreams of gold, the American West has often been characterized as "wild." Its population today is a study in contrasts. Some people have moved there to avoid city life and have an anti-government bias. Other Westerners are interested in water rights and seek governmental solutions to their problems.

Significant differences in attitude also arise in rural versus urban areas. Those in rural areas are much more conservative than those in large cities.[5] One need only look at a map of the vote distribution in the 2012 presidential election to see stark differences in candidate appeal. Barack Obama carried almost every large city in America; Mitt Romney carried 60 percent of the rural voters as well as most of America's heartland.[6] Republicans won the South, the West, and much of the Midwest; Democrats carried the Northeast and West Coast.

☐ Family and Family Size

In the past, familial gender roles were clearly defined. Women did housework and men worked in the fields. Large families were imperative; children were a source of cheap farm labor. Industrialization and knowledge of birth control methods, however, began to put a dent in the size of American families by the early 1900s. No longer needing children to work for survival of the household, couples began to limit family size.

In 1949, 49 percent of those polled thought that four or more children constituted the "ideal" family size; by 2011, 58 percent responded that no children to two children was "best." and only 33 percent preferred to have more than three children.[7] In 1940, nine of ten households were traditional family households. By 2010, just 69 percent of children under eighteen lived with both parents. In fact, over 25 percent of children under eighteen lived with just one of their parents; the majority of those lived with their mother. Moreover, more than 31 percent of all households consisted of a single person, a trend that reflects, in part, the aging American population and declining marriage rate.[8]

Even the institution of marriage has undergone tremendous change. In 2012, nine states plus the District of Columbia allowed same sex couples to marry. In 2010, the

WHAT DOES THE TYPICAL AMERICAN FAMILY LOOK LIKE?

As the demographics of American society change over time, the composition of American families has become increasingly heterogeneous. Here, the characters in the sitcom *Modern Family* exemplify the age, ethnic, and sexual diversity in families today, making the "typical American family" difficult to describe.

political ideology
The coherent set of values and beliefs about the purpose and scope of government held by groups and individuals.

District of Columbia issued more licenses for same-sex marriages than marriages between a man and a woman.

These changes in composition of households, lower birthrates, marriage, and the prevalence of single-parent families affect the kinds of demands people place on government. Single-parent families, for example, may be more likely to support government-subsidized day care or after-school programs.

Political Ideology

1.6 Assess the role of political ideology in shaping American politics.

On September 11, 2001, nineteen terrorists, all of Middle Eastern origin and professing to be devout Muslims engaged in a "holy war" against the United States, hijacked four airplanes and eventually killed over 3,000 people. The terrorists' self-described holy war, or *jihad,* targeted Americans, whom they considered infidels. Earlier, in 1995, a powerful bomb exploded outside the Murrah Federal Building in Oklahoma City, killing nearly 170 people, including many children. This terrorist attack was launched not by those associated with radical Islam but by those with an American anti-government brand of neo-Nazism. Its proponents hold the U.S. government in contempt and profess a hatred of Jews and others they believe are "inferior" ethnic groups and races.

These are but two extreme examples of the powerful role of **political ideology**—the coherent set of values and beliefs people hold about the purpose and scope of government—in the actions of individuals.[9] Ideologies are sets or systems of beliefs that shape the thinking of individuals and how they view the world, especially in regard to issues of "race, nationality, the role and function of government, the relations between men and women, human responsibility for the natural environment, and many other matters."[10] Observers increasingly have recognized these beliefs as a potent political force. Isaiah Berlin, a noted historian and philosopher, stated that two factors above all others shaped human history in the twentieth century: "one is science and technology; the other is ideological battles—totalitarian tyrannies of both right and left and the explosions of nationalism, racism, and religious bigotry that the most perceptive social thinkers of the nineteenth century failed to predict."[11]

It is easier to understand how ideas turn into action when we examine the four functions political scientists attribute to ideologies. These include:

1. *Explanation.* Ideologies can offer reasons why social and political conditions are the way they are, especially in time of crisis. Knowing that Kim Jong-Un rules North Korea as a totalitarian society helps explain, at least in part, why other countries remain concerned by his continued threats to use nuclear force.
2. *Evaluation.* Ideologies can provide standards for evaluating social conditions and political institutions and events. Americans' belief in the importance of individual ability and personal responsibility helps explain the opposition of some people to the Obama administration's health care reforms.
3. *Orientation.* Much like a compass, ideologies provide individuals with an orientation toward issues and a position within the world. When many African American women, Oprah Winfrey among them, decided to campaign for Barack Obama and not Hillary Rodham Clinton in the 2008 Democratic presidential primary, their identity as African Americans may have trumped their identity as women.
4. *Political Program.* Ideologies help people make political choices and guide their political actions. Thus, since the Republican Party is identified with a steadfast opposition to abortion, anyone with strong pro-life views would find the party's stance on this issue a helpful guide in voting.

Finding Your Political Ideology

The four functions of ideology discussed above clearly have real-world implications. Religious, philosophical, and cultural beliefs can become cohesive ideologies that create natural groups within society and lead to political conflict. In America, we often hear about conservative, liberal, and moderate political ideologies (see Figure 1.3).

CONSERVATIVES According to William Safire's *New Political Dictionary*, a **conservative** "is a defender of the status quo who, when change becomes necessary in tested institutions or practices, prefers that it come slowly, and in moderation."[12] Conservatives tend to believe that limited government is best, especially in terms of regulating the economy. Conservatives favor local and state action over federal intervention, and they emphasize fiscal responsibility, most notably in the form of balanced budgets. Conservatives are also likely to believe that the private sector is better equipped than the government to address domestic problems such as homelessness, poverty, and discrimination.

Since the 1970s, a growing number of **social conservative** voters (many with religious ties to the evangelical or Religious Right) increasingly have affected politics and policies in the United States. Social conservatives believe that moral decay must be stemmed and that government should support and further traditional moral teachings. These voters favor government intervention to regulate sexual and social behavior and have mounted effective efforts to restrict contraceptives, abortion, and same-sex marriage. While a majority of social conservatives are evangelical Protestants, Mormons, and Roman Catholics, some Jews and many Muslims are also social conservatives. Others are not affiliated with a traditional religion.

LIBERALS A **liberal** is one who seeks to use the government to change the political, economic, and social status quo and foster the development of equality and the well-being of individuals.[13] The meaning of the word "liberal" has changed over time, but in the modern United States, liberals generally value equality over other aspects of shared political culture. They support well-funded government social welfare programs that seek to protect individuals from economic disadvantages or to correct past injustices, and they generally oppose government efforts to regulate private behavior or infringe on civil rights and liberties.

conservative
One who favors limited government intervention, particularly in economic affairs.

social conservative
One who believes that the government should support and further traditional moral teachings.

liberal
One who favors greater government intervention, particularly in economic affairs and in the provision of social services.

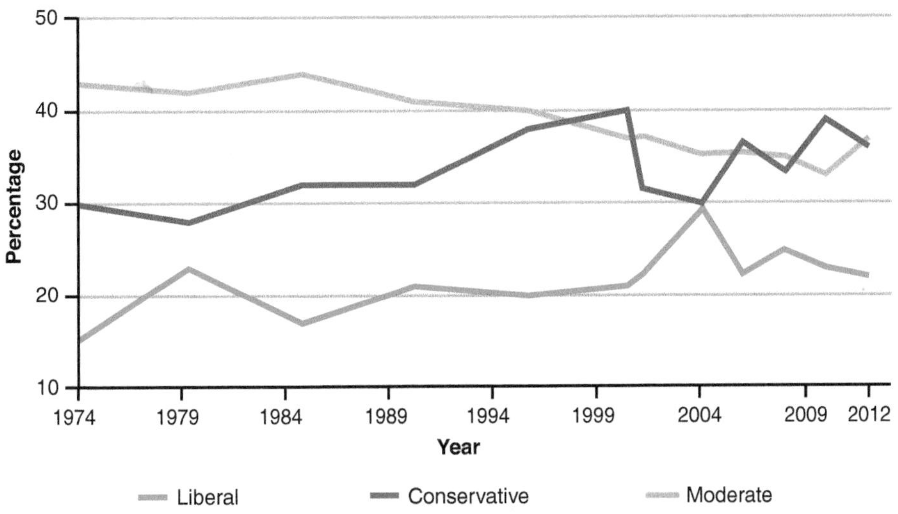

FIGURE 1.3 WHAT ARE AMERICANS' POLITICAL IDEOLOGIES?

Americans' political ideologies have shifted dramatically over time. What was once a largely moderate nation has today become much more closely divided between liberals, conservatives, and moderates. These divisions can make governing particularly challenging and lead to gridlock in our political institutions.

SOURCE: Roper Center for Public Opinion Research and Pew Research Center 2012 Values Survey.

Take a Closer Look

The Nolan Chart, created by Libertarian Party leader David Nolan, is a political ideology chart that helps to classify citizens' political beliefs on two key dimensions—economic and personal freedom. Out of the intersection of citizens' views toward government intervention in each of these areas, Nolan identified five key political ideologies: liberal, moderate, conservative, libertarian, and statist.

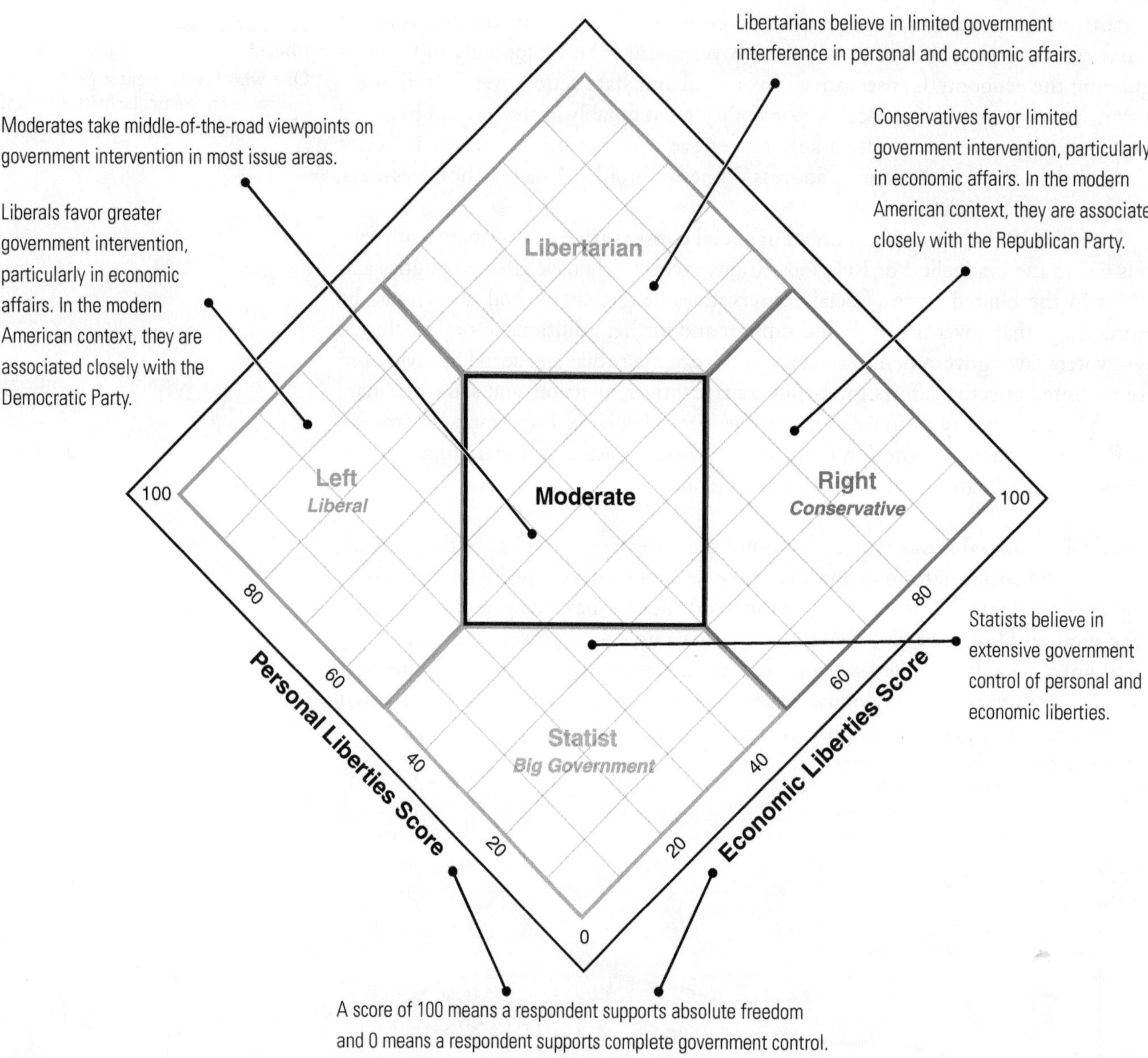

Libertarians believe in limited government interference in personal and economic affairs.
Moderates take middle-of-the-road viewpoints on government intervention in most issue areas.
Conservatives favor limited government intervention, particularly in economic affairs. In the modern American context, they are associated closely with the Republican Party.
Liberals favor greater government intervention, particularly in economic affairs. In the modern American context, they are associated closely with the Democratic Party.
Libertarian
Left
Liberal
Moderate
Right
Conservative
Statist
Big Government
100
80
60
40
20
0
Personal Liberties Score
Economic Liberties Score
Statists believe in extensive government control of personal and economic liberties.
A score of 100 means a respondent supports absolute freedom and 0 means a respondent supports complete government control.

SOURCE: Advocates for Self Government.

CRITICAL THINKING QUESTIONS

1. How does reducing political ideology to two dimensions—economic and personal freedom—help to simplify our understandings of politics? What information does it leave out?
2. What famous (or notorious) political leaders can you think of to exemplify each of these political ideologies?
3. What is your political ideology? Take an online ideology quiz such as the "World's Smallest Political Quiz" to determine where you stand.

MODERATES In general, a **moderate** takes a relatively centrist view on most political issues. Aristotle actually favored moderate politics, believing that domination in the center was better than any extremes, whether dealing with issues of wealth, poverty, or the role of government. Approximately 35 percent of the population today consider themselves political moderates.

moderate
A person who takes a relatively centrist or middle-of-the-road view on most political issues.

statist
One who believes in extensive government control of personal and economic liberties.

libertarian
One who believes in limited government interference in personal and economic liberties.

politics
The study of who gets what, when, and how—or how policy decisions are made.

American dream
An American ideal of a happy, successful life, which often includes wealth, a house, a better life for one's children, and, for some, the opportunity to grow up to be president.

Problems with Ideological Labels

In a perfect world, liberals would be liberal and conservatives would be conservative. Studies reveal, however, that many people who call themselves conservative actually take fairly liberal positions on many policy issues. In fact, anywhere from 20 percent to 60 percent of people will hold a traditionally conservative view on one issue and a traditionally liberal view on another.[14] People who take conservative stances against "big government," for example, often support increases in spending for the elderly, education, or health care. It is also not unusual to encounter a person who could be considered a liberal on social issues such as abortion and civil rights but a conservative on economic or pocketbook issues.

Some critics also charge that a simple left-to-right continuum cannot capture the full complexity of most citizens' political ideologies. They suggest that the ideologies of most are better represented by a spectrum measuring individuals' viewpoints on government interference in both economic and personal liberties. This spectrum includes not only liberal, conservative, and moderate ideologies but also other perspectives such as **statist** (pro-governmental interference) and **libertarian** (anti-governmental interference).

Toward Reform: People and Politics

1.7 Characterize changes in Americans' attitudes toward and expectations of government.

As the American population has changed over time, so has the American political process. **Politics** is the study of who gets what, when, and how—the process by which policy decisions are made. The evolving nature of the American citizenry deeply affects this process. Competing demands often lead to political struggles, which create winners and losers within the system. A loser today, however, may be a winner tomorrow in the ever-changing world of politics. The political ideologies of those in control of Congress, the executive and state houses also have a huge impact on who gets what, when, and how.

Nevertheless, American political culture continues to bind citizens together. Many Americans also share the common goal of achieving the **American dream**—an American ideal of a happy and successful life, which often includes wealth, a house, a better life for one's children, and, for some, the opportunity to grow up to be president. A 2011 poll revealed that 60 percent of Americans believe they are working towards the American dream, despite weak economic conditions.[15]

Redefining Our Expectations

In roughly the first 150 years of our nation's history, the federal government had few responsibilities, and citizens had few expectations of it beyond national defense, printing money, and collecting tariffs and taxes. The state governments were generally far more powerful than the federal government in matters affecting the everyday lives of Americans.

As the nation and its economy grew in size and complexity, the federal government took on more responsibilities, such as regulating some businesses, providing

Is the American Dream a Reality?

The American Dream has long been the aspirational goal of many American people. Traditionally, this dream included visions of home ownership and a life better than that of previous generations. Examine the visual below to consider how understandings of the American Dream are changing in our modern world.

THE AMERICAN DREAM IS MORE IMPORTANT TO YOUNGER GENERATIONS

How important is it to you to achieve the American Dream in your lifetime?

15%
35%
36%
14%
3%
17%
47%
33%
2%
12%
44%
42%
1%
10%
34%
55%
Not at all important
Not very important
Somewhat important
Very important
SILENT GENERATION
BABY BOOMERS
GENERATION X
GENERATION Y

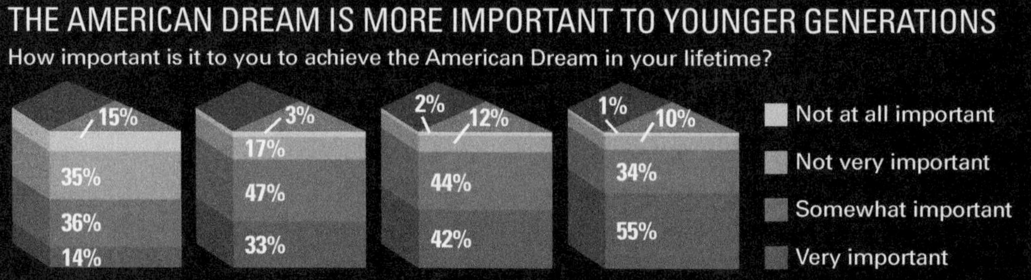

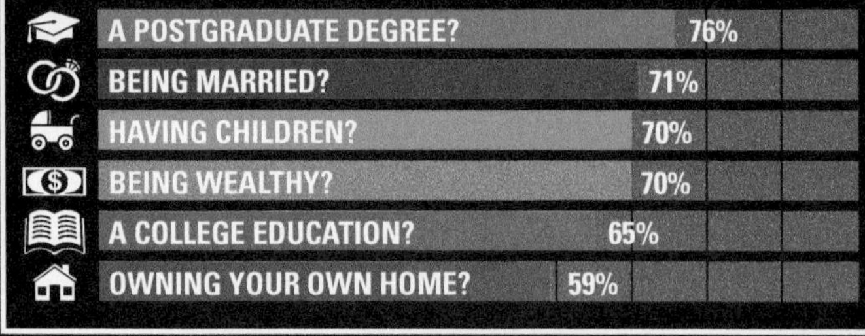

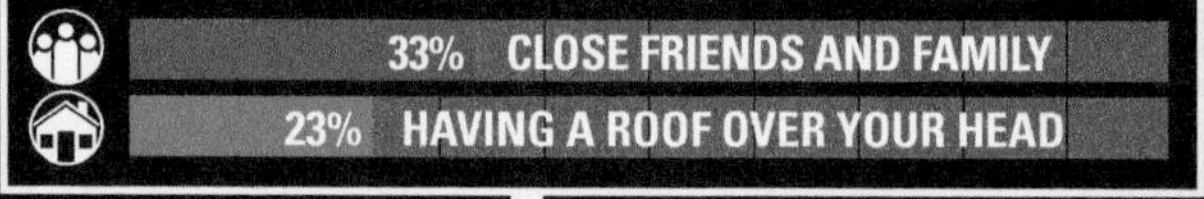

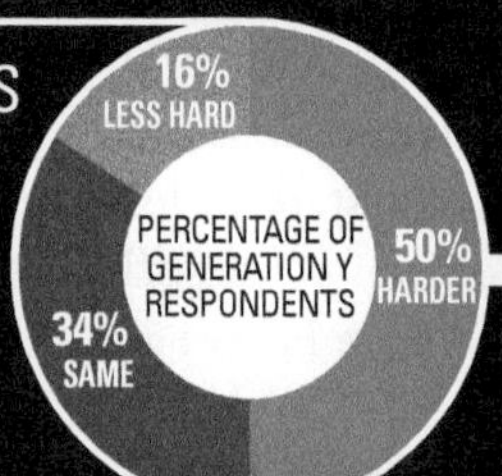

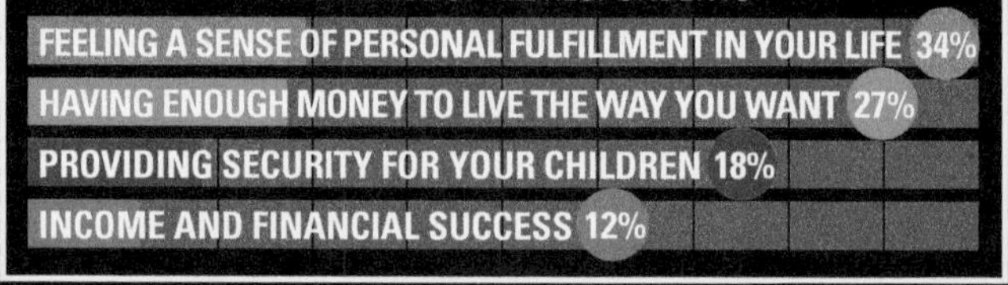

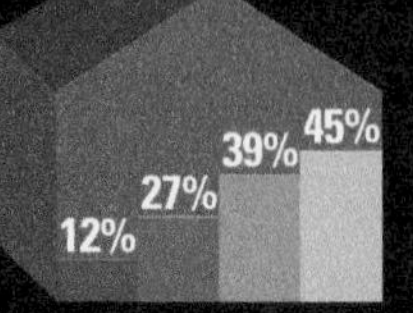

TRADITIONAL MILESTONES ARE NOT ESSENTIAL

Is it possible to achieve the American Dream without...

PERCENTAGE OF ALL RESPONDENTS WHO SAID "YES"

A POSTGRADUATE DEGREE? 76%
BEING MARRIED? 71%
HAVING CHILDREN? 70%
BEING WEALTHY? 70%
A COLLEGE EDUCATION? 65%
OWNING YOUR OWN HOME? 59%

FRIENDS AND FAMILY ARE MOST IMPORTANT TO YOUNG PEOPLE

In the current economic climate, which of the following is more important to you?

PERCENTAGE OF GENERATION Y RESPONDENTS

33% CLOSE FRIENDS AND FAMILY
23% HAVING A ROOF OVER YOUR HEAD

HALF OF ALL YOUNG AMERICANS SAY THEY WORK HARDER THAN THEIR PARENTS

Do you think you're working as hard, harder, or less hard than your parents when they were your age?

16%
LESS HARD
PERCENTAGE OF GENERATION Y RESPONDENTS
50%
HARDER
34%
SAME

AMERICANS VALUE PERSONAL FULFILLMENT OVER MONEY

What is the key to achieving the American Dream?

PERCENTAGE OF ALL RESPONDENTS

FEELING A SENSE OF PERSONAL FULFILLMENT IN YOUR LIFE 34%
HAVING ENOUGH MONEY TO LIVE THE WAY YOU WANT 27%
PROVIDING SECURITY FOR YOUR CHILDREN 18%
INCOME AND FINANCIAL SUCCESS 12%

AND MAKE MORE OF AN EFFORT TO BE SUCCESSFUL

Which of the following would you be willing to do to achieve the American Dream?

Silent Generation
Generation X
Baby Boomers
Generation Y
12%
27%
39%
45%
TAKE A JOB FOR WHICH YOU ARE OVERQUALIFIED
6%
23%
41%
48%
GET ADDITIONAL JOB TRAINING
10%
27%
34%
40%
RELOCATE TO ANOTHER CITY/STATE
5%
18%
37%
45%
GO BACK TO SCHOOL
9%
20%
34%
30%
START YOUR OWN BUSINESS
3%
21%
35%
26%
CHANGE INDUSTRIES

SOURCE: 2011 MetLife Study of the American Dream.

CRITICAL THINKING QUESTIONS

1. What, according to this visual, is the modern American Dream?
2. How do visions of the American Dream differ across generations? Why might these differences exist?
3. How might the trends you observe in this visual affect the demands that citizens place on their government? How might they affect politics?

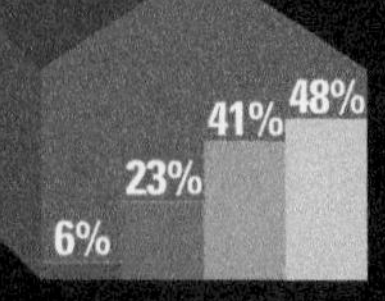

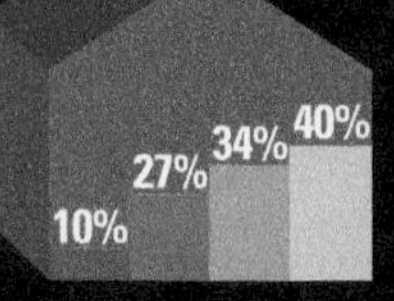

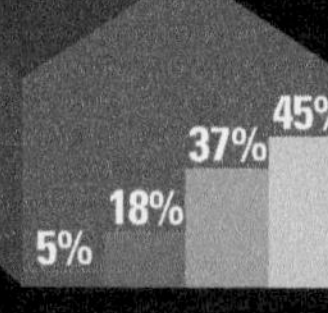

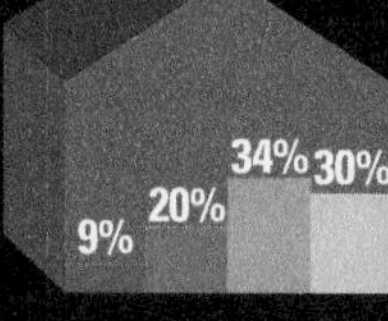

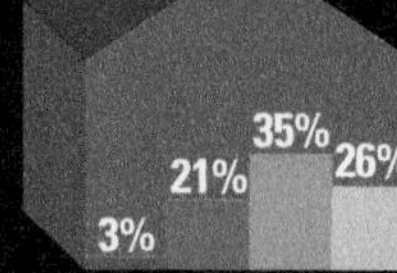

poverty relief, and inspecting food. With these new roles come greater demands on government.

Today, many Americans lack faith in the country's institutions (see Figure 1.4). And, a 2012 poll revealed that more than seven in ten Americans think the country is headed in the wrong direction.[16] These concerns make it even easier for citizens to blame the government for all kinds of woes—personal as well as societal—or to fail to credit it for those things it does well. Many Americans, for example, enjoy a remarkably high standard of living, and much of it is due to governmental programs and protections.

Even in the short time between when you get up in the morning and when you leave for classes or work, the government—its rulings or regulations—pervades your life. National or state governments, for example, set the standards for whether you wake up on Eastern, Central, Mountain, or Pacific time. The national government regulates the airwaves and licenses the radio and TV broadcasts you might listen to as you eat and get dressed. States, too, regulate and tax telecommunications. Whether the water you use to brush your teeth contains fluoride is a state or local governmental issue. The federal Food and Drug Administration inspects your breakfast meat and sets standards for the advertising on your cereal box, orange juice carton, and other food packaging.

The current frustration and dissatisfaction with politics and government may be just another phase, as the changing American body politic seeks to redefine its ideas about and expectations of government and how to reform it. This process is likely to define politics well into the future, but the individualistic nature of the American system will have long-lasting effects on how to accomplish that redefinition. Many Americans say they want less government, but as they get older, they don't want less Social Security. They want lower taxes and better roads, but they don't want to pay road tolls. They want better education for their children, but lower expenditures on schools. They want greater security at airports, but low fares and quick boarding. Some clearly want less for others but not themselves, a demand that puts politicians in the position of nearly always disappointing some voters.

In this text, we present you with the tools needed to understand how our political system has evolved and to understand changes yet to come. Approaching the study of American government and politics with an open mind should help you become a better citizen. We hope that you learn to ask questions, to comprehend how various issues have come to be important, and to see why a particular law was enacted, how it was

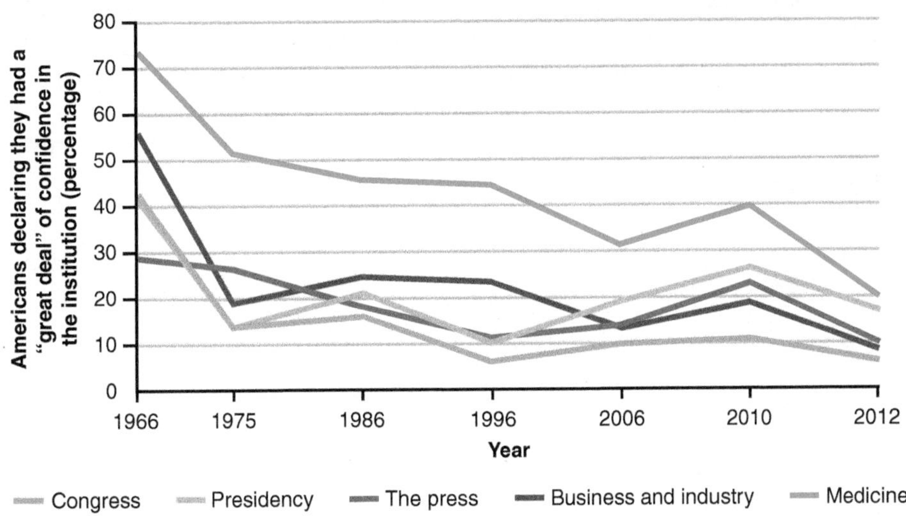

FIGURE 1.4 DO AMERICANS HAVE CONFIDENCE IN POLITICAL INSTITUTIONS?

The line graph below shows the percentages of Americans declaring they had a "great deal" of confidence in American institutions. Note the declining trend of trust in all political institutions, as well as Americans' record low levels of trust in institutions such as Congress and the press.

SOURCE: *Newsweek* (January 8, 1996):32; *Public Perspective 8* (February/March 1994): 4; Lexis-Nexis RPOLL; *Washington Post* (June 13, 2006): A2; www.pollingreport.com; www.gallup.com/poll/1597/confidence-institutions.aspx.

1.1
1.2
1.3
1.4
1.5
1.6
1.7

WHAT IS THE ROLE OF AMERICAN GOVERNMENT?

The most important responsibility of American government is to protect citizens. Thus, despite their disillusionment with the government, citizens in a time of need often turn to political leaders for support. Here, President Barack Obama comforts victims of Superstorm Sandy in New Jersey, just days before the 2012 election.

implemented, and if it needs reform. We further hope that you will learn not to accept at face value everything you see on the TV news, hear on the radio, or read in the newspaper and on the Internet, especially in the blogosphere. Work to understand your government, and use your vote and other forms of participation to help ensure that your government works for you.

We recognize that the discourse of politics has changed dramatically even in the past few years: it is easier than ever before to become informed about the political process and to get involved in campaigns and elections. We also believe that a thorough understanding of the workings of government will allow you to question and think about the political system—the good parts and the bad—and decide for yourself whether possible changes and reforms are advantageous or disadvantageous. Equipped with such an understanding, you likely will become a better informed and more active participant in the political process.

Review the Chapter

Listen to **Chapter 1** on **MyPoliSciLab**

Roots of American Government: We the People

1.1 Trace the origins of American government, p. 5.

American government is rooted in the cultures and experiences of early European colonists as well as interactions with the indigenous populations of the New World. The first colonists sought wealth. Later pilgrims came for religious freedom. The colonies set up systems of government that differed widely in terms of form, role, and function. As they developed, they sought more independence from the British monarchy.

Types of Government

1.2 Evaluate the different types of governments countries may employ, p. 7.

Aristotle classifies the types of governments according to who rules, and in whose interest. Types of governments include monarchy, totalitarianism, aristocracy, oligarchy, polity, and democracy. Fears about mob rule and the vast size of the United States led the Framers to create a republican democracy that relies on the role of representatives to filter citizens' viewpoints.

Functions of American Government

1.3 Explain the functions of American government, p. 9.

The functions of American government include establishing justice, ensuring domestic tranquility, providing for the common defense, promoting the general welfare, and securing the blessings of liberty.

American Political Culture and the Basic Tenets of American Democracy

1.4 Describe American political culture, and identify the basic tenets of American democracy, p. 10.

Political culture is a group's commonly shared attitudes, beliefs, and core values about how government should operate. Key tenets of Americans' shared political culture are liberty and equality; popular consent, majority rule and popular sovereignty; individualism; and religious freedom.

The Changing American Public

1.5 Analyze the changing characteristics of the American public, p. 13.

Several characteristics of the American electorate can help us understand how the system continues to evolve and change. Among these are changes in size and population, racial and ethnic composition, age, religious beliefs, regional growth and expansion, and family and family size.

Political Ideology

1.6 Assess the role of political ideology in shaping American politics, p. 18.

Ideologies, the belief systems that shape the thinking of individuals and how they view the world, affect people's ideas about government. The major categories of political ideology in America are conservative, liberal, and moderate.

Toward Reform: People and Politics

1.7 Characterize changes in Americans' attitudes toward and expectations of government, p. 21.

Shifts in population have created controversy in the American electorate throughout America's history. Americans have high and often unrealistic expectations of government, yet often fail to appreciate how much their government actually does for them. Americans' failing trust in institutions also explains some of the apathy among the American electorate.

Learn the Terms

Study and **Review** the **Flashcards**

American dream, p. 21
conservative, p. 19
democracy, p. 8
direct democracy, p. 8
government, p. 5
indirect democracy, p. 9
liberal, p. 19
libertarian, p. 21
majority rule, p. 12

moderate, p. 21
monarchy, p. 7
natural law, p. 12
oligarchy, p. 8
personal liberty, p. 10
political culture, p. 10
political equality, p. 12
political ideology, p. 18
politics, p. 21
popular consent, p. 12
popular sovereignty, p. 12
republic, p. 9
social conservative, p. 19
statist, p. 21
totalitarianism, p. 7

Test Yourself

Study and **Review** the **Practice Tests**

1. Before the Pilgrims traveled to the New World on the *Mayflower*, the most common reason for settlement in North America was

- **a.** religious freedom.
- **b.** fatal diseases in their homeland.
- **c.** commerce.
- **d.** independence from the crown.
- **e.** to create "a city on a hill."

2. Which of the following settlements was not founded for primarily religious reasons?

- **a.** Connecticut
- **b.** Portsmouth
- **c.** Jamestown
- **d.** Massachusetts Bay Colony
- **e.** Boston

3. As the population of the New World increased, the town meeting form of government was gradually replaced with an indirect democratic system colonists called a(n)

- **a.** direct democracy.
- **b.** monarchy.
- **c.** oligarchy.
- **d.** republic.
- **e.** democracy.

4. Which of the following is NOT a function of American government listed in the Preamble?

- **a.** Establish justice
- **b.** Promote equality
- **c.** Provide for the common defense
- **d.** Secure the blessings of liberty
- **e.** Ensure domestic tranquility

5. Which American ideal, central to the Declaration of Independence, was derived from the social contract theory?

- **a.** Majority rule
- **b.** Popular consent
- **c.** Religious freedom
- **d.** Natural law
- **e.** Political equality

6. Which of these is a major contributor to American population growth since 1940?

- **a.** Longer life expectancy
- **b.** Western European immigration
- **c.** Industrial growth
- **d.** New states added to the United States
- **e.** Higher birthrates

7. Which of the following statements best describes recent demographic trends in the United States?

- **a.** Population has grown largely in Midwestern and Mid-Atlantic states.
- **b.** African Americans have consistently composed the second largest minority group.
- **c.** Couples favor having more children than in the mid-twentieth century.
- **d.** The average age of Americans has increased.
- **e.** More than 50 percent of American children today live with only one parent.

8. According to political scientists, which of the following is NOT considered a function of political ideologies?

- **a.** Political program
- **b.** Evaluation
- **c.** Orientation
- **d.** Explanation
- **e.** Partisanship

9. Which political ideology is most associated with a limited role of government in personal and economic affairs?

- **a.** Liberal
- **b.** Conservative
- **c.** Moderate
- **d.** Libertarian
- **e.** Statist

10. For most Americans, the definition of achieving the American Dream includes obtaining

- **a.** incredible wealth.
- **b.** a job in business.
- **c.** a job in government.
- **d.** a happy and successful life.
- **e.** children.

Explore Further

Ball, Terence, and Richard Dagger. *Political Ideologies and the Democratic Ideal,* 8th ed. New York: Longman, 2010.

Dahl, Robert A. *Polyarchy: Participation and Opposition.* New Haven, CT: Yale University Press, 1972.

Estlund, David M. *Democratic Authority: A Philosophical Framework.* Princeton, NJ: Princeton University Press, 2012.

Fiorina, Morris P., Samuel J. Abrams, and Jeremy C. Pope. *Culture War? The Myth of a Polarized America,* 3rd ed. New York: Longman, 2010.

Ghosh, Cyril. *The Politics of the American Dream: Democratic Inclusion in Contemporary American Political Culture.* New York: Palgrave Macmillan, 2013.

Hobbes, Thomas. *Leviathan.* Ed. Richard Tuck. New York: Cambridge University Press, 1996.

Jamieson, Kathleen Hall. *Everything You Think You Know About Politics . . . and Why You're Wrong.* New York: Basic Books, 2000.

Kazin, Michael. *American Dreamers: How the Left Changed a Nation.* New York: Vintage, 2012.

Locke, John. *Two Treatises of Government.* Ed. Peter Lasleti. New York: Cambridge University Press, 1988.

Nye, Joseph S., Jr. *The Paradox of American Power: Why the World's Superpower Can't Go It Alone.* New York: Oxford University Press, 2002.

Putnam, Robert D., and David E. Campbell. *American Grace: How Religion Divides Us and Unites Us.* New York: Simon and Schuster, 2010.

Rosenfeld, Michael J. *The Age of Independence: Interracial Unions, Same Sex Unions, and the Changing American Family.* Cambridge, MA: Harvard University Press, 2009.

Smith, Hedrick. *Who Stole the American Dream? Can We Get It Back?* New York: Random House, 2012.

Verba, Sidney, Kay Schlozman, and Henry Brady. *Voice and Equality: Civic Volunteerism in American Politics,* 2nd ed. Cambridge, MA: Harvard University Press, 2002.

Wolfe, Alan, and Ira Katznelson, eds. *Religion and Democracy in the United States: Danger or Opportunity?* Princeton, NJ: Princeton University Press, 2012.

To learn more about shifts in the American population, go to the U.S. Census Bureau at **www.census.gov.**

To learn more about Americans' attitudes and expectations of government, go to the Pew Research Center at **www .pewresearch.org.**

To learn about the policy positions and attitudes of American conservatives, go to the American Conservative Union at **www.conservative.org.**

To learn more about the policy positions and attitudes of American liberals, go to the Liberal Oasis at **www.liberaloasis.com.**

Listen to Chapter 2 on MyPoliSciLab

2

The Constitution

t age eighteen, all American citizens are eligible to vote in state and national elections. This has not always been the case. It took an amendment to the U.S. Constitution—one of only seventeen that have been added since ratification of the Bill of Rights in 1791—to guarantee the vote in national elections to those younger than twenty-one years of age.

In 1942, during World War II, Representative Jennings Randolph (D–WV) proposed a constitutional amendment that would lower the voting age to eighteen, believing that since young men were old enough to be drafted, to go to war, and to fight and die for their country, they also should have the right to vote. He continued to reintroduce his proposal during every session of Congress, and in 1954, President Dwight D. Eisenhower endorsed the idea in his State of the Union Address. Presidents Lyndon B. Johnson and Richard M. Nixon—men who had also called upon the nation's young men to fight on foreign shores—echoed his appeal.[1]

During the 1960s, the campaign to lower the voting age took on a new sense of urgency as the draft sent hundreds of thousands of young men to fight in the unpopular war in Vietnam, and thousands of men and women were killed in action. "Old Enough to Fight, Old Enough to Vote" was one popular slogan of the day. By 1970, four states—the U.S. Constitution allows states to set the eligibility requirements for their voters—had lowered their voting ages to eighteen. Later that year, Congress passed legislation that designated eighteen as the voting age in national, state, and local elections.

The state of Oregon, however, challenged the constitutionality of the law in court, arguing that the Constitution did not give Congress the authority to establish a uniform voting age in state and local government elections. The U.S. Supreme Court agreed.[2] The decision from the divided Court meant that those under age twenty-one could vote in national elections but that the states were free to prohibit them from voting in state and local elections. The decision presented the states with a logistical nightmare. Setting the voting age at twenty-one would force states to keep two sets of registration books: one for voters twenty-one and over and one for voters under twenty-one.

2.1 Trace the historical developments that led to the colonists' break with Great Britain and the emergence of the new American nation, p. 31.

2.2 Identify the key components of the Articles of Confederation and the reasons why it failed, p. 37.

2.3 Outline the issues and compromises that were central to the writing of the U.S. Constitution, p. 40.

2.4 Analyze the underlying principles of the U.S. Constitution, p. 44.

2.5 Explain the conflicts that characterized the drive for ratification of the U.S. Constitution, p. 51.

2.6 Distinguish between the methods for proposing and ratifying amendments to the U.S. Constitution, p. 55.

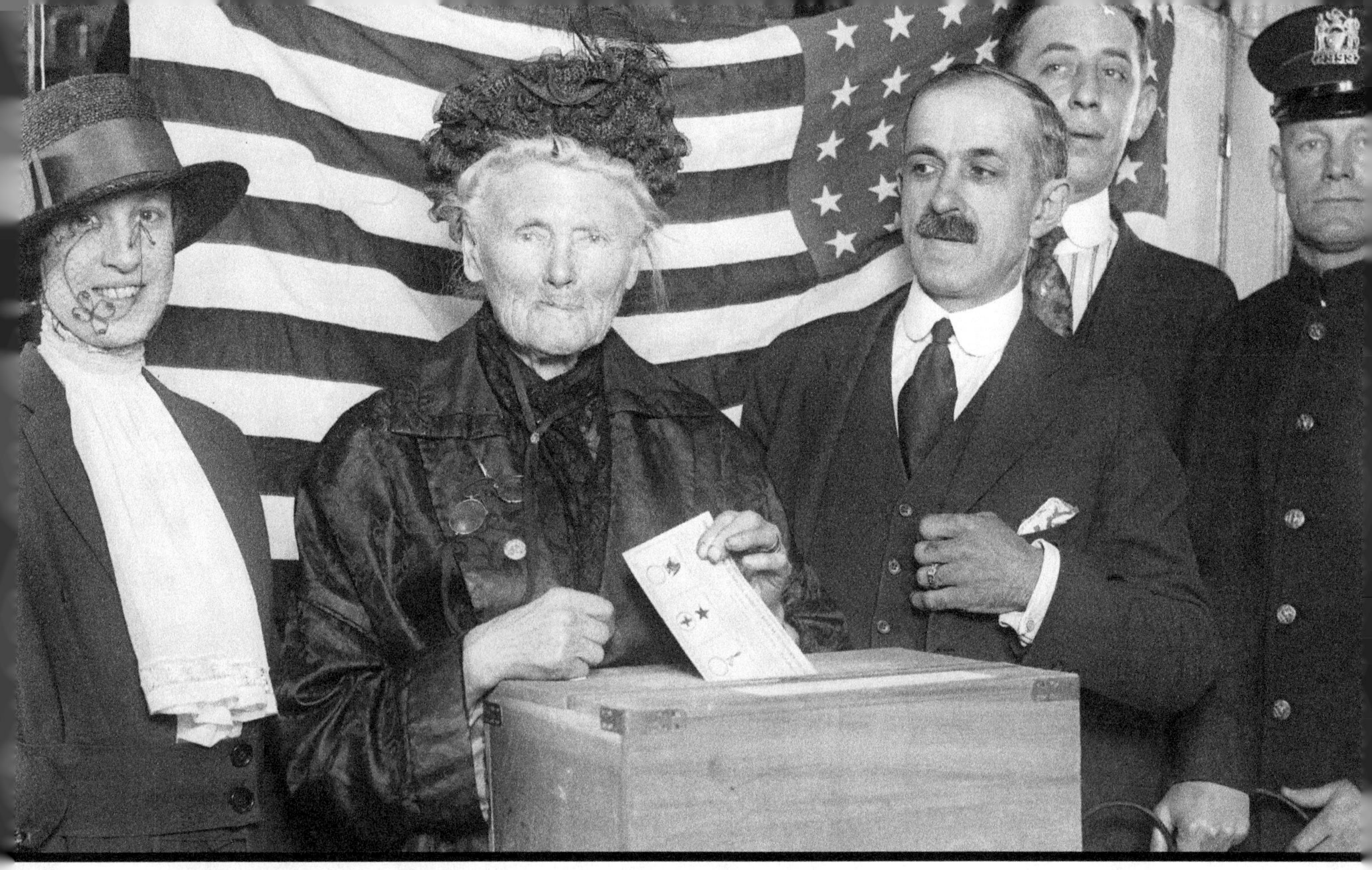

MANY CONSTITUTIONAL AMENDMENTS HAVE ADDRESSED VOTING RIGHTS Above, women cast a ballot after the ratification of the Nineteenth Amendment in 1920. Below, a young voter uses an electronic voting machine in a recent election.

The Big Picture Discover why what the Constitution does not say is just as important as what it does say. Author Alixandra B. Yanus considers how the government refers to the Constitution for answers to current questions that it does not explicitly address, thereby leaving plenty of room for interpretation.

The Basics What is the purpose of a constitution? In this video, you will discover the reasons why the Framers wrote the Constitution and how the Constitution sets up checks and balances, the protection of liberties, and the framework we need for a functioning democracy.

In Context Why is it unusual that the U.S. Constitution has governed so long in its present form? Fordham University political scientist Costas Panagopolos explains why the Constitution is such a rarity and how it has succeeded in an evolving American society.

Thinking Like a Political Scientist How do the institutions created by the U.S. Constitution operate and how has their role changed over time? Fordham University political scientist Costas Panagopolos examines this and other emerging issues in the research and in the study of the Constitution.

In the Real World How well does the system of checks and balances in the United States work, and is it actually fair? Real people voice their opinions on whether or not they believe it is constitutional for Congress to check the power of the president—and vice versa.

So What? The United States has changed a lot in the past two hundred years; so why have we always been governed by the same document? In this video, author Alixandra B. Yanus explains the unique features of the U.S. Constitution that have allowed it to remain effective for so long.

Jennings Randolph, by then a senator from West Virginia, reintroduced his proposed amendment to lower the national voting age to eighteen.[3] Within three months of the Supreme Court's decision, Congress sent the proposed Twenty-Sixth Amendment to the states for ratification. The required three-fourths of the states approved the amendment within three months—making its adoption on June 30, 1971, the quickest in the history of the constitutional amending process.

While young people have not traditionally exercised their Twenty-Sixth Amendment rights in large numbers, voter turnout among those 18 to 29 does seem to be on the rise. Record numbers of young voters went to the polls in the 2012 presidential election; many credited discussions on Facebook and other social networking sites for their political interest and activism. The votes of young people played a decisive role in electing Barack Obama. Young people not only made up 19 percent of all voters—a higher percentage than those age 65 and older—but 60 percent of those age 18 to 29 also voted for Obama.

•••

The Framers never intended the U.S. Constitution to be easily changed. They made the amendment process time consuming and difficult. Over the years, thousands of amendments—including those to prohibit child labor, provide equal rights for women, grant statehood to the District of Columbia, balance the federal budget, and ban flag burning—have been debated or sent to the states for approval, only to die slow deaths. Only twenty-seven amendments have made their way into the Constitution. What the Framers wrote in Philadelphia has continued to work, in spite of increasing demands on and dissatisfaction with our national government. Although Americans often clamor for reform, perhaps they are happier with the system of government created by the Framers than they realize. The ideas that went into the making of the Constitution and the ways that it has evolved to address the problems of a growing and changing nation form the core of our discussion in this chapter.

Roots of the New American Nation

2.1 Trace the historical developments that led to the colonists' break with Great Britain and the emergence of the new American nation.

Beginning in the early seventeenth century, colonists came to the New World for a variety of reasons. Often, they wished to escape religious persecution. Others sought a new start on a continent where land was plentiful or saw business opportunities to be gained in the New World. The independence and diversity of the settlers in the New World complicated the question of how best to rule the new colonies. More than merely an ocean separated Great Britain from the colonies; the colonists were independent people, and it soon became clear that the crown could not govern its subjects in the colonies with the same close rein used at home. King James I thus allowed some local participation in decision making through arrangements such as the first elected colonial assembly, the Virginia House of Burgesses, formed in 1619, and the elected General Court that governed the Massachusetts Bay Colony after 1629. Almost all of the colonists agreed that the king ruled by divine right, but British monarchs allowed the colonists significant liberties in terms of self-government, religious practices, and economic organization. For 140 years, this system worked fairly well.[4]

By the early 1760s, however, a century and a half of physical separation, development of colonial industry, and relative self-governance by the colonies led to weakening ties with—and loyalties to—the crown. By this time, each of the thirteen colonies had drafted its own constitution, which provided the fundamental rules or laws by which it operated. Moreover, many of the most oppressive British traditions—feudalism, a rigid

mercantilism
An economic theory designed to increase a nation's wealth through the development of commercial industry and a favorable balance of trade.

Stamp Act Congress
Meeting of representatives of nine of the thirteen colonies held in New York City in 1765, during which representatives drafted a document to send to the king that listed how their rights had been violated.

class system, and the absolute authority of the king—were absent in the colonies. Land was abundant. The guild and craft systems that severely limited entry into many skilled professions in Great Britain were not part of life in the colonies. And, although religion was central to the lives of most colonists, no single state church existed, so the colonists did not follow the British practice of compulsory tithing (giving a fixed percentage of one's earnings to the state-sanctioned and -supported church).

Trade and Taxation

Mercantilism, an economic theory designed to increase a nation's wealth through the development of commercial industry and a favorable balance of trade, justified Britain's maintenance of strict import/export controls on the colonies. After 1650, for example, the British Parliament passed a series of navigation acts to prevent its chief rival, Holland, from trading with the British colonies. From 1650 until well into the 1700s, Britain tried to control colonial imports and exports, believing it critical to export more goods than it imported as a way of increasing the gold and silver in its treasury. Britain found it difficult to enforce these policies, however, and the colonists, seeing little self-benefit in their operation, widely ignored them. Thus, for years, an unwritten agreement existed. The colonists relinquished to the crown and the British Parliament the authority to regulate trade and conduct international affairs, but they retained the right to levy their own taxes.

This fragile agreement was soon put to the test. The French and Indian War, fought from 1756 to 1763 on the western frontier of the colonies and in Canada, was part of a global war initiated by the British, then the greatest power in the world. This American phase of what was called the Seven Years War was fought between Britain and France with Indian allies. To raise money to pay for the war as well as the expenses of administering the colonies, Parliament enacted the Sugar Act in 1764. This act placed taxes on sugar, wine, coffee, and other products commonly exported to the colonies. A postwar colonial depression heightened resentment of the tax. Major protest, however, failed to materialize until imposition of the Stamp Act by the British Parliament in 1765. This law required that all paper items, from playing cards to books, bought and sold in the colonies carry a stamp mandated by the crown. The colonists did not find the tax itself offensive. However, they feared this act would establish a precedent for the British Parliament not only to control commerce in the colonies but also to raise revenues from the colonists without approval of the colonial governments. The political cry "no taxation without representation" rang out across the colonies. To add insult to injury, in 1765, Parliament passed the Quartering Act, which required colonists to furnish barracks or provide living quarters within their own homes for British troops.

Most colonists, especially those in New England, where these acts hit merchants hardest, were outraged. Men throughout the colonies organized the Sons of Liberty, under the leadership of Samuel Adams and Patrick Henry. Women formed the Daughters of Liberty. Protests against the Stamp Act were violent and loud. Riots, often led by the Sons of Liberty, broke out. These were especially violent in Boston, where an angry mob burned the colonial governor's home and protesters threatened British stamp agents charged with collecting the tax. The outraged colonists also organized a boycott of goods needing the stamps, as well as of British imports.

John Singleton Copley (1738–1815), "Samuel Adams," ca. 1772. Oil on canvas, 49 1/2 x 39 1/2 in. (125.7 cm x 100.3 cm). Deposited by the City of Boston, 30.76c. Courtesy, Museum of Fine Arts, Boston. Reproduced with permission.

WHY WAS SAMUEL ADAMS IMPORTANT?

Samuel Adams (1722–1803), cousin of President John Adams, was an early leader against the British and loyalist oppressors. He played a key role in developing the Committees of Correspondence, and was active in Massachusetts and colonial politics. Today he is known for the beer that bears his name, which is ironic, considering he bankrupted his family's brewery business.

First Steps Toward Independence

In 1765, at the urging of Samuel Adams, nine of the thirteen colonies sent representatives to a meeting in New York City, where they drafted a detailed list of crown violations of the colonists' fundamental rights. Known as the **Stamp Act Congress,** this gathering was the first official meeting of the colonies and the first step toward creating a unified nation. Attendees defined what they thought to be the proper relationship between colonial governments and the British Parliament; they ardently believed Parliament had no authority to tax them without colonial representation in that body, yet they still remained loyal to the king. In contrast, the British believed that direct representation of the colonists was impractical and that members of Parliament represented the best interests of all the British, including the colonists who were British subjects.

The Stamp Act Congress and its petitions to the crown did little to stop the onslaught of taxing measures. Parliament did, however, repeal the Stamp Act and revise the Sugar Act in 1766, largely because of the uproar made by British merchants who were losing large sums of money as a result of the boycotts. Rather than appeasing the colonists, however, these actions emboldened them to increase their resistance. In 1767, Parliament enacted the Townshend Acts, which imposed duties on all kinds of colonial imports, including tea. Responses from the Sons and Daughters of Liberty came immediately. Protesters announced another boycott of tea, and almost all colonists gave up their favorite drink in a united show of resistance to the tax and British authority.[5] Tensions continued to run high, especially after the British sent 4,000 troops to Boston. On March 5, 1770, British troops opened fire on an unruly mob that included disgruntled dockworkers, whose jobs had been taken by British soldiers, and members of the Sons of Liberty, who were taunting the soldiers and throwing objects at British sentries stationed in front of the Boston Customs House. The troops killed five colonists in what became known as the Boston Massacre. Following this confrontation, Parliament lifted all duties except those on tea. The tea tax, however, continued to be a symbolic

WHAT REALLY HAPPENED AT THE BOSTON MASSACRE?

Paul Revere's famous engraving of the Boston Massacre played fast and loose with the facts. While the event occurred on a cold winter's night, the engraving features a clear sky and no ice or snow. Crispus Attucks, the Revolution's first martyr, was African American, although the engraving depicts him as a white man. Popular propaganda such as this engraving—and even dubbing the incident a "massacre"—did much to stoke anti-British sentiment in the years leading up to the Revolutionary War.

2.1

2.2

2.3

2.4

2.5

2.6

Committees of Correspondence
Organizations in each of the American colonies created to keep colonists abreast of developments with the British; served as powerful molders of public opinion against the British.

First Continental Congress
Meeting held in Philadelphia from September 5 to October 26, 1774, in which fifty-six delegates (from every colony except Georgia) adopted a resolution in opposition to the Coercive Acts.

Second Continental Congress
Meeting that convened in Philadelphia on May 10, 1775, at which it was decided that an army should be raised and George Washington of Virginia was named commander in chief.

irritant. In 1772, at the suggestion of Samuel Adams, colonists created **Committees of Correspondence** to keep each other abreast of developments with the British. These committees also served as powerful molders of public opinion against the British.

Meanwhile, despite dissent in Britain over treatment of the colonies, Parliament passed another tea tax designed to shore up the sagging sales of the East India Company, a British exporter of tea. The colonists' boycott had left that trading company with more than 18 million pounds of tea in its warehouses. To rescue British merchants from disaster, in 1773, Parliament passed the Tea Act, granting a monopoly to the financially strapped East India Company to sell tea imported from Britain. This act allowed the company to funnel business to American merchants loyal to the crown, thereby undercutting dissident colonial merchants, who could sell only tea imported from other nations. This practice drove down the price of tea and hurt colonial merchants, who were forced to buy tea at higher prices from other sources.

When the next shipment of tea arrived in Boston from Great Britain, the colonists responded by throwing the Boston Tea Party; other colonies held similar tea parties. When the news reached King George III, he flew into a rage against the actions of his disloyal subjects. "The die is now cast," the king told his prime minister. "The colonies must either submit or triumph."

King George's first act of retaliation was to persuade Parliament to pass the Coercive Acts of 1774. Known in the colonies as the Intolerable Acts, they contained a key provision calling for a total blockade of Boston Harbor, cutting off Bostonians' access to many foodstuffs, until restitution was made for the tea. Another provision reinforced the Quartering Act. It gave royal governors the authority to house British soldiers in the homes of local Boston citizens, allowing Britain to send an additional 4,000 soldiers to patrol Boston.

☐ The First Continental Congress

The British could never have guessed how the cumulative impact of these actions would unite the colonists. Samuel Adams's Committees of Correspondence spread the word, and the people of Boston received food and money from all over the thirteen colonies. The tax itself was no longer the key issue; now the extent of British authority over the colonies presented the far more important question. At the request of the colonial assemblies of Massachusetts and Virginia, all but Georgia's colonial assembly agreed to select a group of delegates to attend a continental congress authorized to communicate with the king on behalf of the now-united colonies.

The **First Continental Congress,** comprising fifty-six delegates, met in Philadelphia from September 5 to October 26, 1774. The colonists had yet to think of breaking with Great Britain; at this point, they simply wanted to iron out their differences with the king. By October, they had agreed on a series of resolutions to oppose the Coercive Acts and to establish a formal organization to boycott British goods. The Congress also drafted a Declaration of Rights and Resolves, which called for colonial rights of petition and assembly, trial by peers, freedom from a standing army, and the selection of representative councils to levy taxes. The Congress further agreed that if the king did not capitulate to its demands, it would meet again in Philadelphia in May 1775.

☐ The Second Continental Congress

King George III refused to yield, tensions continued to rise, and a **Second Continental Congress** was deemed necessary. Before it could meet, fighting broke out in the early morning of April 19, 1775, at Lexington and Concord, Massachusetts, with what American writer and philosopher Ralph Waldo Emerson later called "the shot heard 'round the world." Eight colonial soldiers, called Minutemen, were killed, and 16,000 British troops besieged Boston.

When the Second Continental Congress convened in Philadelphia on May 10, 1775, delegates were united by their increased hostility to Great Britain. In a final attempt to avert conflict, the Second Continental Congress adopted the Olive Branch Petition on July 5, 1775, asking the king to end hostilities. King George III rejected the petition and sent an additional 20,000 troops to quell the rebellion; he labeled all in attendance traitors to the king and subject to death. As a precautionary measure, the Congress already had appointed George Washington of Virginia as commander in chief of the Continental Army. The selection of a southern leader was a strategic decision, because up to that time the Northeast had borne the brunt of British oppression. In fact, the war essentially had begun with the shots fired at Lexington and Concord.

In January 1776, Thomas Paine, with the support and encouragement of Benjamin Franklin, issued (at first anonymously) *Common Sense*, a pamphlet forcefully arguing for independence from Great Britain. In frank, easy-to-understand language, Paine denounced the corrupt British monarchy and offered reasons to break with Great Britain. "The blood of the slain, the weeping voice of nature cries 'Tis Time to Part,'" wrote Paine. *Common Sense*, widely read throughout the colonies, helped to change minds in a very short time. In its first three months of publication, the forty-seven-page *Common Sense* sold 120,000 copies. One copy of *Common Sense* was in distribution for every thirteen people in the colonies—a truly astonishing number, given the low literacy rate.

Common Sense galvanized the American public against reconciliation with Great Britain. On May 15, 1776, Virginia became the first colony to call for independence, instructing one of its delegates to the Second Continental Congress to introduce a resolution to that effect. On June 7, 1776, Richard Henry Lee of Virginia rose to move "that these United Colonies are, and of right ought to be, free and independent States, and that all connection between them and the State of Great Britain is, and ought to be, dissolved." His three-part resolution—which called for independence, the formation of foreign alliances, and preparation of a plan of confederation—triggered hot debate among the delegates. A proclamation of independence from Great Britain constituted treason, a crime punishable by death. Although six of the thirteen colonies had already instructed their delegates to vote for independence, the Second Continental Congress was suspended to allow its delegates to return home to their respective colonial legislatures for final instructions. Independence was not a move the colonists would take lightly.

Declaration of Independence
Document drafted largely by Thomas Jefferson in 1776 that proclaimed the right of the American colonies to separate from Great Britain.

☐ The Declaration of Independence

The Congress set up committees to consider each point of Richard Henry Lee's proposal. The Committee of Five began work on the **Declaration of Independence.** Committee members included Benjamin Franklin of Pennsylvania, John Adams of Massachusetts, Robert Livingston of New York, and Roger Sherman of Connecticut. Adams lobbied hard for the addition of Thomas Jefferson, a Southerner, to add balance. Jefferson's writings, which revealed a "peculiar felicity of expression," had also impressed Adams. Thus, the Congress chose Jefferson of Virginia as chair.

On July 2, 1776, twelve of the thirteen colonies (with New York abstaining) voted for independence. Two days later, the Second Continental Congress voted to adopt the Declaration of Independence, largely penned by Jefferson. On July 9, 1776, the Declaration, now with the approval of New York, was read aloud in Philadelphia.[6]

In simple but eloquent language, the Declaration set out the reasons for separation of the colonies from Great Britain. Most of its stirring rhetoric drew heavily on the works of seventeenth- and eighteenth-century political philosophers, particularly the English philosopher John Locke. Locke had written South Carolina's first constitution, a colonial charter drawn up in 1663. In fact, many words in the opening of the Declaration of Independence closely resemble passages from Locke's *Second Treatise of Civil Government.*

Locke was a proponent of social contract theory, which holds that governments exist based on the consent of the governed. According to Locke, people agree to set up a government largely for the protection of property rights, to preserve life and liberty, and to establish justice. Furthermore, argued Locke, individuals who give their consent to be governed have the right to resist or remove rulers who deviate from those purposes. Such a government exists for the good of its subjects and not for the benefit of those who govern. Thus, rebellion is the ultimate sanction against a government that violates the rights of its citizens.

Take a Closer Look

The Declaration of Independence is arguably one of the most sacred American documents. In clear, concise prose, Thomas Jefferson states the colonists' rationale for their split from Great Britain. But, the document was not always as articulate and powerful as it is today. After Thomas Jefferson submitted his "Rough Draught" to the Committee of Five, other members, including John Adams and Benjamin Franklin, made significant revisions to the document.

The Declaration originally began:

> When in the course of human events it becomes necessary for a people to advance that subordination in which they have hitherto remained, and to assume among the powers of the earth the equal and independant station to which the laws of nature and of nature's god entitle them, a decent respect to the opinions of mankind requires that they should declare the causes which impel them to the change.

The committee changed this to state:

> When in the Course of human events, it becomes necessary for one people to dissolve the political bands which have connected them with another, and to assume among the powers of the earth, the separate and equal station to which the Laws of Nature and of Nature's God entitle them, a decent respect to the opinions of mankind requires that they should declare the causes which impel them to the separation.

Here, Jefferson's phrase "sacred and undeniable" became "self-evident."

The original draft stated that

> ...all men are created equal and independant, that from that equal creation they derive rights inherent and inalienable, among which are the preservation of life, and liberty, and the pursuit of happiness.

In the final draft, however, Jefferson stated,

> that they are endowed by their Creator with certain unalienable Rights, that among these are Life, Liberty and the pursuit of Happiness.

CRITICAL THINKING QUESTIONS

1. Why do you think committee members made revisions such as the ones you see here? What factors may have influenced their changes?
2. Are any edits that appear to weaken the document seen here? Why do you prefer the original language? Why do you think it was not ultimately used?
3. Who was the audience for the Declaration? How did this influence the authors' arguments?

It is easy to see the colonists' debt to John Locke. In stirring language, the Declaration of Independence proclaims:

> We hold these truths to be self-evident, that all men are created equal, that they are endowed by their Creator with certain unalienable Rights, that among these are Life, Liberty and the pursuit of Happiness.

Jefferson and others in attendance at the Second Continental Congress wanted to have a document that would stand for all time, justifying their break with Great Britain and clarifying their notions of the proper form of government. So, the Declaration continued:

> That to secure these rights, Governments are instituted among Men, deriving their just powers from the consent of the governed. That whenever any Form of Government becomes destructive of these ends, it is the Right of the People to alter or abolish it, and to institute new Government, laying its foundation on such Principles and organizing its Powers in such form, as to them shall seem most likely to effect their Safety and Happiness.

After this stirring preamble, the Declaration enumerates the wrongs suffered by the colonists under British rule. All pertain to the denial of personal rights and liberties, many of which would later be guaranteed by the U.S. Constitution through the Bill of Rights.

After the Congress signed and transmitted the Declaration to the king, the Revolutionary War raged with greater vengeance. At a September 1776 peace conference on Staten Island (New York), British General William Howe demanded revocation of the Declaration of Independence. Washington's Continental Army refused, and the war raged on while the Continental Congress struggled to fashion a new united government.

Articles of Confederation

The compact between the thirteen original colonies that created a loose league of friendship, with the national government drawing its powers from the states.

confederation

Type of government in which the national government derives its powers from the states; a league of independent states.

The First Attempt at Government: The Articles of Confederation

2.2 Identify the key components of the Articles of Confederation and the reasons why it failed.

The British had no written constitution. Delegates to the Second Continental Congress were attempting to codify many arrangements that had never before been expressed in legal terminology. To make matters more complicated, the delegates had to arrive at these decisions in a wartime atmosphere. Nevertheless, in late 1777, the Congress passed the **Articles of Confederation,** creating a loose "league of friendship" between the thirteen sovereign, or independent, colonies (some that even called themselves separate countries), and presented the Articles to the states for ratification.

The Articles created a type of government called a **confederation** or confederacy. Unlike Great Britain's unitary system, wherein all governmental powers reside in the national government, the national government in a confederation derives all its powers directly from the states. Thus, the national government in a confederacy is weaker than the sum of its parts, and the states often consider themselves independent nation-states linked together only for limited purposes, such as national defense. So, the Articles of Confederation proposed the following:

- A national government with a Congress empowered to make peace, coin money, appoint officers for an army, control the post office, and negotiate with Indian tribes.
- Each state's retention of its independence and sovereignty, or ultimate authority, to govern within its territories.
- One vote in the legislature, the Congress of the Confederation for each state, regardless of size.
- The vote of nine states to pass any measure (a unanimous vote for any amendment).
- The selection and payment of delegates to the Congress by the states.

The Articles, finally ratified by all thirteen states in March 1781, fashioned a government that reflected the political philosophy of the times.[7] Although it had its flaws, the government under the Articles of Confederation saw the nation through the Revolutionary War. However, once the British surrendered in 1781, and the new nation found itself no longer united by the war effort, the government quickly fell into chaos.

Problems Under the Articles of Confederation

More than 250 years ago, Americans had great loyalties to their states and often did not even think of themselves as Americans. This lack of national identity or loyalty in the absence of a war to unite the citizenry fostered a reluctance to give any power to the national government. By 1784, just one year after the Revolutionary Army was disbanded, governing the new nation under the Articles of Confederation proved unworkable.[8] In fact, historians refer to the chaotic period from 1781 to 1789, when the former colonies were governed under the Articles, as the critical period. Congress rarely could assemble the required quorum of nine states to conduct business. Even when it did meet, states found it difficult to agree on any policies. To raise revenue to pay off war debts and run the government, Congress proposed various land, poll, and liquor taxes. But, since it had no specific power to tax, all these proposals were rejected. At one point, Congress was even driven out of Philadelphia (then the capital of the new national government) by its own unpaid army.

Although the national government could coin money, it had no resources to back up the value of its currency. Continental dollars were worth little, and trade between states grew chaotic as some of them began to coin their own money. Another weakness was that the Articles of Confederation did not allow Congress to regulate commerce among the states or with foreign nations. As a result, individual states attempted to enter into agreements with other countries, and foreign nations were suspicious of trade agreements made with the Congress of the Confederation. In 1785, for example, Massachusetts banned the export of goods in British ships, and Pennsylvania levied heavy duties on ships of nations that had no treaties with the U.S. government.

Fearful of a chief executive who would rule tyrannically, the drafters of the Articles made no provision for an executive branch of government that would be responsible for executing, or implementing, laws passed by the legislative branch. Instead, the president was merely the presiding officer at meetings. John Hanson, a former member of the Maryland House of Delegates and of the First Continental Congress, was the first person to preside over the Congress of the Confederation. Therefore, he is sometimes referred to as the first president of the United States.

The Articles of Confederation, moreover, had no provision for a judicial system to handle the growing number of economic conflicts and boundary disputes among the individual states. Several states claimed the same lands to the west, and Pennsylvania and Virginia went to war with each other.

The Articles' greatest weakness, however, was its failure to provide for a strong central government. Although states had operated independently before the war, during the war they acceded to the national government's authority to wage armed conflict. Once the war was over, however, each state resumed its sovereign status and was unwilling to give up rights, such as the power to tax, to an untested national government. Consequently, the government could not force states to abide by the provisions of the second Treaty of Paris, signed in 1783, which officially ended the Revolutionary War. For example, states passed laws to allow debtors who owed money to Great Britain to postpone payment. States also opted not to restore property to citizens who had remained loyal to Britain during the war. Both actions violated the treaty.

A series of bad harvests kept farmers in debt and worsened the crumbling economy. George Washington and Alexander Hamilton, both interested in the questions of trade and frontier expansion, soon saw the need for a stronger national government with the authority to step in and solve some of these problems. They were not alone. In 1785 and 1786, some state governments began to discuss ways to strengthen the national government.

☐ Shays's Rebellion

Before concerned states and individuals could take action to strengthen the government, new unrest broke out in America. In 1780, Massachusetts had adopted a constitution that appeared to favor the interests of the wealthy. Property-owning requirements barred the lower and middle classes from voting and office holding. And, as the economy of Massachusetts declined, banks foreclosed on the farms of many Massachusetts Continental Army veterans who were waiting for promised bonuses that the national government had no funds to pay. The last straw came in 1786, when the Massachusetts legislature enacted a new law requiring the payment of all debts in cash. Frustration and outrage at the new law incited Daniel Shays, a former Continental Army captain, and 1,500 armed, disgruntled farmers to march to the government arsenal in Springfield, Massachusetts. This group obstructed the entrance to the state court located there, thus preventing the court from foreclosing on the mortgages on their farms.

The Congress of the Confederation immediately authorized the secretary of war to call for a new national militia. Congress made a $530,000 appropriation for this purpose, but every state except Virginia refused the request for money. The governor of Massachusetts then tried to raise a state militia, but because of the poor economy, the state treasury lacked the necessary funds to support his action. A militia finally was assembled after frantic attempts to collect private financial support. By February 4, 1787, this privately paid force ended what was called **Shays's Rebellion.** The failure of the Congress to muster an army and quell the rebellion provided a dramatic example of the weaknesses inherent in the Articles of Confederation and shocked the nation's leaders into recognizing the new national government's inadequacies. It finally prompted several states to join together and call for a convention in Philadelphia in 1787.

Shays's Rebellion
A rebellion in which an army of 1,500 disgruntled and angry farmers led by Daniel Shays marched to Springfield, Massachusetts, and forcibly restrained the state court from foreclosing mortgages on their farms.

WHAT WAS THE RESULT OF SHAYS'S REBELLION?

With Daniel Shays in the lead, a group of farmers who had served in the Continental Army marched to Springfield, Massachusetts, to stop the state court from foreclosing on the veterans' farms. The rebellion illustrated many of the problems of the national government under the Articles of Confederation and is widely thought to have influenced the proceedings of the Constitutional Convention.

2.1

2.2

2.3

2.4

2.5

2.6

constitution
A document establishing the structure, functions, and limitations of a government.

The Miracle at Philadelphia: Writing the U.S. Constitution

2.3 Outline the issues and compromises that were central to the writing of the U.S. Constitution.

On February 21, 1787, in the throes of economic turmoil and with domestic tranquility gone haywire, the Congress passed an official resolution. It called for a Constitutional Convention in Philadelphia for "the sole and express purpose of revising the Articles of Confederation." However, many delegates who gathered in sweltering Philadelphia on May 25, 1787, were prepared to take potentially treasonous steps to preserve the union. For example, on the first day the convention was in session, Edmund Randolph and James Madison of Virginia proposed fifteen resolutions creating an entirely new government (later known as the Virginia Plan). Their enthusiasm, however, was not universal. Many delegates, including William Paterson of New Jersey, considered these resolutions to be in violation of the convention's charter, and proposed the New Jersey Plan, which took greater steps to preserve the Articles.

These proposals met heated debate on the convention's floor. Eventually the Virginia Plan triumphed following a declaration from Randolph that, "When the salvation of the Republic is at stake, it would be treason not to propose what we found necessary."

Although the delegates had established the basic structure of the new government, the work of the Constitutional Convention was not complete. Remaining differences were resolved through a series of compromises, and less than one hundred days after the meeting convened, the Framers had created a new government to submit to the electorate for its approval.

☐ The Characteristics and Motives of the Framers

The fifty-five delegates who attended the Constitutional Convention labored long and hard that hot summer. Owing to the high stakes of their action, they conducted all of the convention's work behind closed doors. George Washington of Virginia, who was unanimously elected the convention's presiding officer, cautioned delegates not to reveal details of the convention even to family members. The delegates agreed to accompany Benjamin Franklin of Pennsylvania to all of his meals. They feared that the normally gregarious gentleman might get carried away with the mood or by liquor and inadvertently let news of the proceedings slip from his tongue.

All of the delegates to the Constitutional Convention were men; hence, they often are called the "Founding Fathers." This text generally refers to them as the Framers, because their work provided the framework for the new government of the United States. Most of them were quite young, many in their twenties and thirties, and only one—Franklin at eighty-one—was rather old. Seventeen owned slaves, with George Washington, George Mason, and John Rutledge owning the most. Thirty-one went to college, and seven signed both the Declaration of Independence and the Constitution.

The Framers brought with them a vast amount of political, educational, legal, and business experience. Clearly, they were an exceptional lot who ultimately produced a brilliant **constitution,** or document establishing the structure, functions, and limitations of a government.

However, debate about the Framers' motives filled the air during the ratification struggle and has provided grist for the mill of historians and political scientists over the years. In his *Economic Interpretation of the Constitution of the United States* (1913), Charles A. Beard argued that the 1780s were a critical period not for the nation as a whole, but rather for business owners who feared that a weak, decentralized government could harm their economic interests.[9] Beard argued that merchants wanted a strong national government to promote industry and trade, to protect private property, and to ensure payment of the public debt—much of which was owed to them. Therefore, according to

Who Were the Framers?

The Framers of the Constitution spent a summer in Philadelphia in nearly complete secrecy, drafting our nation's supreme code of laws. But, who really were these men? They came from varied jobs, cultures, and viewpoints; some men were slaveholders, many were lawyers, and others had little political experience. These differences influenced many of the compromises seen in the final version of the Constitution.

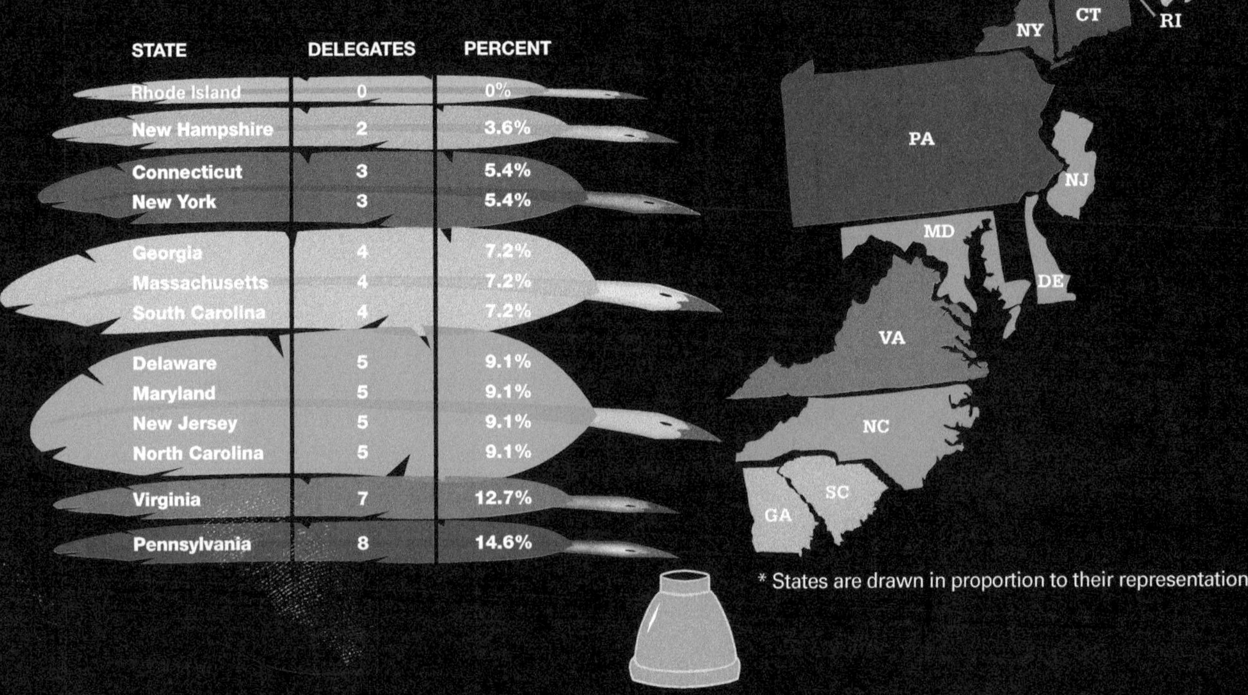

STATE	DELEGATES	PERCENT
Rhode Island	0	0%
New Hampshire	2	3.6%
Connecticut	3	5.4%
New York	3	5.4%
Georgia	4	7.2%
Massachusetts	4	7.2%
South Carolina	4	7.2%
Delaware	5	9.1%
Maryland	5	9.1%
New Jersey	5	9.1%
North Carolina	5	9.1%
Virginia	7	12.7%
Pennsylvania	8	14.6%

* States are drawn in proportion to their representation.

More than just a name

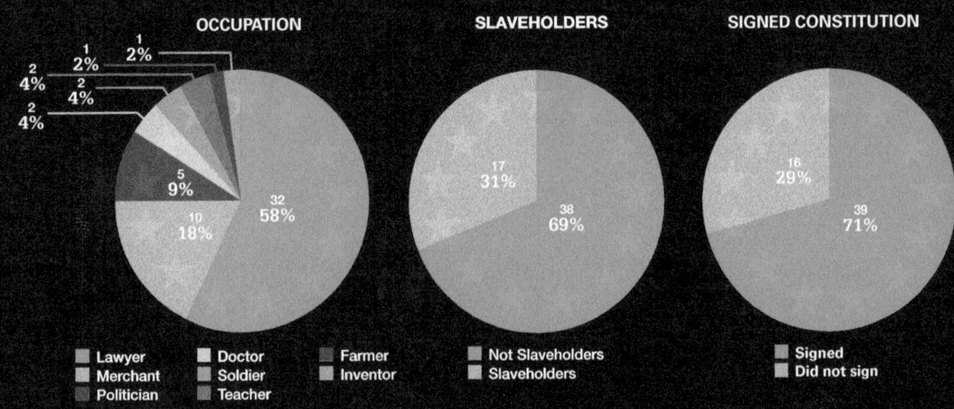

Rhode Island sent no one.

Only 71% of attendees signed the final document.

CRITICAL THINKING QUESTIONS

1. Analyze the occupations of the Framers. Were they a fair representation of the American population at that time? Should more delegates have come from the working class?
2. Examine the percentages of Framers who owned slaves and those who did not. How might these numbers have shaped constitutional compromises on the issue of slavery?
3. Can the words of these Framers, written more than 225 years ago, continue to serve as a framework for government today, or should the Constitution change alongside the nation? Explain your answer.

Virginia Plan
The first general plan for the Constitution offered in Philadelphia. Its key points were a bicameral legislature, as well as an executive and a judiciary chosen by the national legislature.

New Jersey Plan
A framework for the Constitution proposed by a group of small states. Its key points were a one-house legislature with one vote for each state, a Congress with the ability to raise revenue, and a Supreme Court with members appointed for life.

Beard, the Constitution represents "an economic document drawn with superb skill by men whose property interests were immediately at stake."[10]

By the 1950s, Beard's view had fallen into disfavor when other historians were unable to find direct links between wealth and the Framers' motives for establishing the Constitution. Others faulted Beard's failure to consider the impact of religion and individual views about government.[11] In the 1960s, however, another group of historians began to argue that social and economic factors were, in fact, important motives for supporting the Constitution. In *The Anti-Federalists* (1961), Jackson Turner Main posited that while the Constitution's supporters might not have been the united group of creditors suggested by Beard, they were wealthier, came from higher social strata, and had greater concern for maintaining the prevailing social order than the general public.[12] In 1969, Gordon S. Wood's *The Creation of the American Republic* resurrected this debate. Wood deemphasized economics to argue that major social divisions explained different groups' support for (or opposition to) the new Constitution. He concluded that the Framers were representative of a class that favored order and stability over some of the more radical ideas that had inspired the American Revolutionary War and the break with Britain.[13]

☐ The Virginia and New Jersey Plans

The less populous states were concerned with being lost in any new system of government in which states were not treated as equals regardless of population. It is not surprising, therefore, that a large state and then a small one, Virginia and New Jersey, respectively, weighed in with ideas about how the new government should operate.

The **Virginia Plan,** proposed by Edmund Randolph and written by James Madison, called for a national system based heavily on the European nation-state model, wherein the national government derives its powers from the people and not from the member states.

Its key features included:

- Creation of a powerful central government with three branches—the legislative, executive, and judicial.
- A two-house legislature with one house elected directly by the people, the other chosen from among persons nominated by the state legislatures.
- A legislature with the power to select the executive and the judiciary.

In general, smaller states such as New Jersey and Connecticut felt comfortable with the arrangements under the Articles of Confederation. These states offered another model of government, the **New Jersey Plan.** Its key features included:

- Strengthening the Articles, not replacing them.
- Creating a one-house legislature with one vote for each state and with representatives chosen by state legislatures.
- Giving Congress the power to raise revenue from duties on imports and from postal service fees.
- Creating a Supreme Court with members appointed for life by the executive.

☐ Constitutional Compromises

A series of compromises shaped the final Constitution; three of these were particularly important. Below, we discuss the Great Compromise, which concerned the form of the new government, the issue of slavery, and the Three-Fifths Compromise, which dealt with representation.

THE GREAT COMPROMISE The most serious disagreement between the Virginia and New Jersey Plans concerned state representation in Congress. When a deadlock loomed, Connecticut offered its own compromise. Representation in the lower house would be determined by population, and each state would have an equal vote in the upper house. Again, a stalemate occurred.

A committee to work out an agreement soon reported back what became known as the **Great Compromise.** Taking ideas from both the Virginia and New Jersey Plans, it recommended:

- A two-house, or bicameral, legislature.
- In one house of the legislature (later called the House of Representatives), representatives would number fifty-six—no more than one representative for every 30,000 inhabitants. The people would directly elect representatives.
- That house would have the power to originate all bills for raising and spending money.
- In the second house of the legislature (later called the Senate), each state would have an equal vote, and state legislatures would select the representatives.
- In dividing power between the national and state governments, national power would be supreme.[14]

Benjamin Franklin summarized it in this way:

> The diversity of opinions turns on two points. If a proportional representation takes place, the small states contend that their liberties will be in danger. If an equality of votes is to be put in its place, large states say that their money will be in danger. . . . When a broad table is to be made and the edges of a plank do not fit, the artist takes a little from both sides and makes a good joint. In like manner, both sides must part with some of their demands, in order that they both join in some accommodating position.[15]

The Great Compromise ultimately met with the approval of all states in attendance. The smaller states were pleased because they received equal representation in the Senate; the larger states were satisfied with the proportional representation in the House of Representatives. The small states then would dominate the Senate, while the large states, such as Virginia and Pennsylvania, would control the House. But, because both houses had to pass any legislation, neither body could dominate the other.

THE ISSUE OF SLAVERY The Great Compromise dealt with one major concern of the Framers—how best to address the differences in large and small states—but other problems stemming largely from regional differences remained. Slavery, which formed the basis of much of the southern states' cotton economy, was one of the thorniest issues to tackle. To reach an agreement on the Constitution, the Framers had to craft a compromise that balanced southern commercial interests with comparable northern concerns. Eventually, the Framers agreed that Northerners would support continuation of the slave trade for twenty more years, as well as a twenty-year ban on taxing exports to protect the cotton trade, while Southerners consented to a provision requiring only a majority vote on navigation laws. The Framers also gave the national government the authority to regulate foreign commerce and agreed that the Senate would have the power to ratify treaties by a two-thirds majority, which assuaged the fears of southern states, who made up more than one-third of the nation.

THE THREE-FIFTHS COMPROMISE One major conflict had yet to be resolved: how to determine state population with regard to representation in the House of Representatives. Slaves could not vote, but the southern states wanted them included in the determination of population numbers. After considerable dissension, the delegates decided that population for purposes of representation and the apportionment of direct taxes would be calculated by adding the "whole Number of Free Persons" to "three-fifths of all other Persons." "All other Persons" was the delegates' euphemistic way of referring to slaves. Known as the **Three-Fifths Compromise,** this highly political deal ensured that the South would hold 47 percent of the House—enough to prevent attacks on slavery but not so much as to foster the spread of slavery northward.

☐ Unfinished Business: The Executive Branch

The Framers next turned to fashioning an executive branch. While they agreed on the idea of a one-person executive, they could not settle on the length of the term of office or on the procedure for choosing the chief executive. With Shays's Rebellion still fresh

Great Compromise
The final decision of the Constitutional Convention to create a two-house legislature, with the lower house elected by the people and with powers divided between the two houses. It also made national law supreme.

Three-Fifths Compromise
Agreement reached at the Constitutional Convention stipulating that each slave was to be counted as three-fifths of a person for purposes of determining population for representation in the U.S. House of Representatives.

in their minds, the delegates feared putting too much power, including selection of a president, into the hands of the lower classes. At the same time, representatives from the smaller states feared that selection of the chief executive by the legislature would put additional power into the hands of the large states.

Amid these fears, the Committee on Unfinished Portions conducted its sole task: ironing out problems and disagreements concerning the office of chief executive. The committee recommended that the presidential term of office be fixed at four years instead of seven, as had earlier been proposed. The committee also made it possible for a president to serve more than one term.

In addition, the Framers created the Electoral College as a mechanism for selecting the chief executive of the new nation. The Electoral College system gave individual states a key role, because each state would choose electors equal to the number of representatives it had in the House and Senate. This step was a vague compromise that removed election of the president and vice president from both the Congress and the people and placed it in the hands of electors whose method of selection would be left to the states. As Alexander Hamilton noted in *Federalist No. 68,* the Framers fashioned the Electoral College to avoid the "tumult and disorder" that they feared could result if the masses were allowed to vote directly for president. Instead, the task of choosing the president fell to a small number of men (the Electoral College) who "possess[ed] the information and discernment requisite" to decide, in Hamilton's words, the "complicated" business of selecting the president.

In drafting the new Constitution, the Framers also took care to provide for removal of the chief executive. The House of Representatives assumed the sole responsibility of investigating and charging a president or vice president with "Treason, Bribery, or other high Crimes and Misdemeanors." A majority vote then would result in issuing articles of impeachment against the president or vice president. In turn, the Senate took on the sole responsibility of trying the president or vice president on the charges issued by the House. To convict and remove the president or vice president from office required a two-thirds vote of the Senate. The chief justice of the United States was to preside over the Senate proceedings in place of the vice president (that body's constitutional leader) to prevent any conflict of interest on the vice president's part.

The U.S. Constitution

2.4 Analyze the underlying principles of the U.S. Constitution.

The U.S. Constitution's opening line, "We the People," ended, at least for the time being, the question of the source of the government's power: it came directly from the people. The Constitution then explained the need for the new outline of government: "in Order to form a more perfect Union" indirectly acknowledged the weaknesses of the Articles of Confederation in governing a growing nation. Next, the optimistic goals of the Framers for the new nation were set out: to "establish Justice, insure domestic Tranquility, provide for the common defence, promote the general Welfare, and secure the Blessings of Liberty to ourselves and our Posterity," followed by the formal creation of a new government: "do ordain and establish this Constitution for the United States of America."

On September 17, 1787, the delegates approved the Constitution. While the completed document did not satisfy all delegates, of the fifty-five delegates who attended some portion of the meetings, thirty-nine ultimately signed it. The sentiments uttered by Benjamin Franklin probably well reflected those of many others: "Thus, I consent, Sir, to this Constitution because I expect no better, and because I am not sure that it is not the best."[16]

☐ The Basic Principles of the Constitution

The structure of the proposed new national government owed much to the writings of the French philosopher Montesquieu (1689–1755), who advocated distinct functions for

Explore Your World

Written in 1787, the U.S. Constitution is the world's shortest and oldest national constitution still in use. In fact, around the world, the average life span of a constitution written since 1789 is about seventeen years. A lasting, stable constitution may be advantageous for a state, but it may also pose unique challenges; more recent constitutions are able to address modern problems such as civil rights, government bureaucracy, and global trade.

The Constitution of the Kingdom of Norway

(Adopted May 17, 1814)

Section A. Form of Government and Religion

Section B. The Executive Power, the King, and the Royal Family

Section C. Rights of the Citizens and the Legislative Power

Section D. The Judicial Pow

Section E. General Provisic

Both constitutions lay out a basic structure of government that includes three branches: executive, legislative, and judicial.

The Norwegian Constitution is the world's second oldest. It created a unitary system of government led by a constitutional monarch. This constitution endures in part because it can easily be amended to add and delete provisions. In 2012, for example, the legislature passed an amendment separating church and state, thereby nullifying part of the Norwegian Constitution's first section.

THE CONSTITUTION OF THE RUSSIAN FEDERATION

(Adopted December 12, 1993)

SECTION ONE

Chapter 1. The Fundamentals of the Constitutional System
Chapter 2. The Rights and Liberties of Man and Citizen
Chapter 3. The Russian Federation
Chapter 4. The President of the Russian Federation
Chapter 5. The Federal Assembly
Chapter 6. The Government of the Russian Federation
Chapter 7. The Judiciary
Chapter 8. Local Self-Government
Chapter 9. Constitutional Amendments and Revisions

SECTION TWO

Concluding and Transitional Provisions

The Russian Constitution, written after the fall of the Soviet Union, creates a federal system of government. Accordingly, the document contains a high level of detail about the role and powers of state and local governments. It also clearly reserved rights to the people, as articulated in its first section.

CRITICAL THINKING QUESTIONS

1. What are the key differences you observe between these two documents? Are these differences likely the result of temporal, cultural, or political differences?
2. Which elements of the Norwegian Constitution may have enabled it to survive for almost 200 years? How do these elements reflect the era in which it was written?
3. Which elements of the Russian Constitution are particularly striking? How do these elements enable the state to thrive in a globalized, modern world?

separation of powers
A way of dividing the power of government among the legislative, executive, and judicial branches, each staffed separately, with equality and independence of each branch ensured by the Constitution.

checks and balances
A constitutionally mandated structure that gives each of the three branches of government some degree of oversight and control over the actions of the others.

federal system
System of government in which the national government and state governments share power and derive all authority from the people.

each branch of government, called **separation of powers,** with a system of **checks and balances** between each branch. The Constitution's concern with the distribution of power between states and the national government also reveals the heavy influence of political philosophers, as well as the colonists' experience under the Articles of Confederation.[17]

FEDERALISM The question before and during the convention concerned how much power states would give up to the national government. Given the nation's experiences under the Articles of Confederation, the Framers believed that a strong national government was necessary for the new nation's survival. However, they were reluctant to create a powerful government after the model of Great Britain, the country from which they had just won their independence. The colonists did not even consider Great Britain's unitary system. Instead, they fashioned a way (now known as a **federal system**) to divide the power of government between a strong national government and the individual states, with national power being supreme. This system was based on the principle that the federal, or national, government derived its power from the citizens, not the states, as the national government had done under the Articles of Confederation.

Opponents of this system feared that a strong national government would infringe on their liberty. But, supporters of a federal system, such as James Madison, argued that a strong national government with distinct state governments could, if properly directed by constitutional arrangements, actually be a source of expanded liberties and national unity. The Framers viewed the division of governmental authority between the national government and the states as a means of checking power with power, and providing the people with double security against governmental tyranny. Later, the passage of the Tenth Amendment, which stated that powers not given to the national government were reserved by the states or the people, further clarified the federal structure.

SEPARATION OF POWERS James Madison and many of the Framers clearly feared putting too much power into the hands of any one individual or branch of government. Madison's famous words, "Ambition must be made to counteract ambition," were widely believed at the Constitutional Convention.

Separation of powers is simply a way of parceling out power among the three branches of government. Its three key features are:

- Three distinct branches of government: the legislative, the executive, and the judicial.
- Three separately staffed branches of government to exercise these functions.
- Constitutional equality and independence of each branch.

As illustrated in Figure 2.1, the Framers carefully created a system in which law-making, law-enforcing, and law-interpreting functions were assigned to independent branches of government. Only the legislature has the authority to make laws; the chief executive enforces laws; and the judiciary interprets them. Moreover, initially, members of the House of Representatives, members of the Senate, the president, and members of the federal courts were selected by, and therefore responsible to, different constituencies. Madison believed that the scheme devised by the Framers would divide the offices of the new government and their methods of selection among many individuals, providing each office holder with the "necessary means and personal motives to resist encroachment" on his or her power. The Constitution originally placed the selection of senators directly with state legislators, making them more accountable to the states. The Seventeenth Amendment, ratified in 1913, however, called for direct election of senators by the voters, which made them directly accountable to the people and the system thereby more democratic.

The Framers could not have foreseen the intermingling of governmental functions that has since evolved. In Article I of the Constitution, the legislative power is vested in Congress. But, the president also has a role in the legislative process; in order for a bill to become law, he must sign the legislation. If he disagrees with the content of a bill, he may also veto the legislation, although a two-thirds vote in Congress can override his veto. Judicial interpretation also helps to clarify the language or implementation of legislation enacted through this process.

LEGISLATIVE BRANCH POWERS
Pass all federal laws
Pass the federal budget
Declare war
Establish lower federal courts and the number of judges

Legislative Checks on the Executive
Impeach the president
Reject legislation or funding the president wants
Refuse to confirm nominees or approve treaties*
Override the president's veto by a two-thirds vote

Executive Checks on the Legislative
Veto legislation
Call Congress into special session
Implement (or fail to implement) laws passed by Congress

EXECUTIVE BRANCH POWERS
Enforce federal laws and court orders
Propose legislation to Congress
Make foreign treaties
Nominate officers of the U.S. government and federal judges
Serve as commander in chief of the armed forces
Pardon people convicted in federal courts or grant reprieves

Judicial Checks on the Legislative
Rule federal and state laws unconstitutional

Legislative Checks on the Judicial
Change the number and jurisdiction of federal courts
Impeach federal judges
Propose constitutional amendments to override judicial decisions

JUDICIAL BRANCH POWERS
Interpret federal laws and U.S. Constitution
Review the decisions of lower state and federal courts

Judicial Checks on the Executive
Declare executive branch actions unconstitutional
Chief justice presides over impeachment trials

Executive Checks on the Judicial
Appoint federal judges
Refuse to implement decisions

*This power belongs to the Senate only.

FIGURE 2.1 WHAT ARE THE SEPARATION OF POWERS AND HOW DO CHECKS AND BALANCES WORK UNDER THE U.S. CONSTITUTION?

Drawing inspiration from Montesquieu, the Framers crafted a political system of checks and balances and separation of powers. Each of the three branches—executive, legislative, and judicial—has distinct powers, and each branch has powers that intersect with the powers of each of the other branches. This system prevents any one branch from becoming too powerful.

So, instead of a pure system of separation of powers, a symbiotic, or interdependent, relationship among the three branches of government has existed from the beginning. Or, as one scholar has explained, there are "separated institutions sharing powers."[18] While Congress still is entrusted with making the laws, the president, as a single person who can easily capture the attention of the media and the electorate, retains tremendous power in setting the agenda and proposing legislation. And, although the Supreme Court's major function is to interpret the Constitution, its involvement in the 2000 presidential election, which effectively decided the election in favor of George W. Bush, and its decisions affecting criminal procedure, reproductive rights, health care, and other issues have led many critics to charge that it has surpassed its constitutional authority and become, in effect, a law-making body.

CHECKS AND BALANCES The separation of powers among the three branches of the national government is not complete. According to Montesquieu and the Framers, the powers of each branch (as well as the powers of the two houses of the national legislature and the powers between the states and the national government) could be used to check those of the other two governmental branches. The power of each branch of government is checked, or limited, and balanced because the legislative, executive, and judicial branches share some authority, and no branch has exclusive domain over any single activity. The creation of this system allowed the Framers to minimize the threat of tyranny from any one branch. Thus, for almost every power granted to one branch, the Framers established an equal control in the other two branches. For example, although President George W. Bush, as the commander in chief, had the power to deploy American troops to Iraq in 2003, he needed authorization from Congress, under the War Powers Resolution passed in 1973, to keep the troops in the Middle East for longer than ninety days. Similarly, to pay for this mission, the president had to ask Congress to appropriate funds, which it did repeatedly.

☐ The Articles of the Constitution

The document finally signed by the Framers condensed numerous resolutions into a Preamble and seven separate articles remedying many of the deficiencies within the Articles of Confederation (see Table 2.1). The first three articles established the three branches of government, defined their internal operations, and clarified their relationships with one another. The Framers technically considered all branches of government equal, yet some initially appeared more powerful than others. The order of the articles, as well as the detail contained in the first three, reflects the Framers' concern that these branches of government might abuse their powers. The four remaining articles define the relationships between the states, declare national law to be supreme, and set out methods of amending and ratifying the Constitution.

TABLE 2.1 HOW DO THE ARTICLES OF CONFEDERATION AND THE U.S. CONSTITUTION COMPARE TO ONE ANOTHER?

	Articles of Confederation	Constitution
Formal name of the nation	The United States of America	Not specified, but referred to in the Preamble as "the United States of America"
Legislature	Unicameral, called Congress	Bicameral, called Congress, divided into the House of Representatives and the Senate
Members of Congress	Between two and seven members per state	Two senators per state, representatives apportioned according to population of each state
Voting in Congress	One vote per state	One vote per representative or senator
Appointment of members	All appointed by state legislatures, in the manner each legislature directed	Representatives elected by popular vote; senators appointed by state legislatures
Term of legislative office	One year	Two years for representatives; six for senators
Term limit for legislative office	No more than three of every six years	None
When Congress is not in session	A Committee of States had the full powers of Congress	The president of the United States can call on Congress to assemble
Chair of legislature	President of Congress	Speaker of the House of Representatives; vice president is president of the Senate
Executive	None	President
National judiciary	Maritime judiciary established—other courts left to states	Supreme Court established, as well as other courts Congress deems necessary
Adjudicator of disputes between states	Congress	Supreme Court
New states	Admitted upon agreement of nine states (special exemption provided for Canada)	Admitted upon agreement of majority of Congress
Amendment	When agreed upon by all states	When agreed upon by three-fourths of the states
Navy	Congress authorized to build a navy; states authorized to equip warships to counter piracy	Congress authorized to build a navy; states not allowed to keep ships of war
Army	Congress to decide on size of force and to requisition troops from each state according to population	Congress authorized to raise and support armies
Power to coin money	United States and the states	United States only
Taxes	Apportioned by Congress, collected by the states	Levied and collected by Congress
Ratification	Unanimous consent required	Consent of nine states required

ARTICLE I: THE LEGISLATIVE BRANCH Article I vests all legislative powers in the Congress and establishes a bicameral legislature, consisting of the Senate and the House of Representatives. It also sets out the qualifications for holding office in each house, the terms of office, the methods of selection of representatives and senators, and the system of apportionment among the states to determine membership in the House of Representatives. Article I, section 2, specifies that an "enumeration" of the citizenry must take place every ten years in a manner to be directed by the U.S. Congress.

One of the most important sections of Article I is section 8. It carefully lists those powers the Framers wished the new Congress to possess. These specified, or **enumerated, powers** contain many key provisions that had been denied to the Continental Congress under the Articles of Confederation. For example, one major weakness of the Articles was Congress's lack of authority to deal with trade wars. The Constitution remedied this problem by authorizing Congress to "regulate Commerce with foreign Nations, and among the several States." Congress was also given the authority to coin and raise money.

After careful enumeration of seventeen powers of Congress in Article I, section 8, a final, general clause authorizing Congress to "make all Laws which shall be necessary and proper for carrying into Execution the foregoing Powers" completes Article I. Often referred to as the elastic clause, the **necessary and proper clause** has been a source of tremendous congressional activity never anticipated by the Framers, including the passage of laws that regulate the environment, welfare programs, education, and communication.

The necessary and proper clause is the basis for the **implied powers** that Congress uses to execute its other powers. Congress's enumerated power to regulate commerce has been linked with the necessary and proper clause in a variety of U.S. Supreme Court cases. As a result, laws banning prostitution where travel across state lines is involved, regulating trains and planes, establishing federal minimum wage and maximum hour laws, and mandating drug testing for certain workers have passed constitutional muster under the implied powers.

enumerated powers
The powers of the national government specifically granted to Congress in Article I, section 8 of the Constitution.

necessary and proper clause
The final paragraph of Article I, section 8, of the Constitution, which gives Congress the authority to pass all laws "necessary and proper" to carry out the enumerated powers specified in the Constitution; also called the elastic clause.

implied powers
The powers of the national government derived from the enumerated powers and the necessary and proper clause.

ARTICLE II: THE EXECUTIVE BRANCH Article II vests the executive power, that is, the authority to execute the laws of the nation, in a president of the United States. Section 1 sets the president's term of office at four years and explains the Electoral College. It also states the qualifications for office and describes a mechanism to replace the president in case of death, disability, or removal from office. Article II also limits the presidency to natural-born citizens.

The powers and duties of the president are set out in section 3. Among the most important of these are the president's role as commander in chief of the armed forces, the authority to make treaties with the consent of the Senate, and the authority to "appoint Ambassadors, other public Ministers and Consuls, the Judges of the supreme Court, and all other Officers of the United States." Other sections of Article II instruct the president to report directly to Congress "from time to time," in what has come to be known as the State of the Union Address, and to "take Care that the Laws be faithfully executed." Section 4 provides the mechanism for removal of the president, vice president, and other officers of the United States for "Treason, Bribery, or other high Crimes and Misdemeanors."

ARTICLE III: THE JUDICIAL BRANCH Article III establishes a Supreme Court and defines its jurisdiction. During the Philadelphia meeting, the small and large states differed significantly regarding both the desirability of an independent judiciary and the role of state courts in the national court system. The smaller states feared that a strong unelected judiciary would trample on their liberties. In compromise, the Framers permitted Congress to establish lower national courts but did not require it. Thus, state courts and the national court system would exist side by side with distinct areas of authority. Federal courts had authority to decide cases arising under federal law and the U.S. Constitution. The U.S. Supreme Court also assumed the power to settle disputes between states, or between a state and the national government. Ultimately, it was up to the Supreme Court to determine what the provisions of the Constitution actually meant.

2.1

2.2

2.3

2.4

2.5

2.6

full faith and credit clause
Section of Article IV of the Constitution that ensures judicial decrees and contracts made in one state will be binding and enforceable in any other state.

supremacy clause
Portion of Article VI of the Constitution mandating that national law is supreme to (that is, supersedes) all other laws passed by the states or by any other subdivision of government.

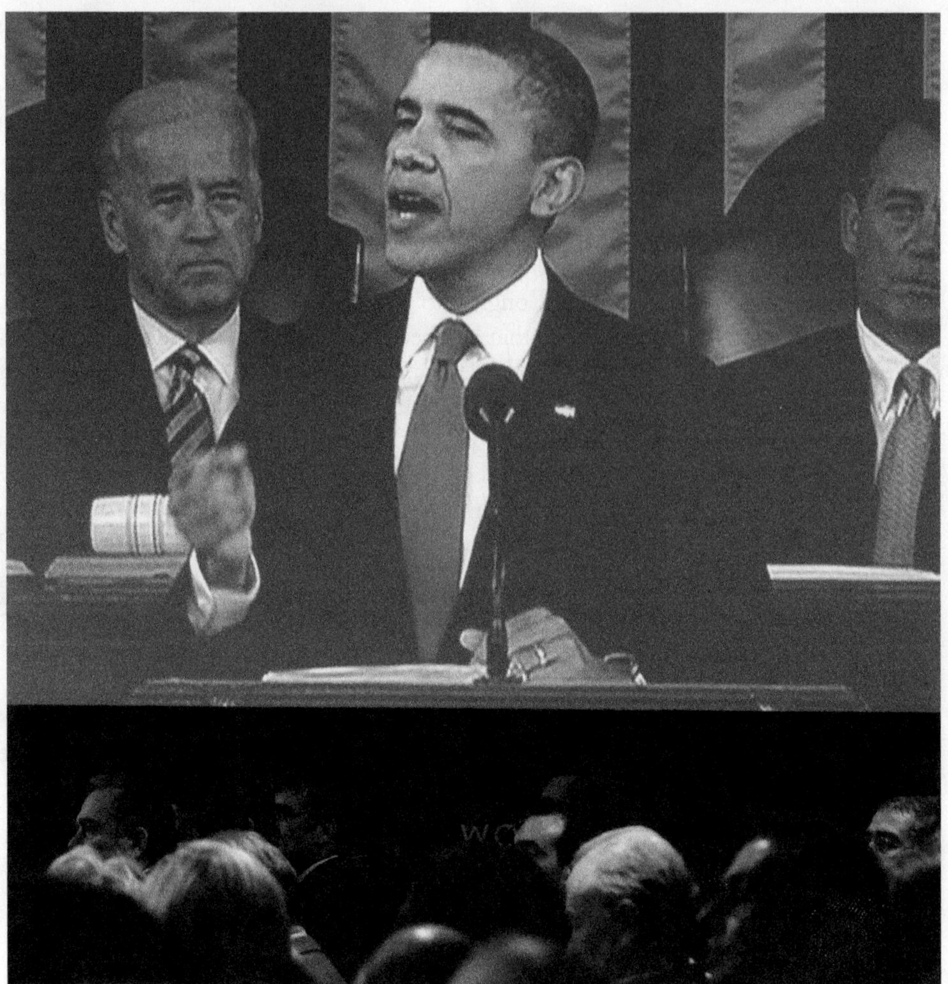

WHY DOES THE PRESIDENT DELIVER A STATE OF THE UNION ADDRESS?

In Article II of the Constitution, the Framers required the president to report directly to Congress "from time to time" about the affairs of the state. Today, the speech has become a media event; the president's address is carried live on television, radio, and the Internet. Here, viewers watch President Obama deliver his 2012 State of the Union address. Vice President Joe Biden and Speaker of the House John Boehner sit behind him.

Although some delegates to the convention urged that the president have authority to remove federal judges, ultimately judges received appointments for life, presuming "good behavior." And, like the president's, their salaries cannot be lowered while they hold office, thereby ensuring that the legislature not attempt to punish the Supreme Court or any other judges for unpopular decisions.

ARTICLES IV THROUGH VII The remainder of the articles in the Constitution attempted to anticipate problems that might occur in the operation of the new national government as well as its relations to the states. Article IV begins with what is called the **full faith and credit clause,** which mandates that states honor the laws and judicial proceedings of other states. Article IV also includes the mechanisms for admitting new states to the union.

Article V (discussed in greater detail on MyPoliSciLab) specifies how amendments can be added to the Constitution. The Bill of Rights, which added ten amendments to the Constitution in 1791, was one of the first items of business when the First Congress met in 1789.

Article VI contains the supremacy clause, which asserts the basic primacy of the Constitution and national law over state laws and constitutions. The **supremacy clause** provides that the "Constitution, and the laws of the United States" as well as all treaties are to be the supreme law of the land. All national and state officers and judges are bound by national law and take oaths to support the federal Constitution above any state law or constitution. Because of the supremacy clause, any legitimate exercise of national power supersedes any state laws or action, in a process called preemption. Without the supremacy clause and the federal courts' ability to invoke it, the national government would have little actual enforceable power; thus, many commentators call the supremacy clause the linchpin of the entire federal system.

Mindful of the potential problems that could occur if church and state were too enmeshed, the Framers specified in Article VI that no religious test shall be required for holding any office. This mandate is strengthened by the separation of church and state guarantee that became part of the Constitution when the First Amendment was ratified.

The seventh and final article of the Constitution concerns the procedures for ratifying the new Constitution: nine of the thirteen states would have to agree to, or ratify, its new provisions before it would become the supreme law of the land.

Federalists
Those who favored a stronger national government and supported the proposed U.S. Constitution; later became the first U.S. political party.

The Drive for Ratification of the U.S. Constitution

2.5 Explain the conflicts that characterized the drive for ratification of the U.S. Constitution.

While delegates to the Constitutional Convention labored in Philadelphia, the Congress of the Confederation continued to govern the former colonies under the Articles of Confederation. The day after the delegates signed the Constitution, William Jackson, the secretary of the Constitutional Convention, left for New York City, then the nation's capital, to deliver the official copy of the document to the Congress. He also took with him a resolution of the delegates calling upon each of the states to vote on the new Constitution. Anticipating resistance from representatives in the state legislatures, however, the Framers required the states to call special ratifying conventions to consider the proposed Constitution.

Explore on MyPoliSciLab Simulation: You Are a Founder

Jackson carried a letter from General George Washington along with the proposed Constitution. In a few eloquent words, Washington summed up the sentiments of the Framers and the spirit of compromise that had permeated the long weeks in Philadelphia:

> That it will meet the full and entire approbation of every state is not perhaps to be expected, but each [state] will doubtless consider, that had her interest alone been consulted, the consequences might have been particularly disagreeable or injurious to others; that it is liable to as few exceptions as could reasonably have been expected, we hope and believe; that it may promote lasting welfare of that country so dear to us all, and secure her freedom and happiness is our ardent wish [19]

The Congress of the Confederation immediately accepted the work of the convention and forwarded the proposed Constitution to the states for their vote It was by no means certain, however, that the states would adopt the new Constitution. From the fall of 1787 to the summer of 1788, debate over the proposed Constitution raged around the nation State politicians understandably feared a strong central government. Farmers and other working-class people feared a distant national government. And, those who had accrued substantial debts during the economic chaos following the Revolutionary War feared that a new government with a new financial policy would plunge them into even greater debt. The public in general was very leery of taxes—these were the same people who had revolted against the king's taxes. At the heart of many of their concerns lay an underlying apprehension of the massive changes that a new system would create. Favoring the Constitution were wealthy merchants, lawyers, bankers, and those who believed that the new nation could not continue to exist under the Articles of Confederation. For them, it all boiled down to one simple question offered by James Madison: "Whether or not the Union shall or shall not be continued."

Federalists Versus Anti-Federalists

During the debate over whether to ratify the Constitution, those who favored the new strong national government chose to call themselves **Federalists.** They were well aware

Explore on MyPoliSciLab

How Long Did It Take to Ratify the Constitution?

Americans today generally support the principles of the Constitution, but after the Framers adjourned on September 17, 1787, three years passed before all thirteen states approved the document. The ensuing ratification debate was an inherently political game of multiple moves, in which the Constitution was kept alive by relatively narrow majorities, particularly in two strategically located states.

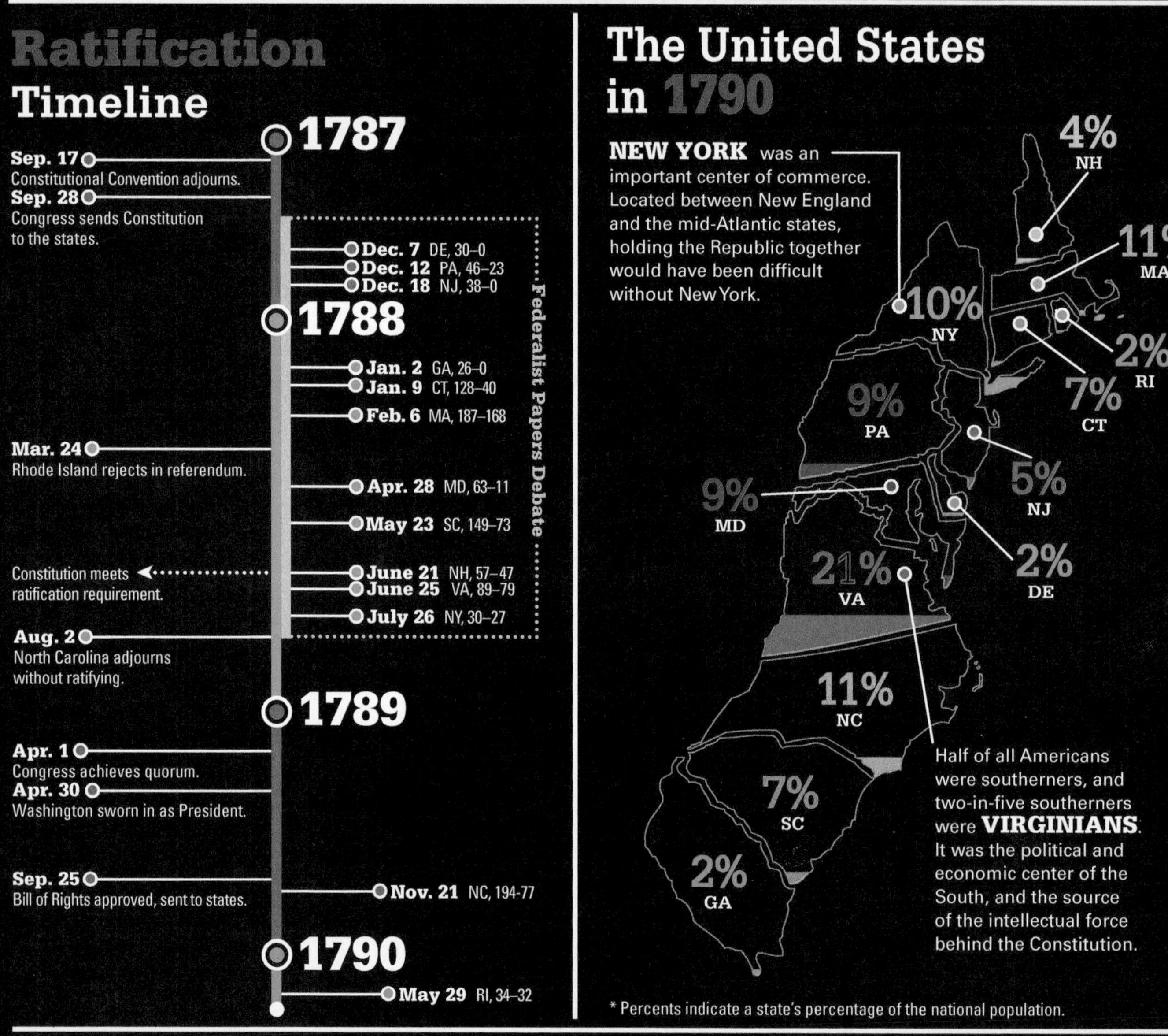

Investigate Further

Concept Why did it take three years for all thirteen states to ratify the Constitution? The first states to ratify the Constitution did so with a strong majority of support for the document. But as those states signed on, opposition in remaining states grew, and the ratification debate intensified.

Connection Which states were most closely divided on ratification? The debate intensified in two strategic states: New York and Virginia. Ratification in those two holdout states was necessary in order to lend legitimacy to the new government.

Cause What were the issues of the debate? Written in support of the new government, *The Federalist Papers* addressed New Yorkers' concerns about federal power. For Virginians, the sticking point was a Bill of Rights, which James Madison promised to introduce in the new Congress.

TABLE 2.2 WHAT WERE THE DIFFERENCES BETWEEN THE FEDERALISTS AND THE ANTI-FEDERALISTS?

	Federalists	Anti-Federalists
Who were they?	Property owners, landed rich, merchants of Northeast and Mid-Atlantic	Small farmers, shopkeepers, laborers
Political philosophy	Elitist; saw themselves and those of their class as most fit to govern (others were to be governed)	Believed in the decency of "the common man" and in participatory democracy; viewed elites as corrupt; sought greater protection of individual rights
Type of government favored	Powerful central government; two-house legislature; upper house (six-year term) further removed from the people, whom they distrusted	Wanted stronger state governments (closer to the people) at the expense of the powers of the national government; sought smaller electoral districts, frequent elections, referendum and recall, and a large unicameral legislature to provide for greater class and occupational representation
Alliances	Pro-British, anti-French	Anti-British, pro-French

that many people still generally opposed the notion of a strong national government. They did not want to risk being labeled nationalists, so they tried to get the upper hand in the debate by nicknaming their opponents **Anti-Federalists.** As noted in Table 2.2, Anti-Federalists argued that they simply wanted to protect state governments from the tyranny of a too powerful national government.[20]

Anti-Federalists
Those who favored strong state governments and a weak national government; opposed ratification of the U.S. Constitution.

The Federalist Papers
A series of eighty-five political essays written by Alexander Hamilton, James Madison, and John Jay in support of ratification of the U.S. Constitution.

Federalists and Anti-Federalists participated in the mass meetings held in state legislatures to discuss the pros and cons of the new plan. Tempers ran high at these meetings, and fervent debates were discussed at town hall meetings and published in newspapers, which played a powerful role in the adoption process. Just two days after the convention's end, in fact, the *Pennsylvania Packet* printed the entire Constitution. Other major papers quickly followed suit. Soon, opinion pieces on both sides of the adoption issue began to appear around the nation, often written under pseudonyms such as "Caesar" or "Constant Reader," as was the custom of the day.

☐ *The Federalist Papers*

One name stood out from all the rest: "Publius" (Latin for "the people"). Between October 1787 and May 1788, eighty-five essays written under that pen name routinely appeared in newspapers in New York, a state where ratification was in doubt. Alexander Hamilton and James Madison wrote most of them. Hamilton, a young, fiery New Yorker born in the British West Indies, wrote fifty-one; Madison, a Virginian who later served as the fourth president, authored twenty-six; jointly they penned another three. John Jay, also of New York, and later the first chief justice of the United States, wrote five of the pieces. These eighty-five essays became known as ***The Federalist Papers.***

Today, *The Federalist Papers* are considered masterful explanations of the Framers' intentions as they drafted the new Constitution. At the time, although they were reprinted widely, they were far too theoretical to have much impact on those who would ultimately vote on the proposed Constitution. Dry and scholarly, they lacked the fervor of much of the political rhetoric then in use. *The Federalist Papers* did, however, highlight the reasons for the new government's structure and its benefits. According to *Federalist No. 10,* for example, the new Constitution was called "a republican remedy for the disease incident to republican government." These musings of Madison, Hamilton, and Jay continue to stand as the clearest articulation of the political theories and philosophies that lie at the heart of our Constitution.

Forced on the defensive, the Anti-Federalists responded to *The Federalist Papers* with their own series of letters written under the pen names "Brutus" and "Cato," two ancient Romans famous for their intolerance of tyranny. These letters (actually essays) undertook a line-by-line critique of the Constitution, as did other works.

Anti-Federalists argued that a strong central government would render the states powerless.[21] They stressed the strengths granted to the government under the Articles of Confederation and maintained that the Articles, not the proposed Constitution, created a true federal system. Moreover, they believed that the strong national government would tax heavily, that the U.S. Supreme Court would overwhelm the states by invalidating state laws, and that the president eventually would have too much power as commander in chief of a large and powerful army.[22]

In particular, Anti-Federalists feared the power of the national government to run roughshod over the liberties of the people. They proposed that the taxing power of Congress be limited, that the executive be curbed by a council, that the military consist of state militias rather than a national force, and that the jurisdiction of the Supreme Court be limited to prevent it from reviewing and potentially overturning the decisions of state courts. But, their most effective argument concerned the absence of a bill of rights in the Constitution. James Madison answered these criticisms in *Federalist Nos. 10* and *51*. In *Federalist No. 10*, Madison pointed out that the voters would not always succeed in electing "enlightened statesmen" as their representatives. The greatest threat to individual liberties would therefore come from factions within the government, who might place narrow interests above broader national interests and the rights of citizens. While recognizing that no form of government could protect the country from unscrupulous politicians, Madison argued that the organization of the new government would minimize the effects of political factions. The great advantage of a federal system, Madison maintained, was that it created the "happy combination" of a national government too large for any single faction to control and several state governments that would be smaller and more responsive to local needs. Moreover, he argued in *Federalist No. 51* that the proposed federal government's separation of powers would prohibit any one branch from either dominating the national government or violating the rights of citizens.

☐ Ratifying the Constitution

Debate continued in the thirteen states as votes were taken from December 1787 to June 1788, in accordance with the ratifying process laid out in Article VII of the proposed Constitution. Three states acted quickly to ratify the new Constitution. Two small states, Delaware and New Jersey, voted to ratify before the large states could rethink the notion of equal representation of the states in the Senate. Pennsylvania, where Federalists were well organized, was also one of the first three states to ratify. Massachusetts assented to the new government but tempered its support by calling for an immediate addition of amendments, including one protecting personal rights. New Hampshire became the crucial ninth state to ratify on June 21, 1788. This action completed the ratification process outlined in Article VII of the Constitution and marked the beginning of a new nation. But, New York and Virginia, which at that time accounted for more than 40 percent of the new nation's population, had not yet ratified the Constitution. Thus, the practical future of the new nation remained in doubt.

Hamilton in New York and Madison in Virginia worked feverishly to convince delegates to their state conventions to vote for the new government. In New York, sentiment against the Constitution ran high. In Albany, fighting broke out over ratification and resulted in injuries and death. When news of Virginia's acceptance of the Constitution reached the New York convention, Hamilton was able to convince a majority of those present to follow suit by a margin of three votes. Both states also recommended the addition of a series of structural amendments and a bill of rights.

North Carolina and Rhode Island continued to hold out against ratification. Both had recently printed new currencies and feared that values would plummet in a federal system that authorized the Congress to coin money. On August 2, 1788, North Carolina became the first state to reject the Constitution on the grounds that no Anti-Federalist amendments were included. Soon after, in September 1789, owing much to the Anti-Federalist pressure for additional protections from the national government, Congress submitted the Bill of Rights to the states for their ratification. North Carolina then ratified the Constitution by a vote of 194–77. Rhode Island, the only state that had not sent representatives to Philadelphia, remained out of the new nation until 1790. Finally, under threats from its largest cities to secede from the state, the legislature called a convention that ratified the Constitution by only two votes (34–32)—one year after George Washington became the first president of the United States.

The Bill of Rights

Once the Constitution was ratified, elections took place. When Congress convened, it immediately sent a set of amendments to the states for ratification. An amendment authorizing the enlargement of the House of Representatives and another to prevent members of the House from raising their own salaries failed to garner favorable votes in the necessary three-fourths of the states. The remaining ten amendments, known as the **Bill of Rights,** were ratified by 1791 in accordance with the procedures set out in the Constitution. Sought by Anti-Federalists as a protection for individual liberties, they offered numerous specific limitations on the national government's ability to interfere with a wide variety of personal liberties, some of which many state constitutions had already guaranteed. These include freedom of expression, speech, press, religion, and assembly, guaranteed by the First Amendment. The Bill of Rights also contains numerous safeguards for those accused of crimes. The Ninth Amendment notes that these enumerated rights are not inclusive, meaning they are not the only rights to be enjoyed by the people, and the Tenth Amendment states that powers not given to the national government are reserved by the states or the people.

Bill of Rights
The first ten amendments to the U.S. Constitution, which largely guarantee specific rights and liberties.

Toward Reform: Methods of Amending the U.S. Constitution

2.6 Distinguish between the methods for proposing and ratifying amendments to the U.S. Constitution.

The Framers did not want to fashion a government subject to the whims of the people. Therefore, they made the formal amendment process a slow one to guard against impulsive amendment of the Constitution. In keeping with this intent, only seventeen amendments have been added since the Bill of Rights. However, informal amendments, prompted by judicial interpretation, cultural and social change, and technological change, have had a tremendous impact on the Constitution.

Formal Methods of Amending the Constitution

Article V of the Constitution creates a two-stage amendment process: proposal and ratification. The Constitution specifies two ways to accomplish each stage. As illustrated in Figure 2.2, amendments to the Constitution can be proposed by: (1) a vote of two-thirds of the members in both houses of Congress; or, (2) a vote of two-thirds of the state legislatures specifically requesting Congress to call a national convention to propose amendments.

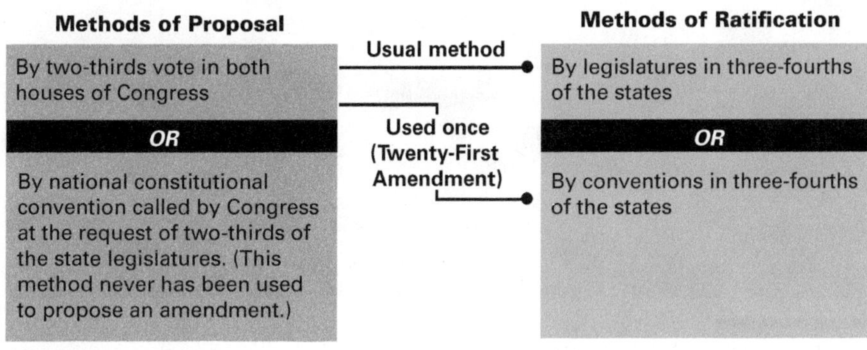

FIGURE 2.2 HOW CAN THE U.S. CONSTITUTION BE AMENDED?

There are two stages to the amendment process: proposal and ratification. An amendment can be proposed by two-thirds of either both houses of Congress or the state legislatures. It can be ratified by three-fourths of the state legislatures or special ratifying conventions called in each of the states.

The second method has never been used. Historically, it has served as a fairly effective threat, forcing Congress to consider amendments it might otherwise never have debated. In the 1980s, for example, several states called on Congress to enact a balanced budget amendment. To forestall a special constitutional convention, in 1985, Congress enacted the Gramm-Rudman-Hollings Act, which called for a balanced budget by the 1991 fiscal year. A three-judge district court later ruled the act unconstitutional on the grounds that the law violated separation of powers principles.

The ratification process is fairly straightforward. When Congress votes to propose an amendment, the Constitution specifies that the ratification process must occur in one of two ways: (1) a favorable vote in three-fourths of the state legislatures; or, (2) a favorable vote in specially called ratifying conventions in three-fourths of the states.

The Constitution itself was ratified by the favorable vote of nine states in specially called ratifying conventions. The Framers feared that the power of special interests in state legislatures would prevent a positive vote on the new Constitution. Since ratification of the Constitution, however, only one ratifying convention has been called. The Eighteenth Amendment, which outlawed the sale of alcoholic beverages nationwide, was ratified by the first method—a vote in state legislatures. Millions of people broke the law, others died from drinking homemade liquor, and still others made their fortunes selling bootleg or illegal liquor. After a decade of these problems, Congress decided to act. It proposed an additional amendment—the Twenty-First—to repeal the Eighteenth Amendment. Congress sent the amendment to the states for ratification, but with a call for ratifying conventions, not a vote in state legislatures.[23] Members of Congress correctly predicted that the move to repeal the Eighteenth Amendment would encounter opposition in the state houses, which conservative rural legislators largely controlled. Thus, Congress's decision to use the convention method led to quick approval of the Twenty-First Amendment.

WHICH IS THE ONLY CONSTITUTIONAL AMENDMENT TO BE REPEALED?

For all its moral support from groups such as the Women's Christian Temperance Union (WCTU), whose members invaded bars to protest the sale of alcoholic beverages, the Eighteenth (Prohibition) Amendment was a disaster. Among its side effects was the rise of powerful crime organizations responsible for illegal sales of alcoholic beverages. Once proposed, it took only ten months to ratify the Twenty-First Amendment, which repealed the Prohibition Amendment.

The Congress, whenever two thirds of both houses shall deem it necessary, shall propose amendments to this Constitution, or, on the application of the legislatures of two thirds of the several states, shall call a convention for proposing amendments, which, in either case, shall be valid to all intents and purposes, as part of this Constitution, when ratified by the legislatures of three fourths of the several states, or by conventions in three fourths thereof, as the one or the other mode of ratification may be proposed by the Congress. —ARTICLE V

With this article, the Framers acknowledged the potential need to change or amend the Constitution. This article provides for two methods to propose amendments: by a two-thirds vote of both houses of Congress or by a two-thirds vote of the state legislatures. It also specifies two alternative methods of ratification of proposed amendments: by a three-quarters vote of the state legislatures, or by a similar vote in specially called state ratifying conventions.

During the Constitutional Convention in Philadelphia, the Framers were divided as to how frequently or how easily the Constitution was to be amended. The original suggestion was to allow the document to be amended "when soever it shall seem necessary." Some delegates wanted to entrust this authority to the state legislatures; however, others feared that it would give states too much power. James Madison alleviated these fears by suggesting that both Congress and the states have a role in the process.

In the late 1960s and early 1970s, leaders of the new women's rights movement sought passage of the Equal Rights Amendment (ERA). Their efforts were rewarded when the ERA was approved in the House and Senate by overwhelming majorities in 1972 and then sent out to the states for their approval. In spite of tremendous lobbying, a strong anti-ERA movement emerged and the amendment failed to gain approval in three-quarters of the state legislatures.

The failed battles for the ERA as well as other amendments, including one to prohibit child labor and another to grant statehood to the District of Columbia, underscore how difficult it is to amend the Constitution. Thus, unlike the constitutions of individual states or many other nations, the U.S. Constitution rarely has been amended. Still, the ERA has been proposed in every session of Congress since 1923.

CRITICAL THINKING QUESTIONS

1. What would it take to get an equal rights amendment added to the U.S. Constitution?
2. Does your state already have an equal rights amendment? What does it guarantee?

The intensity of efforts to amend the Constitution has varied considerably, depending on the nature of the change proposed. Whereas the Twenty-First Amendment took only ten months to ratify, the Equal Rights Amendment (ERA) was introduced in every session of Congress from 1923 until 1972, when Congress finally voted favorably for it. Even then, years of lobbying by women's groups were insufficient to garner necessary state support. By 1982, the congressionally mandated date for ratification, only thirty-five states—three short of the number required—had voted favorably on the amendment.[24] Yet, it has been reintroduced every session in a somewhat symbolic move.

☐ Informal Methods of Amending the Constitution

The formal amendment process is not the only way the Constitution has been altered over time. Judicial interpretation, cultural and social change, and the growth of technology also have had a major impact on how the Constitution has evolved.

JUDICIAL INTERPRETATION As early as 1803, the Supreme Court declared in *Marbury* v. *Madison* that federal courts had the power to nullify acts of the nation's government when the courts found such acts to conflict with the Constitution.[25] Over the years, this check on the other branches of government and on the states has increased the authority of the Court and significantly altered the meaning of various provisions of the Constitution. This fact prompted President Woodrow Wilson to call the Supreme Court "a constitutional convention in continuous session," a role demonstrated by recent decisions in civil liberties, civil rights, and economic regulation.

Today, some analysts argue that the original intent of the Framers—as evidenced in *The Federalist Papers,* as well as in private notes taken by James Madison at the Constitutional Convention—should govern judicial interpretation of the Constitution.[26] Others argue that the Framers knew a changing society needed an elastic, flexible document that could adapt to the ages.[27] In all likelihood, the vagueness of the document was purposeful. Those in attendance in Philadelphia recognized that they could not agree on everything and that it was wiser to leave interpretation to future generations.

SOCIAL AND CULTURAL CHANGE Even the most far-sighted of those in attendance at the Constitutional Convention could not have anticipated the vast changes that have occurred in the United States. For example, although many people were uncomfortable with the Three-Fifths Compromise and others hoped for the abolition of slavery, none could have imagined that an African American would one day become president of the United States. Likewise, few of the Framers could have anticipated the diverse roles that women would play in American society. The Constitution has evolved to accommodate such social and cultural changes. Thus, although no specific amendment guarantees women equal protection under the law, federal courts have interpreted the Constitution to prohibit many forms of gender discrimination, thereby recognizing cultural and societal change.

Social change has also caused alterations in the way institutions of government act. As problems such as the Great Depression appeared national in scope, Congress took on more and more power at the expense of states. In fact, Yale law professor Bruce Ackerman argues that extraordinary times call for extraordinary measures such as the New Deal that, in effect, amend the Constitution. Thus, congressional passage (and the Supreme Court's eventual acceptance) of sweeping New Deal legislation that altered the balance of power between the national government and the states truly changed the Constitution without benefit of amendment.[28]

TECHNOLOGICAL CHANGE Technological advances of the twenty-first century bring up new questions concerning privacy and our rights under the Constitution, including regulation of television airwaves and Internet content, as well as the need for security surveillance systems. The development and growth of social media has also redefined free speech in the classroom and the workplace; online posts can be grounds for firing employees or expelling students. In 2011, for example, an employee of Hispanics United of Buffalo, a nonprofit organization that provides social services for low income clients, posted Facebook comments concerning the performance of another employee. Upon discovery of these comments, the five people involved were fired according to the company's policy of zero tolerance for cyber harassment. Although the employees were ultimately reinstated, the case calls into question our understanding of the scope and application of the Bill of Rights.

Changes in technology have also led our political institutions to expand into areas never imagined by the Framers. The Constitution, for example, does not explicitly empower Congress to create a Social Security system. But, in an effort to address growing poverty among senior citizens during the Great Depression, Congress created this program in 1935. Today, owing in part to advances in medical technology and greater life expectancies, the program issues $52.5 million per month to retirees, dependents, and the disabled.[29] In spite of such massive modifications, the Constitution survives, changed and ever changing after more than 200 years.

On MyPoliSciLab

Review the Chapter

 Listen to Chapter 2 on MyPoliSciLab

Roots of the New American Nation

2.1 Trace the historical developments that led to the colonists' break with Great Britain and the emergence of the new American nation, p. 31.

Settlers came to the New World for a variety of reasons, but most of these early inhabitants remained loyal to Great Britain and considered themselves subjects of the king. Over the years, as new generations of Americans were born on colonial soil, those ties weakened. A series of taxes levied by the British crown ultimately led colonists to convene the Second Continental Congress and to declare their independence.

The First Attempt at Government: The Articles of Confederation

2.2 Identify the key components of the Articles of Confederation and the reasons why it failed, p. 37.

The Articles of Confederation (1781) created a loose league of friendship between the new national government and the states. Numerous weaknesses in the new government quickly became apparent. Among the major flaws were Congress's inability to tax or regulate commerce, the absence of an executive to administer the government, the lack of a strong central government, and no judiciary.

The Miracle at Philadelphia: Writing the U.S. Constitution

2.3 Outline the issues and compromises that were central to the writing of the U.S. Constitution, p. 40.

When weaknesses of the Articles of Confederation became apparent, the states called for a meeting to reform them. The Constitutional Convention (1787) threw out the Articles of Confederation and fashioned a new, more workable form of government. The U.S. Constitution resulted from a series of compromises, including those over representation, issues involving large and small states, slavery, and how to determine population. The delegates also made compromises on how members of each branch of government were to be selected. They created the Electoral College to give states a key role in the selection of the president.

The U.S. Constitution

2.4 Analyze the underlying principles of the U.S. Constitution, p. 44.

The proposed U.S. Constitution created a federal system that drew heavily on Montesquieu's ideas about separation of powers. These ideas concerned a way of parceling out power among the three branches of government. A system of checks and balances also prevented any one branch from having too much power.

The Drive for Ratification of the U.S. Constitution

2.5 Explain the conflicts that characterized the drive for ratification of the U.S. Constitution, p. 51.

The drive for ratification became a fierce fight between Federalists and Anti-Federalists. Federalists lobbied for the strong national government created by the Constitution; Anti-Federalists favored greater state power.

Toward Reform: Methods of Amending the U.S. Constitution

2.6 Distinguish between the methods for proposing and ratifying amendments to the U.S. Constitution, p. 55.

The Framers did not want the whims of the people to sway the government unduly. Therefore, they designed a deliberate two-stage, formal amendment process that required approval on both federal and state levels; this process has rarely been used. However, informal amendments, prompted by judicial interpretation, cultural and social changes, and technological change, have had a tremendous impact on the Constitution.

Learn the Terms

 Study and Review the Flashcards

Anti-Federalists, p. 53
Articles of Confederation, p. 37
Bill of Rights, p. 55
checks and balances, p. 46
Committees of Correspondence, p. 34
confederation, p. 37
constitution, p. 40
Declaration of Independence, p. 35
enumerated powers, p. 49

federal system, p. 46
The Federalist Papers, p. 53
Federalists, p. 51
First Continental Congress, p. 34
full faith and credit clause, p. 50
Great Compromise, p. 43
implied powers, p. 49
mercantilism, p.32
necessary and proper clause, p. 49
New Jersey Plan, p. 42
Second Continental Congress, p. 34
separation of powers, p. 46
Shays's Rebellion, p. 39
Stamp Act Congress, p. 32
supremacy clause, p. 50
Three-Fifths Compromise, p. 43
Virginia Plan, p. 42

Test Yourself

Study and **Review** the **Practice Tests**

1. Which organization functioned as a powerful molder of public opinion against the British?

a. Stamp Act Congress
b. Committees of Correspondence
c. First Continental Congress
d. Second Continental Congress
e. The Boston Massacre

2. The first major gathering of the colonies was the

a. Committees of Correspondence
b. First Continental Congress
c. Second Continental Congress
d. Stamp Act Congress
e. Congress of the Confederation

3. The Declaration of Independence was most directly influenced by which political philosopher?

a. John Locke
b. Thomas Hobbes
c. Isaac Newton
d. Montesquieu
e. Jean-Jacques Rousseau

4. Why did the Articles of Confederation create a national system of government whose power was derived from the states?

a. Disagreements in the Continental Congress necessitated a compromise between those who wanted a strong national government and those who supported strong state governments.
b. The Articles formalized the system of government proposed by the Declaration of Independence.
c. The Framers sought to create a system similar to that of other democracies.
d. It was a reaction to Great Britain's unitary system of government.
e. The states wanted to cede power to a stronger national authority.

5. What was the greatest weakness of the Articles of Confederation?

a. Congress had no specific power to tax.
b. Congress was allowed to regulate only international trade.
c. The central government was too strong.
d. There was no provision for a legislative branch.
e. There was no provision for a judicial system.

6. What was the major difference between the Virginia Plan and the New Jersey Plan?

a. The Virginia Plan created a two-house legislature, while the New Jersey Plan created a one-house legislature.
b. The Virginia Plan proposed a new national government deriving its powers from the people, while the New Jersey Plan proposed revising the Articles to maintain a government deriving its power from the states.
c. The Virginia Plan gave the legislature the power to select the executive and the judiciary, and the New Jersey Plan created an elected president and Supreme Court.
d. The Virginia Plan created a unicameral legislature, while the New Jersey Plan created a bicameral legislature.
e. The Virginia Plan created a government that favored small states, while the New Jersey Plan created a government that favored larger states

7. When James Madison wrote the famous words "ambition must be made to counteract ambition," he was describing what?

a. The bicameral legislature
b. Creating a nonpartisan judiciary
c. The separation of powers and checks and balances between the three branches of the national government
d. The division of state and national power under the Articles of Confederation
e. Citizens' role in electing public officials

8. What does Article III of the U.S. Constitution address?

a. The supremacy of the Constitution
b. The executive branch
c. Procedures for ratification
d. The legislative branch
e. The judicial branch

9. Which of the following exemplifies the Anti-Federalists' views?

- **a.** The most elite groups of society are the most fit to govern.
- **b.** A strong central government could strip powers away from the states.
- **c.** Separation of powers will prevent any one group from dominating the national government.
- **d.** The United States should pursue alliances with the French.
- **e.** The U.S. Constitution, in its original form, provided sufficient protections for the citizens.

10. In which of the following ways has the U.S. Constitution NOT been amended?

- **a.** Ratification of an amendment by legislatures in three-fourths of the states
- **b.** Judicial interpretation
- **c.** Social and cultural change
- **d.** Ratification by conventions called in one-fourth of the states
- **e.** Proposal by two-thirds vote in both houses of Congress

Explore Further

Ackerman, Bruce. *The Failure of the Founding Fathers: Jefferson, Marshall, and the Rise of Presidential Democracy,* new ed. Cambridge, MA: Belknap Press, 2007.

Amar, Akhil Reed. *America's Unwritten Constitution: The Precedents and Principles We Live By.* New York: Basic Books, 2012.

Beard, Charles A. *An Economic Interpretation of the Constitution of the United States,* reissue ed. Mineola, NY: Dover, 2004.

Beeman, Richard. *Plain, Honest Men: The Making of the American Constitution.* New York: Random House, 2009.

Bowen, Catherine Drinker. *Miracle at Philadelphia.* Boston: Little, Brown, 1986.

Breyer, Stephen. *Active Liberty: Interpreting Our Democratic Constitution.* New York: Vintage, 2007.

Brinkley, Alan, Nelson W. Polsby, and Kathleen M. Sullivan. *New Federalist Papers: Essays in Defense of the Constitution.* New York: Norton, 1997.

Dahl, Robert A. *How Democratic Is the American Constitution?* 2nd ed. New Haven, CT: Yale University Press, 2004.

Hamilton, Alexander, James Madison, and John Jay. *The Federalist Papers.* New York: Bantam Books, 1989 (first published in 1788).

Main, Jackson Turner. *The Anti-Federalists: Critics of the Constitution, 1781–1788.* Chapel Hill: University of North Carolina Press, 2004.

Sabato, Larry J. *A More Perfect Constitution.* New York: Walker, 2008.

Stewart, David O. *The Summer of 1787: The Men Who Invented the Constitution.* New York: Simon and Schuster, 2007.

Storing, Herbert J. *What the Anti-Federalists Were For.* Chicago: University of Chicago Press, 1981.

Tushnet, Mark V. *Why the Constitution Matters.* New York: Cambridge University Press, 2011.

Wood, Gordon S. *The Creation of the American Republic, 1776–1787,* reissue ed. Chapel Hill: University of North Carolina Press, 1998.

To learn more about the founding of the United States, the Articles of Confederation, and the writing and ratification of the Constitution, go to the educational resources page of the House of Representatives at **www.house.gov/house/Educate.shtml.**

To learn more about the Declaration of Independence, the Constitution, the Bill of Rights, and the Framers, go to the National Archives site at **www.archives.gov/exhibits/charters/charters.html.**

To learn more about the eighteenth-century documents related to the national founding and the Revolutionary War, go to the Avalon Project at Yale Law School at **http://avalon.law.yale.edu/subject_menus/18th.asp.**

To learn more about *The Federalist Papers,* go to the Library of Congress at **thomas.loc.gov.**

3

Listen to Chapter 3 on MyPoliSciLab

The Federal System

The Supreme Court is often called upon to resolve conflicts between the national and state government. During its 2012 term, for example, the Court considered whether states have the authority to enact immigration law that goes above and beyond federal statutes. The case arose out of a law passed by the state of Arizona in 2010. The statue was widely considered the most restrictive immigration law in the land. Intended to discourage the entry and employment of illegal immigrants, the sweeping law authorized a wide range of investigatory powers for local law enforcement. Perhaps most controversially, it permitted police officers to stop and question anyone they suspected to be in the country illegally, and required those who were detained to produce evidence of either citizenship or legal residency.

The cries against the law were loud, even before it was enacted. Hispanic rights advocates, local politicians, and even President Barack Obama spoke out against the legislation. The president's involvement, especially, was unexpected, as the executive branch rarely interferes with state legislative actions. However, President Obama stated that the bill's provisions undermined "basic notions of fairness that we cherish as Americans, as well as the trust between police and our communities that is so crucial to keeping us safe."[1] He also directed his Justice Department to sue to stop enforcement of the law.

Two years later, in 2012, the case of *Arizona v. United States* reached the United States Supreme Court. In a controversial and widely discussed decision, the justices decided much of the case in favor of federal power, striking down provisions of the act that made illegal immigration and seeking employment while in the United States unlawfully crimes under state law. They also struck down a third provision authorizing the arrest of suspected illegal immigrants without a warrant. In each of these cases, the Court ruled that the state had come into conflict with existing federal law and, according to the U.S. Constitution, federal law must always be supreme.[2]

However, the Court upheld a fourth provision requiring state and local police to verify the citizenship of illegal immigrants. As a result, many Arizona legislators, as well as Republican Governor Jan Brewer, declared the Court's decision a victory for state powers. Supporters further argued that

IMMIGRATION IS AN INTERGOVERNMENTAL PROBLEM Public policy on immigration—and balancing an individual's liberty of movement with the country's security—requires the cooperation of local, state, national, and international governments. Above, European immigrants are screened for entry at Ellis Island, New York, in the 1890s. Below, Hmong immigrants receive health certifications before immigrating to the United States in the present day.

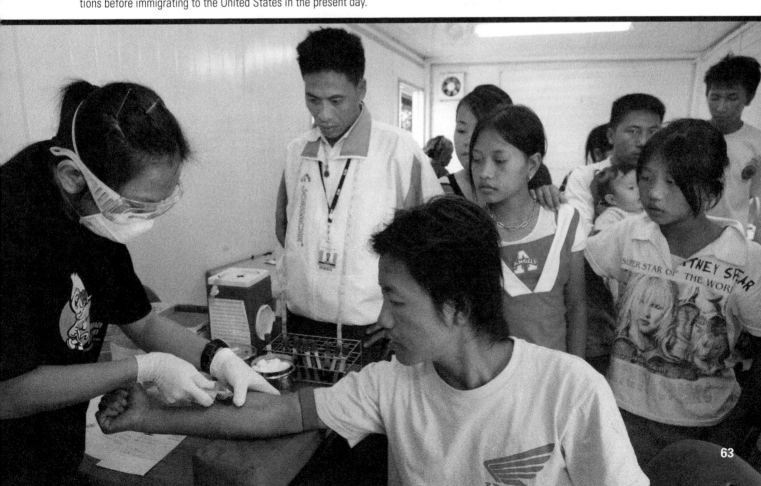

Thinking Like a Political Scientist Find answers to the most current questions that scholars of federalism are raising in the areas of welfare reform and state rights. Barnard College political scientist Scott L. Minkoff explores the challenges faced by state-rights advocates once they are elected to Congress

In the Real World Should the federal government be allowed to mandate health care reform or should that power belong to the states? Hear supporters and detractors of Obamacare explain their opinions, and learn about the recent Supreme Court decision that handed this power to the federal government.

So What? How is a public school in Arkansas different from a public school in New Hampshire? Author Karen O'Connor discusses why—until recently—there were no national standards for public schools in the United States, and why the system of federalism creates these and other differences between states.

the experience of local law enforcement makes the state government more equipped to handle modern immigration than the national government. These comments reflected one of the enduring debates in the federal system, and one considered throughout this chapter.

•••

State and local governments are, to some degree, the lynchpins of the federal system. They have existed since the first settlers arrived at Plymouth and Jamestown and quickly recognized that rules or laws were necessary to keep order even within these small communities. State and local governments thus predate the existence of the national government in every one of the original thirteen colonies.

During the Constitutional Convention, many of the Framers believed that, although a national government was necessary, it should have limited powers. As a result, in the federal system created by the Framers, the states reserved significant powers and authority in a wide array of issues from health to education to administering elections. The national government, in contrast, was given power in areas such as conducting foreign affairs, regulating interstate commerce, and coining money. The governments shared power in other areas, creating a system of checks and balances not only between the executive, legislative, and judicial branches of government, but also between the national government and the states. The Framers further stipulated that the people would be the ultimate source of power for both the national and state governments.

Today, the Constitution ultimately binds a diverse array of governments at the national, state, and local levels. The Constitution lays out the duties, obligations, and powers of national and state governments; states establish and charter local governments. Throughout history, however, crises, historical evolution, public opinion, and judicial interpretation have continually reshaped these relationships. All of these forces have had tremendous influence on policy decisions affecting your daily life. Because there is only one national government, for example, you do not need a passport to travel from Texas to Oklahoma. Only one national currency exists, as does a national minimum wage, although states may set higher hourly wages. But, the laws of various states exhibit many differences. The age at which you may marry is a state issue, as are laws governing divorce, child custody, and criminal justice, including how—or if—the death penalty is applied. Local governments often set liquor or smoking laws. Other policies or programs, such as wars or air traffic regulation, lie solely within the province of the national government. In areas such as education, however, the national, state, and local governments work together in a system of shared powers.

federal system
System of government in which the national government and state governments share power and derive all authority from the people.

confederation
Type of government in which the national government derives its powers from the states; a league of independent states.

unitary system
System of government in which the local and regional governments derive all authority from a strong national government

Roots of the Federal System

3.1 Trace the roots of the federal system and the Constitution's allocation of powers between the national and state governments.

The United States became the first country to adopt a **federal system** of government (although the word "federal" never appears in the U.S. Constitution). The Framers designed this system, wherein the national and state governments share power and derive all authority from the people, to remedy many of the problems experienced under the Articles of Confederation. Under the Articles, the United States was governed as a **confederation,** whereby the national government derived all of its powers from the states. This arrangement led to a weak national government often unable to respond to even localized crises, such as Shays's Rebellion.

Explore on MyPoliSciLab Simulation: You Are a Federal Judge

The new system of government also had to be different from the **unitary system** found in Great Britain, where local and regional governments derived all of their power from a strong national government (see Figure 3.1) Having been under the rule of English kings, whom they considered tyrants, the Framers feared centralizing power in one government or institution. Therefore, they made both the state and the federal governments accountable to the people. While the governments shared some powers, each government was supreme in some spheres, as described in the following section.

3.1

3.2

3.3

3.4

3.5

3.6

3.7

enumerated powers
The powers of the national government specifically granted to Congress in Article I, section 8 of the Constitution.

implied powers
The powers of the national government derived from the enumerated powers and the necessary and proper clause.

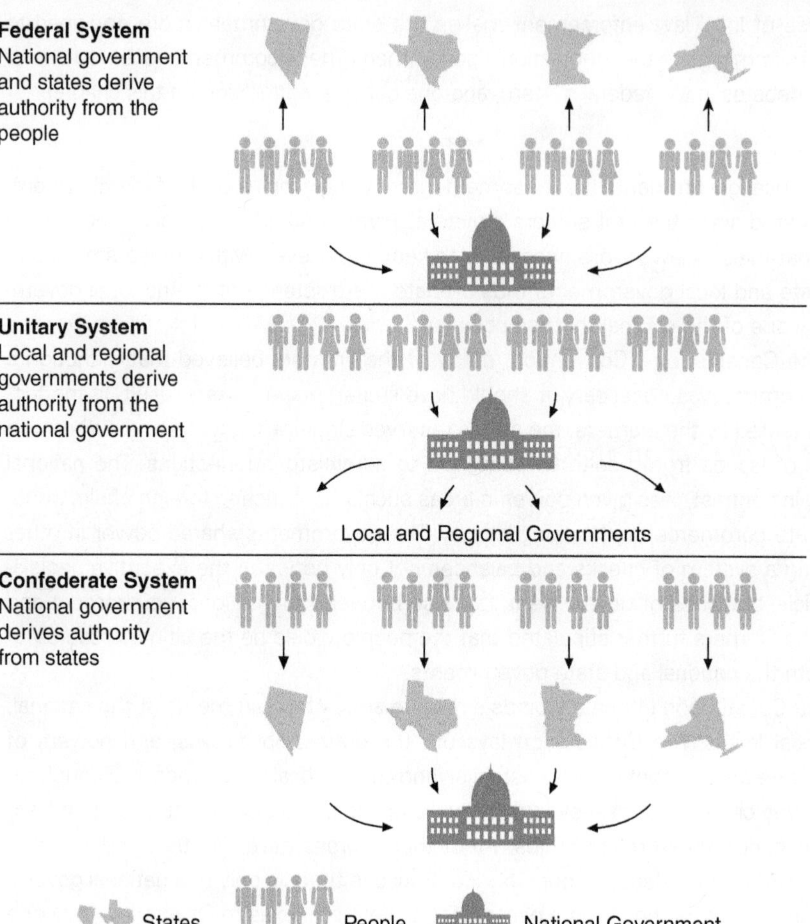

Federal System
National government and states derive authority from the people
Unitary System
Local and regional governments derive authority from the national government
Local and Regional Governments
Confederate System
National government derives authority from states
States
People
National Government

FIGURE 3.1 WHAT IS THE SOURCE OF GOVERNMENTAL AUTHORITY?

The source of governmental authority varies between federal, unitary, and confederate systems. Having experienced the challenges of both unitary and confederate systems, the Framers of the Constitution chose a federal system, in which the power of both state and national governments derives from the people.

National Powers Under the Constitution

All of the powers specifically stated in Article I, section 8, of the Constitution are called **enumerated powers**. Chief among these exclusive powers of the national government are the authorities to coin money, conduct foreign relations, provide for an army and navy, and declare war. In addition, Article I, section 8, contains the necessary and proper clause (also called the elastic clause), which gives Congress the authority to enact laws "necessary and proper" for exercising any of its enumerated powers. These powers derived from enumerated powers and the necessary and proper clause are known as **implied powers**.

The Constitution also clearly set out the federal government's right to collect duties and excises. The Framers wanted to avoid the financial problems experienced by the national government under the Articles of Confederation. If they wished to create a strong new national government, they had to make its power to raise revenue unquestionable. Allowing the new national government to collect tariffs, or taxes on imported goods, was one way to assert this power. And, giving the national government the exclusive power to do so eliminated the financial wars between states that had occurred under the Articles.

Article VI of the federal Constitution underscores the notion that the national government is supreme in situations of conflict between state and national law. It declares that the U.S. Constitution, the laws of the United States, and its treaties are "the supreme Law of the Land; and the Judges in every State shall be bound thereby."

In spite of this explicit language, the courts have consistently been called upon to clarify the meaning of the supremacy clause. In 1920, for example, Missouri sought to prevent a U.S. game warden from enforcing the Migratory Bird Treaty Act of 1918, which

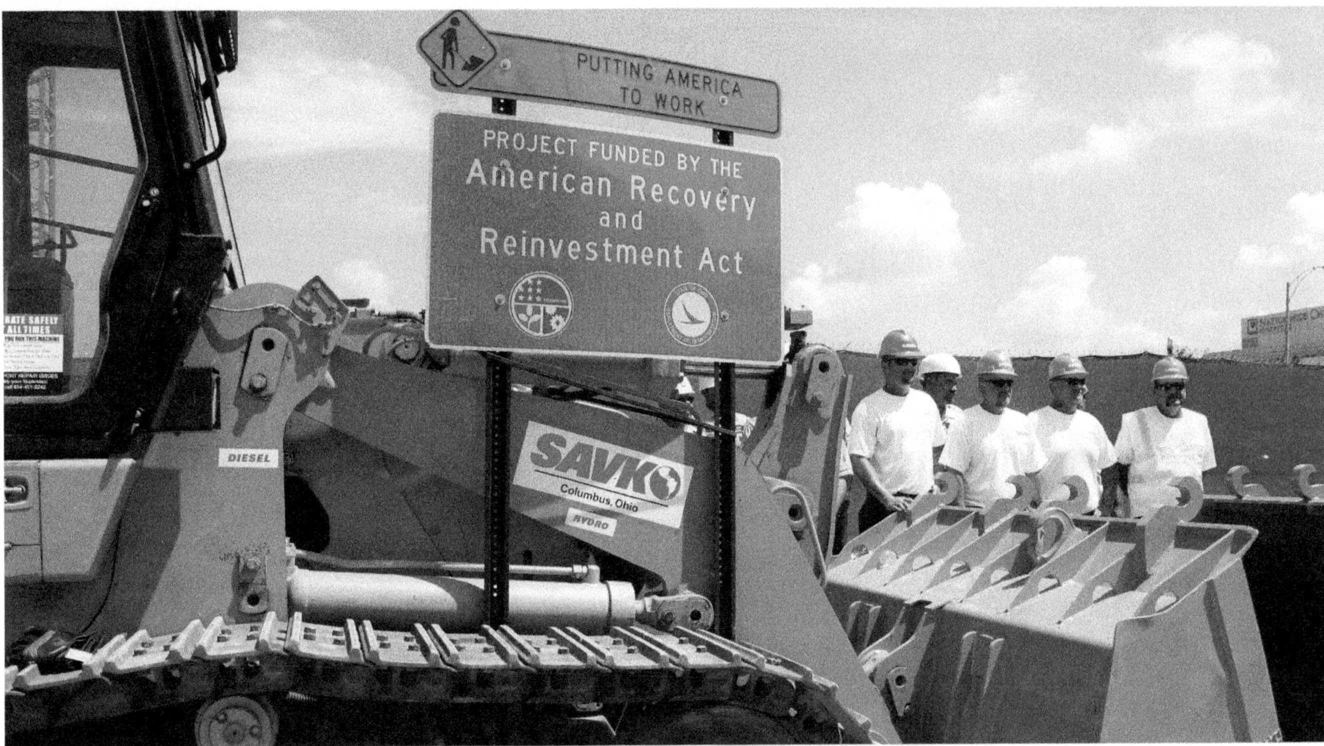

WHEN DO NATIONAL AND STATE GOVERNMENTS WORK TOGETHER?

Intergovernmental cooperation is required to implement many public policies, such as the recent American Recovery and Reinvestment Act, which was enacted as part of the effort to stimulate the economy and create jobs in 2009. Here, work begins on a road construction project jointly funded by the national government and the state of Ohio.

prohibited the killing or capturing of many species of birds as they made their annual migration across the international border from Canada to parts of the United States.[3] Missouri argued that the Tenth Amendment, which reserved a state's powers to legislate for the general welfare of its citizens, allowed Missouri to regulate hunting. But, the Court ruled that since the treaty was legal, it must be considered the supreme law of the land (see the discussion of *McCulloch* v. *Maryland* [1819] that follows later in this chapter).

Tenth Amendment
The final part of the Bill of Rights that defines the basic principle of American federalism in stating that the powers not delegated to the national government are reserved to the states or to the people.

reserved powers
Powers reserved to the states by the Tenth Amendment that lie at the foundation of a state's right to legislate for the public health and welfare of its citizens.

State Powers Under the Constitution

Because states held all the power at the time the Constitution was written, the Framers felt no need, as they did for the new national government, to list and restate all of the powers of the states, although some are specified throughout the Constitution. Article I of the U.S. Constitution not only notes that each state is entitled to two senators; it also leaves to the states the times, places, and manner of elections. Thus, the states may enact their own restrictions on who can and cannot vote. Some states, for example, deny felons the franchise, while other states allow them to retain this right. Article II requires that each state appoint electors to vote for president. And, Article IV guarantees each state a "Republican Form of Government," meaning one that represents the citizens of the state.

Not until the **Tenth Amendment,** the final part of the Bill of Rights, were the states' powers described in greater detail: "The powers not delegated to the United States by the Constitution, nor prohibited by it to the States, are reserved to the States respectively, or to the people." These powers, often called the states' **reserved powers,** include the ability to legislate for the public health, safety, and morals of their citizens. Today, the states' rights to legislate under their reserved powers provide the rationale for many states' restrictions on abortion, for example. Reserved powers also form the basis for state criminal laws, including those concerning the death penalty. As long as the U.S. Supreme Court continues to find the death penalty not in violation of the U.S. Constitution, the states may impose it, whether by lethal injection, gas chamber, electric chair, hanging, or firing squad.

NATIONAL POWERS (ENUMERATED POWERS)	CONCURRENT POWERS	STATE POWERS (RESERVED POWERS)
	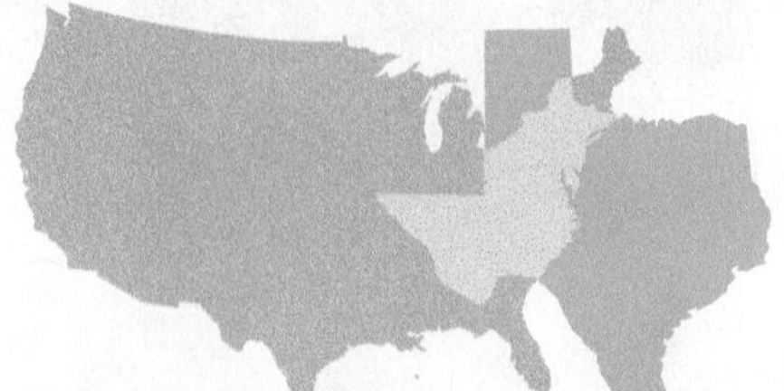	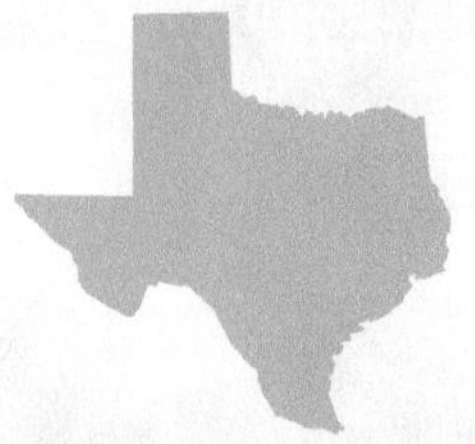
Collect duties, imposts, and excises Regulate commerce with foreign nations, among the states, and with Indian tribes Establish rules of naturalization Coin money Establish a post office Declare and conduct war Provide for an army and a navy Make laws necessary and proper to carry out Article I powers	Tax Borrow money Establish courts Make and enforce laws Charter banks and corporations Spend money for the general welfare	Set times, places, and manner of elections and appoint electors Ratify amendments to the U.S. Constitution Take measures for public health, safety, and morals Exert powers the Constitution does not delegate to the national government or prohibit the states from using Establish local governments Regulate commerce within a state

FIGURE 3.2 HOW IS GOVERNMENTAL POWER DISTRIBUTED IN THE FEDERAL SYSTEM?
The Constitution divides power between the national and state governments. It gives the national government a list of enumerated powers, while many state powers are captured in the reserved powers clause of the Tenth Amendment. The national and state governments also share some powers, known as concurrent powers.

concurrent powers
Powers shared by the national and state governments.

bill of attainder
A law declaring an act illegal without a judicial trial.

***ex post facto* law**
Law that makes an act punishable as a crime even if the action was legal at the time it was committed.

☐ Concurrent Powers Under the Constitution

As revealed in Figure 3.2, national and state powers overlap. The area in which the systems overlap represents **concurrent powers**—powers shared by the national and state governments. States already had the power to tax; the Constitution extended this power to the national government as well. Other important concurrent powers include the rights to borrow money, establish courts, charter banks, and spend money for the general welfare. In illustration of concurrent powers, most individuals must file both state and federal tax returns. States have also allowed local governments to pass a variety of taxation measures, including property taxes for schools and sales taxes on goods such as food and clothing.

☐ Powers Denied Under the Constitution

Article I of the Constitution explicitly denies some powers to the national government or states. Congress, for example, is barred from favoring one state over another in regulating commerce, and it cannot lay duties on items exported from any state. Article I also prohibits the national government from granting titles of nobility, and government employees may not accept salaries or gifts from foreign heads of state.

State governments (as well as the national government) are denied the authority to take arbitrary actions affecting constitutional rights and liberties. Neither national nor state governments may pass a **bill of attainder,** a law declaring an act illegal without a judicial trial. The Constitution also bars national and state governments from passing ***ex post facto* laws,** those that make an act punishable as a crime even if the action was legal at the time it was committed.

☐ Interstate Relations Under the Constitution

In addition to delineating the relationship between states and the national government, the Constitution provides a mechanism for resolving interstate disputes and facilitating relations among states. To avoid any sense of favoritism, it arranges for disputes between

Full Faith and Credit shall be given in each State to the public Acts, Records, and judicial Proceedings of every other State. —ARTICLE IV, SECTION 1

The full faith and credit clause of Article IV of the Constitution rests on principles borrowed from international law that require one country to recognize contracts made in another country, absent a compelling public policy reason to the contrary. In the United States, this principle applies to the relationship between states.

The full faith and credit clause requires a state to recognize public acts and court proceedings of another state. In 1997, the Supreme Court ruled that the full faith and credit clause mandates that state courts always honor the judgments of other state courts, even if it entails going against state public policy or existing state laws. Failure to do so would allow a single state to "rule the world," said Supreme Court Justice Ruth Bader Ginsburg during oral argument.[a]

For the most part, interpretation of the full faith and credit clause has not been controversial. That is changing, however, as advocates of same-sex marriage have suggested that marriages of same-sex couples performed and legally sanctioned in one state must be recognized in another state, as is the case with heterosexual marriages.

In the mid-1990s, the possible legalization of marriage between same-sex couples threw numerous state legislatures and the U.S. Congress into a virtual frenzy. Twenty-five states passed laws in 1996 and 1997 to bar legal recognition of same-sex marriages. The U.S. Congress also got involved by passing what is called the Defense of Marriage Act (DOMA), which President Bill Clinton signed into law in 1996. This federal law aimed to undercut possible state recognition of same-sex marriages by permitting states to disregard such marriages even if they are legal in other states. The constitutionality of this law, however, is questionable. The U.S. Constitution does not formally give Congress legislative authority to create exceptions to the full faith and credit clause. As a result, some observers believe that such an exception would require a constitutional amendment. The Obama administration, moreover, has stated that it does not support DOMA and believes it is unconstitutional.

CRITICAL THINKING QUESTIONS

1. How could a same-sex couple married in one state be granted a divorce in a state that does not recognize same-sex marriage?
2. Should states or the federal government be allowed to create public policy exceptions to the full faith and credit clause?

[a]Oral argument in *Baker* v. *General Motors Corporation,* 522 U.S. 222 (1998), noted in Linda Greenhouse, "Court Weighs Whether One State Must Obey Another's Courts," *New York Times* (October 16, 1997): A25.

states to be settled directly by the U.S. Supreme Court under its original jurisdiction as mandated by Article III (see the discussion of the judiciary). Moreover, Article IV requires that each state give "Full Faith and Credit . . . to the public Acts, Records, and judicial Proceedings of every other State." The **full faith and credit clause** ensures that judicial decrees and contracts made in one state will be binding and enforceable in another, thereby facilitating trade and other commercial relationships. Full faith and credit cases continue to make their way through the judicial system. For example, a state's refusal to honor same-sex marriage contracts poses interesting constitutional questions.

Article IV also contains the **privileges and immunities clause,** guaranteeing that the citizens of each state have the same rights as citizens of all other states. In addition, Article IV includes the **extradition clause,** which requires states to extradite, or return, criminals to states where they have been convicted or are to stand trial.

To facilitate relations among states, Article I, section 10, clause 3, of the U.S. Constitution sets the legal foundation for interstate cooperation in the form of **interstate compacts**, contracts between states that carry the force of law. Currently, more than 200 interstate compacts exist. While some deal with rudimentary items such as state boundaries, others help states carry out their policy objectives and administrative functions. Although several bistate compacts exist, others have as many as fifty signatories.[4] For example, all fifty states signed the Drivers License Compact to facilitate nationwide recognition of licenses issued in the respective states.

full faith and credit clause
Section of Article IV of the Constitution that ensures judicial decrees and contracts made in one state will be binding and enforceable in any other state.

privileges and immunities clause
Part of Article IV of the Constitution guaranteeing that the citizens of each state are afforded the same rights as citizens of all other states.

extradition clause
Part of Article IV of the Constitution that requires states to extradite, or return, criminals to states where they have been convicted or are to stand trial.

interstate compacts
Contracts between states that carry the force of law; generally now used as a tool to address multistate policy concerns.

Dillon's Rule
A premise articulated by Judge John F. Dillon in 1868 which states that local governments do not have any inherent sovereignty and instead must be authorized by state governments that can create or abolish them.

charter
A document that, like a constitution, specifies the basic policies, procedures, and institutions of local government. Charters for local governments must be approved by state legislatures.

county
The basic administrative unit of local government.

municipality
City governments created in response to the emergence of relatively densely populated areas.

special district
A local government that is restricted to a particular function.

☐ Local Governments Under the Constitution

Local governments have no express power under the U.S. Constitution. A description of the relationship between states and local governments comes from Judge John F. Dillon, who in 1868 articulated a premise known as **Dillon's Rule.** Dillon's Rule states that all local governments—whether towns, villages, cities, or counties, or some other form—do not have any inherent sovereignty and instead must be authorized by state governments, which can create or abolish them.

Local governments, therefore, need a **charter**—a document that, like a constitution, specifies the basic policies, procedures, and institutions that are acceptable to the state legislature. States issue charters that establish the authority and procedures defining a municipality, and all amendments to these charters require approval by state governments. The responsibilities of local governments described in these charters vary widely and include public health and safety, education, jobs, and economic vitality, zoning land for particular uses, and assistance to those in need. Local governments are of several types, as highlighted in Figure 3.3.

COUNTIES **Counties** are the basic administrative units of local government. Every state has counties, although in Louisiana they are called parishes, and in Alaska, boroughs. With few exceptions, counties have very broad responsibilities and are used by state governments for welfare and environmental programs, courts, and the registration of land, births, and deaths.

MUNICIPALITIES **Municipalities** are city governments created in response to the emergence of relatively densely populated areas. State governments do not establish them arbitrarily but, instead, municipalities emerge as people locate in a particular place. Some of the most intense struggles among governments within the United States are over the boundaries, scope of authority, and sources of revenue for municipal governments.

County and municipal boundaries may overlap. State actions have merged city and county into a consolidated government in several areas, including San Francisco, California; Denver, Colorado; Honolulu, Hawaii; and Jacksonville, Florida.

TOWNS The term is used generally today to refer to smaller communities, often run by a mayor and town council. The definition of a town varies considerably from state to state. In some states, for example, towns and municipalities may be virtually indistinguishable, while other states set specific restrictions on the size of each type of government.

SPECIAL DISTRICTS Among forms of government, special districts are the most numerous. A **special district** is a local government restricted to a particular function. These districts exist for services such as libraries, sewage, water, and parks and are governed through a variety of structures. Some have elected heads, and others, appointed. Some of these jurisdictions levy a fee to generate their revenues, whereas others depend on appropriations from a state, city, or county. One reason for the proliferation of special districts is the desire to avoid restrictions on funds faced by municipalities or other jurisdictions. The creation of a special park district, for example, may enable the park to have an independent budget and sources of funding.

School districts, the most common form of special districts, exist to provide free public education to students. They frequently cross town lines for purposes of practicality. They have their own budgets and must persuade those without children in a district to agree to help fund schools and extracurricular programs. Most school districts also receive assistance from states or the federal government for some specialized programs, including free or subsidized school lunches. School boards, whose members are usually elected in nonpartisan elections, administer school districts and supervise the officials who are responsible for the day-to-day operations of the school.

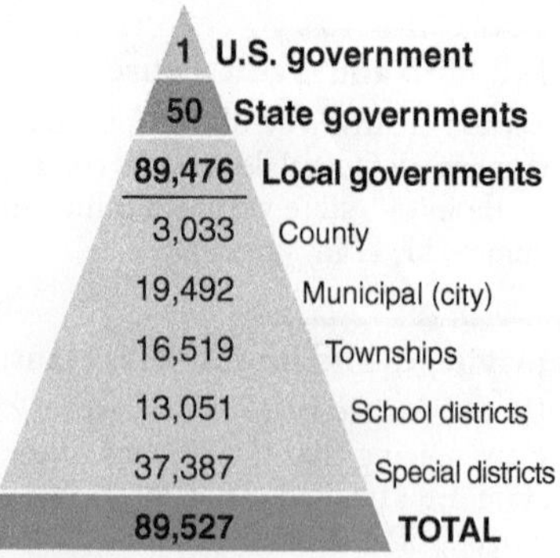

1 **U.S. government**
50 **State governments**
89,476 **Local governments**
3,033 County
19,492 Municipal (city)
16,519 Townships
13,051 School districts
37,387 Special districts
89,527 **TOTAL**

FIGURE 3.3 HOW MANY GOVERNMENTS EXIST IN THE UNITED STATES?

More than 89,000 governments exist in the United States. Most of these governments are found at the local level, and are divided between municipal governments, towns, and special districts, such as school districts. The most common form of government is the special district.

SOURCE: U.S. Census Bureau, www.census.gov/govs/cog/GovOrgTab033ss.html

Federalism and the Marshall Court

3.2 Determine the impact of the Marshall Court on federalism.

The nature of federalism, including its allocation of power between the national government and the states, has changed dramatically over the past 200 years. Much of this change has resulted from rulings of the U.S. Supreme Court, which has played a major role in defining the nature of the federal system. Few Supreme Courts have had a greater impact on the federal–state relationship than the one headed by Chief Justice John Marshall (1801–1835). In a series of decisions, he and his associates carved out an important role for the Court in defining the balance of power between the national government and the states. Three rulings in the early 1800s, *McCulloch* v. *Maryland* (1819), *Gibbons* v. *Ogden* (1824), and *Barron* v. *Baltimore* (1833), were particularly important.

McCulloch v. _Maryland_ (1819)
The Supreme Court upheld the power of the national government and denied the right of a state to tax the federal bank, using the Constitution's supremacy clause. The Court's broad interpretation of the necessary and proper clause paved the way for later rulings upholding expansive federal powers.

Gibbons v. _Ogden_ (1824)
The Supreme Court upheld broad congressional power to regulate interstate commerce. The Court's broad interpretation of the Constitution's commerce clause paved the way for later rulings upholding expansive federal powers.

Defining National Power: *McCulloch* v. *Maryland* (1819)

***McCulloch* v. *Maryland* (1819)** was the first major Supreme Court decision to define the relationship between the national and state governments. In 1816, Congress chartered the Second Bank of the United States. (The charter of the First Bank had been allowed to expire.) In 1818, the Maryland state legislature levied a tax requiring all banks not chartered by Maryland (that is, the Second Bank of the United States) to: (1) buy stamped paper from the state on which their bank notes were to be issued; (2) pay the state $15,000 a year; or, (3) go out of business. James McCulloch, the head cashier of the Baltimore branch of the Bank of the United States, refused to pay the tax, and Maryland brought suit against him. After losing in a Maryland state court, McCulloch appealed the decision to the U.S. Supreme Court by order of the U.S. secretary of the treasury. In a unanimous opinion, the Court answered the two central questions presented to it: Did Congress have the authority to charter a bank? And, if it did, could a state tax it?

Chief Justice John Marshall's answer to the first question—whether Congress had the right to establish a bank or another type of corporation—continues to stand as the classic exposition of the doctrine of implied powers and as a statement of the authority of a strong national government. Although the word "bank" does not appear in the Constitution, the Constitution enumerates powers that give Congress the authority to levy and collect taxes, issue a currency, and borrow funds. From these enumerated powers, Marshall found, it was reasonable to imply that Congress had the power to charter a bank, which could be considered "necessary and proper" to the exercise of its aforementioned enumerated powers.

Marshall next addressed whether any state government could tax a federal bank. To Marshall, this was not a difficult question. The national government depended on the people, not the states, for its powers. In addition, Marshall noted, the Constitution specifically called for the national law to be supreme. "The power to tax involves the power to destroy," wrote the chief justice.[5] Thus, the state tax violated the supremacy clause because individual states cannot interfere with operations of the national government, whose laws are supreme.

The Court's decision in *McCulloch* has far-reaching consequences even today. Lawmakers use the necessary and proper clause to justify federal action in many areas, including social welfare problems. Furthermore, had Marshall allowed the state of Maryland to tax the federal bank, states possibly could have attempted to tax all federal agencies located within their boundaries, a costly proposition that could have driven the federal government into insurmountable debt.[6]

Affirming National Power: *Gibbons* v. *Ogden* (1824)

Shortly after *McCulloch,* the Marshall Court had another opportunity to rule in favor of a broad interpretation of the scope of national power. ***Gibbons* v. *Ogden* (1824)**

Explore Your World

The United States has a federal system of government in which national and subnational political units known as states share power. A number of other countries, including Canada, Switzerland, India, and Nigeria, also have federal systems of government. However, most of the world's nations, including Great Britain, France, China, Japan, and Iran, have unitary systems, with authority concentrated in the central government. Although federal systems are relatively few in number, they tend to be large and politically important. This world map illustrates countries with federal systems of government in green. Countries with other systems of government are shown in gray.

Some subnational units in Brazil are based on cultural boundaries that precede Portuguese colonization. Other subnational units have been created for economic or administrative purposes.

Russia, the world's largest country by landmass, has a federal system comprised of 83 subnational units. The government was formed in 1993 after the dissolution of the Soviet Union.

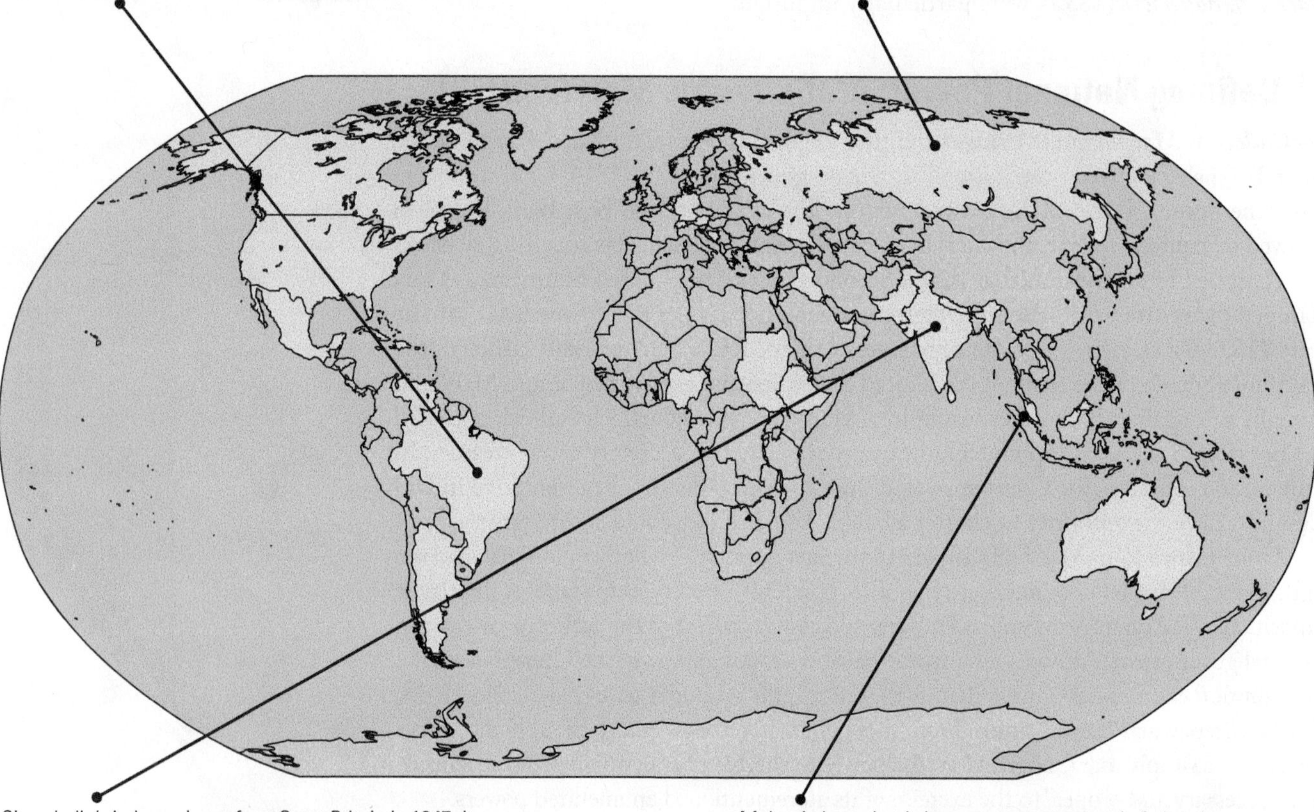

Since India's independence from Great Britain in 1947, its federal system has united citizens speaking thousands of languages and from a variety of diverse religions.

Malaysia has what is known as an asymmetric federation. Some subnational units have more power than others.

CRITICAL THINKING QUESTIONS

1. Study the map to identify what economic, cultural, and political characteristics the countries with federal systems have in common. Why might these characteristics have led to the adoption of federal systems?
2. Examine countries such as India, Nigeria, and Germany. What challenges might these countries face in maintaining a federal system in a region where most other countries choose a different form of government?
3. What other countries might be likely candidates for adopting federal systems in the future? Why do you think these countries are particularly good candidates?

involved a dispute that arose after the New York state legislature granted to Robert Fulton the exclusive right to operate steamboats on the Hudson River.[7] Simultaneously, Congress licensed a ship to sail on the same waters. By the time the case reached the Supreme Court, it was complicated both factually and procedurally. Suffice it to say that both New York and New Jersey wanted to control shipping on the lower Hudson River. But, *Gibbons* actually addressed one simple, very important question: What was the scope of Congress's authority under the commerce clause? The states argued that "commerce," as mentioned in Article I, should be interpreted narrowly to include only direct dealings in products. In *Gibbons,* however, the Supreme Court ruled that Congress's power to regulate interstate commerce included the power to regulate commercial activity as well, and that the commerce power had no limits except those specifically found in the Constitution. Thus, New York had no constitutional authority to grant a monopoly to a single steamboat operator, an action that interfered with interstate commerce.[8]

Barron v. _Baltimore_ (1833)
The Supreme Court ruled that the due process clause of the Fifth Amendment did not apply to the actions of states. This decision limited the Bill of Rights to the actions of Congress alone.

dual federalism
The belief that having separate and equally powerful levels of government is the best arrangement, often referred to as layer-cake federalism.

☐ Limiting the Bill of Rights: *Barron* v. *Baltimore* (1833)

In 1833, in one of Chief Justice Marshall's last major cases on the federal–state relationship, ***Barron* v. *Baltimore* (1833)**, the Court addressed the issue of whether the due process clause of the Fifth Amendment applied to actions of the states.[9] John Barron, a Baltimore businessman, ran a successful docking business off the city's wharf. As the city entered a period of extensive construction, dirt was deposited onto Barron's wharf. In addition, sand and silt drifted to his section of the wharf, making it unusable as a harbor for ships. Barron sued the city and state for damages, arguing that the city took his lands "without just compensation," as guaranteed by the Fifth Amendment of the U.S. Constitution. The Marshall Court ruled that Barron had no federal claim because enumerated rights contained in the Bill of Rights bound only the national government.[10]

Dual Federalism: States' Rights, the Civil War, and Reconstruction

3.3 Describe the emergence and decline of dual federalism.

In the early to mid-1800s, a national crisis began over the division of power between the states and the federal government. One major battleground in this struggle was the issue of slavery, which the pro-states' rights southern states fought to maintain. In contrast, many northern states, where commercial and manufacturing interests were more powerful, favored greater national power. Chief Justice Roger B. Taney (1835–1863), who succeeded John Marshall, saw the Court as an arbiter of those competing state and nationalist views. In a series of cases involving the scope of Congress's power under the commerce clause, the Taney Court further developed the nationalist doctrines first enunciated by Marshall but also emphasized the authority of states to make laws "necessary to their well being and prosperity."[11]

Over time, Chief Justice Taney and the Court also began to articulate further the notions of concurrent power and **dual federalism.** Dual federalism posits that having separate and equally powerful state and national governments is the best constitutional arrangement. Adherents of this theory typically believe that the national government should not exceed its constitutionally enumerated powers, and as stated in the Tenth Amendment, all other powers are, and should be, reserved to the states or to the people.

3.1

3.2

3.3

3.4

3.5

3.6

3.7

nullification
The right of a state to declare void a federal law.

***Dred Scott* v. *Sandford* (1857)**
The Supreme Court concluded that the U.S. Congress lacked the constitutional authority to bar slavery in the territories. This decision narrowed the scope of national power, while it enhanced that of the states.

☐ The States Assert Their Powers: Nullification

While the courts worked to carve out the appropriate roles for each level of government in the federal system, the political debate over states' rights swirled in large part over what is called **nullification,** the right of a state to declare a federal law void. As early as 1798, Congress approved the very unpopular Alien and Sedition Acts, which were passed by the Federalist Congress to prevent criticism of the national government. Thomas Jefferson, James Madison, and others who opposed the acts suggested that states had the right to nullify any federal law that, in the opinion of the states, violated the Constitution. The U.S. Supreme Court, however, never decided the issue, because the Alien and Sedition Acts expired before the Court could hear a challenge to them.

The question of nullification arose again in 1828, when the national government enacted a tariff act, most commonly referred to as the "Tariff of Abominations," that raised duties on raw materials, iron, hemp, and flax and reduced protections against imported woolen goods. John C. Calhoun, who served as vice president from 1825 to 1832 under President Andrew Jackson, broke with Jackson over the tariff bill because it badly affected his home state of South Carolina. Not only did South Carolinians have to pay more for raw materials because of the tariff bill, but it was also becoming increasingly difficult for them to sell their dwindling crops abroad for a profit. Calhoun thus resurrected arguments made by some of the Framers and formulated the theory of nullification to justify South Carolina's refusal to abide by the federal tariff law. Later, he used the same nullification theory in justifying the southern states' resistance to national actions to limit slavery.

Calhoun theorized that the federal government functioned merely as the agent of the states (the people and the individual state governments) and that the Constitution was simply a compact providing instructions on how the agent was to act. Thus, according to Calhoun, the U.S. Supreme Court could not pass judgment on the constitutional validity of acts of Congress. Calhoun posited that if the people of any individual state did not like an act of Congress, they could hold a convention to nullify that act. If a state contested an act, the law would have no force until three-fourths of all the states ratified an amendment expressly giving Congress that power. Then, if the nullifying state still did not wish to be bound by the new provision, it could secede, or withdraw, from the union.

☐ States' Rights and the *Dred Scott* Decision

Debate over nullification only forestalled debate on the inevitable slavery issue. By the 1850s, the country could wait no longer. In cases such as ***Dred Scott* v. *Sandford* (1857),** the Court tried to manage the slavery issue by resolving questions of ownership, the status of fugitive slaves, and slavery in the new territories.[12] The Court generally settled these cases in favor of slavery and states' rights within the framework of dual federalism.

Dred Scott, for example, was born into slavery about 1795. In 1833, his original owners sold him to a family in Missouri. Later he tried to buy his freedom. His ability to take this action was questioned, so abolitionists gave money to support a test case seeking Scott's freedom. They believed his prior residence with a family living in free states and the Wisconsin Territory, which prohibited slavery, made Scott a free man, even though he now lived in a slave state, Missouri. In 1857, after many delays, the U.S. Supreme Court ruled 7–2 that Scott was not a citizen of the United States. "Slaves," said the Court, "were never thought of or spoken of except as property." The Court also found that Congress lacked the authority to ban slavery in the territories. In so doing, this decision narrowed the scope of national power, while it enhanced that of the states. Eventually, however, no form of federalism could accommodate the existence of slavery, and the nation marched toward inevitable war with itself.

☐ Reconstruction and the Transformation of Dual Federalism

The Civil War forever changed the nature of federalism. The concepts of nullification and dual federalism, as well as their emphasis on the role of the states, were destroyed along with the southern states' attempt at a confederacy. In the aftermath of the Civil War and the addition of the Thirteenth, Fourteenth, and Fifteenth Amendments to the Constitution, a profound change occurred in the reunited nation's concept of federalism.

The Civil War had an especially profound impact in the South. After the Civil War, former Confederate states were required to "reconstruct," or adopt new state constitutions approved by the nationalist Congress in Washington, D.C., and endure a range of punishments for their actions. The Reconstruction-era constitutions typically provided former male slaves with considerable power and disenfranchised white men who had been active in the Confederacy. However, because these constitutions divorced political power from economic wealth and social status, and formal authority from informal influence, white communities simply ignored federal rules and governed themselves informally as much as possible. After less than ten years, with the formal end of Reconstruction, whites reasserted political control in the South and rewrote their state constitutions.

The Supreme Court, however, often stepped in to limit state powers in favor of a stronger national government. The Court also recognized the need for national involvement in projects such as railroad construction, canal building, and the development of new technology, such as the telegraph.[13] And, beginning in the 1880s, the Court allowed Congress to regulate many aspects of economic relationships, such as outlawing monopolies, a type of regulation formerly considered to exist exclusively in the realm of the states. By the 1890s, passage of laws such as the Interstate Commerce Act and the Sherman Anti-Trust Act allowed Congress to establish itself as the supreme player in a growing national economy.

Some boundaries to this growing national role did exist, however. In 1895, for example, the United States filed suit against four sugar refiners, alleging that the sale of those four companies would give their buyer control of 98 percent of the U.S. sugar-refining business. The Supreme Court ruled that congressional efforts to control monopolies (through passage of the Sherman Anti-Trust Act) did not grant Congress the authority to prevent the sale of these sugar-refining businesses, because manufacturing was not commerce. Therefore, the Court found the companies and their actions to lie beyond the scope of Congress's regulatory authority.[14] Later that same year, the U.S. Supreme Court declared a congressional effort to tax personal incomes unconstitutional, although an earlier Court had found a similar tax levied during the Civil War constitutional.[15]

HOW DID THE RELATIONSHIP BETWEEN STATE AND NATIONAL GOVERNMENTS CHANGE AFTER THE CIVIL WAR?

Construction of coast-to-coast transportation systems, such as the intercontinental railroad, shown here, necessitated a greater role for the national government. These changes also helped to doom the system of dual federalism, which dominated for the first one hundred years of the nation's history.

Sixteenth Amendment
Amendment to the U.S. Constitution that authorized Congress to enact a national income tax.

Seventeenth Amendment
Amendment to the U.S. Constitution that made senators directly elected by the people, removing their selection from state legislatures.

cooperative federalism
The intertwined relationship between the national, state, and local governments that began with the New Deal, often referred to as marble-cake federalism.

☐ Amending the National–State Relationship

In response to the Court's ruling on the income tax, Congress and the state legislatures were moved to ratify the **Sixteenth Amendment.** The Sixteenth Amendment gave Congress the power to levy and collect taxes on incomes without apportioning them among the states. The revenues taken in by the federal government through taxation of personal income "removed a major constraint on the federal government by giving it access to almost unlimited revenues."[16] If money is power, the income tax and the revenues it generated greatly enhanced the power of the federal government and its ability to enter policy areas in which it formerly had few funds to spend.

The **Seventeenth Amendment,** ratified in 1913, similarly enhanced the power of the national government at the expense of the states. This amendment terminated the state legislatures' election of senators and placed their election in the hands of the people. With senators no longer directly accountable to the state legislatures, states lost their principal protectors in Congress.

While the ratification of the Sixteenth and Seventeenth Amendments set the stage for expanded national government, the catalyst for dual federalism's demise was a series of economic events that ended in the cataclysm of the Great Depression:

- Throughout the 1920s, bank failures were common.
- In 1921, the nation experienced a severe slump in agricultural prices.
- In 1926, the construction industry went into decline.
- In the summer of 1929, inventories of consumer goods and automobiles were at an all-time high.
- On October 29, 1929, stock prices, which had risen steadily since 1926, crashed, taking with them the entire national economy.

Despite the severity of these indicators, Presidents Calvin Coolidge and Herbert Hoover took little action, believing that the national depression comprised an amalgamation of state economic crises better dealt with by state and local governments. It would take the election of President Franklin D. Roosevelt in 1932 to both respond to this crisis and forever change the relationship between state and national governments.

Cooperative Federalism: The Growth of National Government

3.4 Explain how cooperative federalism led to the growth of the national government at the expense of the states.

Most political scientists likened the federal system before the 1930s to a layer cake: in most policy areas, each level or layer of government—national, state, and local—had clearly defined powers and responsibilities. By contrast, the metaphor of marble-cake federalism refers to what political scientists call **cooperative federalism,** a term that describes the intertwined relations among the national, state, and local governments that began during this period. States began to take a secondary, albeit important, cooperative role in the scheme of governance, as did many cities. One political scientist described the new balance of power as:

> Wherever you slice through it you reveal an inseparable mixture of differently colored ingredients. . . . Vertical and diagonal lines almost obliterate the horizontal ones, and in some places there are unexpected whirls and an imperceptible merging of colors, so that it is difficult to tell where one ends and the other begins.[17]

This landmark legislation that marked the beginning of this new era in national–state relations was a program of relief, recovery, and reform designed to bring the nation out of the Great Depression, known as the **New Deal.**

New Deal
The name given to the program of "Relief, Recovery, Reform" begun by President Franklin D. Roosevelt in 1933 to bring the United States out of the Great Depression.

☐ A Need for National Action Arises: The New Deal

Rampant unemployment (historians estimate it was as high as 40 to 50 percent) was the hallmark of the Great Depression. In 1933, to combat severe problems facing the nation, newly elected President Franklin D. Roosevelt (FDR) proposed a variety of innovative programs, collectively called the New Deal, and ushered in a new era in American politics. FDR used the full power of the presidency, as well as his highly effective communication skills, to sell the American public and Congress on a new level of government intervention intended to stabilize the economy and reduce personal suffering. Most politicians during the New Deal period (1933–1939) agreed that to find national solutions to the Depression, which was affecting citizens of every state in the union, the national government would have to exercise tremendous authority.

In the first few weeks of the legislative session after FDR's inauguration, Congress passed a series of acts creating new federal agencies and programs proposed by the president. These new agencies, often known by their initials, created what many termed an alphabetocracy. Among the more significant programs were the Federal Housing Administration (FHA), which provided federal financing for new home construction; the Civilian Conservation Corps (CCC), a work relief program for farmers and homeowners; and the Agricultural Adjustment Administration (AAA) and National

HOW DID FDR'S PUBLIC ACTIONS CHANGE CONCEPTIONS ABOUT FEDERALISM?

This cartoon illustrates FDR's difficulties garnering support from the Supreme Court for the economic and social programs he believed were necessary to end the Great Depression. To coerce support from the Court to transform the federal–state relationship, FDR proposed his Court-packing plan, which was met with great opposition. The plan, however, seemed to convince a majority of justices to overturn the Court's earlier decisions and to support the constitutionality of New Deal programs.

How Has the Federal-State Relationship Evolved?

The balance of power between the national and state governments has evolved over time. In the early years of the new republic, the nation maintained a system of dual federalism, often referred to as layer cake federalism. This relationship transformed into a marble cake form of federalism known as cooperative federalism during the 1930s with the passage of President Franklin D. Roosevelt's New Deal. This image illustrates the changing national–state relationship, building on the cake metaphor.

PROGRESSIVE FEDERALISM

The modern relationship between the states and federal government is both cooperative and coercive, depending on the issue area.

NEW FEDERALISM AND THE DEVOLUTION REVOLUTION

Republican President Ronald Reagan and Republicans in Congress demanded that the national government return some administrative authority to state governments.

2010s

THE GREAT SOCIETY

One of the hallmarks of President Lyndon B. Johnson's Great Society program was offering federal financial aid to states in the form of grants-in-aid.

1980s

THE NEW DEAL AND COOPERATIVE FEDERALISM

The Great Depression and the New Deal signaled the beginning of a new era in federalism where the state and national governments worked together to address a broad array of policy issues, including job creation, health and welfare.

1960s

GROWING NATIONAL INTERVENTION IN THE ECONOMY

The needs of a growing and more technologically advanced nation required the intervention of the national government in economic affairs such as regulating business and constructing roads, railroads, and ports.

1930s

1880s

CIVIL WAR AND RECONSTRUCTION

The Civil War and the defeat of the states' rights South began to alter the division of power between state and national governments.

1860s

DUAL FEDERALISM

The division of national and state powers envisioned by the Framers; each government had separate spheres of authority dictated by the Constitution.

1800s

CRITICAL THINKING QUESTIONS

1. What kinds of events appear to be catalysts for changes in the federal system?
2. Consider the progression from layer to layer. Between which layers did the most change occur? Why was this change more definitive than that between the other layers?
3. How have changes to the federal system affected the lives of citizens? How are these changes seen in the everyday functions of government?

Recovery Administration (NRA), which imposed restrictions on production in agriculture and many industries while also providing subsidies to farmers.

New Deal programs forced all levels of government to work cooperatively with one another. Local governments, especially those of cities, were embraced as equal partners in an intergovernmental system for the first time and became players in the national political arena because many members of Congress wanted to bypass state legislatures, where urban interests usually were underrepresented. FDR also relied on big-city Democratic political machines to turn out voters to support his programs.

Those who feared these unprecedented changes in the federal system quickly challenged the constitutionality of the programs in court. And, at least initially, the U.S. Supreme Court often agreed with them. Through the mid-1930s, the Court continued to rule that certain aspects of New Deal programs went beyond the authority of Congress to regulate commerce. A series of decisions ruling various aspects of New Deal programs unconstitutional reflected the Court's *laissez-faire,* or hands-off, attitude toward the economy, which the justices viewed as a state problem.

FDR and Congress were livid. FDR's frustration with the Court prompted him to suggest what ultimately was nicknamed his "Court-packing plan." Knowing that he could do little to change the minds of those already on the Court, FDR suggested enlarging its size from nine to thirteen justices. This plan would have given him the opportunity to pack the Court with a majority of justices predisposed toward the constitutional validity of the New Deal.

Even though Roosevelt was popular, the Court-packing plan was not.[18] Congress and the public expressed outrage over even the suggestion of tampering with an institution of government. Even the Court appeared to respond to this threat. In 1937, it reversed its series of anti–New Deal decisions, concluding that Congress (and therefore the national government) had broad authority to legislate in any area as long as what was regulated affected commerce in any way. The Court also upheld the constitutionality of most of the massive New Deal relief programs, including the National Labor Relations Act of 1935, which authorized collective bargaining between unions and employees;[19] the Fair Labor Standards Act of 1938, which set a national minimum wage; and the Agricultural Adjustment Act of 1938, which provided crop subsidies to farmers.[20] Congress then used these newly recognized powers to legislate in a wide range of areas, including maximum hour laws and regulation of child labor.

Federal Grants to State and Local Governments

3.5 Describe how the federal budget is used to further influence state and local governments' policies.

President Franklin D. Roosevelt's New Deal programs increased the flow of national dollars to the states for a variety of public works programs, including building and road construction. In the boom times of World War II, when the nation needed most able-bodied Americans to work, even more new federal programs were introduced. These programs often redefined national–state relationships and made the national government a major player in domestic policy. Until the 1960s, however, the national government constructed most federal grant programs in cooperation with the states, with emphasis on assisting the states in fulfilling their traditional responsibilities to protect the health, welfare, and safety of their citizens.

Today, the national government provides grants from its general revenues to states, local governments, nonprofit organizations, and even individuals. These programs range from grants to support state programs aiding needy families to Pell

3.1

3.2

3.3

3.4

3.5

3.6

3.7

categorical grant
Grant that appropriates federal funds to states for a specific purpose.

New Federalism
Federal–state relationship proposed by Reagan administration during the 1980s; hallmark is returning administrative powers to the state governments.

block grant
A large grant given to a state by the federal government with only general spending guidelines.

grants giving students help to fund their educations. These grants are given for a number of purposes including: (1) providing state and local governments with additional funds; (2) setting national standards for national problems, such as clean air and water; and (3) attempting to financially equalize rich and poor states and localities. Federal grants are of several types. These include categorical grants, block grants, and programmatic requests.

☐ Categorical Grants

Categorical grants are grants for which Congress appropriates funds for specific purposes. Categorical grants allocate federal dollars by a precise formula, often based on population. They are subject to detailed conditions imposed by the national government. Often they are made available on a matching basis; that is, states must contribute money to match federal funds, although the national government may pay as much as 90 percent of the total. Categorical grants may be used by the national government to alter states' policy priorities or to coerce states to adopt particular policy objectives. With large sums of money at stake, states will often neglect their own wants and needs to follow the leadership of the national government. For example, states allocate about 15 percent of their budgets to Medicaid, a categorical grant aimed at providing health care for low-income and disabled Americans. Other federal categorical grants fund pollution control, economic development, and law enforcement.

These grants became more prominent mechanisms of coercion in 1964, when President Lyndon B. Johnson launched his Great Society program, which included what LBJ called a "War on Poverty." The Great Society program was a broad attempt to combat poverty and discrimination through urban renewal, education reform, and unemployment relief. In a frenzy of activity in Washington not seen since the New Deal, the national government channeled federal funds to states, to local governments, and even to citizen action groups. Funding these nonprofit organizations allowed liberal members of Congress to bypass not only conservative state legislatures but also conservative mayors and councils in the South and in cities such as Chicago, who were perceived as disinclined to help their poor, often African American, constituencies.

☐ Block Grants

In 1980, former California Republican Governor Ronald Reagan became president, pledging to advance what he called **New Federalism** and a return of power to the states. The hallmark of this action was the consolidation of many categorical grants into fewer, less restrictive **block grants**—large amounts of money given to states with only general spending guidelines. Many of these went to education and health care.[21]

Perhaps not surprisingly, these reforms were popular with governors, who urged the consolidation of even more programs into block grants. Calls to revamp the welfare system, in particular, were popular with citizens and governments alike. These reforms were ultimately realized during the mid-1990s, when a Republican-controlled Congress under Speaker of the House Newt Gingrich (R–GA) and President Bill Clinton replaced the existing federal welfare program with a program known as Temporary Assistance for Needy Families (TANF). TANF returned much of the administrative power for welfare programs to the states and became a hallmark of what became known as the "devolution revolution."

☐ Unfunded Mandates

Another component of Congress' efforts to devolve greater authority back to the state governments during the 1990s was the passage of the Unfunded Mandates Reform Act of 1995. This act prevented Congress from passing costly federal programs without debate on how to fund them and addressed a primary concern of state governments, many of which held the view that federal programs were encompassing a growing part of their state budgets and were in violation of their sovereign policy-making

Explore on MyPoliSciLab

Which States Win and Lose the Federal Aid Game?

The national government collects taxes from everyone, but it doesn't always spend money in the state where it gets it. Instead, the federal government transfers wealth from state to state. Recipient states receive more money than they pay in federal taxes, while donor states pay more in federal taxes than they receive. In 2007, there were 19 donor states and 31 recipient states. The political explanation for which states were donors and recipients is surprising.

Who pays?

DELAWARE, MINNESOTA, NEW JERSEY, and CONNECTICUT all paid at least $6,000 more in federal taxes per person than they received in federal aid. 15 other states were net donors.

Net Donor: Over $5,000 Per Person			
Connecticut $6,241	New Jersey $6,644	Minnesota $7,431	Delaware $12,285

Net Donor: Between $1 and $5,000 per person			
Ohio $49	North Carolina $1,108	Massachusetts $2,133	Rhode Island $2,732
Georgia $434	California $1,466	Colorado $2,176	Illinois $3,640
Washington $773	Nevada $1,616	Nebraska $2,850	New York $4,502
Wisconsin $1,000	Arkansas $1,723	Texas $2,243	

Who receives?

ALASKA took in twice the federal money in 2007 that it paid in taxes. 31 states are recipient states. Of the top six recipient states, four are southern.

Net Recipient: Over $5,000 Per Person					
Alaska -$7,448	New Mexico -$7,143	Mississippi -$6,765	Virginia -$6,239	West Virginia -$5,820	Alabama -$5,130

Net Recipient: Between $1 and $5,000 per person				
Hawaii -$4983	South Carolina -$3,756	Arizona -$1,976	Utah -$792	Pennsylvania -$385
North Dakota -$4,856	Kentucky -$3,012	Idaho -$1,281	Indiana -$723	Oklahoma -$376
South Dakota -$4,414	Maryland -$3,010	Wyoming -$1,205	Tennessee -$603	New Hampshire -$349
Maine -$4,221	Vermont -$2,854	Missouri -$1,190	Florida -$581	Michigan -$171
Montana -$4,149	Louisiana -$2,180	Iowa -$1,075	Oregon -$474	Kansas -$154

SOURCE: Data from United States Internal Revenue Service; *Statistical Abstract of the United States 2012;* and *U.S. Census of Population and Housing, 2010.*

Who are the Recipient States?

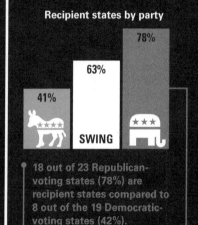

Recipient states by party

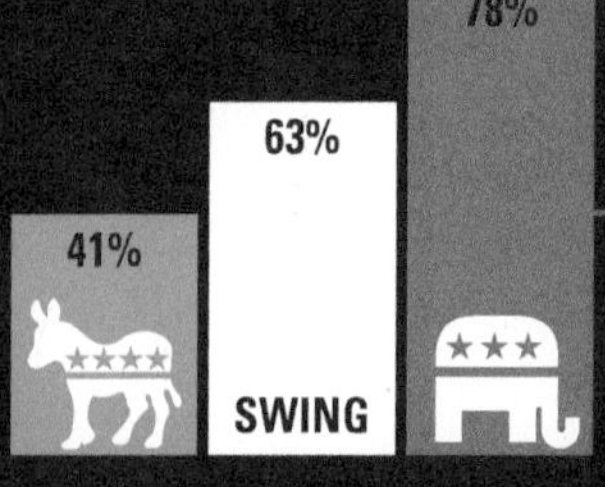

18 out of 23 Republican-voting states (78%) are recipient states compared to 8 out of the 19 Democratic-voting states (42%).

Recipient states by poverty level

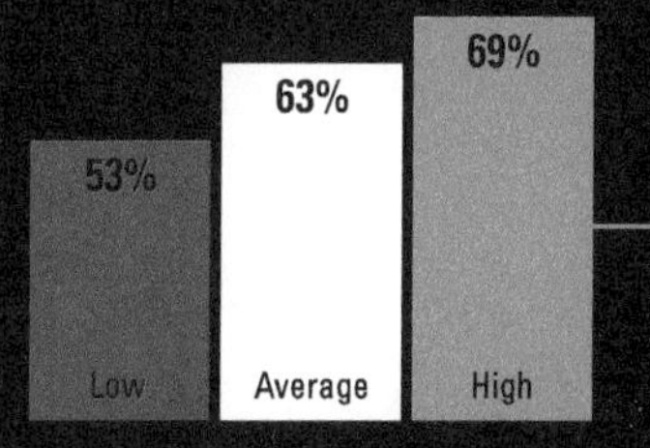

9 of 13 states with high poverty levels are recipient states (69%), while only 9 of 17 states with low poverty levels are recipient states (53%).

Investigate Further

Concept How do we determine donor and recipient states? Per person, we subtract the federal aid dollars sent to a state from the federal tax dollars paid in a state. If the result is positive, a state is a donor state, otherwise it's a recipient state.

Connection What relationship exists between politics and whether a state is a recipient or donor? Recipient states are most often Republican in national politics, while donor states tend to be more Democratic in national politics.

Cause Is there a policy explanation for which states are recipient states? The federal government fights poverty by moving money around the country. Recipient states usually have higher poverty levels and lower average incomes. Therefore, they tend to pay less federal tax than they receive per person.

3.1

3.2

3.3

3.4

3.5

3.6

3.7

programmatic request
Federal funds designated for special projects within a state or congressional district.

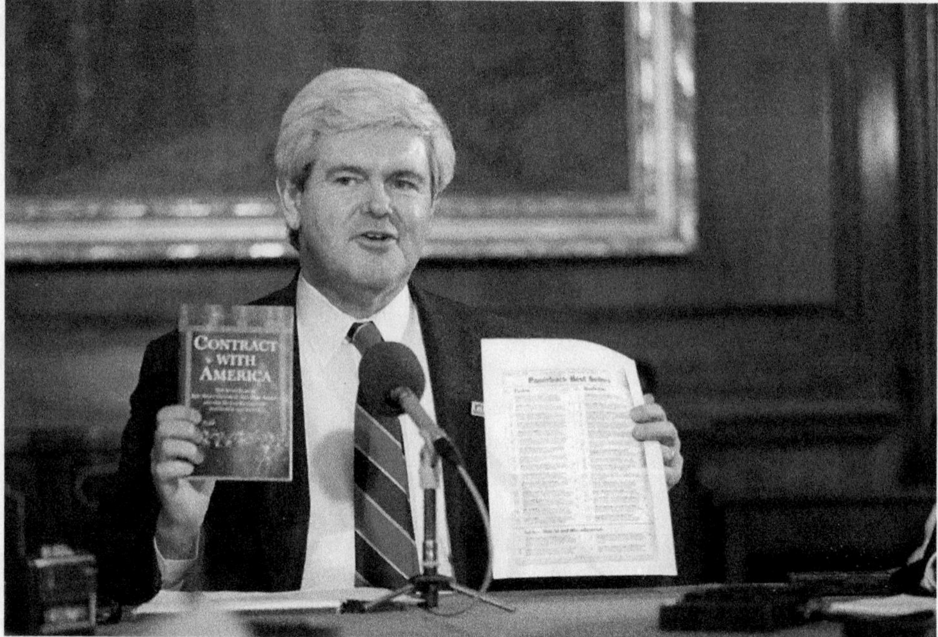

WHO SUPPORTED SCALING BACK THE FEDERAL GOVERNMENT AND INCREASING THE USE OF BLOCK GRANTS?

The devolution of policy-making authority to state and local governments was a popular policy proposal with Republican leaders during the 1980s and 1990s; many Republicans continue to support these goals today. Here, Newt Gingrich, who served as Speaker of the House during the 1990s and as a Republican presidential candidate in 2012, advocates for these goals in the form of a "Contract with America." The Contract was a program of government reform supported by most Republican congressional candidates in 1994.

authority. However, the Unfunded Mandates Reform Act has proved notoriously difficult to enforce, and many states charge the national government with continuing to create federal programs with insufficient funding.

One common example is the No Child Left Behind Act (NCLB) of 2001, now part of the amended Elementary and Secondary Education Act of 1965, which imposed a host of federal requirements on everything from class size to accountability testing.[22] Although the federal government set these increased standards, states charge that Congress did not consider the cost of these dramatic adjustments, which were passed on to the states, localities, and people. As a result, many states and localities have attempted to pass legislation opting out of all or some of the provisions of NCLB.

☐ Programmatic Requests

Informally known as earmarks, **programmatic requests** are federal funds designated for special projects within a state or congressional district that direct specific exemptions from taxes or mandated fees. Federal funds have been provided for special projects since the first Congress. In 1790, money was earmarked to finish a lighthouse at the request of a Massachusetts representative. In 1817, John C. Calhoun suggested monies be used to fund a national highway, but President James Madison said such requests were unconstitutional. In the 1950s, however, President Dwight D. Eisenhower used two earmarks to fund building the massive national highway system.

The use of these grants has exploded in the past two decades. The transportation budget, in particular, has benefited from earmarks; from 1996 to 2005, it increased by 1,150 percent. Programmatic requests are not competitively awarded, and have thus become very controversial owing to the use of paid political lobbyists who try to secure federal funds for their clients, be they states, cities, universities, or nonprofit groups. Members of Congress also attempt to secure these funds to bring programs and economic development back to their home districts. During one recent Congress, members requested 40,000 earmarks worth more than $100 billion directed to their home districts and states for transportation projects alone.[23]

Take a Closer Look

Federal grants have become an increasingly important part of state budgets. While these grant programs may help states to develop new initiatives or implement federal programs, they may also create intergovernmental dependency that can have disastrous consequences. Unlike the national government, most state governments are required to balance their budgets. So, when federal revenues decline, they must often be accompanied by cuts in state government programs and services. To better understand the nature and consequences of this dependency, examine the pie graph and photo below.

Sources of State Government Revenue, 2010

As this pie graph from the Census Bureau indicates, two-thirds of state revenues came from taxes, service charges, and other sources, with the balance between the three varying from state to state.

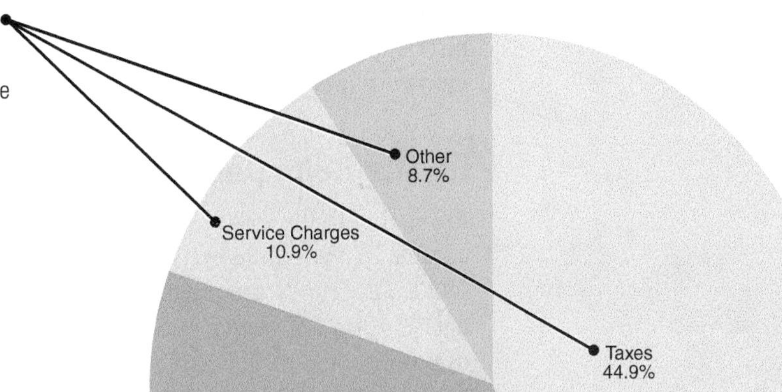

States, on average, received over one-third, or about 35.5% of their revenues from the federal government.

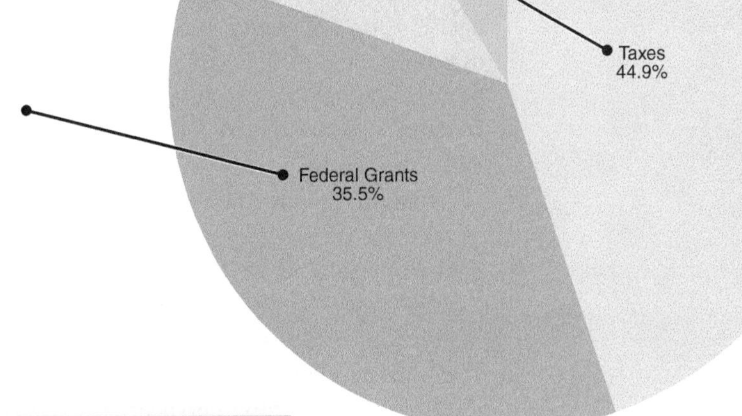

Source: U.S. Census Bureau. 2010 Annual Survey of State Government Finances.

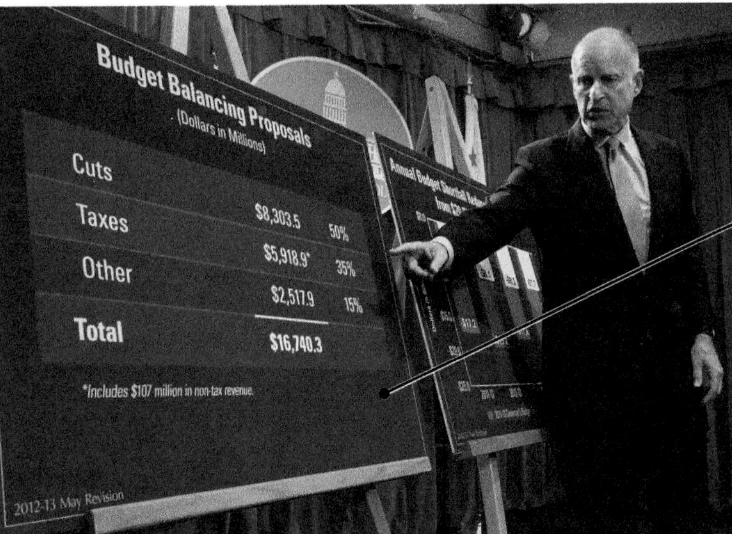

Depending on the federal government for funds can have significant implications for states. When fewer federal dollars flow, states are forced to cut programs. Here, California Governor Jerry Brown (D) discusses a number of ways to address his state's projected $16 billion budget shortfall in 2012.

CRITICAL THINKING QUESTIONS

1. Are state governments too dependent on federal dollars? Should they be required to find other ways to raise revenues? What mechanisms seem most equitable?
2. Should federal governments be required to fully fund any mandates they pass along to state governments? What are the pros and cons of such an arrangement?
3. How do you think cuts in federal dollars affect the demands that state governments place on local governments such as municipalities and special districts?

Judicial Federalism

3.6 Explore the role of the judiciary as arbiter of federal–state conflicts.

The U.S. Supreme Court has always played an important role as the umpire of the federal system. When governmental powers, especially those of the state and national governments, come into conflict, it is the Court's job to determine which government is supreme. As detailed throughout this chapter, the Court has played the role of umpire at many transformational times in American history, including the founding, the Civil War, and during the Great Depression. The modern Supreme Court is no exception.

The Rehnquist Court

From the 1930s until the 1980s, the Court made its federalism decisions largely outside of the public eye. While the Court under Chief Justice Earl Warren in the 1950s and 1960s attracted a great deal of attention, it was largely for the justices' decisions on civil rights and liberties issues, not the Court's decisions on the balance of power between the state and national governments. Through the process of incorporation, which bound state governments to the provisions of the U.S. Constitution, however, many of these decisions had the result—intended or not—of expanding federal power at the expense of subnational units.

Beginning in the late 1980s, however, the Court's willingness to allow Congress to regulate in a variety of areas waned. This revolution was led by a group of new justices appointed by President Ronald Reagan. These judges, including Justices Sandra Day O'Connor, Antonin Scalia, and Anthony Kennedy, were committed to the notion of states' rights and to rolling back federal intervention in many areas. The leadership of a conservative chief justice William H. Rehnquist, only served to intensify the changing perspective.

According to one observer, the federalism decisions made by the Rehnquist Court in the 1980s and 1990s were "a reexamination of the country's most basic constitutional arrangements."[24] The Court's decisions largely agreed with the Republican states' rights view evident in the policies of the Reagan administration and the Contract with America Congresses. For example, in *U.S.* v. *Lopez* (1995), which involved the conviction of a student charged with carrying a concealed handgun onto school property, a five-person majority of the Court ruled that Congress lacked constitutional authority under the commerce clause to regulate guns within 1,000 feet of a school.[25] The majority concluded that, however well-intentioned, gun control laws, even those involving schools, were not substantially related to interstate commerce. Thus, they were a state, not a federal, matter.

The Roberts Court

In 2005, following the death of Chief Justice Rehnquist, President George W. Bush appointed Chief Justice John Roberts to head the Supreme Court. A number of other changes in the composition of the Court, including the appointment of conservative Justice Samuel Alito and liberal Justices Sonia Sotomayor and Elena Kagan (by President Barack Obama) followed soon after.

In its early years, the Roberts Court appeared tentative to address high-profile federalism cases. However, during its 2011 term, the Court thrust itself into the federalism debate, deciding a series of visible cases related to the balance of national and state power. These cases considered issues such as immigration (discussed in the opening vignette), redistricting, and health care.[26] Much to the surprise of many Court-watchers, in both the immigration and health care cases, the Roberts Court sided with the power of the national government. Whether these decisions are a temporary departure from the norm or a harbinger of a new era in federalism remains to be seen. Like the Court's federalism decisions of previous eras, they may also simply be the result of a strategic Court seeking to maintain its institutional prestige by following the will of the people.

preemption
A concept that allows the national government to override state or local actions in certain policy areas.

progressive federalism
A pragmatic approach to federalism that views relations between national and state governments as both coercive and cooperative.

Toward Reform: Attempts to Balance National and State Power

3.7 Assess the challenges in balancing national and state powers and the consequences for policy making.

As we have seen throughout this chapter, attempting to find equilibrium between the powers and responsibilities of national and state governments is one of the greatest challenges of a federal system. The roles and relative strengths of the national and state governments in the United States have changed over time and continue to evolve today. Here, we explore the current status of this relationship, and examine its consequences for policy making.

The Price of Federalism

In 1995, political scientist Paul E. Peterson published his seminal exploration of the balance between state and national powers, *The Price of Federalism*.[27] In this book, Peterson considered how governments should best divide policy-making responsibility into two broad issue areas: redistributive and developmental policies. Redistributive policies are those whereby the government collects money (usually through taxation) from one group of citizens to finance a service, such as health care or welfare, for another group of citizens. In contrast, developmental policies are those designed to strengthen a government's economic standing, such as building roads and other infrastructure. The national government's greater financial resources and ability to ensure a uniform standard, Peterson argued, made it better suited to handle redistributive programs. In contrast, developmental programs would be best left to state governments, which are closer to the people and better able to assess and address regional needs.

The problem with this arrangement—and the price of American federalism—is that, historically, the division of power has not followed this pattern. The national government and members of Congress in particular have had reelection incentives to create and fund programs that have a direct impact on constituents. As a result, administration of redistributive policies often fell to the states, perhaps with federal financial assistance.

In more recent years, however, the federal government, while not totally abandoning developmental projects, has begun to take greater responsibility for redistributive policies. One such example is the passage of the No Child Left Behind Act of 2001 (NCLB), the first comprehensive federal education legislation, discussed earlier in this chapter.

States are not entirely satisfied with these steps toward policy efficiency. Under the Tenth Amendment, state and local governments traditionally have controlled education policy. Many states and localities view NCLB as an unprecedented **preemption** of state and local powers.

Progressive Federalism

During his first term, President Barack Obama appeared receptive to a pragmatic movement known as **progressive federalism.** Advocates of progressive federalism view the relationship between the states and the national government as both coercive and cooperative.[28] The form taken by the relationship depends chiefly on the political environment at each level of government. The best and first option is when the federal government is able to reach consensus and establish a national standard.

"Stop! Wait! Government's no longer the problem—it's the solution."

HOW DO VIEWS ON THE ROLE OF GOVERNMENT CHANGE?

Depending on the party in power and the political climate, the national government may be viewed as either a necessary evil or simply evil. Progressive federalism acknowledges both of these viewpoints, taking a pragmatic approach to balancing the authority of state and national governments.

However, failing the national government's ability to enact a particular proposal, national policy makers may embrace states' efforts to address that policy issue, particularly when those in power agree with the outcome of the state policy-making process. This approach allows policy makers to achieve their goals gradually and encourages states to act as what U.S. Supreme Court Justice Louis Brandeis called "laboratories of democracy."

Perhaps the most visible attempt by the Obama administration to create a national mandate was the passage of the 2010 Patient Protection and Affordable Care Act, which established a variety of mechanisms to ensure that nearly all Americans had access to health insurance. Part of this health care reform legislation also included significant changes in the Medicaid program administered by the state governments. Almost immediately after the ink was dry on the president's signature on the act, a group of state governments challenged the constitutionality of the act. They charged that it exceeded the federal government's power to regulate interstate commerce. The Supreme Court, however, upheld the constitutionality of the law, citing the federal government's power to tax as a justification for Congress' authority to enact the health care reform legislation.

In other areas, the Obama administration permitted state governments to take the lead. In 2009, for example, Obama allowed the state of California to impose stricter limits on greenhouse gas emissions from cars and trucks than those established by the Environmental Protection Agency (EPA). This resolved a long-standing conflict between the states and the federal government and opened the door for a number of other states to follow California's lead.

Not everyone views progressive federalism positively. Critics, including the U.S. Chamber of Commerce, have called progressive federalism "free-for-all federalism." They charge that the emission standards, in particular, will lead to a costly "patchwork of laws impacting a troubled [automotive] industry."[29] Complying with a variety of state standards, they note, is more costly than meeting one national standard. It is also more expensive to monitor and lobby the legislatures of fifty states than it is to address only the EPA.

Review the Chapter

 Listen to Chapter 3 on MyPoliSciLab

Roots of the Federal System

3.1 Trace the roots of the federal system and the Constitution's allocation of powers between the national and state governments, p. 65.

The national government has both enumerated and implied powers under the Constitution. National and state governments share an additional group of concurrent powers. Other powers are reserved to the states or the people, or expressly denied to both governments. The powers of the national government are ultimately declared supreme. Local governments are not expressly mentioned in the constitution but are formed when state governments delegate their sovereign authority.

Federalism and the Marshall Court

3.2 Determine the impact of the Marshall Court on federalism, p. 71.

The Supreme Court under the leadership of John Marshall played a key role in defining the relationship and powers of the national government through its broad interpretations of the supremacy and commerce clauses.

Dual Federalism: States' Rights, the Civil War, and Reconstruction

3.3 Describe the emergence and decline of dual federalism, p. 73.

Dual federalism was characterized by a system of separate but equally powerful state and national governments. This system was exemplified by states' authority to regulate issues such as slavery, evident in the doctrine of nullification and the Supreme Court's decision in *Dred Scott* v. *Sanford* (1857). The Civil War changed forever the nature of federalism. A further departure from dual federalism became evident with the ratification of the Sixteenth and Seventeenth Amendments in 1913.

Cooperative Federalism: The Growth of National Government

3.4 Explain how cooperative federalism led to the growth of the national government at the expense of the states, p. 76.

The notion of equally powerful but separate national and state governments met its demise in the wake of the Great Depression. Franklin D. Roosevelt's New Deal ushered in an era of cooperative federalism, in which the powers of the national and state and local governments became more integrated, working together to solve shared problems.

Federal Grants to State and Local Governments

3.5 Describe how the federal budget is used to further influence state and local governments' policies, p. 79.

The federal government provides money to states in a number of ways, including categorical grants, block grants, and programmatic requests. Problems may result when the federal government creates programs without providing sufficient funds These are called unfunded mandates.

Judicial Federalism

3.6 Explore the role of the judiciary as an arbiter of federal–state conflicts, p. 84.

The Supreme Court has always been an important arbiter of the relationship between national and state governments. While many of the decisions of the Rehnquist Court favored state governments, more recent decisions by the Roberts Court have favored national power in areas such as immigration and health care.

Toward Reform: Attempts to Balance National and State Power

3.7 Assess the challenges in balancing national and state powers and the consequences for policy making, p. 85.

The roles and relative strengths of the national and state governments have changed over time. Some political scientists argue that the national government is best suited for redistributive policy and the states for developmental policy. Progressive approaches to federalism combine coercion and cooperation to achieve desired policy objectives.

Learn the Terms

Barron v. *Baltimore* (1833), p. 73
bill of attainder, p. 68
block grant, p. 80
categorical grant, p. 80
charter, p. 70
concurrent powers, p. 68
confederation, p. 65
cooperative federalism, p. 76
county, p. 70
Dillon's Rule, p. 70
Dred Scott v. *Sandford* (1857), p. 74
dual federalism, p. 73
enumerated powers, p. 66
ex post facto law, p. 68
extradition clause, p. 69
federal system, p. 65
full faith and credit clause, p. 69
Gibbons v. *Ogden* (1824), p. 71
implied powers, p. 66
interstate compacts, p. 69
McCulloch v. *Maryland* (1819), p. 71
municipality, p. 70
New Deal, p. 77
New Federalism, p. 80
nullification, p. 74
preemption, p. 85
privileges and immunities clause, p. 69
programmatic requests, p. 82
progressive federalism, p. 85
reserved powers, p. 67
Seventeenth Amendment, p. 76
Sixteenth Amendment, p. 76
special district, p. 70
Tenth Amendment, p. 67
unitary system, p. 65

Test Yourself

Study and **Review** the **Practice Tests**

1. Under the Constitution, both the national and state governments

a. are totally autonomous.
b. do not share any powers.
c. are accountable to the people.
d. can regulate interstate commerce.
e. are able to establish local governments.

2. The Tenth Amendment provides for

a. states' reserved powers.
b. states' implied powers.
c. concurrent state and federal powers.
d. enumerated federal powers.
e. taking private property for public purposes.

3. In *Gibbons* v. *Ogden,* the U.S. Supreme Court

I. articulated an expansive view of congressional powers.
II. gave Robert Fulton the exclusive right to operate steamships on the Hudson River.
III. concluded that commerce should be given a broad definition.
IV. declared that the states had sole authority to regulate commerce.

a. I only
b. II and III
c. I and II
d. III and IV
e. I and III

4. The Supreme Court held in *Barron* v. *Baltimore* that

a. Congress had broad powers to regulate interstate commerce.
b. the Bill of Rights did not apply to state governments.
c. Congress lacked the ability to ban slavery.
d. the city of Baltimore could not nullify laws passed by Congress.
e. states could not tax the federal bank.

5. Nullification

a. was used to justify South Carolina's refusal to abide by federal tariff laws.
b. is a political maneuver in which Congress purposefully invalidates state laws by passing national laws.
c. is a principle that allows states to invalidate laws from other states.
d. played no part in the development of the Civil War.
e. was deemed unconstitutional after the Supreme Court invalidated the Alien and Sedition Acts.

6. The Great Depression led to

a. a variety of innovative programs to combat terrorism.
b. greater adherence to the philosophy of dual federalism.
c. a growth in national government activity.
d. a provision allowing the election of President Franklin D. Roosevelt for four terms.
e. the increased use of unfunded mandates.

7. New Federalism favors ____ over ____ grants.

a. block/categorical
b. categorical/block
c. funded mandates/categorical
d. block/unfunded mandates
e. block/funded mandates

8. In general, the Rehnquist Court's federalism decisions empowered:

a. both state and national governments.
b. the state governments at the expense of the national government.
c. the national government at the expense of the states.
d. neither the state nor the national government.
e. local governments at the expense of the state and national governments

9. The No Child Left Behind Act is an example of

a. a block grant.
b. returning power to the states.
c. a funded mandate.
d. preemption.
e. a categorical grant.

10. According to the text, which of the following best exemplifies the cooperative aspects of progressive federalism?

a. Bailing out the failing automobile industry
b. Health care reform
c. Allowing states to set emissions standards
d. Creating of the U.S. Department of Education
e. Reforming Social Security and Medicare

Explore Further

Bowman, Ann O'Meara, and Richard C. Kearney. *State and Local Government*, 8th ed. Belmont, CA: Wadsworth, 2010.

Chemerinsky, Erwin. *Enhancing Government: Federalism for the 21st Century*. Stanford, CA: Stanford Law Books, 2008.

Ebel, Robert D., and John E. Petersen. *The Oxford Handbook of State and Local Government*. New York: Oxford University Press, 2012.

Gerston, Larry N. *American Federalism: A Concise Introduction*. Armonk, NY: M. E. Sharpe, 2007.

Gray, Virginia, Russell L. Hanson, and Thad Kousser, eds. *Politics in the American States: A Comparative Analysis*, 10th ed. Washington, DC: CQ Press, 2012.

Grodzins, Morton. *The American System: A View of Government in the United States*. Chicago: Rand McNally, 1966.

LaCroix, Alison. *The Ideological Origins of American Federalism*. Cambridge, MA: Harvard University Press, 2010.

Mayer, M. H. *Homeland Security and Federalism: Protecting America from Outside the Beltway*. New York: Praeger, 2009.

Nugent, John D. *Safeguarding Federalism: How States Protect Their Interests in National Policymaking*. Norman: University of Oklahoma Press, 2009.

O'Toole, Laurence L., ed. *American Intergovernmental Relations: Foundations, Perspectives, and Issues*, 4th ed. Washington, DC: CQ Press, 2007.

Peterson, Paul E. *The Price of Federalism*. Washington, DC: Brookings Institution, 1995.

Rivlin, Alice, Timothy J. Conlan, and Paul Posner. *Intergovernmental Management for the 21st Century*. Washington, DC: Brookings Institution, 2007.

Smith, Kevin B., ed. *State and Local Government, 2013–2014 ed.* Washington, DC: CQ Press, 2012.

Smith, Kevin B., Alan Greenblatt, and Michele Mariani Vaughn. *Governing States and Localities*, 3rd ed. Washington, DC: CQ Press, 2010.

Stephens, G. Ross, and Nelson Wikstrom. *American Intergovernmental Relations: A Fragmented Federal Polity*. New York: Oxford University Press, 2006.

To learn more about federalism, go to the American Council on Intergovernmental Relations at **govinfo.library.unt.edu/amcouncil/federalism.html.**

To learn more about state and local governments, go to State and Local Government on the Net at **www.statelocalgov.net/.**

To learn more about Supreme Court cases on federalism, go to the Oyez Project at **www.oyez.org.**

Listen to **Chapter 4** on **MyPoliSciLab**

4

Civil Liberties

The Bill of Rights, written in 1789, set forth to define the natural rights of the citizens of the United States. It was also intended to limit the new national government's ability to overstep its authority. The Fourth Amendment, for example, guards against unreasonable search and seizure. Specifically, the amendment states that it protects "the right of people to be secure in their persons, houses, papers, and effects." The Fourth Amendment also provides guidelines regarding obtaining a warrant in order to conduct a search.

Through this amendment, the government ensured that the people of the United States were guaranteed both their privacy and autonomy. However, interpreting the Fourth Amendment—as well as many other amendments—has posed significant challenges for the modern judiciary. Determining what constitutes an "unreasonable" search or when a law enforcement officer has "probable cause," especially, prove difficult in practice. Constantly evolving technology and social and political norms can also pose unique challenges for the criminal justice system.

Two cases decided during the Supreme Court's 2012 term illustrate the ongoing challenges of the Fourth Amendment. In the first case, the Court was asked to rule on whether or not law enforcement officers could plant GPS tracking devices on a suspected criminal's vehicle. The Court ultimately decided that, although the purpose of the search, monitoring a suspected criminal's activity, was the same as an extended investigation, implanting a tracking device on the suspect's vehicle compromised the suspect's expectation of privacy. Though the Court did not explicitly state that a warrant was necessary, observers noted that the ruling was construed in such a way that using a GPS device to track a suspect's activity without a warrant would be unlikely to stand up to legal challenge.[1]

In a second case, the Court considered whether invasive strip searches could be performed on all individuals entering a prison. In this case, the justices acknowledged the diversity of problems facing the criminal justice system today, including concealed weapons, gang tattoos, and

JUDICIAL INTERPRETATION HAS REDEFINED THE FOURTH AMENDMENT Vehicles are one Fourth Amendment issue that has continuously troubled the Supreme Court. Above, police officers search a vehicle during the Prohibition Era. Below, a Department of Homeland Security agent uses technological devices to search a van at the U.S.-Mexico border.

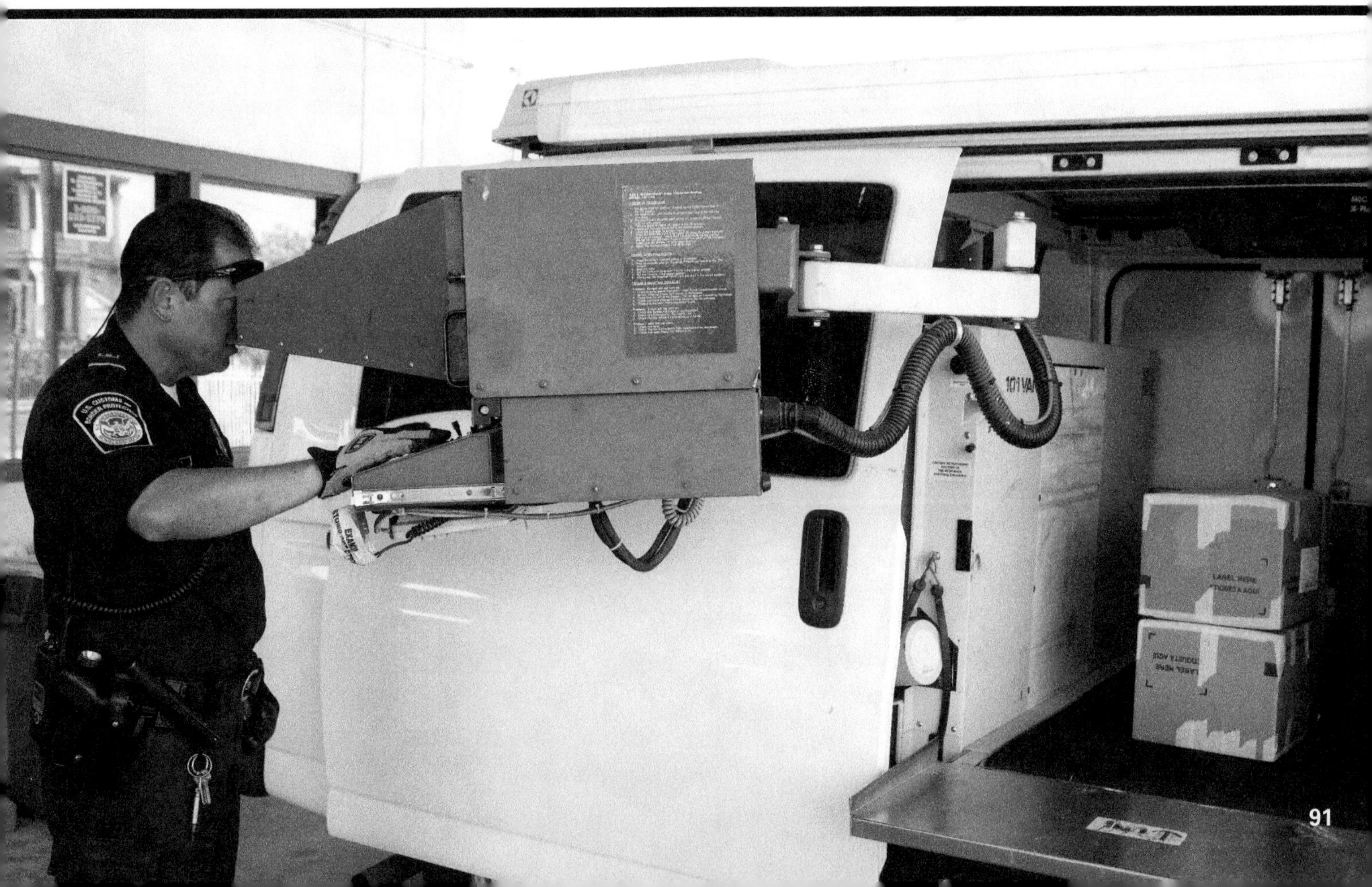

MyPoliSciLab Videos

The Big Picture Find out how the events of September 11, 2001 transformed civil liberties in the United States. Author Alixandra B. Yanus reviews the acts that were passed by the government after that day, and demonstrates why it can be troubling to accept civil liberties for all people.

The Basics What are civil liberties and where do they come from? In this video, you will learn about our First Amendment guarantees and about protections the Bill of Rights provides those accused of crimes. In the process, you'll discover how our liberties have changed over time to reflect our changing values and needs.

In Context Uncover the importance of civil liberties in a changing American society. University of Massachusetts at Boston political scientist Maurice T. Cunningham identifies the origins of our civil liberties and evaluates the clash between national security and civil liberties in a post 9/11 age.

Think Like a Political Scientist What are some of the challenges facing political scientists in regards to civil liberties? In this video University of Massachusetts at Boston political scientist Maurice T. Cunningham raises some of the thought-provoking questions regarding civil liberties that have arisen during the last decade.

In the Real World The American legal system and the American people have both struggled over whether the death penalty should be imposed in this country In this segment, we'll hear what citizens have to say about the death penalty.

So What? Like having the freedom to read whatever book or magazine you want without censorship? In this video, author Alixandra B. Yanus lays out the civil liberties Americans enjoy (and take for granted) and explains how these liberties can sometimes run into conflict with each other.

smuggled drugs or other illegal substances. In so doing, they noted that if any suspected criminal was entering the general prison population, law enforcement officers had an interest in ensuring the safety of the prison and of society. Thus, performing a general strip search, even without a warrant, was permissible.[2]

In each of these cases, the Supreme Court was asked to consider issues related to the Fourth Amendment that the Framers could never have imagined. The brilliance of the civil liberties codified by the First Congress is that the Bill of Rights remains a relatively stable statement of our natural rights as Americans, even as technology has evolved. With judicial interpretation, the sentiments expressed more than 200 years ago still apply to the modern world.

•••

civil liberties
The personal guarantees and freedoms that the government cannot abridge by law, constitution, or judicial interpretation.

civil rights
The government-protected rights of individuals against arbitrary or discriminatory treatment by governments or individuals.

Civil liberties are the personal guarantees and freedoms that government cannot abridge, by law, constitution, or judicial interpretation. As guarantees of "freedom to" action, they place limitations on the power of the government to restrain or dictate an individual's actions. **Civil rights,** in contrast, provide freedom from arbitrary or discriminatory treatment by government or individuals.

Questions of civil liberties often present complex problems. We must decide how to determine the boundaries of speech and assembly—or, how much control over our personal liberties we give to police or other law enforcement officials. Moreover, during times of war, it is important to consider the liberties accorded to those who oppose war or are suspected of anti-government activities.

Resolution of civil liberties questions often falls to the judiciary, which must balance the competing interests of the government and the people. Thus, in many of the cases discussed in this chapter, a conflict arises between an individual or group of individuals seeking to exercise what they believe to be a liberty and the government, be it local, state, or national, seeking to control the exercise of that liberty in an attempt to keep order and preserve the rights (and safety) of others. In other cases, two liberties clash, such as a physician's and her patients' right to easy access to a medical clinic such as Planned Parenthood versus a pro-life advocate's liberty to picket that clinic. In this chapter, we explore the various dimensions of civil liberties guarantees contained in the U.S. Constitution and the Bill of Rights.

Roots of Civil Liberties: The Bill of Rights

4.1 Trace the constitutional roots of civil liberties.

In 1787, most state constitutions explicitly protected a variety of personal liberties, such as speech, religion, freedom from unreasonable searches and seizures, and trial by jury. The new federal system established by the Constitution would redistribute power between the national government and the states. Without an explicit guarantee of specific civil liberties, could the national government be trusted to uphold the freedoms already granted to citizens by their states?

Recognition of the increased power of the new national government led Anti-Federalists to stress the need for a bill of rights. Anti-Federalists and many others were confident they could control the actions of their own state legislators, but they did not trust the national government to protect civil liberties.

The notion of including a bill of rights in the Constitution was not popular at the Constitutional Convention. When George Mason of Virginia suggested adding such a bill to the preface of the proposed Constitution, representatives unanimously

Bill of Rights
The first ten amendments to the U.S. Constitution, which largely guarantee specific rights and liberties.

Ninth Amendment
Part of the Bill of Rights that makes it clear that enumerating rights in the Constitution or Bill of Rights does not mean that others do not exist.

Tenth Amendment
The final part of the Bill of Rights that defines the basic principle of American federalism in stating that the powers not delegated to the national government are reserved to the states or to the people.

due process clause
Clause contained in the Fifth and Fourteenth Amendments; over the years, it has been construed to guarantee a variety of rights to individuals.

substantive due process
Judicial interpretation of the Fifth and Fourteenth Amendments' due process clauses that protects citizens from arbitrary or unjust state or federal laws.

defeated his resolution.[3] In subsequent ratification debates, Federalists argued that a bill of rights was unnecessary, putting forward three main arguments in opposition.

1. A bill of rights was unnecessary in a constitutional republic founded on the idea of popular sovereignty and inalienable, natural rights. Moreover, most state constitutions contained bills of rights, so federal guarantees were unnecessary.
2. A bill of rights would be dangerous. According to Alexander Hamilton in *Federalist No. 84,* since the national government was one of enumerated powers (that is, it had only the powers listed in the Constitution), "Why declare that things shall not be done which there is no power to do?"
3. A national bill of rights would be impractical to enforce. Its validity would largely depend on public opinion and the spirit of the people and government.

Some Framers, however, came to support the idea. After the Philadelphia convention, James Madison conducted a lively correspondence with Thomas Jefferson about the need for a national bill of rights. Jefferson supported such guarantees far more quickly than did Madison. But, the reluctant Madison soon found himself in a close race against James Monroe for a seat in the House of Representatives in the First Congress. The district was largely Anti-Federalist. In an act of political expediency, Madison issued a new series of public letters similar to *The Federalist Papers,* in which he vowed to support a bill of rights. Once elected to the House, Madison made good on his promise and became the prime author of the Bill of Rights. Still, he considered Congress to have far more important matters to handle and viewed his work on the Bill of Rights as "a nauseous project."[4]

With fear of political instability running high, Congress worked quickly to approve Madison's draft. The proposed Bill of Rights was sent to the states for ratification in 1789, the same year the first Congress convened. By 1791, the states had approved most of its provisions.

The **Bill of Rights,** the first ten amendments to the Constitution, contains numerous specific guarantees against encroachment by the new government, including those of free speech, press, and religion. The Ninth and Tenth Amendments, favored by the Federalists, note that the Bill of Rights is not exclusive. The **Ninth Amendment** makes clear that this special listing of rights does not mean that others do not exist. The **Tenth Amendment** reiterates that powers not delegated to the national government are reserved to the states or to the people.

□ The Incorporation Doctrine: The Bill of Rights Made Applicable to the States

The Framers intended the Bill of Rights to limit the national government's power to infringe on the rights and liberties of the citizenry. In *Barron* v. *Baltimore* (1833), the Supreme Court ruled that the Bill of Rights limited only the actions of the U.S. government and not those of the states.[5] In 1868, however, the Fourteenth Amendment was added to the U.S. Constitution. Its language suggested that some or even all protections guaranteed in the Bill of Rights might be interpreted to prevent state infringement of those rights. Section 1 of the Fourteenth Amendment reads: "No State shall . . . . deprive any person of life, liberty, or property, without due process of law." Questions about the scope of "liberty" as well as the meaning of "due process of law" continue even today to engage legal scholars and jurists.

Until nearly the turn of the twentieth century, the Supreme Court steadfastly rejected numerous arguments for interpreting the **due process clause** in the Fourteenth Amendment in such a way as to make various provisions in the Bill of Rights applicable to the states. In 1897, however, the Court began to increase its jurisdiction over the states by holding them to a **substantive due process** standard whereby they had the legal burden to prove that their laws constituted a valid exercise of power to regulate the health, welfare, or public morals of citizens.[6] Interference with state power,

WHEN DID THE COURT FIRST ARTICULATE THE DOCTRINE OF SELECTIVE INCORPORATION?

Until *Gitlow v. New York* (1925), involving Benjamin Gitlow (shown on the right testifying before Congress), the executive secretary of the Socialist Party, it generally was thought that, despite the Fourteenth Amendment, the limitations of the Bill of Rights did not apply to the states. After *Gitlow*, the Court gradually bound states to most of these provisions through a process known as selective incorporation.

however, was rare, and states passed sedition laws (laws that made it illegal to speak or write any political criticism that threatened to diminish respect for the government, its laws, or public officials), anticipating that the U.S. Supreme Court would uphold their constitutionality. When Benjamin Gitlow, a member of the Socialist Party, printed 16,000 copies of a manifesto in which he urged workers to overthrow the U.S. government, he was convicted of violating a New York state law that prohibited such advocacy. Although his conviction was upheld, in *Gitlow* v. *New York* (1925), the U.S. Supreme Court noted that states were not completely free to limit forms of political expression, saying:

> For present purposes we may and do assume that freedom of speech and of the press—which are protected by the First Amendment from abridgement by Congress—are among the *fundamental personal rights and "liberties"* protected by the due process clause of the Fourteenth Amendment from impairment by the states [emphasis added].[7]

Gitlow, with its finding that states could not abridge free speech protections, was the first decision to clearly articulate the **incorporation doctrine.** In *Near* v. *Minnesota* (1931), the U.S. Supreme Court further developed this doctrine by holding that a state law violated the First Amendment's freedom of the press: "The fact that the liberty of the press may be abused by miscreant purveyors of scandal does not make any the less necessary the immunity of the press from previous restraint by the state."[8]

incorporation doctrine
An interpretation of the Constitution holding that the due process clause of the Fourteenth Amendment requires state and local governments to guarantee the rights stated in the Bill of Rights.

selective incorporation
A judicial doctrine whereby most, but not all, protections found in the Bill of Rights are made applicable to the states via the Fourteenth Amendment.

Selective Incorporation and Fundamental Freedoms

The Supreme Court has not made all specific guarantees in the Bill of Rights applicable to the states through the due process clause of the Fourteenth Amendment, as shown in Table 4.1. Instead, the Court has used the process of **selective incorporation** to limit

4.1

4.2

4.3

4.4

4.5

4.6

4.7

fundamental freedoms
Those rights defined by the Court as essential to order, liberty, and justice and therefore entitled to the highest standard of review.

TABLE 4.1 HOW HAS SELECTIVE INCORPORATION MADE THE BILL OF RIGHTS APPLICABLE TO THE STATES?

Amendment	Right	Date	Case Incorporated
I	Speech	1925	*Gitlow* v. *New York*
	Press	1931	*Near* v. *Minnesota*
	Assembly	1937	*DeJonge* v. *Oregon*
	Religion	1940	*Cantwell* v. *Connecticut*
II	Bear arms	2010	*McDonald* v. *City of Chicago*
III	No quartering of soldiers		Not incorporated
IV	No unreasonable searches or seizures	1949	*Wolf* v. *Colorado*
	Exclusionary rule	1961	*Mapp* v. *Ohio*
V	Just compensation	1897	*Chicago, B&Q R.R. Co.* v. *Chicago*
	Self-incrimination	1964	*Malloy* v. *Hogan*
	Double jeopardy	1969	*Benton* v. *Maryland*
	Grand jury indictment		Not incorporated
VI	Public trial	1948	*In re Oliver*
	Right to counsel	1963	*Gideon* v. *Wainwright*
	Confrontation of witnesses	1965	*Pointer* v. *Texas*
	Impartial trial	1966	*Parker* v. *Gladden*
	Speedy trial	1967	*Klopfer* v. *North Carolina*
	Compulsory trial	1967	*Washington* v. *Texas*
	Criminal trial	1968	*Duncan* v. *Louisiana*
VII	Civil jury trial		Not incorporated
VIII	No cruel and unusual punishment	1962	*Robinson* v. *California*
	No excessive bail	1971	*Schilb* v. *Kuebel*

the rights of states by protecting against abridgement of **fundamental freedoms.** These freedoms—defined by the Court as essential to order, liberty, and justice—are subject to the Court's most rigorous standard of review.

The Court set out the rationale for selective incorporation in *Palko* v. *Connecticut* (1937).[9] Frank Palko was charged with first-degree murder for killing two Connecticut police officers, found guilty of a lesser charge of second-degree murder, and sentenced to life imprisonment. Connecticut appealed. Palko was retried, found guilty of first-degree murder, and sentenced to death. Palko then appealed his second conviction, arguing that it violated the Fifth Amendment's prohibition against double jeopardy because the due process clause of the Fourteenth Amendment had made the Fifth Amendment applicable to the states.

The Supreme Court disagreed. In an opinion written by Justice Benjamin Cardozo, the Court ruled that the due process clause bound states only to those rights that were "of the very essence of a scheme of ordered liberty." The Fifth Amendment's double jeopardy clause was not, in the Court's view, among these rights. The Court overruled its decision in 1969.[10]

Today, selective incorporation requires states to respect freedoms of press, speech, and assembly, among other liberties. The Court has not incorporated other guarantees, such as those contained in the Third and Seventh Amendments (housing of soldiers and jury trials in civil cases), because it has yet to consider them sufficiently fundamental to national notions of liberty and justice.

First Amendment Guarantees: Freedom of Religion

4.2 Describe the First Amendment guarantee of freedom of religion.

The **First Amendment** to the Constitution begins, "Congress shall make no law respecting an establishment of religion, or prohibiting the free exercise thereof." This statement sets the boundaries of governmental action. The **establishment clause** directs the national government not to sanction an official religion. The **free exercise clause** ("or prohibiting the free exercise thereof") guarantees citizens that the national government will not interfere with their practice of religion. These guarantees, however, are not absolute. In the mid-1800s, Mormons traditionally practiced and preached polygamy, the taking of multiple wives. In 1879, when the Supreme Court was first called on to interpret the free exercise clause, it upheld the conviction of a Mormon man under a federal law barring polygamy. The Court reasoned that to do otherwise would provide constitutional protections to a full range of religious beliefs, including those as extreme as human sacrifice. "Laws are made for the government of actions," noted the Court, "and while they cannot interfere with mere religious belief and opinions, they may with practices."[11] Later, in 1940, the Supreme Court observed that the First Amendment "embraces two concepts—freedom to believe and freedom to act. The first is absolute, but in the nature of things, the second cannot be. Conduct remains subject to regulation of society."[12]

First Amendment
Part of the Bill of Rights that imposes a number of restrictions on the federal government with respect to civil liberties, including freedom of religion, speech, press, assembly, and petition.

establishment clause
The first clause of the First Amendment; it directs the national government not to sanction an official religion.

free exercise clause
The second clause of the First Amendment; it prohibits the U.S. government from interfering with a citizen's right to practice his or her religion.

***Lemon* test**
Three-part test created by the Supreme Court for examining the constitutionality of religious establishment issues.

The Establishment Clause

The separation of church and state has always generated controversy in American politics. A majority of Americans clearly value the moral teachings of their own religions, especially Christianity. U.S. coins are embossed with "In God We Trust." The U.S. Supreme Court asks for God's blessing on the Court. Every session of the U.S. House and Senate begins with a prayer, and both the House and Senate have their own chaplains. Through the years, the Court has been divided over the interpretation of the establishment clause. Does this clause erect a total wall between church and state, as favored by Thomas Jefferson, or does it allow some governmental accommodation of religion? While the Supreme Court has upheld the constitutionality of many kinds of church/state entanglements, such as public funding to provide sign language interpreters for deaf students in religious schools,[13] the Court has held fast to the rule of strict separation between church and state when issues of mandatory prayer in school are involved. In *Engel* v. *Vitale* (1962), for example, the Court ruled that the recitation in public school classrooms of a brief nondenominational prayer drafted by the local school board was unconstitutional.[14] One year later, in *Abington School District* v. *Schempp* (1963), the Court ruled that state-mandated Bible reading or recitation of the Lord's Prayer in public schools was also unconstitutional.[15]

The Court has gone back and forth in its effort to find a workable way to deal with church/state questions. In 1971, in *Lemon* v. *Kurtzman,* the Court tried to carve out a three-part test for laws dealing with religious establishment issues. According to the ***Lemon* test,** a practice or policy was constitutional if it: (1) had a legitimate secular purpose; (2) neither advanced nor inhibited religion; and, (3) did not foster an excessive government entanglement with religion.[16] But, the Supreme Court often has sidestepped the *Lemon* test altogether and has appeared more willing to lower the wall between church and state as long as school prayer is not involved. In 1981, for example, the Court ruled unconstitutional a Missouri law prohibiting the use of state university buildings and grounds for "purposes of religious worship." The law had been used to ban religious groups from using school facilities.[17]

In 1995, the Court signaled that it was willing to lower the wall even further. In a case involving the University of Virginia, a 5–4 majority held that the university violated the free speech rights of a fundamentalist Christian group when it refused to fund the group's student magazine. Justice David Souter highlighted the importance of this decision in his dissent: "The Court today, for the first time, approves direct funding of core religious activities by an arm of the state."[18] The Court under Chief Justice John Roberts, however, has demonstrated that boundaries to these accommodations exist. In 2010, in *Christian Legal Society* v. *Martinez*, the Court ruled that the University of California Hastings College of Law could deny recognition and therefore funding to the Christian Legal Society because the group limited its membership to those who shared a common faith orientation.

For more than a quarter-century, the Supreme Court basically allowed "books only" as an aid to religious schools, noting that the books go to children, not to schools. But, in 2000, the Court voted 6–3 to uphold the constitutionality of a federal aid provision that allowed the government to lend books and computers to religious schools.[19] And, in 2002, by a bitterly divided 5–4 vote, the Supreme Court concluded that governments can give parents money to send their children to private or religious schools.[20] Basically, the Court now appears willing to support programs as long as they provide aid to religious and nonreligious schools alike, and the money goes to persons who exercise free choice over how it is used.

Prayer in school also continues to be an issue. In 1992, the Court persisted in its unwillingness to allow organized prayer in public schools by finding unconstitutional the saying of prayer at a middle school graduation.[21] And, in 2000, the Court ruled that student-led, student-initiated prayer at high school football games violated the establishment clause.

Establishment issues, however, do not always focus on education. In 2005, for example, the Supreme Court, in a 5–4 decision, narrowly upheld the *Lemon* test by ruling that a privately donated courthouse display, which included the Ten Commandments and 300 other historical documents illustrating the evolution of American law, violated the First Amendment's establishment clause.[22]

But, in 2010, the Court appeared to reverse course. In a 5–4 decision, the Court ruled that a white cross erected on a World War I memorial on federal lands in the Mojave Desert was constitutional. According to Justice Anthony Kennedy, who wrote the majority

SHOULD CHILDREN BE REQUIRED TO PRAY IN PUBLIC SCHOOLS?

School prayer is just one of the thorny questions the Supreme Court has addressed under the establishment clause. Though the Court has usually decided against prayer in schools, even when it is student-led, many educational institutions maintain this practice.

opinion, the cross "is not merely a reaffirmation of Christian beliefs" but a symbol "often used to honor and respect" heroism. This opinion leaves state and local governments to ponder what kind of religious displays in public settings will be constitutional.[23]

☐ The Free Exercise Clause

The free exercise clause of the First Amendment proclaims that "Congress shall make no law . . . prohibiting the free exercise [of religion]." Although the free exercise clause of the First Amendment guarantees individuals the right to be free from governmental interference in the exercise of their religion, this guarantee, like other First Amendment freedoms, is not absolute.

The free exercise clause may also pose difficult questions for the courts to resolve. In the area of free exercise, the Court often has had to confront questions of "What is a god?" and "What is a religious faith?"—questions that theologians have grappled with for centuries. In 1965, for example, in a case involving three men who were denied conscientious objector deferments during the Vietnam War because they did not subscribe to "traditional" organized religions, the Court ruled unanimously that belief in a supreme being was not essential for recognition as a conscientious objector.[24] Thus, the men were entitled to the deferments because their views paralleled those who objected to war and who belonged to traditional religions. In contrast, despite the Court's having ruled that Catholic, Protestant, Jewish, and Buddhist prison inmates must be allowed to hold religious services,[25] as early as 1987, the Court ruled that Islamic prisoners could be denied the same right for security reasons.[26]

Furthermore, when secular law conflicts with religious law, the right to exercise one's religious beliefs is often denied—especially if a minority or an unpopular or "suspicious" group hold the religious beliefs in question. Thus, the U.S. Supreme Court has interpreted the Constitution to mean that governmental interests can outweigh free exercise rights. The Court has upheld as constitutional state statutes barring the use of certain illegal drugs (such as peyote), snake handling, and polygamy—all practices once part of some religious observances—when states have shown compelling reasons to do so.[27]

Congress has mightily objected to many of the Court's rulings on religious freedom. In 2000, it responded by passing the Religious Freedom Restoration Act, which specifically made the use of peyote in American Indians' religious services legal.[28] As a result, in 2006, the U.S. Supreme Court found by a vote of 8–0 that the use of hoasca tea, well known for its hallucinogenic properties, was a permissible free exercise of religion for members of a Brazilian-based church. The Court noted that Congress had overruled its earlier decision and specifically legalized the use of other sacramental substances, including peyote. Regarding the religious uses of hoasca tea and peyote, Justice Ruth Bader Ginsburg queried, "if the government must accommodate one, why not the other?"[29]

First Amendment Guarantees: Freedoms of Speech, Press, Assembly, and Petition

4.3 Outline the First Amendment guarantees of and limitations on freedom of speech, press, assembly, and petition.

The Supreme Court has, to varying degrees, scrutinized the remaining guarantees protected by the First Amendment. During times of war, for example, the Court generally has allowed Congress and the chief executive extraordinary leeway in limiting First Amendment freedoms. Below, we provide historical background and current judicial interpretations of the freedoms of speech, press, assembly, and petition.

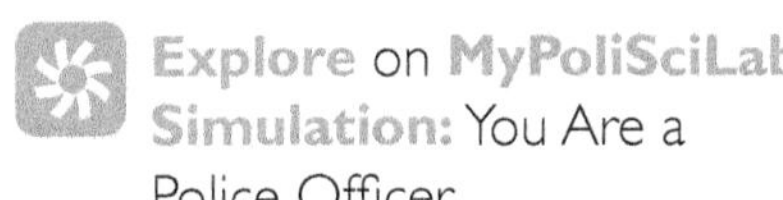

prior restraint
Constitutional doctrine that prevents the government from prohibiting speech or publication before the fact; generally held to be in violation of the First Amendment.

Freedoms of Speech and the Press

A democracy depends on a free exchange of ideas, and the First Amendment shows that the Framers were well aware of this fact. Historically, one of the most volatile issues of constitutional interpretation has centered on the First Amendment's mandate that "Congress shall make no law . . . abridging the freedom of speech or of the press." As with the establishment and free exercise clauses of the First Amendment, the Court has not interpreted speech and press clauses as absolute bans on government regulation. This leeway in interpretation has led to thousands of cases seeking both broader and narrower judicial interpretations of the scope of the amendment. Over the years, the Court has employed a hierarchical approach in determining what the government can and cannot regulate, with some liberties getting greater protection than others. Generally, the Court has granted thoughts the greatest protection and actions or deeds the least. Words have fallen somewhere in the middle, depending on their content and purpose.

THE ALIEN AND SEDITION ACTS When the states ratified the First Amendment in 1791, it was considered to protect against **prior restraint** of speech or expression, or to guard against the prohibition of speech or publication before the fact. Faced with increasing criticism of the Federalist government by Democratic-Republicans in 1798, the Federalist Congress, with President John Adams's blessing, enacted the Alien and Sedition Acts. These acts banned any criticism of the Federalist government by the growing numbers of Democratic-Republicans, making the publication of "any false, scandalous writing against the government of the United States" a criminal offense. Although the law clearly flew in the face of the First Amendment's ban on prior restraint, the Adams administration successfully prosecuted and partisan Federalist judges imposed fines and jail terms on at least ten Democratic-Republican newspaper editors. The acts became a major issue in the 1800 presidential election campaign, which led to the election of Thomas Jefferson, a vocal opponent of the acts. He quickly pardoned all who had been convicted under their provisions, and the Democratic-Republican Congress allowed the acts to expire before the Federalist-controlled U.S. Supreme Court had an opportunity to rule on the constitutionality of these First Amendment infringements.

SLAVERY, THE CIVIL WAR, AND RIGHTS CURTAILMENTS After the public outcry over the Alien and Sedition Acts, the national government largely refrained from regulating speech. But, in its place, the states, which were not yet bound by the Bill of Rights through selective incorporation, began to prosecute those who published articles critical of governmental policies. In the 1830s, at the urging of abolitionists (those who sought an end to slavery), the publication or dissemination of any positive information about slavery became a punishable offense in the North. In the opposite vein, in the South, supporters of slavery enacted laws to prohibit publication of any antislavery sentiments. Southern postmasters, for example, refused to deliver northern abolitionist newspapers, a step that amounted to censorship of the U.S. mail.

During the Civil War, President Abraham Lincoln took several steps that actually were unconstitutional. He made it unlawful to print any criticisms of the national government or of the Civil War, effectively suspending the free press protections of the First Amendment. Lincoln went so far as to order the arrest of several newspaper editors critical of his conduct of the war and ignored a Supreme Court decision saying that these practices were unconstitutional.

After the Civil War, states also began to prosecute individuals for seditious speech if they uttered or printed statements critical of the government. Between 1890 and 1900, for example, more than one hundred state prosecutions for sedition took place.[30] Moreover, by the dawn of the twentieth century, public opinion in the United States had grown increasingly hostile toward the commentary of Socialists and Communists who attempted to appeal to growing immigrant populations. Groups espousing socialism and communism became the targets of state laws curtailing speech and the written word (see the earlier discussion of *Gitlow* v. *New York*).

WORLD WAR I AND ANTI-GOVERNMENTAL SPEECH The next major efforts to restrict freedom of speech and the press did not occur until Congress, at the urging of President Woodrow Wilson during World War I, passed the Espionage Act in 1917. The government convicted nearly 2,000 Americans of violating its various provisions, especially prohibitions on urging resistance to the draft or distributing anti-war leaflets. In *Schenck* v. *U.S.* (1919), the Supreme Court upheld this act, ruling that Congress had a right to restrict speech "of such a nature as to create a clear and present danger that will bring about the substantive evils that Congress has a right to prevent."[31] Under this **clear and present danger test** the circumstances surrounding an incident are important. Anti-war leaflets, for example, may be permissible during peacetime, but during World War I they were considered too dangerous. *Schenck* is also famous for Chief Justice Oliver Wendell Holmes's comment that the false cry of "Fire!" in a crowded theater would not be protected speech.

Still, for decades, the Supreme Court wrestled with what constituted a danger. Finally, in *Brandenburg* v. *Ohio* (1969), the Court fashioned a new test for deciding whether the government could regulate certain kinds of speech: the **direct incitement test.** Now, the government could punish the advocacy of illegal action only if "such advocacy is directed to inciting or producing imminent lawless action and is likely to incite or produce such action."[32] The requirement of "imminent lawless action" makes it more difficult for the government to punish speech and publication and is consistent with the Framers' notion of the special role played by these elements in a democratic society.

clear and present danger test
Test articulated by the Supreme Court in *Schenck* v. *U.S.* (1919) to draw the line between protected and unprotected speech; the Court looks to see "whether the words used" could "create a clear and present danger that they will bring about substantive evils" that Congress seeks "to prevent."

direct incitement test
Test articulated by the Supreme Court in *Brandenburg* v. *Ohio* (1969) holding that the First Amendment protects advocacy of illegal action unless imminent lawless action is intended and likely to occur.

symbolic speech
Symbols, signs, and other methods of expression generally considered to be protected by the First Amendment.

☐ Protected Speech and Press

The expression of ideas through speech and the press is a cornerstone of a free society. In line with this thinking, the U.S. Supreme Court has accorded constitutional protection to a number of aspects of speech and the press, even though the content of such expression may be objectionable to some citizens or the government. Here, we discuss the implications of this protection with respect to prior restraint, symbolic speech, and hate speech.

LIMITING PRIOR RESTRAINT As we have seen with the Alien and Sedition Acts, although Congress attempted to limit speech before the fact as early as 1798, the U.S. Supreme Court did not take a firm position on this issue until the 1970s. In *New York Times Co.* v. *U.S.* (1971), also called the Pentagon Papers case, the Supreme Court ruled that the U.S. government could not block the publication of secret Department of Defense documents illegally furnished to the *Times* by anti-war activists.[33] In 1976, the U.S. Supreme Court went even further, noting in *Nebraska Press Association* v. *Stuart* that any attempt by the government to prevent expression carried "'a heavy presumption' against its constitutionality."[34] In this case, a trial court issued a gag order barring the press from reporting the lurid details of a crime. In balancing the defendant's constitutional right to a fair trial against the press's right to cover a story, the Nebraska trial judge concluded that the defendant's right had greater weight. The Supreme Court disagreed, holding the press's right to cover the trial paramount. Still, judges often have leeway to issue gag orders affecting parties to a lawsuit or to limit press coverage of a case.

SYMBOLIC SPEECH In addition to the general protection accorded to pure speech, the Supreme Court has extended the reach of the First Amendment to **symbolic speech,** a means of expression that includes symbols or signs. In the words of Justice John Marshall Harlan, these kinds of speech are part of the "free trade in ideas."[35] Perhaps the most visible example of symbolic speech is the burning of the American flag as an expression of protest.

The Supreme Court first acknowledged that symbolic speech was entitled to First Amendment protection in *Stromberg* v. *California* (1931).[36] In that case, the Court overturned a communist youth camp director's conviction under a state statute prohibiting the display of a red flag, a symbol of opposition to the U.S. government. In a similar vein,

4.1
4.2
4.3
4.4
4.5
4.6
4.7

Explore Your World

Free speech and free press are central values in most industrialized democracies such as the United States. In these countries, citizens and the media act as powerful watchdogs over the government's actions. However, in other countries such as Russia in the 1920s and North Korea in 2012, the government controls and monitors the media. This means that the government's message—as illustrated in the posters below—may be the only viewpoint citizens can learn, understand, and espouse.

This Russian poster was created during the 1920s. It illustrates the rise of the Russian economy and advocates for the Russian goverment's Five Year Plan. Note the images of prominent Russian Communist Party leaders, including Joseph Stalin, on the engine.

This propaganda poster from North Korea in 2012 depicts the image of a fist coming down on two people. The words on the poster, roughly translated, state, "Let's strike them with a single blow." This photo was taken at a rally against the South Korean president. Note how many people in the crowd have responded by raising a single fist.

CRITICAL THINKING QUESTIONS

1. How do these posters represent their country of origin? How do they represent other countries? What message does this send about global politics?
2. How do these posters use emotional appeals to induce support from citizens? Is this an appropriate tactic?
3. Can you think of any examples in which the U.S. government (or other western governments) employed tactics such as those seen in these posters? How were they similar, and how were they different?

the right of high school students to wear black armbands to protest the Vietnam War was upheld in *Tinker* v. *Des Moines Independent Community School District* (1969).[37]

In recent years, however, the Court has appeared less willing to support the standards established in *Tinker*. In a case commonly referred to as the "Bong Hits 4 Jesus" case, the Court ruled that a student's free speech rights were not violated when a school suspended him for displaying what the Court characterized as a "sophomoric" banner at an Olympic torch relay parade.[38]

hate speech
Any communication that belittles a person or group on the basis of characteristics.

HATE SPEECH "As a thumbnail summary of the last two or three decades of speech issues in the Supreme Court," wrote eminent First Amendment scholar Harry Kalven Jr. in 1966, "we may come to see the Negro as winning back for us the freedoms the Communists seemed to have lost for us."[39] Still, says noted African American studies scholar Henry Louis Gates Jr., Kalven would be shocked to see the stance that some now take toward the First Amendment, which once protected protests, rallies, and agitation in the 1960s: "The byword among many black activists and black intellectuals is no longer the political imperative to protect free speech; it is the moral imperative to suppress '**hate speech**,'" any communication that belittles a person or group on the basis of characteristics.[40]

In the 1990s, a particularly thorny First Amendment issue emerged as cities and universities attempted to prohibit what they viewed as hate speech. In *R.A.V.* v. *City of St. Paul* (1992), a St. Paul, Minnesota, ordinance that made it a crime to engage in speech or action likely to arouse "anger," "alarm," or "resentment" on the basis of race, color, creed, religion, or gender was at issue. The Court ruled 5–4 that a white teenager who burned a cross on a black family's front lawn, thereby committing a hate crime under the ordinance, could not face charges under that law because the First Amendment prevents governments from "silencing speech on the basis of its content."[41] In 2003, the Court narrowed this definition, ruling that state governments could constitutionally restrict cross burning when it occurred with the intent of racial intimidation.[42]

Three-quarters of colleges and universities have banned a variety of forms of speech or conduct that create or foster an intimidating, hostile, or offensive environment on

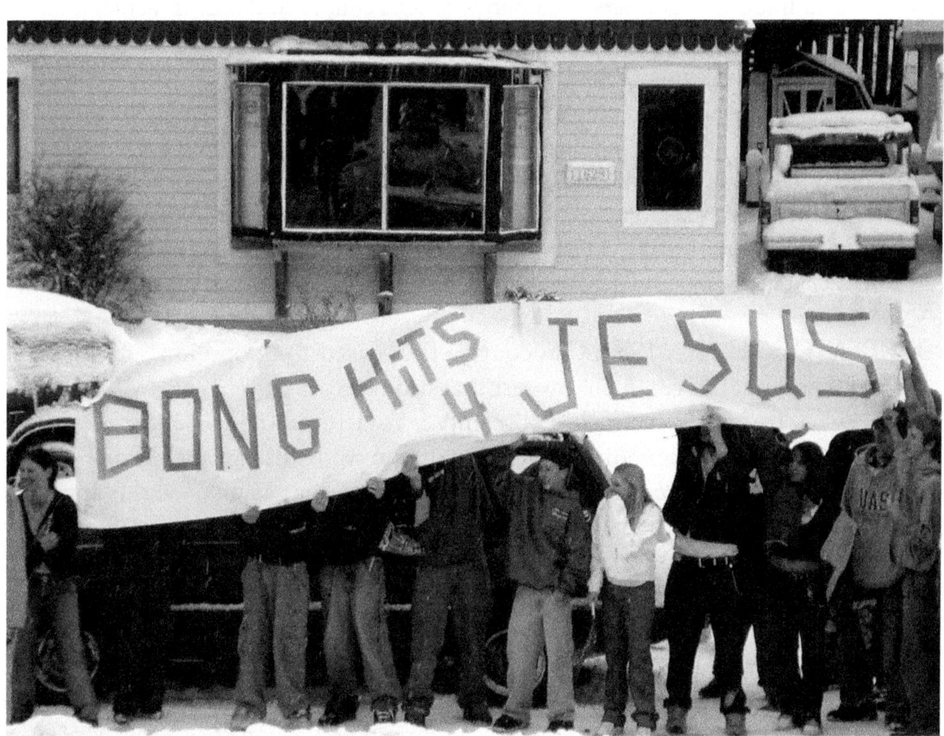

HOW BROAD IS THE RIGHT TO SYMBOLIC SPEECH?

In a 2007 case, the Supreme Court ruled that a school district was within its rights to suspend a student for displaying this banner, because it was intended to promote illegal drug use, even though it occurred off school property.

libel
False written statement that defames a person's character.

slander
Untrue spoken statements that defame the character of a person.

***New York Times Co.* v. *Sullivan* (1964)**
Case in which the Supreme Court concluded that "actual malice" must be proven to support a finding of libel against a public figure.

fighting words
Words that "by their very utterance inflict injury or tend to incite an immediate breach of peace." Fighting words are not subject to the restrictions of the First Amendment.

campus. To prevent disruption of university activities, some universities have also established free speech zones that restrict the time, place, or manner of speech. Critics, including the American Civil Liberties Union, charge that free speech zones imply the limitation of speech on other parts of the campus, which they see as a violation of the First Amendment. They have filed a number of suits in district court, but to date the Supreme Court has heard none of these cases.

Unprotected Speech and Press

Although the Supreme Court has allowed few governmental bans on most types of speech, some forms of expression lack protection. In 1942, the Supreme Court set forth the rationale by which it would distinguish between protected and unprotected speech. According to the Court, libel, fighting words, and obscenity are not protected by the First Amendment because "such expressions are no essential part of any exposition of ideals, and are of such slight social value as a step to truth that any benefit that may be derived from them is clearly outweighed by the social interest in order and morality."[43]

LIBEL AND SLANDER **Libel** is a false written statement that defames the character of a person. If the statement is spoken, it is **slander.** In many nations—such as Great Britain, for example—suing someone for libel is relatively easy. In the United States, however, the standards of proof reach much higher. A person who believes that he or she has been a victim of libel must show that the statements made were untrue. Truth is an absolute defense against the charge of libel, no matter how painful or embarrassing the revelations.

Individuals that the U.S. Supreme Court considers "public persons or public officials" often find it more difficult to sue for libel or slander. ***New York Times Co.* v. *Sullivan* (1964)** was the first major libel case considered by the Supreme Court.[44] An Alabama state court found the *Times* guilty of libel for printing a full-page advertisement accusing Alabama officials of physically abusing African Americans during various civil rights protests. (Civil rights activists, including former First Lady Eleanor Roosevelt, paid for the ad.) The Supreme Court overturned the conviction and established that a finding of libel against a public official could stand only if "actual malice," or a knowing disregard for the truth, was shown. Proof that the statements were false or negligent was not sufficient to demonstrate actual malice. Later the Court ruled that even intentional infliction of emotional distress was not sufficient.[45]

FIGHTING WORDS In 1942, the Court stated that **fighting words,** or words that "by their very utterance inflict injury or tend to incite an immediate breach of peace," are not subject to the restrictions of the First Amendment.[46] Federal and state governments can therefore regulate fighting words, which include "profanity, obscenity, and threats."

OBSCENITY Through 1957, U.S. courts often based their opinions of what was obscene on an English common-law test that had been set out in 1868: "Whether the tendency of the matter charged as obscenity is to deprive and corrupt those whose minds are open to such immoral influences and into whose hands a publication of this sort might fall."[47] In *Roth* v. *U.S.* (1957), however, the Court abandoned this approach and held that, to be considered obscene, the material in question had to be "utterly without redeeming social importance," and articulated a new test for obscenity: "whether to the average person, applying contemporary community standards, the dominant theme of the material taken as a whole appeals to the prurient interests."[48]

In many ways, the *Roth* test brought with it as many problems as it attempted to solve. Throughout the 1950s and 1960s, "prurient" remained hard to define, as the Supreme Court struggled to find a standard for judging actions or words. Moreover, showing that a book or movie was "*utterly* without redeeming social value" proved a difficult task. Even some hardcore pornography passed muster under the *Roth* test, prompting some critics to argue that the Court fostered the increased number of sexually oriented publications designed to appeal to those living during the sexual revolution.

Richard M. Nixon made the growth in pornography a major issue when he ran for president in 1968. Nixon pledged to appoint to federal judgeships only those who would uphold law and order and stop coddling criminals and purveyors of porn. Once elected president, Nixon appointed four justices to the Supreme Court, including Chief Justice Warren E. Burger, who wrote the opinion in *Miller* v. *California* (1973). In that case, the Court set out a test redefining obscenity. To make it easier for states to regulate obscene materials, the justices concluded that lower courts must ask, "whether the work depicts or describes, in a patently offensive way, sexual conduct specifically defined by state law." The courts also would determine "whether the work, taken as a whole, lacks serious literary, artistic, political, or scientific value." The Court also noted that local standards might affect its assessment of obscenity, under the rationale that what the citizens of New York City find acceptable might not be the case in Maine or Mississippi.[49]

Time and contexts clearly have altered the Court's and, indeed, much of America's perceptions of what works are obscene. But, the Supreme Court has allowed communities great leeway in drafting statutes to deal with obscenity and, even more importantly, other forms of questionable expression. In 1991, for example, the Court voted 5–4 to allow Indiana to ban totally nude erotic dancing, concluding that the statute furthered a substantial governmental interest in creating order in society and regulating morals, and therefore did not violate the First Amendment.[50]

While lawmakers have been fairly effective in restricting the sale and distribution of obscene materials, Congress has found it difficult to monitor the Internet. Since 1996, Congress has passed several laws designed to prohibit the transmission of obscene or "harmful" materials over the Internet to anyone under age eighteen. For many years, the Supreme Court repeatedly found these laws unconstitutional.[51] But, in 2008, a seven-justice majority decided that the PROTECT Act, which outlawed the sale or transmission of child pornography, was not overly broad and did not abridge the freedom of speech guaranteed by the First Amendment.[52]

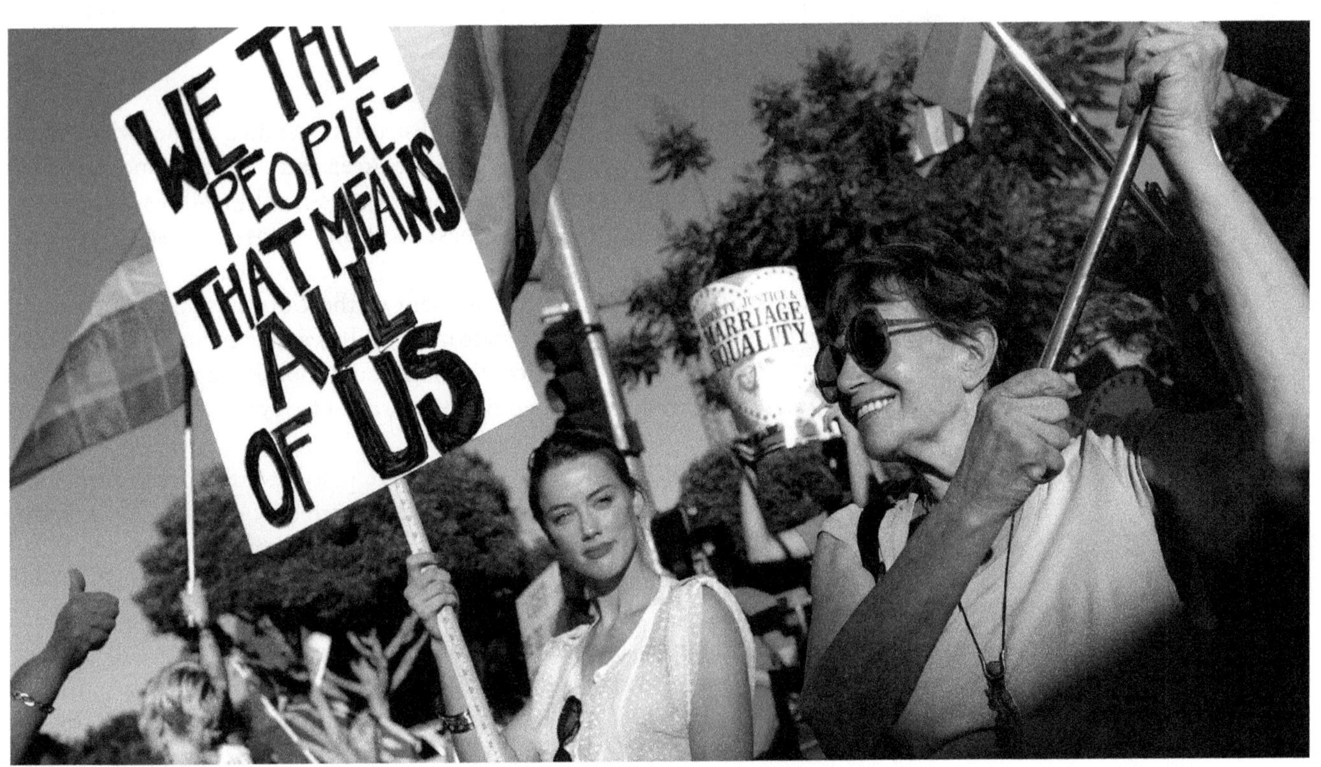

HOW DO WE USE OUR RIGHT TO ASSEMBLE?

The First Amendment rights to assembly and petition are often seen in the form of protests, marches, and rallies. Here, protestors in California march in support of gay marriage rights following a federal appellate court's ruling on that issue.

4.1

4.2

4.3

4.4

4.5

4.6

4.7

Freedoms of Assembly and Petition

"Peaceful assembly for lawful discussion cannot be made a crime," Chief Justice Charles Evans Hughes wrote in the 1937 case of *DeJonge* v. *Oregon,* which incorporated the First Amendment's freedom of assembly clause.[53] Despite this clear assertion, and an even more ringing declaration in the First Amendment, the fundamental freedoms of assembly and petition have been among the most controversial, especially in times of war. As with other First Amendment freedoms, the Supreme Court often has become the arbiter between the freedom of the people to express dissent and government's authority to limit controversy in the name of national security.

Because the freedom to assemble hinges on peaceful conduct, the freedoms of assembly and petition relate directly to those of speech and the press. If the words spoken or actions taken at any event cross the line of constitutionality, the First Amendment may no longer protect events such as parades or protests. Absent that protection, leaders and attendees may be subject to governmental regulation and even arrest, incarceration, or civil fines.

The U.S. Supreme Court has rarely addressed the question of the right to petition the government. But, in 2010, the Court heard a case questioning the constitutionality of Washington State's Public Records Act. This law allowed the government to release the names of citizens who had signed a petition in support of a ballot initiative that would have banned gay couples from adopting children. The plaintiffs who signed the "Preserve Marriage, Protect Children" petition did not want their names released because they feared harassment. The Court, however, ruled that disclosure of these names did not violate the First Amendment.[54]

The Second Amendment: The Right to Keep and Bear Arms

4.4 Summarize changes in the interpretation of the Second Amendment right to keep and bear arms.

During colonial times, the colonists' distrust of standing armies was evident. Most colonies required all white men to keep and bear arms, and deputized these men to defend their settlements against Indians and European powers. The colonists viewed these local militias as the best way to keep order and protect liberty.

The Framers added the Second Amendment to the Constitution to ensure that Congress could not pass laws to disarm state militias. This amendment appeased Anti-Federalists, who feared that the new Constitution would abolish the right to "keep and bear arms." It also preserved an unstated right—the right to revolt against governmental tyranny.

Through the early 1920s, few state statutes were passed to regulate firearms (and generally these laws dealt with the possession of firearms by slaves). The Supreme Court's decision in *Barron* v. *Baltimore* (1833), which refused to incorporate the Bill of Rights to the state governments, prevented federal review of those state laws.[55] Moreover, in *Dred Scott* v. *Sandford* (1857), Chief Justice Roger B. Taney listed the right to own and carry arms as a basic right of citizenship.[56]

In 1934, Congress passed the National Firearms Act in response to the explosion of organized crime in the 1920s and 1930s, which stemmed from Prohibition. The act imposed taxes on automatic weapons and sawed-off shotguns. In *U.S.* v. *Miller* (1939), a unanimous Court upheld the constitutionality of the act, stating that the Second Amendment was intended to protect a citizen's right to own ordinary militia weapons, which did not include sawed-off shotguns.[57] For nearly seventy years following *Miller,* the Court did not directly address the Second Amendment. Then, in *D.C.* v. *Heller*

How Do States Restrict the Right to Bear Arms?

The scope and application of the Second Amendment is a contentious and sensitive issue in American politics. Can, for example, citizens carry concealed weapons for self-protection? Does this right extend to possession of a rapid-fire submachine gun? As the image below illustrates, interstate variations in the number and severity of regulations on gun ownership are significant.

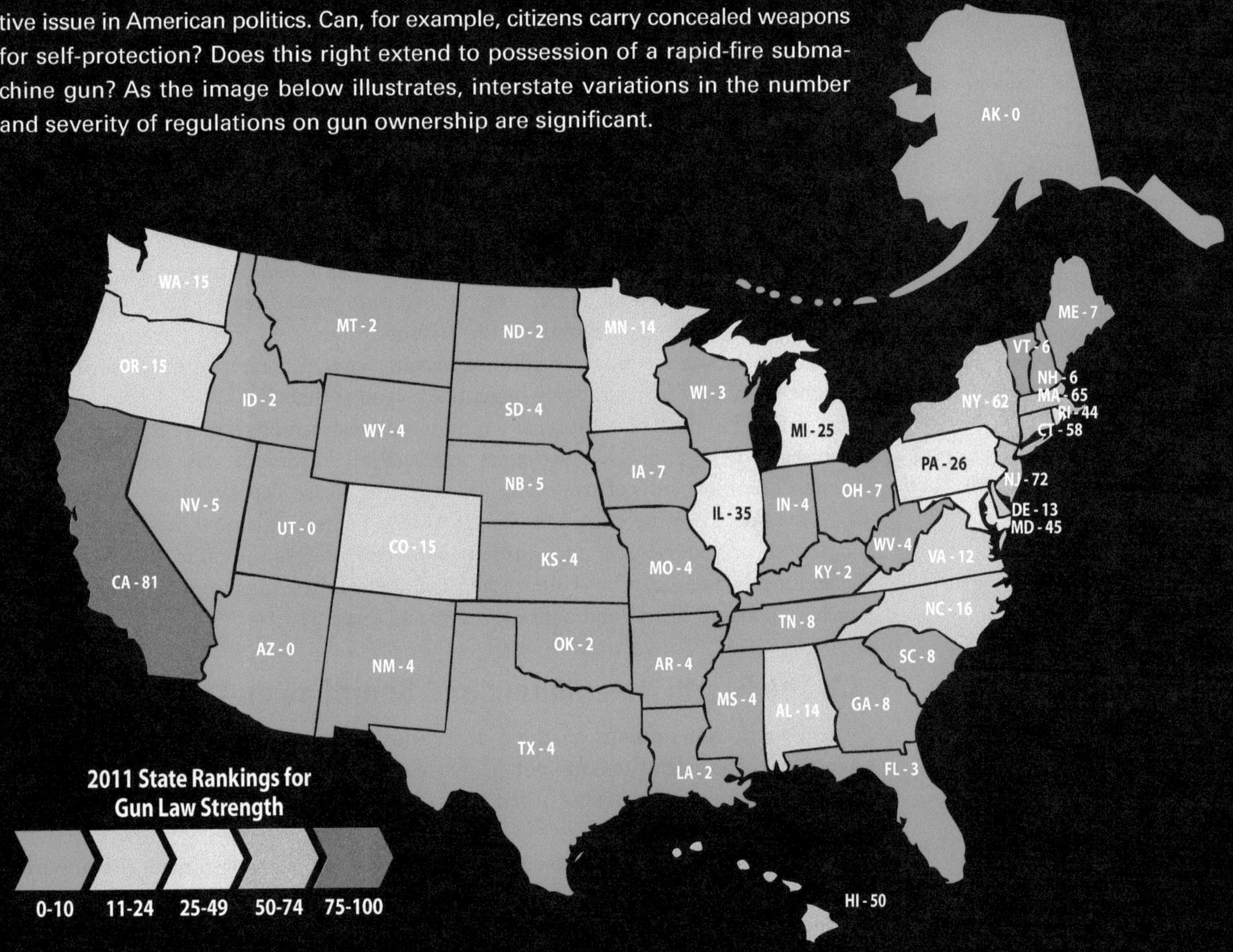

AK - 0
WA - 15
MT - 2
ND - 2
MN - 14
ME - 7
VT - 6
NH - 6
MA - 65
RI - 44
CT - 58
OR - 15
ID - 2
SD - 4
WI - 3
NY - 62
MI - 25
WY - 4
PA - 26
NJ - 72
IA - 7
NB - 5
NV - 5
IL - 35
IN - 4
OH - 7
DE - 13
MD - 45
UT - 0
CO - 15
WV - 4
VA - 12
KS - 4
MO - 4
KY - 2
CA - 81
NC - 16
TN - 8
OK - 2
AZ - 0
AR - 4
SC - 8
NM - 4
MS - 4
AL - 14
GA - 8
TX - 4
LA - 2
FL - 3
HI - 50

2011 State Rankings for Gun Law Strength

0-10 | 11-24 | 25-49 | 50-74 | 75-100

State Laws Governing Firearms

CRITICAL THINKING QUESTIONS

1. How do gun control laws vary across the nation? What geographic patterns do you observe? Why do you observe these patterns?
2. Which gun control laws are most and least common? How do you explain these variations?
3. Should the national government have broader latitude to control ownership, sale, use, and manufacture of guns and firearms? Is it permissible under the constitution? Should this be a state responsibility?

SOURCES: Legal Community Against Violence's Web site and reports were the primary sources used for determining points awarded for each state. Visit www.LCAV.org. National Rifle Association Institute for Legislative Action, "Compendium of State Laws Governing Firearms."

4.1 4.2 4.3 4.4 4.5 4.6 4.7

writs of *habeas corpus*
Petition requesting that a judge order authorities to prove that a prisoner is being held lawfully and that allows the prisoner to be freed if the government's case does not persuade the judge. *Habeas corpus* rights imply that prisoners have a right to know what charges are being made against them.

***ex post facto* law**
Law that makes an act punishable as a crime even if the action was legal at the time it was committed.

bill of attainder
A law declaring an act illegal without a judicial trial.

Fourth Amendment
Part of the Bill of Rights that reads: "The right of the people to be secure in their persons, houses, papers, and effects, against unreasonable searches and seizures, shall not be violated, and no Warrants shall issue, but upon probable cause, supported by Oath or affirmation, and particularly describing the place to be searched, and the persons or things to be seized."

(2008), the Court offered some clarification, ruling that the Second Amendment protected an individual's right to own a firearm for personal use in Washington, D.C.[58]

In light of the Court's ruling, the D.C. City Council adopted new gun control laws requiring gun registration and prohibiting assault weapons and large-capacity magazines. A U.S. District Court ruled that these laws were valid and within the scope of the *Heller* decision.[59] And, in 2010, the Supreme Court broadened the ownership rights in *Heller* to include citizens of all states. It also incorporated the Second Amendment.[60]

The Rights of Criminal Defendants

4.5 Analyze the rights of criminal defendants found in the Bill of Rights.

rticle I of the Constitution guarantees a number of rights for persons accused of crimes. Among those are **writs of *habeas corpus*,** or court orders in which a judge requires authorities to prove they are holding a prisoner lawfully and that allow the prisoner to be freed if the government's case does not persuade the judge. In addition, *habeas corpus* rights imply that prisoners have a right to know what charges are being made against them.

Article I of the Constitution also prohibits ***ex post facto* laws,** those that make an act punishable as a crime even if the act was legal at the time it was committed. And, Article I prohibits **bills of attainder,** laws declaring an act illegal without a judicial trial.

The Fourth, Fifth, Sixth, and Eighth Amendments supplement these rights with a variety of procedural guarantees, often called due process rights. In this section, we examine how the courts have interpreted and applied these guarantees in an attempt to balance personal liberty and national safety and security.

The Fourth Amendment and Searches and Seizures

The **Fourth Amendment** to the Constitution protects people from unreasonable searches by the federal government. Moreover, it sets forth in some detail what may not be searched unless a warrant is issued, underscoring the Framers' concern with preventing government abuses.

The purpose of this amendment was to deny the national government the authority to make general searches. Over the years, in a number of decisions, the Supreme Court has interpreted the Fourth Amendment to allow the police to search: (1) the person arrested; (2) things in plain view of the accused person; and, (3) places or things that the arrested person could touch or reach or that are otherwise in the arrestee's immediate control.

Warrantless searches often occur if police suspect that someone is committing or is about to commit a crime. In these situations, police may stop and frisk the individual under suspicion. In 1989, the Court ruled that "reasonable suspicion" presented sufficient justification for stopping a suspect—a much lower standard than probable cause.[61]

Searches can also be made without a warrant if police obtain consent. In the case of homes, this consent must come from all occupants present at the time of the search. The police cannot conduct a warrantless search of a home if one of the occupants objects.[62] In contrast, under the open fields doctrine first articulated by the Supreme Court in 1924, if you own a field, and even if you post "No Trespassing" signs, the police can search your field without a warrant to see if you are engaging in illegal activity, such as growing marijuana, because you cannot reasonably expect privacy in an open field.[63]

In situations involving no arrests, police must obtain search warrants from a "neutral and detached magistrate" prior to conducting more extensive searches of houses, cars, offices, or any other place where an individual would reasonably have some expectation of privacy.[64] Thus, firefighters can enter your home to fight a fire without a warrant. But, if they decide to investigate the cause of the fire, they must obtain a warrant before they reenter.[65]

Cars have proven problematic for police and the courts because of their mobile nature. As noted by Chief Justice William H. Taft as early as 1925, "the vehicle can quickly be moved out of the locality or jurisdiction in which the warrant must be sought."[66] Historically, then, the Court has been lenient about the scope of automobile searches. In 2002, for example, an unusually unanimous Court ruled that the totality of the circumstances had to be considered in evaluating whether a border patrol officer acted lawfully in stopping a suspicious minivan. This ruling gave law enforcement officers more leeway to pull over suspicious motorists.[67] And, courts do not require search warrants in possible drunk driving situations. Thus, police in some states can require a Breathalyzer test to determine whether you have been driving with a blood alcohol level in excess of legal limits.[68]

More recently, the Roberts Court has attempted to limit law enforcement's power in some situations. In 2009, for example, the Court ruled that a warrantless vehicle search conducted after the driver voluntarily left his car and entered into police control was not legal. For a warrantless vehicle search to be legal, it needed to be both narrowly construed and the defendant needed to be able to access his vehicle.[69] And, in 2012, the Supreme Court limited law enforcement's ability to use GPS tracking devices on criminal suspects' vehicles.[70]

Testing for drugs, too, is an especially thorny search and seizure issue. While many private employers and professional athletic organizations routinely require drug tests upon application or as a condition of employment, governmental requirements present constitutional questions about the scope of permissible searches and seizures. In 1989, the Supreme Court ruled that mandatory drug and alcohol testing of employees involved in accidents was constitutional.[71] In 1995, the Court declared random drug testing of public high school athletes constitutional.[72] And, in 2002, the Court upheld the constitutionality of a Tecumseh, Oklahoma, policy that required mandatory drug testing of high school students participating in any extracurricular activities. Thus, prospective band, choir, debate, or drama club members were subject to the same kind of random drug testing undergone by athletes.[73]

Fifth Amendment
Part of the Bill of Rights that imposes a number of restrictions on the federal government with respect to the rights of persons suspected of committing a crime. It provides for indictment by a grand jury and protection against self-incrimination, and prevents the national government from denying a person life, liberty, or property without the due process of law. It also prevents the national government from taking property without just compensation.

The Fifth Amendment: Self-Incrimination and Double Jeopardy

The **Fifth Amendment** provides a variety of guarantees protecting those charged with a crime. It requires, for example, that individuals accused in the most serious cases be allowed to present their case before a grand jury, a group of citizens charged with determining whether enough evidence exists for a case to go to trial. The Fifth Amendment also states that "No person shall be . . . compelled in any criminal case to be a witness against himself." "Taking the Fifth" is shorthand for exercising one's constitutional right not to self-incriminate. The Supreme Court has interpreted this guarantee to be "as broad as the mischief against which it seeks to guard," finding that criminal defendants do not have to take the stand at trial to answer questions, nor can a judge make mention of their failure to do so as evidence of guilt.[74] Moreover, lawyers cannot imply that a defendant who refuses to take the stand must be guilty or have something to hide.

This right not to incriminate oneself also means that prosecutors cannot use as evidence in a trial any of a defendant's statements or confessions that he or she did not make voluntarily. As is the case in many areas of law, however, judicial interpretation of the term "voluntary" has changed over time.

In earlier times, it was not unusual for police to beat defendants to obtain their confessions. In 1936, however, the Supreme Court ruled that convictions for murder based solely on confessions given after physical beatings were unconstitutional.[75] Police then began to resort to other measures for forcing confessions. Defendants, for example, faced questioning for hours on end with no sleep or food, or threats of physical violence until they were mentally beaten into giving confessions. In other situations, police threatened family members. In one case, authorities told a young mother accused of marijuana possession that her welfare benefits would be terminated and her children taken away if she failed to talk.[76]

***Miranda* v. *Arizona* (1966)** was the Supreme Court's response to coercive efforts used in obtaining confessions that were not truly voluntary. On March 3, 1963, an eighteen-year-old girl was kidnapped and raped on the outskirts of Phoenix, Arizona. Ten days later, police arrested Ernesto Miranda, a poor, mentally disturbed man with a ninth-grade education. In a police-station lineup, the victim identified Miranda as her attacker. Police then took Miranda to a separate room and questioned him for two hours. At first he denied guilt. Eventually, however, he confessed to the crime and wrote and signed a brief statement describing the crime and admitting his guilt. At no time did police tell him that he did not have to answer any questions or that he could be represented by an attorney.

After Miranda's conviction, his case was appealed on the grounds that his Fifth Amendment right not to incriminate himself had been violated because the police had coerced his confession. Writing for the Court, Chief Justice Earl Warren, himself a former district attorney and a former California state attorney general, noted that because police have a tremendous advantage in any interrogation situation, the law must grant criminal suspects greater protection. A confession obtained in the manner of Miranda's was not truly voluntary; thus, it was inadmissible at trial.

To provide guidelines for police to implement *Miranda,* the Court mandated that: "Prior to any questioning, the person must be warned that he has a right to remain silent, that any statements he does make may be used as evidence against him, and that he has a right to the presence of an attorney, either retained or appointed."[77] In response to this mandate from the Court, police routinely began to read suspects what are now called their ***Miranda* rights,** a practice you undoubtedly have seen repeated over and over in movies and TV police dramas.

Although the Burger Court did not enforce the reading of *Miranda* rights as vehemently as had the Warren Court, Chief Justice Warren E. Burger, Warren's successor, acknowledged that they had become an integral part of established police procedures.[78] The more conservative Rehnquist and Roberts Courts, however, have been more willing to weaken *Miranda* rights, allowing coerced confessions and employing much more flexible standards for the admission of evidence.[79]

The Fifth Amendment also mandates: "nor shall any person be subject for the same offense to be twice put in jeopardy of life or limb." Called the **double jeopardy clause,** it protects individuals from being tried twice for the same crime in the same jurisdiction. Thus, if a jury acquits a defendant of a murder charge, the defendant cannot be retried in that jurisdiction for the offense even if new information is unearthed that could further point to guilt. But, if a defendant was tried in a state court, he or she could still face charges in a federal court or vice versa. This provision is relatively clear and embedded in the law; the Court has heard little litigation on this issue in the past forty years.

☐ The Fourth and Fifth Amendments and the Exclusionary Rule

In *Weeks* v. *U.S.* (1914), the U.S. Supreme Court adopted the **exclusionary rule,** which bars the use of illegally seized evidence at trial. Thus, although the Fourth and Fifth Amendments do not prohibit the use of evidence obtained in violation of their provisions, the exclusionary rule is a judicially created remedy to deter constitutional violations. In *Weeks,* for example, the Court reasoned that allowing police and prosecutors to use the "fruits of a poisonous tree" (a tainted search) would only encourage that activity.[80]

In balancing the need to deter police misconduct against the possibility that guilty individuals could go free, the Warren Court decided that deterring police misconduct was more important. In *Mapp* v. *Ohio* (1961), the Warren Court ruled "all evidence obtained by searches and seizures in violation of the Constitution, is inadmissible in a state court."[81] This historic and controversial case put law enforcement officers on notice that if they violated any constitutional rights in the search for evidence, their efforts would be for naught because federal or state trials could not accept tainted evidence.

***Miranda* v. *Arizona* (1966)**
A landmark Supreme Court ruling holding that the Fifth Amendment requires individuals arrested for a crime to be advised of their right to remain silent and to have counsel present.

***Miranda* rights**
Statements required of police that inform a suspect of his or her constitutional rights protected by the Fifth Amendment, including the right to an attorney provided by the court if the suspect cannot afford one.

double jeopardy clause
Part of the Fifth Amendment that protects individuals from being tried twice for the same offense in the same jurisdiction.

exclusionary rule
Judicially created rule that prohibits police from using illegally seized evidence at trial.

WHY WAS ERNESTO MIRANDA IMPORTANT TO THE DEVELOPMENT OF DEFENDANTS' RIGHTS?

Even though Ernesto Miranda's confession was not admitted as evidence at his retrial, the testimony of his ex-girlfriend and the victim was enough to convince the jury of his guilt. He served nine years in prison before he was paroled. After his release, he routinely sold autographed cards inscribed with what are called the *Miranda* rights now read to all suspects. In 1976, four years after his release, Miranda was stabbed to death during a card game. Two *Miranda* cards were found on his body, and the person who killed him was read his *Miranda* rights upon his arrest.

In 1976, the Court noted that the exclusionary rule "deflects the truth-finding process and often frees the guilty."[82] Since then, the Court has carved out a variety of limited "good faith exceptions" to the exclusionary rule, allowing the use of tainted evidence in a variety of situations, especially when police have a search warrant and, in good faith, conduct the search on the assumption that the warrant is valid, even though it is subsequently found invalid. Since the purpose of the exclusionary rule is to deter police misconduct, and in this situation no police misconduct exists, the courts have permitted introduction of the seized evidence at trial. Another exception to the exclusionary rule is "inevitable discovery." Courts may allow illegally seized evidence if such evidence would likely have been discovered in the course of continuing investigation.

The Court has continued to uphold the exclusionary rule. In a 2006 victory for advocates of defendants' rights, the Court ruled unanimously that the Fourth Amendment requires that any evidence collected under an anticipatory warrant—one presented by the police yet not authorized by a judge—would be inadmissible at trial as a violation of the exclusionary rule.[83]

Sixth Amendment
Part of the Bill of Rights that sets out the basic requirements of procedural due process for federal courts to follow in criminal trials. These include speedy and public trials, impartial juries, trials in the state where the crime was committed, notice of the charges, the right to confront and obtain favorable witnesses, and the right to counsel.

☐ The Sixth Amendment and the Right to Counsel

The **Sixth Amendment** guarantees to an accused person "the Assistance of Counsel in his defense." In the past, this guarantee meant only that an individual could hire an attorney to represent him or her in court. Since most criminal defendants are too poor to hire private lawyers, this provision gave little assistance to many who found themselves on trial. Recognizing this, Congress required federal courts to provide an attorney for defendants who could not afford one. Capital cases (in which the death penalty is a possibility) were the first to require this provision;[84] eventually, in all federal criminal cases, the poor received legal counsel.[85] The Court also began to expand the right to counsel to other state offenses but did so in a piecemeal fashion that gave the states little direction. Given the high cost of legal counsel, this ambiguity often made it cost-effective for the states not to provide counsel at all.

These ambiguities came to an end with the Court's decision in *Gideon* v. *Wainwright* (1963).[86] Clarence Earl Gideon, a fifty-one-year-old drifter, was charged with breaking into a Panama City, Florida, pool hall and stealing beer, wine, and some change from a vending machine. At his trial, he asked the judge to appoint a lawyer for him because he was too poor to hire one. The judge refused, and Gideon was convicted and given a five-year prison term for petty larceny. The case against Gideon had not been strong, but as a layperson unfamiliar with the law and with trial practice and procedure, he was unable to point out its weaknesses.

The apparent inequities in the system that had resulted in Gideon's conviction continued to bother him. Eventually, he requested some paper from a prison guard, consulted books in the prison library, and then drafted and mailed a writ of *certiorari* to the U.S. Supreme Court, asking it to overrule his conviction.

In a unanimous decision, the Supreme Court agreed with Gideon and his court-appointed lawyer, Abe Fortas, a future associate justice of the Court. Writing for the Court, Justice Hugo Black explained, "lawyers in criminal courts are necessities, not luxuries." Therefore, the Court concluded, the state must provide an attorney to indigent defendants in felony cases. In emphasis of the Court's point, the jury acquitted Gideon when he was retried with a lawyer to argue his case.

The Burger and Rehnquist Courts gradually expanded the *Gideon* rule. The justices first applied this standard to cases that were not felonies[87] and, later, to many cases in which probation and future penalties were possibilities. In 2008, the Court also ruled that the right to counsel began at the accused's first appearance before a judge.[88]

The issue of legal representation also extends to questions of competence. Various courts have held that lawyers who fell asleep during trial, failed to put forth a defense, or were drunk during the proceedings were "adequate." In 2005, however, the Supreme Court ruled that the Sixth Amendment's guarantees required lawyers to take reasonable steps to prepare for their clients' trial and sentencing, including examination of their prior criminal history.[89]

Take a Closer Look

The due process rights contained in the Fourth, Fifth, Sixth, and Eighth Amendments to the U.S. Constitution provide a variety of protections for those accused of a crime. Perhaps nowhere are these privileges on display more than in the American courtroom, as shown in the photo below.

The Sixth Amendment provides a right to a trial by jury. This is the jury box.

The Sixth Amendment provides for a right to counsel for the accused. The defense sits to the judge's right, and the prosecution to the left.

The Sixth Amendment provides for a right to a speedy, public, and impartial trial in a court of law. According to the Fifth Amendment, however, no one may be tried twice for the same crime.

The Fifth Amendment prevents defendants from self-incrimination, but they may voluntarily take the stand. The Sixth Amendment provides for the right to confront witnesses.

The judge plays a crucial role in the sentencing process. The Eighth Amendment protects against excessive fines and bail, as well as cruel and unusual punishment.

CRITICAL THINKING QUESTIONS

1. Do the accused have any rights beyond those highlighted in this photo? Are those rights reflected or protected anywhere in the courtroom?
2. What observations can you make about the geography of the courtroom? How does the utilization of space reflect the goals of the American judicial system?
3. Does the American judicial system provide too many protections for those accused of a crime? Should suspected criminals be guilty until proven innocent?

The Sixth Amendment and Jury Trials

The Sixth Amendment (and, to a lesser extent, Article III of the Constitution) provides that a person accused of a crime shall enjoy the right to a speedy and public trial by an impartial jury—that is, a trial in which a group of the accused's peers act as a fact-finding, deliberative body to determine guilt or innocence. It also gives defendants the right to confront witnesses against them. The Supreme Court has held that jury trials must be available if a prison sentence of six or more months is possible.

Impartiality is a requirement of jury trials that has undergone significant change, with the method of jury selection being the most frequently challenged part of the process. Historically, lawyers had used peremptory challenges (those for which no cause needs to be given) to exclude minorities from juries, especially when the defendant was a member of a minority group. In 1954, for example, the U.S. Supreme Court ruled that Hispanics were entitled to a jury trial that included other Hispanics.[90] And, in 1986, the Court ruled that the use of peremptory challenges specifically to exclude African American jurors violated the equal protection clause of the Fourteenth Amendment.[91]

In 1994, the Supreme Court answered the major remaining question about jury selection: can lawyers exclude women from juries through their use of peremptory challenges? This question arose frequently because in rape trials and sex discrimination cases, one side or another often considers it advantageous to select jurors on the basis of their sex. The Supreme Court ruled that the equal protection clause prohibits discrimination in jury selection on the basis of gender. Thus, lawyers cannot strike all potential male jurors because of the belief that males might be more sympathetic to the arguments of a man charged in a paternity suit, a rape trial, or a domestic violence suit, for example.[92]

The right to confront witnesses at trial also is protected by the Sixth Amendment. In 1990, however, the Supreme Court ruled that this right was not absolute, and the testimony of a six-year-old alleged child abuse victim via one-way closed-circuit TV was permissible. The clause's central purpose, said the Court, was to ensure the reliability of testimony by subjecting it to rigorous examination in an adversarial proceeding.[93] In this case, the child was questioned out of the presence of the defendant, who was in communication with his defense and prosecuting attorneys. The defendant, along with the judge and jury, watched the testimony.

The Eighth Amendment and Cruel and Unusual Punishment

Among its protections, the **Eighth Amendment** prohibits "cruel and unusual punishments," a concept rooted in the English common-law tradition. Today the United States is the only western nation to put people to death for committing crimes. Not surprisingly, tremendous state-by-state differences exist in the imposition of the death penalty. Texas leads the nation in the number of executions each year.

The death penalty was in use in all colonies at the time they adopted the U.S. Constitution, and its constitutionality went unquestioned. In fact, in two separate cases in the late 1800s, the Supreme Court ruled that deaths by public shooting[94] and electrocution were not "cruel and unusual" forms of punishment in the same category as "punishments which inflict torture, such as the rack, the thumbscrew, the iron boot, the stretching of limbs and the like."[95]

In the 1960s, the NAACP (National Association for the Advancement of Colored People) Legal Defense and Educational Fund (LDF), believing that African Americans received the death penalty more frequently than members of other groups, orchestrated a carefully designed legal attack on its constitutionality.[96] Public opinion polls revealed that in 1971, on the eve of the LDF's first major death sentence case to reach the Supreme Court, public support for the death penalty had fallen below 50 percent. With the timing just right, in *Furman* v. *Georgia* (1972), the Supreme Court effectively put an end to capital punishment, at least in the short run.[97] The Court ruled that because the death penalty often was imposed in an arbitrary manner, it constituted cruel and unusual punishment in violation of the Eighth and Fourteenth Amendments.

Eighth Amendment
Part of the Bill of Rights that states: "Excessive bail shall not be required, nor excessive fines imposed, nor cruel and unusual punishments inflicted."

HOW DO STATES VARY IN THEIR APPLICATION OF THE DEATH PENALTY?

This cartoon offers a social commentary on the frequent administration of the death penalty in Texas, which leads the nation in the number of executions. The state of Texas has accounted for a third of the nation's executions since 1976, a fact that is particularly remarkable after considering that the death penalty is illegal in sixteen states and rarely used in many others.

Following *Furman,* several state legislatures enacted new laws designed to meet the Court's objections to the arbitrary nature of the sentence. In 1976, in *Gregg* v. *Georgia,* the Supreme Court in a 7–2 decision ruled that Georgia's rewritten death penalty statute was constitutional.[98]

This ruling did not deter the NAACP LDF from continuing to bring death penalty cases before the Court. In 1987, a 5–4 Court ruled that imposition of the death penalty—even when it appeared to discriminate against African Americans—did not violate the equal protection clause.[99] The Court noted that even if statistics show clear discrimination, reversal of an individual sentence required demonstration of racial discrimination in that particular case.

Four years later, a case involving the same defendant produced an equally important ruling on the death penalty and criminal procedure from the U.S. Supreme Court. In the second case, the Court held that new issues could not be raised on appeal, even if some state error existed. The case, *McCleskey* v. *Zant* (1991), produced new standards designed to make the filing of repeated appeals much more difficult for death-row inmates. Justice Lewis Powell, one of those in the five-person majority, said, after his retirement, that he regretted his vote and should have voted the other way.[100]

Although as recently as 2008 the Supreme Court has upheld the constitutionality of the death penalty by lethal injection,[101] it has made some exceptions. The Court, for example, has exempted two key classes of people from the death penalty: those who are what the law calls mentally retarded and those under the age of eighteen.[102]

PROTECTING THE WRONGFULLY CONVICTED At the state level, a move to at least stay executions gained momentum in March 2000, when Governor George Ryan (R–IL) ordered a moratorium on all executions. Ryan, a death penalty proponent, became disturbed by new evidence collected as a class project by Northwestern University students. The students unearthed information that led to the release of

 Explore on MyPoliSciLab

Should the Government Apply the Death Penalty?

The United States is the only advanced democracy that practices capital punishment. Proponents argue that the death penalty is a deterrent to violent crimes, but since 1992, public support for it has declined. A majority of Americans still believe the death penalty should exist, but there are racial differences among supporters.

Death Penalty Supporters by Race

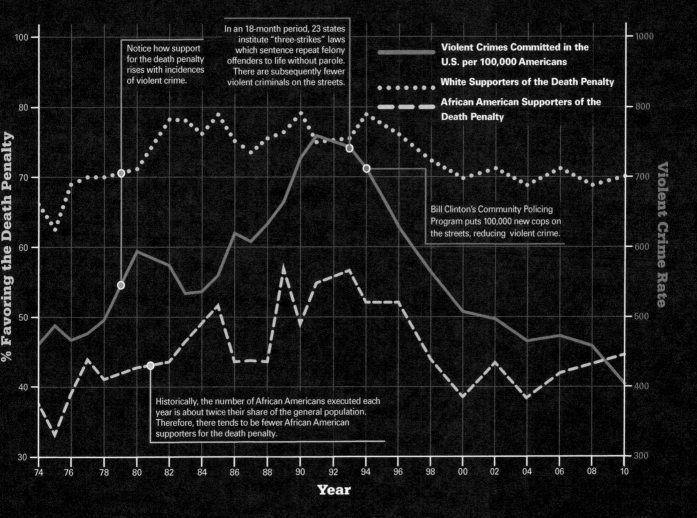

In an 18-month period, 23 states institute "three-strikes" laws which sentence repeat felony offenders to life without parole. There are subsequently fewer violent criminals on the streets.
Violent Crimes Committed in the U.S. per 100,000 Americans

Bill Clinton's Community Policing Program puts 100,000 new cops on the streets, reducing violent crime.

74 76 78 80 82 84 86 88 90 92 94 96 98 00 02 04 06 08 10

SOURCE: Data from General Social Survey, 1972-2010; Bureau of Justice Statistics, U.S. Department of Justice.

Investigate Further

Concept How widespread is American support for using the death penalty? A majority of Americans endorse capital punishment, but support is stronger among whites than African Americans. The racial disparities are due in part to the fact that African Americans are more likely to be on death row than non-Hispanic whites.

Connection Is support for the death penalty related to lower crime rates? When violent crime goes up nationally, so does support for the death penalty because supporters believe it will decrease the crime rate. However, this effect is contested by death penalty opponents and those who see other explanations for less crime.

Cause Are there any competing explanations for the decline of crime, besides the death penalty? There are at least two non-death penalty related reasons for the decline of crime: increased federal spending to put more cops on the street, and states using stiffer sentencing for repeat felony offenders.

right to privacy
The right to be left alone; a judicially created principle encompassing a variety of individual actions protected by the penumbras cast by several constitutional amendments, including the First, Third, Fourth, Ninth, and Fourteenth Amendments.

thirteen men on the state's death row. The specter of allowing death sentences to continue in the face of evidence indicating so many wrongful convictions prompted Ryan's much publicized action. Soon thereafter, the Democratic governor of Maryland followed suit after receiving evidence that blacks were much more likely to be sentenced to death than whites; however, the Republican governor who succeeded him lifted the stay.

Before leaving office in January 2003, Illinois Governor Ryan continued his anti–death-penalty crusade by commuting the sentences of 167 death-row inmates, giving them life in prison instead. This action constituted the single largest anti–death-penalty action since the Court's decision in *Gregg,* and it spurred national conversation on the death penalty, which, in recent polls, has seen its lowest levels of support since 1978.

In another effort to verify that those on death row are not there in error, several states offer free DNA testing to death-row inmates. The U.S. Supreme Court recognized the potential exculpatory power of DNA evidence in *House* v. *Bell* (2006). In this case, the Court ruled that a Tennessee death-row inmate who had exhausted other federal appeals was entitled to an exception to more stringent federal appeals rules because DNA and related evidence suggested his innocence.[103] The Supreme Court, further, has ruled that although inmates do not have an automatic right to DNA testing, it is within their civil rights to file a lawsuit seeking this relief.[104]

The Right to Privacy

4.6 Explain the origin and significance of the right to privacy.

To this point, we have discussed rights and freedoms that have been derived from specific guarantees contained in the Bill of Rights. However, the U.S. Supreme Court also has given protection to rights not enumerated specifically in the Constitution. Although silent about the **right to privacy,** the Bill of Rights contains many indications that the Framers expected some areas of life to be off limits to governmental regulation. The liberty to practice one's religion guaranteed in the First Amendment implies the right to exercise private, personal beliefs. The guarantee against unreasonable searches and seizures contained in the Fourth Amendment similarly suggests that persons are to be secure in their homes and should not fear that police will show up at their doorsteps without cause. As early as 1928, Justice Louis Brandeis hailed privacy as "the right to be left alone—the most comprehensive of rights and the right most valued by civilized men."[105] Not until 1965, however, did the Court attempt to explain the origins of this right.

Birth Control

Today, most Americans take access to birth control for granted. Grocery stores sell condoms, and some TV stations air ads for them. Easy access to birth control, however, was not always the case. Many states often barred the sale of contraceptives to minors, prohibited the display of contraceptives, or even banned their sale altogether. One of the last states to do away with these kinds of laws was Connecticut. It outlawed the sale of all forms of birth control and even prohibited physicians from discussing it with their married patients until the Supreme Court ruled its restrictive laws unconstitutional.

Griswold v. *Connecticut* (1965) involved a challenge to the constitutionality of an 1879 Connecticut law prohibiting the dissemination of information about and/or the sale of contraceptives.[106] In *Griswold,* seven justices decided that various portions of the Bill of Rights, including the First, Third, Fourth, Ninth, and Fourteenth Amendments, cast what the Court called "penumbras" (unstated liberties on the fringes or in the shadow of more explicitly stated rights), thereby creating zones of privacy, including a

WHAT WAS THE OUTCOME OF GRISWOLD V. CONNECTICUT (1965)?

In this photo, Estelle Griswold (left), executive director of the Planned Parenthood League of Connecticut, and Cornelia Jahncke, its president, celebrate the Supreme Court's ruling in *Griswold* v. *Connecticut* (1965). *Griswold* invalidated a Connecticut law that made selling contraceptives or disseminating information about contraception to married couples illegal.

married couple's right to plan a family. Thus, the Connecticut statute was ruled unconstitutional because it violated marital privacy, a right the Court concluded could be read into the U.S. Constitution through interpreting several amendments.

Later, the Court expanded the right to privacy to include the right of unmarried individuals to have access to contraceptives. "If the right of privacy means anything," wrote Justice William J. Brennan Jr., "it is the right of the individual, married or single, to be free from unwarranted governmental intrusion into matters so fundamentally affecting a person as the decision to bear or beget a child."[107] This right to privacy formed the basis for later decisions from the Court, including the right to secure an abortion.

☐ Abortion

In the early 1960s, two groups of birth-related tragedies occurred. European women who had taken the drug thalidomide while pregnant gave birth to severely deformed babies, and, in the United States, a nationwide measles epidemic resulted in the birth of babies with major health problems. The increasing medical safety of abortions and the growing women's rights movement combined with these tragedies to put pressure on the legal and medical establishments to support laws guaranteeing a woman's access to a safe and legal abortion.

By the late 1960s, fourteen states had voted to liberalize their abortion policies, and four states decriminalized abortion in the early stages of pregnancy. But, many women's rights activists wanted more. They argued that the decision to carry a pregnancy to term was a woman's fundamental right. In 1973, in one of the most controversial decisions ever handed down, seven members of the Court agreed with this position.

The woman whose case became the catalyst for pro-choice and pro-life groups was Norma McCorvey, an itinerant circus worker. The mother of a toddler she was unable to care for, McCorvey could not leave another child in her mother's care. So, she decided to terminate her second pregnancy. She was unable to secure a legal abortion, and the conditions she found when seeking an illegal abortion frightened her. McCorvey turned to two young Texas lawyers who were aiming to challenge Texas's

> *The enumeration in the Constitution, of certain rights, shall not be construed to deny or disparage others retained by the people.* –NINTH AMENDMENT

This amendment simply reiterates the belief that rights not specifically enumerated in the Bill of Rights exist and are retained by the people. It was added to assuage the concerns of Federalists, such as James Madison, who feared that the enumeration of so many rights and liberties in the first eight amendments to the Constitution would result in the denial of rights that were not enumerated.

Until 1965, the Ninth Amendment was rarely mentioned by the Court. In that year, however, it was used for the first time by the Court as a positive affirmation of a particular liberty—marital privacy. Although privacy is not mentioned in the Constitution, it was—according to the Court—one of those fundamental freedoms that the drafters of the Bill of Rights implied as retained. Since 1965, the Court has ruled in favor of a host of fundamental liberties guaranteed by the Ninth Amendment, often in combination with other specific guarantees, including the right to have an abortion.

CRITICAL THINKING QUESTIONS

1. **How can the U.S. justice system dictate the definition of a fundamental right if the Constitution does not specifically enumerate that right?**
2. **Are there other implied rights that should be protected by the Ninth Amendment?**

***Roe* v. *Wade* (1973)**
The Supreme Court found that a woman's right to an abortion was protected by the right to privacy that could be implied from specific guarantees found in the Bill of Rights applied to the states through the Fourteenth Amendment.

restrictive statute and were looking to bring a lawsuit with just such a plaintiff. McCorvey, who was unable to obtain a legal abortion, later gave birth and put the baby up for adoption. Nevertheless, she allowed her lawyers to proceed, with her as their plaintiff. Her lawyers used the pseudonym Jane Roe for McCorvey in their challenge of the Texas law as enforced by Henry Wade, the district attorney for Dallas County, Texas.

When the case finally came before the Supreme Court, Justice Harry A. Blackmun, a former lawyer at the Mayo Clinic, relied heavily on medical evidence to rule that the Texas law violated a woman's constitutionally guaranteed right to privacy, which, he argued, included her decision to terminate a pregnancy. Writing for the majority in ***Roe* v. *Wade* (1973),** Blackmun divided pregnancy into three stages. In the first trimester, a woman's right to privacy gave her an absolute right (in consultation with her physician), free from state interference, to terminate her pregnancy. In the second trimester, the state's interest in the health of the mother gave it the right to regulate abortions, but only to protect the woman's health. Only in the third trimester—when the fetus becomes potentially viable—did the Court find that the state's interest in potential life outweighed a woman's privacy interests. Even in the third trimester, however, the Court ruled that abortions to save the life or preserve the health of the mother were legal.[108]

Roe v. *Wade* unleashed a torrent of political controversy. Pro-life groups, caught off guard, scrambled to recoup their losses in Congress. Representative Henry Hyde (R–IL) persuaded Congress to ban the use of Medicaid funds for abortions for poor women, and the Supreme Court upheld the constitutionality of the Hyde Amendment in 1977 and again in 1980.[109] The issue soon became political—it was incorporated into the Republican Party's platform in 1980—and quickly polarized both major political parties.

Since that time, well-organized pro-life groups have attacked the right to an abortion and its constitutional underpinnings in the right to privacy. The administrations of Ronald Reagan and George Bush strongly opposed abortions, and their Justice Departments regularly urged the Court to overrule *Roe*. They came close to victory in *Webster* v. *Reproductive Health Services* (1989).[110] In *Webster*, the Court upheld state-required fetal viability tests in the second trimester, even though these tests increased the cost of an abortion considerably. The Court also upheld Missouri's refusal to allow abortions to be performed in state-supported hospitals or by state-funded doctors or nurses. Perhaps most noteworthy, however, was that four justices seemed willing to overrule *Roe* v. *Wade* and that Justice Antonin Scalia publicly rebuked his colleague, Justice Sandra Day O'Connor, then the only woman on the Court, for failing to provide the critical fifth vote to overrule *Roe*.

After *Webster*, states began to enact more restrictive legislation. In *Planned Parenthood of Southeastern Pennsylvania* v. *Casey* (1992), Justices Sandra Day O'Connor, Anthony Kennedy, and David Souter, in a jointly authored opinion, wrote that Pennsylvania could limit abortions as long as its regulations did not pose "an undue burden" on pregnant women.[111] The narrowly supported standard, by which the Court upheld a twenty-four-hour waiting period and parental consent requirements, did not overrule *Roe*, but clearly limited its scope by abolishing its trimester approach and substituting the undue burden standard for the trimester approach used in *Roe*.

In the early 1990s, newly elected pro-choice President Bill Clinton appointed two supporters of abortion rights, Ruth Bader Ginsburg and Stephen Breyer, to the Supreme Court. Meanwhile, Republican-controlled Congresses made repeated attempts to restrict abortion rights. In March 1996 and again in 1998, Congress passed and sent to President Clinton a bill to ban—for the first time—a specific procedure used in late-term abortions. The president repeatedly vetoed the federal Partial Birth Abortion Ban Act. Many state legislatures, nonetheless, passed their own versions of the law. In 2000, the Supreme Court, however, ruled 5–4 in *Stenberg* v. *Carhart* that a Nebraska partial birth abortion statute was unconstitutionally vague because it failed to contain an exemption for a woman's health. The law, therefore, was unenforceable and called into question the partial birth abortion laws of twenty-nine other states.[112]

But, by October 2003, Republican control of the White House and both houses of Congress facilitated passage of the federal Partial Birth Abortion Ban Act. Pro-choice groups immediately filed lawsuits challenging the constitutionality of this law. The Supreme Court heard oral arguments on the challenge to the federal ban the day after the 2006 midterm elections. In a 5–4 decision, *Gonzales* v. *Carhart* (2007), the Roberts Court revealed the direction it was heading in abortion cases. Over the strong objections of Justice Ginsburg, Justice Kennedy's opinion for the majority upheld the federal act, although, like the law at issue in *Stenberg*, it contained no exceptions for the health of the mother. Observers viewed this ruling as a significant step toward reversing *Roe* v. *Wade* altogether.

The Court's decision in *Gonzales* has empowered states to enact abortion regulations with new gusto. In 2010, for example, Nebraska enacted legislation prohibiting most abortions after twenty weeks. Other states, such as Oklahoma, have laws or are considering legislation that requires doctors to show women an ultrasound image of the fetus before they are allowed to abort. And, in Utah, a new law categorizes self-induced abortions as homicide.[113]

The implementation of these and other restrictions on access to abortion are currently the subject of significant litigation. There are, for example, more than ten cases related to the twenty-week ban winding their way through the judicial system. The U.S. Supreme Court is expected to rule on—and likely uphold—these limits as failing to impose an "undue burden" on a pregnant woman.

WHICH CASE LED TO GREATER DISCUSSION OF GAY RIGHTS ISSUES?

Tyron Garner (left) and John Geddes Lawrence (center), the plaintiffs in *Lawrence* v. *Texas* (2003), are shown here with their attorney. The ruling in this case proved to be a huge victory for advocates of gay and lesbian rights, as it deemed anti-sodomy laws unconstitutional. Following this decision, states began to debate laws related to marriage and other rights for same-sex couples.

☐ Homosexuality

Not until 2003 did the U.S. Supreme Court rule that an individual's constitutional right to privacy, which provided the basis for the *Griswold* (contraceptives) and *Roe* (abortion) decisions, prevents states from criminalizing private sexual behavior. This monumental decision invalidated the laws of fourteen states.

In *Lawrence* v. *Texas* (2003), six members of the Court overruled its decision in *Bowers* v. *Hardwick* (1986), which had upheld anti-sodomy laws. They found the Texas law unconstitutional; five justices found it violated fundamental privacy rights.[114]

Justice O'Connor agreed that the law was unconstitutional, but concluded it was an equal protection violation. Although Justice Antonin Scalia issued a stinging dissent, charging, "the Court has largely signed on to the so-called homosexual agenda," the majority of the Court was unswayed.

Toward Reform: Civil Liberties and Combating Terrorism

4.7 Evaluate how reforms to combat terrorism have affected civil liberties.

After September 11, 2001, the George W. Bush administration, Congress, and the courts all operated in what Secretary of State Condoleezza Rice dubbed "an alternate reality," in which Bill of Rights guarantees were suspended in a time of war, just as they had been in the Civil War and in World Wars I and II.[115] The USA PATRIOT Act, the Military Commissions Act, and a series of secret Department of Justice memos all altered the state of civil liberties in the United States. Here, we detail the provisions of these actions, as well as subsequent actions by the Barack Obama administration, and explain how they have affected the civil liberties discussed in this chapter.

☐ The First Amendment

Both the 2001 USA PATRIOT Act and the 2006 Military Commissions Act contain a variety of major and minor interferences with the civil liberties that Americans, as well as those visiting our shores, have come to expect. The USA PATRIOT Act, for example, violates the First Amendment's free speech guarantees by barring those who have been subject to search orders from telling anyone about those orders, even in situations in which no need for secrecy can be proven. It also authorizes the Federal Bureau of Investigation (FBI) to investigate citizens who choose to exercise their freedom of speech, without demonstrating that any parts of their speech might be labeled illegal.

Another potential infringement of the First Amendment occurred right after the September 11, 2001, terrorist attacks, when it was made clear that members of the media were under strong constraints to report on only positive aspects of U.S. efforts to combat terrorism. And, while the Bush administration decried any leaks of information about its deliberations or actions, the administration selectively leaked information that led to conservative columnist Robert Novak's disclosure of the identity of Valerie Plame, a CIA operative.

In addition, respect for religious practices fell by the wayside in the wake of the war on terrorism. For example, many Muslim detainees captured in Iraq and Afghanistan were fed pork, a violation of basic Islamic dietary laws. Some were stripped naked in front of members of the opposite sex, another religious violation.

☐ The Fourth Amendment

The USA PATRIOT Act enhances the ability of the government to curtail specific search and seizure restrictions in four areas. First, it allows the government to examine an individual's private records held by third parties. This empowers the FBI to force anyone, including physicians, libraries, bookshops, colleges and universities, and Internet service providers, to turn over all records on a particular individual. Second, it expands the government's right to search private property without notice to the owner. Third, according to the ACLU, the act "expands a narrow exception to the Fourth Amendment that had been created for the collection of foreign intelligence information."[116] Finally, the act expands an exception for spying that collects "addressing information" about where and to whom communications are going, as opposed to what is contained in the documents.

Judicial oversight of these governmental powers is virtually nonexistent. Proper governmental authorities need only certify to a judge, without any evidence, that the requested search meets the statute's broad criteria. Moreover, the legislation deprives judges of the authority to reject such applications.

Other Fourth Amendment violations include the ability to conduct searches without a warrant. The government also does not have to demonstrate probable cause that a person has, or might, commit a crime. Thus, the USA PATRIOT Act also goes against key elements of the due process rights guaranteed by the Fifth Amendment.

☐ Due Process Rights

Illegal incarceration and torture are federal crimes, and the Supreme Court ruled in 2004 that detainees have a right of *habeas corpus*.[117] However, the Bush administration argued that under the Military Commissions Act of 2006, alien victims of torture had significantly reduced rights of *habeas corpus*. The Military Commissions Act also eliminated the right to challenge "detention, transfer, treatment, trial, or conditions of confinement" of detainees. It allowed the government to declare permanent resident aliens to be enemy combatants and enabled the government to jail these people indefinitely without any opportunity to file a writ of *habeas corpus*. In 2008, in a surprising setback for the Bush administration, the Roberts Court ruled parts of the act unconstitutional, finding that any detainees could challenge their extended incarceration in federal court.[118]

Secret offshore prisons, known as black sites, have also held many suspected terrorists against their will. In September 2006, President Bush acknowledged the existence of these facilities, moving fourteen such detainees to the detention facility at Guantanamo Bay, Cuba. The conditions of this facility sparked intense debate, as opponents cited numerous accusations of torture as well as possible violations of human rights. Those in support of the continued use of Guantanamo declared the detainees unlawful combatants and not war criminals subject to the provisions of the Geneva Convention. After President Barack Obama took office in 2009, he vowed to close Guantanamo by January 2010 and move detainees to a facility in Illinois. By the end of 2012, however, Guantanamo Bay remained open.

Recent federal activity has also curtailed the Sixth Amendment right to trial by jury. Those people detained as enemy combatants often do not have access to the evidence against them and are subject to coercion or torture in the gathering of additional evidence. Trials of enemy combatants are closed, and people tried in these courts do not have a right to an attorney of their choosing. The Supreme Court limited the federal government's activity in these tribunals, but the Military Commissions Act returned these powers to the executive branch.[119] The Obama administration, to the surprise of many observers, also has done little to restore the rights revoked by these acts, and has, in fact, further limited some detainees' ability to challenge their incarceration.

Finally, great controversy has surrounded the Eighth Amendment's prohibition on cruel and unusual punishment. Since shortly after the terrorist attacks of September 11, 2001, rumors abounded that many prisoners detained by the U.S. government faced inhumane treatment. In 2004, for example, photos of cruel treatment of prisoners held by the U.S. military in Abu Ghraib, Iraq surfaced. These photos led to calls for investigations at all levels of government. On the heels of this incident, the Justice Department declared torture "abhorrent" in a December 2004 legal memo. That position lasted but a short time. After Alberto Gonzales was sworn in as attorney general in February 2005, the Department of Justice issued a secret memo endorsing harsh interrogation techniques. According to one Justice Department memo, interrogation practices were not considered illegal unless they

WHAT ARE LIVING CONDITIONS LIKE FOR DETAINEES?

Prisoners of the war on terrorism live in maximum security prisons where their civil liberties are often compromised. Here, military police escort a detainee to his cell at Guantanamo Bay Detention Camp.

produced pain equivalent to that with organ failure or death. Among the techniques authorized by the government were combinations of "painful physical and psychological tactics, including head-slapping, simulated drowning, and frigid temperatures."[120] The most controversial of these techniques is waterboarding, which simulates drowning. Although the Obama administration has harshly attacked the use of such tactics and techniques, it announced that those who committed these acts during the Bush administration would not be prosecuted.[121]

Review the Chapter

 Listen to Chapter 4 on MyPoliSciLab

Roots of Civil Liberties: The Bill of Rights

4.1 Trace the constitutional roots of civil liberties, p. 93.

Most of the Framers originally opposed the Bill of Rights. Anti-Federalists, however, continued to stress the need for a bill of rights during the drive for ratification of the Constitution, and some states tried to make their ratification contingent on the addition of a bill of rights. Thus, during its first session, Congress sent the first ten amendments to the Constitution, the Bill of Rights, to the states for their ratification. Later, the addition of the Fourteenth Amendment allowed the Supreme Court to apply some of the amendments to the states through a process called selective incorporation.

First Amendment Guarantees: Freedom of Religion

4.2 Describe the First Amendment guarantee of freedom of religion, p. 97.

The First Amendment guarantees freedom of religion. The establishment clause, which prohibits the national government from establishing a religion, does not, according to Supreme Court interpretation, create an absolute wall between church and state. While the national and state governments may generally not give direct aid to religious groups, the Court has held that many forms of aid, especially those that benefit children, are constitutionally permissible. In contrast, the Court has generally barred mandatory prayer in public schools. The Court has allowed some governmental regulation of religious practices under the free exercise clause.

First Amendment Guarantees: Freedoms of Speech, Press, Assembly, and Petition

4.3 Outline the First Amendment guarantees of and limitations on freedom of speech, press, assembly, and petition, p. 99.

Historically, one of the most volatile subjects of constitutional interpretation has been the First Amendment's mandate that "Congress shall make no law . . . abridging the freedom of speech or of the press." As with the establishment and free exercise clauses of the First Amendment, the Court has not interpreted the speech and press clauses as absolute bans against government regulation. The Supreme Court has ruled against prior restraint, thus protecting freedom of the press. The Court has also protected symbolic speech and hate speech as long as they do not become action. Areas of speech and publication unprotected by the First Amendment include libel, fighting words, and obscenity and pornography. The freedoms of peaceable assembly and petition are directly related to the freedoms of speech and the press. As with other First Amendment rights, the Supreme Court has become the arbiter between the people's right to dissent and the government's need to promote security.

The Second Amendment: The Right to Keep and Bear Arms

4.4 Summarize changes in the interpretation of the Second Amendment right to keep and bear arms, p. 106.

Initially, the right to bear arms was envisioned in terms of state militias. Over the years, states and Congress have enacted various gun ownership restrictions with little Supreme Court interpretation. However, the Court ruled in *D.C.* v. *Heller* (2008) and *McDonald* v. *City of Chicago* (2010) that the Second Amendment protects an individual's right to own a firearm.

The Rights of Criminal Defendants

4.5 Analyze the rights of criminal defendants found in the Bill of Rights, p. 108.

The Fourth, Fifth, Sixth, and Eighth Amendments provide a variety of procedural guarantees to individuals accused of crimes. The Fourth Amendment prohibits unreasonable searches and seizures, and the Court has generally refused to allow evidence seized in violation of this safeguard to be used at trial. The Fifth Amendment protects those who have been charged with crimes. It mandates the use of grand juries in cases of serious crimes. It also guarantees that "no person shall be compelled to be a witness against himself." The Supreme Court has interpreted this provision to require the government to inform the accused of his or her right to remain silent. The Court has also interpreted this provision to require exclusion of illegally obtained confessions at trial. Finally, the Fifth Amendment's double jeopardy clause protects individuals from being tried twice for the same crimes in the same jurisdiction. The Court's interpretation of the Sixth Amendment's guarantee of "assistance of counsel" stipulates that the government provide counsel to defendants unable to pay for it in cases subject to prison sentences. The Sixth Amendment also requires an impartial jury, although the meaning of impartial continues to evolve through judicial interpretation. The judicial view is that the Eighth Amendment's ban against "cruel and unusual punishments" does not bar imposition of the death penalty.

The Right to Privacy

4.6 Explain the origin and significance of the right to privacy, p. 116.

The right to privacy is a judicially created right carved from the penumbras (unstated liberties implied by more explicitly stated rights) of several amendments, including the First, Third, Fourth, Ninth, and Fourteenth Amendments. The Court has found statutes that limit access to birth control, prohibit abortion, and ban homosexual acts to be unconstitutional under this right.

Toward Reform: Civil Liberties and Combating Terrorism

4.7 Evaluate how reforms to combat terrorism have affected civil liberties, p. 120.

After the terrorist attacks of September 11, 2001, Congress and the executive branch enacted reforms that dramatically altered civil liberties in the United States. Critics charge that the changes have significantly compromised a host of constitutional guarantees, while supporters say that they are necessary to protect national security in a time of war.

Learn the Terms

Study and **Review** the **Flashcards**

bill of attainder, p. 108
Bill of Rights, p. 94
civil liberties, p. 93
civil rights, p. 93
clear and present danger test, p. 101
direct incitement test, p. 101
double jeopardy clause, p. 110
due process clause, p. 94
Eighth Amendment, p. 113
establishment clause, p. 97
exclusionary rule, p. 110
ex post facto law, p. 108
Fifth Amendment, p. 109
fighting words, p. 104
First Amendment, p. 97
Fourth Amendment, p. 108
free exercise clause, p. 97
fundamental freedoms, p. 96
hate speech, p. 103
incorporation doctrine, p. 95
Lemon test, p. 97
libel, p. 104
Miranda rights, p. 110
Miranda v. *Arizona* (1966), p. 110
New York Times Co. v. *Sullivan* (1964), p. 104
Ninth Amendment, p. 94
prior restraint, p. 100
right to privacy, p. 116
Roe v. *Wade* (1973), p. 118
selective incorporation, p. 95
Sixth Amendment, p. 111
slander, p. 104
substantive due process, p. 94
symbolic speech, p. 101
Tenth Amendment, p. 94
writ of *habeas corpus*, p. 108

Test Yourself

Study and **Review** the **Practice Tests**

1. Which amendment did the Court use to make some provisions of the Bill of Rights applicable to the states?

a. Fifth
b. Tenth
c. Eleventh
d. Fourteenth
e. Fifteenth

2. Which of the following was NOT used as an argument against adding a bill of rights to the Constitution?

a. A constitutional republic is founded upon the idea of popular sovereignty and inalienable rights.
b. Federal guarantees were unnecessary because most state constitutions contained their own bills of rights.
c. The government should not enumerate what it could not do.
d. A national bill of rights would be nearly impossible to enforce.
e. The Constitution already contained protections for individual rights.

3. The U.S. Supreme Court has interpreted the establishment clause to mean that

a. reciting prayer in classrooms is constitutional, as long as the prayer is nondenominational.
b. state university grounds cannot be used for worship.
c. a privately owned display of the Ten Commandments in a courthouse is unconstitutional.
d. faculty-led prayer at high school football games is constitutional.
e. governments may provide aid to religious schools as long as the aid goes to children and not to religious goals.

4. Which form of speech is protected under the First Amendment?

a. Libel
b. Symbolic speech
c. Slander
d. Fighting words
e. Obscenity

5. Which is NOT considered a protected form of speech?

- **a.** Carrying a "Bong Hits 4 Jesus" banner during a school-sanctioned parade
- **b.** Wearing black armbands to protest a war
- **c.** Publishing secret documents in a newspaper
- **d.** Displaying a symbol of opposition to the U.S. government
- **e.** Burning the American flag

6. The U.S. Supreme Court first ruled that the Second Amendment protects an individual's right to own a firearm in certain jurisdictions

- **a.** in the early 1800s, when laws were passed to limit possession of firearms by slaves.
- **b.** when Justice Roger B. Taney considered the right to own and carry arms a basic right of citizenship.
- **c.** in *D.C.* v. *Heller* in 2008.
- **d.** when a law that made sawed-off shotguns illegal was overturned in the 1930s.
- **e.** in *Barron* v. *Baltimore* in 1833.

7. Traditionally, the Supreme Court has ruled that the Fourth Amendment requires a warrant for police to search

- **a.** the person arrested.
- **b.** things in plain view of the accused.
- **c.** employees of the federal or state government.
- **d.** places or things in the arrestee's immediate control.
- **e.** the home of the accused.

8. When suspects are arrested and read their *Miranda* rights, the authorities are informing them of their ____ Amendment rights.

- **a.** Second
- **b.** Third
- **c.** Fourth
- **d.** Fifth
- **e.** Seventh

9. The U.S. Supreme Court ruled that the controversial 2003 federal Partial Birth Abortion Ban Act was

- **a.** a law that could be passed only by the states.
- **b.** unconstitutional because it contained no health exceptions for the mother.
- **c.** constitutional despite its lack of a health exception for the mother.
- **d.** unconstitutional because it violated the three-trimester approach created by *Roe* v. *Wade* (1973).
- **e.** constitutional based on the precedent established in *Planned Parenthood of Southeastern Pennsylvania* v. *Casey* (1992).

10. The major act passed in the aftermath of September 11, 2001, to combat terrorism in the United States was the

- **a.** Military Commissions Act.
- **b.** JUSTICE Act.
- **c.** Detention and Retention Act.
- **d.** Habeas Corpus Act.
- **e.** USA PATRIOT Act.

Explore Further

Abrams, Floyd. *Speaking Freely: Trials of the First Amendment.* New York: Viking, 2006.

Ackerman, Bruce. *Before the Next Attack: Preserving Civil Liberties in an Age of Terrorism.* New Haven, CT: Yale University Press, 2007.

Baird, Robert M., and Stuart E. Rosenbaum. *Death Penalty: Debating the Moral, Legal, and Political Issues.* Amherst, NY: Prometheus Books, 2010.

Cole, David, and James X. Dempsey. *Terrorism and the Constitution: Sacrificing Civil Liberties in the Name of National Security,* 3rd ed. Washington, DC: First Amendment Foundation, 2006.

Darmer, M. Katherine B., Robert M. Baird, and Stuart E. Rosenbaum, eds. *Civil Liberties vs. National Security in a Post 9/11 World.* Amherst, NY: Prometheus, 2004.

Gates, Henry Louis, Jr., ed. *Speaking of Race, Speaking of Sex: Hate Speech, Civil Rights, and Civil Liberties.* New York: New York University Press, 1995.

Ivers, Gregg, and Kevin T. McGuire, eds. *Creating Constitutional Change.* Charlottesville: University Press of Virginia, 2004.

Lane, Frederick S. *American Privacy: The 400-Year History of Our Most Contested Right.* Boston: Beacon Press, 2009.

Lendler, Marc. *Gitlow* v. *New York: Every Idea an Incitement.* Lawrence, University Press of Kansas, 2012.

Lewis, Anthony. *Gideon's Trumpet,* reissue ed. New York: Vintage Books, 1989.

———. *Make No Law: The Sullivan Case and the First Amendment,* reprint ed. New York: Random House, 1992.

O'Connor, Karen. *No Neutral Ground: Abortion Politics in an Age of Absolutes.* Boulder, CO: Westview, 1996.

Romero, Anthony D., and Dina Temple-Raston. *In Defense of Our America: The Fight for Civil Liberties in the Age of Terror.* New York: William Morrow, 2007.

Sando, Philippe. *Torture Teams: Rumsfeld's Memo and the Betrayal of American Values.* New York: Palgrave Macmillan, 2008.

Wheeler, Leigh Anne. *How Sex Became a Civil Liberty.* New York: Oxford University Press, 2012.

To learn more about differing views on civil liberties, go to the home pages for the following groups:
American Civil Liberties Union at **www.aclu.org**
People for the American Way at **www.pfaw.org**
American Center for Law and Justice at **www.aclj.org**
The Federalist Society at **www.fed-soc.org**

To learn more about the Supreme Court cases discussed in this chapter, go to Oyez: U.S. Supreme Court Media at **www.oyez.org,** and search on the case name. Or, go to the Legal Information Institute of Cornell University's Law School at **www.law.cornell.edu/supct/cases/topic.htm,** where you can search cases by topic.

To learn more about civil liberties protections for homosexuals, go to Human Rights Campaign at **www.hrc.org,** and Lambda Legal at **www.lambdalegal.org.**

Listen to Chapter 5 on MyPoliSciLab

5

Civil Rights

Walmart stores are the nation's largest employer, with more than 2 million employees. Of those employees, two-thirds are women. Management at Walmart stores, however, is 86 percent male.

Beginning in 2000, Betty Dukes, a Walmart worker from California, attempted to address this gap in hiring—as well as the resultant gap in men's and women's wages—by filing a case alleging that Walmart engaged in systematic sex discrimination. Dukes claimed that, despite six years of work for the company, she was repeatedly denied opportunities to attend management training seminars. As a result, she was unable to advance from her hourly work to a salaried, better-paying position within the company.

Eventually Dukes joined forces with other female Walmart employees who felt discriminated against on the basis of their sex. Among these was Christine Kwapnoski, a Walmart worker from New Hampshire who, when she asked why she had not been promoted in fifteen years, was told, "Blow the cobwebs off your makeup" and "doll up." Eventually, cases like those filed by Dukes and Kwapnoski reached class action status. Ultimately, the litigants claimed to represent more than 1.6 million women who had worked at Walmart since 1998.

It took more than ten years for the women's case to reach the Supreme Court. In 2011, however, the Court heard and decided the case of *Walmart* v. *Dukes*. Ultimately, in a 5-4 decision, the Court reached no conclusion on the merits of the women's sex discrimination or pay equity claims. Instead, the Court ruled that a group of 1.6 million women was simply too large and too diverse for the suit to move forward as a class action lawsuit. The individual plaintiffs were encouraged to begin litigation again, working on their own to show discrimination by Walmart stores.

Plaintiffs such as Dukes and Kwapnoski have continued to fight in individual suits. But, they are not alone. Experts estimate that more that 12,000 sex discrimination lawsuits against Walmart are still ongoing. In the meantime, critics charge, so is the discrimination and corporate culture that makes at 1.6 million-person class action lawsuit fathomable.

But, pay equity isn't only an issue at Walmart. Across the country, women only make about 75 to 80 cents for every dollar that similarly situated men earn. Despite the passage of well-intentioned legislation such as the Equal Pay Act of 1963, Title VII of the Civil Rights Act of 1964, and the Lilly Ledbetter Fair Pay Act of 2009, many women lack the courage or the ability to speak

5.1 Trace the efforts from 1800 to 1890 of African Americans and women to win the vote, p. 129.

5.2 Outline developments in African Americans' and women's push for equality from 1890 to 1954, p. 135.

5.3 Analyze the civil rights movement and the effects of the Civil Rights Act of 1964, p. 141.

5.4 Assess statutory and constitutional remedies for discrimination pursued and achieved by the women's rights movement, p. 147.

5.5 Describe how other groups have mobilized in pursuit of their own civil rights, p. 153.

5.6 Evaluate the ongoing debate concerning civil rights and affirmative action, p. 163.

WOMEN IN THE WORKPLACE The tasks performed by women in the workplace have changed over time. Above, women work in the knitting mills of Lowell, Massachusetts during the mid-1800s. Below, a female employee stocks shelves at a modern Walmart store.

MyPoliSciLab Videos

The Big Picture How did groups in America realize that they were being discriminated against? And what have they chosen to do about it? Author Karen O'Connor explains why the ongoing struggle for civil rights continues to be a major topic of discussion in American politics.

The Basics Discover whether we have always had civil rights and whether all American citizens have them. Watch as ordinary people answer questions about where our civil rights come from and how we won them. Consider what equal treatment and protection under the law means today.

In Context Discover how civil rights issues have permeated our society since the United States was founded. In the video, University of Oklahoma political scientist Alisa H. Fryar talks about how civil rights has expanded in scope since the Civil Rights Movement of the twentieth century.

Thinking Like a Political Scientist Where are we headed in terms of civil rights research in the United States? University of Oklahoma political scientist Alisa H. Fryar discusses how current research on voting rights, municipal election methods, and education address civil rights issues.

In the Real World The Defense of Marriage Act declares that the federal government does not recognize same-sex marriage. Is that constitutional? Hear real people argue both sides as they discuss their beliefs about same-sex marriage, and find out how public opinion has changed dramatically over the years

So What? Why do women pay more for dry cleaning than men? Author Karen O'Connor dispels the myth that discrimination no longer exists in the United States by looking at the ways men and women are treated, and argues that there is still more to be done to reach equality.

up against sex discrimination. When the livelihoods of families and children depend on a paycheck from a working woman, something—even when it is less than what a male counterpart might make—often seems better than nothing. Thus, the issue of pay equity, like other civil rights issues discussed in this chapter, can often be a difficult one for policymakers to tackle.[1]

civil rights
The government-protected rights of individuals against arbitrary or discriminatory treatment by governments or individuals.

•••

Since the Framers wrote the Constitution, concepts of **civil rights**—the government-protected rights of individuals against arbitrary or discriminatory treatment by governments or individuals based on categories such as race, sex, national origin, age, religion, or sexual orientation—have changed dramatically. The Fourteenth Amendment, one of three Civil War Amendments ratified from 1865 to 1870, introduced the notion of equality into the Constitution by specifying that a state could not deny "any person within its jurisdiction equal protection of the laws." Throughout history, the Fourteenth Amendment's equal protection guarantees have been the lynchpin of efforts to expand upon the original intent of the amendment. Today, this amendment protects a variety of groups from discrimination.

The Fourteenth Amendment has generated more litigation to determine and specify its meaning than any other provision of the Constitution. Within a few years of its ratification, women—and later African Americans and other minorities and disadvantaged groups—took to the courts, seeking expanded civil rights in all walks of life. But, these groups did not limit their struggle to the courts. The arsenal of those seeking equality has also included public protest, civil disobedience, legislative lobbying, and appeals to public opinion.

Since passage of the Civil War Amendments, the expansion of civil rights to more and more groups has followed a fairly consistent pattern. In this chapter, we will explore how notions of equality and civil rights have changed in the United States.

Roots of Suffrage: 1800–1890

5.1 Trace the efforts from 1800 to 1890 of African Americans and women to win the vote.

Today, we take for granted the voting rights—or suffrage—of women and African Americans. Since 1980, women have outvoted men in presidential elections; at present, African Americans and women are core groups of the Democratic Party. But, it wasn't always this way. The period from 1800 to 1890 was one of tremendous change and upheaval in America. Despite the Civil War and the freeing of slaves, the promise of equality guaranteed to African Americans by the Civil War Amendments failed to become a reality. Woman's rights activists also began to make claims for equality, often using the arguments enunciated for the abolition of slavery, but they, too, fell far short of their goals.

Slavery and Congress

Congress banned the slave trade in 1808, after expiration of the twenty-year period specified by the Constitution. In 1820, blacks made up 25 percent of the U.S. population and formed the majority in some southern states. By 1840, that figure had fallen to 20 percent. After introduction of the cotton gin (a machine invented in 1793 that separated seeds from cotton very quickly), the South became even more dependent on agriculture, such as cotton, tobacco, and rice, with cheap slave labor as its economic base. At the same time, technological advances were turning the northern states into an increasingly industrialized region, which deepened the cultural and political differences, as well as the animosity, between North and South.

As the nation grew westward in the early 1800s, conflicts between northern and southern states intensified over the free versus slave status of new states admitted to the union. The first major crisis occurred in 1820, when Missouri applied for admission to the union as a slave state—that is, one in which slavery would be legal. Missouri's admission would have weighted the Senate in favor of slavery and therefore was opposed by northern senators. To resolve this conflict, Congress passed the Missouri Compromise of 1820. The Compromise prohibited slavery north of the geographical boundary at 36 degrees latitude. This act allowed the union to admit Missouri as a slave state. To maintain the balance of slave and free states, Maine was carved out of a portion of Massachusetts.

☐ The First Civil Rights Movements: Abolition and Women's Rights

The Missouri Compromise solidified the South in its determination to keep slavery legal, but it also fueled the fervor of those opposing it. William Lloyd Garrison, a white New Englander, galvanized the abolitionist movement in the early 1830s. A newspaper editor, Garrison (along with Arthur Tappan) founded the American Anti-Slavery Society in 1833; by 1838, it had more than 250,000 members. Given the U.S. population today, the National Association for the Advancement of Colored People (NAACP) would need 3.8 million members to have the same kind of overall proportional membership. (In 2013, NAACP membership was approximately 300,000.)

Slavery was not the only practice that people began to question in the decades following the Missouri Compromise. In 1840, for example, Garrison and Frederick Douglass, a well-known black abolitionist writer, left the Anti-Slavery Society when it refused to accept their demand that women be allowed to participate equally in all its activities. Custom dictated that women not speak out in public, and most laws explicitly made women second-class citizens. In most states, for example, women could not divorce their husbands or keep their own wages and inheritances. And, of course, they could not vote.

Elizabeth Cady Stanton and Lucretia Mott, who were to found the first woman's rights movement, attended the 1840 meeting of the World Anti-Slavery Society in London with their husbands. In spite of their long journey, they were not permitted to participate in the convention because they were women. As they sat in a mandated area apart from the male delegates, they compared their status to that of the slaves they sought to free. They concluded that women were not much better off than slaves, and they resolved to address this issue. In 1848, they finally sent out a call for the first woman's rights convention. Three hundred women and men, including Frederick Douglass, attended the first meeting for woman's rights, held in Seneca Falls, New York.

The Seneca Falls Convention in 1848 attracted people from other states as well as New York. Attendees passed resolutions demanding the abolition of legal, economic, and social discrimination against women. All of the resolutions reflected the attendees' dissatisfaction with contemporary moral codes; divorce and criminal laws; and the limited opportunities for women in education, the church, medicine, law, and politics. Ironically, only the call for "woman suffrage"—a call to give women the right to vote—failed to win unanimous approval. Most who attended the Seneca Falls Convention continued to press for woman's rights along with the abolition of slavery. Similar conventions took place later across the Northeast and Midwest. At an 1851 meeting in Akron, Ohio, for example, former slave Sojourner Truth delivered her famous "Ain't I a Woman?" speech, calling on women to recognize the plight of their black sisters.

☐ The 1850s: The Calm Before the Storm

By 1850, much had changed in America: the Gold Rush had spurred westward migration, cities grew as people were lured from their farms, railroads and the telegraph increased mobility and communication, and immigrants flooded into the United States. The woman's movement gained momentum, and slavery continued to tear the nation apart. Harriet Beecher Stowe's *Uncle Tom's Cabin,* a novel that depicted the evils of slavery, further inflamed the country. *Uncle Tom's Cabin* sold more than 300,000 copies in 1852. Equivalent sales today would top 4 million copies.

WHO WAS ELIZABETH CADY STANTON?

Elizabeth Cady Stanton was one of the founders of the woman suffrage movement. She was also a key organizer of the first woman's rights convention at Seneca Falls, New York, in 1848. Though she never lived to exercise her right to vote, the actions of Stanton and her fellow suffragists, including Lucretia Mott (seated behind her on the podium) and Susan B. Anthony, paved the way for the ratification of the Nineteenth Amendment.

The tremendous national reaction to *Uncle Tom's Cabin,* which later prompted President Abraham Lincoln to call Stowe "the little woman who started the big war," had not yet faded when a new controversy over the Missouri Compromise became the lightning rod for the first major civil rights case addressed by the U.S. Supreme Court. In *Dred Scott* v. *Sandford* (1857), the Court ruled that the Missouri Compromise, which prohibited slavery north of a set geographical boundary, was unconstitutional. Furthermore, the Court added that slaves were not U.S. citizens and, as a consequence, could not bring suits in federal court.

5.1
5.2
5.3
5.4
5.5
5.6

☐ The Civil War and Its Aftermath: Civil Rights Laws and Constitutional Amendments

The Civil War had many causes, but slavery was clearly a key issue. During the war (1861–1865), abolitionists continued to press for an end to slavery. They were partially rewarded when President Abraham Lincoln issued the Emancipation Proclamation, which provided that all slaves in states still in active rebellion against the United States would be freed automatically on January 1, 1863. Designed as a measure to gain favor for the war in the North, the Emancipation Proclamation did not free all slaves—it freed only those who lived in the Confederacy. Complete abolition of slavery did not occur until congressional passage and ultimate ratification of the Thirteenth Amendment in 1865.

The **Thirteenth Amendment** was the first of the three Civil War Amendments. It banned all forms of "slavery [and] involuntary servitude." Although the federal government required the southern states to ratify the Thirteenth Amendment as a condition of readmission to the Union after the war, most former Confederate states passed laws designed to restrict opportunities for newly freed slaves. These **Black Codes** denied most legal rights to newly freed slaves by prohibiting African Americans from voting, sitting on juries, or even appearing in public places. Although Black Codes differed from state to state, all empowered local law enforcement officials to arrest unemployed blacks, fine them for vagrancy, and hire them out to employers to satisfy their fines. Some state codes even required African Americans to work on plantations or as domestics. The Black Codes laid the groundwork for Jim Crow laws, which later would institute segregation in all walks of life in the South.

An outraged Congress enacted the Civil Rights Act of 1866 to invalidate some state Black Codes. President Andrew Johnson vetoed the legislation, but—for the first time in history—Congress overrode a presidential veto. The Civil Rights Act formally made African Americans citizens of the United States and gave Congress and the federal courts the power to intervene when states attempted to restrict the citizenship rights of male African Americans in matters such as voting. Congress reasoned that African Americans were unlikely to succeed if they had to file discrimination complaints in state courts, where most judges were elected. Passage of a federal law allowed African Americans to challenge discriminatory state practices in federal courts, where the president appointed judges for life.

Because controversy remained over the constitutionality of the act (since the Constitution gives states the right to determine qualifications of voters), Congress proposed the **Fourteenth Amendment** simultaneously with the Civil Rights Act to guarantee, among other things, citizenship to all freed slaves. Other key provisions of the Fourteenth Amendment barred states from abridging "the privileges or immunities of citizenship" or depriving "any person of life, liberty, or property, without due process of law." Finally, the Fourteenth Amendment includes the **equal protection clause,** which prohibits states from denying "any person within its jurisdiction the equal protection of the laws."

Unlike the Thirteenth Amendment, which had near-unanimous support in the North, the Fourteenth Amendment faced opposition from many women because it failed to guarantee them suffrage. During the Civil War, woman's rights activists put aside their claims for expanded rights for women, most notably the right to vote, and threw their energies into the war effort. They were convinced that once the government freed the slaves and gave them the right to vote, women would receive this same right. They were wrong.

In early 1869, after ratification of the Fourteenth Amendment (which specifically added the word "male" to the Constitution for the first time), woman's rights activists met in Washington, D.C., to argue against passage of any new amendment that would extend suffrage to black males and not to women. The convention resolved that "a man's government is worse than a white man's government, because, in proportion as you increase the tyrants, you make the condition of the disenfranchised class more hopeless and degraded."

Thirteenth Amendment
One of the three Civil War Amendments; specifically bans slavery in the United States.

Black Codes
Laws denying most legal rights to newly freed slaves; passed by southern states following the Civil War.

Fourteenth Amendment
One of the three Civil War Amendments; guarantees equal protection and due process of the law to all U.S. citizens.

equal protection clause
Section of the Fourteenth Amendment that guarantees all citizens receive "equal protection of the laws."

Neither slavery nor involuntary servitude, except as a punishment for crime whereof the party shall have been duly convicted, shall exist within the United States, or any place subject to their jurisdiction. —THIRTEENTH AMENDMENT, SECTION 1

This amendment, the first of three Civil War Amendments, abolished slavery throughout the United States and its territories. It also prohibited involuntary servitude.

Based on his wartime authority, in 1863, President Abraham Lincoln issued the Emancipation Proclamation abolishing slavery in the states that were in rebellion against the United States. Abolishing slavery in the Union, however, proved more challenging. Congress could not end this practice by statute. Thus, the proposed Thirteenth Amendment was forwarded to the states on February 1, 1865. With its adoption, said one of its sponsors, it relieved Congress "of sectional strifes."

Initially, some doubted if any groups other than newly freed African slaves were protected by the provisions of the amendment. Soon, however, the Supreme Court went on to clarify this question by noting: "If Mexican peonage or the Chinese coolie labor system shall develop slavery of the Mexican or Chinese race within our territory, this amendment may safely be trusted to make it void."[a]

In the early 1900s, the Supreme Court was called on several times to interpret section 1 of the amendment, especially in regard to involuntary servitude. Thus, provisions of an Alabama law that called for criminal sanctions and jail time for defaulting sharecroppers were considered unconstitutional, and Congress enacted a law banning this kind of involuntary servitude.

More recently, the Thirteenth Amendment has been invoked to seek a stop to the estimated 100,000 to 300,000 American children and teens forced into sex trafficking each year. Like some slaves, many of the children are forced to have sex multiple times at the will and for the financial benefit of their "owners." Still, most federal and state programs target helping adults and not the young.

CRITICAL THINKING QUESTIONS

1. **Is forcing prison inmates to work as part of a "chain gang" a form of involuntary servitude? Why or why not?**
2. **Why have the federal and state governments largely failed to stop or minimize the sex trafficking of minors?**

[a] *The Slaughterhouse Cases*, 83 U.S. 36 (1873).

In spite of these arguments, Congress passed the **Fifteenth Amendment** in early 1869. It guaranteed the "right of citizens" to vote regardless of their "race, color or previous condition of servitude." Sex was not mentioned.

Fifteenth Amendment
One of the three Civil War Amendments; specifically enfranchised newly freed male slaves.

Woman's rights activists were shocked. Abolitionists' continued support of the Fifteenth Amendment prompted many woman's rights supporters to leave the abolition movement and to work solely for the cause of woman's rights. Twice burned, Susan B. Anthony (who had joined the women's movement in 1852) and Elizabeth Cady Stanton decided to form their own group, the National Woman Suffrage Association (NWSA), to achieve that goal and other woman's rights. Another more conservative group, the American Woman Suffrage Association, was founded at the same time to pursue the sole goal of suffrage. In spite of the NWSA's opposition, however, the states ratified the Fifteenth Amendment in 1870.

Civil Rights, Congress, and the Supreme Court

Continued southern resistance to African American equality led Congress to pass the Civil Rights Act of 1875, designed to grant equal access to public accommodations such as theaters, restaurants, and transportation. The act also prohibited the exclusion of African Americans from jury service. By 1877, however, national interest in the legal condition of African Americans waned. Most white Southerners

Jim Crow laws
Laws enacted by southern states that required segregation in public schools, theaters, hotels, and other public accommodations.

***Civil Rights Cases* (1883)**
Name attached to five cases brought under the Civil Rights Act of 1875. In 1883, the Supreme Court decided that discrimination in a variety of public accommodations, including theaters, hotels, and railroads, could not be prohibited by the act because such discrimination was private, not state, discrimination.

poll tax
A tax levied in many southern states and localities that had to be paid before an eligible voter could cast a ballot.

and even some Northerners never had believed in true equality for "freedmen," as former slaves were called. Any rights that freedmen received had been contingent on federal enforcement. And, federal occupation of the South (known as Reconstruction) ended in 1877. National troops were no longer available to guard polling places and to prevent whites from excluding black voters, and southern states quickly moved to limit African Americans' access to the ballot. Other forms of discrimination also came about by judicial decisions upholding **Jim Crow laws,** which required segregation in public schools and facilities, including railroads, restaurants, and theaters. Some Jim Crow laws, specifically known as miscegenation laws, barred interracial marriage.

All these laws, at first glance, appeared to conflict with the Civil Rights Act of 1875. In 1883, however, a series of cases decided by the Supreme Court severely damaged the vitality of the 1875 act. The ***Civil Rights Cases* (1883)** were five separate cases involving convictions of private individuals found to have violated the Civil Rights Act by refusing to extend accommodations to African Americans in theaters, a hotel, and a railroad.[2] In deciding these cases, the Supreme Court ruled that Congress could prohibit only state or governmental action, but not private acts of discrimination. The Court thus concluded that Congress had no authority to outlaw private discrimination in public accommodations. The Court's opinion in the *Civil Rights Cases* provided a moral reinforcement for the Jim Crow system. Southern states viewed the Court's ruling as an invitation to gut the reach and intent of the Thirteenth, Fourteenth, and Fifteenth Amendments.

In devising ways to make certain that African Americans did not vote, southern states had to sidestep the intent of the Fifteenth Amendment. This amendment did not guarantee suffrage; it simply said that states could not deny anyone the right to vote on the basis of race or color. To exclude African Americans in a way that seemed racially neutral, southern states used three devices before the 1890s: (1) **poll taxes** (small taxes on the right to vote that often came due when poor African American sharecroppers had the least amount of money on hand); (2) some form of property-owning qualifications; and, (3) "literacy" or "understanding" tests, which allowed local voter registration officials to administer difficult reading-comprehension tests to potential voters whom they did not know. For example, some potential voters were asked to rewrite entire sections of the Constitution by hand as the registrar dictated its text.

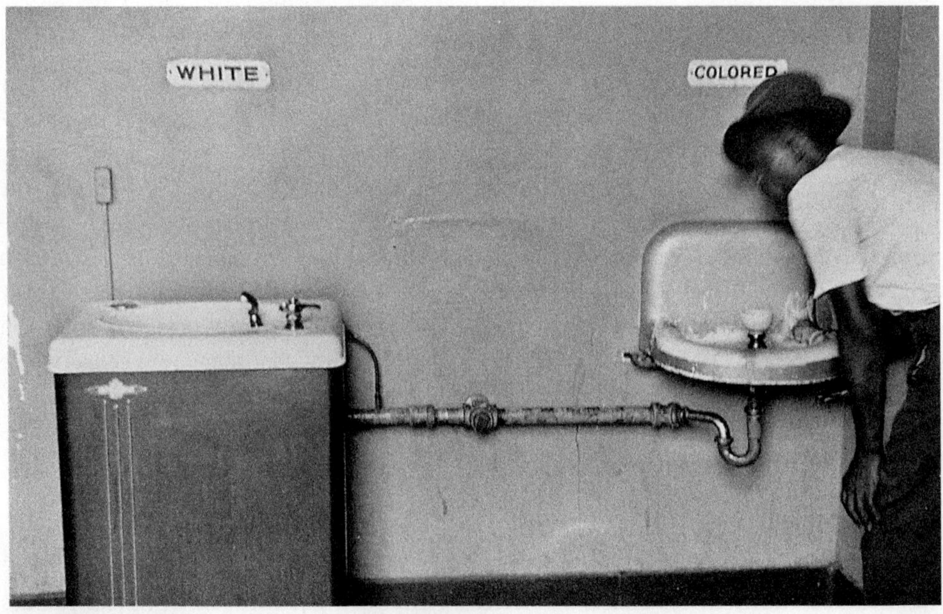

WHAT DID JIM CROW LAWS DO?

Throughout the South, examples of Jim Crow laws abounded. As noted in the text, there were Jim Crow schools, restaurants, hotels, and businesses. Some buildings even had separate "white" and "colored" facilities, such as the public drinking fountains shown here. Notice the obvious difference in quality.

These voting restrictions had an immediate impact. By the late 1890s, black voting fell by 62 percent from the Reconstruction period, while white voting fell by only 26 percent. To make certain these laws did not further reduce the numbers of poor or uneducated white voters, many southern states added a **grandfather clause** to their voting qualification provisions, granting voting privileges to those citizens who failed to pass a wealth or literacy test only if their grandfathers had voted before Reconstruction. Grandfather clauses effectively denied the descendents of slaves the right to vote.

grandfather clause
Voter qualification provision in many southern states that allowed only those citizens whose grandfathers had voted before Reconstruction to vote unless they passed a wealth or literacy test.

***Plessy* v. *Ferguson* (1896)**
Supreme Court case that challenged a Louisiana statute requiring that railroads provide separate accommodations for blacks and whites. The Court found that separate-but-equal accommodations did not violate the equal protection clause of the Fourteenth Amendment.

5.1
5.2
5.3
5.4
5.5
5.6

The Push for Equality, 1890–1954

5.2 Outline developments in African Americans' and women's push for equality from 1890 to 1954.

The Progressive era (1890–1920) was characterized by a concerted effort to reform political, economic, and social affairs. Evils such as child labor, the concentration of economic power in the hands of a few industrialists, limited suffrage, political corruption, business monopolies, and prejudice against African Americans all were targets of progressive reform. Distress over the inferior legal status of African Americans increased with the U.S. Supreme Court's decision in ***Plessy* v. *Ferguson* (1896),** a case that some commentators point to as the Court's darkest hour.[3]

In 1892, a group of African Americans in Louisiana decided to test the constitutionality of a Louisiana law mandating racial segregation on all public trains. This meant that certain undesirable cars at the rear of the train were reserved for blacks. They convinced Homer Plessy, a man who was one-eighth black, to board a train in New Orleans and proceed to the "whites only" car.[4] He was arrested when he refused to take a seat in the car reserved for African Americans, as required by state law. Plessy challenged the law, arguing that the Fourteenth Amendment prohibited racial segregation.

The Supreme Court disagreed. After analyzing the history of African Americans in the United States, the majority concluded that the Louisiana law was constitutional. The justices based the decision on their belief that separate facilities for blacks and whites provided equal protection of the laws. After all, they reasoned, the Louisiana statute did not prevent Plessy from riding the train; it required only that the races travel separately. Justice John Marshall Harlan was the lone dissenter. He argued that "the Constitution is colorblind" and that it was senseless to hold constitutional a law "which, practically, puts the badge of servitude and degradation upon a large class of our fellow citizens."

Not surprisingly, the separate-but-equal doctrine enunciated in *Plessy* v. *Ferguson* soon came to mean only separate, as new legal avenues to discriminate against African Americans made their way into law throughout the South. The Jim Crow system soon expanded and became a way of life and a rigid social code in the American South. Journalist Juan Williams notes in *Eyes on the Prize:*

> There were Jim Crow schools, Jim Crow restaurants, Jim Crow water fountains, and Jim Crow customs—blacks were expected to tip their hats when they walked past whites, but whites did not have to remove their hats even when they entered a black family's home. Whites were to be called "sir" and "ma'am" by blacks, who in turn were called by their first names by whites. People with white skin were to be given a wide berth on the sidewalk; blacks were expected to step aside meekly.[5]

By 1900, equality for African Americans was far from the promise first offered by the Civil War Amendments. Again and again, the Supreme Court nullified the intent of the amendments and sanctioned racial segregation; southern states avidly followed its lead.[6] Yet, the Supreme Court did take a step toward progress when it ruled that peonage laws, which often affected poor blacks, amounted to debt bondage or indentured servitude and were unconstitutional.[7]

WHY WAS THE NIAGARA MOVEMENT FOUNDED?

W.E.B. Du Bois (second from left in the second row, facing right) is pictured with the other original leaders of the Niagara Movement. This 1905 photo was taken on the Canadian side of Niagara Falls because no hotel on the American side would accommodate the group's African American members. The meeting detailed a list of injustices suffered by African Americans.

The Founding of the National Association for the Advancement of Colored People

In 1909, a handful of individuals active in a variety of progressive causes, including woman suffrage and the fight for better working conditions for women and children, met to discuss the idea of a group devoted to addressing the problems of the "Negro." Major race riots had occurred in several American cities, and progressive reformers were concerned about these outbreaks of violence and the possibility of others. Oswald Garrison Villard, the influential publisher of the *New York Evening Post*—and the grandson of William Lloyd Garrison—called a conference to discuss the matter. This group soon evolved into the National Association for the Advancement of Colored People (NAACP). Along with Villard, its first leaders included W.E.B. Du Bois, a founder of the Niagara Movement, a group of African American intellectuals who took their name from their first meeting place, in Niagara Falls, Ontario, Canada.

Key Woman's Groups

The struggle for woman's rights was revitalized in 1890, when the National and American Woman Suffrage Associations merged. The new organization, the National American Woman Suffrage Association (NAWSA), was headed by Susan B. Anthony.

Unlike NWSA, which had sought a wide variety of expanded rights for women, this new association largely devoted itself to securing woman suffrage. The proliferation of woman's groups during the Progressive era greatly facilitated its task. In addition to the rapidly growing temperance movement—whose members pressed to ban the sale of alcohol, which many women blamed for a variety of social ills—woman's groups sprang up to seek goals such as maximum hour or minimum wage laws for women, improved sanitation, public morals, and education.

One of the most active groups lobbying on behalf of women during this period was the National Consumers League (NCL), which successfully lobbied the state of Oregon for legislation limiting women to ten hours of work a day. Soon after the law was enacted, Curt Muller was charged with and convicted of employing women more than ten hours a day in his small laundry. When he appealed his conviction to the U.S. Supreme Court, the NCL sought permission from the state to conduct the defense of the statute.

At the urging of NCL attorney and future U.S. Supreme Court Justice Louis Brandeis, NCL members guided by Josephine Goldmark (Brandeis's sister-in-law, whose name also appears on the legal brief submitted to the U.S. Supreme Court) amassed an impressive array of sociological and medical data that were incorporated into what became known as the Brandeis brief. This document contained only three pages of legal argument. More than a hundred pages were devoted to nonlegal, sociological data used to convince the Court that Oregon's statute was constitutional. In agreeing with the NCL in *Muller* v. *Oregon* (1908), the Court relied heavily on these data to document women's unique status and to justify their differential legal treatment. Specifically, the justices argued that long hours at work could impair a woman's reproductive capabilities.[8]

Women seeking suffrage then used reasoning reflecting the Court's opinion in *Muller*. Discarding earlier notions of full equality, NAWSA based its claim to the right to vote largely on the fact that women, as mothers, should be enfranchised. The new woman's movement—called the **suffrage movement** because of its focus on voting rights—soon took on racist and nativist overtones. Suffragists argued that if undereducated African American men and immigrants could vote, why couldn't women?

By 1917, the new woman's movement had more than 2 million members. In 1920, a coalition of woman's groups, led by NAWSA and the newer, more radical National Woman's Party, was able to secure ratification of the **Nineteenth Amendment** to the

suffrage movement
The drive for voting rights for women that took place in the United States from 1890 to 1920.

Nineteenth Amendment
Amendment to the Constitution that guaranteed women the right to vote.

MR. PRESIDENT, HOW LONG MUST WOMEN WAIT FOR LIBERTY?

Members of the National Woman's Party engaged in a number of radical protest tactics in order to win the right to vote. Here, they are shown protesting in front of the White House; eventually, these demonstrators were arrested, jailed, and even force-fed in an attempt to stop their resistance.

Explore on MyPoliSciLab

Are All Forms of Discrimination the Same?

In *Loving* v. *Virginia* (1967), the Supreme Court ruled unconstitutional all laws that restricted marriage based solely on race. Today, a similar debate revolves around marriage for same-sex couples. Public opposition to interracial marriage declined dramatically after the Court's decision — as shown in the 1972 and 1988 data. Has opinion about same-sex marriage changed in a similar way?

"Should Interracial Marriage Be Legal?"

1972

REGION	YES	NO
Northeast	71%	26%
Midwest	61%	35%
South	43%	53%
Rocky Mountains	54%	41%
Pacific Coast	74%	24%

1988

REGION	YES	NO
Northeast	85%	11%
Midwest	76%	21%
South	62%	35%
Rocky Mountains	89%	11%
Pacific Coast	87%	12%

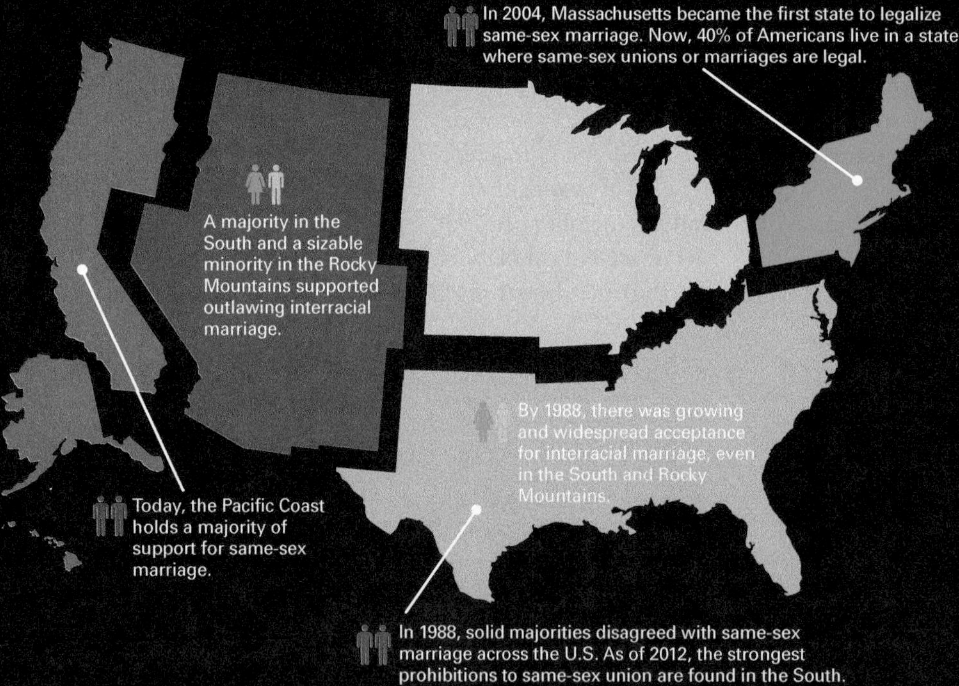

In 2004, Massachusetts became the first state to legalize same-sex marriage. Now, 40% of Americans live in a state where same-sex unions or marriages are legal.
A majority in the South and a sizable minority in the Rocky Mountains supported outlawing interracial marriage.
By 1988, there was growing and widespread acceptance for interracial marriage, even in the South and Rocky Mountains.
Today, the Pacific Coast holds a majority of support for same-sex marriage.
In 1988, solid majorities disagreed with same-sex marriage across the U.S. As of 2012, the strongest prohibitions to same-sex union are found in the South.

"Should Same-Sex Marriage Be Legal?"

1988

REGION	YES	NO
Northeast	12%	63%
Midwest	12%	66%
South	8%	78%
Rocky Mountains	12%	63%
Pacific Coast	16%	62%

2010

REGION	YES	NO
Northeast	54%	30%
Midwest	50%	41%
South	38%	46%
Rocky Mountains	45%	44%
Pacific Coast	52%	33%

SOURCE: General Social Survey data from 1972, 1988, and 2010.

Investigate Further

Concept How do we measure discrimination of interracial and same-sex marriage? Pollsters ask if a person agrees or disagrees with policy proposals, such as laws that recognize same-sex or interracial marriage. By watching the responses over time, we are able to determine change in public opinion.

Connection How does geography help predict public opinion on interracial marriage and same-sex marriage? The American South and Rocky Mountains are historically more conservative regions, and more resistant to changing definitions of marriage. But, even in these regions, opinion on interracial and same-sex marriage has become more liberal over time.

Cause Does opinion about marriage influence policy or vice versa? After the Supreme Court settled the matter of interracial marriage in 1967, public opinion followed suit across the country. Support for same-sex marriage has also changed over time, but policies vary by state. Legalization is more common where public opinion is most favorable, and bans are most common where support lags.

Constitution through rallies, protest marches, and the support of President Woodrow Wilson. The Nineteenth Amendment guaranteed all women the right to vote—fifty years after the Fifteenth Amendment had enfranchised African American males.

After passage of the suffrage amendment in 1920, the fragile alliance of diverse woman's groups that had come together to fight for the vote quickly disintegrated. Women returned to their home groups, such as the NCL or the Woman's Christian Temperance Union, to pursue their individualized goals. In fact, after the tumult of the suffrage movement, organized activity on behalf of women's rights did not reemerge in national politics until the 1960s. In the meantime, the NAACP continued to fight racism and racial segregation. Its activities and those of others in the civil rights movement would later give impetus to a new women's movement.

☐ Litigating for Equality

During the 1930s, leaders of the NAACP began to sense that the time was right to launch a full-scale challenge to the constitutionality of *Plessy*'s separate-but-equal doctrine in the federal courts. Clearly, the separate-but-equal doctrine and the proliferation of Jim Crow laws barred any hope of full equality for African Americans. Traditional legislative channels were unlikely to work, given African Americans' limited or nonexistent political power. Thus, the federal courts and a litigation strategy were the NAACP's only hopes. The NAACP mapped out a long-range plan that would first target segregation in professional and graduate education.

TEST CASES The NAACP opted first to challenge the constitutionality of Jim Crow law schools. In 1935, all southern states maintained fully segregated elementary and secondary schools. Colleges and universities also were segregated, and most states did not provide for postgraduate education for African Americans. NAACP lawyers chose to target law schools because they were institutions that judges could well understand, and integration there would prove less threatening to most whites.

Lloyd Gaines, a graduate of Missouri's all-black Lincoln University, sought admission to the all-white University of Missouri Law School in 1936. The school immediately rejected him. In the separate-but-equal spirit, the state offered to build a law school at Lincoln (although no funds were allocated for the project) or, if he did not want to wait, to pay his tuition at an out-of-state law school. Gaines rejected the offer, sued, lost in the lower courts, and appealed to the U.S. Supreme Court.

The attorneys filed Gaines's case at a promising time. As our discussion of federalism illustrates, a constitutional revolution of sorts occurred in Supreme Court decision making in 1937. Prior to this, the Court was most receptive to, and interested in, the protection of economic liberties. In 1937, however, the Court began to regard the protection of individual freedoms and personal liberties as important issues. Thus, in 1938, Gaines's lawyers pleaded his appeal to a far more sympathetic Supreme Court. NAACP attorneys argued that the creation of a separate law school of a laughable lesser caliber than that of the University of Missouri would not and could not afford Gaines an equal education. The justices agreed and ruled that Missouri had failed to meet the separate-but-equal requirements of *Plessy*. The Court ordered Missouri either to admit Gaines to the school or to set up a law school for him.[9]

Recognizing the importance of the Court's ruling, the NAACP, in 1939, created a separate, tax-exempt legal defense fund to devise a strategy that would build on the Missouri case and bring about equal educational opportunities for all African American children. The first head of the NAACP Legal Defense and Educational Fund, commonly referred to as the LDF, was Thurgood Marshall, who later became the first African American to serve on the U.S. Supreme Court. Sensing that the Court would be more amenable to the NAACP's broader goals if it were first forced to address a variety of less threatening claims to educational opportunity, Marshall and the LDF brought a series of carefully crafted test cases to the Court. These cases attracted attention across the United States and helped to raise the visibility of civil rights issues.

5.1

5.2

5.3

5.4

5.5

5.6

***Brown* v. *Board of Education* (1954)**

U.S. Supreme Court decision holding that school segregation is inherently unconstitutional because it violates the Fourteenth Amendment's guarantee of equal protection.

The first case involved H.M. Sweatt, a forty-six-year-old African American mail carrier who applied for admission to the all-white University of Texas Law School in 1946. Rejected on racial grounds, Sweatt sued. The judge gave the state six months to establish a law school or to admit Sweatt to the university. The state legislature then authorized $3 million for the creation of the Texas State University for Negroes. One hundred thousand dollars of that money was allotted for a new law school in Austin across the street from the state capitol building. It consisted of three small basement rooms, a library of 10,000 books, access to the state law library, and three part-time first-year instructors as the faculty. Sweatt declined the opportunity to attend the substandard university and instead chose to continue his legal challenge.

While working on the Texas case, the LDF also decided to pursue a case involving George McLaurin, a retired university professor who had been denied admission to the doctoral program in education at the University of Oklahoma. Marshall reasoned that McLaurin, at age sixty-eight, would be immune from the charges that African Americans wanted integration so they could intermarry with whites, an act that was illegal in most southern states. After a lower court ordered McLaurin's admission, the university reserved a dingy alcove in the cafeteria for him to eat in during off-hours, and he was given his own table in the library behind a shelf of newspapers. In what surely "was Oklahoma's most inventive contribution to legalized bigotry since the adoption of the 'grandfather clause,'" McLaurin was forced to sit outside classrooms while lectures and seminars were conducted inside.[10]

The Supreme Court handled these two cases together.[11] The eleven southern states filed an *amicus curiae* (friend of the court) brief, in which they argued that *Plessy* should govern both cases. The LDF received assistance, however, from an unexpected source—the U.S. government. In a dramatic departure from the past, President Harry S Truman directed his Department of Justice to file an *amicus* brief urging the Court to overrule *Plessy*. Earlier, Truman had issued an executive order desegregating the military.

Since the late 1870s, the U.S. government never had sided against the southern states in a civil rights matter and never had submitted an *amicus* brief supporting the rights of African American citizens. President Truman believed that because so many African Americans had fought and died for their country in World War II, this kind of executive action was not only proper but honorable as well.

Although the Court did not overrule *Plessy,* the justices found that measures taken by the states in each case failed to live up to the strictures of the separate-but-equal doctrine. The Court unanimously ruled that the remedies to each situation were inadequate to afford a sound education. In the *Sweatt* case, for example, the Court declared that the "qualities which are incapable of objective measurement but which make for greatness in a law school . . . includ[ing] the reputation of the faculty, experience of the administration, position and influence of the alumni, standing in the community, traditions and prestige" made it impossible for the state to provide an equal education in a segregated setting.[12]

In 1950, after the Court had handed down these decisions, the LDF concluded that the time had come to launch a full-scale attack on the separate-but-equal doctrine. The Court's decisions were encouraging, and the position of the U.S. government and the population in general (and especially outside the South) appeared more receptive to an outright overruling of *Plessy.*

BROWN V. BOARD OF EDUCATION ***Brown* v. *Board of Education* (1954)** actually was five cases brought from different areas of the South and border states involving public elementary or high school systems that mandated separate schools for blacks and whites.[13] In *Brown,* LDF lawyers, again led by Thurgood Marshall, argued that the equal protection clause of the Fourteenth Amendment made *Plessy*'s separate-but-equal doctrine unconstitutional, and that if the Court was still reluctant to overrule *Plessy,* the only way to equalize the schools was to integrate them. A major component of the LDF's strategy was to prove that the intellectual, psychological, and financial damage done to African Americans as a result of segregation prevented any court from finding that the separate-but-equal policy was consistent with the intent of the Fourteenth Amendment's equal protection clause.

In *Brown*, the LDF presented the Supreme Court with evidence of the harmful consequences of state-imposed racial discrimination. To buttress its claims, the LDF introduced the now-famous doll study, conducted by Kenneth and Mamie Clark, two prominent African American sociologists who had long studied the negative effects of segregation on African American children. Their research revealed that black children not only preferred white dolls when shown black dolls and white dolls, but that many added that the black doll looked "bad." The LDF attorneys used this information to illustrate the negative impact of racial segregation and bias on an African American child's self-image.

The LDF supported its legal arguments with important *amicus curiae* briefs submitted by the U.S. government, major civil rights groups, labor unions, and religious groups decrying racial segregation. On May 17, 1954, Chief Justice Earl Warren delivered the fourth opinion of the day, *Brown* v. *Board of Education*. Writing for the Court, Warren stated:

> To separate [some school children] from others . . . solely because of their race generates a feeling of inferiority as to their status in the community that may affect their hearts and minds in a way very unlikely ever to be undone. We conclude, unanimously, that in the field of public education the doctrine of "separate but equal" has no place.

Brown was, without doubt, the most important civil rights case decided in the twentieth century.[14] It immediately evoked an uproar that shook the nation. Some segregationists gave the name Black Monday to the day the decision was handed down. The governor of South Carolina denounced the decision, saying, "Ending segregation would mark the beginning of the end of civilization in the South as we know it."[15] The LDF lawyers who had argued these cases, as well as the cases leading to *Brown*, however, were jubilant.

Remarkable changes had occurred in the civil rights of Americans since 1890. Women won the right to vote, and after a long and arduous trail of litigation in the federal courts, the Supreme Court finally overturned its most racist decision of the era, *Plessy* v. *Ferguson*. The Court boldly proclaimed that separate but equal (at least in education) would no longer pass constitutional muster. The question then became how *Brown* would be interpreted and implemented. Could it be used to invalidate other Jim Crow laws and practices? Would African Americans ever be truly equal under the law?

The Civil Rights Movement

5.3 Analyze the civil rights movement and the effects of the Civil Rights Act of 1964.

lthough it did not create immediate legal change, *Brown* served as a catalyst for a civil rights movement across the United States, and especially in the South. The decision emboldened activists and gave them faith that the government might one day change its segregationist policies in all areas of the law.[16]

School Desegregation After *Brown*

One year after *Brown*, in a case referred to as *Brown* v. *Board of Education II* (1955), the Court ruled that racially segregated systems must be dismantled "with all deliberate speed."[17] To facilitate implementation, the Court placed enforcement of *Brown* in the hands of appointed federal district court judges, whom it considered more immune to local political pressures than elected state court judges.

The NAACP and its LDF continued looking to the courts for implementation of *Brown*, while the South entered into a near conspiracy to avoid the mandates of *Brown II*.

WHAT ROLE DID CIVIL DISOBEDIENCE PLAY IN THE CIVIL RIGHTS MOVEMENT?

Here, Rosa Parks is fingerprinted by a Montgomery, Alabama, police officer after her arrest for violating a city law requiring segregation on public buses. Parks refused to give up her seat to accommodate a white man, starting a city-wide bus boycott. Parks is just one of many citizens who engaged in these nonviolent acts of resistance to unjust laws.

In Arkansas, for example, Governor Orval Faubus, who was facing a reelection bid, announced that he would not "be a party to any attempt to force acceptance of change to which people are overwhelmingly opposed."[18] The day before school was to begin, he declared that National Guardsmen would surround Little Rock's Central High School to prevent African American students from entering. While the federal courts in Arkansas continued to order desegregation, the governor remained adamant. Finally, President Dwight D. Eisenhower sent federal troops to Little Rock to protect the rights of the nine African American students attending Central High.

In reaction to the governor's illegal conduct, the Court broke with tradition and issued a unanimous decision in *Cooper* v. *Aaron* (1958), which was filed by the Little Rock School Board and asked the federal district court for a delay of two and one-half years in implementing desegregation plans. Each justice signed the opinion individually, underscoring his own support for the notion that "no state legislator or executive or judicial officer can war against the Constitution without violating his undertaking to support it."[19] The state's actions thus were ruled unconstitutional and its "evasive schemes" illegal.

☐ A New Move for African American Rights

In 1955, soon after *Brown II,* the civil rights movement took another step forward—this time in Montgomery, Alabama. Rosa Parks, the local NAACP's Youth Council adviser, decided to challenge the constitutionality of the segregated bus system. First, Parks and other NAACP officials began to raise money for litigation and made speeches around town to garner public support. Then, on December 1, 1955, Rosa Parks made history when she refused to leave her seat in the front of the colored section of the bus to make room for a white male passenger without a seat. Police arrested her for violating an Alabama law banning integration of public facilities, including buses. After being freed on bond, Parks and the NAACP decided to enlist city clergy to help her cause. At the same time, they distributed 35,000 handbills calling for African Americans to boycott the Montgomery bus system on the day of Parks's trial. Black ministers used Sunday services to urge their members to support the boycott. On

Monday morning, African Americans walked, carpooled, or used black-owned taxicabs. That night, local ministers decided the boycott should continue. A new, twenty-six-year-old minister, the Reverend Martin Luther King Jr., was selected to lead the newly formed Montgomery Improvement Association.

As the boycott dragged on, Montgomery officials and local business owners (who were suffering negative economic consequences) began to harass the city's African American citizens. The black residents held out, despite suffering personal hardship for their actions, ranging from harassment to job loss to bankruptcy. In 1956, a federal court ruled that the segregated bus system violated the equal protection clause of the Fourteenth Amendment. After a year-long boycott, African American Montgomery residents ended their protest when city officials ordered the public transit system to integrate. The first effort at nonviolent protest had been successful. Organized boycotts and other forms of nonviolent protest, including sit-ins at segregated restaurants and bus stations, were to follow.

☐ Formation of New Groups

The recognition and respect earned by the Reverend Martin Luther King Jr. within the African American community helped him launch the Southern Christian Leadership Conference (SCLC) in 1957, soon after the end of the Montgomery Bus Boycott. Unlike the NAACP, which had northern origins and had come to rely largely on litigation as a means of achieving expanded equality, the SCLC had a southern base and was rooted more closely in black religious culture. The SCLC's philosophy reflected King's growing belief in the importance of nonviolent protest and civil disobedience.

On February 1, 1960, a few students from the all-black North Carolina Agricultural and Technical College in Greensboro participated in the first sit-in for civil rights. The students went to a local lunch counter, sat down, and ordered cups of coffee. They were not served, but stayed until closing. After the national wire services picked up the story, over the next several days, the students were joined by hundreds of others from the Greensboro area. When the students refused to leave, the police arrested and jailed them, rather than their white tormentors. Soon thereafter, African American college students around the South did the same. The national media extensively covered their actions.

Over spring break 1960, with the assistance of an $800 grant from the SCLC, 200 student delegates—black and white—met at Shaw University in Raleigh, North Carolina, to consider recent sit-in actions and to plan for the future. Later that year, the Student Nonviolent Coordinating Committee (SNCC) was formed.

Whereas the SCLC generally worked with church leaders in a community, SNCC was much more of a grassroots organization. Always perceived as more radical than the SCLC, SNCC tended to focus its organizing activities on the young, both black and white.

In addition to joining the sit-in bandwagon, SNCC also came to lead what were called freedom rides, designed to shine the spotlight on segregated public accommodations. Bands of college students and other civil rights activists traveled by bus throughout the South in an effort to force bus stations to desegregate. Often these protesters faced angry mobs of segregationists and brutal violence, as local police chose not to defend the protesters' basic constitutional rights to free speech and peaceful assembly. African Americans were not the only ones to participate in freedom rides; increasingly, white college students from the North began to play an important role in SNCC.

While SNCC continued to sponsor sit-ins and freedom rides, in 1963 King launched a series of massive nonviolent demonstrations in Birmingham, Alabama, long considered a major stronghold of segregation. Thousands of blacks and whites marched to Birmingham in a show of solidarity. Peaceful marchers were met there by the Birmingham police commissioner, who ordered his officers to use dogs, clubs, and fire hoses on the marchers. Americans across the nation were horrified as they witnessed on television the brutality and abuse heaped on the protesters. As the marchers had hoped, the shocking scenes helped convince President John F. Kennedy to propose important civil rights legislation.

Take a Closer Look

Throughout history, literature has played a significant role in raising the public's awareness of important civil rights issues. Movements for greater rights for African Americans, women, Hispanics, and American Indians, among others, have all been aided by the power of prose. Although some of these texts were works of fiction, and others nonfiction, all helped to energize and mobilize a growing social movement.

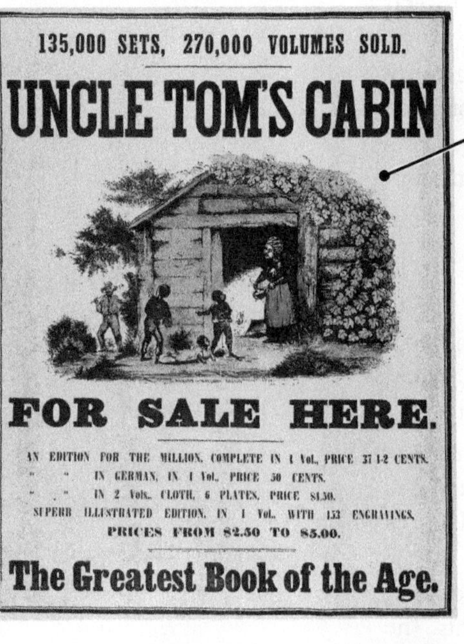

Uncle Tom's Cabin, written by Harriet Beecher Stowe in 1852, is one of the most widely circulated texts of all time. It depicted the realities of slavery, helped to inspire the abolition movement, and was a catalyst for the Civil War.

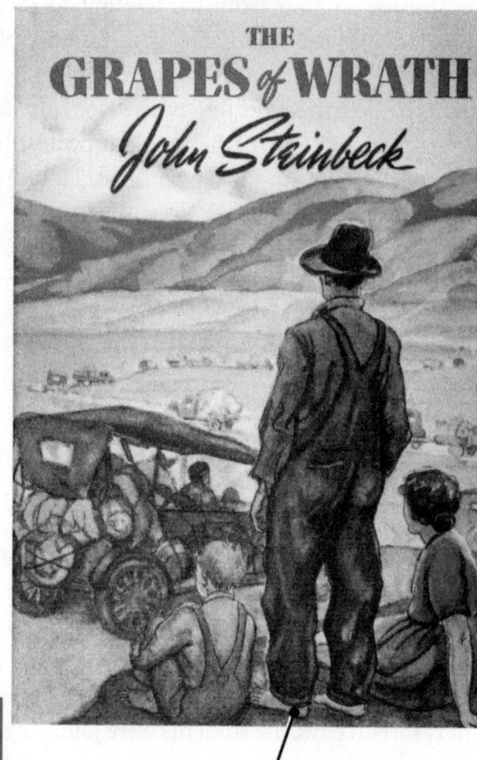

The Grapes of Wrath, written by John Steinbeck in 1939, did not focus on a Hispanic family. However, its story of California tenant farmers struggling to survive resonated with many Hispanic rights activists and helped to motivate movements for farm workers' rights.

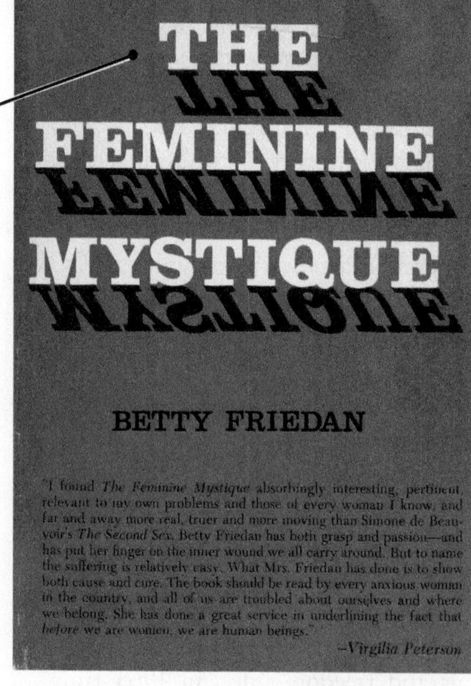

Betty Friedan's *The Feminine Mystique* was first published in 1963. It played an important role in helping housewives and other women realize that they were not alone in their feelings of discontent. As a result, it served as one of the inspirations for the 1960's women's movement.

CRITICAL THINKING QUESTIONS

1. How do the visuals of these texts depict the plight and despair faced by minority groups?
2. What other texts have been significant in mobilizing social and political change for disadvantaged groups? How are they similar to and different from the books shown here?
3. Why do you think literature has been so effective in mobilizing citizens for social change? What does writing add that everyday life cannot? How will the Internet change this?

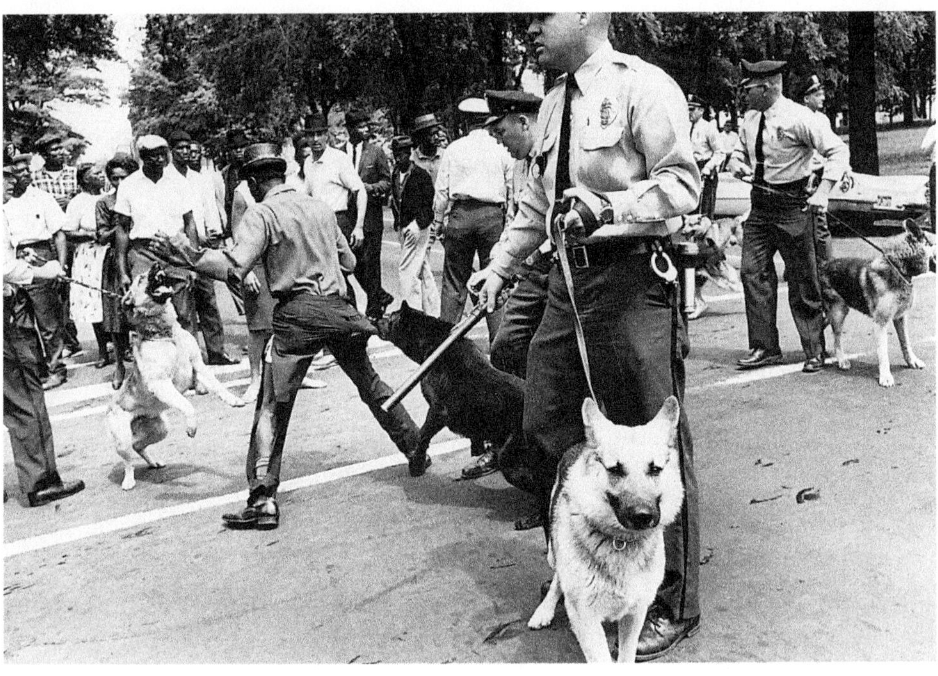

WHEN IS A PICTURE WORTH MORE THAN A THOUSAND WORDS?

During the spring of 1963, civil rights demonstrators descended on Birmingham, Alabama, to challenge racial segregation. This famous photograph of menacing German Shepherds "controlled" by local police, yet attacking citizens, was taken in May 1963. It was frequently reprinted and also discussed on the floor of Congress during debates over the Civil Rights Act of 1964.

The Civil Rights Act of 1964

Both the SCLC and SNCC sought full implementation of U.S. Supreme Court decisions dealing with race and an end to racial segregation and discrimination. The cumulative effect of collective actions including sit-ins, boycotts, marches, and freedom rides—as well as the tragic bombings, lynchings, and other deaths inflicted in retaliation—led Congress to pass the first major piece of civil rights legislation since the post–Civil War era, the Civil Rights Act of 1964, followed the next year by the Voting Rights Act of 1965. Several events led to consideration of the two pieces of legislation.

In 1963, President John F. Kennedy requested that Congress pass a law banning discrimination in public accommodations. Seizing the moment, the Reverend Martin Luther King Jr. called for a monumental march on Washington, D.C., to demonstrate widespread support for far-ranging anti-discrimination legislation. It was clear that national legislation outlawing discrimination was the only answer: southern legislators would never vote to repeal Jim Crow laws. The March on Washington for Jobs and Freedom was held in August 1963, only a few months after the Birmingham demonstrations. More than 250,000 people heard King deliver his famous "I Have a Dream" speech from the Lincoln Memorial. Before Congress had the opportunity to vote on any legislation, however, President Kennedy was assassinated on November 22, 1963, in Dallas, Texas.

When Vice President Lyndon B. Johnson, a southern-born, former Senate majority leader, succeeded Kennedy as president, he put civil rights reform at the top of his legislative priority list, and civil rights activists gained a critical ally. Thus, through the 1960s, the movement subtly changed its focus from peaceful protest and litigation to legislative lobbying. Its scope broadened from integration of school and public facilities and voting rights to preventing housing and job discrimination and alleviating poverty.

Changes in public opinion helped the push for civil rights legislation in the halls of Congress. Between 1959 and 1965, southern attitudes toward integrated schools changed enormously. The proportion of Southerners who responded that they would not mind their child's attendance at a racially balanced school doubled.

Civil Rights Act of 1964
Wide-ranging legislation passed by Congress to outlaw segregation in public facilities and discrimination in employment, education, and voting; created the Equal Employment Opportunity Commission.

***de jure* discrimination**
Racial segregation that is a direct result of law or official policy.

***de facto* discrimination**
Racial discrimination that results from practice (such as housing patterns or other social or institutional, nongovernmental factors) rather than the law.

In spite of strong presidential support and the sway of public opinion, the Civil Rights Act of 1964 did not sail through Congress. Southern senators, led by South Carolina's Strom Thurmond, a Democrat who later switched to the Republican Party, conducted the longest filibuster in the history of the Senate. For eight weeks, Thurmond led the effort to hold up voting on the civil rights bill. Once passed, the **Civil Rights Act of 1964:**

- Outlawed arbitrary discrimination in voter registration and expedited voting rights lawsuits.
- Barred discrimination in public accommodations engaged in interstate commerce.
- Authorized the Department of Justice to initiate lawsuits to desegregate public facilities and schools.
- Provided for the withholding of federal funds from discriminatory state and local programs.
- Prohibited discrimination in employment on grounds of race, creed, color, religion, national origin, or sex.
- Created the Equal Employment Opportunity Commission (EEOC) to monitor and enforce the bans on employment discrimination.

As practices thought to be in violation of the law continued, other changes continued to sweep the United States. African Americans in the North, who believed that their brothers and sisters in the South were making progress against discrimination, found themselves frustrated. Northern blacks, too, were experiencing high unemployment, poverty, and discrimination, and had little political clout. Some, including African American Muslim leader Malcolm X, even argued that, to survive, African Americans must separate themselves from white culture in every way. These increased tensions resulted in violent race riots in many major cities from 1964 to 1968, when many African Americans in the North took to the streets, burning and looting to vent their rage. The assassination of the Reverend Martin Luther King Jr. in 1968 triggered a new epidemic of race riots.

Statutory Remedies for Race Discrimination

Many Southerners adamantly believed that the Civil Rights Act of 1964 was unconstitutional because it went beyond the scope of Congress's authority to legislate under the Constitution, and they quickly brought lawsuits to challenge its scope. In 1964, on expedited review, the Supreme Court upheld its constitutionality, finding that Congress had operated within the legitimate scope of its commerce power as outlined in Article I.[20]

EDUCATION One of the key provisions of the Civil Rights Act of 1964 authorized the Department of Justice to bring actions against school districts that failed to comply with *Brown* v. *Board of Education*. By 1964, a full decade after *Brown,* fewer than 1 percent of African American children in the South attended integrated schools.

In *Swann* v. *Charlotte-Mecklenburg School District* (1971), the Supreme Court ruled that all vestiges of state-imposed segregation, called ***de jure* discrimination,** or discrimination by law, must be eliminated at once. The Court also ruled that lower federal courts had the authority to fashion a wide variety of remedies, including busing, racial quotas, and the pairing of schools, to end dual, segregated school systems.[21]

In *Swann,* the Court was careful to distinguish *de jure* from ***de facto* discrimination,** which is discrimination that results from practice, such as housing patterns or private acts, rather than the law. The Court noted that its approval of busing was a remedy for intentional, government-imposed or -sanctioned discrimination only.

Over the years, forced, judicially imposed busing found less and less favor with the Supreme Court, even in situations where *de jure* discrimination had existed. In 2007, in a contentious 5–4 opinion, the Supreme Court abolished the use of voluntary school desegregation plans based on race.[22]

EMPLOYMENT Title VII of the Civil Rights Act of 1964 prohibits employers from discriminating against employees for a variety of reasons, including race, sex, age, and national origin. (In 1978, the act was amended to bar discrimination based on pregnancy.) In 1971, in one of the first major cases decided under the act, the Supreme Court ruled that employers could be found liable for discrimination if their employment practices had the effect of excluding African Americans from certain positions.[23] The Court allowed African American employees to use statistical evidence showing the Duke Power Company had excluded them from all but one department, because it required employees to have a high school education or pass a special test to be eligible for promotion.

The Supreme Court ruled that although the tests did not appear to discriminate against African Americans, their effects—that no African American employees were in any other departments—were sufficient to shift to the employer the burden of proving that no discrimination occurred. Thus, the Duke Power Company would have to prove that the tests were a business necessity that had a "demonstrable relationship to successful performance" of a particular job.

The notion of "business necessity," as set out in the Civil Rights Act of 1964 and interpreted by the federal courts, had special importance for women. They had long been kept out of many occupations on the strength of the belief that customers preferred to deal with male personnel. Conversely, because airlines believed that passengers preferred being served by young, attractive women, they barred males from flight-attendant positions. Similarly, many large factories, manufacturing establishments, and police and fire departments avoided hiring women by subjecting them to arbitrary height and weight requirements. Like the tests declared illegal by the Court, a relation between these requirements and job performance often could not be shown, and the federal courts eventually ruled them illegal.

The Women's Rights Movement

5.4 Assess statutory and constitutional remedies for discrimination pursued and achieved by the women's rights movement.

As in the abolition movement of the 1800s, women from all walks of life participated in the civil rights movement. Women were important members of new groups such as SNCC and the SCLC, as well as more traditional groups such as the NAACP, yet they often found themselves treated as second-class citizens. At one point during an SNCC national meeting, its male chair proclaimed: "The only position for women in SNCC is prone."[24] Statements and attitudes such as these led some women to found early women's liberation groups that generally were quite radical but small in membership. Others established more traditional groups, such as the National Organization for Women (NOW).

Three key events helped to forge a new movement for women's rights in the early 1960s. In 1961, soon after his election, President John F. Kennedy created the President's Commission on the Status of Women, headed by former First Lady Eleanor Roosevelt. The commission's report, *American Women,* released in 1963, documented pervasive discrimination against women in all areas of life. In addition, the civil rights movement and the publication of Betty Friedan's *The Feminine Mystique* (1963), which led some women to question their lives and status in society, enhanced many women's dawning recognition that something was wrong.[25] Soon after, the Civil Rights Act of 1964 prohibited discrimination based not only on race but also on sex. Ironically, southern Democrats had added that provision to Title VII of the act. These senators saw a prohibition against sex discrimination in employment as a joke, and viewed its addition as a means to discredit the entire act and ensure its defeat. Thus, it was added at the last minute, and female members of Congress seized the opportunity to garner additional support for the measure.

Equal Rights Amendment
Proposed amendment to the Constitution that states "Equality of rights under the law shall not be denied or abridged by the United States or any state on account of sex."

In 1966, after the Equal Employment Opportunity Commission failed to enforce the law as it applied to sex discrimination, female activists formed the National Organization for Women. NOW was modeled closely after the NAACP. Its founders sought to work within the political system to prevent discrimination. Initially, they directed most of this activity toward two goals: achievement of equality either by passage of an equal rights amendment to the Constitution or by judicial decisions intended to broaden the scope of the equal protection clause of the Fourteenth Amendment.

□ The Equal Rights Amendment

Not all women agreed with the concept of full equality for women. Members of the National Consumers League, for example, feared that an equal rights amendment would invalidate protective legislation of the kind specifically ruled constitutional in *Muller* v. *Oregon* (1908). Nevertheless, from 1923 to 1972, a proposal for an equal rights amendment was made in every session of every Congress. Every president between Harry S Truman and Richard M. Nixon backed it, and by 1972 public opinion favored its ratification.

Finally, in 1972, in response to pressure from NOW, the National Women's Political Caucus, and a wide variety of other feminist groups, Congress voted in favor of the **Equal Rights Amendment** (ERA) by overwhelming majorities (84–8 in the Senate; 354–24 in the House). The amendment provided that:

> Equality of rights under the law shall not be denied or abridged by the United States or by any state on account of sex.
>
> The Congress shall have the power to enforce, by appropriate legislation, the provisions of this article.

Within a year, twenty-two states ratified the amendment, most by overwhelming margins, but the tide soon turned. In *Roe* v. *Wade* (1973), the Supreme Court decided that women had a constitutionally protected right to privacy that included the right to terminate a pregnancy. Almost overnight, *Roe* provided the ERA's opponents with political fuel. Although privacy rights and the ERA have nothing to do with each other, opponents effectively persuaded many people in states that had yet to ratify the amendment that the two were linked. They also claimed that the ERA and feminists were anti-family and that the ERA would force women out of their homes and into the workforce because husbands would no longer be responsible for supporting their wives financially.

These arguments and the amendment's potential to make women eligible for the unpopular military draft brought the ratification effort to a near standstill. In 1974 and 1975, the amendment only squeaked through the Montana and North Dakota legislatures, and two states—Nebraska and Tennessee—voted to rescind their earlier ratifications. By 1978, one year before the expiration deadline for ratification, thirty-five states had voted for the amendment—three short of the three-fourths necessary for ratification. Efforts in key states such as Illinois and Florida failed as opposition to the ERA intensified. Faced with the prospect of defeat, ERA supporters heavily lobbied Congress to extend the deadline for ratification. Congress extended the ratification period by three years, but to no avail. No additional states ratified the amendment, and three more rescinded their votes.

What began as a simple correction to the Constitution turned into a highly controversial proposed change. Even though large percentages of the public favored the ERA, opponents needed to stall ratification in only thirteen states, while supporters had to convince legislators in thirty-eight. Ironically, the success of women's rights activists in the courts was hurting the effort. When women first sought the ERA in the late 1960s, the Supreme Court had yet to rule that women were protected from any kind of discrimination by the Fourteenth Amendment's equal protection clause, thus highlighting the need for an amendment. But, as the Court widened its interpretation of the Constitution to protect women from some sorts of discrimination, many felt the

Explore Your World

Good fences make good neighbors, or so the adage goes. Throughout history, many countries have adopted this perspective. Beginning in the seventh century B.C., for example, China fortified its borders by constructing the Great Wall. And, following World War II, Germans built the Berlin Wall to divide the city of Berlin into East (communist) and West (democratic). Today, many politicians call for the construction of a "fence" or a "wall" between the United States and Mexico to stem illegal immigration and drug trafficking. Building a fence, however, poses a dilemma; although it may increase domestic security, it may also strain relations with allies around the world.

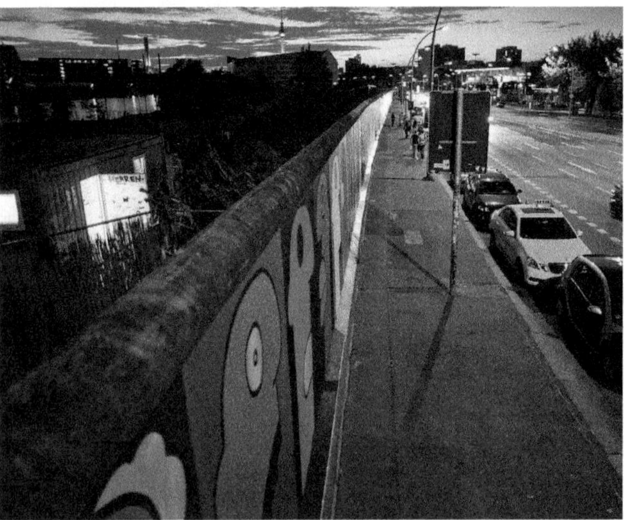

This photo of the Berlin Wall, taken after the reunification of Germany, illustrates the lasting effects of the division of the German capital. Note the contrast between the vibrancy of the West and the desertion of the East.

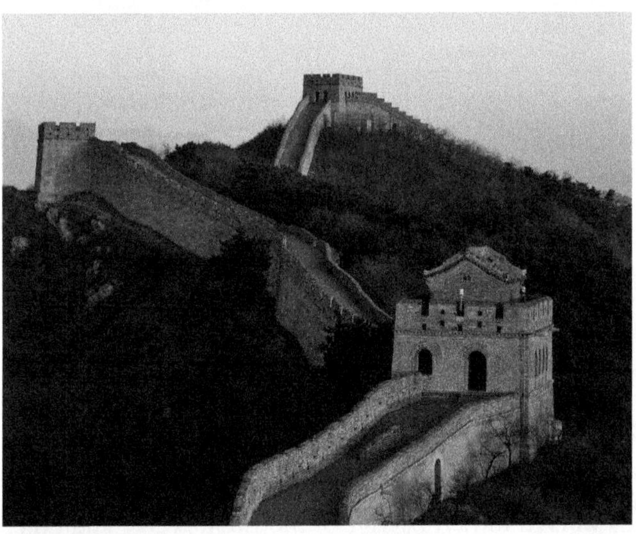

Construction on the Great Wall of China began as early as 700 B.C. It extends for more than 13,000 miles along the border of China and Mongolia.

This photo illustrates a small section of the fence between the United States and Mexico in the American Southwest. The fence remains an ongoing debate; more than 300 miles of fence have been constructed in California, Arizona, and New Mexico. Work continues in these states, as well as Texas.

CRITICAL THINKING QUESTIONS

1. What similarities do you see between the walls or fences depicted here? What important differences do you observe?
2. Does each of these walls have the same implications for domestic and foreign policy? Why or why not?
3. Is a border fence constitutional? What combination of physical boundaries and legal constraints should the United States use to protect its borders from illegal immigrants? What about the civil rights of immigrants?

5.1
5.2
5.3
5.4
5.5
5.6

suspect classification
Category or class, such as race, that triggers the highest standard of scrutiny from the Supreme Court.

strict scrutiny
A heightened standard of review used by the Supreme Court to determine the constitutional validity of a challenged practice.

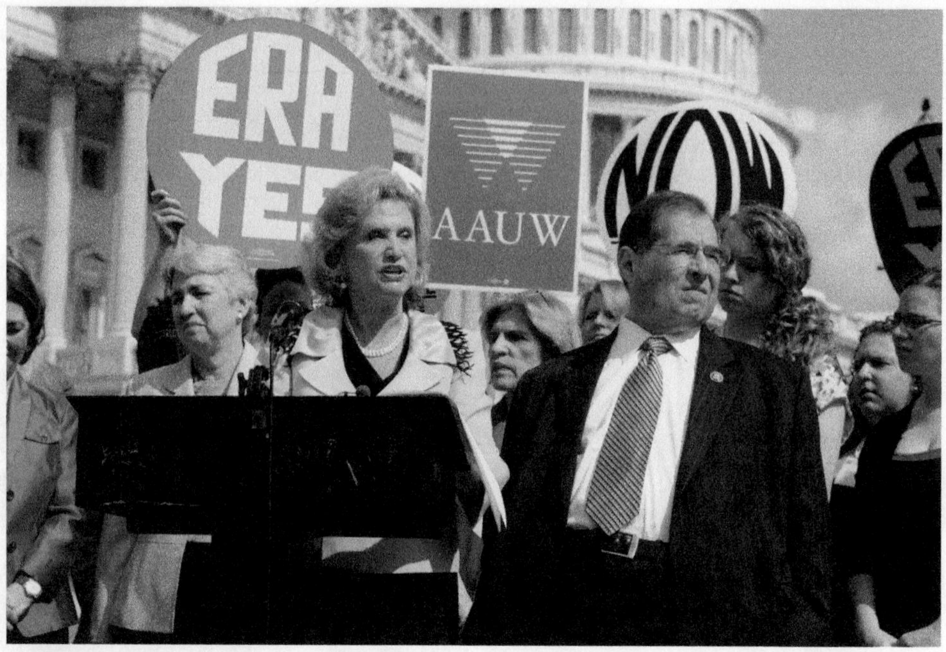

WHO CONTINUES TO FIGHT FOR THE ERA?

Members of Congress led by Representative Carolyn Maloney (D–NY) have reintroduced the Equal Rights Amendment in all recent sessions of Congress. Here, Representative Maloney (at the podium), her bipartisan co-sponsors, and women's group leaders, hold a press conference announcing the reintroduction of the ERA in the 111th Congress.

need for a new amendment was less urgent. The proposed amendment died without ratification on June 30, 1982. Since 1982, the amendment has been reintroduced in every session of Congress.

□ The Equal Protection Clause and Constitutional Standards of Review

While several women's groups worked toward passage of the ERA, NOW and other groups, including the American Civil Liberties Union (ACLU), formed litigating arms to pressure the courts. But, women faced an immediate roadblock in the Supreme Court's interpretation of the equal protection clause of the Fourteenth Amendment.

The Fourteenth Amendment protects all U.S. citizens from state action that violates equal protection of the laws. Most laws, though, are subject to what is called the rational basis or minimum rationality test. This lowest level of scrutiny means that governments must show a rational foundation for any distinctions they make. As early as 1937, however, the Supreme Court recognized that certain freedoms were so fundamental that a very heavy burden would fall on any government seeking to restrict those rights. When fundamental freedoms such as those guaranteed by the First Amendment or **suspect classifications** such as race are involved, the Court uses a heightened standard of review called **strict scrutiny** to determine the constitutional validity of the challenged practices, as detailed in Table 5.1.

Beginning with *Korematsu* v. *U.S.* (1944), which involved a constitutional challenge to the internment of Japanese Americans as security risks during World War II, Justice Hugo Black noted that "all legal restrictions which curtail the civic rights of a single racial group are immediately suspect," and should be given "the most rigid scrutiny."[26] In *Brown* v. *Board of Education* (1954), the Supreme Court again used the strict scrutiny standard to evaluate the constitutionality of race-based distinctions. In legal terms, this means that if a statute or governmental practice makes a classification based on race, the statute is presumed to be unconstitutional unless the state can provide "compelling affirmative justifications"—that is, unless the state can prove that the law in question is necessary to accomplish a permissible goal and that it is the least restrictive means of accomplishing that goal. (In *Korematsu*,

TABLE 5.1 WHAT ARE THE STANDARDS OF REVIEW FASHIONED BY THE COURT UNDER THE EQUAL PROTECTION CLAUSE?

Type of Classification: *What kind of statutory classification is at issue?*	**Standard of Review:** *What standard of review will be used?*	**Test:** *What does the Court ask?*	**Example:** *How does the Court apply the test?*
Fundamental freedoms (including religion, speech, assembly, press), suspect classifications (including race, alienage, and national origin)	Strict scrutiny or heightened standard	Is the classification necessary to the accomplishment of a permissible state goal? Is it the least restrictive way to reach that goal?	*Brown* v. *Board of Education* (1954): Racial segregation not necessary to accomplish the state's goal of educating its students.
Gender	Intermediate standard	Does the classification serve an important governmental objective, and is it substantially related to those ends?	*Craig* v. *Boren* (1976): Keeping drunk drivers off the roads may be an important governmental objective, but allowing eighteen- to twenty-one-year-old women to drink alcoholic beverages while prohibiting men of the same age from drinking is not substantially related to that goal.
Others (including age, wealth, mental capacity, and sexual orientation)	Minimum rationality standard	Is there any rational foundation for the discrimination?	*Romer* v. *Evans* (1996): Colorado state constitutional amendment denying equal rights to homosexuals is unconstitutional.

the Court concluded that the national risks posed by Japanese Americans, Italian Americans, and German Americans were sufficient to justify their internment.)

During the 1960s and into the 1970s, the Court routinely struck down as unconstitutional practices and statutes that discriminated on the basis of race. The Court ruled that "whites-only" public parks and recreational facilities, tax-exempt status for private schools that discriminated, and statutes prohibiting interracial marriage were unconstitutional. In contrast, the Court refused to consider whether the equal protection clause might apply to discrimination against women. Finally, in a case argued in 1971 by Ruth Bader Ginsburg (later an associate justice of the Supreme Court) as director of the Women's Rights Project of the ACLU, the Supreme Court ruled that an Idaho law granting a male parent automatic preference over a female parent as the administrator of their deceased child's estate violated the equal protection clause of the Fourteenth Amendment. *Reed* v. *Reed* (1971), the Idaho case, turned the tide in terms of constitutional litigation. Although the Court did not rule that sex was a suspect classification, it concluded that the equal protection clause of the Fourteenth Amendment prohibited unreasonable classifications based on sex.[27]

In 1976, the Court ruled that sex discrimination complaints would be judged according to a new, judicially created intermediate standard of review a step below strict scrutiny.[28] In *Craig* v. *Boren* (1976), the Court carved out a new test for examining claims of sex discrimination alleged to violate the U.S. Constitution: "to withstand constitutional challenge, . . . classifications by gender must serve important governmental objectives and must be substantially related to achievement of those objectives." According to the Court, it created an intermediate standard of review within what previously was a two-tier distinction—strict scrutiny and rational basis.

Men, too, can use the Fourteenth Amendment to fight gender-based discrimination. Since 1976, the Court has applied the intermediate standard of constitutional review to most claims involving gender that it has heard. Thus, the Court has found the following practices in violation of the Fourteenth Amendment:

- Single-sex public nursing schools.[29]
- Laws that consider males adults at twenty-one years but females adults at eighteen years.[30]
- Laws that allow women, but not men, to receive alimony.[31]
- State prosecutors' use of peremptory challenges to reject male or female potential jurors to create more sympathetic juries.[32]
- Virginia's maintenance of an all-male military college, the Virginia Military Institute.[33]

5.1

5.2

5.3

5.4

5.5

5.6

Equal Pay Act of 1963
Legislation that requires employers to pay men and women equal pay for equal work.

In contrast, the Court has upheld the following governmental practices and laws:

- Draft registration provisions for males only.[34]
- State statutory rape laws that apply only to female victims.[35]
- Different requirements for a child's acquisition of citizenship based on whether the citizen parent is a mother or a father.[36]

The level of review used by the Court is crucial. Clearly, a statute excluding African Americans from draft registration would be unconstitutional. But, because gender is not subject to the same higher standard of review used in racial discrimination cases, the Court ruled the exclusion of women from requirements of the Military Selective Service Act permissible because it considered the government policy to serve "important governmental objectives."[37]

This history perhaps clarifies why women's rights activists continue to argue that until the passage of the Equal Rights Amendment, women will never enjoy the same rights as men. An amendment would raise the level of scrutiny applied by the Court to gender-based claims, although indications are clear that the Supreme Court of late favors requiring states to meet a tougher test than *Craig* and show "exceedingly persuasive justifications" for their actions.[38]

☐ Statutory Remedies for Sex Discrimination

In part because of the limits of the intermediate standard of review and the fact that the equal protection clause applies only to governmental discrimination, women's rights activists began to look for statutory solutions to discrimination. The **Equal Pay Act of 1963,** the first such piece of legislation, requires employers to pay women and men equal pay for equal work. Women have won important victories under the act, but a large wage gap between women and men continues to exist, even beginning with the first paycheck issued to men and women with equal jobs, education, and experience. Women's earnings in 2012 equaled about 75 to 80 percent of men's earnings, depending on location and occupation.

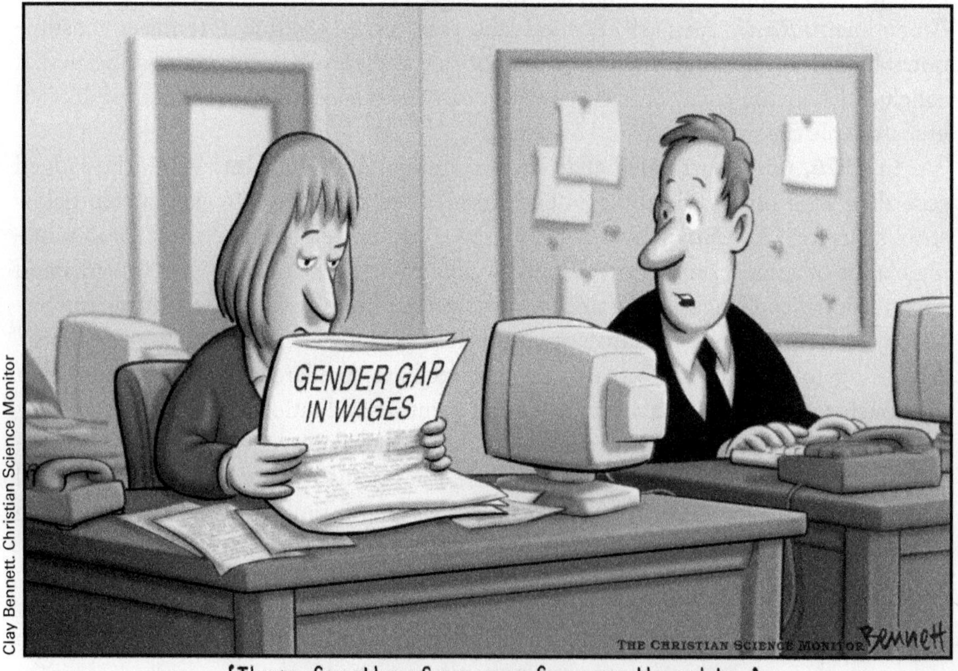

Clay Bennett. Christian Science Monitor

WHAT ARE THE PRACTICAL CONSEQUENCES OF PAY EQUITY?

This cartoon pokes fun at a serious issue in gender equality: pay equity. In 2012, women earned between 75 and 80 cents for every $1.00 earned by their similarly situated male counterparts.

In 2007, the U.S. Supreme Court tested the boundaries of the Equal Pay Act. The justices heard the case of Lilly Ledbetter, the lone female supervisor at a Goodyear tire factory in Alabama. Ledbetter charged that sex discrimination throughout her career had led her to earn substantially less than her male counterparts. In a 5–4 decision, the Court ruled that Ledbetter and other women could not seek redress of grievances under the provisions of the Equal Pay Act for discrimination that had occurred over a period of years. Justice Ruth Bader Ginsburg, the only woman on the Court at the time, took the uncommon action of reading her dissent from the bench. Speaking for herself and Justices David Souter, John Paul Stevens, and Stephen Breyer, she angrily noted, "In our view, the court does not comprehend, or is indifferent to, the insidious way in which women can be victims of pay discrimination."[39] In 2009, the first official act of President Barack Obama was to sign the Lilly Ledbetter Fair Pay Act, which overruled the Court's decision bearing her name.

Title IX
Provision of the Education Amendments of 1972 that bars educational institutions that receive federal funds from discriminating against female students.

Another important piece of legislation is Title VII of the Civil Rights Act of 1964, which prohibits gender discrimination by private (and, after 1972, public) employers. Much litigation has focused on this act, too. Key victories under Title VII include:

- Consideration of sexual harassment as sex discrimination.[40]
- Inclusion of law firms, which many argued were private partnerships, in the coverage of the act.[41]
- A broad definition of what can be considered sexual harassment, including same-sex harassment.[42]
- Allowance of voluntary programs to redress historical discrimination against women.[43]

Finally, **Title IX** of the Education Amendments of 1972 bars educational institutions that receive federal funds from discriminating against female students. Title IX, which parallels Title VII, greatly expanded the opportunities for women in elementary, secondary, and postsecondary institutions. Most of today's college students do not go through school being excluded from home economics or technology education classes because of their sex. Nor, probably do many attend schools that have no team sports for females. Yet, this was commonly the case in the United States prior to passage of Title IX.[44] Nevertheless, sport facilities, access to premium playing times, and quality equipment remain unequal in many high schools and colleges. Major rulings by the U.S. Supreme Court that uphold the provisions of Title IX include:

- Holding school boards or districts responsible for both student-on-student harassment and harassment of students by teachers.[45]
- Allowing retaliatory lawsuits by coaches on behalf of their sports teams denied equal treatment by school boards.[46]

Other Groups Mobilize for Rights

5.5 Describe how other groups have mobilized in pursuit of their own civil rights.

African Americans and women are not the only groups that have suffered unequal treatment under the law. Denial of civil rights has led other disadvantaged groups to mobilize. Their efforts parallel in many ways the efforts made by African Americans and women. Not only did popular books galvanize some groups, many also recognized that litigation and the use of test-case strategies would be key to further civil rights gains. Others have opted for more direct, traditional forms of activism.

5.1

5.2

5.3

5.4

5.5

5.6

□ Hispanic Americans

Hispanics are the largest minority group in the United States. But, Hispanic population growth in the United States is not a new phenomenon. In 1910, the Mexican Revolution forced Mexicans seeking safety and employment into the United States. And, in 1916, New Mexico entered the union officially as a bilingual state—the only one in the United States.

Early Hispanic immigrants, many of whom were from families who had owned land when parts of the Southwest were still under Mexico's control, formed the League of United Latin American Citizens (LULAC) in 1929. LULAC continues to be the largest Hispanic organization in the United States, with local councils in every state and Puerto Rico. Hispanics returning home from fighting in World War II also formed the American G.I. Forum in Texas to fight discrimination and improve their legal status.

As large numbers of immigrants from Mexico and Puerto Rico entered the United States, they quickly became a source of cheap labor, with Mexicans initially tending to settle in the Southwest, where they most frequently found employment as migratory farm workers, and Puerto Ricans mainly moving to New York City. Both groups gravitated to their own neighborhoods, where life revolved around the Roman Catholic Church and the customs of their homeland, and both groups largely lived in poverty. Still, in 1954, the same year as *Brown,* Hispanics won a major victory when, in *Hernandez* v. *Texas,* the Supreme Court struck down discrimination based on race and ethnicity.[47] In *Hernandez,* the Court ruled unanimously that Mexican Americans had the right to a jury that included other Mexican Americans.

A push for greater Hispanic rights began in the mid-1960s, just as a wave of Cuban immigrants started to establish homes in Florida, dramatically altering the political and social climate of Miami and neighboring towns and cities in South Florida. This new movement, marked by the establishment of the National Council of La Raza in 1968, incorporated many tactics drawn from the African American civil rights movement, including sit-ins, boycotts, marches, and other activities designed to heighten publicity for their cause. In one earlier example, in 1965, Cesar Chavez and Dolores Huerta organized migrant workers into the United Farm Workers Union, which would become the largest such union in the nation, and led them in a strike against produce growers in California. Organizers eventually coupled this strike with a national boycott of various farm products, including lettuce and grapes. After several years, declining sales led producers to give in to some of the workers' demands.

Hispanics also have relied heavily on litigation to secure legal change. Key groups are the Mexican American Legal Defense and Educational Fund (MALDEF) and the Puerto Rican Legal Defense and Education Fund (renamed LatinoJustice PRLDEF). MALDEF began its life in 1968 after members of LULAC met with NAACP LDF leaders and, with their assistance, secured a $2.2-million start-up grant from the Ford Foundation. The founders of MALDEF originally created it to bring test cases before the Supreme Court with the intent to force school districts to allocate more funds to schools with predominantly low-income minority populations, to implement bilingual education programs, to require employers to hire Hispanics, and to challenge election rules and apportionment plans that undercount or dilute Hispanic voting power.

MALDEF has been successful in expanding voting rights and electoral opportunities to Hispanic Americans under the Voting Rights Act of 1965 (renewed in 2006 for ten years) and the U.S. Constitution's equal protection clause. In 1973, for example, it won a major victory when the Supreme Court ruled that multimember electoral districts (in which more than one person represents a single district) in Texas discriminated against African Americans and Hispanics.[48] In multimember systems, legislatures generally add members to larger districts instead of drawing smaller districts in which a minority candidate could garner a majority of the votes necessary to win.

The organization's success in educational equity cases came more slowly. In 1973, for example, in *San Antonio Independent School District* v. *Rodriguez,* the Supreme Court refused to find that a Texas law under which the state appropriated a set dollar amount

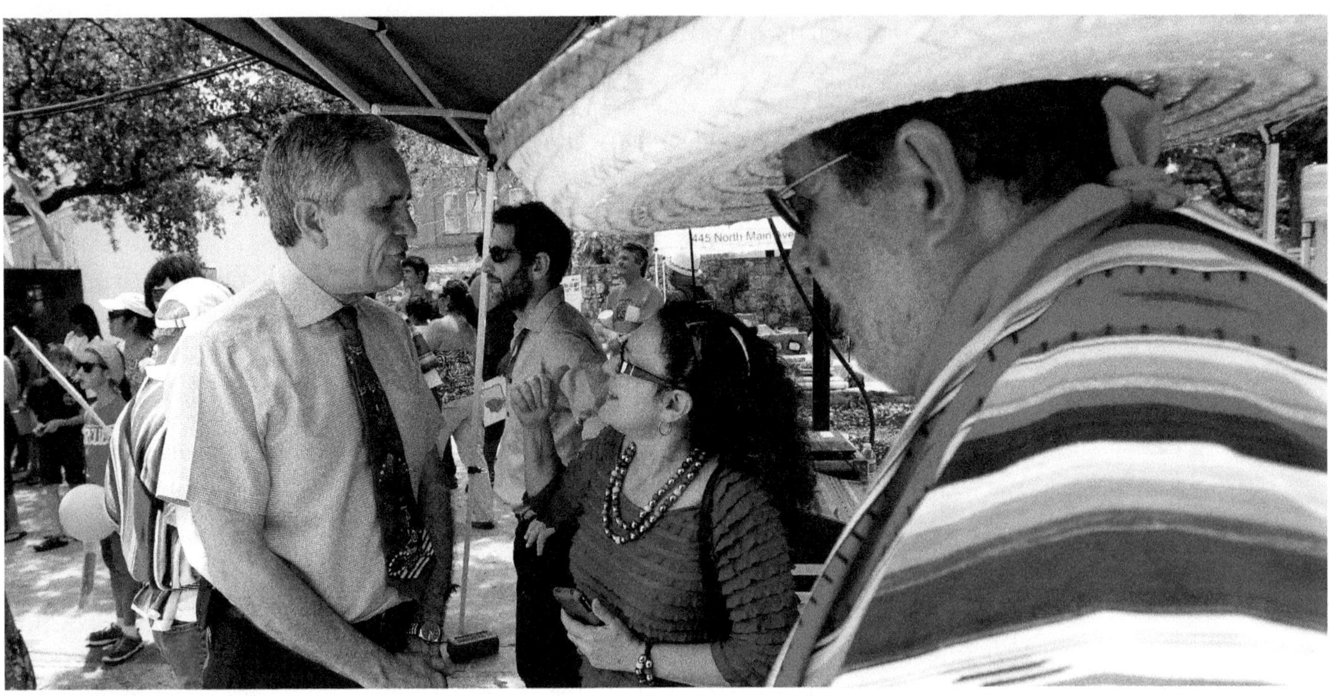

WHO REPRESENTS HISPANIC AMERICANS IN CONGRESS?

Interest groups such as MALDEF have worked to assure greater Hispanic representation in Congress and other political institutions. However, the efforts of these groups have not been entirely successful; even drawing majority-Hispanic congressional districts does not guarantee that a Hispanic will be elected. Such is the case in Texas, where white Representative Lloyd Doggett (D), defeated several Hispanic candidates in the state's 35th district.

to each school district per pupil, while allowing wealthier districts to enrich educational programs from other funds, violated the equal protection clause of the Fourteenth Amendment.[49] In 1989, however, MALDEF won a case in which a state district judge elected by the voters of only a single county declared the state's entire method of financing public schools to be unconstitutional under the state constitution.[50] And, in 2004, it entered into a settlement with the state of California in a case brought four years earlier to address, in MALDEF's words, "the shocking inequities facing public school children across the state."[51]

MALDEF continues to litigate in a wide range of areas of concern to Hispanics. High on its agenda today are affirmative action, the admission of Hispanic students to state colleges and universities, health care for undocumented immigrants, and challenging redistricting practices that make it more difficult to elect Hispanic legislators. To ensure that Hispanics are adequately represented, it also litigates to challenge many state redistricting plans. MALDEF and other Hispanic rights groups, for example, have played a major role in challenging redistricting plans in the state of Texas. As a result of these legal challenges, the U.S. Supreme Court has repeatedly found unconstitutional redistricting plans that divide geographically compact Hispanic populations into many congressional districts, thus diluting Hispanic representation.[52]

MALDEF also stands at the fore of legislative lobbying for expanded rights. Since 2002, it has worked to oppose restrictions concerning driver's license requirements for undocumented immigrants, to gain greater rights for Hispanic workers, and to ensure that redistricting plans do not silence Hispanic voters. MALDEF also focuses on the rights of Hispanic immigrants and workers.

□ American Indians

American Indians are the first true Americans, and their status under U.S. law is unique. The U.S. Constitution considers Indian tribes distinct governments, a situation that has affected the treatment of these Americans by Congress and the Supreme Court.

For years, Congress and the courts manipulated the law to promote westward expansion of the United States. The Northwest Ordinance of 1787, passed by the Continental Congress, specified that "good faith should always be observed toward the Indians; their lands and property shall never be taken from them without their consent, and their property rights, and liberty, they shall never be invaded or disturbed, unless in just and lawful wars authorized by Congress." The federal government did not follow this pledge. During the eighteenth and nineteenth centuries, it isolated American Indians on reservations as it confiscated their lands and denied them basic political rights. The U.S. government administered Indian reservations, and American Indians often lived in squalid conditions.

With passage of the Dawes Act in 1887, however, the government switched policies, promoting assimilation over separation. This act gave each American Indian family land within the reservation; the rest was sold to whites, thus reducing Indian lands from about 140 million acres to about 47 million. Moreover, to encourage American Indians to assimilate, the act mandated sending their children to boarding schools off the reservation. It also banned native languages and rituals. American Indians did not become U.S. citizens, nor were they given the right to vote, until 1924.

At least in part because tribes were small and scattered (and the number of members declining), American Indians formed no protest movement in reaction to these drastic policy changes. Not until the 1960s did American Indians began to mobilize. During this time, American Indian activists, many trained by the American Indian Law Center at the University of New Mexico, began to file hundreds of test cases in the federal courts involving tribal fishing rights, tribal land claims, and taxation of tribal profits. The Native American Rights Fund (NARF), founded in 1970, became the NAACP LDF of the American Indian rights movement.

American Indians have won some very important victories concerning hunting, fishing, and land rights. Tribes all over the country have sued to reclaim lands they maintain the United States stole from them, often more than 200 years ago. These land rights allow American Indians to host gambling casinos across the country, frequently on tribal lands abutting cities and states where gambling is illegal. This phenomenon has resulted in billions of dollars of revenue for Indian tribes. These improvements in American Indians' economic affairs have helped to increase their political clout. Tribes are donating to political campaigns of candidates predisposed to policies favorable to tribes. The Agua Caliente Band of Cahuilla Indians, for example, donated $7.5 million to political campaigns in just one year alone. These large

HOW WERE AMERICAN INDIANS TREATED BY THE U.S. GOVERNMENT?

Indian children were forcibly removed from their homes beginning in the late 1800s and sent to boarding schools where they were pressured to give up their cultural traditions and tribal languages. Here, girls from the Yakima Nation in Washington State are pictured in front of such a school in 1913.

expenditures, American Indians claim, are legal, because as sovereign nations they are immune from federal and state campaign finance disclosure laws. The political involvement of Indian tribes will most likely continue to grow as their casinos—and the profits of those ventures—proliferate.

Despite these successes, Indian tribes still found themselves locked in a controversy with the Department of the Interior over its handling of Indian trust funds, which are to be paid to Indians for the use of their lands. In 1996, several Indian tribes filed suit to force the federal government to account for the billions of dollars it has collected over the years for its leasing of American Indian lands, which it took from the Indians and has held in trust since the late nineteenth century.[53] As the result of years of mismanagement, the trust, administered by the Department of the Interior, has no records of monies taken in or how they were disbursed. The original class action lawsuit included 50,000 American Indians, who claimed the government owed them more than $10 billion. The trial judge found massive mismanagement of the funds, which generated up to $500 million a year. After years of litigation that at one time threatened to hold the secretary of the interior in contempt, the case was finally settled. In 2009, the tribes accepted a $3.4 billion settlement. The settlement establishes a $2 billion trust for anyone willing to sell tribal lands. The Department of the Interior also agreed to set aside 5 percent of the land's value for scholarships for American Indian children.

American Indians have also not fared particularly well in other policy areas, such as religious freedom. The Supreme Court used the rational basis test to rule that a state could infringe on religious exercise (use of peyote as a sacrament in religious ceremonies) as long as it served a compelling state interest.[54] Congress attempted to restore some of those rights through passage of the Religious Freedom Restoration Act in 1993. The Supreme Court, however, later declared parts of the law unconstitutional.[55]

Like the civil rights and women's rights movements, the movement for American Indian rights has had a radical as well as a more traditional branch. In 1973, for example, national attention centered on the plight of Indians when members of the radical American Indian Movement took over Wounded Knee, South Dakota, the site of the U.S. Army's massacre of 150 Indians in 1890. Just two years before the protest, the treatment of Indians had been highlighted in Dee Brown's best-selling *Bury My Heart at Wounded Knee,* which in many ways served to mobilize public opinion against the oppression of American Indians in the same way *Uncle Tom's Cabin* had against slavery.[56]

☐ Asian and Pacific Island Americans

One of the most significant difficulties for Asian and Pacific Island Americans has been finding a Pan-Asian identity. Originally, Asian and Pacific Island Americans were far more likely to identify with their individual Japanese, Chinese, Korean, or Filipino heritage.[57] Not until 1977 did the U.S. government decide to use "Asian and Pacific Island" for all of these origins. Some subgroups have even challenged this identity; in the 1990s, native Hawaiians unsuccessfully requested to be categorized with American Indians, with whom they felt greater affinity.

Discrimination against Asian and Pacific Island immigrants developed over time in the United States. In 1868, Congress passed a law allowing free migration from China, because workers were needed to complete building an intercontinental railroad. But in 1882, Congress passed the Chinese Exclusion Act, which was the first act to restrict the immigration of any identifiable nationality. This legislation implicitly invited more discriminatory laws against the Chinese, which closely paralleled the Jim Crow laws affecting African Americans.

Several Supreme Court cases also slowed the progress of Asian and Pacific Island Americans. This began to change in 1886, when the Court decided the landmark case of *Yick Wo* v. *Hopkins,* using the rational basis test highlighted in Table 5.1. A number of events precipitated this decision. Discriminatory provisions in the California Constitution prevented Chinese people from practicing many professions. However,

HOW WERE JAPANESE AMERICANS TREATED DURING WORLD WAR II?
The internment of Japanese Americans during World War II was a low point in American history. In *Korematsu* v. *U.S.* (1944), the U.S. Supreme Court upheld the constitutionality of this action.

the Chinese in California were allowed to open laundries. And, many immigrants did. In response to this growing trend, the city of San Francisco passed a ban on laundries operating in wooden buildings, two-thirds of which were owned by persons of Chinese ancestry. The Court in *Yick Wo* found that the law violated the Fourteenth Amendment in its application since one ethnic group was being targeted.[58]

In 1922, the Court took a step backward, ruling that Asian and Pacific Island Americans were not white and therefore not entitled to full citizenship rights.[59] Conditions became even worse, especially for those of Japanese descent, after the Japanese attack on Pearl Harbor in 1941. In response to the attack, President Franklin D. Roosevelt issued Executive Order 9066, which led to the internment of over 130,000 Japanese Americans, Italian Americans, and German Americans, some of whom were Jewish refugees. More than two-thirds of those confined to internment camps were U.S. citizens. The Supreme Court upheld the constitutionality of these camps in *Korematsu* v. *U.S.* (1944). The justices applied the strict scrutiny standard of review and ruled that these internments served a compelling governmental objective and were not discriminatory on their face. According to Justice Hugo Black:

> Korematsu was not excluded from the Military Area because of hostility to him or his race. He was excluded because we are at war with the Japanese Empire, because the properly constituted military authorities feared an invasion of our West Coast and felt constrained to take proper security measures, because they decided that the military urgency of the situation demanded that all citizens of Japanese ancestry be segregated from the West Coast temporarily, and, finally, because Congress, reposing its confidence in this time of war in our military leaders—as inevitably it must—determined that they should have the power to do just this.[60]

In sharp contrast, as a goodwill gesture to an ally, the U.S. government offered Chinese immigrants the opportunity to apply for U.S. citizenship. At the end of the war, President Harry S Truman extended the same privilege to Filipino immigrants, many of whom had aided in the war effort.

During the 1960s and 1970s, Asian and Pacific Island Americans, like many other groups discussed in this chapter, began to organize for equal rights. Filipino farm workers, for example, joined with Mexicans to form the United Farm Workers Union. In 1973, the Movement for a Free Philippines emerged to oppose the government of Ferdinand Marcos, the president of the Philippines. Soon, it joined forces with the Friends of Filipino People, also founded in 1973. These groups worked with the Free Legal Assistance Group (FLAG) to openly oppose the Vietnam War and, with the aid of the Roman Catholic Church, established relief organizations for Filipinos in the United States and around the world.

In the 1970s and 1980s, Japanese Americans also mobilized, lobbying the courts and Congress for reparations for their treatment during World War II. In 1988, Congress passed the Civil Liberties Act, which apologized to the interned and their descendents and offered reparations to them and their families.

Today, myriad Asian and Pacific Island Americans are the fastest-growing minority group. They target diverse political venues. In California, in particular, they have enjoyed success in seeing more men and women elected at the local and state levels.

☐ Gays and Lesbians

Until very recently, gays and lesbians have experienced many challenges in achieving anything approximating equal rights.[61] However, gays and lesbians have, on average, far higher household incomes and educational levels than other minority groups, and they are beginning to convert these advantages into political clout at the ballot box. They have also recently benefited from changes in public opinion. Like African Americans and women, gays and lesbians have worked through the courts to achieve incremental legal change. In the late 1970s, gay and lesbian activists dedicated to ending legal restrictions on the civil rights of homosexuals founded Lambda Legal, the National Center for Lesbian Rights, and Gay and Lesbian Advocates and Defenders (GLAD).[62] These groups have won important legal victories concerning HIV/AIDS discrimination, insurance policy survivor benefits, and even some employment issues. However, progress in other areas has relied on changing voters' and policymakers' hearts and minds.[63]

In 1993, for example, President Bill Clinton tried to ban discrimination against homosexuals in the armed services. Eventually, Clinton compromised with congressional and military leaders on what was called the "Don't Ask, Don't Tell" (DADT) policy. The military would no longer ask gays and lesbians if they were homosexual, but it barred them from revealing their sexual orientation under threat of discharge. Despite the compromise, the armed services discharged thousands on the basis of their sexual orientation. Government officials called the policy into question as the wars in Iraq and Afghanistan increased America's need for active-duty military personnel.

In 2010, a federal district court judge ruled the "Don't Ask" policy unconstitutional. She also issued an injunction directing the Department of Defense to refrain from enforcing the policy. As a result of these rulings and increasing public pressure, in late 2010, Congress passed and President Barack Obama signed into law a formal repeal of DADT. In September 2011, the policy officially ended, paving the way for many military members to openly acknowledge their homosexuality.

Changes in public opinion have also opened the door for greater legal and constitutional protection for gay and lesbian rights.[64] In 1996, for example, the U.S. Supreme Court ruled that an amendment to the Colorado Constitution that denied homosexuals the right to seek protection from discrimination was unconstitutional under the equal protection clause of the Fourteenth Amendment.

Less than ten years later, these sentiments were reflected in the Court's decision in *Lawrence* v. *Texas* (2003). In this case, the Court reversed an earlier ruling, finding a Texas statute banning sodomy to be unconstitutional. Writing for the majority, Justice Anthony Kennedy stated, "[homosexuals'] right to liberty under the due process clause gives them the full right to engage in their conduct without intervention of the government."[65]

5.1

5.2

5.3

5.4

5.5

5.6

Following the Court's ruling in *Lawrence,* many Americans were quick to call for additional rights for homosexuals. A good number of corporations responded to this amplified call. For example, Walmart announced it would ban job discrimination based on sexual orientation. In addition, editorial pages across the country praised the Court's ruling, arguing that the national view toward homosexuality had changed.[66] In November 2003, the Massachusetts Supreme Court further agreed when it ruled that denying homosexuals the right to civil marriage was unconstitutional under the commonwealth's constitution. The U.S. Supreme Court later refused to hear an appeal of this case, paving the way for legality of same-sex marriage.

While voters, legislators, and courts in more liberal states took action to legalize these unions, the Religious Right mobilized against them. In 2004, many conservative groups and Republican politicians made same-sex marriage a key issue. Initiatives or referenda prohibiting same-sex marriage were placed on eleven state ballots, and voters overwhelmingly passed all of them. The 2006 mid-term elections also saw same-sex marriage bans on several state ballots, but the issue seemed to lack the emotional punch of the 2004 effort in the context of plummeting presidential approval and the ongoing war in Iraq.

In 2008, California and Connecticut joined Massachusetts in legalizing same-sex marriages. Same-sex couples traveled to California, especially, to legally marry. But, in November 2008, California voters passed a ballot proposition amending the state constitution to make same-sex marriages illegal again. This provision, however, did not pass legal muster in U.S. district court.

While other states and the District of Columbia have legalized same-sex marriage in recent years, California's Proposition 8 has been mired in litigation. On February 8, 2012, a three-judge panel of the Ninth Circuit Court of Appeals declared Proposition 8 unconstitutional in a 2–1 ruling. Backers of the ban on same-sex marriage, Protect Marriage, asked the Ninth Circuit to grant an *en banc* review to reconsider its ruling.[67]

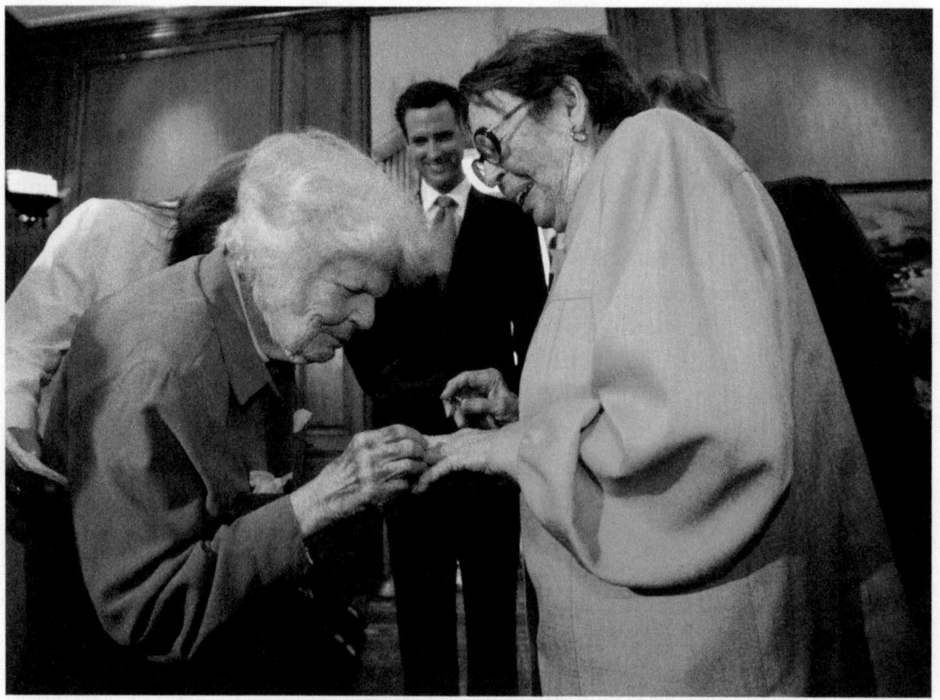

WHY IS SAME-SEX MARRIAGE CONTROVERSIAL?

The legalization of same-sex marriage in California in 2008 allowed gay couples committed to one another for decades to tie the knot. Here, lesbian activists Del Martin (age 87) and Phyllis Lyon (age 83)—partners for more than 50 years—are married by San Francisco Mayor Gavin Newsom. Unions such as this face opposition by many religious conservatives, who believe homosexuality is a sin and support only the rights of heterosexual couples to marry. Martin died in August 2008, only a few months after her wedding.

How Do Governments Regulate Same-Sex Marriage?

Under the federal system of government created by the Framers, marriage has historically been a state responsibility. Thus, in the past ten years, states have been very active in passing legislation on this issue. State legislatures and voters have chosen to adopt a wide array of laws, with some states fully supporting same-sex marriages, others refusing all unions, and many choosing legislation between the two extremes.

CRITICAL THINKING QUESTIONS

1. How do the numbers of states allowing and prohibiting same-sex unions vary? What may be the cause of these differences?
2. What are the differences between the tiers of each cake? Why might states adopt laws that vary so widely?
3. Should the United States move toward full marriage equality for homosexual couples? Why or why not?

5.1

5.2

5.3

5.4

5.5

5.6

Ongoing litigation also focuses on the constitutionality of the 1996 Defense of Marriage Act (DOMA), a federal law defining marriage as between one man and one woman. Several district courts around the nation have declared the law to be an unconstitutional violation of the Fourteenth Amendment's equal protection clause. It is likely to take a Supreme Court decision to settle the issue.[68]

☐ Americans with Disabilities

Americans with disabilities also have lobbied hard for anti-discrimination legislation as well as equal protection under the Constitution. In the aftermath of World War II, many veterans returned to a nation unequipped to handle their disabilities. The Korean and Vietnam Wars made the problems of disabled veterans all the more clear. These veterans saw the successes of African Americans, women, and other minorities, and they, too, began to lobby for greater protection against discrimination.[69] In 1990, in coalition with other disabled people, veterans finally convinced Congress to pass the Americans with Disabilities Act (ADA). The statute defines a disabled person as someone with a physical or mental impairment that limits one or more "life activities," or who has a record of such impairment. It thus extends the protections of the Civil Rights Act of 1964 to all citizens with physical or mental disabilities. It guarantees access to public facilities, employment, and communication services. Furthermore, it requires employers to acquire or modify work equipment, adjust work schedules, and make existing facilities accessible to those with disabilities. For example, people in

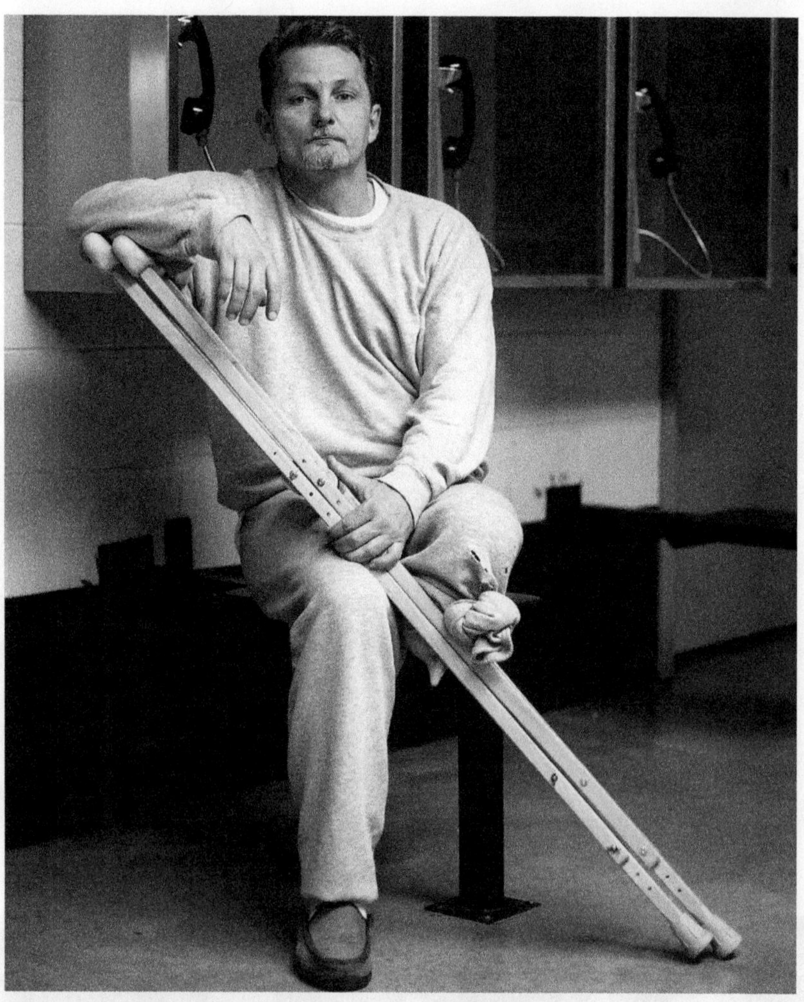

WHOM DOES THE AMERICANS WITH DISABILITIES ACT PROTECT?

George Lane was the appellant in *Tennessee* v. *Lane* (2004), concerning the scope of the Americans with Disabilities Act, which guarantees the disabled access to public buildings, among other protections. Lane was forced to crawl up two flights of stairs to attend a state court hearing on a misdemeanor charge. Had he not, he could have been jailed.

wheelchairs must have ready access to buildings, and deaf employees must have telecommunication devices made available to them.

In 1999, the U.S. Supreme Court issued a series of four decisions redefining and limiting the scope of the ADA. The cumulative impact of these decisions dramatically limited the number of people who can claim coverage under the act. Moreover, these cases "could profoundly affect individuals with a range of impairments—from diabetes and hypertension to severe nearsightedness and hearing loss—who are able to function in society with the help of medicines or aids but whose impairments may still make employers consider them ineligible for certain jobs."[70] Thus, pilots who need glasses to correct their vision cannot claim discrimination when employers fail to hire them, even though their vision is correctable.[71] In the 2004 case of *Tennessee* v. *Lane,* however, the Court ruled 5–4 that disabled persons could sue states that failed to make reasonable accommodations to ensure that courthouses are handicapped accessible.[72]

The largest national nonprofit organization lobbying for expanded civil rights for the disabled is the American Association of People with Disabilities (AAPD). Acting on behalf of over 56 million Americans who suffer from some form of disability, it works in coalition with other disability organizations to make certain that the ADA is implemented fully. The activists who founded AAPD lobbied for the ADA and recognized that "beyond national unity for ADA and our civil rights, people with disabilities did not have a venue or vehicle for working together for common goals."[73]

affirmative action
Policies designed to give special attention or compensatory treatment to members of a previously disadvantaged group.

5.1 5.2 5.3 5.4 5.5 5.6

Toward Reform: Civil Rights and Affirmative Action

5.6 Evaluate the ongoing debate concerning civil rights and affirmative action.

Many civil rights debates center on the question of equality of opportunity versus equality of results. Most civil rights and women's rights organizations argue that taking race and gender into account in fashioning remedies for discrimination is the only way to overcome the lingering and pervasive burdens of racism and sexism, respectively. They argue that the Constitution is not, and should not be, blind to color or sex.

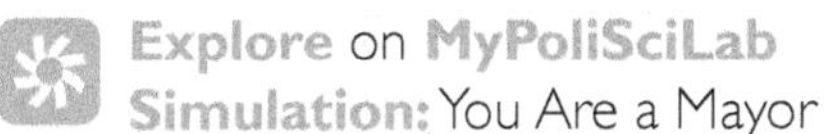

Other groups believe that if the use of labels to discriminate against a group was once wrong, the use of those same labels to help a group should likewise be wrong. They argue that laws should be neutral, or color-blind. According to this view, quotas and other forms of **affirmative action,** policies designed to give special attention or compensatory treatment to members of a previously disadvantaged group, are unconstitutional.

The debate over affirmative action and equality of opportunity became particularly intense during the presidential administration of Ronald Reagan Shortly before his election, the Court generally decided in favor of affirmative action in two cases. In 1978, the Supreme Court for the first time fully addressed the issue of affirmative action. Alan Bakke, a thirty-one-year-old paramedic, sought admission to several medical schools, which rejected him because of his age. The next year, he applied to the University of California at Davis and was placed on its waiting list. The Davis Medical School maintained two separate admission committees—one for white students and another for minority students. The school did not admit Bakke, although his grades and standardized test scores were higher than those of all African American students admitted to the school. In *Regents of the University of California* v. *Bakke* (1978), a sharply divided Court concluded that Bakke's rejection had been illegal because the use of strict quotas was inappropriate.[74] The medical school, however, was free to "take race into account," said the Court.

Bakke was followed by a 1979 case in which the Court ruled that a factory and a union could voluntarily adopt a quota system in selecting black workers over more senior white workers for a training program.[75] These kinds of programs outraged blue-collar Americans, who traditionally had voted for the Democratic Party. In 1980, they abandoned the party in droves to support Ronald Reagan, an ardent foe of affirmative action.

For a time, despite the addition of Reagan-appointed Justice Sandra Day O'Connor to the Court, the justices continued to uphold affirmative action plans, especially when clear-cut evidence of prior discrimination was present. In 1987, for example, the Court ruled for the first time that a public employer could use a voluntary plan to promote women even if no judicial finding of prior discrimination existed.[76]

In all these affirmative action cases, the Reagan administration strongly urged the Court to invalidate the plans in question, but to no avail. Changes on the Court, however, including the 1986 elevation of William H. Rehnquist, a strong opponent of affirmative action, to chief justice, signaled an end to advances in civil rights law. In a three-month period in 1989, the Supreme Court handed down five civil rights decisions limiting affirmative action programs and making it harder to prove employment discrimination.

In February 1990, congressional and civil rights leaders unveiled legislation designed to overrule the Court's decisions, which, according to the bill's sponsor, "were an abrupt and unfortunate departure from its historic vigilance in protecting the rights of minorities."[77] The bill passed both houses of Congress but was vetoed by President Reagan's successor, George Bush, and Congress failed to override the veto. In late 1991, however, Congress and the White House reached a compromise on a weaker version of the civil rights bill, which passed by overwhelming majorities in both houses of Congress. The Civil Rights Act of 1991 overruled all five Supreme Court rulings.

The Supreme Court, however, has not remained silent on the issue. In 1995, the Court ruled that Congress, like the states, must show that affirmative action programs meet the strict scrutiny test.[78] In 1996, the Court of Appeals for the Fifth Circuit also declared as unconstitutional the University of Texas Law School's affirmative action admissions program, throwing the college and university admissions programs in Texas, Oklahoma, and Mississippi into turmoil. Later that year, the U.S. Supreme Court refused to hear the case, thereby allowing the decision by the Court of Appeals to stand.[79]

By 2002, the U.S. Supreme Court once again found the affirmative action issue ripe for review. In *Grutter* v. *Bollinger* (2003), the Court voted to uphold the constitutionality of the University of Michigan's Law School admissions policy, which gave preference to minority applicants.[80] However, in *Gratz* v. *Bollinger* (2003), the Court struck down Michigan's undergraduate point system, which gave minority applicants twenty automatic points simply because they were minorities.[81]

Together, these cases set the stage for a new era in affirmative action in the United States. Although the use of strict quotas and automatic points is not constitutional, the Court clearly believes that some preferential treatment has its place, at least until greater racial and ethnic parity is achieved. However, as Justice Sandra Day O'Connor noted in *Grutter*, "a program must remain flexible enough to ensure that each applicant is evaluated as an individual and not in a way that makes an applicant's race or ethnicity the defining feature of his or her application."

In 2012, however, the Court called even this standard into question by accepting a case involving a white applicant denied admission at the University of Texas at Austin. A ruling is expected during the Court's 2012-13 term.[82]

Review the Chapter

 **Listen to Chapter 5 on MyPoliSciLab**

Roots of Suffrage: 1800–1890

5.1 Trace the efforts from 1800 to 1890 of African Americans and women to win the vote, p. 129.

When the Framers tried to compromise on the issue of slavery, they only postponed dealing with a volatile question that eventually would rip the nation apart. Ultimately, the Civil War brought an end to slavery. Among its results were the triumph of the abolitionist position and the adoption of the Thirteenth, Fourteenth, and Fifteenth Amendments. During this period, women also sought expanded rights, especially the right to vote, to no avail.

The Push for Equality, 1890–1954

5.2 Outline developments in African Americans' and women's push for equality from 1890 to 1954, p. 135.

Although the Civil War Amendments became part of the Constitution, the Supreme Court limited their application. As legislatures throughout the South passed Jim Crow laws, the NAACP was founded in the early 1900s to press for equal rights for African Americans. Woman's groups also were active during this period, successfully lobbying for passage of the Nineteenth Amendment, which ensured them the right to vote. Groups such as the National Consumers League (NCL) began to view litigation as a means to an end and went to court to argue for the constitutionality of legislation protecting women workers.

The Civil Rights Movement

5.3 Analyze the civil rights movement and the effects of the Civil Rights Act of 1964, p. 141.

In 1954, the U.S. Supreme Court ruled in *Brown* v. *Board of Education* that racially segregated state school systems were unconstitutional. This victory empowered African Americans as they sought an end to other forms of pervasive discrimination. Bus boycotts, sit-ins, freedom rides, pressure for voting rights enforcement, and massive nonviolent demonstrations became common tactics. These efforts culminated in passage of the Civil Rights Act of 1964, which gave African Americans another weapon in their legal arsenal.

The Women's Rights Movement

5.4 Assess statutory and constitutional remedies for discrimination pursued and achieved by the women's rights movement, p. 147.

After passage of the Equal Pay Act of 1963 and the Civil Rights Act of 1964, a new women's rights movement arose. Several women's rights groups were created. Some sought a constitutional amendment (the Equal Rights Amendment) as a remedy for discrimination; it would elevate the standard of review for sex-based claims. In general, strict scrutiny, the most stringent standard, is applied to race-based claims and cases involving fundamental freedoms. The Court developed an intermediate standard of review to assess the constitutionality of sex discrimination claims. All other claims are subject to the rational basis test.

Other Groups Mobilize for Rights

5.5 Describe how other groups have mobilized in pursuit of their own civil rights, p. 153.

Building on the successes of African Americans and women, other groups, including Hispanics, American Indians, Asian and Pacific Island Americans, gays and lesbians, and those with disabilities, organized to litigate for expanded civil rights and to lobby for anti-discrimination laws.

Toward Reform: Civil Rights and Affirmative Action

5.6 Evaluate the ongoing debate concerning civil rights and affirmative action, p. 163.

All of the groups discussed in this chapter have yet to reach full equality. Affirmative action, a policy designed to remedy education and employment discrimination, continues to generate controversy.

Learn the Terms

affirmative action, p. 163
Black Codes, p. 132
Brown v. *Board of Education* (1954), p. 140
civil rights, p. 129
Civil Rights Act of 1964, p. 146
Civil Rights Cases (1883), p. 134
de facto discrimination, p. 146
de jure discrimination, p. 146
Equal Pay Act of 1963, p. 152
equal protection clause, p. 132
Equal Rights Amendment, p. 148
Fifteenth Amendment, p. 133
Fourteenth Amendment, p. 132
grandfather clause, p. 135
Jim Crow laws, p. 134
Nineteenth Amendment, p. 137
Plessy v. *Ferguson* (1896), p. 135
poll tax, p. 134
strict scrutiny, p. 150
suffrage movement, p. 137
suspect classification, p. 150
Thirteenth Amendment, p. 132
Title IX, p. 153

Test Yourself

Study and **Review** the **Practice Tests**

1. The Fourteenth Amendment, which provided legal protection for the rights of citizens, did NOT include

a. African Americans.
b. those with a "previous condition of servitude."
c. women.
d. those over twenty-one years old.
e. immigrants.

2. Why did Elizabeth Cady Stanton and Lucretia Mott found the first woman's rights movement in the nineteenth century?

a. They escaped from slavery and joined forces with William Lloyd Garrison.
b. After attending an abolitionist meeting, they concluded that women were not much better off than slaves.
c. They were jailed for attempting to hold a woman's rights convention in Seneca Falls in 1848.
d. William Lloyd Garrison and Frederick Douglass encouraged them to leave the abolition movement to pursue their own causes.
e. Their husbands and sons made comments implying women were undeserving of suffrage rights.

3. Which law(s), passed after the Civil War Amendments, reverted many African Americans back to conditions similar to those characterizing their previous lifestyles?

a. Equal protection clause
b. Civil Rights Act of 1875
c. Fifteenth Amendment
d. Civil Rights Act of 1866
e. Black Codes

4. Women's rights advocates won the right to vote with the ratification of the

a. Eighteenth Amendment.
b. Nineteenth Amendment.
c. Twentieth Amendment.
d. Seventeenth Amendment.
e. Sixteenth Amendment.

5. *Brown* v. *Board of Education* (1954) ruled that segregation in schools is unconstitutional because:

a. there were not enough law schools for African Americans.
b. all schools should be integrated.
c. it violates the Fourteenth Amendment's guarantee of equal protection.
d. postgraduate programs were not offered to African Americans
e. African Americans had fought in World War II and should therefore be afforded adequate schooling.

6. The Civil Rights Act of 1964 did all of the following EXCEPT:

a. create a commission to monitor workplace discrimination.
b. prohibit discrimination in employment based on race, creed, color, religion, national origin, or sex.
c. allow discrimination in voter registration.
d. allow the withholding of federal funds from discriminatory programs.
e. establish Department of Justice monitoring of southern elections.

7. Which standard of review does the U.S. Supreme Court apply to practices involving alleged gender discrimination?

- **a.** Strict scrutiny
- **b.** Heightened standard
- **c.** Intermediate standard
- **d.** Minimum rationality
- **e.** Suspect class scrutiny

8. Which of these issues has NOT been a subject of litigation and lobbying on behalf of Hispanic rights groups?

- **a.** Education
- **b.** Immigration
- **c.** Workers' rights
- **d.** Driver's licensing
- **e.** Protection of native lands

9. Which group did President Franklin D. Roosevelt's executive order NOT force into internment camps after the attack on Pearl Harbor?

- **a.** German Americans
- **b.** Irish Americans
- **c.** Italian Americans
- **d.** Jewish refugees
- **e.** Japanese Americans

10. Which of the following statements is true about affirmative action programs in the United States?

- **a.** Affirmative action programs are widespread with virtually no limitations.
- **b.** Affirmative action programs have been deemed unconstitutional.
- **c.** Affirmative action programs can be used, but they must pass the strict scrutiny test.
- **d.** Numerical quotas are the only means by which affirmative action can be applied.
- **e.** Racial and ethnic parity has made affirmative action programs obsolete.

Explore Further

Anderson, Terry H. *The Pursuit of Fairness: A History of Affirmative Action*. New York: Oxford University Press, 2005.

Delgado, Richard. *Justice at War: Civil Liberties and Civil Rights During Times of Crisis*. New York: New York University Press, 2005.

Freeman, Jo. *The Politics of Women's Liberation*. New York: Backinprint.com, 2000.

Klarman, Michael. *From the Closet to the Altar: Courts, Backlash, and the Struggle for Same-Sex Marriage.* New York, Oxford University Press, 2012.

Longmore, Paul, and Lauri Umansky. *The New Disability History: American Perspectives*. New York: New York University Press, 2001.

Lovell, George I. *This is Not Civil Rights: Discovering Rights Talk in 1939 America.* Chicago: University of Chicago Press, 2012.

Mansbridge, Jane J. *Why We Lost the ERA*. Chicago: University of Chicago Press, 1986.

McClain, Paula D., and Joseph Stewart Jr. *"Can We All Get Along?": Racial and Ethnic Minorities in American Politics,* 5th ed. Boulder, CO: Westview, 2009.

McGlen, Nancy E., Karen O'Connor, Laura Van Assendelft, and Wendy Gunther-Canada. *Women, Politics, and American Society,* 5th ed. New York: Longman, 2010.

Reed, Adolph, Jr., ed. *Without Justice for All: The New Liberalism and Our Retreat from Racial Equity*. Boulder, CO: Westview, 2001.

Rodriguez, Marc. *Rethinking the Chicano Movement.* New York: Routledge, 2013.

Wilkins, David E. and Heidi Kiiwetinepinesiik Stark. *American Indian Politics and the American Political System,* 3rd ed. New York: Rowman and Littlefield, 2010.

Williams, Juan. *Eyes on the Prize: America's Civil Rights Years, 1954–1965*. New York: Penguin, 1987.

Wilson, William Julius. *The Bridge over the Racial Divide: Rising Inequality and Coalition Politics,* 2nd ed. Berkeley: University of California Press, 2001.

Zia, Hellen. *Asian American Dreams: The Emergence of an American People*. New York: Farrar, Straus and Giroux, 2000.

To learn more about civil rights issues in the United States, go to the Leadership Conference on Civil and Human Rights at **www.civilrights.org,** where a coalition of 150 civil rights organizations provides coverage of a host of civil rights issues as well as links to breaking news related to civil rights.

To learn more about the ACLU Women's Rights Project, go to its website at **www.aclu.org/womensrights/index.html.**

To learn more about ongoing efforts to achieve greater rights for gay and lesbian Americans, see **http://lambdalegal.org.**

To learn more about disability advocacy groups, go to the website for the American Association of People with Disabilities at **www.aapd.com.**

Listen to Chapter 6 on MyPoliSciLab

6 Congress

The U.S. Constitution creates Congress as the legislative branch of government. Its primary goals are to make the laws of the nation, as well as to represent citizens' interests in national politics. However, in recent Congresses, neither of these objectives has been particularly apparent.

As a result, the modern Congress has a serious image problem. Its approval ratings reached a new low in August of 2012, when only 10 percent of Americans said they approved of the institution. The 112th House of Representatives and Senate have passed a staggeringly low number of pieces of legislation—and many of the laws that have passed have been ceremonial or simple renewals of existing programs. As a result, the legislative branch—once the most powerful political institution in the world—has been branded as a "do-nothing" institution, fraught with political conflict and weakened by partisan gridlock.

The lack of legislation passed by Congress, critics note, does not owe to a lack of important issues facing the nation. When Congress adjourned for the election in September 2012, the issues facing the institution were staggering. Farmers in the Midwest faced serious droughts and a need for governmental relief. The national debt was swelling by the minute. Unemployment was hovering near 10 percent. Questions remained about the persistence of President George W. Bush's tax cuts for the middle class. And, no budget had been passed for the upcoming fiscal year, skirting the issues of funding for programs as varied and significant as Medicare, Medicaid, and national defense. Moreover, the American people—and the presidential candidates—appeared to demand action on a range of other issues, including education, student grants and loans, access to abortion and contraceptives, gay marriage, and the implementation of health care reform.

What caused such dramatic inactivity in the 112th Congress? To some degree, that depends on whom you ask. Democratic Party officials, including House Democratic Leader Nancy Pelosi (D-CA), very vocally blamed the Republican majority in the House for failing to schedule debates and votes on significant pieces of legislation. They noted the accomplishments of recent Democratic-controlled Congresses

6.1 Trace the roots of the legislative branch outlined by the U.S. Constitution, p. 171.

6.2 Characterize the demographic attributes of members of Congress, and identify factors that affect their chances for reelection, p. 175.

6.3 Assess the role of the committee system, political parties, and congressional leadership in organizing Congress, p. 179.

6.4 Identify three of the most significant powers of Congress, p. 187.

6.5 Analyze the factors that influence how members of Congress make decisions, p. 195.

6.6 Evaluate the strategic interactions between Congress, the president, the courts, and the people, p. 199.

CONGRESS FUNCTIONS AS THE NATION'S LAWMAKING BODY The basic structure, rules, and procedures of Congress have changed very little since the 1940s, shown above. However, the interpersonal dynamics, policy issues, and role of the media have led to dramatically different outcomes in the modern Congress, shown below.

MyPoliSciLab Videos

Watch on MyPoliSciLab

The Big Picture Is Congress actually representative of the American people? Author Alixandra B. Yanus compares what Congress is supposed to do with what it actually does, and offers some suggestions as to why Americans have become increasingly disillusioned with their representatives.

The Basics Why do we have two houses of Congress? This video reveals the answer to this question and explores the differences between the two houses in their organization and procedures. You will also learn how a bill becomes a law, how Congress is organized, and how members of Congress represent you.

In Context Discover the role that the Framers expected Congress to serve in the U.S. government. Columbia University political scientist Greg Wawro discusses how Congress has become more expansive in its powers. Listen as Greg Wawro also delves into the process of creating coalitions in Congress to achieve policy results.

Think Like a Political Scientist Why has the United States become more polarized in the last decade? Columbia University political scientist Greg Wawro examines this central question and explains why polarization may be correlated to the income gap between the wealthy and the poor. He also explores recent research on the Senate as a super-majoritarian institution.

In the Real World Congress today is the most divided it has been since the end of World War II. It is also the least effective. Is compromise the answer? Real people consider the benefits and the dangers of compromise, and they discuss issues—like abortion—where compromise seems impossible

So What? Want to change the way your government operates? In this video, author Alixandra B. Yanus reveals why Congress may actually listen to what you have to say. Find out how you can get involved in your state government and how Congress can help you accomplish your goals.

as evidence for the fact that the problem was particularistic to the politics of the Republican Party and Speaker of the House John Boehner's (R-OH) unwillingness to compromise.

Republicans, on the other hand, blamed the Democrats in the Senate. They accused Majority Leader Harry Reid (D-NV) for the lack of legislative output, noting that even when the House passes or considers legislation, Reid and the Democrats are often unwilling to discuss the issue in the Senate. This resistance, they noted, is particularly evident when it comes to issues of the budget and financial reform—some of the most important issues facing the country today.

Ironically, it may be exactly this type of hyperpartisanship and finger-pointing that has produced such a low approval rating among the American people. To these citizens, many of whom are not especially interested in politics, an unwillingness to compromise for the good of the nation often looks a lot like a failure of representation. Increasingly, therefore, citizens ask why members of Congress are so focused on dividing into Democrats and Republicans—rather than uniting as Americans.

•••

The Framers' original conception of Congress's authority was much narrower than it is today. Those in attendance at the Constitutional Convention wished to create a legislative body that would be able to make laws as well as raise and spend revenues. Over time, Congress has attempted to maintain these roles, but changes in demands made on the national government have allowed the executive and judicial branches to gain powers at the expense of the legislative branch. Moreover, the power and the importance of individual members have grown.

Today, members of Congress must combine and balance the roles of lawmaker, budgeter, and policy maker with acting as a representative of their district, their state, their party, and sometimes their race, ethnicity, or gender. Not surprisingly, this balancing act often results in role conflict.

In this chapter, we analyze the powers of Congress and the competing roles members play as they represent the interests of their constituents, make laws, and oversee actions of the other two branches of government. We also show that as these functions have changed throughout U.S. history, so has Congress itself.

Roots of the Legislative Branch of Government

6.1 Trace the roots of the legislative branch outlined by the U.S. Constitution.

rticle I of the Constitution describes the structure of the legislative branch of government. The Great Compromise at the Constitutional Convention resulted in the creation of a lower house, the House of Representatives, and an upper house, the Senate. Any two-house legislature, such as the one created by the Framers, is called a **bicameral legislature.** The population of any given state determines the number of representatives that state sends to the House of Representatives. In contrast, two senators represent each state in the Senate, regardless of the state's population.

bicameral legislature
A two-house legislature.

The U.S. Constitution sets forth the formal, or legal, requirements for membership in the House and Senate. As agreed to at the Constitutional Convention, House members must be at least twenty-five years of age; senators, thirty. Members of the House must be citizens of the United States for at least seven years; those elected to the Senate, at least nine years. Both representatives and senators must be legal residents of the states from which they are elected. Historically, many members of Congress have moved to their states specifically to run for office. In 1964, U.S. Attorney General Robert Kennedy moved to New York to launch a successful campaign for the Senate, as did Hillary Clinton in 2000. Less successful was former Republican presidential hopeful Alan Keyes, who moved from Maryland to run unsuccessfully for a U.S. Senate seat in Illinois against Barack Obama in 2006.

The eligible electorate in each congressional district votes to elect members of the House of Representatives to two-year terms. The Framers expected that House members would be more responsible to the people, both because they were elected directly by them

apportionment
The process of allotting congressional seats to each state according to its proportion of the population, following the decennial census.

bill
A proposed law.

and because they were up for reelection every two years. The U.S. Constitution requires that a census, which entails the counting of all Americans, be conducted every ten years. Until the first census could be taken, the Constitution fixed the number of representatives in the House of Representatives at sixty-five. In 1790, one member represented about 30,000 people. But, as the population of the new nation grew and states were added to the union, the House became larger and larger. In 1910, it expanded to 435 members, and in 1929, its size was fixed at that number by statute. When Alaska and Hawaii became states in the 1950s, however, the number of seats increased to 437. The number reverted to 435 in 1963. In 2012, the average number of people in a district was 713,000.

Each state is granted its share of these 435 representatives on the basis of its population. After each U.S. Census, a constitutionally mandated process called **apportionment** adjusts the number of seats allotted to each state. After seats are apportioned, state legislatures must redraw congressional districts to reflect population shifts, thereby ensuring that each member in Congress represents approximately the same number of residents. This process of redrawing congressional districts to reflect increases or decreases in the number of seats allotted to a state, as well as population shifts within a state, is called redistricting. It is discussed in greater detail later in this chapter.

Senators are elected to six-year terms, and originally state legislatures chose them because the Framers intended senators to represent their states' interests in the Senate. State legislators lost this influence over the Senate with the ratification of the Seventeenth Amendment in 1913, which provides for the direct election of senators by voters. Then, as now, one-third of all senators are up for reelection every two years.

The Constitution specifically gives Congress its most important powers: the authorities to make laws and raise and spend revenues. No **bill,** or proposed law, can become law without the consent of both houses. Examples of other powers shared by both houses include the power to declare war, raise an army and navy, coin money, regulate commerce, establish the federal courts and their jurisdiction, set forth rules of immigration and naturalization, and "make all Laws which shall be necessary and proper for carrying into Execution the foregoing Powers." As interpreted by the U.S. Supreme Court, the necessary and proper clause, found at the end of Article I, section 8, when coupled with one or more of the specific powers enumerated in Article I, section 8, has allowed Congress to increase the scope of its authority, often at the expense of the states and into areas not necessarily envisioned by the Framers (see Table 6.1).

HOW LONG ARE MEMBERS' TERMS?

Members of the Senate serve six-year terms, while members of the House of Representatives serve for two years. There are no term limits, so members may run for reelection for an unlimited number of terms. The advantages of incumbency make turnover in Congress very low; new members such as Tammy Duckworth (D-IL), a disabled Iraq War veteran, constitute only a small percentage of representatives.

> *The Congress shall have power ... to establish a uniform Rule of Naturalization.*
>
> —ARTICLE I, SECTION 8, CLAUSE 4

This clause places authority to draft laws concerning naturalization in the hands of Congress. The power of Congress over naturalization is exclusive—meaning that no state can bestow U.S. citizenship on anyone. Citizenship is a privilege, and Congress may make laws limiting or expanding the criteria.

The word "citizen" was not defined constitutionally until ratification in 1868 of the Fourteenth Amendment, which sets forth two kinds of citizenship: by birth and through naturalization. Throughout American history, Congress has imposed a variety of limits on naturalization, originally restricting it to "free, white persons." "Orientals" were excluded from eligibility in 1882. At one time, those affiliated with the Communist Party and those who lacked "good moral character" (a phrase that was construed to bar homosexuals, drunkards, gamblers, and adulterers) were deemed unfit for citizenship. These restrictions no longer carry the force of law, but they do underscore the power of Congress in this matter.

Congress continues to retain the right to naturalize large classes of individuals, as it did in 2000, when it granted automatic citizenship rights to all minor children adopted abroad as long as at least one adoptive parent was an American citizen. Naturalized citizens, however, do not necessarily possess the full rights of citizenship enjoyed by other Americans, such as the right to run for president. Congress at any time, subject only to Supreme Court review, can limit the rights and liberties of naturalized citizens, especially in times of national crisis. In the wake of the September 11, 2001, terrorist attacks, when it was revealed that one-third of the forty-eight al-Qaeda–linked operatives who took part in some sort of terrorist activities against the United States were lawful permanent residents or naturalized citizens, Congress called for greater screening by the U.S. Bureau of Citizenship and Immigration Services for potential terrorists.

CRITICAL THINKING QUESTIONS

1. Is Congress the appropriate institution to have the power over immigration and naturalization? Why or why not?
2. Is racial profiling by the U.S. Bureau of Citizenship and Immigration Services and other government entities an appropriate action in the name of national security? Why or why not?

TABLE 6.1 WHAT ARE THE POWERS OF CONGRESS?

The powers of Congress, found in Article I, section 8, of the Constitution, include the powers to:
Lay and collect taxes and duties.
Borrow money.
Regulate commerce with foreign nations and among the states.
Establish rules for naturalization (the process of becoming a citizen) and bankruptcy.
Coin money, set its value, and fix the standard of weights and measures.
Punish counterfeiting.
Establish a post office and post roads.
Issue patents and copyrights.
Define and punish piracies, felonies on the high seas, and crimes against the law of nations.
Create courts inferior to (below) the U.S. Supreme Court.
Declare war.
Raise and support an army and navy and make rules for their governance.
Provide for a militia (reserving to the states the right to appoint militia officers and to train militias under congressional rules).
Exercise legislative powers over the seat of government (the District of Columbia) and over places purchased to be federal facilities (forts, arsenals, dockyards, and "other needful buildings").
"Make all Laws which shall be necessary and proper for carrying into Execution the foregoing Powers, and all other Powers vested by this Constitution in the government of the United States."

impeachment
The power delegated to the House of Representatives in the Constitution to charge the president, vice president, or other "civil officers," including federal judges, with "Treason, Bribery, or other high Crimes and Misdemeanors." This is the first step in the constitutional process of removing government officials from office.

The Constitution gives formal law-making powers to Congress alone. But, it is important to remember that presidents issue proclamations and executive orders with the force of law; bureaucrats issue quasi-legislative rules and are charged with enforcing laws, rules, and regulations; and the Supreme Court and lower federal courts render opinions that generate principles also having the force of law.

Reflecting the different constituencies and size of each house of Congress (as well as the Framers' intentions), Article I gives special, exclusive powers to each house in addition to their shared role in law-making. For example, as noted in Table 6.2, the Constitution specifies that all revenue bills must originate in the House of Representatives.

Over the years, however, this mandate has become less clear, and it is not unusual to see budget bills being considered simultaneously in both houses. Ultimately, each house must approve all bills. The House also has the power of **impeachment,** or to charge the president, vice president, or other "civil officers," including federal judges, with "Treason, Bribery, or other high Crimes and Misdemeanors." But, only the Senate has authority to conduct impeachment trials, with a two-thirds yea vote being necessary to remove a federal official, such as the president or a judge, from office.

While the House and Senate share in the impeachment process, the Senate has the sole authority to approve major presidential appointments, including federal judges, ambassadors, and Cabinet- and sub–Cabinet-level positions. The Senate, too, must approve all presidential treaties by a two-thirds vote. Failure by the president to court the Senate can be costly. At the end of World War I, for example, President Woodrow Wilson worked hard to persuade other nations to accept the Treaty of Versailles, which contained the charter of the proposed League of Nations. He overestimated his support in the Senate, however. That body refused to ratify the treaty, dealing Wilson and his international stature a severe setback.

TABLE 6.2 WHAT ARE THE KEY DIFFERENCES BETWEEN THE HOUSE OF REPRESENTATIVES AND THE SENATE?

Constitutional Differences	
House	**Senate**
435 voting members (apportioned by population)	100 voting members (two from each state)
Two-year terms	Six-year terms (one-third up for reelection every two years)
Initiates all revenue bills	Offers "advice and consent" on many major presidential appointments
Initiates impeachment procedures and passes articles of impeachment	Tries impeached officials
	Approves treaties
Differences in Operation	
House	**Senate**
More centralized, more formal; stronger leadership	Less centralized, less formal; weaker leadership
Committee on Rules fairly powerful in controlling time and rules of debate (in conjunction with the Speaker of the House)	No rules committee; limits on debate come through unanimous consent or cloture of filibuster
More impersonal	More personal
Power distributed less evenly	Power distributed more evenly
Members are highly specialized	Members are generalists
Emphasizes tax and revenue policy	Emphasizes foreign policy
Changes in the Institution	
House	**Senate**
Power centralized in the Speaker's inner circle of advisers	Senate workload increasing and institution becoming more formal; threat of filibusters more frequent than in the past
Procedures becoming more efficient	Becoming more difficult to pass legislation
Turnover is relatively high, although those seeking reelection almost always win	Turnover is moderate

The Members of Congress

6.2 Characterize the demographic attributes of members of Congress, and identify factors that affect their chances for reelection.

Today, many members of Congress find the job exciting in spite of public criticism of the institution. But, it wasn't always so. Until Washington, D.C., got air-conditioning and drained its swamps, it was a miserable town. Most representatives spent as little time there as possible, viewing Congress, especially the House, as a stepping stone to other political positions back home. Only after World War I did most House members become congressional careerists who viewed their work in Washington as long term.[1]

Members must attempt to appease several constituencies—party leaders, colleagues and lobbyists in Washington, D.C., and voters at home.[2] In attempting to do so, members spend full days at home as well as in D.C. (see Table 6.3). According to one study of House members, average representatives made about forty trips back home to their districts each year.[3] One journalist has aptly described a member's days as a

> kaleidoscopic jumble: breakfast with reporters, morning staff meetings, simultaneous committee hearings to juggle, back-to-back sessions with lobbyists and constituents, phone calls, briefings, constant buzzers interrupting office work to make quorum calls and votes on the run, afternoon speeches, evening meetings, receptions, fund-raisers, all crammed into four days so they can race home for a weekend gauntlet of campaigning. It's a rat race.[4]

Congressional Demographics

Congress is better educated, richer, more male, and whiter than the general population. Over two-thirds of the members of the House and Senate also hold advanced degrees.[5]

Many members of both houses have significant inherited wealth, but given their educational attainment, which is far higher than the average American's, it is not surprising to find so many wealthy members of Congress. Almost half of all members of Congress are millionaires. The Senate, in fact, is often called the Millionaires Club. In

TABLE 6.3 WHAT IS A TYPICAL DAY LIKE FOR A MEMBER OF CONGRESS?

5:00 a.m.	Arrive at office.
7:00 a.m.	Give a tour of the U.S. Capitol to constituents.
8:00 a.m.	Eat breakfast with the House Shipbuilding Caucus.
9:00 a.m.	Meet with Speaker of the House and other members of Congress.
10:00 a.m.	Attend House Armed Services Committee hearing.
11:00 a.m.	Prepare for afternoon press conference, return phone calls, and sign constituent mail.
12:00 p.m.	Meet with constituents who want the member to join a caucus that may benefit the district.
1:00 p.m.	Read one of nine newspapers to keep track of current events.
2:00 p.m.	Attend Homeland Security Subcommittee hearing.
3:00 p.m.	Attend floor vote.
3:30 p.m.	Meet with group of high school students on front steps of Capitol.
4:15 p.m.	Return to office to sign more constituent mail and to meet with the American Heart Association.
5:00 p.m.	Attend Sustainable Energy and Environment Caucus meeting.
7:00 p.m.	Eat dinner with fellow members.
9:00 p.m.	Return to office to sign more constituent mail and read more newspapers.
11:00 p.m.	Leave office to go home.

SOURCE: Adapted from Bob Clark, "A Day in the Life ..." *Evening Tribune* (October 7, 2009), www.eveningtribune.com (accessed October 20, 2010).

incumbency
Already holding an office.

2011, the average net worth of a House member was $4.7 million, while the average net worth of a senator was $13.9 million.

The average age of House members is fifty-seven; Representative Aaron Schock (R–IL) was first elected to the House in 2008 at age twenty-eight and is still the youngest member of Congress. The average age of senators in the 112th Congress is sixty-three. Michael Lee (R–UT) is the youngest senator; he was first elected in 2010 at the age of thirty-nine.

The 2012 elections saw a record number of women, African Americans, and other minorities elected to Congress. By the 113th Congress, the total number of women members rose to seventy-seven in the House and twenty in the Senate. The number of African Americans in the House remained steady at forty-four. No African Americans currently serve in the Senate. Thirty-one Hispanics served in Congress. Also serving in the 112th Congress are eleven members of Asian or Pacific Island American heritage, and one American Indian, Tom Cole (R–OK). A record number—five—openly homosexual members and one bisexual served in the House; one homosexual woman, Tammy Baldwin (D-WI) served in the Senate.

□ Running for and Staying In Office

Despite the long hours and hard work required of senators and representatives, thousands of people aspire to these jobs every year. Yet, only 535 men and women (plus seven nonvoting members from American Samoa, the District of Columbia, Guam, the U.S. Virgin Islands, and Puerto Rico) actually serve in the U.S. Congress. Membership in one of the two major political parties is almost always a prerequisite for election, because election laws in various states often discriminate against independents (those without party affiliation) and minor-party candidates. The ability to raise money often is key to any member's victory, and many members spend nearly all of their free time on the phone, dialing for dollars, or attending fundraisers. Incumbency and redistricting also affect members' chances at reelection.

INCUMBENCY **Incumbency** helps members stay in office once they are elected.[6] It is often very difficult for outsiders to win because they don't have the advantages

WHO ARE THE NONVOTING MEMBERS REPRESENTING WASHINGTON, D.C.?

Shadow Senators Paul Strauss (rear) and Michael Brown (left) and Delegate Eleanor Holmes Norton (center), all Democrats, represent Washington, D.C., in the Senate and the House, respectively. When Democrats held the House, Norton was allowed to cast votes in committee, a privilege she lost in 2011 when Republicans gained control of the House. D.C.'s two shadow senators have no voting rights or legal standing.

The People's House?

The Framers intended the House of Representatives to be the people's house. At least in theory, it is the more democratic of the two houses of Congress, and its members are intended to be closer to and more representative of the American population. Critics, however, charge that it is difficult for all citizens' interests to be heard in an institution whose members overrepresent some groups, while underrepresenting others, as shown in the infographic below.

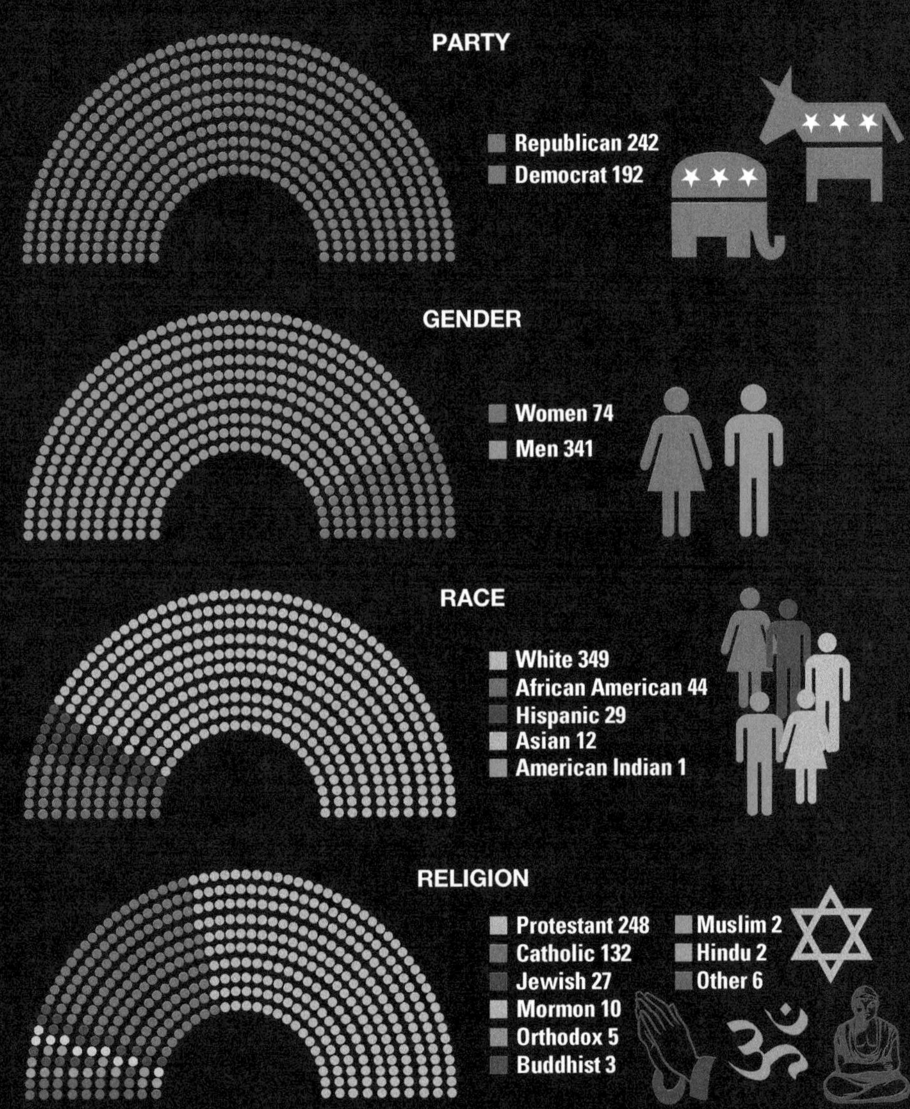

SOURCE: Data from Jennifer E. Manning, "Membership of the 112th Congress: A Profile," *Congressional Research Service,* accessed online August 1, 2012.

CRITICAL THINKING QUESTIONS

1. Which demographic groups are most over and unde1rrepresented in Congress, compared to the population?
2. Can members provide substantive policy representation for citizens even if they are descriptively different? Why or why not?
3. Should actions be taken to make the House look more like the American people? Why or why not? What positives and negatives might result from these actions?

6.1

6.2

6.3

6.4

6.5

6.6

redistricting
The process of redrawing congressional districts to reflect increases or decreases in seats allotted to the states, as well as population shifts within a state.

gerrymandering
The drawing of congressional districts to produce a particular electoral outcome without regard to the shape of the district.

TABLE 6.4 WHAT ARE THE ADVANTAGES OF INCUMBENCY?

Name recognition. Members' names have been on the ballot before, and voters may associate their names with programs or social services they have brought to the district.
Credit claiming. Members may claim to be responsible for federal money brought to the district.
Casework. Members and their staffs help constituents solve problems with the government, including navigating red tape and tracking down federal aid.
Franking privilege. Members may send mail or newsletters for free by using their signature in place of a stamp.
Access to media. Members and their staffs may have relationships with reporters and may find it easy to spin stories or give quotes.
Ease in fund-raising. Incumbents' high reelection rates make them a safe bet for individuals or groups wanting to give donations in exchange for access.
Experience in running a campaign. Members have already put together a campaign staff, made speeches, and come to understand constituent concerns.
Redistricting. In the House, a member's district may be drawn to enhance electability.

enjoyed by incumbents, including name recognition, access to free media, an inside track on fund-raising, and a district drawn to favor the incumbent (see Table 6.4).

It is not surprising, then, that, on average, 96 percent of incumbents who seek reelection win their primary and general election races.[7] In 2012, only about 20 incumbent House members lost their reelection bids. The majority of those who lost were Republicans, and many of those members had been first elected in 2010.[8] In the Senate, however, only two members, Scott Brown (R-MA) and Richard Lugar (R-IN) ran for reelection and lost.

REDISTRICTING The process of redrawing congressional districts to reflect increases or decreases in seats allotted to the states, as well as population shifts within a state, is called **redistricting.** Redistricting is a largely political process. In most states, partisan state legislatures draw district lines. As a result, the majority party in the state legislature uses the redistricting process as an opportunity to ensure formation of voting districts that protect their majority. The process of drawing congressional districts can, therefore, become highly contentious. In recent years, redistricting battles in many states have become increasingly personal, with members of some state legislatures even walking out during the process. Hoping to avoid this sort of political high theater, some states, including Iowa and Arizona, appoint nonpartisan commissions or use some other independent means of drawing district lines. Although the processes vary in detail, most states require legislative approval of redistricting plans.

The redistricting process often involves **gerrymandering**—the drawing of congressional districts to produce a particular electoral outcome without regard to the shape of the district. Because of enormous population growth, the partisan implications of redistricting, and the requirement under the Voting Rights Act of 1965 for minorities to have an equal chance to elect candidates of their choice, legislators end up drawing oddly shaped districts to elect more members of their party.[9] Redistricting plans routinely meet with court challenges across the country (see Figure 6.1).

For a long time, the U.S. Supreme Court considered redistricting based on partisan considerations to be a political question not within the scope of constitutional law, but, rather, one worked out through the regular political process.[10] But, in recent years the Supreme Court has involved itself in some such cases and has ruled that:

- Congressional as well as state legislative districts must be apportioned on the basis of population.[11]
- District lines must be contiguous; one must be able to draw the boundaries of the district with a single unbroken line.[12]
- Purposeful gerrymandering of a congressional district to dilute minority strength is illegal under the Voting Rights Act of 1965.[13]
- Redrawing districts to enhance minority representation is constitutional if race is not the "predominate" factor.[14]
- States may redistrict more frequently than every ten years.[15]

The Original "Gerrymander" Cartoon, 1812

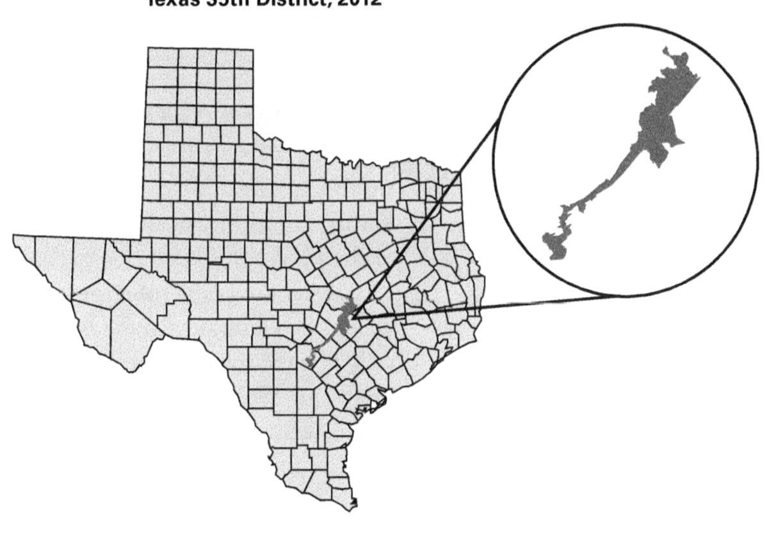

FIGURE 6.1 WHAT IS GERRYMANDERING?

Two drawings—one a mocking cartoon, the other all too real—show the bizarre geographical contortions that result from gerrymandering. The term was coined by combining the last name of the Massachusetts governor first credited with politicizing the redistricting process, Elbridge Gerry, and the word "salamander," which looked like the oddly shaped district that Gerry created.

SOURCES: David Van Biema, "Snakes or Ladders?" *Time* (July 12, 1993) © 1993, Time Inc. Reprinted by permission.

How Congress Is Organized

6.3 Assess the role of the committee system, political parties, and congressional leadership in organizing Congress.

majority party
The political party in each house of Congress with the most members.

minority party
The political party in each house of Congress with the second most members.

party caucus (or conference)
A formal gathering of all party members.

As demonstrated in Figure 6.2, the organization of both houses of Congress is closely tied to political parties and their strength in each house. The basic division in Congress is between majority and minority parties. The **majority party** in each house is the party with the most members. The **minority party** in each house is the party with the second most members (see Figure 6.2).

At the beginning of each new Congress—the 113th Congress, for example, will sit in two sessions, one in 2013 and one in 2014—the members of each party formally gather in their **party caucus (or conference)** (see Figure 6.3 for the partisan composition of Congress). Historically, these caucuses have enjoyed varied powers, but today the party caucuses—now called caucus by House and Senate Democrats and conference by House and Senate Republicans—have several roles, including nominating or electing party officers, reviewing committee assignments, discussing party policy, imposing party discipline, setting party themes, and coordinating media, including talk radio. Conference and caucus chairs are recognized party leaders who work with other leaders in the House or Senate.[16]

Each caucus or conference has specialized committees that fulfill certain tasks. House Republicans, for example, have a Committee on Committees that makes committee assignments. The Democrats' Steering Committee performs this function. Each party also has congressional campaign committees to assist members in their reelection bids.

Leadership in the House of Representatives

Even in the first Congress in 1789, the House of Representatives was almost three times larger than the Senate. It is not surprising, then, that from the beginning the House has shown tighter organization, more elaborate structure, and governance by stricter rules. Traditionally, loyalty to party leadership and voting along party lines have been more common in the House than in the Senate. House leaders also play a key role

Speaker of the House
The only officer of the House of Representatives specifically mentioned in the Constitution; the chamber's most powerful position; traditionally a member of the majority party.

in moving the business of the House along. Historically, the Speaker of the House, the majority and minority leaders, and the Republican and Democratic House whips have made up the party leadership that runs the institution.

THE SPEAKER OF THE HOUSE The **Speaker of the House,** the chamber's most powerful position, is the only officer of the House of Representatives specifically mentioned in the Constitution. The office follows a model similar to the British Parliament—the Speaker was the one who spoke to the king and conveyed the wishes of the House of Commons to the monarch.[17]

The entire House of Representatives elects the Speaker at the beginning of each new Congress. Traditionally, the Speaker is a member of the majority party. Although typically not the member with the longest service, the Speaker generally has served in the House for a long time and in other House leadership positions as an apprentice. Speaker John Boehner (R–OH) was in office twenty years before being elected to the position.

The Speaker presides over the House of Representatives, oversees House business, and is the official spokesperson for the House, as well as being second in the line of presidential succession (after the vice president). The Speaker is also expected to smooth the passage of party-backed legislation through the House. To aid in this process, the Speaker generally has great political influence within the chamber and in policy negotiations with the president.

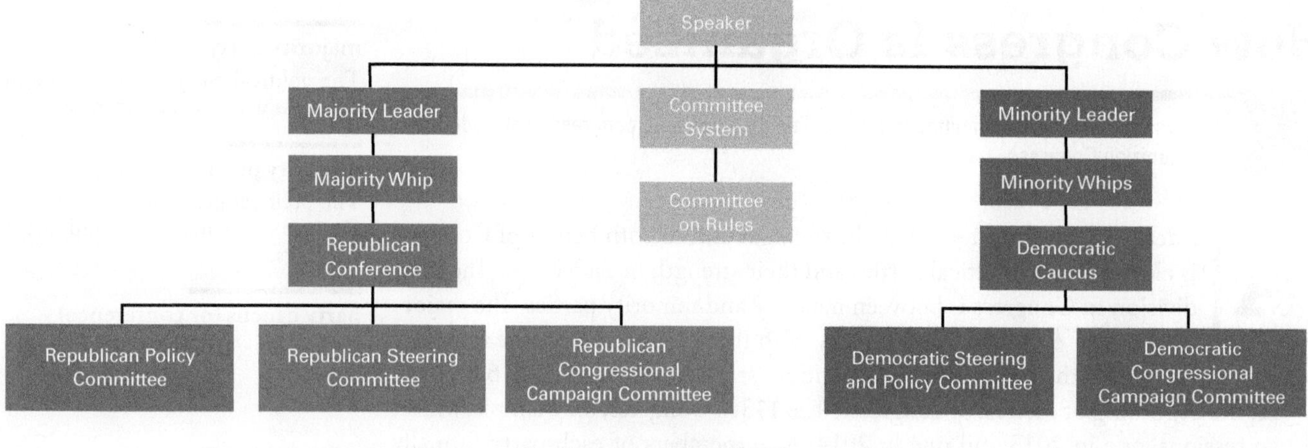

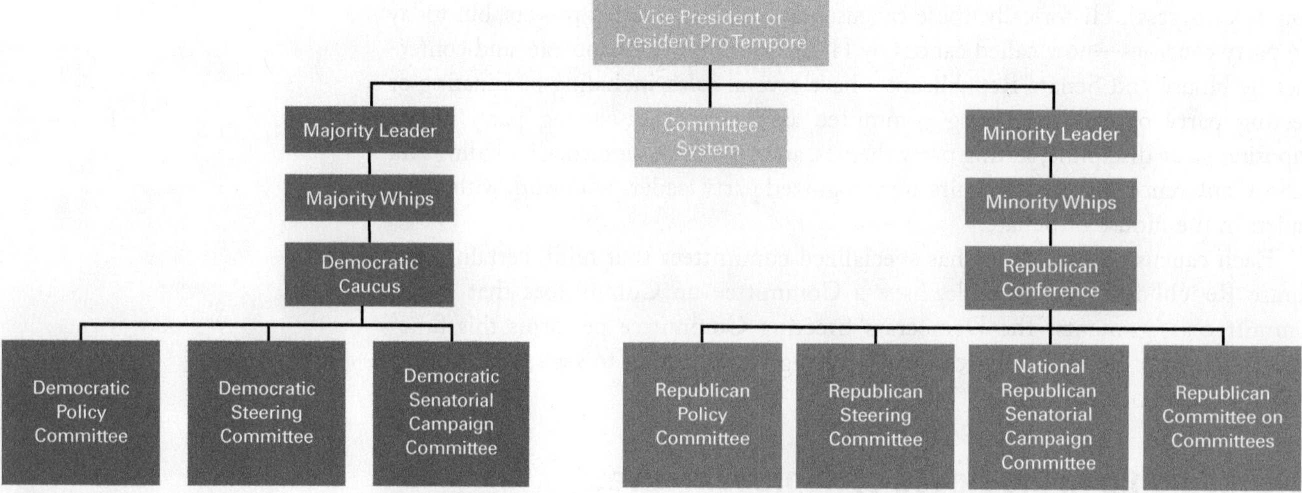

FIGURE 6.2 HOW ARE THE HOUSE OF REPRESENTATIVES AND THE SENATE ORGANIZED?
Parties play a very important role in organizing both the House and Senate. The majority and minority leaders are chosen by the party caucus or conference, as are other key leaders in the party hierarchy. This structure helps to organize operations and conflict in each of the institutions.

SOURCE: Adapted from Roger H. Davidson and Walter J. Oleszek, *Congress and Its Members*, 10th ed. (Washington, DC: CQ Press, 2006.) Updated by the authors.

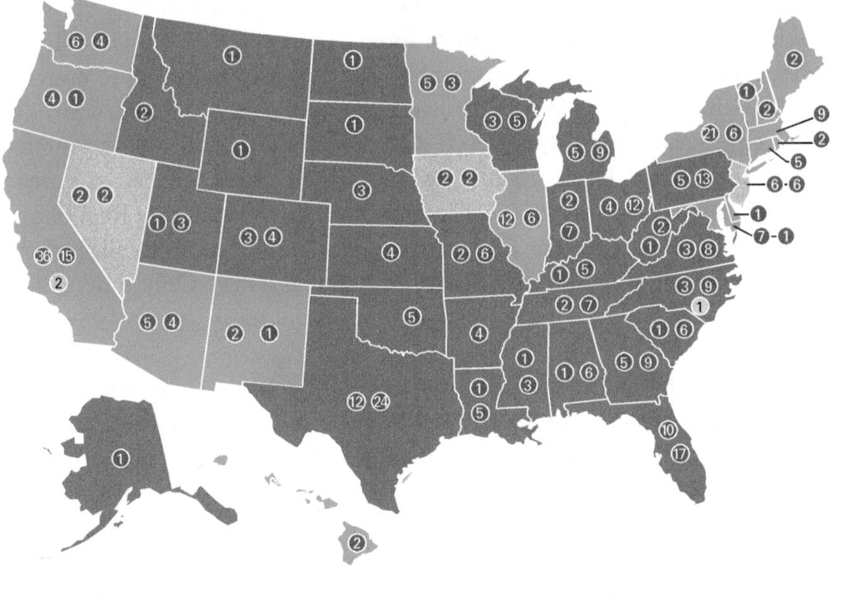

House of Representatives

- Republican seats
- Democratic seats
- Undecided seats*
- Republican majority
- Democratic majority
- Equal party membership

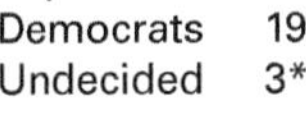

Total

Republicans 234
Democrats 198
Undecided 3*

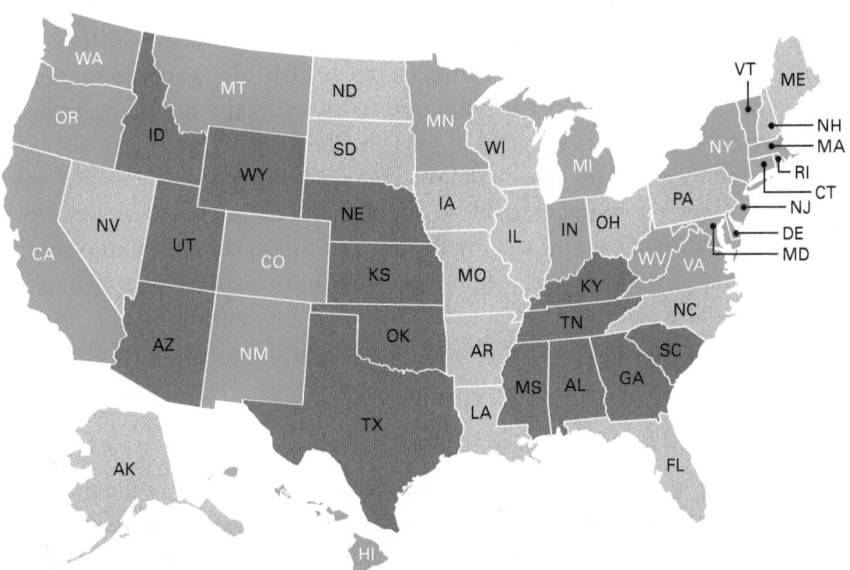

Senate

- Democratic
- Republican
- Split

Total

Democrats 53
Republicans 44
Independents 3

*As of mid-November 2012.

FIGURE 6.3 WHAT IS THE PARTISAN COMPOSITION OF THE 113TH CONGRESS?

The partisan composition of the 113th Congress is quite similar to that of the 112th Congress, with Republicans holding the majority in the House of Representatives and Democrats holding the majority in the Senate. Democrats made small gains in each of the houses, but it was not enough to switch overall control.

SOURCE: CNN Races and Results, http://www.cnn.com/election/2012/results/race/house and http://www.cnn.com/election/2012/results/race/senate.

The first powerful Speaker was Henry Clay (R–KY). Serving in Congress at a time when turnover was high, he was elected to the position in 1810, his first term in office. He held the post of Speaker of the House for a total of six terms—longer than anyone else in the nineteenth century.

By the late 1800s, the House ceased to have a revolving door, and the length of members' average stays increased. With this new professionalization of the House came professionalization in the position of Speaker. Between 1896 and 1910, a series of Speakers initiated changes that brought more power to the office as the Speaker largely took control of committee assignments and the appointing of committee chairs. Institutional and personal rule reached its height during the 1903–1910 tenure of Speaker Joe Cannon (R–IL).

Negative reaction to those strong Speakers eventually led to a revolt in 1910 and 1911 in the House and to a reduction of the formal powers of the Speaker. As a consequence, many Speakers between Cannon and Newt Gingrich (R-GA), who became Speaker in 1995, often relied on more informal powers derived from their personal ability to persuade

majority leader
The head of the party controlling the most seats in the House of Representatives or the Senate; is second in authority to the Speaker of the House and in the Senate is regarded as its most powerful member.

minority leader
The head of the party with the second highest number of elected representatives in the House of Representatives or the Senate.

whip
Party leader who keeps close contact with all members of his or her party, takes vote counts on key legislation, prepares summaries of bills, and acts as a communications link within a party.

members of their party. Gingrich, the first Republican Speaker in forty years, convinced fellow Republicans to return important formal powers to the position. These formal changes, along with his personal leadership skills, allowed Gingrich to exercise greater control over the House and its agenda than any other Speaker since the days of Cannon.

Current Speaker John Boehner (R–OH) faced many challenges trying to control members of his party during his first two years as Speaker; he received a great deal of criticism for his often conflictual leadership style. After retaining a Republican majority during the 113th Congress, Boehner vowed to become a more collaborative leader, seeking greater compromise on a variety of political issues. Only time will tell if his governing style lives up to this promise.

LEADERSHIP TEAMS After the Speaker, the next most powerful people in the House are the majority and minority leaders, who are elected in their individual party caucuses or conferences. The **majority leader** is the head of the party controlling the most seats in the House; his or her counterpart in the party with the second highest number of seats is the **minority leader.** The majority leader helps the Speaker schedule proposed legislation for debate on the House floor.

The Republican and Democratic **whips,** who are elected by party members in caucuses, assist the Speaker and majority and minority leaders in their leadership efforts. The position of whip originated in the British House of Commons, where it was named after the "whipper in," the rider who keeps the hounds together in a fox hunt. Party whips—first designated in the U.S. House of Representatives in 1899—do, as their name suggests, try to whip fellow Democrats or Republicans into line on partisan issues. They try to maintain close contact with all members on important votes, prepare summaries of content and implications of bills, take vote counts during debates and votes, and in general persuade members to toe the party line. Whips and their deputy whips also serve as communications links, distributing word of the party line from leaders to rank-and-file members and alerting leaders to concerns in the ranks.

Leadership in the Senate

Organization and formal rules never have played the same role in the Senate as in the House. Through the 1960s, the Senate was a gentlemen's club whose folkways—unwritten rules of behavior—governed its operation. One such folkway, for example,

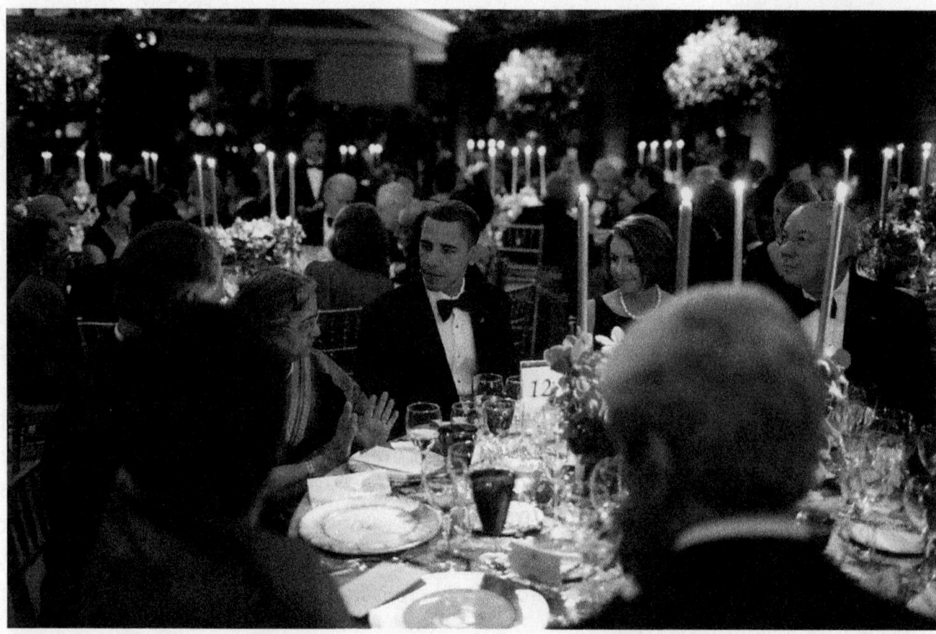

WHO WAS THE FIRST FEMALE SPEAKER OF THE HOUSE?

Nancy Pelosi, shown here at a State Dinner with President Barack Obama and General Colin Powell, was the first woman Speaker. A strong Speaker, she was known for her ability to count votes before allowing any bill on the floor, resulting in the highest levels of party unity in modern Congresses.

Explore Your World

The structure of the U.S. Capitol reflects not only the bicameral legislature created by the Framers in Article I but also American culture. For example, the designer of the Capitol "Americanized" some of the columns on the building by sculpting ears of corn instead of traditional European acanthus leaves. Examine each of the photos below and consider how they reflect the characteristics of the state they represent.

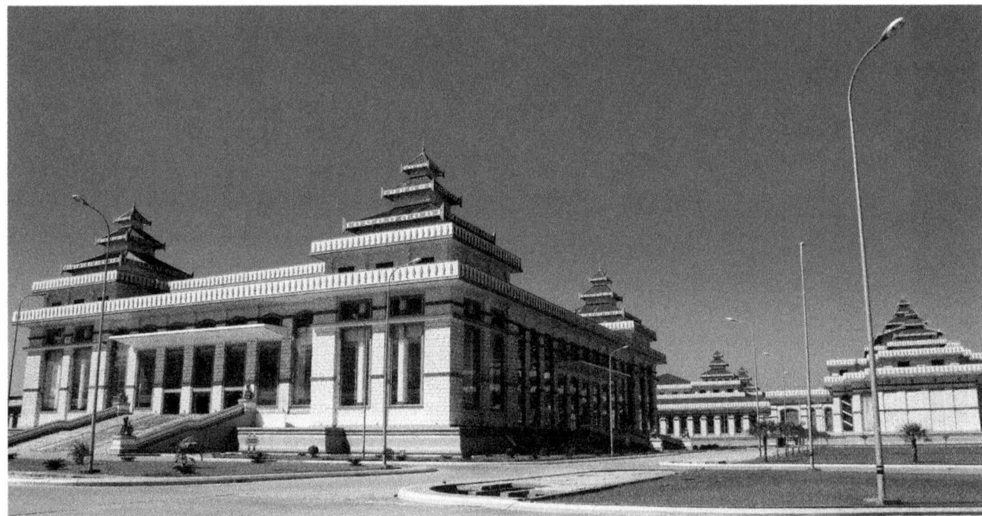

Myanmar's (Burma) legislative building is one of the newest in the world, opening in 2010 after decades of controversy in that country gave way to parliamentary elections. The building's architecture echos the style of many Burmese temples in the region, but this lavish complex has spurred controversy, as the perfectly manicured lawns and brand new buildings contrast sharply with the poverty of many of the country's residents.

The most prominent feature of the U.S. Capitol is its dome, which is located in the center of the building. The wings on either side of the dome are home to the House of Representatives and the Senate.

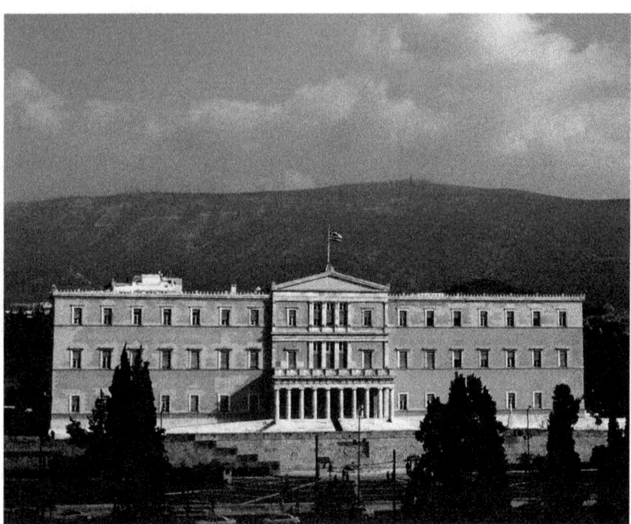

The Hellenic Parliament meets in the Parliament House in Athens, Greece. The building sits elevated on a hill, above Constitution Square. Although the legislature is unicameral today, it was bicameral during some parts of the country's history.

CRITICAL THINKING QUESTIONS

1. What similarities and differences did you notice in the physical structures of the legislative buildings?
2. Why do you think each legislature looks the way it does? How has the country's governmental system influenced each building's appearance? How have cultural influences affected each building's appearance?
3. Assume two new countries have just been established: one has a unicameral legislature, and the other has a bicameral legislature. If you were to design a legislative building for each of these countries, how would each look and why?

6.1

6.2

6.3

6.4

6.5

6.6

president pro tempore
The official chair of the Senate; usually the most senior member of the majority party.

stipulated that political disagreements not become personal criticisms. A senator who disliked another referred to that senator as "the able, learned, and distinguished senator." A member who really could not stand another called that senator "my very able, learned, and distinguished colleague."

In the 1960s and 1970s, senators became increasingly active on a variety of issues on and off the Senate floor, and extended debates often occurred on the floor without the rigid rules of courtesy that had once prevailed. These changes have made the majority leader's role as coalition-builder extraordinarily challenging.[18]

PRESIDING OFFICER The Constitution specifies that the presiding officer of the Senate is the vice president of the United States. Because he is not a member of the Senate, he votes only in the case of a tie.

The official chair of the Senate is the **president pro tempore,** or pro tem, whom the majority party selects and who presides over the Senate in the absence of the vice president. The position of pro tem today is primarily an honorific office generally awarded to the most senior senator of the majority party. Once elected, the pro tem stays in that office until the majority party in the Senate changes. Since presiding over the Senate can be a rather perfunctory duty, neither the vice president nor the president pro tempore actually performs the task very often. Instead, this particular duty rotates among junior members of the majority party of the chamber, allowing more senior members to attend meetings of greater importance.

MAJORITY LEADER The true leader of the Senate is the majority leader, elected to the position by the majority party. Because the Senate is a smaller and more collegial body, the majority leader is not nearly as powerful as the Speaker of the House. Senate Majority Leader Harry Reid (D–NV) discovered the many difficulties that may face a Senate leader trying to coordinate members of his party and ensure party loyalty, even in times of high partisanship. Most of Reid's troubles resulted from struggles to ensure the loyalty of moderate Democratic members on important votes dealing with economic recovery and health care reform. As a result of these challenges, but also because of high unemployment and foreclosure rates in his home state of Nevada, Reid appeared to be one of the most vulnerable members of the Senate during the 2010 election. He ultimately defeated Tea Party member Sharron Angle with help from many labor unions.

LEADERSHIP TEAMS The minority leader and the Republican and Democratic whips round out the leadership positions in the Senate and perform functions similar to those of their House counterparts. But, leading and whipping in the Senate can be quite a challenge. Senate rules always have given tremendous power to individual senators; in most cases senators can offer any kind of amendments to legislation on the floor, and an individual senator can bring all work on the floor to a halt indefinitely through a filibuster unless three-fifths of the senators vote to cut him or her off.[19]

□ The Committee System

The saying "Congress in session is Congress on exhibition, whilst Congress in its committee rooms is Congress at work" may not be as true today as it was when Woodrow Wilson wrote it in 1885.[20] Still, "the work that takes place in the committee and subcommittee rooms of Capitol Hill is critical to the productivity and effectiveness of Congress."[21] Standing committees are the first and last places to which most bills go. Usually, committee members play key roles in floor debate about the merits of bills that have been introduced. When the House and Senate pass different versions of a bill, a conference committee with members of both houses meets to iron out the differences. Committee organization and specialization are especially important in the House of Representatives because of its size. The establishment of subcommittees allows for even greater specialization.

TYPES OF COMMITTEES Congressional committees are of four types: (1) standing; (2) joint; (3) conference; and, (4) select (or special).[22]

1. **Standing committees** are those to which bills are referred for consideration; they are so called because they continue from one Congress to the next.
2. **Joint committees** are standing committees that include members from both houses of Congress and are set up to conduct investigations or special studies. They focus public attention on major matters, such as the economy, taxation, or scandals.
3. **Conference committees** are special joint committees created to reconcile differences in bills passed by the House and Senate. A conference committee comprises members from the House and Senate committees that originally considered the bill.
4. **Select (or special) committees** are temporary committees appointed for specific purposes, such as investigating the September 11, 2001, terrorist attacks.

In the 112th Congress, the House had twenty standing committees, as shown in Table 6.5, each with an average of thirty-one members. Together, these standing committees had roughly ninety subcommittees that collectively acted as the eyes, ears, and

standing committee
Committee to which proposed bills are referred; continues from one Congress to the next.

joint committee
Standing committee that includes members from both houses of Congress set up to conduct investigations or special studies.

conference committee
Special joint committee created to reconcile differences in bills passed by the House and Senate.

select (or special) committee
Temporary committee appointed for a specific purpose.

TABLE 6.5 WHAT WERE THE COMMITTEES OF THE 112TH CONGRESS?

Standing Committees	
House	**Senate**
Agriculture	Agriculture, Nutrition, and Forestry
Appropriations	Appropriations
Armed Services	Armed Services
Budget	Banking, Housing, and Urban Affairs
Education and the Workforce	Budget
Energy and Commerce	Commerce, Science, and Transportation
Ethics	Energy and Natural Resources
Financial Services	Environment and Public Works
Foreign Affairs	Finance
Homeland Security	Foreign Relations
House Administration	Health, Education, Labor, and Pensions
Judiciary	Homeland Security and Governmental Affairs
Commercial and Administrative Law	Judiciary
The Constitution, Civil Rights, and Civil Liberties	*Administrative Oversight and the Courts*
Courts and Competition Policy	*Antitrust, Competition Policy, and Consumer Rights*
Crime, Terrorism, and Homeland Security	*The Constitution*
Immigration, Citizenship, Refugees, Border Security, and International Law	*Crime and Drugs*
Task Force on Antitrust	*Human Rights and the Law*
Natural Resources	*Immigration, Refugees, and Border Security*
Oversight and Government Reform	*Terrorism, Technology, and Homeland Security*
Rules	Rules and Administration
Science, Space, and Technology	Small Business and Entrepreneurship
Small Business	Veterans Affairs
Transportation and Infrastructure	
Veterans' Affairs	
Ways and Means	

Select, Special, and Other Committees		
House	**Senate**	**Joint Committees**
Intelligence	Select Ethics	Economics
	Select Intelligence	Taxation
	Special Aging	Library
	Indian Affairs	Printing

NOTE: The subcommittees of the House and Senate Judiciary Committees during the 112th Congress are listed in italics.

6.1

6.2

6.3

6.4

6.5

6.6

discharge petition
Petition that gives a majority of the House of Representatives the authority to bring an issue to the floor in the face of committee inaction.

seniority
Time of continuous service on a committee.

hands of the House. They considered issues roughly parallel to those of the departments represented in the president's Cabinet. For example, there were committees on agriculture, education, the judiciary, veterans' affairs, transportation, and commerce.

Although most committees in one house parallel those in the other, the House Committee on Rules, for which no counterpart in the Senate exists, plays a major role in the House's law-making process. As an indication of this committee's importance, the Speaker directly appoints its chair and majority party members. This committee reviews most bills after they come from a committee and before they go to the full chamber for consideration. Performing a traffic cop function, the Committee on Rules gives each bill what is called a rule, which contains the date the bill will come up for debate and the time that will be allotted for discussion, and often specifies what kinds of amendments can be offered. Bills considered under a closed rule cannot be amended.

Standing committees have considerable power. They can kill bills, amend them radically, or hurry them through the process. In the words of former President Woodrow Wilson, once a bill is referred to a committee, it "crosses a parliamentary bridge of sighs to dim dungeons of silence whence it never will return."[23] Committees report out to the full House or Senate only a small fraction of the bills assigned to them. A **discharge petition** signed by a majority (218) of the House membership can force bills out of a House committee.

In the 112th Congress, the Senate had sixteen standing committees ranging in size from fifteen to twenty-nine members. It also had roughly seventy subcommittees, which allowed all majority party senators to chair at least one.

In contrast to members of the House, who hold few committee assignments (an average of 1.8 standing and three subcommittees), senators each serve on an average of three to four committees and seven subcommittees. Whereas the committee system allows House members to become policy or issue specialists, Senate members often are generalists.

Senate committees have the same power over framing legislation that House committees do, but the Senate, as an institution more open to individual input than the House, gives less deference to the work done in committees. In the Senate, legislation is more likely to be rewritten on the floor, where all senators can generally participate and add amendments.

COMMITTEE CHAIRS Committee chairs enjoy tremendous power and prestige, with authorization to select all subcommittee chairs, call meetings, and recommend majority members to sit on conference committees. Committee chairs may even opt to kill a bill by refusing to schedule hearings on it. They also have a large committee staff at their disposal and are often recipients of favors from lobbyists, who recognize the chair's unique position of power. Interpersonal skills, influence, and expertise are a chair's best resources.

Historically, committee chairs were the majority party members with the longest continuous service on the committee. Committee chairs in the House, unlike the Senate, are no longer selected by **seniority,** or time of continuous service on the committee. Instead, to ensure that candidates demonstrate party loyalty, party leaders interview potential chairs. Six years of service on a particular committee is the limit on all committee chairs.

COMMITTEE MEMBERSHIP Many newly elected members of Congress set their sights on certain committee assignments. Others are more flexible. Many legislators who desire particular committee assignments inform their party's selection committee of their preferences. They often request assignments based on their own interests or expertise or on a particular committee's ability to help their prospects for reelection. One political scientist has noted that members view committee assignments the way investors view stocks—they seek to acquire those that will add to the value of their portfolios.[24]

Some committees, such as Energy and Commerce, facilitate reelection by giving House members influence over decisions that affect large campaign contributors. Other committees, such as Education and the Workforce or Judiciary, attract members eager to work on the policy responsibilities assigned to the committee even if the appointment does them little good at the ballot box. Another motivator for certain committee assignments is the desire to have power and influence within the chamber. The Appropriations and Budget

Committees provide that kind of reward for some members, given the monetary impact of the committees. Congress can approve programs, but unless money for them is appropriated in the budget, they are largely symbolic.

In both the House and the Senate, committee membership generally reflects party distribution within that chamber. For example, at the outset of the 113th Congress, Republicans held a majority of House seats and thus claimed about a 55 percent share of the seats on several committees. On committees more critical to the operation of the House or to the setting of national policy, the majority often takes a disproportionate share of the slots. Since the Committee on Rules regulates access to the floor for legislation approved by other standing committees, control by the majority party is essential for it to manage the flow of legislation. For this reason, no matter how narrow its margin in the chamber, the majority party makes up more than two-thirds of the Committee on Rules' membership.

Powers of Congress

6.4 Identify three of the most significant powers of Congress.

The Framers wished to ensure that the national government had sufficient power to govern the states. Thus, Article I, section 7, of the Constitution details the procedures by which Congress can make laws and raise revenues. Article I, section 8, also details Congress's power to tax, spend, regulate commerce, coin money, and make "all Laws which shall be necessary and proper for carrying into Execution" those powers.

Today, Congress not only makes laws dealing with substantive policy but also spends significant time negotiating and trying to pass the nation's budget. In addition, in accordance with the system of checks and balances, it has a key oversight role. Through the War Powers Resolution, congressional review, approval of nominations, and impeachment, Congress can check the power of the executive and judicial branches.

The Law-making Function

Congress's law-making power allows it to affect the day-to-day lives of all Americans and set policy for the future. Although proposals for legislation—be they about terrorism, Medicare, or tax policy—can come from the president, executive agencies, committee staffs, interest groups, or even private individuals, only members of the House or Senate can formally submit a bill for congressional consideration (although lobbyists initially draft many of them). Once a member of Congress introduces a bill, it usually reaches a dead end. Of the approximately 10,500 bills introduced during the 112th session, Congress voted fewer than 150 into law, making it the least productive Congress in modern history.

A bill must survive several stages before it becomes a law. One or more standing committees and both chambers must approve it, and if House and Senate versions differ, each house must accept a conference report resolving those differences. Multiple stopping points provide many opportunities for legislation to die or members to revise the content of legislation and may lead representatives to alter their views on a particular piece of legislation several times over. Thus, it is much easier to defeat a bill than to pass one (see Figure 6.4). The ongoing debates on the budget process are particularly illustrative of this problem.

COMMITTEE REFERRAL The House and Senate have parallel processes, and often the same bill is introduced in each chamber at the same time. One member of Congress must introduce a bill, but several other members (called co-sponsors) often sponsor a bill, in an attempt to show support for its aims. Once introduced, the bill is sent to the clerk of the chamber, who gives it a number (for example, HR 1 or S 1—indicating House or Senate bill number one, respectively). The bill is then printed, distributed, and sent to the appropriate committee or committees for consideration.

Take a Closer Look

Much of the work of Congress is accomplished in committee hearings and private meetings and negotiations. The activity that occurs on the floor of the U.S Senate and House of Representatives is, as a result, more informal than many citizens might expect. While one member is speaking in support of or opposition to a piece of legislation, other members—if they are even in the chamber—may be casting votes, talking with colleagues, or even milling around. Still, the floor proceedings of the U.S. Congress play an important role in the legislative process.

Each senator has a desk in the chamber, with Republicans on the left hand side of the presiding officer and Democrats on the right. Senators, however, rarely sit at these desks.

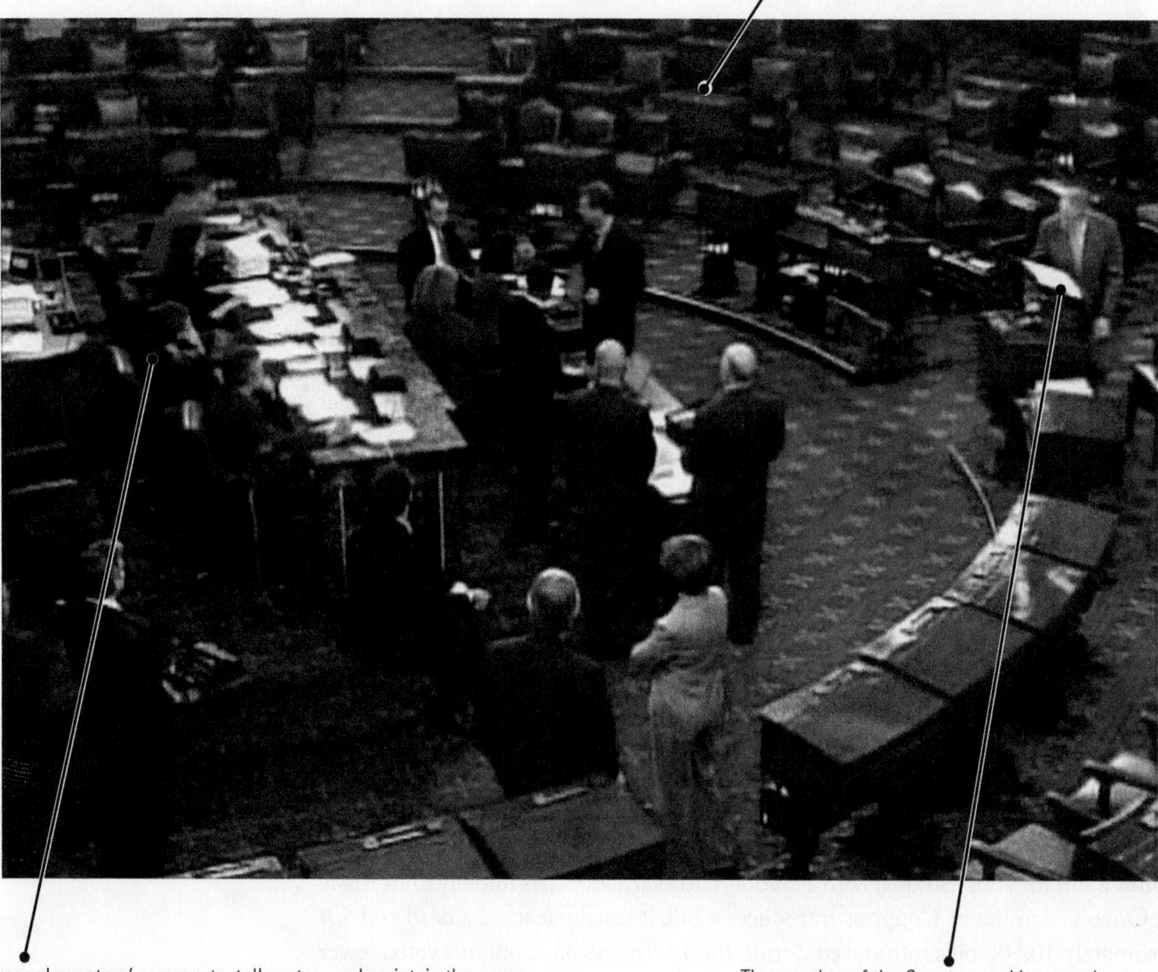

Clerks record senators' comments, tally votes, and maintain the operations of the institution. Behind the clerks sits a presiding officer. Officially, this member should be the vice president or the president pro tempore, but in practice, it is usually a junior member.

The member of the Senate speaking stands at a podium at the front and center of the chamber.

CRITICAL THINKING QUESTIONS

1. Why are formal legislative sessions important to the governmental process, even if little actual work is accomplished during this time?
2. Should members be required to spend more time in the chamber listening to their colleagues' speeches and participating in the legislative process? What would be the positives and negatives of this requirement?
3. Should some of the work traditionally accomplished on the floor of the House and Senate, such as voting and giving speeches, move online in the interest of efficiency? Why or why not?

The committee usually refers the bill to one of its subcommittees, whose staff researches the proposed legislation, and then the chair decides whether or not to hold hearings. The subcommittee hearings provide an opportunity for those on both sides of the issue to voice their opinions. Since the 1970s, most hearings have been open to the public. After the hearings, the subcommittee revises the bill and then votes to approve or defeat it. If the subcommittee votes in favor of the bill, it is returned to the full committee. There, it goes through **markup,** a session during which committee members can offer changes to a bill before it goes to the floor. The full committee may also reject the bill before it goes to the floor in either house.

markup
A session in which committee members offer changes to a bill before it goes to the floor.

FLOOR DEBATE The second stage of action takes place on the House or Senate floor. As previously discussed, in the House, before a bill may be debated on the floor, the Committee on Rules must approve it and give it a rule and a place on the calendar,

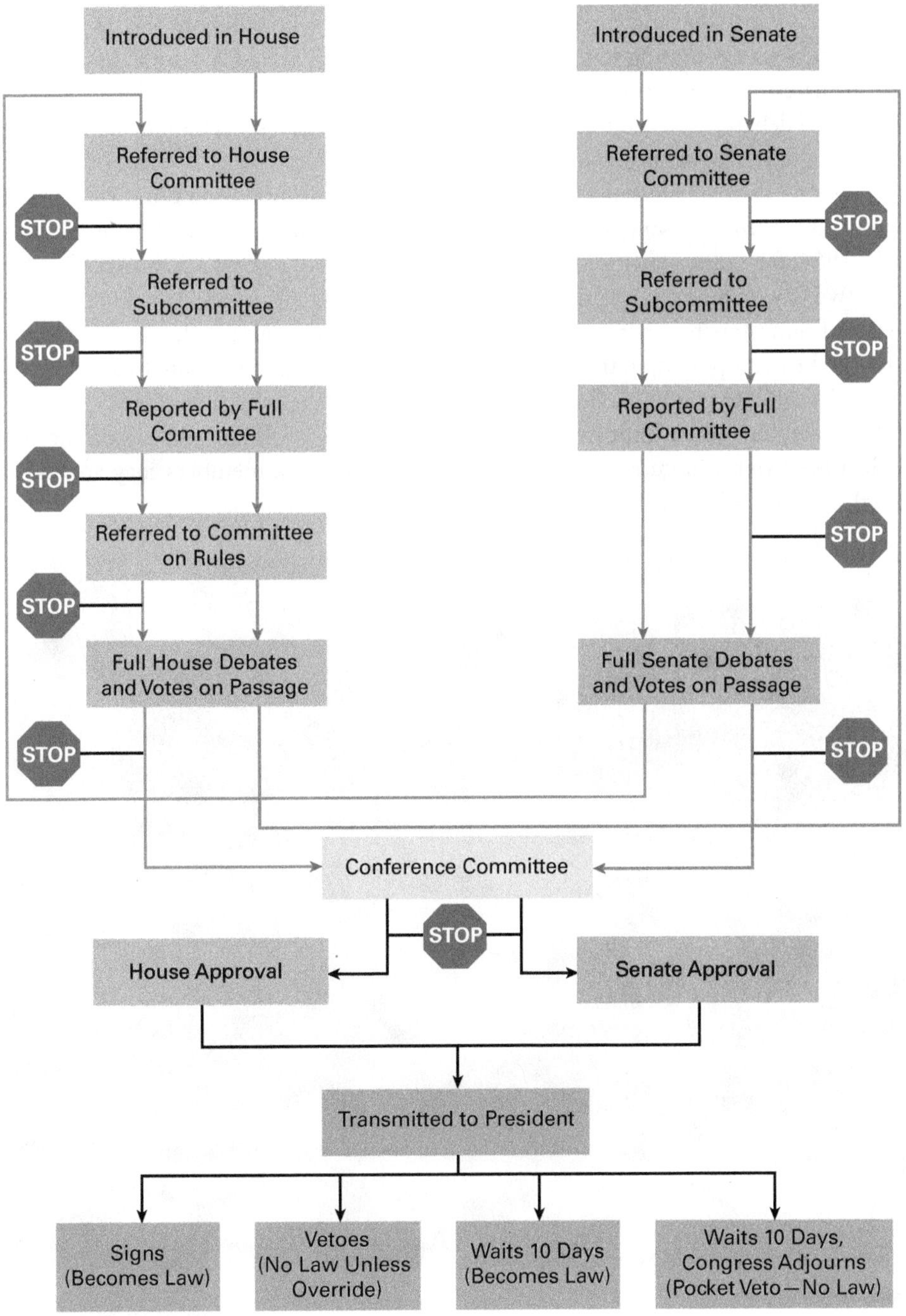

Introduced in House
Referred to House Committee
STOP
Referred to Subcommittee
STOP
Reported by Full Committee
STOP
Referred to Committee on Rules
STOP
Full House Debates and Votes on Passage
STOP

Introduced in Senate
Referred to Senate Committee
STOP
Referred to Subcommittee
STOP
Reported by Full Committee
STOP
Full Senate Debates and Votes on Passage
STOP

Conference Committee
STOP
House Approval
Senate Approval
Transmitted to President
Signs (Becomes Law)
Vetoes (No Law Unless Override)
Waits 10 Days (Becomes Law)
Waits 10 Days, Congress Adjourns (Pocket Veto—No Law)

FIGURE 6.4 HOW DOES A BILL BECOME A LAW?

A bill must go through a carefully prescribed process in both the House of Representatives and the Senate in order to be enacted into law. After a bill has passed both houses, differences must be reconciled and the proposed legislation must meet with the president's approval. As a result, though many bills are introduced, few actually become law.

hold
A procedure by which a senator asks to be informed before a particular bill or nomination is brought to the floor. This request signals leadership that a member may have objections to the bill (or nomination) and should be consulted before further action is taken.

filibuster
A formal way of halting Senate action on a bill by means of long speeches or unlimited debate.

cloture
Mechanism requiring the vote of sixty senators to cut off debate.

or schedule. (House budget bills, however, do not go to the Committee on Rules.) In the House, the rule given to a bill determines limits on the floor debate and specifies what types of amendments, if any, may be attached to the bill. Once the Committee on Rules considers the bill, it is added to the calendar.

When the day arrives for floor debate, the House may choose to form a Committee of the Whole. This procedure allows the House to deliberate with only one hundred members present to expedite consideration of the bill. During this time, members may offer amendments, and the full House ultimately takes a vote. If the bill survives, it goes to the Senate for consideration if that body did not consider it simultaneously.

Unlike the House, whose size necessarily limits debate, the Senate may hold up bills by a hold or a filibuster. A **hold** is a procedure by which a senator asks to be informed before a particular bill (or nomination) is brought to the floor. This request signals the Senate leadership and the sponsors of the bill that a colleague may have objections to the bill (or nomination) and should be consulted before further action is taken. A hold may be anonymous or public and can be placed for any reason—including reviewing, negotiating changes, or attempting to kill a bill. Holds can be lifted by a senator at any time.

Filibusters, a formal way of halting Senate action on a bill by means of long speeches or unlimited debate, grew out of the absence of rules to restrict speech in the Senate. The content of a filibuster has no limits as long as a senator keeps talking. A senator may read from a phone book, recite poetry, or read cookbooks to delay a vote. Often, a team of senators takes turns speaking to continue the filibuster in the hope of tabling or killing a bill. In 1964, for example, a group of northern liberal senators kept a filibuster alive for eighty-two days in an effort to prevent amendments that would weaken a civil rights bill. The use of filibusters has increased in recent years. Moreover, simply the threat of a filibuster can be quite potent; in the modern Senate, it often takes the assured votes of sixty senators for a bill to come to a final vote because of the threat of a filibuster.

Senators may end a filibuster in only one way. Sixty of them must sign a motion for **cloture.** After a cloture motion passes the Senate floor, members may spend no more than thirty additional hours debating the legislation at issue.

WHAT IS THE PRESIDENT'S ROLE IN LAWMAKING?

After a bill has won the approval of both houses of Congress, the president has the final opportunity to approve the law or veto it, sending it back to Congress for a potential veto override. Here, President Barack Obama, surrounded by Vice President Joe Biden and legislative leaders, signs into law the Patient Protection and Affordable Care Act of 2010, which reformed health care in the United States.

FINAL APPROVAL The third stage of action takes place when the two chambers of Congress approve different versions of the same bill. When this happens, they establish a conference committee to iron out the differences between the two versions. The conference committee, whose members are from the original House and Senate committees, hammers out a compromise, which is returned to each chamber for a final vote. Sometimes the conference committee fails to agree and the bill dies there. No changes or amendments to the compromise version are allowed. If the bill does not pass in both houses, it dies. If the bill passes, it is sent to the president, who has ten days to consider a bill. He has four options:

1. The president can sign the bill, at which point it becomes law.
2. The president can **veto** the bill, which is more likely to occur when the president is of a different party from the majority in Congress; Congress may override the president's veto with a two-thirds vote in each chamber, a very difficult task.
3. The president can wait the full ten days, at the end of which time the bill becomes law without his signature if Congress is still in session.
4. If Congress adjourns before the ten days are up, the president can choose not to sign the bill, which is called a **pocket veto.** To become law, the bill then has only one path: to be reintroduced in the next session of Congress and put through the process all over again.

veto
The formal, constitutional authority of the president to reject bills passed by both houses of Congress, thus preventing them from becoming law without further congressional action.

pocket veto
If Congress adjourns during the ten days the president has to consider a bill passed by both houses of Congress, the bill is considered vetoed without the president's signature.

Congressional Budget Act of 1974
Act that established the congressional budgetary process by laying out a plan for congressional action on the annual budget resolution, appropriations, reconciliation, and any other revenue bills.

☐ The Budgetary Function

Since the writing of the Constitution, Congress has enjoyed authority over the budgetary process. For much of American history, however, congressional budgets were piecemeal and made without an eye toward setting the course of public policy. By the 1920s, as a result of growing federal regulation and the bureaucracy, many policy makers sensed a need for greater centralization and order in the budgetary process. Thus, Congress passed and President Warren G. Harding signed into law the Budget and Accounting Act of 1921. This legislation required the president—for the first time—to submit a budget to Congress. The president's proposal would include the prior year's spending, projections, and proposals for the next year. Congress, in turn, could alter the allocation of appropriations but could not increase the total level of spending proposed by the president. To aid the executive branch in this role, the act also created the Bureau of the Budget. In 1970, the name of this agency was changed to the Office of Management and Budget.

This process continued relatively unfettered until the early 1970s, when tension between a Democratic-controlled Congress and a Republican president, Richard M. Nixon, exposed several shortcomings in the system. For example, although Congress authorized the expenditure of funds for many social problems, President Nixon refused to spend appropriated money on them. Angered and frustrated by Nixon's flagrant use of executive power, Congress solidified its role in the budgetary process by passing the Congressional Budget Act of 1974.

CONGRESSIONAL BUDGET ACT OF 1974 The **Congressional Budget Act of 1974** established the congressional budgetary process we use today. The act also created the Congressional Budget Office (CBO), a nonpartisan agency to help members make accurate estimations of revenues and expenditures and to lay out a plan for congressional action on the annual budget resolution, appropriations, reconciliation, and any other revenue bills. In general, these bills and resolutions establish levels of spending for the federal government and its agencies during the next fiscal year. (The federal government's fiscal year runs from October 1 of one year to September 30 of the next. Thus, the 2014 fiscal year runs from October 1, 2013, to September 30, 2014.) Although these levels rarely change dramatically from year to year, the programs and policies that receive increases and decreases in federal spending make a powerful statement about the goals of Congress and the president. For fiscal year 2013, for example, President Obama's initial budget proposal suggested cuts to the defense budget and increased spending on health care.

6.1

6.2

6.3

6.4

6.5

6.6

reconciliation
A procedure that allows consideration of controversial issues affecting the budget by limiting debate to twenty hours, thereby ending threat of a filibuster.

pork
Legislation that allows representatives to bring money and jobs to their districts in the form of public works programs, military bases, or other programs.

programmatic requests
Federal funds designated for special projects within a state or congressional district.

One special process detailed by the Congressional Budget Act of 1974 is **reconciliation.** The reconciliation procedure allows consideration of controversial issues affecting the budget by limiting debate to twenty hours, thereby ending the threat of a filibuster in the Senate. This process received a great deal of attention in 2010, when members of Congress used it to pass the health care reform bill.

The Congressional Budget Act of 1974 also includes a timetable intended to make sure that action on the budget occurs without unnecessary delay (see Table 6.6). Under this constraint, Congress must complete initial action on the budget resolution by April 15 of the preceding fiscal year. The budget resolution—or one or more continuing resolutions allowing the government to spend money at the same rates as the previous fiscal year—must receive approval by the start of the new fiscal year on October 1. When this does not occur, the federal government may shut down, as happened in 1995 when a Republican-controlled Congress and President Bill Clinton, a Democrat, could not agree on spending levels. As a result, all federal offices, buildings, and services did not operate for twenty-two days. Note that although this is the formal process for passing a budget, Congress has not passed a full budget since 2001. In the past ten years, Congress has passed eight temporary budgets to keep government running. During this time, members have made only minor adjustments to spending. At the beginning of the 113th Congress, both Republicans and Democrats in Congress vowed to prioritize budget reform and reducing the national debt. Whether the parties can compromise on these issues, however, remains to be seen.

PORK AND PROGRAMMATIC REQUESTS Representatives often seek to win appropriations known as **pork,** legislation that allows representatives to bring money and jobs to their districts in the form of public works programs, military bases, or other programs. Many of these programs, once called earmarks but now called **programmatic requests,** are funds that an appropriations bill designates for specific projects within a state or congressional district. Legislators who bring jobs and new public works programs back to their districts are hard to defeat when up for reelection. But, ironically, these programs also attract much of the public criticism directed at the federal government in general and Congress in particular.

☐ The Oversight Function

Historically, Congress has performed its oversight function by holding committee hearings in which members question bureaucrats to determine if they are enforcing and interpreting the laws as intended by Congress. These hearings, now routinely televised, are among Congress's most visible and dramatic actions. Congress uses them not only to gather information but also to focus on particular executive-branch actions. They often signal that Congress believes an agency needs to make changes in policy or

TABLE 6.6 WHAT IS THE TIMELINE FOR THE CONGRESSIONAL BUDGETARY PROCESS?

Date	Action
First Monday in February	**President submits budget to Congress**—President's budget is prepared by the Office of Management and Budget; includes requested levels of spending for the next fiscal year.
February 15	**Budget outlooks**—Congressional Budget Office submits economic projections to the House and Senate Budget Committees.
April 15	**Budget resolution**—Congress must complete action on the initial version of a budget resolution.
May 15	**Appropriation begins**—House begins to consider appropriations bills.
June 10	**Appropriations Committee**—House Appropriations Committee should conclude consideration of appropriations issues.
June 15	**Reconciliation ends**—House must handle any reconciliation bills by this date.
June 30	**Appropriation ends**—Full House should conclude consideration of all appropriations bills.
October 1	**Fiscal year begins**—Government's fiscal year runs from October 1 to September 30.

performance before it next comes before the committee to justify its budget or actions. Congress also uses hearings to improve program administration.

Congress may also exercise its oversight powers in a number of other ways. It may, for example, use its powers under the War Powers Resolution or the Congressional Review Act of 1996 to examine actions taken by the president. The Senate also has the authority to offer advice and consent on executive and judicial branch nominees. Congress's ultimate oversight power, however, is the power to impeach other federal officials and remove them from office.

THE WAR POWERS RESOLUTION After years of playing second fiddle to a series of presidents from Theodore Roosevelt to Richard M. Nixon, a "snoozing Congress" was "aroused" and seized for itself the authority and expertise necessary to exercise its full foreign policy oversight powers over the chief executive.[25] In a delayed response to Lyndon B. Johnson's conduct of the Vietnam War, in 1973 Congress passed the **War Powers Resolution** over President Nixon's veto. The resolution permits the president to send troops into action only with the authorization of Congress or if the United States, its territories, or the armed forces are attacked. It also requires the president to notify Congress within forty-eight hours of committing troops to foreign soil. In addition, the president must withdraw troops within sixty days unless Congress votes to declare war. The president also must consult with Congress, if at all possible, prior to committing troops.

War Powers Resolution
Passed by Congress in 1973; the president is limited in the deployment of troops overseas to a sixty-day period in peacetime (which can be extended for an extra thirty days to permit withdrawal) unless Congress explicitly gives its approval for a longer period.

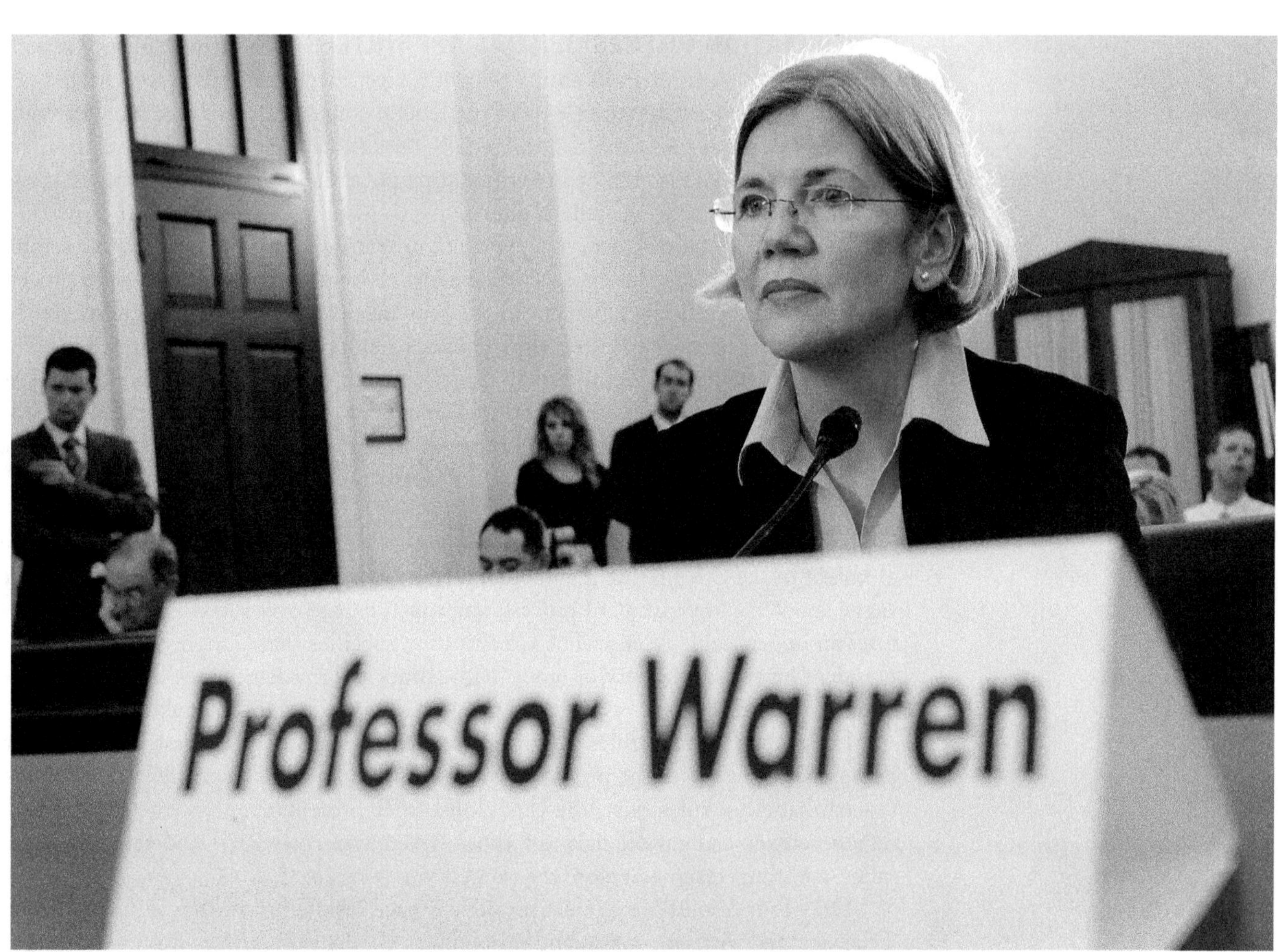

ON WHAT ISSUES DOES CONGRESS CONDUCT OVERSIGHT HEARINGS?

In 2008, Congress created the Troubled Assets Relief Program (TARP) to aid in restoring order and liquidity to the nation's financial system. It also created an Oversight Panel to assure that this program was working efficiently and effectively. Law Professor Elizabeth Warren, who in 2012 was elected to the Senate representing Massachusetts, chaired this committee. She is shown here testifying to the House Budget Committee.

congressional review
A process whereby Congress can nullify agency regulations by a joint resolution of legislative disapproval.

senatorial courtesy
A process by which presidents generally allow senators from the state in which a judicial vacancy occurs to block a nomination by simply registering their objection.

The War Powers Resolution, however, has had limited effectiveness in claiming an oversight role for Congress in international crisis situations. Presidents Gerald R. Ford, Jimmy Carter, and Ronald Reagan never consulted Congress in advance of committing troops, citing the need for secrecy and swift movement, although each president did notify Congress shortly after the deployment of troops abroad. They contended that the War Powers Resolution was probably unconstitutional because it limits presidential prerogatives as commander in chief.

CONGRESSIONAL REVIEW The Congressional Review Act of 1996 allows Congress to exercise its oversight powers by nullifying agency regulations. Under the home rule charter of the District of Columbia, the House and Senate may also nullify actions of the Washington, D.C. City Council. This process is called **congressional review.**[26] If using this oversight power, Congress has sixty days after the implementation of an administrative action to pass a joint resolution of legislative disapproval. The president must also have signed the resolution.

Historically, congressional review has been used rather infrequently. Since its passage, Congress has introduced only about seventy-five joint resolutions of legislative disapproval, and only once has a resolution succeeded.[27] In 2001, Congress and President George W. Bush reversed Clinton administration ergonomics regulations, which were intended to prevent job-related repetitive stress injuries. However, during the 112th Congress, House Republicans pledged to make greater use of the act, questioning a record eleven regulations in the first nine months of 2011.[28]

CONFIRMATION OF PRESIDENTIAL APPOINTEES The Senate plays a special oversight function through its ability to confirm key members of the executive branch, as well as presidential appointments to the federal courts. Although the Senate generally confirms most presidential nominees, it does not always do so. A wise president considers senatorial reaction before nominating potentially controversial individuals to his administration or to the federal courts.

In the case of federal district court appointments, senators often have considerable say in the nomination of judges from their states through **senatorial courtesy,** a process by which presidents generally defer to the senators who represent the state where the vacancy occurs. Through the "blue slip" process, senators may submit a favorable or unfavorable review of a nominee; they may also choose not to comment. Despite this procedure, the judicial nominees of recent presidents have encountered particularly hostile Senates. "Appointments have always been the battleground for policy disputes," says one political scientist. But now, "what's new is the rawness of it—all of the veneer is off."[29]

IMPEACHMENT As discussed earlier, the impeachment process is Congress's ultimate oversight of the U.S. president and federal court judges. The U.S. Constitution is quite vague about the impeachment process, and much debate over it concerns what constitutes an impeachable offense. The Constitution specifies that Congress can impeach a president for treason, bribery, or other "high crimes and misdemeanors." Most commentators agree that the Framers intended this phrase to mean significant abuses of power.

House and Senate rules control how the impeachment process operates. Yet, because Congress uses the process so rarely, and under such disparate circumstances, few hard and fast rules exist. The U.S. House of Representatives has voted to impeach only seventeen federal officials. Of those, seven were convicted and removed from office, and three resigned before the process was completed.

Only four resolutions against presidents have resulted in further action: (1) John Tyler, charged with corruption and misconduct in 1843; (2) Andrew Johnson, charged with serious misconduct in 1868; (3) Richard M. Nixon, charged with obstruction of justice and the abuse of power in 1974; and, (4) Bill Clinton, charged with perjury and obstruction of justice in 1998. The House rejected the charges against Tyler; the Senate acquitted Johnson by a one-vote margin; Nixon resigned before the full House voted on the articles of impeachment; and the Senate acquitted Clinton by a vote of 55–45 after the House voted for impeachment.

How Members Make Decisions

6.5 Analyze the factors that influence how members of Congress make decisions.

trustee
Role played by an elected representative who listens to constituents' opinions and then uses his or her best judgment to make a final decision.

delegate
Role played by an elected representative who votes the way his or her constituents would want, regardless of personal opinions.

politico
An elected representative who acts as a trustee or as a delegate, depending on the issue.

divided government
The political condition in which different political parties control the presidency and Congress.

Explore on MyPoliSciLab Simulation: You Are a Consumer Advocate

Over the years, political theorists have offered various ideas about how any legislative body can best represent constituents' interests. Does it make a difference if the members of Congress come from or are members of a particular group? Are they bound to vote the way their constituents expect them to vote even if they personally favor another policy? Your answer to these questions may depend on your view of the representative function of legislators.

British political philosopher Edmund Burke (1729–1797), who also served in the British Parliament, believed that although he was elected from Bristol, it was his duty to represent the interests of the entire nation. He reasoned that elected officials were obliged to vote as they personally thought best. According to Burke, a representative should be a **trustee** who listens to the opinions of constituents and then can be trusted to use his or her own best judgment to make final decisions.

A second theory of representation holds that a representative should be a **delegate.** True delegates are representatives who vote the way their constituents would want them to, regardless of their own opinions. Delegates, therefore, must be ready and willing to vote against their conscience or personal policy preferences if they know how their constituents feel about a particular issue.

Not surprisingly, members of Congress and other legislative bodies generally do not fall neatly into either category. It is often unclear how constituents regard a particular issue, or conflicting opinions may arise within a single constituency. With these difficulties in mind, a third theory of representation holds that a **politico** alternately dons the hat of a trustee or delegate, depending on the issue. On matters of great concern to their constituents, representatives most likely will vote as delegates; on other matters, perhaps those less visible, representatives will act as trustees and use their own best judgment.[30]

In addition to weighing their representational role, members of Congress consider a number of other factors when deciding how to vote on a piece of legislation. Among these are political parties, constituents, interest groups and lobbyists, and staff and support agencies.

Political Parties

The influence of political parties on members' votes cannot be overstated. In fact, congressional party unity, a measure of the solidarity of the members of a political party, has reached historically high levels in recent years. Members of both the Democratic and Republican Parties in the House and Senate vote together on approximately 90 percent of all legislation considered by those bodies.

The incentives for members to vote with their party also rarely have been higher—or more creative. In addition to lending members campaign support through party organizations or member-to-member political action committees (PACs), leadership in both houses may also offer committee assignments or chairs as rewards to members who toe the party line. The rejuvenated use of many of these tools as mechanisms of party control can be traced back to former Representative Tom DeLay (R–TX), an effective majority whip.

DeLay earned the nickname "The Hammer" for his relentless persuasion of colleagues during a time of **divided government,** when different political parties controlled the presidency and Congress. For example, President Bill Clinton was surprised to learn that moderate Republicans on whom he had counted to vote against his impeachment were "dropping like flies." The reason? DeLay had threatened Republicans with the denial of coveted committee assignments and with the prospect of strong Republican challengers in the next primary season unless they voted with the party.

Explore on MyPoliSciLab

Can Congress Get Anything Done?

A government cannot operate without a budget, revenue, or appropriations. But over the past thirty years, members of Congress have grown so polarized that they cannot agree on a budget or much of anything else. Polarization occurs when members of both parties move away from the moderate middle and share increasingly less common ground. Since 2001, Congress failed to pass a budget eight times, succeeding only in approving temporary budgets to keep government running. As the parties grow more polarized, Congress is less able to pass a permanent budget and the national debt increases.

Party Polarization

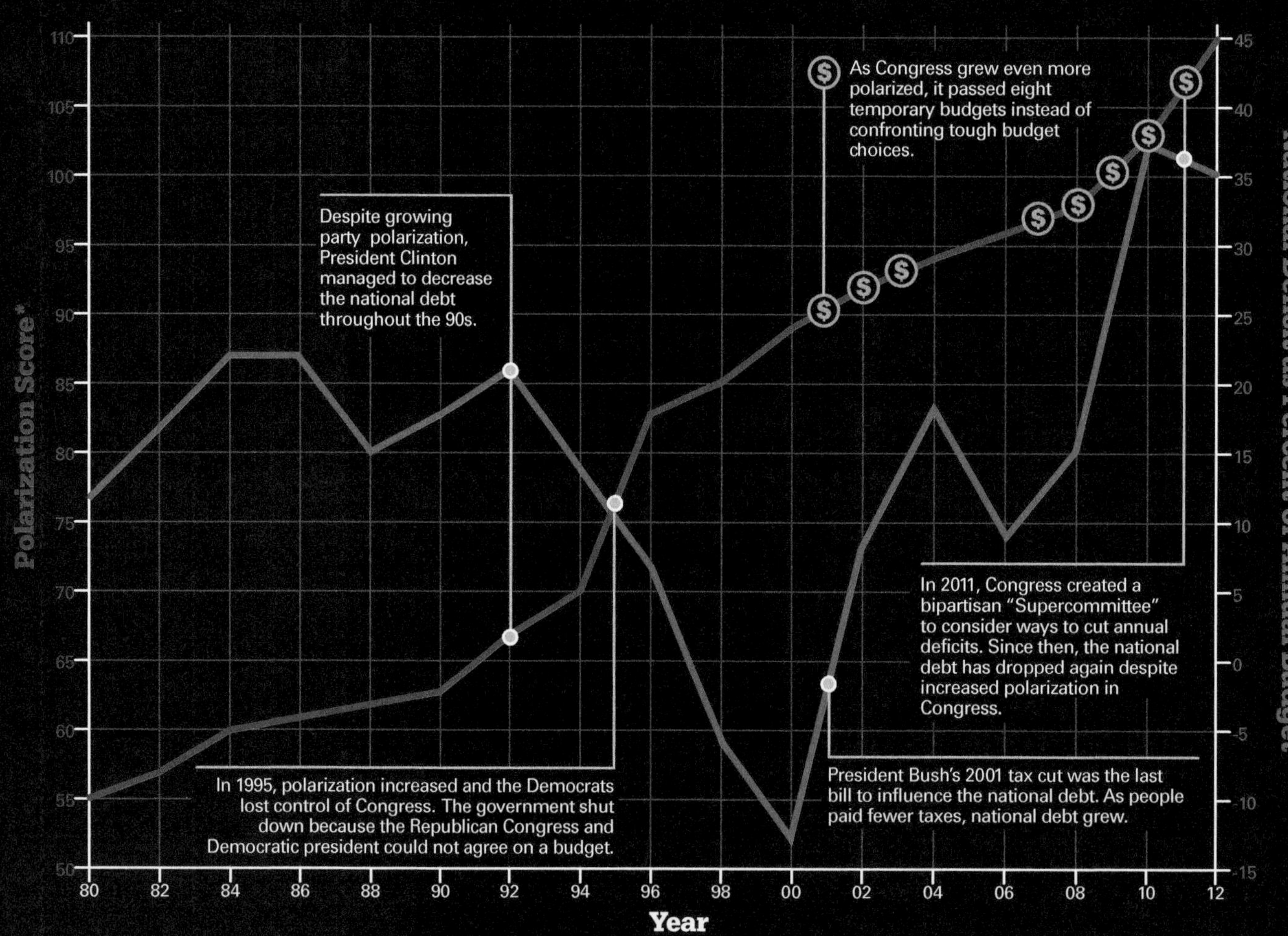

Polarization Score *
National Deficit as Percent of Annual Budget
Year
110
105
100
95
90
85
80
75
70
65
60
55
50
45
40
35
30
25
20
15
10
5
0
-5
-10
-15
80
82
84
86
88
90
92
94
96
98
00
02
04
06
08
10
12
As Congress grew even more polarized, it passed eight temporary budgets instead of confronting tough budget choices.
Despite growing party polarization, President Clinton managed to decrease the national debt throughout the 90s.
In 2011, Congress created a bipartisan "Supercommittee" to consider ways to cut annual deficits. Since then, the national debt has dropped again despite increased polarization in Congress.
In 1995, polarization increased and the Democrats lost control of Congress. The government shut down because the Republican Congress and Democratic president could not agree on a budget.
President Bush's 2001 tax cut was the last bill to influence the national debt. As people paid fewer taxes, national debt grew.

*** Polarization is measured as the distance between the two parties' ideological scores as computed from data at Voteview.com.**
SOURCE: Data from Voteview and the U.S. Government Accountability Office.

Investigate Further

Concept What is political polarization? Polarization occurs when members of both political parties consistently vote along ideological lines. Political scientists track polarization because it has nearly doubled in the past thirty years, and it tends to impede the government's ability to function.

Connection Is polarization related to greater annual debt? On a yearly basis, polarization is largely independent of the debt incurred by the United States—notice, for example, during the Clinton presidency how polarization grew even as debt decreased. However, as a long-term trend, national debt and polarization in Congress increase together.

Cause Does polarization impede Congress's ability to create annual budgets? Yes. The more polarized Congress becomes, the more likely the disagreements over permanent budget solutions lead to temporary resolutions that barely stave off government shutdown.

The president may also act as chief of the party and attempt to coerce members to support his legislative package. This is particularly true in times of **unified government,** when the presidency and Congress are controlled by members of the same party and share a similar policy agenda. During the health care reform debates, for example, President Barack Obama visited the districts of members who were on the fence about supporting the proposal in an apparent attempt to mobilize constituent opinion. Showing his dedication to the cause, Obama even offered to wash one Democratic member's car in exchange for a vote.

unified government
The political condition in which the same political party controls the presidency and Congress.

☐ Constituents

When they are voting, members of Congress always have in mind their constituents—the people who live and vote in a representative's home district or state. Studies by political scientists show that members vote in conformity with prevailing opinion in their districts about two-thirds of the time. On average, Congress passes laws that reflect national public opinion at about the same rate.[31] It is rare for a legislator to vote against the wishes of his or her constituents regularly, particularly on issues of social welfare, domestic policy, or other crucial issues. For example, during the 1960s, representatives from southern states could not hope to keep their seats for long if they voted in favor of proposed civil rights legislation. During modern times, members from districts disproportionately populated by the elderly are careful to support Social Security and Medicare.

Gauging how voters regard any particular issue often is not easy. Because it is virtually impossible to know how the folks back home feel on all matters, a representative's perception of his or her constituents' preferences is important. Even when voters

HOW DO MEMBERS OF CONGRESS LEARN ABOUT THEIR CONSTITUENTS' OPINIONS ON POLITICAL ISSUES?

Members and their staffs spend a substantial portion of their time meeting with constituents in Washington, D.C., and in their district offices; they also monitor calls, letters, e-mail, and social media. Failure to remain in touch with their constituents at home may decrease a member's likelihood of winning another term in Congress. Here, Senator Kay Hagan (D–NC) meets with High Point University students in her D.C. office.

logrolling
Vote trading; voting to support a colleague's bill in return for a promise of future support.

have opinions, legislators may receive little guidance if they come from a narrowly divided district. Abortion is an issue about which many voters feel passionate, but a legislator whose district has roughly equal numbers of pro-choice and pro-life advocates can satisfy only a portion of his or her constituents.

In short, legislators tend to act on their own preferences as trustees when dealing with topics that have come through the committees on which they serve or with issues they know about as a result of experience in other contexts, such as their vocation. On items of little concern in their district or when they have limited first-hand knowledge, legislators tend to turn to other sources for voting cues. But, members are always keenly aware of the consequences of voting against their constituents' views on "wedge issues"—topics like same-sex marriage, insurance coverage for contraceptives, and flag burning—that tend to drive a wedge between voters.

☐ Colleagues and Caucuses

The range and complexity of issues confronting Congress means that no one can be up to speed on more than a few topics. When members must vote on bills concerning issues about which they know very little, they often turn for advice to colleagues who have served on the committee that handled the legislation. On issues that are of little interest to a legislator, **logrolling,** or vote trading, often occurs. Logrolling often takes place on specialized bills targeting money or projects to selected congressional districts. An unaffected member may exchange a yea vote now for the promise of a future yea vote on a similar piece of specialized legislation.

Members may also look to other representatives who share common interests. Special-interest caucuses created around issues, home states, regions, congressional class, or other commonalities facilitate this communication. Prior to 1995, these groups were more powerful. Several caucuses enjoyed formal status and were provided staff, office space, and budgets, which the Republican takeover ended. Today, however, all caucuses are informal in nature, although some, such as the Black and Hispanic Caucuses, are far more organized than others. The Congressional Caucus for Women's Issues, for example, has formal elections of its Republican and Democratic co-chairs and vice chairs, its members provide staff to work on issues of common concern to caucus members, and staffers meet regularly to facilitate support for legislation of interest to women.

☐ Interest Groups, Lobbyists, and Political Action Committees

A primary function of most lobbyists, whether they work for interest groups, trade associations, or large corporations, is to provide information to supportive or potentially supportive legislators, committees, and their staffs. It is likely, for example, that a representative knows the National Rifle Association's (NRA's) position on gun control legislation. What the legislator needs from the NRA is information and substantial research on the feasibility and impact of such legislation. How could the states implement such legislation? Is it constitutional? Will it really have an impact on violent crime or crime in schools? Organized interests can persuade undecided legislators or confirm the support of their friends by providing information that legislators use to justify the position they have embraced. They also can supply direct campaign contributions, volunteers, and publicity to members seeking reelection.

The high cost of campaigning has made members of Congress, especially those without huge personal fortunes, attentive to those who help pay the tab for such expenses. Political action committees (PACs) organized by interest groups are a major source of most members' campaign funding. When an issue arises that is of little consequence to a member's constituents, that member, not surprisingly, tends to support the positions of those interests who helped pay for the last campaign. After all, who wants to bite the hand that feeds him or her?

Interest groups also use grassroots appeals to pressure legislators by urging their members in a particular state or district to call, write, fax, e-mail, text, or tweet their senators or representatives. Lobbyists cannot vote, but constituents back home can and do.

TABLE 6.7 WHAT ARE THE CONGRESSIONAL SUPPORT AGENCIES?

Congressional Research Service (CRS)	Government Accountability Office (GAO)	Congressional Budget Office (CBO)
Created in 1914 as the Legislative Research Service (LRS), CRS is administered by the Library of Congress. It responds to more than a quarter-million congressional requests for information each year. Its staff conducts nonpartisan studies of public issues, as well as major research projects for committees at the request of members. CRS also prepares summaries and tracks the progress of all bills introduced.	The Government Accountability Office (GAO) was established in 1921 as an independent regulatory agency for the purpose of auditing the financial expenditures of the executive branch and federal agencies. The GAO performs four additional functions: it sets government standards for accounting; it provides a variety of legal opinions; it settles claims against the government; and it conducts studies upon congressional request.	The CBO was created in 1974 to evaluate the economic effect of different spending programs and to provide information on the cost of proposed policies. It is responsible for analyzing the president's budget and economic projections. The CBO provides Congress and individual members with a valuable second opinion to use in budget debates.

Staff and Support Agencies

Members of Congress rely heavily on their staffs for information on pending legislation.[32] House members have an average of fifteen staffers; senators, an average of thirty-five. Staff is divided between D.C. and district offices. When a bill is nonideological or one on which the member has no real position, staff members can be very influential. In many offices, they are the greatest influence on their boss's votes, and lobbyists are just as likely to contact key staffers as they are members.

Congressional committees and subcommittees also have their own dedicated staff to assist committee members. Additional help for members comes from support personnel at the Congressional Research Service (CRS) at the Library of Congress, the Government Accountability Office (GAO), and the Congressional Budget Office (CBO) (see Table 6.7).

Toward Reform: Balancing Institutional Power

6.6 Evaluate the strategic interactions between Congress, the president, the courts, and the people.

The Framers envisioned that the Congress, the president, and the judiciary would have discrete powers, and that one branch would be able to hold the others in check. These checks and balances would also allow citizens to influence their government but temper the will of the people. Especially since the 1930s, the president often has held the upper hand in institutional power. In times of crisis or simply when it was unable to meet public demands for solutions, Congress has willingly handed over its authority to the chief executive. Even though the inherent powers of the chief executive give the president greater latitude, Congress does, of course, retain ultimate legislative authority to question executive actions and to halt administration activities by cutting off funds for programs a president wants. Similar checks and balances affect relations between Congress and the courts.

Congress and the Executive

The balance of power between Congress and the president has fluctuated over time. The post–Civil War Congress tried to regain control of the vast executive powers that the recently slain President Abraham Lincoln had assumed. Angered at the refusal of Lincoln's successor, Andrew Johnson, to go along with its radical "reforms" of the South, Congress passed the Tenure of Office Act, which prevented the president, under threat of civil penalty, from removing any Cabinet-level appointees of the previous administration. Johnson accepted the challenge and fired Lincoln's secretary of war, who many believed guilty of heinous war crimes. The House voted to impeach Johnson, but the desertion of a handful of Republican senators prevented him from being removed from office. (The effort fell short by one vote.) Nonetheless, this attempt to remove the president greatly weakened his power, and the Congress again became the center of power and authority in the federal government.

Beginning in the early 1900s, however, a series of strong presidents acted at the expense of congressional power. Theodore Roosevelt, Franklin D. Roosevelt, and Lyndon B. Johnson viewed the presidency as carrying with it enormous powers. Especially since the presidency of Franklin D. Roosevelt, Congress has ceded to the president a major role in the legislative process.

☐ Congress and the Judiciary

As part of our system of checks and balances, the power of judicial review gives the Supreme Court the ability to review the constitutionality of acts of Congress. Historically, the Court has used this power very carefully. From 1787 to 1987, the Supreme Court struck down only 127 federal laws, for an average of less than one law per term. However, in recent years, the Court has struck down congressional legislation, at a rate of nearly three laws per term. Thus, Congress must be increasingly mindful of the Court's reaction when it enacts new laws for the nation.[33]

Congress also interacts with the judiciary in a number of other ways. No matter how busy federal judges are, it is ultimately up to Congress to determine the number of judges on each court, as well as the boundaries of judicial districts and circuits. Congress also sets the jurisdiction of the federal courts. During recent Congresses, for example, several members, unhappy with Supreme Court actions on abortion and gay rights, pushed for a bill to prevent federal courts from hearing challenges related to these civil liberties issues. When Congress threatens the Court's jurisdiction, it is signaling its belief that federal judges have gone too far.

☐ Congress and the People

Congress, at least conceptually, is the people's branch of government. The people elect the members, who then are supposed to serve in the citizens' best interest. In recent years, however, citizens have increasingly questioned members' dedication to their representational role. In 2012, as shown in Figure 6.5, the congressional approval rate reached an all-time low of 10 percent; even individual members of Congress, who have generally had higher approval ratings than Congress as a whole, received a dismal 41 percent approval rating. These low approval numbers mirror the frustrations of the American people over the increasing partisanship and unproductivity of the institution.

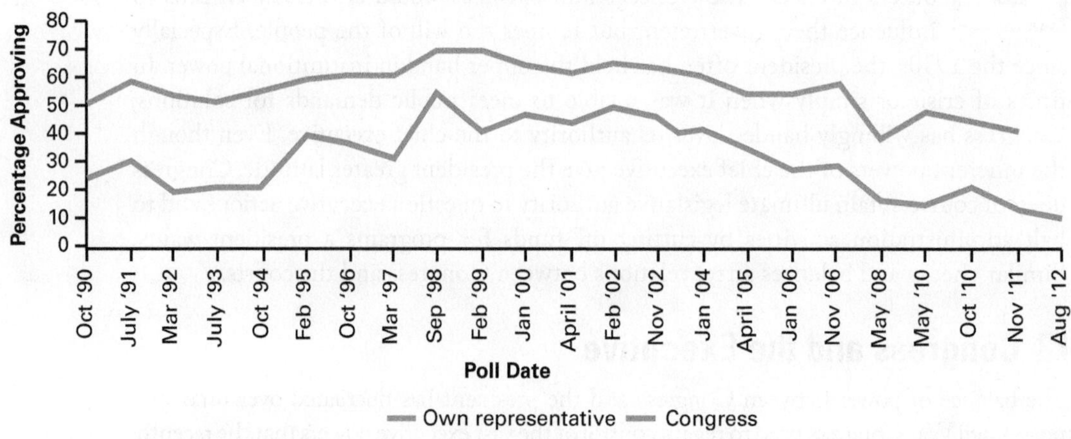

FIGURE 6.5 WHAT DO AMERICANS THINK ABOUT CONGRESS?

This graph shows the American public's views on Congress as an institution and individual members. Poll respondents were asked, "Do you approve or disapprove of the way Congress is handling its job?" and "Do you approve or disapprove of the way the representative from your district is handling his or her job?"

SOURCE: http://www.ropercenter.uconn.edu/data_access/tag/congressional_approval.html#.UDp_QERZt8ohttp; http://www.gallup.com/poll/156662/congress-approval-ties-time-low.aspx

Review the Chapter

 **Listen** to **Chapter 6** on **MyPoliSciLab**

Roots of the Legislative Branch of Government

6.1 Trace the roots of the legislative branch outlined by the U.S. Constitution, p. 171.

The Constitution created a bicameral legislature with members of each body to be elected differently, and thus to represent different constituencies. Article I of the Constitution sets forth qualifications for office, states age minimums, and specifies how legislators are to be distributed among the states. The Constitution also requires that seats in the House of Representatives be apportioned by population. Thus, after every U.S. Census, state legislatures must redraw district lines to reflect population shifts. In addition, the Constitution also provides a vast array of enumerated and implied powers to Congress. Both houses of Congress share some, such as lawmaking and oversight, but not others, such as confirmation of presidential appointees.

The Members of Congress

6.2 Characterize the demographic attributes of members of Congress, and identify factors that affect their chances for reelection, p. 175.

Members of Congress live in two worlds—in their home districts and in the District of Columbia. They must attempt to appease two constituencies: party leaders, colleagues, and lobbyists in Washington, D.C., on the one hand, and constituents in their home districts, on the other. In general, members of Congress are better educated, richer, more likely to be male, and more likely to be white than the general population, in terms of its makeup, and membership in one of the two major parties is almost always a prerequisite for election, as is the ability to raise money. When it comes to reelection, incumbency and redistricting also affect members' chances.

How Congress Is Organized

6.3 Assess the role of the committee system, political parties, and congressional leadership in organizing Congress, p. 179.

Political parties play a major role in the way Congress is organized. The Speaker of the House is traditionally a member of the majority party, and the parties also control other leadership roles, such as majority and minority leaders and whips. In addition to the party leaders, Congress has a labyrinth of committees and subcommittees that cover the entire range of government policies, often with a confusing tangle of shared responsibilities. In these environments, many policies take shape and members make their primary contributions to solving public problems.

Powers of Congress

6.4 Identify three of the most significant powers of Congress, p. 187.

The three most significant powers of Congress are its lawmaking, budgetary, and oversight functions. The road to enacting a bill into law is long and strewn with obstacles, and only a small share of the proposals introduced become law. The Congressional Budget Act of 1974 solidified Congress's role in the budgetary process. Congress conducts oversight in a number of ways, including through hearings. Congress also offers advice and consent on executive and judicial branch nominees and has the power to impeach federal officials and remove them from office.

How Members Make Decisions

6.5 Analyze the factors that influence how members of Congress make decisions, p. 195.

Members' view of their representational role—as trustees, delegates, or politicos—influences how they make policy decisions. Legislators may also consider a number of other factors, including political party; constituents; colleagues and caucuses; staff and support agencies; and interest groups, lobbyists, and political action committees. When a bill is nonideological or one on which a member has no real position, staff members may have the greatest influence on how a member of Congress votes.

Toward Reform: Balancing Institutional Power

6.6 Evaluate the strategic interactions between Congress, the president, the courts, and the people, p. 199.

The balance of power between Congress and the executive branch has fluctuated tremendously over time. Congress was most powerful in the early years of U.S. history, but since the New Deal, the president has played an important role in proposing legislation and spending. An ongoing power struggle also characterizes legislative–judicial relations. Although the judiciary can declare acts of Congress unconstitutional, Congress also exercises control over the judiciary in a variety of ways. The people also hold an important check on all political institutions.

Learn the Terms

apportionment, p. 172
bicameral legislature, p. 171
bill, p. 172
cloture, p. 190
conference committee, p. 185
Congressional Budget Act of 1974, p. 191
congressional review, p. 194
delegate, p. 195
discharge petition, p. 186
divided government, p. 195
filibuster, p. 190
gerrymandering, p. 178
hold, p. 190
impeachment, p. 174
incumbency, p. 176
joint committee, p. 185
logrolling, p. 198
majority leader, p. 182
majority party, p. 179
markup, p. 189
minority leader, p. 182
minority party, p. 179
party caucus (or conference), p. 179
pocket veto, p. 191
politico, p. 195
pork, p. 192
president pro tempore, p. 184
programmatic requests, p. 192
reconciliation, p. 192
redistricting, p. 178
select (or special) committee, p. 185
senatorial courtesy, p. 194
seniority, p. 186
Speaker of the House, p. 180
standing committee, p. 185
trustee, p. 195
unified government, p. 197
veto, p. 191
War Powers Resolution, p. 193
whip, p. 182

Test Yourself

Study and **Review** the **Practice Tests**

1. Which power is NOT granted to Congress in Article I?

- **a.** Regulating commerce with foreign nations and between the states
- **b.** Declaring war
- **c.** Raising and supporting an army and navy
- **d.** Overruling Supreme Court decisions
- **e.** Establishing rules for naturalization

2. All of these describe the House of Representatives EXCEPT:

- **a.** initiates all revenue bills.
- **b.** two-year terms served by members.
- **c.** low turnover in membership.
- **d.** decentralized power.
- **e.** powerful Committee on Rules.

3. Much of the controversy surrounding redistricting comes from a process called:

- **a.** gerrymandering.
- **b.** reallocation.
- **c.** census review.
- **d.** incumbency.
- **e.** demography.

4. The official who oversees House business and is second in line for presidential succession is

- **a.** minority leader.
- **b.** Speaker of the House.
- **c.** vice president.
- **d.** president pro tempore.
- **e.** conference chair

5. A party whip is

- **a.** any new member of the majority party in the House
- **b.** a moderate member of any party.
- **c.** a leader responsible for mobilizing party support.
- **d.** a member designated to speak to the media on behalf of the party.
- **e.** the longest serving member of each party.

6. The practice of halting Senate action on a bill through unlimited debate or long speeches is called a

- **a.** hold.
- **b.** filibuster.
- **c.** veto.
- **d.** cloture.
- **e.** pocket veto.

7. Which of these is NOT a power of Congress that limits the president's power?

- **a.** War Powers Resolution
- **b.** Congressional review
- **c.** Appointment
- **d.** Senatorial courtesy
- **e.** Oversight

8. Members of Congress rely heavily on all of these groups to educate them on specific political issues EXCEPT:

- **a.** caucuses.
- **b.** newspaper editors.
- **c.** interest groups.
- **d.** political parties.
- **e.** lobbyists.

9. Political parties' influence on the votes of members of Congress is

a. decreasing rapidly.
b. decreasing slowly.
c. about the same as during the 1960s.
d. increasing.
e. almost nonexistent.

10. Which of the following statements is true regarding congressional approval?

a. Congressional approval is at historic highs.
b. Citizens generally think more highly of Congress than of their individual members.
c. Approval of Congress is higher than approval of all other political institutions.
d. Despite declining approval, members of Congress continue to be reelected at high rates.
e. Congressional approval has declined in every year since Watergate.

Explore Further

Adler, E. Scott, and John S. Lapinski, eds. *The Macropolitics of Congress.* Princeton, NJ: Princeton University Press, 2006.

Cox, Gary W., and Mathew D. McCubbins. *Setting the Agenda: Responsible Party Government in the U.S. House of Representatives.* New York: Cambridge University Press, 2005.

Davidson, Roger H., Walter J. Oleszek, and Frances E. Lee. *Congress and Its Members,* 13th ed. Washington, DC: CQ Press, 2011.

Dodd, Lawrence C. *Thinking About Congress: Essays on Congressional Change.* New York: Routledge, 2011.

Dodd, Lawrence C., and Bruce I. Oppenheimer, eds. *Congress Reconsidered,* 9th ed. Washington, DC: CQ Press, 2008.

Fenno, Richard F., Jr. *Home Style: House Members in Their Districts,* reprint ed. New York: Longman, 2009.

Mayhew, David R. *Congress: The Electoral Connection,* 2nd ed. New Haven, CT: Yale University Press, 2004.

Miler, Kristina C. *Constituency Representation in Congress: The View from Capitol Hill.* New York: Cambridge University Press, 2010.

Oleszek, Walter J. *Congressional Procedures and the Policy Process,* 8th ed. Washington, DC: CQ Press, 2010.

Price, David E. *The Congressional Experience: A View from the Hill,* 3rd ed. Boulder, CO: Westview Press, 2005.

Quirk, Paul J., and Sarah A. Binder, eds. *Institutions of American Democracy: The Legislative Branch.* New York: Oxford University Press, 2006.

Schickler, Eric, and Frances E. Lee, eds. *The Oxford Handbook of the American Congress.* New York: Oxford University Press, 2011.

Smith, Steven S. *Party Influence in Congress.* New York: Cambridge University Press, 2007.

Straus, Jacob R. *Party and Procedure in the United States Congress.* Lanham, MD: Rowman and Littlefield, 2012.

Theriault, Sean M. *Party Polarization in Congress.* New York: Cambridge University Press, 2008.

To learn more about the Senate, go to its official Web site at **www.senate.gov.**

To learn more about the House of Representatives, go to its official Web site at **www.house.gov.**

To learn more about the legislative branch, go to the Library of Congress's home page, named Thomas, in honor of President Thomas Jefferson, at **thomas.loc.gov.**

To learn more about members of Congress, go to the Congressional Biographical Directory at **bioguide.congress.gov**

Listen to Chapter 7 on MyPoliSciLab

7 The Presidency

When Ronald Reagan died on June 5, 2004, many Americans first in California and then in Washington, D.C., lined up for hours to pay their respects to the man who had been the fortieth president of the United States. Many people could see, for the first time in recent memory, the grandeur of a presidential state funeral. The first president to lie in state in the Rotunda of the Capitol since Lyndon B. Johnson died in January 1973, Reagan was one of only nine American presidents to receive that honor.

Presidential funerals underscore the esteem that most Americans accord the office of the president, regardless of its occupant. Just before the first president, George Washington died, he made it known that he wanted his burial to be a quiet one, "without parade or funeral oration." He also requested a three-day delay of his burial—a common request at the time because of the fear of being buried alive. Despite these requests, Washington's funeral was a state occasion as hundreds of soldiers, with their rifles held backward, marched to Mount Vernon, Virginia, where he was interred. Across the nation, imitation funerals took place, and the military wore black armbands for six months.[1]

When President Abraham Lincoln was assassinated in 1865, his funeral became a nationwide event. He lay in state in the East Room of the White House, where more than 25,000 mourners came to pay their respects. Black cloth draped the room, and two dozen Union soldiers formed an honor guard. Following the funeral, a parade to the Capitol was held in Washington, D.C. Thousands of free blacks escorted Lincoln to the Rotunda, where he lay in state for another day. The body of the deceased president then embarked on a national train tour to his burial site in Springfield, Illinois, allowing Americans across the country an opportunity to grieve.

Today, one of the first things a president does upon taking office is to consider funeral plans. The military has a 138-page book devoted to the kind of ceremony and traditions so evident in the Reagan funeral: a horse-drawn caisson, a riderless horse with boots hung backward in the stirrups to indicate that the deceased will ride no more, a twenty-one-gun salute, and a flyover by military aircraft. Each president's family, however, has personalized their private, yet also public,

7.1 Trace the development of the presidency and the provisions for choosing and replacing presidents, p. 207.

7.2 Identify and describe the constitutional powers of the president, p. 212.

7.3 Evaluate the development and expansion of presidential power, p. 217.

7.4 Outline the structure of the presidential establishment and the functions of each of its components, p. 221.

7.5 Explain the concept of presidential leadership and analyze the importance of public opinion, p. 225.

7.6 Assess the president's role as policy maker, p. 229.

PRESIDENTIAL FUNERALS ARE OCCASIONS FOR NATIONAL MOURNING Above, the nation mourns President Abraham Lincoln, the first American president to be assassinated. Below, former presidents and vice presidents and their wives attend a funeral service for President Ronald Reagan in the National Cathedral in Washington, D.C., prior to his interment in California.

In Context Uncover the historical context that led the Framers to fear a strong executive. In this video University of Oklahoma political scientist Glen Krutz not only reveals the reason behind the Framers' apprehension, but also explores how this fear still restricts presidents today as they struggle to create new policies.

Think Like a Political Scientist Why do presidents try to persuade you to support their policies? In this video, University of Oklahoma political scientist Glen Krutz discloses why persuasion is vital to a president's success and how technology has created obstacles and opportunities for presidents.

In the Real World Should President Obama have used an executive order to change immigration policy? The president bypassed Congress to implement his own agenda. Find out why some people believe the president abused his powers and others think he was entirely justified.

So What? Find out what it takes to become president of the United States. In this video, author Alixandra B. Yanus explains the future of the presidency, and considers what ethnicities and demographics we can expect to hold the office in the coming years.

opportunity to mourn. The Reagan family, for example, filed a 300-page plan for the funeral in 1989 and updated it regularly. President Gerald R. Ford filed a plan that was implemented after his death in 2006. Presidents Jimmy Carter and George Bush have also filed formal plans; Bill Clinton, George W. Bush, and Barack Obama have yet to do so.

The Reagan funeral also created a national time-out from the news of war, and even presidential campaigns halted in respect for the deceased president. One historian commented that the event gave Americans the opportunity to "rediscover . . . what holds us together instead of what pulls us apart."[2] This is often the role of presidents—in life or in death.

•••

The authority granted to the president by the U.S. Constitution and through subsequent congressional legislation makes it a position with awesome power and responsibility. Not only did the Framers not envision such a powerful role for the president, but they also could not have foreseen the skepticism with which the modern media greet many presidential actions.

The modern media, used by successful presidents to help advance their agendas, have brought us closer to our presidents and made them seem more human, a mixed blessing for those trying to lead. Only two photographs exist of President Franklin D. Roosevelt in a wheelchair, his paralysis kept a closely guarded secret. Seven decades later, presidential candidate Mitt Romney was asked on national TV what he wore to bed.

Public opinion and confidence greatly affect a president's ability to get his programs adopted and his vision of the nation implemented. As one political scientist has noted, the president's power often rests on the power to persuade.[3] To persuade, he must have the capacity to forge links with members of Congress as well as gain the support of the American people and the respect of foreign leaders. The tension between public expectations about the presidency and the formal powers of the president permeate our discussion of how the office has evolved from its humble origins in Article II of the Constitution to its current stature.

Roots of the Office of President of the United States

7.1 Trace the development of the presidency and the provisions for choosing and replacing presidents.

The earliest example of executive power in the colonies was the position of royal governor. The king of England appointed a royal governor to each British colony and normally entrusted them with the "powers of appointment, military command, expenditure, and—within limitations—pardon, as well as with large powers in connection with the powers of law making."[4] Royal governors often found themselves at odds with the colonists and especially with elected colonial legislatures. The people, many of whom had fled from Great Britain to escape royal domination, distrusted and disdained the governors as representatives of the crown. Other colonists, generations removed from England, no longer felt strong ties to the king and his power over them.

When the colonists declared their independence from Great Britain in 1776, their distrust of a strong chief executive remained. Most state constitutions reduced the once-powerful office of governor to a symbolic post elected annually by the legislature. However, some states did entrust wider powers to their chief executives. In New York, the people directly elected the governor. Perhaps because the people could then hold him accountable, they gave him the power to pardon, the duty to faithfully execute the laws, and the power to act as commander in chief of the state militia.

Under the Articles of Confederation, no executive branch of government existed; the eighteen different men who served as the president of the Continental Congress of the United States of America were president in name only—they held no actual authority or power in the new nation. When the delegates to the Constitutional Convention met in Philadelphia to fashion a new government, the need for an executive branch to implement

7.1
7.2
7.3
7.4
7.5
7.6

the laws made by Congress created little dissent. Although some delegates suggested that multiple executives would be preferable, the Framers eventually agreed that executive authority should be vested in one person. This agreement was relatively easy because the Framers felt certain that George Washington—whom they had trusted with their lives during the Revolutionary War—would become the first president of the new nation.

The Framers also concurred on a title for the new office. Borrowing from the title used at several American colleges and universities, the Framers called the new chief executive "the president." How the president was to be chosen and by whom created a major stumbling block. James Wilson of Philadelphia suggested that the people should elect the president, who should remain "independent of the legislature." Wilson also suggested giving the executive an absolute veto over the acts of Congress. "Without such a defense," he wrote, "the legislature can at any moment sink it [the executive] into non-existence."[5]

The manner of the president's election troubled the Framers for some time. Their solution to the dilemma was the creation of the Electoral College. We leave the resolution of that issue aside for now and turn instead to details of the issues the Framers resolved quickly.

□ Presidential Qualifications and Terms of Office

The Constitution requires the president (and the vice president, whose major function is to succeed the president in the event of his death or disability) to be a natural-born citizen of the United States, at least thirty-five years old, and a resident of the United States for fourteen years or longer. In the 1700s, those engaged in international diplomacy often traveled out of the country for substantial periods of time, and the Framers wanted to make sure that prospective presidents spent significant time on this country's shores before running for its highest elective office. While the Constitution does not bar a woman or member of a minority group from seeking the presidency, Barack Obama is the only nonwhite male thus far to win election to this office (see Table 7.1).

Although only two of the last six presidents failed to win a second term, at one time the length of a president's term created controversy. Various delegates to the Constitutional Convention suggested four-, seven-, and eleven-year terms with no eligibility for reelection. The Framers ultimately reached agreement on a four-year term with eligibility for reelection.

WHO HAS SERVED AS PRESIDENT OF THE UNITED STATES?

Before Barack Obama, all of the people who served as president were white men. Here, four former presidents—George W. Bush, Bill Clinton Jimmy Carter, and George Bush—gather to celebrate the opening of the Clinton Presidential Library in 2004.

TABLE 7.1 WHO WERE THE U.S. PRESIDENTS?

President	Place of Birth	Higher Education	Occupation	Years in Congress	Years as Governor	Years as Vice President	Age at Becoming President
George Washington	VA	William & Mary	Military/surveyor	2	0	0	57
John Adams	MA	Harvard	Farmer/lawyer	5	0	4	61
Thomas Jefferson	VA	William & Mary	Farmer/lawyer	5	3	4	58
James Madison	VA	Princeton	Farmer	15	0	0	58
James Monroe	VA	William & Mary	Farmer/lawyer	7	4	0	59
John Quincy Adams	MA	Harvard	Lawyer	0[a]	0	0	58
Andrew Jackson	SC	None	Military/Lawyer	4	0	0	62
Martin Van Buren	NY	None	Lawyer	8	0	4	55
William H. Harrison	VA	Hampden-Sydney	Military	0	0	0	68
John Tyler	VA	William & Mary	Lawyer	12	2	0	51
James K. Polk	NC	North Carolina	Lawyer	14	3	0	50
Zachary Taylor	VA	None	Military	0	0	0	65
Millard Fillmore	NY	None	Lawyer	8	0	1	50
Franklin Pierce	NH	Bowdoin	Lawyer	9	0	0	48
James Buchanan	PA	Dickinson	Lawyer	20	0	0	65
Abraham Lincoln	KY	None	Lawyer	2	0	0	52
Andrew Johnson	NC	None	Tailor	14	4	0	57
Ulysses S. Grant	OH	West Point	Military	0	0	0	47
Rutherford B. Hayes	OH	Kenyon	Lawyer	3	6	0	55
James A. Garfield	OH	Williams	Educator/lawyer	18	0	0	50
Chester A. Arthur	VT	Union	Lawyer	0	0	1	51
Grover Cleveland	NJ	None	Lawyer	0	2	0	48
Benjamin Harrison	OH	Miami (Ohio)	Lawyer	6	0	0	56
Grover Cleveland	NJ	None	Lawyer	0	2	0	53
William McKinley	OH	Allegheny	Lawyer	14	4	0	54
Theodore Roosevelt	NY	Harvard	Lawyer/author	0	2	1	43
William H. Taft	OH	Yale	Lawyer	0	0	0	52
Woodrow Wilson	VA	Princeton	Educator	0	2	0	56
Warren G. Harding	OH	Ohio Central	Newspaper editor	6	0	0	56
Calvin Coolidge	VT	Amherst	Lawyer	0	2	3	51
Herbert Hoover	IA	Stanford	Engineer	0	0	0	55
Franklin D. Roosevelt	NY	Harvard/Columbia	Lawyer	0	4	0	49
Harry S Truman	MO	None	Clerk/store owner	10	0	0	61
Dwight D. Eisenhower	TX	West Point	Military	0	0	0	63
John F. Kennedy	MA	Harvard	Writer	14	0	0	43
Lyndon B. Johnson	TX	Texas State	Educator	24	0	3	55
Richard M. Nixon	CA	Whittier/Duke	Lawyer	6	0	8	56
Gerald R. Ford	NE	Michigan/Yale	Lawyer	25	0	2	61
Jimmy Carter	GA	Naval Academy	Farmer/business owner	0	4	0	52
Ronald Reagan	IL	Eureka	Actor	0	8	0	69
George Bush	MA	Yale	Business owner	4	0	8	64
Bill Clinton	AR	Georgetown/Yale	Lawyer, law professor	0	12	0	46
George W. Bush	CT	Yale/Harvard	Business owner	0	6	0	54
Barack Obama	HI	Columbia/Harvard	Community organizer, law professor	3	0	0	48

[a]Adams served in the U.S. House for six years after leaving the presidency.

SOURCE: Adapted from *Presidential Elections Since 1789*, 4th ed. (Washington, DC: CQ Press, 1987), 4; Norman Thomas, Joseph Pika, and Richard Watson, *The Politics of the Presidency*, 3rd ed. (Washington, DC: CQ Press, 1993), 490; Harold W. Stanley and Richard G. Niemi, eds., *Vital Statistics on American Politics 2001–2002* (Washington, DC: CQ Press, 2001). Updated by the authors.

7.1

7.2

7.3

7.4

7.5

7.6

Twenty-Second Amendment
Adopted in 1951; prevents a president from serving more than two terms, or more than ten years if he came to office via the death, resignation, or impeachment of his predecessor.

impeachment
The power delegated to the House of Representatives in the Constitution to charge the president, vice president, or other "civil officers," including federal judges, with "Treason, Bribery, or other high Crimes and Misdemeanors." This is the first step in the constitutional process of removing government officials from office.

executive privilege
An implied presidential power that allows the president to refuse to disclose information regarding confidential conversations or national security to Congress or the judiciary.

***U.S. v. Nixon* (1974)**
Supreme Court ruling on power of the president, holding that no absolute constitutional executive privilege allows a president to refuse to comply with a court order to produce information needed in a criminal trial.

The first president, George Washington (1789–1797), sought reelection only once, and a two-term limit for presidents became traditional. Although Ulysses S. Grant unsuccessfully sought a third term, the two terms established by Washington remained the standard for 150 years, avoiding the Framers' much-feared "constitutional monarch," a perpetually reelected tyrant. In the 1930s and 1940s, however, Franklin D. Roosevelt ran successfully in four elections as Americans fought first the Great Depression and then World War II. Despite Roosevelt's popularity, negative reaction to his long tenure in office led to passage (and ratification in 1951) of the **Twenty-Second Amendment.** It limits presidents to two four-year terms. A vice president who succeeds a president due to death, resignation, or impeachment is eligible for a maximum of ten years in office: two years of a president's remaining term and two elected terms, or more than two years of a president's term followed by one elected term.

The Framers paid little attention to the office of vice president beyond the need to have an immediate official stand-in for the president. Initially, for example, the vice president's one and only function was to assume the office of president in the case of the president's death or some other emergency. After further debate, the delegates made the vice president the presiding officer of the Senate (except in cases of presidential impeachment). They feared that if the Senate's presiding officer were chosen from the Senate itself, one state would be short a representative. The delegates gave the vice president authority to vote in that body in the event of a tie. These are his only constitutional powers.

During the Constitutional Convention, Benjamin Franklin staunchly supported inclusion of a provision allowing for **impeachment,** the first step in a formal process to remove a specified official from office. He noted that "historically, the lack of power to impeach had necessitated recourse to assassination."[6] Not surprisingly, then, Franklin urged the rest of the delegates to formulate a legal mechanism to remove the president and vice president. Impeachment is that mechanism.

Each house of Congress was given a role in the impeachment process to ensure that the chief executive could be removed only for "Treason, Bribery, or other high Crimes and Misdemeanors." The Framers empowered the House to impeach the president by a simple majority vote. The Senate then acts as a court of law and tries the president for the charged offenses, with the chief justice of the U.S. Supreme Court presiding. A two-thirds majority vote in the Senate on any count contained in the articles of impeachment is necessary to remove the president from office. The House of Representatives has impeached only two presidents, Andrew Johnson and Bill Clinton. The Senate removed neither man, however, from office.

In 1974, President Richard M. Nixon resigned from office rather than face the certainty of impeachment, trial, and removal from office for his role in covering up details about a break-in at the Democratic Party's national headquarters in the Watergate office complex. What came to be known simply as Watergate also produced a major decision from the Supreme Court on the scope of what is termed **executive privilege.** In ***U.S. v. Nixon* (1974),** the Supreme Court ruled unanimously that no overriding executive privilege sanctioned the president's refusal to comply with a court order to produce information for use in the trial of the Watergate defendants. Since then, presidents have varied widely in their claim to executive privilege. President Bill Clinton asserted it several times, especially during the impeachment proceedings against him. President George W. Bush made such claims less frequently, instead often arguing that he and the vice president had what he called "constitutional prerogatives."[7]

☐ Rules of Succession

Through 2013, eight presidents have died in office from illness or assassination. William H. Harrison was the first president to die in office—he caught a cold at his inauguration in 1841 and died one month later. John Tyler thus became the first vice president to succeed to the presidency. In 1865, Abraham Lincoln became the first assassinated president.

Knowing that a system of orderly transfer of power was necessary, the Framers created the office of the vice president. To further clarify presidential succession, in

> *Whenever there is a vacancy in the office of the Vice President, the President shall nominate a Vice President who shall take office upon confirmation by a majority vote of both Houses of Congress.*
> —TWENTY-FIFTH AMENDMENT, SECTION 2

This clause of the Twenty-Fifth Amendment allows a president to fill a vacancy in the office of vice president with the consent of a simple majority of both Houses of Congress. The purpose of this amendment, which also deals with vacancies in the office of the president, was to remedy some structural flaws in Article II. When this amendment to the Constitution was proposed in 1965 (it was ratified in 1967), seven vice presidents had died in office and one had resigned. For over 20 percent of the nation's history, no vice president had been available to assume the office of the president in case of his death or infirmity. When John F. Kennedy was assassinated, Vice President Lyndon B. Johnson became president and the office of vice president was vacant. Since Johnson had suffered a heart attack as vice president, members of Congress were anxious to remedy the problems that might occur should no vice president be able to step in.

Richard M. Nixon followed Johnson as president, and during Nixon's presidency, the office of the vice president became empty twice. First, Vice President Spiro T. Agnew was forced to resign in the wake of charges of bribe taking, corruption, and income-tax evasion while an elected official in Maryland. His replacement was popular House Minority Leader Gerald R. Ford (R–MI), who had no trouble gaining a majority vote in both houses of Congress to confirm his nomination. When Nixon resigned rather than face certain impeachment, Ford became president and selected the former governor of New York, Nelson A. Rockefeller, to be his vice president. This chain of events set up for the first time in U.S. history a situation in which neither the president nor the vice president had been elected to those positions.

CRITICAL THINKING QUESTIONS

1. Why wasn't the Twenty-Fifth Amendment proposed until 1965? Why might a vice president be more necessary today than in the past?
2. Is it appropriate in a representative democracy to ever have a situation in which both the president and the vice president have not been popularly elected?

1947, Congress passed the Presidential Succession Act, which lists—in order—those in line to succeed the president (see Table 7.2).

The Succession Act has never been used because a vice president has always been available to take over when a president died in office. To ensure this will continue to be the case, the **Twenty-Fifth Amendment,** in fact, became part of the Constitution in 1967 as a response to the death of President John F. Kennedy. Should a vacancy occur in the office of the vice president, the Twenty-Fifth Amendment directs the president to appoint a new vice president, subject to the approval (by a simple majority) of both houses of Congress.

The Twenty-Fifth Amendment also contains a section that allows the vice president and a majority of the Cabinet (or some other body determined by Congress) to deem a president unable to fulfill his duties. It sets up a procedure to permit the vice president to become acting president if the president is incapacitated. The

Twenty-Fifth Amendment
Adopted in 1967 to establish procedures for filling vacancies in the office of president and vice president as well as providing for procedures to deal with the disability of a president.

TABLE 7.2 WHAT IS THE PRESIDENTIAL LINE OF SUCCESSION?

1. Vice President	10. Secretary of Commerce
2. Speaker of the House	11. Secretary of Labor
3. President Pro Tempore of the Senate	12. Secretary of Health and Human Services
4. Secretary of State	13. Secretary of Housing and Urban Development
5. Secretary of the Treasury	14. Secretary of Transportation
6. Secretary of Defense	15. Secretary of Energy
7. Attorney General	16. Secretary of Education
8. Secretary of the Interior	17. Secretary of Veterans Affairs
9. Secretary of Agriculture	18. Secretary of Homeland Security

Cabinet
The formal body of presidential advisers who head the fifteen executive departments. Presidents often add others to this body of formal advisers.

president also can voluntarily relinquish his power. Twice, for example, President George W. Bush made Vice President Dick Cheney acting president while he underwent colonoscopies.

The Constitutional Powers of the President

7.2 Identify and describe the constitutional powers of the president.

Explore on MyPoliSciLab Simulation: You Are a First-Term President

In contrast to Article I's laundry list of enumerated powers for the Congress, Article II details few specific presidential powers. Perhaps the most important section of Article II is its first sentence: "The executive Power shall be vested in a President of the United States of America." Nonetheless, the president's combined powers, discussed below, make him a major player in the policy process.

The Appointment Power

To help the president enforce laws passed by Congress, the Constitution authorizes him to appoint, with the advice and consent of the Senate, "Ambassadors, other public Ministers and Consuls, judges of the supreme Court, and all other Officers of the United States, whose Appointments are not herein otherwise provided for, and which shall be established by Law." Although this section of the Constitution deals only with appointments, behind that language lies a powerful policy-making tool. The president has the authority to make nearly 3,500 appointments to his administration (of which about 1,125 require Senate confirmation).[8] He also holds the power to remove many of his appointees at will. In addition, he technically appoints more than 75,000 military personnel. Many of these appointees are in positions to wield substantial authority over the course and direction of public policy. And, especially in the context of his ability to make appointments to the federal courts, his influence can last far past his term of office.

It is not surprising, then, that the president has, as one of his most important tasks, the selection of the right people. Presidents look for a blend of loyalty, competence, and integrity. Identifying these qualities in people constitutes a major challenge that every new president faces. Recent presidents have made an effort to create staffs that are more diverse, or, in President Bill Clinton's words, look "more like America."

In the past, when a president forwarded nominations to the Senate for its approval, the Senate traditionally gave his selections great respect—especially those for the **Cabinet,** an advisory group chosen by the president to help him make decisions and execute laws. In fact, until the Clinton administration, the Senate confirmed the vast majority (97 percent) of all presidential nominations.[9] This is no longer the case, as investigations into nominees' pasts and political wrangling in the Senate can delay the approval of nominees for months.

WHO HELPS THE PRESIDENT CONDUCT FOREIGN AFFAIRS?

The president has a large number of aides who help him craft foreign policy. These aides are often held accountable for a president's policy-making failures. Here, President George W. Bush quite literally shows Secretary of Defense Donald Rumsfeld the door following Republican losses in the 2006 midterm elections. These defeats were at least in part attributable to Rumsfeld's failures in the conduct of wars in Afghanistan and Iraq.

Delay or rejection of nominees can have a major impact on the course of an administration. Rejections leave a president without first choices, affect a president's relationship with the Senate, and influence how the public perceives the president. One method presidents have for persuading Congress to approve or disapprove nominees quickly is to make temporary appointments while Congress is in recess (thus, without congressional approval). For example, after Congress delayed confirmation of sixty-three of his nominees, President Barack Obama threatened to use recess appointments. Congress subsequently confirmed twenty-seven nominees in one day.

The Power to Convene Congress

The Constitution requires the president to inform the Congress periodically of "the State of the Union" and authorizes the president to convene either one or both houses of Congress on "extraordinary Occasions." In *Federalist No. 77,* Hamilton justified the latter by noting that because the Senate and the chief executive enjoy concurrent powers to make treaties, "It might often be necessary to call it together with a view to this object, when it would be unnecessary and improper to convene the House of Representatives." The power to convene Congress had more importance when Congress did not sit in nearly year-round sessions.

executive agreements
Formal international agreements entered into by the president that do not require the advice and consent of the U.S. Senate.

veto
The formal, constitutional authority of the president to reject bills passed by both houses of Congress, thus preventing them from becoming law without further congressional action.

☐ The Power to Make Treaties

The president's power to make treaties with foreign nations is checked by the Constitution's stipulation that at least two-thirds of the members of the Senate must approve all treaties. The chief executive can also "receive ambassadors," wording that has been interpreted to allow the president to recognize the existence of other nations.

Historically, the Senate ratifies about 90 percent of the treaties submitted by the president.[10] Through 2012, the Senate has rejected only twenty-one treaties put to a vote, often under highly partisan circumstances. Perhaps the most notable example of such a refusal was the Senate's defeat of the Treaty of Versailles submitted by President Woodrow Wilson in 1919. The treaty was an agreement among the major nations to end World War I. At Wilson's insistence, it also called for the creation of the League of Nations—a precursor of the United Nations—to foster continued peace and international disarmament. In struggling to gain international acceptance for the League, Wilson had taken American support for granted. This was a dramatic miscalculation. Isolationists, led by Senator Henry Cabot Lodge (R–MA), opposed U.S. participation in the League on the grounds that the League would place the United States in the center of every major international conflict. Proponents countered that, League or no League, the United States had emerged from World War I as a world power and that membership in the League of Nations would enhance its new role. The vote in the Senate for ratification was very close, but the isolationists prevailed—the United States stayed out of the League, and Wilson was devastated.

The Senate also may require substantial amendment of a treaty prior to its approval. When President Jimmy Carter proposed the controversial Panama Canal Treaty in 1977 to turn the canal over to Panama, for example, the Senate demanded settlement of several conditions before approving the canal's return.

Presidents may also "unsign" treaties, a practice often met with dismay from other signatories. For example, the George W. Bush administration formally withdrew its support for the International Criminal Court (ICC), the first permanent court to prosecute war crimes, genocide, and other crimes against humanity. Critics of this action now charge that President Bush and Vice President Dick Cheney should face prosecution for the treatment of detainees held by the United States.[11]

When trade agreements are at issue, presidents often must consider the wishes of both houses of Congress. Congressional "fast track" authority protects a president's ability to negotiate trade agreements with confidence that Congress will not alter the accords. Trade agreements submitted to Congress under fast track procedures bar amendments and require an up or down vote in Congress within ninety days of introduction.

Presidents also often use **executive agreements** to try sidestepping the constitutional "advice and consent" of the Senate requirement for ratification of treaties and the congressional approval requirement for trade agreements. Executive agreements allow the president to form secret and highly sensitive arrangements with foreign nations, without Senate approval. Presidents have used these agreements since the days of George Washington, and the courts have upheld their use. Although executive agreements are not binding on subsequent administrations, since 1900, many presidents have favored them over treaties. President George Bush, for example, concluded forty-four such agreements. More recent presidents have used only a fraction of this number.

☐ The Veto Power

Presidents can affect the policy process through **veto** power, the authority to reject bills passed by both houses of Congress. The threat of a presidential veto often prompts members of Congress to fashion legislation they know will receive presidential acquiescence,

7.1
7.2
7.3
7.4
7.5
7.6

Take a Closer Look

The president of the United States is asked to wear many hats. A good number of these roles extend from the powers the Framers enumerated in Article II of the U.S. Constitution. Others have evolved out of necessity over time. As a result, the modern president fulfills at least six different professional roles: chief law enforcer, leader of the party, commander in chief, shaper of public policy, key player in the legislative process, and chief of state. Examine the examples, shown below, of recent presidents as they fulfilled these roles.

CHIEF LAW ENFORCER:

Troops sent by President Dwight D. Eisenhower enforce a federal court decision ordering the integration of public schools in Little Rock, Arkansas.

LEADER OF THE PARTY:

President Ronald Reagan mobilizes conservatives at the Republican National Convention, changing the nature of the party.

COMMANDER IN CHIEF:

President Barack Obama meets with members of the armed forces.

SHAPER OF PUBLIC POLICY:

President Richard M. Nixon cheers on the efforts of Apollo 11 astronauts as he celebrates U.S. space policy.

KEY PLAYER IN THE LEGISLATIVE PROCESS:

President Bill Clinton celebrates newly passed legislation at a bill-signing ceremony.

CHIEF OF STATE:

President John F. Kennedy and his wife Jacqueline pose for cameras with the president of France and his wife during the Kennedys' widely publicized 1961 trip to that nation.

CRITICAL THINKING QUESTIONS

1. Which of these presidential roles is most important? Why?
2. How are these roles derived from the enumerated powers of the presidency? How are they enhanced by the president's inherent powers?
3. How has the balance of power between these roles changed over time? Which roles have become more and less important, and why?

if not support. Thus, simply threatening to veto legislation often gives a president another way to influence law-making.

During the Constitutional Convention, proponents of a strong executive argued that the president should have an absolute and final veto over acts of Congress. Opponents of this idea, including Benjamin Franklin, countered that in their home states, the executive veto "was constantly made use of to extort money" from legislators. James Madison made the most compelling argument for a compromise on the issue:

> Experience has proven a tendency in our governments to throw all power into the legislative vortex. The Executives of the States are in general little more than Ciphers, the legislatures omnipotent. If no effectual check be devised for restraining the instability and encroachments of the latter, a revolution of some kind or other would be inevitable.[12]

In keeping with the system of checks and balances, then, the Framers gave the president veto power, but only as a "qualified negative." Although the president had the authority to veto any act of Congress (with the exception of joint resolutions that propose constitutional amendments), the Framers gave Congress the authority to override an executive veto by a two-thirds vote in each house. Congress, however, cannot usually muster enough votes to override a veto. Thus, of the approximately 2,500 presidential vetoes that have occurred in over 200 years, Congress has overridden only about a hundred (see Table 7.3).

As early as 1873, in his State of the Union message, President Ulysses S. Grant proposed a constitutional amendment to give presidents a **line-item veto,** the power to disapprove of individual items within a spending bill rather than the bill in its entirety. Many governors have this authority. Over the years, 150 resolutions calling for a line-item veto were introduced in Congress. Finally, in 1996, Congress enacted legislation that gave the president this authority. The city of New York soon challenged the line-item veto law when President Bill Clinton used it to stop payment of some congressionally authorized funds to the city. In *Clinton* v. *City of New York* (1998), the U.S. Supreme Court ruled that the line-item veto was unconstitutional because it gave powers to the president denied him by the U.S. Constitution. Significant alterations of executive–congressional powers, said the Court, require constitutional amendment.[13]

line-item veto

The authority of a chief executive to delete part of a bill passed by the legislature that involves taxing or spending. Ruled unconstitutional by the U.S. Supreme Court.

War Powers Resolution

Passed by Congress in 1973; requires the authorization of Congress to deploy troops overseas and limits the time of their deployment.

The Power to Preside over the Military as Commander in Chief

One of the most important executive powers is that over the military. Article II states that the president is "Commander in Chief of the Army and Navy of the United States." While the Constitution specifically grants Congress the authority to declare war, presidents since Abraham Lincoln have used the commander in chief clause in conjunction with the chief executive's duty to "take Care that the Laws be faithfully executed" to wage war (and to broaden various powers).

Modern presidents continually clash with Congress over the ability to declare war. The Vietnam War, in which 58,000 American soldiers were killed and 300,000 were wounded, was conducted (at a cost of $150 billion) without a congressional declaration of war. In fact, acknowledging President Lyndon B. Johnson's claim to war-making authority, in 1964 Congress passed—with only two dissenting votes—the Gulf of Tonkin Resolution, which authorized a massive commitment of U.S. forces in South Vietnam.

During that highly controversial war, Presidents Johnson and Richard M. Nixon routinely assured members of Congress that victory was near. In 1971, however, publication of what were called *The Pentagon Papers* revealed what many people had suspected all along: the Johnson administration had systematically altered casualty figures and distorted key facts to place the progress of the war in a more positive light. Angered that this misinformation had led Congress to defer to the executive in the conduct of the Vietnam War, in 1973, Congress passed the **War Powers Resolution** to limit the president's authority to introduce American troops into hostile foreign lands without congressional approval. President Nixon vetoed the resolution, but both houses of Congress overrode it by a two-thirds majority.

7.1

7.2

7.3

7.4

7.5

7.6

TABLE 7.3 HOW MANY PRESIDENTIAL VETOES HAVE THERE BEEN?

President	Regular Vetoes	Pocket Vetoes	Total Vetoes	Vetoes Overridden
Washington	2	.....	2	.....
J. Adams	.....	.....	.....	.....
Jefferson	.....	.....	.....	.....
Madison	5	2	7	.....
Monroe	1	.....	1	.....
J. Q. Adams	.....	.....	.....	.....
Jackson	5	7	12	.....
Van Buren	.....	1	1	.....
W. H. Harrison	.....	.....	.....	.....
Tyler	6	4	10	1
Polk	2	1	3	.....
Taylor	.....	.....	.....	.....
Fillmore	.....	.....	.....	.....
Pierce	9	.....	9	5
Buchanan	4	3	7	.....
Lincoln	2	5	7	.....
A. Johnson	21	8	29	15
Grant	45	48	93	4
Hayes	12	1	13	1
Garfield	.....	.....	.....	.....
Arthur	4	8	12	1
Cleveland	304	110	414	2
B. Harrison	19	25	44	1
Cleveland	42	128	170	5
McKinley	6	36	42	.....
T. Roosevelt	42	40	82	1
Taft	30	9	39	1
Wilson	33	11	44	6
Harding	5	1	6	.....
Coolidge	20	30	50	4
Hoover	21	16	37	3
F. Roosevelt	372	263	635	9
Truman	180	70	250	12
Eisenhower	73	108	181	2
Kennedy	12	9	21	.....
L. Johnson	16	14	30	.....
Nixon	26	17	43	7
Ford	48	18	66	12
Carter	13	18	31	2
Reagan	39	39	78	9
Bush[a]	29	15	44	1
Clinton	36	1	37	2
G. W. Bush	10	.....	10	3
Obama[b]	2	.....	2	.....
Total	1,496	1,066	2,563	109

[a]President George Bush attempted to pocket veto two bills during intrasession recess periods. Congress considered the two bills enacted into law because of the president's failure to return the legislation. The bills are not counted as pocket vetoes in this table.
[b]As of October 2012.

SOURCE: Clerk of the House, http://artandhistory.house.gov/house_history/vetoes.aspx.

Presidents since Nixon have continued to insist that the War Powers Resolution is an unconstitutional infringement on their executive power. Still, in 2001, President George W. Bush complied with the resolution when he sought, and both houses of Congress approved, a joint resolution authorizing the use of force against "those responsible for the recent [September 11] attacks launched against the United States." This resolution actually gave the president more open-ended authority to wage war than President Johnson had received from the Gulf of Tonkin Resolution in 1964. In October 2002, after President Bush declared Iraq to be a "grave threat to peace," the House (296–133) and Senate (77–23) also voted overwhelmingly to allow the president to use force in Iraq "as he determines to be necessary and appropriate," thereby conferring tremendous authority on Bush and future presidents to wage war.

pardon
An executive grant providing restoration of all rights and privileges of citizenship to a specific individual charged or convicted of a crime.

☐ The Pardoning Power

Presidents can exercise a check on judicial power through their constitutional authority to grant reprieves or pardons. A **pardon** is an executive grant releasing an individual from the punishment or legal consequences of a crime before or after conviction, and restores all rights and privileges of citizenship. Presidents exercise complete pardoning power for federal offenses except in cases of impeachment, which cannot be pardoned. President Gerald R. Ford gave the most famous presidential pardon of all to former President Richard M. Nixon—who had not been formally charged with any crime—"for any offenses against the United States, which he, Richard Nixon, has committed or may have committed while in office." This unilateral, absolute pardon unleashed a torrent of public criticism against Ford and raised questions about whether Nixon had discussed the pardon with Ford before resigning. Many analysts attribute Ford's defeat in the 1976 election to that pardon.

Even though pardons generally apply to a specific individual, presidents have also used them to offer general amnesties. Presidents George Washington, John Adams, James Madison, Abraham Lincoln, Andrew Johnson, Theodore Roosevelt, Harry S Truman, and Jimmy Carter used general pardons to grant amnesty to large classes of individuals for illegal acts. Carter, for example, incurred the wrath of many veterans' groups when he made an offer of unconditional amnesty to approximately 10,000 men who had fled the United States or gone into hiding to avoid the draft for military service in the Vietnam War.

The Development and Expansion of Presidential Power

7.3 Evaluate the development and expansion of presidential power.

Every president brings to the position not only a vision of America but also expectations about how to use presidential authority. But, most presidents find accomplishing their goals much more difficult than they envisioned. As he was leaving office, for example, President Harry S Truman mused about what surprises awaited his successor, Dwight D. Eisenhower, a former general: "He'll sit here and he'll say, 'Do this! Do that!' And nothing will happen. Poor Ike—it won't be a bit like the army. He'll find it very frustrating."[14]

The formal powers enumerated in Article II of the Constitution and the Supreme Court's interpretation of those constitutional provisions limit a president's authority. The times in which the president serves, his confidantes and advisers, and his personality and leadership abilities all affect how he wields these powers. The 1950s postwar Era of Good Feelings and economic prosperity presided over by the grandfatherly Eisenhower, for instance, called for a very different leader from the one needed by the Civil War–torn

inherent powers
Powers that belong to the president because they can be inferred from the Constitution.

nation governed by Abraham Lincoln. Furthermore, not only do different times call for different kinds of leaders; they also often provide limits or, conversely, wide opportunities for whomever serves as president at the time. Crises, in particular, trigger expansions of presidential power. The danger to the union posed by the Civil War in the 1860s required a strong leader to take up the reins of government. Because of his leadership during this crisis, Lincoln was ranked the best president in a survey of historians from across the political spectrum (see Table 7.4).

☐ Establishing Presidential Authority: The First Presidents

When President George Washington was sworn in on a cold, blustery day in New York City on April 30, 1789, he took over an office and a government yet to be created. Eventually, the government hired a few hundred postal workers and Washington appointed a small group of Cabinet advisers and clerks. During Washington's two terms, the entire federal budget was only about $40 million, or approximately $10 for every citizen in America. In contrast, in 2012, the federal budget was $3.55 trillion, or $11,500 for every person.

George Washington set several important precedents for future presidents:

- He took every opportunity to establish the primacy of the national government. In 1794, for example, Washington used the militia of four states to put down the Whiskey Rebellion, an uprising of 3,000 western Pennsylvania farmers opposed to a federal excise tax on liquor. To emphasize the significance of the action, Washington, along with Secretary of the Treasury Alexander Hamilton, led the 15,000 troops into battle himself. Washington's action helped establish the idea of federal supremacy and the authority of the executive branch to collect taxes levied by Congress.
- He began the practice of regular meetings with his advisers, thus establishing the Cabinet system.
- He asserted the chief executive's prominent role in the conduct of foreign affairs. He sent envoys to negotiate the Jay Treaty to end continued hostilities with Great Britain. Then, over senatorial objection, he continued to wield his authority first to negotiate treaties and then simply to submit them to the Senate for approval. Washington made it clear that the Senate's function was limited to approval of treaties and did not include negotiation with foreign powers.
- He claimed the powers of the presidency as the basis for establishing a policy of strict neutrality when the British and French were at war. Although the Constitution is silent about a president's authority to declare neutrality, Washington's supporters argued that the Constitution granted the president **inherent powers**—that is, powers belonging to the president because they can be inferred from the Constitution, such as that authorizing him to conduct diplomatic relations.

Like Washington, the next two presidents, John Adams and Thomas Jefferson, acted in ways critical to the development of the presidency as well as to the president's role in

TABLE 7.4 WHO WERE THE BEST U.S. PRESIDENTS?

According to Historians ...	According to American People ...
1. Lincoln	1. Reagan
2. Washington	2. Lincoln
3. F. Roosevelt	3. Clinton
4. T. Roosevelt	4. Kennedy
5. Truman	5. Washington
6. Kennedy	6. F. Roosevelt
7. Jefferson	7. Obama
8. Eisenhower	8. No opinion
9. Wilson	9. G. W. Bush (tie)
10. Reagan	9. Jefferson (tie)

SOURCE: C-SPAN 2009 Historians Survey of Presidential Leadership; Gallup Poll, February 2–5, 2011.

HOW DID ABRAHAM LINCOLN EXPAND PRESIDENTIAL POWERS?

During the Civil War, Lincoln assumed inherent powers that no president before him had claimed. He argued that these actions were necessary for the preservation of the union. After the war, the president's powers never returned to their previous levels. Here, Lincoln is shown meeting with military leaders following the battle of Antietam, one of the bloodiest battles of the Civil War.

the political system. Adams's poor leadership skills, for example, heightened the divisions between Federalists and Anti-Federalists and probably hastened the development of political parties. Jefferson took critical steps to expand the role of the president in the legislative process. Like Washington, he claimed that certain presidential powers were inherent and used such powers to justify his expansion of the size of the nation through the Louisiana Purchase in 1803.

□ Incremental Expansion of Presidential Powers: 1809–1933

Although the first three presidents made enormous contributions to the office of the chief executive, the way government functioned in its formative years caused the balance of power to be heavily weighted in favor of a strong Congress. Americans routinely had close contacts with their representatives in Congress, while to most citizens the president seemed a remote figure. By the end of Jefferson's first term, it was clear that the Framers' initial fear of an all-powerful, monarchical president was unfounded. The strength of Congress and the relatively weak presidents who came after Jefferson allowed Congress quickly to assert itself as the most powerful branch of government.

President Andrew Jackson was the first strong national leader who represented more than just a landed, propertied elite. By the time Jackson ran for president in 1828, eleven new states had been added to the union, and the number of white males eligible to vote had increased dramatically, as nearly all states had removed property requirements for voting. The election of Jackson from Tennessee, as the seventh president, signaled the end of an era: he was the first president to be neither a Virginian nor an Adams. Jackson personified the western, frontier, egalitarian spirit, and his election launched the beginning of Jacksonian democracy. The masses loved him, and legends arose around his down-to-earth image. Jackson, for example, once was asked to give a position to a soldier who had lost his leg on the battlefield and needed the job to

7.1

7.2

7.3

7.4

7.5

7.6

support his family. When told that the man hadn't voted for him, Jackson responded: "If he lost his leg fighting for his country, that is vote enough for me."[15]

Jackson used his image and personal power to buttress the developing party system by rewarding loyal followers of his Democratic Party with presidential appointments. Frequently at odds with Congress, he made use of the veto power against twelve bills, surpassing the combined total of ten vetoes used by his six predecessors. Jackson also reasserted the supremacy of the national government (and the presidency) by facing down South Carolina's nullification of a federal tariff law.

Abraham Lincoln's approach to the presidency was similar to Jackson's. To combat the unprecedented emergency of the Civil War, Lincoln assumed powers that no president before him had claimed. Because Lincoln believed he needed to act quickly for the very survival of the nation, he frequently took action without first obtaining the approval of Congress. Among many of Lincoln's legally questionable acts were:

- He suspended the writ of *habeas corpus,* which allows those in prison to petition for release, citing the need to jail persons suspected of disloyal practices.
- He expanded the size of the U.S. Army above congressionally mandated ceilings.
- He ordered a blockade of southern ports without the approval of Congress.
- He closed the U.S. mail to treasonable correspondence.

Lincoln argued that the inherent powers of his office allowed him to circumvent the Constitution in a time of war or national crisis. Since the Constitution conferred on the president the duty to make sure that the laws of the United States are faithfully executed, reasoned Lincoln, these acts were constitutional. He simply refused to allow the nation to crumble because of what he viewed as technical requirements of the Constitution.

Creating the Modern Presidency

Since the 1930s, the general trend has been for presidential—as opposed to congressional—decision making to assume greater importance. The start of this trend can be traced to the four-term presidency of Franklin D. Roosevelt (FDR), who led the nation through several crises. This growth of presidential power, as well as of the federal government and its programs in general, is now criticized by many. To understand the basis for a large number of today's calls for reform of the political system, it is critical to learn how the government and the role of the president grew.[16]

FDR took office in 1933 in the midst of the Great Depression, a major economic crisis in which a substantial portion of the U.S. workforce was unemployed. Noting the sorry state of the national economy in his inaugural address, FDR concluded: "This nation asks for action and action now." To jump-start the American economy, FDR asked Congress for and was given "broad executive powers to wage a war against the emergency, as great as the power that would be given to me if we were in fact invaded by a foreign foe."[17]

Just as Abraham Lincoln had taken bold steps upon his inauguration, Roosevelt also acted quickly. He immediately fashioned a plan for national recovery called the New Deal, a package of bold and controversial programs designed to invigorate the failing American economy.

Roosevelt served an unprecedented twelve years in office; he was elected to four terms but died shortly after the beginning of the fourth. During his years in office, the nation went from the economic war of the Great Depression to the real international conflict of World War II. The institution of the presidency changed profoundly and permanently with the creation of new federal agencies to implement the New Deal.

Not only did FDR create a new bureaucracy to implement his pet programs, but he also personalized the presidency by establishing a new relationship between the president and the people. In his radio addresses, or fireside chats, as he called them, he spoke directly to the public in a relaxed and informal manner about serious issues.

To his successors, FDR left the modern presidency, including a burgeoning federal bureaucracy, an active and usually leading role in both domestic and foreign policy and legislation, and a nationalized executive office that used technology—first radio, then TV, and now the Internet—to bring the president closer to the public than ever before.

The Presidential Establishment

7.4 Outline the structure of the presidential establishment and the functions of each of its components.

As the responsibilities and scope of presidential authority grew over the years, so did the executive branch, including the number of people working directly for the president in the White House. The presidential establishment includes the vice president and his staff, the Cabinet, the first lady and her staff, the Executive Office of the President, and the White House staff. All help the president fulfill his duties as chief executive.

The Vice President

For many years, political observers considered the vice presidency a sure place for a public official to disappear into obscurity. When John Adams wrote to his wife, Abigail, about his position as America's first vice president, he said it was "the most insignificant office that was the invention of man . . . or his imagination conceived."[18]

Historically, presidents chose their vice presidents largely to balance—politically, geographically, or otherwise—the presidential ticket, with little thought given to the possibility that the vice president could become president. Franklin D. Roosevelt, for example, a liberal New Yorker, selected John Nance Garner, a conservative Texan, to be his running mate in 1932. After serving two terms, Garner—who openly disagreed with Roosevelt over many policies, including Roosevelt's decision to seek a third term—unsuccessfully sought the 1940 presidential nomination himself.

In 2008, President Barack Obama, accused of lacking foreign policy experience, chose Senator Joe Biden (D–DE) to balance the Democratic ticket. Obama and Biden ran for reelection in 2012. They were challenged by former Governor Mitt Romney and Representative Paul Ryan (R-WI). One of the main reasons Romney selected Ryan as his running mate was to energize social conservatives who had not been firmly behind Romney. Ryan, as chair of the House Budget Committee, also provided the Republican ticket with expertise in federal financial matters.

How much power a vice president has depends on how much the president is willing to give. Jimmy Carter was the first president to grant his vice president, Walter Mondale, more than ceremonial duties. In fact, Mondale was the first vice president to have an office in the White House. The last two vice presidents, Dick Cheney and Joe Biden, have attained significant powers and access to the president, elevating the office to new heights.

The Cabinet

The Cabinet, which has no official basis in the Constitution but is implied by Article II, section 2, is an informal institution based on practice and precedent whose membership is determined by tradition and presidential discretion. By custom, this advisory group selected by the president includes the heads of major executive departments. Presidents today also include their vice presidents in Cabinet meetings, as well as any other agency heads or officials to whom they would like to accord Cabinet-level status.

As a body, the Cabinet's major function is to help the president execute the laws and assist him in making decisions. Although the Framers discussed the idea of some form of national executive council, they did not include a provision for one in the Constitution. They did recognize, however, the need for departments of government and departmental heads.

Over the years, the Cabinet has grown alongside the responsibilities of the national government. As interest groups, in particular, pressured Congress and the president to recognize their demands for services and governmental action, they often were rewarded by the creation of an executive department. Since a secretary heading an executive department automatically became a member of the president's Cabinet, powerful clientele groups, including farmers (Agriculture), business people (Commerce), workers (Labor), and teachers (Education), saw the creation of a department as a way to expand their access to the national government.

While the size of the president's Cabinet has increased over the years, the reliance of most presidents on their Cabinet secretaries has decreased. Some individual members of a president's Cabinet, however, may be very influential.

☐ The First Lady

From the time of Martha Washington, first ladies (a term coined in 1849) have assisted presidents as informal advisers while making other, more public, and significant contributions to American society. Abigail Adams, for example, was a constant sounding board for her husband, John. An early feminist, in 1776 she cautioned him "to Remember the Ladies" in any new code of laws.

Edith Bolling Galt Wilson was probably the most powerful first lady. When President Woodrow Wilson collapsed and was left partly paralyzed in 1919, she became his surrogate and decided whom and what the stricken president saw. Her detractors dubbed her "Acting First Man."

Eleanor Roosevelt also played a powerful and much criticized role in national affairs. Not only did she write a nationally syndicated daily newspaper column, but also she traveled and lectured widely, worked tirelessly on countless Democratic Party matters, and raised six children. After FDR's death, she shone in her own right as U.S.

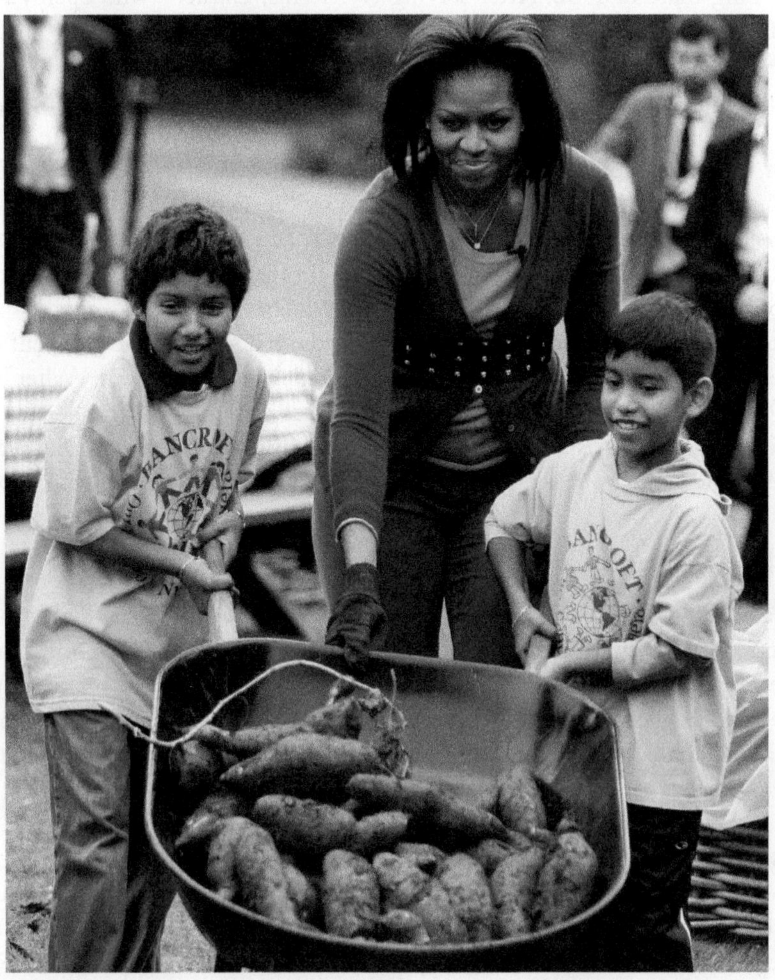

WHAT DO FIRST LADIES DO?

First ladies often take on important policy initiatives and charitable causes. First Lady Michelle Obama, for example, has prioritized childhood health and fitness. She has been active in the "Let's Move!" campaign, even challenging late night television host Jimmy Fallon to a series of physical fitness tests in the White House. She is shown here helping students harvest the White House vegetable garden.

delegate to the United Nations, where she headed the commission that drafted the covenant on human rights. Later, she headed President John F. Kennedy's Commission on the Status of Women.

More recently, First Lady Michelle Obama, a lawyer who was an administrator at the University of Chicago Medical Center, has prioritized health and physical fitness. From planting an organic White House vegetable garden to visiting schools around the country, she has stressed the importance of healthy lunches and fresh food and encouraged children to make nutritious choices, viewing childhood obesity and childhood diabetes as a serious problem and policy priority.

Executive Office of the President (EOP)
A mini-bureaucracy created in 1939 to help the president oversee the executive branch bureaucracy.

☐ The Executive Office of the President (EOP)

In 1939, FDR established the **Executive Office of the President (EOP)** to oversee his New Deal programs. Its purpose was to provide the president with a general staff to help him direct the diverse activities of the executive branch. In fact, it is a mini-bureaucracy of several advisers and offices located in the ornate Eisenhower Executive Office Building next to the White House on Pennsylvania Avenue, as well as in the White House itself, where the president's closest advisers often are located.

The EOP has expanded to include several advisory and policy-making agencies and task forces. Over time, the units of the EOP have become the prime policy makers in their fields of expertise, as they play key roles in advancing the president's policy preferences. Among the EOP's most important members are the National Security Council, the Council of Economic Advisers, the Office of Management and Budget, the Office of the Vice President, and the Office of the U.S. Trade Representative.

The National Security Council (NSC) was established in 1947 to advise the president on American military affairs and foreign policy. The NSC comprises the president; the vice president; and the secretaries of state, defense, and treasury. The chair of the Joint Chiefs of Staff and the director of the Central Intelligence Agency also participate. Others, such as the White House chief of staff and the general counsel, may attend. The national security adviser runs the staff of the NSC, coordinates information and options, and advises the president.

Although the president appoints the members of each of these bodies, they must perform their tasks in accordance with congressional legislation. As with the Cabinet, depending on who serves in pivotal positions, these mini-agencies may not be truly responsible or responsive to the president.

Presidents can clearly indicate their policy preferences by the kinds of offices they include in the EOP. President Barack Obama's addition of an Economic Recovery Advisory Board to the EOP showed his concern about the economy and a desire to find ways to bring the country out of recession. President Obama has also appointed an unprecedented number of "czars," administrators given authority by the president over important policy priorities. The rise in the number of czars can be partially explained by the ever-growing number of organizations and groups now managed by the government, including those involving health, energy, and technology issues. Examples of Obama administration czars include the "California Water Czar" and the "Drug Czar." These two men, as well as the other czars, report directly to the president with updates concerning their target areas. This delegation of authority allows the president to oversee special interests while spending his time on the pressing issues of state.

☐ The White House Staff

Often more directly responsible to the president are the members of the White House staff: the personal assistants to the president, including senior aides, their deputies, assistants with professional duties, and clerical and administrative aides. As personal assistants, these advisers are not subject to Senate confirmation, nor do they have divided loyalties. Their power derives from their personal relationship with the president, and they have no independent legal authority.

What Does the West Wing Say About the Presidency?

The White House, also known as the "President's Palace" or "Executive Mansion," is both a national symbol and a unique private residence. The West Wing of the White House also serves as office space for some of the president's closest advisors. It was added to the White House in 1902 and has been redesigned several times since then to serve the needs of the president. Most recently, for example, the White House swimming pool, added at the behest of President Franklin D. Roosevelt, was converted into the press room. Examine the diagram of the West Wing and consider how its layout reflects individuals' power and the president's policy priorities.

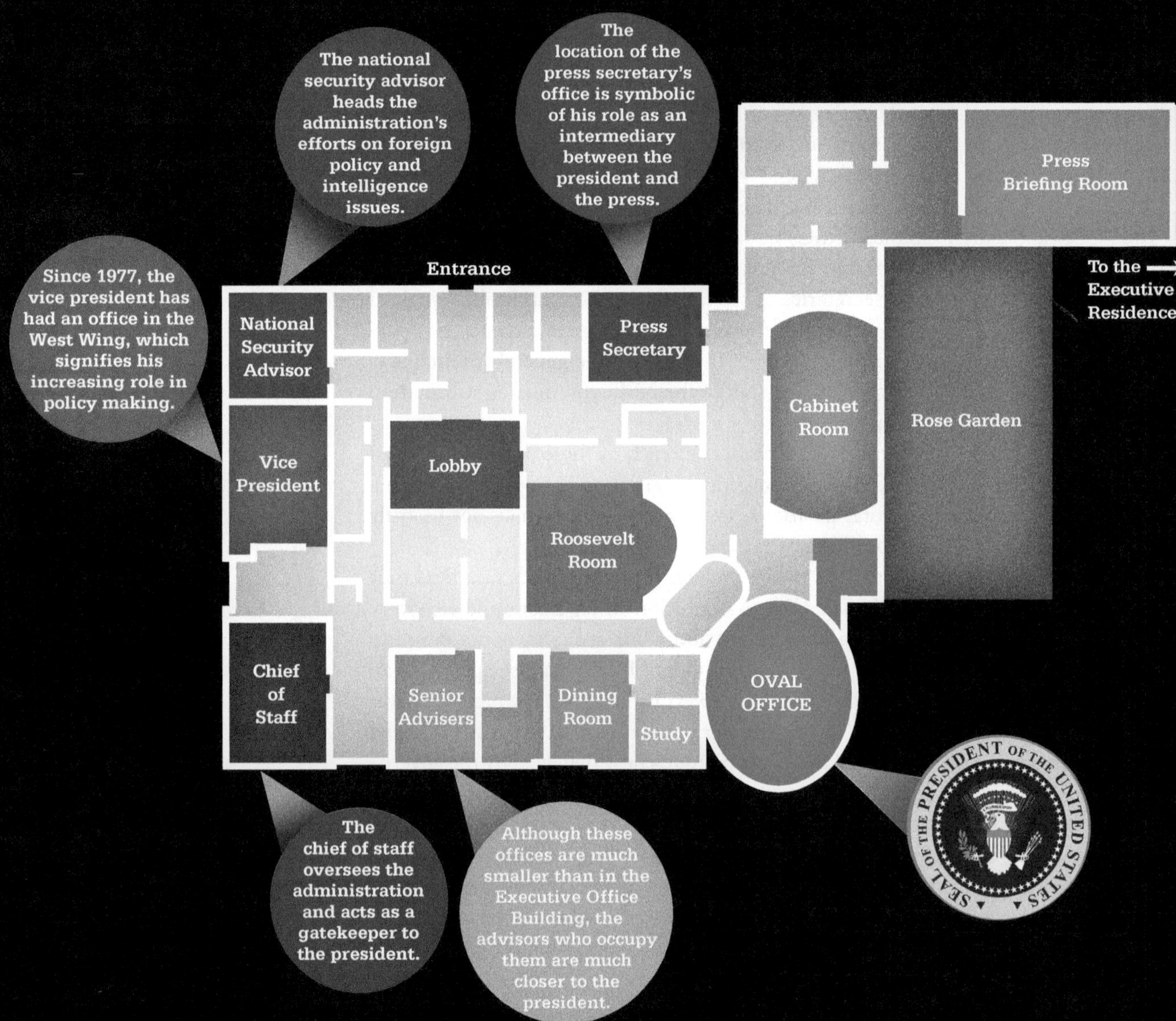

The national security advisor heads the administration's efforts on foreign policy and intelligence issues.
The location of the press secretary's office is symbolic of his role as an intermediary between the president and the press.
Since 1977, the vice president has had an office in the West Wing, which signifies his increasing role in policy making.
Entrance
National Security Advisor
Press Secretary
Press Briefing Room
To the Executive Residence
Cabinet Room
Rose Garden
Vice President
Lobby
Roosevelt Room
Chief of Staff
Senior Advisers
Dining Room
Study
OVAL OFFICE
SEAL OF THE PRESIDENT OF THE UNITED STATES
The chief of staff oversees the administration and acts as a gatekeeper to the president.
Although these offices are much smaller than in the Executive Office Building, the advisors who occupy them are much closer to the president.

CRITICAL THINKING QUESTIONS

1. Whose offices are closest to the president? What statement does this make about these individuals' power and authority?
2. Whose offices are notably missing from the West Wing? Where are their offices located, and what statement does this make about these individuals' power and authority?
3. How might the allocation of West Wing office space vary from one administration to the next? Why might these variations occur?

Although presidents organize the White House staff in different ways, they typically have a chief of staff whose job is to facilitate the smooth running of the staff and the executive branch of government. Successful chiefs of staff also have protected the president from mistakes and helped implement policies to obtain the maximum political advantage for the president. Other important White House aides include domestic, foreign, and economic policy strategists; the communications staff; the White House counsel; and a liaison between the president and Congress.

As presidents have tried to consolidate power in the White House, and as public demands on the president have grown, the size of the White House staff has increased—from fifty-one in 1943, to 247 in 1953, to a high of 583 in 1972. Since that time, staffs have been trimmed, generally running around 500. The Obama White House has approximately 490 staffers.

Presidential Leadership and the Importance of Public Opinion

7.5 Explain the concept of presidential leadership and analyze the importance of public opinion.

A president's success in having his programs adopted or implemented depends on many factors, including his leadership capabilities, his personality and powers of persuasion, his ability to mobilize public opinion in support of his actions, the public's perception of his performance, and Congress's perception of his public support.

☐ Presidential Leadership and Personality

Leadership is not easy to exercise, and it remains an elusive concept for scholars to identify and measure, but it is important to all presidents seeking support for their programs and policies. Moreover, ideas about the importance of effective leaders have deep roots in our political culture. Frequently, the difference between great and mediocre presidents centers on their ability to grasp the importance of leadership style. Truly great presidents, such as Lincoln and FDR, understood that the White House was a seat of power from which decisions could flow to shape the national destiny. They recognized that their day-to-day activities and how they went about them should be designed to bolster support for their policies and to secure congressional and popular backing that could translate their intuitive judgment into meaningful action. Mediocre presidents, on the other hand, have tended to regard the White House as "a stage for the presentation of performances to the public" or a fitting honor to cap a career.[19]

Political scientist Richard E. Neustadt calls the president's ability to influence members of Congress and the public "the power to persuade." Neustadt believes this power is crucial to presidential leadership because it enables presidents to get their policy goals enacted and win support for their policies in the electorate.[20] Persuasion may come from a variety of sources, including a president's natural charisma or ability to make people do things they would not ordinarily do.

At least one prominent psychologist has suggested that a president's personality may influence his success in the White House. Specifically, this scholar proposes that presidents with mood disorders may be best suited to lead when crises arise. Mania, for example, may lend itself to creative solutions in trying times. Similarly, political scientists and historians have long discussed Lincoln's melancholy and how it affected his ability to keep the nation together.[21]

President Barack Obama is generally credited with having a charismatic leadership style. This was particularly evident in his early emphasis on cross-cultural governing, a deviation from presidential norms. While most presidents tend to stay at home during the early days of their term, during his first six months in office, President Obama traveled abroad more than any other president. His goal was to rebuild the international reputation of the United States. Both he and Secretary of State Hillary Clinton went out of their way to embrace international values, especially in the Middle East. This leadership left many Americans feeling sour, and believing that the president had neglected the many domestic problems facing the United States, including jobs, the economy, and health care reform.

☐ Going Public

Even before radio, TV, and the Internet, presidents tried to reach out to the public to gain support for their programs through what President Theodore Roosevelt called the bully pulpit. The development of commercial air travel, radio, newsreels, TV, computers, cell phones, and social media has made direct communication to larger numbers of voters easier. Presidents, first ladies, and other presidential advisers travel the world over to publicize their views and to build support on a personal level as well for administration programs.

Direct presidential appeals to the electorate, such as those often made by recent presidents, are referred to as "going public."[22] Going public means that a president bypasses the heads of members of Congress to gain support from the people, who can then place pressure on their elected officials in Washington.

Bill Clinton was keenly aware of the importance of maintaining his connection with the public. Beginning with his 1992 campaign, Clinton often appeared on *Larry King Live* on CNN. Even after becoming president, Clinton continued to take his case directly to the people. He launched his health care reform proposals, for example, on a prime-time edition of *Nightline* hosted by Ted Koppel. Moreover, at a black-tie dinner honoring radio and TV correspondents, Clinton responded to criticisms leveled against him for not holding traditional press conferences by pointing out how clever he was to ignore the traditional press. "You know why I can stiff you on the press conferences? Because Larry King liberated me from you by giving me to the American people directly."[23]

WHAT ROLE DO PRESIDENTIAL SPEECHES SERVE?

Presidents carefully chose favorable audiences that enable them to mobilize support for key initiatives. Here, President Barack Obama speaks to students and faculty at the University of North Carolina—Chapel Hill, encouraging them to lobby members of Congress against raising student loan interest rates.

Barack Obama continued the tradition of going directly to the people, becoming the first sitting president to appear on *The Late Show with David Letterman* and later on *The View*. He also chose favorable audiences for his speeches. For example, in May 2012, Obama visited several college campuses urging students to pressure lawmakers not to increase interest rates on student loans. "Tweet them!" the president said, "Urge your parents to Tweet!"[24]

☐ The President and Public Opinion

Presidents and other public figures often use approval ratings as tacit measures of their political capital: their ability to enact public policy simply because of their name and their office. People assume that presidents who have high approval ratings—as President George W. Bush did in the immediate aftermath of the September 11, 2001, terrorist attacks—are more powerful leaders with a mandate for action that comes largely by virtue of high levels of public support. These presidents are often able to use their clout to push controversial legislation, such as the USA PATRIOT Act, through Congress. A public appearance from a popular president can even deliver a hotly contested congressional seat or gubernatorial contest to the president's party.

In sharp contrast, low approval ratings often cripple presidents in the policy arena. Their low ratings can actually prevent favored policies from being enacted on Capitol Hill, even when their party controls the legislature, as many of their partisans locked in close elections shy away from being seen or affiliated with an unpopular president.

Presidential popularity, though, generally follows a cyclical pattern. These cycles have been recorded since 1938, when pollsters first began to track presidential popularity. Typically, presidents enjoy their highest level of public approval at the beginning of their terms and try to take advantage of this honeymoon period to get their programs passed by Congress as soon as possible (see Figure 7.1). Each action a president takes,

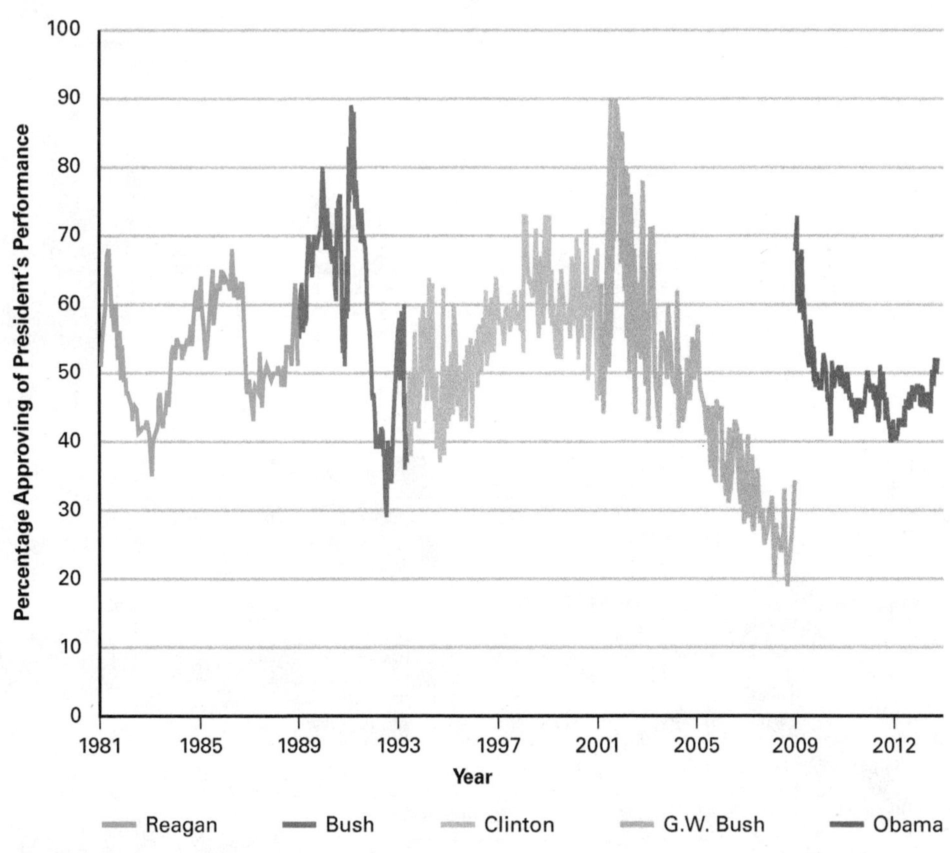

FIGURE 7.1 HOW DO PRESIDENTIAL APPROVAL RATINGS VARY OVER TIME?

Examine the line graph, which shows the percentage of the American public approving of the president's performance from 1981 through 2012. When is the president's approval the highest? The lowest? How does the president's approval rating change over his term? Based on partisanship?

SOURCE: http://www.gallup.com/poll/124922/presidential-approval-center.aspx

Explore on MyPoliSciLab

What Influences a President's Public Approval?

Political scientists watch a president's approval rating because it shows how much political capital is available to him, indicates how the public views the executive's performance, and helps us relate popular support to policy success, such as dealing with foreign crises or managing the economy. Gallup approval ratings of two recent presidents are shown below; you can see how presidential approval is shaped by the economy and by events.

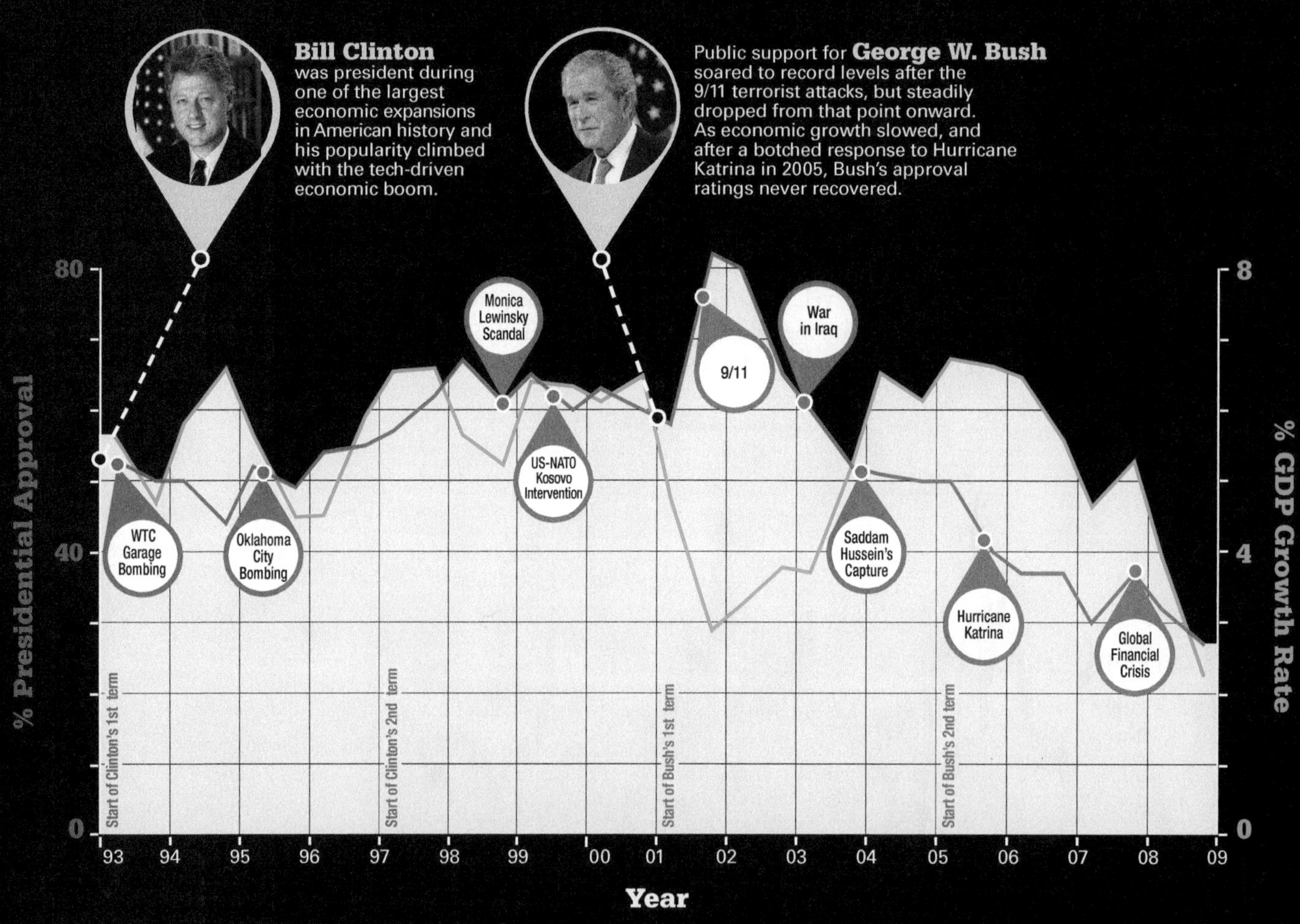

SOURCE: Data from the Gallup Presidential Job Approval Center.

Investigate Further

Concept Do presidents gain or lose popularity over the course of their term? For President Clinton, an initial loss of popularity—due in part to economic recession—was followed by durable gains in public support. George W. Bush's popularity peaked with the 9/11 attacks then systematically fell off.

Connection Is popularity tied to economic performance? Clearly Bill Clinton's popularity moved with the economy. As it grew, so too did Clinton's job approval. For President Bush, there may be correlation between economic approval and popularity, but it is masked for much of his term by the effects of war on public opinion.

Cause How do events shape the popularity of President Bush? The 9/11 terrorist attacks led to a rally-round-the-flag effect which defined George W. Bush's presidency. For a brief period, success in the Iraq war boosted Bush's popularity until war fatigue and failure to manage other crises pulled his approval ratings to record low levels.

however, is divisive—some people will approve, and others will disapprove. Disapproval tends to have a negative cumulative effect on a president's approval rating. Since Lyndon B. Johnson's presidency, only four presidents have left office with approval ratings of more than 50 percent. Many people attribute this trend to events such as Vietnam, the Iraq War, and economic recessions that have made the public increasingly skeptical of presidential performance.

However, recent presidents have experienced a surge in their approval ratings during the course of their presidencies. Popularity surges usually allow presidents to achieve some policy goals they believe will benefit the nation, even though the policies are unpopular with the public. Often coming on the heels of a domestic or international crisis such as the 1991 Persian Gulf War or the 9/11 terrorist attacks, these increased approval ratings generally do not last long, as the cumulative effects of governing once again catch up with the president.

Toward Reform: The President as Policy Maker

7.6 Assess the president's role as policy maker.

When President Franklin D. Roosevelt sent his first legislative package to Congress, he broke the traditional model of law-making.[25] As envisioned by the Framers, the responsibility of making laws fell to Congress. Now FDR was claiming a leadership role for the president in the legislative process. Said the president of this new relationship: "It is the duty of the President to propose and it is the privilege of the Congress to dispose."[26] With those words and the actions that followed, FDR shifted the presidency into a law- and policy maker role. Now the president and the executive branch not only executed the laws but generally suggested them and proposed budgets to Congress to fund those proposals.

The President's Role in Proposing and Facilitating Legislation

Modern presidents play a major role in setting the legislative agenda, especially in an era when the House and Senate are narrowly divided along partisan lines. Without working majorities, "merely placing a program before Congress is not enough," as President Lyndon B. Johnson once explained. "Without constant attention from the administration, most legislation moves through the congressional process at the speed of a glacier."[27]

However, presidents have a hard time persuading Congress to pass their programs. Recent research by political scientists shows that presidents are much more likely to win on bills central to their announced agendas, such as President Barack Obama's victory on health care reform, than to secure passage of legislation proposed by others.[28]

Because presidents generally experience declining support for policies they advocate throughout their terms, it is important for a president to propose key plans early in his administration. Even President Lyndon B. Johnson, who was able to push nearly 60 percent of his programs through Congress, noted: "You've got to give it all you can, that first year . . . before they start worrying about themselves. . . . You can't put anything through when half the Congress is thinking how to beat you."[29]

A president can also bolster support for his legislative package by calling on his political party. As the informal leader of his party, he should take that advantage to build coalitions in Congress, where party loyalty is very important. This strategy works

Explore Your World

Executive mansions and palaces are often among the most ornate homes in the world. These homes exemplify the importance and prominence of the head of government. They may represent the state's culture or values. Their structure and functions may also vary, depending on whether the state has a presidential or a parliamentary system. Examine the structures shown below, with an eye toward these themes.

Christiansborg Palace in Copenhagen, Denmark, is the only building in the world that houses all three branches of a state's government. It is home to the prime minister, the Danish Supreme Court, and the Folketing, the Danish legislature.

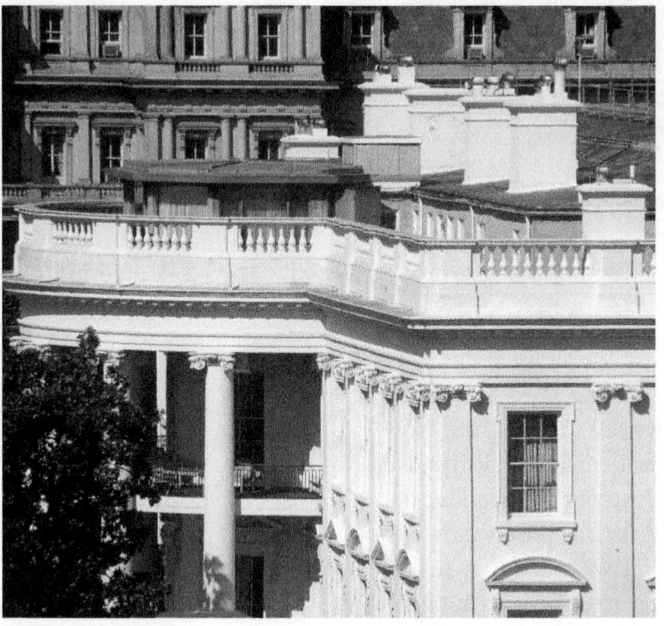

Though the White House, home of the American president, may appear modest on the outside, the residence area of the White House alone boasts 132 rooms, thirty-five bathrooms, and twenty-eight fireplaces.

Until 2002, the prime minister of Japan lived in the small brick residence, shown in the back right hand side of this photo. However, the prime minister's residence has recently been upgraded to the larger glass building in the foreground.

CRITICAL THINKING QUESTIONS

1. How does each of these structures reflect the history and governmental system of the state it represents?
2. In states with parliamentary systems, how would you expect the residence of the head of government, the prime minister, to compare to the residence of the head of state, who is often a monarch? How does the combination of these roles affect the structure and functions of presidential residences?
3. Should presidents and prime ministers be provided an official residence at the citizens' expense? Why or why not?

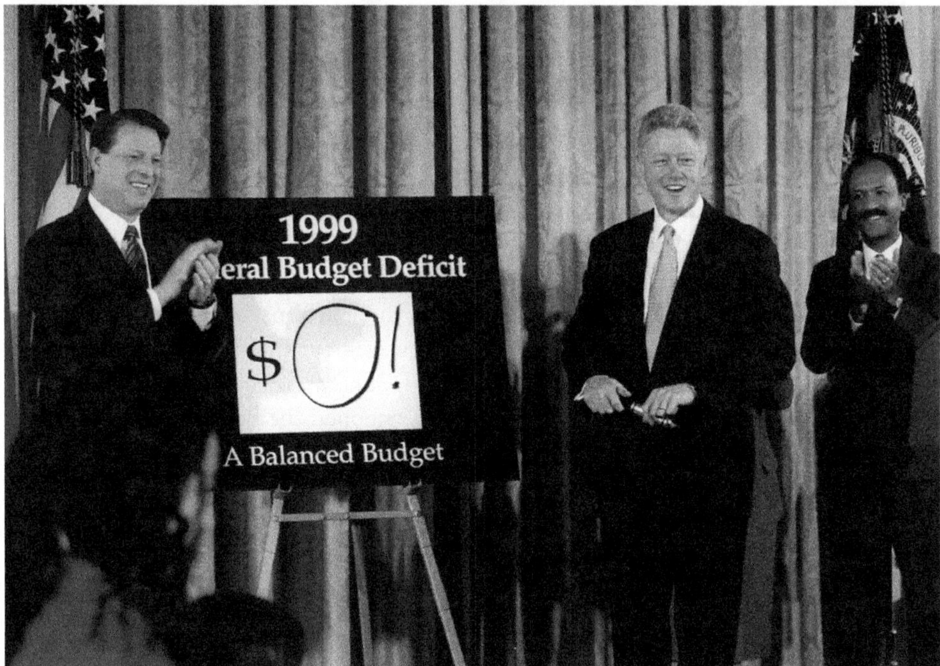

HOW IMPORTANT IS A BALANCED BUDGET?

President Bill Clinton and Vice President Al Gore celebrate the first balanced budget in years, a feat not likely to be repeated soon.

Office of Management and Budget (OMB)
The office that prepares the president's annual budget proposal, reviews the budget and programs of the executive departments, supplies economic forecasts, and conducts detailed analyses of proposed bills and agency rules.

best when the president has carried members of his party into office on his coattails as well as when his party has a majority in the legislature.

The Budgetary Process and Legislative Implementation

Closely associated with a president's ability to have legislation passed is his capacity to secure funding for new and existing programs. A president sets national policy and priorities through his budget proposals and his continued insistence on their congressional passage. The budget proposal not only outlines the programs he wants but also indicates the importance of each program by the amount of funding requested for each and for its associated agency or department.

Because the Framers gave Congress the power of the purse, Congress had primary responsibility for the budgetary process until 1930. The economic disaster set off by the stock market crash of 1929, however, gave FDR the opportunity to involve himself in the congressional budgetary process, just as he inserted himself into the legislative process. In 1939, the Bureau of the Budget, which had been created in 1921 to help the president inform Congress of the amount of money needed to run the executive branch of government, was made part of the newly created Executive Office of the President. In 1970, President Nixon changed its name to the **Office of Management and Budget (OMB)** to clarify its function in the executive branch.

The OMB works exclusively for the president and employs hundreds of budget and policy experts. Major OMB responsibilities include preparing the president's annual budget proposal; assessing the costs of the president's proposals; and reviewing the progress, budget, and program proposals of the executive department agencies. It also supplies economic forecasts to the president and conducts detailed analyses of proposed bills and agency rules. OMB reports allow the president to attach price tags to his legislative proposals and defend his budget.

executive order
Rule or regulation issued by the president that has the effect of law. All executive orders must be published in the *Federal Register*.

signing statements
Occasional written comments attached to a bill signed by the president.

7.1

7.2

7.3

7.4

7.5

7.6

☐ Policy Making Through Executive Order

Proposing legislation and using the budget to advance policy priorities are not the only ways that presidents can affect the policy process, especially in times of highly divided government when the policies of the president and Congress may differ. Presidents may institute major policy changes by issuing an **executive order,** a rule or regulation set forth by the president that has the effect of law without congressional approval. Presidents Franklin D. Roosevelt and Harry S Truman used executive orders to seize mills, mines, and factories whose production was crucial to World War II and Korean War efforts. Roosevelt and Truman argued that these actions were necessary to preserve national security. The Supreme Court, however, eventually disagreed with the Truman administration in *Youngstown Sheet and Tube* v. *Sawyer* (1952). In that case, the Court unequivocally stated that Truman had overstepped the boundaries of his office as provided by the Constitution.[30]

While many executive orders help clarify or implement legislation enacted by Congress, others have the effect of making new policy. President Truman also used an executive order to end segregation in the military, and affirmative action was institutionalized as national policy through Executive Order 11246, issued by Lyndon B. Johnson in 1966.

Presidents may also issue **signing statements,** occasional written comments attached to a bill, when signing legislation. Often these written statements merely comment on the bill signed, but they sometimes include controversial claims by the president that some part of the legislation is unconstitutional and that he intends to disregard it or to implement it in other ways.

President George W. Bush used signing statements to express his belief that portions of more than 1,200 laws were unconstitutional. "Among the laws Bush said he [could] ignore [were] military rules and regulations, affirmative action provisions, requirements that Congress be told about immigration services problems, 'whistle-blower' protections for nuclear regulator officials, and safeguards against political interference in federally funded research."[31]

After taking office, President Barack Obama sent out a memorandum instructing agencies not to follow directives from previous administrations without first seeking the approval of the Department of Justice.[32] And yet, much like Bush, Obama has issued several signing statements raising constitutional concerns about bills he signed into law, including the 2012 appropriations for the Department of Defense.[33]

Signing statements, thus, have become another way for the president to use his informal powers to make and influence public policy. For example, these statements invite litigation and may delay policy implementation. Because signing statements happen at the end of the legislative process, they also represent a largely unchecked way for the president to assert himself in the ongoing power struggle with Congress.

Review the Chapter

Listen to Chapter 7 on MyPoliSciLab

Roots of the Office of President of the United States

7.1 Trace the development of the presidency and the provisions for choosing and replacing presidents, p. 207.

To keep any one president from becoming too powerful, the Framers created an executive office with limited powers. They mandated that a president be at least thirty-five years old, a natural-born citizen, and a resident of the United States for fourteen years or more, and they opted not to limit the president's term of office. To further guard against tyranny, they made provisions for the removal of the president.

The Constitutional Powers of the President

7.2 Identify and describe the constitutional powers of the president, p. 212.

The Framers gave the president a variety of specific constitutional powers in Article II, including the powers to appoint, to convene Congress, and to make treaties. The Constitution also gives the president the capacity to grant pardons and to veto acts of Congress. In addition, the president derives considerable power from being commander in chief of the military.

The Development and Expansion of Presidential Power

7.3 Evaluate the development and expansion of presidential power, p. 217.

The development of presidential power has depended on the personal force of those who have held the office. George Washington, in particular, took several actions to establish the primacy of the president in national affairs and as chief executive of a strong national government. With only a few exceptions, subsequent presidents often let Congress dominate in national affairs. Franklin D. Roosevelt (FDR), however, took more power for the office of the president, and made more decisions in national and foreign affairs.

The Presidential Establishment

7.4 Outline the structure of the presidential establishment and the functions of each of its components, p. 221.

As the responsibilities of the president have grown, so has the executive branch of government. FDR established the Executive Office of the President to help him govern. Perhaps the most important policy advisers are those closest to the president: the vice president, the White House staff, some members of the Executive Office of the President, and the first lady.

Presidential Leadership and the Importance of Public Opinion

7.5 Explain the concept of presidential leadership and analyze the importance of public opinion, p. 225.

To gain support for his programs or proposed budget, the president uses a variety of skills, including personal leadership and direct appeals to the public. The president's leadership and personal style, which are affected by his character and his ability to persuade, determine how he goes about winning support. Since the 1970s, however, the American public has been increasingly skeptical of presidential actions, and few presidents have enjoyed the extended periods of popularity needed to help win support for programmatic change.

Toward Reform: The President as Policy Maker

7.6 Assess the president's role as policy maker, p. 229.

Since FDR, the public has looked to the president to propose legislation to Congress. Through proposing legislation, advancing budgets, involvement in the regulatory process, and executive orders and agreements, presidents make policy.

Learn the Terms

Study and Review the Flashcards

Cabinet, p. 212
executive agreements, p. 213
Executive Office of the President (EOP), p. 223
executive order, p. 232
executive privilege, p. 210
impeachment, p. 210
inherent powers, p. 218
line-item veto, p. 215
Office of Management and Budget (OMB), p. 231
pardon, p. 217
signing statements, p. 232
Twenty-Fifth Amendment, p. 211
Twenty-Second Amendment, p. 210
U.S. v. *Nixon* (1974), p. 210
veto, p. 213
War Powers Resolution, p. 215

Test Yourself

Study and Review the Practice Tests

1. Which of the following is a requirement to become president of the United States?

a. Be at least 35 years old
b. No prior criminal record
c. Have a valid U. S. passport
d. Be a resident of the United States for at least thirty years
e. Have previous government experience

2. Which of the following is a constitutional duty of the vice president?

a. In the event of an emergency, the vice president must stand in for the president.
b. The vice president is the director of foreign policy, often meeting with delegates from other nations and addressing international crises.
c. The vice president functions as the head of the Supreme Court, voting in the event of a tie.
d. The vice president is the president's official legislative liaison.
e. All of the above

3. Which of the following is NOT a role fulfilled by the modern president?

a. Chief of state
b. Commander in chief
c. Chief of party
d. Chief legislator
e. Chief of education

4. When creating treaties, the president must:

a. make binding treaties only with permission from the Supreme Court.
b. seek the approval of the Senate.
c. host delegates and ambassadors, but only with Senate approval.
d. rely only on the House of Representatives to negotiate all treaties related to international commerce.
e. operate only within the framework established by the United Nations.

5. The president's authority is defined by:

a. Supreme Court interpretation of international law.
b. the powers granted to the president by the Senate and the House of Representatives.
c. the implied and inherent powers extending from Article II of the Constitution.
d. the powers enumerated in the Bill of Rights.
e. the powers given to the president by Congress upon his appointment to office.

6. Which of the following is NOT selected by the president?

a. The Speaker of the House
b. The Cabinet
c. The vice president
d. The first lady
e. The national security advisor

7. Cabinet secretaries

a. may also serve simultaneously in Congress.
b. are elected by the American people.
c. have decreased in number and importance in the American political system.
d. may not identify with a particular political party.
e. have become less important presidential advisors over time.

8. How, according to political scientists, can American presidents best demonstrate their ability to lead?

a. By spending time abroad with foreign leaders
b. By increasing public attention to particular issues
c. By attending all sessions of Congress
d. By maintaining a wholesome family life
e. By visiting low-income constituencies across the country

9. What is the typical trend of a president's approval ratings throughout his tenure in office?

a. The rating usually remains consistent, regardless of the decisions made.
b. The rating is higher when entering office than the rating when leaving office.
c. The rating is lower when entering office than the rating when leaving office.
d. The rating is sporadic, based on the decisions made, and no pattern can be found.
e. Each president has had a unique rating pattern, and no systematic differences can be observed.

10. Which of the following is NOT a method that the president can use to make and influence public policy?

a. Signing statements to comment on bills
b. Suggesting changes to legislation
c. Using the budget to advance policy priorities
d. Issuing an executive order
e. Amending the Constitution

Explore Further

Barber, James David. *The Presidential Character: Predicting Presidential Performance in the White House,* 5th ed. New York: Longman, 2008.

Cronin, Thomas E., and Michael A. Genovese. *The Paradoxes of the American Presidency,* 3rd ed. New York: Oxford University Press, 2009.

Ghaemi, Nassir. *A First Rate Madness: Uncovering the Links Between Leadership and Mental Illness.* New York: Penguin, 2011.

Greenstein, Fred I. *The Presidential Difference: Leadership Style from FDR to Barack Obama,* 3rd ed. Princeton, NJ: Princeton University Press, 2009.

Han, Lori Cox. *New Directions in the American Presidency.* New York: Routledge, 2010.

Neustadt, Richard E. *Presidential Power and the Modern Presidents.* New York: Free Press, 1991.

Pfiffner, James P. *The Character Factor: How We Judge America's Presidents.* College Station: Texas A&M University Press, 2004.

______. *The Modern Presidency,* 6th ed. Belmont, CA: Wadsworth, 2010.

Pika, Joseph A., and John Anthony Maltese. *The Politics of the Presidency,* 8th ed. Washington, DC: CQ Press, 2012.

Rozell, Mark J. *Executive Privilege: Presidential Power, Secrecy, and Accountability.* Lawrence: University Press of Kansas, 2010.

Shesol, Jeff. *Supreme Power: Franklin Roosevelt vs. the Supreme Court.* New York: W.W. Norton, 2010.

Skowronek, Stephen. *The Politics Presidents Make: Leadership from John Adams to Bill Clinton.* Cambridge, MA: Harvard University Press, 1997.

Warshaw, Shirley Anne. *The Co-Presidency of Bush and Cheney.* Stanford, CA: Stanford University Press, 2009.

Wood, B. Dan. *The Politics of Economic Leadership: The Causes and Consequences of Presidential Rhetoric.* Princeton, NJ: Princeton University Press, 2007.

To learn more about the office of the president, go to the official White House Web site at **www.whitehouse.gov.** There you can track current presidential initiatives and legislative priorities, read press briefings, and learn more about presidential nominations and executive orders.

To learn more about past presidents, go to the National Archives Web site at **www.archives.gov/index.html.** There you can learn about the presidential libraries, view presidential documents, and hear audio of presidents speaking.

To learn more about the office of the vice president, go to **www.whitehouse.gov/vicepresident.**

To learn more about the initiatives favored by the first lady, go to **www.whitehouse.gov/firstlady.**

8

Listen to Chapter 8 on MyPoliSciLab

The Executive Branch and the Federal Bureaucracy

On the afternoon of May 2, 2011, United States Navy SEAL Team Six performed the most significant counterterrorism assassination in the history of United States. Two helicopters flew from Afghanistan to al-Qaeda founder Osama bin Laden's compound in Abbottabad, Pakistan. Despite difficulties with the first helicopter, the SEAL Team successfully landed and entered the compound. Several gunmen, including bin Laden's son, Khalid, confronted them immediately; the SEALs rebuffed the gunmen's attack. Reaching the third floor of the house, one member of the SEAL Team saw an armed man look outside a door. The SEAL fired on the male assailant, injuring him with the first shot; additional shots were fired, and the assailant was soon dead. When prompted, a child identified the man on the floor by name: Osama bin Laden.

The SEAL Team immediately relayed their victorious message to their commander in chief, President Barack Obama, and his Cabinet. In military language, they stated: "For God and country, I pass Geronimo, Geronimo, E.K.I.A." which meant, "Osama bin Laden, Enemy Killed In Action."

Although the SEAL Team carried out the on-the-ground attack that ultimately took bin Laden's life, their actions were supported by years of research and data collection by intelligence analysts in a variety of government agencies. Perhaps no bureaucrat was more dedicated to the cause than a Central Intelligence Agency employee known only as Miss One-Hundred Percent. In the

BUREAUCRATS PLAY AN IMPORTANT ROLE AS ADVISORS TO THE PRESIDENT Above, President John F. Kennedy meets with his national security team in the wake of the Cuban Missile Crisis. Below, President Barack Obama and his national security team watch live coverage of the capture of Osama bin Laden.

MyPoliSciLab Videos

Watch on MyPoliSciLab

The Big Picture From the IRS to the Department of Defense, bureaucracy exists to help Americans—so why does everyone hate it? Author Karen O'Connor defends public bureaucrats against the charges that they are lazy and inefficient, and provides some explanations for why they are so underappreciated.

The Basics What does the bureaucracy do? What is its role in our democracy? In this video, you will listen to what people think about bureaucrats and the job they do. You will also learn why the bureaucracy can have such a big impact on your life.

2
What does the bureacracy do? Is it effective?

3

In Context Why is the bureaucracy important in the policy-making process? In this video, University of North Texas political scientist Matthew Eshbaugh-Soha talks about not only the bureaucracy and its importance at the federal level, but also the role the federal bureaucracy plays in cooperation with state and local bureaucracies.

Thinking Like a Political Scientist Are bureaucracies democratic? And if so, how are they democratic? University of North Texas political scientist Matthew Eshbaugh-Soha tackles this question and also looks at political appointments and other important research topics associated with bureaucracies.

In the Real World Is the federal bureaucracy too big and too powerful? Real people weigh in on this question and discuss whether they feel reducing the size of the bureaucracy is worth losing the protections that those agencies provide.

So What? Discover how bureaucracy affects you. Author Karen O'Connor examines a typical day in the life of a student, and highlights the ways that bureaucracy is present—from the water temperature of your shower to the brand of clothing that you wear.

days leading up to the attack, Miss One-Hundred Percent briefed the SEAL Team. During these meetings, she shared information about bin Laden's compound, the location of the target within the compound, and the amount of time they would have to execute their orders. Once they returned to their base in Afghanistan, Miss One-Hundred Percent not only debriefed the SEALs, but she also identified bin Laden's body on behalf of the U.S. government, shedding tears for the success of her career's greatest mission.

Without the cooperation of Miss One-Hundred Percent and others like her at the Central Intelligence Agency, Federal Bureau of Investigation, Department of Defense, and National Security Agency, just to name a few, the mission to capture and ultimately kill bin Laden would have been impossible. Employing this type of cooperation to solve large-scale national problems is the hallmark of the federal bureaucracy. The diverse programs and agencies that comprise the bureaucracy also enable government officials to work efficiently on many issues at once. In so doing, the executive branch can carry out orders handed down from officials in each of the three branches of government. For example, the mission to capture bin Laden, officially called Operation Neptune Spear, was confirmed and ordered by the president of the United States, acting as commander in chief of the armed forces. Funds appropriated by Congress were essential to its completion, and the U.S. Supreme Court may review its constitutionality.[1]

•••

The **federal bureaucracy,** or the thousands of federal government agencies and institutions that implement and administer federal laws and programs, is frequently called the "fourth branch of government." Critics often charge that the bureaucracy is too large, too powerful, and too unaccountable to the people or even to elected officials. Many politicians, elected officials, and voters complain that the federal bureaucracy is too wasteful. However, few critics discuss the fact that state and local bureaucracies and bureaucrats, whose numbers are proportionately far larger, also implement laws and policies and are often far less accountable than those working for the federal government.

federal bureaucracy
The thousands of federal government agencies and institutions that implement and administer federal laws and programs.

Many Americans—as evidenced by the success of the Tea Party movement—are uncomfortable with the prominent role of the federal government in their lives. Nevertheless, recent studies show that most users of federal agencies rate quite favorably the agencies and services they receive. Most of those polled drew sharp distinctions between particular agencies and the government as a whole. For example, only 20 percent of Americans in one poll expressed positive views toward federal agencies, whereas 61 percent of respondents voiced satisfaction with the agencies with which they have dealt.[2]

Harold D. Lasswell once defined political science as the "study of who gets what, when, and how."[3] Those questions of "what, when, and how" can perhaps best be answered by examining what the bureaucracy is, how it works, and how it is controlled—the topics in this chapter.

Roots of the Federal Bureaucracy

8.1 Trace the growth and development of the federal bureaucracy.

In 1789, three executive departments existed under the Articles of Confederation: Foreign Affairs, War, and Treasury, which President George Washington inherited as his Cabinet. A secretary headed each department, and the Department of State almost immediately became the new name for Foreign Affairs. To provide the president with legal advice, Congress also created the office of attorney general. From the beginning, individuals appointed as Cabinet secretaries (as well as the attorney general) were subject to approval by the U.S. Senate, but the president alone could remove them from office. Even the first Congress realized how important it was for a president to be surrounded by those in whom he had complete confidence and trust.

spoils system
The firing of public-office holders of a defeated political party to replace them with loyalists of the newly elected party.

patronage
Jobs, grants, or other special favors that are given as rewards to friends and political allies for their support.

merit system
A system of employment based on qualifications, test scores, and ability, rather than party loyalty.

Pendleton Act
Reform measure that established the principle of federal employment on the basis of open, competitive exams and created the Civil Service Commission.

civil service system
The merit system by which many federal bureaucrats are selected.

From 1816 to 1861, the size of the federal executive branch and the bureaucracy grew as existing departments faced increased demands and new departments were created. The Post Office, for example, which Article I constitutionally authorized Congress to create, had to enlarge to meet the needs of a growing and westward-expanding population. President Andrew Jackson removed the Post Office from the jurisdiction of the Department of the Treasury in 1829 and promoted the postmaster general to Cabinet rank.

The Post Office quickly became a major source of jobs President Jackson could fill by presidential appointment, as every small town and village in the United States had its own postmaster. In commenting on Jackson's wide use of political positions to reward friends and loyalists, one fellow Jacksonian Democrat commented: "to the victors belong the spoils." From that statement came the term **spoils system,** which describes an executive's ability to fire public-office holders of the defeated political party and replace them with party loyalists. The spoils system was a form of **patronage**—jobs, grants, or other special favors given as rewards to friends and political allies for their support.

The Civil War and the Growth of Government

The Civil War (1861–1865) permanently changed the nature of the federal bureaucracy. As the nation geared up for war, President Abraham Lincoln authorized the addition of thousands of new employees to existing departments. The Civil War also spawned the need for new government agencies in response to a series of poor harvests and distribution problems. President Lincoln (who understood that well-fed troops are necessary to conduct a war) created the Department of Agriculture in 1862, although it was not given full Cabinet-level status until more than twenty years later.

Congress also created the Pension Office in 1866 to pay benefits to the thousands of Union veterans who had fought in the war (more than 127,000 veterans initially were eligible for benefits). Justice, headed by the attorney general, became a Cabinet department in 1870, and Congress and the president added other departments through 1900. Agriculture became a full-fledged department in 1889 and began to play an important part in informing farmers about the latest developments in soil conservation, livestock breeding, and planting.

From the Spoils System to the Merit System

By the time James A. Garfield, a former distinguished Civil War officer, was elected president in 1880, many reformers were calling for changes in the patronage system. Garfield's immediate predecessor, Rutherford B. Hayes, had favored the idea of replacing the spoils system with a **merit system,** a system of employment based on qualifications, test scores, and ability, rather than loyalty. Congress, however, failed to pass the legislation he proposed. Possibly because potential job seekers wanted to secure positions before Congress had the opportunity to act on an overhauled civil service system, thousands pressed Garfield for positions. This siege prompted Garfield to record in his diary: "My day is frittered away with the personal seeking of people when it ought to be given to the great problems which concern the whole country."[4] Garfield resolved to reform the civil service, but his life was cut short by the bullets of an assassin who, ironically, was a frustrated job seeker.

Public reaction to Garfield's death and increasing criticism of the spoils system prompted Congress to pass the Civil Service Reform Act in 1883, more commonly known as the **Pendleton Act.** It established a merit system of federal employment on the basis of open, competitive exams and created a bipartisan three-member Civil Service Commission, which operated until 1978. Initially, the law covered only about 10 percent of positions in the federal **civil service system,** but later laws and executive orders extended coverage of the act to over 90 percent of all federal employees.

WHICH U.S. PRESIDENT POPULARIZED THE SPOILS SYSTEM?

Here, a political cartoonist depicts how President Andrew Jackson might have been immortalized for his use of the spoils system. Note that President Jackson is shown riding a pig, rather than a horse. Words written in the ground below the animal include "fraud," "bribery," and "plunder."

independent regulatory commission
An entity created by Congress outside a major executive department.

Regulating Commerce

As the nation grew, so did the bureaucracy (see Figure 8.1). In the wake of the tremendous growth of big business (especially railroads), widespread price fixing, and other unfair business practices that occurred after the Civil War, Congress created the Interstate Commerce Commission (ICC) in 1887. In doing so, Congress was reacting to public outcries over exorbitant rates charged by railroad companies for hauling freight. It became the first **independent regulatory commission,** an entity outside a major executive department. Congress creates independent regulatory commissions such as the ICC, which generally focus on particular aspects of the economy. Commission members are appointed by the president and hold their jobs for fixed terms, but the president cannot remove them unless they fail to uphold their oaths of office. The creation of the ICC also marked a shift in the focus of the bureaucracy from service to regulation, giving the government—in the shape of the bureaucracy—vast powers over individual and property rights.

Theodore Roosevelt, a progressive Republican, became president in 1901, and he strengthened the movement toward governmental regulation of the economic sphere. When he asked Congress, and it agreed, to establish and oversee employer-employee relations, the size of the bureaucracy grew further. At the turn of the twentieth century, many workers toiled long hours for low wages in substandard conditions. Many employers refused to recognize the rights of workers to join unions, and many businesses had grown so large and powerful they could force workers to accept substandard conditions and wages. Progressives wanted new government regulations to cure some of the ills suffered by workers and to control the power of increasingly monopolistic corporations.

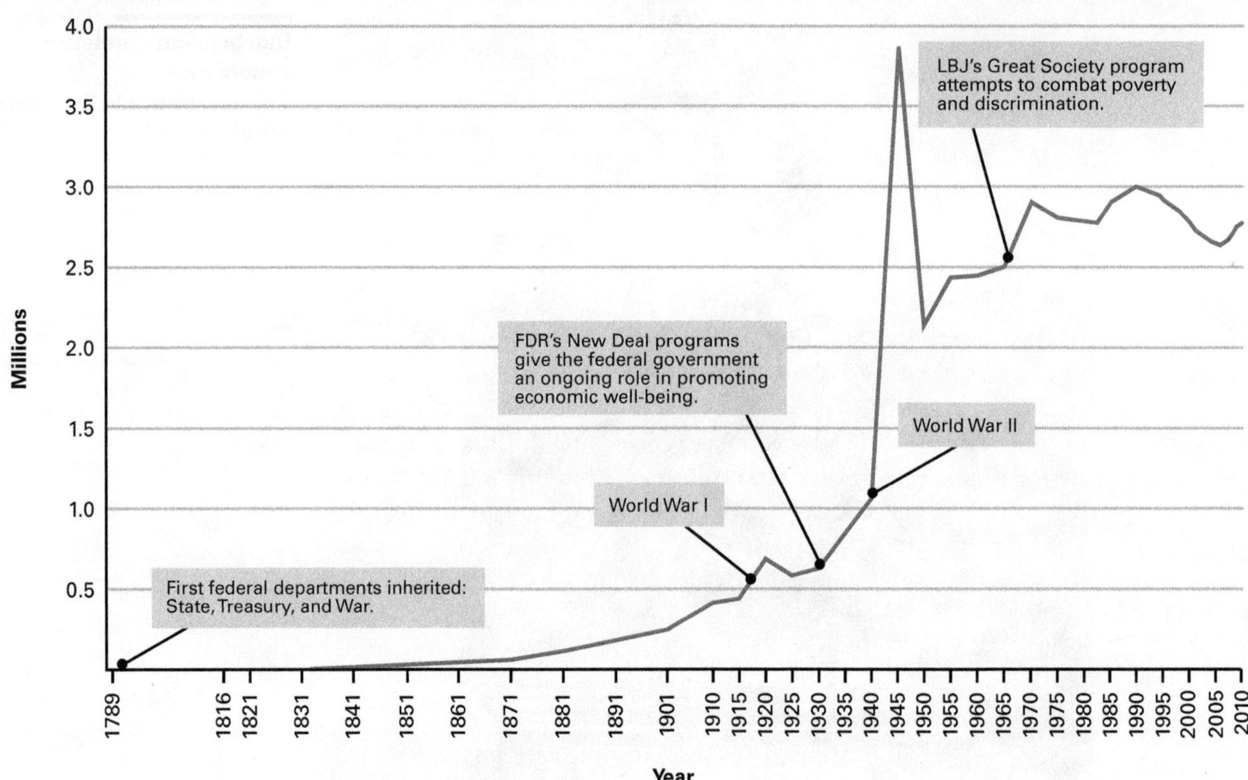

FIGURE 8.1 HOW MANY EMPLOYEES WORK IN THE FEDERAL EXECUTIVE BRANCH?

The size of the federal executive branch has fluctuated with the needs of the nation. The line graph above tracks these changes from the country's creation to the twenty-first century. Notice the overall growth marked by periods of decline. What events may have caused these fluctuations?

SOURCE: Office of Personnel Management, http://www.opm.gov/feddata/historicaltables/totalgovernmentsince1962.asp.

In 1913, when it became clear that one agency could not represent the interests of both employers and employees, President Woodrow Wilson divided the Department of Commerce and Labor, creating two separate departments. One year later, Congress created the Federal Trade Commission (FTC) to protect small businesses and the public from unfair competition, especially from big business.

The ratification of the Sixteenth Amendment to the Constitution in 1913 also affected the size and growth potential of government. It gave Congress the authority to implement a federal income tax to supplement the national treasury and provided a huge infusion of funds to support new federal agencies, services, and programs.

☐ The World Wars and the Growth of Government

The economy appeared to boom as U.S. involvement in World War I caused an increase in manufacturing, but ominous events loomed just over the horizon. Farmers were in trouble after a series of bad harvests, the nation experienced a severe slump in agricultural prices, the construction industry went into decline, and, throughout the 1920s, bank failures became common. After stock prices crashed in 1929, the nation plunged into the Great Depression. To combat the resultant high unemployment and weak financial markets, President Franklin D. Roosevelt (who was first elected in 1932) created hundreds of new government agencies to regulate business practices and various aspects of the national economy. Roosevelt believed that a national economic depression called for national intervention. Thus, the president proposed, and the Congress enacted, far-ranging economic legislation. The desperate mood of the nation supported these moves, as most Americans began to reconsider their ideas about the proper role of government and the provision of governmental services. Formerly, most Americans had believed in a hands-off approach; now they considered it the federal government's job to get the economy going and get Americans back to work.

As the nation struggled to recover from the Great Depression, the Japanese attack on U.S. ships at Pearl Harbor, Hawaii, on December 7, 1941, forced the United States into World War II. The war immediately affected the economy: healthy, eligible men went to war, and women went to work at factories or in other jobs to replace the men. Factories operated around the clock to produce the armaments, material, and clothes necessary to equip, shelter, and dress an army.

During World War II, the federal government also continued to grow tremendously to meet the needs of a nation at war. Tax rates were increased to support the war, and they never again fell to prewar levels. After the war, this infusion of new monies and veterans' demands for services led to a variety of new programs and a much bigger government. The G.I. (Government Issue) Bill, for example, provided college loans for returning veterans and reduced mortgage rates to enable them to buy homes. The national government's involvement in these programs not only affected more people but also led to its greater involvement in more regulation. Homes bought with Veterans Housing Authority loans, for example, had to meet certain specifications. With these programs, Americans became increasingly accustomed to the national government's role in entirely new areas, such as affordable middle-class housing and scholarships that allowed lower- and middle-class men who fought in World War II their first opportunities for higher education.

Within two decades after World War II, the civil rights movement and President Lyndon B. Johnson's Great Society program produced additional growth in the bureaucracy. The Civil Rights Act of 1964 brought about creation of the Equal Employment Opportunity Commission (EEOC) in 1965. Congress also created the Departments

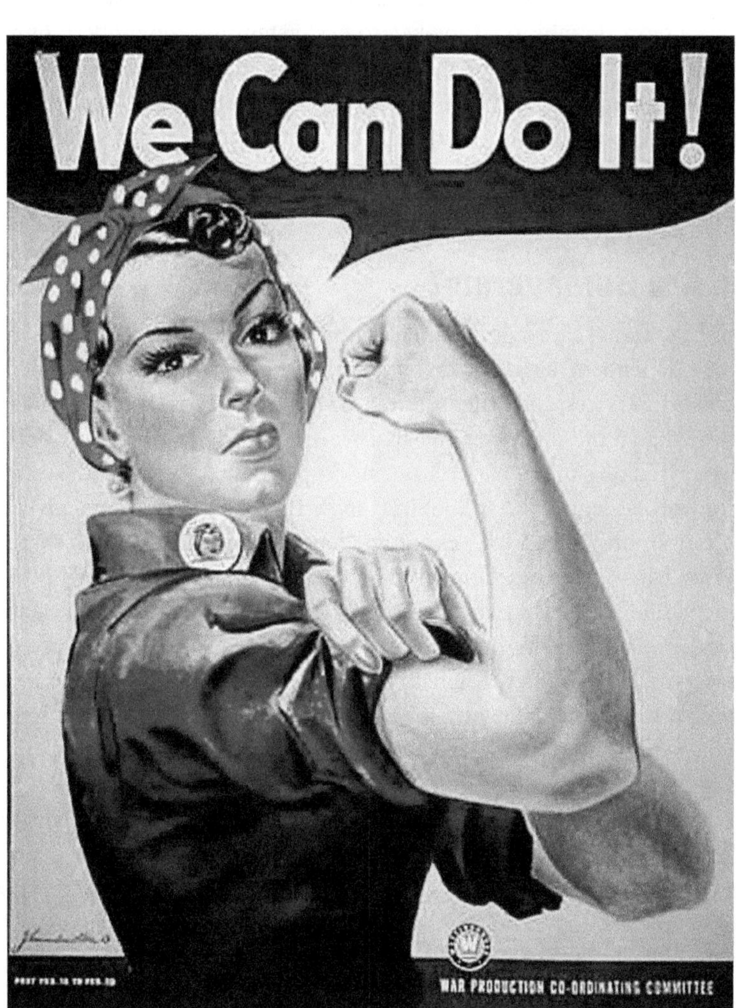

HOW DID WORLD WAR II CHANGE GOVERNMENT?

During World War II, the size of the federal government grew dramatically. Men went off to war, and women were encouraged to work in factories at home in order to help the war effort, as exemplified by this famous poster of Rosie the Riveter. When the war ended, veterans returned to their jobs.

of Housing and Urban Development (HUD) and Transportation in 1965 and 1966, respectively. These expansions of the bureaucracy corresponded to increases in the president's power and his ability to persuade Congress that new commissions and departments would prove an effective way to solve pressing social problems.

The Modern Bureaucracy

8.2 Describe modern bureaucrats, and outline the structure of the modern bureaucracy.

The national government differs from private business in numerous ways. Governments exist for the public good, not to make money. Businesses are driven by a profit motive; government leaders, but not bureaucrats, are driven by reelection. Businesses earn their money from customers; the national government raises revenue from taxpayers. Bureaucracies also differ from businesses because it is difficult to determine to whom bureaucracies are responsible. Is it the president? Congress? The people?

The different natures of government and business have a tremendous impact on the way the bureaucracy operates. Because all of the incentive in government "is in the direction of not making mistakes," public employees view risks and rewards very differently from their private-sector counterparts.[5] Government employees have little reason to take risks or go beyond their assigned job tasks. In contrast, private employers are far more likely to reward ambition. One key to understanding the modern bureaucracy is to learn who bureaucrats are, how the bureaucracy is organized, how organization and personnel affect each other, and how bureaucrats act within the political process. It also is important to recognize that government cannot be run entirely like a business. An understanding of these facts and factors can help in the search for ways to motivate positive change in the bureaucracy.

Who Are Bureaucrats?

Federal bureaucrats are career government employees who work in Cabinet-level departments and independent agencies that comprise more than 2,000 bureaus, divisions, branches, offices, services, and other subunits of the federal government. Federal workers number more than 3 million. Over one-quarter of all civilian employees work in the U.S. Postal Service, making it the nation's second largest employer behind Walmart. Small percentages work as legislative and judicial staff. The remaining federal civilian workers are spread out among the various executive departments and agencies throughout the United States. Most of these federal employees are paid according to what is called the "General Schedule" (GS). They advance within fifteen GS grades (as well as steps within those grades), moving into higher GS levels and salaries as their careers progress.

At the lower levels of the U.S. Civil Service, competitive examinations are used to fill most positions. These usually involve a written test. Mid-level to upper ranges of federal positions do not normally require tests; instead, applicants submit résumés online. Personnel departments then evaluate potential candidates and rank them according to how well they fit a particular job opening. The personnel department then forwards to the agency filling the vacancy only the names of those deemed "qualified." This can be a time-consuming process; it often takes six to nine months to fill a position in this manner.

Persons not covered by the civil service system make up the remaining 10 percent of the federal workforce. Their positions generally fall into three categories:

1. *Appointive policy-making positions.* Nearly 3,500 people are presidential appointees. Some of these, including Cabinet secretaries and under- and assistant secretaries, are subject to Senate confirmation. These appointees, in turn, are responsible for appointing high-level policy-making assistants who form the top of the bureaucratic hierarchy. These are called "Schedule C" political appointees.[6]

2. *Independent regulatory commissioners.* Although each president has the authority to appoint as many as one hundred commissioners, they become independent of his direct political influence once they take office.
3. *Low-level, nonpolicy patronage positions.* These types of positions generally concern administrative assistants to policy makers.

More than 15,000 job skills are represented in the federal government. Government employees, whose average age is forty-seven, have a length of service averaging sixteen years. They include forest rangers, FBI agents, foreign service officers, computer programmers, security guards, librarians, administrators, engineers, plumbers, lawyers, doctors, postal carriers, and zoologists, among others. The diversity of jobs in the government mirrors that in the private sector. The federal workforce, itself, is also diverse but underrepresents Hispanics, in particular, and the overall employment of women lags behind that of men. Women make up 64 percent of the lowest GS levels but only 34 percent of the highest GS levels.[7]

About 303,000 federal workers are found in the nation's capital; the rest are located in regional, state, and local offices scattered throughout the country. To enhance efficiency, the United States is divided into ten regions, with most agencies having regional offices in at least one city in that region (see Figure 8.2). The decentralization of the bureaucracy facilitates accessibility to the public. The Social Security Administration, for example, has numerous offices so that its clients can have a place nearby to take their paperwork, questions, and problems. Decentralization also helps distribute jobs and incomes across the country.

A major concern about the federal workforce is the high rate of turnover in many of the most important positions. This turnover rate has become especially true in the Department of Homeland Security. Many employees of its Transportation Security Administration, for example, leave after only a short time on the job for more lucrative careers outside government. At the Department of State, which once boasted many of the most highly coveted jobs in the federal bureaucracy, the dangers associated with postings in Iraq and Afghanistan, as well as elsewhere in the Middle East, are making it harder to find well-qualified people to staff critical positions.[8] Consequently, the military has enlisted private contractors at unprecedented rates to fill many bureaucratic positions in these potentially dangerous sites. Many of these private contractors are former government employees who can make almost twice the amount of money working for private companies. While

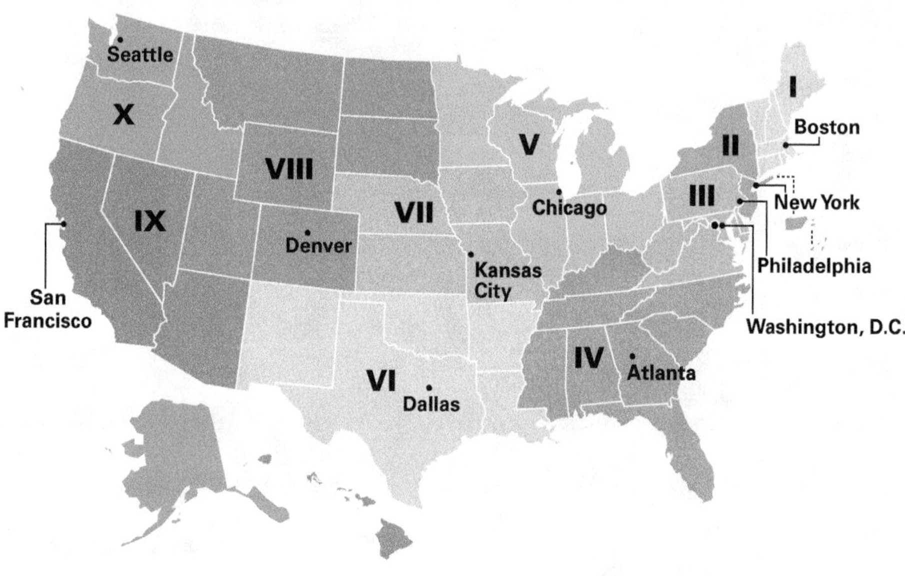

FIGURE 8.2 WHAT ARE THE FEDERAL AGENCY REGIONS, AND WHERE ARE THEIR HEADQUARTERS LOCATED?

To bring the federal bureaucracy closer to citizens and increase the efficiency of providing government services, the federal agencies maintain an office in Washington, D.C. and in ten other regional locations across the country. These cities are shown on the map above.

SOURCE: Department of Health and Human Services, www.hhs.gov/images/regions.gif.

Who Are Federal Workers?

The federal government employs over 3 million people in a diverse range of jobs, from administrative assistant to scientist. But bureaucrats do not necessarily match the demographics of America. Older Americans and men are overrepresented at the highest levels of the federal workforce, while other groups, such as Hispanics and African Americans, are underrepresented. Examine the demographics of the federal workforce in greater detail in the infographic below.

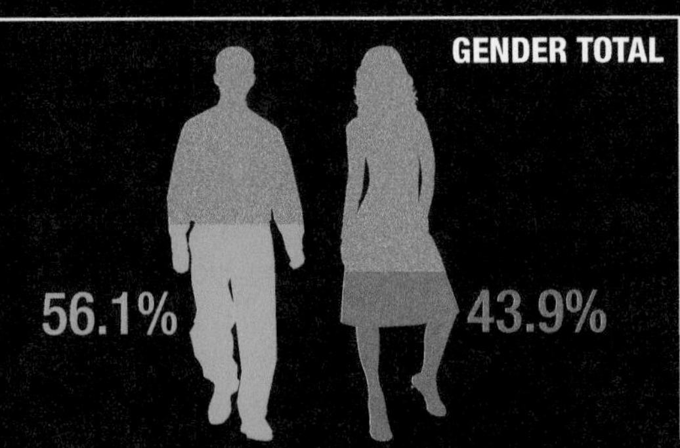

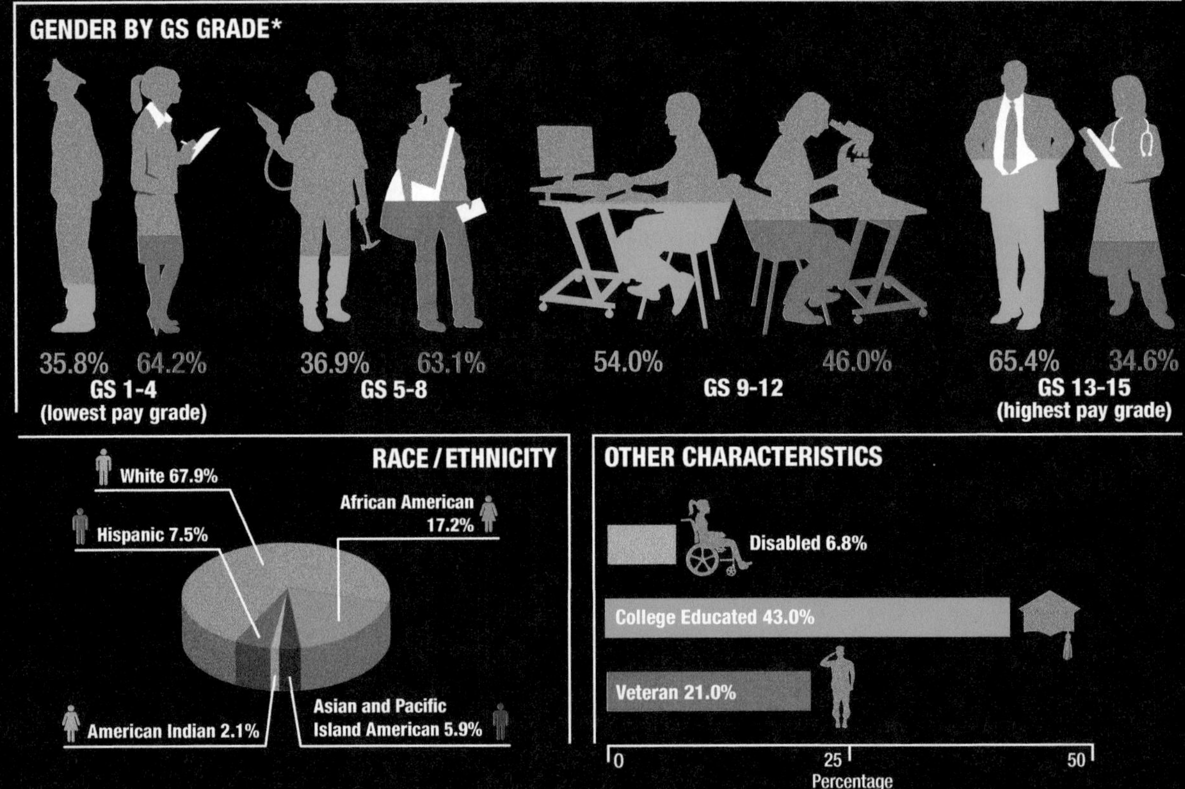

*GS stands for "General Schedule" and indicates the pay scale for U.S. civil service employees

SOURCES: Office of Personnel Management, www.opm.gov; and Equal Employment Opportunity Commission, http://www1.eeoc.gov/eeoc.gov/eeoc/newsroom/release/3-21-12.cfm

CRITICAL THINKING QUESTIONS

1. Compare the male to female ratio at each GS level. How do the percentages change as the GS levels increase? What does this suggest about gender equity in the federal workforce?
2. Which race and ethnicity categories appear to be over- and underrepresented in the federal workforce? Does the federal government appear to be an equal opportunity employer?
3. Why are so many federal workers college educated and veterans? How might these demographic characteristics affect policy outcomes?

the exact number of private contractors is unknown, it is estimated that $536 billion of the federal budget was spent on government contractors in 2011. More than $177 billion was spent in Iraq and Afghanistan alone.[9]

The graying of the federal workforce is another concern. More than two-thirds of those in the highest nonpolitical positions, as well as a large number of mid-level managers, are eligible to retire.[10] Many in government hope that the Presidential Management Fellows Program, which began in 1977 to hire and train future managers and executives, will be enhanced to make up for the shortfall in experienced managers that the federal government now faces. Agencies even are contemplating ways to pay the college loans of prospective recruits, while at the same time trying to improve benefits to attract older workers.[11]

departments
Major administrative units with responsibility for a broad area of government operations. Departmental status usually indicates a permanent national interest in a particular governmental function, such as defense, commerce, or agriculture.

Formal Organization

At least 1,150 civilian agencies are in existence. But, even experts cannot agree on the exact number of separate governmental agencies, commissions, and departments that make up the federal bureaucracy.[12] A distinctive feature of the executive bureaucracy is its traditional division into areas of specialization. For example, the Occupational Safety and Health Administration (OSHA) handles occupational safety, and the Department of State specializes in foreign affairs. It is normal, however, for more than one agency to be involved in a particular issue or for one agency to be involved in many issues. The largest department, the Department of Homeland Security, with its vast authority and range of activities, is probably the best example of this phenomenon. In fact, numerous agencies often have authority in the same issue areas, making administration even more difficult.

Agencies fall into four general categories: (1) Cabinet departments; (2) government corporations; (3) independent executive agencies; and, (4) independent regulatory commissions.

CABINET DEPARTMENTS The fifteen Cabinet **departments** are major administrative units that have responsibility for conducting broad areas of government operations (see Figure 8.3). Cabinet departments account for about 60 percent of the federal workforce.

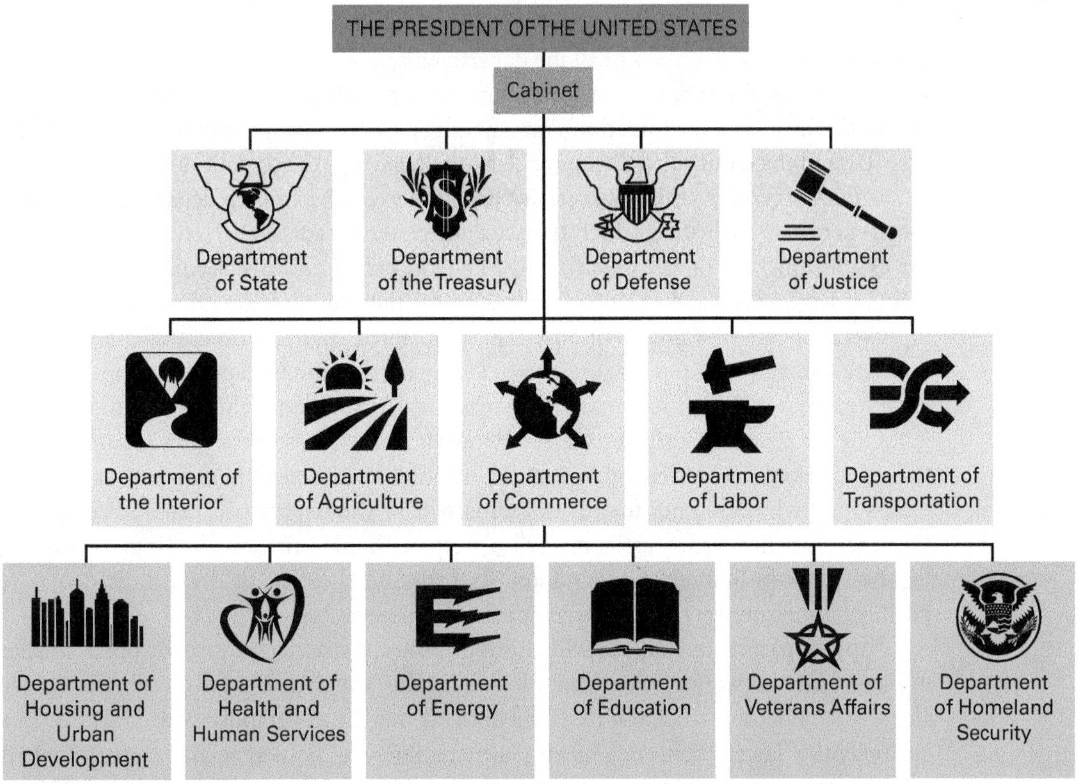

FIGURE 8.3 WHAT ARE THE CABINET DEPARTMENTS?

Cabinet departments reflect the government's permanent interest in a particular issue area. The modern Cabinet includes fifteen agencies focusing on issues ranging from commerce and foreign affairs to education and health.

The President . . . may require the Opinion, in writing, of the principal Officer in each of the executive Departments, upon any subject relating to the Duties of their respective Office. —ARTICLE II, SECTION 2, CLAUSE 1

This clause, along with additional language designating that the president shall be the commander in chief, notes that the heads of departments are to serve as advisers to the president. The Constitution does not directly mention a Cabinet.

This meager language is all that remains of the Framers' initial efforts to create a council to guide the president. Those in attendance at the Constitutional Convention largely favored the idea of a council but could not agree on who should be part of that body. Some actually wanted to follow the British parliamentary model and create the Cabinet from members of the House and Senate, who would rotate into the bureaucracy; most, however, appeared to support the idea of the heads of departments along with the chief justice, who would preside when the president was unavailable. The resulting language above depicts a one-sided arrangement whereby the heads of executive departments must simply answer in writing any questions put to them by the president.

The Cabinet of today differs totally from the structure envisioned by the Framers. George Washington was the first to convene a meeting of what he called his Cabinet. Some presidents have used their Cabinets as trusted advisers; others have used them as a demonstration of their commitment to political, racial, ethnic, or gender diversity, and have relied more on White House aides than particular Cabinet members. Who is included in the Cabinet, as well as how it is used, is solely up to the discretion of the sitting president, with the approval of the U.S. Senate, although both houses of Congress must approve the creation or abolishment of executive departments.

CRITICAL THINKING QUESTIONS

1. **What issues arise from requiring senatorial approval for Cabinet positions, and how does the Constitution remedy these issues?**
2. **Can you think of any new constituencies or issues that are sufficiently important to be elevated to Cabinet-level status?**

The vice president, the heads of all the departments, as well as the U.S. Ambassador to the United Nations, the U.S. Trade Representative, the president's chief of staff, and the heads of the Environmental Protection Agency (EPA), Office of Management and Budget (OMB), and the Council of Economic Advisors make up the formal Cabinet.

Cabinet members called secretaries head the executive branch departments (except the Department of Justice, which the attorney general leads). A secretary is responsible for establishing his or her department's general policy and overseeing its operations. Cabinet secretaries are directly responsible to the president but are often viewed as having two masters—the president and citizens affected by the business of their departments. Cabinet secretaries also are tied to Congress through the appropriations, or budgetary, process and their role in implementing legislation and making rules and policy.

One or more undersecretaries or deputies assist the secretary by taking part of the administrative burden off his or her shoulders, and several assistant secretaries lend support by directing major programs within the department. In addition, each secretary has numerous assistants who help with planning, budgeting, personnel, legal services, public relations, and key staff functions. Some of these individuals are political appointees while others are career civil servants.

Most departments are subdivided into bureaus, divisions, sections, or other smaller units, and the real work of each agency is done at this level. Subdivision usually takes place along functional lines, but the basis for division may be geography, work processes (for example, the Transportation Security Administration is housed in the Department of Homeland Security), or clientele (such as the Bureau of Indian Affairs in the Department of the Interior). Clientele agencies representing clearly defined interests are particularly subject to outside lobbying. These organized interests are also active at the regional level, where the agencies conduct most of their program implementation.

INDEPENDENT EXECUTIVE AGENCIES **Independent executive agencies** closely resemble Cabinet departments but have narrower areas of responsibility. Generally speaking, independent agencies perform services rather than regulatory functions. The president appoints the heads of these agencies, and they serve, like Cabinet secretaries, at his pleasure.

independent executive agencies
Governmental units that closely resemble a Cabinet department but have narrower areas of responsibility and perform services rather than regulatory functions.

Independent agencies exist apart from executive departments for practical or symbolic reasons. The National Aeronautics and Space Administration (NASA), for example, could have been placed within the Department of Defense. Such positioning, however, might have conjured up thoughts of a space program dedicated solely to military purposes, rather than to civilian satellite communication or scientific exploration. Similarly, the Department of the Interior could have been home to the Environmental Protection Agency (EPA); instead, Congress created the EPA as an independent agency in 1970 to administer federal programs aimed at controlling pollution and protecting the nation's environment. As an independent agency, the EPA is less indebted to the president on a day-to-day basis than if it were within a Cabinet department, although the president still has the power to appoint its director and often intervenes in high-profile environmental issues and decisions. Most presidents have also given the EPA director informal Cabinet-level status.

INDEPENDENT REGULATORY COMMISSIONS As noted earlier, independent regulatory commissions are agencies created by Congress to exist outside the major departments and regulate a specific economic activity or interest. Because of the complexity of modern economic issues, Congress sought to create commissions that could develop expertise and provide continuity of policy with respect to economic issues because neither Congress nor the courts have the time or specific talents to do so. Examples include the National Labor Relations Board (NLRB), the Federal Reserve Board, the Federal Communications Commission (FCC), and the Securities and Exchange Commission (SEC).[13]

Older boards and commissions, such as the SEC and the Federal Reserve Board, generally are charged with overseeing a certain industry. Most were created specifically to be free from partisan political pressure. Each has five to seven members (always an odd number, to avoid tie votes) selected by the president, and confirmed by the Senate, for fixed, staggered terms to increase the chances of a bipartisan board. Unlike the case

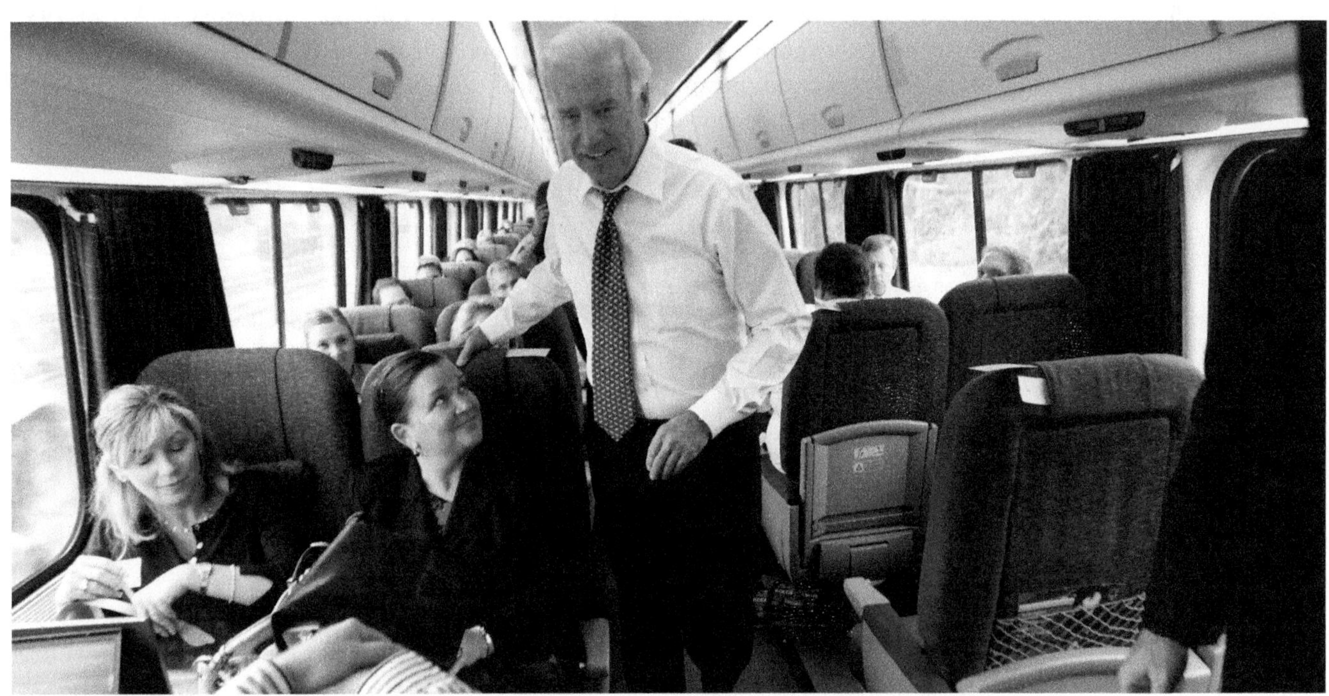

WHAT DO GOVERNMENT CORPORATIONS DO?

Amtrak provides train service across the United States. Its most profitable line runs through the Northeast Corridor from Boston to Washington, D.C. Thousands of travelers use these train lines to navigate the important business centers and congested airspace of the Northeast. Vice President Joe Biden is among these commuters; he frequently takes the train from the nation's capital to his home in Wilmington, Delaware.

8.1

8.2

8.3

8.4

government corporations
Businesses established by Congress to perform functions that private businesses could provide.

Hatch Act
The 1939 act to prohibit civil servants from taking activist roles in partisan campaigns. This act prohibited federal employees from making political contributions, working for a particular party, or campaigning for a particular candidate.

of executive department heads, the president cannot easily remove them. In 1935, the U.S. Supreme Court ruled that in creating independent commissions, Congress had intended them to be independent panels of experts sequestered, as far as possible, from immediate political pressures.[14]

Regulatory boards established since the 1960s concern themselves with how the business sector relates to public health and safety. The Occupational Safety and Health Administration (OSHA), for example, promotes job safety. These boards and commissions often lack autonomy and freedom from political pressures; they are generally headed by a single administrator who is subject to removal by the president. Thus, they are far more susceptible to the political wishes of the president who appoints them.[15]

GOVERNMENT CORPORATIONS **Government corporations** are the most recent addition to the bureaucracy. Dating from the early 1930s, they are businesses established by Congress to perform functions that private businesses could provide. Some of the better known government corporations include the United States Postal Service, Amtrak, and the Federal Deposit Insurance Corporation (FDIC). Unlike other governmental agencies, government corporations charge a fee for their services. The Tennessee Valley Authority (TVA), for example, provides electricity at reduced rates to millions of Americans in Appalachia.

The government often forms corporations when the financial incentives for private industry to provide services are minimal. The area served by the TVA demonstrates this point; it was a poor region of Appalachia that had failed to attract private companies. In other cases, Congress intervenes to salvage valuable public assets. For example, when passenger rail service in the United States became unprofitable, Congress stepped in to create Amtrak, nationalizing the passenger-train industry to keep passenger trains running, especially along the Northeast Corridor.

☐ Government Workers and Political Involvement

As the number of federal employees and agencies grew during the 1930s, many Americans began to fear that members of the civil service would play major roles not only in implementing public policy but also in electing members of Congress and even the president. Consequently, Congress enacted the Political Activities Act of 1939, commonly known as the **Hatch Act.** It prohibited federal employees from becoming directly involved in working for political candidates. Although this act allayed many critics' fears, other people argued that the Hatch Act was too extreme.

TABLE 8.1 WHAT DOES THE LIBERALIZED HATCH ACT STIPULATE?

Federal Employees May	Federal Employees May Not
Be candidates for public office in nonpartisan elections	Use their official authority or influence to interfere with an election
Assist in voter registration drives	Collect political contributions unless both individuals are members of the same federal labor organization or employee organization and the one solicited is not a subordinate employee
Express opinions about candidates and issues	Knowingly solicit or discourage the political activity of any person who has business before the agency
Contribute money to political organizations	Engage in political activity while on duty
Attend political fund-raising functions	Engage in political activity in any government office
Attend and be active at political rallies and meetings	Engage in political activity while wearing an official uniform
Join and be active members of a political party or club	Engage in political activity while using a government vehicle
Sign nominating petitions	Solicit political contributions from the general public
Campaign for or against referendum questions, constitutional amendments, and municipal ordinances	Be candidates for public office in partisan elections
Campaign for or against candidates in partisan elections	
Make campaign speeches for candidates in partisan elections	
Distribute campaign literature in partisan elections	
Hold office in political clubs or parties	

SOURCE: U.S. Special Counsel's Office.

In 1993, the Hatch Act was liberalized to allow employees to run for public office in nonpartisan elections, contribute money to political organizations, and campaign for or against candidates in partisan elections. Federal employees still, however, are prohibited from engaging in political activity while on duty, soliciting contributions from the general public, and running for office in partisan elections (see Table 8.1). The act, however, has proved difficult to enforce. For example, government employees are not allowed to display photos of themselves with elected officials, unless it is an official photo. However, even if it is an official photo, it must be in its original, unaltered state, with no modifications such as horns or halos.[16]

implementation
The process by which a law or policy is put into operation.

iron triangles
The relatively ironclad relationships and patterns of interaction that occur among agencies, interest groups, and congressional committees or subcommittees.

issue networks
The loose and informal relationships that exist among a large number of actors who work in broad policy areas.

How the Bureaucracy Works

8.3 Determine how the bureaucracy makes policy.

German sociologist Max Weber believed bureaucracies were a rational way for complex societies to organize themselves. Model bureaucracies, said Weber, exhibit certain features, including:

Explore on MyPoliSciLab Simulation: You Are Head of FEMA

1. A chain of command in which authority flows from top to bottom.
2. A division of labor whereby work is apportioned among specialized workers to increase productivity.
3. Clear lines of authority among workers and their superiors
4. A goal orientation that determines structure, authority, and rules.
5. Impersonality, whereby all employees are treated fairly based on merit and all clients are served equally, without discrimination, according to established rules.
6. Productivity, whereby all work and actions are evaluated according to established rules.[17]

Clearly, this Weberian idea is somewhat idealistic, and even the best run government agencies do not always work this way, but most try to do so.

When Congress creates any kind of department, agency, or commission, it is actually delegating some of its powers listed in Article I, section 8, of the U.S. Constitution. Therefore, the laws creating departments, agencies, corporations, or commissions carefully describe their purpose and give them the authority to make numerous policy decisions, which have the effect of law. Congress recognizes that it does not have the time, expertise, or ability to involve itself in every detail of every program; therefore, it sets general guidelines for agency action and then allows the agency to work out the details. How agencies execute congressional wishes is called **implementation,** the process by which a law or policy is put into operation.

Historically, in attempting to study how the bureaucracy made policy, political scientists investigated what they termed **iron triangles,** the relatively ironclad relationships and patterns of interaction that occur among federal workers in agencies or departments, interest groups, and relevant congressional committees and subcommittees. Today, iron triangles no longer dominate most policy processes. Some do persist, however, such as the relationships between the Department of Veterans Affairs, the House Committee on Veterans Affairs, and the American Legion and the Veterans of Foreign Wars, the two largest veterans groups (see Figure 8.4).

Many political scientists who examine external influences on the modern bureaucracy prefer to study **issue networks.** In general, issue networks, like iron triangles, include agency officials, members of Congress (and committee staffers), and interest group lobbyists. But, they also include lawyers, consultants, academics, public relations specialists, and sometimes even the courts. Unlike iron triangles, issue networks constantly are changing as members with technical expertise or newly interested parties become involved in issue areas and others phase out.

interagency councils
Working groups created to facilitate coordination of policy making and implementation across a host of governmental agencies.

policy coordinating committees
Subcabinet-level committees created to facilitate interactions between agencies and departments to handle complex policy problems.

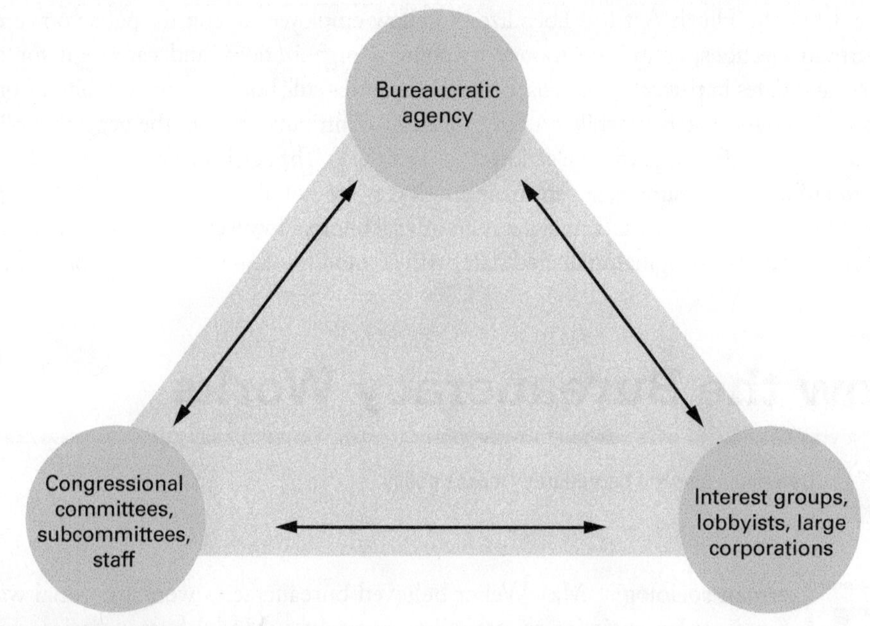

FIGURE 8.4 WHAT CONSTITUTES AN IRON TRIANGLE?

Iron triangles are the relatively stable relationships formed between bureaucratic agencies, congressional committees, and interest groups. Cooperation between these three policy actors may make policy making in some issue areas, such as veterans' affairs, an insular process confined to a small clientele.

As a result of the increasing complexity of many policy domains, a number of alliances have also arisen within the bureaucracy. One such example is **interagency councils,** working groups established to facilitate the coordination of policy making and implementation across a host of agencies. Depending on the amount of funding these councils receive, they can be the prime movers of administration policy in any area where an interagency council exists. The U.S. Interagency Council on Homelessness, for example, works to coordinate the activities of the more than fifty governmental agencies and programs that work to alleviate homelessness.

In areas marked by extraordinarily complex policy problems, recent presidential administrations have set up **policy coordinating committees** (PCCs) to facilitate interaction among agencies and departments at the subcabinet level. These PCCs gained increasing favor after the September 11, 2001, terrorist attacks. For example, the Homeland Security Council PCC (the HSC-PCC) oversees multiple agencies and executive departments to ensure the creation and implementation of consistent, effective homeland security policies, as well as the coordination of such policies with state and local agencies. Composed of representatives from various executive departments as well as the FBI, CIA, Federal Emergency Management Agency (FEMA), and the vice president's office, among others, the HSC-PCC works with and advises the White House on its agenda to combat terrorism.

☐ Making Policy

The main purpose of all of these decision-making bodies is policy making. Policy making and implementation take place on both informal and formal levels. From a practical standpoint, many decisions are left to individual government employees on a day-to-day basis. Department of Justice lawyers, for example, make daily decisions about whether or not to prosecute suspects. Similarly, street-level Internal Revenue Service agents make many decisions during personal audits. These street-level bureaucrats make policy on two levels. First, they exercise broad judgment in decisions concerning citizens with whom they interact. Second, taken together, their individual actions add up to agency behavior.[18] Thus, how bureaucrats interpret and how they apply (or choose not to apply) various policies are equally important parts of the policy-making process.

Take a Closer Look

Interagency councils are working groups established to facilitate the coordination of policy making and implementation across a number of agencies. One such group is the U.S. Interagency Council on Homelessness, which was formed in 1987 as a partnership between nearly all of the Cabinet departments and a number of other executive branch agencies, including the Executive Office of the President. The diagram below, taken from the group's "Federal Strategic Plan to Prevent and End Homelessness," shows the interagency scope of the causes and solutions to homelessness in the United States.

The scope and causes, as well as goals and strategies, illustrated in this diagram show the need for multiple agency involvement in addressing the problem of homelessness.

The problem-solving process illustrated in this diagram is typical of policy making in the United States.

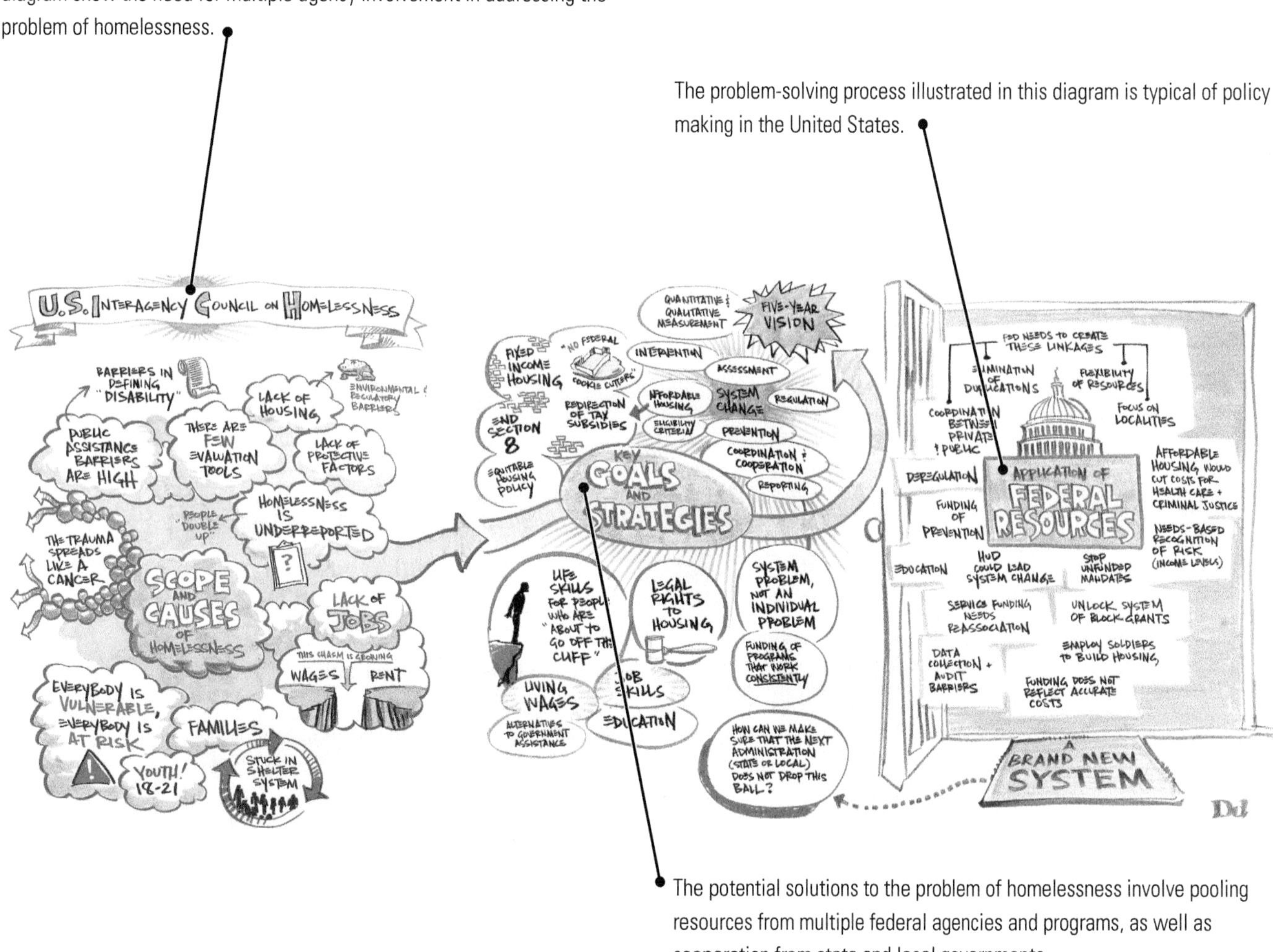

The potential solutions to the problem of homelessness involve pooling resources from multiple federal agencies and programs, as well as cooperation from state and local governments.

SOURCE: Input from the New York Stakeholders' Meeting is captured in a graphic format by Art of Hosting volunteer Drew Dernavich, http://www.usich.gov/PDF/OpeningDoors_2010_FSPPreventEndHomeless.pdf.

CRITICAL THINKING QUESTIONS

1. How do the causes, goals, and solutions illustrated in the diagram show the need for interagency cooperation to solve the problem of homelessness?
2. How does this diagram reveal some of the challenges of interagency cooperation?
3. How might similar cooperation help to solve other policy problems facing the United States today? What agencies would you need to bring together to address these problems?

8.1

8.2

8.3

8.4

administrative discretion
The ability of bureaucrats to make choices concerning the best way to implement congressional or executive intentions.

rule making
A quasi-legislative process resulting in regulations that have the characteristics of a legislative act.

regulations
Rules governing the operation of all government programs that have the force of law.

Administrative discretion, the ability of bureaucrats to make choices concerning the best way to implement congressional or executive intentions, also allows decision makers (whether they are in a Cabinet-level position or at the lowest GS levels) a tremendous amount of leeway. Bureaucrats exercise administrative discretion through two formal procedures: rule making and administrative adjudication.

RULE MAKING **Rule making** is a quasi-legislative process resulting in regulations that have the characteristics of a legislative act. **Regulations** are the rules that govern the operation of all government programs and have the force of law. In essence, then, bureaucratic rule makers often act as lawmakers as well as law enforcers when they make rules or draft regulations to implement various congressional statutes. Some political scientists say that rule making "is the single most important function performed by agencies of government" (see Figure 8.5).[19]

Because regulations often involve political conflict, the 1946 Administrative Procedures Act established rule-making procedures to give everyone the chance to participate in the process. The act requires that: (1) public notice of the time, place, and nature of the rule-making proceedings be provided in the *Federal Register;* (2) interested parties be given the opportunity to submit written arguments and facts relevant to the rule; and, (3) the statutory purpose and basis of the rule be stated. After rules are published, thirty days generally must elapse before they take effect.

Sometimes the law requires an agency to conduct a formal hearing before issuing rules. A committee helps staffers collect evidence and calls interested parties and interest groups to testify on the issue. The process can take weeks, months, or even years, at

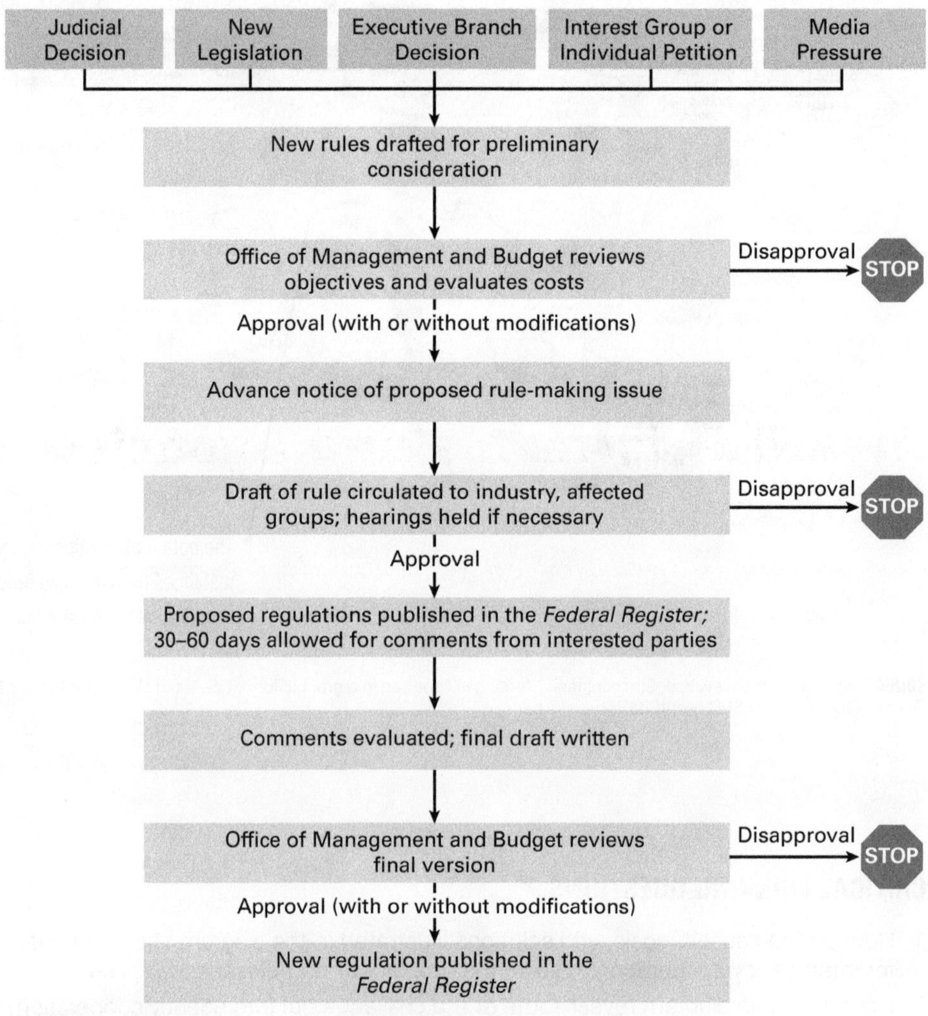

FIGURE 8.5 HOW IS A REGULATION MADE?

The 1946 Administrative Procedures Act spells out a specific process for rule making in the federal bureaucracy. Similar to the process of making legislation, a proposed rule has many opportunities to fail to be implemented. Affected citizens also have a number of opportunities to offer their opinions of a proposed rule.

TABLE 8.2 HOW MANY COMMENTS DO AGENCIES RECEIVE ON PROPOSED RULES?

Agency	Subject	Comments
Food and Nutrition Service	Nutrition in school lunches	54,468
Federal Motor Carrier Safety Administration	Hours of service for drivers	27,333
Centers for Medicare and Medicaid Services	Physical fee schedule	20,280
National Oceanic and Atmospheric Agency	Annual fish catch limits	14,681
Environmental Protection Agency	Greenhouse gas emissions	5,028

SOURCE: Gregory Korte, "Comments Slow Down Rules Process." *USA Today* (May 25, 2011): A5; and www.regulations.gov.

administrative adjudication
A quasi-judicial process in which a bureaucratic agency settles disputes between two parties in a manner similar to the way courts resolve disputes.

the end of which agency administrators must review the entire record and then justify the new rules. Although cumbersome, the process has reduced criticism of some rules and bolstered the deference given by the courts to agency decisions.

Many Americans are unaware of their opportunity to influence government through the rule-making process. All private citizens with interest in potential rules have the right to submit comments. Presidents George W. Bush and Barack Obama have taken efforts to make commenting easier for citizens by using the government's regulations.gov portal. As a result, the average rule receives about eighty comments, but some rules may receive thousands of comments from citizens (see Table 8.2).

ADMINISTRATIVE ADJUDICATION Agencies regularly find that persons or businesses are not in compliance with the federal laws the agencies are charged with enforcing, or that they are in violation of an agency rule or regulation. To force compliance, some agencies resort to **administrative adjudication,** a quasi-judicial process in which a bureaucratic agency settles disputes between two parties in a manner similar to the way courts resolve disputes. Administrative adjudication is referred to as quasi-judicial, because adjudication by any body other than the judiciary would be a violation of the constitutional principle of separation of powers.

Several agencies and boards employ administrative law judges to conduct hearings. Although employed by the agencies, these judges are strictly independent and cannot be removed except for gross misconduct. Their actions, however, are reviewable in the federal courts, as are the findings of judges in agencies such as the Equal Employment Opportunity Commission and Social Security Administration.

Toward Reform: Making Agencies Accountable

8.4 Evaluate controls designed to make agencies more accountable.

Although many critics of the bureaucracy argue that federal employees should be responsive to the public interest, the public interest is difficult to define. As it turns out, several factors control the power of the bureaucracy, and to some degree, the same kinds of checks and balances that operate among the three branches of government serve to rein in the bureaucracy (see Table 8.3).

Many political scientists argue that the president should take charge of the bureaucracy because it is his responsibility to see that popular ideas and expectations are translated into administrative action. But, under our constitutional system, the president is not the only actor in the policy process. Congress creates the agencies, funds them, and establishes the broad rules of their operation. Moreover, Congress continually reviews the various agencies through oversight committee investigations, hearings, and its power of the purse. And, the federal judiciary, as in most other matters, has the ultimate authority to review administrative actions.

TABLE 8.3 HOW ARE AGENCIES MADE ACCOUNTABLE?

The President Has the Authority to:	The Congress Has the Authority to:	The Judiciary Has the Authority to:
Appoint and remove agency heads and other top bureaucrats.	Pass legislation that alters the bureaucracy's activities.	Rule on whether bureaucrats have acted within the law and require policy changes to comply with the law.
Reorganize the bureaucracy (with congressional approval).	Abolish existing programs and agencies.	Force agencies to respect the rights of individuals through hearings and other proceedings.
Make changes in an agency's annual budget proposals.	Refuse to appropriate funds for certain programs.	Rule on the constitutionality of all challenged rules and regulations.
Ignore legislative initiatives originating within the bureaucracy.	Investigate agency activities and compel bureaucrats to testify about them.	
Initiate or adjust policies that would, if enacted by Congress, alter the bureaucracy's activities.	Influence presidential appointments of agency heads and other top bureaucratic officials.	
Issue executive orders.	Write legislation to limit bureaucratic discretion.	
Reduce an agency's annual budget.		

☐ Executive Control

As the size and scope of the American national government, in general, and of the executive branch and bureaucracy, in particular, have grown, presidents have delegated more and more power to bureaucrats. But, most presidents have continued to try to exercise some control over the bureaucracy. They have often found that task more difficult than first envisioned. President John F. Kennedy, for example, once lamented that to give anyone at the Department of State an instruction was comparable to putting your request in a dead-letter box.[20] No response would ever be forthcoming.

Recognizing these potential problems, presidents try to appoint the best possible people to carry out their wishes and policy preferences. Presidents make hundreds of appointments to the executive branch; in doing so, they have the opportunity to appoint individuals who share their views on a range of policies. Although presidential appointments account for a very small proportion of all federal jobs, presidents or the Cabinet secretaries usually appoint most top policy-making positions. Executive control over these positions can be severely hampered when Congress refuses to approve nominees. At one point during the administration of President George W. Bush, for example, 138 of 575 top positions were vacant.[21]

With the approval of Congress, presidents can reorganize the bureaucracy. They also can make changes in an agency's annual budget requests and ignore legislative initiatives originating within the bureaucracy. Several presidents have made a priority of trying to tame the bureaucracy to increase its accountability. Thomas Jefferson, the first president to address the issue of accountability, attempted to cut waste and bring about a "wise and frugal government." The government began to seriously consider calls for reform during the Progressive era (1890–1920). Later, President Calvin Coolidge urged spending cuts and other reforms. His Correspondence Club aimed to reduce bureaucratic letter writing by 30 percent.[22]

Presidents also can shape policy and provide direction to bureaucrats by issuing executive orders.[23] Executive orders are rules or regulations issued by the president that have the effect of law; the *Federal Register* must publish all executive orders. A president can direct an agency to act, but it may take some time to carry out the order. Given their many jobs, few presidents can ensure that the government will implement all their orders or will like all the rules that have been made, For example, even before Congress acted to protect women from discrimination by the federal government, the National Organization for Women convinced President Lyndon B. Johnson to sign a 1967 executive order that added the category of "gender" to an earlier order prohibiting discrimination on the basis of race, color, religion, or national origin in the awarding of federal contracts. Although the president signed the order, the Office of Federal

Explore Your World

A key function of the bureaucracy is to represent the U.S. government to foreign states. One way the Department of State accomplishes this goal is by sending diplomats and bureaucrats to other countries to establish relationships with foreign leaders. Diplomatic offices are of two types: consulates and embassies. Consulates are smaller and are found in large cities that attract tourists; they help U.S. citizens with visas, international law, and identification. Embassies are large, usually located in a foreign capital, and work directly with foreign governments. The structure and functions of an embassy may be telling about the quality of U.S. relations with a particular country. Examine the U.S. embassies shown below and consider the variations in their appearance.

The U.S. Embassy in Paris, France, is the U.S.'s first diplomatic mission. It is located near the Champs-Élysées in the heart of the capital city.

U.S. embassies and consulates are occasionally targets for anti-American sentiment. On September 11, 2012, and for several days thereafter, U.S. diplomatic missions throughout the Muslim world were attacked in a series of protests. This photo shows the embassy in Tunis, Tunisia after these acts of violence. In total, at least 75 people, including the U.S. ambassador to Libya, were killed and hundreds of others were injured.

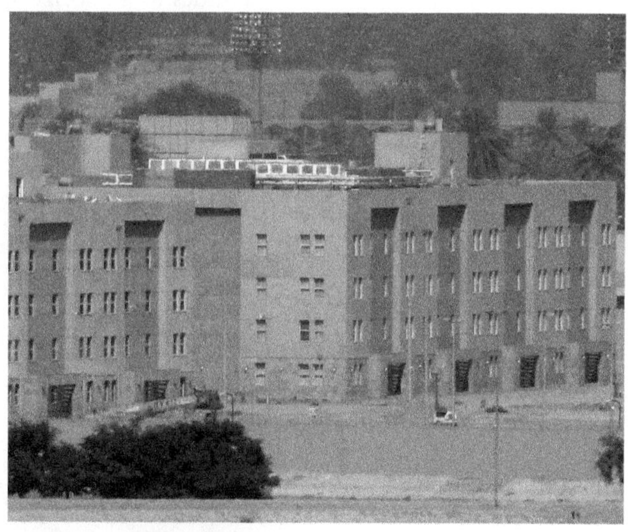

The U.S. Embassy in Iraq was constructed in the past several years. It is the largest, most fortified embassy in the world. It is located in the International (or "Green") Zone of Baghdad.

CRITICAL THINKING QUESTIONS

1. What do these buildings say about the importance of a U.S. embassy in these states?
2. Consider our relationship with each of these governments. Do we maintain strong relationships with these countries, or are we struggling in our efforts to remain friendly? How is the role of an American embassy in an "ally" country different from that of an embassy in a nation where we are constantly in conflict?
3. How do the security and location of embassies vary across states? How might this reflect the quality of a country's relationship with the United States?

Contract Compliance, part of the Department of Labor's Employment Standards Administration, failed to draft appropriate guidelines for implementation of the order until several years later.[24]

☐ Congressional Control

Congress can confirm (or reject) nominees to top bureaucratic positions and has also played an important role in checking the power of the bureaucracy. Constitutionally, it possesses the authority to create or abolish departments and agencies. It may also transfer agency functions, and expand or contract bureaucratic discretion, as was the case in the creation of the Department of Homeland Security.

Congress can also use its investigatory powers to conduct program evaluations or hold oversight hearings. It is not at all unusual for a congressional committee or subcommittee to conduct hearings on a particular problem and then direct the relevant agency to study the problem or find ways to remedy it. Representatives of the agencies also appear before these committees on a regular basis to inform members about agency activities, ongoing investigations, and budget requests.

Political scientists distinguish between two different forms of congressional oversight. One is proactive and allows Congress to set its own agenda for programs or agencies to review. A second kind of oversight is reactive and generally involves a congressional response to a complaint filed by a constituent, a politically significant actor, or the media. For example, in the aftermath of an oil rig explosion and ensuing oil spill in the Gulf of Mexico in 2010, a host of congressional committees held hearings to investigate the cause of what has been called the worst environmental disaster in U.S. history. Members of Congress from both houses grilled executives from British Petroleum (BP), the oil drilling company Transocean, the service contractor Halliburton, and others to determine not only who was responsible for the accident but also what efforts were being made to contain it.[25]

Congress also has the power of the purse. To control the bureaucracy, it can use its abilities to authorize spending and appropriate funds for an agency's activities, much like the proverbial carrot and stick. Money can be a powerful tool to coerce bureaucrats into making particular policies.

HOW DOES GOVERNMENT OVERSEE ENVIRONMENTAL DISASTERS?

Congressional oversight hearings examined the causes of a massive oil spill in the Gulf of Mexico in 2010. The results of these hearings helped the U.S. Coast Guard, the National Oceanic and Atmospheric Administration, and numerous other agencies to design ways to minimize the effects of this spill and craft strategies to prevent future disasters.

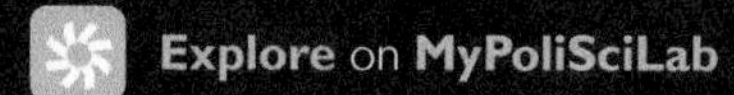

What Puts the "Big" in Big Government?

The national government is actually not as big as it once was. Since 1962, the total number of government employees has fallen due to a reduction in the number of military personnel after Vietnam and the Cold War. The number of civilians employed directly by the government has also declined since the 1980s. However, even as the size of government has grown smaller, its spending has increased to the point that one-fourth of the U.S. economy comes from government funded programs, contracts, and benefits.

Size of the Government Workforce*

* In Thousands

	EXECUTIVE	MILITARY	LEGISLATIVE AND JUDICIAL	TOTAL
1962	2,485	2,840	30	5,355
1972	2,823	2,360	42	5,225
1982	2,770	2,147	55	4,972
1992	3,017	1,848	66	4,931
2002	2,630	1,456	66	4,152
2012	2,500	1,602	64	4,166

Government as Percent of GDP

1962

Government consumed just under one-fifth of the total economy and paid for that consumption with income such as taxes.

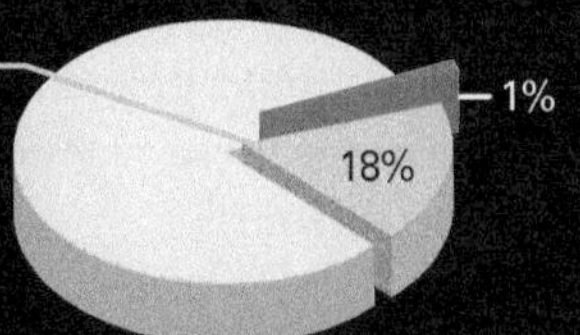

2012

Government consumed one-fourth of the total economy and paid a larger portion of it by borrowing instead of by taxing.

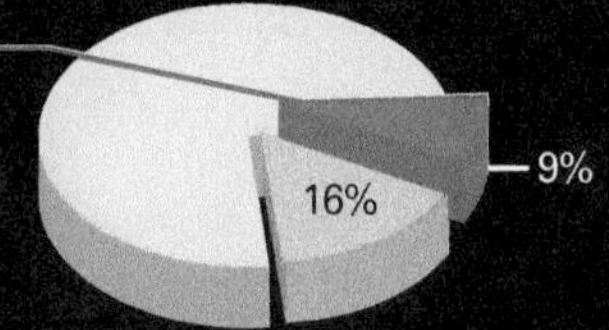

■ Government Spending Through Taxing
■ Government Spending Through Borrowing

SOURCE: Data from Voteview and U.S. Office of Management and Budget.

Investigate Further

Concept Is the federal government growing larger? The number of federal employees has actually decreased by over one million in a half-century. Since the late 1960s, the main difference in the size of its workforce is due to a smaller military and greater use of outside contractors.

Connection Do fewer federal employees mean smaller government? While the number of employees may be smaller, the federal government's share of the country's gross domestic product has grown every decade since the 1960s.

Cause If the government employs fewer people, how is it "bigger" than it was in 1962? Even with fewer people, the government implements more expensive programs that contribute to the total U.S. economy. Higher salaries, more expensive defense programs, larger entitlement programs, and increased spending to pay for past debt drive up costs.

The first step in the funding process is authorization. Budget authorization originates in the various legislative committees that oversee particular agencies (such as Agriculture, Veterans Affairs, Education, and Labor) and sets the maximum amounts that agencies can spend on particular programs. While some authorizations, such as those for Social Security, are permanent, others, including Departments of State and Defense procurements, are watched closely and are subject to annual authorizations.

Once Congress authorizes programs, it requires specific allocation, or appropriation, of funds before they can be spent. Such appropriations originate with the House Appropriations Committee, not the specialized legislative committees. Thus, the House Appropriations Committee routinely holds hearings to allow agency heads to justify their budget requests.

To help Congress oversee the bureaucracy's financial affairs, in 1921 Congress created the General Accounting Office, now called the Government Accountability Office (GAO). The GAO is Congress's watchdog over executive branch spending. At the same time, the Office of the Budget, now the Office of Management and Budget (OMB), was set up in the executive branch to help with creating the president's budget. The GAO, the Congressional Research Service (CRS), and the Congressional Budget Office (CBO) provide Congress with its own bureaucracy to research and monitor what the executive branch and bureaucracy are doing. Today, the GAO not only tracks how money is spent by the executive branch but also monitors how policies are implemented. If the GAO uncovers problems with an agency's work, it notifies Congress immediately.

Legislators also augment their formal oversight of the executive branch by allowing citizens to appeal adverse bureaucratic decisions to agencies, Congress, and even the courts. Congressional review, a procedure adopted by the 104th Congress, by which joint resolutions of legislative disapproval can nullify agency regulations, is another method of exercising congressional oversight. This form of oversight is discussed in greater detail in our discussion of Congress.

☐ Judicial Control

Whereas the president and Congress have direct ongoing control over the actions of the bureaucracy, the judiciary's oversight function is less apparent, but equally important. Still, federal judges, for example, can issue injunctions or orders to an executive agency even before a rule is publicized, giving the federal judiciary a potent check on the bureaucracy.

The courts also have ruled that agencies must give all affected individuals their due process rights guaranteed by the U.S. Constitution. The Social Security Administration cannot stop a recipient's checks, for example, unless that individual receives reasonable notice and an opportunity for a hearing. These types of cases make up the largest proportion of cases filed in federal district courts.

On a more informal, indirect level, litigation, or even the threat of litigation, often exerts a strong influence on bureaucrats. Injured parties can bring suit against agencies for their failure to enforce a law and can challenge agency interpretations of any law. In general, however, the courts give great weight to the opinions of bureaucrats and usually defer to their expertise.[26]

The development of specialized courts, however, has altered the relationship of some agencies with the federal courts, apparently resulting in less judicial deference to agency rulings. Research by political scientists reveals that specialized courts such as the Court of International Trade, because of its jurists' expertise, defer less to agency decisions than do more generalized federal courts. Conversely, reversal of decisions from executive agencies is more likely than reversal of decisions from more specialized independent regulatory commissions.[27]

Review the Chapter

Listen to **Chapter 8** on **MyPoliSciLab**

Roots of the Federal Bureaucracy

8.1 Trace the growth and development of the federal bureaucracy, p. 239.

The federal bureaucracy has changed dramatically since President George Washington's time, when the executive branch had only three departments—State, War, and Treasury. The size of the federal bureaucracy increased significantly following the Civil War. As employment opportunities within the federal government expanded, a civil service system was created to ensure that more and more jobs were filled according to merit and not by patronage. By the late 1800s, reform efforts led to further growth of the bureaucracy, as independent regulatory commissions came into existence. In the wake of the Great Depression, President Franklin D. Roosevelt's New Deal created many new agencies to get the national economy back on course.

The Modern Bureaucracy

8.2 Describe modern bureaucrats, and outline the structure of the modern bureaucracy, p. 244.

The modern bureaucracy has more than 3 million civilian workers from all walks of life. In general, bureaucratic agencies fall into four categories: departments, independent agencies, independent regulatory commissions, and government corporations. The Hatch Act regulates the political activity of employees in the federal government.

How the Bureaucracy Works

8.3 Determine how the bureaucracy makes policy, p. 251.

The bureaucracy is responsible for implementing many laws passed by Congress. A variety of formal and informal mechanisms, such as rule making and administrative adjudication, help bureaucrats make policy.

Toward Reform: Making Agencies Accountable

8.4 Evaluate controls designed to make agencies more accountable, p. 255.

Agencies enjoy considerable discretion, but they are also subject to many formal controls that help make them more accountable. The president, Congress, and the judiciary all exercise various degrees of control over the bureaucracy through oversight, funding, or litigation.

Learn the Terms

Study and **Review** the **Flashcards**

administrative adjudication, p. 255
administrative discretion, p. 254
civil service system, p. 240
departments, p. 247
federal bureaucracy, p. 239
government corporations, p. 250
Hatch Act, p. 250
implementation, p. 251
independent executive agencies, p. 249
independent regulatory commission, p. 241
interagency councils, p. 252
iron triangles, p. 251
issue networks, p. 251
merit system, p. 240
patronage, p. 240
Pendleton Act, p. 240
policy coordinating committees, p. 252
regulations, p. 254
rule making, p. 254
spoils system, p. 240

Test Yourself

1. What was the primary goal of the spoils system?

a. To reward political allies for their support
b. To increase pay for certain workers
c. To increase loyalty among members of the opposition party
d. To give soldiers additional food rations
e. To hire federal workers on the basis of their previous experience and credentials

2. Which act of Congress established a merit system of federal employment?

a. Federal Employees Act
b. Pendleton Act
c. Dawes Act
d. Hatch Act
e. Political Activities Act

3. Bureaucratic agencies representing areas of permanent national interest whose heads are appointed directly by the president are known as:

a. government corporations.
b. independent regulatory commissions.
c. independent executive agencies.
d. policy coordinating committees.
e. Cabinet departments.

4. Why did Congress initially create independent regulatory commissions such as the Interstate Commerce Commission?

a. To better address foreign affairs issues
b. To maintain checks and balances in the government
c. To serve the Cabinet departments
d. To regulate specific economic interests
e. To perform functions that could be provided by private businesses

5. The Hatch Act regulates:

a. the creation of federal regulatory commissions.
b. job safety.
c. the use of government contractors.
d. the political activity of government employees.
e. hiring and firing government employees for poor performance.

6. Iron triangles are made up of:

a. the president, Congress, and bureaucrats.
b. interest groups, lobbyists, and bureaucrats.
c. bureaucratic agencies, interest groups, and congressional committees.
d. the vice president, Supreme Court, and Congress.
e. bureaucratic agencies, congressional committees, and the president.

7. Why were interagency councils created?

a. To develop nonpartisan solutions to partisan problems
b. To decrease government spending
c. To give interest groups greater access to the policy-making process
d. To improve relations between the executive and legislative branches
e. To facilitate policy making in complex issue areas

8. Which of the following does the 1946 Administrative Procedures Act NOT require?

a. Giving everyone a chance to participate in the rule-making process
b. Providing public notice of the time, place, and nature of the rule-making proceedings in the *Federal Register*
c. The Office of Management and Budget must review proposed rules.
d. Proposed rules must state the statutory purpose and basis of the provision.
e. The president must sign a rule for it to become law.

9. Which of the following must be published in the *Federal Register* in order to become law?

a. Executive orders
b. Regulations
c. Administrative adjudications
d. Supreme Court decisions
e. Proposed bills

10. The president can check the power of executive branch agencies by:

a. amending the Constitution.
b. issuing executive orders.
c. confirming or rejecting nominees.
d. holding oversight hearings.
e. issuing injunctions before rules are published.

Explore Further

Anderson, James E. *Public Policymaking: An Introduction,* 7th ed. Belmont, CA: Wadsworth Publishing, 2010.

Dolan, Julie A., and David H. Rosenbloom. *Representative Bureaucracy: Classic Readings and Continuing Controversies.* Armonk, NY: M. E. Sharpe, 2003.

Durant, Robert F., ed. *The Oxford Handbook of American Bureaucracy*. New York: Oxford University Press, 2012.

Etzioni-Halevy, Eva. *Bureaucracy and Democracy*. New York: Routledge, 2012.

Gormley, William T., and Steven J. Balla. *Bureaucracy and Democracy: Accountability and Performance,* 3rd ed. Washington, DC: CQ Press, 2012.

Hood, Christopher. *The Blame Game? Spin, Bureaucracy, and Self-Preservation in Government.* Princeton, NJ: Princeton University Press, 2010.

Ingraham, Patricia Wallace, and Laurence E. Lynn Jr. *The Art of Governance: Analyzing Management and Administration*. Washington, DC: Georgetown University Press, 2004.

Kane, John, and Haig Patapan. *The Democratic Leader: How Democracy Defines, Empowers, and Limits Its Leaders.* New York: Oxford University Press, 2012.

Kerwin, Cornelius M., and Scott R. Furlong. *Rulemaking: How Government Agencies Write Law and Make Policy,* 4th ed. Washington, DC: CQ Press, 2010.

Meier, Kenneth J., and Laurence O'Toole. *Bureaucracy in a Democratic State: A Governance Perspective*. Baltimore: Johns Hopkins University Press, 2006.

Nigro, Lloyd G., Felix A. Nigro, and J. Edward Kellough. *The New Public Personnel Administration,* 6th ed. Belmont, CA: Wadsworth, 2006.

Peters, B. Guy. *The Politics of Bureaucracy,* 6th ed. New York: Routledge, 2009.

Stivers, Camilla. *Gender Images in Public Administration: Legitimacy and the Administrative State,* 2nd ed. Thousand Oaks, CA: Sage, 2002.

Twight, Charlotte. *Dependent on DC: The Rise of Federal Control over the Lives of Ordinary Americans.* New York: Palgrave Macmillan, 2002.

Wilson, James Q. *Bureaucracy: What Government Agencies Do and Why They Do It,* reprint ed. New York: Basic Books, 2000.

To learn more about federal employees, go to the Office of Personnel Management Web site at **www.opm.gov** or to the page listing demographic information, **www.opm.gov/feddata/factbook/.**

To learn more about rules, proposed rules, and notices of federal agencies and organizations, go to the Web site of the *Federal Register* at **www.gpoaccess.gov/fr/index.html.**

To view or comment on a proposed regulation, go to **www.regulations.gov.**

To learn more about the Government Accountability Office, go to **www.gao.gov.**

9

Listen to Chapter 9 on MyPoliSciLab

The Judiciary

In the summer of 2005, President George W. Bush was given an opportunity to shape the future of the U.S. Supreme Court. The death of Chief Justice William H. Rehnquist, who had presided over the Court for over twenty-five years, left an important vacancy on the high Court. To fill Chief Justice Rehnquist's seat, President Bush nominated an appeals court judge named John Roberts. Roberts's record in the lower courts had been conservative, and observers expected that his ideology would deviate little from that of his predecessor. Less clear was the new chief justice's ability to lead his fellow justices in a similar direction.

Seven years after his nomination, the legacy of the Roberts Court is taking shape. Despite the more recent additions of Justices Sonia Sotomayor and Elena Kagan—both of whom are moderate-to-liberal females appointed by a Democratic president—the Roberts Court is building a reputation as a conservative body dedicated to expanding the institutional power of the Supreme Court.

This legal strategy with an eye toward judicial power has prompted many Court-watchers to draw comparisons between Chief Justice Roberts and one of the Court's most legendary leaders, Chief Justice John Marshall. Chief Justice Marshall, who served on the Court in the early 1800s, is said to have done more for the power and the legacy of the Court and the federal government than any other justice before or since his tenure.

Only time will tell whether the Roberts Court is able to continue on its current trajectory. The personalities and politics of the eight other justices, who are appointed by the president and serve for life terms with good behavior, certainly, will play significant roles. But, if recent decisions on health care, criminal rights, and campaign finance, just to name a few, are any indication, the Roberts Court is forming its own identity, one that is quite separate from that of the chief justices who have immediately preceded him.

IDEOLOGY ISN'T THE ONLY THING THAT HAS CHANGED Above, members of the liberal Warren Court (1953–1969), which decided a host of civil rights and liberties cases. Below, members of the modern, conservative Roberts Court, which has been especially active in economic and criminal procedure cases.

MyPoliSciLab Videos

Watch on MyPoliSciLab

The Big Picture What kinds of cases make it to the Supreme Court? Author Karen O'Connor explains why the court rarely makes decisions on cases that affect only the parties involved, and discusses why so much attention is paid to the cases that the Supreme Court chooses to rule on.

The Basics Do you have confidence in the U.S. court system? Watch this video to discover what the founders did to make sure the federal judiciary would be independent of political influence. You'll also learn about an important check the Supreme Court has on the other two branches of U.S. government.

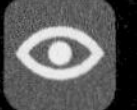

How do cases get to the Supreme Court?

In Context Discover how the Supreme Court gained a check on the other two branches after the U.S. Constitution was written. East Central University political scientist Christine Pappas discusses *Marbury* v. *Madison* and analyzes how the power of judicial review has impacted campaign finance law.

Thinking Like a Political Scientist Why do legal scholars and political scientists disagree over how judges make decisions? East Central University political scientist Christine Pappas analyzes this and other questions scholars study. She explains how the other branches of government limit the role of the judiciary in public policy making, and discusses research on how public opinion influences the courts.

In the Real World Should the Supreme Court have the power to knock down popular laws? This segment uses the Supreme Court's decision in *U.S.* v. *Arizona* (2012) to illustrate the tension between protecting the law and having a government that's run by the people.

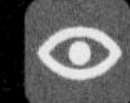

So What? What is the Supreme Court doing for you? Author Karen O'Connor demonstrates how the Supreme Court's decisions have affected everything from your student newspaper to your birth control, which is why it is important to be engaged and informed about the decisions the courts are making.

•••

In 1787, when writing *The Federalist Papers,* Alexander Hamilton urged support for the U.S. Constitution. He firmly believed that the judiciary would prove to be "the least dangerous" branch of government. The judicial branch seemed so inconsequential that when the young national government made its move to the District of Columbia in 1800, Congress actually forgot to include any space to house the justices of the Supreme Court! Last-minute conferences with Capitol architects led to the allocation of a small area in the basement of the Senate wing of the Capitol building for a courtroom. Noted one commentator, "A stranger might traverse the dark avenues of the Capitol for a week, without finding the remote corner in which justice is administered to the American Republic."[1]

Today, the role of the courts, particularly the Supreme Court of the United States, differs significantly from what the Framers envisioned. The "least dangerous branch" now is perceived by many people as having too much power.

Historically, Americans have remained unaware of the political power held by the courts. As part of their upbringing, they learned to regard the federal courts as above the fray of politics. That, however, has never been the case. Elected presidents nominate judges to the federal courts and justices to the Supreme Court, and elected senators ultimately confirm (or decline to confirm) presidential nominees to the federal bench. The process by which cases ultimately get heard—if they are heard at all—by the Supreme Court often is political as well. Interest groups routinely seek out good test cases to advance their policy positions. Even the U.S. government, generally through the Department of Justice and the U.S. solicitor general (a political appointee in that department), seeks to advance its position in court. Interest groups then often line up on opposing sides to advance their positions, much in the same way lobbyists do in Congress.

We offer a note on terminology: in referring to the "Supreme Court," the "Court," or the "high Court" here, we always mean the U.S. Supreme Court, which sits at the pinnacle of the federal and state court systems. The Supreme Court is referred to by the name of the chief justice who presided over it during a particular period. For example, the Marshall Court is the Court presided over by John Marshall from 1801 to 1835, and the Roberts Court is the current Court that began in 2005. When we use the term "courts," we refer to all federal or state courts unless otherwise noted.

jurisdiction
Authority vested in a particular court to hear and decide the issues in a particular case.

original jurisdiction
The jurisdiction of courts that hear a case first, usually in a trial. These courts determine the facts of a case.

Roots of the Federal Judiciary

9.1 Trace the development of the federal judiciary and the origins of judicial review.

The detailed notes James Madison took at the Constitutional Convention in Philadelphia make it clear that the Framers devoted little time to writing Article III, which created the judicial branch of government. The Framers believed that a federal judiciary posed little threat of tyranny. One scholar has even suggested that, for at least some delegates to the Constitutional Convention, "provision for a national judiciary was a matter of theoretical necessity . . . more in deference to the maxim of separation [of powers] than in response to clearly formulated ideas about the role of a national judicial system and its indispensability."[2]

The Framers also debated the need for any federal courts below the Supreme Court. Some argued in favor of deciding all cases in state courts, with only appeals going before the Supreme Court. Others argued for a system of federal courts. A compromise left the final choice to Congress, and Article III, section 1, begins simply by vesting "The judicial Power of the United States . . . in one supreme Court, and in such inferior Courts as the Congress may from time to time ordain and establish."

Article III, section 2, specifies the judicial power of the Supreme Court. It also discusses the types of cases the Court can hear, or its **jurisdiction** (see Table 9.1). Courts have two types of jurisdiction: original and appellate. **Original jurisdiction**

appellate jurisdiction
The power vested in particular courts to review and/or revise the decision of a lower court.

Judiciary Act of 1789
Legislative act that established the basic three-tiered structure of the federal court system.

TABLE 9.1 WHAT KINDS OF CASES DOES THE U.S. SUPREME COURT HEAR?

The following are the types of cases the Supreme Court was given the jurisdiction to hear as initially specified in Article III, section 2, of the Constitution:
All cases arising under the Constitution and laws or treaties of the United States
All cases of admiralty or maritime jurisdiction
Cases in which the United States is a party
Controversies between a state and citizens of another state (later modified by the Eleventh Amendment)
Controversies between two or more states
Controversies between citizens of different states
Controversies between citizens of the same state claiming lands under grants in different states
Controversies between a state, or the citizens thereof, and foreign states or citizens thereof
All cases affecting ambassadors or other public ministers

refers to a court's authority to hear disputes as a trial court; these courts determine the facts of a case. The Supreme Court has original jurisdiction in cases involving the state governments or public officials. **Appellate jurisdiction** refers to a court's ability to review and/or revise cases already decided by a trial court. The Supreme Court has appellate jurisdiction in all other cases. This section also specifies that all federal crimes, except those involving impeachment, shall be tried by jury in the state in which the crime was committed. The third section of the article defines treason and mandates that at least two witnesses appear in such cases.

Had the Framers viewed the Supreme Court as the potential policy maker it is today, they most likely would not have provided for life tenure with "good behavior" for all federal judges in Article III. The Framers agreed on this feature because they did not want the justices (or any federal judges) subject to the whims of politics, the public, or politicians. Moreover, Alexander Hamilton argued in *Federalist No. 78* that the "independence of judges" was needed "to guard the Constitution and the rights of individuals."

The Constitution nonetheless did include some checks on the power of the judiciary. One such check gives Congress the authority to alter the Court's ability to hear certain kinds of cases. Congress can also propose constitutional amendments that, if ratified, can effectively reverse judicial decisions, and it can impeach and remove federal judges. In one further check, it is the president who, with the "advice and consent" of the Senate, appoints all federal judges.

The Court can, in turn, check the presidency by presiding over presidential impeachment. Article I, section 3, notes in discussing impeachment, "When the President of the United States is tried, the Chief Justice shall preside."

☐ The Judiciary Act of 1789 and the Creation of the Federal Judicial System

In spite of the Framers' intentions, the pervasive role of politics in the judicial branch quickly became evident with the passage of the Judiciary Act of 1789. Congress spent nearly the entire second half of its first session deliberating the various provisions of the act to give form and substance to the federal judiciary. As one early observer noted, "The convention has only crayoned in the outlines. It left it to Congress to fill up and colour the canvas."[3]

The **Judiciary Act of 1789** established the basic three-tiered structure of the federal court system. At the bottom were the federal district courts—at least one in each state. If people participating in a lawsuit (called litigants) were unhappy with the district court's verdict, they could appeal their case to the circuit courts, constituting the second tier. Each circuit court, initially created to function as a trial court for important cases, originally comprised one district court judge and two Supreme Court justices who met as a circuit court twice a year. Not until 1891 did circuit courts (or, as we know them today, courts of appeals) take on their exclusively appellate function and begin to focus solely on reviewing the findings of lower courts. The third tier of the federal judicial system defined by the Judiciary Act of 1789 was the Supreme Court of the United

The Judges both of the supreme and inferior Courts, shall . . . receive for their services, a compensation, which shall not be diminished during their continuance in office. —ARTICLE III, SECTION 1

This section of Article III guarantees that the salaries of all federal judges will not be reduced during their service on the bench. At the Constitutional Convention, considerable debate raged over how to treat the payment of federal judges. Some believed that Congress should have an extra check on the judiciary by being able to reduce their salaries. This provision was a compromise after James Madison suggested that Congress have the authority to bar increases as well as decreases in the salaries of these unelected jurists. The delegates recognized that decreases, as well as no opportunity for raises, could negatively affect the perks associated with life tenure.

This clause of the Constitution has not elicited much controversy. When the federal income tax was first enacted, some judges unsuccessfully challenged it as a diminution of their salaries. Much more recently, Chief Justices William H. Rehnquist and John Roberts repeatedly urged Congress to increase salaries for federal judges. As early as 1989, Rehnquist noted that "judicial salaries are the single greatest problem facing the federal judiciary today." Roberts, in his first state of the judiciary message, pointed out that the comparatively low salaries earned by federal judges drive away many well-qualified and diverse lawyers, compromising the independence of the American judiciary.

Increasing numbers of federal judges are leaving the bench for more lucrative private practice. While a salary of $223,500 (for the chief justice) or $213,900 (for the other justices) may sound like a lot to most people, lawyers in large urban practices routinely earn more than double and triple that amount annually. Supreme Court clerks, moreover, now regularly receive $250,000 signing bonuses (in addition to large salaries) from law firms anxious to pay for their expertise.

CRITICAL THINKING QUESTIONS

1. How does prohibiting Congress from diminishing the salaries of judges reduce political influences on the judiciary?
2. How do justices' salaries compare to the average income of a worker in your area? Do you agree with Chief Justice Roberts's contention that judges are underpaid? Why or why not?

States. Although the Constitution mentions "the supreme Court," it did not designate its size. In the Judiciary Act, Congress set the size of the Supreme Court at six—the chief justice plus five associate justices. After being reduced to five members in 1801, Congress expanded and contracted the Court's size until it was fixed at nine in 1869.

When the justices met in their first public session in New York City in 1790, they were garbed magnificently in black and scarlet robes in the English fashion. The elegance of their attire, however, could not compensate for the relative ineffectiveness of the Court. Its first session—presided over by John Jay, who was appointed chief justice of the United States by President George Washington—initially had to be adjourned when fewer than half the justices attended. Later, once a sufficient number of justices assembled, the Court decided only one major case. Moreover, as an indication of its lowly status, one associate justice left the Court to become chief justice of the South Carolina Supreme Court. (Although today we might consider such a move as a step down, keep in mind that in the early years of the United States, many people viewed the states, and thus their courts, as more important than the national government.)

Hampered by frequent changes in personnel, limited space for its operations, no clerical support, and no system of reporting its decisions, the early Court did not impress many people. From the beginning, the circuit court duties of the Supreme Court justices presented problems for the prestige of the Court. Few good lawyers were willing to accept nominations to the high Court because circuit court duties entailed a substantial amount of travel—most of it on horseback over poorly maintained roads. Southern justices often rode as many as 10,000 miles a year on horseback. President George Washington tried to prevail on several friends and supporters to fill vacancies on the Court, but most refused the "honor." John Adams, the second president of the United

judicial review
Power of the courts to review acts of other branches of government and the states.

States, ran into similar problems. When Adams asked John Jay to resume the position of chief justice after Jay resigned to become governor of New York, Jay declined the offer.

In spite of these problems, in its first decade, the Court took several actions to mold the new nation. First, by declining to give George Washington advice on the legality of some of his actions, the justices attempted to establish the Supreme Court as an independent, nonpolitical branch of government. Although John Jay frequently gave the president private advice, the Court refused to answer questions Washington posed to it concerning the construction of international laws and treaties.

The early Court also tried to advance principles of nationalism and to maintain the national government's supremacy over the states. As circuit court jurists, the justices rendered numerous decisions on such matters as national suppression of the Whiskey Rebellion, which occurred in 1794 after imposition of a national excise tax on whiskey, and the constitutionality of the Alien and Sedition Acts, which made it a crime to criticize national governmental officials or their actions.

During the ratification debates, Anti-Federalists had warned that Article III extended federal judicial power to controversies "between a State and Citizens of another State"—meaning that a citizen of one state could sue any other state in federal court, a prospect unthinkable to defenders of state sovereignty. Although Federalists, including Alexander Hamilton and James Madison, had scoffed at the idea, the nationalist Supreme Court quickly proved them wrong in *Chisholm* v. *Georgia* (1793). In *Chisholm*, the justices interpreted the Court's jurisdiction under Article III, section 2, to include the right to hear suits brought by a citizen against a state in which he did not reside. Writing in *Chisholm*, Justice James Wilson denounced the "haughty notions of state independence, state sovereignty, and state supremacy."[4] The states' reaction to this perceived attack on their authority led to passage and ratification in 1798 of the Eleventh Amendment to the Constitution, which specifically limited judicial power by stipulating that the authority of the federal courts could not "extend to any suit . . . commenced or prosecuted against one of the United States by citizens of another State."

The Marshall Court: *Marbury* v. *Madison* (1803) and Judicial Review

John Marshall, who headed the Court from 1801 to 1835, brought much-needed respect and prestige to the Court. President John Adams appointed Marshall chief justice in 1800, three years after he declined to accept a nomination as associate justice. An ardent Federalist, Marshall is considered the most important justice to serve on the high Court. Part of his reputation results from the duration of his service and the historical significance of this period in our nation's history.

As chief justice, Marshall helped to establish the role and power of the Court. The Marshall Court, for example, discontinued the practice of *seriatim* (Latin for "in a series") opinions, which was the custom of the King's Bench in Great Britain. Prior to the Marshall Court, the justices delivered their individual opinions in order of seniority. For the Court to take its place as an equal branch of government, Marshall believed, the justices needed to speak as a Court and not as six individuals. In fact, during Marshall's first four years in office, the Court routinely spoke as one, and the chief justice wrote twenty-four of its twenty-six opinions.

The Marshall Court also established the authority of the Supreme Court over the judiciaries of the various states.[5] In addition, the Court established the supremacy of the federal government and Congress over state governments through a broad interpretation of the necessary and proper clause in *McCulloch* v. *Maryland* (1819).[6]

Finally, the Marshall Court claimed the right of **judicial review**, the power of the courts to review acts of other branches of government and of the states. The Supreme Court derives much of its day-to-day power and impact on the policy process from this right. This claim established the Court as the final arbiter of constitutional questions, with the right to declare congressional acts void.[7]

Alexander Hamilton first publicly endorsed the idea of judicial review in *Federalist No. 78*, noting, "Whenever a particular statute contravenes the Constitution, it will be

WHY IS JOHN MARSHALL IMPORTANT TO THE DEVELOPMENT OF JUDICIAL AUTHORITY?

A single person can make a major difference in the development of an institution. Such was the case with John Marshall (1755–1835), who dominated the Supreme Court during his thirty-four years as chief justice. More of a politician than a lawyer, Marshall served as a delegate to the Virginia legislature and played an instrumental role in Virginia's ratification of the U.S. Constitution in 1787. He became secretary of state in 1800 under John Adams. When Oliver Ellsworth resigned as chief justice of the United States in 1800, Adams nominated Marshall. Marshall served on the Court until the day he died, participating in more than 1,000 decisions and authoring more than 500 opinions.

the duty of the judicial tribunals to adhere to the latter and disregard the former." Nonetheless, because the U.S. Constitution does not mention judicial review, the actual authority of the Supreme Court to review the constitutionality of acts of Congress was an unsettled question. But, in ***Marbury* v. *Madison* (1803)**, Chief Justice John Marshall claimed this sweeping authority for the Court by asserting that the Constitution's supremacy clause implies the right of judicial review.[8]

Marbury v. *Madison* arose amid a sea of political controversy. In the final hours of his administration, John Adams appointed William Marbury as the justice of the peace for the District of Columbia. But, in the confusion of winding up matters, Adams's secretary of state failed to deliver Marbury's commission. Marbury then asked James Madison, Thomas Jefferson's secretary of state, for the commission. Under direct orders from Jefferson, who was irate over the Adams administration's last-minute appointment of several Federalist judges (quickly confirmed by the Federalist Senate), Madison refused to turn over the commission. Marbury and three other Adams appointees who were in the same situation then filed a writ of *mandamus* (a legal motion) asking the Supreme Court to order Madison to deliver their commissions.

Political tensions ran high as the Court met to hear the case. Jefferson threatened to ignore any order of the Court. Marshall realized that a refusal of the executive branch to comply with the decision could devastate both him and the prestige of the Court. Responding to this challenge, in a brilliant opinion that in many sections reads more like a lecture to Jefferson than a discussion of the merits of Marbury's claim, Marshall concluded that although Marbury and the others were entitled to their commissions, the Court lacked the power to issue the writ sought by Marbury. In *Marbury* v. *Madison,* Marshall further ruled that those parts of the Judiciary Act of 1789 that extended the original jurisdiction of the Court to allow it to issue writs of *mandamus* were inconsistent with the Constitution and therefore unconstitutional.

Although the immediate effect of the decision was to deny power to the Court, its long-term effect was to establish the implied power of judicial review. Said Marshall, writing for the Court, "it is emphatically the province and duty of the judicial department to say what the law is." Since *Marbury,* the Court has routinely exercised the power of judicial review to determine the constitutionality of acts of Congress, the executive branch, and the states.

***Marbury* v. *Madison* (1803)**
Case in which the Supreme Court first asserted the power of judicial review by finding that the congressional statute extending the Court's original jurisdiction was unconstitutional.

trial court
Court of original jurisdiction where cases begin.

appellate court
Court that generally reviews only findings of law made by lower courts.

constitutional courts
Federal courts specifically created by the U.S. Constitution or by Congress pursuant to its authority in Article III.

legislative courts
Courts established by Congress for specialized purposes, such as the Court of Appeals for Veterans Claims.

The Federal Court System

9.2 Explain the organization of the federal court system.

The judicial system in the United States can best be described as a dual system consisting of the federal court system and the judicial systems of the fifty states. Cases may arise in either system. Both systems are basically three-tiered. At the bottom of the system are **trial courts**, where litigation begins. In the middle are **appellate courts**; these courts generally review only findings of law made by trial courts. At the top of both the federal and state court systems sits a court of last resort (see Figure 9.1). In the federal court system, trial courts are called district courts, appellate courts are termed courts of appeals, and the Supreme Court is the court of last resort.

The federal district courts, courts of appeals, and the Supreme Court are called **constitutional (or Article III) courts** because Article III of the Constitution either established them or authorized Congress to establish them. The president nominates (with the advice and consent of the Senate) judges who preside over these courts, and they serve lifetime terms, as long as they engage in "good behavior."

In addition to constitutional courts, **legislative courts** are set up by Congress, under its implied powers, generally for special purposes. The U.S. territorial courts (which hear federal cases in the territories) and the U.S. Court of Appeals for Veterans

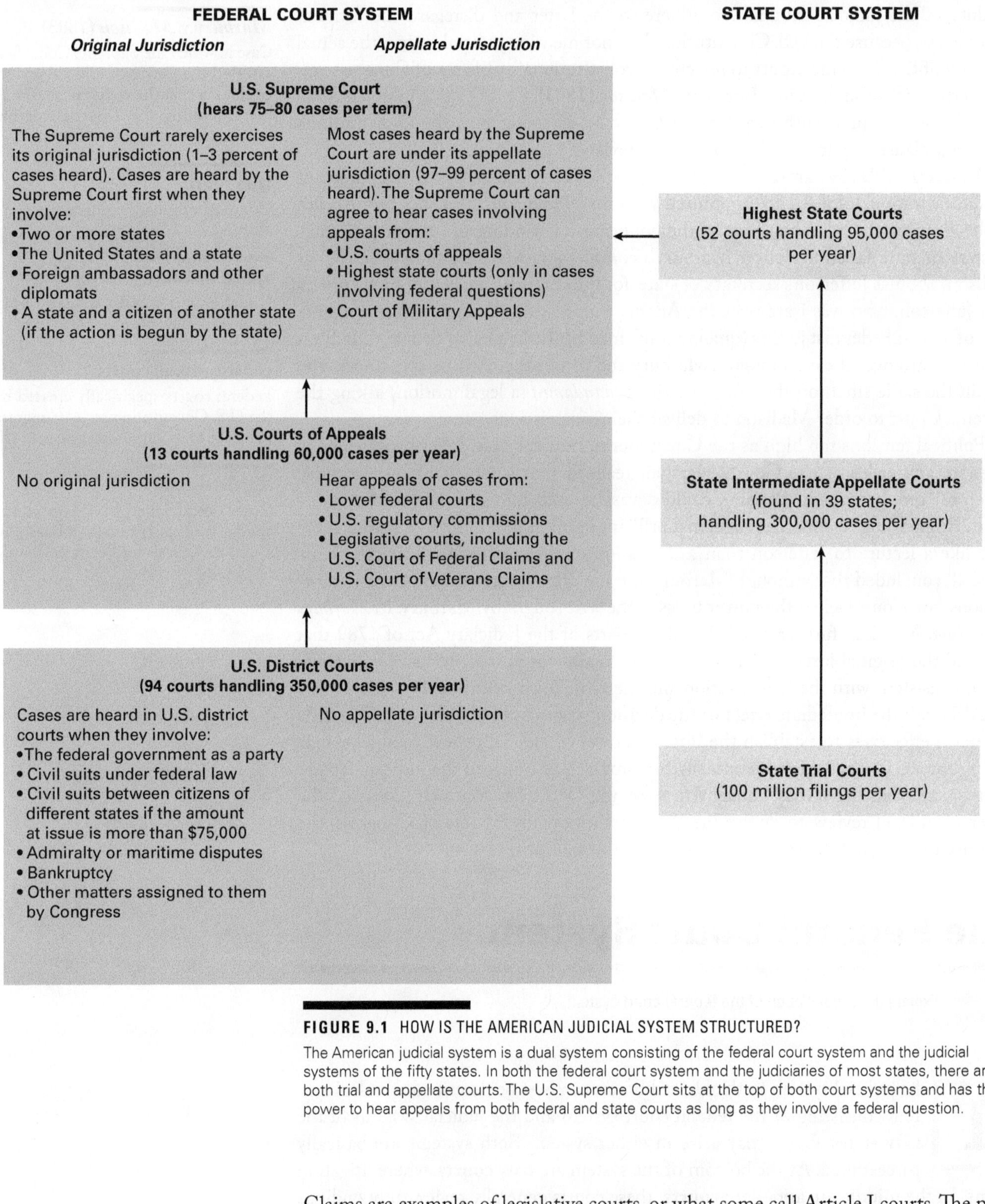

9.1
9.2
9.3
9.4
9.5
9.6

FEDERAL COURT SYSTEM

Original Jurisdiction | *Appellate Jurisdiction*

STATE COURT SYSTEM

U.S. Supreme Court
(hears 75–80 cases per term)

The Supreme Court rarely exercises its original jurisdiction (1–3 percent of cases heard). Cases are heard by the Supreme Court first when they involve:
- Two or more states
- The United States and a state
- Foreign ambassadors and other diplomats
- A state and a citizen of another state (if the action is begun by the state)

Most cases heard by the Supreme Court are under its appellate jurisdiction (97–99 percent of cases heard). The Supreme Court can agree to hear cases involving appeals from:
- U.S. courts of appeals
- Highest state courts (only in cases involving federal questions)
- Court of Military Appeals

U.S. Courts of Appeals
(13 courts handling 60,000 cases per year)

No original jurisdiction

Hear appeals of cases from:
- Lower federal courts
- U.S. regulatory commissions
- Legislative courts, including the U.S. Court of Federal Claims and U.S. Court of Veterans Claims

U.S. District Courts
(94 courts handling 350,000 cases per year)

Cases are heard in U.S. district courts when they involve:
- The federal government as a party
- Civil suits under federal law
- Civil suits between citizens of different states if the amount at issue is more than $75,000
- Admiralty or maritime disputes
- Bankruptcy
- Other matters assigned to them by Congress

No appellate jurisdiction

Highest State Courts
(52 courts handling 95,000 cases per year)

State Intermediate Appellate Courts
(found in 39 states; handling 300,000 cases per year)

State Trial Courts
(100 million filings per year)

FIGURE 9.1 HOW IS THE AMERICAN JUDICIAL SYSTEM STRUCTURED?

The American judicial system is a dual system consisting of the federal court system and the judicial systems of the fifty states. In both the federal court system and the judiciaries of most states, there are both trial and appellate courts. The U.S. Supreme Court sits at the top of both court systems and has the power to hear appeals from both federal and state courts as long as they involve a federal question.

Claims are examples of legislative courts, or what some call Article I courts. The president appoints (subject to Senate confirmation) the judges who preside over these federal courts; they serve fixed, fifteen-year renewable terms.

□ The District Courts

As we have seen, Congress created U.S. district courts when it enacted the Judiciary Act of 1789. District courts are federal trial courts. Currently, the federal district courts number ninety-four. No district court cuts across state lines. Every state has at least one federal district court, and the most populous states—California, Texas, and New York—each have four (see Figure 9.2).[9]

Federal district courts, in which the bulk of the judicial work takes place in the federal system, have original jurisdiction over only specific types of cases. Although

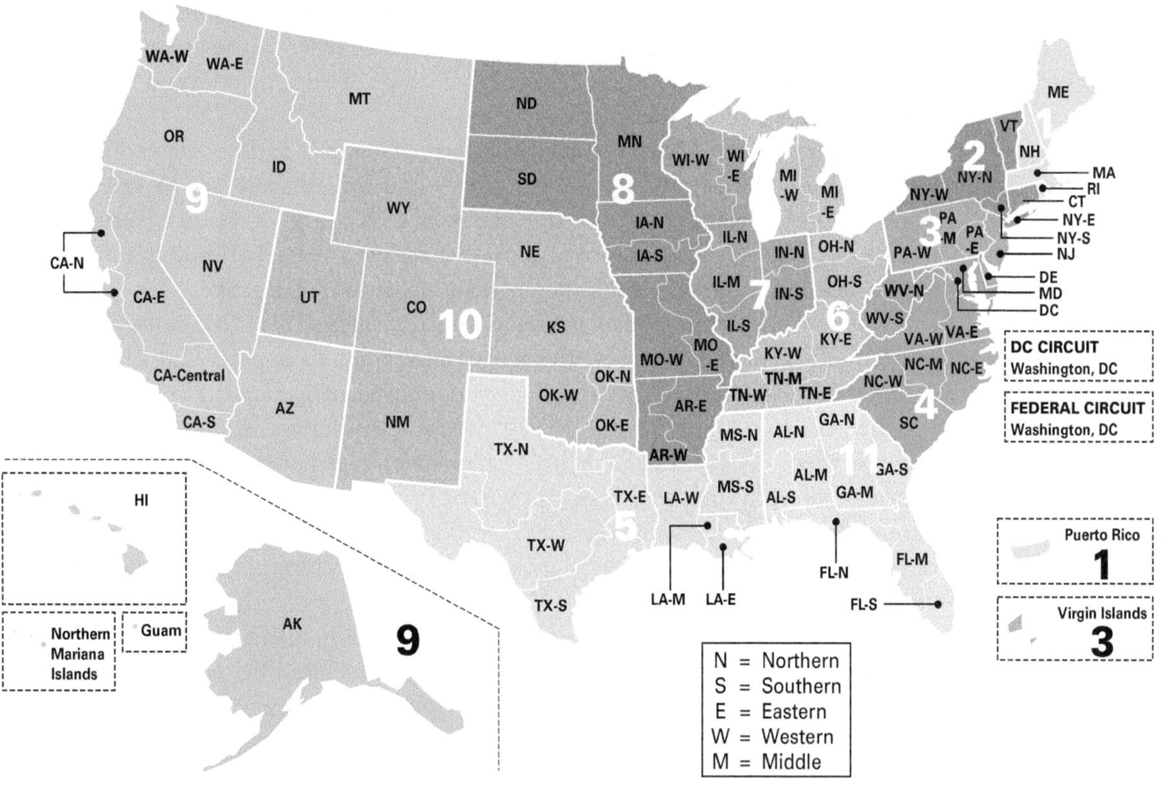

FIGURE 9.2 WHAT ARE THE BOUNDARIES OF FEDERAL DISTRICT COURTS AND COURTS OF APPEALS?

This map shows the location of each U.S. court of appeals and the boundaries of the federal district courts in states with more than one district. Note that there are eleven numbered and two unnumbered courts of appeals. There are also ninety-four district courts. States are divided into between one and four districts; no district court crosses state lines.

rules governing district court jurisdiction can be complex, cases, which are heard in federal district courts by a single judge (with or without a jury), generally fall into one of three categories:

1. They involve the federal government as a party.
2. They present a federal question based on a claim under the U.S. Constitution, a treaty with another nation, or a federal statute. This is called federal question jurisdiction and it can involve criminal or civil law.
3. They involve civil suits in which citizens are from different states, and the amount of money at issue is more than $75,000.[10]

Each federal judicial district has a U.S. attorney, nominated by the president and confirmed by the Senate. The U.S. attorney in each district is that district's chief law enforcement officer. U.S. attorneys have a considerable amount of discretion regarding whether they pursue criminal or civil investigations or file charges against individuals or corporations. They also have several assistants to help them in their work. The number of assistant U.S. attorneys in each district depends on the amount of litigation.

☐ The Courts of Appeals

The losing party in a case heard and decided in a federal district court can appeal the decision to the appropriate court of appeals. The U.S. courts of appeals (known as the circuit courts of appeals prior to 1948) are the intermediate appellate courts in the federal system and were established in 1789 to hear appeals from federal district courts. Currently, eleven numbered courts of appeals exist. A twelfth, the U.S. Court of Appeals for the D.C. Circuit, handles most appeals involving federal regulatory commissions

brief
A document containing the legal written arguments in a case filed with a court by a party prior to a hearing or trial.

precedent
A prior judicial decision that serves as a rule for settling subsequent cases of a similar nature.

stare decisis
In court rulings, a reliance on past decisions or precedents to formulate decisions in new cases.

and agencies, including, for example, the National Labor Relations Board and the Securities and Exchange Commission. The thirteenth federal appeals court is the U.S. Court of Appeals for the Federal Circuit, which deals with patents and contract and financial claims against the federal government.

The number of judges within each court of appeals varies—depending on the workload and the complexity of the cases—and ranges from six to nearly thirty. Supervising each court is a chief judge, the most senior judge in terms of service below the age of sixty-five, who can serve no more than seven years. In deciding cases, judges are divided into rotating three-judge panels, made up of the active judges within the court of appeals, visiting judges (primarily district judges from the same court), and retired judges. In rare cases, all the judges in a court of appeals may choose to sit together (*en banc*) to decide a case of special importance by majority vote.

The courts of appeals have no original jurisdiction. Rather, Congress has granted these courts appellate jurisdiction over two general categories of cases: appeals from criminal and civil cases from the district courts, and appeals from administrative agencies. Criminal and civil case appeals constitute about 90 percent of the workload of the courts of appeals; those from administrative agencies constitute about 10 percent.

Once a federal court of appeals makes a decision, a litigant no longer has an automatic right to an appeal. The losing party may submit a petition to the U.S. Supreme Court to hear the case, but the Court grants few of these requests. The courts of appeals, then, are the courts of last resort for almost all federal litigation. Keep in mind, however, that most cases, if they actually go to trial, go no further than the district court level.

In general, courts of appeals try to correct errors of law and procedure that have occurred in lower courts or administrative agencies. Courts of appeals hear no new testimony; instead, lawyers submit written arguments in what is called a **brief** (also submitted in trial courts), and they then appear to present and argue the case orally to the court. Decisions of any court of appeals are binding on only the courts within its geographic confines.

☐ The Supreme Court

The U.S. Supreme Court is often at the center of highly controversial issues that the political process has yet to resolve successfully. It reviews cases from the U.S. courts of appeals and state supreme courts (as well as other courts of last resort) and acts as the final interpreter of the U.S. Constitution.

Since 1869, the U.S. Supreme Court has consisted of eight associate justices and one chief justice, whom the president nominates specifically for that position. The number nine holds no special significance, and the Constitution does not specify the size of the Court. Between 1789 and 1869, Congress periodically altered the size of the Court. The lowest number of justices on the Court was six; the most, ten. Through December 2012, only 112 justices had served on the Court, with only seventeen chief justices.

Compared with the president or Congress, the Supreme Court operates with few support staff. Along with the four clerks each justice employs, the Supreme Court has only about 400 staff members.

Decisions of the U.S. Supreme Court, however, are binding throughout the nation and establish national **precedents**, or rules for settling subsequent cases of similar nature. This reliance on past decisions or precedents to formulate decisions in new cases is called ***stare decisis*** (a Latin phrase meaning "let the decision stand"). The principle of *stare decisis* allows for continuity and predictability in our judicial system. Although *stare decisis* can be helpful in predicting decisions, at times judges carve out new ground and ignore, decline to follow, or even overrule precedents to reach a different conclusion in a case involving similar circumstances. This is a major reason why so much litigation exists in America today. Parties to a suit know that the outcome of a case is not always predictable; if such prediction were possible, there would be little reason to go to court.

Explore Your World

Judiciaries enjoy a unique role in the political systems of many states. They are the ultimate arbiters of the law and the Constitution, and wield significant power in determining innocence, guilt, and liability. Judges also play an important role in maintaining the rule of law and enforcing appropriate punishments for crimes committed. It is only appropriate, then, that judicial officers around the world are outfitted in a way that conveys the honor and responsibility of the position they hold. Most judicial robes are red or black. This tradition may have its roots in the mourning robes worn to pay respect during medieval times.

Judicial dress is a contentious issue in Pakistan. Some Pakistani judges, such as the one shown at right in this photo, dress in the English tradition and wear robes with wigs. Others, especially Muslim judges, choose to wear more traditional Nehru-style jackets with hats.

American Chief Justice William H. Rehnquist, seen here presiding over the 1999 impeachment trial of President Bill Clinton, added embellishments to his traditional black robe in the form of four gold stripes on each sleeve.

Red robes are traditional on the German Federal Constitutional Court. These robes are based on those worn by Italian judges during the Renaissance. Though the hat is officially part of the uniform, it has largely been eliminated in recent years.

CRITICAL THINKING QUESTIONS

1. How does each of these modes of dress reflect the culture and traditions of the countries they represent?
2. How might you expect judges in other countries—for example, Australia or Italy—to dress? What influences your expectation?
3. Does requiring a particular "uniform" accord judges additional power and respect? Should other political leaders, such as members of the legislature, wear uniform dress?

9.1

9.2

9.3

9.4

9.5

9.6

senatorial courtesy

A process by which presidents generally allow senators from the state in which a judicial vacancy occurs to block a nomination by simply registering their objection.

How Federal Court Judges Are Selected

9.3 Outline the criteria and process used to select federal court judges.

The selection of federal judges is often a highly political process with important political ramifications because the president must nominate judges and the U.S. Senate must confirm them. Presidents, in general, try to select well-qualified men and women for the bench. But, these appointments also provide a president with the opportunity to put his philosophical stamp on the federal courts (see Table 9.2).

In selecting his nominees, the president may look for guidance from members of Congress, advisers, confidantes, or other high-ranking party officials.[11] The U.S. Constitution, for example, mandates that presidents receive advice and consent from the Senate. Historically, presidents have screened their nominees through a process known as **senatorial courtesy**. This is the process by which presidents generally allow senators from the state in which a judicial vacancy occurs to block a nomination by simply registering their objection. One way senators may voice their opposition is through an informal process known as the "blue slip." When a judicial nomination is forwarded to the Senate Judiciary Committee, senators from the state in which a vacancy occurs are sent a letter, usually printed on light blue paper, asking them to register their support or opposition to a nominee. How seriously senators take the blue slips varies from one Congress to the next.[12]

Who Are Federal Judges?

Typically, federal district court judges have held other political offices, such as state court judge or prosecutor. Most have been involved in politics, which is what usually brings them into consideration for a position on the federal bench. Griffin Bell, a former federal court of appeals judge (who later became U.S. attorney general in the Carter administration), once remarked, "For me, becoming a federal judge wasn't very difficult. I managed John F. Kennedy's presidential campaign in Georgia."[13]

TABLE 9.2 HOW DOES A PRESIDENT AFFECT THE FEDERAL JUDICIARY?

President	Appointed to Supreme Court	Appointed to Courts of Appeals[a]	Appointed to District Courts[b]	Total Appointed	Total Number of Judgeships[c]	Percentage of Judgeships Filled by President
Carter (1977–1981)	0	56	203	259	657	39
Reagan (1981–1989)	3	83	290	376	740	50
Bush (1989–1993)	2	42	148	192	825	22
Clinton (1993–2001)	2	66	305	373	841	44
G.W. Bush (2001–2009)	2	61	261	324	866	37
Obama (2009–)[d]	2	30	130	162	874	19

[a]Does not include the U. S. Court of Appeals for the Federal Circuit.
[b]Includes district courts in the territories.
[c]Total judgeships authorized in president's last year in office.
[d]Barack Obama data through October 2012.

SOURCE: "Imprints on the Bench," *CQ Weekly Report* (January 19, 2001): 173. Reprinted by permission of Copyright Clearance Center on behalf of Congressional Quarterly, Inc. Updated by authors. Obama data from Senate Judiciary Committee, www.judiciary.senate.gov/nominations/112thCongress.cfm and www.judiciary.senate.gov/nominations/111thCongress.cfm.

Most recent nominees have had prior judicial experience. White males continue to dominate the federal courts, but since the 1970s, most presidents have pledged (with varying degrees of success) to do their best to appoint more African Americans, Hispanics, women, and other underrepresented groups to the federal bench.

☐ Nomination Criteria

Justice Sandra Day O'Connor once remarked that "You have to be lucky" to be appointed to the judiciary.[14] Although luck certainly factors in, over the years a variety of reasons have accounted for nominations to the bench. Depending on the timing of a vacancy, a president may or may not have a list of possible candidates or even a specific individual in mind. Until recently, presidents often looked within their circle of friends or their administration to fill a vacancy. Nevertheless, whether the nominee is a friend or someone known to the president only by reputation, at least six criteria are especially important: experience, ideology or policy preferences, rewards, pursuit of political support, religion, and race and gender.

EXPERIENCE Most nominees have had at least some judicial, legal, or governmental experience. For example, John Jay, the first chief justice, was one of the authors of *The Federalist Papers* and was active in New York politics. In 2012, all nine sitting Supreme Court justices but one—former Solicitor General Elena Kagan—had prior judicial experience (see Table 9.3). Many of the sitting justices also served as law professors; notably, Justice Kagan was dean of the Harvard Law School.

IDEOLOGY OR POLICY PREFERENCES Most presidents also seek to appoint individuals who share their policy preferences, and almost all have political goals in mind when they appoint a judge or justice. Presidents Franklin D. Roosevelt, Richard M. Nixon, and Ronald Reagan achieved success in molding the federal judiciary to their own political beliefs. Most presidents select judges and justices of their own party affiliation. Chief Justice John Roberts and Justice Samuel Alito, for example, both Republicans, worked in the Department of Justice during the Reagan and George Bush administrations. Roberts also served as associate White House counsel under Reagan.

TABLE 9.3 WHO ARE THE JUSTICES OF THE SUPREME COURT IN 2012?

Justices	Year of Birth	Year Appointed	Political Party	Law School	Appointing President	Religion	Prior Judicial Experience	Prior Government Experience
John Roberts	1955	2005	R	Harvard	G. W. Bush	Roman Catholic	U.S. Court of Appeals	Dept. of Justice, associate White House counsel
Antonin Scalia	1936	1986	R	Harvard	Reagan	Roman Catholic	U.S. Court of Appeals	Assistant attorney general, Office of Legal Counsel
Anthony Kennedy	1936	1988	R	Harvard	Reagan	Roman Catholic	U.S. Court of Appeals	None
Clarence Thomas	1948	1991	R	Yale	Bush	Roman Catholic	U.S. Court of Appeals	Chair, Equal Employment Opportunity Commission
Ruth Bader Ginsburg	1933	1993	D	Columbia/ Harvard	Clinton	Jewish	U.S. Court of Appeals	None
Stephen Breyer	1938	1994	D	Harvard	Clinton	Jewish	U.S. Court of Appeals	Chief counsel, Senate Judiciary Committee
Samuel Alito	1950	2006	R	Yale	G. W. Bush	Roman Catholic	U.S. Court of Appeals	Dept. of Justice, U.S. attorney
Sonia Sotomayor	1954	2009	D	Yale	Obama	Roman Catholic	U.S. Court of Appeals	Assistant attorney general, City of New York
Elena Kagan	1960	2010	D	Harvard	Obama	Jewish	None	U.S. solicitor general, associate White House counsel

Who Are Federal Judges?

Judicial appointments provide presidents with an opportunity to make a lasting impact on public policy. Recent presidents, including Bill Clinton, George W. Bush, and Barack Obama, have also used them as an opportunity to increase the diversity of individuals serving at the highest levels of the U.S. government and to curry favor with traditionally underrepresented groups. Though a diverse federal judiciary has a definite symbolic effect on American politics, its policy impact is less clear.

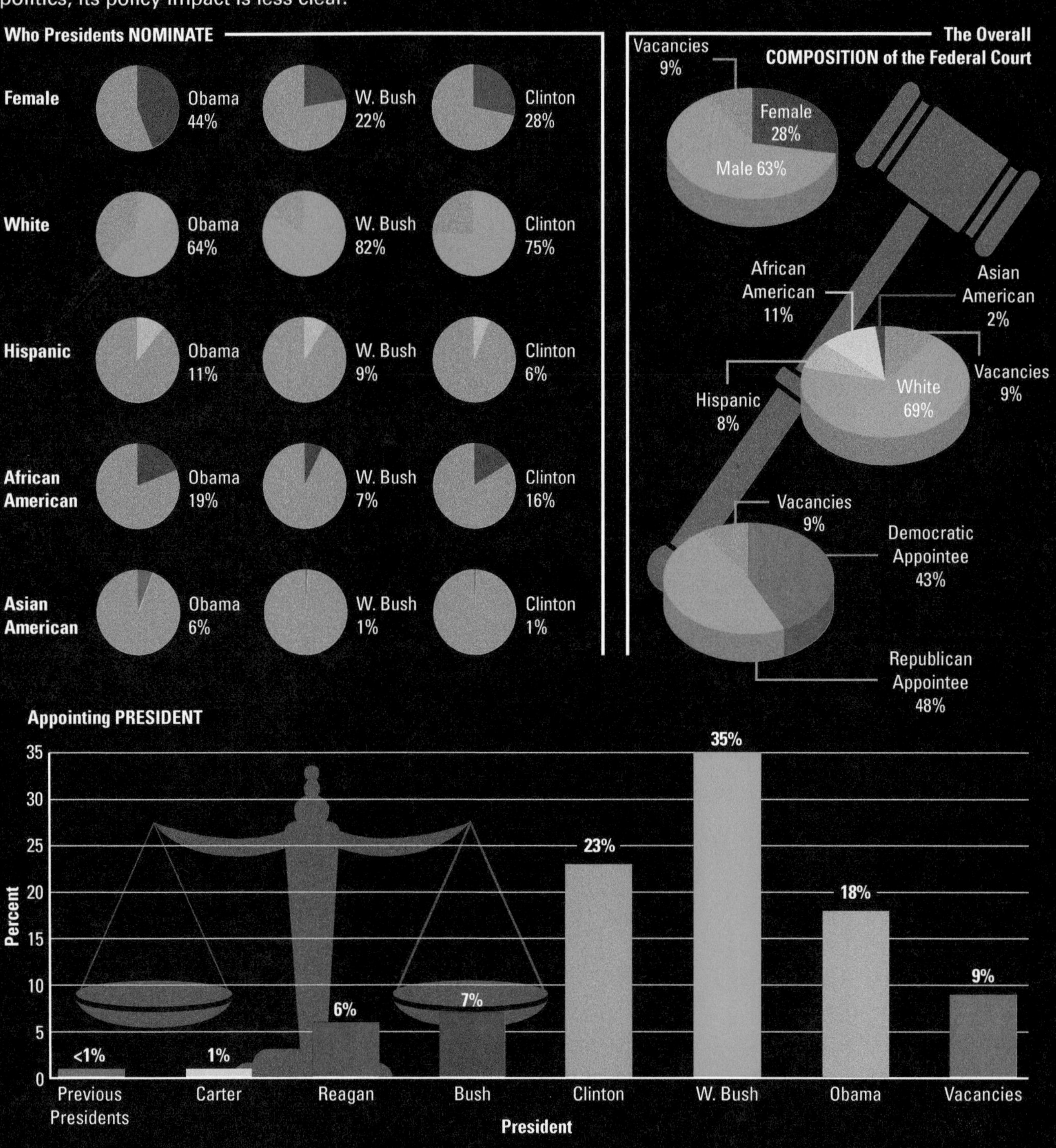

SOURCE: Data from Federal Judicial Center, Biographical Directory of Federal Judges

CRITICAL THINKING QUESTIONS

1. Which groups are over- and underrepresented in the federal judiciary?
2. What differences, if any, exist between judges nominated by Republican presidents and those appointed by Democratic presidents?
3. Should gender, race, and ethnicity matter in the federal courts? Why or why not?

REWARDS Historically, many of those appointed to the judiciary have been personal friends of presidents. Lyndon B. Johnson, for example, appointed his longtime friend Abe Fortas to the bench.

PURSUIT OF POLITICAL SUPPORT During Ronald Reagan's successful campaign for the presidency in 1980, some of his advisers feared that the gender gap would hurt him. Polls repeatedly showed that he was far less popular with female voters than with men. To gain support from women, Reagan announced during his campaign that should he win, he would appoint a woman to fill the first vacancy on the Supreme Court. When Justice Potter Stewart, a moderate, announced his retirement from the bench, under pressure from women's rights groups, President Reagan nominated Sandra Day O'Connor of the Arizona Court of Appeals to fill the vacancy.

RELIGION Through late 2012, of the 112 justices who have served on the Court, almost all have been members of traditional Protestant faiths. Only twelve have been Roman Catholic, and only eight have been Jewish.[15] Today, more Catholics—Roberts, Scalia, Kennedy, Thomas, Alito, and Sotomayor—serve on the Court than at any other point in history. Three Jewish justices—Breyer, Ginsburg, and Kagan—round out the Court. At one time, no one could have imagined that Catholics would someday make up a majority of the Court, or that no members of any Protestant faiths would serve.

RACE, ETHNICITY, AND GENDER Through 2012 only two African Americans and four women have served on the Court. Race was undoubtedly a critical issue in the appointment of Clarence Thomas to replace Thurgood Marshall, the first African American justice. But, President George Bush refused to acknowledge his wish to retain a black seat on the Court. Instead, he announced that he was "picking the best man for the job on the merits," a claim that was met with considerable skepticism by many observers.

As the ethnic diversity of the United States has increased, presidents have faced greater pressure to nominate a Hispanic justice to the Supreme Court. Early in his presidency, President Barack Obama fulfilled these expectations by nominating Sonia Sotomayor. A Puerto Rican and self-proclaimed "wise Latina woman" who grew up in the Bronx, New York, Sotomayor became the first Hispanic Supreme Court justice at the height of a fierce immigration debate.

Although the role of gender was crucial to the nomination of Sandra Day O'Connor, when O'Connor resigned, George W. Bush nominated Judge John Roberts to replace her. When Chief Justice William H. Rehnquist died soon after, Bush nominated Roberts to fill the vacant chief justice position. O'Connor's vacancy eventually was filled by Judge Samuel Alito, much to O'Connor's public chagrin. The departing justice noted that one woman on the Supreme Court was hardly proportional to women's representation within the legal profession.[16] President Barack Obama attempted to remedy this situation with the appointments of Justices Sotomayor and Kagan.

☐ The Confirmation Process

The Constitution gives the Senate the authority to approve all nominees to the federal bench. Ordinarily, nominations are referred to the Senate Judiciary Committee. This committee investigates the nominees, holds hearings, and votes on its recommendation for Senate action. At this stage, the committee may reject a nominee or send the nomination to the full Senate for a vote. The full Senate then deliberates on the nominee before voting. A simple majority vote is required for confirmation.

INVESTIGATION As a president proceeds to narrow the list of possible nominees for a judicial vacancy, White House staff begin an investigation into their personal and professional backgrounds. The Federal Bureau of Investigation also receives names of potential nominees for background checks. In addition, the names are forwarded to the American Bar Association (ABA), the politically powerful organization that represents

9.1

9.2

9.3

9.4

9.5

9.6

the interests of the legal profession. Republican President Dwight D. Eisenhower started this practice, believing it helped "insulate the process from political pressure."[17] After its own investigation, the ABA rates each nominee, based on his or her qualifications, as Well Qualified (previously "Highly Qualified"), Qualified, or Not Qualified.

After a formal nomination is made and sent to the Senate, the Senate Judiciary Committee embarks on its own investigation. To start, the Senate Judiciary Committee asks each nominee to complete a lengthy questionnaire detailing previous work (dating as far back as high school summer jobs), judicial opinions written, judicial philosophy, speeches, and even all interviews ever given to members of the press. Committee staffers also contact potential witnesses who might offer testimony concerning the nominee's fitness for office.

LOBBYING BY INTEREST GROUPS Many organized interests show keen interest in the nomination process. Interest groups are particularly active in Supreme Court nominations. In 1987, for example, the nomination of Judge Robert H. Bork to the Supreme Court led liberal groups to launch an extensive radio, TV, and print media campaign against the nominee. These interest groups decried Bork's actions as solicitor general, especially his firing of the Watergate special prosecutor at the request of President Richard M. Nixon, as well as his political beliefs. As a result of this outcry, the Senate rejected Bork's nomination by a 42–58 vote (see Table 9.4).

More and more, interest groups are also involving themselves in district court and court of appeals nominations. They recognize that these appointments often pave the way for future nominees to the Supreme Court. For example, a coalition of conservative evangelical Christian organizations, including Focus on the Family and the Family Research Council, have held a series of "Justice Sunday" events featuring televangelists and politicians promoting the confirmation of judges with politically conservative and religious records.

THE SENATE COMMITTEE HEARINGS AND SENATE VOTE Not all nominees inspire the kind of intense reaction that kept Bork from the Court and almost blocked the confirmation of Clarence Thomas. Until 1929, all but one Senate Judiciary Committee hearing on a Supreme Court nominee were conducted in executive session—that is, closed to the public. The 1916 hearings on Louis Brandeis, the first Jewish justice, took place in public and lasted nineteen days, although Brandeis

TABLE 9.4 HOW MANY INTEREST GROUPS SUBMIT TESTIMONY TO THE SENATE JUDICIARY COMMITTEE?

Nominee	Year	Support	Oppose	ABA Rating	Senate Vote
O'Connor	1981	7	4	Well-Q	99–0
Scalia	1986	10	14	Well-Q	98–0
Bork	1987	21	17	Well-Q[a]	42–58
Kennedy	1987	10	14	Well-Q	98–0
Souter	1990	20	17	Well-Q	90–9
Thomas	1991	21	32	Q[b]	52–48
Ginsburg	1993	4	6	Well-Q	96–3
Breyer	1994	3	3	Well-Q	87–9
Roberts	2005	19	50	Well-Q	78–22
Alito	2005	6	66	Well-Q	58–42
Sotomayor	2009	210	8	Well-Q	68–31
Kagan	2010	48	8	Well-Q	63-37

[a]Four ABA committee members evaluated him as Not Qualified.
[b]Two ABA committee members evaluated him as Not Qualified.

SOURCE: Amy Harder and Charlie Szymanski, "Sotomayor in Context: Unprecedented Input from Interest Groups," *National Journal* (August 5, 2009), ninthjustice.nationaljournal.com/2009/08/sotomayor-in-context-recordbre.php. Updated by the authors.

WHAT ROLE DOES THE SENATE JUDICIARY COMMITTEE PLAY IN THE JUDICIAL NOMINATION PROCESS?

The Senate Judiciary Committee plays an important role in the process of advice and consent on presidential nominees to the judiciary. As part of this process, they hold confirmation hearings where potential justices appear before the committee. Here, Clarence Thomas testifies before the committee following his nomination in 1991. He was subsequently confirmed to serve on the Supreme Court.

himself never was called to testify. In 1925, Harlan Fiske Stone became the first nominee to testify before the committee.

Since the 1980s, it has become standard for senators to ask the nominees probing questions. Most nominees have declined to answer many of these questions on the grounds that the issues raised ultimately might come before the courts.

After the conclusion of hearings, the Senate Judiciary Committee usually makes a recommendation to the full Senate. Any rejections of presidential nominees to the Supreme Court generally occur only after the Senate Judiciary Committee has recommended against a nominee's appointment. Few recent confirmations have been close, although current Supreme Court Justices Clarence Thomas and Samuel Alito were confirmed by margins of less than ten votes.

☐ Appointments to the U.S. Supreme Court

Justice Oliver Wendell Holmes once remarked that a justice should be a "combination of Justinian, Jesus Christ and John Marshall."[18] However, as with other federal court judges, the president must nominate and the Senate must confirm the justices of the Supreme Court. Presidents always have realized the importance of Supreme

Court appointments to their ability to achieve all or many of their policy objectives. But, even though most presidents have tried to appoint jurists with particular political or ideological philosophies, they often have erred in their assumptions about their appointees. President Dwight D. Eisenhower, a moderate conservative, for example, was appalled by the liberal opinions written by his appointee to chief justice, Earl Warren, concerning criminal defendants' rights.

Historically, because of the critical role the Supreme Court enjoys in our constitutional system, its nominees have encountered more opposition than have district court or court of appeals nominees. As the role of the Court has expanded over time, so, too, has the amount of attention given to nominees. With this increased attention has come greater opposition, especially to nominees with controversial views.

The Supreme Court Today

9.4 Evaluate the Supreme Court's process for accepting, hearing, and deciding cases.

Explore on MyPoliSciLab Simulation: You Are a Supreme Court Clerk

iven the judicial system's vast size and substantial, although often indirect, power over so many aspects of our lives, it is surprising that so many Americans know very little about the judicial system in general and the U.S. Supreme Court in particular.

Even after the attention the Court received surrounding many of its recent controversial decisions, two-thirds of those Americans surveyed in 2012 could not name one member of the Court. Virtually no one could name all nine members of the Court. As revealed in Table 9.5, Chief Justice John Roberts was the best-known justice. Still, only about 20 percent of those polled could name him.

While the American public's lack of interest can take the blame for much of this ignorance, the Court has also taken great pains to ensure its privacy and sense of decorum. The Court's rites and rituals contribute to its mystique and encourage a "cult of the robe."[19] Consider, for example, the way the Supreme Court conducts its proceedings. Oral arguments are not televised, and utmost secrecy surrounds deliberations concerning the outcome of cases. In contrast, C-SPAN brings us daily coverage of various congressional hearings and floor debate on bills and important national issues, and CNN and sometimes other networks provide extensive coverage of many important state court trials. The Supreme Court, however, remains adamant in its refusal to televise its proceedings—including public oral arguments, although it now allows the release of same-day audio recordings of oral arguments.

TABLE 9.5 CAN AMERICANS NAME THE JUSTICES OF THE SUPREME COURT?

Supreme Court Justice	Percentage Who Could Name
John Roberts	20
Clarence Thomas	16
Antonin Scalia	16
Ruth Bader Ginsburg	13
Sonia Sotomayor	13
Anthony Kennedy	10
Samuel Alito	5
Elena Kagan	4
Stephen Breyer	3

SOURCE: © 2012 Findlaw & Thomson Reuters business. Reprinted by permission.

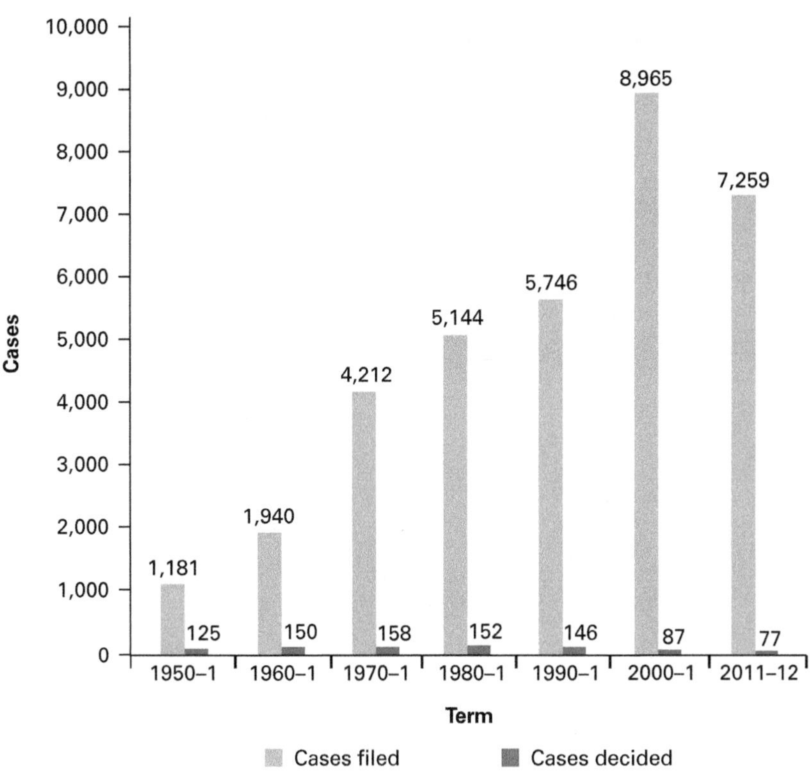

FIGURE 9.3 HOW MANY CASES DOES THE SUPREME COURT HANDLE?

The modern Supreme Court is asked to hear over 7,000 cases per year (represented by orange bars); of these cases, it reaches a final decision in about 1 percent, or 75 cases (represented by red bars). This is about half of the total number of decisions the Court handed down twenty years ago.

SOURCE: Administrative Office of the Courts; Supreme Court Public Information Office.

Deciding to Hear a Case

Over 7,250 cases were filed at the Supreme Court during its 2011-12 term; 79 were heard, and 77 decisions were issued. In contrast, from 1790 to 1801, the Court received only 87 total cases under its appellate jurisdiction. In the Court's early years, most of the justices' workload involved their circuit-riding duties.[20] As recently as the 1940s, fewer than 1,000 cases were filed annually. Filings increased at a dramatic rate until the mid-1990s, shot up again in the late 1990s, and generally have now leveled off (see Figure 9.3).

The content of the Court's docket is every bit as significant as its size. During the 1930s, cases requiring the interpretation of constitutional law began to account for a growing portion of the Court's workload, leading the Court to assume a more important role in the policy-making process. At that time, only 5 percent of the Court's cases involved questions concerning the Bill of Rights. By the late 1950s, one-third of filed cases involved such questions; by the 1960s, half did.[21]

Justices can also exercise a significant role in policy making and politics by opting not to hear a case. In early 2012, for example, the Supreme Court refused to revisit a case concerning prayer in school. The "Doe" family sued the Indian River School Board for including Christian prayer during the school day, at graduation, and during meetings. When the school board attempted to return to the Court, the justices refused, allowing the prior ruling to continue to govern precedent regarding prayer in school.[22]

writ of *certiorari*
A request for the Supreme Court to order up the records from a lower court to review the case.

WRITS OF *CERTIORARI* AND THE RULE OF FOUR Since 1988, nearly all appellate cases that have gone to the Supreme Court arrived there on a petition for a **writ of *certiorari*** (from the Latin "to be informed"), which is a request for the Supreme Court—at its discretion—to order up the records of the lower courts for purposes of review (see Figure 9.4).

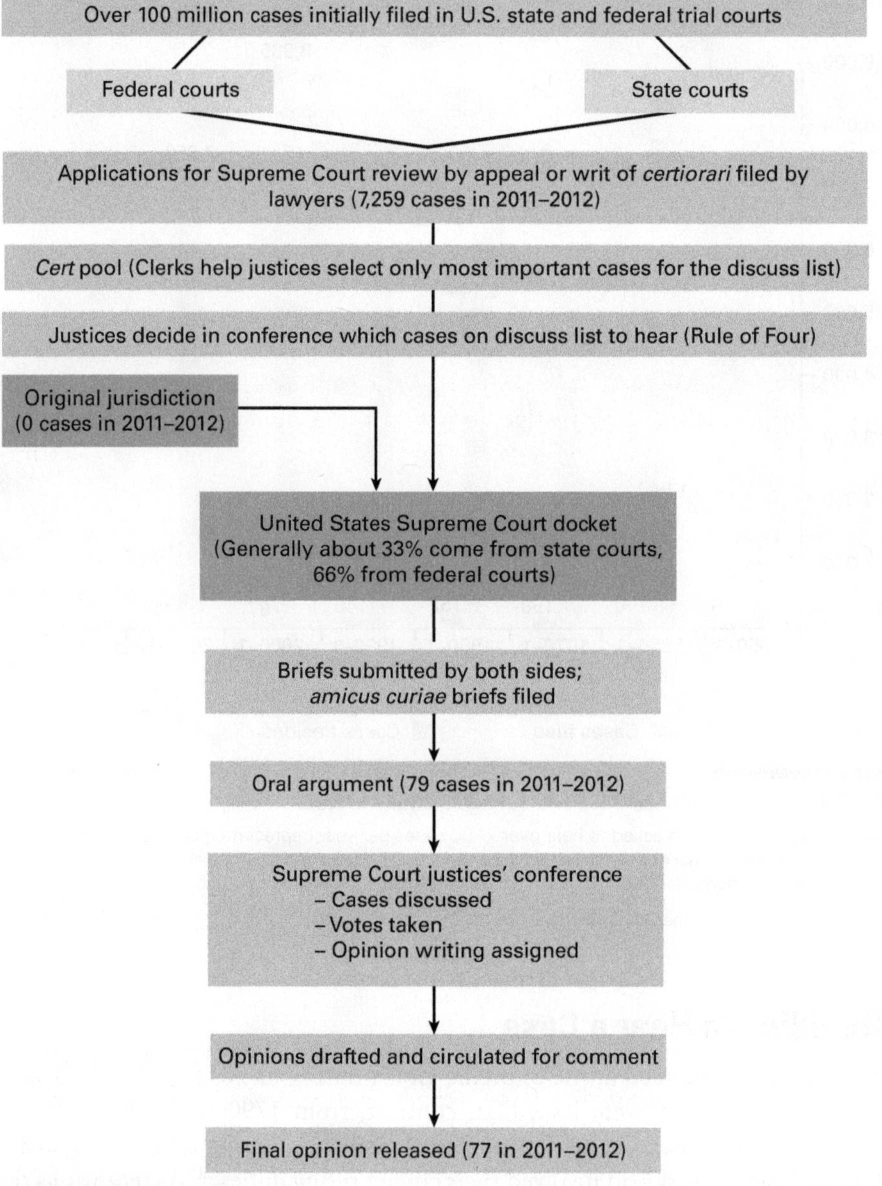

FIGURE 9.4 HOW DOES A CASE GET TO THE SUPREME COURT?

This figure illustrates both how cases get on the Court's docket and what happens after a case is accepted for review. A case may take several years to wind its way through the federal judiciary and another year or two to be heard and decided by the Supreme Court, if the justices decide to grant *certiorari*.

The Supreme Court controls its own caseload through the *certiorari* process, deciding which cases it wants to hear and rejecting most cases that come to it. All petitions, or writs of *certiorari,* must meet two criteria:

1. The case must come from a U.S. court of appeals, a court of military appeals, district court, or a state court of last resort.
2. The case must involve a federal question. Thus, the case must present questions of federal constitutional law or involve a federal statute, action, or treaty. The reasons that the Court should accept the case for review and legal argument supporting that position are set out in the petitioner's writ of *certiorari.*

The clerk of the Court transmits petitions for writs of *certiorari* first to the chief justice's office, where his clerks review the petitions, and then to the individual justices' offices. On the Roberts Court, all of the justices except Justice Samuel Alito (who allows his clerks great individual authority in selecting the cases for him to review) participate in what is called the *cert* pool. Pool participants review their assigned fraction of petitions and share their notes with each other. Those cases deemed noteworthy by the justices then make it onto what is called the discuss list prepared by the chief justice's clerks and are circulated to the chambers of the other justices. All other petitions are dead listed and go no further. Only about 30 percent of submitted petitions make it to the discuss list. During one of their weekly conference meetings, the justices review the cases on the discuss list. The chief justice speaks first, then the rest of the justices, according to seniority. The decision process ends when the justices vote, and by custom, *certiorari* is granted according to the **Rule of Four**—when at least four justices vote to hear a case.

Rule of Four
At least four justices of the Supreme Court must vote to consider a case before it can be heard.

THE ROLE OF CLERKS As early as 1850, the justices of the Supreme Court beseeched Congress to approve the hiring of a clerk to assist each justice. Congress denied the request, so when Justice Horace Gray hired the first law clerk in 1882, he paid the clerk himself. Justice Gray's clerk was a top graduate of Harvard Law School whose duties included cutting Justice Gray's hair and running personal errands. Finally, in 1886, Congress authorized each justice to hire a stenographer clerk for $1,600 a year.

Clerks typically are selected from candidates at the top of the graduating classes of prestigious law schools. They perform a variety of tasks, ranging from searching arcane facts to playing tennis or taking walks with the justices. Clerks spend most of their time researching material, reading and summarizing cases, and helping justices write opinions. Clerks also make the first pass through the petitions that come to the Court, undoubtedly influencing which cases get a second look. They often help draft opinions and serve as informal conduits for communication between the justices' chambers. Just how much assistance they provide in the writing of opinions is unknown.[23]

Over time, the number of clerks employed by the justices has increased. Through the 1946 to 1969 terms, most justices employed two clerks. By 1970, most had three clerks, and by 1980, all but three justices had four clerks. In 2010, the nine active justices and three retired justices employed approximately forty clerks. This growth in the

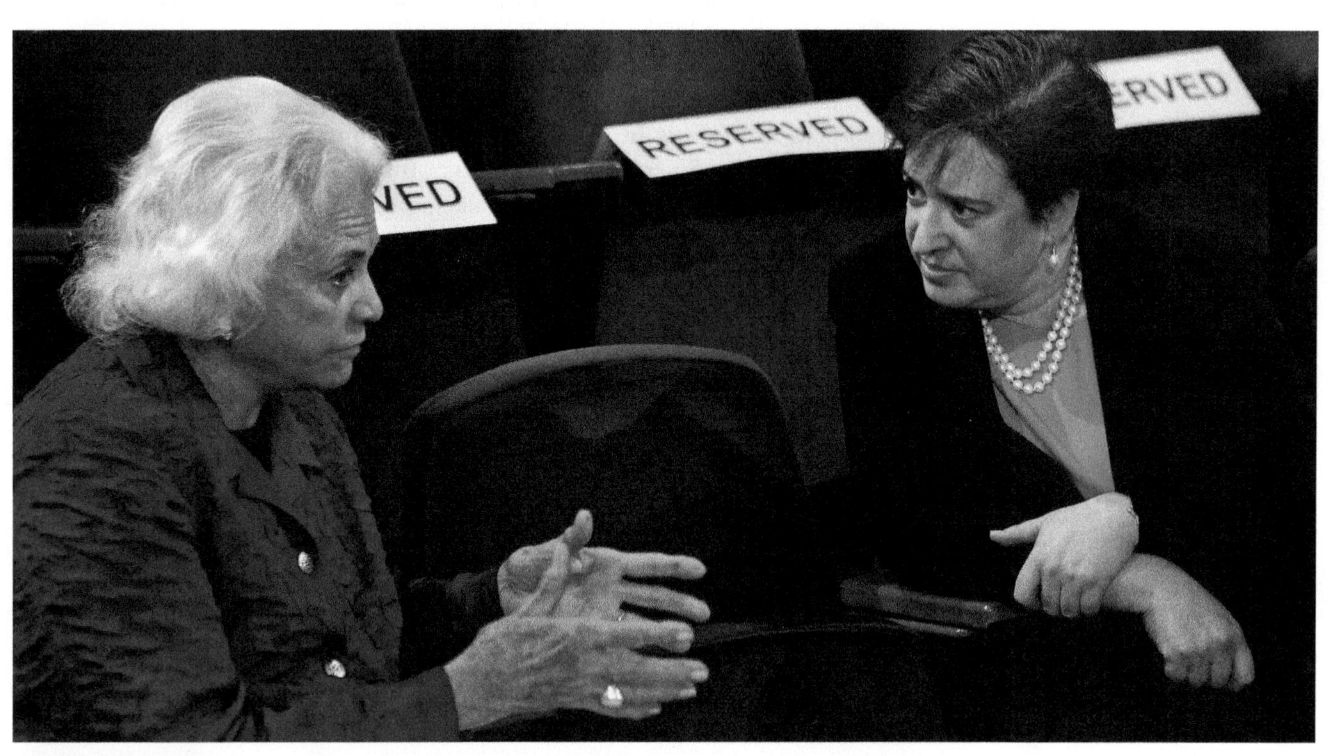

WHY ARE SUPREME COURT CLERKSHIPS IMPORTANT?

Supreme Court clerkships are awarded to a small number of elite law school graduates each year. In addition to providing valuable experience at the Court, clerkships can open doors to opportunities in government and private practice. Justice Elena Kagan (right, seated with former Justice Sandra Day O'Connor) served as a law clerk to Justice Thurgood Marshall. She later went on to serve as White House counsel, Harvard Law School dean, solicitor general, and, ultimately, Supreme Court justice.

9.1

9.2

9.3

9.4

9.5

9.6

solicitor general
The fourth-ranking member of the Department of Justice; responsible for handling nearly all appeals on behalf of the U.S. government to the Supreme Court.

amicus curiae
"Friend of the court"; *amici* may file briefs or even appear to argue their interests orally before the court.

number of clerks has had many interesting ramifications for the Court. As the number of clerks has grown, so has the length of the Court's written opinions.[24]

☐ How Does a Case Survive the Process?

It can be difficult to determine why the Court decides to hear a particular case. The Court does not offer reasons, and "the standards by which the justices decide to grant or deny review are highly personalized and necessarily discretionary," noted former Chief Justice Earl Warren.[25] Political scientists nonetheless have attempted to determine the characteristics of the cases the Court accepts. Among the cues are the following:

- The federal government is the party asking for review.
- The case involves conflict among the courts of appeals.
- The case presents a civil rights or civil liberties question.
- The case involves the ideological or policy preferences of the justices.
- The case has significant social or political interest, as evidenced by the presence of interest group *amicus curiae* briefs.

FEDERAL GOVERNMENT One of the most important cues for predicting whether the Court will hear a case is the solicitor general's position. The **solicitor general**, appointed by the president, is the fourth-ranking member of the Department of Justice and is responsible for handling nearly all appeals on behalf of the U.S. government to the Supreme Court. The solicitor's staff resembles a small, specialized law firm within the Department of Justice. But, because this office has such a special relationship with the Supreme Court, even having a suite of offices within the Supreme Court building, the solicitor general often is called the Court's "ninth and a half member."[26] Moreover, the office of the solicitor general, on behalf of the U.S. government, appears as a party or as an ***amicus curiae,*** or friend of the court, in more than 50 percent of the cases heard by the Court each term.

This special relationship helps to explain the overwhelming success the solicitor general's office enjoys before the Supreme Court. The Court generally accepts 70 to 80 percent of cases in which the U.S. government is the petitioning party, compared with about 5 percent of all others.[27] But, because of this special relationship, the solicitor general often ends up playing two conflicting roles: representing in Court both the president's policy interests and the broader interests of the United States. At times, solicitors find these two roles difficult to reconcile. Former Solicitor General Rex E. Lee (1981–1985), for example, noted that on more than one occasion he refused to make arguments in Court that had been advanced by the Reagan administration (a stand that ultimately forced him to resign from his position).[28]

CONFLICT AMONG THE COURTS OF APPEALS Conflict among the lower courts is another reason justices take cases. When interpretations of constitutional or federal law are involved, justices seem to want consistency throughout the federal court system. Often these conflicts occur when important civil rights or civil liberties questions arise. Political scientists have noted that justices' ideological leanings play a role.[29] It is not uncommon to see conservative justices voting to hear cases to overrule liberal lower court decisions, or vice versa. Justices also take cases when several circuit courts disagree over a main issue.

INTEREST GROUP PARTICIPATION A quick way for justices to gauge the ideological ramifications of a particular civil rights or liberties case is by the nature and amount of interest group participation. Richard C. Cortner has noted that "Cases do not arrive on the doorstep of the Supreme Court like orphans in the night."[30] Instead, most cases heard by the Supreme Court involve interest group participation. This participation may come in a number of forms.

Well-funded liberal groups, such as the American Civil Liberties Union, People for the American Way, or the NAACP Legal Defense and Educational Fund, and conservative groups, including the Washington Legal Foundation, Concerned Women for America, and the American Center for Law and Justice, routinely sponsor cases before the Supreme Court. Sponsorship implies that a group has helped to devise the legal strategy, pay the costs of litigation, and shepherd the case through the court system. It can be very costly and time-consuming.

Other groups participate as *amicus curiae*, or a friend of the Court. *Amicus* participation has increased dramatically since the 1970s. Because litigation is so expensive, few individuals have the money, time, or interest to sponsor a case all the way to the U.S. Supreme Court. All sorts of interest groups, then, find that joining ongoing cases through *amicus* briefs is a useful way to advance their policy preferences. Major cases addressing issues of great national importance, such as campaign finance, health care, or affirmative action attract large numbers of *amicus* briefs as part of interest groups' efforts to lobby the judiciary and bring about desired political objectives (see Table 9.6).[31]

The *amicus curiae* briefs filed by interested parties, especially interest groups or other parties potentially affected by the outcome of the case, often echo or expand the positions of both parties in a case and often provide justices with additional information about the potential consequences of a case. Research by political scientists has found that "not only does [an *amicus*] brief in favor of *certiorari* significantly improve the chances of a case being accepted, but two, three, and four briefs improve the chances even more."[32] Clearly, it's the more the merrier, whether the briefs are filed for or against granting review.

Finally, interest groups also support litigants' efforts by holding practice oral arguments during mock court sessions. In these sessions, the lawyer who will argue the case

TABLE 9.6 WHICH GROUPS PARTICIPATED AS *AMICUS CURIAE* IN *CITIZENS UNITED* V. *FEC* (2010)?

For the Petitioner (Committee for Truth in Politics)		
Alliance Defense Fund	Cato Institute	Michigan Chamber of Commerce
American Civil Liberties Union	Center for Competitive Politics	National Rifle Association
American Civil Rights Union	Center for Constitutional Jurisprudence	Pacific Legal Foundation
AFL-CIO	Fidelis Center	Reporters Committee for Freedom of the Press
American Justice Partnership	Former FEC Commissioners	Senator Mitch McConnell
California Broadcasters Association	Free Speech Defense & Education Fund	Seven Former Chairmen and One Former Commissioner of the Federal Election Commission
California First Amendment Coalition	Institute for Justice	U.S. Chamber of Commerce
Campaign Finance Scholars	Judicial Watch	Wyoming Liberty Group et al.
For the Respondent (Center for Political Accountability et al.)		
American Independent Business Alliance	Justice at Stake	Norman Ornstein
Campaign Legal Center et al.	League of Women Voters	Rep. Chris Van Hollen et al.
Center for Independent Media et al.	Program on Corporations, Law & Democracy et al.	Senator John McCain et al.
Committee for Economic Development	Public Good	The Sunlight Foundation
Democratic National Committee		
For Neither Party		
Former Officials of the American Civil Liberties Union	Independent Sector	Montana et al.
Hachette Book Group, Inc., and HarperCollins Publishers L.L.C.		

9.1

9.2

9.3

9.4

9.5

9.6

before the justices participates in several complete rehearsals, with prominent lawyers and law professors role playing the various justices.

☐ Hearing and Deciding the Case

Once the Court accepts a case for review, a flurry of activity begins. Lawyers on both sides of the case prepare their written arguments for submission to the Court. In these briefs, lawyers cite prior case law and make arguments regarding why the Court should find in favor of their client.

ORAL ARGUMENTS After the Court accepts a case and each side has submitted briefs and *amicus* briefs, oral argument takes place. The Supreme Court's annual term begins the first Monday in October, as it has since the late 1800s, and generally runs through mid-June. Justices hear oral arguments from the beginning of the term until early April. Special cases, such as *U.S.* v. *Nixon* (1974)—which involved President Richard M. Nixon's refusal to turn over tapes of Oval Office conversations to a special prosecutor investigating a break-in at the Democratic Party headquarters in the Watergate complex—have been heard even later in the year.[33] During the term, "sittings," periods of about two weeks in which cases are heard, alternate with "recesses," also about two weeks long. Justices usually hear oral arguments Monday through Wednesday.

Generally, only the immediate parties in the case take part in oral argument, although it is not uncommon for the U.S. solicitor general or one of his or her deputies to make an appearance to argue orally as an *amicus curiae*. Oral argument at the Court is fraught with time-honored tradition and ceremony. At precisely ten o'clock every morning when the Court is in session, the Court marshal, dressed in a formal morning coat, emerges to intone "Oyez! Oyez! Oyez!" as the nine justices emerge from behind a reddish-purple velvet curtain to take their places on the raised and slightly angled bench. The chief justice sits in the middle. The remaining justices sit to the left and right, alternating in seniority.

Almost all attorneys are allotted one half-hour to present their cases, including the time required to answer questions from the bench. As a lawyer approaches the mahogany lectern, a green light goes on, indicating that the attorney's time has begun. A white light flashes when five minutes remain. When a red light goes on, Court practice mandates that counsel stop immediately. One famous piece of Court lore told to all attorneys concerns a counsel who continued talking and reading from his prepared argument after the red light went on. When he looked up, he found an empty bench—the justices had risen quietly and departed while he continued to talk. On another occasion, Chief Justice Charles Evans Hughes stopped a leader of the New York Bar in the middle of the word "if."

Although many Court watchers have tried to figure out how a particular justice will vote based on the questioning at oral argument, most researchers find that the nature and number of questions asked do not help much in predicting the outcome of a case. Nevertheless, oral argument has several important functions. First, it is the only opportunity for even a small portion of the public (who may attend the hearings) and the press to observe the workings of the Court. Second, it assures lawyers that the justices have heard the parties' arguments, and it forces lawyers to focus on arguments believed important by the justices. Last, it provides the Court with additional information, especially concerning the Court's broader political role, an issue not usually addressed in written briefs. For example, the justices can ask how many people might be affected by its decision or where the Court (and country) would be heading if a case were decided in a particular way. Justice Stephen Breyer also notes that oral arguments are a good way for the justices to try to highlight certain issues for other justices.

THE CONFERENCE AND THE VOTE The justices meet in closed conference twice a week when the Court is hearing oral arguments. Since the ascendancy of Chief Justice Roger B. Taney to the Court in 1836, the justices have begun each conference session with a round of handshaking. Once the door to the conference room closes, no others

Take a Closer Look

The Supreme Court hears oral argument in most cases in which it reaches a final decision. Scholars have found that oral argument serves a number of important functions. For example, it provides an opportunity for the justices to highlight important case themes and to ask questions about the impact of a case that go beyond what is detailed in the party or *amicus curiae* briefs. Review the illustration of arguments before the Supreme Court during one of the 2012 cases that decided the constitutionality of the health care reform bill.

No cameras are allowed in the Supreme Court during oral arguments. Thus, we have only illustrations of what oral arguments look like in our nation's highest court.

The justices are seated on a curved bench at the front of the courtroom in order of seniority. The chief justice sits in the center, with the most senior associate justice at his right hand side. The second most senior associate justice sits on the chief's left hand side, and so on.

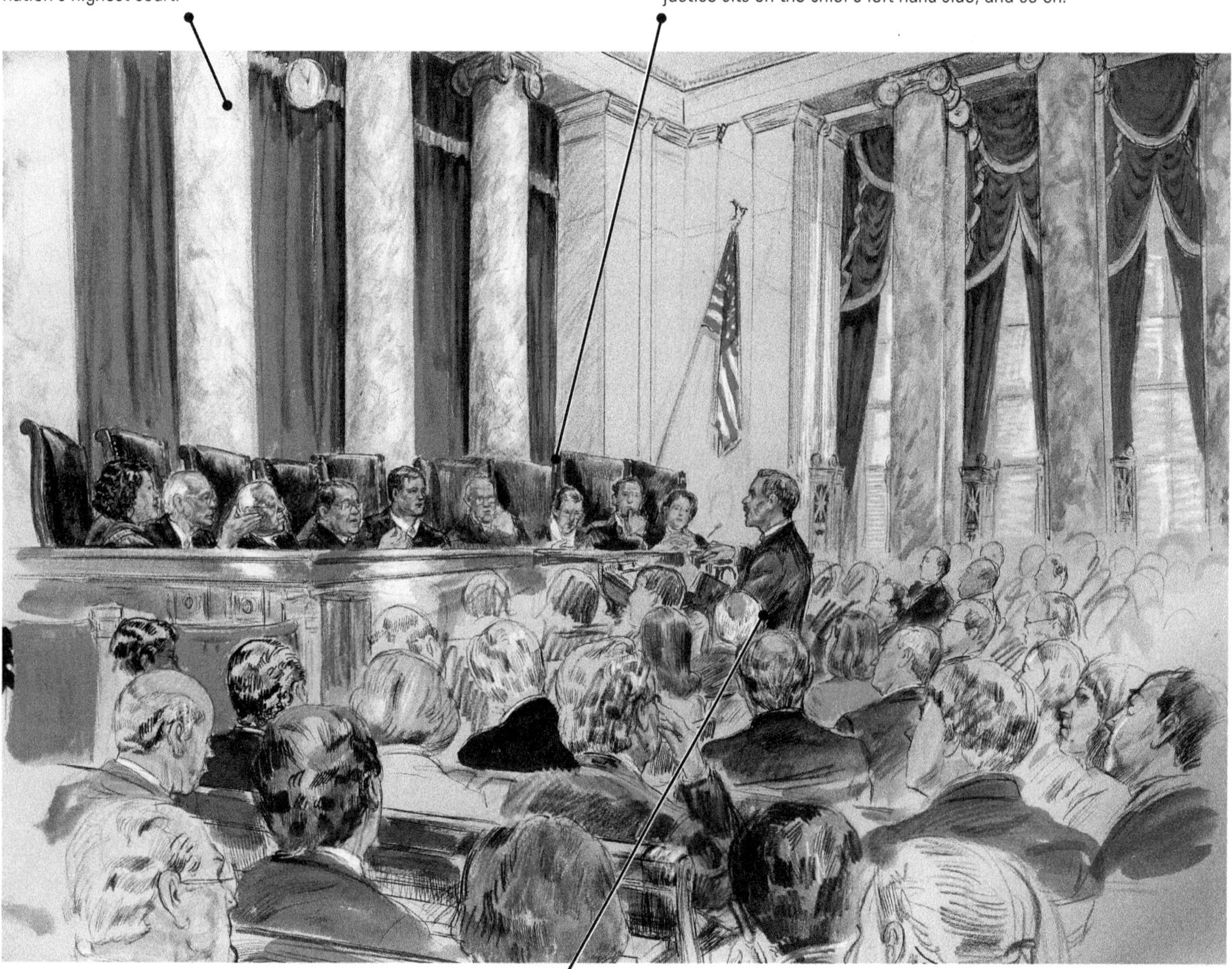

Lawyers are typically allowed to present thirty minutes of oral argument before the Court. However, this time is usually more like a question- and-answer session with the justices than a prepared speech.

CRITICAL THINKING QUESTIONS

1. Why do oral arguments remain important to the Court? How might a discussion between the justices and the parties' attorneys advance and improve judges' decision making?
2. How might the attorney representing a party in a case affect the case's outcome?
3. Should the Supreme Court allow cameras and video recordings in the courtroom? Why or why not?

are allowed to enter. The justice with the least seniority acts as the doorkeeper for the other eight, communicating with those waiting outside to fill requests for documents, water, and any other necessities.

Conferences highlight the importance and power of the chief justice, who presides over them and makes the initial presentation of each case. Each individual justice then discusses the case in order of his or her seniority on the Court, with the most senior justice speaking next. Most accounts of the decision-making process reveal that at this point some justices try to change the minds of others, but that most enter the conference room with a clear idea of how they will vote on each case.

During the Rehnquist Court, the justices generally voted at the same time they discussed each case, with each justice speaking only once. Initial conference votes were not final, and justices were allowed to change their minds before final votes were taken later. The Roberts Court is much more informal than the Rehnquist Court. The justices' regular conferences now last longer and, unlike the conferences headed by Rehnquist, Roberts encourages discussion.[34]

WRITING OPINIONS After the Court has reached a decision in conference, the justices must formulate a formal opinion of the Court. If the chief justice is in the majority, he selects the justice who will write the opinion. This privilege enables him to wield tremendous power and is a very important strategic decision; the author of the decision may determine the tone and content of the Court's opinion. If the chief justice is in the minority, the assignment falls to the most senior justice in the majority.

The opinion of the Court can take several different forms. Most decisions are reached by a majority opinion written by one member of the Court to reflect the views of at least five justices. This opinion usually sets out the legal reasoning justifying the decision, and this legal reasoning becomes a precedent for deciding future cases. The reasoning behind any decision is often as important as the outcome. Under the system of *stare decisis,* both are likely to be relied on as precedent later by lower courts confronted with cases involving similar issues.

In the process of creating the final opinion of the Court, informal caucusing and negotiation often take place, as justices may hold out for word changes or other modifications as a condition of their continued support of the majority opinion. This negotiation process can lead to divisions in the Court's majority. When this occurs, the Court may be forced to decide cases by plurality opinions, which attract the support of three or four justices. While these decisions do not have the precedential value of majority opinions, they nonetheless have been used by the Court to decide many major cases. Justices who agree with the outcome of the case, but not with the legal rationale for the decision, may file concurring opinions to express their differing approach.

Justices who do not agree with the outcome of a case file dissenting opinions. Although these opinions have little direct legal value, they can be an important indicator of legal thought on the Court and are an excellent platform for justices to note their personal and legal disagreements with other members of the Court. Justice Antonin Scalia is often noted for writing particularly stinging dissents.

Judicial Philosophy and Decision Making

9.5 Analyze the factors that influence judicial decision making.

Justices do not make decisions in a vacuum. Principles of *stare decisis* dictate that the justices follow the law of previous cases in deciding cases at hand. But, a variety of legal and extra-legal factors have also been found to affect Supreme Court decision making.

☐ Judicial Philosophy, Original Intent, and Ideology

One of the primary issues concerning judicial decision making focuses on judicial philosophy, particularly what is called the activism/restraint debate. Advocates of **judicial restraint** argue that courts should allow the decisions of other branches to stand, even when they offend a judge's own principles. Restraintists defend their position by asserting that unelected judges make up the federal courts, which renders the judicial branch the least democratic branch of government. Consequently, the courts should defer policy making to other branches of government as much as possible.

Restraintists refer to *Roe* v. *Wade* (1973), the case that liberalized abortion laws, as a classic example of **judicial activism** run amok. They maintain that the Court should have deferred policy making on this sensitive issue to the states or to the elected branches of the federal government.

Advocates of judicial restraint generally agree that judges should be **strict constructionists**; that is, they should interpret the Constitution as the Framers wrote and originally intended it. They argue that in determining the constitutionality of a statute or policy, the Court should rely on the explicit meanings of the clauses in the document, which can be clarified by looking at founding documents.

Advocates of judicial activism contend that judges should use their power broadly to further justice. Activists argue that it is appropriate for courts to correct injustices committed by other branches of government. Implicit in this argument is the notion that courts need to protect oppressed minorities.[35]

Although judicial activists are often considered politically liberal and restraintists politically conservative, in recent years a new brand of conservative judicial activism has become prevalent. Liberal activist decisions often expanded the rights of political and legal minorities. But, conservative activist judges view their positions as an opportunity to issue broad rulings that impose their own political beliefs and policies on the country at large.

judicial restraint
A philosophy of judicial decision making that posits courts should allow the decisions of other branches of government to stand, even when they offend a judge's own principles.

judicial activism
A philosophy of judicial decision making that posits judges should use their power broadly to further justice.

strict constructionist
An approach to constitutional interpretation that emphasizes interpreting the Constitution as it was originally written and intended by the Framers.

☐ Public Opinion

Many political scientists have examined the role of public opinion in Supreme Court decision making. Not only do the justices read legal briefs and hear oral arguments, but they also read newspapers, watch TV, and have some knowledge of public opinion—especially on controversial issues.

Whether or not public opinion actually influences justices (see Table 9.7), it can act as a check on the power of the courts. Activist periods on the Supreme Court generally have corresponded to periods of social or economic crisis. For example, in the early, crisis-ridden years of the republic, the Marshall Court supported a strong national

TABLE 9.7 DO SUPREME COURT DECISIONS ALIGN WITH THE VIEWS OF THE AMERICAN PUBLIC?

Issues	Case	Court Decision	Public Opinion Before Decision
Is the death penalty constitutional?	*Gregg* v. *Georgia* (1976)	Yes	Yes (72% favor)
Should homosexual relations between consenting adults be legal?	*Lawrence* v. *Texas* (2003)	Yes	Maybe (50% favor)
Should state and local governments be able to pass laws that ban the possession or sale of handguns?	*McDonald* v. *City of Chicago* (2010)	No	Maybe (50% oppose)
Is donating money a form of free speech protected by the First Amendment?	*Citizens United* v. *FEC* (2010)	Yes	Yes (62% favor)
Is the Patient Protection and Affordable Care Act constitutional?	*National Federation of Independent Businesses* v. *Sebelius* (2012)	Yes	No (48% oppose)

SOURCE: Lexis-Nexis RPOLL.

Explore on MyPoliSciLab

Who Are the Activist Judges?

In practice, an activist judge—liberal or conservative—is one who overturns a law as unconstitutional. Even though the current Roberts Court has handed down fewer decisions than earlier courts, 19 out of 408 decisions declared laws unconstitutional between 2005 and 2010. The data below shows which judges are most responsible for these controversial decisions.

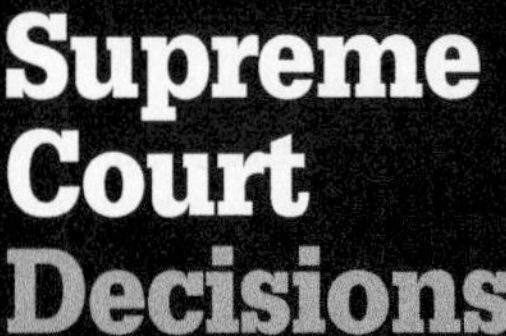

Supreme Court Decisions

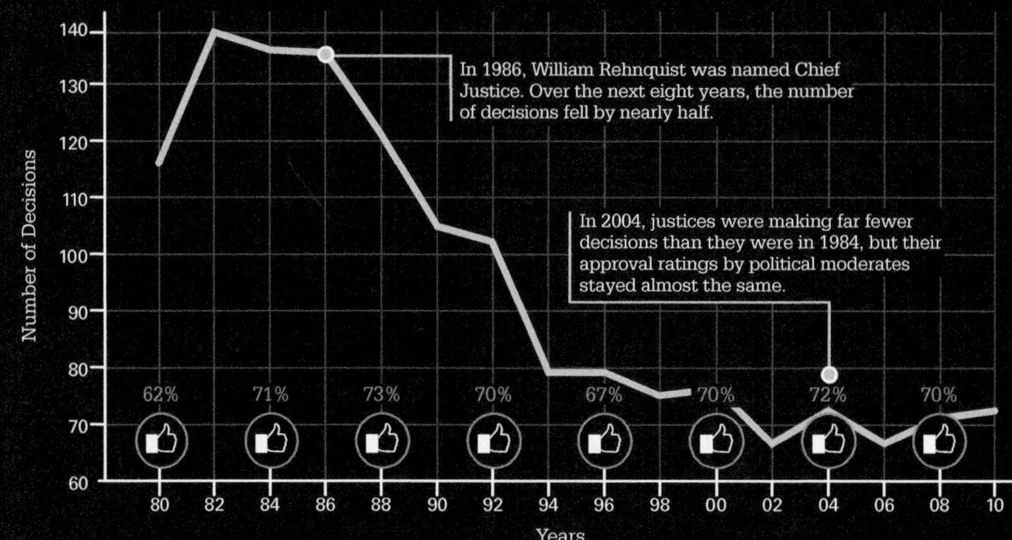

In 1986, William Rehnquist was named Chief Justice. Over the next eight years, the number of decisions fell by nearly half.
In 2004, justices were making far fewer decisions than they were in 1984, but their approval ratings by political moderates stayed almost the same.

Judicial Activism on the Roberts Court

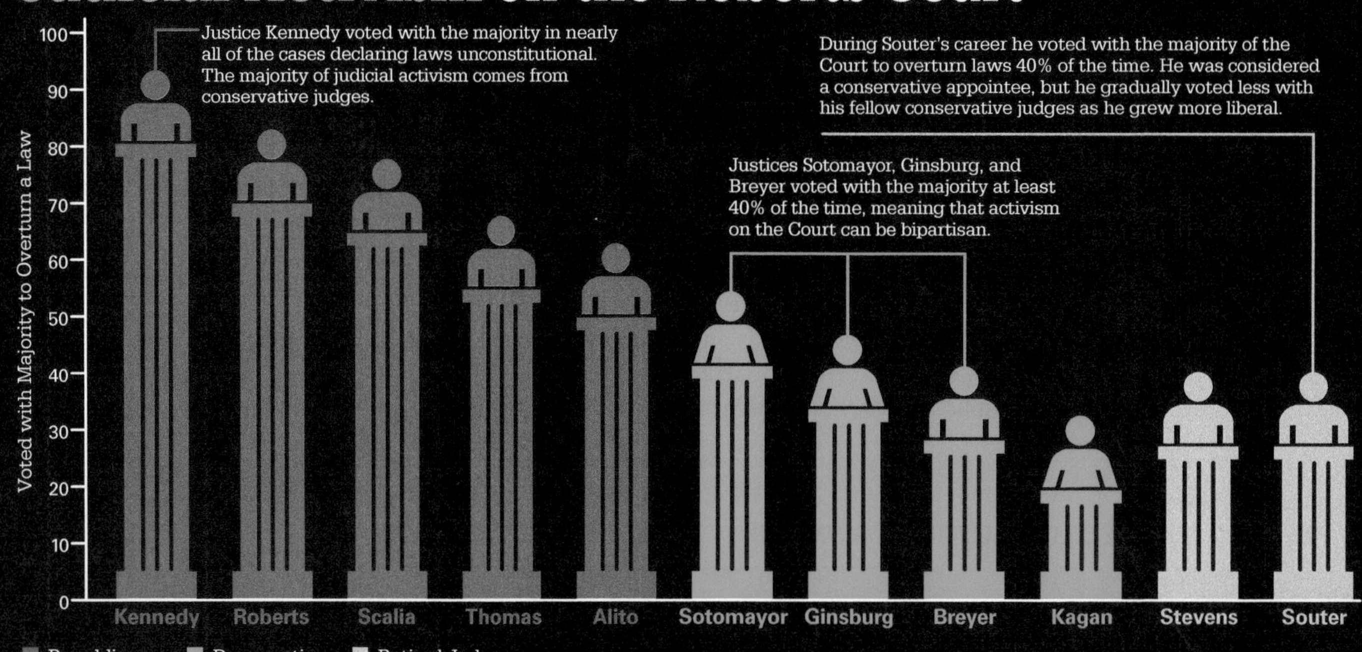

Voted with Majority to Overturn a Law
100
90
80
70
60
50
40
30
20
10
0
Justice Kennedy voted with the majority in nearly all of the cases declaring laws unconstitutional. The majority of judicial activism comes from conservative judges.
During Souter's career he voted with the majority of the Court to overturn laws 40% of the time. He was considered a conservative appointee, but he gradually voted less with his fellow conservative judges as he grew more liberal.
Justices Sotomayor, Ginsburg, and Breyer voted with the majority at least 40% of the time, meaning that activism on the Court can be bipartisan.
Kennedy
Roberts
Scalia
Thomas
Alito
Sotomayor
Ginsburg
Breyer
Kagan
Stevens
Souter
Republican
Democratic
Retired Judges

SOURCE: Data from the United States Supreme Court and the General Social Survey, 1980-2010.

Investigate Further

Concept Why is judicial activism controversial? By declaring a law unconstitutional, judicial activism overturns legislation that is a product of the democratic process. It sets precedents for controversial or divisive issues, and it limits future legislation.

Connection Does judicial activism affect public confidence? Over two-thirds of American moderates continued to express confidence in the Court, even as it handed down fewer decisions and became more conservative in the 2000s.

Cause Is judicial activism conservative or liberal? On the Roberts Court, the decisions that overturn laws can be bipartisan, but they are usually decided by the conservative justices.

government, much to the chagrin of a series of pro-states' rights Democratic-Republican presidents. Similarly, the Court capitulated to political pressures and public opinion when, after 1936, it reversed many of its earlier decisions that had blocked President Franklin D. Roosevelt's New Deal programs.

The courts, especially the Supreme Court, also can be the direct target of public opinion. When *Webster* v. *Reproductive Health Services* (1989) was about to come before the Supreme Court, unprecedented lobbying of the Court took place as groups and individuals on both sides of the abortion issue marched and sent appeals to the Court. Mail at the Court, which usually averaged about 1,000 pieces a day, rose to an astronomical 46,000 pieces per day, virtually paralyzing normal lines of communication.

The Supreme Court also appears to affect public opinion. Political scientists have found that the Court's initial rulings on controversial issues such as abortion or capital punishment positively influence public opinion in the direction of the Court's opinion. However, this research also finds that subsequent decisions have little effect.[36]

The Court also is dependent on the public for its prestige as well as for compliance with its decisions. In times of war and other emergencies, for example, the Court frequently has decided cases in ways that commentators have attributed to the sway of public opinion and political exigencies. In *Korematsu* v. *U.S.* (1944), for example, the high court upheld the obviously unconstitutional internment of Japanese, Italian, and German American citizens during World War II.[37] Moreover, Chief Justice William H. Rehnquist once suggested that the Court's restriction on presidential authority in *Youngstown Sheet & Tube Co.* v. *Sawyer* (1952), which invalidated President Harry S Truman's seizure of the nation's steel mills, was largely attributable to Truman's unpopularity in light of the Korean War.[38]

Public confidence in the Court, as with other institutions of government, has ebbed and flowed. Public support for the Court was highest after the Court issued *U.S.* v. *Nixon* (1974).[39] At a time when Americans lost faith in the presidency because of the Watergate scandal, they could at least look to the Supreme Court to do the right thing. Although the percentage of Americans with confidence in the courts has fluctuated over time, in 2012, an all-time low of 52 percent of Americans approved of the way the Supreme Court was doing its job.[40]

Toward Reform: Power, Policy Making, and the Court

9.6 Assess the role of the Supreme Court in the policy-making process.

ll judges, whether they recognize it or not, make policy. The decisions of the Supreme Court, in particular, have a tremendous impact on American politics and policy. Over the past 250 years, the justices have helped to codify many of the major rights and liberties guaranteed to the citizens of the United States. Although justices need the cooperation of the executive and legislative branches to implement and enforce a good number of their decisions, it is safe to say that many policies we take for granted in the United States would not have come to fruition without support of the Supreme Court.[41] These include the right to privacy and equal rights for African Americans, women, Hispanics, gays and lesbians, and other minority groups.

Several Courts have played particularly notable roles in the development of the judiciary's policy-making role. As discussed earlier in the chapter, the Marshall Court

9.1

9.2

9.3

9.4

9.5

9.6

played an important role in establishing the role and power of the Supreme Court, including the power of judicial review in *Marbury* v. *Madison* (1803). The Warren Court decided a number of civil rights cases that broadly expanded civil and political rights. These decisions drew a great deal of criticism but played a major role in broadening public understanding of the Court as a policy maker. The Rehnquist Court made numerous decisions related to federalism, which caused observers to take note of the Court's ability to referee conflicts between the federal government and the states. And, the Roberts Court reversed the general trend of the Court's agreement with executive actions during times of war by finding in 2008 that the Bush administration's denial of *habeas corpus* rights to prisoners being held at Guantanamo Bay was an unconstitutional exercise of presidential power.[42]

☐ Policy Making

One measure of the power of the courts and their ability to make policy is that more than one hundred federal laws have been declared unconstitutional. Although many of these laws have not been particularly significant, others have. In 2012, the Roberts Court struck down portions of an Arizona state law regulating immigration on the grounds that it violated the Constitution's supremacy clause.[43]

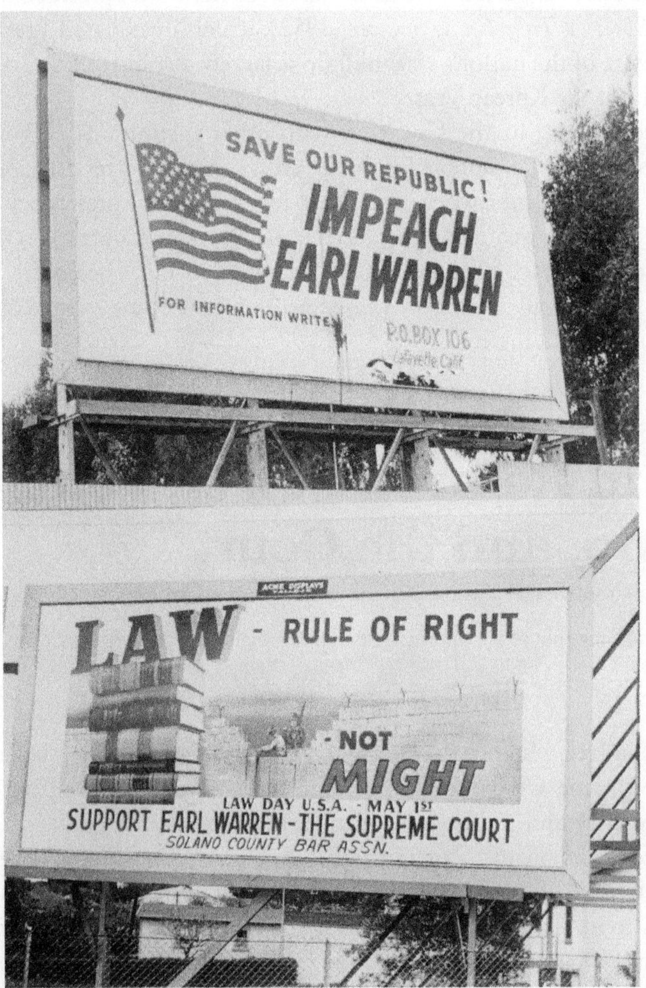

DO UNPOPULAR SUPREME COURT RULINGS THREATEN THE NATION?

The Warren Court's broad expansions of civil and political rights led to a great deal of criticism, including a movement to impeach the chief justice. Here, two California billboards present contrasting views of Warren's performance.

Another measure of the policy-making power of the Supreme Court is its ability to overrule itself. Although the Court generally abides by the informal rule of *stare decisis,* by one count, it has overruled itself in more than 200 cases.[44] *Brown* v. *Board of Education* (1954), for example, overruled *Plessy* v. *Ferguson* (1896), thereby reversing years of constitutional interpretation concluding that racial segregation was not a violation of the Constitution. Moreover, in the past few years, the Court repeatedly has reversed earlier decisions in the areas of criminal defendants' rights, reproductive rights, and free speech, revealing its powerful role in determining national policy.

A measure of the growing power of the federal courts is the degree to which they now handle issues that had been considered political questions more appropriately settled by the other branches of government. Prior to 1962, for example, the Court refused to hear cases questioning the size (and population) of congressional districts, no matter how unequal they were.[45] The boundary of a legislative district was considered a political question. Then, in *Baker* v. *Carr* (1962), Justice William Brennan, writing for the Court, concluded that simply because a case involved a political issue, it did not necessarily involve a political question. This opened the floodgates to cases involving a variety of issues that the Court formerly had declined to address.[46]

judicial implementation
How and whether judicial decisions are translated into actual public policies affecting more than the immediate parties to a lawsuit.

☐ Implementing Court Decisions

President Andrew Jackson, annoyed about a particular decision handed down by the Marshall Court, is alleged to have said, "John Marshall has made his decision; now let him enforce it." Jackson's statement raises a question: how do Supreme Court rulings translate into public policy? In fact, although judicial decisions carry legal and even moral authority, all courts must rely on other units of government to carry out their directives. If the president or members of Congress, for example, do not like a particular Supreme Court ruling, they can underfund programs needed to implement a decision or seek only lax enforcement. **Judicial implementation** refers to how and whether judicial decisions are translated into actual public policies affecting more than the immediate parties to the lawsuit.

How well a decision is implemented often depends on how well crafted or popular it is. Hostile reaction in the South to *Brown* v. *Board of Education* (1954) and the absence of precise guidelines to implement the decision meant that the ruling went largely unenforced for years. The *Brown* experience also highlights how much the Supreme Court needs the support of both federal and state courts as well as other governmental agencies to carry out its judgments. For example, you probably graduated from high school after 1992, when the Supreme Court ruled that public middle school and high school graduations could not include a prayer, yet your own commencement ceremony may have included one.[47]

The implementation of judicial decisions involves what political scientists call an implementing population and a consumer population.[48] The implementing population consists of those people responsible for carrying out a decision. Depending on the policy and issues in question, the implementing population can include lawyers, judges, public officials, police officers and police departments, hospital administrators, government agencies, and corporations. In the case of school prayer, the implementing population could include teachers, school administrators, or school boards. The consumer population consists of those people who might be directly affected by a decision—in this case, students and parents.

For effective implementation of a judicial decision, the first requirement is for members of the implementing population to show they understand the original decision. For example, the Supreme Court ruled in *Reynolds* v. *Sims* (1964) that every person should have an equally weighted vote in electing governmental representatives.[49] This "one person, one vote" rule might seem simple enough at first glance, but in practice it can be very difficult to understand. The implementing population in this case consists chiefly of state legislatures and local governments, which determine voting districts for federal, state, and local offices. If a state legislature draws districts in such a way that African American or Hispanic voters are spread thinly across a number of separate constituencies, the chances are slim that any particular district will elect a representative who is especially sensitive to minority concerns. Does that violate "equal representation"? (In practice, courts and the Department of Justice have intervened in many cases to ensure that elected officials would include minority representation, only ultimately to be overruled by the Supreme Court.)

The second requirement is that the implementing population actually must follow Court policy. Thus, when the Court ruled that men could not be denied admission to a state-sponsored nursing school, the implementing population—in this case, university administrators and the state board of regents governing the nursing school—had to enroll qualified male students.[50]

Implementation of judicial decisions is most likely to be smooth if a few highly visible public officials, such as the president or a governor, shoulder the responsibility of seeing to the task. By the same token, these officials also can thwart or impede judicial intentions. Recall, for example, the effect of Governor Orval Faubus's initial refusal to allow black children to attend all-white public schools in Little Rock, Arkansas.

The third requirement for implementation is for the consumer population to be aware of the rights that a decision grants or denies them. Teenagers seeking an abortion, for example, are consumers of the Supreme Court's decisions on abortion and contraception. They need to know that most states require them to inform their parents of their intention to have an abortion or to get parental permission to do so. Similarly, criminal defendants and their lawyers are consumers of Court decisions and need to know, for instance, the implications of recent Court decisions for evidence presented at trial, sentencing guidelines, and prison reform.

Review the Chapter

 **Listen** to **Chapter 9** on **MyPoliSciLab**

Roots of the Federal Judiciary

9.1 Trace the development of the federal judiciary and the origins of judicial review, p. 267.

Many Framers viewed the judicial branch of government as little more than a minor check on the other two branches, ignoring Anti-Federalist concerns about an unelected judiciary and its potential for tyranny. The Judiciary Act of 1789 established the basic federal court system we have today. It was the Marshall Court (1801–1835), however, that interpreted the Constitution to include the Court's major power, that of judicial review.

The Federal Court System

9.2 Explain the organization of the federal court system, p. 271.

The federal court system is made up of constitutional and legislative courts. Federal district courts, courts of appeals, and the Supreme Court are constitutional courts.

How Federal Court Judges Are Selected

9.3 Outline the criteria and process used to select federal court judges, p. 276.

District court, court of appeals, and Supreme Court justices are nominated by the president and must also win Senate confirmation. Important criteria for selection include competence, ideology, rewards, pursuit of political support, religion, race, ethnicity, and gender.

The Supreme Court Today

9.4 Evaluate the Supreme Court's process for accepting, hearing, and deciding cases, p. 282.

Several factors influence the Court's decision to hear a case. Not only must the Court have jurisdiction, but at least four justices must vote to hear the case. Cases with certain characteristics are most likely to be heard. Once a case is set for review, briefs and *amicus curiae* briefs are filed and oral argument is scheduled. The justices meet in conference after oral argument to discuss the case; votes are taken; and opinions are written, circulated, and then announced.

Judicial Philosophy and Decision Making

9.5 Analyze the factors that influence judicial decision making, p. 290.

Judges do not make decisions in a vacuum. In addition to following the law of previous cases, other factors, including personal philosophy and ideology, have an extraordinary impact on how judges decide cases. Public opinion may also play a role in some cases.

Toward Reform: Power, Policy Making, and the Court

9.6 Assess the role of the Supreme Court in the policy-making process, p. 293.

The Supreme Court is an important participant in the policy-making process. The power to interpret laws gives the Court a tremendous policy-making power never envisioned by the Framers. However, if the president or members of Congress oppose a particular Supreme Court ruling, they can underfund programs needed to implement a decision or seek only lax enforcement.

Learn the Terms

 **Study** and **Review** the **Flashcards**

amicus curiae, p. 286
appellate court, p. 271
appellate jurisdiction, p. 268
brief, p. 274
constitutional courts, p. 271
judicial activism, p. 291
judicial implementation, p. 295
judicial restraint, p. 291
judicial review, p. 270
Judiciary Act of 1789, p. 268
jurisdiction, p. 267
legislative courts, p. 271
Marbury v. *Madison* (1803), p. 271
original jurisdiction, p. 267
precedent, p. 274
Rule of Four, p. 285
senatorial courtesy, p. 276
solicitor general, p. 286
stare decisis, p. 274
strict constructionist, p. 291
trial court, p. 271
writ of *certiorari*, p. 283

Test Yourself

Study and **Review** the **Practice Tests**

1. Which of the following is NOT one of Congress's constitutional powers over the judiciary?

- **a.** Authority to alter the Court's jurisdiction
- **b.** Impeach and remove federal judges
- **c.** Veto a Supreme Court decision
- **d.** Offer advice and consent on presidential appointments
- **e.** Propose constitutional amendments

2. Which of the following paved the way for the courts to become a co-equal branch?

- **a.** Writ of *certiorari*
- **b.** *McCulloch* v. *Maryland* (1819)
- **c.** The Judiciary Act of 1789
- **d.** Judicial review
- **e.** *Federalist No. 78*

3. Courts of original jurisdiction are most often known as:

- **a.** appellate courts.
- **b.** courts of appeals.
- **c.** trial courts.
- **d.** legislative courts.
- **e.** constitutional courts.

4. Which of the following types of courts handles the bulk of the caseload in the federal system?

- **a.** District courts
- **b.** Courts of appeals
- **c.** Special purpose courts
- **d.** Legislative courts
- **e.** Supreme Court

5. Which of the following is NOT true of the courts of appeals?

- **a.** Cases may be heard by multiple judges.
- **b.** Judges try to correct errors in law.
- **c.** They are the highest courts in the federal system.
- **d.** Judges hear no new testimony.
- **e.** Their decisions are binding only within their geographic confines.

6. According to the Constitution, who must offer advice and consent on a presidential appointment to the Supreme Court?

- **a.** Current justices
- **b.** Constituents
- **c.** President
- **d.** Senate
- **e.** House of Representatives

7. All of the following are criteria that would help get a case heard by the Supreme Court EXCEPT:

- **a.** The case presents a civil rights question.
- **b.** The federal government is the party asking for review.
- **c.** The case involves a conflict among the courts of appeals.
- **d.** The case has significant social or political issues.
- **e.** The case presents a lack of evidence.

8. What does it mean if the Court grants a petition for a writ of *certiorari*?

- **a.** They have decided to review a lower court's decision.
- **b.** They are throwing out a case.
- **c.** They have decided that a case is unconstitutional.
- **d.** They have reached a unanimous decision.
- **e.** The court cannot come to a clear decision.

9. Which of the following does NOT appear to affect Supreme Court justices' decisions?

- **a.** *Stare decisis*
- **b.** Political circumstances
- **c.** Judicial philosophy
- **d.** Public opinion
- **e.** Economic impact

10. Which of the following is the best way to measure the power of the courts in policy making?

- **a.** The number of cases heard
- **b.** How many days the court is in session
- **c.** How long justices serve on the court
- **d.** The number of laws declared unconstitutional
- **e.** Popularity of judicial decisions

Explore Further

Baird, Vanessa. *Answering the Call of the Court: How Justices and Litigants Set the Supreme Court Agenda.* Charlottesville: University of Virginia Press, 2008.

Baum, Lawrence. *Judges and Their Audiences: A Perspective on Judicial Behavior.* Princeton, NJ: Princeton University Press, 2005.

Bonneau, Chris W., and Melinda Gann Hall. *In Defense of Judicial Elections.* New York: Routledge, 2009.

Collins, Paul M., Jr. *Friends of the Supreme Court: Interest Groups and Decision Making.* New York: Oxford University Press, 2008.

Epstein, Lee, Jeffrey A. Segal, Harold J. Spaeth, and Thomas G. Walker. *The Supreme Court Compendium: Data, Decisions, and Developments,* 6th ed. Washington, DC: CQ Press, 2012.

Gibson, James L. *Electing Judges: The Surprising Effects of Campaigning on Judicial Legitimacy.* Chicago: University of Chicago Press, 2012.

Greenhouse, Linda. *The U.S. Supreme Court: A Very Short Introduction.* New York: Oxford University Press, 2012.

Hall, Kermit L., ed. *The Oxford Companion to the Supreme Court of the United States,* 2nd ed. New York: Oxford University Press, 2005.

Lazarus, Edward. *Closed Chambers: The First Eyewitness Account of the Epic Struggles Inside the Supreme Court.* New York: Times Books, 1998.

O'Brien, David M. *Storm Center: The Supreme Court in American Politics,* 9th ed. New York: Norton, 2012.

Perry, H. W. *Deciding to Decide: Agenda Setting in the United States Supreme Court,* reprint ed..Cambridge, MA: Harvard University Press, 2005.

Sunstein, Cass R., David Schkade, Lisa M. Ellman, and Andres Sawicki. *Are Judges Political? An Empirical Analysis of the Federal Judiciary.* Washington, DC: Brookings Institution, 2006.

Ward, Artemus, and David L. Weiden. *Sorcerer's Apprentices: 100 Years of Law Clerks at the United States Supreme Court.* New York: New York University Press, 2006.

Whittington, Keith E. *Political Foundations of Judicial Supremacy: The Presidency, the Supreme Court, and Constitutional Leadership in U.S. History.* Princeton, NJ: Princeton University Press, 2007.

Woodward, Bob, and Scott Armstrong. *The Brethren: Inside the Supreme Court,* 2nd reprint ed. New York: Avon, 2005.

To learn more about the U.S. Supreme Court and examine current cases on the Court's docket, go to **www.supremecourt.gov.**

To learn more about the workings of the U.S. justice system, go to the Department of Justice's Web site at **www.usdoj.gov.**

To learn more about the U.S. Senate Judiciary Committee and judicial nominations currently under review, go to the Senate's Web site at **www.senate.gov.**

To learn more about past and current U.S. Supreme Court cases, go to **www.oyez.org** to hear streaming audio of oral arguments before the Court.

10

Listen to Chapter 10 on MyPoliSciLab

Public Opinion and Political Socialization

In 1863, Abraham Lincoln proudly summarized American government as one "of the people, by the people, and for the people." Though this sentiment has always been true to some degree, our modern political landscape has given this old idea new perspective.

Today, we know more about what "the people" want from their government than ever before. Much of this knowledge comes from our increasing ability to collect representative data on aggregate public opinion. The tools available to pollsters, including the Internet, robocalls, and computer programs, make data collection, analysis, and dissemination easier than ever.

However, there can be dangerous consequences to having so much data. Just about anything can be proven—or disproven—with a public opinion poll. Moreover, the volume of polls conducted and information available about these studies makes them an attractive topic for news coverage. This phenomenon is especially prevalent during election season. And, while on one hand, it may be interesting to examine the relationship between events and citizens' evaluations of political leaders, on the other hand, constant reports of the results of the latest poll only serve to intensify the horse-race atmosphere of the campaign. More importantly, it may also distract from the true issues of the election and obscure citizens' understanding of the political process.

Consider, for example, a three-week period in September 2012. On August 31, 2012, a Gallup tracking poll reported that 48 percent of registered voters intended to vote for President Barack Obama; 45 percent supported the Republican candidate, Governor Mitt Romney. About a week

10.1 Trace the development of modern public opinion research, p. 303.

10.2 Describe the methods for conducting and analyzing different types of public opinion polls, p. 306.

10.3 Assess the potential shortcomings of polling, p. 312.

10.4 Analyze the process by which people form political opinions, p. 315.

10.5 Evaluate the effects of public opinion on politics, p. 321.

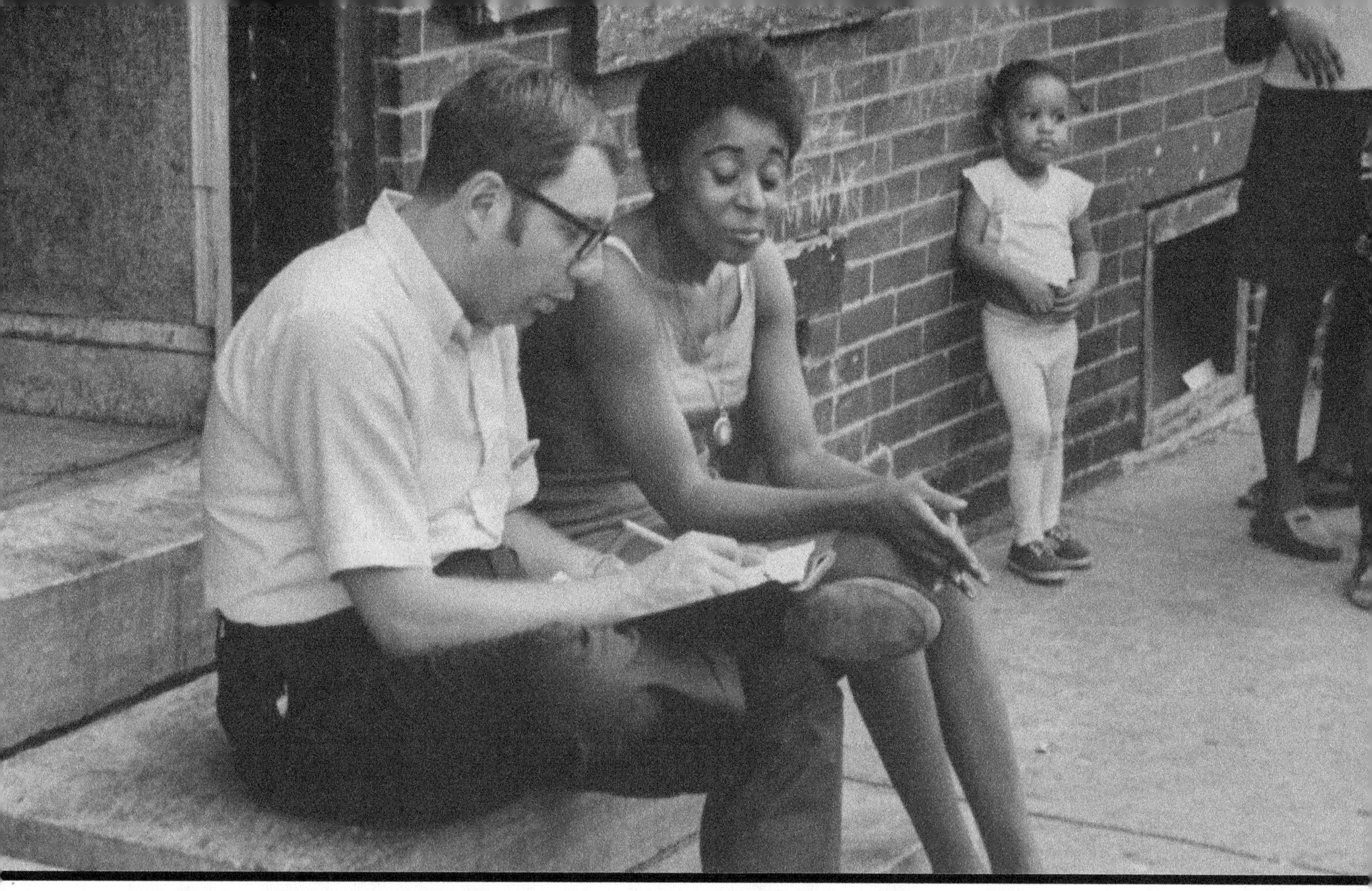

PUBLIC OPINION PLAYS AN IMPORTANT ROLE IN PRESIDENTIAL ELECTIONS Above, a Gallup Poll worker conducts face-to-face interviews during the 1968 presidential election. Below, pollsters use Google search results to track interest in the 2012 presidential candidates, Governor Mitt Romney and President Barack Obama.

MyPoliSciLab Videos

Watch on MyPoliSciLab

The Big Picture What do Americans think? Author Larry J. Sabato explains why public opinion polls may not be the most accurate way to learn how Americans feel about issues, and he reveals how experts can make pretty accurate guesses on how you will vote—without ever having met you.

The Basics How do people form opinions? In this video, we examine how we know what opinions the public holds, and how they come by those opinions. As we go along, you'll discover that Americans aren't always well-informed about government and policies, but that they share core values.

Are average folks informed about their government?

In Context How did the emergence of scientific polling in the twentieth century change our democracy? In this video, Columbia University political scientist Robert Y. Shapiro outlines the history of polling and the emergence of public opinion as a major factor in American politics.

Thinking Like a Political Scientist Uncover some of the new questions being asked by political scientists regarding public opinion. In this video, Columbia University political scientist Robert Y. Shapiro examines some of the new public opinion trends that are being researched.

In the Real World Should politicians listen more to their constituents (who may not be educated about all of the issues), or to their own sense of what is right and wrong? Hear real people weigh in on this question, and learn how presidents have dealt with it in the past.

So What? Does a good president listen to his people or to his principles? Author Larry J. Sabato discusses why presidents sometimes need to choose their gut over public opinion—especially because figuring out what the public wants is never an exact science.

later, on the heels of a successful Democratic Convention, President Obama
to 50 percent of registered voters. Obama's boost was short-lived. On Se
lowing the murders of U.S. Ambassador Christopher Stevens and two
Consulate in Libya, only 47 percent of registered voters said they would su
Obama in November.

In a close election such as 2012, these small shifts are often portrayed by the media dramatic sea changes in the tides of public opinion. And indeed, if these changes were real alterations of the entire population's beliefs, they could have been the difference between an Obama victory and a Romney victory. However, public opinion polls are based on a sample of the American public, and have a margin of error of plus or minus 4 percent. Thus, although the media made much of these shifting values, it is actually possible that public opinion did not change at all during this period. On Election Day, the final popular vote reflected a similarly small margin of victory in the popular vote. Although President Obama won a near landslide in the Electoral College, he won the popular vote by just 3 percent, securing 51 percent of the vote compared to Romney's 48 percent.

•••

In 1787, John Jay wrote glowingly of the sameness of the American people. He and the other authors of *The Federalist Papers* believed that Americans had more in common than not. Wrote Jay in *Federalist No. 2*, we are "one united people—a people descended from the same ancestors, speaking the same language, professing the same religion, attached to the same principles of government, very similar in manners and customs." Many of those who could vote in Jay's time were of English heritage; almost all were Christian. Moreover, most believed that certain rights—such as freedom of speech, association, and religion—were rights that could not be revoked. Jay also spoke of shared public opinion and of the need for a national government that reflected American ideals.

Today, however, Americans are more diverse, and the growth of modern public opinion research has helped us to better understand Americans' views on political issues and how our varying experiences, values, and heritage shape them. In part, this is attributable to the pervasiveness of polls. Not a week goes by that major cable news networks, major newspapers, foundations, or colleges and universities do not poll Americans on something—from views on political issues, such as the environment, race, and health care, to their emotions, including happiness and stress. Polling is so common now that the public needs the ability to interpret often-conflicting poll results. In this chapter, we explore how polls are conducted and analyzed, as well as how Americans' demographic and cultural experiences define public opinion.

Roots of Public Opinion Research

10.1 Trace the development of modern public opinion research.

t first glance, **public opinion** seems to be a straightforward concept: it is what the public thinks about a particular issue or set of issues at any point in time. In government and politics, for example, researchers measure citizens' views on candidates, political institutions, and policy proposals. Since the 1930s, governmental decision makers have relied heavily on **public opinion polls**—interviews with samples of citizens that estimate the feelings and beliefs of larger populations, such as all Americans or all women. According to George Gallup (1901–1983), an Iowan who is considered the founder of modern-day polling, polls have played a key role in defining issues of concern to the public, shaping administrative decisions, and helping "speed up the process of democracy" in the United States.[1]

Gallup further contended that leaders must constantly take public opinion—no matter how short-lived—into account. This practice does not mean that leaders

he public's view slavishly; it does mean, however, that they should
e appraisal of public opinion and consider it in reaching their deci-
may find this process challenging when public opinion appears

llup, as a pollster, undoubtedly had a vested interest in fostering
on polls, his sentiments accurately reflect the views of many
must f... ncerning the role of public opinion in governance. Some com-
ha... gue that the government should do what a majority of the public wants
. Others argue that the public as a whole doesn't have consistent day-to-day opinions on issues but that subgroups within the public often hold strong views on some issues. These pluralists believe that the government must allow for the expression of minority opinions and that democracy works best when different voices are allowed to fight it out in the public arena, echoing James Madison in *Federalist No. 10*.

straw poll
Unscientific survey used to gauge public opinion on a variety of issues and policies.

sample
A subset of the ... selected to be ... poses of pr...

The Earliest Public Opinion Research

As early as 1824, one Pennsylvania newspaper tried to predict the winner of that year's presidential contest, showing Andrew Jackson leading over John Quincy Adams. In 1883, the *Boston Globe* sent reporters to selected election precincts to poll voters as they exited voting booths, in an effort to predict the results of key contests. Public opinion polling as we know it today really began to develop in the 1930s. Walter Lippmann's seminal work, *Public Opinion* (1922), prompted much of this growth. In this book, Lippmann observed that research on public opinion was far too limited, especially in light of its importance. Researchers in a variety of disciplines, including political science, heeded Lippmann's call to learn more about public opinion. Some tried to use scientific methods to measure political thought through the use of surveys or polls. As methods for gathering and interpreting data improved, survey data began to play an increasingly significant part in all walks of life, from politics to retailing.

Literary Digest, a popular magazine that first began national presidential polling in 1916, was a pioneer in the use of the **straw poll**, an unscientific survey used to gauge public opinion, to predict the popular vote, which it did, for Woodrow Wilson. Its polling methods were hailed widely as "amazingly right" and "uncannily accurate."[2] In 1936, however, its luck ran out. *Literary Digest* predicted that Republican Alfred M. Landon would beat incumbent President Franklin D. Roosevelt by a margin of 57 percent to 43 percent of the popular vote. Roosevelt, however, won in a landslide election, receiving 62.5 percent of the popular vote and carrying all but two states.

Literary Digest's 1936 straw poll had three fatal errors. First, it drew its **sample**, a subset of the whole population selected to be questioned for the purposes of prediction or gauging opinion, from telephone directories and lists of automobile owners. This technique oversampled the upper middle class and the wealthy, groups heavily Republican in political orientation. Moreover, in 1936, voting polarized along class lines. Thus, the oversampling of wealthy Republicans was particularly problematic because it severely underestimated working class Democratic voters, who had neither cars nor telephones.

Literary Digest's second problem was timing. The magazine mailed its questionnaires in early September. This did not allow the *Digest* to measure the changes in public sentiment that occurred as the election drew closer.

Its third error occurred because of a problem we now call self-selection. Only highly motivated individuals sent back the cards—a mere 22 percent of those surveyed responded. Those who answer mail surveys (or today, online surveys) are quite different from the general electorate; they often are wealthier and better educated and care more fervently about issues. *Literary Digest,* then, failed to observe one of the now well-known cardinal rules of survey sampling: "One cannot allow the respondents to select themselves into the sample."[3]

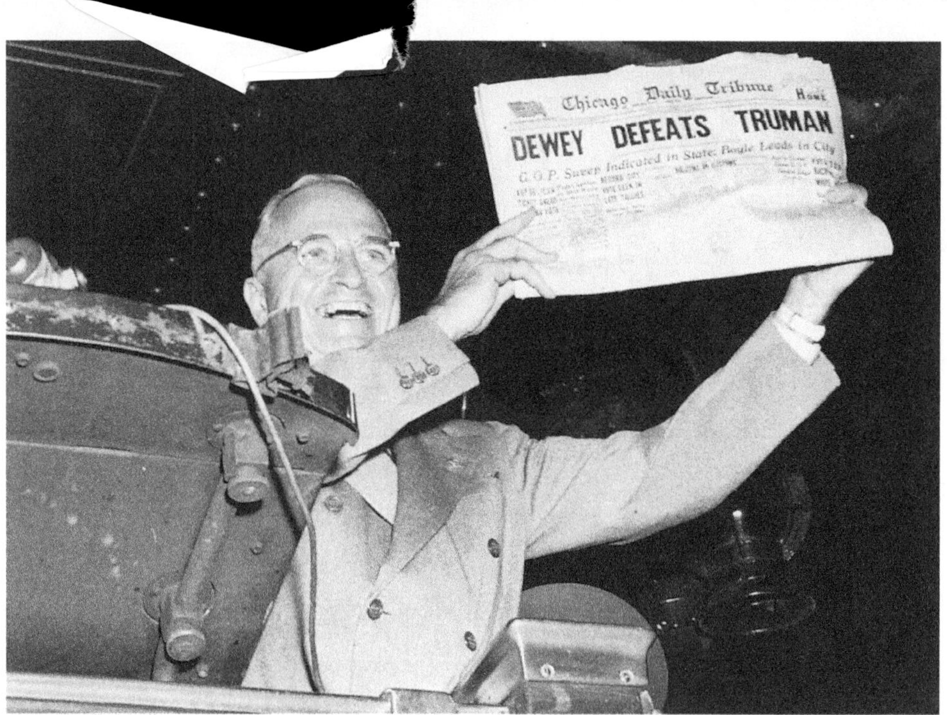

IS POLLING ALWAYS ACCURATE?

Not only did advance polls in 1948 predict that Republican nominee Thomas E. Dewey would defeat Democratic incumbent President Harry S Truman, but on the basis of early and incomplete vote tallies, some newspapers' early editions published the day after the election declared Dewey the winner. Here a triumphant Truman holds aloft the *Chicago Daily Tribune*.

☐ The Gallup Organization

At least one pollster, however, correctly predicted the results of the 1936 election: George Gallup. Gallup had written his dissertation in psychology at the University of Iowa on how to measure the readership of newspapers. He then expanded his research to study public opinion about politics. He was so confident about his methods that he gave all of his newspaper clients a money-back guarantee: if his poll predictions weren't closer to the actual election outcome than those of the highly acclaimed *Literary Digest,* he would refund their money. Although Gallup underpredicted Roosevelt's victory by nearly 7 percent, the fact that he got the winner right was what everyone remembered, especially given *Literary Digest*'s dramatic miscalculation.

Through the late 1940s, polling techniques increased in sophistication. The number of polling groups also dramatically rose, as businesses and politicians began to rely on polling information to market products and candidates. But, in 1948, the polling industry suffered a severe, although fleeting, setback when Gallup and many other pollsters incorrectly predicted that Thomas E. Dewey would defeat President Harry S Truman.

Nevertheless, as revealed in Figure 10.1, the Gallup Organization continues to predict the winners of the presidential popular vote successfully. In 2012, for example, Gallup's final poll of registered voters correctly predicted that Barack Obama would win the popular vote.

☐ The American National Election Studies

Recent efforts to measure public opinion also have benefited from social science surveys such as the American National Election Studies (ANES). The ANES have been conducted by researchers at the University of Michigan and Stanford University since 1952. Since 1977, they have been funded largely by the national government through the

10.1

10.2

10.3

10.4

10.5

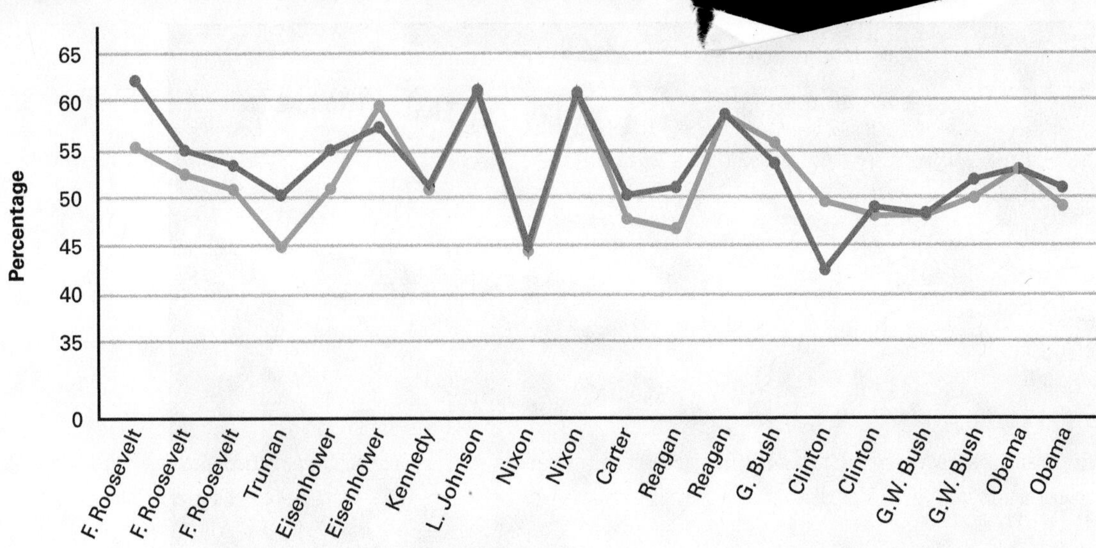

FIGURE 10.1 HOW SUCCESSFUL HAS THE GALLUP POLL BEEN?

As seen here, Gallup's final predictions have been remarkably accurate. Furthermore, in each of the years in which a significant discrepancy exists between Gallup's prediction and the election's outcome, a prominent third candidate factored in. In 1948, Strom Thurmond ran on the Dixiecrat ticket; in 1980, John Anderson ran as the American Independent Party candidate; in 1992, Ross Perot ran as an independent.

SOURCES: Marty Baumann, "How One Polling Firm Stacks Up," *USA Today* (October 27, 1992): 13A; 1996 data from Mike Mokrzycki, "Pre-election Polls' Accuracy Varied," *Atlanta Journal and Constitution* (November 8, 1996): A12; 2000 data from Gallup Organization, "Poll Releases," November 7, 2000; 2004, 2008, and 2012 data from *USA Today* and CNN/Gallup Tracking Poll, www.usatoday.com.

National Science Foundation. Focusing on the political attitudes and behavior of the electorate, ANES surveys include questions about how respondents voted, their party affiliation, and their opinions of major political parties and candidates. In addition, ANES surveys contain questions about interest in politics and political participation.

Researchers conduct ANES surveys before and after mid-term and presidential elections, often including many of the same questions. This format enables researchers to compile long-term studies of the electorate and facilitates political scientists' understanding of how and why people vote and participate in politics.

Conducting and Analyzing Public Opinion Polls

10.2 Describe the methods for conducting and analyzing different types of public opinion polls.

Explore on **MyPoliSciLab** **Simulation:** You Are a Polling Consultant

The polling process most often begins when someone says, "Let's find out about X and Y." Potential candidates for local office may want to know how many people have heard of them (the device used to find out is called a "name recognition survey"). Better-known candidates contemplating a run for higher office might wish to discover how they might fare against an incumbent. Polls also can help gauge how effective particular ads are or how well (or negatively) the public perceives a candidate. Political scientists have found that public opinion polls are critical to successful presidents and their staffs, who use polls to "create favorable legislative environment(s) to pass the presidential agenda, to win reelection, and to be judged favorably by history."[4]

Explore Your World

Public opinion polls have become an increasingly common tool for gauging public opinion not only in the United States but also around the world. These global public opinion surveys help us to understand the commonalities and differences across international contexts, and also reflect the social, cultural, and political variations of different states. To think more deeply about these trends, examine the results of four questions from the 2012 Pew Global Attitudes Survey that assess the attitudes toward global powers held by citizens in a sample of countries.

Russia, the European Union, China, and the United States are four significant global powers. Each has significant influence in international politics and world affairs. They also have unique allies and enemies.

Citizens from Russia, China, and the United States are most positive toward their respective states. Citizens from states with long-standing rivalries with each of these countries are the least positive.

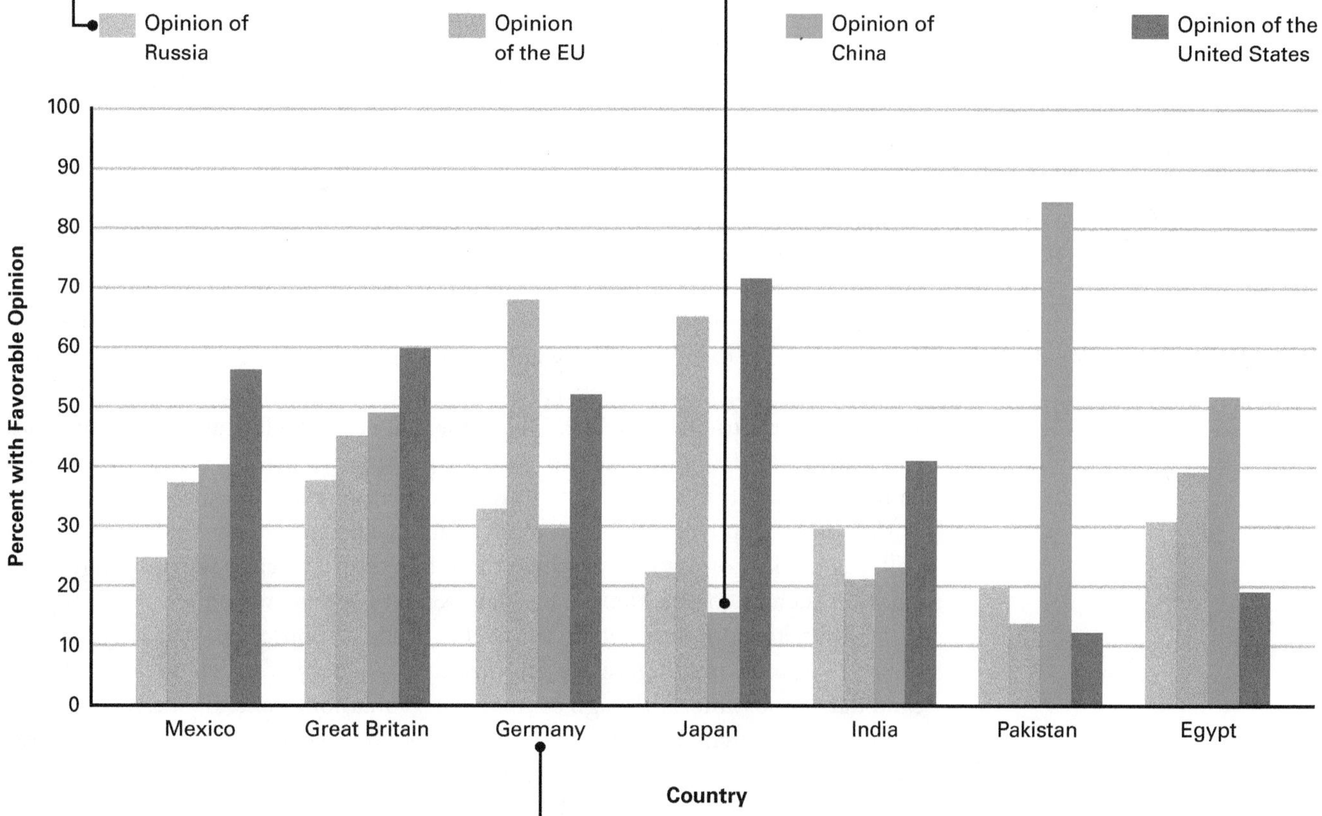

Opinion of Russia
Opinion of the EU
Opinion of China
Opinion of the United States

Percent with Favorable Opinion

100
90
80
70
60
50
40
30
20
10
0

Mexico
Great Britain
Germany
Japan
India
Pakistan
Egypt

Country

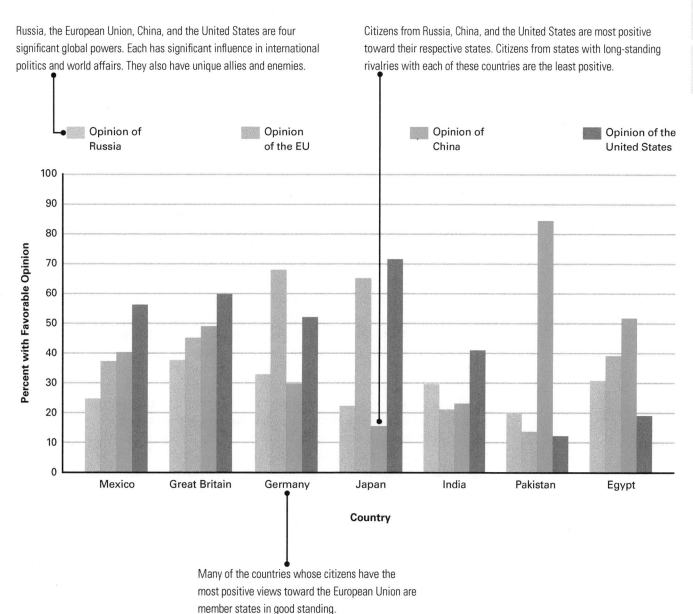

Many of the countries whose citizens have the most positive views toward the European Union are member states in good standing.

CRITICAL THINKING QUESTIONS

1. How do citizens' ratings in these surveys reflect—and not reflect—political and geographic alliances?
2. Which countries' citizens are most and least positive across the board? Why do you think this is the case?
3. What might be some of the challenges in measuring and comparing cross-national public opinion?

push polls
Polls taken for the purpose of providing information on an opponent that would lead respondents to vote against that candidate.

population
The entire group of people whose attitudes a researcher wishes to measure.

random sampling
A method of poll selection that gives each person in a group the same chance of being selected.

stratified sampling
A variation of random sampling; the population is divided into subgroups and weighted based on demographic characteristics of the national population.

☐ Designing the Survey and Sample

No matter the type of poll, serious pollsters or polling firms must make several decisions before undertaking the process. These include determining the content and phrasing of the questions, selecting the sample from the public, and deciding how to go about contacting respondents.

DETERMINING THE CONTENT AND PHRASING THE QUESTIONS The first matter candidates, political groups, or news organizations must consider when deciding to use a poll concerns what questions they want answered. Determining the content of a survey is critical to obtaining the desired results, and for that reason, candidates, companies, and news organizations generally rely on pollsters. Polls may ask, for example, about job performance, demographics, and specific issue areas.

Special care must be taken in constructing the questions. For example, if your professor asked you, "Do you think my grading procedures are fair?" rather than asking, "In general, how fair do you think the grading is in your American Politics course?" you might give a slightly different answer. The wording of the first question tends to put you on the spot and personalize the grading style; the second question is more neutral. Even more obvious differences appear in the real world of polling, especially when interested groups want a poll to yield particular results. Responses to highly emotional issues, such as abortion, same-sex marriage, and affirmative action, often are skewed depending on the phrasing of a particular question. Even in unbiased polls, how a question is worded can unintentionally skew results.

All good polls for political candidates contain questions intended to yield information that helps campaigns judge their own strengths and weaknesses as well as those of their opponents. They might, for example, ask if you would be more likely to vote for candidate X if you knew he or she was a strong environmentalist. These kinds of questions are accepted as an essential part of any poll, but concerns arise over where to draw the line. Questions that cross the line are called **push polls** and often result from ulterior motives.[5] The intent of push polls is to give respondents some negative or even untruthful information about a candidate's opponent so that they will move away from that candidate and toward the one paying for the poll. Reputable polling firms eschew these tactics. A typical push poll might ask a question such as "If you knew Candidate X beat his wife, would you vote for him?" Push poll takers do not even bother to record the responses because they are irrelevant; the questions themselves are meant to push away as many voters from a candidate as possible. Although campaign organizations generally deny conducting push polls, research shows that this type of polling has targeted more than three-quarters of political candidates. Push poll calls are made to thousands; legitimate polls survey much smaller samples.

SELECTING THE SAMPLE After deciding to conduct a poll, pollsters must determine the **population**, or the entire group of people whose attitudes a researcher wishes to measure. This universe could be all Americans, all voters, all city residents, all Hispanics, or all Republicans. In a perfect world, the poll would ask every individual to give an opinion, but such comprehensive polling is not practical. Consequently, pollsters take a sample of the population that interests them. One way to obtain this sample is by **random sampling.** This method of selection gives each potential voter or adult approximately the same chance of being selected.

Simple random, nonstratified samples, however, are not very useful for predicting voting because they may undersample or oversample key populations not likely to vote. To avoid such problems, reputable polling organizations use **stratified sampling** (the most rigorous sampling technique) based on U.S. Census data that provide the number of residences in an area and their location. Researchers divide the population into several sampling regions. They then randomly select subgroups to sample in proportion to

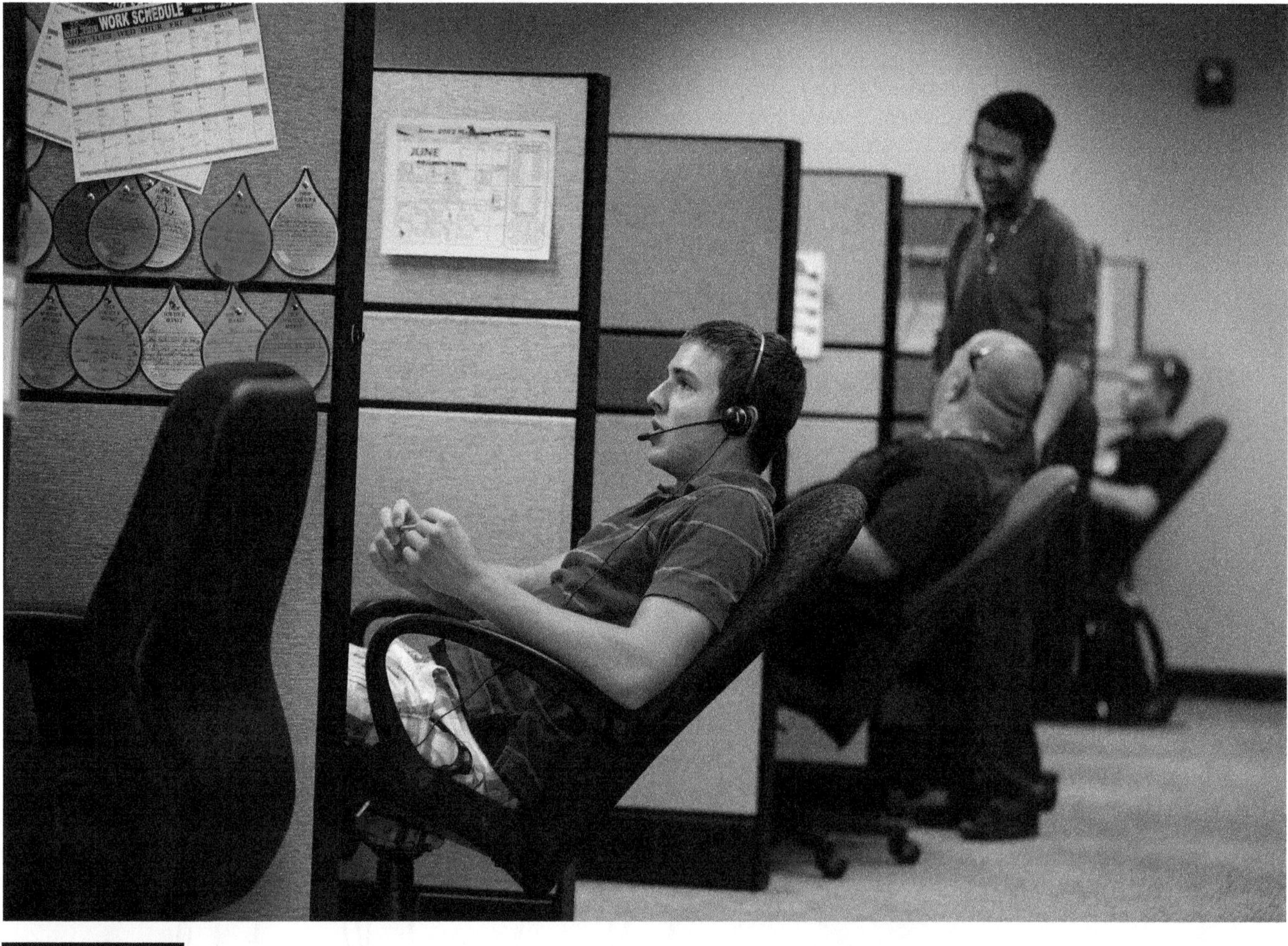

HOW ARE POLLS CONDUCTED?

The most common method of conducting a public opinion poll is via telephone. These polls are often administered by survey researchers working at large phone banks, such as the one shown here.

the total national population. These selected primary sampling units often are used for many years, because it is cheaper for polling companies to train interviewers to work in fixed areas.

The pollsters choose about twenty respondents from each primary sampling unit for interviewing; the total is 600 to 1,000 respondents. Large, sophisticated surveys such as the American National Election Studies and the University of Chicago's General Social Survey attempt to sample from lists of persons living in each household in a sampling unit. A key to the success of the stratified sampling method is not to let people volunteer to be interviewed—volunteers often have different opinions from those who do not volunteer.

☐ Contacting Respondents

After selecting the poll's methodology, the next decision is how to contact those to be surveyed. Political polling today takes a variety of forms, including telephone polls, in-person interviews, and Internet polls.

TELEPHONE POLLS Telephone polls are the most frequently used mechanism by which to gauge the mood of the electorate. The most common form of telephone polls is the random-digit dialing survey, in which a computer randomly selects telephone numbers for dialing. In spite of some problems (such as the fact that many people do not want to be bothered or do not have landline phones), most polls done for

Take a Closer Look

The emergence of a growing number of public opinion research firms means that citizens, the media, and political leaders know more than ever before about how voters perceive political issues and candidates. This information may be useful for promoting a more democratic and representative government. But, it may also be notoriously mercurial, marked by dramatic fluctuations from week to week or even day to day, as illustrated in the political cartoon below.

Public opinion polls may fluctuate dramatically from day to day. Especially during the election season, tracking these fluctuations is a form of political sport.
KYLE'S UP, ETHAN'S DOWN. HOLD ON, ETHAN'S UP AND KYLE'S DOWN!.... WAIT....
MIKE LUCKOVICH ATLANTA JOURNAL-CONSTITUTION
© AJC.com 4/04
FUTURE POLLSTER....
A record number of polling firms tracked the results of the 2012 presidential election.
The seesaw metaphor is a useful comparison when thinking about how the media, in particular, discusses the political horse race.

CRITICAL THINKING QUESTIONS

1. Why do so many agencies and organizations want to collect public opinion data? How do the data help them advocate for their cause?
2. How might frequent fluctuations in the results of public opinion polls both help and hurt candidates?
3. Is there too much public opinion data in modern politics? Why or why not?

newspapers and news magazines operate in this way. Pollsters are exempt from federal and state do-not-call lists because poll taking is a form of constitutionally protected speech.

During the 1992 presidential elections, the introduction of **tracking polls**, which were taken on a daily basis via phone by some news organizations, allowed presidential candidates to monitor short-term campaign developments and the effects of their campaign strategies. Today, tracking polls involve small samples (usually of registered voters contacted at certain times of the day) and take place every twenty-four hours. Pollsters then combine the results into moving three- to five-day averages (see Figure 10.2).

tracking polls
Continuous surveys that enable a campaign or news organization to chart a candidate's daily rise or fall in support.

exit polls
Polls conducted as voters leave selected polling places on Election Day.

IN-PERSON INTERVIEWS Some polls, such as the American National Election Studies, perform individual, person-to-person interviews. In-person surveys allow surveyors to monitor respondents' body language and to interact on a more personal basis; thus, they may yield higher rates of completion. However, the unintended influence of the questioner or pollster may lead to interviewer bias. How the pollster dresses, relates to the person being interviewed, and asks the questions can affect responses.

Exit polls, a special form of in-person poll, are conducted as voters leave selected polling places on Election Day. Generally, large news organizations send pollsters to selected precincts to sample every tenth voter as he or she emerges from the polling site. The results of these polls help the media predict the outcome of key races, often just a few minutes after the polls close in a particular state and generally before voters in other areas—sometimes in a later time zone—have cast their ballots. By asking a series of demographic and issue questions, these polls also provide an independent assessment of why voters supported particular candidates.

INTERNET POLLS Well-established pollster John Zogby was among the first to use a scientific Internet survey. Zogby regularly queries over 3,000 representative volunteers (selected using the sampling techniques discussed later in this chapter) on a host of issues. Zogby, Harris Interactive, and other Internet pollsters using scientific

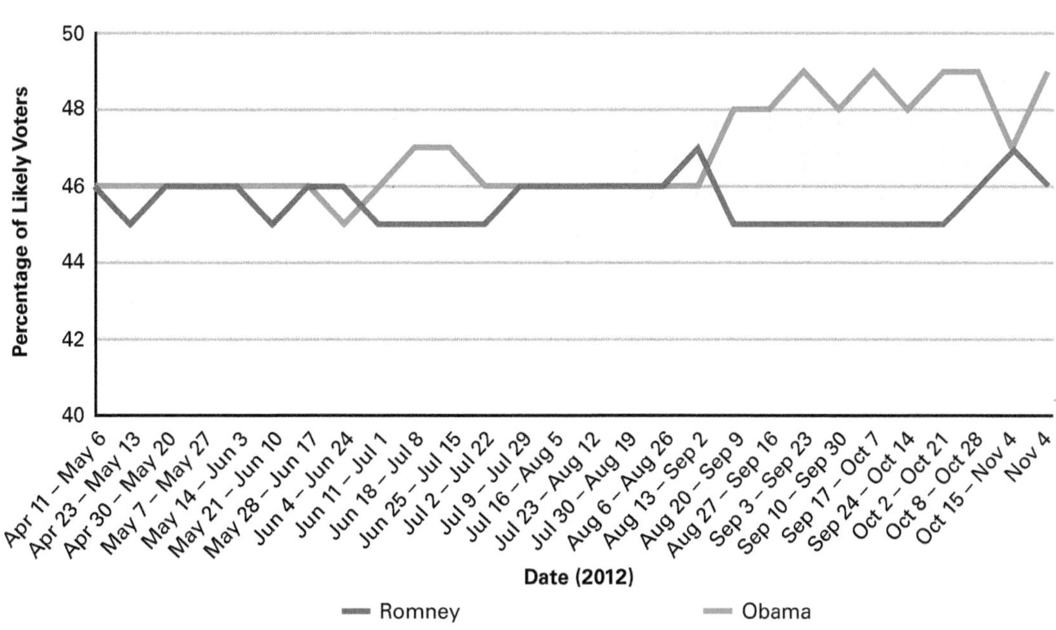

FIGURE 10.2 WHAT DOES A DAILY TRACKING POLL LOOK LIKE?

Day-to-day fluctuations in public opinion on electoral contests are often shown through tracking polls. This figure shows the ups and downs of the 2012 presidential election. President Barack Obama led for much of the race, although the polling data generally remained within the margin of error. Note, particularly, Mitt Romney's gains after the first presidential debate.

SOURCE: *USA Today* and CNN/Gallup Poll results, http://www.gallup.com/poll/154559/US-Presidential-Election-Center.aspx?ref=interactive.

margin of error
A measure of the accuracy of a public opinion poll.

sampling strategies have established relatively effective records in predicting election outcomes and gauging opinions on numerous issues of importance to the American public. Political scientists, too, use online polling to collect survey research data. The biannual Cooperative Congressional Election Study conducted by a consortium of universities is one example of this kind of research.

Contrasting sharply with scientific Internet surveys are unscientific Web polls that allow anyone to weigh in on a topic. Such polls are common on many Web sites, such as CNN.com and ESPN.com. These polls resemble a straw poll in terms of sampling and thus produce results that are largely inconclusive and of interest only to a limited number of people.

Analyzing the Data

Analyzing the collected data is a critical step in the polling process. Analysis reveals the implications of the data for public policy and political campaigns. Data are entered into a computer program, where answers to questions are recorded and analyzed. Often, analysts pay special attention to subgroups within the data, such as Democrats versus Republicans, men versus women, age groups, or political ideology, among others. Reporting the results of this analysis can happen in a variety of ways, such as by news organizations or campaigns.

Shortcomings of Polling

10.3 Assess the potential shortcomings of polling.

Information derived from public opinion polls has become an important part of governance. When the results of a poll are accurate, they express the attitudes of the electorate and help guide policy makers. However, when the results of a poll are inaccurate, disastrous consequences can result. For example, during the 2000 presidential election, Voter News Service (VNS), the conglomerate organization that provided the major networks with their exit poll data, made a host of errors in estimating the results of the presidential vote in Florida, which led news organizations to call the election for Al Gore. Not only did VNS fail to estimate the number of voters accurately, but it also used an inaccurate exit poll model and incorrectly estimated the number of African American and Cuban voters in Florida. Polls may be inaccurate for a number of reasons. These include survey error, limited respondent options, lack of information, difficulty measuring intensity, and lack of interest.

Survey Error

All polls contain errors. They may come about from natural errors in statistical measurement that arise from using a sample to extrapolate the opinions of the general public, known as the margin of error. They may also result from drawing an improper sample, known as sampling error.

MARGIN OF ERROR Typically, the margin of error in a sample of 1,000 will be about 4 percent. If you ask 1,000 people, "Do you like ice cream?" and 52 percent say yes and 48 percent say no, the results are too close to tell whether more people like ice cream than not. Why? Because the **margin of error** implies that somewhere between 56 percent (52 + 4) and 48 percent (52 – 4) of the people like ice cream, while between 52 percent (48 + 4) and 44 percent (48 – 4) do not. The margin of error in a close election makes predictions very difficult.

Explore on MyPoliSciLab

What Do Young People Think About Politics Today?

In recent years, attention has focused on the potential power of the youth vote. But in 2012, polls show that individuals between the ages of 18 and 25 are cynical about political leadership as well as their own ability to influence government. In a time when many are taking to the streets with the Tea Party and Occupy Wall Street movements, most young voters are not gravitating to either group. Here is how they responded to questions about leadership and participation.

How 18- to 25-Year-Olds Responded

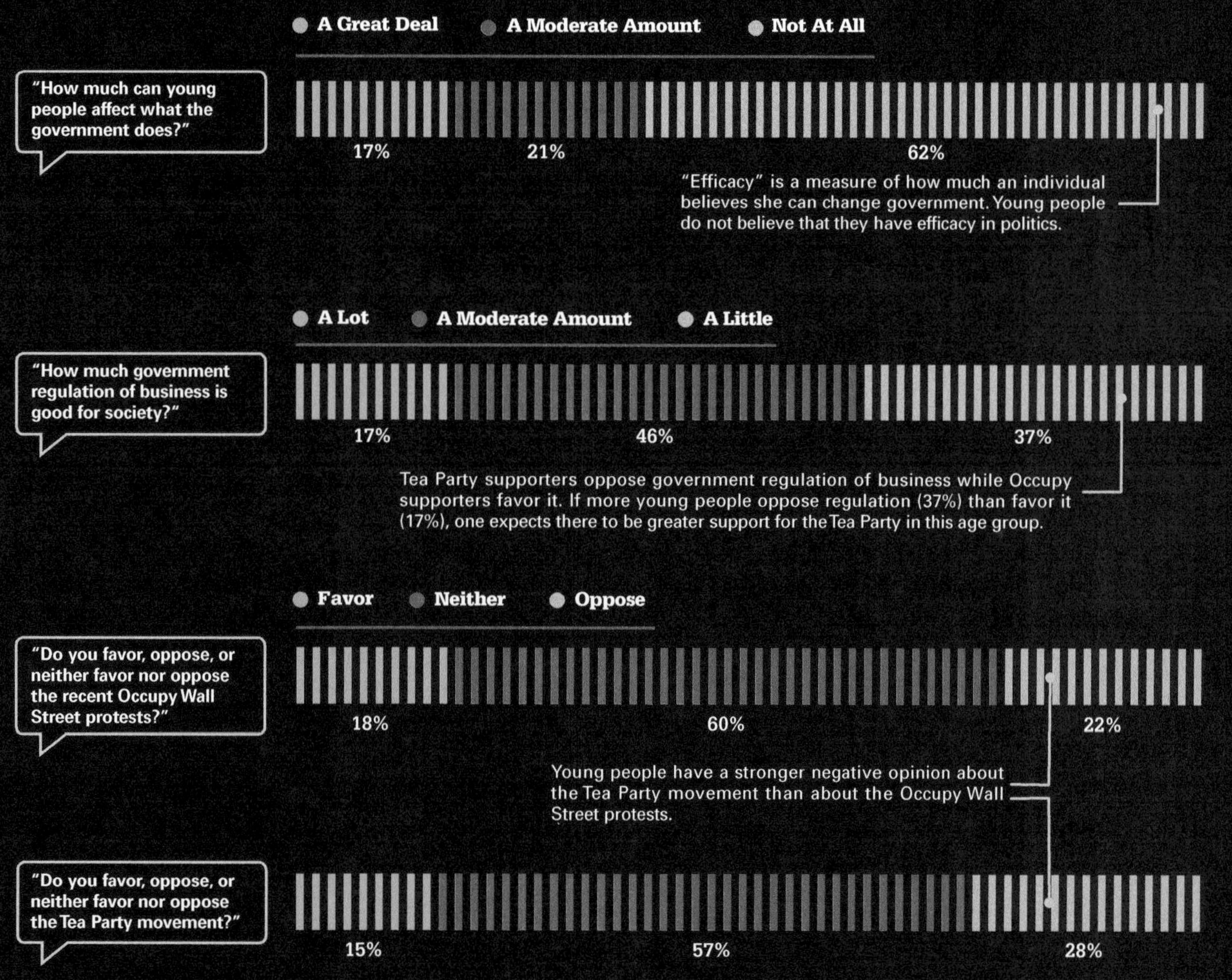

A Great Deal
A Moderate Amount
Not At All
"How much can young people affect what the government does?"
17%
21%
62%
"Efficacy" is a measure of how much an individual believes she can change government. Young people do not believe that they have efficacy in politics.
A Lot
A Moderate Amount
A Little
"How much government regulation of business is good for society?"
17%
46%
37%
Tea Party supporters oppose government regulation of business while Occupy supporters favor it. If more young people oppose regulation (37%) than favor it (17%), one expects there to be greater support for the Tea Party in this age group.
Favor
Neither
Oppose
"Do you favor, oppose, or neither favor nor oppose the recent Occupy Wall Street protests?"
18%
60%
22%
Young people have a stronger negative opinion about the Tea Party movement than about the Occupy Wall Street protests.
"Do you favor, oppose, or neither favor nor oppose the Tea Party movement?"
15%
57%
28%

SOURCE: Data from American National Election Study, "Evaluations of Government and Society Study," Release Wave 4, Winter 2012.

Investigate Further

Concept Why does efficacy matter? Questions that measure efficacy among Americans indicate that it is low among young voters because this group thinks they have no voice. This disengaged attitude is not indicative of a healthy democracy.

Connection Do opinions about Occupy Wall Street and the Tea Party relate to young people's economic beliefs? Like the Tea Party, young voters tend to oppose government regulation, while Occupy supporters favor government involvement. However, this shared belief between young people and the Tea Party does not translate to stronger Tea Party support.

Cause Does low efficacy among 18- to 25-year-olds fuel their desire to influence government and join popular political movements? No. Even though Occupy Wall Street is viewed more positively than the Tea Party among today's youth, feelings of low efficacy do not lead to widespread support for either movement.

SAMPLING ERROR The accuracy of any poll depends on the quality of the sample. Small samples, if properly drawn, can be very accurate if each unit in the universe has an equal opportunity to be sampled. If a pollster, for example, fails to sample certain populations, his or her results may reflect that shortcoming. Often polls underrepresent the opinions of the poor and homeless because pollsters give insufficient attention to representatively sampling these groups.

☐ Limited Respondent Options

Famed political scientist V.O. Key Jr. was among the first social scientists to note the problem of limited respondent options. He cautioned students of public opinion to be certain their questions adequately allowed respondents the appropriate range in which they could register their opinions. Simple yes-no (or approve-disapprove) questions may not be sufficient to "take the temperature" of the public. For example, if someone asks you, "How do you like this class?" and then gives only like or dislike options, your full sentiments may not be tapped if you like the class very much or feel only so-so about it.

Thus, the American National Election Studies use "feeling thermometer" questions, wherein respondents provide a response from 0 to 100 measuring how they "feel" about a particular issue. These types of questions, however, are too lengthy and unwieldy for polling organizations that seek quick answers.

☐ Lack of Information

Public opinion polls may also be inaccurate when they attempt to gauge attitudes toward issues about which the public has little information. Most academic public opinion research organizations, such as the American National Election Studies, use some kind of filter question that first asks respondents whether or not they have thought about the question. These screening procedures generally allow survey researchers to exclude as many as 20 percent of their respondents, especially on complex issues such as the federal budget. Questions on more personal issues, such

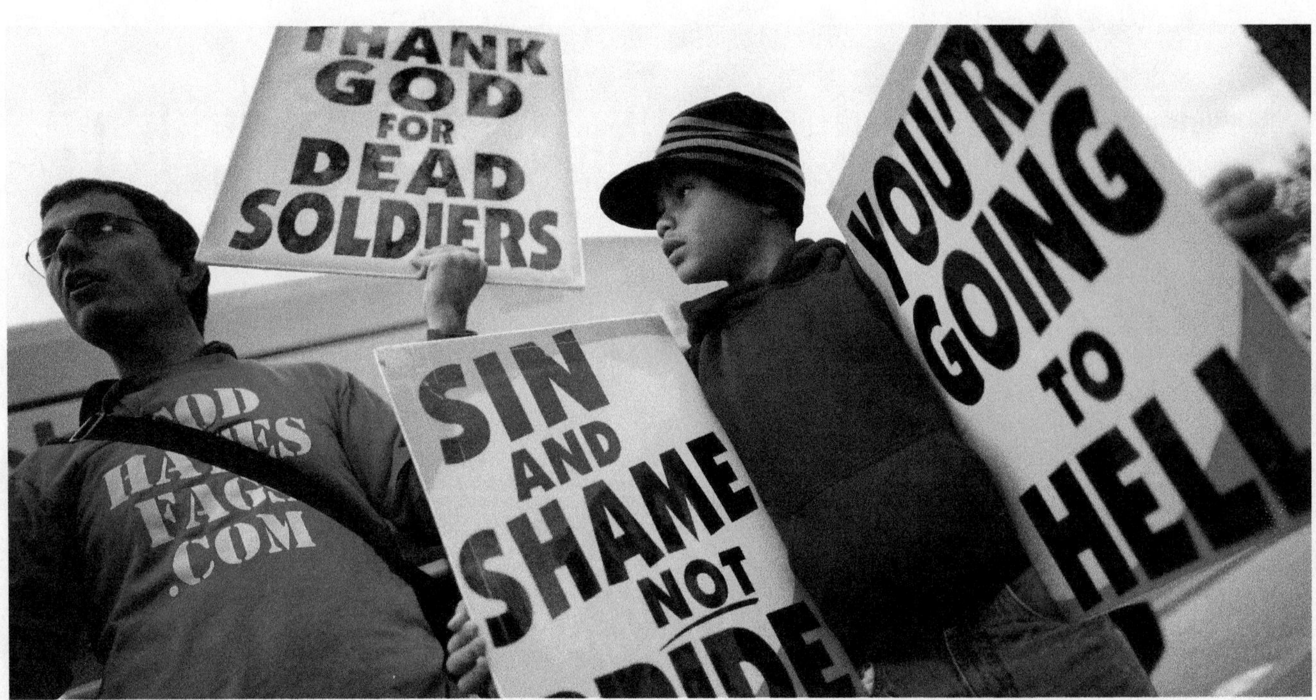

CAN POLLS MEASURE INTENSITY OF OPINION?

One of the greatest shortcomings of most public opinion polls is that they measure direction of public opinion, but not intensity. Here, members of Westboro Baptist Church demonstrate intense opposition to homosexuality by protesting outside the Supreme Court.

as moral values, drugs, crime, race, and women's role in society, receive far fewer "no opinion" or "don't know" responses.

political socialization
The process through which individuals acquire their political beliefs and values.

☐ Difficulty Measuring Intensity

Another shortcoming of polls concerns their inability to measure intensity of feeling about particular issues. Whereas a respondent might answer affirmatively to any question, it is likely that his or her feelings about issues such as big government, the death penalty, or support for the war on terrorism are much more intense than are those about the Electoral College or absentee ballot laws.

☐ Lack of Interest in Political Issues

When we face policies that do not affect us personally and do not involve moral issues, we often have difficulty forming an opinion. This phenomenon is especially true with regard to foreign policy. Most Americans often know little of the world around them. Unless major issues of national importance take center stage, American public opinion on foreign affairs is likely to be volatile in the wake of any new information. In contrast, most Americans are more interested in domestic policy issues, such as health care, bank bailouts, and employment, issues that have greater impact on their daily lives.

Forming Political Opinions

10.4 Analyze the process by which people form political opinions.

Political scientists believe that many of our attitudes about issues are grounded in our political values. The process through which individuals acquire their beliefs is known as **political socialization.**[6] Demographic characteristics, family, school, peers, the mass media, and political leaders often act as important influences or agents of political socialization.

☐ Demographic Characteristics

Individuals have little control over most demographic characteristics. But, at birth, these characteristics begin to affect you and your political values. Some of the major demographic characteristics that pollsters routinely expect will affect political opinions include gender, race and ethnicity, age, and religion.

GENDER From the time of the earliest public opinion polls, women have held more liberal attitudes than men about social issues, such as education, poverty, capital punishment, and the environment. Public opinion polls have also found that women's views about war and military intervention are more negative than men's. Some analysts suggest that women's more nurturing nature and their role as mothers influence their more liberal attitudes on issues affecting the family or children. Research by political scientists, however, finds no support for a maternal explanation (see Table 10.1).[7]

RACE AND ETHNICITY Another reliable predictor of people's political attitudes is their race or ethnicity. Differences in political socialization appear at a very early age. Young African American children, for example, generally show very positive feelings about American society and political processes, but this attachment lessens considerably over time. Historically, black children have had less positive views of the president and other public officials than have white children.[8]

TABLE 10.1 DO MEN AND WOMEN THINK DIFFERENTLY ABOUT POLITICAL ISSUES?

	Men (%)	Women (%)
Labor unions are necessary to protect the working person	59	68
Best way to ensure peace is through military strength	57	50
School boards ought to have the right to fire teachers who are known homosexuals	24	19
Women get fewer opportunities than men for good jobs	45	52
We should restrict and control people coming to our country more than we do now	69	68
Voted for Barack Obama in 2012	45[a]	55[a]

[a]CNN Exit Polls, November 6, 2012.

SOURCE: Pew Research Center, 2012 American Values Survey, www.people-press.org/values-questions.

Race and ethnicity are exceptionally important factors in the study of public opinion. The direction and intensity of African American and Hispanic opinions on a variety of issues often are quite different from those of whites. For example, blacks and Hispanics are more likely than whites to support laws and regulations protecting the environment. Minorities are also more likely to favor government-sponsored health insurance. And, Hispanics are also more likely than other groups to support liberalized immigration policies.[9]

AGE Age seems to have a decided effect on political socialization. Our view of the proper role of government, for example, often depends on the era in which we were born and our individual experiences with a variety of social, political, and economic forces. Older people, for example, continue to be affected by having lived through the hard economic times of the Great Depression and World War II.

One political scientist predicts that as Baby Boomers age, the age gap in beliefs about political issues, especially governmental programs, will increase.[10] Young people, for example, resist higher taxes to fund Medicare, while the elderly resist all efforts to limit Medicare or Social Security. In states such as Florida, to which many northern retirees have flocked, seeking relief from cold winters and high taxes, the elderly have voted as a bloc to defeat school tax increases and to pass tax breaks for themselves.

RELIGION Political scientists have found significant evidence that religion affects the political beliefs and behaviors of the American citizenry. Many American ideals, including hard work and personal responsibility, are rooted in our nation's Protestant heritage. These ideals have affected the public policies adopted by government; they may be one reason why the United States has a less developed welfare state than many other industrialized democracies.

Religious beliefs also shape individual attitudes toward political issues. Evangelical Christians and Roman Catholics, for example, may support programs that provide aid to parochial schools, even if it comes at the expense of lowering the wall of separation between church and state. Similarly, Jewish Americans are more likely to favor aid to Israel—a policy at odds with Muslim Americans' support for a Palestinian state. How strictly we practice and follow religious doctrine may affect political beliefs, as well. For example, strict Roman Catholics, Orthodox Jews, Mormons, and evangelical Christians believe that abortion should be illegal in all cases; they also believe in more traditional roles for women.

☐ Family, Peers, and School

The influence of the family on political socialization can be traced to two factors: communication and receptivity. Children, especially during their preschool years, spend tremendous amounts of time with their parents; early on, they learn their

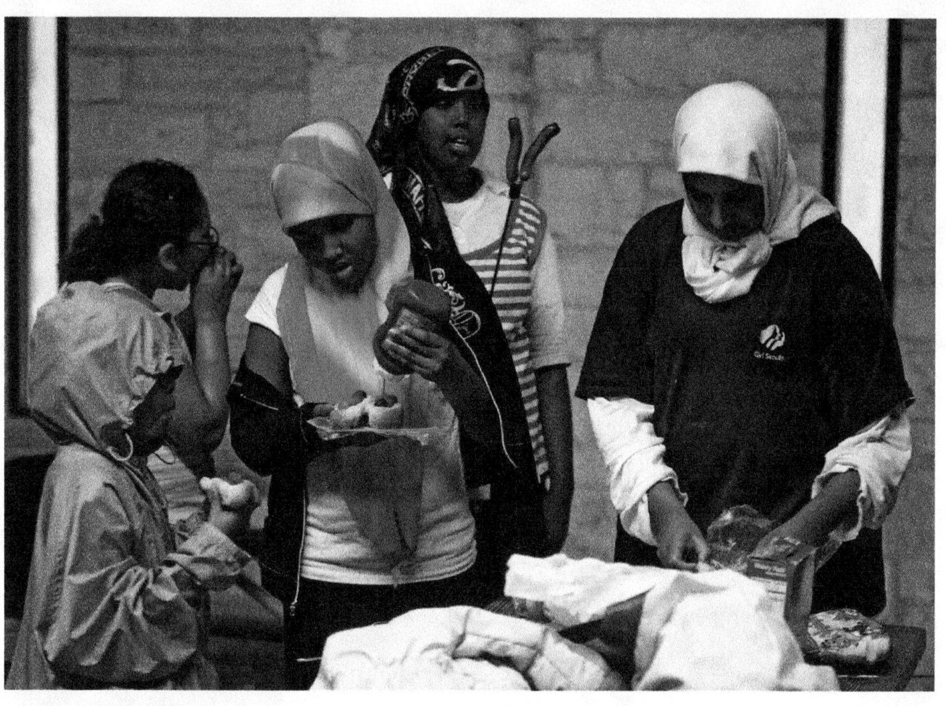

HOW DO YOU ENCOURAGE YOUNG WOMEN TO THINK ABOUT CAREERS IN POLITICS?

Researchers find that women are more reluctant than similarly qualified men to think about running for office. In an attempt to change this norm, the Girl Scouts of the USA offers a Ms. President badge for social action. Farheen Hakeem, shown right, leads a Girl Scout troop in Minneapolis.

parents' political values, even though these concepts may be vague. One study of first graders, for example, found that they already had developed political orientations consistent with those of their parents.[11] And, by the age of ten or eleven, children become more selective in their perceptions of the president. By this age, children raised in Democratic households are much more likely to cast a critical eye on a Republican president than are those raised in Republican households, and vice versa.

A child's peers—that is, children about the same age—also seem to have an important effect on the socialization process. While parental influences are greatest from birth to age five, beyond that point a child's peer group becomes increasingly important, especially as he or she enters middle school or high school. Groups such as the Girl Scouts of the USA recognize the effect of peer pressure and are trying to influence more young women to participate in, and have a positive view of, politics. The Girl Scouts' Ms. President patch encourages girls as young as five to learn "herstory" and to emulate women leaders.

Researchers report mixed findings concerning the role of schools in the political socialization process. There is no question that, in elementary school, children are taught respect for their nation and its symbols. Most school days begin with the Pledge of Allegiance, and patriotism and respect for country are important components of most school curricula. Support for flag and country creates a foundation for national allegiance that prevails despite the negative views about politicians and government institutions that many Americans develop later in life.

For decades, the *Weekly Reader*, read by elementary school students nationwide, attempted to foster political awareness and a sense of civic duty among young people. In presidential election years, students had the opportunity to vote for actual presidential candidates in the nationwide *Weekly Reader* election. These elections were remarkably accurate in predicting the winner. *Weekly Reader* was wrong only once, in the 1992 election of Bill Clinton. These returns were skewed by children's support for prominent independent candidate Ross Perot. *Weekly Reader* was folded into *Scholastic News* in

How Do Demographic Characteristics Affect Public Opinion?

Demographic characteristics, as discussed in the text, have a powerful impact on the way citizens view government, political leaders, and public policies. These gaps may be the result of gender, race, age, party, and religion, among other factors. They endure as a result of cultural norms, socialization, and differing value systems. Examine the variations in the attitudes of each of these groups on the questions asked below.

The Federal Government Controls Too Much of Our Daily Lives

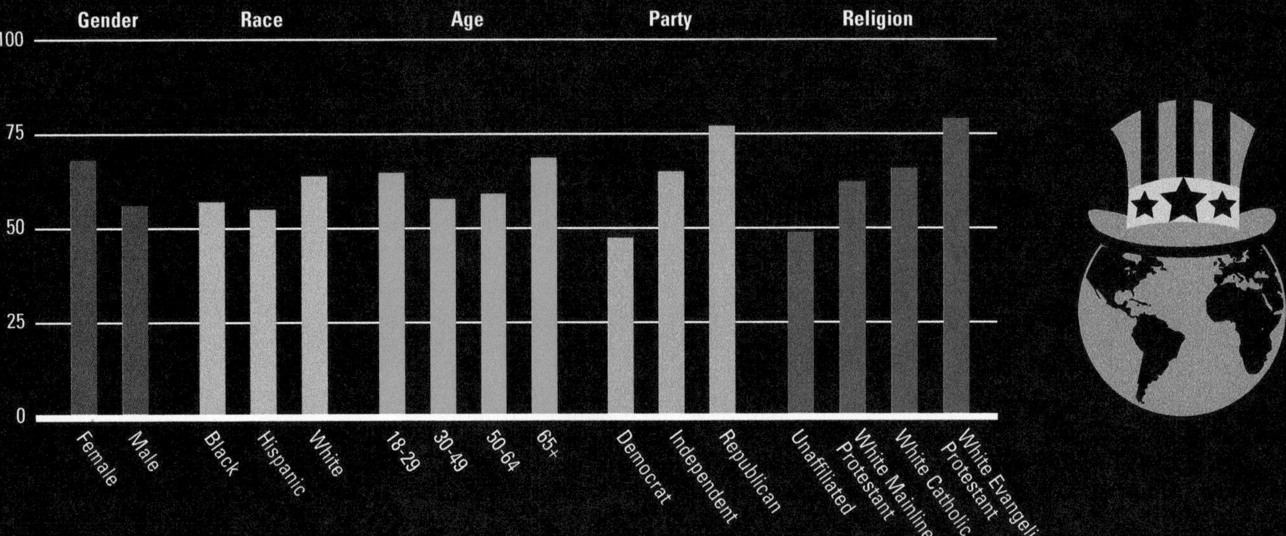

The Government Should Guarantee Every Citizen Enough to Eat and a Place to Sleep

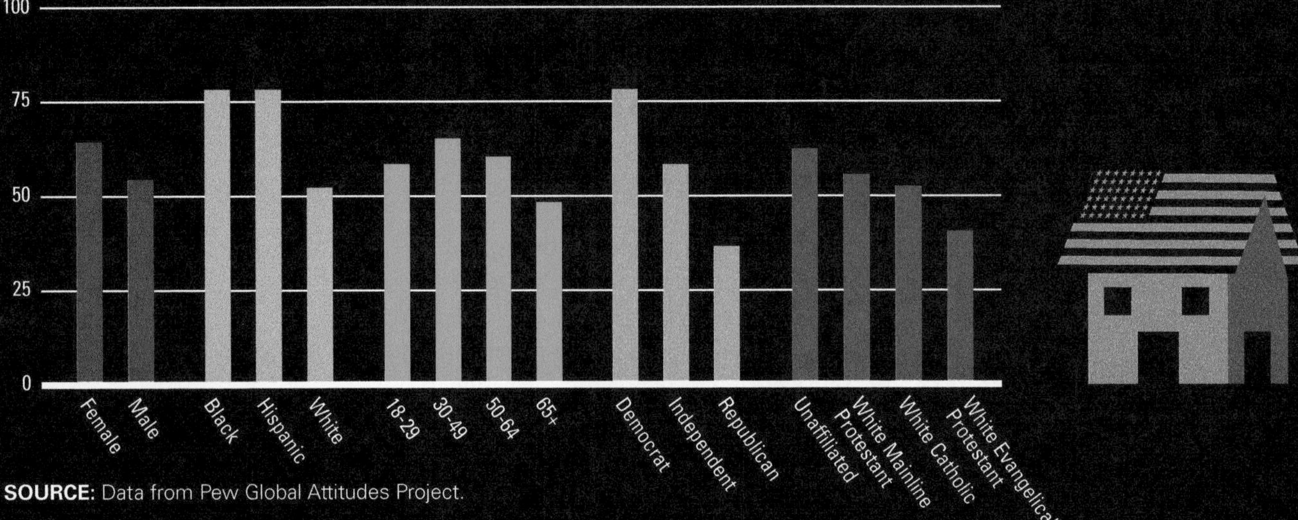

SOURCE: Data from Pew Global Attitudes Project.

CRITICAL THINKING QUESTIONS

1. Which gaps are largest? Smallest? Why do you think these differences exist?
2. Why do you think Republicans are more likely than Democrats and Independents to believe that government controls too much of our daily lives?
3. How might citizens' views on these questions differ as a result of other demographic characteristics, such as income and education?

2012; in a poll designed by Zogby International, students predicted that President Barack Obama would win reelection.

High schools also can be important agents of political socialization. They continue the elementary school tradition of building good citizens and often reinforce textbook learning with trips to the state or national capital. They also offer courses on current U.S. affairs. Many high schools impose a compulsory service-learning requirement, which some studies report positively affects later political participation.[12]

At the college level, teaching style often changes. Many college courses and texts like this one are designed in part to provide the information necessary for thinking critically about issues of major political consequence. It is common in college for students to be called on to question the appropriateness of certain political actions or to discuss underlying reasons for certain political or policy decisions. Therefore, most researchers believe that college has a liberalizing effect on students. Since the 1920s, studies have shown that students become more liberal each year they are in college (see Figure 10.3).

☐ The Mass Media

Over the years, more and more Americans have turned away from traditional news sources, such as nightly news broadcasts on the major networks and daily newspapers, in favor of different outlets. TV talk shows, talk radio, online magazines, and blogs are important sources of political news for many people. Cable news, the Internet, and social media are almost omnipresent in the lives of modern Americans. American teenagers, for example, consume almost eleven hours of media content each day.[13]

Cable and Internet news sources are often skewed. Consuming slanted views may affect the way citizens process political information, form opinions on public policy, obtain political knowledge, and receive new ideas. One recent study, for

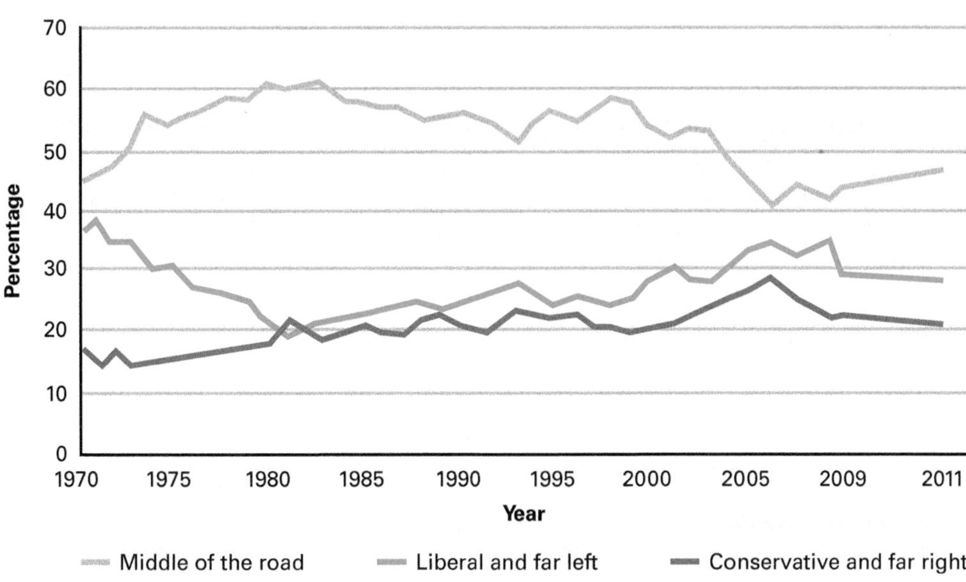

FIGURE 10.3 WHAT ARE THE IDEOLOGICAL SELF-IDENTIFICATIONS OF FIRST-YEAR COLLEGE STUDENTS?

Nearly a majority of first-year college students describe themselves as middle of the road. The percentage of students identifying as conservative or liberal has remained relatively consistent since the 1990s. Liberal and far left students make up slightly higher proportions of first-year students than do conservatives.

SOURCES: Cooperative Institutional Research Program, http://heri.ucla.edu/PDFs/pubs/TFS/Norms/Monographs/TheAmericanFreshman2011.pdf.

example, revealed that Americans who get most of their news from cable news outlets such as Fox News and MSNBC are even less knowledgeable about political issues than citizens who consume no political news. Individuals who rely on alternative sources such as *The Daily Show* and *The Colbert Report,* as well as Sunday morning talk shows and National Public Radio, are generally more knowledgeable.[14]

☐ Cues from Leaders or Opinion Makers

Given the visibility of political leaders and their access to the media, it is easy to see the important role they play in influencing opinion formation. Political leaders, members of the news media, and a host of other experts have regular opportunities to affect public opinion because of the lack of deep conviction with which most Americans hold many of their political beliefs.

The president, especially, is often in a position to mold public opinion through effective use of the bully pulpit. The president derives this power from the majesty of his office and his singular position as head of state. Thus, presidents often take to TV in an effort to drum up support for their programs.[15] President Barack Obama, for example, presented his case for economic reform and job creation directly to the public, urging citizens to support his efforts.

☐ Political Knowledge

Political knowledge and political participation have a reciprocal effect on one another—an increase in one will increase the other. Knowledge about the political system is essential to successful political involvement, which, in turn, teaches citizens about politics and expands their interest in public affairs. And, although few citizens know everything about all of the candidates and issues in a particular election, they can, and often do, know enough to impose their views and values on the general direction the nation should take.

This observation is true despite the fact that most Americans' level of knowledge about history and politics is quite low. According to the U.S. Department of Education, today's college graduates have less civic knowledge than high school graduates did fifty years ago. Americans also do not appear to know much about foreign policy; some critics even argue that many Americans are geographically illiterate (see Table 10.2).[16]

Gender differences in political knowledge are also significant. On many traditional measures of political knowledge, women lag behind their male counterparts. However, on issues of interest to women—such as representation in the legislature—women do as well or better than their male counterparts.[17] The gender gap in political knowledge also appears to be affected by education, age, number of children, and marital status.[18]

TABLE 10.2 WHAT IS THE EXTENT OF AMERICANS' POLITICAL KNOWLEDGE?

Can You Identify the Following?	Percentage Unable to Identify
Majority party in the House of Representatives	57
Speaker of the House	56
British prime minister	62
Photo of Justice Sonia Sotomayor	35
Israel on a map	43

SOURCES: Pew Research Center, "What the Public Knows," (November 7, 2011): www.people-press.org/2011/11/07/what-the-public-knows-in-words-and-pictures/?src=iq-quiz.

The Senate of the United States shall be composed of two Senators from each State, chosen by the Legislature thereof, for six Years; and each Senator shall have one Vote. —ARTICLE I, SECTION 3, CLAUSE 1

The Senate of the United States shall be composed of two Senators from each State, elected by the people thereof, for six years; and each Senator shall have one vote. —SEVENTEENTH AMENDMENT

The Framers of the Constitution were skeptical of the influence public opinion might have on politics. This is one of the reasons that they crafted such a deliberate system of government with both separation of powers and checks and balances. It was also the primary motivating factor behind the creation of the Electoral College to select the president.

One additional way the Framers tried to temper the influence of public opinion on politics was by placing the selection of senators in the hands of state legislators, as stipulated in Article I, section 3, clause 1 of the Constitution. Legislators, the Framers believed, would be more experienced in political activity and less subject to the effects of campaigning and the whims of the citizenry; thus, they would be more deliberate in their selection of qualified individuals to serve in the Senate.

But, experience proved that this was not always the case. Senators often were chosen on the basis of partisanship and other political alliances. In the early 1900s, Progressive reformers lobbied for an amendment to the Constitution that would remove the selection of senators from the state legislatures and place it in the hands of the citizens. This reform was eventually enacted as the Seventeenth Amendment.

Today, members of both the House of Representatives and the Senate are elected (and reelected) directly by the people. As a result, members of Congress closely monitor their constituents' opinions on a range of political issues. They use phone calls, letters, and e-mails from citizens, as well as the results of public opinion polls conducted nationally and within their states and districts to help them accomplish this task.

Despite this attention to public opinion, representatives and senators continue to fulfill the deliberate role envisioned by the Framers. They do not always enact the policies that public opinion seems to favor. For example, majorities of Americans oppose U.S. engagement abroad. Yet, complete withdrawal of all peacekeeping and ground troops remains a distant possibility. Similarly, majorities favor insurance coverage for contraceptives and equal pay for women, yet Congress cannot agree on these issues.

CRITICAL THINKING QUESTIONS

1. How closely should members of Congress monitor public opinion? How much weight should these opinions have on their voting behavior?
2. Should public opinion matter more in some issue areas than others? If so, on which issues should it matter more? Less?

Toward Reform: The Effects of Public Opinion on Politics

10.5 Evaluate the effects of public opinion on politics.

As early as the founding period, the authors of *The Federalist Papers* noted that "all government rests on public opinion," and as a result, public opinion inevitably influences the actions of politicians and public officials. In many swing states, the public's view of who could best handle the economy, for example, was the driving force behind the victory of Barack Obama in the 2012 presidential campaign.

Andrew Kohut, president of the Pew Research Center, argues that the public has become more of a critical player in national and international politics in the past three decades for a variety of reasons. Key among them is the rise in the number of polls regularly conducted and reported upon.

According to Kohut, it is impossible to find any major policy proposal for which polling has not "played a significant, even critical role."[19] Another observer of public opinion polls says, "Polls have become more important and necessary in news writing and presentation, to the point that their significance overwhelms the phenomena they are supposed to be measuring or supplementing."[20] Kohut offers several well-known cases that show the interaction between public opinion, as reported in polling data, and policy and politics. These include President Bill Clinton's high public opinion ratings in the midst of the Monica Lewinsky sex scandal. When it appeared that the public was rallying to Clinton's side, Republicans' popularity fell. In another example, on the campaign trail in 2012, President Barack Obama deemphasized his work on health care reform, in part due to the deep divisions in public opinion on the issue. Examples such as these show how the public's views, registered through public opinion polls, can affect policy.

On MyPoliSciLab

Review the Chapter

Listen to **Chapter 10** on **MyPoliSciLab**

Roots of Public Opinion Research

10.1 Trace the development of modern public opinion research, p. 303.

Public opinion is what the public thinks about an issue or a particular set of issues. Polls are used to estimate public opinion. Almost since the beginning of the United States, various attempts have been made to influence public opinion about particular issues or to sway elections. *Literary Digest* first began national presidential polling in 1916, using unscientific straw polls. Modern-day polling did not begin until the 1930s. George Gallup was the first to use scientific polling methods to determine public opinion.

Conducting and Analyzing Public Opinion Polls

10.2 Describe the methods for conducting and analyzing different types of public opinion polls, p. 306.

Those who conduct polls must first determine what questions they want answered and how to phrase those questions. Then they must determine the sample, or subset, of the group whose attitudes they wish to measure, and finally they must determine the method for contacting respondents. The different types of polls include telephone polls, in-person interviews, and Internet polls. Once the poll results are in, they must undergo analysis.

Shortcomings of Polling

10.3 Assess the potential shortcomings of polling, p. 312.

Polls may have several shortcomings that create inaccuracies. These include survey errors, not having enough respondent options to reflect public opinion on an issue, polling those who lack the information necessary to accurately respond, inability to measure the intensity of public opinion on an issue, and the public's lack of interest in political issues.

Forming Political Opinions

10.4 Analyze the process by which people form political opinions, p. 315.

The first step in forming opinions occurs through a process known as political socialization. Demographic characteristics—including gender, race, ethnicity, age, and religion—as well as family, school, and peers all affect how we view political events and issues. The views of other people, the media, and cues from leaders and opinion makers also influence our ultimate opinions about political matters.

Toward Reform: The Effects of Public Opinion on Politics

10.5 Evaluate the effects of public opinion on politics, p. 321.

Politicians often use knowledge of the public's views on issues to tailor campaigns or to drive policy decisions.

Learn the Terms

Study and **Review** the **Flashcards**

exit polls, p. 311
margin of error, p. 312
political socialization, p. 315
population, p. 308
public opinion, p. 303
public opinion polls, p. 303
push polls, p. 308
random sampling, p. 308
sample, p. 304
stratified sampling, p. 308
straw polls, p. 304
tracking polls, p. 311

Test Yourself

Study and Review the Practice Tests

1. What was one of the three fatal errors of *Literary Digest*'s 1936 straw poll?

- **a.** Questionnaires were mailed too late.
- **b.** The sample was biased toward blue collar workers.
- **c.** The response rate was low.
- **d.** The margin of error was too large.
- **e.** The citizens surveyed were not interested in politics.

2. What is the correct term for an unscientific survey used to gauge public opinion on a variety of issues and policies?

- **a.** Exit poll
- **b.** Gallup poll
- **c.** Straw poll
- **d.** Tracking poll
- **e.** Internet poll

3. The in-person interviews conducted every two years and used by political scientists to conduct empirical analysis are known as the

- **a.** *Literary Digest* Poll.
- **b.** Gallup Poll.
- **c.** Harris Interactive Poll.
- **d.** American National Election Studies.
- **e.** Tracking Poll.

4. Which of the following is NOT a traditional poll used by reputable polling organizations?

- **a.** Telephone poll
- **b.** In-person interviews
- **c.** Push poll
- **d.** Tracking poll
- **e.** Exit poll

5. Which of the following is NOT a benefit of stratified sampling?

- **a.** It gives each potential voter or adult approximately the same chance of being selected.
- **b.** It avoids undersampling or oversampling key populations.
- **c.** It is relatively inexpensive.
- **d.** It can be conducted at a polling place on Election Day.
- **e.** It allows for a broad, random sample of participants.

6. Which of the following is a shortcoming of polling discussed in your text?

- **a.** Too many respondent options
- **b.** Limited interviewer knowledge
- **c.** Oversampling
- **d.** Inaccurate results
- **e.** Margin of error

7. One measure of the accuracy of a public opinion poll is referred to as the

- **a.** margin of error.
- **b.** tracking error.
- **c.** voting error.
- **d.** information gap.
- **e.** stratified sampling.

8. Which of the following is an accurate description of the different political views of men and women?

- **a.** Women are more conservative on education.
- **b.** Men are more liberal on capital punishment.
- **c.** Men are more supportive of wars and military intervention.
- **d.** Men are more liberal on health care.
- **e.** Women are more conservative on family and children's issues.

9. Which political leader has the greatest influence on public policy?

- **a.** Member of Congress from your district
- **b.** President
- **c.** Supreme Court
- **d.** Governor
- **e.** Attorney general

10. The number of public opinion polls conducted has

- **a.** decreased in recent years.
- **b.** stayed about the same.
- **c.** increased in campaigns, but decreased in government.
- **d.** increased overall.
- **e.** grown in the 1990s, but decreased recently.

Explore Further

Aldrich, John H., and Kathleen M. McGraw. *Improving Public Opinion Surveys: Interdisciplinary Innovation and the American National Election Studies*. Princeton, NJ: Princeton University Press, 2012.

Asher, Herbert. *Polling and the Public: What Every Citizen Should Know*, 8th ed. Washington, DC: CQ Press, 2010.

Atkeson, Lonna Rae, and Cherie D. Maestas. *Catastrophic Politics: How Extraordinary Events Redefine Perceptions of Government*. New York: Cambridge University Press, 2012.

Bardes, Barbara A., and Robert Oldendick. *Public Opinion: Measuring the American Mind*, 4th ed. Lanham, MD: Rowman & Littlefield, 2012.

Best, Samuel J., and Brian S. Krveger. *Exit Polls: Surveying the American Electorate*. Washington, DC: CQ Press, 2012.

Clawson, Rosalee A., and Zoe M. Oxley. *Public Opinion: Democratic Ideals, Democratic Practice*, 2nd ed. Washington, DC: CQ Press, 2012.

Erikson, Robert S., James A. Stimson, and Michael B. MacKuen. *The Macro Polity*. New York: Cambridge University Press, 2002.

Erikson, Robert S., and Kent L. Tedin. *American Public Opinion: Its Origins, Contents, and Impact*, 8th ed. New York: Longman, 2010.

Key, V. O., Jr. *Public Opinion and American Democracy*. New York: Knopf, 1961.

Manza, Jeff, Fay Lomax Cook, and Benjamin I. Page, eds. *Navigating Public Opinion: Polls, Policy, and the Future of American Democracy*. New York: Oxford University Press, 2002.

Norrander, Barbara, and Clyde Wilcox. *Understanding Public Opinion*, 3rd ed. Washington, DC: CQ Press, 2009.

Persily, Nathan, Jack Citrin, and Patrick J. Egan, eds. *Public Opinion and Constitutional Controversy*. New York: Oxford University Press, 2008.

Sniderman, Paul M., and Benjamin Highton. *Facing the Challenge of Democracy: Explorations in the Analysis of Public Opinion and Political Participation*. Princeton, NJ: Princeton University Press, 2012.

Stimson, James A. *Tides of Consent: How Public Opinion Shapes American Politics*. New York: Cambridge University Press, 2004.

Zaller, John. *The Nature and Origins of Mass Opinions*. New York: Cambridge University Press, 1992.

To learn more about the history of the Gallup Organization and poll trends, go to **www.gallup.com.**

To learn more about state and national political polling results, go to Real Clear Politics at **www.realclearpolitics.com/polls/**.

To learn more about the American National Election Studies (ANES), including the history of this public opinion research project, go to **www.electionstudies.org.**

To learn more about the most recent Roper Center polls, go to the Roper Center's public opinion archives at **www.ropercenter.uconn.edu.**

11

Listen to Chapter 11 on MyPoliSciLab

Political Parties

In August 2012, at their quadrennial national convention in Tampa, the Republican Party nominated Governor Mitt Romney as its candidate for president of the United States. He was joined on the ticket by Representative Paul Ryan, the Republican Party's nominee for vice president. A week later, in Charlotte, the Democratic Party formally renominated President Barack Obama and Vice President Joe Biden as the standard bearers for their ticket.

In many ways, the Republican and Democratic conventions were a study in the dramatic differences that exist between two major parties. For example, the keynote speakers who appeared at each of the conventions were designed to appeal to the each party's base of supporters. Actor Clint Eastwood and former Secretary of State Condoleezza Rice spoke at the Republican National Convention, while former President Bill Clinton and First Lady Michelle Obama were featured at the Democratic National Convention.

The issue positions taken by the parties' platforms similarly reflected the often-opposing identities of the Democrats and the Republicans. The Democratic Party's platform, for example, advocated for a woman's right to choose if she wishes to have an abortion. It also supported the legalization of same-sex marriage and cutting the defense budget. The Republican Party's platform, in contrast, took a pro-life stance on abortion, advocated for a constitutional amendment to ban same-sex marriage, and called for maintaining federal spending on national defense.

Despite these differences in content and emphasis, the essential purposes of the Republican and Democratic conventions were quite similar. First, the conventions served as a venue to formally nominate the parties' candidates for president of the United States. Second, the gatherings were designed to engage the party faithful and energize them for the general election campaign. And finally, the conventions were an attempt to increase voters' interest in the upcoming contest. The parties' decision to hold their conventions in the swing states of Florida and North Carolina clearly reflected this goal.

11.1 Trace the evolution of the two-party system in the United States, p. 329.

11.2 Outline the structure of American political parties at the national, state, and local levels, p. 333.

11.3 Identify the functions performed by American political parties, p. 337.

11.4 Analyze how political socialization and group affiliations shape party identification, p. 344.

11.5 Evaluate the role of minor parties in the American two-party system, p. 347.

11.6 Assess party polarization in the modern era, p. 350.

CONVENTIONS ARE PEP RALLIES FOR THE PARTY FAITHFUL Above, delegates celebrate the nomination of Wendell Willkie at the Republican Party convention in Philadelphia in 1940. Below, Michigan delegates show their support for Mitt Romney in 2012.

MyPoliSciLab Videos

Watch on MyPoliSciLab

The Big Picture Learn what purpose the major political parties serve in American politics—and why there are only two of them. Author Larry J. Sabato analyzes the party system in the United States, and weighs what it is able to accomplish against the problems it creates.

The Basics Why do we have political parties in America? In this video, you will learn about the rise of political parties in the United States, the reasons why the two-party system continues to dominate American politics, and how the major parties differ from one another.

In Context Trace the development of political parties in the United States from the time of the ratification of the Constitution. Oklahoma State University political scientist Jeanette M. Mendez explains why political parties emerged and what role they play in our democratic system.

Thinking Like a Political Scientist How can we tell that Americans are increasingly polarized and what are the implications of this trend? In this video, Oklahoma State University political scientist Jeanette M. Mendez reveals how scholars measure party polarization at the elite and mass level and who is behind this phenomenon.

In the Real World Why do Americans only have two party choices—Democrats and Republicans? Real people evaluate the effectiveness of the "winner takes all" electoral system in the United States, and they weigh in on whether third parties—such as the Libertarians and the Green Party—should have more representation in national elections.

So What? Who is in the middle of American politics and why do we see so few of our politicians appealing to them? Author Larry J. Sabato argues that more moderate politicians, who are willing to compromise, must enter politics if anything is ever going to get done.

•••

At the most basic level, a **political party** is an organized effort by office holders, candidates, activists, and voters to pursue their common interests by gaining and exercising power through the electoral process. The goal, of course, is to win office in order to influence public policy. Nominating candidates to run under the party label is, notably, the key differentiating factor between political parties and interest groups. However, as we will discuss later in this text, political parties and interest groups now work together so closely that it may be difficult to tell where one stops and the other begins.

political party
An organized group with shared goals and ideals that joins together to run candidates for office and exercise political and electoral power.

Political scientists sometimes describe political parties as consisting of three separate but related entities: (1) the office holders who organize themselves and pursue policy objectives under a party label (the governmental party); (2) the workers and activists who make up the party's formal organization structure (the organizational party); and, (3) the voters who consider themselves allied or associated with the party (the party in the electorate).[1]

In this chapter, we will address contemporary party politics from each of these vantage points. We will trace parties from their roots in the late 1700s to today and will cover reforms to party politics that have been sought throughout American history. A discussion of the increasing polarization of American political parties will conclude the chapter.

Roots of the Two-Party System

11.1 Trace the evolution of the two-party system in the United States.

merican political parties have been inclusive and pragmatic since the founding of the republic. By tracing the history and development of political parties, we will see that even as dramatic shifts in party coalitions and reforms have taken place to democratize the electoral process, the competitive two-party system has always featured prominently in the United States.

The Development of Political Parties, 1800–1824

Though the Framers warned against a government ruled by permanent political alliances, these alliances actually had their roots in the creation of the U.S. Constitution. Those who supported the stronger central government fashioned in the new Constitution identified with what eventually became the Federalist Party, while the future Democratic-Republicans favored a system of greater state authority similar to that created by the Articles of Confederation. These alliances, however did not codify into permanent groups until President George Washington stepped off the national stage. To win the presidency in 1796, his vice president, John Adams, narrowly defeated archrival Thomas Jefferson. According to the Constitution, Jefferson became vice president. Over the course of Adams's single term, the Federalists and Democratic-Republicans became increasingly organized around these clashing men and their principles. In the presidential election of 1800, the Federalists supported Adams's bid for a second term, but this time the Democratic-Republicans prevailed with their nominee, Jefferson, who became the first U.S. president elected as the nominee of a political party.

WHERE DID THE PARTY SYMBOLS ORIGINATE?

In 1874, the cartoonist Thomas Nast published a cartoon depicting the upcoming election at the Central Park Zoo. The elephant was labeled "The Republican Vote" running away from the donkey, which was the symbol chosen by Andrew Jackson for his campaign, after being known as "the jackass."

Jefferson was deeply committed to the ideas of his party but not nearly as devoted to the idea of a party system. He regarded his party as a temporary measure necessary to defeat Adams, not a long-term political tool or an essential element of democracy. As a result, Jefferson's party never achieved widespread loyalty among the nation; rather, it drew most of its support from the agrarian South. The Federalists, too, remained a regional party, drawing their support from the commercial New England states. No broad-based national party organizations existed to mobilize popular support.[2] Just as the nation was in its infancy, so, too, was the party system.

political machine

A party organization that recruits voter loyalty with tangible incentives and is characterized by a high degree of control over member activity.

□ Jacksonian Democracy, 1824–1860

After the spirited confrontations of the republic's early years, political parties faded somewhat in importance for a quarter of a century. By 1820, the Federalist Party dissolved. James Monroe's presidency from 1817 to 1825 produced the so-called Era of Good Feelings, when party competition was nearly nonexistent at the national level (see Figure 11.1).

Party organizations, however, continued to develop at the state level, fueled in part by the enormous growth in the electorate that took place between 1820 and 1840. During this twenty-year period, the United States expanded westward and most states abolished property requirements as a condition of white male suffrage. The number of votes cast in presidential contests rose from 300,000 to more than 2 million.

Party membership broadened along with the electorate. Formed around President Andrew Jackson's popularity, the Democratic Party, which succeeded the old Jeffersonian Democratic-Republicans, attracted most of the newly enfranchised voters, who were drawn to Jackson's charismatic style. Jackson's strong personality polarized many people, and opposition to the president coalesced into the Whig Party. Among the Whig Party's early leaders was Henry Clay, Speaker of the House from 1811 to 1820.

The incumbent Jackson, having won a first term as president in 1828, defeated Clay in the 1832 presidential contest. This election was the first in which the party's nominee was chosen at a large party convention rather than the small undemocratic caucuses popular until that time. Thus, Jackson was the first chief executive to win the White House as the nominee of a truly national, popularly based political party.

The Whigs and the Democrats continued to strengthen after 1832. Their competition usually proved fierce and closely matched, and they brought the United States the first broadly supported two-party system in the Western world.[3] Unfortunately for the Whigs, the issue of slavery sharpened the many divisive tensions within the party, which led to its gradual dissolution and replacement by the new Republican Party. Formed in 1854 by anti-slavery activists, the Republican Party set its sights on the abolition (or at least containment) of slavery. After a losing presidential effort for John C. Frémont in 1856, the party was able to assemble enough support primarily from former Whigs and anti-slavery northern Democrats to win the presidency for Abraham Lincoln in a fragmented 1860 vote. From the presidential election of 1860 to this day, the same two major parties, the Republicans and the Democrats, have dominated elections in the United States, and control of an electoral majority has seesawed between them.

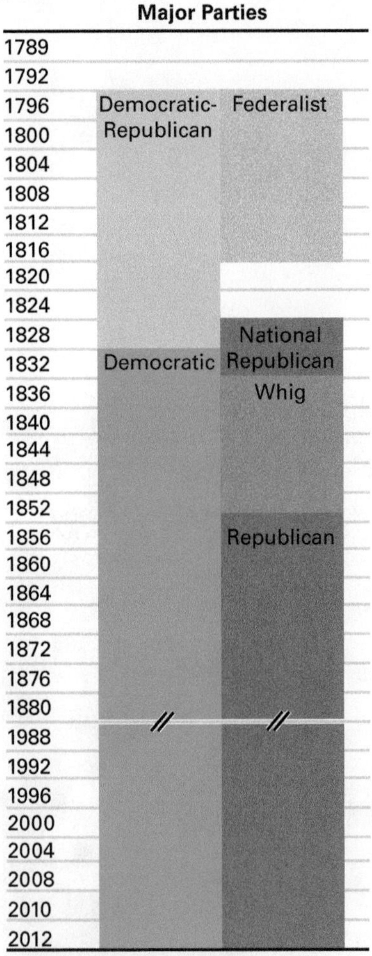

Major Parties

1789, 1792, 1796, 1800, 1804, 1808, 1812, 1816, 1820, 1824, 1828, 1832, 1836, 1840, 1844, 1848, 1852, 1856, 1860, 1864, 1868, 1872, 1876, 1880, 1988, 1992, 1996, 2000, 2004, 2008, 2010, 2012

Democratic-Republican | Federalist

Democratic | National Republican | Whig | Republican

FIGURE 11.1 HOW HAS THE TWO-PARTY SYSTEM DEVELOPED?

The United States has had two political parties for much of its existence. Though the names of these parties have changed over time, the central controversies over the role of government in citizens' lives have remained constant. The two parties we know today, the Democrats and Republicans, have existed since 1856.

SOURCE: Harold W. Stanley and Richard G. Niemi, *Vital Statistics on American Politics, 2007–2008* (Washington, DC: CQ Press, 2007). Updated by the authors.

□ The Golden Age, 1860–1932

Party stability, the dominance of party organizations in local and state governments, and the impact of those organizations on the lives of millions of voters were the central traits of the era called the "Golden Age" of political parties. This era, from the end of post–Civil War Reconstruction until the reforms of the Progressive era, featured remarkable stability in the identity of both the Republican and Democratic Parties. Such stability has been exceptionally rare in democratic republics around the world.

Political machines, organizations that use tangible incentives such as jobs and favors to win loyalty among voters, were a central element of life for millions of people in the United States during the Golden Age. In fact, for city-dwellers, and particularly immigrants from European countries such as Ireland, Italy, and Germany, party and government were virtually interchangeable during this time. In addition to providing housing, employment, and even food to many voters, parties in most major cities offered entertainment by organizing torchlight parades, weekend picnics, socials, and other community events. Many citizens—even those who were not particularly "political"—attended, thereby forming some allegiance to one party or the other.

The parties also gave citizens the opportunity for upward social mobility as they rose in the organization. As a result, parties generated intense loyalty and devotion among their supporters and office holders, which helped to produce startlingly high levels of voter turnout—75 percent or better in all presidential elections from 1876 to 1900—compared with today's 50–60 percent.[4]

candidate-centered politics
Politics that focus on the candidates, their particular issues, and character rather than party affiliation.

The Modern Era

Between 1900 and the 1930s, the government gradually took over a number of important functions previously performed by the parties, such as printing ballots, conducting elections, and providing social welfare services. These changes had a major impact on party loyalty and strength. Beginning in the 1930s with Franklin D. Roosevelt's New Deal, social services began to be regarded as a right of citizenship rather than as a privilege extended in exchange for a person's support of a party. The flow of immigrants also slowed dramatically in the 1920s, causing party machines to lose even greater power in many places.

In the post–World War II era, extensive social changes continued to contribute to the move away from strong parties. A weakening of the party system gave rise to **candidate-centered politics**, which focus on candidates, their particular issues, and character, rather than party affiliation. Parties' diminished control over issues and campaigns also has given candidates considerable power in how they conduct themselves during election season and how they seek resources. Interest groups and lobbyists have stepped into the void that weaker parties have left behind. Candidates today compete for endorsements and contributions from a variety of multi-issue as well as single-issue organizations.

The population shift from urban to suburban locales has also weakened parties. During the post–World War II era, millions of people moved from the cities to the suburbs, where a sense of privacy and detachment can deter even the most energetic party organizers. In addition, population growth in the last half-century has created legislative districts with far more people, making it less feasible to knock on every door or shake every hand.

It is difficult to imagine modern American politics without political parties, but where in the text of the Constitution do we find the provision to establish them?

Nowhere in the Constitution do we find a provision establishing political parties. Some might point out that the First Amendment sets forth the right to assemble as a constitutional right, and this right certainly helps to preserve and protect parties from governmental oppression during rallies and conventions. However, the right to assemble is not the same as permission for two organizations to mediate elections. Furthermore, James Madison, in *Federalist No. 10*, feared that a majority tyranny created by the domination of a single faction fighting for one set of interests posed one of the greatest dangers to the new American republic. For that reason, he hoped that extending the sphere of representation among many members of Congress would prevent a majority of representatives from coming together to vote as a bloc.

How well the modern Democratic and Republican Parties embody Madison's ideal is an open question. On one hand, the members of Congress who represent each of the parties are not monolithic blocs. Regional, religious, and ethnic variations, to name a few, characterize these individuals. On the other hand, we have heard growing cries in Washington, D.C., in recent years regarding the difficulties of being a political moderate; longtime Senator Olympia Snowe (R–ME), for example, cited the growing partisanship of Congress as a key reason behind her decision not to seek reelection in 2012. The growing polarization of the parties in government is discussed throughout this chapter.

CRITICAL THINKING QUESTIONS

1. How could the Constitution be amended to officially establish political parties as an institution of government? Would this be a good idea? Why or why not?
2. Are modern political parties inclusive enough of varied citizen interests? Why or why not?

party realignment
Dramatic shifts in partisan preferences that drastically alter the political landscape.

critical election
An election that signals a party realignment through voter polarization around new issues and personalities.

secular realignment
The gradual rearrangement of party coalitions, based more on demographic shifts than on shocks to the political system.

□ Citizen Support and Party Realignment

Periodically, voters make dramatic shifts in partisan preference that drastically alter the political landscape. During these **party realignments**, existing party affiliations are subject to upheaval: many voters may change parties, and the youngest age group of voters may permanently adopt the label of the newly dominant party.[5]

Preceding a major realignment are one or more **critical elections**, which may polarize voters around new issues and personalities in reaction to crucial developments, such as a war or an economic depression. Three tumultuous eras in particular have produced significant critical elections. First, Thomas Jefferson, in reaction against the Federalist Party's agenda of a strong, centralized federal government, formed the Democratic-Republican Party, which won the presidency and Congress in 1800. Second, in reaction to the growing crisis over slavery, the Whig Party gradually dissolved and the Republican Party gained strength and ultimately won the presidency in 1860. Third, the Great Depression caused large numbers of voters to repudiate Republican Party policies and embrace the Democratic Party in 1932 (see Figure 11.2). Each of these cases resulted in fundamental and enduring alterations in the party's base of supporters. During the New Deal realignment, for example, blue-collar workers, labor union members, white Southerners, and the poor gravitated toward the Democratic Party.

A critical election is not the only occasion when changes in partisan affiliation are accommodated. More gradual shifts in party coalitions, called **secular realignments**, may also change voters' loyalties.[6] This piecemeal process depends not on convulsive shocks to the political system but on slow, barely discernible demographic shifts—the shrinking of one party's base of support and the enlargement of the other's, for example—or simple generational replacement (that is, the dying off of the older generation and the maturing of the younger generation).

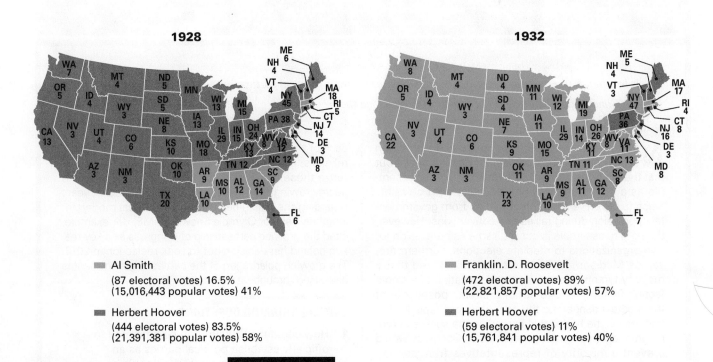

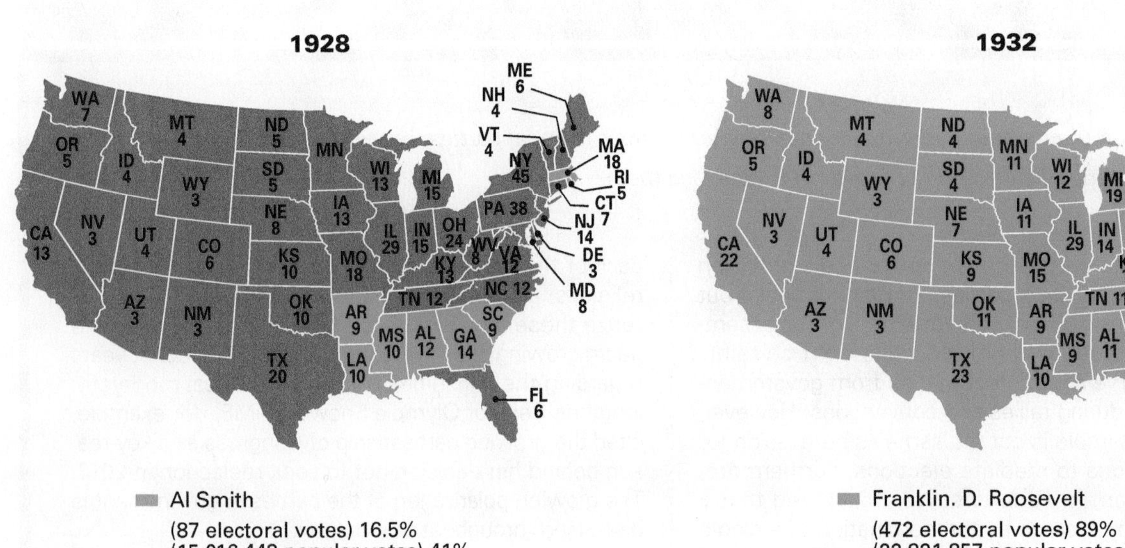

FIGURE 11.2 WHAT DOES A REALIGNMENT LOOK LIKE?

The map on the left shows the Electoral College results of the 1928 election, won by Republican Herbert Hoover. The map on the right shows the results of the 1932 election, won by Democrat Franklin D. Roosevelt. The numbers in the maps represent the number of Electoral College votes allocated to each state. Note the obvious increase in the number and percentage of "blue states."

The most significant recent example of this phenomenon occurred during the late 1980s and early 1990s, when the southern states, traditionally Democratic stalwarts since the Civil War, shifted dramatically toward the Republican Party. Many factors contributed to this gradual regional shift in party allegiance. Southern Democrats were the most conservative of the New Deal coalition, favoring the social status quo and opposing civil rights reform and affirmative action. As the Democratic Party turned toward more liberal social causes, such as civil rights and social spending, many southern voters and politicians shifted their allegiance toward the Republicans.[7]

The Organization of American Political Parties

11.2 Outline the structure of American political parties at the national, state, and local levels.

Despite significant changes in their structure and functions, the two major parties remain fairly well organized. Parties organize conflict and represent citizens' interests in Washington, D.C., state capitals, and local governments throughout the nation (see Figure 11.3). They also engage in many of the fund-raising activities necessary to run candidates for political office and provide the manpower and electoral expertise to deliver voters on Election Day. Examining the national, state, and local parties separately should not lead us to overlook the increasing integration of these party units, however.

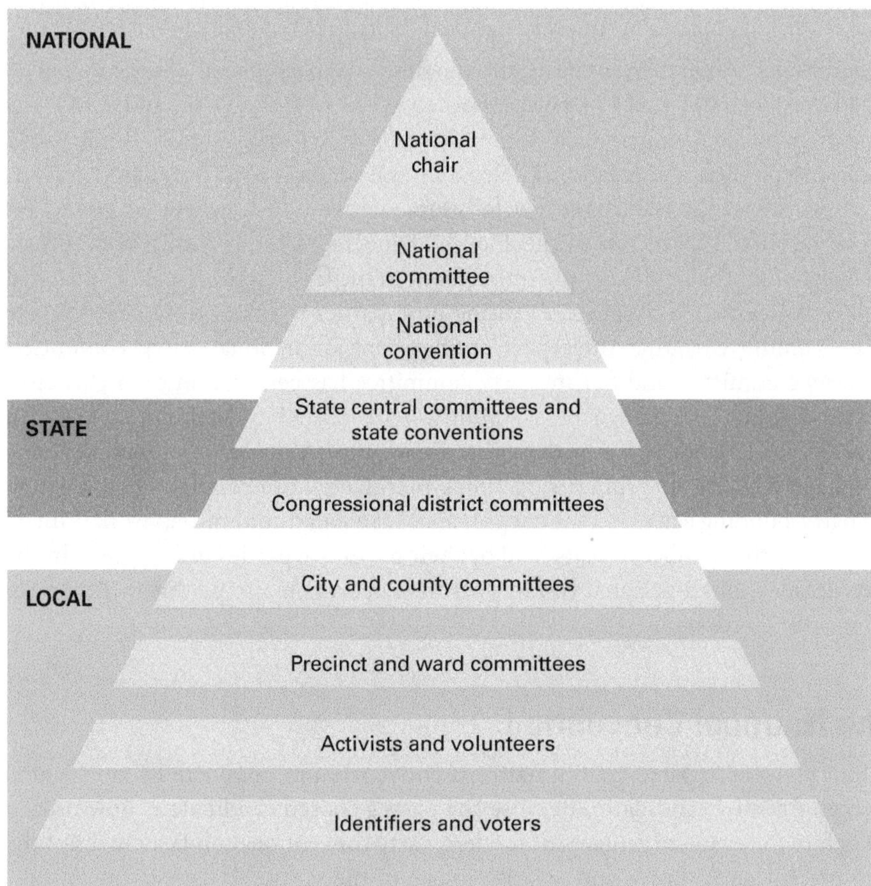

FIGURE 11.3 HOW ARE POLITICAL PARTIES ORGANIZED?

American political parties are national in scope, but their real roots—and power—lie in state and local party organizations. Thus, the organization of political parties in America is often presented as a pyramid, with identifiers and voters as the "base" and the national chair as the "pinnacle."

national convention

A party meeting held in the presidential election year for the purposes of nominating a presidential and vice presidential ticket and adopting a platform.

☐ The National Party

The national party organization sits at the pinnacle of the party system in the United States. Its primary function is to establish a cohesive vision for partisan identifiers nationwide and to disseminate that vision to party members and voters. A chairperson, who serves as the head of the national committee, leads the national party. Every four years, the national committee organizes a convention designed to reevaluate policies and nominate a candidate for the presidency.

THE NATIONAL CHAIRPERSON The key national party official is the chair of the national committee. The chair is usually selected by the sitting president or newly nominated presidential candidate, who is accorded the right to name the individual for at least the duration of his or her campaign. The national committee may also choose the chair when the election has ended and the party has been defeated.

The chair is the primary spokesperson and arbitrator for the party during the four years between elections. He or she has the responsibility of damping down factionalism, negotiating candidate disputes, and preparing the machinery for the next presidential election. Perhaps most critically, the chair is called upon to raise funds and keep the party financially strong. Balancing the interests of all potential party candidates is a particularly difficult job, and strict neutrality is normally expected from the chair. In 2012, the chair of the Republican National Committee was Reince Priebus. His Democratic counterpart was Representative Debbie Wasserman-Schultz (D-FL).

THE NATIONAL COMMITTEE The first national party committees were skeletal and formed some years after the first presidential nominating conventions in the 1830s. First the Democrats in 1848 and then the Republicans in 1856 established national governing bodies—the Democratic National Committee, or DNC, and the Republican National Committee, or RNC—to make arrangements for the national conventions and to coordinate the subsequent presidential campaigns.

In addition, to serve their interests, the congressional party caucuses in both houses organized their own national committees, loosely allied with the DNC and RNC. The National Republican Congressional Committee (NRCC) originated in 1866, when the Radical Republican congressional delegation was feuding with Abraham Lincoln's moderate successor, President Andrew Johnson, and wanted a counterweight to his control of the RNC. At the same time, House Democrats set up a similar committee.

Ratification of the Seventeenth Amendment to the Constitution in 1913 initiated the popular election of U.S. senators causing both parties to organize separate Senate campaign committees. This three-part arrangement of national party committee, House party committee, and Senate party committee has persisted in both parties to the present day, and each party's three committees are located in Washington, D.C. An informal division of labor, however, does exist among the national committees. Whereas the DNC and RNC focus primarily on aiding presidential campaigns and conducting general party-building activities, the congressional campaign committees work primarily to maximize the number of seats held by their respective parties in Congress. In the past two decades, all six national committees have become major players in American campaigns and elections.[8]

☐ The National Convention

Every four years, each party holds a **national convention** to nominate its presidential and vice presidential candidates. Because the party's chosen candidate is now usually known before the event, organizers of modern party conventions can heavily script the event to present an inclusive and positive image of the party. Modern party conventions, therefore, serve an important role as pep rallies to mobilize supporters and engage more casual observers. The convention also fulfills its function as the ultimate governing body for the party. The rules adopted and the party platform that is passed serve as durable guidelines to steer the party until the next convention.

Delegates, or representatives to the party conventions, do much of the work at these events. Delegates are no longer selected by party leaders, but by citizens participating in primary elections and grassroots caucuses. The apportionment of delegates to presidential candidates varies by party. A Democratic Party rule decrees that a state's delegates be apportioned in proportion to the votes cast in support of each candidate in the state primary or caucus (so that, for example, a candidate who receives 30 percent of the vote gains about 30 percent of the convention delegates). In contrast, the Republican Party allows states to choose between this proportional system or a winner-take-all system.

delegate
Representative to the party convention.

superdelegate
Delegate to the Democratic Party's national convention that is reserved for a party official and whose vote at the convention is unpledged to a candidate.

The Democratic Party also allows party officials to serve as **superdelegates**. Superdelegates are not pledged to a candidate and thus may support whichever candidate they choose. Superdelegates allow the party to maintain some level of control over the selection process, while still allowing most delegates to be pledged by the people.

Who the delegates are, a topic of less importance today than when delegates enjoyed more power in the selection process, still reveals interesting differences between political parties. Both parties draw their delegates from an elite group whose income and educational levels are far above the average American's. About 40 percent of delegates at the 2012 Democratic convention were minorities, and half were women. Only 13 percent of the delegates to the 2012 Republican convention were racial and ethnic minorities. Although this number may seem small when compared to the Democrats, it represents an increase in minority representation from 2008, when 7 percent of the delegates were minorities.

☐ State and Local Parties

Although national committee activities attract most of the media attention, the roots of the party lie not in Washington, D.C., but in the states and localities. Virtually all government regulation of political parties falls to the states. Most importantly, the vast majority of party leadership positions are filled at subnational levels.

The arrangement of party committees provides for a broad base of support. The smallest voting unit, the precinct, usually takes in a few adjacent neighborhoods and is the fundamental building block of the party. The United States has more than 100,000 precincts. The precinct committee members are the foot soldiers of any party, and their efforts are supplemented by party committees above them in the wards, cities, counties, towns, villages, and congressional districts.

The state governing body supervising this collection of local party organizations is usually called the state central (or executive) committee. Its members come from all major geographic units, as determined by and selected under state law. Generally, state parties are free to act within the limits set by their state legislatures without interference from the national party. One key exception is the selection and seating of presidential convention delegates. Here, the national committee may establish quotas or mandates regarding type, number, or manner of electing delegates.

Increased fund-raising, campaign events, registration drives, publicity, and distribution of campaign literature have also enabled parties to become more effective political actors over the past three decades.[9]

☐ Informal Groups

Numerous official and semi-official groups also attempt to affect the formal party organizations. Both the DNC and RNC have affiliated organizations of state and local party women (the National Federation of Democratic Women and the National Federation of Republican Women), as well as numerous college campus organizations, including the College Democrats of America and the College Republican National Committee. The youth divisions (the Young Democrats of America and the Young Republican National Federation) have a generous definition of "young," up to and including age thirty-five. State governors in each party have their own party associations, too (the Democratic Governors Association and the Republican Governors Association). Each of these organizations provides loyal and energetic foot soldiers for campaigns and voter mobilization.

Explore Your World

Political parties are the building blocks of governmental systems across the globe. They are a fundamental representation of the values and ideals of the people, and are essential for the long-term development of emerging democracies. Countries use party systems to shape and maintain their chosen system of government, with varying degrees of effectiveness. While the United States has only two major parties, other states may have as few as one or more than fifty political parties. Review the table below for information on parties in the legislatures of several other countries.

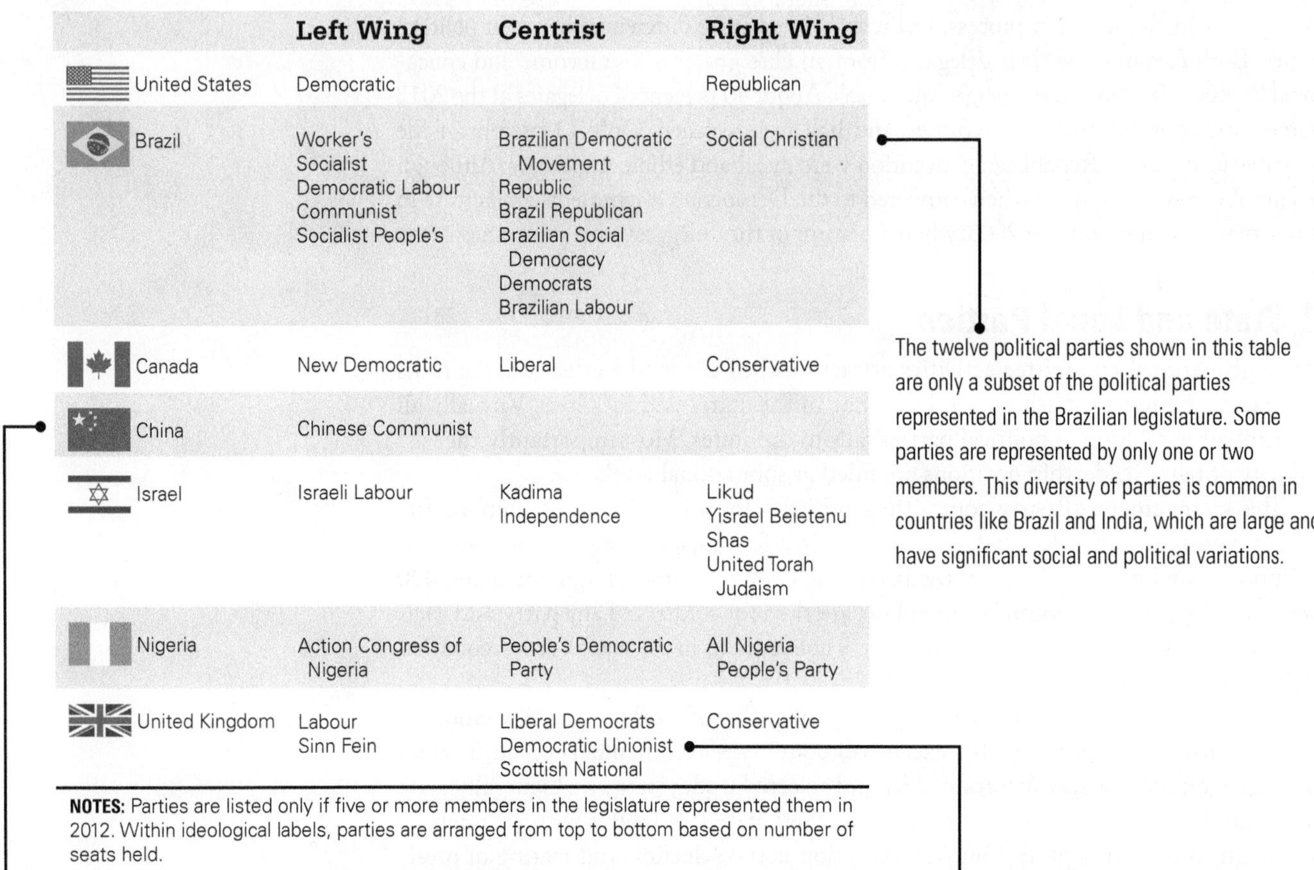

	Left Wing	Centrist	Right Wing
United States	Democratic		Republican
Brazil	Worker's Socialist Democratic Labour Communist Socialist People's	Brazilian Democratic Movement Republic Brazil Republican Brazilian Social Democracy Democrats Brazilian Labour	Social Christian
Canada	New Democratic	Liberal	Conservative
China	Chinese Communist		
Israel	Israeli Labour	Kadima Independence	Likud Yisrael Beitenu Shas United Torah Judaism
Nigeria	Action Congress of Nigeria	People's Democratic Party	All Nigeria People's Party
United Kingdom	Labour Sinn Fein	Liberal Democrats Democratic Unionist Scottish National	Conservative

NOTES: Parties are listed only if five or more members in the legislature represented them in 2012. Within ideological labels, parties are arranged from top to bottom based on number of seats held.

The twelve political parties shown in this table are only a subset of the political parties represented in the Brazilian legislature. Some parties are represented by only one or two members. This diversity of parties is common in countries like Brazil and India, which are large and have significant social and political variations.

In some states, such as China, only one political party is allowed to exist upon order of the government. The Chinese Communist Party is the world's largest political party, claiming over 80 million members.

Many states, like the United Kingdom, have significant nationalist or regional parties represented in their legislatures. Sinn Fein, the Democratic Unionist, and the Scottish National Parties all represent this ideal in the United Kingdom.

CRITICAL THINKING QUESTIONS

1. What geographic and political factors do you think contribute to the number of political parties in each state?
2. How are common words such as "democratic" used differently across political systems? Why do you think these variations exist?
3. Do you feel that your views can be adequately represented by the two-party system in the United States? Do you completely agree with the views of one party, or do you find yourself more moderate in your opinions?

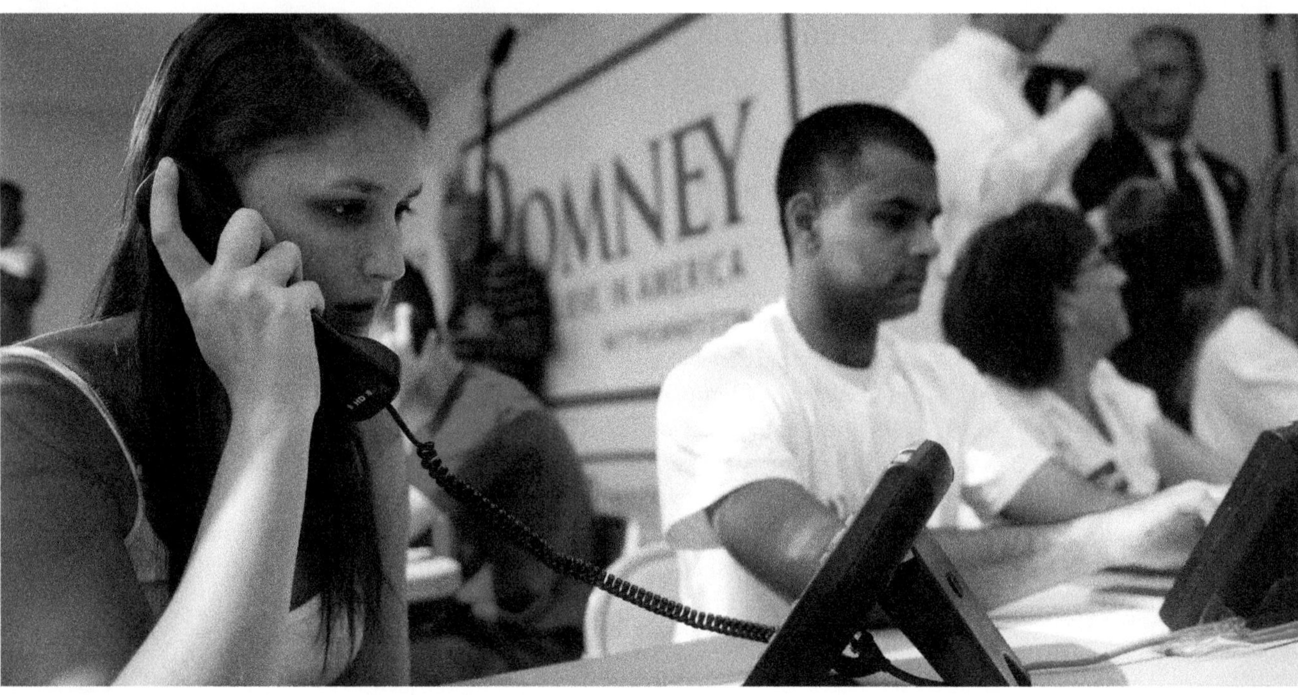

HOW DO COLLEGE STUDENTS HELP POLITICAL PARTIES?

College students can be important volunteers for political parties and candidates. Here, students volunteer to make phone calls on behalf of 2012 Republican presidential candidate Mitt Romney.

think tank
Institutional collection of policy-oriented researchers and academics who are sources of policy ideas.

Just outside the party orbit are the supportive interest groups and associations that often provide money, labor, or other forms of assistance to the parties. Labor unions, progressive groups, teachers, African American and women's groups, and Americans for Democratic Action are some of the Democratic Party's most important supporters. Businesses, the U.S. Chamber of Commerce, evangelical Christian organizations, and some pro-life groups work closely with the Republicans.

Each U.S. party also has several institutionalized sources of policy ideas. Though unconnected to the parties in any official sense, these **think tanks**, or institutional collections of policy-oriented researchers and academics who are sources of policy ideas, influence party positions and platforms. Republicans have dominated the world of think tanks, with prominent conservative groups including the Hudson Institute, American Enterprise Institute, and Heritage Foundation. And, the libertarian Cato Institute is closely aligned with the Republican Party. While generally fewer in number, prominent think tanks that generally align with the Democratic Party include the Center for National Policy and Open Society Institute. The Brookings Institution, founded in 1916, prides itself on a scholarly and nonpartisan approach to public policy.

Activities of American Political Parties

11.3 Identify the functions performed by American political parties.

For over 200 years, the two-party system has served as the mechanism American society uses to organize and resolve social and political conflict. Political parties often are the chief agents of change in our political system. They provide vital services to society, and it would be difficult to envision political life without them.

☐ Running Candidates for Office

The election, proclaimed author H. G. Wells, is "democracy's ceremonial, its feast, its great function," and the political parties assist in this ceremony in essential ways. First, the parties help to raise money for candidates. Second, parties help to recruit candidates, mobilize public support, and get out the vote.

RAISING MONEY Political parties, particularly during mid-term and presidential election years, spend a great deal of time raising and disseminating money for candidates. Historically, Republicans enjoyed greater fund-raising success than Democrats, due in large part to a significant number of wealthy identifiers and donors. However, in recent years, Democrats have caught up, even out-raising Republicans during the 2008 presidential election (see Figure 11.4).

The parties can raise so much money because they have developed networks of donors accessed by a variety of methods. Both parties have highly successful mail, phone, and e-mail solicitation lists. They also use Internet sites, online advertisements, and social media such as Facebook and Twitter to help reach supporters and raise money for their candidates' electoral pursuits.

The Republican effort to reach donors through the mail dates back to the early 1960s and accelerated in the mid-1970s, when postage and production costs were relatively low. Throughout the election, Republican and Democratic Party activists received emails and phone calls soliciting donations. Democrats received emails from a wide variety of celebrities and political figures, including former President Bill Clinton and singer Beyonce, while Republicans received most of their emails directly from Mitt Romney.

MOBILIZING SUPPORT AND GETTING OUT THE VOTE The parties take a number of steps to broaden citizens' knowledge of candidates and campaigns in the days leading up to the election. Parties, for example, spend millions of dollars for national, state, and local public opinion surveys. In important contests, the parties also commission tracking polls to chart the daily rise or fall of public support for a candidate. The information provided in these polls is invaluable to developing campaign strategy in the tense concluding days of an election.

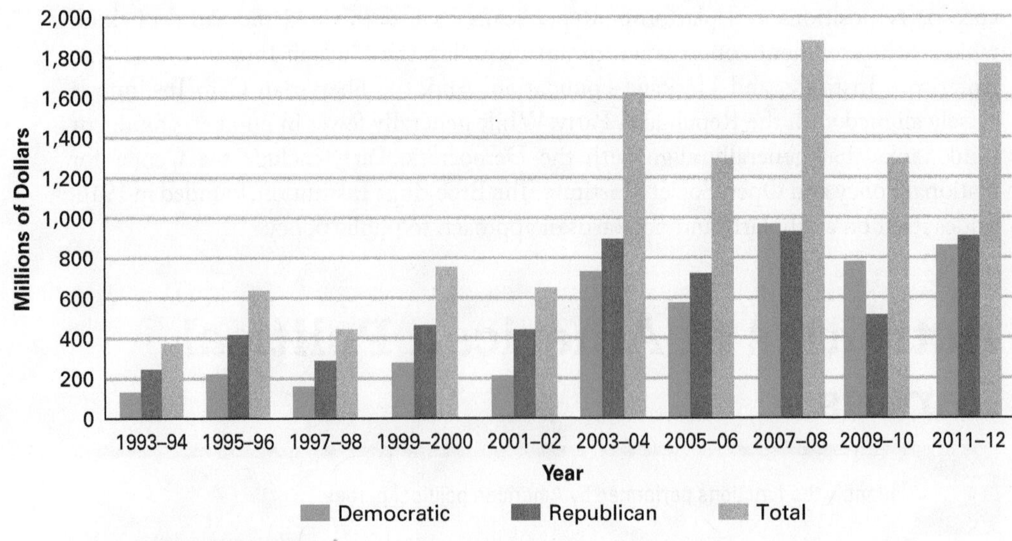

FIGURE 11.4 HOW MUCH MONEY DO PARTIES RAISE?

Changes in political campaigns and campaign finance laws have allowed both political parties to raise increasing amounts of money over the past twenty years. Historically, the Republican Party's fund-raising dwarfed that of their Democratic counterparts, but in recent years, the Democratic Party has come much closer to and even surpassed Republicans' fund-raising in 2008.

SOURCES: 2003–2012 from Center for Responsive Politics, www.opensecrets.org, and earlier years from Harold W. Stanley and Richard Niemi, *Vital Statistics on American Politics, 2003–2004* (Washington, DC: CQ Press, 2004).

Both parties also operate sophisticated media divisions that specialize in the design and production of TV advertisements for party nominees at all levels. And, both parties train the armies of political volunteers and paid operatives who run the candidates' campaigns. Early in each election cycle, the national parties also help prepare voluminous research reports on opponents, analyzing their public statements, votes, and attendance records.

Finally, both parties greatly emphasize their duty to "get out the vote" (GOTV) on Election Day. One tactic used by modern parties is "micro-targeting," a practice derived from the field of consumer behavior. With data obtained from a growing volume of government census records and marketing firms, parties use advanced computer models to identify potential voters based on consumer preferences, personal habits, and past voting behavior. Once identified, these voters' names are stored in a database—Republicans call theirs the Voter Vault—and shared with individual campaigns, whose volunteers contact voters by phone and personal visits. The detailed information accessed from these databases allows campaigns to carefully tailor their messages to individual voters. The voter turnout drive culminates during the final seventy-two hours of the campaign, when party operatives personally contact voters and remind them to vote. During the 2012 election, Democrats attributed much of their victory in the presidential election to their successful GOTV efforts—or ground game—which led to Democrats out-voting Republicans by significant margins in most states.

national party platform
A statement of the general and specific philosophy and policy goals of a political party, usually promulgated at the national convention.

☐ Formulating and Promoting Policy

The **national party platform** is the most visible instrument that parties use to formulate, convey, and promote public policy. Every four years, each party writes a lengthy platform explaining its positions on key issues. In a two-party system, a party's platform argues why its preferences are superior to those of the rival party. This is particularly true for contentious social issues that have little room for compromise and that divide the electorate, such as abortion and same-sex marriage.

Scholarship suggests that about two-thirds of the promises in the victorious party's presidential platform are completely or mostly implemented. Moreover, about one-half or more of the pledges of the losing party also tend to find their way into public policy, a trend no doubt reflecting the effort of both parties to support broad policy positions that enjoy widespread support in the general public.[10] For example, in 2012, both party platforms supported budget reform, an issue that Democrats and Republicans in Congress vowed to quickly address (see Table 11.1).

TABLE 11.1 WHAT DO PARTY PLATFORMS SAY?

Issue	Democratic Platform	Republican Platform
Abortion	Strongly supports *Roe* v. *Wade* (1973) and a woman's right to choose.	Upholds the "sanctity of human life"; believes unborn children have "individual right to life."
Defense	Supports reductions in federal defense spending.	Believes that cuts in defense spending would be "disaster" for national security.
Medicare	Opposes any movement toward privatization of or vouchers for Medicare.	Believes in "premium-support" model for Medicare.
Public-Employee Unions	Opposes attacks on collective bargaining undertaken by some Republican governors.	Supports Republican governors' efforts to reform laws governing unions.
Same-Sex Marriage	Supports marriage equality and equal treatment under law for same-sex couples.	Supports constitutional amendment defining marriage as between one man and one woman.

SOURCES: "Moving America Forward: 2012 Democratic National Platform," http://www.democrats.org/democratic-national-platform; and http://www.gop.com/2012-republican-platform_home.

11.1

11.2

11.4

11.5

11.6

☐ Organizing Government

Political parties are able to implement their policy agendas in part because they play such a significant role in organizing the operations of government and providing structure for political conflict within and between the branches. Here, we consider the role of parties in the legislative, executive, and judicial branches at the federal and state levels.

PARTIES IN CONGRESS Nowhere is the party more visible or vital than in the Congress. In this century, political parties have dramatically increased the sophistication and impact of their internal congressional organizations. Prior to the beginning of every session, the parties in both houses of Congress gather (or "caucus") separately to select party leaders and to arrange for the appointment of members of each chamber's committees. In effect, then, the parties organize and operate Congress.

Congressional party leaders enforce discipline among party members in various ways. These leaders can, for example, award committee assignments and chairs to the loyal, or withhold them from the rebellious, regardless of seniority. Pork-barrel projects—government projects yielding rich patronage benefits that sustain many legislators' electoral survival—may be included or deleted during the appropriations process. Small favors and perquisites (such as the allocation of desirable office space or the scheduling of floor votes for the convenience of a member) can also be useful levers.

Perhaps as a response to these increased incentives, party labels have become the most powerful predictor of congressional voting. In the past few years, party-line voting has increased noticeably, as reflected in the upward trend in both Democrats' and Republicans' party unity, shown in Figure 11.5. Although not invariably predictive, a member's party affiliation proved to be the best indicator of his or her votes. In 2011, party unity among both parties in the House and Senate topped 85 percent. The House Republicans and the Senate Democrats—who controlled their houses of Congress—set records for party unity at 91 and 92 percent, respectively.[11]

THE PRESIDENTIAL PARTY Among the many roles assigned to the president is that of informal party leader. This means that he is often the public face of his party's agenda. He may find it is his responsibility to bring together an often divided party and wrangle votes in Congress for important political battles, as Barack Obama did on health care reform in 2010. Presidents reciprocate the support they receive from members of Congress by appointing many activists to office, recruiting candidates, raising money for the party treasury, and campaigning extensively for party nominees during election seasons.

Some presidents have taken their party responsibilities more seriously than have others.[12] Democrats Woodrow Wilson and Franklin D. Roosevelt dedicated themselves to building their party in both the electorate and in government. Republicans Ronald Reagan and George W. Bush also exemplified the "pro-party" presidency. Most of President George W. Bush's major policy initiatives and legislative victories depended on support from his own party and prompted near-unanimous opposition from the Democrats. This emphasis on satisfying core GOP voters was instrumental in encouraging the party's base to turn out to vote, albeit with mixed electoral success.

PARTIES IN THE FEDERAL COURTS Although federal judges do not run for office under a party label, judges are creatures of the political process, and their posts are considered patronage plums. Judges are often chosen not only for their abilities but also as representatives of a certain philosophy or approach to government. Most recent presidents have appointed judges overwhelmingly from their own party. Democratic executives tend to select more liberal judges who are friendly to social programs or labor interests. Republican executives generally lean toward conservatives, hoping they will be tough on criminal defendants, opposed to abortion, and supportive of business interests. These opposing ideals may lead to conflict between the president and the

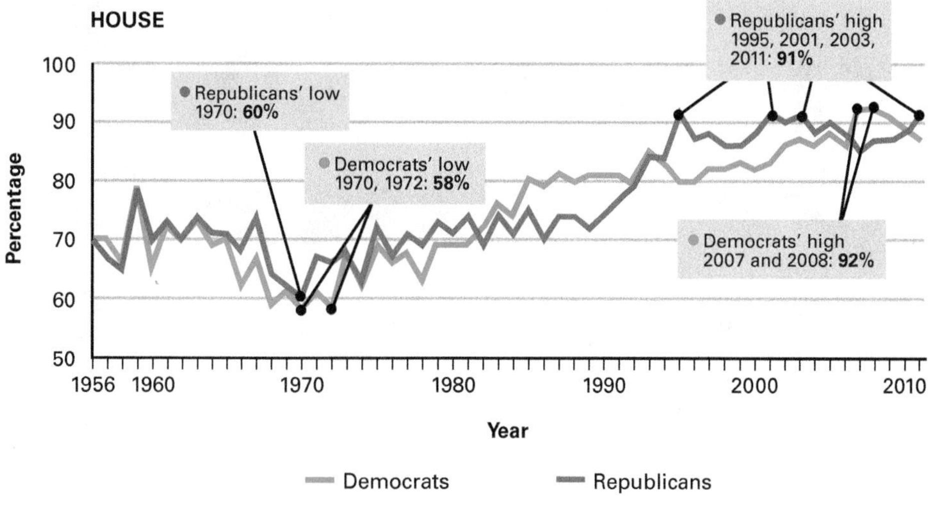

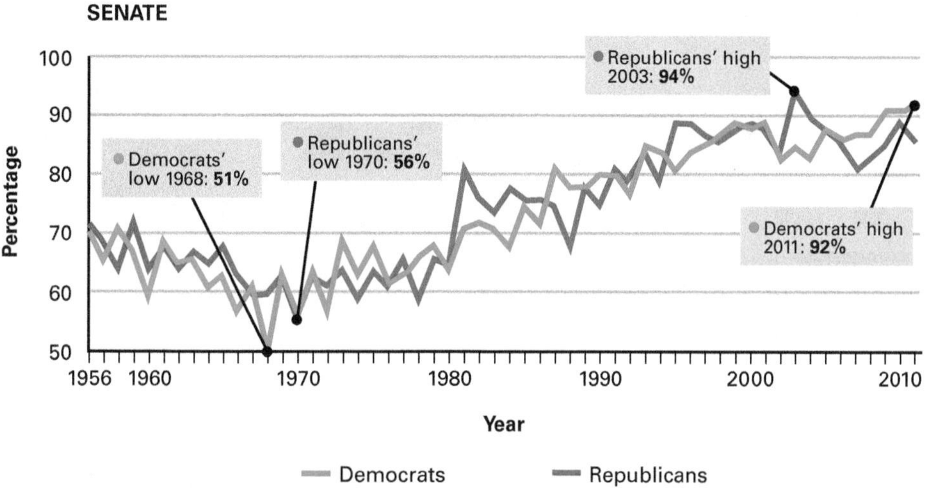

FIGURE 11.5 HOW HAVE PARTY UNITY SCORES CHANGED?

Party unity scores have increased dramatically over time. As the two parties have become increasingly homogenized and polarized, their unity on important issues has risen accordingly, upwards of 90 percent in some recent Congresses.

SOURCE: http://media.cq.com/media/2011/votestudy_2011/graphics/

Senate. President Barack Obama, for example, has seen many of his judicial appointments blocked by Senate Republicans, who refused to allow a vote on the nominations. This tactic is an attempt to forestall ideological changes that can last far beyond the next election cycle.

PARTIES IN STATE GOVERNMENT Most of the conclusions discussed about the parties' relationships to the national legislative, executive, and judicial branches apply to those branches at the state level as well. State legislators, however, depend on their state and local parties for election assistance much more than do their congressional counterparts. Whereas members of Congress have significant support from interest groups and large government-provided staffs to assist (directly or indirectly) their reelection efforts, state legislative candidates need party workers and, increasingly, the party's financial support and technological resources at election time.

Governors in many states hold greater influence over their parties' organizations and legislators than do presidents. Many governors have more patronage positions at their command than the president, and these material rewards and incentives give governors added clout with party activists and office holders. In addition, tradition in some states permits the governor to play a part in selecting the legislature's committee chairs and party floor leaders, and some state executives even attend and help direct the party legislative caucuses, activities no president would ever undertake.

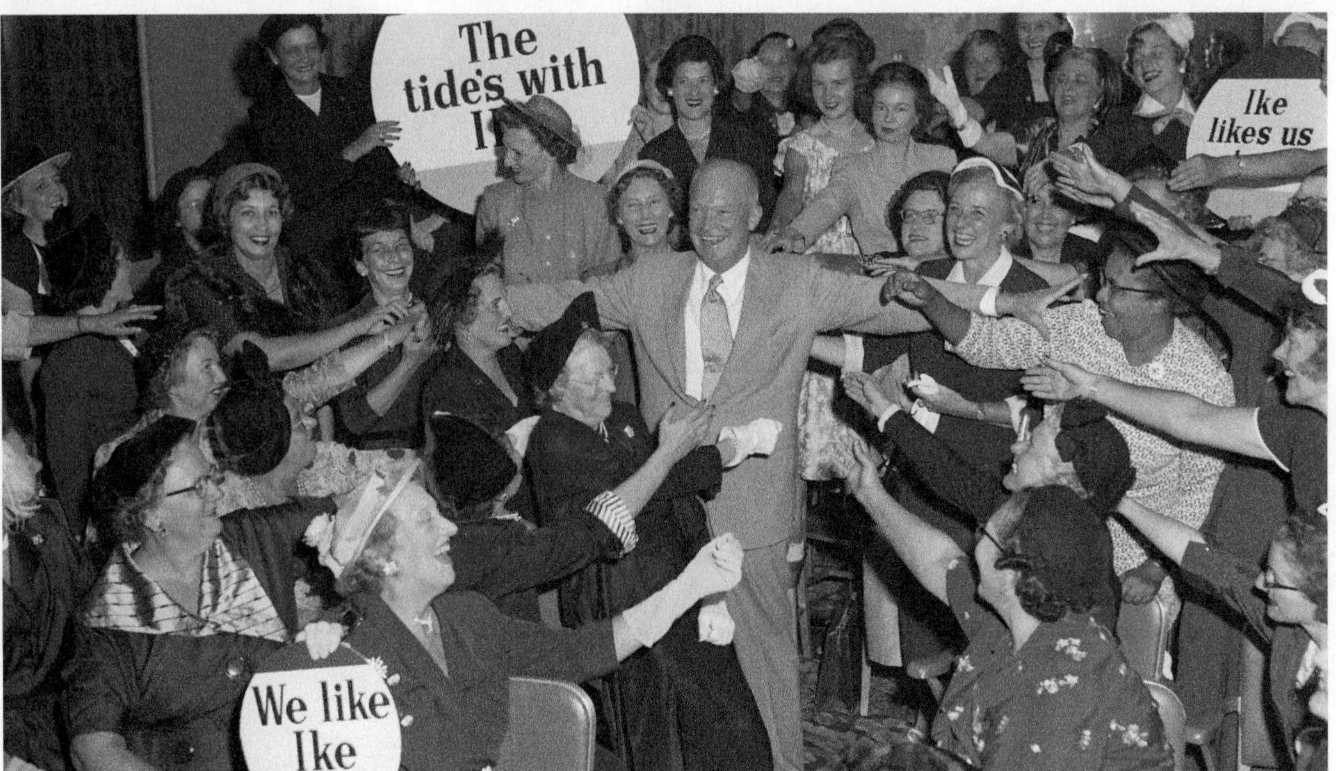

WHAT DOES A NONPARTISAN PRESIDENT LOOK LIKE?

President Dwight D. Eisenhower, a former military general and World War II hero, is as close to a nonpartisan president as modern America has ever had. Though he was very popular personally, his moderate agenda and unwillingness to work with party leaders translated into little support for the Republican Party.

The influence of party organizations in state judiciaries varies tremendously. Some states have taken dramatic actions to ensure that their supreme court judges can make independent decisions. Many of these states use a selection system called the Missouri Plan, which relies on a nonpartisan judicial nominating commission, to choose appointed state court judges. But, in other states (and in many local judicial elections), supreme court judges run as party candidates. These partisan elections have received a great deal of criticism in recent years, as they have become more costly and personal. Many commentators argue that they are contrary to the ideal of blind justice.

☐ Furthering Unity, Linkage, and Accountability

Parties, finally, are the glue that holds together the disparate elements of the U.S. governmental and political apparatus. The Framers designed a system that divides and subdivides power, making it possible to preserve individual liberty but difficult to coordinate and initiate action in a timely fashion. Parties help compensate for this drawback by linking the branches of government. Although rivalry between the branches is inevitable, the partisan and ideological affiliations of the leaders of each branch constitute a common basis for cooperation, as the president and his fellow party members in Congress usually demonstrate daily. Not surprisingly, presidential candidates and presidents are also inclined to push policies similar to those advocated by their party's congressional leaders.

Even within each branch, party affiliation helps bring together members of the House of Representatives and the Senate, or the president and the department heads in the bureaucracy. Similarly, the division of national, state, and local governments, while always an invitation to struggle, is made more workable by the intersecting party relationships that exist among office holders at all levels. Party affiliation, in other words, provides a basis for mediation and negotiation laterally among the branches of government and vertically among national, state, and local layers.

Which Party Governs Better?

When asked which party governs better, Americans are guided by partisanship—Democrats and Republicans each think government runs better when their party is in charge. Even so, general dissatisfaction with both major parties is substantial, and many Americans believe that a third party option is needed in the United States.

Your Level of Trust Depends on Your Party

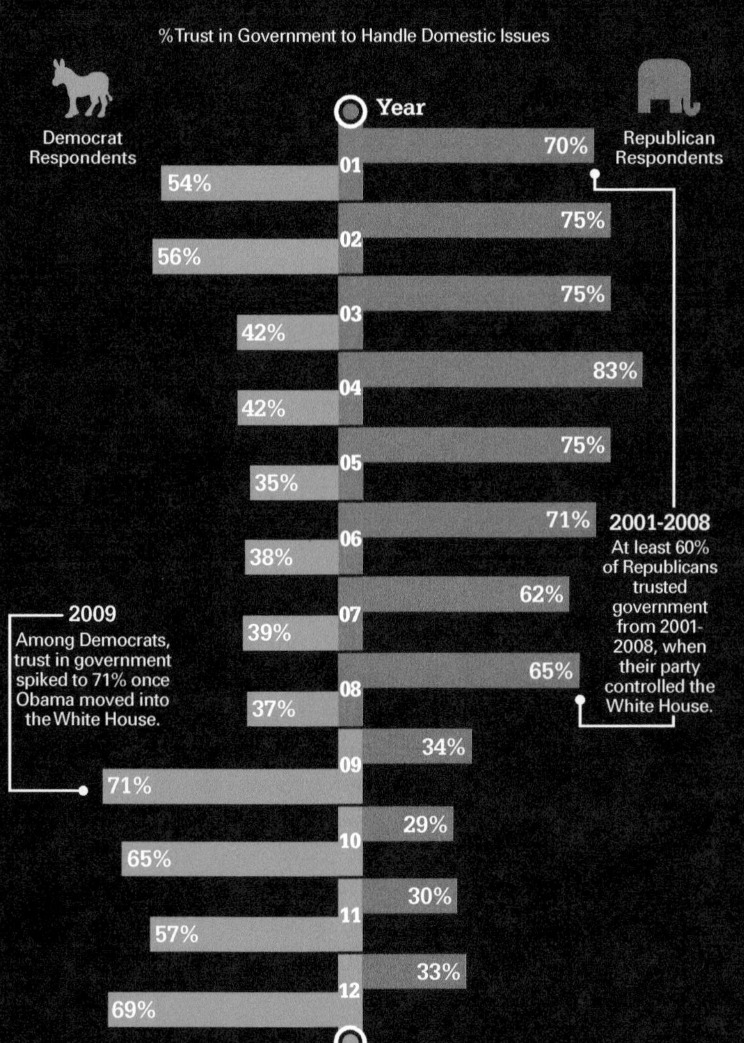

% Trust in Government to Handle Domestic Issues
Democrat Respondents

Republican Respondents

2001-2008
At least 60% of Republicans trusted government from 2001-2008, when their party controlled the White House.

Among Democrats, trust in government spiked to 71% once Obama moved into the White House.

SOURCE: Data from Gallup.

Does the United States Need a Third Party?

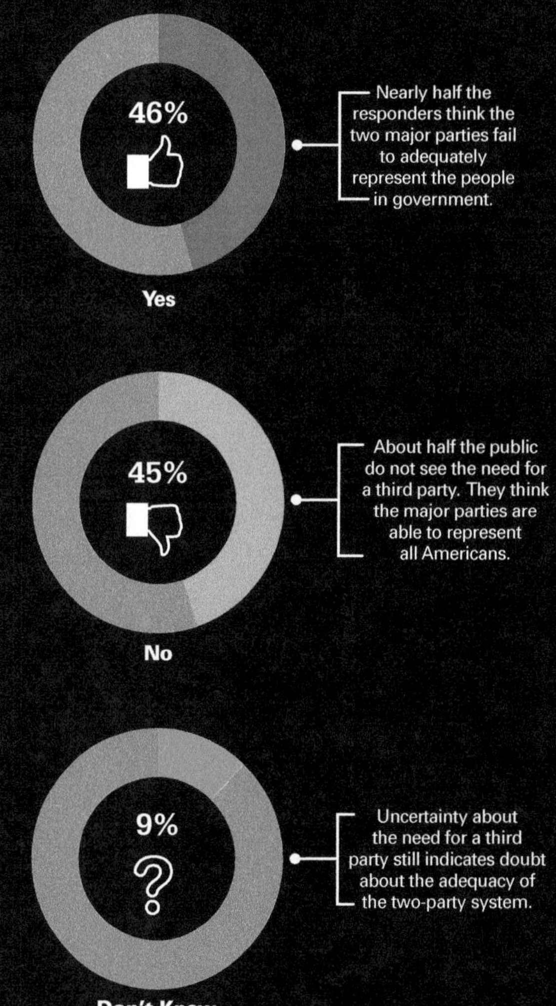

46%
Yes
Nearly half the responders think the two major parties fail to adequately represent the people in government.
45%
No
About half the public do not see the need for a third party. They think the major parties are able to represent all Americans.
9%
Don't Know
Uncertainty about the need for a third party still indicates doubt about the adequacy of the two-party system.

Investigate Further

Concept How do we measure which party governs better? Survey research allows us to track public opinion on party performance on certain issues. Historically, when it comes to trusting government, partisans trust their party to govern, but not the other. Partisanship is a lens through which voters evaluate and determine trust of parties and government.

Connection Which party do Americans think governs better? Voters think *their* party governs better. Democrats think we are governed better when Democrats rule. Republicans think the same when Republicans rule. The parties represent different governing philosophies, so each party has a different definition of what it means to "govern better."

Cause When do third parties become viable? Third parties become viable when major parties fail on divisive issues that matter to the public, like the economy or racial issues. Third parties emerge to address those issues and often capture a lot of support. However, the third party is usually absorbed by a major party that co-opts their issues and supporters.

party identification
A citizen's personal affinity for a political party, usually expressed by a tendency to vote for the candidates of that party.

The party's linkage function does not end there. Party identification and organization foster communication between the voter and the candidate, as well as between the voter and the office holder. The party connection represents one means of increasing accountability in election campaigns and in government. Candidates on the campaign trail and elected party leaders are required from time to time to account for their performance at party-sponsored forums, nominating primaries, and on Election Day.

Party Identification

11.4 Analyze how political socialization and group affiliations shape party identification.

Explore on MyPoliSciLab Simulation: You Are a Voter

The party in the electorate—the mass of potential voters who identify with a party label—is a crucial element of the political party. But, in some respects, it is the weakest component of the U.S. political party system. Although **party identification,** or a citizen's affinity for a political party, tends to be a reliable indicator of likely voting choices, the trend is for fewer voters to declare loyalty to a party; 29 percent of voters called themselves independents on Election Day in 2012.

For those Americans who do firmly adopt a party label, their party often becomes a central political reference symbol and perceptual screen. For these partisans, party identification is a significant aspect of their political personality and a way of defining and explaining themselves to others. The loyalty generated by the label can be as intense as any enjoyed by sports teams and alma maters.

Political Socialization

Not surprisingly, parents are the single greatest influence in establishing a person's first party identification. Parents who are politically active and share the same party identification raise children who will be strong party identifiers, whereas parents without party affiliations or with mixed affiliations produce offspring more likely to be independents.

Early socialization is hardly the last step in an individual's acquisition and maintenance of a party identity; marriage, economic status, and other aspects of adult life can change one's loyalty. Charismatic political personalities, particularly at the national level (such as Franklin D. Roosevelt and Ronald Reagan), can influence party identification, as can cataclysmic events (the Civil War and the Great Depression are the best examples). Hot-button social issues (for instance, abortion and same-sex marriage), sectionalism, and candidate-oriented politics may also influence party ties.

Group Affiliations

Just as individuals vary in the strength of their partisan choice, so do groups vary in the degree to which they identify with the Democratic Party or the Republican Party. Variations in party identification are particularly noticeable when geography, gender, race and ethnicity, age, social and economic status, religion, and marital status are examined (see Table 11.2).

GEOGRAPHY Many modern states, particularly in the Mid-Atlantic, Rust Belt, and Southwest, are rather closely contested between the parties; these states are often referred to as "swing states" in electoral politics. Democrats, however, dominate in the Northeast and California, while Republicans are strongest in the South and Midwest. In 2011, the most Democratic states were Hawaii, Maryland, Connecticut,

TABLE 11.2 WHO IDENTIFIES AS A DEMOCRAT? A REPUBLICAN?

		Democratic Identifiers	Independents	Republican Identifiers
Region	Northeast	35	46	20
	Midwest	33	44	23
	South	32	39	29
	West	33	39	28
Gender	Male	27	48	26
	Female	38	35	26
Race	Black	70	28	3
	Hispanic	40	46	13
	Asian	33	44	22
	White	28	42	31
Age	<30	31	48	21
	30–49	32	45	23
	50+	34	37	28
Income	<30,000	36	45	20
	30,000–74,999	33	42	25
	75,000+	30	40	31
Education	High School or Less	38	40	23
	College	30	42	28
	Advanced Degree	33	42	25
Religion	Protestant	31	34	35
	Catholic	36	43	21
	Jewish	48	30	22
Evangelical Christian	Yes	31	33	37
	No	32	43	25
Ideology	Conservative	18	37	45
	Moderate	31	52	18
	Liberal	65	31	4

NOTE: Due to rounding, not all rows equal 100 percent.

SOURCE: Pew Research Center, January 2012 Political Survey.

and New York. In contrast, the most Republican states were Utah, Idaho, Wyoming, and Alaska.[13]

GENDER Some political scientists argue that the difference in the way men and women vote first emerged in 1920, when newly enfranchised women registered overwhelmingly as Republicans. Not until the 1980 presidential election, however, did scholars observe a noticeable and possibly significant gender gap in party identification. This pattern continues to play an important role in politics. Today, 38 percent of women identify as Democrats, and 26 percent as Republicans.

Most researchers, however, now explain the gender gap by focusing not on the Republican Party's difficulties in attracting female voters, but rather on the Democratic Party's inability to attract the votes of men. As one study notes, the gender gap exists because of the lack of support for the Democratic Party among men and the corresponding male preference for the Republican Party. These differences stem largely from divergences of opinions about social welfare and military issues.[14]

RACE AND ETHNICITY Race is a significant indicator of party identification. African Americans, for example, are overwhelmingly Democratic in their partisan identification.

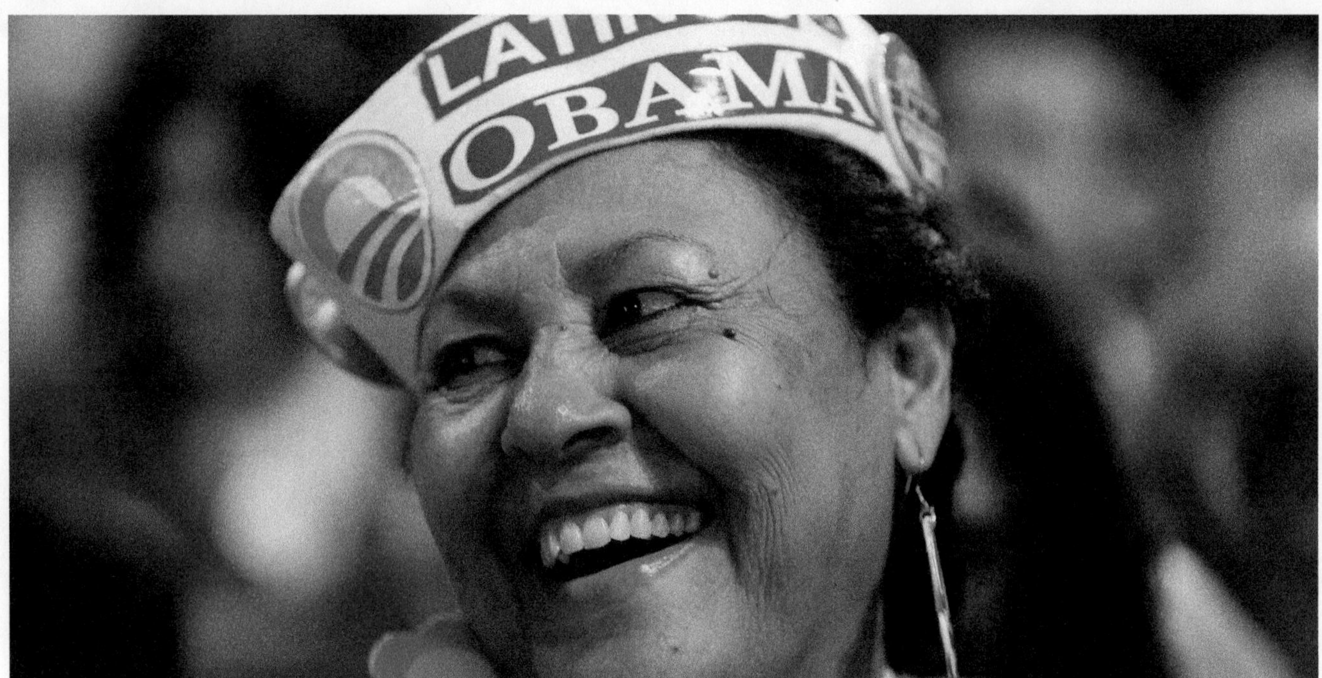

WHICH POLITICAL PARTY DO HISPANICS SUPPORT?

Hispanic voters increasingly support Democratic candidates, although this may vary with an individual's country of origin. Here, a Hispanic delegate to the Democratic National Convention shows her support for President Barack Obama.

The 65-percent-plus advantage they offer the Democrats in party affiliation dwarfs the edge given to either party by any other significant segment of the electorate, and their proportion of strong Democrats is three times that of whites.

Hispanics supplement African Americans as Democratic stalwarts; by more than two-thirds, Hispanics prefer the Democratic Party. Some divisions do exist by country of origin. Voting patterns of Puerto Ricans are very similar to those of African Americans, while Mexican Americans favor the Democrats by smaller margins. An exception is the Cuban American population, whose anti–Communist tilt translates into support for the Republican Party.

As the Hispanic population has increased rapidly in recent years and now exceeds that of African Americans, Republicans have fought to make inroads with Hispanic voters. During the 2012 Republican National Convention, for example, the party showcased a number of visible Hispanic leaders, including Senator Marco Rubio (FL) and Governor Susana Martinez (NM). Still, debates and proposals regarding immigration and the DREAM Act continue to reveal how difficult it is for Republicans to appeal to a potentially supportive new voting bloc while also satisfying their conservative base with immigration restrictions and increased enforcement.

AGE Political socialization creates a strong relationship between age and party identification. Today, middle-aged voters disproportionately favor the Republican Party. These voters, often at the height of their career and, consequently, their earning potential, tend to favor the low taxes championed by Republicans.[15] In contrast, the Democratic Party's more liberal positions on social issues tend to resonate with today's moderate but socially progressive young adults. The nation's oldest voters, who were alive during the Great Depression, also tend to favor the Democratic Party and its support for social insurance programs.

SOCIAL AND ECONOMIC FACTORS Occupation, income, and education are closely related, so many of the same partisan patterns appear in all three classifications. Democratic support drops as one climbs the income scale. The same pattern is generally evident with regard to education, although those with advanced degrees tend to be Democrats.[16] The GOP remains predominant among executives, professionals, and white-collar workers, whereas the Democrats lead substantially among trial lawyers, educators, and blue-collar workers. Labor union members are also Democrats by nearly two to one. Women who do not work outside the home tend to be conservative and favor the Republicans.

RELIGION Religion can be evaluated based on both denomination and religiosity, or how frequently an individual engages in activities such as prayer and church attendance. With respect to religious denomination, Catholic and, even more so, Jewish voters tend to favor the Democratic Party, while Mormons and white Protestants—especially Methodists, Presbyterians, and Episcopalians—align with the Republicans. The Republican Party has also made gains among the most religious identifiers of all sects; between 2008 and 2011, the Pew Research Center observed a 9 percent increase in support for the GOP among both practicing Catholics and Jews. These increases may reflect the party's visible support for socially conservative viewpoints, including opposition to abortion and contraception.[17]

MARITAL STATUS Even marital status reveals something about partisan affiliation. People who are married tend to favor the Republican Party, while single people who have never married tend to identify with the Democratic Party. Taken as a group, the widowed lean toward the Democrats, probably because these voters are older and there are many more widows than widowers; here, the age and gender gaps are again expressing themselves. The divorced and the separated, who may be experiencing economic hardship, appear to be more liberal than the married population.[18]

Minor Parties in the American Two-Party System

11.5 Evaluate the role of minor parties in the American two-party system.

To this point, our discussion has focused largely on the activities of the two major political parties, the Democrats and the Republicans. This is not an entirely complete picture of the political system. Although minor parties face a challenge in surviving and thriving in the American political system, these parties continue to make important contributions to the political process, revealing sectional and political divides and bringing to light new issues.

The Formation and Role of Minor Parties

The decision to form a political party can be a difficult one. Most parties are rooted in social movements made up of activists and groups whose primary goal is to influence public policy. Parties aim to accomplish the same goal, but they also run candidates for elective office. Making this transition requires a substantial investment of financial and human resources, as well as a broad base of political support to compete in elections. Throughout history, therefore, very few social movements have evolved into parties. Those that have succeeded in this mission have had the support of political elites and uninhibited access to the ballot.

For example, during the 1840s and 1850s, the Liberty and Free Soil Parties formed around the abolition issue. The parties' leaders were well-educated Northerners who accounted for a significant proportion of the electorate at the time. In contrast, when civil rights issues emerged on the agenda again in the early twentieth century, it was

Take a Closer Look

Although minor parties have enjoyed only limited electoral success in the United States, they have been successful in bringing to the table many new issues ripe for consideration. In recent elections, the Libertarian Party, the United States' third largest and fastest growing party, has enjoyed this type of success. Though its candidates have won few electoral victories, the party's emphases on small government, laissez-faire economics, and personal liberty have received increasing attention from supporters of the Tea Party movement. Republican presidential candidate and Representative Ron Paul also advocated for many of these positions.

The Libertarian Party's platform seeks an "America at peace with the world" and supports an end to "the current U.S. government policy of foreign intervention, including military and economic aid."

The Libertarian Party's platform argues that all individuals should enjoy their natural rights. It further argues that "sexual orientation, preference, gender, or gender identity should have no impact on the government's treatment of individuals."

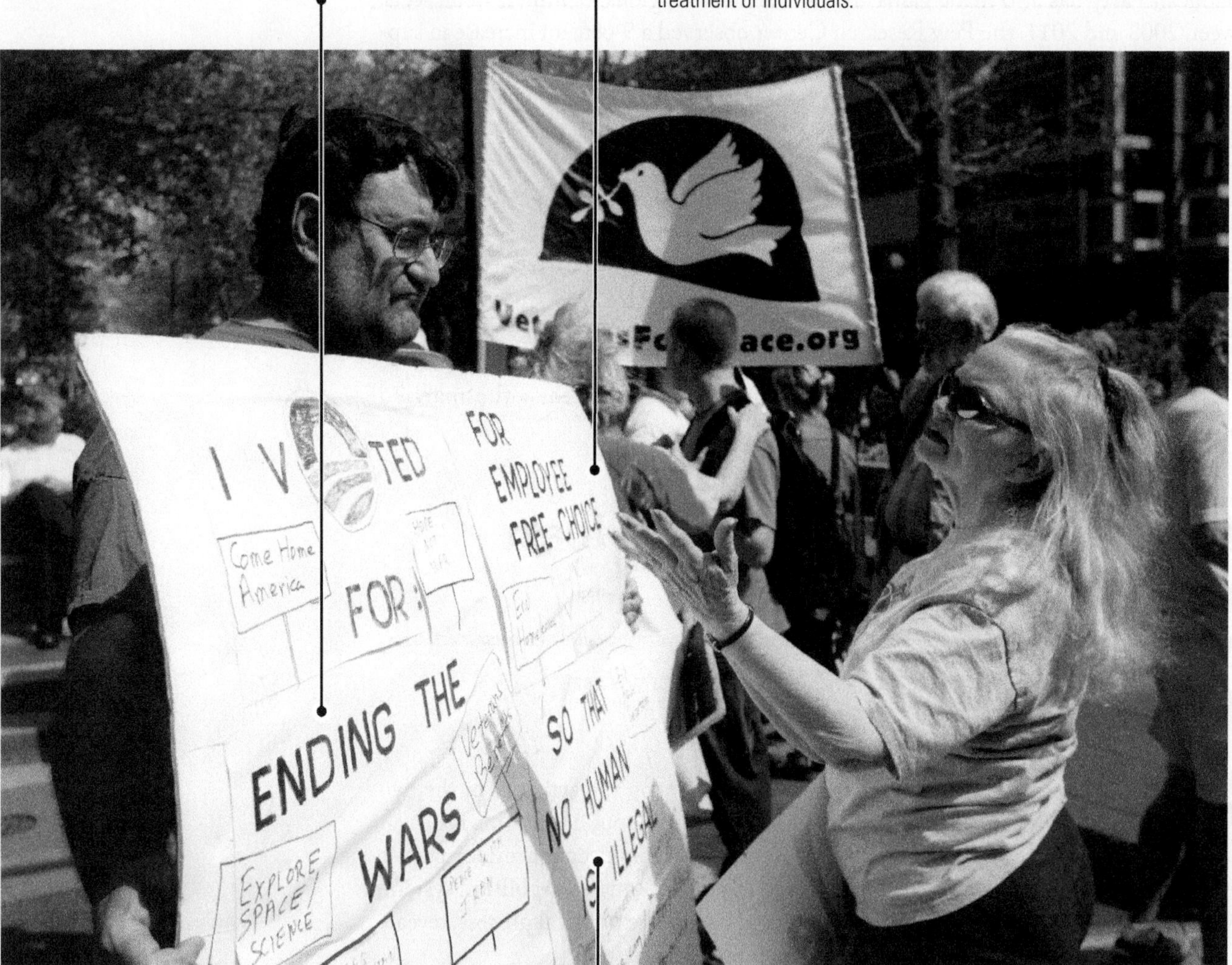

The Libertarian Party advocates for personal liberty in all aspects of life. The platform states that "individuals should be free to make choices for themselves and to accept responsibility for the consequences of the choices they make."

CRITICAL THINKING QUESTIONS

1. How are the Libertarian Party's ideas similar to and different from those of the Republican and Democratic Parties?
2. Why do so few Americans know about and understand the positions of minor parties such as the Libertarian Party?
3. Can the Libertarian Party become a major party in the United States? What changes would be necessary to the U.S. electoral system in order for this to happen?

TABLE 11.3 WHAT ARE SOME OF AMERICA'S MINOR PARTIES?

Minor Party	Year Founded	Primary Purpose
Liberty/Free-Soil	1840	Abolition of slavery
Prohibition	1880	Prohibition of alcohol sale and consumption
Progressive/Bull Moose	1912	Factionalism in Republican Party; gave Theodore Roosevelt the platform to run for the presidency
American Independent	1968	States' rights; opposition to desegregation
Libertarian	1971	Opposition to governmental intervention in economic and social policy
Reform	1996	Economic issues; tax reform, national debt, federal deficit
Green	2000	Environmentalism and social justice

proportional representation
A voting system that apportions legislative seats according to the percentage of the vote won by a particular political party.

winner-take-all system
An electoral system in which the party that receives at least one more vote than any other party wins the election.

through a social movement led by activists in groups such as the NAACP. One reason why this social movement did not become a party was the fact that black voters in areas where segregation had the most significant impact were largely denied the franchise and thus could not have voted for potential party candidates. The ability of the current Tea Party movement to develop into a full-fledged third party will hinge on many of these same variables. To date, it appears the group has become a faction—albeit highly vocal—within the larger Republican Party. It has, however, had success in controlling the party's agenda and demanding budget cuts.

Minor parties based on causes neglected by the major parties have significantly affected American politics (see Table 11.3). These parties find their roots in sectionalism (as did the Southern states' rights Dixiecrats, who broke away from the Democrats in 1948); in economic protest (such as the agrarian revolt that fueled the Populists, an 1892 prairie-states party); in specific issues (such as the Green Party's support of the environment); in ideology (the Socialist, Communist, and Libertarian Parties are examples); and in appealing, charismatic personalities (Theodore Roosevelt's affiliation with the Bull Moose Party in 1912 is perhaps the best example).

Minor parties achieve their greatest successes when they incorporate new ideas or alienated groups or nominate attractive candidates as their standard-bearers. They also thrive when declining trust in the two major political parties plagues the electorate. Usually, though, minor parties' ideas are co-opted by one of the two major parties, each of them eager to take the politically popular issue that gave rise to the minor party and make it their own in order to secure the allegiance of the minor party's supporters. For example, the Republicans of the 1970s absorbed many of the states' rights planks of George Wallace's 1968 presidential bid. Both major parties have also more recently attempted to attract independent voters by sponsoring reforms of the governmental process.

☐ Barriers to Minor-Party Success

Many European countries use **proportional representation**, a voting system that apportions legislative seats according to the percentage of votes a political party receives. However, the United States has a single-member, plurality electoral system, often referred to as a **winner-take-all system**, or a system in which the party that receives at least one more vote than any other party wins the election. To paraphrase the legendary football coach Vince Lombardi, finishing first is not everything, it is the *only* thing in U.S. politics; placing second, even by one vote, doesn't count. The winner-take-all system encourages the grouping of interests into as few parties as possible (the democratic minimum being two).

The Electoral College system and the rules of public financing for American presidential elections also make it difficult for minor parties to seriously complete. Not only must a candidate win popular votes, but the candidate also must win majorities in states that allow him or her to gain a total of 270 electoral votes.

polarization
The presence of increasingly conflicting and divided viewpoints between the Democratic and Republican Parties.

Toward Reform: Red States and Blue States

11.6 Assess party polarization in the modern era.

In recent years, the existence, consequences, and causes of partisan **polarization**, or the increasingly conflicting and divided viewpoints of the Democratic and Republican Parties, has incited much debate. In this section, we detail each of these factors, making a careful distinction between elite polarization, or divergence among members of the party in government and the most engaged citizens, and mass polarization, or division among members of the general public.[19]

United or Divided?

Scholars have noted increasing partisan divisions between members of Congress over the past two decades. As northern liberal Republicans, and particularly, southern conservative Democrats have become increasingly rare, the parties have retreated in two separate directions, with the Republican caucus appearing to move rightward and their Democratic counterparts appearing to shift to the left. These changes have created a Congress with a bimodal distribution of members' ideologies, and few members left in the center. It is, however, important to note that the parties are not equally polarized—Republicans in Congress are further right and more homogeneous than their Democratic counterparts.

What is less clear is whether this polarization in government has also led to polarization of the American people. Most Americans still identify as politically moderate. However, the issue positions of the most politically active citizens seem to suggest a growing division among these members of the electorate. Some scholars contend that this is not polarization—a term carrying a negative connotation—but, rather, party sorting, which means that parties develop clear issue positions that more efficiently and effectively cue the electorate to identify with a particular label.

Causes of Polarization

Following the 2004 presidential election, a graphic playing on the Electoral College results of the contest between President George W. Bush and Senator John Kerry made its rounds on the Internet. This visual depicted the northern Democratic, or "blue" states, the states in which a majority of citizens had voted for Kerry, as "The United States of Canada." The remaining Republican, or "red" states, the states where a majority of citizens had supported Bush, were labeled "Jesusland." To some degree, this visual represents a major cause of our belief that we live in a polarized nation: our own perception. This perception is fed by the 24-hour and Internet news cycles, which constantly need to sell a story to fill the voluminous airtime and attract viewers in a market-driven media environment. The idea that we might live in a world of "red states" and "blue states" is one such story that has provided the media with much fodder for discussion.

The perception of deep division not only in Congress but in the mass electorate also has its roots in changing political campaigns. As parties have increasingly used microtargeting to identify partisans, we have created stereotypes of party identifiers in our heads. Republicans, for example, are thought to drive American-made pickup trucks, watch NASCAR, and be card-carrying members of the National Rifle Association. In contrast, Democrats drive Volvos, drink Starbucks coffee, and shop at their local organic markets. Though these stereotypes may harbor some truth, they are not perfect archetypes, and create unnecessary divisions among people.

Are American Political Parties Polarized?

In the past ten years, scholars have hotly debated the question of whether American political parties are polarized. As we have argued in the text, the answer to this question appears to vary based on our definition of the political party. The ideological distribution of the party in government and the party in the electorate varies dramatically, as shown below. These differences may have consequences for how Americans view the political parties.

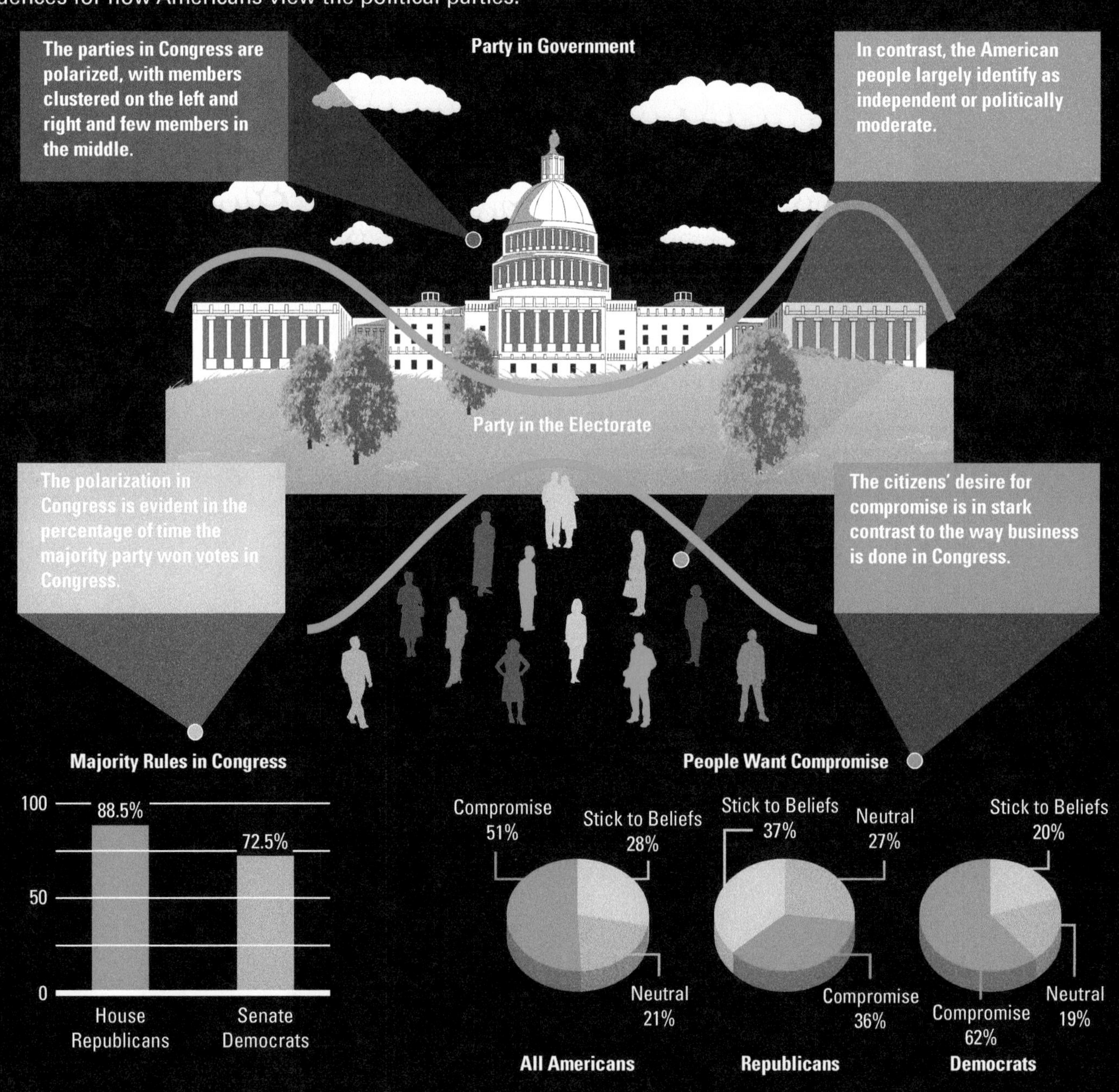

The parties in Congress are polarized, with members clustered on the left and right and few members in the middle.
Party in Government
In contrast, the American people largely identify as independent or politically moderate.
Party in the Electorate
The polarization in Congress is evident in the percentage of time the majority party won votes in Congress.
The citizens' desire for compromise is in stark contrast to the way business is done in Congress.
Majority Rules in Congress
100
88.5%
72.5%
50
0
House Republicans
Senate Democrats
People Want Compromise
Compromise 51%
Stick to Beliefs 28%
Neutral 21%
All Americans
Stick to Beliefs 37%
Neutral 27%
Compromise 36%
Republicans
Stick to Beliefs 20%
Neutral 19%
Compromise 62%
Democrats

SOURCE: Data from www.gallup.com and media.cq.com.

CRITICAL THINKING QUESTIONS

1. How does the party in government compare to the party in the electorate? Why do you think these differences exist?
2. How does polarization affect the way that citizens view the Democratic and Republican Parties? What are the consequences of these views?
3. Will growing polarization in Congress eventually translate into greater polarization in the electorate? Why or why not?

11.1

11.2

11.3

11.4

11.5

11.6

Finally, polarization between the parties is also rooted in the clearer articulation of party positions on a range of issues, from national defense and foreign policy to economic affairs to so-called cultural "wedge issues." These cultural issues—summarized by some commentators as "guns, God, and gays"—include such matters as religious freedom, same-sex marriage, and abortion and contraception, on which the parties have taken increasingly opposing viewpoints in recent years. Today, for example, being pro-choice on abortion is a litmus test for Democratic candidates in most areas of the country.

☐ Consequences of Polarization

The consequences of the growing division between the two parties in government have been on clear display in recent Congresses. These Congresses have been among the least productive in history. The lack of moderate members, lower incentives to compromise and cross party lines, and the close margins by which the parties have held both the House and the Senate have made it nearly impossible to enact important policy proposals.

The consequences of potential polarization in the electorate, however, are less obvious. Some commentators have suggested that forcing the generally moderate American people to choose between two clearly divided political parties will lead to increased political apathy and lower rates of participation and engagement in politics and government. Other scholars charge that polarization actually encourages political participation by giving citizens clear choices and cues. Empirical evidence to date has been mixed. But, as Congress grows increasingly divided, monitoring the electorate for changes in partisan identification, issue positions, and political activity becomes significant for the health of American democracy.

On MyPoliSciLab

Review the Chapter

Listen to **Chapter 11** on **MyPoliSciLab**

Roots of the Two-Party System

11.1 Trace the evolution of the two-party system in the United States, p. 329.

Political parties have been a presence in American politics since the nation's infancy. The Federalists and the Democratic-Republicans were the first two parties to emerge in the late 1700s. In 1832, the Democratic Party (which succeeded the Democratic-Republicans) held the first national presidential nomination convention, and the Whig Party formed around opposition to President Andrew Jackson. The Democratic and Whig Parties strengthened for several years until the issue of slavery led to the Whig Party's gradual dissolution and replacement by the Republican Party (formed by anti-slavery activists to push for the containment of slavery). From 1860 to this day, the same two political parties, Democratic and Republican, have dominated elections in the United States.

The Organization of American Political Parties

11.2 Outline the structure of American political parties at the national, state, and local levels, p. 333.

The national party organization sits at the top of the party system. A chairperson leads the national party, and every four years the national committee of each party organizes a national convention to nominate a candidate for the presidency. The state and local parties are the heart of party activism, as virtually all government regulation of political parties falls to the states. The state governing body, generally called the state central or executive committee, supervises the collection of local party organizations.

Activities of American Political Parties

11.3 Identify the functions performed by American political parties, p. 337.

For over 200 years, the two-party system has served as the mechanism by which American society organizes and resolves social and political conflict. The two major parties provide vital services to society, including running candidates for office, proposing and formulating policy, organizing government, and furthering unity, linkage, and accountability.

Party Identification

11.4 Analyze how political socialization and group affiliations shape party identification, p. 344.

Most American voters have a personal affinity for a political party, which summarizes their political views and preferences and is expressed by a tendency to vote for the candidates of that party. This party identification begins with political socialization; parents are the single greatest influence on a person's political leanings. However, different group affiliations, including geographic region, gender, race and ethnicity, age, social and economic factors, religion, and marital status, also affect individuals' loyalties to political parties, and these may change over the course of a lifetime.

Minor Parties in the American Two-Party System

11.5 Evaluate the role of minor parties in the American two-party system, p. 347.

Minor parties have often significantly affected American politics. Ideas of minor parties that become popular with the electorate are often co-opted by one of the two major parties eager to secure supporters. Minor parties make progress when the two major parties fail to incorporate new ideas or alienated groups or if they do not nominate attractive candidates for office. However, many of the institutional features of American politics, including the winner-take-all system and the Electoral College, encourage the grouping of interests into as few parties as possible.

Toward Reform: Red States and Blue States

11.6 Assess party polarization in the modern era, p. 350.

In recent years, scholars have debated the presence and origins of growing polarization between the two political parties. Though the cause of these growing divisions can in part be attributed to the 24-hour news cycle, clear differences also exist between the parties' positions both in government and in the most active segments of the electorate. The divide between the two parties can make it difficult to create policy in American political institutions.

Learn the Terms

 Study and Review the Flashcards

candidate-centered politics, p. 331
critical election, p. 332
delegate, p. 335
national convention, p. 334
national party platform, p. 339
party identification, p. 344
party realignment, p. 332
polarization, p. 350
political machine, p. 330
political party, p. 329
proportional representation, p. 349
secular realignment, p. 332
superdelegate, p. 335
think tank, p. 337
winner-take-all system, p. 349

Test Yourself

 Study and Review the Practice Tests

1. Who was the first president to win election as the nominee of a truly national, popularly based political party?

- **a.** Thomas Jefferson
- **b.** Andrew Jackson
- **c.** John Adams
- **d.** James Monroe
- **e.** Andrew Johnson

2. Which of the following was true of the Golden Age of political parties?

- **a.** Parties were unstable.
- **b.** There was very little political activity in local communities.
- **c.** Very few candidates ran for office.
- **d.** Party organizations dominated local and state governments.
- **e.** Citizens were dissatisfied with national party organizations.

3. Which of the following is NOT a way that the chair of the national committee comes to the position?

- **a.** Selected by the sitting president
- **b.** Chosen by the national committee when the election has ended and the party has been defeated
- **c.** Picked by the newly nominated presidential candidate
- **d.** Nominated by the vice president with presidential approval
- **e.** None of the above

4. What is/are the ultimate governing body/bodies for political parties?

- **a.** The national chair
- **b.** Identifiers and voters
- **c.** The national committee
- **d.** Congressional and district committees
- **e.** State central committees and state conventions

5. Which of the following is NOT a function performed by modern American political parties?

- **a.** Organizing Congress
- **b.** Job creation
- **c.** Running candidates for office
- **d.** Furthering unity, linkage, and accountability
- **e.** Formulating policy

6. What is the most powerful predictor of congressional call voting?

- **a.** Tenure in office
- **b.** Age
- **c.** Gender
- **d.** Party affiliation
- **e.** Race/ethnicity

7. What is party identification?

- **a.** A citizen's affinity for a political party
- **b.** A rule that requires a citizen to vote for their party's candidates after they have registered as a member of that party
- **c.** The number of times a person has voted for a particular party
- **d.** The chance an independent will choose to vote for a certain party in a presidential election
- **e.** How often a citizen votes in his or her party's primary elections

8. Which of the following groups of people tend to favor the Republican Party?

- **a.** Catholics
- **b.** Women
- **c.** Young people
- **d.** Cuban Americans
- **e.** Northerners

9. Why do some observers say minor parties benefit the American political system?

- **a.** Minor parties often win election to office and lead to greater diversity in politics.
- **b.** Minor parties increase voter turnout.
- **c.** Minor parties promote change in electoral rules.
- **d.** Minor parties can bring attention to new issue areas.
- **e.** Minor parties lead to compromise between the Democrats and the Republicans.

10. Where are American political parties most polarized?

- **a.** Electorate
- **b.** Supreme Court
- **c.** Local party organizations
- **d.** Executive branch
- **e.** Legislative branch

Explore Further

Abramowitz, Alan I. *The Disappearing Center: Engaged Citizens, Polarization, and American Democracy*. New Haven, CT: Yale University Press, 2010.

Aldrich, John H. *Why Parties? A Second Look*. Chicago: University of Chicago Press, 2011.

Bullock, Charles S., and Mark J. Rozell, eds. *The New Politics of the Old South: An Introduction to Southern Politics,* 4th ed. Lanham, MD: Rowman and Littlefield, 2009.

Green, Donald J. *Third Party Matters: Politics, Presidents, and Third Parties in American History*. New York: Praeger, 2010.

Green, John C., and Daniel Coffey. *The State of the Parties,* 6th ed. Lanham, MD: Rowman and Littlefield, 2010.

Fiorina, Morris P. *Culture War? The Myth of a Polarized America,* 3rd ed. New York: Longman, 2010.

Hershey, Marjorie Randon. *Party Politics in America,* 15th ed. New York: Pearson Longman, 2012.

Key, V. O., Jr. *Southern Politics in State and Nation*, new edition. Knoxville: University of Tennessee Press, 1984.

———. *Politics, Parties, and Pressure Groups,* 5th ed. New York: Crowell, 1964.

Maisel, L. Sandy, Jeffrey M. Berry, and George C. Edwards III, eds. *The Oxford Handbook of American Political Parties and Interest Groups*. New York: Oxford University Press, 2010.

Mayhew, David R. *Electoral Realignments*. New Haven, CT: Yale University Press, 2004.

Sabato, Larry J., and Bruce Larson. *The Party's Just Begun: Shaping Political Parties for America's Future,* 2nd ed. New York: Longman, 2009.

Schaffner, Brian F. *Politics, Parties, and Elections in America,* 7th ed. Boston, MA: Thomson Wadsworth, 2011.

Schattschneider, E. E. *Party Government*. New York: Holt, Rinehart and Winston, 1942.

Skocpol, Theda, and Vanessa Williamson. *The Tea Party and the Remaking of Republican Conservatism*. New York: Oxford University Press, 2012.

White, John Kenneth, and Daniel M. Shea. *New Party Politics: From Jefferson and Hamilton to the Information Age,* 2nd ed. Boston, MA: Thomson Wadsworth, 2003.

To learn more about the Democratic and Republican Parties, go to **www.dnc.org** and **www. rnc.org**.

To learn more about campaign contributions to political parties, go to the Center for Responsive Politics's Web site at **www.opensecrets.org/**.

To learn more about the ideology and party identification of the American electorate, go to the Web site of the Pew Research Center for the People and the Press at **www.people-press.org**.

To learn more about minor parties, go to their Web sites at **www.gp.org, www.lp.org**, and **www.reformparty.org**.

Listen to Chapter 12 on MyPoliSciLab

12 Elections and Voting

The nation headed into the 2012 elections with a fiercely divided electorate; a White House and Senate controlled by the Democratic Party; and the U.S. House of Representatives solidly controlled by the Republican Party. At the congressional level, in several states, conservative factions within the Republican Party seemed to have little tolerance for candidates--even incumbents–if they were perceived as moderate or left of center. In Indiana, for example, Republican Senator Richard Lugar, who had served in the chamber for over thirty-five years, lost the party's nomination to the more conservative State Treasurer Richard Mourdock.

But, both the Democrats and the Republicans expressed confidence that in 2012 their party would win majorities in both houses of Congress. Democrats forecast that they would win the House and retain control of the Senate by appealing to young, female, and minority voters. Republicans believed that the struggling economy under the Democratic president would be enough to help them hold the House and pick up enough seats to win control of the Senate.

After all the votes were counted and despite spending a record-breaking more than $6 billion on the elections, the composition of both houses of Congress was virtually identical. Democrats gained just two seats in the Senate and five in the House. Ultimately, party control did not shift in either the House or the Senate.

Such results might provoke a cynical response that individual voters are powerless to affect major change in government, but on close inspection the results of 2012 highlight several notable facts about American voters.

On Election Day, voters clearly rejected representation by candidates who appeared out of step with their beliefs. In Missouri, for example, incumbent Democratic Senator Claire McCaskill, who was not expected to win reelection, ultimately defeated her challenger, Representative Todd Akin, after he made comments about "legitimate rape," which garnered

12.1 Trace the roots of American elections, and distinguish among the four different types of elections, p. 359.

12.2 Outline the electoral procedures for presidential and general elections, p. 362.

12.3 Compare and contrast congressional and presidential elections, and explain the incumbency advantage, p. 368.

12.4 Identify seven factors that influence voter choice, p. 372.

12.5 Identify six factors that affect voter turnout, p. 376.

12.6 Explain why voter turnout is low, and evaluate methods for improving voter turnout, p. 380.

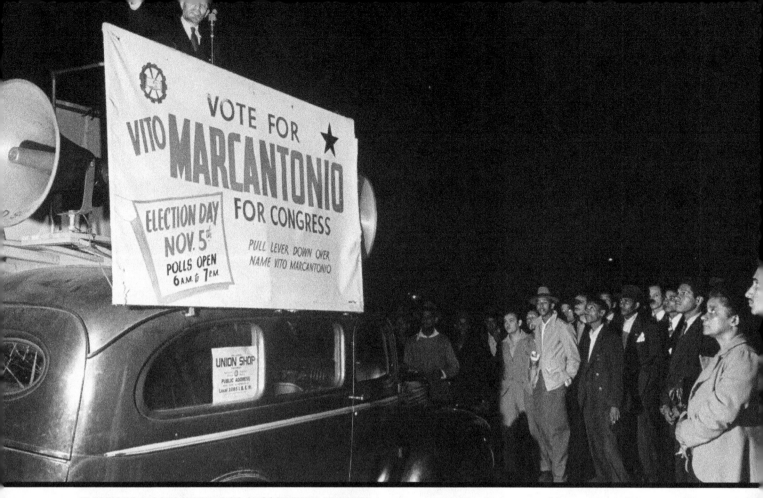

ELECTIONS ALLOW CITIZENS TO CHOOSE THEIR LEADERS In order to be elected to Congress, candidates must convince voters to turn out on Election Day. Above, Representative Vito Marcantonio (Labor-NY) campaigns for office in the 1940s. Below, Senator Elizabeth Warren (D-MA) asks voters for support in 2012.

Think Like a Political Scientist Why has the United States experienced a surge in voter turnout? Columbia University political scientist Donald P. Green analyzes voter turnout trends, and takes a look at how research conducted by political scientists on this subject has contributed to increased voter turnout.

In the Real World Not every citizen of the United States has a photo ID. Should everyone be required to have one when they vote? Real people discuss the issue of voter fraud, and whether it is a serious enough problem to warrant possibly disenfranchising a large segment of the population.

So What? Make your vote count. Larry J. Sabato shares his reasons why students and young adults should care more about politics than any other age group, and he explains why politicians rarely cater to younger voters.

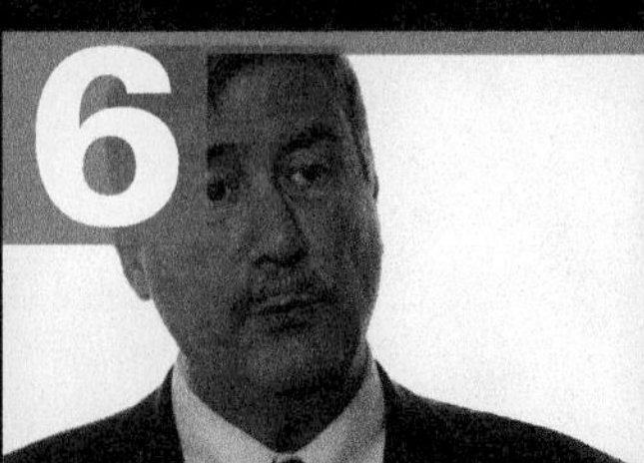

negative attention in the national media and among Missouri voters. Similarly, in Indiana, State Treasurer Mourdock ultimately lost his bid for the Senate to Democratic Representative Joe Donnelly after making similar comments that even Republican presidential nominee Mitt Romney disavowed.

In Massachusetts, where two years earlier Republican Senator Scott Brown achieved a surprising victory in a majority Democratic state, Senator Brown was defeated for reelection by Democratic candidate Elizabeth Warren. In the most expensive Senate race of the year, Warren became the first woman ever elected to the U.S. Senate from Massachusetts. In the 113th Congress, she will serve in a Senate that counts a record-breaking twenty women among its ranks.

Though it may seem contrary to the deep party divisions in Washington, D.C., the results of the 2012 election also highlighted how ideologically moderate most American voters are. This highlights a growing need for candidates who speak to voters not at the extremes of their political parties, but in the middle. The absence, for example, of socially liberal and economically conservative candidates provides an opportunity for growth and change in American politics.

•••

Every year, on the Tuesday following the first Monday in November, a plurality of voters, simply by casting ballots peacefully across a continent-sized nation, reelects or replaces politicians at all levels of government—from the president of the United States to members of the U.S. Congress to state legislators. Americans tend to take this process for granted, but in truth it is a marvel. Many other countries do not enjoy the benefit of competitive elections and the peaceful transition of political power made possible through the electoral process.

Americans hold frequent elections at all levels of government for more offices than any other nation on earth. And, the number of citizens eligible to participate in these elections has grown steadily over time. Despite increased access to the ballot box, however, voter participation remains historically low. After all the blood spilled and energy expended to expand voting rights, only about half of eligible voters bother to go to the polls.

This chapter focuses on elections and voting in the United States. We will explore both presidential and congressional contests, and examine the range of factors that affect vote choice and voter turnout. We will also assess the shortcomings of the democratic process in the United States, including low rates of participation in American elections.

Roots of American Elections

12.1 Trace the roots of American elections, and distinguish among the four different types of elections.

Elections are responsible for most political changes in the United States. Regular free elections guarantee mass political action and enable citizens to influence the actions of their government. Societies that cannot vote their leaders out of office are left with little choice other than to force them out by means of strikes, riots, or *coups d'état*.

☐ Purposes of Elections

Popular election confers on government a legitimacy that it can achieve no other way. Elections confirm the concept of popular sovereignty, the idea that legitimate political power derives from the consent of the governed, and they serve as the bedrock for democratic governance. At fixed intervals, the **electorate**—citizens eligible to vote—is called on to judge those in power. Even though the majority of office holders in the United States win reelection, some inevitably lose power, and all candidates are accountable to the voters. The threat of elections keeps policy makers focused on public opinion and promotes ethical behavior.

electorate
The citizens eligible to vote.

mandate
A command, indicated by an electorate's votes, for the elected officials to carry out a party platform or policy agenda.

primary election
Election in which voters decide which of the candidates within a party will represent the party in the general election.

closed primary
A primary election in which only a party's registered voters are eligible to cast a ballot.

open primary
A primary election in which party members, independents, and sometimes members of the other party are allowed to participate.

crossover voting
Participation in the primary election of a party with which the voter is not affiliated.

runoff primary
A second primary election between the two candidates receiving the greatest number of votes in the first primary.

general election
Election in which voters decide which candidates will actually fill elective public offices.

initiative
An election that allows citizens to propose legislation or state constitutional amendments by submitting them to the electorate for popular vote.

In addition, elections are the primary means to fill public offices and to organize and staff the government. Because candidates advocate certain policies, elections also provide a choice of direction on a wide range of issues, from abortion to civil rights to national defense to the environment. If current office holders are reelected, they may continue their policies with renewed resolve. Should office holders be defeated and their challengers elected, a change in policies will likely result. Either way, the winners will claim a **mandate** (literally, a command) from the people to carry out a party platform or policy agenda.

☐ Types of Elections

The United States is almost unrivaled in the variety and number of elections it holds. Under the Constitution, the states hold much of the administrative power over these elections, even when national office holders are being elected. Thus, as we will see, states have great latitude to set the date and type of elections, determine the eligibility requirements for candidates and voters, and tabulate the results.

The electoral process has two stages: primary and general elections. In most jurisdictions, candidates for state and national office must compete in both of these races. Some states (but not the national government) also use the electoral process to make public policy and remove office holders. These processes are known as the initiative, referendum, and recall.

PRIMARY ELECTIONS In **primary elections,** voters decide which candidates within a party will represent the party in the general elections. Primary elections take on a number of different forms, depending on who is allowed to participate. **Closed primaries** allow only a party's registered voters to cast a ballot. In **open primaries,** however, independents and sometimes members of the other party are allowed to participate. Closed primaries are considered healthier for the party system because they prevent members of one party from influencing the primaries of the opposition party. Studies of open primaries indicate that **crossover voting**—participation in the primary of a party with which the voter is not affiliated—occurs frequently.[2] Nevertheless, research suggests that these crossover votes are usually individual decisions; little evidence exists for organized attempts by voters of one party to influence the primary results of the other party.[3]

In eight states, when none of the candidates in the initial primary secures a majority of the votes, there is a **runoff primary,** a contest between the two candidates with the greatest number of votes.[4] Louisiana has a novel twist on the primary system. There, all candidates for office appear on the ballot on the day of the national general election. If one candidate receives over 50 percent of the vote, the candidate wins and no further action is necessary. If no candidate wins a majority of the vote, the top two candidates, even if they belong to the same party, face each other in a runoff election. Such a system blurs the lines between primary and general elections.

GENERAL ELECTIONS Once the parties have selected their candidates for various offices, each state holds its general election. In the **general election,** voters decide which candidates will actually fill elective public offices. These elections take place at many levels, including municipal, county, state, and national. Whereas primaries are contests between the candidates within each party, general elections are contests between the candidates of opposing parties.

INITIATIVE AND REFERENDUM Taken together, the initiative and referendum processes are collectively known as ballot measures; both allow voters to enact public policy. They are used by some state and local governments, but not the national government.

An **initiative** is a process that allows *citizens* to propose legislation or state constitutional amendments by submitting them to the electorate for popular vote, provided the initiative supporters receive a certain number of signatures on petitions supporting the placement of the proposal on the ballot. Twenty-four states and the District of

Columbia use the initiative process. A **referendum** is an election whereby the *state legislature* submits proposed legislation or state constitutional amendments to the voters for approval. Legislators often use referenda when they want to spend large sums of money or address policy areas for which they do not want to be held accountable in the next election cycle.

referendum
An election whereby the state legislature submits proposed legislation or state constitutional amendments to the voters for approval.

Ballot measures have been the subject of heated debate in the past decades. Critics charge that ballot measures—intended to give citizens more direct control over policy making—are now unduly influenced by interest groups and "the initiative industry—law firms that draft legislation, petition management firms that guarantee ballot access, direct-mail firms, and campaign consultants who specialize in initiative contests."[5] Critics also question the ability of voters to deal with the numerous complex issues that appear on a ballot. In addition, the wording of a ballot measure can have an enormous impact on the outcome. In some cases, a "yes" vote will bring about a policy change; in other cases, a "no" vote will cause a change.[6] Moreover, ballot initiatives are not subject to the same campaign contribution limits applied to donations in

HOW ARE BALLOT MEASURES USED?

Citizens and state legislators use ballot measures to make public policy on a wide range of controversial issues. Here, a sign expresses opposition to Amendment One, a 2012 North Carolina ballot measure that prohibited same-sex marriage in that state.

recall
An election in which voters can remove an incumbent from office prior to the next scheduled election.

12.1

12.2

12.3

12.4

12.5

12.6

candidate campaigns. Consequently, a single wealthy individual can bankroll a ballot measure and influence public policy in a manner that is not available to the individual through the normal policy process.

Supporters of ballot measures argue that critics have overstated their case, and that the process has historically been used to champion popular issues that were resisted at the state level by entrenched political interests. Citizens have used initiatives, for example, in popular progressive causes such as banning child labor, promoting environmental laws, expanding suffrage to women, and passing campaign finance reform. The process has also been instrumental in passing popular conservative proposals such as tax relief and banning gay marriages.[7] Furthermore, supporters point out that ballot measures can heighten public interest in elections and can increase voter participation.

RECALL **Recall** elections—or deelections—allow voters to remove an incumbent from office prior to the next scheduled election. Recall elections are historically very rare, and sometimes they are thwarted by an official's resignation or impeachment prior to the vote. In recent years, however, recall has become a more popular technique to challenge officials at the state and local levels. In fact, 65 percent of all recalls of state legislators have taken place in the past 30 years. In 2011, alone, voters attempted to recall the mayors of Miami and Omaha, sixteen Wisconsin state senators, and the entire Bell, California, city council. And, in 2012, voters unsuccessfully attempted to recall Wisconsin Governor Scott Walker, who had fallen under fire for cutting state employees' bargaining rights. Observers attribute this growing use of recall to the development of new technologies, such as the Internet, that make fund-raising and signature gathering easier. Online news sources, too, may turn local recall elections into national news.[8]

Presidential Elections

12.2 Outline the electoral procedures for presidential and general elections.

No U.S. election can compare to the presidential contest. This spectacle, held every four years, brings together all the elements of politics and attracts the most ambitious and energetic politicians to the national stage. Voters in a series of state contests that run through the winter and spring of the election year select delegates who will attend each party's national convention. Following the national convention for each party, held in late summer, a final set of fifty separate state elections to select the president are held on the Tuesday after the first Monday in November. This lengthy process exhausts candidates and voters alike, but it allows the diversity of the United States to be displayed in ways a shorter, more homogeneous presidential election process could not.

Primaries and Caucuses

The state party organizations use several types of methods to elect the national convention delegates who will ultimately select the candidates running against each other in the general election:

1. *Winner-take-all primary.* Under this system the candidate who wins the most votes in a state secures all of that state's delegates. While Democrats no longer permit its use because they view it as less representative than a proportional system, Republicans generally prefer this process, as it enables a candidate to amass a majority of delegates quickly and shortens the divisive primary season.
2. *Proportional representation primary.* Under this system, candidates who secure a threshold percentage of votes are awarded delegates in proportion to the number

How Does the Iowa Caucus Work?

Caucuses are the oldest and most traditional method of choosing a party's nominee for political office. Rates of participation in caucuses, however, may be lower than in primary elections because of the investment of time required by this method of choosing a nominee, as well as citizens' lack of familiarity with the process of caucusing. Examine the infographic below to learn more about how caucuses are conducted in the first caucus state, Iowa, as well as many other states.

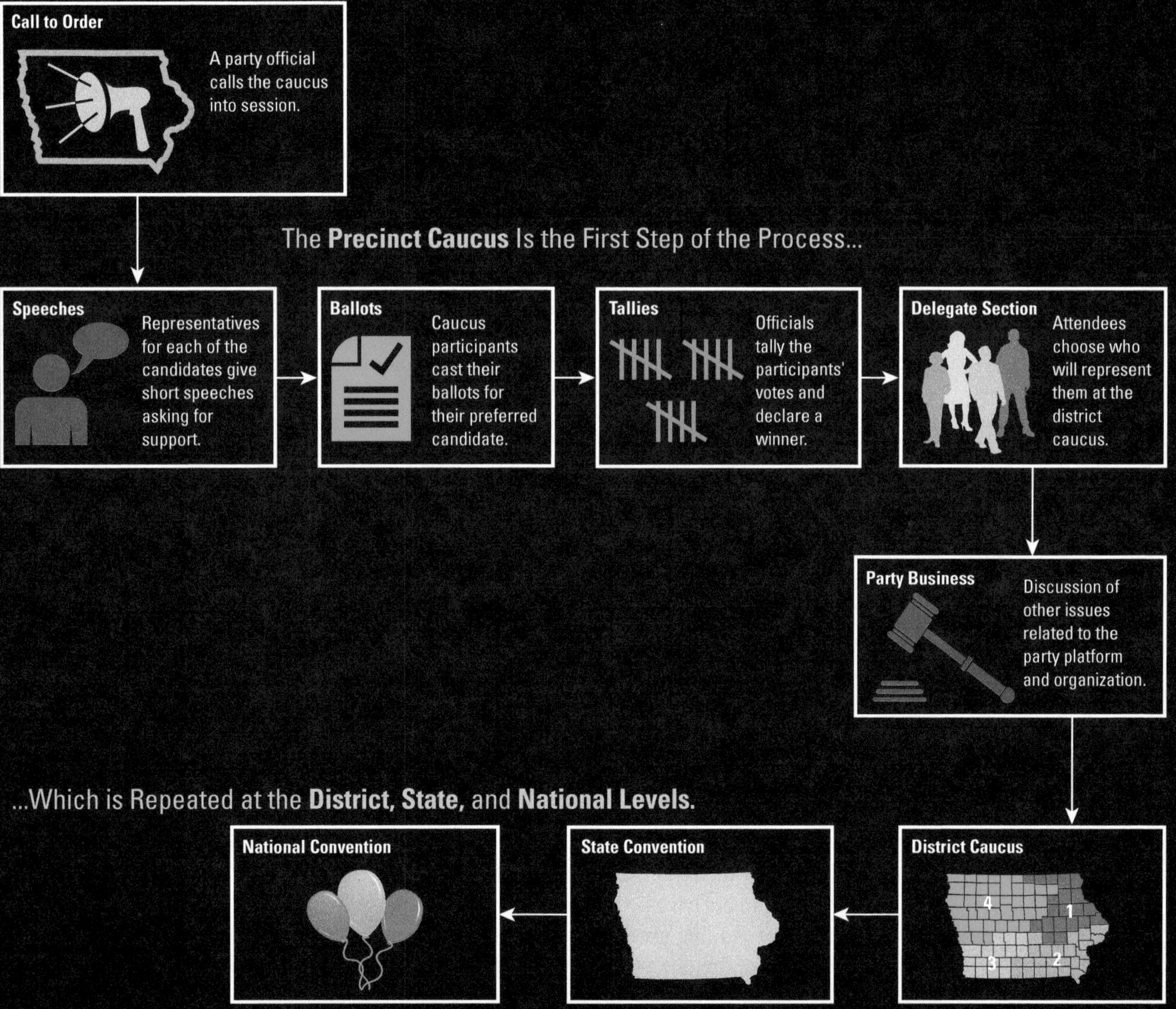

Call to Order
A party official calls the caucus into session.
The Precinct Caucus Is the First Step of the Process...
Speeches
Representatives for each of the candidates give short speeches asking for support.
Ballots
Caucus participants cast their ballots for their preferred candidate.
Tallies
Officials tally the participants' votes and declare a winner.
Delegate Section
Attendees choose who will represent them at the district caucus.
Party Business
Discussion of other issues related to the party platform and organization.
...Which is Repeated at the District, State, and National Levels.
District Caucus
4
1
3
2
State Convention
National Convention

SOURCE: *Des Moines Register*, "How the Iowa Caucuses Work," http://caucuses.desmoinesregister.com/how-to-caucus/.

CRITICAL THINKING QUESTIONS

1. How does the caucus process enable citizens to learn more about the candidates before they cast their ballot? What are the advantages and disadvantages of such a system?
2. What types of voters are most likely to participate in caucuses? How does this affect the ultimate selection of a party's candidate for office?
3. What would a diagram of a primary election look like? What are the similarities and differences between these two methods of delegate selection?

front-loading
The tendency of states to choose an early date on the nomination calendar.

of popular votes won. Democrats now use this system in many state primaries, where they award delegates to anyone who wins more than 15 percent of the vote in any congressional district. Although proportional representation is probably the fairest way of allocating delegates to candidates, its downside is that it renders majorities of delegates more difficult to accumulate and thus can lengthen the presidential nomination contest.

3. *Caucus.* The caucus is the oldest, most party-oriented method of choosing delegates to the national conventions. Traditionally, the caucus was a closed meeting of party activists in each state who selected the party's choice for presidential candidate. Today, caucuses (in Iowa, for example) are more open and attract a wider range of the party's membership. Indeed, new participatory caucuses more closely resemble primary elections than they do the old, exclusive party caucuses.[9] At a caucus, participants spend several hours learning about politics and the party. They listen to speeches by candidates or their representatives and receive advice from party leaders and elected officials, then cast a well-informed vote.

SELECTING A SYSTEM The mix of preconvention contests has changed over the years, with the most pronounced trend being the shift from caucuses to primary elections. Only seventeen states held presidential primaries in 1968; in 2012, thirty-seven states chose this method. In recent years, the vast majority of delegates to each party's national convention have been selected through the primary system.

Many people support the increase in number of primaries because they believe that primaries are more democratic than caucuses. Primaries are accessible not only to party activists but also to most of those registered to vote. Thus, although both primaries and caucuses attract the most ideologically extreme voters in each party, primaries nominate more moderate and appealing candidates—those that primary voters believe can win in the general election. Primaries are also more similar to the general election and thus constitute a rigorous test for the candidates and a chance to display, under pressure, some of the skills needed to be a successful president.

Critics believe that the qualities tested by the primary system are by no means a complete list of those needed by a successful president. For instance, skill at handling national and local media representatives is by itself no guarantee of an effective presidency. The exhausting primary schedule may be a better test of a candidate's stamina than of his or her brain power. In addition, critics argue that although primaries may attract more participants than do caucuses, this quantity does not substitute for the quality of information held by caucus participants.

FRONT-LOADING The role of primaries and caucuses in the presidential election has been altered by **front-loading,** the tendency of states to choose an early date on the nomination calendar (see Figure 12.1). This trend is hardly surprising, given the added press emphasis on the first contests and the voters' desire to cast their ballots before the competition is decided. Front-loading has important effects on the nomination process. First, a front-loaded schedule generally benefits the front-runner, since opponents have little time to turn the contest around once they fall behind. Second, front-loading gives an advantage to the candidate who wins the "invisible primary," that is, the one who can raise the bulk of the money *before* the nomination season begins. Once primaries and caucuses begin, less opportunity is available to raise money to finance campaign efforts simultaneously in many states.

However, Internet fund-raising has emerged as a means to soften the advantage of a large campaign fund going into a primary battle, since it allows candidates to raise large sums from many small donors nationwide virtually overnight. All of the major 2012 presidential candidates relied on online donations to finance their campaigns. President Obama's technology team received such acclaim for their innovative fund-raising efforts that, in a twist of irony, they found themselves headlining fundraisers attracting other campaign strategists who wanted to learn from their record-breaking fund-raising efforts.[10]

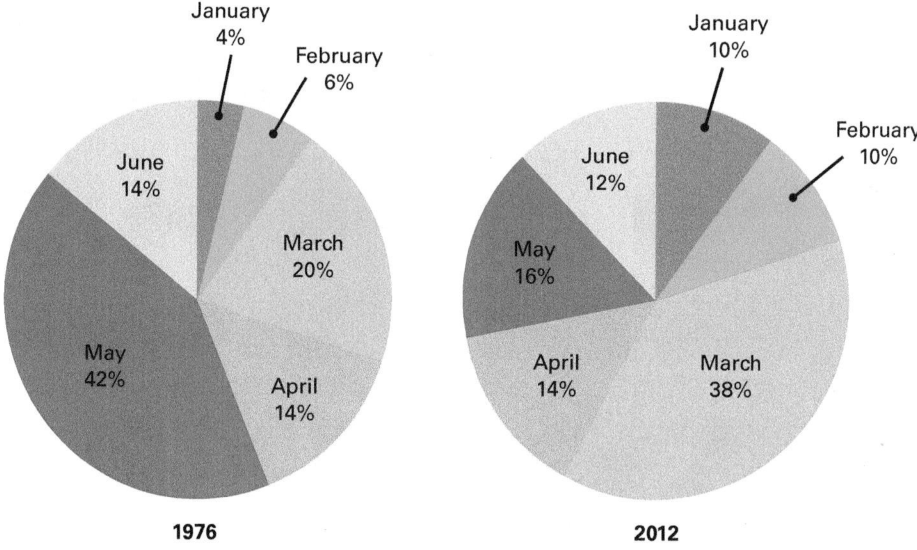

FIGURE 12.1 WHEN DO STATES CHOOSE THEIR NOMINEE FOR PRESIDENT?

These pie graphs show when Republican Party caucuses and primary elections were held in 1976 and 2012. The trend toward front-loading is evident. In 2012, for example, most states held their primaries and caucuses in March; in comparison, in 1976, most states held their nominating contests in May.

SOURCE: Joshua T. Putnam, frontloading.blogspot.com.

Electoral College
Representatives of each state who cast the final ballots that actually elect a president.

elector
Member of the Electoral College.

reapportionment
The reallocation of the number of seats in the House of Representatives after each decennial census.

Electing a President: The Electoral College

Given the enormous amount of energy, money, and time expended to nominate two major-party presidential contenders, it is difficult to believe that the general election could be more arduous than the nominating contests, but it usually is. The process of campaigning for the presidency (and other offices) is described in another chapter, but the object of the exercise is clear: winning a majority of the **Electoral College.** This uniquely American institution consists of representatives of each state who cast the final ballots that actually elect a president. The total number of **electors**—the members of the Electoral College—for each state is equivalent to the number of senators and representatives that state has in the U.S. Congress. The District of Columbia is accorded three electoral votes, making 538 the total number of votes cast in the Electoral College. Thus, the magic number for winning the presidency is 270 votes.

Keep in mind that through **reapportionment,** representation in the House of Representatives and consequently in the Electoral College is altered every ten years to reflect population shifts. Reapportionment is simply the reallocation of the number of seats in the House of Representatives that takes place after each decennial census. After the 2010 Census, for example, the Electoral College map was redrawn to reflect a sizeable population shift from the Midwest and the Democratic-dominated Northeast to the South and West, where Republicans are much stronger (see Figure 12.2). Texas, for example, gained four congressional districts, and therefore four additional seats in the House of Representatives and four additional votes in the Electoral College. Florida gained two seats and two votes, while six other states gained one. New York and Ohio both lost two seats and two votes, and eight states lost a single seat and electoral vote. Thus, if Barack Obama wins the same states in 2012 that he won in 2008, he will win six fewer electoral votes.

HISTORICAL CHALLENGES The Electoral College resulted from a compromise between those Framers who argued for selection of the president by the Congress and those who favored selection by direct popular election. Three points are essential to understanding the Framers' design of the Electoral College. The system was constructed to: (1) work without political parties; (2) cover both the nominating and electing phases of presidential selection; and (3) produce a nonpartisan president.

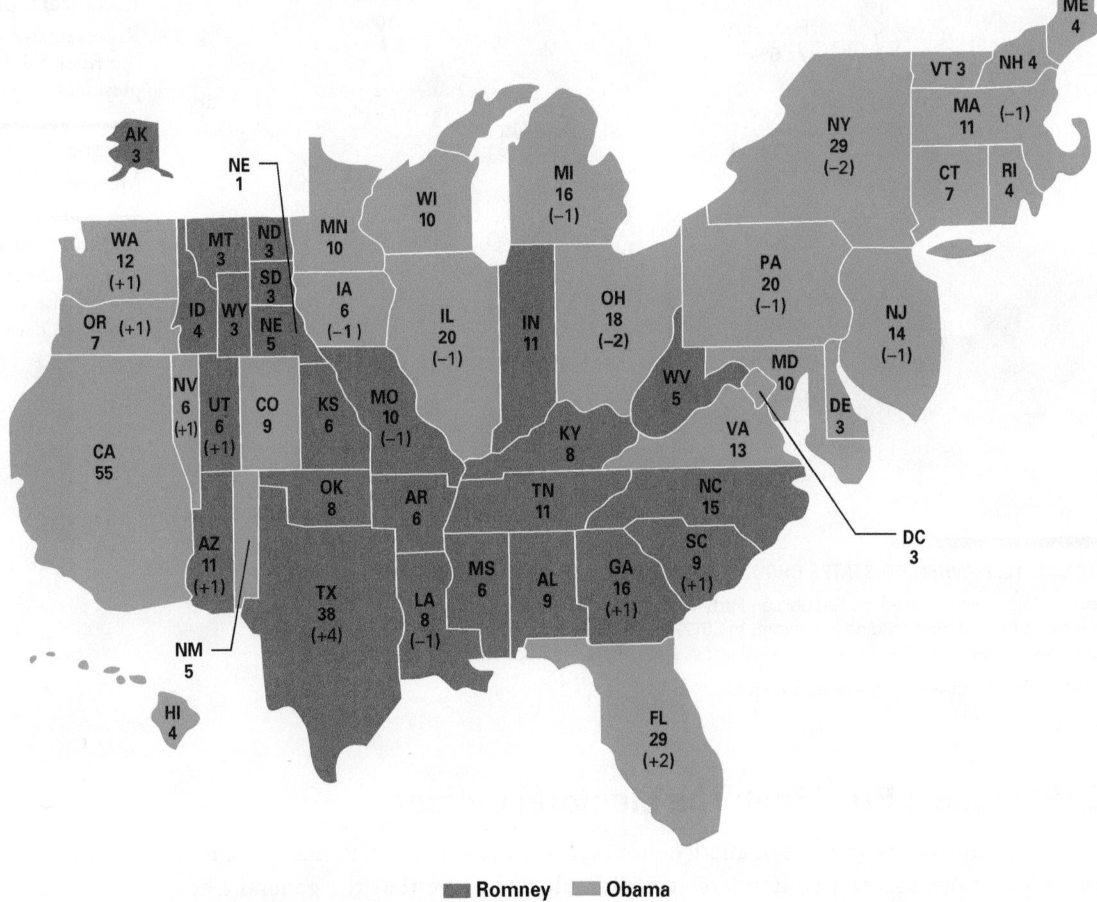

FIGURE 12.2 HOW IS VOTING POWER APPORTIONED IN THE ELECTORAL COLLEGE?

This map visually represents the respective electoral weights of the fifty states in the 2012 presidential election. For each state, the gain or loss of Electoral College votes based on the 2010 Census is indicated in parentheses. Note the loss of seats in the Northeast and the gains in the South and West.

SOURCE: CNN, http://www.cnn.com/election/2012/results/race/president.

THE ELECTORAL VOTE.
Now let us look at it from another point of view.

HOW WAS THE 1876 PRESIDENTIAL ELECTION RESOLVED?

This cartoon from the 1876 presidential contest between Republican Rutherford B. Hayes and Democrat Samuel J. Tilden describes the frustration of many Americans with interpreting the constitutional procedures for resolving Electoral College disputes. An electoral commission formed by Congress to decide the matter awarded all disputed electors to Hayes, giving him the victory even though he had lost the popular vote by a 51–48 percent margin.

Most of the challenges faced by the Electoral College are the result of changes in presidential elections that have occurred over time.

For example, because the Framers expected partisanship to have little influence, they originally designed the Electoral College to elect the president and vice president from the same pool of candidates; the one who received the most votes would become president and the runner-up would become vice president. To accommodate this system, each elector was given two votes. Following the development of the first party system, the republic's fourth presidential election soon revealed a flaw in this plan. In 1800, Thomas Jefferson and Aaron Burr were, respectively, the presidential and vice presidential candidates advanced by the Democratic-Republican Party, whose supporters controlled a majority of the Electoral College. Accordingly, each Democratic-Republican elector cast one of his two votes for Jefferson and the other one for Burr. Since there was no way under the constitutional arrangements for electors to earmark their votes separately for president and vice president, the presidential election resulted in a tie between Jefferson and Burr. Even though most understood Jefferson to be the actual choice for president, the Constitution mandated that a tie be decided by the House of Representatives, which the Federalists controlled. The controversy was settled in Jefferson's favor, but only after much energy was expended to persuade Federalists not to give Burr the presidency.

The Twelfth Amendment, ratified in 1804 and still the constitutional foundation for presidential elections today, attempted to remedy the confusion between the selection of vice presidents and presidents that beset the election of 1800. The amendment provided for separate elections for each office. In the event of a tie or when no candidate received a majority of the total number of electors, the election still went to the House

Each State shall appoint, in such Manner as the Legislature thereof may direct, a Number of Electors, equal to the whole Number of Senators and Representatives to which the State may be entitled in the Congress: but no Senator or Representative, or Person holding an Office of Trust or Profit under the United States, shall be appointed an Elector. —ARTICLE II, SECTION 1, CLAUSE 2

This clause of the Constitution creates what is called the Electoral College, the representative body of citizens formally responsible for choosing the president of the United States. This body was created as a compromise between some Framers who favored allowing citizens to directly choose their president and other Framers who feared that directly electing a president could lead to tyranny. As stipulated in the Constitution, each state has a number of votes in the Electoral College that is equivalent to the number of senators and representatives that state has in the U.S. Congress.

Since the ratification of the Twelfth Amendment to the Constitution in 1824, the Electoral College has remained relatively unchanged, save for the addition of electors as the size of the House of Representatives and Senate grew. However, one major change in the Electoral College occurred when Congress enacted and the states ratified the Twenty-Third Amendment to the Constitution. This amendment gave the District of Columbia, which had evolved from a dismal swampland to a growing metropolitan area, representation in the Electoral College. The amendment set the number of electors representing the District as equal to the number of electors representing the smallest state, regardless of the District's population. Today, the District has three electors, making it equal with small-population states such as Delaware and Wyoming.

This provision could become problematic if the population of the District grows from its present level of 618,000. Then, if the District were to have voting power in the Electoral College equal to its population, it would require at least one additional elector. Republicans in Congress, however, have resisted modifying this provision, as well as giving the District a voting member (or members) of Congress, in part because the District is one of the most heavily Democratic areas of the nation. In 2012, for example, more than 91 percent of the District's residents voted for Barack Obama.

CRITICAL THINKING QUESTIONS

1. **Should the Electoral College continue to play a role in the selection of the president? Why or why not?**
2. **Should the District of Columbia have representation in the Electoral College equal to its population? Why or why not?**

of Representatives; now, however, each state delegation would have one vote to cast for one of the three candidates who had received the greatest number of electoral votes.

The Electoral College modified by the Twelfth Amendment has fared better than the College as originally designed, but it has not been problem free. On three occasions during the nineteenth century, the electoral process resulted in the selection of a president who received fewer votes than his opponent. In 1824, neither John Quincy Adams nor Andrew Jackson secured a majority of electoral votes, throwing the election into the House. Although Jackson had more electoral and popular votes than Adams, the House selected the latter as president. In the 1876 contest between Republican Rutherford B. Hayes and Democrat Samuel J. Tilden, no candidate received a majority of electoral votes; the House decided the election in Hayes's favor even though he had 250,000 fewer popular votes than Tilden. In the election of 1888, President Grover Cleveland secured about 100,000 more popular votes than did Benjamin Harrison, yet Harrison won a majority of the Electoral College vote, and with it the presidency.

No further Electoral College crises have occurred. However, the 2000 presidential election once again brought the Electoral College to the forefront of voters' minds. Throughout the 2000 presidential campaign, many analysts foresaw that the election would likely be the closest since the 1960 race between John F. Kennedy and Richard M. Nixon. Few observers realized, however, that the election would be so close that the winner would not be officially declared for more than five weeks after Election Day. And, no one could have predicted that the Electoral College winner, George W. Bush, would lose the popular vote and become president after the Supreme Court's controversial decision in *Bush* v. *Gore* (2000) stopped a recount of votes cast in Florida. With the margin of the Electoral College results so small (271 for Bush, 267 for Gore), a Gore victory in any number of closely contested states could have given him a majority in the Electoral College.

SHOULD THE ELECTORAL COLLEGE BE REFORMED? Following the 2000 election, many political observers suggested that the system of electing a president needed reform. Two major proposals were put forward and are discussed in this section. To date, however, no changes have been made, and it will likely take another major electoral crisis to reopen the debate.

First, and perhaps most simply, some observers have suggested using the national popular vote to choose the president. While this is the most democratic reform, it is by far the least likely to be enacted, given that the U.S. Constitution would have to be amended to abolish the Electoral College. Even assuming that the House of Representatives could muster the two-thirds majority necessary to pass an amendment, the proposal would almost certainly never pass the Senate. Small states have the same representation in the Senate as populous ones, and the Senate thus serves as a bastion of equal representation for all states, regardless of population—a principle generally reinforced by the existing configuration of the Electoral College, which ensures disproportionate electoral influence for the smallest states.

Another proposed reform is known as the congressional district plan. This plan would retain the Electoral College but give each candidate one electoral vote for each congressional district that he or she wins in a state, and the winner of the overall popular vote in each state would receive two bonus votes (one for each senator) for that state. Two states currently use the congressional district plan: Maine and Nebraska.

One advantage of the congressional district plan is that it can be adopted without constitutional amendment. Any state that wants to split its Electoral College votes need only pass a law to this effect. It may also promote more diffuse political campaigns; instead of campaigning only in states that are "in play" in the Electoral College, candidates might also have to campaign in competitive districts in otherwise safe states.

But, the congressional district plan also has some unintended consequences. First, the winner of the popular vote might still lose the presidency. Under this plan, Richard M. Nixon would have won the 1960 election instead of John F. Kennedy. Second, this reform would further politicize the congressional redistricting process. If electoral votes were at stake, parties would seek to maximize the number of safe electoral districts for their presidential nominee while minimizing the number of competitive districts. Finally, although candidates would not ignore entire states, they would quickly learn to focus their campaigning on competitive districts while ignoring secure districts, thereby eliminating some of the democratizing effect of such a change. During the 2012 election, another proposal to reform the Electoral College came to light. Eight states and Washington, D.C. have signed the National Popular Vote Interstate Compact. The signatories vow that they will pledge their electoral votes to the winner of the popular vote, regardless of the state's winner. The compact will take effect when states with 270 electoral votes—a majority—agree to support its provisions.

Congressional Elections

12.3 Compare and contrast congressional and presidential elections and explain the incumbency advantage.

ompared with presidential elections, congressional elections receive scant national attention. Unlike major-party presidential contenders, most candidates for Congress labor in relative obscurity. Some nominees for Congress are celebrities—television stars, sports heroes, and even local TV news anchors. The vast majority of party nominees for Congress, however, are little-known state legislators and local office holders who receive remarkably limited coverage in many states and communities. For them, just establishing name identification in the electorate is the biggest battle.

incumbency
Already holding an office.

The Incumbency Advantage

The current system enhances the advantages of **incumbency,** or already holding an office. Those people in office tend to remain in office. In a "bad" year such as the Republican wave of 2010, "only" 87 percent of House incumbents won reelection. Senatorial reelection rates can be much more mercurial. In 2006, only 79 percent of senators seeking reelection were victorious. In 2010, only two incumbents were not reelected. To the political novice, these reelection rates might seem surprising, as public trust in government and satisfaction with Congress has remained remarkably low during the very period that reelection rates have been on the rise. To understand the nature of the incumbency advantage, it is necessary to explore its primary causes: staff support, visibility, and the "scare-off" effect.

STAFF SUPPORT Members of the U.S. House of Representatives are permitted to hire eighteen permanent and four nonpermanent aides to work in their Washington and district offices. Senators typically enjoy far larger staffs, with the actual size determined by the number of people in the state they represent. Both House and Senate members also enjoy the additional benefits provided by the scores of unpaid interns who assist with office duties. Many activities of staff members directly or indirectly

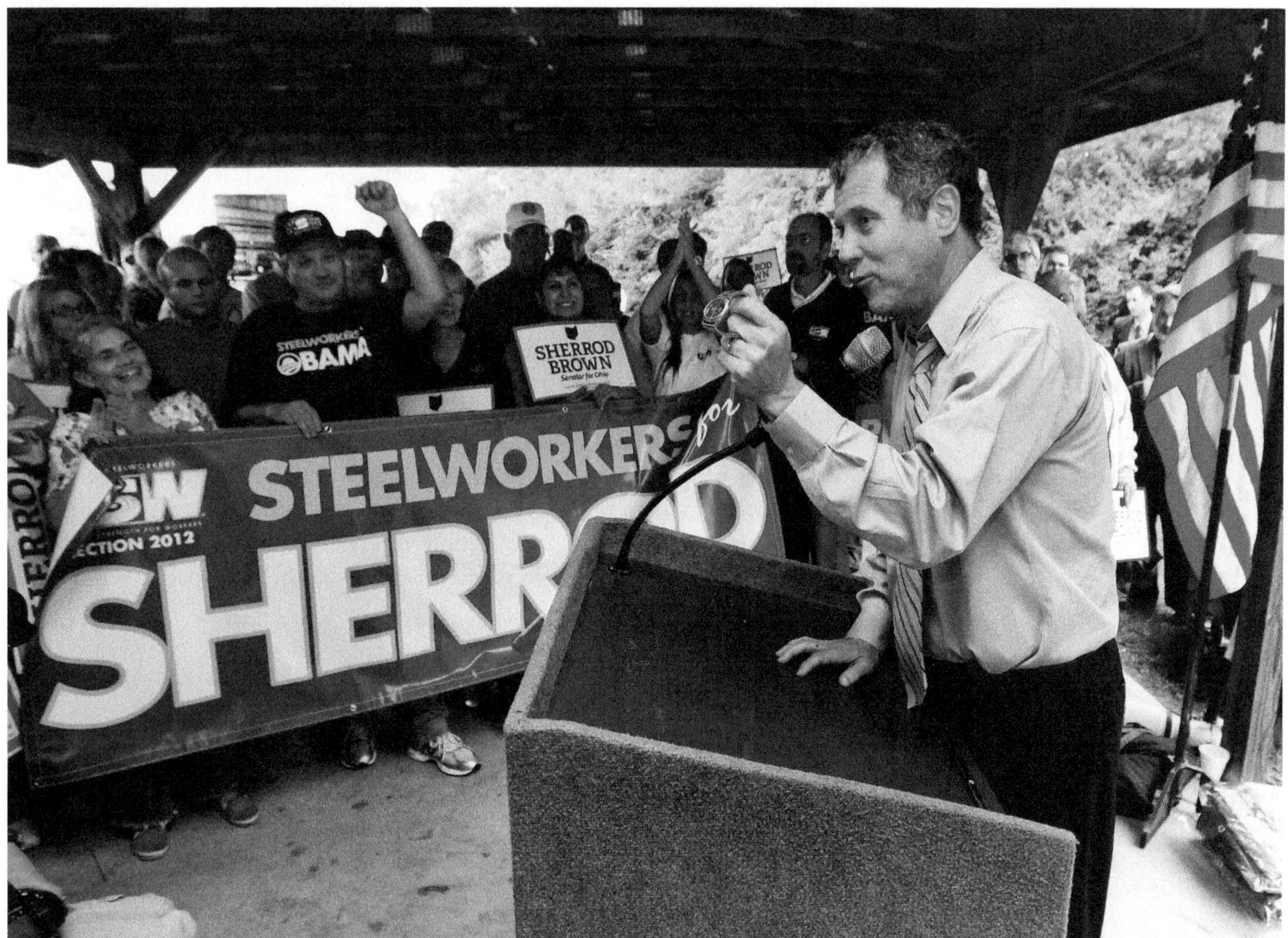

WHAT ARE SOME OF THE ADVANTAGES OF INCUMBENCY?

Incumbent office holders enjoy many advantages on Election Day, including credit claiming, name recognition, staff and support, and, in some cases, district lines that are drawn to enhance their electability. Here, Senator Sherrod Brown (D-OH) asks steelworkers for their support during his 2012 reelection bid. Key to Brown's victory were policies he had supported while in Congress, including restrictions on trade with China, popular with manufacturing workers and unions in his home state.

promote the legislator through constituency services, the wide array of assistance provided by members of Congress to voters in need. Constituent service may include tracking a lost Social Security check, helping a veteran receive disputed benefits, or finding a summer internship for a college student. Research has shown that if a House incumbent's staff helped to solve a problem for a constituent, that constituent rated the incumbent more favorably than constituents who were not assisted by the incumbent,[11] therefore providing the incumbent a great advantage over any challenger.

VISIBILITY Most incumbents are highly visible in their districts. They have easy access to local media, cut ribbons galore, attend important local funerals, and speak frequently at meetings and community events. Moreover, convenient schedules and generous travel allowances increase the local availability of incumbents. Nearly a fourth of the people in an average congressional district claim to have met their representative, and about half recognize their legislator's name without prompting. This visibility has an electoral payoff, as research shows district attentiveness is at least partly responsible for incumbents' electoral safety.[12]

THE "SCARE-OFF" EFFECT Research also identifies an indirect advantage of incumbency: the ability of the office holder to fend off challenges from quality challengers, something scholars refer to as the "scare-off" effect.[13] Incumbents have the ability to scare off these opponents because of the institutional advantages of office, such as high name recognition, large war chests, free constituent mailings, staffs attached to legislative offices, and overall experience in running a successful campaign. Potential strong challengers facing this initial uphill battle will often wait until the incumbent retires rather than challenge him or her.[14]

☐ Why Incumbents Lose

While most incumbents win reelection, in every election cycle some members of Congress lose their positions to challengers. Members lose their reelection bids for four major reasons: redistricting, scandals, presidential coattails, and mid-term elections.

REDISTRICTING At least every ten years, state legislators redraw congressional district lines to reflect population shifts, both in the state and in the nation at large. This political process itself may be used to secure incumbency advantage by creating "safe" seats for members of the majority party in the state legislature. But, it can also be used to punish incumbents in the out-of-power party. Some incumbents can be put in the same districts as other incumbents, or other representatives' base of political support can be weakened by adding territory favorable to the opposition party. The number of incumbents who actually lose their reelection bids because of redistricting is lessened by the strategic behavior of redistricted members—who often choose to retire rather than wage an expensive reelection battle.[15]

SCANDALS Modern scandals come in many varieties. The old standby of financial impropriety has been supplemented by other forms of career-ending incidents, such as sexual improprieties. Incumbents implicated in scandals typically do not lose reelections—because they simply choose to retire rather than face defeat.[16] Representative Anthony Weiner (D–NY), for example, resigned from office in 2011 after admitting he had sent several sexually explicit photos on his official House Twitter account during the three preceding years.

PRESIDENTIAL COATTAILS The defeat of a congressional incumbent can also occur as a result of presidential coattails. Successful presidential candidates usually carry into office congressional candidates of the same party in the year of their election. The strength of the coattail effect has, however, declined in modern times, as party identification has weakened and the powers and perks of incumbency have grown. Whereas Harry S Truman's party gained seventy-six House seats and nine

TABLE 12.1 HOW DOES THE PRESIDENT AFFECT CONGRESSIONAL ELECTIONS?

Gain (+) or Loss (–) for President's Party					
	Presidential Election Years		Mid-Term Election Years		
President/Year	**House**	**Senate**	**Year**	**House**	**Senate**
Truman (D): 1948	+76	+9	1950	–28	-5
Eisenhower (R): 1952	+24	+2	1954	–18	–1
Eisenhower (R): 1956	–2	0	1958	–47	–13
Kennedy (D): 1960	–20	–2	1962	–2	+4
L. Johnson (D): 1964	+38	+2	1966	–47	-3
Nixon (R): 1968	+7	+5	1970	–12	+1
Nixon (R): 1972	+13	–2	*Ford* (R): 1974	–48	-3
Carter (D): 1976	+2	0	1978	–15	-3
Reagan (R): 1980	+33	+12	1982	–26	–1
Reagan (R): 1984	+15	-2	1986	-5	-8
Bush (R): 1988	–3	–1	1990	–10	–1
Clinton (D): 1992	–10	0	1994	–52	–9[a]
Clinton (D): 1996	+10	–2	1998	+3	0
G. W. Bush (R): 2000	–2	–4	2002	+8	+2
G. W. Bush (R): 2004	+3	+4	2006	–30	-6
Obama (D): 2008	+21	+8	2010	–63	-6
Obama (D): 2012	+5	+2			

[a]Includes the switch from Democrat to Republican of Alabama U.S. Senator Richard Shelby one day after the election.

SOURCE: *Congressional Quarterly Guide to U.S. Elections*, 6th ed. Washington, DC: CQ Press: 2010. Updated by the authors.

mid-term election
An election that takes place in the middle of a presidential term.

additional Senate seats in 1948, Barack Obama's party gained only twenty-one House members and eight senators in 2008. The gains can be minimal even in presidential landslide reelection years, such as 1972 (Nixon) and 1984 (Reagan) (see Table 12.1).

MID-TERM ELECTIONS Elections in the middle of presidential terms, called **mid-term elections,** present a threat to incumbents of the president's party. Just as the presidential party usually gains seats in presidential election years, it usually loses seats in off years. The problems and tribulations of governing normally cost a president some popularity, alienate key groups, or cause the public to want to send the president a message of one sort or another. An economic downturn or presidential scandal can underscore and expand this circumstance, as the continuing recession in 2010 demonstrated. All in all, Democrats lost more seats than either party has in an election since 1938.

Also apparent is the tendency of voters to punish the president's party much more severely in the sixth year of an eight-year presidency. After only two years, voters may still be willing to "give the guy a chance," but after six years, voters are often restless for change. In what many saw as a referendum on President George W. Bush's policy in Iraq, for example, the Republican Party lost control of both chambers of Congress in the 2006 election. This mid-term election was typical of the sixth-year itch, with voters looking for a change and punishing the incumbent president's party in Congress.

Senate elections are less inclined to follow these off-year patterns than are House elections. The idiosyncratic nature of Senate contests is due to their intermittent scheduling (only one-third of the seats come up for election every two years) and the existence of well-funded, well-known candidates who can sometimes swim against whatever political tide is rising. In the 2010 mid-term elections, Democrats were able to retain control of the Senate despite huge losses in the House. The impact of the Tea Party movement was far less powerful in statewide elections, and some Senate Democrats in close elections were able to win reelection; among them Senators Patty Murray (D–WA) and Michael Bennet (D–CO).

Patterns in Vote Choice

12.4 Identify seven factors that influence voter choice.

conventional political participation
Activism that attempts to influence the political process through commonly accepted forms of persuasion such as voting or letter writing.

unconventional political participation
Activism that attempts to influence the political process through unusual or extreme measures, such as protests, boycotts, and picketing.

The act of voting is the most common form of **conventional political participation,** or activism that attempts to influence the political process through commonly accepted forms of persuasion. Other examples of conventional political participation include writing letters and making campaign contributions. Citizens may also engage in **unconventional political participation,** or activism that attempts to influence the political process through unusual or extreme measures. Examples include participating in protests, boycotts, and picketing.

A number of factors affect citizens' choices about which candidate to support. Party affiliation and ideology stand at the forefront of these predictors. Other important factors are income and education, race and ethnicity, gender, religion, and political issues (see Figure 12.3).

☐ Party Identification

Party identification remains the most powerful predictor of vote choice. Stated simply, self-described Democrats tend to vote for Democratic candidates and self-described Republicans tend to vote for Republican candidates. This trend is particularly obvious

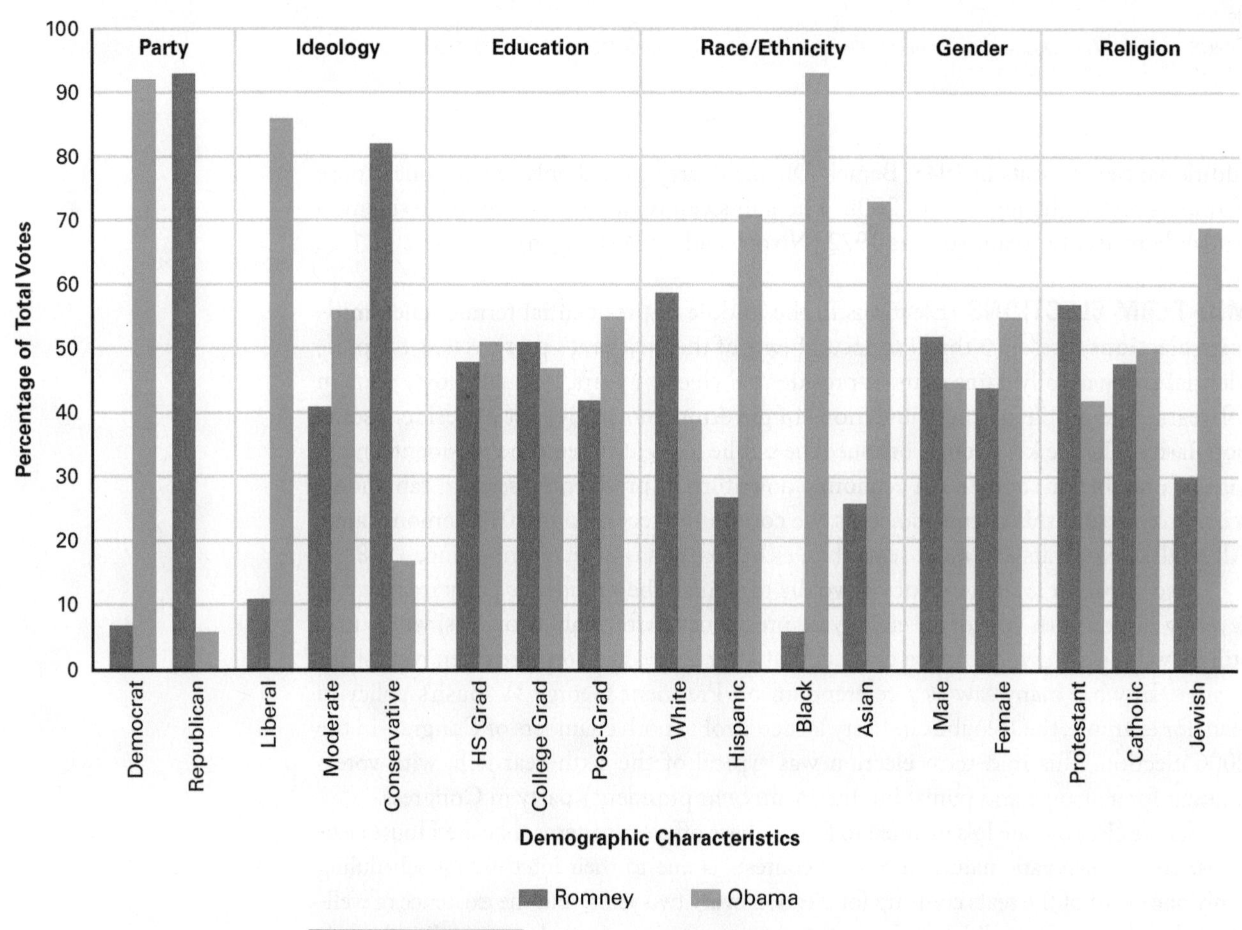

FIGURE 12.3 HOW DO DEMOGRAPHIC CHARACTERISTICS AFFECT VOTERS' CHOICES?

Demographic characteristics can be powerful predictors of citizens' choices at the voting booth. Partisanship is the most significant predictor of these decisions. In 2012, for example, 92 percent of Democrats voted for President Barack Obama and 93 percent of Republicans voted for Mitt Romney.

SOURCE: http://www.cnn.com/election/2012/results/race/president#exit-polls.

in less-visible elections, where voters may not know anything about the candidates and need a cue to help them cast their ballot. However, even in presidential elections, a high correlation exists between vote choice and party affiliation. In 2012, for example, 92 percent of self-identified Democrats voted for President Barack Obama, and 93 percent of self-identified Republicans voted for Mitt Romney.

In recent years, observers have noted higher levels of **ticket-splitting**, voting for candidates of different parties for various offices in the same election.[17] Scholars have posited several potential explanations for ticket-splitting. One is that voters split their tickets, consciously or not, because they trust neither party to govern. Under this interpretation, ticket-splitters are aware of the differences between the two parties and split their tickets to augment the checks and balances already present in the U.S. Constitution.[18] Alternatively, voters split their tickets possibly because the growth of issue- and candidate-centered politics has made party less important as a voting cue.[19]

ticket-splitting
Voting for candidates of different parties for various offices in the same election.

☐ Ideology

Ideology represents one of the most significant divisions in contemporary American politics. Liberals, generally speaking, favor government involvement in social programs and are committed to the ideals of tolerance and social justice. Conservatives, on the other hand, are dedicated to the ideals of individualism and market-based competition, and they tend to view government as a necessary evil rather than an agent of social improvement. Moderates lie somewhere between liberals and conservatives on the ideological spectrum; they favor conservative positions on some issues and liberal positions on others.

Not surprisingly, ideology is very closely related to vote choice. Liberals tend to vote for Democrats, and conservatives tend to vote for Republicans. In 2012, 86 percent of self-described liberals voted for President Obama, whereas only 11 percent voted for Romney. Conservatives, on the other hand, voted for Romney over Obama at a rate of 82 to 17 percent.[20]

☐ Income and Education

Over the years, income has been a remarkably stable correlate of vote choice. The poor vote more Democratic; the well-to-do vote heavily Republican.[21] The 2012 election was, to some extent, consistent with these trends. Sizeable majorities of those making less than $50,000 annually supported Obama, with 60 percent of those making less than $50,000 annually leading the way. All other income classes were a virtual toss-up, with Obama and Romney each carrying between 40 and 50 percent of the electorate. It can be said, however, that Romney, as the Republican candidate, performed better with voters in middle-class and high-income brackets than he did with poorer voters.

Since income and education are highly correlated—more educated people tend to make more money—it should be no surprise that education follows a somewhat similar pattern. The most educated and the least educated citizens are more inclined to vote Democratic, and those in the middle—for example, with a bachelor's degree—tend to vote Republican.

☐ Race and Ethnicity

Racial and ethnic groups also are likely to vote in distinct patterns. While whites have shown an increasing tendency to vote Republican, African American voters remain overwhelmingly Democratic in their voting decisions. Despite the best efforts of the Republican Party to garner African American support, this pattern shows no signs of waning. In 2012, Obama's candidacy accentuated this trend, and 93 percent of African Americans voted for him. Romney received a mere 6 percent of the African American vote.[22]

Hispanics also are likely to identify with and vote for Democrats, although not as monolithically as African Americans. In 2012, for example, Obama received 71 percent of the votes cast by Hispanics; Romney received only 27 percent.

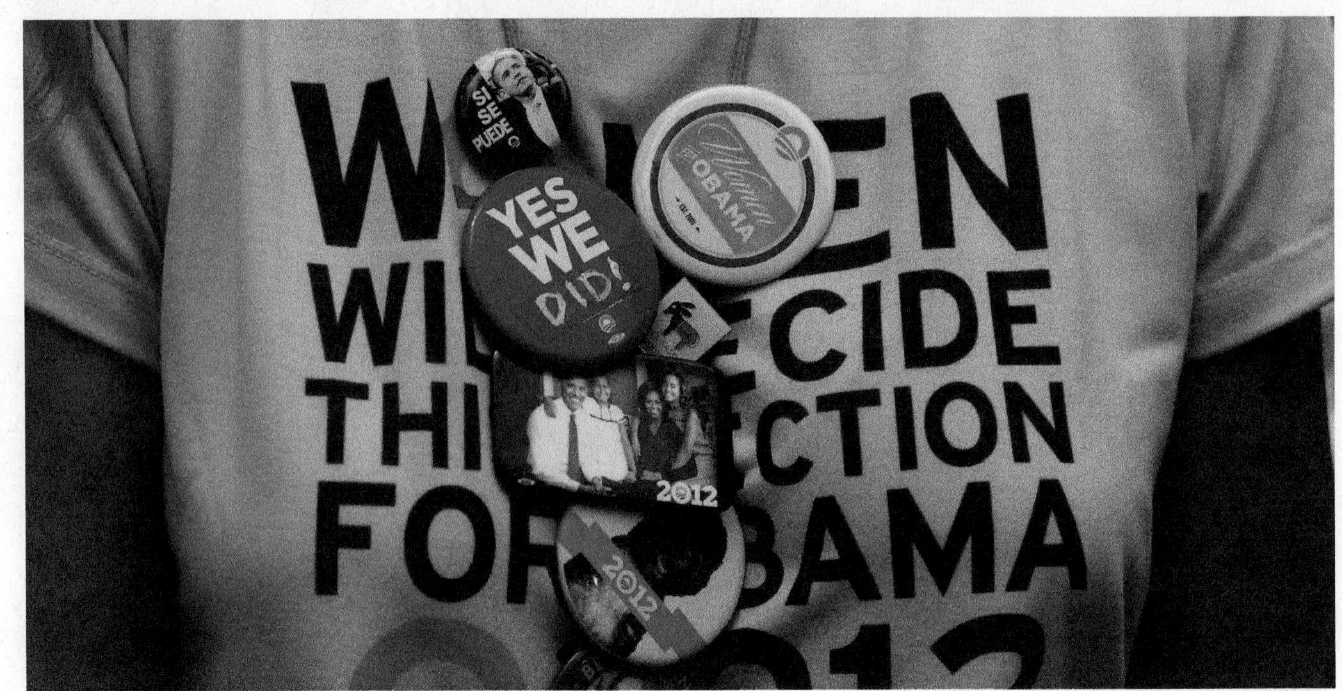

HOW DOES GENDER INFLUENCE ELECTORAL OUTCOMES?

The gender gap is one of the most powerful and consistent patterns in American elections. Women are significantly more likely to support Democratic candidates than their male counterparts. Thus, as reflected in this t-shirt, which declares, "Women will decide the election for Obama," female voters received much of the credit for Democrats' victories in 2012.

Asian and Pacific Island Americans are more variable in their voting than either the Hispanic or the African American community. The considerable political diversity within this group is worth noting: Chinese Americans tend to prefer Democratic candidates, but Vietnamese Americans, with strong anti-communist leanings, tend to support Republicans. A typical voting split for the Asian and Pacific Island American community runs about 60 percent Democratic and 40 percent Republican, though it can reach the extreme of a 50–50 split, depending on the election.[23] In the 2012 election, 73 percent of Asian American voters supported Obama and 26 percent of Asian American voters supported Romney.

□ Gender

Since 1980, the gender gap—the difference between the voting choices of men and women—has become a staple of American politics. In general, women are more likely to support Democratic candidates and men are more likely to support Republicans. The gender gap varies considerably from election to election, though normally it is between 5 and 7 percentage points. That is, women support the average Democrat 5 to 7 percent more than men. In 2012, Obama won 55 percent of the female vote, but only 45 percent of the male vote.[24]

A gender gap in vote choice is confined not only to contests between Democrats and Republicans but is frequently apparent in intraparty contests as well. In the 2012 Republican primaries and caucuses, Republican women were more likely than Republican men to support Mitt Romney. In the Arizona primary, for example, women supported Romney over his competitor, Rick Santorum, by a nearly two to one margin.[25]

□ Religion

Religious groups also have tended to vote in distinct patterns, but some of these traditional differences have declined considerably in recent years. The most cohesive of religious groups has been Jewish voters, a majority of whom have voted for every Democratic presidential candidate since the New Deal realignment. In 2012, 69 percent of Jewish voters supported Obama.

Explore on MyPoliSciLab

Who Votes and Who Doesn't?

Political scientists analyze voting patterns by group to find out why certain people are and are not voting. Hispanics, school dropouts, low-income citizens, and youth consistently vote less frequently than other Americans. New policies, such as photo identification requirements, make voting harder and might reinforce non-voting in these groups.

Who Didn't Vote in 2008?

		Percent
Race	Hispanic	40%
	White	25%
	Black	25%
	Other	28%
Education	Some High School or Less	51%
	High School Degree	31%
	Some College	25%
	College Degree	13%
	Post-Grad	10%
Household Income	Under $25K	44%
	Over $25K	21%
Age	18-25	44%
	25-40	37%
	40-60	23%
	Over 60	15%

Percent (axis: 10, 20, 30, 40, 50)

Hispanic citizens have lower rates of voter registration than African Americans and non-Hispanic whites because they move homes more often than most Americans.

A person with some high school or less is over three times more likely to not vote than someone with a college degree.

Lower-income citizens are more likely to move in a given year, and as such, they are less likely to register and vote.

Almost half of American citizens under 25 did not vote in 2008, and one in five moved in the previous 12 months.

Who Doesn't Have Photo ID in Texas?

A 2012 federal court trial challenging Texas's voter photo identification requirements found that African American and Hispanic Texans are nearly twice as likely as non-Hispanic whites to lack necessary photo identification.

Percent Without Photo ID

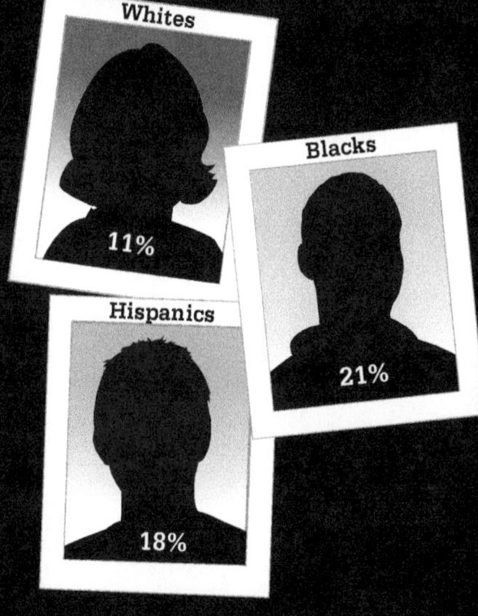

SOURCE: Data from General Social Survey, 2008; U.S. Census Bureau; and *State of Texas v. Holder*, 12-cv-128, District Court for the District of Columbia (2012).

Investigate Further

Concept Why does voting participation among groups matter? Members of groups have common experiences or circumstances that help us understand why they do or don't vote. For example, southern Jim Crow laws kept black voting rates low for decades.

Connection What do non-voting groups share in common? Hispanics, the poor, and the young are more likely to move from year to year, and less likely to be registered. Less-educated Americans confront literacy barriers to political information which also makes them

Cause How might voter photo identification laws lead to less voting? Minority voters are less likely to have photo identification. In addition, members of highly mobile groups are less likely to have identification with a correct address.

12.1

12.2

12.3

12.4

12.6

retrospective judgment
A voter's evaluation of a candidate based on past performance on a particular issue.

prospective judgment
A voter's evaluation of a candidate based on what he or she pledges to do about an issue if elected.

turnout
The proportion of the voting-age public that casts a ballot.

In contrast, Protestants are increasingly Republican in their vote choice. This increased support owes largely to the rise of social conservatives, as well as the Republican emphasis on personal responsibility.[26] In 2012, 57 percent of Protestants supported Romney. Republican support is even stronger among evangelical Protestants. Among those voters who self-identified as "born again," 78 percent supported Romney.

Catholic voters are a much more divided group. Historically, Catholic voters tended to identify with the Democratic Party and its support of social justice issues and anti-poverty programs. But, since the 1970s and the rise of the abortion issue, Catholic voters have cast their votes for Republican candidates in larger numbers. In the past several presidential elections, the Catholic vote has consistently aligned with the winning party. In 2004, 52 percent of Catholic voters supported Republican President George W. Bush. In 2012, 50 percent of Catholic voters supported Democratic President Obama.

☐ Issues

In addition to the underlying influences on vote choice discussed above, individual issues can have important effects in any given election year. One of the most important driving forces is the state of the economy.[27] Voters tend to reward the party in government, usually the president's party, during good economic times and punish that party during periods of economic downturn. When this occurs, the electorate is exercising **retrospective judgment;** that is, voters are rendering judgment on the party in power based on past performance on particular issues, in this case the economy. At other times, voters might use **prospective judgment;** that is, they vote based on what a candidate pledges to do about an issue if elected.

The 2012 election provides an example of how both retrospective and prospective judgments helped voters reach their ballot decisions. Voters in key swing states such as Ohio used retrospective judgment to credit President Barack Obama with bailing out automotive companies and saving American manufacturing jobs. Similarly, many voters, especially women, used prospective judgment to bolster their support for Obama, expressing concern about the future of their access to contraception and other reproductive medicine under a Romney administration. This combination, along with other major issues in the election, helped to deliver a second victory for the president.

Voter Turnout

12.5 Identify six factors that affect voter turnout.

Explore on MyPoliSciLab Simulation: You Are a Voting Registration Volunteer

Turnout is the proportion of the voting-age public that casts a ballot. In general, all citizens who are age eighteen or older are eligible to vote. States add a number of different regulations to limit the pool of eligible voters, such as restricting felons' participation and requiring voter identification (see Table 12.2).

Although about 58 percent of eligible voters turned out in 2012, average voter turnout in general elections in the United States is much lower than in other industrialized democracies: approximately 40 percent. An additional 25 percent are occasional voters, and 35 percent rarely or never vote. Some factors known to influence voter turnout include income and education, race and ethnicity, gender, age, civic engagement, and interest in politics.

☐ Income and Education

A considerably higher percentage of citizens with annual incomes over $65,000 vote than do citizens with incomes under $35,000. Wealthy citizens are more likely than poor ones to think that the system works for them and that their votes make a difference.

TABLE 12.2 HOW DO STATES REGULATE VOTER ELIGIBILITY?

Restrict felons' ability to vote after completion of their sentence	13 states
Allow incarcerated felons to vote from prison	2 states
Require all voters to show some form of identification to vote	30 states
Require all voters to show a photo identification to vote	9 states
Require no voter registration	1 state
Allow Election Day registration	11 states and DC
Require voters to register to vote at least 30 days prior to an election	14 states and DC
Allow no-excuse absentee balloting	27 states and DC
Allow early voting	34 states

SOURCES: Pew Center on the States, www.pewcenteronthestates.org, National Council on State Legislatures, www.ncsl.org, and CIRCLE, www.civicyouth.org.

People with higher incomes are also more likely to recognize their direct financial stake in the decisions of the government, thus spurring them into action.[28] In contrast, lower-income citizens often feel alienated from politics, possibly believing that conditions will remain the same no matter who holds office. As a result, these people are less likely to believe that their vote will make a difference and are more reluctant to expend the effort to turn out and vote.

As with vote choice, income and education are highly correlated; a higher income is often the result of greater educational attainment. Thus, all other things being equal, college graduates are much more likely to vote than those with less education, and people with advanced degrees are the most likely to vote. People with more education tend to learn more about politics, are less hindered by registration requirements, and are more self-confident about their ability to affect public life.[29]

☐ Race and Ethnicity

Despite substantial gains in voting rates among minority groups, race remains an important factor in voter participation. Whites still tend to vote more regularly than do African Americans, Hispanics, and other minority groups (see Figure 12.4).

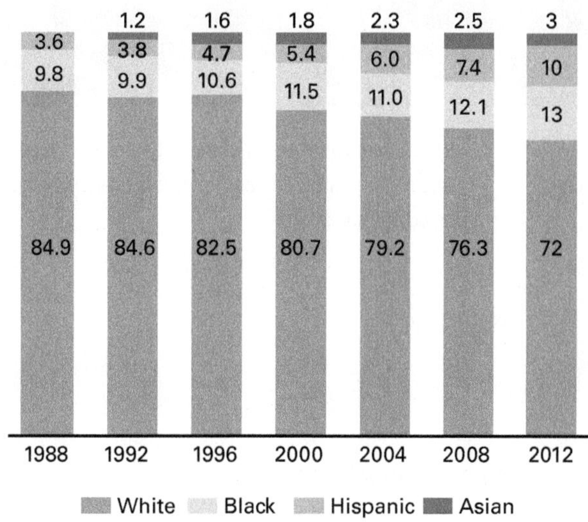

FIGURE 12.4 HOW HAS THE RACIAL AND ETHNIC COMPOSITION OF VOTERS CHANGED?

Although white Americans continue to constitute a majority of the U.S. electorate, black, Hispanic, and Asian voters have accounted for significant percentages of the electorate during recent campaigns. This diversity alters both the voices heard from the voting booth and the demands placed on government.

SOURCE: Data from Pew Research Center, "Dissecting the 2008 Electorate: Most Diverse in U.S. History," April 30, 2009. www.pewresearch.org; and http://www.cnn.com/election/2012/results/race/president#exit-polls.

Take a Closer Look

Political scientists have observed a number of discernible patterns in voter turnout and vote choice. Many of these patterns are affected by individuals' demographic characteristics. Examine the voters waiting in line to cast their ballot in Fort Lauderdale, Florida, and consider what we might predict about how each of these people will vote based on what we can observe from this photo.

Politically engaged individuals, such as those who volunteer on behalf of candidates, are more likely than other citizens to turn out to vote.

Women, particularly married ones, are more likely to turn out to vote than men. Although women in general favor Democratic candidates, married women are more likely than their single counterparts to vote for Republicans.

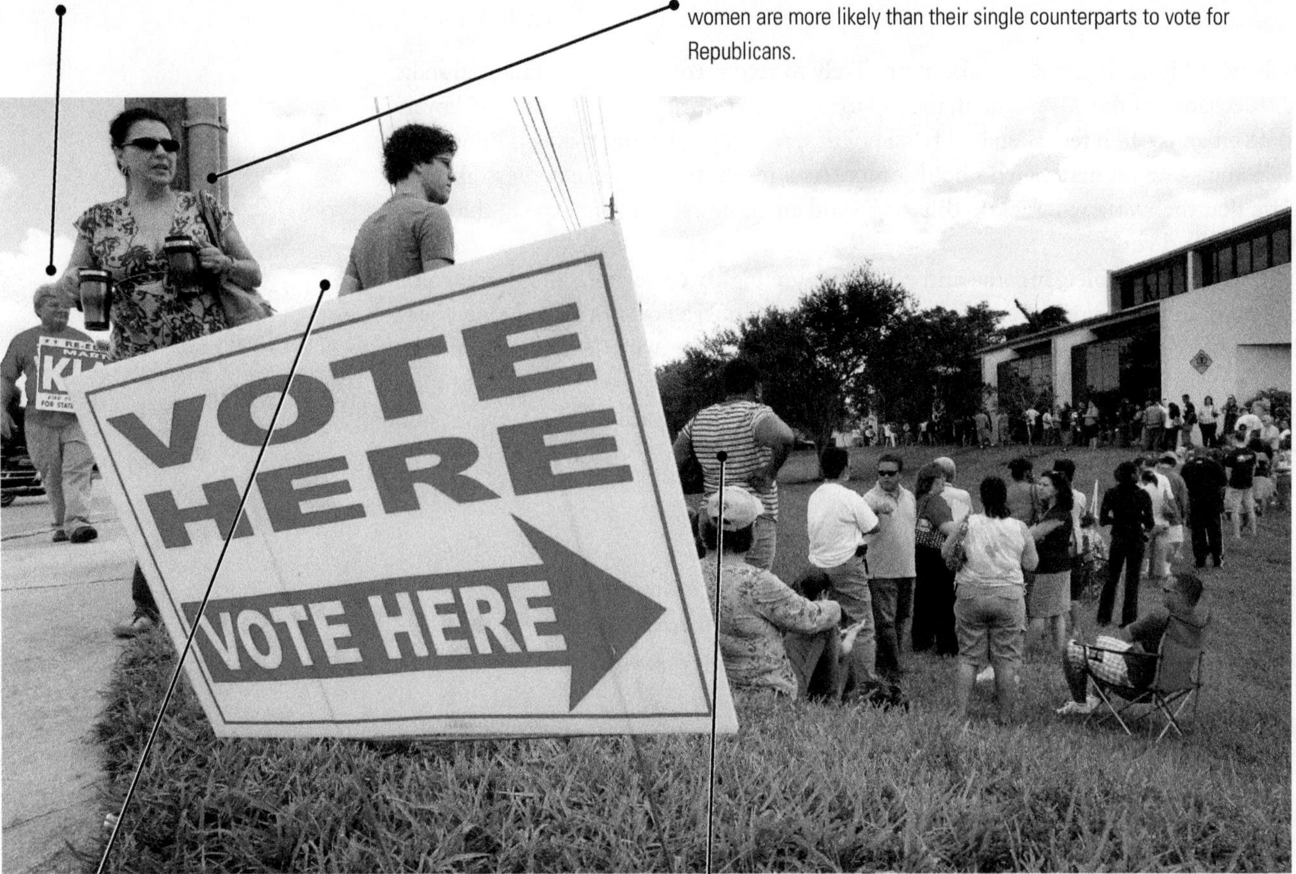

Source To Come

Young people, both male and female, have historically been less likely to turn out to vote. More young people vote for Democrats than Republicans.

African Americans and other minority groups vote at lower rates than their white counterparts. African Americans overwhelmingly support Democratic candidates.

CRITICAL THINKING QUESTIONS

1. How might you predict that other individuals shown in this photo would vote based on their demographic characteristics?
2. What other demographic characteristics might help you to better understand the voter turnout and vote choices of the people shown in this photo?
3. How do voter turnout and vote choices affect the policy priorities of American political institutions? How might altering the composition of the voting population alter the government's agenda?

Several factors help to explain these persistent differences. One reason is the relative income and educational levels of the two racial groups. Many racial and ethnic minorities tend to be poorer and to have less formal education than whites; as mentioned earlier, both of these factors affect voter turnout. Significantly, though, highly educated and wealthier African Americans are more likely to vote than whites of similar background.[30]

Another explanation focuses on the long-term consequences of the voting barriers that African Americans historically faced in the United States, especially in areas of the Deep South. In the wake of Reconstruction, the southern states made voter registration extremely difficult for African Americans, and only a small percentage of the eligible African American population was registered throughout the South until the 1960s. The Voting Rights Act (VRA) of 1965 helped change this situation by targeting states that once used literacy or morality tests or poll taxes to exclude minorities from the polls. The act bans any voting device or procedure that interferes with a minority citizen's right to vote, and it requires approval for any changes in voting qualifications or procedures in certain areas where minority registration is not in proportion to the racial composition of the district. It also authorizes the federal government to monitor all elections in areas where discrimination was practiced or where less than 50 percent of the voting-age public was registered to vote in the 1964 election. As a result of the VRA and other civil rights reforms, turnout among African Americans has increased dramatically.

The Hispanic community in the United States is now slightly larger than the African American community; thus, Hispanics have the potential to wield enormous political power. In California, Texas, Florida, Illinois, and New York, five key electoral states, Hispanic voters have emerged as powerful allies for candidates seeking office. Moreover, their increasing presence in New Mexico, Arizona, Colorado, and Nevada,—the latter two of which were key battleground states in the 2012 presidential election, has forced candidates of both parties to place more emphasis on issues that affect Hispanics. However, turnout among Hispanics is much lower than that among whites and African Americans. In 2012, Hispanics accounted for almost 12 percent of the U.S. population but 10 percent of those who turned out to vote.

☐ Gender

With passage of the Nineteenth Amendment in 1920, women gained the right to vote in the United States. While early polling numbers are not reliable enough to shed light on the voting rate among women in the period immediately following ratification of the Nineteenth Amendment, it is generally accepted that women voted at a lower rate than men. Recent polls suggest that today women vote at a slightly higher rate than their male counterparts. Since women constitute slightly more than 50 percent of the U.S. population, they now account for a majority of the American electorate.

☐ Age

A strong correlation exists between age and voter turnout. The Twenty-Sixth Amendment to the Constitution, ratified in 1971, lowered the voting age to eighteen. While this amendment obviously increased the number of eligible voters, it did so by enfranchising the group that is least likely to vote. A much higher percentage of citizens age thirty and older vote than do citizens younger than thirty, although voter turnout decreases over the age of seventy, primarily due to the difficulties some older voters experience in getting to their polling locations. Regrettably, only about 50 percent of eligible eighteen- to twenty-nine-year-olds are even registered to vote.[31] The most plausible reason is that younger people are more mobile; they have not put down roots in a community. Because voter registration is not automatic, people who relocate have to make an effort to register. As young people marry, have children, and settle down in a community, the likelihood that they will vote increases.[32]

Civic Engagement

Individuals who are members of civic organizations, trade and professional organizations, and labor unions are more likely to vote and participate in politics than those who are not members of these or similar types of groups. People who more frequently attend church or other religious services, moreover, also are more inclined to vote than people who rarely attend or do not belong to religious institutions.

Many of these organizations emphasize community involvement, which often encourages voting and exposes members to requests for support from political parties and candidates. These groups also encourage participation by providing opportunities for members to develop organizational and communication skills relevant to political activity. Union membership is particularly likely to increase voting turnout among people who, on the basis of their education or income, are less likely to vote.[33]

Interest in Politics

People who are highly interested in politics constitute only a small minority of the U.S. population. The most politically active Americans—party and issue-group activists—make up less than 5 percent of the country's more than 313 million people. Those who contribute time or money to a party or a candidate during a campaign make up only about 10 percent of the total adult population. Although these percentages appear low, they translate into millions of Americans who are reliable voters and also contribute more than just votes to the system.

Toward Reform: Problems with Voter Turnout

12.6 Explain why voter turnout is low, and evaluate methods for improving voter turnout.

Inspiring citizens to turn out to vote is particularly important in the United States because of the winner-take-all electoral system. In theory, in such a system, any one vote could decide the outcome of the election. Although the importance of individual votes has been showcased in close elections such as the 2008 Minnesota race for the U.S. Senate, which was decided by only 312 votes, voter turnout in the United States remains quite low. In mid-term elections, only 40 to 45 percent of the eligible electorate turns out to vote; that amount rises to 50 or 60 percent in presidential elections. The following sections discuss the causes of, and potential remedies for, low voter turnout in the United States.

Why Don't Americans Turn Out?

People may choose not to participate in elections for many reasons. Nonparticipation may be rooted in something as complicated as an individual's political philosophy or something as simple as the weather—voter turnout tends to be lower on rainy Election Days. Here, we discuss some of the most common reasons for nonvoting: other commitments, difficulty of registration, difficulty of voting, the number of elections, voter attitudes, and the weakened influence of political parties (see Figure 12.5).

OTHER COMMITMENTS According to the U.S. Census Bureau, 17.5 percent of registered nonvoters reported in 2008 that they did not vote because they were too busy or had conflicting work or school schedules. Another 14.9 percent said they did not vote because they were ill or disabled, or had a family emergency. While these

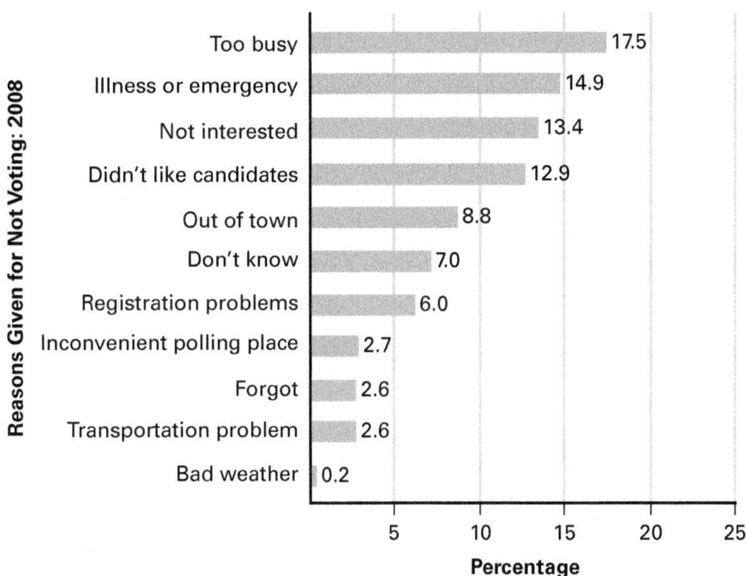

FIGURE 12.5 WHY DON'T PEOPLE VOTE?

During November of each federal election year, the U.S. Census Bureau conducts a Current Population Survey that asks a series of questions related to voting and registration. In the November 2008 survey, respondents were asked whether they voted in the 2008 election and, if not, what their reasons were for not voting. The most common reason for not voting was being too busy.

SOURCE: U.S. Census Bureau, Current Population Survey, November 2008.

reasons account for a large portion of the people surveyed, they also reflect the respondents' desire not to seem uneducated about the candidates and issues or apathetic about the political process. Although some would-be voters are undoubtedly busy, infirm, or otherwise unable to make it to the polls, it is likely that many of these nonvoters are offering an easy excuse and have another reason for failing to vote.

DIFFICULTY OF REGISTRATION A major reason for lack of participation in the United States remains the relatively low percentage of the adult population that is registered to vote. Requiring citizens to take the initiative to register is an American invention; nearly every other democratic country places the burden of registration on the government rather than on the individual. Thus, the cost (in terms of time and effort) of registering to vote is higher in the United States than in other industrialized democracies.

The National Voter Registration Act of 1993, commonly known as the Motor Voter Act, was a significant national attempt to ease the bureaucratic hurdles associated with registering to vote. The law requires states to provide the opportunity to register through driver's license agencies, public assistance agencies, and the mail. Researchers estimate that this law has increased voter registration by 5 to 9 percent, and some scholars hypothesize that the law is at least partially responsible for the increases in voter participation experienced in recent elections.

Eleven states now also allow online voter registration. Although some critics have expressed concerns about the security of this process, it has proved an effective way to increase registration. In Arizona, the first state to implement the online option in 2003, voter registration increased by almost 10 percent as a result of the law.[34]

DIFFICULTY OF VOTING Stringent ballot access laws are another factor affecting voter turnout in the United States. Voters in thirty states, for example, must provide some form of identification to cast a ballot. In nine of these states, that identification must include a photo. Though supporters charge that voter identification laws are simply intended to prevent voter fraud, opponents argue that this legislation may disproportionately limit the ballot access of a number of groups, including women, racial and ethnic minorities, the poor, the elderly, and the disabled.[35] As a result of concerns about the constitutionality of these laws, courts in some states, including Pennsylvania, stopped enforcement of the provisions for the 2012 election. Similar laws in other states, particularly the South, continue to be reviewed by the courts.

Citizens who plan to be out of state on Election Day or who are physically unable to go to the polls may also face challenges in casting an absentee ballot. Many states, for instance, require citizens to apply in person for absentee ballots, a burdensome requirement given that a person's inability to be present in his or her home state is often the reason for absentee balloting in the first place. Recent literature in political science links liberalized absentee voting rules and higher turnout.[36]

NUMBER OF ELECTIONS Another explanation for low voter turnout in the United States is the sheer number and frequency of elections. According to a study by the International Institute for Democracy and Electoral Assistance, the United States typically holds twice as many national elections as other Western democracies, a consequence of the relatively short two-year term of office for members of the House of Representatives.[37] American federalism, with its separate elections at the local, state, and national levels, and its use of primary elections for the selection of candidates, also contributes to the number of elections in which Americans are called on to participate. With so many elections, even the most active political participants may skip part of the electoral process from time to time.

VOTER ATTITUDES Voter attitudes also affect the low rates of voter turnout observed in the United States. Some voters are alienated, and others are just plain

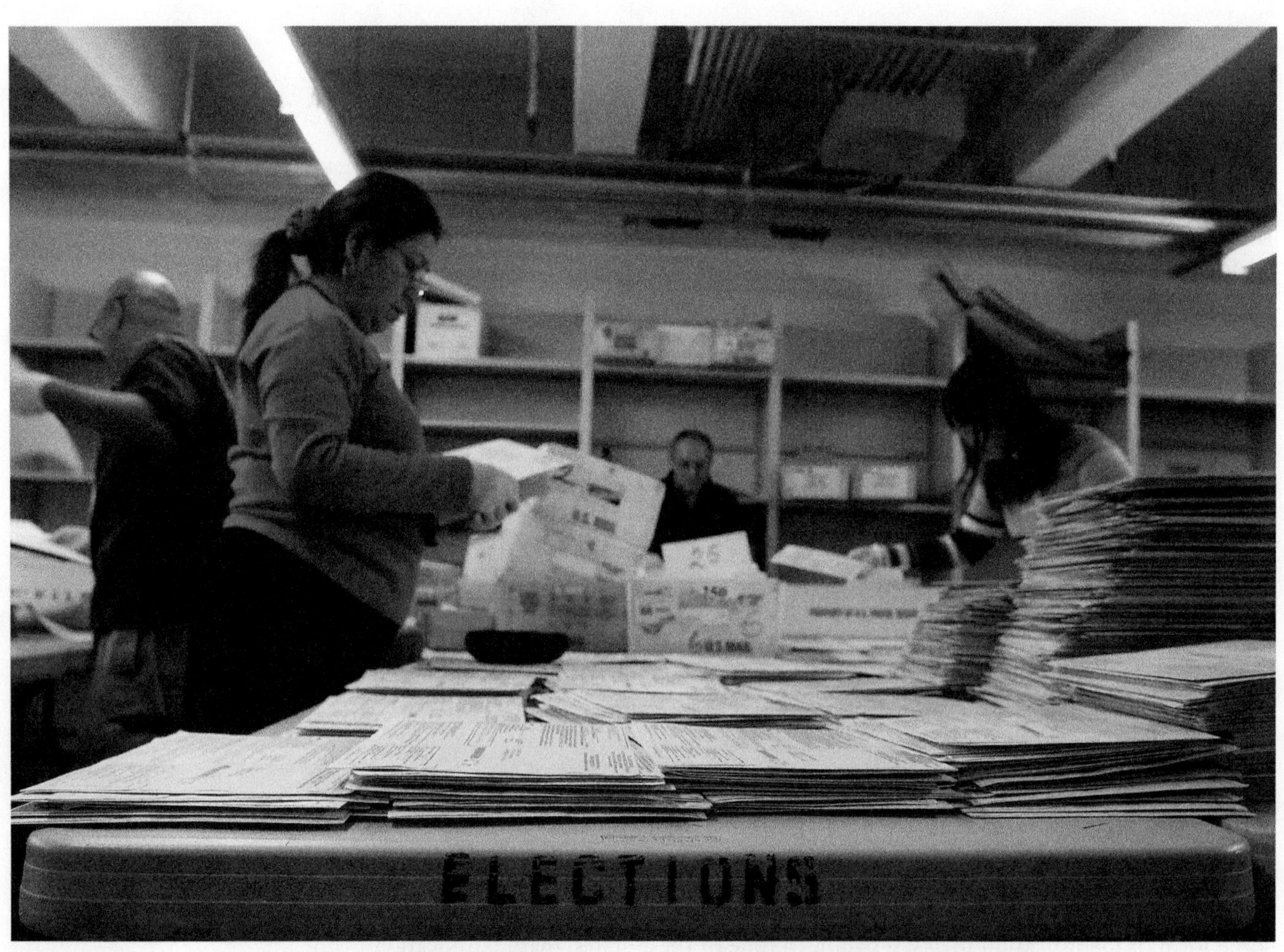

HOW DO CITIZENS VOTE BY ABSENTEE BALLOT?

Citizens who will be unable to make it to the polls on Election Day may file an application to vote by absentee ballot. Local Boards of Elections mail ballots to these individuals; citizens fill out the ballot and return them by mail. Here, election officials sort and organize completed absentee ballots.

apathetic, possibly because of a lack of pressing issues in a particular year, satisfaction with the status quo, or uncompetitive elections. Furthermore, many citizens may be turned off by the quality of campaigns in a time when petty issues and personal mudslinging are more prevalent than ever. In 2008, 12.4 percent of registered nonvoters reported they were not interested in the election. Another 12.9 percent said they did not like the issues or candidates.

WEAKENED INFLUENCE OF POLITICAL PARTIES Political parties today are not as effective as they once were in mobilizing voters, ensuring they are registered, and getting them to the polls. The parties at one time were grassroots organizations that forged strong party–group links with their supporters. Today, candidate- and issue-centered campaigns and the growth of expansive party bureaucracies have resulted in somewhat more distant parties with which fewer people identify very strongly. While efforts have been made in recent elections to bolster the influence of parties—in particular, through sophisticated get-out-the-vote efforts—the parties' modern grassroots activities still pale in comparison to their earlier efforts.

☐ Ways to Improve Voter Turnout

Reformers have proposed many ideas to increase voter turnout in the United States. Always on the list is raising the political awareness of young citizens, a reform that inevitably must involve our nation's schools. The rise in formal education levels among Americans has had a significant effect on voter turnout.[38] No less important, and perhaps simpler to achieve, are institutional reforms such as making Election Day a holiday, easing constraints on voter registration, allowing mail and online voting, modernizing the ballot, and strengthening political parties.

MAKE ELECTION DAY A HOLIDAY Since elections traditionally are held on Tuesdays, the busy workday is an obstacle for many would-be voters. Some reformers have, therefore, proposed that Election Day should be a national holiday. This strategy could backfire if people used the day off to extend vacations or long weekends. The tradition of Tuesday elections, however, should reduce this risk.

ENABLE EARLY VOTING In an attempt to make voting more convenient for citizens who may have other commitments on Election Day, thirty-four states (largely in the West, Midwest, and South) currently allow voters to engage in a practice known as early voting. Several additional states allow voters with a valid excuse to cast a ballot early. Early voting allows citizens to cast their ballot up to a month before the election—the time frame varies by state—either by mail or at a designated polling location. Many citizens have found early voting to be a preferable way to cast their ballot; during the 2012 election, approximately 25 percent of eligible voters took advantage of early voting.

Critics of early voting, however, charge that the method decreases the importance of the campaign. They also fear that voters who cast early ballots may later come to regret their choices. It is possible, for example, that a voter could change his or her mind after hearing new information about candidates just prior to Election Day, or that a voter could cast a ballot for a candidate who subsequently withdraws from the race.

PERMIT MAIL AND ONLINE VOTING Reformers have also proposed several ways that citizens could vote from their own homes. For example, citizens of Oregon, Washington, and some California counties vote almost entirely by mail-in ballots. These systems have been credited with increasing voter turnout rates in those states. But, voting by mail has its downside: concerns about decreased ballot security and increased potential for fraud with mail-in elections. Another problem is that it may delay election results as the Board of Elections waits to receive all ballots.

Internet voting may be a more instantaneous way to tally votes. Some states, including Arizona and Michigan, have already experimented with using this

Explore Your World

The act of casting a secret ballot to choose a political leader is something that many Americans take for granted. However, many people around the world have never experienced the privilege of expressing their views on who should govern. Even citizens who have won the right to vote may cast their ballots in ways that are fundamentally different from those we use in the United States.

Afghanistan held its first presidential elections in 2004; allowing women to vote in these elections marked a sea change for the largely Islamic nation. Voters cast secret ballots that were hand tabulated by election officials.

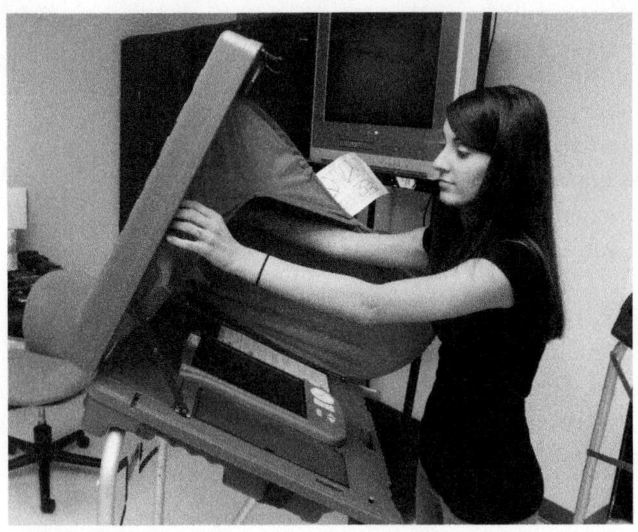

All voters in the United States are given the opportunity to cast a secret ballot and vote for the candidate of their choice without threat or intimidation. The method of voting varies, though an increasing number of jurisdictions use computers to tabulate the results of each election.

In some states, or cantons, in Switzerland, citizens still vote in person in town meetings. Other Swiss citizens vote by mail, at traditional polling locations, or online.

CRITICAL THINKING QUESTIONS

1. How might the type of ballot used in an election affect voters who turn out to cast a ballot? The results of the election?
2. Should all voters be allowed to cast a secret ballot? Why or why not?
3. What steps should be taken to ensure that all citizens have access to the ballot?

method to cast ballots in primary elections. In addition, military members and their families from thirty-two states and Washington, D.C., used Internet voting to cast absentee ballots in the 2012 elections.[39] However, Internet voting booths have been slow to catch on with the general public because many voters are wary of the security of this method and worry about online hackers and an inability to prevent voter fraud. Other observers fear that an all-online system could unintentionally disenfranchise poor voters, who may be less likely to have access to an Internet connection.

MAKE REGISTRATION EASIER Registration laws vary by state, but in most states, people must register prior to Election Day. Among the eleven states that permit Election Day registration, turnout is generally higher. In fact, the top four states in voter turnout in 2008—Minnesota, Wisconsin, Maine, and New Hampshire—all allow same-day registration. Other states, such as North Carolina and Louisiana, have seen turnout increase after moving to a same-day system. Turnout has averaged about 11 percentage points higher in recent elections than in other states, supporting the long-held claim by reformers that voter turnout could be increased if registering to vote were made simpler for citizens.[40] Better yet, all U.S. citizens could be registered automatically at the age of eighteen. Critics, however, argue that such automatic registration could breed even greater voter apathy and complacency.

Increasing voter registration drives in areas where many citizens are not registered to vote may also increase voter turnout. One recent study of college students, for example, demonstrated that students who registered to vote in on-campus voter registration drives were much more likely to turn out to vote than other Americans age eighteen to twenty-four.[41]

MODERNIZE THE BALLOT Following the 2000 election, when the outcome of the presidential election in Florida, and by extension the nation, hinged on "hanging chads"—punch-card ballots that had not been fully separated—legislators and other observers called for reforms to modernize the ballot. The federal government even enacted the Help America Vote Act (HAVA) to aid states in upgrading voting equipment. Reformers hoped that these changes would make the process of voting easier, more approachable, and more reliable.

States and localities have made significant upgrades to the types of ballots they use as a result of the HAVA. Traditional, hand-counted, paper ballots are now used in fewer than 10 percent of jurisdictions. In thirty-two states, citizens mark paper ballots, but their votes are computer tabulated. In another eleven states, and large percentages of other states, voting is entirely electronic, often done on touch-screen voting machines.[42] States have also experimented with other new technologies for casting ballots. In Oregon, for example, disabled residents were able to vote with iPads; several other states are exploring expanded use of this technology.[43]

Supporters of electronic voting believe that training poll workers, administrators, and voters on how to effectively use the new equipment is vital. Critics maintain that lack of a paper trail leaves electronic machines vulnerable to fraud and worry that the machines could crash during an election. Still other critics cite the expense of the machines. All, however, agree that updating election equipment and ensuring fair elections across the country should be a legislative priority. As Charles M. Vest, the president of the Massachusetts Institute of Technology, noted, "A nation that can send a man to the moon, that can put a reliable ATM machine on every corner, has no excuse not to deploy a reliable, affordable, easy-to-use voting system."[44]

STRENGTHEN PARTIES Reformers have long argued that strengthening political parties would increase voter turnout, because parties have historically been the most successful at mobilizing citizens to vote in the United States. During the late 1800s and early 1900s, the country's "Golden Age" of powerful political parties, one of their primary activities was getting out the vote on Election Day. Even today, the parties' Election Day get-out-the-vote drives increase voter turnout by several million people in national contests. The challenge is how to go about enacting reforms that strengthen parties. One way would be to allow political parties to raise and spend greater sums of money during the campaign process. Such a reform, however, raises ethical questions about the role and influence of money in politics. Another potential change would be to enact broader systemic reforms that allow for a multiparty system and facilitate greater party competition. But, these reforms would be very difficult to pass into law.

Ultimately, the solution to ensuring greater voter turnout may lie in encouraging the parties to enhance their get-out-the-vote efforts. Additional voter education programs, too, may show voters what is at stake in elections and thereby inspire higher turnout in future elections.

Review the Chapter

 **Listen** to **Chapter 12** on **MyPoliSciLab**

Roots of American Elections

12.1 Trace the roots of American elections, and distinguish among the four different types of elections, p. 359.

Elections are responsible for most political changes in the United States. Regular elections guarantee mass political action, create governmental accountability, and confer legitimacy on regimes. Elections in the United States are of four major types: primary elections, general elections, initiatives and referenda, and recall elections.

Presidential Elections

12.2 Outline the electoral procedures for presidential and general elections, p. 362.

No U.S. election can compare to the presidential contest, held every four years. The parties select presidential candidates through either primary elections or caucuses, with the primary process culminating in each party's national convention, after which the general election campaign begins. The American political system uses indirect electoral representation in the form of the Electoral College.

Congressional Elections

12.3 Compare and contrast congressional and presidential elections, and explain the incumbency advantage, p. 368.

In congressional elections, incumbents have a strong advantage over their challengers because of staff support, the visibility they get from being in office, and the "scare-off" effect. Redistricting, scandals, presidential coattails, and mid-term elections serve as countervailing forces to the incumbency advantage and are the main sources of turnover in Congress.

Patterns in Vote Choice

12.4 Identify seven factors that influence voter choice, p. 372.

Seven factors that affect vote choice are party identification, ideology, income and education, race and ethnicity, gender, religion, and issues. Democrats, liberals, those who are poor or uneducated, African Americans, women, younger Americans, and Jews tend to vote Democratic. Republicans, conservatives, those who are wealthy and moderately educated, whites, men, older Americans, and Protestants tend to vote Republican.

Voter Turnout

12.5 Identify six factors that affect voter turnout, p. 376.

Voter turnout in the United States is much lower than in other industrialized democracies. It is higher, however, among citizens who are white, older, more educated, have higher incomes, belong to civic organizations, and attend religious services more frequently. Whether they are casting ballots in congressional or presidential elections, partisan identification is the most powerful predictor of voter choice.

Toward Reform: Problems with Voter Turnout

12.6 Explain why voter turnout is low, and evaluate methods for improving voter turnout, p. 380.

Americans do not vote for several reasons, including other commitments, difficulty registering to vote, difficulty voting, the number of elections, voter attitudes, and the weakened influence of political parties. Suggestions for improving voter turnout include making Election Day a holiday, enabling early voting, allowing for mail and online voting, making the registration process easier, modernizing the ballot, and strengthening political parties. Each of these suggested reforms has both pros and cons associated with it.

Learn the Terms

 **Study** and **Review** the **Flashcards**

closed primary, p. 360
conventional political participation, p. 372
crossover voting, p. 360
elector, p. 365
Electoral College, p. 365
electorate, p. 359
front-loading, p. 364
general election, p. 360
incumbency, p. 369
initiative, p. 360
mandate, p. 360
mid-term election, p. 371
open primary, p. 360
primary election, p. 360
prospective judgment, p. 376
reapportionment, p. 365
recall, p. 362
referendum, p. 361
retrospective judgment, p. 376
runoff primary, p. 360
ticket-splitting, p. 373
turnout, p. 376
unconventional political participation, p. 372

Test Yourself

 **Study** and **Review** the **Practice Tests**

1. In what type of election do candidates run against members of their own party?

a. General
b. Initiative
c. Referendum
d. Primary
e. Mid-term

2. Which of the following is true of primary elections?

a. Primaries nominate more moderate candidates than do caucuses.
b. Political parties have historically preferred primary elections to caucuses.
c. Primary election voters usually know more about the candidates than do caucus participants.
d. Primary elections involve a greater time commitment on behalf of voters than do caucuses.
e. Scheduling an early primary lessens a state's impact on the process of selecting a presidential nominee.

3. Abolishing the Electoral College

a. has been ruled unconstitutional by the Supreme Court.
b. would require a constitutional amendment.
c. is supported by the Republican Party.
d. would be likely to pass the Senate but not the House.
e. receives significant support from smaller states.

4. Which of the following is NOT a reason for why many incumbents lose reelection?

a. Redistricting
b. Scandals
c. Partisanship
d. Presidential coattails
e. Mid-term elections

5. Which of the following is true of mid-term elections?

a. Mid-term elections have higher voter turnout than presidential elections
b. The president's party usually loses seats in a mid-term election year.
c. Issues rarely affect the outcome of mid-term elections.
d. Senate elections are more affected by mid-term election forces than are House elections.
e. Campaign spending is higher in mid-term elections than presidential elections

6. The most powerful predictor of vote choice is:

a. age.
b. party identification.
c. gender.
d. race.
e. ethnicity.

7. Which of the following is NOT a major predictor of a person's vote choice?

a. Gender
b. Income
c. Education
d. Type of ballot
e. Party

8. In general, voter turnout is higher among those who are

a. older and wealthier.
b. less educated with a moderate income.
c. male.
d. African American.
e. age eighteen to twenty-four.

9. The most common reason why people don't vote is:

a. they were not contacted by a political party.
b. they experienced difficulties with absentee voting.
c. they are too busy.
d. they are uninterested.
e. they are disabled or ill.

10. Which of the following is NOT a way to improve voter turnout?

a. Make Election Day a holiday
b. Enable early voting
c. Permit online voting
d. Make registration easier
e. Weaken political parties

Explore Further

Brennan, Jason. *The Ethics of Voting*. Princeton, NJ: Princeton University Press, 2012.

Campbell, Angus, Philip E. Converse, Warren E. Miller, and Donald E. Stokes. *The American Voter*, reprint ed. Chicago: University of Chicago Press, 1980.

Flanigan, William H., and Nancy H. Zingale. *Political Behavior of the American Electorate*, 12th ed. Washington, DC: CQ Press, 2010.

Gelman, Andrew. *Red State, Blue State, Rich State, Poor State: Why Americans Vote the Way They Do*, expanded ed. Princeton, NJ: Princeton University Press, 2009.

Gilens, Martin. *Affluence and Influence: Economic Inequality and Political Power in America*. Princeton, NJ: Princeton University Press, 2012.

Hall, Thad E., R. Michael Alvarez, and Lonna Rae Atkinson, eds. *Confirming Elections: Creating Confidence and Integrity Through Election Auditing*. New York: Palgrave Macmillan, 2012.

Hanmer, Michael J. *Discount Voting: Voter Registration Reforms and Their Effects*. New York: Cambridge University Press, 2012.

Herrnson, Paul S. *Congressional Elections: Campaigning at Home and in Washington*, 6th ed. Washington, DC: CQ Press, 2012.

Jacobson, Gary C. *The Politics of Congressional Elections*, 8th ed. New York: Prentice Hall, 2012.

Leighley, Jan E., ed. *The Oxford Handbook of American Elections and Political Behavior*. New York: Oxford University Press, 2010.

Lewis-Beck, Michael S., Helmut Norpoth, William G. Jacoby, and Herbert F. Weisberg. *The American Voter Revisited*. Ann Arbor: University of Michigan Press, 2008.

Mayer, William G. *The Swing Voter in American Politics*. Washington, DC: Brookings Institution, 2007.

Sabato, Larry J. *Get in the Booth! A Citizen's Guide to the 2010 Elections*. New York: Longman, 2011.

Streb, Matthew J. *Rethinking American Electoral Democracy*, 2nd ed. New York: Routledge, 2011.

Wattenberg, Martin P. *Is Voting for Young People?* 3rd ed. New York: Longman, 2012.

To learn more about elections, go to CNN at **www.cnn.com/elections**.

To learn more about election reform, go to the Pew Center on the States at **www.electiononline.org**.

To learn more about civic learning and engagement, go to CIRCLE at **www.civicyouth.org**.

To learn more about voting, go to Project Vote Smart at **www.vote-smart.org**.

((**Listen** to **Chapter 13** on **MyPoliSciLab**

13

The Campaign Process

President Barack Obama faced no internal challenges for the Democratic nomination for president in 2012. This gave President Obama an immediate advantage in the presidential election because he did not have to focus his efforts on competition within the party. As a result, he was able to build on the successful infrastructure he had created in 2008 and focus his efforts on fundraising and building an on-the-ground game, particularly in swing states.

On the Republican side, more than ten candidates engaged in a several month-long primary battle. At various points, former Senator Rick Santorum, former Speaker of the House Newt Gingrich, and a range of other candidates, including Herman Cain and Michele Bachmann were the frontrunners for the nomination. In April 2012, at long last, the GOP chose former Massachusetts Governor Mitt Romney. If there was residual angst in the Republican Party over Governor Romney's selection to fill the top spot on the GOP ticket, it seemed to fade after the selection of Representative Paul Ryan as Romney's running mate. Following the party's convention, Republicans appeared to unite in their efforts to hold President Obama to a single term as president.

With the economy as the dominant issue, both candidates emphasized experience as the key to being successful over the next four years. The President claimed his leadership was responsible for getting the nation's economy back on track, while Mitt Romney argued that there had been little improvement and touted his experience as a successful businessman as key selling points with voters.

The election, ultimately, would turn on the question of whether the American people believed conditions were getting better or worse. Would they blame the sitting president for the nation's problems and turn him out of office in favor of a candidate with business experience, or would they trust that the president was delivering and moving forward, albeit slowly, on his promise of "Change" four years earlier?

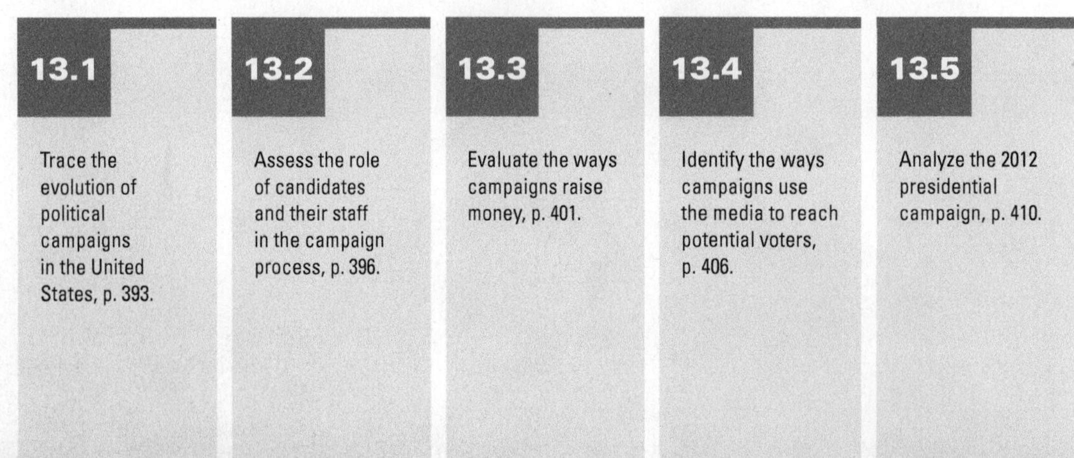

13.1
Trace the evolution of political campaigns in the United States, p. 393.
13.2
Assess the role of candidates and their staff in the campaign process, p. 396.
13.3
Evaluate the ways campaigns raise money, p. 401.
13.4
Identify the ways campaigns use the media to reach potential voters, p. 406.
13.5
Analyze the 2012 presidential campaign, p. 410.

PRESIDENTIAL CAMPAIGNS LEAVE INDELIBLE MARKS ON THE NATION Above, Theodore Roosevelt gives a campaign speech from the back of a train in 1912. Below, President Barack Obama celebrates his 2012 reelection with his wife, Michelle, and daughters, Sasha and Malia.

MyPoliSciLab Videos

Watch on MyPoliSciLab

The Big Picture Are politicians always campaigning? Author Larry J. Sabato singles out the characteristics political parties are looking for in the candidates they nominate for office, and he proves why the economy—more than any other issue—is what interests voters the most.

The Basics Do you have trouble figuring out when all the elections are and who you should vote for? If you do, you are not alone. This video will help you understand why the United States has so many types of elections, what purposes they serve, and whether money and campaign staff is vital to campaign victories.

2
Do you think money is important in elections?

3

In Context Discover why voting and elections are essential to a democracy. In this video, Fordham University political scientist Costas Panagopolos discusses why voting is important in the United States. He also explains how electoral reforms have expanded the voting population throughout the years.

Thinking Like a Political Scientist Discover how scholars respond when voter turnout—even in presidential elections—declines, as it did during the last half of the twentieth century. Fordham University political scientist Costas Panagopolos explorers the research behind this issue, recent trends, and factors that may explain these outcomes.

In the Real World In its controversial Citizens United decision, the Supreme Court ruled that money is speech and thus the courts cannot put a limit on the amount of money an individual—or a corporation—spends on an election. Real people decide whether or not they agree with that decision, and they consider some of its long-term implications

So What? Learn how the election system works—and how you can improve it. Author Larry J. Sabato reflects on the ways social media and smartphone technology could change how campaigns are conducted in the future, even if face-to-face communication is still the most effective way to win voters.

Both campaigns vigorously pursued electors in all key battleground states, and both campaigns included grassroots organizing in all fifty states, relying on extensive use of technology and social networking sites such as Twitter, Facebook, and emails. Romney's campaign banked on a strategy that would require him to win back many of the states that Obama took in 2008 but that George W. Bush had carried in 2004. These included states like Indiana, as well as key swing states such as Virginia, Ohio, Colorado, Nevada, New Hampshire and North Carolina.

Obama's campaign believed that if they could convince voters to turn out and support them as they had in 2008, the path to reelection would be smooth. This strategy proved successful when, on Election Day, the Obama campaign held together a coalition of women, African Americans, Hispanics, and young voters to secure a second term for the president.

With the exception of Indiana and North Carolina, which supported Mitt Romney, Obama carried every other state he had won in 2008. Shortly before midnight, networks projected Ohio for the Democrats and Obama secured the necessary 270 Electoral College votes to be declared the winner of the 2012 presidential election.

Ultimately, after securing victory in Florida on the Saturday after the election, President Obama won a total of 332 votes in the Electoral College to Romney's 206. No doubt, many Democrats will claim that this significant victory in the Electoral College gives Obama a mandate for his second term in office. However, Republicans point to Obama's comparatively smaller margin of victory—3 percent—in the popular vote and claim that Americans are more divided than the Electoral College results indicate.

•••

Modern political campaigns have become high-stakes, high-priced extravaganzas, but the basic purpose of modern electioneering remains intact: one person asking another for support. The art of modern campaigning involves the management of a large budget and staff, the planning of sophisticated voter outreach efforts, and the creation of high-tech Internet and social media sites that provide continuous communication updates and organize voter and donor support. Campaigning also involves the diplomatic skill of unifying disparate individuals and groups to achieve a fragile electoral majority. How candidates perform these exquisitely difficult tasks is the subject of this chapter.

nomination campaign
Phase of a political campaign aimed at winning a primary election.

Roots of Modern Political Campaigns

13.1 Trace the evolution of political campaigns in the United States.

ampaigns are dynamic, unpredictable, and exciting. No two political campaigns are the same. Despite the unique qualities of each race, however, most electoral contests are similar in structure, consisting of a nomination campaign and a general election campaign.

☐ The Nomination Campaign

The **nomination campaign**, the phase of a political campaign aimed at winning a primary election, begins as soon as the candidate has decided to run for office. This may be years prior to the actual election. During the nomination campaign, the candidates target party leaders and interest groups. They test out themes, slogans, and strategies, and learn to adjust to the pressure of being in the spotlight day in and day out. This is the time for candidates to learn that a single careless phrase could end the campaign or guarantee a defeat. The press and public take much less notice of gaffes at this time than they will later, in the general election campaign.

general election campaign
Phase of a political campaign aimed at winning election to office.

13.2

13.3

13.4

13.5

A danger not always heeded by candidates during the nomination campaign is that, in the quest to win the party's nomination, a candidate can move too far to the right or left and appear too extreme to the electorate in November. Party activists are generally more ideologically extreme than party-identified voters in the general electorate, and activists participate in primaries and caucuses at a relatively high rate. If a candidate tries too hard to appeal to the interests of party elites, he or she jeopardizes the ultimate goal of winning the election. Conservative Barry Goldwater, the 1964 Republican nominee for president, and liberal George McGovern, the 1972 Democratic nominee for president, both fell victim to this phenomenon in seeking their party's nomination—Goldwater going too far right, and McGovern going too far left—and they were handily defeated in the general elections by Presidents Lyndon B. Johnson and Richard M. Nixon, respectively.

☐ The General Election Campaign

After earning the party's nomination, candidates embark on the **general election campaign**, or the phase of a political campaign aimed at winning election to office. Unlike the nomination campaign, in which candidates must run against members of their own political party, during the general election campaign, candidates in partisan elections

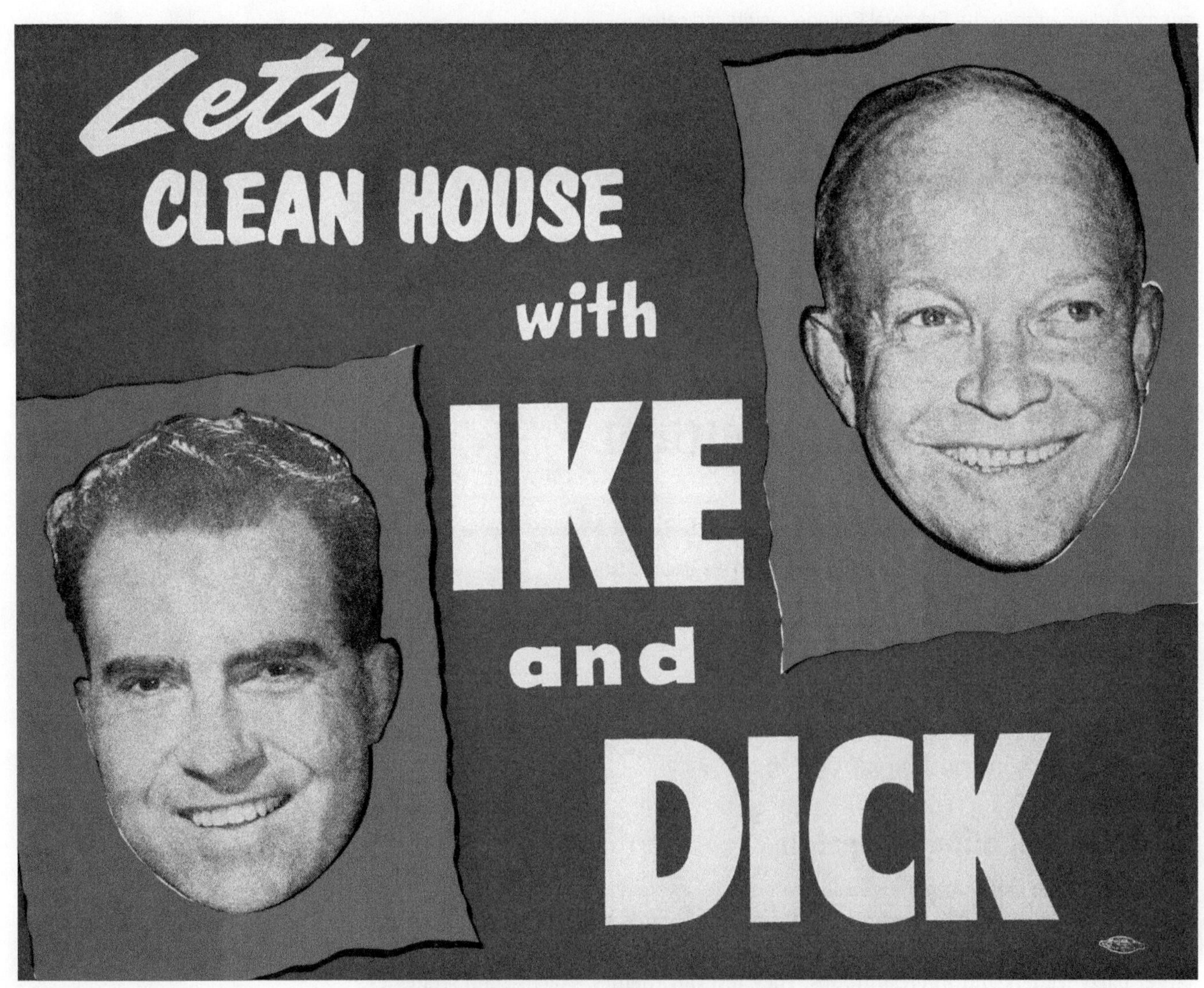

WHY ARE POLITICAL CAMPAIGNS IMPORTANT?

Political campaigns help voters to make informed choices on Election Day. They do this through a complex set of political tools, including media signs and slogans. Here, a sign encourages voters to endorse Dwight D. Eisenhower and Richard M. Nixon for president and vice president, respectively, in 1952.

Explore Your World

Political candidates ultimately become lawmakers and policy makers. As a result, many states around the world have identified a need to make their candidate pools more representative of the country's population at large. One way of achieving this goal is by adopting quotas that mandate a certain percentage of candidates come from traditionally underrepresented groups, such as women or ethnic or religious minorities. Examine the chart below to consider whether candidate quotas translate into greater representation in government; this example focuses on women as candidates and members of the lower house of each country's legislature.

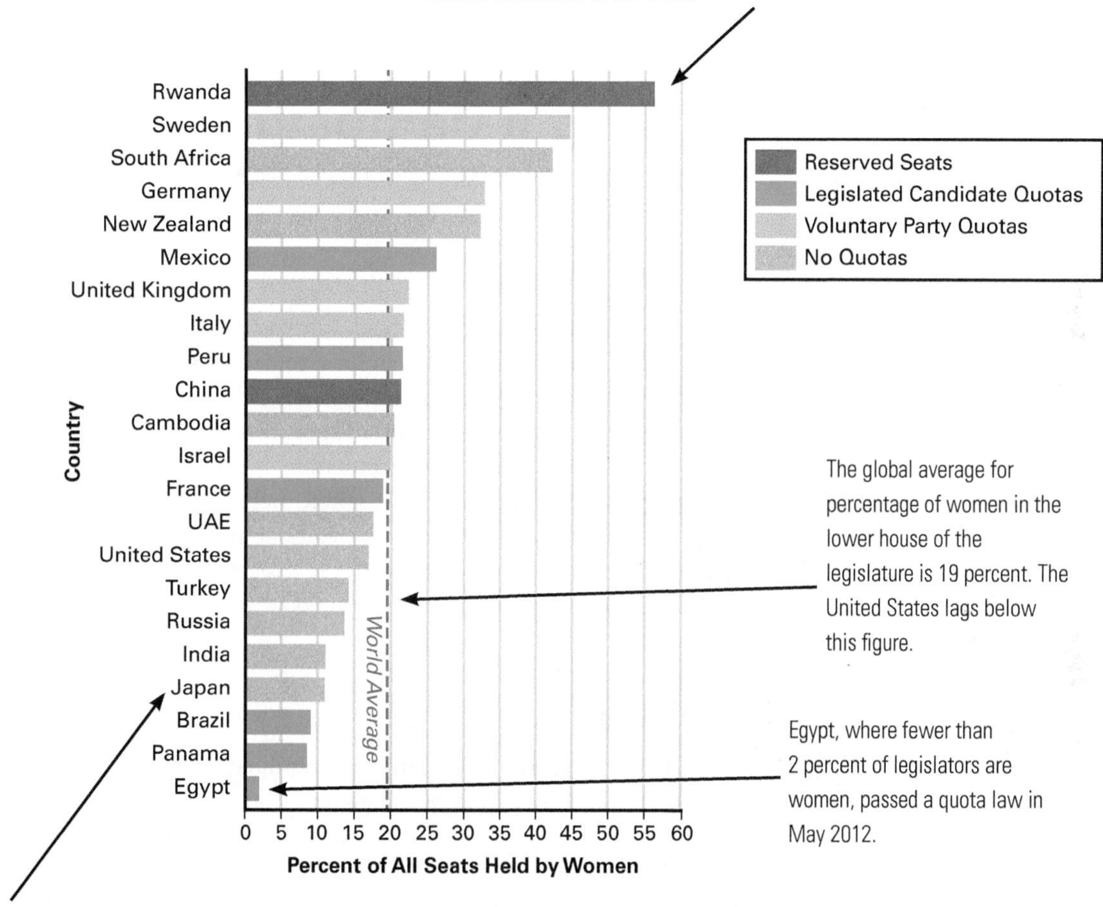

Women played an active role in writing the Rwandan constitution adopted after the late 1990s genocide. They demanded that seats be reserved for women in the legislature; today Rwanda has the highest percentage of female lawmakers in the world.
Rwanda
Sweden
South Africa
Germany
New Zealand
Mexico
United Kingdom
Italy
Peru
China
Cambodia
Israel
France
UAE
United States
Turkey
Russia
India
Japan
Brazil
Panama
Egypt
Country
World Average
0 5 10 15 20 25 30 35 40 45 50 55 60
Percent of All Seats Held by Women
Reserved Seats
Legislated Candidate Quotas
Voluntary Party Quotas
No Quotas
The global average for percentage of women in the lower house of the legislature is 19 percent. The United States lags below this figure.
Egypt, where fewer than 2 percent of legislators are women, passed a quota law in May 2012.
Japanese women lag behind their male counterparts in both public and private leadership positions. The government has recently considered adopting quota laws to narrow these gaps.

SOURCE: "Focus: Women in Parliament," *The Economist* (May 9, 2012): http://www.economist.com/blogs/graphicdetail/2012/05/focus-1; The Quota Project, www.quotaproject.org. Data as of March 31, 2012.

CRITICAL THINKING QUESTIONS

1. Does there appear to be a relationship between quota laws and percentages of women in government?
2. How might quota laws improve the representation of women's issues in government and politics? In what ways might they be ineffective?
3. Should the United States adopt a law requiring that a certain percentage of political candidates be women? Why or why not?

run against nominees from other political parties. All eligible voters, regardless of political party, have the opportunity to vote in these elections. For this reason, most political scientists suggest that candidates running in general elections have an incentive to move their positions on political issues toward the ideological center. These scholars argue that candidates representing the two major parties are unlikely to lose the votes of party loyalists. The citizens whose votes are "up for grabs" are often political moderates, and choosing middle-of-the-road positions on controversial issues may help to attract the votes of these individuals.

The length of the general election campaign varies widely from state to state, depending on the date of the primary elections. In states that hold primary elections in January, the general election campaign can be quite long. However, in states that hold primary elections in September, the general election campaign is quite short. The length of this campaign season affects how candidates structure their campaigns, how they raise money, whom they meet along the campaign trail, and even their advertising strategies.

Assembling a Campaign Staff

13.2 Assess the role of candidates and their staff in the campaign process.

andidates are the center of political campaigns. While a candidate may not make all of the decisions, or even have the expertise or knowledge to handle the wide variety of issues and concerns that affect the campaign, it is ultimately the candidate's name that appears on the ballot. And, on Election Day, voters hold only the candidate truly accountable.

Candidates employ a wide variety of people to help them run an effective campaign. Most candidates for higher offices hire a campaign manager, finance chair, and communications staff. They may also contract the assistance of a variety of political consultants. In addition, candidates rely on networks of grassroots volunteers to spread the campaign's message and to get out the vote.

☐ The Candidate

Before there can be a campaign, there must be a candidate. Candidates run for office for any number of reasons, including personal ambition, the desire to promote ideological objectives or pursue specific public policies, or simply because they think they can do a better job than their opponents.[1] In any case, to be successful, candidates must spend a considerable amount of time and energy in pursuit of their desired office, and all candidates must be prepared to expose themselves and often their families to public scrutiny and the chance of rejection by the voters.

In an effort to show voters they are hardworking, thoughtful, and worthy of the office they seek, candidates try to meet as many citizens as possible in the course of a campaign. To some degree, such efforts are symbolic, especially for presidential candidates, since it is possible to have direct contact with only a small fraction of the millions of people who are likely to vote in a presidential contest. But, one should not discount the value of visiting numerous localities both to increase media coverage and to motivate local activists who are working for the candidate's campaign.

Thus, a typical candidate maintains an exhausting schedule. The day may begin at 5:00 a.m. at the entrance gate to an auto plant with an hour or two of handshaking, followed by similar glad-handing at subway stops until 9:00 a.m. Strategy sessions with key advisers and preparation for upcoming presentations and forums may fill the rest of the morning. A luncheon talk, afternoon fundraisers, and a series of media interviews crowd the afternoon agenda. Cocktail parties are followed by a dinner speech, perhaps telephone or neighborhood canvassing of voters, and a civic forum or two. Meetings with advisers and planning for the next day's events can easily take a candidate past midnight. After only a few hours of sleep, the candidate starts all over again.

The hectic pace of campaigning can strain the candidate's family life and leaves little time for reflection and long-range planning. After months of this grueling pace, candidates may be functioning on automatic pilot and often commit gaffes, from referring to the wrong city's sports team to fumbling an oft-repeated stump speech. Candidates also are much more prone to lose their tempers, responding sharply to criticism from opponents and even the media when they believe they have been characterized unfairly. These frustrations and the sheer exhaustion only get worse when a candidate believes he or she is on the verge of defeat and the end of the campaign is near.

campaign manager
The individual who travels with the candidate and coordinates the campaign.

The Campaign Staff

Paid staff, political consultants, and dedicated volunteers work behind the scenes to support the candidate. Collectively, they plan general strategy, conduct polls, write speeches, craft the campaign's message, and design a communications plan to disseminate that message in the form of TV advertisements, radio spots, Web sites, and direct mail pieces. Others are responsible for organizing fund-raising events, campaign rallies, and direct voter contacts.

It is important to note that the campaign staff varies significantly in size and nature, depending on the type of race. Presidential, senatorial, and gubernatorial races employ large professional staffs and a number of different consultants and pollsters. In contrast, races for state legislatures will likely have only a paid campaign manager and rely heavily on volunteer workers (see Figure 13.1).

CAMPAIGN MANAGER A **campaign manager** runs nearly every campaign at the state and national level. The campaign manager travels with the candidate and coordinates the campaign. He or she is the person closest to the candidate who makes the essential day-to-day decisions, such as whom to hire and when to air TV and radio

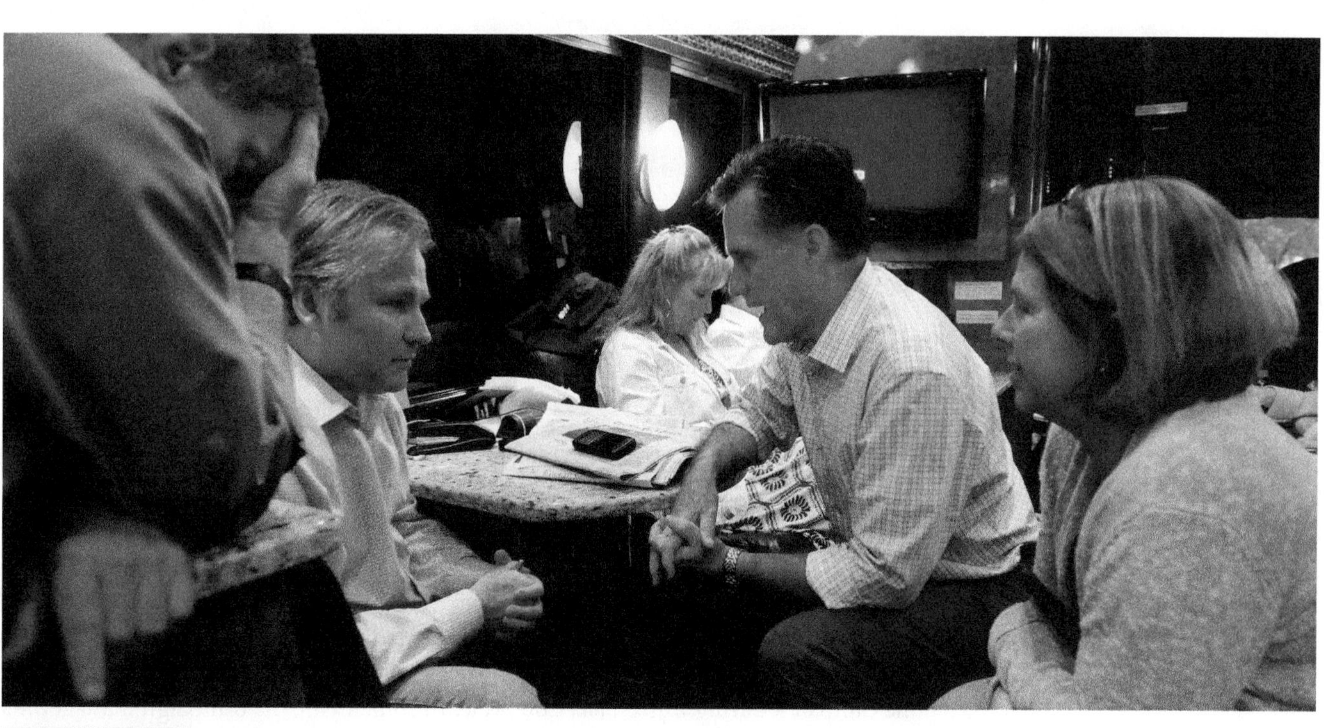

WHAT ROLE DO CAMPAIGN STAFF PLAY?

Staff assist the candidate with much of the day-to-day work of running a political campaign. Here, presidential candidate Mitt Romney holds a meeting on his campaign bus with senior advisors Stuart Stevens and Eric Ferhnstrom and campaign manager Beth Myers.

finance chair
The individual who coordinates the financial business of the campaign.

President Barack Obama's Campaign Organization
Obama for America

Senior Campaign Staff
Campaign Manager: Jim Messina
Consultant: David Axelrod
Senior Advisors: Robert Gibbs, Jim Margolis
Director of Opinion Research: David Simas
Deputy Campaign Managers: Jen Dillon O'Malley, Juliana Smoot, Stephanie Cutter, Steve Hildebrand

Operations
Chief Operating Officer: Ann Marie Habershaw
Director of State Operations: David Levine
Chief Financial Officer: Mary Beth Schulz
General Counsel: Bob Bauer

Finance
Finance Director: Rufus Gifford
Deputy Finance Director: Elizabeth Lowery
Director of Grassroots Fundraising: Yolanda Magallanes
National Finance Chair: Matthew Barzun

Communications
Senior Communications Advisor: David Axelrod
Communications Director: Brent Colburn
National Press Secretary: Ben LaBolt
Traveling Press Secretary: Jen Psaki
Scheduling and Advance: Lisa Kohnke
Director of Rapid Response: Lis Smith
Director of Speechwriting: Stephen Krupin

Internet and Information Technology
Chief Technology Officer: James Harper Reed
Digital Director: Teddy Goff
Online Organizer: Betsy Hoover
Social Media Content Manager: Jessi Langsen
Video: Stephen Muller
E-mail: Caitlin Mitchell
Internet Advertising: Andrew Bleeker

Political
Political Director: Katherine Archuleta
Deputy National Political Director: Yohannes Abraham
Youth Vote Director: Valeisha Butterfield-Jones

Policy
Policy Director: James Kvaal
Senior Policy Strategist: Joel Benenson
Healthcare Policy Director: Christen Linke Young
National Security Coordinator: Marie Harf

Research and Polling
Research Director: Elizabeth Jarvis-Shean
Lead Pollster/Senior Strategist: Joel Benenson

Field
Field Director: Jeremy Bird
Battleground States Director: Mitch Stewart

Joseph R. Biden Staff
Chief of Staff: Sheila Nix
Deputy Chief of Staff: Scott Mulhauser
Communications Director: Sam B. King
Press Secretary: Amy Dudley

Michelle Obama Staff
Senior Advisor and Chief of Staff: Allyson Laackman
Communications Director: Olivia Alair

FIGURE 13.1 HOW IS A CAMPAIGN STAFF ORGANIZED?

Presidential candidates have large staffs that help them run the day-to-day operations of their lengthy campaigns to be the chief executive of the United States. Among these officers are the campaign manager, finance chair, communications director, and a large number of professional political consultants. The diagram below shows the staff of the 2012 Barack Obama campaign.

SOURCE: Updated with data from http://www.p2012.org/candidates/obamaorg.html.

advertisements. The campaign manager also helps to determine the campaign's overall strategy and works to keep the campaign on message throughout the race. He or she works directly for the campaign; therefore, campaign managers can usually run only one campaign during a given election cycle. In some cases, the campaign manager may be the only full-time employee of the campaign.

FINANCE CHAIR The major role of the **finance chair** is to coordinate the financial efforts of the campaign. This job includes raising money, keeping records of funds

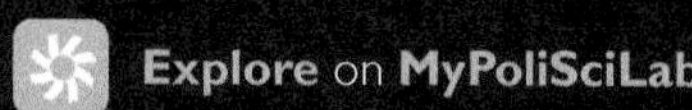

How Are People Involved in Politics?

There are a lot of ways to participate in politics. According to the 2008 American National Election Study, most Americans have attended a city council meeting, participated in a school board meeting, or signed a paper petition. But many have not protested, given money to political organizations, or distributed political information. How people engage in politics—and how often—is in part a function of efficacy, or whether or not individuals believe they have a say in government.

Political Activity

Activity	Percent
Signed a paper petition	56%
Attended a city council or school board meeting	55%
Gave money to a social/political organization	42%
Attended meeting on a political or social issue	34%
Distributed social/political group information	21%
Joined a protest rally or march	19%

Do You Have a Say in Government?

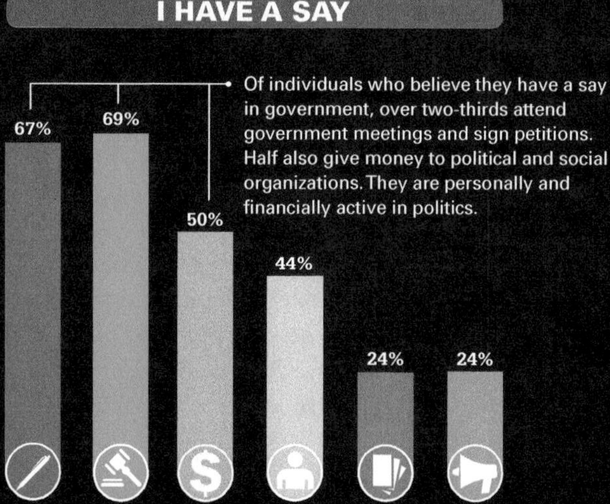

I HAVE A SAY
67%
69%
50%
44%
24%
24%
Of individuals who believe they have a say in government, over two-thirds attend government meetings and sign petitions. Half also give money to political and social organizations. They are personally and financially active in politics.

I DON'T HAVE A SAY

51%
46%
33%
24%
17%
17%

Less than 20% of individuals who do NOT believe they have a say in government take part in protests or disseminate information. They are generally less active than people who think they have a say.

SOURCE: Data from the American National Election Studies, 2008 Time Series Studies, post-election interview responses only.

Investigate Further

Concept What are the most frequent forms of participation? Americans most frequently participate by attending local government meetings and signing paper petitions. Attending protests and rallies and distributing political information are less common.

Connection How are city council and school board meetings different from protests and petitions? Council and board meetings can make policy for government. Protests and petitions are ways of communicating information about issues to people with authority to make policy.

Cause How is participation related to efficacy? Those who believe they don't have a say in government are generally less active, while those who do think they have a say are more likely to engage. Regardless of their perceived influence, people are more likely to interact with institutions than to protest or disseminate information.

communications director
The person who develops the overall media strategy for the candidate.

press secretary
The individual charged with interacting and communicating with journalists on a daily basis.

campaign consultant
A private-sector professional who sells to a candidate the technologies, services, and strategies required to get that candidate elected.

pollster
A campaign consultant who conducts public opinion surveys.

voter canvass
The process by which a campaign reaches individual voters, either by door-to-door solicitation or by telephone.

get-out-the-vote (GOTV)
A push at the end of a political campaign to encourage supporters to go to the polls.

received and spent, and filing the required paperwork with the Federal Election Commission, the bureaucratic agency in charge of monitoring campaign activity. As the cost of campaigns has risen and fund-raising has become more important, the finance chair has also grown in prestige and significance. Although a volunteer accountant may fill the role of finance chair in state and local elections, candidates for most federal offices hire someone to fill this position.

COMMUNICATIONS STAFF A **communications director**, who develops the overall media strategy for the campaign, heads the communications staff. It is the communications director's job to stay apprised of newspaper, TV, radio, and Internet coverage, as well as supervise media consultants who craft campaign advertisements. Coordinating these many media sources can be challenging, as we will discuss later in this chapter.

In many campaigns, the communications director works closely with the **press secretary.** The press secretary interacts and communicates with journalists on a daily basis and acts as the spokesperson for the campaign. It is the press secretary's job to be quoted in news coverage, to explain the candidate's issue positions, and to react to the actions of opposing candidates. He or she also has the job of delivering bad news and responding to attacks from opponents or interest groups. (It is better not to have the candidate doing the dirty work of the campaign.)

An increasingly significant part of the campaign's communications staff is the Internet team, which manages the campaign's online communications, outreach, and fund-raising. Members of the Internet team post on blogs advocating for the candidate and create candidate profiles on social networking sites. They may organize Web chats or real-world meet-ups and grassroots events. They also act as important liaisons with the campaign's volunteers.

CAMPAIGN CONSULTANTS **Campaign consultants** are the private-sector professionals and firms who sell the technologies, services, and strategies many candidates need to get elected. The number of consultants has grown exponentially since they first appeared in the 1930s, and their specialties and responsibilities have increased accordingly, to the point that campaign consultants are now an important part of many campaigns at the state and national level.[2]

Candidates generally hire specialized consultants who focus on only one or two areas, such as fund-raising, polling, media relations, Internet outreach, and speech writing. Media consultants, for example, design advertisements for distribution on TV, the Internet, radio, billboards, and flyers. They work with the communications director to craft the campaign's message and spin key issues.

Pollsters, on the other hand, are campaign consultants who conduct public opinion surveys. These studies gather opinions from a candidate's potential constituents. They are useful because they can tell a candidate where he or she stands relative to opponents, or can provide useful information about the issues and positions important to voters. Pollsters may also work with the media staff to gauge the potential impact of proposed radio or TV advertisements.

VOLUNTEERS Volunteers are the lifeblood of every national, state, and local campaign. Volunteers answer phone calls, staff candidate booths at festivals and county fairs, copy and distribute campaign literature, and serve as the public face of the campaign. They go door to door to solicit votes, or use computerized telephone banks to call targeted voters with scripted messages, two basic methods of **voter canvass**. Most canvassing, or direct solicitation of support, takes place in the month before the election, when voters are most likely to be paying attention. Closer to Election Day, volunteers begin vital **get-out-the-vote (GOTV)** efforts, contacting supporters to encourage them to vote and arranging for their transportation to the polls if necessary. In recent years, the Internet and social networking sites such as Facebook and Twitter have been important tools used by volunteers to get out the vote and energize supporters.

Raising Money

13.3 Evaluate the ways campaigns raise money.

Successful campaigns require a great deal of money. In 2012, for example, nearly $2 billion was raised by the Democratic and Republican Parties. Presidential candidates raised nearly $1 billion in additional support for their campaigns. And, candidates for the Senate raised $644 million. Candidates for the House, in contrast, raised over $1 billion. Recall, however, that there are more candidates for House than Senate.[3]

Efforts to regulate this type of campaign spending are nothing new. They are also far from settled. As spending from individuals, political parties, political action committees (PACs), and other sources continues to rise, it is likely that calls for reform will also continue. The sections that follow detail the current regulations and their implications for candidates running for political office.

Regulating Campaign Finance

The United States has struggled to regulate campaign spending for well over one hundred years. One early attempt to regulate the way candidates raise campaign resources was enacted in 1883, when Congress passed civil service reform legislation that prohibited solicitation of political funds from federal workers, attempting to halt a corrupt and long-held practice. In 1907, the Tillman Act prohibited corporations from making direct contributions to candidates for federal office. The Corrupt Practices Acts (1910, 1911, and 1925), Hatch Act (1939), and Taft-Hartley Act (1947) all attempted to regulate the manner in which federal candidates finance their campaigns and, to some extent, limit the corrupting influence of campaign spending.

Congress did not enact serious, broad campaign finance regulation, however, until the 1970s, in the wake of the Watergate scandal. The Federal Election Campaign Act (FECA) and its amendments established disclosure requirements; the Presidential Public Funding Program provided partial public funding for presidential candidates who meet certain criteria; and the Federal Election Commission (FEC), an independent federal agency, was created to enforce the nation's election laws. Although these provisions altered the campaign landscape, by 2002, it became clear that they were insufficient to regulate ever-increasing campaign expenditures in the United States. Behind the leadership of Senators John McCain (R–AZ) and Russell Feingold (D–WI), Congress enacted and President George W. Bush signed into law a new set of campaign finance regulations known as the Bipartisan Campaign Reform Act (BCRA) (see Table 13.1).

BCRA regulates political advertising and funding. The act, as it was originally passed, limited the broadcast of issue advocacy ads within thirty days of a primary election and sixty days of a general election, and set hard limits on campaign contributions from a number of sources, including individuals, political parties, political action committees, and members of Congress. Opponents of BCRA, including Senator Mitch

TABLE 13.1 WHAT ARE THE INDIVIDUAL CONTRIBUTION LIMITS UNDER BCRA?

	Contribution Limit
To candidate, per election	$2,500[a]
To national party committee, per year	$30,800[a]
To state/local party committee, per year	$10,000
To other political committee, per year	$5,000
Total contributions, per 2-year cycle	$117,000[a]

[a] These limits are for 2011–2012. BCRA limits are adjusted in odd-numbered years to account for inflation.

SOURCE: Federal Election Commission, www.fec.gov.

McConnell (R–KY) and the National Rifle Association, wasted little time in challenging its limits as an infringement on their right to free speech. In a 2003 decision, the Supreme Court disagreed, holding that the government's interest in preventing corruption overrides the free speech rights to which the parties would otherwise be entitled. Thus, BCRA's restrictions on individual expenditures were upheld.[4]

The Supreme Court has, however, declared other sections of BCRA unconstitutional. In 2007, for example, the Court held that the thirty- and sixty-day limits placed on issue advocacy ads were unconstitutional, thus opening the door to these electioneering communications throughout the election cycle.[5] And, in 2008, the Court overturned another provision of the act that had attempted to limit the amount of a candidate's own money that could be spent on running for office.[6] More recently, in 2010, the Court handed down a decision in *Citizens United* v. *FEC* that declared unconstitutional BCRA's ban on electioneering communications made by corporations and unions.[7] This decision struck a significant blow to BCRA's provisions and has had a dramatic effect on the power of interest groups and corporations in campaigns and elections. As a result of these rulings, campaign spending surpassed all recent records, spending approximately $6 billion on the 2012 election.

The cumulative result of these decisions—and the Supreme Court's willingness to equate money with speech—has been to effectively gut campaign finance law in the United States. Though limits still exist on individuals' expenditures to parties and candidates, independent expenditures, or funds spent to advocate for the election of a candidate without coordinating with that candidate's campaign committee, are virtually unlimited. To date, efforts to advance further campaign finance reforms have met with little success in Congress.

☐ Sources of Campaign Funding

As mentioned previously, the Bipartisan Campaign Reform Act regulates campaign contributions from a number of sources, including individuals, political parties, members of Congress, personal savings, and political action committees. The Federal Election Commission regulates, records, and discloses these expenditures. The FEC also monitors infractions of campaign finance rules and acts as a quasi-judicial arbiter of conflicts.

BCRA and more recent judicial interpretations of the law have also opened the door to a number of other actors in political campaigns. Immediately following enactment of the law, 527 political committees became active in the campaign process. Following the Supreme Court's 2007 actions to lift the limits on issue advocacy ads, 501(c) groups increased their role in electoral politics. Most recently, after the *Citizens United* decision, Super PACs have become important players in the 2012 elections.

INDIVIDUALS Individual contributions are donations from independent citizens. The maximum allowable contribution under federal law for congressional and presidential elections was $2,500 per election to each candidate in 2011–2012, with primary and general elections considered separately. Individuals in 2011–2012 were also limited to a total of $117,500 in gifts to all candidates, political action committees, and parties combined per two-year election cycle. These limits rise at the rate of inflation each election cycle. Most candidates receive a majority of all funds directly from individuals, and most individual gifts are well below the maximum level. In one recent election, researchers found that individual donors accounted for 60 percent of contributions to candidates for the House of Representatives, 75 percent of contributions to candidates for the Senate, and 85 percent of contributions to presidential candidates.[8] In 2012, the vast majority of Barack Obama's $600 million fund-raising effort came from individuals. Of those donations, almost 34 percent came from small money donors.[9]

POLITICAL PARTIES Candidates receive substantial donations from the national and state committees of the Democratic and Republican Parties. Under the current rules, national parties can give up to $5,000 per election to a House candidate and

$43,100 to a Senate candidate. In 2012, the Republican and Democratic Parties raised nearly $2 billion. In competitive races, the parties may provide almost 20 percent of their candidates' total campaign funds.

political action committees (PACs)
Officially recognized fund-raising organizations that represent interest groups and are allowed by federal law to make contributions directly to candidates' campaigns.

PERSONAL SAVINGS The U.S. Supreme Court ruled in *Buckley* v. *Valeo* (1976) that no limit could be placed on the amount of money candidates can spend from their own families' resources, since such spending is considered a First Amendment right of free speech.[10] For wealthy politicians, this allowance may mean personal spending in the millions. For example, in 2012, former WWE chief executive officer Linda McMahon spent $40 million of her own money to run unsuccessfully for the Senate in Connecticut. Other self-financed candidates also ran for the House and Senate. Interestingly, in 2012, most of these self-financed candidates did not win their bids for office. While self-financed candidates often garner a great deal of attention, most candidates commit much less than $100,000 in family resources to their election bids.

POLITICAL ACTION COMMITTEES (PACs) **Political action committees (PACs)** are officially recognized fund-raising organizations allowed by federal law to make contributions directly to candidates' campaigns. A wide variety of groups, including labor unions, corporations, trade unions, ideological issue groups, and even members of Congress seeking to build their party's membership in Congress, may create them. Under current rules, a PAC can give no more than $5,000 per candidate per election, and $15,000 each year to each of the national party committees.

Although a good number of PACs of all persuasions existed prior to the 1970s, it was during the 1970s—the decade of campaign finance reform—that the modern PAC era began. PACs grew in number from 113 in 1972 to a peak of 4,268 in 1988. Today, approximately 4,000 PACs are registered with the FEC. These political committees have historically played a major role, particularly in congressional elections. However, in the 2012 election, the role of PACs significantly declined at the expense of other forms of outside spending. PACs spent only $32 million on the 2012 elections. Approximately 61 percent of these funds went to Republican candidates, while 39 percent of these funds went to Democratic candidates (see Figure 13.2).[11]

PACs remain one of the most controversial parts of the campaign financing process. Some observers claim that PACs are the embodiment of corrupt special interests that use campaign donations to buy the votes of legislators. Studies, in fact, have confirmed this suspicion. PACs effectively use contributions to punish legislators and affect policy, at least in the short run.[12] Legislators who vote contrary to the wishes of a PAC see their donations withheld, but those who are successful in legislating as the PAC wishes gain the reward of even greater donations.[13]

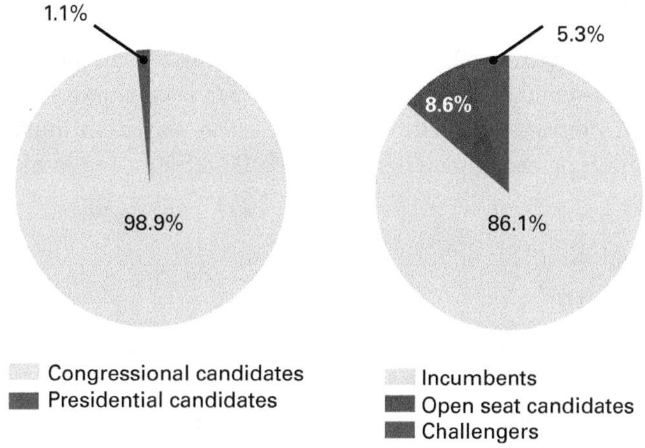

FIGURE 13.2 HOW DO PACS ALLOCATE THEIR CAMPAIGN CONTRIBUTIONS?

Political action committees are major players in American elections. Most PAC money goes to incumbent candidates running for the House of Representatives or the Senate.

SOURCE: Center for Responsive Politics, www.opensecrets.org/lobby, 2008.

527 political committee
Organizations created with the primary purpose of influencing electoral outcomes; the term is typically applied only to freestanding interest groups that do not explicitly advocate for the election of a candidate.

501(c) group
Interest groups whose primary purpose is not electoral politics.

Super PACs
Political action committees established to make independent expenditures.

independent expenditures
Spending for campaign activity that is not coordinated with a candidate's campaign.

public funds
Donations from general tax revenues to the campaigns of qualifying presidential candidates.

matching funds
Donations to presidential campaigns whereby every dollar raised from individuals in amounts less than $251 is matched by the federal treasury.

527 POLITICAL COMMITTEES Named for the section of the tax code from which they draw their name, **527 political committees** are organizations created with the primary purpose of influencing electoral outcomes. Although 527s technically include candidate campaign committees and party committees, the term is typically applied only to freestanding interest groups that do not explicitly advocate for the election of a candidate. Many unions and partisan organizations such as the College Republican National Committee have formed 527s.

527s are subject to very limited government regulation. The Federal Election Commission monitors the contributions given to these groups. However, no limits are set on how much an individual or other organization may contribute or on how much a group may spend on electoral activities. Thus, during the 2012 campaign, 527 groups spent approximately $343 million. These expenditures narrowly favored Democratic candidates. Notable 527s participating in the 2012 election included ActBlue and EMILY's List on the Democratic side of the aisle and Citizens United on the Republican side of the aisle.[14]

501(c) GROUPS **501(c) groups** are interest groups whose primary purpose is not electoral politics. Federal rules, in fact, mandate that no more than half of a 501(c) group's budget be spent on campaign politics. Like 527s, they take their name from the section of the tax code under which they are established. These groups first became significantly involved in electoral politics after the Supreme Court lifted BCRA's ban on issue advocacy. Thus, most of their electoral activity focuses on raising awareness of candidates' positions on issues of interest to the group.

These groups are not required to disclose the source of their donations. However, they spend significant sums of money on campaigns. In the 2012 election cycle, 501(c) groups spent roughly as much as did 527s. Unlike 527s, however, most of these contributions favored Republican candidates. Examples of notable 501(c) groups include American Values Action and the America's Not Stupid both of which lean Republican, and many state chapters of Planned Parenthood, which tend to lean Democratic in their contributions.[15]

SUPER PACS The fastest-growing and arguably most significant external actor in the 2012 elections, **Super PACs** are a special kind of political action committee established to make **independent expenditures**, or spending for campaign activity that is not coordinated with a candidate's campaign. Unlike traditional PACs, they may not give money directly to candidates or party committees. However, they may advocate on behalf of candidates.

Though Super PACs must disclose the sources of their contributions to the FEC, they may take money from any person or organization interested in influencing the political process. They also are not subject to contribution or expenditure limits, which was abundantly clear in the 2012 elections. Super PACs spent more than $600 million on the 2012 presidential election, with a larger percentage going to Republican Mitt Romney than President Barack Obama. They also played an important role in the 2012 Republican primary, spending close to $100 million, and in many congressional elections.

☐ Public Funds

Public funds are donations from general tax revenues to the campaigns of qualifying candidates. On the federal level, only presidential candidates are eligible to receive public funds, although in recent years, few candidates have chosen to accept them. Some states also offer public funds to qualifying individuals running for particular offices, especially within the judiciary.

A candidate for president can become eligible to receive public funds during the nomination campaign by raising at least $5,000 in individual contributions of $250 or less in each of twenty states. The candidate can then apply for federal **matching funds**,

How Has Campaign Financing Changed Over Time?

Campaign financing has changed dramatically in the last ten years. Following the passage of the Bipartisan Campaign Reform Act (BCRA) in 2002, some expenditures traditionally used in political campaigns were outlawed. But, BCRA, and subsequent interpretations of the law by the Supreme Court, opened the door for other forms of money to play increasingly large roles in the political process. The rise of Super PACs has been one such change. These political action committees came under a great deal of fire during the 2012 election because of the unlimited sums of money they raised and spent from wealthy donors, potentially silencing the voices of average citizens.

What Unleashed Outside Spending?

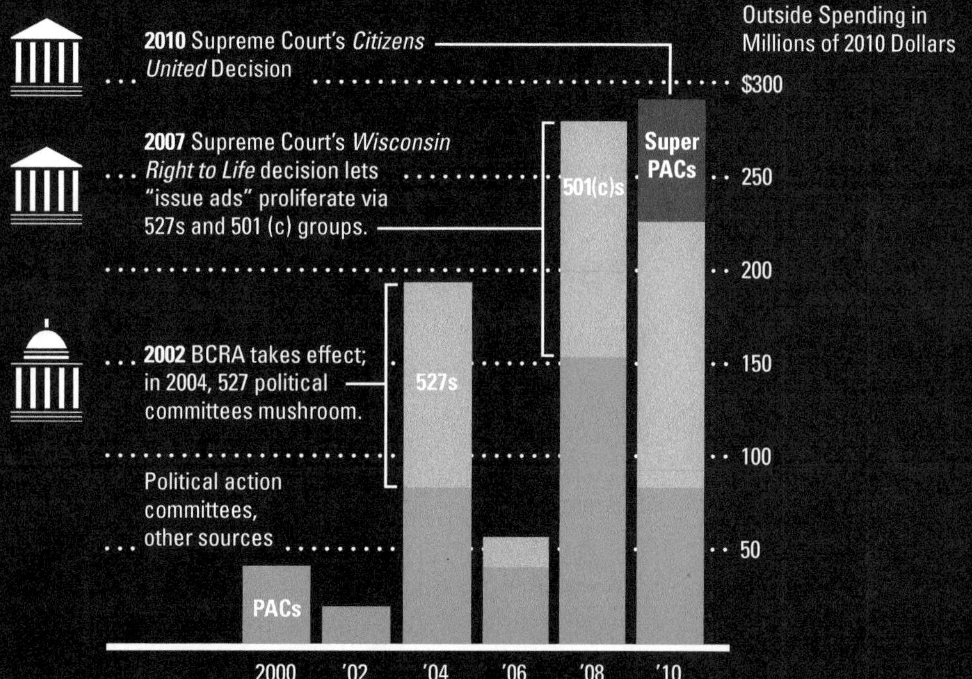

The Top 5 Super PAC Spenders in 2012 Were...

$142,645,946 Restore Our Future

$91,115,402 American Crossroads

$33,564,920 Americans for Prosperity

$66,482,084 Priorities USA Action

Republican National Committee $40,166,559

SOURCE: Data from the Center for Responsive Politics and the Federal Election Commission.

CRITICAL THINKING QUESTIONS

1. How have the sources of outside funds changed over the last several elections? What events explain these changes?
2. Why do you think Republican groups spent larger sums of money than Democratic groups? How do Democrats raise and spend money for campaigns?
3. Is further campaign finance reform necessary? Why or why not?

whereby every dollar raised from individuals in amounts less than $251 is matched by the federal treasury on a dollar-for-dollar basis. Of course, this assumes the Presidential Election Campaign Fund has enough money to do so. Taxpayers who designate $3 of their taxes for this purpose each year when they send in their federal tax returns provide the money for the fund. (Only about 20 percent of taxpayers check off the appropriate box, even though participation does not increase their tax burden.)

During the general election campaign, the two major-party presidential nominees can accept a $91.2 million lump-sum payment from the federal government after the candidate accepts his or her nomination. If the candidate accepts the money, it becomes the sole source for financing the campaign. A candidate may refuse the money and be free from the spending cap the government attaches to it. In 2008, Barack Obama was the first presidential candidate to opt out of the public financing system. In 2012, both major-party candidates chose not to accept the public funding in favor of raising unrestricted amounts of private donations. This trend will likely continue into the future.

A third-party candidate receives a smaller amount of public funds proportionate to his or her November vote total, if that candidate gains a minimum of 5 percent of the vote. Note that in such a case, the money goes to third-party campaigns only *after* the election is over; no money is given in advance of the general election. Only two third-party candidates have qualified for public campaign funding: John Anderson in 1980, after gaining 7 percent of the vote, and Texas billionaire Ross Perot in 1992, after gaining 19 percent of the vote.

Reaching Voters

13.4 Identify the ways campaigns use the media to reach potential voters.

Explore on MyPoliSciLab Simulation: You Are a Campaign Strategist

The media play a large role in determining what voters actually see and hear about the candidate. Media can take a number of different forms; among these are traditional media, new media, and campaign advertisements.

Traditional media coverage of a political campaign includes content appearing in newspapers and magazines as well as on radio and TV. New media coverage includes content that appears on the Internet, in blogs, and on social media sites. Both traditional and new media can be very difficult for a campaign to control. Campaigns, however, have a great deal of control over the content they include in their campaign advertisements.

Traditional Media

During campaign season, the news media constantly report political news. What they report is largely based on news editors' decisions of what is newsworthy or "fit to print." The press often reports what candidates are doing, such as giving speeches, holding fundraisers, or meeting with party leaders. Reporters may also investigate rumors of a candidate's misdeeds or unflattering personal history, such as run-ins with the law, alleged use of drugs, or alleged sexual improprieties.

Although this free media attention may help candidates increase their name recognition, it may prove frustrating for campaigns, which do not control the content of the coverage. For example, studies have shown that reporters are obsessed with the horse-race aspect of politics—who is ahead, who is behind, and who is gaining—to the detriment of the candidates' issues and ideas. Public opinion polls, especially tracking polls, many of them taken by news outlets, dominate coverage on network TV in particular. This horse-race coverage can have an effect on how the public views the candidates. Using poll data, journalists often predict the margins by which they expect contenders to win or lose. A projected margin of victory of 5 percentage points can be judged a setback if the candidate had been expected to win by 12 or 15 points. The tone of the media coverage, that a candidate is either gaining or losing support in polls, can also affect whether people decide to give money and other types of support to a candidate.[16]

STRATEGIES TO CONTROL MEDIA COVERAGE Candidates and their media consultants use various strategies in an effort to obtain favorable press coverage. First, campaign staff members often seek to isolate the candidate from the press, thus reducing the chances that reporters will bait a candidate into saying something that might damage his or her cause. Naturally, journalists are frustrated by such a tactic, and they demand open access to candidates.

Second, the campaign stages media events: activities designed to include brief, clever quotes called sound bites and staged with appealing backdrops so that they will be covered on the TV news and in the newspaper. In this fashion, the candidate's staff can successfully fill the news hole reserved for campaign coverage.

Third, campaign staff and consultants have cultivated a technique termed spin—they put forward the most favorable possible interpretation for their candidate (and the most negative for their opponent) on any circumstance occurring in the campaign. They also work the press to sell their point of view or at least to ensure it is included in the reporters' stories.

Fourth, candidates and their representatives have found ways to circumvent traditional reporters by appearing on talk shows such as *The View, Ellen,* and *The Five,* in which they have an opportunity to present their views and answer questions. They also make regular appearances on comedy shows, such as *Saturday Night Live, The Late Show, The Daily Show,* and *The Colbert Report.*

CANDIDATE DEBATES The first face-to-face presidential debate in U.S. history did not occur until 1960, and debates did not become a regular part of presidential campaigns until the 1980s. However, they are now an established feature of presidential campaigns as well as races for governor, U.S. senator, and many other offices.

Candidates and their staffs recognize the importance of debates as a tool not only for consolidating their voter base but also for correcting misperceptions about the candidate's suitability for office. However, while candidates have complete control over what they say in debates, they cannot control what the news media will highlight and focus on after the debates. Therefore, even though candidates prepare themselves by rehearsing their responses, they cannot avoid the perils of spontaneity. Errors or slips

HOW HAVE THE RULES AND FORMAT FOR PRESIDENTIAL DEBATES CHANGED SINCE THE FIRST TELEVISED DEBATES?

Presidential debates have come a long way since an ill-at-ease Richard M. Nixon was visually bested by John F. Kennedy in the first set of televised debates. In 2012, President Barack Obama sparred with Governor Mitt Romney in a series of three debates, including one focusing on domestic policy, shown here.

of the tongue in a debate can affect election outcomes. President Gerald R. Ford's erroneous insistence during an October 1976 debate with Jimmy Carter that Poland was not under Soviet domination (when in fact it was) may have cost him a close election. George Bush's bored expression and repeated glances at his watch during his 1992 debate with Bill Clinton certainly did not help Bush's electoral hopes. In most cases, however, debates do not alter the results of an election, but rather increase knowledge about the candidates and their respective personalities and issue positions, especially among voters who had not previously paid attention to the campaign.

□ New Media

Contemporary campaigns have an impressive new array of weapons at their disposal: faster printing technologies, reliable databases, instantaneous Internet publishing and mass e-mail, social media sites, autodialed pre-recorded messages, and enhanced telecommunications and teleconferencing. As a result, candidates can gather and disseminate information more quickly and effectively than ever.

One outcome of these changes is the ability of candidates to employ "rapid-response" techniques: the formulation of prompt and informed responses to changing events on the campaign trail. In response to breaking news of a scandal or issue, for example, candidates can conduct background research, implement an opinion poll and tabulate the results, devise a containment strategy and appropriate spin, and deliver a reply. This capability contrasts strongly with techniques used in earlier campaigns, which took much longer to prepare and had little of the flexibility enjoyed by the contemporary e-campaign.[17]

The use of new media takes a number of forms. The most widely used tool is, of course, the Internet. The first use of the Internet in national campaigning came in 1992, when the Democratic presidential ticket of Bill Clinton and Al Gore maintained a Web site that stored electronic versions of their biographical summaries, speeches, press releases, and position papers. The Internet remained something of a virtual brochure until the 2000 elections, when candidates began using e-mail and their Web sites as vehicles for fund-raising, recruiting volunteers, and communicating with supporters. By 2006, most campaign Web sites featured downloadable and streaming video and were integrated into the candidate's overall communication and mobilization strategy. In 2012, all of the major candidates running for president and over 90 percent of Democratic and Republican congressional candidates maintained a campaign Web site.

The growth of online social media sites, such as Facebook, Twitter, and YouTube, has also helped candidates to disseminate their message to citizens. In August 2012, for example, President Barack Obama participated in Reddit.com's Ask Me Anything chat series. He received more than 10,000 questions from citizens and answered ten, including those focusing on the challenges of being president and the role of money in politics. Although these sites have been effective in reaching the politically engaged, early evidence suggests that they do not inspire new demographic groups to become engaged in electoral politics.[18]

Many candidates also use new media to target specific constituencies. One way campaigns may do this is through recorded phone messages, or robo-calling. These calls may both raise money and rally supporters for the candidate and spread negative (and sometimes false) information about an opponent. Robo-calls are remarkably efficient; campaign consultants can reach up to 2,500 telephones per minute at only pennies per call.

During the 2012 election, candidates also experimented with using smartphone technology to advertise to particular groups of people. Smartphones use GPS technology to determine users' locations and provide them with appropriate advertisements when they surf the Internet on their mobile browsers. Potential advertisers may buy ad space in targeted locations; candidates are no exception. Tech-savvy campaign consultants thus used this strategy to purchase mobile Internet advertisements centered on ballparks, fairs, voting locations, or other places where they might find particularly sympathetic or engaged constituencies.[19]

Take a Closer Look

A clear and classic example of negative campaign advertising aired during the 1964 presidential campaign. In an attempt to reinforce the view that his Republican challenger, Senator Barry Goldwater, held extreme views and would be reckless in office, President Lyndon B. Johnson's campaign produced a television ad called "Peace Little Girl" that was considered so shocking and unfair, it was pulled after only one broadcast. Considerable discussion of the ad in the media, however, ensured that its point was made repeatedly to the electorate. Review the stills of the ad below to consider its impact on politics.

The ad began with a serene scene depicting a young girl counting the petals she was picking off a daisy.

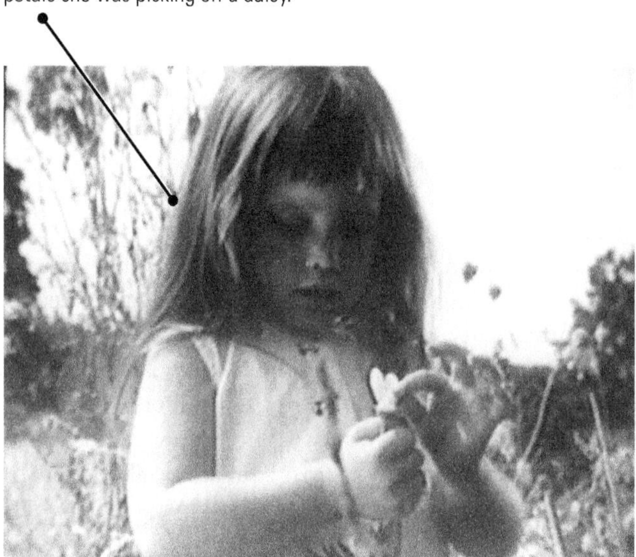

Once the girl said the number nine, a voice-over started counting down a missile launch that ended in images of a nuclear explosion and a mushroom cloud. The viewer then heard the president's voice saying, "These are the stakes."

CRITICAL THINKING QUESTIONS

1. What was this ad trying to imply?
2. Why do you think this ad was considered so shocking and unfair?
3. What types of ads would generate similar controversy today? Explain your answer.

positive ad
Advertising on behalf of a candidate that stresses the candidate's qualifications, family, and issue positions, with no direct reference to the opponent.

negative ad
Advertising on behalf of a candidate that attacks the opponent's character or platform.

contrast ad
Ad that compares the records and proposals of the candidates, with a bias toward the candidate sponsoring the ad.

inoculation ad
Advertising that attempts to counteract an anticipated attack from the opposition before the attack is launched.

☐ Campaign Advertisements

Candidates and their media consultants may choose to buy airtime in the form of campaign advertisements. These ads may take a number of different forms. **Positive ads** stress the candidate's qualifications, family, and issue positions with no direct reference to the opponent. The incumbent candidate usually favors positive ads. **Negative ads** attack the opponent's character or platform. And, with the exception of the candidate's brief, legally required statement that he or she approved the ad, a negative ad may not even mention the candidate who is paying for the airing. **Contrast ads** compare the records and proposals of the candidates, with a bias toward the candidate sponsoring the ad.

Although the number of negative advertisements has increased dramatically during the past two decades, negative advertisements have been a part of American campaigns almost since the nation's founding. In 1796, Federalists portrayed losing presidential candidate Thomas Jefferson as an atheist and a coward. In Jefferson's second bid for the presidency in 1800, Federalists again attacked him, this time spreading a rumor that he was dead. The effects of negative advertising are well documented. Rather than voting *for* a candidate, voters frequently vote *against* a candidate by voting for the opponent, and negative ads can provide the critical justification for such a decision.

Before the 1980s, well-known incumbents usually ignored negative attacks from their challengers, believing that the proper stance was to rise above the fray. But, after some well-publicized defeats of incumbents in the early 1980s in which negative TV advertising played a prominent role,[20] incumbents began attacking their challengers in earnest. The new rule of politics became "An attack unanswered is an attack agreed to." In a further attempt to stave off criticisms from challengers, incumbents began anticipating the substance of their opponents' attacks and airing **inoculation ads** early in the campaign to protect themselves in advance from the other side's spots. Inoculation advertising attempts to counteract an anticipated attack from the opposition before such an attack is launched. For example, a senator who fears a broadside about her voting record on veterans' issues might air advertisements that feature veterans or their families in praise of her support.

Although paid advertising remains the most controllable aspect of a campaign's strategy, the news media are increasingly having an impact on it. Major newspapers throughout the country have taken to analyzing the accuracy of TV advertisements aired during campaigns—a welcome and useful addition to journalists' scrutiny of politicians.

Toward Reform: The 2012 Presidential Campaign

13.5 Analyze the 2012 presidential campaign.

In the American political system, any election that includes an incumbent president inevitably becomes a referendum on the previous four years. If the American electorate is satisfied with his policies, the road to reelection can be relatively assured. However, if voters are uncertain or dissatisfied with a president's first term in office, they may select a new occupant for the White House–regardless of whether or not the incumbent was directly responsible for their dissatisfaction. That was the primary question that confronted voters in the 2012 presidential race between the Democratic incumbent President Barack Obama and the Republican nominee, Mitt Romney, a former governor of the commonwealth of Massachusetts.

The Nomination Campaign

Unlike 2008, Barack Obama did not face any opposition for the Democratic nomination. It was a different story for Republicans. Selection of the Republican nominee proved to be a long and contentious process featuring some of the same candidates who had sought the nomination four years earlier. The contest began in 2011 with a wide field of candidates, including Romney, who had been preparing to run again for president since his unsuccessful bid in 2008. Also seeking the nomination were former Minnesota Governor Tim Pawlenty, Representative Michele Bachmann (MN), Georgia entrepreneur Herman Cain, former Speaker of the House Newt Gingrich (GA), former Utah Governor Jon Huntsman, Texas Governor Rick Perry, former U.S. Senator Rick Santorum (PA), and Representative Ron Paul (TX). In total, 2,286 delegates were at stake and the winning candidate would need the support of 1,144 of them to become the Republican nominee.

THE DEMOCRATIC RACE With no opponent, President Barack Obama avoided the entire primary campaign trail and spent much of the spring and summer of 2012 raising money for his campaign as the Republicans battled one another for their party's nomination.

THE REPUBLICAN RACE Few observers expected the 2012 Republican contest to be as long and dramatic as it was. Through twenty debates over the course of a year, each candidate sought to portray himself or herself as the conservative best able to win an election in an economic climate that historically would have favored the ouster of an incumbent president (see Figure 13.3).

Many observers assumed that Mitt Romney would be an early favorite among Republicans. However, as in 2008, there was no widespread movement toward Romney among social conservatives, with many expressing concerns over his record as a moderate former governor of Massachusetts. They and others also expressed concern with Romney's Mormon faith.

Prior to the start of the Republican primaries and caucuses, several contenders showed early promise in polls. When the official contests began in the late winter and early spring of 2012, the first three states with primaries and caucuses delivered three different winners. Rick Santorum narrowly defeated Romney in the Iowa caucuses. Mitt Romney carried New Hampshire, a neighboring state to his home in Massachusetts, and Newt Gingrich carried South Carolina less than two weeks later.

Following his victory in Iowa, Santorum went on to win three more states before Super Tuesday, March 6, 2012, on which ten states voted. Of the Super Tuesday contests, Romney carried six states to Santorum's three, and Newt Gingrich won his home state of Georgia. As twelve other states and territories held primaries and caucuses later in March, Mitt Romney and Rick Santorum emerged as the only remaining viable candidates. After Santorum won in Kansas, he also took three southern states—Alabama, Mississippi, and Tennessee. Yet, despite Santorum's handful of victories, Mitt Romney carried the majority of the March contests, and by early April it became apparent that he had enough votes to win the Republican nomination for president. One week after Governor Romney won primaries in Wisconsin, Maryland, and Washington, D.C., he became the presumptive Republican nominee. Rick Santorum officially suspended his campaign on April 10th, and the other remaining candidates followed soon after.

The Interim Period

A gap of almost two months separated the end of the primary season and the opening of the Republican and Democratic National Conventions. Both campaigns were relatively quiet during the interim period, choosing instead to prepare for the general election. Several notable events that influenced the general election, however, did occur during the summer months.

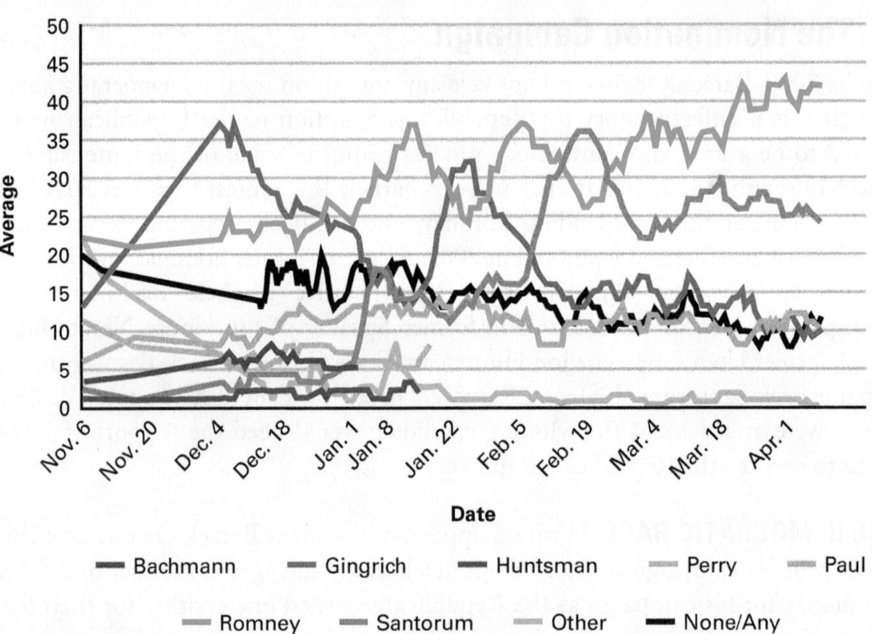

FIGURE 13.3 HOW DID THE FRONTRUNNER CHANGE THROUGHOUT THE 2012 REPUBLICAN PRIMARY?

Reflecting the diversity of the Republican field, many candidates appeared to be the "flavor of the week" during the nomination campaign. From November 2011 to April 2012, however, three candidates separated themselves from the field—Mitt Romney, Newt Gingrich, and Rick Santorum. This figure tracks the rise and fall of each candidate's popularity, as well as that of several other Republican candidates.

SOURCE: Data from http://www.gallup.com/poll/154337/2012-republican-presidential-nomination-race.aspx.

President Obama received encouraging news on June 28 when the U.S. Supreme Court upheld a legal challenge to the signature legislative accomplishment of his first term, the Patient Protection and Affordable Care Act, which Republicans had labeled "Obamacare." The Obama campaign viewed the ruling as an important legal and political victory, even as the Romney campaign vowed to use the issue against the president in the general election. Another moment troubled Obama for the duration of the campaign came in mid-July when the President told a large crowd in Roanoke, Virginia, " if you've got a business, you didn't build that; somebody else made that happen." The remark was carried in national news and received heated criticism from conservative commentators. The comments would be featured in several national television ads against the president in the fall.

Governor Romney faced his own political challenges during that summer when he made several verbal gaffes during an overseas trip to Europe and the Middle East prior to the opening of the 2012 Summer Olympics in London. Romney, who had chaired the 2002 Winter Olympic Games in Salt Lake City, Utah, angered many in London when he questioned whether the city was prepared for the start of the games. Later on that same trip, he also upset Palestinians by making remarks suggesting that Israelis are economically more successful than Palestinians because of cultural differences.

National polls at the start of August showed President Obama generally leading his Republican opponent. On Saturday, August 11, the Romney campaign, sensing the need to make headlines prior to the start of the Republican convention at the end of the month, announced the selection of 42-year-old Representative Paul Ryan of Wisconsin as Romney's running mate.

Romney's announcement generated great excitement among the Republican base. The six-term member of Congress and chair of the House Budget Committee hailed from what was expected to be a battleground state in the general election. Ryan had gained considerable respect among the Republican base after he and other House Republicans challenged Democrats and the Obama White House with several high-profile legislative proposals aimed at fiscal responsibility and reducing the nation's debt. Romney's selection of Ryan as his running mate was widely viewed as an attempt to

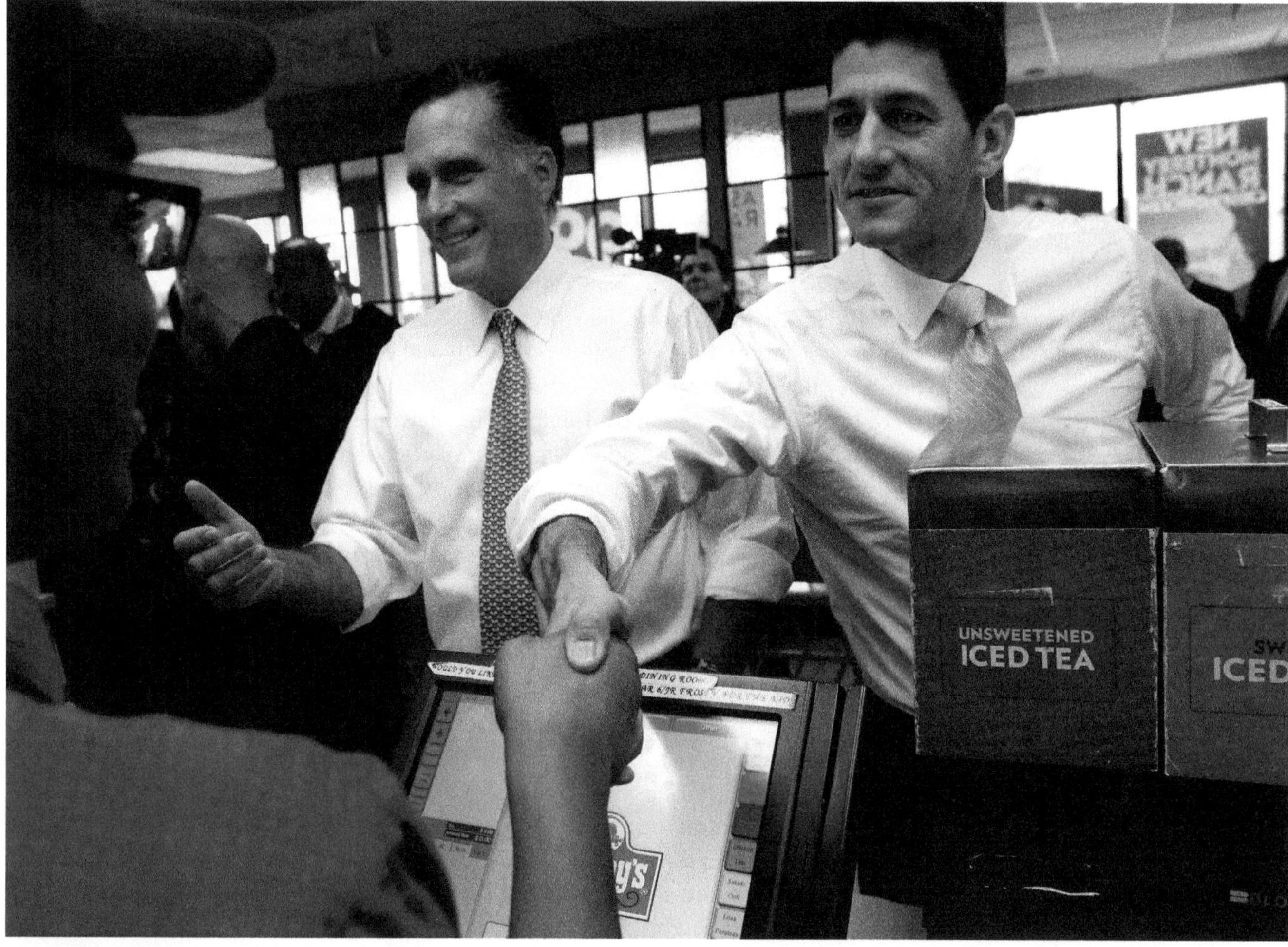

HOW DOES A PRESIDENTIAL CANDIDATE CHOOSE A RUNNING MATE?

Governor Mitt Romney chose Representative Paul Ryan, chair of the House Budget Committee, because he believed Ryan would help to shore up support with the conservative base. He also hoped that Ryan would help to deliver votes in his home state of Wisconsin, which many commentators viewed as a swing state.

shore up any remaining skepticism about his conservative credentials among the Republican base, and as a strategic effort to make Wisconsin a more competitive in the November election.

☐ The Party Conventions

The Republican National Convention was held August 27-30 in Tampa, Florida. Due to the threat of Hurricane Isaac, which loomed just off Florida's West Coast, the order of the convention was changed and most official activity on the opening day of the convention was suspended, with the exception of the unveiling of a debt clock that displayed and updated in real time, the nation's rising national debt. Tuesday, August 28 marked the start of the convention featuring speeches by New Jersey Governor Chris Christie and a primetime address by Ann Romney, wife of the presidential nominee. Her speech was designed as a personal address to the nation aimed specifically at appealing to women voters and presenting her husband as relatable and likeable person. On Wednesday, vice presidential nominee Paul Ryan accepted his nomination and delivered a rousing speech to the convention delegates that was highly critical of the Obama administration, but was widely challenged by the media for numerous factual errors.

One of the most bizarre moments of the 2012 Republican Convention came on the final day, when actor Clint Eastwood took to the stage in primetime with an empty chair meant to represent President Obama. The unscripted presentation of Eastwood speaking to the empty chair was received well within the convention hall, but met mixed reviews among the viewing public and the media. The next day, in an unexpected move on Twitter, President Obama responded to Eastwood's skit by posting a picture of himself sitting in a chair marked "The President" with the message: "This seat's taken."

The Republican Convention concluded with Mitt Romney's acceptance speech, viewed by an estimated 30.3 million people. The speech mixed personal stories with his assessment of the state of the American economy, his plans to build economic growth, move the country toward greater energy independence, and a promise to the American people that if elected President, he would "help you and your family."

The 2012 Democratic National Convention followed less than a week later on September 4-6 in Charlotte, North Carolina. Controversy erupted on the opening day of the convention when it was reported that the 2012 Democratic Party Platform omitted multiple references to God, and that language affirming Jerusalem as the capital of Israel had been removed. The following day, amendments reinserting the stricken language were offered and adopted, but only after three attempts by the Convention Chair to gauge whether the voice-vote by the convention delegates met the necessary two-thirds support for passage under convention rules.

First Lady Michelle Obama delivered the convention's opening night primetime address. Like Ann Romney's speech at the Republican convention, the first lady's remarks were laced with passionate and personal stories of how she and President Obama met and raised a family. The speech was well-received by viewers and produced a standing ovation among the tightly packed delegates in the convention hall.

One of the most highly anticipated speeches came on the second night of the convention, when former President Bill Clinton officially nominated President Obama for reelection. Clinton electrified the convention delegates with a message that the Obama administration was on the right track toward economic recovery and prosperity. Clinton's speech received high praise from the media for making complex economic problems sound simple without talking down to the American people.

The following night, President Obama's acceptance of the nomination was originally scheduled to occur in a 72,000-seat football stadium, similar to a setting that had worked well for at the Democratic convention in Denver in 2008. However, rain and the threat of severe weather led party officials to move the finale back to the convention hall with additional seating to accommodate an audience of approximately 20,000. Many felt that Clinton's remarks the night before would be a tough act for the president to follow, and it was made all the more challenging by news of the venue change.

Vice President Joe Biden spoke first, touting his middle-class upbringing and challenging Republican assertions about the direction of the previous four years. Then, President Obama delivered a rousing acceptance speech viewed by 35.7 million people. In his comments, he offered a forceful argument that it was his administration that rescued the American economy from catastrophe and set the country on a path to recovery.

☐ The General Election Campaign

After the party conventions, the general election campaign kicked off in full force. As the candidates entered the home stretch, the key issue driving both campaigns was the state of the American economy and which candidate would achieve sustained recovery. As the incumbent president, Obama continued to receive considerable blame for the slow, at times stagnant, growth of the American economy over the previous four years. Further complicating their choice, voters received mixed messages about the state of the economy: the stock market and other measures of recovery from the Great Recession showed modest improvement, yet unemployment remained stubbornly high at around 8 percent for most of 2012.

On the eleventh anniversary of the September 11 attacks on the Pentagon and the World Trade Center, national security and international affairs came into focus. Terrorists again attacked representatives of the United States overseas, killing Ambassador Christopher Stevens and three others at the U.S. consulate in Benghazi, Libya. Criticism after the incident led the Obama administration to apologize for certain aspects of the administration's handling of the crisis. Governor Romney was also criticized by some for appearing to try to use the crisis to advance his candidacy.

A week later, Romney faced his own scandal when a surreptitious video from a private Republican fundraiser in May was released publicly. In it, Governor Romney was seen suggesting to supporters that "47 percent" of the American people are dependent on government assistance, labeling them as "victims" who "will vote for the president no matter what." As news of the leaked video broke, Governor Romney initially refused to apologize for the remarks, but later stated on national news that his remarks in the video were wrong. The video resurfaced in numerous anti-Romney campaign ads.

Both candidates, as well as their vice presidential running mates, spent the final months of the election traveling across the country, attempting to speak to voters and influence their vote on Election Day. One of the best opportunities for both candidates to speak to the voters about the issues was the series of presidential debates sponsored by the Commission on Presidential Debates.

CANDIDATE DEBATES The first presidential debate occurred on Wednesday, October 3, at the University of Denver and focused on domestic policy, especially job creation and the American economy. The week before the debate, most national polls showed Obama holding a small lead over Romney. Both campaigns attempted to downplay expectations of their respective candidate's likely performance during the debates while also suggesting that the other side would perform much better.

The format of the first debate featured questions posed by moderator Jim Lehrer of PBS, with responses and rebuttals by the candidates. While neither candidate broke new ground on the issues, Romney repeatedly challenged Obama over the cost of the president's signature healthcare reform legislation, which at one point Romney referred to as "Obamacare." It was the first time Romney or any other Republican had spoken the term—which Republicans used a derisive way—in front of the president. Romney turned to the President and apologized, saying he used the word "with all respect." The President responded simply with, "I like it."

But the first debate would be remembered for Obama's lackluster performance, which would haunt him in the days ahead and redefine the race moving forward. The president was widely criticized for seeming disinterested, distracted, unengaged, and even bored. Romney's performance, on the other hand, helped establish credibility for his candidacy and counter images that he did not understand or wasn't sympathetic to the problems facing the American people. The television audience for the first debate was estimated at more than 67 million viewers and nearly every opinion poll in the following days found that viewers believed Romney was the clear winner.

As a result, President Obama's poll numbers fell after the debate, leaving him tied or even trailing Romney in most national surveys. On the day of the first debate, an average of national presidential tracking polls showed Obama was the choice of 49.1 percent of likely voters, while Romney was the choice of 46 percent. By Monday of the following week the Obama-Biden ticket's national average had dropped to 47.9 while Romney-Ryan rose to 47.4. Almost overnight, the race for the White House had become a real contest.

The only vice presidential debate was held on Thursday, October 11 at Centre College in Danville, Kentucky. Fifty-one million viewers watched the faceoff between Vice President Biden and Representative Ryan, far short of the 73 million who had tuned in during 2008 when Biden took on former Alaska Governor Sarah Palin.

The second presidential debate was held on Tuesday, October 16 at Hofstra University in Hempstead, New York. The town hall format focused primarily on domestic affairs, but unlike the first debate, this second conversation included some discussion of foreign policy. Moderator Candy Crowley of CNN asked questions prepared by eighty-two undecided voters from the New York area selected to attend the debate. The stakes were high for both candidates, but especially for Obama, who needed to reclaim lost ground.

With a TV viewing audience of nearly 66 million people, this time the president was significantly more aggressive toward Governor Romney. Among the most notable

13.1

13.2

13.3

13.4

> *No Person except a natural born Citizen, or a Citizen of the United States, at the time of the Adoption of this Constitution, shall be eligible to the Office of President; neither shall any Person be eligible to that Office who shall not have attained to the Age of thirty five Years, and been fourteen Years a Resident within the United States.* —ARTICLE II, SECTION 1, CLAUSE 4

This provision of Article II is referred to as the presidential eligibility clause. It requires that the president be a natural-born citizen, at least thirty-five years old, and a resident of the United States for at least fourteen years. The Framers believed that each of these requirements was necessary to have a reasoned, respected chief executive who was loyal to the United States and familiar with its internal politics. In the 1700s, for example, it was not uncommon for a diplomat to spend years outside the country; without air travel and instantaneous communication, it was easy to become detached from politics at home.

In recent years, however, much of the controversy swirling around this section of the Constitution has centered on the natural-born citizen clause. Successful politicians from both sides of the aisle have been born outside the United States and are thus ineligible to serve as president, even if they have become naturalized citizens.

The natural-born citizen clause was also the subject of much controversy during and following the 2008 presidential election. Some observers questioned the circumstances surrounding the birth of President Barack Obama and wondered if this made him ineligible to serve as president of the United States. Obama was born in Hawaii to an American mother and a Kenyan father. Some critics claimed that his father's British lineage (Kenya was a colony of Great Britain at the time of Obama's birth) governed his citizenship and therefore that he should be ineligible to serve as president. Other critics argued that Obama's birth certificate was inauthentic, even though his official birth certificate filed with the Hawaii Department of Health had been validated.

Even after Obama had spent two years as president, in mid-2010, 27 percent of Americans and 41 percent of Republicans said they did not believe the president was "born in the United States."[a] To attempt to silence the cries of these so-called "birthers," in April 2011, President Obama released to the media a certified copy of his certificate of live birth. However, some Americans still rejected the validity of this birth certificate; the state of Arizona, for example, required that the birth certificate be validated again before the president's name could appear on that state's ballot during the 2012 presidential election.

CRITICAL THINKING QUESTIONS

1. **Are the Framers' concerns about birth and residency as relevant today as they were 200 years ago? Why or why not?**
2. **What documents, if any, should a potential presidential candidate have to present to prove age and citizenship?**

[a]CNN Poll, August 4, 2010, http://politicalticker.blogs.cnn.com/2010/08/04/cnn-poll-quarter-doubt-president-was-born-in-u-s/

quotes by the candidates during the second debate was an oddly phrased statement by Romney that as governor of Massachusetts he has requested and received "binders full of women" qualified to serve in his administration. The phrase was perceived by some as insensitive to women and became widely parodied on the Internet. The general consensus following the second debate was that President Obama's performance was substantially better than in the first debate; most polls agreed.

The final presidential debate was held at Lynn University in Boca Raton, Florida on Monday, October 22. Of the three debates, it was the least watched, with a television viewing audience estimated at 59.2 million. The candidates sat together at a table and veteran CBS correspondent Bob Schieffer moderated the debate. It was planned that the last debate would focus exclusively on foreign policy—and while the candidates did spend much of the time discussing foreign policy issues such as the attack on the U.S. consulate in Benghazi, Libya, the Arab Spring, the Syrian civil war, and Iran's nuclear program—both candidates also used the setting to raise various points about their domestic economic plans on job creation, education, and the national deficit.

As in the second debate, the president was more aggressive, and polls following the debate again suggested that President Obama had outperformed Governor Romney. The Obama campaign, however, appeared to have made only marginal progress in recovering from his disastrous showing in the first debate. Neither candidate showed any significant signs of momentum heading into the final weeks of the campaign, though both sides proclaimed publicly that they were headed to victory. Polls reflected that the race was within the margin of error, with Romney recording a slight lead of 47.9 percent to Obama's 47 percent three days after their final joint appearance on national television.

THE FINAL DAYS Heading into the final push, key swing states such as Colorado, Virginia, New Hampshire, Ohio, Florida, and Wisconsin remained too evenly split for most national polls and news organizations to predict a clear advantage for either candidate, but a natural disaster lingering on the horizon would make a profound difference. Hurricane Sandy had been churning off the Eastern Seaboard of the United States for nearly a week. With landfall imminent, both campaigns were forced to cancel events in Virginia, North Carolina, and the Washington, D.C. area to avoid the appearance of campaigning while a storm lingered, and also to ensure that campaign events did not cause law enforcement and other first responders to be diverted from storm preparation efforts.

One week before Election Day, the megastorm slammed into Atlantic City, New Jersey and the Delmarva Peninsula on Monday, October 29. In terms of size, Hurricane Sandy was one of the largest to strike the United States in modern recorded history. At

HOW DO CANDIDATES REACH OUT TO VOTERS FOR SUPPORT?

Candidates hold large speeches, rallies and events in an attempt to energize potential supporters. Here, President Obama speaks to a gathering in Madison, Wisconsin, in the weeks before the election.

the time of impact, it stretched over 900 miles, an area twice the size of Texas, creating torrential downpours and severe flooding in New York, New Jersey, Virginia, Maryland, Connecticut, Delaware, Maine, Pennsylvania, Vermont, North Carolina, and Rhode Island, along with blizzard conditions and more than two feet of snow in parts of West Virginia, Kentucky, and Tennessee. The full economic impact of the storm would not be realized for months, but most estimates placed the damages well over $50 billion.

The aftermath of the storm created political odd couples just six days before the election, as President Obama toured flood-ravaged areas of the New Jersey coast with that state's Republican Governor Chris Christie, who had advocated against the president's reelection during the Republican convention and throughout the general election campaign. But in the aftermath of the storm, the Republican governor greeted the Democratic president with open arms, welcoming him to the Garden State to assess the damages, and praising the president's efforts to cut through government bureaucracy to deliver timely assistance to the people of New Jersey.

The national spotlight was on President Obama throughout the closing days of the campaign as he traveled from one area to another, examining the damage of the storm. Meanwhile, there was virtually nothing the Romney campaign could do to gain similar attention. Both campaigns suspended partisan campaign events for days after the storm struck, converting what would have been political rallies into "storm relief events" with Romney joining his supporters to collect and pack supplies for delivery to the American Red Cross. Eventually, but with just days remaining until Americans went to the polls, the focus of the national media returned to politics.

☐ Election Results and Analysis

On election night, even as the first returns and exit polls were announced from states in Eastern and Central time zones, it was not immediately clear which candidate would win. Early in the evening, Romney received welcome news when networks projected him as the winner in Indiana, a state that Barack Obama had carried in 2008. Romney's Electoral College totals remained ahead of Obama's for more than two hours after most polling stations closed on the East Coast, but many of the early battleground states there remained too close to call based on early precinct reporting (see Figure 13.4).

The first sign of trouble for the Republicans came just after 9:00 PM Eastern when major news networks projected that Romney would lose in Michigan. Romney had campaigned hard against the Obama bailout of the automobile industry, and few expected him to carry Michigan, despite the fact that he had once lived in the state and his father had served as the state's 43rd governor. Still the results in Michigan were seen as a likely indicator of how Romney might be received in other auto-industry states such as Wisconsin and Ohio.

Fifteen minutes later, Pennsylvania, where Romney had made an eleventh-hour push for support, was projected for Obama. That was quickly followed by declarations that Wisconsin and New Hampshire would also go to the president. As the hours passed, the 2012 map began to look very similar to 2008, as Obama won victories in each of the key battleground states with two exceptions—Indiana and North Carolina—which were called for Romney just after 11:00 PM Eastern. But, the race effectively ended when Ohio was placed in the Democratic column; Obama was projected to have accumulated enough Electoral College votes to win reelection as president of the United States.

Governor Romney held off on conceding the election until after midnight. By then the major networks were projecting that Obama would also take the electoral votes in Colorado, Nevada, and Virginia. Only Florida remained uncalled, and it would be days before official results would be tabulated due to polling glitches and the prolonged process of counting of absentee and provisional ballots primarily in Miami-Dade County—the same county that had encountered problems during the 2000 presidential election. Unlike 2000, however, the final outcome did not hinge on results from the Sunshine State. The only question that remained unanswered on election night was Obama's margin of victory. Romney delivered a gracious concession speech

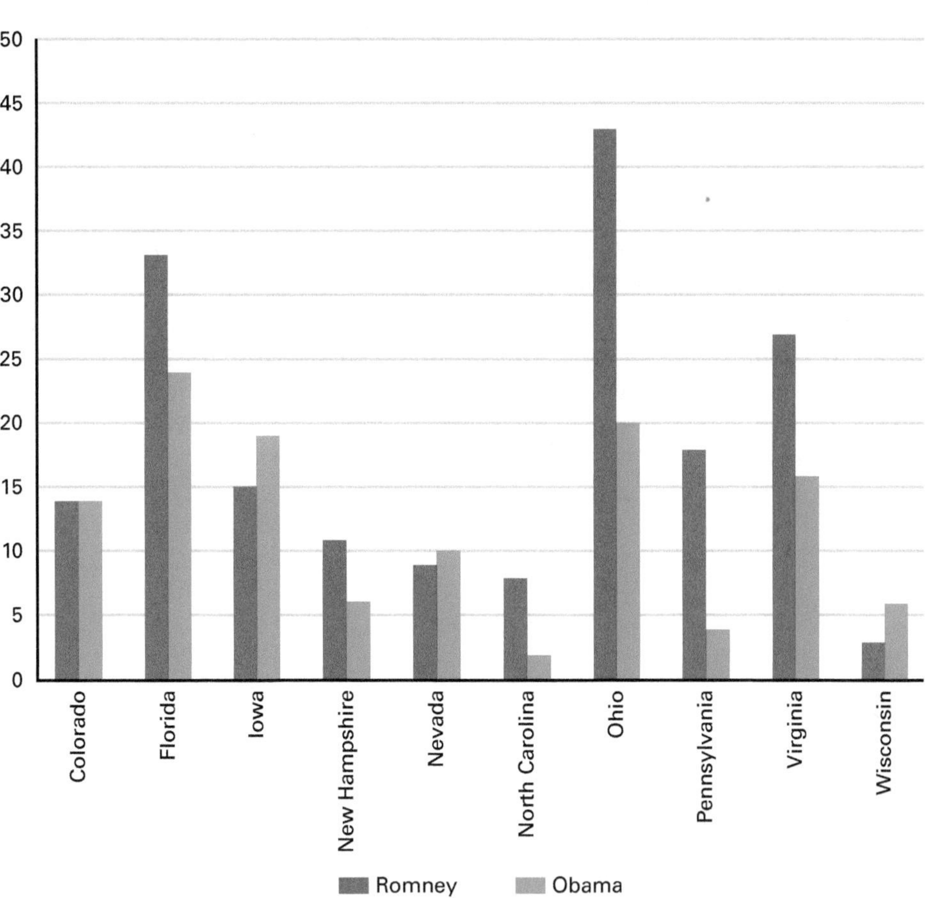

FIGURE 13.4 WHICH STATES WERE THE FOCUS OF THE 2012 PRESIDENTIAL CAMPAIGN?

The majority of candidate visits were concentrated on a small number of swing states that were viewed as up for grabs in the 2012 presidential election. During the campaign, President Obama visited the above ten battleground states 131 times and Mitt Romney visited them 179 times. The remaining 40 states received Obama 81 times and Romney 106 times.

SOURCE: Data from http://www.cnn.com/election/2012/campaign-tracker/.

in front of supporters in Boston. President Obama, whose campaign slogan had been "Forward" followed with his victory speech in Chicago promising supporters, "the best is yet to come."

When polls in the remaining states closed and all the final tallies were in, Obama's victory in the Electoral College was 332 to Romney's 206. It stood as a substantial win—largely due to the support of women, minority, and young voters—though smaller than his landslide victory in 2008.

In the end, it was a slight, unexpected lift provided by Hurricane Sandy that pushed President Obama to victory in the 2012 election. President Obama won the key swing states of Ohio, Colorado, Iowa, Nevada, New Hampshire, Florida, and Virginia, and kept Wisconsin in the Democratic column despite Romney's selection of Representative Paul Ryan as his running mate. Though President Obama received some 8 million fewer votes in 2012 than in 2008 and his Electoral College victory was smaller, the Romney campaign won back only two of the states that voted for Barack Obama in 2008.

The 2012 campaign was a roller-coaster ride for both the candidates and public, especially after Governor Romney dramatically outshone President Obama in the first debate in Denver on October 3. Yet for a challenger to defeat an incumbent, the challenger must deliver game-changing performances again and again, and no challenger has a bully pulpit like that of a sitting president. Ten days before the election, no one could have imagined that a late-season hurricane would play such a dramatic role in the presidential election, or that it would act as a circuit breaker for the Republicans'

13.1

13.2

13.3

13.4

momentum. Not only did the storm cause unprecedented damage along the East Coast and throughout much of New England, but it also pushed Romney off center stage in the last critical days of the campaign, enabling President Obama to dominate as presidential comforter-in-chief, assisted by his new bipartisan friend, Republican Governor Chris Christie.

Adding to the president's good fortune was a final jobs report the Friday before the election that proved helpful only because it wasn't disastrously bad. It showed the unemployment rate failed to jump back above the psychologically damaging level of 8 percent. Had the number been higher, Governor Romney could have used that number to build a crescendo for change. Instead, the final potential obstacle to Obama's reelection passed by as a one-day story. While Governor Romney surged after the first debate, he never quite closed the deal in enough of the key swing states and simply ran out of time.

Review the Chapter

 **Listen** to **Chapter 13** on **MyPoliSciLab**

Roots of Modern Political Campaigns

13.1 Trace the evolution of political campaigns in the United States, p. 393.

In modern campaigns, there is a predictable pathway toward office that involves nomination and general election campaign strategy. At the nomination phase, it is essential for candidates to secure the support of party identifiers, interest groups, and political activists. In the general election, the candidates must focus on the voters and defining their candidacy in terms acceptable to a majority of voters in the district or state.

Assembling a Campaign Staff

13.2 Assess the role of candidates and their staff in the campaign process, p. 396.

The candidate makes appearances, meets voters, raises funds, holds press conferences, gives speeches, and is ultimately responsible for conveying the campaign message and for the success of the campaign. The candidate relies on a campaign manager, professional staff, and political consultants to coordinate the strategy and message of his or her campaign. Volunteer support is also particularly important for mobilizing citizens and getting out the vote.

Raising Money

13.3 Evaluate the ways campaigns raise money, p. 401.

Since the 1970s, campaign financing has been governed by the terms of the Federal Election Campaign Act (FECA). This act was amended in 2002 by the Bipartisan Campaign Reform Act (BCRA). BCRA regulates political advertising and funding from a number of sources from which campaigns raise money. Recently, the Supreme Court has begun to chip away at some of the key tenets of the act. In 2010, the Court in *Citizens United* v. *FEC* declared unconstitutional BCRA's ban on electioneering communications made by corporations and unions, opening the way for an increase in the power of interest groups and corporations in campaigns and elections.

Reaching Voters

13.4 Identify the ways campaigns use the media to reach potential voters, p. 406.

Candidates and campaigns rely on three main strategies for reaching voters: traditional media coverage (newspapers, magazines, TV, and radio), new media coverage (Internet, blogs, and social media sites), and paid campaign advertisements. Traditional media coverage is the most difficult for candidates to control.

Toward Reform: The 2012 Presidential Campaign

13.5 Analyze the 2012 presidential campaign, p. 410.

Incumbent President Barack Obama was unchallenged for the 2012 Democratic nomination for president, while Mitt Romney emerged as the winner of a contentious Republican primary process. Nevertheless, polls indicated that the race for the presidency was consistently within the margin of error. But, the week before Election Day, a disastrous hurricane struck the Eastern Seaboard, putting the president on center stage. With the exception of Indiana and North Carolina, President Obama won reelection with exactly the same states he won in 2008 and largely with the same coalition he had assembled four years earlier.

Learn the Terms

 **Study** and **Review** the **Flashcards**

501(c) group, p. 404
527 political committee, p. 404
campaign consultant, p. 400
campaign manager, p. 397
communications director, p. 400
contrast ad, p. 410
finance chair, p. 398
general election campaign, p. 394
get-out-the-vote (GOTV), p. 400
independent expenditures, p. 404
inoculation ad, p. 410
matching funds, p. 404
negative ad, p. 410
nomination campaign, p. 393
political action committee (PAC), p. 403
pollster, p. 400
positive ad, p. 410
press secretary, p. 400
public funds, p. 404
Super PACs, p. 404
voter canvass, p. 400

Test Yourself

 **Study** and **Review** the **Practice Tests**

1. One of the primary dangers of the nomination campaign is that

a. candidates can become overly cautious and not talk about issues.
b. many candidates ignore their ideological base.
c. candidates may raise too much money.
d. candidates may attract too much media coverage.
e. candidates can become too ideologically extreme.

2. How do candidates generally position themselves ideologically during a general election campaign?

a. Moving to the extreme right or left of their party's identified voters
b. Gaining the support of niche groups to build a coalition
c. Taking positions held by third-party candidates
d. Becoming more ideologically moderate
e. Crossing over to take a wide range of issues held by members of the other party

3. The head of a political campaign is usually called the

a. campaign consultant.
b. political manager.
c. campaign manager.
d. political strategist.
e. political insider.

4. A campaign consultant responsible for assembling public opinion data is known as a

a. finance chair.
b. pollster.
c. direct mail consultant.
d. communications director.
e. campaign manager.

5. Most candidates receive a majority of their campaign contributions from

a. individuals.
b. PACs.
c. one of the political parties.
d. a combination of parties and PACs.
e. foreign corporations

6. Which of the following are not limited by the FEC disclosure rules?

a. Individual expenditures
b. Political parties
c. Independent expenditures
d. PACs
e. Member-to-member donations

7. One of the strategies that campaigns use to control the media is

a. making the candidate more available to the press
b. staging media events
c. ignoring Internet attacks.
d. appearing on the major networks' nightly news shows.
e. holding unrehearsed, spontaneous press conferences.

8. Ads that compare candidates' positions to those of their opponents are known as:

a. negative ads.
b. inoculation ads.
c. free ads.
d. contrast ads.
e. positive ads.

9. During the 2012 presidential elections:

a. The presumptive Republican nominee faced little opposition for the party's nomination.

b. Barack Obama held an early and sustained lead in the Republican primaries.

c. Mitt Romney faced no opposition for the Democratic Party's nomination in 2012.

d. Three different Republican candidates won the first three states in the primary contests.

e. President Barack Obama won all three presidential debates against Mitt Romney.

10. In 2012, Barack Obama:

a. Built a winning coalition of white men, evangelical Christians, and wealthy Americans.

b. Carried all of the swing states on Election Day.

c. Lost campaign momentum due to Hurricane Sandy.

d. Asked Vice President Joe Biden to step aside as his running mate.

e. Lost the support of only two states he had carried in 2008.

Explore Further

Abrajano, Marisa. *Campaigning to the New American Electorate: Advertising to Latino Voters*. Palo Alto, CA: Stanford University Press, 2011.

Baker, Fred W. *Political Campaigns and Political Advertising: A Media Literacy Guide.* Santa Barbara, CA: Greenwood, 2009.

Brewer, Mark D., and L. Sandy Maisel. *The Parties Respond: Changes in American Parties and Campaigns,* 5th ed. Boulder, CO: Westview Press, 2012.

Burton, Michael John, and Daniel M. Shea. *Campaign Craft: The Strategies, Tactics, and Art of Political Campaign Management,* 4th ed. Westport, CT: Praeger, 2010.

Campbell, James E. *The American Campaign: U.S. Presidential Campaigns and the National Vote,* 2nd ed. College Station: Texas A&M University Press, 2008.

Erikson, Robert S., and Christopher Wlezien. *The Timeline of Presidential Elections: How Campaigns Do (and Do Not) Matter.* Chicago: University of Chicago Press, 2012.

Johnson, Dennis W. *No Place for Amateurs: How Political Consultants Are Reshaping American Democracy,* 2nd ed. New York: Routledge, 2007.

Karpf, David. *The MoveOn Effect: The Unexpected Transformation of Political Advocacy.* New York: Oxford University Press, 2012.

Nelson, Candice J., and James A. Thurber. *Campaigns and Elections American Style,* 3rd ed. Boulder, CO: Westview Press, 2009.

Panagopoulos, Costas. *Politicking Online: The Transformation of Election Campaign Communications.* New Brunswick, NJ: Rutgers University Press, 2009.

Sabato, Larry J. *Pendulum Swing.* New York: Pearson, 2011.

Skewes, Elizabeth A. *Message Control: How News Is Made on the Presidential Campaign Trail.* Lanham, MD: Rowman and Littlefield, 2007.

Trent, Judith S., and Robert V. Friedenberg. *Political Campaign Communication: Principles and Practices,* 7th ed. Westport, CT: Praeger, 2011.

Vavreck, Lynn. *The Message Matters: The Economy and Presidential Campaigns.* Princeton, NJ: Princeton University Press, 2009.

West, M. Darrell. *Air Wars: Television Advertising in Election Campaigns 1952–2008,* 5th ed. Washington, DC: CQ Press, 2009.

To learn more about campaign financing, go to the Federal Election Commission at **www.fec.gov**.

To learn more about the 2012 U.S. political campaigns, go to *Politico* at **www.politico.com/2012/**.

To learn more about presidential campaign commercials, go to the Living Room Candidate at **www.livingroomcandidate.org**.

To learn more about campaign Web sites, go to the Library of Congress at **lcweb2.loc.gov/diglib/lcwa.**

14

Listen to Chapter 14 on MyPoliSciLab

The News Media

Campaign fund-raising? There's an app for that. Counting electoral votes? There's an app for that. Aggregating, sharing, and organizing political news? There's an app for that, too.

The Internet, smartphones, and social media have transformed many aspects of Americans' lives, and politics is no exception. Gone are the days of the weekly, and even daily, news cycle. In the modern world, political news is happening—and being reported—almost instantaneously. No longer do newspaper publishers have to typeset every individual letter, as they did in the earliest days of the republic. No longer do journalists file daily reports to be aired on the nightly news, well after a campaign event has occurred. Instead, reporters can post live Twitter updates, complete with photos, tips, and even video, as a campaign event is occurring.

Even the way citizens consume their news has changed. The newspaper, once the lifeblood of American democracy, was supplanted by TV news in the 1960s. Today, TV is still the most popular news source for all Americans, but the Internet is gaining rapidly, even outpacing TV among the youngest Americans. Large percentages of Americans, moreover, report getting political news not only on their computers but also on smartphones and tablets. In an average day, one-quarter of Americans will access news on two or more digital devices.[1]

These changes in the production and consumption of news have affected the way that newsmakers organize their public relations strategies and staffs. Nearly all congressional candidates in 2012 maintained Web sites; most include audio and video Web links. Political leaders maintain Facebook and Twitter sites to stay in touch with their constituents and monitor public opinion. And, with the advent of narrowcasting and infotainment, political leaders can choose to appear in a greater variety of venues than ever before.

While these changes result in many positives for American democracy, and may serve to engage traditionally underserved populations, they also can have negative consequences. As we will discuss throughout this chapter, allowing citizens to become too close to their leaders may

14.1 Trace the historical development of the news media in the United States, p. 427.

14.2 Characterize four major trends in the news media today, p. 433.

14.3 Summarize the ethical standards and federal regulations that govern the news media, p. 439.

14.4 Assess how the news media cover politics, p. 442.

14.5 Evaluate the influence of the news media on public policy and the impact of media bias, p. 445.

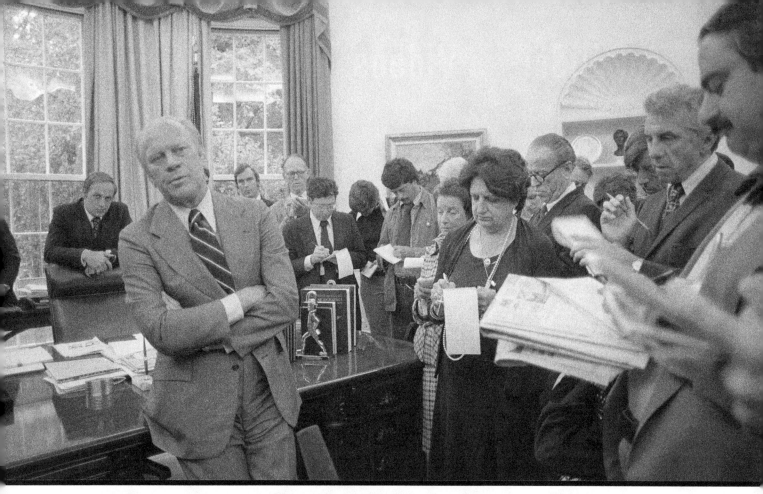

THE MEDIA ACT AS AN INTERMEDIARY BETWEEN CITIZENS AND GOVERNMENT Above, newspaper reporters take pen and paper notes while interviewing President Gerald Ford in the Oval Office during the 1970s. Below, covering the campaign of President Barack Obama in 2012 was a multimedia experience; smartphones and tablet computers were essential tools for any member of the press corps.

In Context Trace the evolution of media outlets from newspapers to the new media that exists today. In this video, University of Oklahoma political scientist Tyler Johnson examines the history of media outlets and the effect of both traditional and new media on the political information and messages that reach the public.

Thinking Like a Political Scientist How does the media shape public opinion? In this video, University of Oklahoma political scientist Tyler Johnson discusses how media framing works and what market factors are influencing this process.

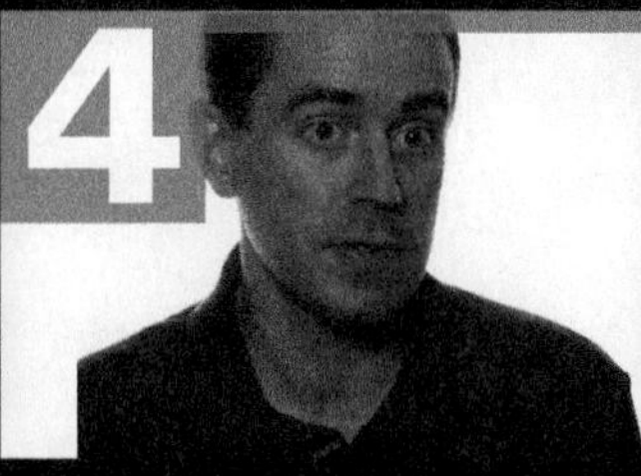

In the Real World What is the ideal relationship between the government and the media? Real people consider whether leaks of confidential government information to the press is good for democracy or whether leaks give the government too much control over the stories being told in the newspapers

So What? Find out what the government is doing behind closed doors. Author Alixandra B. Yanus explains what the role of the media in American politics has been, and considers why it is easier than ever before to be informed about and engaged in the news.

remove some of the filter that the Framers deliberately imposed on the political system. Giving average citizens a glimpse inside the process may strip away too much of the veneer from policy making, leading to disillusionment with government and leaders. And, moving from professional journalists publishing on clear deadlines to a world of citizen journalists and nearly constant updates may weaken the media's traditional watchdog role and adherence to journalistic standards.

•••

The Framers agreed that a free press was necessary to monitor government and ensure the continuation of a democratic society, a tenet they codified in the First Amendment to the U.S. Constitution. Throughout history, the press has fulfilled this watchdog role, acting as an intermediary between citizens and their government. The news media inform the public, giving citizens the information they need to choose their leaders and influence the direction of public policy. As this chapter will discuss, the way the media interact with and report on these political leaders can also significantly influence individuals' views of political issues.

The news media's impact on American politics is so important that it has often been called the "fourth estate," a term harkening back to the British Parliament and implying an integral role for the press in government. This so-called fourth estate comprises a variety of entities, from traditional local news outlets to growing media corporations, and, increasingly, average citizens. It is evident in all facets of American life, from morning newspapers to nightly comedy news shows.

Though the form of the news media has changed significantly since our nation's founding, the media's informational and watchdog roles remain. This chapter traces the development of the news media in the United States, explores recent developments affecting the media, and considers how these changes influence politics and government.

mass media
The entire array of organizations through which information is collected and disseminated to the general public.

news media
Media providing the public with new information about subjects of public interest.

Roots of the News Media in the United States

14.1 Trace the historical development of the news media in the United States.

The **mass media**—the entire array of organizations through which information is collected and disseminated to the general public—have become a colossal enterprise in the United States. The mass media include print sources, movies, TV, radio, and Internet-based material. Collectively, the mass media use broadcast, cable, satellite, and broadband technologies to distribute information that reaches every corner of the United States and the world. A powerful tool for both entertaining and educating the public, they reflect American society but are also the primary lens through which citizens view American culture and politics. The **news media,** one component of the larger mass media, provide new information about subjects of public interest and play a vital role in the political process.[2] Although often referred to as a large, impersonal whole, the media are made up of diverse personalities and institutions, and they form a spectrum of opinion. Through the various outlets composing the news media—from newspapers to social media sites—journalists inform the public, influence public opinion, and affect the direction of public policy in our democratic society.

Throughout American history, technological advances have had a major impact on the way in which Americans receive their news. High-speed presses and more cheaply produced paper made mass-circulation daily newspapers possible. The telegraph and then the telephone enabled easier and much faster newsgathering. When radio became widely available in the 1920s, millions of Americans could hear national politicians instead of merely reading about them. With TV—first introduced in the late 1940s, and nearly a universal fixture in U.S. homes by the early 1960s—citizens could see and hear political candidates and presidents. Now, with the rise of the Internet, access to information has once again changed form. Never before has information been more widely available, and never have the lines between news producer and consumer been less clear.

☐ Print Media

The first example of news media in America took the form of newspapers, which were published in the colonies as early as 1690. The number of newspapers grew throughout the 1700s, as colonists began to realize the value of a press free from government oversight and censorship. The battle between Federalists and Anti-Federalists over ratification of the Constitution played out in various partisan newspapers in the late eighteenth century. Thus, it came as no surprise that one of the Anti-Federalists' demands was a constitutional amendment guaranteeing freedom of the press.

The partisan press eventually gave way to the penny press. In 1833, Benjamin Day founded the *New York Sun,* which cost a penny at the newsstand. Beyond its low price, the *Sun* sought to expand its audience by freeing itself from the grip of a single political party. Inexpensive and politically independent, the *Sun* was the forerunner of modern newspapers, which relied on mass circulation and commercial advertising to produce profit. By 1861, the penny press had so supplanted partisan papers that President Abraham Lincoln announced his administration would have no favored or sponsored newspaper.

Although the print media were becoming less partisan, they were not necessarily gaining in respectability. Mass-circulation dailies sought wide readership, attracting customers with the sensational and the scandalous. The sordid side of politics became the entertainment of the times. One of the best-known examples occurred in the presidential campaign of 1884, when the *Buffalo Evening Telegraph* headlined "A Terrible Tale" about Grover Cleveland, the Democratic nominee.[3] The story alleged that Cleveland, an unmarried man, had fathered a child in 1871, while sheriff of Buffalo, New York. Even though paternity was indeterminate because the child's mother had been seeing other men, Cleveland willingly accepted responsibility, since all the other men were married, and he dutifully paid child support for years. The strict Victorian moral code that dominated American values at the time made the story even more shocking than it would be today. Fortunately for Cleveland, another newspaper, the *Democratic Sentinel,* broke a story that helped offset this scandal: The

Stock Montage, Inc./Historical Pictures Collection

DID THE PRACTICE OF YELLOW JOURNALISM CONTRIBUTE TO THE RISE OF OBJECTIVE JOURNALISM?

In this 1898 cartoon titled "Uncle Sam's Next Campaign—the War Against the Yellow Press," yellow journalism is attacked for its threats, insults, filth, grime, blood, death, slander, gore, and blackmail. The cartoon was published in the wake of the Spanish-American War, and the cartoonist suggests that, having won the war abroad, the government ought to attack yellow journalists at home.

first child of Republican presidential nominee James G. Blaine and his wife had been born just three months after their wedding.

Throughout the nineteenth century, payoffs to the press were common. Andrew Jackson, for instance, gave one in ten of his early appointments to loyal reporters.[4] During the 1872 presidential campaign, the Republicans slipped cash to about 300 newsmen.[5] Wealthy industrialists also sometimes purchased investigative cease-fires for tens of thousands of dollars.

In the late 1800s and early 1900s, prominent publishers such as William Randolph Hearst and Joseph Pulitzer expanded the reach of newspapers in their control by practicing what became pejoratively known as **yellow journalism,** perhaps because both Hearst and Pulitzer published a popular cartoon of the era called "The Yellow Kid." Yellow journalism featured pictures, comics, color, and sensationalized news coverage. These innovations were designed to increase readership and capture a share of the burgeoning immigrant population.

The Progressive movement gave rise to a new type of journalism in the early 1920s. **Muckraking** journalists—so named by President Theodore Roosevelt after a special rake designed to collect manure—devoted themselves to exposing misconduct by government, business, and individual politicians.[6] For Roosevelt, muckraking was a derogatory term used to describe reporters who focused on the carnal underbelly of politics rather than its more lofty pursuits. Nevertheless, much good came from these efforts. Muckrakers stimulated demands for anti-trust regulations—laws that prohibit companies, such as large steel companies, from controlling an entire industry—and exposed deplorable working conditions in factories, as well as outright exploitation of workers by business owners. An unfortunate side effect of this emphasis on crusades and investigations, however, was the frequent publication of gossip and rumor without sufficient proof.

As the news business grew, so did the focus on increasing its profitability. Newspapers became more careful and less adversarial in their reporting, to avoid alienating the advertisers and readers who produced their revenues. Clearer standards were applied in evaluating the behavior of people in power. Journalism also changed during this period as the industry became more professionalized. Reporters learned to adhere to principles of objectivity and balance and to be motivated by a never-ending quest for the "truth."[7]

More recently, faced by an onslaught of competing forms of media, including radio, TV, and the Internet, newspapers have struggled to maintain their circulation. Though some print dailies have moved to online-print hybrids or have created subscription-only Web sites to monetize their content, other papers have failed to adapt to the changing news environment. Since 2007, almost twenty major daily newspapers have completely ended their operations. Others, such as the *New Orleans Times-Picayune*, have eliminated less profitable publication days and gone to a three-day-a-week model, publishing only on Sunday, Wednesday, and Friday. The consequences of these changes for citizens' political knowledge—particularly among older Americans least likely to use new technology—remain to be seen.

yellow journalism

A form of newspaper publishing in vogue in the late nineteenth century that featured pictures, comics, color, and sensationalized news coverage.

muckraking

A form of journalism, in vogue in the early twentieth century, devoted to exposing misconduct by government, business, and individual politicians.

☐ Radio News

The advent of radio in the early twentieth century was a media revolution and a revelation to the average American, who rarely, if ever, had heard the voice of a president, governor, or senator. The radio became the center of most homes in the evening, when national networks broadcast the news as well as entertainment shows. Calvin Coolidge was the first president to speak on radio on a regular basis, but President Franklin D. Roosevelt made the radio broadcast a must-listen by presenting "fireside chats" to promote his New Deal.

News radio, which had begun to take a back seat to TV by the mid-1950s, regained popularity with the advent of AM talk radio in the mid-1980s. Controversial radio host Rush Limbaugh began the trend with his unabashedly conservative views, opening the door for other conservative commentators such as Laura Ingraham, Sean Hannity, and Glenn Beck. Statistics show that these conservative radio hosts resurrected the radio as

Congress shall make no law respecting an establishment of religion, or prohibiting the free exercise thereof; or abridging the freedom of speech, or of the press; or the right of the people peaceably to assemble, and to petition the Government for a redress of grievances. —FIRST AMENDMENT

The Framers knew that democracy is not easy, that a republic requires a continuous battle for rights and responsibilities. One of those rights is freedom of the press, preserved in the First Amendment to the Constitution. The Framers' view of the press, and its required freedom, however, was almost certainly less broad than our conception of press freedom today.

It is difficult to appreciate what a leap of faith it was for the Framers to grant freedom of the press when James Madison brought the Bill of Rights before Congress. Newspapers were largely run by disreputable people, since at the time editors and reporters were judged as purveyors of rumor and scandal.

But, the printed word was one of the few modes of political communication in the young nation—it was critical for keeping Americans informed about issues. Therefore, the Framers hoped that giving the press freedom to print all content, although certain to generate sensational stories, would also produce high-quality, objective reporting.

Not much has changed since the Framers instituted the free press. We still have tabloids and partisan publications in which politicians attack each other, and we still rely on the press to give us important political information that we use to make voting decisions. The simple, enduring protection the Framers created in the First Amendment continues to make possible the flow of ideas that a democratic society relies upon.

CRITICAL THINKING QUESTIONS

1. **Should TV news, which relies on the spoken word, be afforded the same protections given to the written word? Why or why not?**
2. **How relevant to new media are the guarantees enshrined in the First Amendment? Do bloggers, for example, deserve the same constitutional protections as traditional journalists?**

a news medium by giving a strong ideological bent to the information they broadcast. Yet, most truly liberal political talk radio has struggled. Many liberals turn to National Public Radio (NPR), which receives government funding as well as private donations, and does not air solely political content. It also covers a variety of cultural and socially important issues. Studies of the overall political coverage of NPR, moreover, have failed to find any overt liberal bias.[8]

☐ TV News

TV was first demonstrated in the United States at the 1939 World's Fair in New York, but it did not take off as a news source until after World War II. While most homes had TVs by the early 1960s, it took several years more for TV to replace print and radio as the nation's chief news provider. In 1963, most networks provided just fifteen minutes of news per day; only two major networks devoted thirty minutes to news coverage. During this period, a substantial majority of Americans still received most of their news from newspapers. But, in 2011, most Americans received their news from TV or the Internet; this trend was particularly pronounced among young adults eighteen to twenty-four years old, who got the majority of their news from online sources.[9]

An important distinction exists between network and cable news stations. Network news has lost viewers over time. Cable news, however, has increased in viewership, due in large part to the greater availability of cable and satellite services providing twenty-four-hour news channels. Fox News is the most prominent of these channels, drawing an average of almost 2 million prime-time viewers, more than the next two largest competitors—CNN and MSNBC—combined.[10]

Where Do You Get Your Political News?

Politically interested people get their news from four main news outlets—television, the Internet, print, and radio. Among these media sources, no single one dominates the others, but partisan trends do exist. Republicans more often go to Fox News, while more Democrats go to NPR's "All Things Considered".

Americans Go to These News Sources

TV 93%
Internet 78%
Print 77%
Radio 76%
Blogs/ Social Media 41%

FOX NEWS

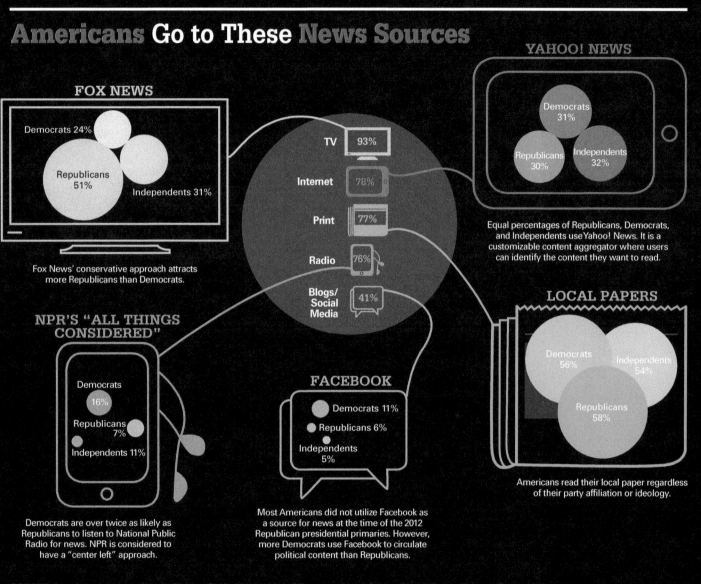

Democrats 24%
Republicans 51%
Independents 31%

Fox News' conservative approach attracts more Republicans than Democrats.

YAHOO! NEWS

Democrats 31%
Republicans 30%
Independents 32%

Equal percentages of Republicans, Democrats, and Independents use Yahoo! News. It is a customizable content aggregator where users can identify the content they want to read.

NPR'S "ALL THINGS CONSIDERED"

Democrats 16%
Republicans 7%
Independents 11%

Democrats are over twice as likely as Republicans to listen to National Public Radio for news. NPR is considered to have a "center left" approach.

FACEBOOK

Democrats 11%
Republicans 6%
Independents 5%

Most Americans did not utilize Facebook as a source for news at the time of the 2012 Republican presidential primaries. However, more Democrats use Facebook to circulate political content than Republicans.

LOCAL PAPERS

Democrats 56%
Independents 54%
Republicans 58%

Americans read their local paper regardless of their party affiliation or ideology.

SOURCE: Data from American National Election Study, "Evaluations of Government and Society Study," Release Wave 4, February 2012.

Investigate Further

Concept Where are people getting their political news? Politically interested Americans go to several types of outlets for political news. Television is still the most popular news source, but the Internet, print, and radio hold substantial ground. Despite widespread popularity among youth, social media—like Facebook—is not a dominant source for political news.

Connection How is politics related to media choices? In general, Americans tend to seek information that reinforces their politics. The rise of cable television and Internet sources compartmentalized information. People can't read or watch all the news, so they choose a few "comfortable" content providers who reinforce their opinions and beliefs.

Cause Do the major party's identifiers exhibit particular media consumption habits? Both parties have certain news sources that they favor over others. For example, Republicans rely more on Fox News while Democrats tend toward NPR's "All Things Considered". However, party crossover in media use does exist, particularly for Internet and social media sources.

Cable and satellite providers also give consumers access to a less glitzy and more unfiltered source of news, C-SPAN, a basic cable channel that offers gavel-to-gavel coverage of congressional proceedings, as well as major political events when Congress is not in session. It also produces some of its own programming, such as *Washington Journal,* which invites scholars and journalists to speak about topics pertaining to their areas of expertise. Because the content of C-SPAN can be erudite, technical, and sometimes downright tedious (such as the fixed camera shot of the Senate during a roll-call vote), audiences tend to be very small, but they are loyal and give C-SPAN its place as a truly content-driven news source.

☐ Online Media

Online media, including Internet news, blogs, and social networking sites, are transforming the relationship between the media and citizens, even challenging our perceptions of what is defined as "media." They also remove many of the traditional filters, such as editors and journalistic standards, which lend credibility to professional news outlets; moreover, they make media more low cost and widely accessible than ever before. The almost instantaneous availability of information through smartphones only enhances these changes.

THE INTERNET The Internet, which began as a Department of Defense project named Advanced Research Projects Agency Network (ARPANET) in the late 1960s, has grown into an unprecedented source of public information for people throughout the world. In 2010, for example, 41 percent of Americans claimed the Internet was their main news source. This percentage—and the diversity of ways that individuals can access information—is growing annually. Smartphone apps and Web sites such as YouTube and Hulu only serve to increase the number of ways individuals can consume news online.[11]

BLOGS Blogs provide an editorial and news outlet for citizens. Increasingly, they are also an opportunity for news organizations to offer updates on emerging news stories, such as the *New York Times* blog, "The Caucus," which gives updates on politics and government. Though blogs often offer more commentary than traditional news sources, they are also important informational tools, linking people with common ideological or issue-specific interests. Most political blogs, for example, are targeted to a sophisticated political elite that is already interested in and knowledgeable about public affairs.

While blogs and their user-generated content seem to offer people a more democratic means of engaging in public discussion, concern is growing that the blogosphere has become dominated by a small elite. Although over 173 million blogs can be found on the Web, only a very small number of sites have a sizeable audience and thus attract most of the advertising dollars available.[12] Moreover, most of the best-known political bloggers are graduates of the nation's top colleges, and many have postgraduate degrees. And, the linking practices common on many blogs and Web sites mean that content produced by the top political bloggers often rises to the top, homogenizing the message received by political sophisticates and policy makers.[13]

SOCIAL MEDIA Social media sites, such as Facebook and Twitter, although not necessarily created to spread political news, have the potential to do just that. More than one-third of the U.S. population has a Facebook page, but as of 2011, fewer than 10 percent of Americans said they often followed Facebook recommendations for news. Politicians and candidates have increasingly realized the growth potential for Facebook to reach citizens and engage them in the political process. During the 2012 election, for example, Facebook was home to a great deal of political debate. Supporters of presidential candidate Barack Obama, especially, established fan pages with millions of Facebook friends. These sites then became ways to organize activists, raise money, and energize young voters.

Many local and national political leaders have also turned to Twitter to reach out to supporters and raise money for political campaigns. President Barack Obama has his own Twitter feeds, @whitehouse and @barackobama, which he uses for presidential and campaign purposes, respectively. In 2011, he used his @whitehouse account to hold an online town hall meeting, something he had previously done using both Facebook and YouTube. During this virtual meeting, the president fielded questions on issues such as national security and the economy, answering citizens' questions with responses that met Twitter's 140-character limit.[14]

With the online service Chirpify, candidates can also use Twitter (like text messaging) as a way to raise instantaneous money for their campaigns. All citizens have to do is set up a profile on Chirpify's site, and then they can make political donations by simply tweeting "Donate $amount to @candidate for Election 2012."[15] The success of the platform fundraising tool has led Chirpify to expand into other online venues, including allowing users to purchase items directly from candidates' or friends' Instagram sites.

Average citizens, too, have used Twitter to spread political news. Users have tweeted from political rallies, offered commentary on the president's State of the Union Address, and used hashtags to mark political issues such as health care, jobs, and the economy as trending topics. Although many "tweeps" may not consider these actions political, they are, in fact, a part of politics.

Sites such as these fundamentally change the media. Politicians can interact directly with citizens, without using reporters and editors as intermediaries. Though this may seem more democratic, critics worry that a growing reliance on social networking sites will weaken the media's role as a filter, educator, and watchdog. They also express increasing concerns that politicians may not engage in deliberative democracy, but may instead make policy decisions designed to placate the mobs of citizens that Madison and the Framers feared would trouble their republican form of government. One commentator, for example, has asked if there would have even been a Constitution if the Framers had tweeted the proceedings of the famously secret Philadelphia Convention.[16]

Current News Media Trends

14.2 Characterize four major trends in the news media today.

A number of ongoing transformations define the news media today. Among these are the growth in corporate ownership and media consolidation; the targeting of programming at specific populations, known as narrowcasting; and infotainment. The people who deliver the news, too, have changed. Media news coverage today increasingly relies both on subject-matter experts and on average citizens.

Taken together, these changes create a news environment in which the boundaries between producers and consumers of news are increasingly blurred. Without the traditional lines of demarcation between news owners and objects of the news, and consumers and producers, the media's informational and watchdog roles are at risk of compromise.

Corporate Ownership and Media Consolidation

Private ownership of the media in the United States has proved to be a mixed blessing. While private ownership ensures media independence, something that cannot be said

Who Owns the News Media?

Since passage of the 1996 Telecommunications Act, media ownership has consolidated. Today, as the figure below indicates, 90 percent of media outlets are owned by just six companies—Comcast, News Corporation, Disney, Viacom, Time Warner, and CBS. This consolidation has consequences for how reporters cover stories, which stories do or do not receive attention, and, by extension, which issues policy makers prioritize.

The Media Has Never Been More Consolidated

1983

In 1983, 90% of American media was owned by 50 companies.

2012

In 2012, that same 90% is controlled by 6 companies.

Comcast owns 15 television stations, NBC, Telemundo, E! Entertainment, NBC Sports, Hulu, and Universal Pictures.

Disney owns 10 television stations, 277 radio stations, ABC, ESPN, A&E, the History Channel, Lifetime, *Discover* Magazine, *Bassmaster* Magazine, Hyperion Publishing, Touchstone Pictures, Pixar Animation, and Miramax Film Corporation.

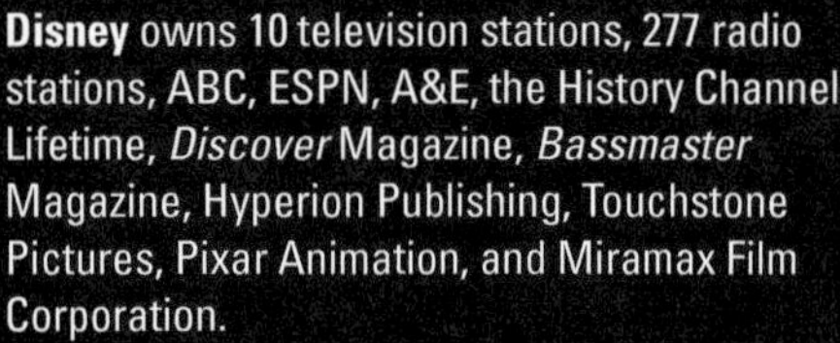

Viacom owns 10 television stations such as Comedy Central, BET, Nickelodeon, TV Land, MTV, VH1, and Paramount Pictures.

CBS owns 30 TV stations, Smithsonian Channel, Showtime, The Movie Channel, and Paramount Network Television.

News Corp. owns 27 television stations, the Fox Network and Fox News Channel, FX, National Geographic Channel, the *Wall Street Journal, TV Guide,* the *New York Post,* DirecTV, HarperCollins Publishers, Twentieth Century Fox, and MySpace.

Time Warner owns HBO, CNN, the Cartoon Network, Warner Bros., *Time* Magazine, Turner Broadcasting, and DC Comics.

SOURCE: Data from Common Cause, www.commoncause.org.

CRITICAL THINKING QUESTIONS

1. How might Comcast's and General Electric's ownership of the NBC family of networks alter the way that reporters with NBC news cover particular stories?
2. What is the next horizon in media consolidation? Do you foresee any of these conglomerates joining together? Why or why not?
3. Should the government take action to end media consolidation? Why or why not?

about state-controlled media in countries such as China, it also brings market pressures to journalism that do not exist in state-run systems. The news media in the United States are multi-billion-dollar, for-profit businesses that ultimately are driven by the bottom line. As with all free market enterprises, the pressure in privately owned media is to increasingly consolidate media ownership, to reap the benefits that come from larger market shares and fewer large-scale competitors.

Consequently, the top six media chains account for more than 90 percent of news media content. Large media conglomerates such as Gannett, Media News Group, and News Corporation own most daily newspapers; fewer than 300 of the approximately 1,400 daily newspapers are independently owned. Only one of the three original TV networks—CBS—remains an independent entity: Comcast owns NBC, and Disney owns ABC. In radio, Cox Communications and Clear Channel far outpace their competitors in terms of both stations and audience.

Unlike traditional industries, in which the primary concern associated with consolidation is price manipulation, consolidation of the media poses far greater potential risks. As the media have increasingly become dominated by a few mega-corporations, observers have grown fearful that these groups could limit the flow of information and ideas that define the essence of a free society and that make democracy possible. These profit-driven media chains, aimed at expanding market shares and pleasing advertisers, may overwhelmingly focus on sensational issues and avoid those that could alienate their audiences, anger executives, or compromise relationships with government regulators. Former *CBS Evening News* anchor Dan Rather, for example, summarizes media consolidation's threat to democracy by saying, "These large corporations, they have things they need from the power structure in Washington, whether it's Republican or Democrat, and of course the people in Washington have things they want the news to report. To put it bluntly, very big business is in bed with very big government in Washington, and has more to do with what the average person sees, hears, and reads than most people know."[17]

narrowcasting
Targeting media programming at specific populations within society.

☐ Narrowcasting

In recent years, fierce competition to attract viewers and the availability of additional TV channels made possible by cable and satellite TV have led media outlets to move toward **narrowcasting**—targeting media programming at specific populations within society. Within the realm of cable news, MSNBC and Fox News are most notable for engaging in this form of niche journalism. The two stations divide audiences by ideology. Fox News emphasizes a conservative viewpoint, and MSNBC stresses a more liberal perspective.

Audiences also divide along partisan lines over other news sources. Republicans, for example, are more likely than Democrats and Independents to listen to AM talk radio.[18] And, while only a small disparity in newspaper reading exists between Republicans and Democrats, newspapers can be categorized by ideology; for instance, the *Washington Times* offers more conservative fare than its rival, the *Washington Post* (see Table 14.1). As a result, political scientists have found that simply knowing where someone gets his or her news can predict party affiliation.[19]

Other narrowcasting targets specific racial, ethnic, or religious groups. Examples include Spanish-language news programs on stations such as Univision and Telemundo, as well as news programming geared toward African American viewers on cable's Black Entertainment Television (BET). For evangelical Christians, Pat Robertson's Christian Broadcasting Network (CBN), with its flagship *700 Club,* has been narrowcasting news for over forty years. The rising use of smartphones and mobile apps, too, has helped narrowcasting to grow.

While narrowcasting can promote the interests specific to segments of the population, especially racial and ethnic minorities who may ordinarily be left out of mainstream media coverage, it comes with a social cost. Narrowcasting increases the chance that group members will rely on news that appeals to their preexisting views.

TABLE 14.1 HOW DO MEDIA OUTLETS RELATE TO PARTY AFFILIATION?

Regularly watch/ read/listen to...	Total %	Republican %	Democrat %	Independent %
Local TV news	50	51	54	48
Daily newspaper	40	45	41	38
Community papers	30	35	30	30
Network evening news	28	27	30	27
Fox News	23	40	15	20
Morning shows	20	18	26	17
CNN	18	12	25	17
Sunday morning shows	11	11	13	11
NPR	11	6	14	14
MSNBC	11	6	16	10
News blogs	9	10	10	9
News magazines	8	7	10	8
CNBC	8	6	11	6
The Daily Show	7	4	9	8
Glenn Beck Program	7	14	2	7
The Colbert Report	6	3	7	7
The New York Times	5	2	8	6
Rush Limbaugh Show	5	13	2	4
USA Today	4	6	4	4
Wall Street Journal	4	6	3	5
C-SPAN	4	3	5	3
The Rachel Maddow Show	3	1	4	3

SOURCE: Pew Research Center, "Americans Spend More Time Following News," (September 12, 2010): http://www.people-press.org/2010/09/12/section-1-watching-reading-and-listening-to-the-news/.

By limiting one's exposure to a broad range of information or competing views, narrowcasting could result in further polarization of public opinion. The polarization made possible by narrowcasting is particularly problematic when it comes to programs that are narrowcasted in a specific ideological direction.[20] These broadcasts may result in what has been called the "Fox effect" or the "CNN effect." These effects result when a network chooses an ideologically favorable storyline—true or untrue—to cover almost *ad nauseam*. In so doing, the network sets the agenda both for partisans, who adopt the storyline being sold, and for other news networks, who feel compelled to address the issue.[21]

Narrowcasting also enables political leaders to avoid particularly hard-hitting news reporters. For example, a Republican candidate may avoid the historically tough questions asked by Sunday morning talk shows such as *Meet the Press* and *Face the Nation*, and choose instead to appear on Fox News, which features a more friendly audience and a comparatively easy-going moderator. This strategy may have electoral consequences, as it limits the visibility of such candidates to people who were already likely supporters, but nonetheless is increasingly popular.[22]

☐ Infotainment

Infotainment—or TV programming that blends political news and information with entertainment—has exploded as a way for citizens to engage with the political process. Different forms of infotainment exist, including late night comedy shows, daytime talk shows, and comedy news shows.

Late night comedy shows, such as *Saturday Night Live* and those hosted by Jay Leno and David Letterman, have mocked politicians and the news for years. What is new, however, is that political leaders have embraced these programs as a way to connect with citizens, both on the campaign trail and while in office. During the 2012 presidential campaign, for example, *Saturday Night Live* sketches spoofed a wide variety of political themes, including the presidential debates, uninformed voters, and the government's response to Hurricane Sandy. And, President Barack and First Lady Michelle Obama have appeared on a number of late night talk shows, including the *Late Show with David Letterman* and *Late Night with Jimmy Fallon*. On Fallon's show, President Obama even slow-jammed the news, and the first lady challenged the host to an obstacle course race through the White House.

Daytime talk shows have also entered the political game. The president and first lady have been frequent guests on these programs, on which they have promoted policy initiatives such as the first lady's "Let's Move" campaign. President Obama also announced his 2008 run for the presidency on *The Oprah Winfrey Show*. Even cable news channels have attempted to create shows that follow the talk show format; Fox News's *The Five* is an example of this phenomenon.

Political leaders see many advantages to appearing on late night and talk shows. These soft news programs give politicians an opportunity to reach much larger and more diverse audiences than do Sunday morning talk shows or cable news channels. In addition, the questions asked by hosts of *Live! With Kelly and Michael* or *The Today Show* are often less technical and hard-hitting than those asked by the traditional news media. And, for a charismatic official, such as President Obama or President Bill Clinton, infotainment programs may also provide a venue to humanize the politician and make viewers connect with him or her on a more personal level.

In addition, the emergence of comedy news shows such as Jon Stewart's *The Daily Show* and Stephen Colbert's *The Colbert Report*—which originated as a satire of Fox News's *The O'Reilly Factor*—has also changed the way Americans receive their political news. These shows present news "freed from the media's preoccupation with balance, the fixation with fairness. They have no obligation to deliver the day's most important news, if that news is too depressing, too complicated or too boring. Their sole allegiance is to comedy."[23] As a result, many viewers find news presented by Stewart or Colbert to be more palatable, and more entertaining, than what they might view on a nightly network news show. The shows are especially popular news sources among younger Americans, who are often jaded by the conventions of traditional journalism and politics.

Infotainment, overall, makes political news and events more accessible to Americans. But, research has shown that the effects of infotainment may be clearest for highly attentive citizens. Watching soft news about politics makes sophisticates' political behavior more consistent. In essence, for these people, infotainment acts as an information shortcut that helps them to better remember facts and figures about the governmental process.[24] The effects of infotainment on less sophisticated audiences, however, are not as clear. Some less politically engaged citizens may also fail to find humor in shows like *Saturday Night Live*'s political coverage or *The Daily Show* because they lack the context in which to process the information provided by the programming; these citizens, however, may connect with a show like *The View*.

☐ Increasing Use of Experts

Most journalists know a little bit about many subjects but do not specialize in any one area and certainly do not possess enough knowledge to fill the hours of airtime made possible by cable TV's twenty-four-hour news cycle. Therefore, especially on cable stations, the news media employ expert consultants from a number of different disciplines ranging from medical ethics to political campaigning. These experts, also referred to as pundits, or the more derogatory term "talking heads," are hired to discuss the dominant issues of the day. For example, during the 2012 presidential campaign, one could not turn on the TV or read a newspaper without encountering a stable full of government officials, campaign consultants, former candidates, academics, and other experts giving their thoughts about the upcoming election.

HOW DO EXPERTS INFLUENCE NEWS COVERAGE?
Pundits bring a sense of credibility and experience to their political commentary. However, the reliance on these experts may blur the lines between producers and consumers of news and weaken democratic deliberation. Here, Republican strategist Ed Gillespie and TV host Rachel Maddow appear on *Meet the Press* with David Gregory.

citizen journalists
Ordinary individuals who collect, report, and analyze news content.

Experts have a significant impact on how we view political news stories. One study, for example, finds that "news from experts or research studies is estimated to have almost as great an impact" as anchorpersons, reporters in the field, or special commentators. These "strong effects by commentators and experts are compatible with a picture of a public that engages in collective deliberation and takes expertise seriously."[25]

However, two main concerns arise about the increasing use of experts in news reporting. First, it is unclear how objective these experts are. Many of the pundits on air during the presidential campaign, for example, had ties to one of the two major candidates. Others were political operatives closely connected to the Democratic and Republican parties and to members of Congress. Second, so-called experts may weaken democratic deliberation, even though they are not particularly accurate in their predictions. But, because many pundits have official-sounding titles such as "strategist" or "former administration official," viewers assign privilege to experts' beliefs and do not take time to form their own political opinions. In many cases, the educated evaluations of citizens would be as accurate as the "expert" opinions they hear on TV or read in newspapers.[26]

☐ Citizen Journalists

In the past, only professionals whose occupation was to cover current events filed news reports. Today, however, much of what we call "news" content is written and filmed by amateur **citizen journalists,** ordinary individuals who collect, report, and analyze news content.

Many citizen journalists use the Internet as a way to reach an interested news audience. Sites such as Associated Content may cover a broad range of issues. Other sites, such as local news and politics blogs, focus on niche issues and local events, such as town meetings, school closings, and recycling initiatives, that often are left out of larger publications. Uploading videos to YouTube may also allow citizens to showcase content not covered by traditional news outlets or provide a location to share common experiences, such as natural disasters. Citizens may also tweet narratives or opinions about newsworthy occurrences.

Many traditional news organizations have embraced the value of citizen journalism. In addition to bringing new perspectives—and perhaps new readers and viewers—into the fold, citizen journalists may reach the scene of important events before news crews. Citizen journalism also has financial benefits for traditional news outlets: using citizen coverage and footage is far cheaper than hiring reporters. This can be a way for news outlets to continue offering coverage of a broad range of issues in an era of decreasing budgets.

Media scholars have hotly debated the value of citizen journalism. On one hand, citizen journalism can act as a democratizing force, allowing more people to participate in setting agendas and framing issues. It can also give more instantaneous coverage than traditional media. On the other hand, citizen journalists are often not trained in the rules and standards of journalism. They may not treat their sources with the same respect or fact-check as thoroughly as professional reporters. Perhaps as a result, research has shown that consumers of citizen journalism score lower on political knowledge than those who rely on professional news organizations.[27] Finally, and perhaps most importantly, citizen journalists once again blur the line between producers and consumers of news, compromising the objectivity of news coverage.

on the record
Information provided to a journalist that can be released and attributed by name to the source.

off the record
Information provided to a journalist that will not be released to the public.

on background
Information provided to a journalist that will not be attributed to a named source.

deep background
Information provided to a journalist that will not be attributed to any source.

Rules Governing the News Media

14.3 Summarize the ethical standards and federal regulations that govern the news media.

Professional journalists may obtain and publish information in a number of ways. They are, however, subject to boundaries in this pursuit. Journalists are primarily limited by the ethical standards of their profession. In some cases, additional governmental regulations may apply.

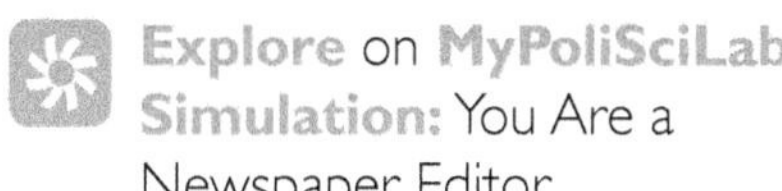
Explore on MyPoliSciLab Simulation: You Are a Newspaper Editor

Journalistic Standards

The heaviest restrictions placed on reporters come from the industry's own professional norms and each journalist's level of integrity, as well as from oversight by editors who are ultimately responsible for the accuracy of the news they produce. To guide the ethical behavior of journalists, the Society of Professional Journalists publishes a detailed "Code of Ethics" that includes principles and standards governing issues such as avoiding conflicts of interest and verifying the information being reported.

One dilemma faced by reporters is how to deal ethically with sources. Informants may speak to reporters in a number of ways. If a session is **on the record,** as in a formal press conference, every word an official utters can be printed. In contrast, a journalist may obtain information **off the record,** which means that nothing the official says may be printed. Reporters may also obtain information **on background**, meaning that none of the information can be attributed to the source by name. Whereas background talks can be euphemistically attributed to sources, such as "unnamed senior officials," information on **deep background** must be completely unsourced, with the reporter giving the reader no hint about the origin. When reporters obtain information in any of these ways, they must take care to respect their source's wishes. Otherwise, not only might that person refuse to talk to them in the future, but other potential sources may do the same.

Journalists also grapple with the competitive nature of the news business. The pressure to get the story right is often weighed against the pressure to get the story first, or at the very least to get it finished before the next deadline. The twenty-four-hour news

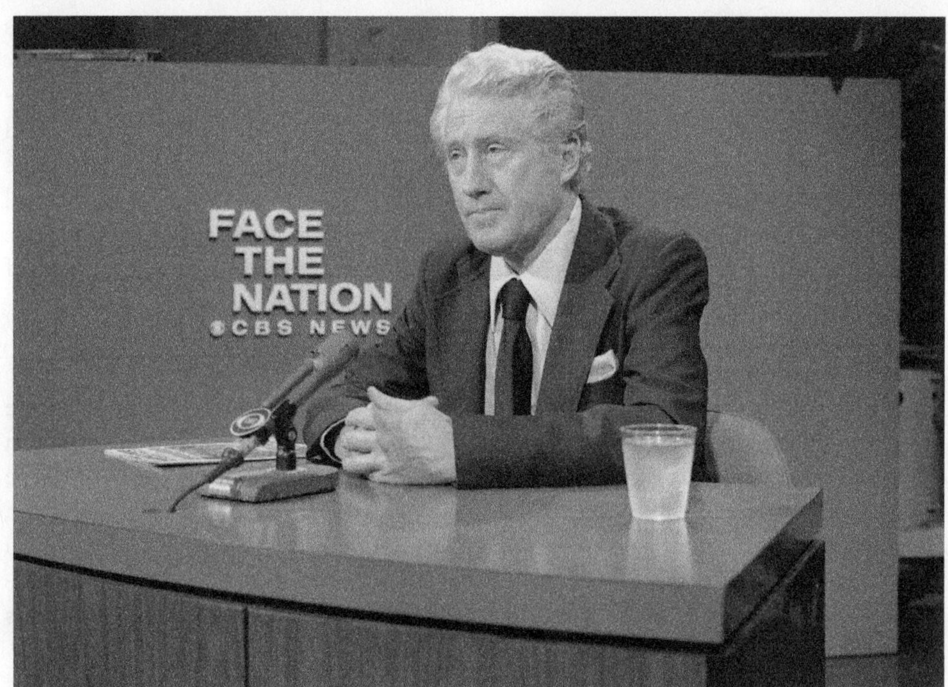

HOW DO JOURNALISTS USE INFORMATION OBTAINED ON DEEP BACKGROUND?

W. Mark Felt, former associate director of the Federal Bureau of Investigation, shown here on *Face the Nation,* spoke to *Washington Post* reporters on deep background during the Watergate scandal. Known only as "Deep Throat," Felt provided information crucial to linking the Richard M. Nixon administration to the break-in at the Watergate Hotel. His true identity was not revealed for more than thirty years, when he went public in 2005.

cycle, brought to life by cable news stations and nourished by the expansion of online media, has heightened the pressure to produce interesting copy in a timely manner.

To ensure professional integrity, several major newspapers and magazines, including the *Washington Post* and the *New York Times,* have hired internal media critics, or ombudsmen, who assess how well their newspaper and its reporters are performing their duties. Some nonprofits, such as the Project for Excellence in Journalism and the Pew Research Center for the People and the Press in Washington, D.C., conduct scientific studies of the news and entertainment media. Other groups, including the conservative watchdog group Accuracy in Media (AIM) and its liberal counterpart Fairness and Accuracy in Reporting (FAIR), critique news stories and attempt to set the record straight on important issues they believe have received biased coverage. All of these organizations have a role in making sure the media treat topics important to citizens in a fair and objective manner.

Government Regulations

The U.S. government regulates media in a number of ways. Some regulations apply to all forms of media. Libel and slander, for example, are illegal in all cases. The Constitution also places a limit on prior restraint—that is, the government may not limit any speech or publications before they actually occur. This principle was clearly affirmed in *New York Times Co.* v. *U.S.* (1971).[28] In this case, the Supreme Court ruled that the government could not prevent publication by the *New York Times* of the Pentagon Papers, classified government documents about the Vietnam War that had been photocopied and sent to the *Times* and the *Washington Post* by Daniel Ellsberg, a government employee. "Only a free and unrestrained press can effectively expose deception in the government," Justice Hugo Black wrote in a concurring opinion for the Court. "To find that the President has 'inherent power' to halt the publication of news by resort to the courts would wipe out the First Amendment."

Government can, however, regulate electronic media such as radio or TV more heavily than print content. Two reasons account for this unequal treatment. First, the airwaves used by the electronic media are considered public property and are leased by the federal government to private broadcasters. Second, those airwaves are in limited supply; without some regulation, the nation's many radio and TV stations would interfere with one another's frequency signals. The scope of government regulation of the Internet remains unclear and has been debated hotly in recent years. Government regulations of electronic media apply in two major areas: ownership and content.

content regulations
Limitations on the substance of the mass media.

equal time rule
The rule that requires broadcast stations to sell air time equally to all candidates in a political campaign if they choose to sell it to any.

MEDIA OWNERSHIP In 1996, Congress passed the sweeping Telecommunications Act, deregulating whole segments of the electronic media. The Telecommunications Act sought to provide an optimal balance of competing corporate interests, technological innovations, and consumer needs. It appeared to offer limitless opportunities for entrepreneurial companies to give consumers enhanced services. This deregulation, however, resulted in the sudden merger of previously distinct kinds of media in order to create a more "multimedia" approach to communicating information and entertainment. This merger paved the way for the formation of multimedia corporations such as Viacom, Time Warner, and Comcast and the media consolidation discussed earlier in this chapter.

Since the initial passage of this act, the Federal Communications Commission (FCC) has continued to relax ownership standards, leading to even greater media consolidation. Today, a single company may own up to 45 percent of media in a given market. Whether a media conglomerate may own both a newspaper and a TV station in a single market, however, continues to be fiercely debated.

CONTENT The government also subjects the electronic media to substantial **content regulations,** or limitations on the substance of the mass media. To ensure that the airwaves "serve the public interest, convenience, and necessity," the FCC has attempted to promote equity in broadcasting. For example, the **equal time rule** requires that broadcast stations sell air time equally to all candidates in a political campaign if they choose to sell it to any, which they are under no obligation to do. An exception to this rule is a political debate: stations may exclude from this event less well known and minor-party candidates.

One more recent controversy over regulation of electronic media content involves the Internet. This controversy centers primarily on limiting users' access to illegal content, such as pirated movies and music. Initially, Internet service providers (ISPs) attempted to limit users' access to this content, slowing the network connections of those suspected of using illegal file-sharing programs. But, following more than a decade of controversy, the FCC ruled in November 2011 that ISPs may not block or slow the transmission of legal content. This Open Internet, or "net neutrality" rule, was a victory for Web-based companies such as Google and Yahoo, which argued that any other ruling would infringe on users' First Amendment rights.

Congressional actions to limit online piracy, however, have continued in earnest. In early 2012, controversy arose over two similar pieces of legislation—the Stop Online Piracy Act (SOPA) and the PROTECT IP Act (PIPA). These acts, which were supported by content producers such as the Recording Industry Association of America and the Motion Picture Association of America, would have given officials the power to shutter entire Internet domains if federal law enforcement officers suspected they were infringing on copyright laws. Opponents of the law, concerned that the government could potentially have the power to shut down any Web site at will, feared the consequences of such a mandate. An Internet "blackout" led by online content providers such as Wikipedia and Google raised citizens' awareness of these bills. During early January 2012, Google estimates that more than 7 million people petitioned Congress, asking members to vote against SOPA and PIPA, ultimately leading to the defeat of both pieces of legislation.[29]

14.1

14.2

14.3

14.4

14.5

press release
A document offering an official comment or position.

press briefing
A relatively restricted session between a press secretary or aide and the press.

press conference
An unrestricted session between an elected official and the press.

How the News Media Cover Politics

14.4 Assess how the news media cover politics.

The news media focus an extraordinary amount of attention on politicians and the day-to-day operations of government. In 2012, over 3,300 reporters were members of the House Radio-Television Correspondents Gallery.[30] The media have a visible presence at the White House as well; these reporters come from traditional and online media outlets and hail from across the country and, increasingly, around the world. Consequently, the media report, then intensively scrutinize and interpret, a politician's every public utterance.

☐ How the Press and Public Figures Interact

Communication between elected officials or public figures and the media takes a number of different forms. A **press release** is a written document offering an official comment or position on an issue or news event; it is usually faxed, e-mailed, or handed directly to reporters. A **press briefing** is a relatively restricted live engagement with the press, with the range of questions limited to one or two specific topics. In a press briefing, a press secretary or aide represents the elected official or public figure, who does not appear in person. In a full-blown **press conference,** an elected official appears in person to talk with the press at great length about an unrestricted range of topics. Press conferences provide a field on which reporters struggle to obtain the answers they need and public figures attempt to retain control of their message and spin the news and issues in ways favorable to them.

Politicians and media interact in a variety of other ways as well. Politicians hire campaign consultants who use focus groups and polling in an attempt to gauge how to present the candidate to the media and to the public. In addition, politicians can attempt to bypass the national news media through paid advertising and by appearing on talk shows and local news programs. Politicians also use the media to attempt to retain a high level of name recognition and to build support for their ideological and policy ideas.

☐ Covering the Presidency

The three branches of the U.S. government—the executive, the legislative, and the judicial—are roughly equal in power and authority. But, in the world of media coverage, the president stands first among equals. The White House beat is one of the most prestigious posts a political reporter can hold. Many of the most famous network news anchors, including NBC's Brian Williams, got their start covering the presidency.

The attention of the press to the White House enables a president to appear even on very short notice and to televise live, interrupting regular programming. The White House's press briefing room is a familiar sight on the evening news, not just because presidents use it fairly often but also because the presidential press secretary has almost daily question and answer sessions there.

The post of press secretary to the president has existed only since Herbert Hoover's administration (1929–1933). The power of this position, however, has grown tremendously over time. Presidents increasingly resist facing the media on their own and leave this task to their press secretary. As a result, press secretaries have a difficult job; they must convince the media of the importance of the president's policy decisions as well as defend any actions taken by the executive branch. In many ways, the prestige and power of the presidency depend on the "spin" of the press secretary and

Take a Closer Look

The James S. Brady Press Briefing Room is a central part of the president's media outreach efforts. Each day, the press secretary meets with members of the media in this room. Reporters have the opportunity to ask questions about presidential policies and activities, which they then report to their viewers, readers, and listeners. Seat assignments in the briefing room—which the White House Correspondents Association makes—have a significant impact on a news agency's ability to be recognized by the press secretary and ask the hard-hitting questions.

The front row, center seat, long reserved for UPI reporter Helen Thomas, is considered the "best seat in the house" because of its proximity to the press secretary. Today, the Associated Press takes this seat.

The press secretary stands at a podium in the front of the room, facing reporters. Shown here is President Obama's second press secretary, Jay Carney.

Brady Briefing Room Seating Chart As of September 2012

Podium

1	National Broadcasting Company	Fox News	Columbia Broadcasting System	Associated Press	American Broadcasting Company	Reuters	Cable News Network
2	*Wall Street Journal*	Columbia Broadcasting System Radio	Bloomberg	National Public Radio	*Washington Post*	*New York Times*	Associated Press Radio
3	Agence France Presse	*USA Today*	McClatchy	American Urban Radio Networks	*Politico*	Tribune	ABC Radio
4	Foreign Pool	Microsoft and the National Broadcasting System	*Washington Times*	*New York Daily News*	*National Journal*	Voice of America	*Congress Daily*
5	*Newsweek*	*Time*	*The Hill*	Hearst	*New York Post*	Fox Radio	*Chicago Sun-Times*
6	*Washington Examiner*	CCH/ United Press International	Salem Radio	Media News Group	*Christian Science Monitor*	Bureau of National Affairs	Dow Jones
7	Talk Radio	*Dallas Morning News*	*Boston Globe/ Roll Call*	Christian Broadcasting Network	*Baltimore Sun*/British Broadcasting Corporation	Scripps	*Financial Times*

Occupying seats farther from the press secretary are foreign news outlets, such as the BBC, and comparatively small daily newspapers, such as the *Dallas Morning News*.

CRITICAL THINKING QUESTIONS

1. What news outlets are you surprised to see seated in the White House press room? What news outlets are missing?
2. How does a daily press briefing help to keep citizens informed and the president accountable?
3. Should the president have to face the media on a daily basis, rather than sending his press secretary? Why or why not?

his or her ability to win over the media. Thus, many presidents choose close aides with whom they have worked previously and who are familiar with their thinking. For example, President Barack Obama's second press secretary, Jay Carney, worked as Vice President Joe Biden's director of communications before being appointed press secretary in 2011.

Covering Congress

With 535 voting members representing distinct geographic areas, covering Congress poses a difficult challenge for the media. Most news organizations solve the size and decentralization problems by concentrating coverage on three groups of individuals. First, the leaders of both parties in both houses receive the lion's share of attention because only they can speak for a majority of their party's members. Usually, the majority and minority leaders in each house and the Speaker of the House are the preferred spokespersons, but the whips also receive a substantial share of air time and column inches. Second, key committee chairs command center stage when subjects in their domain are newsworthy. Heads of the most prominent committees (such as Appropriations or Judiciary) are guaranteed frequent coverage, but even the chairs and members of minor committees or subcommittees can achieve fame when the time and issue are right. For example, a sensational scandal may lead to congressional committee hearings that receive extensive media coverage. Third, local newspapers and broadcast stations normally devote some

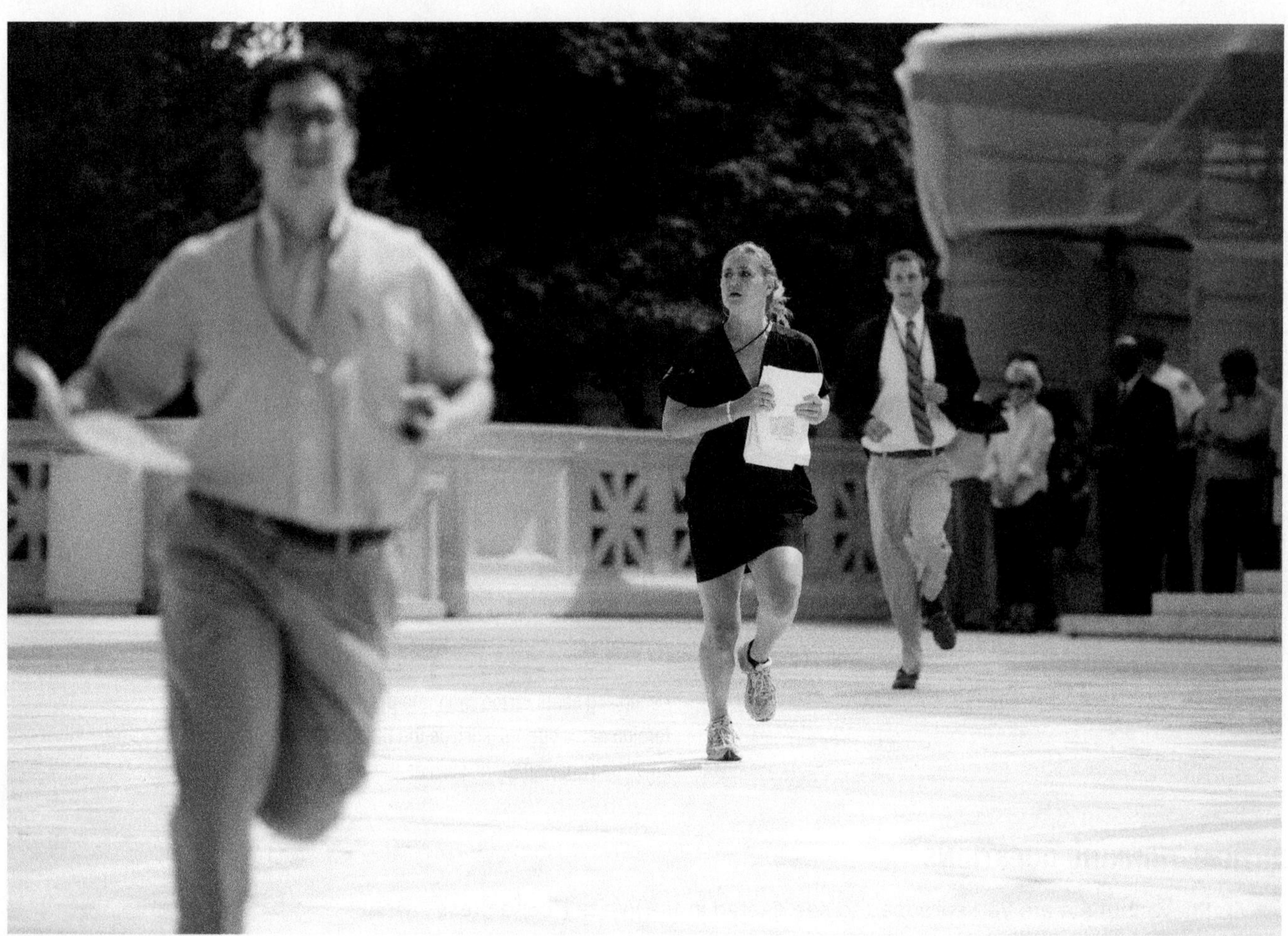

HOW DOES THE MEDIA COVER THE SUPREME COURT?

TV cameras are not allowed inside the Supreme Court. As a result, when the Court hands down an important opinion, such as its health care decision in 2012, it is not uncommon to see journalists sprinting from the courtroom with draft opinions in hand, hoping to be the first news agency to report the Court's decision.

resources to covering local senators and representatives, even when these legislators are junior and relatively lacking in influence.

As with coverage of the president, media coverage of Congress is disproportionately negative. A significant segment of media attention given to the House and Senate focuses on conflict among members. Some political scientists believe that such reporting is at least partially responsible for the public's negative perceptions of Congress.[31]

media effects
The influence of news sources on public opinion.

agenda setting
The process of forming the list of issues to be addressed by government.

14.1 14.2 14.3 14.4

☐ Covering the Supreme Court

While the president and Congress interact with the media on a regular basis, the Supreme Court remains a virtual media vacuum. TV cameras have never been permitted to record Supreme Court proceedings. Print and broadcast reporters, however, are granted access to the Court. Still, fewer than a dozen full-time reporters cover the Supreme Court, and the amount of space dedicated to Court-related news has continued to shrink. Stories involving complex legal issues are not as easy to sell as well-illustrated stories dealing with the Congress or president.[32]

The justices, citing the need to protect the public's perception of the Supreme Court as a nonpolitical and autonomous entity, have given little evidence to suggest they are eager to become more media friendly. Many veteran reporters have criticized this decision. As longtime Court reporter Tony Mauro noted, "Of course we don't want the Supreme Court playing to the crowd, ruling to please the majority. But that does not mean the [C]ourt should be invisible and unaccountable. Clarence Thomas on *Face the Nation*? John Roberts taking questions posted on YouTube? Sam Alito blogging? Why not? Really, why not?"[33]

Toward Reform: News Media Influence, News Media Bias, and Public Confidence

14.5 Evaluate the influence of the news media on public policy and the impact of media bias.

Many important questions pertain to the news media's relationship with the public. For instance, how much influence do the media actually have on the public's understanding of political issues? Do the media have a discernible ideological bent or bias, as some people suggest? Are people able to resist information that is inconsistent with their preexisting beliefs? And, how much confidence does the public have in the news media?

☐ News Media Influence

Some political scientists argue that the content of news coverage accounts for a large portion of the volatility and changes in public opinion and voting preferences of Americans, when measured over relatively short periods of time.[34] These changes are called **media effects**. These effects may be visible in a number of ways.

First, the media can influence the list of issues to be addressed by government through a process known as **agenda setting**. Significant media attention to an issue often increases the salience of that issue with average citizens. These citizens then pressure the government to take action. For example, media coverage of an immigration law enacted by the state of Arizona in 2010 ignited citizens' passions about the matter and made it a hot topic in many congressional campaigns.

Explore Your World

The media act as a filter for citizens' comprehension of political issues, helping them determine which issues are important and fashioning the frame for understanding. However, even the same political event may receive dramatically different coverage, depending on the country and context of the reporters shaping the story. Examine these front pages from around the world on the day after the U.S. military killed Osama bin Laden.

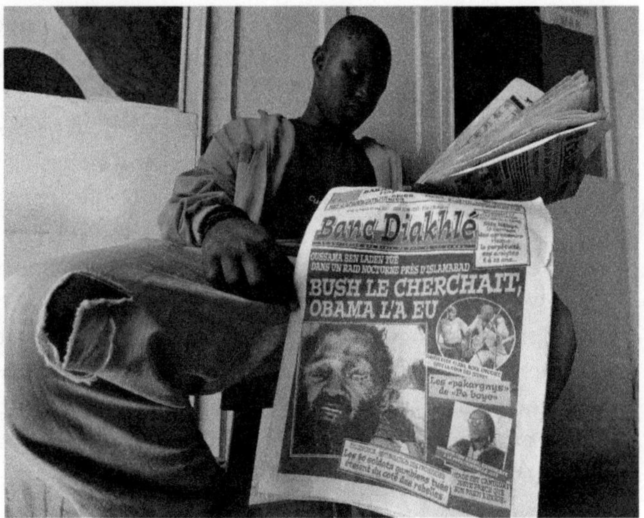

A French-language newspaper in Dakar, Senegal featured a fake illustration of Osama bin Laden. Roughly translated, the headline declares that [President George W.] Bush looked for bin Laden, but [President Barack] Obama found him.

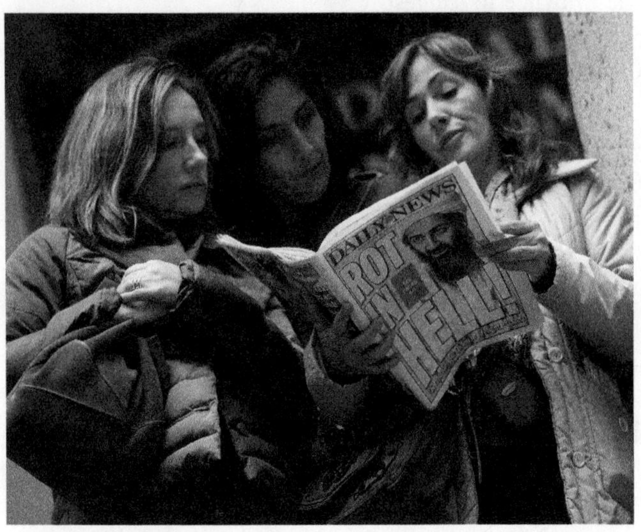

The *New York Daily News*, a tabloid-style paper famous for its sometimes clever and often sensational headlines, declared simply, "Rot in Hell."

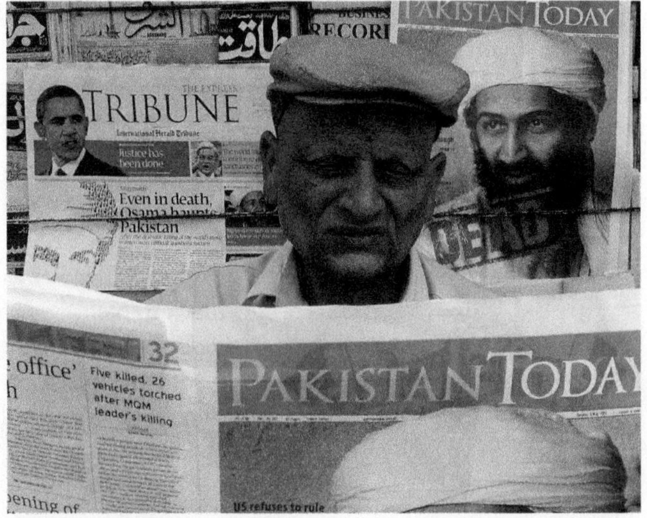

English language newspapers in Pakistan, the country where bin Laden was ultimately captured and killed, report the al Qaeda leader's death with a local focus, noting that "Even in death, Osama haunts Pakistan."

CRITICAL THINKING QUESTIONS

1. How are the front pages similar and different? Why do you think these similarities and differences exist?
2. How does each of these front pages affect the political and cultural viewpoints of the country in which they originated?
3. How do you think media in each of these countries affected public opinion and policy making in their countries?

Second, the media influence public opinion through **framing**—the process by which a news organization defines a political issue and consequently affects opinion about the issue. For example, an experiment conducted by one group of scholars found that if a news story about a Ku Klux Klan rally was framed as a civil rights story (i.e., a story about the right of a group to express its ideas, even if they are unpopular), viewers were generally tolerant of the rally. However, if the story was framed as a law and order issue (i.e., a story about how the actions of one group disrupted a community and threatened public safety), public tolerance for the rally decreased. In either case, the media exert subtle influence over the way people respond to the same information.[35]

framing
The process by which a news organization defines a political issue and consequently affects opinion about the issue.

Third, the media have the power to indirectly influence the way the public views politicians and government. For example, voters' choices in presidential elections often relate to their assessments of the economy. In general, a healthy economy motivates voters to reelect the incumbent president, whereas a weak economy impels them to choose the challenger. Hence, if the media paint a consistently dismal picture of the economy, that picture may well hurt the incumbent president seeking reelection.

Fourth, reporting can sway the public opinion and votes of people who lack strong political beliefs. So, for example, the media have a greater influence on political independents than on strong partisans.[36] That said, the sort of politically unmotivated individual who is subject to media effects may be less likely to engage in political affairs, in which case the media's influence may be more limited.

Finally, the media likely have a greater impact on topics far removed from the lives and experiences of readers and viewers. News reports can probably shape public opinion about events in foreign countries somewhat easily. Yet, what the media say about domestic issues, such as rising food or gas prices, neighborhood crime, or child rearing, may have relatively little effect, because most citizens have personal experience of, and well-formed ideas about, these subjects.

News Media Bias

Are journalists biased? The answer is simple and unavoidable. Of course they are. Journalists, like all human beings, have values, preferences, and attitudes galore—some conscious, others subconscious, but all reflected at one time or another in the subjects covered or the portrayal of events or content communicated. Given that the press is biased, in what ways is it biased, and when and how are the biases shown?

Much of the debate over media bias in contemporary politics has centered on the ideological bias of the people who report the news. Historically, most journalists self-identified as liberal Democrats.[37] Today, however, the percentage of journalists who identify as Democrats is at an all-time low. The debate has now shifted to examining biases of the news business, as commentators increasingly ask whether media consolidation has produced a news environment biased toward corporations and conservative politics. These scholars point to the elite background of the typical journalist, who tends to be white, male, highly educated, and relatively affluent. As a result, many of these journalists, in their reporting, may unconsciously ignore issues important to racial and ethnic minorities, the poor, and others who might be critical of government and big business.[38] They may also look to different sources for expertise to enrich their reporting. One study of the 2012 election, for example, revealed that, even on issues of concern to women, male pundits were four to seven times more likely to be quoted by the news media than their female counterparts.[39]

At the end of the day, the deepest bias among political journalists is the desire to grab a good story. News people know that if they report news with spice and drama, they will increase their audience. The fear of missing a good story shapes how media outlets develop headlines and frame their stories.

In the absence of an intriguing story, news people may attempt to create a horse race where none exists. While the horse-race components of elections are intrinsically interesting, the limited time that TV devotes to politics is disproportionately given to electoral competition, leaving less time for adequate discussion of public policy.[40] Looking at media coverage of the 2012 presidential primaries, one study found that only 9 percent of stories examined issue positions and candidate qualifications.[41]

One other source of bias, or at least of nonobjectivity, is the increasing celebrity status of many people who report the news. In an age of media stardom and blurring boundaries between entertainment and news, journalists in prominent media positions have unprecedented opportunities to attain fame and fortune. And, especially in the case of journalists with highly ideological perspectives, close involvement with wealthy or powerful special-interest groups can blur the line between reporting on policy issues and influencing them. Some journalists find work as political consultants or members of government—which seems reasonable, given their prominence, abilities, and expertise, but which can become problematic when they attempt to straddle both spheres. A good example of this phenomenon is Representative Michele Bachmann (R–MN), who ran for president in 2012 but who also frequently appears as a guest on cable news channels.

□ Public Confidence

Americans' general assessment of the news media is considerably unfavorable and has trended downward since the 1980s. According to a 2011 survey by the Pew Research Center for the People and the Press, a majority of the public gives the media low ratings on a number of indicators. Pew, for example, found 66 percent believed that the press was often inaccurate, 77 percent believed that stories favored one side, and 80 percent believed that powerful people and organizations often influenced coverage. These figures reached their highest levels in two decades.[42]

Despite the increasing displeasure expressed by most Americans about these and other shortcomings, the media have managed to maintain higher approval ratings than other political institutions. Americans also continue to value the media's watchdog role, with 58 percent believing that press scrutiny keeps political leaders from wrongdoing.[43] Thus, while public confidence in media organizations has declined and reforms are certainly warranted, Americans have not wavered in their support for a vigorous free press and for the role of the media in a democratic society.

Review the Chapter

 Listen to Chapter 14 on MyPoliSciLab

Roots of the News Media in the United States

14.1 Trace the historical development of the news media in the United States, p. 427.

News media, a component of the larger mass media, provide the public with key information about subjects of public interest and play a crucial role in the political process. The news media consist of print, broadcast, and new media. The nation's first newspaper was published in 1690. Until the mid- to late 1800s, when independent papers first appeared, newspapers were partisan; that is, they openly supported a particular party. In the twentieth century, first radio in the late 1920s and then TV in the late 1940s revolutionized the transmission of political information. The growth of online media, such as the Internet, blogs, and social media sites, continues to transform the relationship between media and citizens.

Current News Media Trends

14.2 Characterize four major trends in the news media today, p. 433.

Five trends affecting the modern media are: (1) corporate ownership and increasing consolidation of media outlets; (2) narrowcasting in order to capture particular segments of the population; (3) the growth of infotainment; (4) the increasing use of experts; and, (5) the rise of citizen journalists—ordinary individuals who collect, report, and analyze news content. These trends have all altered the news content citizens receive.

Rules Governing the News Media

14.3 Summarize the ethical standards and federal regulations that govern the news media, p. 439.

Journalists are guided in ethical behavior by a detailed "Code of Ethics" published by the Society of Professional Journalists, which includes principles and standards concerning issues such as avoiding conflicts of interest, verifying the information being reported, and dealing ethically with sources. In addition, the U.S. government regulates both media ownership and content. The Telecommunications Act of 1996 deregulated whole segments of the electronic media, paving the way for greater media consolidation. Content regulation such as network neutrality has also been a subject of significant government attention.

How the News Media Cover Politics

14.4 Assess how the news media cover politics, p. 442.

The news media cover every aspect of the political process, including the executive, legislative, and judicial branches of government, though the bulk of attention focuses on the president. Congress, with its 535 members and complex committee system, poses a challenge to the modern media, as does the Supreme Court, with its legal rulings and aversion to media attention. Politicians have developed a symbiotic relationship with the media, both feeding the media a steady supply of news and occasionally being devoured by the latest media feeding frenzy.

Toward Reform: News Media Influence, News Media Bias, and Public Confidence

14.5 Evaluate the influence of the news media on public policy and the impact of media bias, p. 445.

By controlling the flow of information, framing issues in a particular manner, and setting the agenda, the media have the potential to exert influence over the public, though generally they have far less effect than people believe While the media do possess biases, a wide variety of news options are available in the United States, providing news consumers with an unprecedented amount of information from which to choose. Public opinion regarding the media is largely critical, although Americans continue to value the news media's watchdog role.

Learn the Terms

 **Study** and **Review** the **Flashcards**

agenda setting, p. 445
citizen journalists, p. 438
content regulations, p. 441
deep background, p. 439
equal time rule, p. 441
framing, p. 447
mass media, p. 427
media effects, p. 445
muckraking, p. 429
narrowcasting, p. 435
news media, p. 427
off the record, p. 439
on background, p. 439
on the record, p. 439
press briefing, p. 442
press conference, p. 442
press release, p. 442
yellow journalism, p. 429

Test Yourself

 **Study** and **Review** the **Practice Tests**

1. What form of journalism stimulated demands for anti-trust regulations?

a. Yellow journalism
b. Penny press
c. Muckraking
d. TV news
e. Radio news

2. Most people get their information about politics from

a. the radio.
b. newspapers.
c. social media.
d. the Internet.
e. TV.

3. Media consolidation has

a. led to fewer owners in the media sphere.
b. not been allowed by the U.S. Supreme Court.
c. led networks to refrain from any possible kind of bias.
d. led to more news and less entertainment.
e. led to a decline in narrowcasting.

4. The rise of citizen journalism has

a. improved the accuracy of press coverage.
b. democratized political news.
c. polarized public opinion.
d. decreased citizens' reliance on technology.
e. become an important part of infotainment.

5. TV and radio are regulated by the federal government because

a. their content may be offensive to some people.
b. TV and radio are considered dangerous to the spirit of democracy.
c. the airwaves are public property.
d. the Constitution allows it specifically.
e. media profits are not legally allowed to exceed certain levels.

6. Which of these forms of media faces the least government regulation?

a. TV
b. Radio
c. Internet
d. Social media
e. Newspapers

7. Much of the news media's attention to government focuses on

a. the president.
b. Congress.
c. the Supreme Court.
d. the bureaucracy.
e. interest groups.

8. The president's official liaison to the media is known as the

a. communications director.
b. public information officer.
c. press secretary.
d. public relations coordinator.
e. spokesperson.

9. The process of forming and shaping the list of issues addressed by government is known as:

a. agenda setting.
b. media bias.
c. public opinion.
d. socialization.
e. framing.

10. When covering campaigns, most journalists' deepest bias is

a. a liberal bias.
b. a conservative bias.
c. a libertarian bias.
d. a bias to get a good story.
e. total objectivity.

Explore Further

Bennett, W. Lance. *News: The Politics of Illusion,* 9th ed. New York: Longman, 2011.

Dagnes, Alison D. *Politics on Demand: The Effects of 24-Hour News on American Politics.* New York: Praeger, 2010.

Graber, Doris A. *Mass Media and American Politics,* 8th ed. Washington, DC: CQ Press, 2009.

———, ed. *Media Power in Politics,* 6th ed. Washington, DC: CQ Press, 2010.

Hall, Jane. *Media and Politics.* New York: Pearson, 2013.

Iyengar, Shanto, and Jennifer A. McGrady. *Media Politics: A Citizen's Guide,* 2nd ed. New York: Norton, 2011.

Jamieson, Kathleen Hall, and Joseph N. Cappella. *Echo Chamber: Rush Limbaugh and the Conservative Media Establishment,* reprint ed. New York: Oxford University Press, 2010.

Jones, Jeffrey P. *Entertaining Politics: New Political Television and Civic Culture,* 2nd ed. Lanham, MD: Rowman and Littlefield, 2010.

McChesney, Robert W. *The Problem of the Media: U.S. Communication Politics in the Twenty-First Century.* New York: Monthly Review, 2004.

Overholser, Geneva, and Kathleen Hall Jamieson, eds. *The Institutions of American Democracy: The Press.* New York: Oxford University Press, 2005.

Rosenstiel, Tom, Marion Just, Todd Belt, Atiba Pertilla, Walter Dean, and Dante Chinni. *We Interrupt This Newscast: How to Improve Local News and Win Ratings, Too.* New York: Cambridge University Press, 2007.

Sellers, Patrick. *Cycles of Spin: Strategic Communication in the U.S. Congress.* New York: Cambridge University Press, 2009.

Stroud, Natalie Jomini. *Niche News: The Politics of News Choice.* New York: Oxford University Press, 2011.

Tewksbury, David, and Jason Rittenberg. *News on the Internet: Information and Citizenship in the 21st Century.* New York: Oxford University Press, 2012.

Williams, Bruce A., and Michael X. Delli-Carpini. *After Broadcast News: Media Regimes, Democracy, and the New Information Environment.* New York: Cambridge University Press, 2011.

To learn more about the state of the media, go to the Project for Excellence in Journalism at **www.journalism.org**.

To learn more about the public's attitudes about the news media, go to the Pew Research Center for the People and the Press at **www.people-press.org**.

To learn more about the front pages of over a hundred daily newspapers from around the world in their original, unedited form, go to the Web site of the Newseum at **www.newseum.org**.

To learn more about how the media cover specific stories, the broader trends in coverage, ethical dilemmas in the field, and the impact of technology, go to the *American Journalism Review* at **www.ajr.org**.

15 Interest Groups

Listen to Chapter 15 on MyPoliSciLab

In early America, interest groups were largely ad hoc organizations formed in local communities. Following the advent of television, the first national political organizations began to take shape. Today, smartphones and Facebook have once again contributed to changes in the interest group system.

No longer does joining a group imply attending physical meetings or becoming a dues-paying or card-carrying member. Today, joining an interest group or participating in a social movement may be as simple as clicking a "like" button, signing an online petition, or signing up for an email listserv.

As a result, the way we understand interest groups and their role in American politics is also changing. Although some groups still hold in-person marches and protests, the numbers of people attending these events pale in comparison to the number of virtual supporters groups have in cyberspace. Such was the case in 2011 with the Occupy Wall Street movement. Approximately 2,000 protestors gathered in New York City at the height of the movement, but tens of thousands were inspired to hold similar protests across the country, and millions liked the movement on Facebook or followed it on Twitter.

Gone, too, are the days when interest groups' primary roles in electoral politics were to knock on doors and make phone calls on behalf of candidates. Today, groups have found new responsibilities, as decisions such as *Citizens United* v. *Federal Election Commission* (2010) have opened the door for greater involvement by political action committees (PACs) and SuperPACs.

Finally, interest groups are becoming more informal. Stalwart groups such as the Chamber of Commerce continue to play key roles in politics. But, so, too, do nebulous interests organized around race, ethnicity, or class. During the 2012 elections, for example, candidates paid a great deal of attention to the "middle class." Though this group is based more on identity than formal membership, mobilizing a group of Americans around a shared goal and common policy objectives is precisely what interest groups have been doing since the nation's inception.

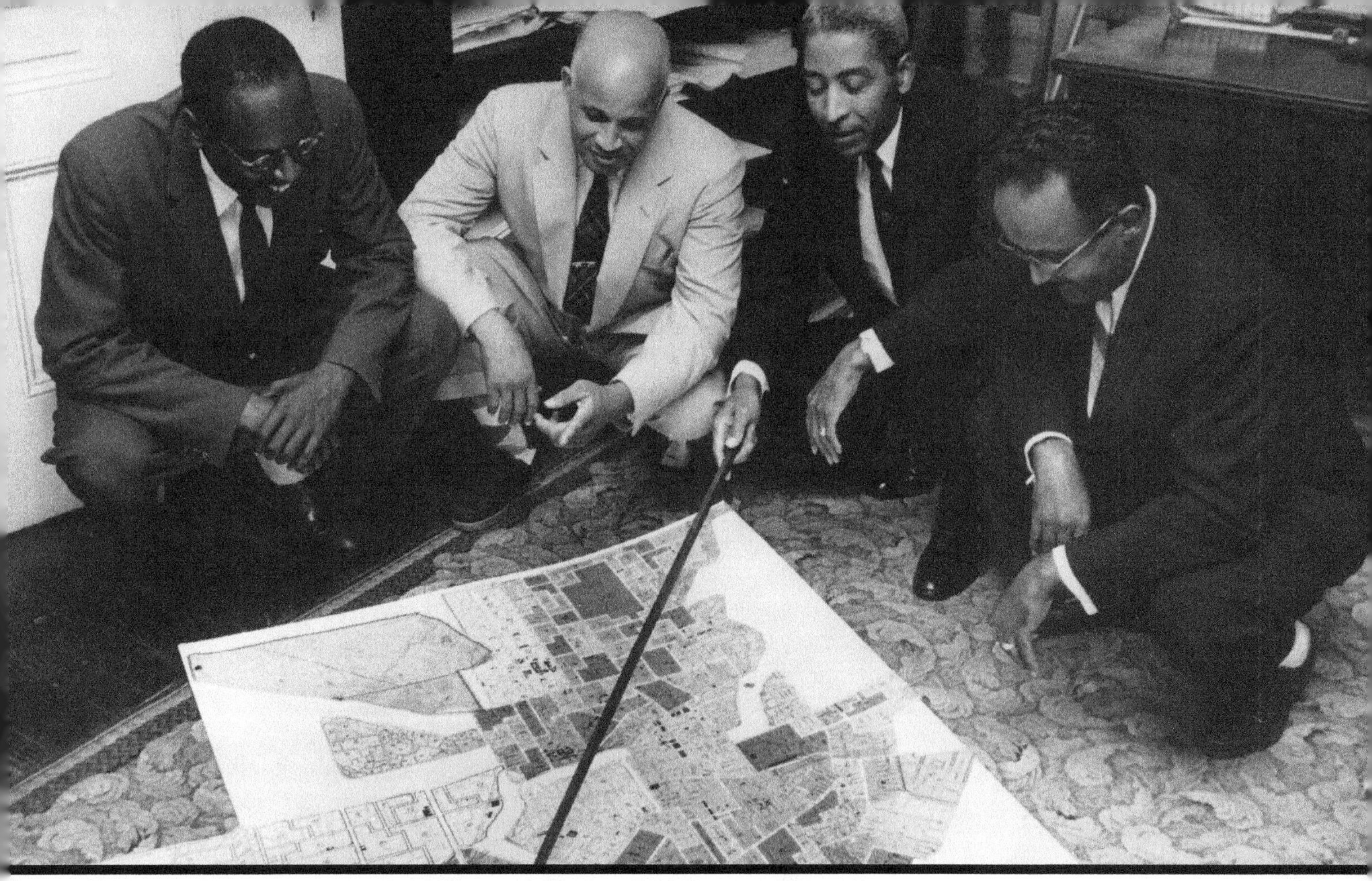

THE ROLE OF INTEREST GROUPS IN ELECTIONS HAS CHANGED Above, members of the NAACP plan a voter targeting campaign during the 1960 presidential election. Below, television host Stephen Colbert and members of Colbert Nation celebrate the creation of a Super PAC for the 2012 election cycle.

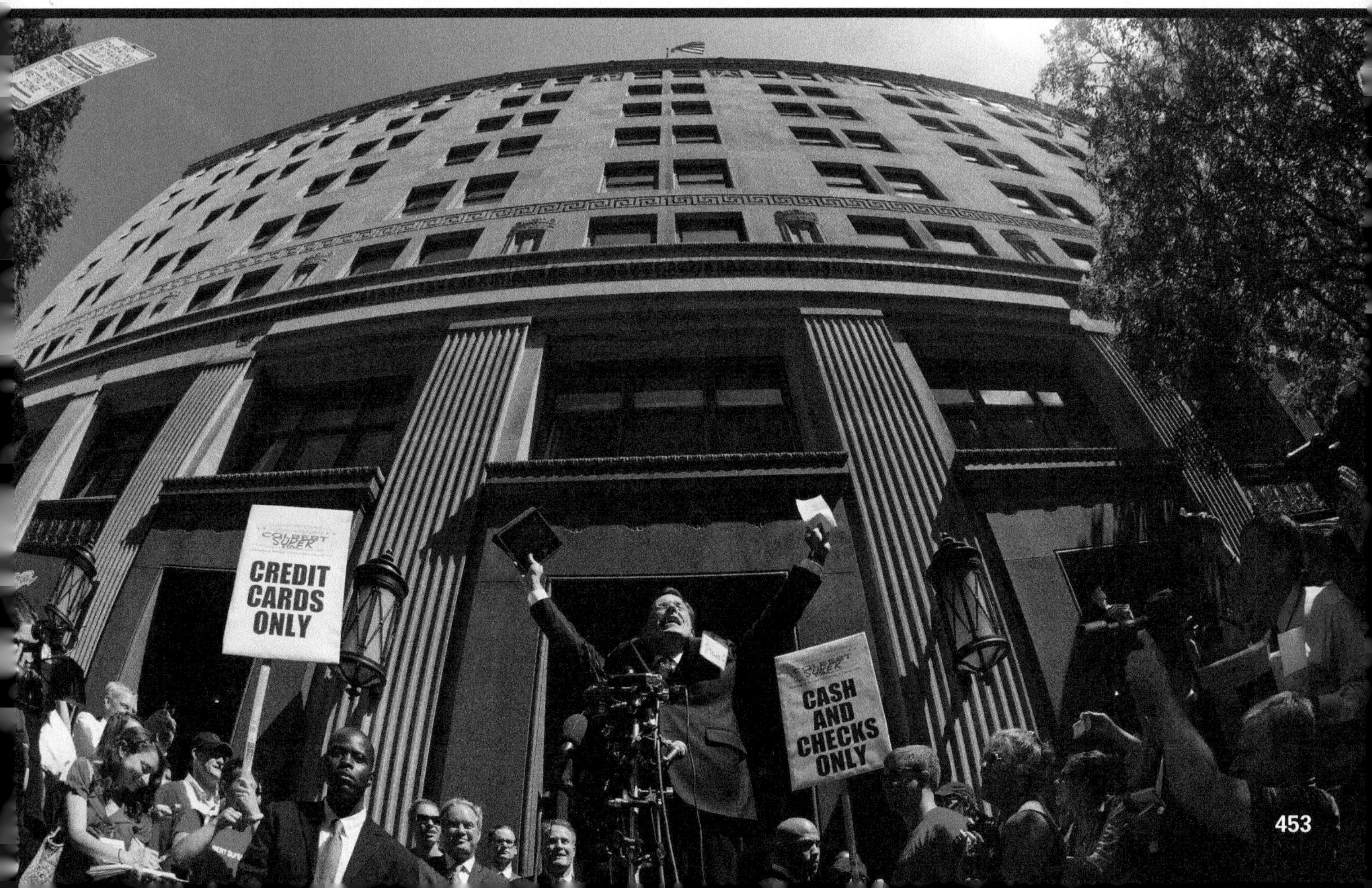

MyPoliSciLab Videos

Watch on MyPoliSciLab

The Big Picture Learn how interest groups influence politicians (and public policy). Author Alixandra B. Yanus discusses the explosive rise of the number of interest groups over the past forty years, and she weighs in on whether these groups are a positive or negative force.

The Basics What are interest groups and what role do they play in our democracy? Listen to real people tackle these and other questions. Learn what types of interest groups exist in our country, what tactics they use to achieve their goals, and why interest groups matter.

In Context Examine the emergence of interest groups in American politics. In this video, Boston College political scientist Kay Lehman Schlozman traces the roots of interest group involvement in American politics and why they are an important part of the political process today.

Thinking Like a Political Scientist Do interest groups have an impact on policy? Boston College political scientist Kay Lehman Schlozman explains why this is not an easy question to answer. She also discusses how scholars determine which groups are represented and which groups are not.

In the Real World Is pizza a vegetable? This video illustrates the difference between elitist and populist theories of interest groups by examining real people's reactions to the recent debate over whether school cafeterias should count pizza sauce as a full serving of vegetables.

So What? What does your Greek organization, your church, and your community service group all have in common? They are all interest groups In this video, author Alixandra B. Yanus explains how interest groups operate, how they influence policy changes, and how they can become dangerous when given too much power.

•••

The face of interest group politics in the United States is changing as quickly as laws, political consultants, and technology allow. Big business and trade groups are increasing their activities and engagement in the political system. At the same time, evidence concerning whether ordinary citizens join political groups is conflicting. Political scientist Robert Putnam, for example, has argued that fewer Americans are joining groups, a phenomenon he labeled "bowling alone."[1] Others disagree, concluding that America is in the midst of an "explosion of voluntary groups, activities and charitable donations [that] is transforming our towns and cities."[2] Although bowling leagues, which were once a common means of bringing people together, have withered, other organizations such as volunteer groups, soccer associations, health clubs, and environmental groups are flourishing. Older organizations, such as the Elks Club and the League of Women Voters, are attracting fewer new members, but this does not mean that people are not joining groups; they are simply joining different groups and online social networks.

Why is this debate so important? Political scientists believe that involvement in community groups and activities with others of like interests enhances the level of **social capital,** "the web of cooperative relationships between citizens that facilitates resolution of collective action problems."[3] The more social capital that exists in a given community, the more citizens are engaged in its governance and well-being, and the more likely they are to work for the collective good.[4] This tendency to form small-scale associations for the public good, or **civic virtue,** as Putnam calls it, creates fertile ground within communities for improved political and economic development.[5] Thus, if Americans truly are joining fewer groups, overall citizen engagement in government and the government's provision of services may suffer. New groups, such as the Tea Party movement, place increased demands on government, even when the demands are for less government.

Interest groups are also important because they give the unrepresented or underrepresented an opportunity to have their voices heard, thereby making the government and its policy-making process more representative of diverse populations and perspectives. In addition, interest groups offer powerful and wealthy interests even greater access to, or influence on, policy makers at all levels of government.

social capital
Cooperative relationships that facilitate the resolution of collective problems.

civic virtue
The tendency to form small-scale associations for the public good.

interest group
A collection of people or organizations that tries to influence public policy.

pluralist theory
The theory that political power is distributed among a wide array of diverse and competing interest groups.

disturbance theory
The theory that interest groups form as a result of changes in the political system.

Roots of the American Interest Group System

15.1 Trace the roots of the American interest group system.

Interest groups are organized collections of people or organizations that try to influence public policy; they have various names: special interests, pressure groups, organized interests, nongovernmental organizations (NGOs), political groups, lobby groups, and public interest groups. Interest groups are differentiated from political parties largely by the fact that interest groups do not run candidates for office.

Theories of Interest Group Formation

Interest group theorists use a variety of theories to explain how interest groups form and how they influence public policy. **Pluralist theory** argues that political power is distributed among a wide range of diverse and competing interest groups. Pluralist theorists such as David B. Truman explain the formation of interest groups through **disturbance theory**. According to this approach, groups form as a result of changes in the political system. Moreover, one wave of groups will give way to another wave representing a contrary perspective (a countermovement). Thus, Truman would argue, all salient issues will be represented in government. The government, in turn, should

transactions theory
The theory that public policies are the result of narrowly defined exchanges or transactions among political actors.

collective good
Something of value that cannot be withheld from a nonmember of a group, for example, a tax write-off or a better environment.

public interest group
An organization that seeks a collective good that will not selectively and materially benefit group members.

15.2

15.3

15.4

15.5

provide a forum in which the competing demands of groups and the majority of the U.S. population can be heard and balanced.[6]

Transactions theory arose out of criticisms of the pluralist approach. Transactions theory argues that public policies are the result of narrowly defined exchanges or transactions among political actors. Transactions theorists offer two main contentions: it is not rational for people to mobilize into groups, and therefore, the groups that do mobilize will represent elites. This idea arises from economist Mancur Olson's *The Logic of Collective Action.*[7] In this work, Olson assumes that individuals are rational and have perfect information upon which to make informed decisions. He uses these assumptions to argue that, especially in the case of **collective goods,** or things of value that may not be withheld from nonmembers, such as a better environment, it makes little sense for individuals to join a group if they can gain the benefits secured by others at no cost and become "free riders." (The problem of free riders is discussed later in this chapter.)

The elite bias that transactionists expect in the interest group system is the result of differences in the relative cost of mobilization for elite and nonelite citizens. Individuals who have greater amounts of time or money available simply have lower transaction costs. Thus, according to one political scientist, "The flaw in the pluralist heaven is that the heavenly chorus sings with a strong upper-class bias."[8]

☐ Kinds of Organized Interests

In this text, we use interest group as a generic term to describe the numerous organized groups that try to influence government policy. They take many forms, including public interest groups, business and economic groups, governmental units such as state and local governments, and political action committees (PACs) (see Table 15.1).

PUBLIC INTEREST GROUPS One political scientist defines **public interest groups** as organizations "that seek a collective good, the achievement of which will not selectively and materially benefit the membership or activists of the organization."[9] For example, many Progressive era groups were created by upper- and middle-class women to solve the varied problems of new immigrants and the poor. Today, civil liberties groups, environmental groups, good government groups, peace groups, church groups, groups that speak out for those who cannot (such as children, the mentally ill, or animals), and even MoveOn.org are examples of public interest groups. Ironically, even though many of these groups are not well funded, they are highly visible and can actually wield more political clout than other better-funded groups.

TABLE 15.1 WHAT ARE THE CHARACTERISTICS OF SELECTED INTEREST GROUPS?

Name (Founded)	Membership	PAC?	Fundraising—2012 Election Cycle[a]
AARP (1958)	40 million	N	n/a
AFL-CIO (1886)	11.5 million	Y	$15,459,582
MoveOn.org (1998)	5 million	Y	$17,011,544
U.S. Chamber of Commerce (1912)	3 million businesses	Y	$276,463
Sierra Club (1892)	1.4 million	Y	$975,775
Human Rights Campaign (1980)	750,000	Y	$1,130,162
Planned Parenthood Federation of America (1916)	700,000	Y	$1,085,867
Christian Coalition (1989)	500,000	N	n/a
National Association for the Advancement of Colored People (NAACP) (1909)	500,000	N	n/a
League of United Latin American Citizens (LULAC) (1929)	115,000	N	n/a
Public Citizen, Inc. (1971)	80,000	N	n/a

[a]Fundraising data through November 9, 2012.

SOURCE: www.opensecrets.org (November 10, 2012).

Take a Closer Look

Interest groups may be formed and sustained for any number of reasons. Among these are citizens seeking to represent the unique economic interests of a country or a particular region. The vast size and geopolitical variation of the United States lends itself well to tremendous variations in organized interests, as the cartoon below illustrates.

The population of the American Southwest has increased dramatically over the past several decades. However, much of this area is dry, desert land, meaning that citizens here often lobby their governments to invent creative solutions to water shortages.

The Rust Belt, a region in the upper Midwest and Northeast, is marked by the flight of industries, such as manufacturing, iron, and steel, which once dominated their economies. With the loss of traditional labor markets, citizens in these states frequently seek capital investments to revitalize communities, job creation programs, and other forms of economic development.

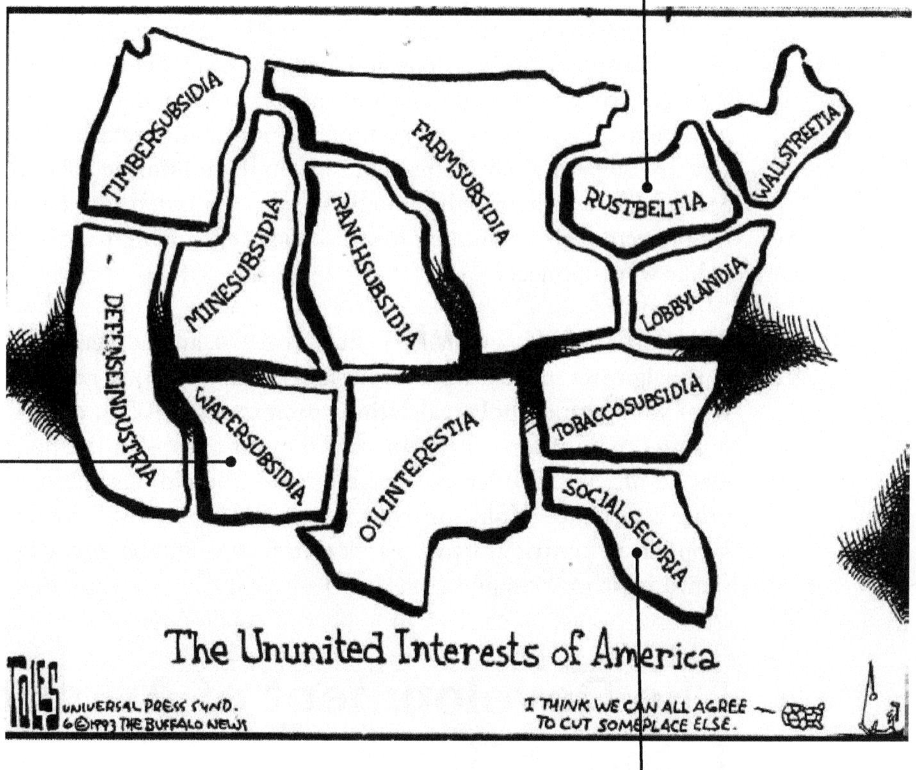

Many retirees have moved from their chilly homes in the Northeast, Midwest, and Mid-Atlantic to southern states, particularly Florida. These retirees demand lower property taxes, maintenance of veterans' benefits, and the continuance of Social Security and Medicare.

CRITICAL THINKING QUESTIONS

1. How do other regions depicted on the map reflect the unique demands citizens place on their governments?
2. What national issues might interest citizens in all areas of the country?
3. How do these regional interests both undermine and enhance the fundamental tenets of American democracy?

economic interest group
A group with the primary purpose of promoting the financial interests of its members.

political action committee (PAC)
Officially recognized fund-raising organizations that represent interest groups and are allowed by federal law to make contributions directly to candidates' campaigns.

ECONOMIC INTEREST GROUPS Most groups have some sort of economic agenda, even if it only involves acquiring enough money in donations to pay the telephone bill or to send out the next mailing. **Economic interest groups** are, however, groups whose primary purpose is to promote the economic interests of their members. Historically, the three largest categories of economic interest groups were business groups (including trade and professional groups, such as the American Medical Association), labor organizations (such as the AFL-CIO), and organizations representing the interests of farmers. The influence of farmers and labor unions is on the decline, however, as big businesses such as General Electric and AT&T spend increasingly large amounts contributing to campaigns and hiring lobbyists.

Groups that mobilize to protect particular economic interests generally are the most fully and effectively organized of all interest group types.[10] They exist to make profits and to obtain economic benefits for their members. To achieve these goals, however, they often find they must resort to political means rather than trust the operation of economic markets to produce favorable outcomes for their members.

GOVERNMENTAL UNITS State and local governments are becoming strong organized interests as they lobby the federal government or even charitable foundations for money to cover a vast array of state and local programs. The big intergovernmental associations as well as state and local governments want to make certain they get their fair share of federal dollars in the form of block grants or pork-barrel projects. Most states, large cities, and even public universities retain lobbyists in Washington, D.C., to advance their interests or to keep them informed about relevant legislation. States seek to influence the amount of money allotted to them in the federal budget for projects such as building roads, schools, enhancing parks or waterways, or other public works projects.

POLITICAL ACTION COMMITTEES In 1974, amendments to the Federal Election Campaign Act made it legal for businesses, labor unions, and interest groups to form what were termed **political action committees (PACs),** officially registered fund-raising organizations that represent interest groups in the political process. Many elected officials also have leadership PACs to help raise money for themselves and other candidates. Unlike interest groups, PACs do not have formal members; they simply have contributors who seek to influence public policy by electing legislators sympathetic to their aims.

The Development of American Interest Groups

15.2 Describe the historical development of American interest groups.

Previous experience led the Framers to tailor a governmental system of multiple pressure points to check and balance political factions. It was their belief that the division of power between national and state governments and across the three branches would prevent any one individual or group of individuals from becoming too influential. They also believed that decentralizing power would neutralize the effect of special interests, who would find it impossible to spread their efforts with any effectiveness throughout so many different levels of government. Thus, the "mischief of faction" feared by James Madison in *Federalist No. 10* could be lessened. But, as farsighted as they were, the Framers could not have envisioned the vast sums of money or the technology that would be available to some interest groups as the nature of these groups evolved over time.

☐ National Groups Emerge (1830–1889)

Although all kinds of local groups proliferated throughout the colonies and in the new states, the first national groups did not emerge until the 1830s when communication networks improved. Many were single-issue groups deeply rooted in the Christian religious revivalism sweeping the nation. Concern with humanitarian issues such as temperance, peace, education, slavery, and woman's rights led to the founding of numerous associations dedicated to addressing these issues. Among the first of these groups was the American Anti-Slavery Society, founded in 1833 by William Lloyd Garrison.

After the Civil War, more groups were founded. For example, the Women's Christian Temperance Union (WCTU) was created in 1874 with the goal of outlawing the sale of liquor. Its members, many of them quite religious, believed that alcohol consumption was an evil injurious to family life because many men drank away their paychecks, leaving no money to feed or clothe their families. The WCTU's activities took conventional and unconventional forms, which included organizing prayer groups, lobbying for prohibition legislation, conducting peaceful marches, and engaging in more violent protests such as the destruction of saloons.

The Grange also was formed during the period after the Civil War. Created as an educational society for farmers, it taught them about the latest agricultural developments. Although its charter formally stated that the Grange was not to involve itself in politics, in 1876 it formulated a detailed plan to pressure Congress into enacting legislation favorable to farmers.

WHAT WERE THE FIRST NATIONAL GROUPS TO EMERGE FOLLOWING THE CIVIL WAR?

One of the first truly national groups was The National Grange of the Order of Patrons of Husbandry or, more simply, the Grange, established in 1867 to educate and disseminate knowledge to farmers. The group also lobbied for farmers' interests in other areas, such as trust-busting.

lobbyist
Interest group representative who seeks to influence legislation that will benefit his or her organization or client through political and/or financial persuasion.

Business interests also began to figure even more prominently in both state and national politics during the late 1800s. A popular saying of the day noted that the Standard Oil Company did everything to the Pennsylvania legislature except refine it. Increasingly large trusts, monopolies, business partnerships, and corporate conglomerations in the oil, steel, and sugar industries became sufficiently powerful to control the votes of many representatives in state and national legislatures.

Perhaps the most effective organized interest of the day was the railroad industry. In a move that could not take place today because of its clear impropriety, the Central Pacific Railroad sent its own **lobbyist** to Washington, D.C., in 1861, where he eventually became the clerk (staff administrator) of the committees of both houses of Congress that were charged with overseeing regulation of the railroad industry. Subsequently, Congress awarded the Central Pacific Railroad (later called the Southern Pacific) vast grants of lands along its route and large subsidized loans. The railroad company became so powerful that it later achieved nearly total political control of the California legislature.

□ The Progressive Era (1890–1920)

By the 1890s, a profound change had occurred in the nation's political and social outlook. Rapid industrialization, an influx of immigrants, and monopolistic business practices created a host of problems, including crime, poverty, squalid and unsafe working conditions, and widespread political corruption. Many Americans began to believe that new measures would be necessary to impose order on this growing chaos and to curb some of the more glaring problems in society. The political and social movement that grew out of these concerns was called the Progressive movement.

Progressive era groups ranged from those rallying for public libraries and kindergartens to those seeking better labor conditions for workers—especially for women and children. Other groups, including the NAACP, were dedicated to ending racial discrimination. Groups seeking woman suffrage also were active during this time.

Not even the Progressives themselves could agree on what the term "progressive" actually meant, but their desire for reform led to an explosion of all types of interest groups, including single-issue, trade, labor, and the first public interest groups. Politically, the movement took the form of the Progressive Party, which sought on many fronts to limit or end the power of the industrialists' near-total control of the steel, oil, railroad, and other key industries.

In response to the pressure applied by Progressive era groups, the national government began to regulate business. Because businesses had a vested interest in keeping wages low and costs down, more business groups organized to consolidate their strength and to counter Progressive moves. Not only did governments have to mediate Progressive and business demands, but they also had to accommodate the role of organized labor, which often allied itself with Progressive groups against big business.

ORGANIZED LABOR Until creation of the American Federation of Labor (AFL) in 1886, no real national union activity had taken place. The AFL brought skilled workers from several trades together into one stronger national organization for the first time. As the AFL grew in power, many business owners began to press individually or collectively to quash the unions. As business interests pushed states for what are called open shop laws to outlaw unions in their factories, the AFL became increasingly political. It also was forced to react to the success of big businesses' use of legal injunctions to prohibit union organization. In 1914, massive lobbying by the AFL and its members led to passage of the Clayton Act, which labor leader Samuel Gompers hailed as the Magna Carta of the labor movement. This law allowed unions to organize free from prosecution and also guaranteed their members' right to strike, a powerful weapon against employers.

BUSINESS GROUPS AND TRADE ASSOCIATIONS The National Association of Manufacturers (NAM) was founded in 1895 by manufacturers who had suffered business losses in the economic panic of 1893 and who believed they were being affected adversely by the growth of organized labor. NAM first became active politically in 1913 when a major tariff bill was under congressional consideration. NAM's tactics were "so insistent and abrasive" and its expenditures so lavish that President Woodrow Wilson was forced to denounce its lobbying tactics as an "unbearable situation."[11] Congress immediately called for an investigation of NAM's activities but found no member of Congress willing to testify that he had ever even encountered a member of NAM (probably because many members of Congress had received illegal contributions and gifts).

The second major business organization, the U.S. Chamber of Commerce, came into being in 1912, with the assistance of the federal government. NAM, the Chamber of Commerce, and other **trade associations,** groups representing specific industries, were effective spokespersons for their member companies. They were unable to defeat passage of the Clayton Act, but organized interests such as cotton manufacturers planned elaborate and successful campaigns to overturn key provisions of the act in the courts.[12] Aside from the Clayton Act, innumerable pieces of pro-business legislation were passed by Congress, whose members continued to insist they had never been contacted by business groups.

trade association
A group that represents a specific industry.

The Rise of the Interest Group State

During the 1960s and 1970s, the Progressive spirit reappeared in the rise of public interest groups. Generally, these groups devoted themselves to representing the interests of African Americans, women, the elderly, the poor, and consumers, or to working on behalf of the environment. Many of their leaders and members had been active in the civil rights and anti–Vietnam War movements of the 1960s. Other groups formed during the Progressive era, such as the American Civil Liberties Union (ACLU) and the NAACP, gained renewed vigor. Many of them had as their patron the liberal Ford Foundation, which helped to bankroll numerous groups, including the Women's Rights Project of the ACLU, the Mexican American Legal Defense and Educational Fund, the Puerto Rican Legal Defense and Education Fund (now called Latino Justice PRLDEF), and the Native American Rights Fund.[13] The American Association of Retired Persons, now simply called AARP, also came to prominence in this era.

The civil rights and anti-war struggles left many Americans feeling cynical about a government that, in their eyes, failed to respond to the will of the majority. They also believed that if citizens banded together, they could make a difference. Thus, two major new public interest groups—Common Cause and Public Citizen—were founded during this time. Common Cause, a good-government group that acts as a watchdog over the federal government, is similar to some of the early Progressive movement's public interest groups. Public Citizen is the collection of groups founded by Ralph Nader (who went on to run as a candidate for president in 1996 and subsequent elections).

CONSERVATIVE RESPONSE: RELIGIOUS AND IDEOLOGICAL GROUPS Conservatives, concerned by the activities of these liberal public interest groups founded during the 1960s and 1970s, responded by forming religious and ideological groups that became a potent force in U.S. politics. In 1978, the Reverend Jerry Falwell founded the first major new religious group, the Moral Majority. The Moral Majority was widely credited with assisting in the election of Ronald Reagan as president in 1980 as well as with the defeats of several liberal Democratic senators that same year. Falwell claimed to have sent 3 to 4 million newly registered voters to the polls.[14]

Pat Robertson, a televangelist, formed the Christian Coalition in 1990. Since then, it has grown in power and influence. The Christian Coalition played an important role in the Republicans winning control of the Congress in 1994. In 2012, the group distributed 30 million voter guides in churches throughout the United States. This voter guide, while not expressly advocating for any one candidate, compared Governor Mitt Romney's and President Barack Obama's stances on a number of key issues ranging from abortion to taxation to health care.

The Christian Coalition is not the only conservative interest group to play an important role in the policy process as well as in elections at the state and national level. The National Rifle Association (NRA), an active opponent of gun control legislation, saw its membership rise in recent years, as well as its importance in Washington, D.C. The NRA and its political action committee spent more than $9 million trying to elect Republican candidates in 2012. And, conservative groups such as Students for Academic Freedom have made their views known in the area of higher education.

BUSINESS GROUPS, CORPORATIONS, AND ASSOCIATIONS Conservative business leaders, unsatisfied with the work of the National Association of Manufacturers and the U.S. Chamber of Commerce, also decided during the 1970s to start new organizations to advance their political and financial interests in Washington, D.C. The Business Roundtable, for example, was created in 1972. The Roundtable, whose members head about 150 large corporations, is "a fraternity of powerful and prestigious business leaders that tells 'business's side of the story' to legislators, bureaucrats, White House personnel, and other interested public officials."[15] It urges its members to engage in direct lobbying to influence the course of policy formation. In 2011, for example, members of the Business Roundtable cautioned the Obama administration against the economic harm that could result from enacting stricter environmental protection legislation related to preservation of the ozone layer.

Most large corporations, in addition to having their own governmental affairs departments, employ D.C.-based lobbyists to keep them apprised of legislation that may affect them, or to lobby bureaucrats for government contracts. Large corporations also channel significant sums of money to favored politicians or political candidates.

ORGANIZED LABOR Membership in labor unions held steady throughout the early and mid-1900s and then skyrocketed toward the end of the Depression. By then,

HOW IS THE FACE OF UNION MEMBERSHIP CHANGING?

Historically, most union members were white, male, blue collar workers and female teachers. In more recent years, however, unions have become more female and more diverse. Part of this change is the result of broadening union membership to include service workers, such as those shown here protesting with the Service Employees Industrial Union.

Who Are Union Members?

Labor unions have a rich history in the United States. During the peak of union labor in the 1950s, almost 30 percent of working Americans were members of a union. However, union membership, especially among private sector employees, has declined dramatically in recent years. These numbers provide a stark comparison to other industrialized democracies, for example, Finland, where 70 percent of workers are members of a union.

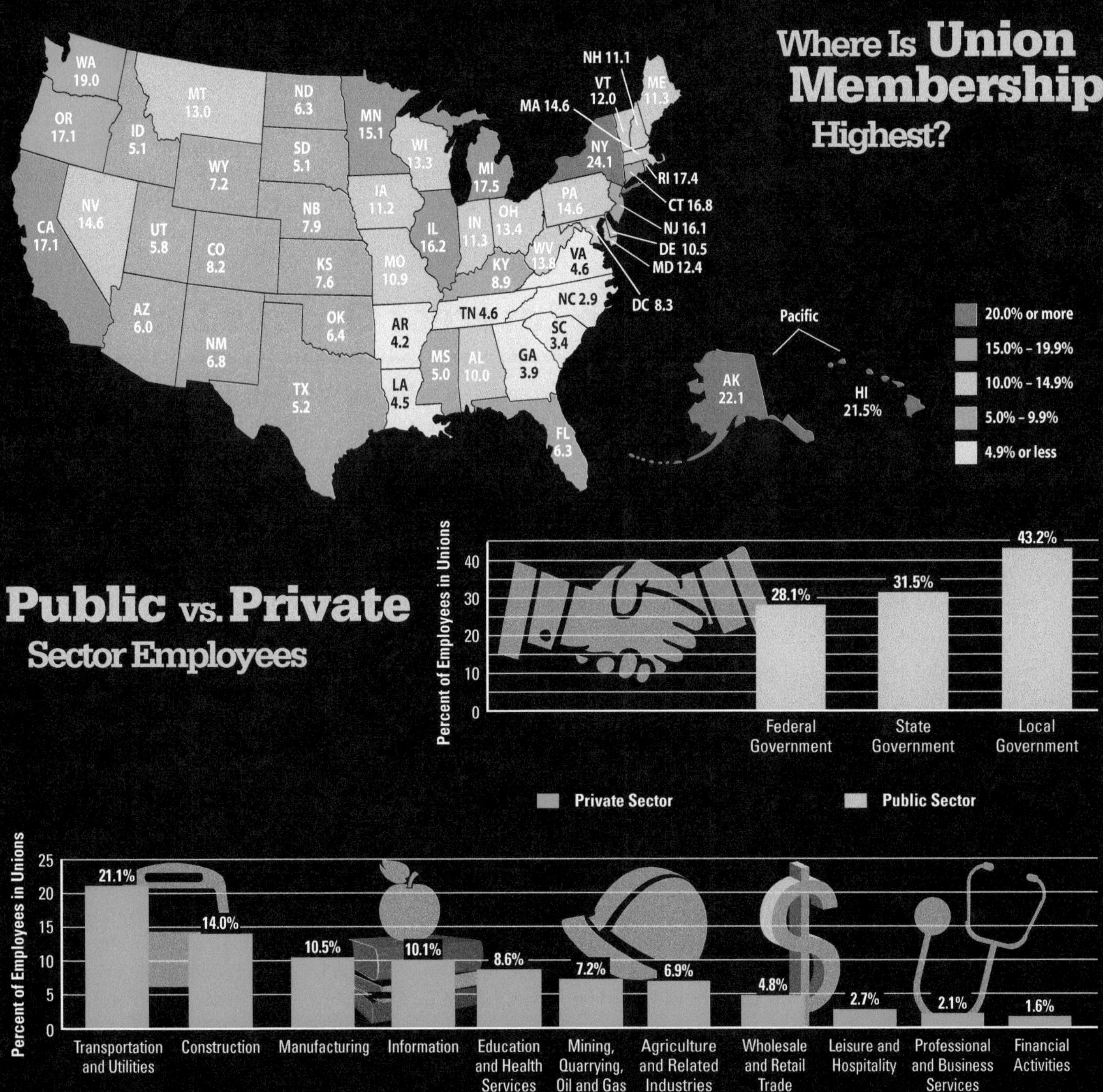

CRITICAL THINKING QUESTIONS

1. How can you explain the regional variations in union membership shown in the map above?
2. Why do you think there are varying rates of union membership between public and private employees and across differing professions?
3. What would be the positives and negatives of increasing (or decreasing) the number of unionized American workers?

organized labor began to wield potent political power, as it was able to turn out its members in support of particular political candidates, many of whom were Democrats.

Labor became a stronger force in U.S. politics when the American Federation of Labor (AFL) merged with the Congress of Industrial Organizations (CIO) in 1955. Concentrating its efforts largely on the national level, the new AFL-CIO immediately channeled its energies into pressuring the government to protect concessions won from employers at the bargaining table and to other issues of concern to its members, including minimum wage laws, the environment, civil rights, medical insurance, and health care.

More recently, the political clout of organized labor has waned at the national level. Membership peaked at about 30 percent of the workforce in the late 1940s. Since that time, union membership has plummeted as the nation changed from a land of manufacturing workers and farmers to a nation of white-collar professionals and service workers.

Even worse for the future of the labor movement, at least in the short run, is the split that occurred at the AFL-CIO's 2005 annual meeting, ironically the fiftieth anniversary of the joining of the two unions. Plagued by reduced union membership and disagreement over goals, seven member unions, including three of its largest, seceded from the AFL-CIO. The head of the Service Employees International Union (SEIU) at that time, Andy Stern, said the AFL-CIO had grown "pale, male, and stale."[16]

What Do Interest Groups Do?

15.3 Identify several strategies and tactics used by organized interests.

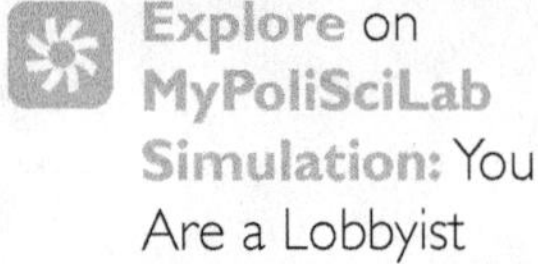

Not all organized interests are political, but they may become politically active when their members believe that a government policy threatens or affects group goals. Interest groups also enhance political participation by motivating like-minded individuals to work toward a common purpose. Legislators often are much more likely to listen to or be concerned about the interests of a group as opposed to the interests of any one individual.

Just as members of Congress are assumed to represent the interests of their constituents in Washington, D.C., interest groups are assumed to represent the interests of their members to policy makers at all levels of government. In the 1950s, for example, the NAACP was able to articulate the interests of African Americans to national decision makers, even though as a group they had little or no electoral clout, especially in the South. Without the efforts of civil rights groups, it is unlikely that either the courts or Congress would have acted as quickly to make discrimination illegal. By banding together with others who have similar interests at a particular time, all sorts of individuals—from railroad workers to women to physical therapists to concerned parents to homosexuals to mushroom growers—can advance their collective interests in Congress, statehouses, communities, and school districts. Gaining celebrity support or hiring a lobbyist to advocate those interests also increases the likelihood that issues of concern will be addressed and acted on favorably.

Interest groups, however, do have a downside. Because groups make claims on society, they can increase the cost of public policies. The elderly can push for more costly health care and Social Security programs; people with disabilities, for improved access to public buildings; industry, for tax loopholes; and veterans, for improved benefits that may be costly to other Americans. Many Americans believe that interest groups exist simply to advance their own selfish interests, with little regard for the rights of other groups or, more importantly, of people not represented by any organized group.

Whether good or bad, interest groups play an important role in U.S. politics. In addition to enhancing the democratic process by providing increased representation and participation, they raise public awareness about important issues, help frame the public agenda, and often monitor programs to guarantee effective implementation. Most often, they accomplish these goals through some sort of lobbying or electoral activities.

Lobbying

Most interest groups place lobbying at the top of their agendas. **Lobbying** is the activities of a group or organization that seek to persuade political leaders to support the group's position. The exact origin of the term is disputed. In mid-seventeenth-century England, there was a room located near the floor of the House of Commons where members of Parliament would congregate and could be approached by their constituents and others who wanted to plead a particular cause. Similarly, in the United States, people often waited outside the chambers of the House and Senate to speak to members of Congress as they emerged. Because they waited in the lobbies to argue their cases, by the nineteenth century they were commonly referred to as lobbyists. An alternate piece of folklore explains that when Ulysses S. Grant was president, he would frequently walk from the White House to the Willard Hotel on Pennsylvania Avenue just to relax in its comfortable and attractive lobby. Interest group representatives and those seeking favors from Grant would crowd into that lobby and try to press their claims. Soon they were nicknamed lobbyists (see Figure 15.1).

lobbying
The activities of a group or organization that seek to persuade political leaders to support the group's position.

Most politically active groups use lobbying to make their interests heard and understood by those who are in a position to influence or change governmental policies. Depending on the type of group and on the role it aims to play, lobbying can take many forms. You probably have never thought of the Boy Scouts or Girl Scouts as political. Yet, when Congress began debating the passage of legislation dealing with discrimination in private clubs, representatives of both organizations testified in the hope of persuading Congress to allow them to remain single-sex organizations.

Lobbyists and organizations can influence policy at the local, state, and national levels in multiple legal ways. Almost all interest groups lobby by testifying at hearings and contacting legislators. Other groups also provide information that decision makers might not have the time, opportunity, or interest to gather on their own. Interest groups also file lawsuits or friend of the court briefs to lobby the courts. And, groups energize grassroots members to contact their representatives or engage in protests or demonstrations.

LOBBYING CONGRESS A wide variety of lobbying activities target members of Congress: congressional testimony on behalf of a group, individual letters or e-mails from

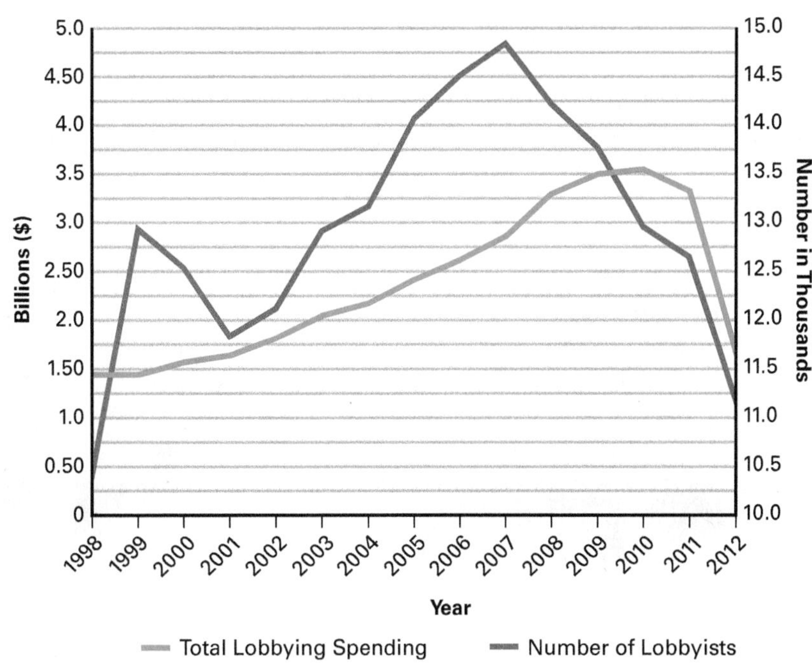

FIGURE 15.1 HOW MANY LOBBYISTS ARE THERE? HOW MUCH DO THEY SPEND?

Each year, more than 10,000 lobbyists attempt to influence public policy in Congress and the federal agencies. This large scale lobbying effort is an expensive industry, costing billions of dollars each year.

SOURCE: Center for Responsive Politics, http://www.opensecrets.org/lobby/index.php.

NOTE: 2012 data is through September 17, 2012.

interested constituents, campaign contributions, or the outright payment of money for votes. Of course, the last activity is illegal, but there exist numerous documented instances of money changing hands for votes.

Lobbying Congress and issue advocacy are skills that many people have developed over the years. In 1869, for example, women gathered in Washington, D.C., for the second annual meeting of the National Woman Suffrage Association and marched to Capitol Hill to hear one of their members (unsuccessfully) ask Congress to pass legislation that would enfranchise women under the terms of the Fourteenth Amendment. Practices such as these floor speeches are no longer permitted.

Today, many effective lobbyists are former members of Congress, staff aides, or other Washington insiders. These connections help them develop close relationships with senators and House members in an effort to enhance their access to the policy-making process. A symbiotic relationship between members of Congress, interest group representatives, and affected bureaucratic agencies often develops. In these iron triangles and issue networks, congressional representatives and their staff members, who face an exhausting workload and legislation they frequently know little about, often look to lobbyists for information. "Information is the currency on Capitol Hill, not dollars," said one lobbyist.[17] One aide reports: "My boss demands a speech and a statement for the *Congressional Record* for every bill we introduce or co-sponsor—and we have a lot of bills. I just can't do it all myself. The better lobbyists, when they have a proposal they are pushing, bring it to me along with a couple of speeches, a *Record* insert, and a fact sheet."[18]

Not surprisingly, lobbyists work most closely with representatives who share their interests.[19] A lobbyist from the NRA, for example, would be unlikely to try influencing a liberal representative who, on record, was strongly in favor of gun control. It is much more effective for a group such as the NRA to provide useful information for its supporters and to those who are undecided. Good lobbyists also can encourage members to file amendments to bills favorable to their interests, as was evident in the recent health care debate. They also can urge their supporters in

WHAT ROLE DO LOBBYISTS PLAY IN CONGRESS?

This cartoon presents one popular view of how legislation gets enacted on Capitol Hill. Political science research, however, reveals that interest groups do not directly "buy" members' votes in a quid pro quo. They do, however, reward loyal supporters in Congress with campaign contributions and other incentives.

> *Congress shall make no law respecting . . . the right of the people peaceably to assemble, and to petition the Government for a redress of grievances.* —FIRST AMENDMENT

This section of the First Amendment prohibits the national government from enacting laws dealing with the right of individuals to join together to make their voices known about their positions on a range of political issues. Little debate on this clause took place in the U.S. House of Representatives, and none was recorded in the Senate.

Freedom of association, a key concept that allows Americans to organize and join a host of political groups, grew out of a series of cases decided by the Supreme Court in the 1950s and 1960s, when many southern states were trying to limit the activities of the National Association for the Advancement of Colored People (NAACP). From the right to assemble and petition the government, along with the freedom of speech, the Supreme Court construed the right of people to come together to support or to protest government actions. First, the Court ruled that states could not compel interest groups to provide their membership lists to state officials. Later, the Court ruled that Alabama could not prohibit the NAACP from urging its members and others to file lawsuits challenging state discriminatory practices. Today, although states and localities can require organized interests to apply for permits to picket or protest, they cannot in any way infringe on their ability to assemble and petition in peaceable ways.

CRITICAL THINKING QUESTIONS

1. **What role has protest played in American history?**
2. **Does requiring a government permit infringe on the right to protest? Under what conditions could a government permit be declined?**

Congress to make speeches (often written by the group) and to pressure their colleagues in the chamber.

A lobbyist's effectiveness depends largely on his or her reputation for fair play and provision of accurate information. No member of Congress wants to look uninformed. As one member noted: "It doesn't take very long to figure out which lobbyists are straightforward, and which ones are trying to snow you. The good ones will give you the weak points as well as the strong points of their case. If anyone ever gives me false or misleading information, that's it—I'll never see him again."[20]

LOBBYING THE EXECUTIVE BRANCH As the executive branch has increasingly concerned itself with shaping legislation, lobbying efforts directed toward the president and the bureaucracy have gained in frequency and importance. Groups often target one or more levels of the executive branch because so many potential access points exist, including the president, White House staff, and numerous levels of the executive branch bureaucracy. Groups try to work closely with the administration to influence policy decisions at their formulation and later implementation stages. As with congressional lobbying, the effectiveness of a group often depends on its ability to provide decision makers with important information and a sense of where the public stands on the issue. The National Women's Law Center, for example, has been instrumental in seeing that Title IX, which Congress passed to mandate educational equity for women and girls, is enforced fully by the Department of Education.

LOBBYING THE COURTS The courts, too, have proved a useful target for interest groups.[21] Although you might think that the courts decide cases affecting only the parties involved or that they should be immune from political pressures, interest groups for years have recognized the value of lobbying the courts, especially the U.S. Supreme Court, and many political scientists view it as a form of political participation.[22]

15.1

15.2

15.3

15.4

15.5

Generally, interest group lobbying of the courts can take two forms: direct sponsorship or the filing of *amicus curiae* briefs. Sponsorship involves providing resources (financial, human, or otherwise) to shepherd a case through the judicial system, and the group may even become a named party, as in *Planned Parenthood of Southeastern Pennsylvania* v. *Casey* (1992). When a case that a group is interested in, but not actually sponsoring, comes before a court, the organization often will file an *amicus* brief—either alone or with other like-minded groups—to inform the justices of the group's policy preferences, generally offered in the guise of legal arguments. Over the years, as the number of both liberal and conservative groups viewing litigation as a useful tactic has increased, so has the number of briefs submitted to the courts. An interest group has sponsored or filed an *amicus curiae* brief in most of the major U.S. Supreme Court cases noted in this text.[23] Interest groups also file *amicus* briefs in lower federal and state supreme courts, but in much lower numbers.

In addition to litigating, interest groups try to influence nominations to the federal courts. For example, they play an important part in judicial nominees' Senate confirmation hearings. In 1991, for example, 112 groups testified or filed prepared statements for or against the controversial nomination of Clarence Thomas to the U.S. Supreme Court.[24] In 2009, 218 groups testified or prepared statements for or against the nomination of Sonia Sotomayor to the Supreme Court. The diversity of groups was astounding, from gun rights groups to pro-choice groups, women's groups, and Hispanic advocacy organizations.[25]

It is also becoming more common for interest groups of all persuasions to pay for trips so that judges may attend "informational conferences" or simply to interact with judges by paying for club memberships and golf outings. In fact, many commentators criticized the absence of Justice Antonin Scalia from the swearing in of Chief Justice John Roberts because Scalia was on a golf outing in Colorado. This outing was part of a legal conference sponsored by the Federalist Society, a conservative group that was highly influential in judicial appointments during the Bush administration.[26]

GRASSROOTS LOBBYING Interest groups regularly try to inspire their members to engage in grassroots lobbying, hoping that lawmakers will respond to those pressures and the attendant publicity.[27] In essence, the goal of many organizations is to persuade ordinary voters to serve as their advocates. In the world of lobbying, few things are more useful than a list of committed supporters. Radio and TV talk-show hosts such as Rush Limbaugh and Rachel Maddow try to stir up their listeners by urging them to contact their representatives in Washington, D.C. Other interest groups use petition drives and carefully targeted and costly TV advertisements pitching one side of an argument. It is also routine for interest groups to e-mail or text message their members and provide a direct Web link as well as suggested text that citizens can use to lobby their legislators.

PROTESTS AND RADICAL ACTIVISM An occasional, though highly visible, tactic used by some groups is protest activity. Although usually a group's members opt for more conventional forms of lobbying or influence policy through the electoral process, when these forms of pressure group activities are unsuccessful, some groups (or individuals within groups) resort to more forceful measures to attract attention to their cause. Since the Revolutionary War, violent, illegal protest has been one tactic of organized interests. The Boston Tea Party, for example, involved breaking all sorts of laws, although no one was hurt physically. Other forms of protest, such as the Whiskey Rebellion, ended in tragedy for some participants.

Today, anti-war activists, animal rights activists, and some pro-life groups, such as Operation Rescue, at times rely on illegal protest activities. Members of the Animal Liberation Front, for example, stalked the wife of a pharmaceutical executive, broke into her car, stole her credit cards, and then made over $20,000 in unauthorized charitable donations.[28] Members of this group also use circus bombings, the sabotage of restaurants, and property destruction to gain attention for their cause.[29] Other radical groups also post on the Internet the names and addresses of those they believe to be engaging in wrongful activity and urge members to take action against these people. Some groups have faced federal terrorism charges for these illegal actions.

☐ Election Activities

In addition to trying to achieve their goals (or at least draw attention to them) by lobbying, many interest groups also become involved more directly in the electoral process. The 2012 Republican and Democratic National Conventions, for example, were the targets of significant fund raising by organized interests. Seizing the opportunity to meet and greet many of the Republican and Democratic Parties' elites in one location, Super PACs, in particular, hosted a wide array of dinners, speeches and events.

CANDIDATE RECRUITMENT AND ENDORSEMENTS Some interest groups recruit, endorse, and/or provide financial or other forms of support to political candidates. EMILY's List (EMILY stands for "Early money is like yeast—it makes the dough rise") was founded to support pro-choice Democratic women candidates, especially during party primary election contests. It now also recruits and trains candidates. In 2012, EMILY's List spent more than $30 million in direct contributions to candidates, volunteer mobilization, hiring campaign consultants, and funding for some direct media.

Candidate endorsements also play a prominent role in focusing voters' attention on candidates who advocate policies consistent with an interest group's beliefs. In addition, endorsements may help mobilize group members. Many members of groups supporting Barack Obama and Mitt Romney in 2012 provided much needed volunteers and enthusiasm.

GETTING OUT THE VOTE Many interest groups believe they can influence public policy by putting like-minded representatives in office. To that end, many groups across the ideological spectrum launch massive get-out-the-vote (GOTV) efforts. These include identifying prospective voters and transporting them to the polls. Well-financed interest groups such as the liberal MoveOn.org and its conservative counterpart, Progress for America, often produce issue-oriented ads for newspapers, radio, TV, and the Internet, designed to educate the public as well as increase voter interest in election outcomes.

RATING THE CANDIDATES OR OFFICE HOLDERS Many ideological groups rate candidates on a scale from 0 to 100 to help their members (and the general public) evaluate the voting records of members of Congress. They use these ratings to help their members and other voters make informed voting decisions. The American Conservative Union (conservative) and Americans for Democratic Action (liberal)—two groups at ideological polar extremes—are just two examples that routinely rate candidates and members of Congress based on their votes on key issues.

CAMPAIGN CONTRIBUTIONS Corporations, labor unions, and interest groups may give money to political candidates in a number of ways. Organized interests are allowed to form political action committees (PACs) to raise money for direct contributions to political candidates in national elections. PAC money plays a significant role in the campaigns of many congressional incumbents, often averaging over half a House candidate's total spending. PACs generally contribute to those who have helped them before and who serve on committees or subcommittees that routinely consider legislation of concern to that group. In 2012, the average Senate candidate received $2.2 million from PACs, and the average House candidate received $745,000 (see Figure 15.2).

Some organized interests may also prefer to make campaign expenditures through Super PACs, 527s, or 501(c) groups. Money raised by these groups may not be given to or spent in coordination with a candidate's campaign. However, it may be used for issue advocacy, which may help a group's preferred candidate indirectly. These groups have been major players in recent elections, spending over $660 million in 2012.

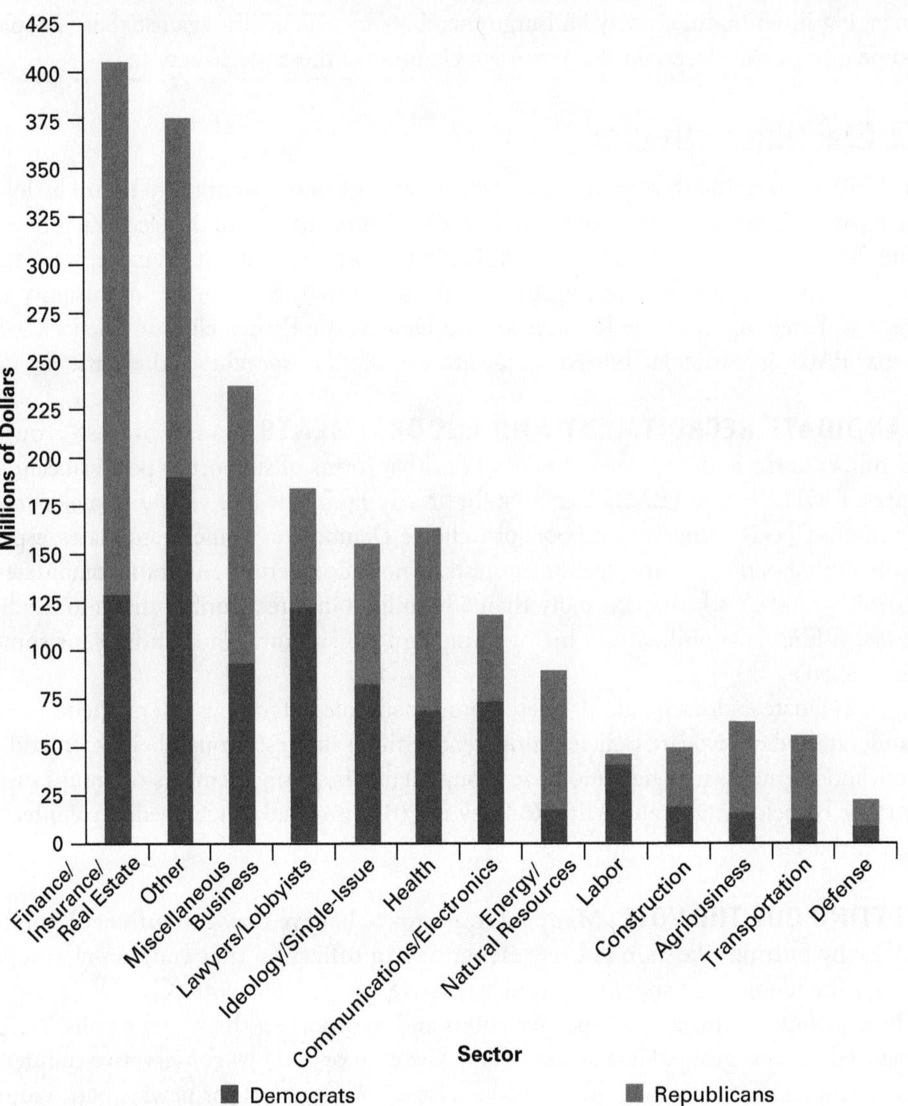

FIGURE 15.2 HOW MUCH MONEY DO INTEREST GROUPS SPEND ON ELECTIONS?
Political action committees play an important role in national elections. The amount of money they spend and how it is allocated between Democrats and Republicans varies widely over interest group sectors.

SOURCE: Data from the Center for Responsive Politics, http://www.opensecrets.org/industries/index.php, accessed November 10, 2012.

What Makes Interest Groups Successful?

15.4 Analyze the factors that make an interest group successful.

All of the groups discussed in this chapter have one characteristic in common: they all want to shape the public agenda, whether by helping to elect candidates, maintaining the status quo, or obtaining favorable legislation or rulings from national, state, and local governments.[30] For powerful groups, simply making sure that certain issues never get discussed may be the goal. In contrast, those opposed to other issues, such the growing wealth gap in the United States, succeed when the issue becomes front-page news and citizens place pressure on government leaders to address the issue.

Explore Your World

Interest groups—often called nongovernmental organizations (NGOs) beyond the boundaries of the United States—play a significant role in world politics. Most states, as well as the European Union, United Nations, and other intergovernmental organizations, face heavy lobbying from corporate interests and citizen activists. Some of these NGOs are specific to the challenges faced within one country. Others transcend national boundaries and work to increase the global standard of living and bring attention to the interconnected nature of our modern world.

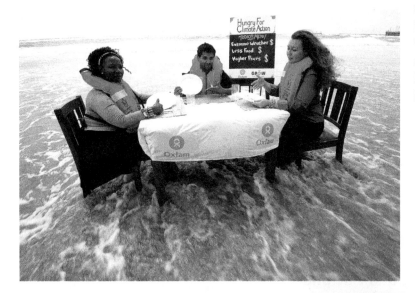

Oxfam was founded in 1942 in Great Britain as the Oxford Committee for Famine Relief. The goal of the organization at its inception was to distribute food to occupied nations during World War II. Today, the organization works to fight poverty and hunger around the world by providing disaster relief, lobbying governments, and increasing food security and water hygiene.

A Shell Oil executive established the Bangladesh Rural Advancement Committee (now known simply as BRAC) in 1972, soon after that country's independence. Today, it is an important development organization, providing microcredit to individuals in Asia, Africa, and the Caribbean. The group also works to combat poverty and improve citizens' standard of living in other ways.

CRITICAL THINKING QUESTIONS

1. How can international NGOs have both positive and negative effects on the citizens they attempt to serve?
2. What lobbying tactics might these groups find most successful in raising attention to their causes? What governmental agencies should they lobby?
3. Can you think of other interest groups that are successful on an international or global scale? What are they, and why are they successful?

15.1

15.2

15.3

15.4

15.5

Groups succeed when they win legislation, court cases, or even elections individually or in coalition with other groups.[31] They also are successful when their leaders become elected officials or policy makers in any of the three branches of the government. For example, Representative Rosa DeLauro (D–CT) was a former political director of EMILY's List. And, President Barack Obama worked as a grassroots community organizer for a variety of Chicago-based groups.

Political scientists have studied several phenomena that contribute in varying degrees—individually and collectively—to particular groups' successes. These include leaders, funding and patrons, and a solid membership base.

☐ Leaders

Interest group theorists frequently acknowledge the key role of leaders in the formation, viability, and success of interest groups while noting that leaders often vary from rank-and-file members on various policies.[32] Without the powerful pen of William Lloyd Garrison in the 1830s, who knows whether the abolition movement would have been as successful? Other notable leaders include Frances Willard of the WCTU; Marian Wright Edelman, who founded the Children's Defense Fund; and Pat Robertson of the Christian Coalition.

The role of an interest-group leader is similar to that of an entrepreneur in the business world. Leaders of groups must find ways to attract members. As in the marketing of a new product, an interest-group leader must offer something attractive to entice members to join. Potential members of the group must be convinced that the benefits of joining outweigh the costs. Union members, for example, must be persuaded that the union's winning higher wages and concessions for them will offset the cost of their union dues.

☐ Funding and Patrons

Advertising, litigating, and lobbying are expensive. Without financiers, few public interest groups could survive their initial start-up periods. To remain in business, many interest groups rely on membership dues, direct-mail solicitations, special events, and patrons.

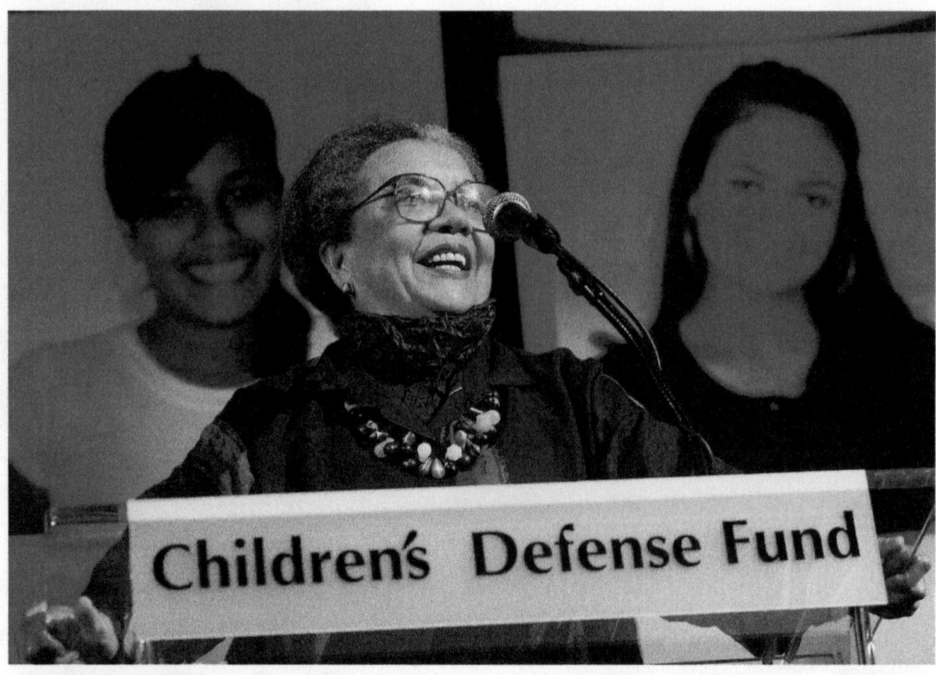

WHO ARE INTEREST-GROUP LEADERS?

As president of the Children's Defense Fund, Marian Wright Edelman continues to fight against child poverty and for better health care. Since the group's establishment in 1973, Edelman has been an active, public face for the cause she represents.

Charismatic leaders often are especially effective fundraisers and recruiters of new members. In addition, governments, foundations, and wealthy individuals can serve as **patrons,** providing crucial start-up funds for groups, especially public interest groups.[33]

patron
A person who finances a group or individual activity.

free rider problem
Potential members fail to join a group because they can get the benefit, or collective good, sought by the group without contributing the effort.

☐ Members

Organizations usually comprise three kinds of members. At the top are a relatively small number of leaders who devote most of their energies to the single group. The second tier of members generally is involved psychologically as well as organizationally. They are the workers of the group—they attend meetings, pay dues, and chair committees to see that things get done. In the bottom tier are the rank-and-file members who don't actively participate. They pay their dues and call themselves group members, but they do little more. Most group members fall into this last category.

Since the 1960s, survey data have revealed that group membership is drawn primarily from people with higher income and education levels.[34] Individuals who are wealthier can afford to belong to more organizations because they have more money and, often, more leisure time. Money and education also are associated with greater confidence that one's actions will bring results, a further incentive to devote time to organizing or supporting interest groups. These elites also are often more involved in politics and hold stronger opinions on many political issues.

People who do belong to groups often join more than one. Overlapping memberships can affect the cohesiveness of a group. Imagine, for example, that you are an officer in the College Republicans. If you call a meeting, people may not attend because they have academic, athletic, or social obligations. Divided loyalties and multiple group memberships frequently affect the success of a group, especially if any one group has too many members who simply fall into the dues-paying category.

Groups vary tremendously in their ability to enroll what are called potential members. According to Mancur Olson, all groups provide a collective good.[35] If one union member at a factory gets a raise, for example, all other workers at that factory will, too. Therefore, those who don't join or work for the benefit of the group still reap the rewards of the group's activity. The downside of this phenomenon is called the **free rider problem**. As Olson asserts, potential members may be unlikely to join a group because they realize that they will receive many of the benefits the group achieves, regardless of their participation. Not only is it irrational for free riders to join any group, but the bigger the group, the greater the free rider problem.

Thus, groups provide a variety of material benefits to convince potential members to join. The American Automobile Association (better known as AAA), for example, offers roadside assistance and trip-planning services to its members. Similarly, AARP offers a wide range of discount programs to its 40 million members over the age of fifty. Many of those members do not necessarily support all of the group's positions but simply want to take advantage of its discounts.

Individuals may also choose to join groups when their rights are threatened. Membership in a group may be necessary to establish credibility in a field, as well. Many lawyers, for example, join local bar associations for this reason.

In addition, groups may form alliances with others to help overcome the free rider problem. These alliances have important implications.[36] For example, farmers and farmers' markets across the country join the Farmers' Market Coalition to raise local and national awareness of the importance of sustainable agriculture.

Interest groups also carve out policy niches to differentiate themselves to potential members as well as policy makers. One study of gay and lesbian groups, for example, found that they avoided direct competition by developing different issue niches.[37] Some concentrate on litigation; others lobby for marriage law reform or open inclusion of gays in the military.

Small groups often have an organizational advantage because, for example, in a small group such as the National Governors Association, any individual's share of the collective good may be great enough to make it rational for him or her to join. Patrons, be they large foundations such as the Koch Family Foundations or individuals such as

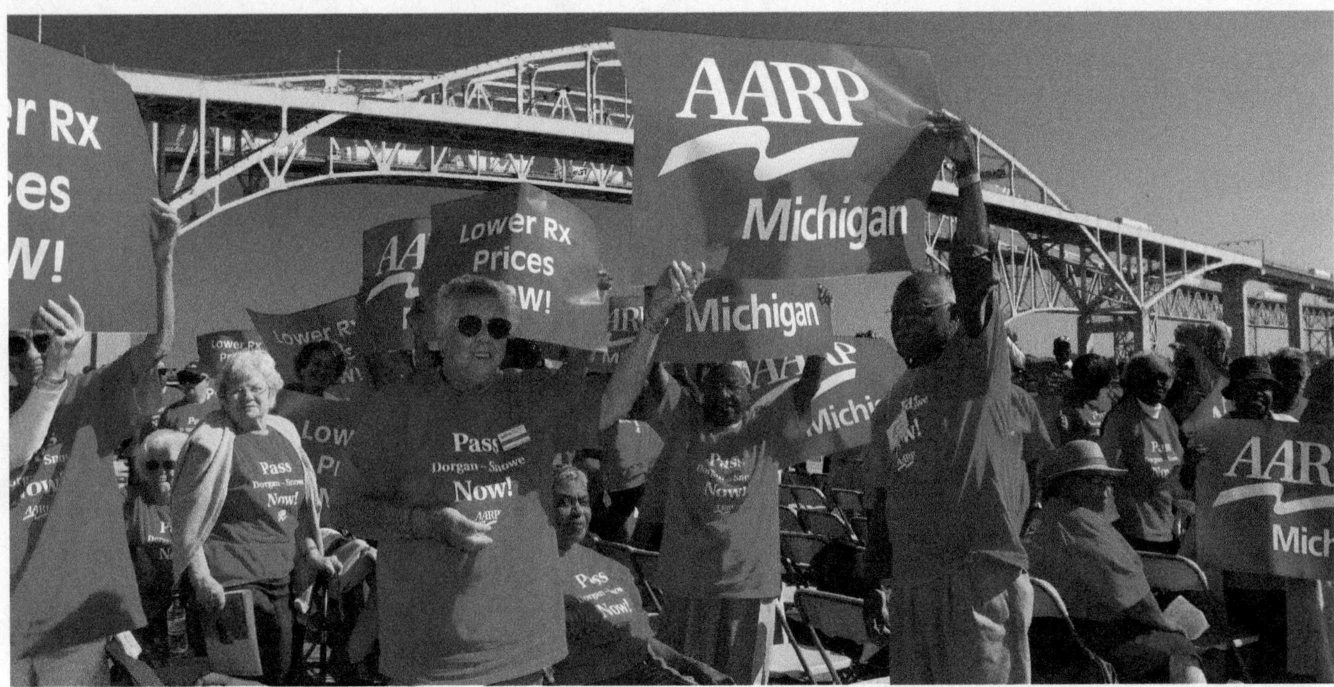

HOW DO INTEREST GROUPS CONVINCE POTENTIAL MEMBERS TO BECOME DUES-PAYING MEMBERS?
AARP has been particularly successful at motivating its pool of potential members to join, in large part because it offers a variety of material benefits. Here, AARP members in Michigan hold a rally advocating the importation of cheaper prescription drugs from Canada, just across the bridge shown in the background.

wealthy financier George Soros, often eliminate the free rider problem for public interest groups.[38] They make the costs of joining minimal because they contribute much of the group's necessary financial support.[39]

Toward Reform: Regulating Interest Groups and Lobbyists

15.5 Explain reform efforts geared toward regulating interest groups and lobbyists.

For the first 150 years of our nation's history, federal lobbying practices went unregulated. While the courts remain largely free of lobbying regulations, reforms have altered the state of affairs in Congress and the executive branch.

☐ Regulating Congressional Lobbyists

In 1946, in an effort to limit the power of lobbyists, Congress passed the Federal Regulation of Lobbying Act, which required anyone hired to lobby any member of Congress to register and file quarterly financial reports. For years, few lobbyists actually filed these reports and numerous good-government groups continued to argue for the strengthening of lobbying laws.

By 1995, public opinion polls began to show that Americans believed the votes of members of Congress were available to the highest bidder. Thus, in late 1995, Congress passed the first effort to regulate lobbying since the 1946 act. The Lobbying Disclosure Act employed a strict definition of lobbyist (one who devotes at least 20 percent of a client's or employer's time to lobbying activities). It also required lobbyists to: (1) register

Can Interest Groups Buy Public Policy?

Interest groups such as banks and labor unions participate in activities that influence legislation their members care about, such as tax policy or social benefits. During the election season, interest groups team up with political action committees (PACs) to finance different campaigns. Directing contributions to the party in power, and specifically to committee members who write legislation, is a common practice in American politics. Both labor unions and banks donate similar amounts of money to candidates, but they have different contribution strategies.

Banks and Labor Unions Have Similar Campaign Funding

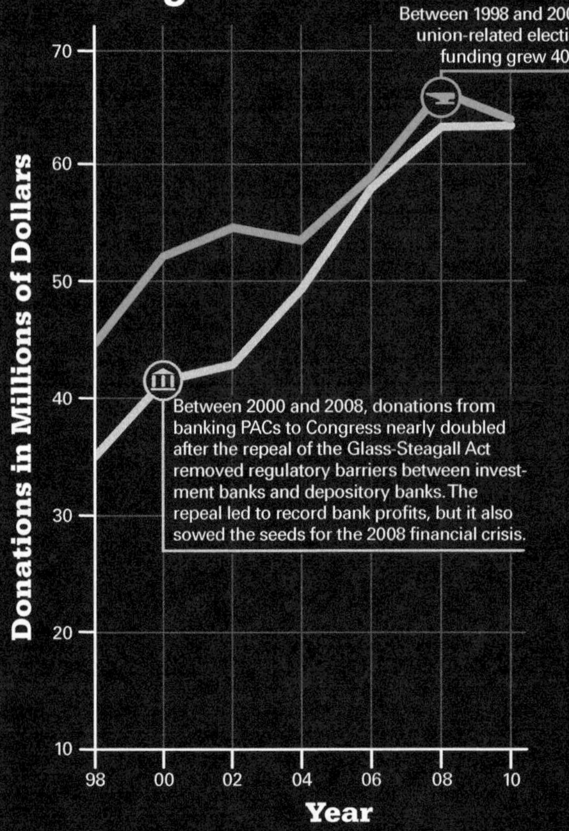

Between 1998 and 2008, union-related election funding grew 40%.
Between 2000 and 2008, donations from banking PACs to Congress nearly doubled after the repeal of the Glass-Steagall Act removed regulatory barriers between investment banks and depository banks. The repeal led to record bank profits, but it also sowed the seeds for the 2008 financial crisis.
Donations in Millions of Dollars
70
60
50
40
30
20
10
98
00
02
04
06
08
10
Year
Labor donations to all candidates
Banking donations to all candidates

SOURCE: Data from the Federal Election Commission, www.fec.gov.

Banks and Labor Unions Have Different Party Priorities

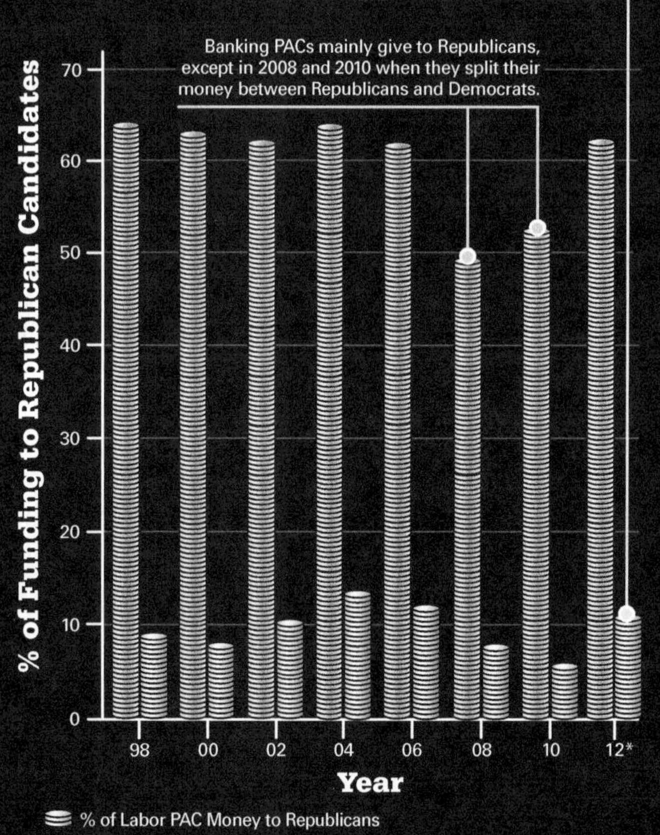

Labor PACs consistently give less than 20% of their money to Republicans no matter which party is in power.
Banking PACs mainly give to Republicans, except in 2008 and 2010 when they split their money between Republicans and Democrats.
% of Funding to Republican Candidates
70
60
50
40
30
20
10
0
98
00
02
04
06
08
10
12*
Year
% of Labor PAC Money to Republicans
% of Banking PAC Money to Republicans

* As of reporting period ending October 1, 2012.

Investigate Further

Concept Are banks or labor unions giving more money to politicians through their PACs? They are giving roughly similar amounts of money. In fact, labor PACs donate more money than banking PACs.

Connection How are labor unions' donation strategies different from those of banks? Labor PACs consistently give the majority of their PAC money to Democrats even when Republicans control Congress. Banking PACs give more strategically. During most years, they focus their money on Republicans, but when Democrats are in power they split their donations between both parties.

Cause How do interest groups buy policy? Interest groups use PACs and campaign financing to reinforce political friendships with legislators. Labor PACs use their donations to support Democrats who share their ideological values, while banking PACs change their donation strategy depending on which party is in power.

15.1

15.2

15.3

15.4

15.5

Honest Leadership and Open Government Act of 2007
Lobbying reform banning gifts to members of Congress and their staffs, toughening disclosure requirements, and increasing time limits on moving from the federal government to the private sector.

with the clerk of the House and the secretary of the Senate; (2) report their clients and issues and the agency or house they lobbied; and (3) estimate the amount they are paid by each client. These reporting requirements made it easier for watchdog groups or the media to monitor lobbying activities. In fact, a comprehensive analysis by the Center for Responsive Politics revealed that by the end of 2011, 12,714 lobbyists were registered. Nearly $6 million was spent on lobbying for every member of Congress.[40]

After lobbyist Jack Abramoff pleaded guilty to extensive corruption charges in 2006, Congress pledged to reexamine the role of lobbyists in the legislative process. After the Democrats took control of both houses of Congress in 2007 in the wake of a variety of lobbying scandals, they were able to pass the **Honest Leadership and Open Government Act of 2007**. Among the act's key provisions were a ban on gifts and honoraria to members of Congress and their staffs, tougher disclosure requirements, and longer time limits on moving from the federal government to the private lobbying sector. Many observers complained, however, that the law did not go far enough. In particular, many commentators were critical of the fact that the ban on gifts applied only to private lobbyists. Thus, state and local agencies and public universities, for example, are still free to offer tickets for football and basketball games, as well as to provide meals and travel.[41]

☐ Regulating Executive Branch Lobbyists

Formal lobbying of the executive branch is governed by some restrictions in the 1995 Lobbying Disclosure Act as well as updates contained in the Honest Leadership and Open Government Act of 2007. Executive branch employees are also constrained by the 1978 Ethics in Government Act. Enacted in the wake of the Watergate scandal, this legislation attempted to curtail questionable moves by barring members of the executive branch from representing any clients before their agency for two years after leaving governmental service. Thus, someone who worked in air pollution policy for the Environmental Protection Agency and then went to work for the Environmental Defense Fund would have to wait two years before lobbying his or her old agency.

More recently, the Obama administration has implemented reforms that bring congressional-style lobbying regulation to the executive branch. In regulations put into place on his first day on the job, Barack Obama limited aides leaving the White House from lobbying executive agencies within two years. He also banned members of the administration from accepting gifts from lobbyists.

☐ Regulating Judicial Branch Lobbyists

There are few formal regulations on interest group participation before the Supreme Court. Though interested parties must ask the Court for permission to file an *amicus curiae* brief, in practice, the great majority of these petitions are granted. In recent years, activists have called for reform to the case sponsorship and oral advocacy processes before the Court, but to no avail. Similarly, a number of nonprofit and good government groups have suggested that there need to be additional restrictions on groups' access to judges in "legal education" sessions—many of which are held at fancy resorts at little to no cost to the judges. Congress and the judiciary have also failed to put these regulations in place.

Review the Chapter

Listen to Chapter 15 on MyPoliSciLab

Roots of the American Interest Group System

15.1 Trace the roots of the American interest group system, p. 455.

An organized interest is a collection of people or groups with shared attitudes who make claims on government. Political scientists approach the development of interest groups from a number of theoretical perspectives, including pluralist theory and the transactions approach. Interest groups can be classified in a variety of ways, based on their functions and membership.

The Development of American Interest Groups

15.2 Describe the historical development of American interest groups, p. 458.

Interest groups did not begin to emerge in the United States until the 1830s. From 1890 to 1920, the Progressive movement dominated. The 1960s saw the rise of a wide variety of liberal interest groups. During the 1970s and 1980s, legions of conservatives formed new groups to counteract those efforts. Business groups, corporations, and unions also established their presence in Washington, D.C., during this time.

What Do Interest Groups Do?

15.3 Identify several strategies and tactics used by organized interests, p. 464.

Interest groups often fill voids left by the major political parties and give Americans opportunities to make organized claims on government. The most common activity of interest groups is lobbying, which takes many forms. Groups routinely pressure members of Congress and their staffs, the president and the bureaucracy, and the courts; they use a variety of techniques to educate and stimulate the public to pressure key governmental decision makers. Interest groups also attempt to influence the outcome of elections; some run their own candidates for office. Others rate elected officials to inform their members how particular legislators stand on issues of importance to them. Political action committees (PACs), a way for some groups to contribute money to candidates for office, are another means of gaining support from elected officials and ensuring that supportive officials stay in office.

What Makes Interest Groups Successful?

15.4 Analyze the factors that make an interest group successful, p. 470.

Interest group success can be measured in a variety of ways, including a group's ability to get its issues on the public agenda, winning key pieces of legislation in Congress or executive branch or judicial rulings, or backing successful candidates. Several factors contribute to interest group success, including leaders and patrons, funding, and committed members.

Toward Reform: Regulating Interest Groups and Lobbyists

15.5 Explain reform efforts geared toward regulating interest groups and lobbyists, p. 474.

Not until 1946 did Congress pass any laws regulating federal lobbying. Those laws were largely ineffective and were successfully challenged as violations of the First Amendment. In 1995, Congress passed the Lobbying Disclosure Act, which required lobbyists to register with both houses of Congress. By 2007, a rash of scandals resulted in sweeping reforms called the Honest Leadership and Open Government Act, which dramatically limited what lobbyists can do. The executive branch is regulated by the 1978 Ethics in Government Act. Lobbying the judiciary is largely unregulated.

Learn the Terms

Study and Review the Flashcards

civic virtue, p. 455
collective good, p. 456
disturbance theory, p. 455
economic interest group, p. 458
free rider problem, p. 473
Honest Leadership and Open Government Act of 2007, p. 476
interest group, p. 455
lobbying, p. 465
lobbyist, p. 460
patron, p. 473
pluralist theory, p. 455
political action committee (PAC), p. 458
public interest group, p. 456
social capital, p. 455
trade association, p. 461
transactions theory, p. 456

Test Yourself

Study and Review the Practice Tests

1. Which theory of group politics emphasizes the distribution of political power among a wide array of diffuse interests?

a. Pluralist theory
b. Transactions theory
c. Social capital theory
d. Elite theory
e. Disturbance theory

2. Interest groups that are formed with the primary goal of engaging in campaigns and elections are known as:

a. citizen campaign associations.
b. public interest groups.
c. economic groups.
d. political action committees.
e. governmental organizations.

3. Many interest groups established in the 1830s shared a common tradition in the

a. women's rights movement.
b. Christian revival.
c. temperance movement.
d. development of the economy.
e. growth of political campaigns.

4. Many Progressive era groups placed pressure on the national government to begin

a. regulating business.
b. funding small businesses.
c. lowering taxes.
d. cutting budgets.
e. increasing political patronage.

5. Interest groups may participate in the courts by:

a. directly lobbying justices.
b. giving campaign contributions to federal judges.
c. filing friend of the court briefs.
d. submitting formal comments on judicial decisions.
e. writing proposed legislation.

6. Which of the following can a political action committee NOT do?

a. Endorse candidates
b. Produce advertisements for like-minded candidates
c. Rate candidates or elected officials
d. Make financial contributions to candidates
e. Coordinate expenditures with a candidate's campaign

7. Most interest group members fall into which of the following categories?

a. Leaders
b. Active participants
c. Lobbyists
d. Those who pay dues, but do not actively participate within the group
e. Politically disengaged

8. What is the term for an individual who reaps the benefits of an interest group's activity without actually having membership in the group?

a. Patron
b. Free rider
c. Lobbyist
d. Constituent
e. Elite

9. Which of the three branches of government still remain largely free of lobbying regulations?

- **a.** Executive
- **b.** Judicial
- **c.** Legislative
- **d.** Executive and legislative
- **e.** Executive and judicial

10. The 1978 Ethics in Government Act was passed as a result of

- **a.** U.S. involvement in the Vietnam War.
- **b.** the economic recession.
- **c.** the Watergate scandal.
- **d.** Great Society legislation.
- **e.** the Arab oil embargo.

Explore Further

Baumgartner, Frank R., Jeffrey M. Berry, Marie Hojnacki, David C. Kimball, and Beth L. Leech. *Lobbying and Policy Change: Who Wins, Who Loses, and Why*. Chicago: University of Chicago Press, 2009.

Berry, Jeffrey M., and Clyde Wilcox. *The Interest Group Society*, 5th ed. New York: Longman, 2008.

Cigler, Allan J., and Burdett A. Loomis, eds. *Interest Group Politics*, 8th ed. Washington, DC: CQ Press, 2011.

Collins, Paul M., Jr. *Friends of the Supreme Court: Interest Groups and Judicial Decision Making*. New York: Oxford University Press, 2008.

Grossman, Matt. *The Not-So-Special Interests: Interest Groups, Public Representation, and American Governance*. Stanford, CA: Stanford University Press, 2012.

Herrnson, Paul S., Christopher J. Deering, and Clyde Wilcox, eds. *Interest Groups Unleashed*. Washington, DC: CQ Press, 2012.

Kollman, Ken. *Outside Lobbying: Public Opinion and Interest Group Strategies*. Princeton, NJ: Princeton University Press, 1998.

Loomis, Burdett A., ed. *CQ Press Guide to Interest Groups and Lobbying in the United States*. Washington, DC: CQ Press, 2011.

Maisel, L. Sandy, and Jeffrey M. Berry. *The Oxford Handbook of American Political Parties and Interest Groups*, reprint ed. New York: Oxford University Press, 2012.

McGlen, Nancy E., Karen O'Connor, Laura Van Assendelft, and Wendy Gunther-Canada. *Women, Politics, and American Society*, 5th ed. New York: Longman, 2010.

Nownes, Anthony J. *Interest Groups in American Politics: Pressure and Power*, 2nd ed. New York: Routledge, 2012.

Olson, Mancur. *The Logic of Collective Action: Public Goods and the Theory of Groups*. Cambridge, MA: Harvard University Press, 1965.

Rozell, Mark J., Clyde Wilcox, and Michael M. Franz. *Interest Groups in American Campaigns: The New Face of Electioneering*, 3rd ed. New York: Oxford University Press, 2012.

Schlozman, Kay Lehman, Sidney Verba, and Henry E. Brady. *The Unheavenly Chorus: Unequal Political Voice and the Broken Promise of American Democracy*. Princeton, NJ: Princeton University Press, 2012.

Truman, David B. *The Governmental Process: Political Interests and Public Opinion*. New York: Knopf, 1951.

To learn more about specific interest groups discussed in this chapter, type the name of the group into an Internet search engine and ask yourself the following questions as you explore the group's Web site:

- What are this group's stated goals?
- What are the requirements to become a member of the group?
- Does the group provide information that can be used by anyone, even someone not interested in formally joining the group?
- On its Web site, does this group explicitly oppose any other interest groups?

To learn more about how interest groups grade your political representatives, go to Project Vote Smart at **www.votesmart.org** and click "Interest Group Ratings" on the home page.

To learn more about interest group fund-raising, go to the Center for Responsive Politics's Web site at **www.opensecrets.org**.

To learn more about lobbying reform efforts, go to Thomas, the legislative information section of the Library of Congress, at **thomas.loc.gov**. Search for the Lobbying Disclosure Act of 1995 and the Honest Leadership and Open Government Act of 2007 in order to find out more about the lobbying restrictions required by this legislation.

16

Listen to Chapter 16 on MyPoliSciLab

Domestic Policy

On the evening of April 20, 2010, an offshore drilling well, leased and run by British Petroleum (BP) and known as Deepwater Horizon, exploded off the coast of the state of Louisiana. The well released methane gas and ignited into flames, killing eleven workers and injuring seventeen others. Two days later, on April 22, the rig completely sank into the ocean, and workers observed an oil slick forming in the Gulf of Mexico. What followed became the greatest environmental disaster in American history, as BP repeatedly tried—and failed—to cap the leak or capture the oil leaking into the Gulf.

The company used a variety of tactics to try to stop the constant flow of oil These included using unmanned underwater robots to close the open valves on the rig, installing containment domes, and attempting to divert the flow away from the fractured pipe. Nearly 2 million gallons of chemical dispersants were applied directly to the well one mile below the surface of the ocean in order to break the oil into tiny droplets. Finally, on July 15, almost three months after the leak had begun, engineers were able to cap the leaking well.

Three years after the spill, estimates of the environmental and economic impact of the BP spill remain imprecise. Although visible short-term damage can be measured, including more than a half million claims by businesses and individuals, over a thousand miles of oiled shoreline, and the deaths of thousands of birds, turtles, and sea mammals, the long-term impact is immeasurable. Large areas of the ocean floor remain covered in oil, and plumes of oil and natural gas have been detected in a ten mile radius, endangering the sensitive growth stages of the entire marine food chain. A total of 88,000 square miles of the Gulf remain closed, off limits to the fishing and oil industries. Scientists question whether the recent increase in the death of young bottlenose dolphins is linked to the spill; more than 150 washed ashore in the first few months of 2012.

It often takes a crisis of this magnitude to prompt changes in public policy, yet controversies about the responsible party, the economic impact of regulations, and scientific and technological uncertainties impede decision making. Many Gulf state politicians initially called on the national government for

16.1	16.2	16.3	16.4	16.5
Trace the stages of the policy-making process, p. 483.	Describe health policy in the United States, p. 495.	Outline education policy in the United States, p. 502.	Explain energy and environmental policy in the United States, p. 506.	Assess the ongoing challenges in U.S. domestic policy, p. 511.

DRILLING FOR OIL HAS BEEN A MAJOR INDUSTRY IN THE UNITED STATES SINCE THE 1850s.
Above, an oil well at Semitropic, California, in the late 1800s. Below, the Deepwater Horizon in the Gulf of Mexico following the 2010 disaster.

MyPoliSciLab Videos

The Big Picture What policies would you implement to improve the government? Author Alixandra B. Yanus traces the public policy process in America and demonstrates how a policy evolves from just an idea or suggestion into a full-fledged law.

The Basics Find out what public policy is, who makes public policy, and how they make it. In this video, you will also explore the major social policy issues we face and consider the role of the federal and state governments in specific areas such as education.

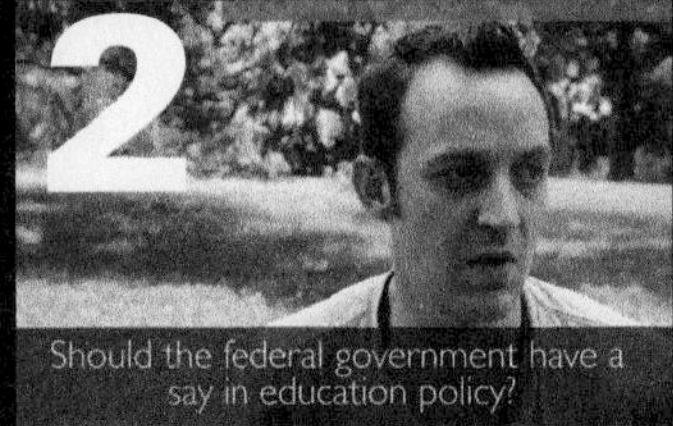

In Context Discover the history of social policy in the United States. In this video, Columbia University political scientist Ester Fuchs discusses why social policy emerged and how the focus of social policy had changed over time.

Thinking Like a Political Scientist What role do political scientists play in policy making? Columbia University political scientist Ester Fuchs examines not only the research of political scientist on public policy, but the impact of this research on the policy making process.

In the Real World In order to reduce unemployment among younger people, the federal government allows companies to pay workers under the age of 20 less than the minimum wage. Real people discuss the larger implications of this law, and whether or not it is beneficial or harmful to young people.

So What? How well is the government working? Author Alixandra B. Yanus demonstrates how public policy affects almost every aspect of your daily life—whether you are aware of it or not—and she explains why the strength of public policies is the best way to measure of the strength of political institutions.

support. Later, however, they criticized the efforts of the Army Corps of Engineers and the Coast Guard to limit the spill. In particular, Louisiana Republican Governor Bobby Jindal said, "We've been frustrated with the disjointed effort to date that has too often meant too little, too late for the oil hitting our coast. . . . It is clear we don't have the resources we need to protect our coast . . . we need more boom, more skimmers, more vacuums, more jack-up barges . . ."[1] Despite U.S. military and administrative involvement in the cleanup efforts, President Barack Obama has claimed that the cost of cleansing affected areas should fall entirely on the shoulders of BP. "We will fight this spill with everything we've got for as long as it takes. We will make BP pay for the damage their company has caused," said President Obama.[2] The oil company, to date, has paid over $6 billion in claims, with a tentative settlement agreement to pay an estimated $7.8 billion in "fairness" for the company's liability. The real policy concern, however, is how to prevent such a disaster in the future. In the short term, President Barack Obama delayed plans for leasing new drilling sites off the coast of mid-Atlantic and southeastern states and in large areas of the eastern Gulf region pending further study.

public policy
An intentional course of action or inaction followed by government in dealing with some problem or matter of concern.

domestic policy
A category of public policy that includes a broad and varied range of government programs affecting the lives of citizens within a country.

•••

Public policy is an intentional course of action or inaction followed by government in dealing with some problem or matter of concern.[3] Public policies are thus governmental policies; they are authoritative and binding on people. Individuals, groups, and even government agencies that do not comply with policies can face penalties of fines, loss of benefits, or even jail terms. The phrase "course of action" implies that policies develop or unfold over time. They involve more than a legislative decision to enact a law or a presidential decision to issue an executive order. Also important is how the law or executive order is carried out. The impact or meaning of a policy depends on whether it is vigorously enforced, enforced only in some instances, or not enforced at all. Government inaction, or the decision not to make policy, also defines public policy.

Domestic policy is a category of public policy that includes a broad and varied range of government programs affecting the lives of citizens within a country. Health care, welfare, education, environment, energy, and public safety are all considered domestic policies, although most public policy today also has global implications. Domestic policies reflect a country's historical experiences, values, and attitudes toward social and economic conditions. This chapter provides in-depth analysis of three domestic policy areas: health care, education, and environment and energy. Each area highlights a different stage of the policy-making process and the conditions that create opportunities for and constraints on reform.

Roots of Domestic Policy in the United States

16.1 Trace the stages of the policy-making process.

The Framers of the Constitution created a decentralized policy-making process with powers shared by Congress, the president, the courts, and the states. In addition, social forces, including attitudes toward the role and size of government, constrain the development of government policies. In the United States, policy making often begins at the state and local levels, where these "laboratories for democracy" set the stage for federal governmental action. Some issues, however, instantly demand policy leadership at the federal level. Which level of government dominates can change over time as issues evolve. Historically, the federal government's involvement in domestic policy making has shifted focus from the immediate economic and national security concerns facing the new nation, to improvement of social and working conditions created by industrialization, to an expanded focus on a broad range of domestic policies, including health care, welfare, education, environment, energy, and public safety.

16.1

16.2

16.3

16.4

16.5

Patient Protection and Affordable Care Act
2010 legislation aimed at reducing the number of uninsured individuals and decreasing health care costs.

As the federal government initially concentrated more on economic policy and national security, states took the lead in addressing poor living and working conditions for Americans. Progressivism called for reforms in response to the industrial revolution, starting at the grassroots level, working up to the states, and eventually capturing the federal government's attention. In the area of child labor, for example, in 1836 Massachusetts required child factory workers under the age of 15 to spend at least three months in school. Other states followed with limits on the length of a child's workday and minimum age laws. The National Child Labor Committee was formed in 1904, but when the first federal child labor law, the Keating-Owen Act, passed in 1916 it was struck down as unconstitutional.[4] The law was revised, reintroduced, and subsequently struck down again. Similarly, states passed protective legislation to improve the working conditions of women. Oregon's maximum hour law, which applied to women but not to men, was declared unconstitutional. When Congress passed a minimum wage law for women and children working in the District of Columbia, it was also struck down. Finally, the 1938 Fair Labor Standards Act created a minimum wage for both women and men and prohibited the employment of minors. The 1930s marked a clear change in the federal government's role in domestic policy making, specifically in the President's role in dominating that process. President Franklin Roosevelt's New Deal created the modern welfare state and the first entitlement programs: Social Security and Aid to Families with Dependent Children. From that point, the federal government, under the direction of strong presidential advocates, continued to expand its role in domestic policy.

☐ The Evolution of Health Care Policy

In the health care field, the federal government's involvement began in 1798 with the establishment of the National Marine Service (NMS) for "the relief of sick and disabled seamen." States and localities primarily were responsible for public health issues, including public sanitation, clean water programs, pasteurization of milk, immunization programs, and other activities designed to reduce the incidence of infectious and communicable diseases. National health insurance first received serious consideration in the 1930s, when Congress was legislating a number of New Deal social programs. But, because of the strong opposition of the American Medical Association (AMA), universal health insurance was not adopted. The AMA and its allies distrusted government intervention in their affairs and feared that regulations would limit their discretion as well as their earnings. In particular, they worried that government intrusion into the health care field would limit physicians' fees, restrict the amount of time approved for specific types of hospital visits, and constrain charges for prescription drugs.

As a result, government health insurance remained on the back burner for many years. It received some consideration during the 1960s, when Congress and the Johnson administration were working to establish Medicare and Medicaid. Health care attracted a great deal of attention in the early 1990s, during the first year of President Bill Clinton's term. Clinton established a health care reform task force led by his wife, Hillary, and attempted to compel Congress to adopt legislation creating universal health coverage in the United States. Ultimately, however, these efforts failed. The phrase "socialized medicine" and horror stories about long wait times for medically necessary services in countries with nationalized health care turned public opinion against Clinton and the Democrats.

Clinton's failure at health care reform, as well as the extended period of Republican legislative control that began in 1995, kept national health insurance off the governmental agenda for the next fifteen years. During this time, health care costs and the number of uninsured Americans rose dramatically. By 2008, more than 45 million Americans had no health insurance coverage, and another 20 million were underinsured.

Thus, during the 2008 presidential election, Democratic candidate Barack Obama ran on a platform that promised to bring much-needed reform to the American health insurance system. After taking office, Obama and the Democratic Congress set to work crafting legislation that accomplished their goal. More than a year later—and after a great deal of political wrangling—on March 23, 2010, President Obama signed into law the **Patient Protection and Affordable Care Act.** This legislation represents a dramatic change in the federal government's role in health care policy. Immediately, states challenged the constitutionality of the law, and in 2012 the Supreme Court voted 5–4 to uphold it.

The Evolution of Education Policy

In the field of public education, the state level also historically took the lead. Following the Revolutionary War, reformers of that era, such as Benjamin Franklin, began to see education as a means of legitimizing democratic institutions in the minds of young people and of establishing social and political order in the United States. In 1787, the Northwest Ordinance specifically set aside land for the establishment of public schools. However, state and local governments controlled development of their education systems, curricula, and goals. In 1852, Massachusetts passed the first compulsory education law, and by 1918 all states had similar laws.

In the late nineteenth and early twentieth century, when immigration was at high levels, education again emerged on the governmental agenda. Many of the social, economic, and political elites of the era came to view education as a tool for assimilating immigrants and for protecting social and political order. Policy making focused on curriculum development. Reforms came about largely through the work of John Dewey (1859–1952), a psychologist by training, who advocated experiential learning rather than relying on passive experience, whereby teachers would inform students of "facts," and students would memorize them. By the mid-twentieth century, the Cold War between the United States and the Soviet Union sparked new curriculum reforms focused on enhancing math and science programs. After the Soviets launched the world's first satellite, known as *Sputnik I,* into space on October 4, 1957, many American policy makers and citizens grew concerned about the capacity of American technology to meet the perceived threat of the Soviet Union and its allies.

WHO WAS JOHN DEWEY?

John Dewey was an influential education reform advocate of the late nineteenth and early twentieth centuries. He advocated active and experiential learning. He also created the numeric Dewey Decimal system for organizing books uniformly throughout the United States.

At the same time, education policy making at the federal level shifted toward access and equality. The Supreme Court's landmark decision in *Brown* v. *Board of Education* (1954) ruled that separate educational facilities for black and white students were inherently unequal. *Brown* established both the road map for racial desegregation in American schools and a national standard for equality of educational opportunity. Under Johnson's War on Poverty, Head Start was initiated in 1964 to provide preschool to at-risk low-income children, and the Elementary and Secondary Education Act of 1965 created Title I programs to improve educational opportunities for low-income K–12 students. These policies marked an important turning point in education policy. Enforcement of civil rights legislation—related to both race and gender, such as Title IX of the Education Amendments of 1972—required the national government to increasingly involve itself in a policy area traditionally reserved for state and local governments.

The Department of Education was created as a Cabinet-level agency in 1979 specifically to guide national education policy, establish education opportunity programs, and construct national examinations for administration in local schools. In 1983, the department released *A Nation at Risk,* including sobering statistics about the quality of education in the United States. Among the report's findings were the following: 13% of all seventeen-year-olds were functionally illiterate; standardized test scores had declined; achievement in math and science had declined; students were spending an average of 6 hours per day for 180 days in school, compared with 8 hours per day for 220 days in other industrialized countries; and most students lacked "higher order" intellectual skills, such as the ability to draw inferences, write persuasive essays, or solve multistep math problems.

States responded with outcome-based education (OBE) reforms in the 1980s, focused on assessment of student learning, while the national government continued providing guidelines. In 1994, Congress passed the Goals 2000: Educate America Act, replacing OBE with standards-based education (SBE). States worked to develop their own standardized curriculums and assessment programs based on federal guidelines, paving the way for more comprehensive reform with the 2002 No Child Left Behind Act (NCLB). NCLB linked standards, testing, and accountability, further increasing the role of the federal government in education policy. While the new federal legislation did not *require* policy change, states had to comply with federal rules if they wanted

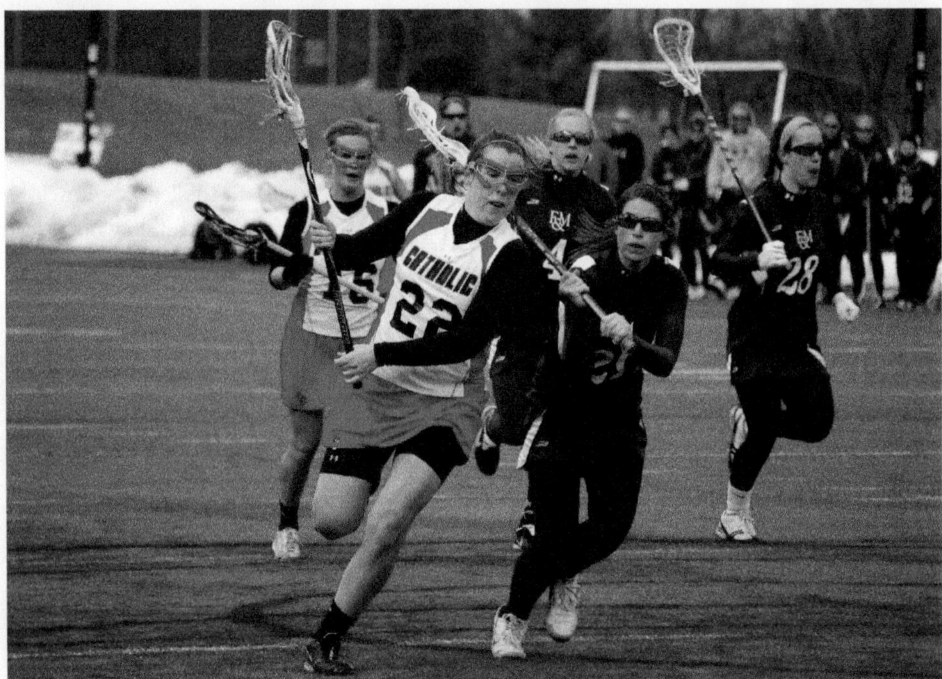

HOW DID TITLE IX CHANGE EDUCATION?

Title IX of the Education Amendments of 1972 greatly expanded educational and athletic opportunities for women. As a result of these gender equity requirements, women's lacrosse is one of the fastest growing collegiate sports.

to receive federal funding. Included in the legislation was a school choice option in the event a school fails to meet standards or make adequate yearly progress. The school choice movement, as well as strong arguments for privatization of elementary and secondary education, reflects the influence of Nobel Prize–winning economist Milton Friedman, who concluded that through private marketplace competition, schools would be forced to either improve student achievement outcomes or face the shuttering of their enterprise. More than a decade after passage of NCLB, states continued to struggle to meet standards. President Barack Obama created the Race to the Top initiative to encourage states to develop their own innovative education reforms. By 2011, math scores were the highest they had been since enactment of NCLB, although reading scores had not measurably improved.[5]

☐ The Evolution of Energy and Environmental Policy

In the areas of environmental and energy policy, issues have successfully demanded national attention and federal government policy leadership until recently. Initial concerns about the environment related to industrialization and laissez-faire attitudes about what individuals and businesses could do with their private property. President Theodore Roosevelt, a Progressive, embraced conservation as a federal government policy, creating the U.S. Forest Service, national parks, national forests, national monuments, and nature preserves. President Franklin D. Roosevelt continued this trend and, in 1937, Congress passed the Pittman-Robertson Federal Aid and Wildlife Restoration Act to protect endangered species and provide conservation funding for state programs.

By the late 1950s and early 1960s, America was in the midst of one of the most robust economic periods in national history. The nation prospered, with vibrant manufacturing and transportation sectors that were bolstered by access to cheap fossil fuels. With the nation's abundant coal supplies and relatively unfettered access to oil, little need arose for government efforts in the area of energy policy. In essence, the issue of energy was largely absent from the government agenda because energy was not seen as a real problem for the United States.[6] However, the effects of intensive energy use on the environment grew more obvious to the nation as a whole. From heavy smog in major cities to thick clouds of smoke in industrial towns, Americans had begun to take notice of deteriorating environmental conditions that related to its industrial might.

In response, the government's agenda shifted from conservation to environmental protection. The 1962 publication of Rachel Carson's *Silent Spring* increased the visibility of environmental damage due to toxic and hazardous waste. Americans' growing concerns about environmental conditions led to the first Earth Day in 1970, when millions of citizens took part in marches and rallies demanding greater government action to protect the environment. This public pressure had tremendous impact on the national and state governments, ushering in the "environmental decade" of the 1970s. The Environmental Protection Agency (EPA) was created in 1970 and the federal government passed major policies affecting water pollution, air pollution, endangered species, and hazardous waste.

At the same time, the United States grew increasingly dependent on oil from foreign sources. In particular, oil from Middle Eastern nations such as Saudi Arabia and Iran accounted for a growing share of the nation's energy sources. While foreign oil remained cheap and abundant, the national government faced little demand to invest itself in major energy initiatives. But, in 1973, the need for action in the area of energy became all too obvious to the American public, and the energy problem abruptly found its way onto the government's agenda. On October 17, 1973, the members of the Organization of Arab Petroleum Exporting Countries (OAPEC) announced an embargo of oil shipments to any nation that supported Israel during its war with Egypt and Syria; this included the United States.[7] The embargo was compounded when the larger Organization of Petroleum Exporting Countries (OPEC) decided to raise oil prices throughout the world.[8] The cumulative impact of these actions was a dramatic increase in the cost of oil in the United States, with a gallon of gasoline rising from 38 cents to 55 cents between May 1973 and May 1974.[9] Soaring prices and shrinking supplies led to the first rationing of gas in the United States since the end of World War II and thrust energy to the front of the government's agenda.

The national government responded with a series of policies designed to reduce consumption of petroleum in the United States, including a national speed limit of 55 miles per hour in order to increase fuel efficiency and an earlier date for the start of daylight savings time in an attempt to lower demand for electricity.[10] It also initiated Corporate Average Fuel Efficiency (CAFE) standards in 1975, which required automakers to meet average fuel efficiency standards for the fleet of cars they sold in the United States. For example, in 1978, General Motors was required to have its domestically sold automobiles average 18 miles per gallon (MPG). This meant GM could sell a large sedan that got 12 MPG if it also sold a smaller car that got 24 MPG.

Besides adopting energy conservation measures, the national government also turned its attention to increasing the availability of energy for the nation. To minimize the short-term impact of oil disruptions, Congress established the Strategic Petroleum Reserve in 1975 as part of the Energy Policy and Conservation Act. The Strategic Petroleum Reserve holds about two months of inventory that can be accessed under a presidential order.

With policy initiatives mounting and the complexity of energy policy growing, the Department of Energy (DOE) was established in 1977.[11] In 1978, Congress expanded the reach of the DOE with passage of the National Energy Act of 1978 (NEA), a comprehensive law including a variety of components related to both energy conservation and the expansion of energy sources. A key component of the 1978 NEA was the Energy Tax Act, providing tax breaks to individuals and companies that used alternative energy sources, such as solar or geothermal power, and penalizing inefficient use of energy by establishing a "gas-guzzler tax" on cars that did not reach a minimum MPG threshold. Although the purpose of the gas-guzzler tax was to reduce the public demand for such vehicles, the law did not make the impact originally anticipated because it did not apply to vehicles over 6,000 pounds. What was originally considered an exemption for businesses that needed vans and trucks to do their work turned out to be a way around the gas-guzzler tax for business owners, who could purchase or lease sport utility vehicles (SUVs) to conduct everyday business activities.

In 1989, the oil tanker *Exxon Valdez* ran aground, spilling 11 million gallons of crude oil into the Prince Edward Sound off the coast of Alaska. The environmental crisis

16.1

16.2

16.3

16.4

16.5

greenhouse gases
Gases in the atmosphere that lead to higher global temperatures.

global warming
The increase in global temperatures due to carbon emissions from burning fossil fuels such as coal and oil.

that followed ultimately prompted congressional passage of the 1990 Oil Pollution Act, improving the EPA's ability to prevent and respond to future oil spills. The law created an Oil Spill Liability Trust Fund to provide funding to clean up oil spills if the responsible party is unable to do so. New rules required oil companies to submit oil spill contingency plans and meet new standards for above-ground storage of oil. The Coast Guard also issued new rules requiring a double-hulled structure for oil tankers. These policies would later prove insufficient, as revealed by the BP incident of 2010, not just in containing an oil spill but in protecting the safety of oil spill cleanup workers, as well.

Global concern for climate change also escalated during the 1980s. Scientists warned that the burning of fossil fuels contributes to increased levels of **greenhouse gases** in the atmosphere, which in turn leads to higher global temperatures. These higher temperatures have a number of significant impacts on the planet, such as melting polar ice caps, increasing sea levels, prolonged droughts, more intense storms, major habitat destruction, and species extinction. These scientific concerns have spurred international action to manage the problem of **global warming.**

However, while most of the world's industrial nations ratified the Kyoto Protocol in 1997, which committed them to reducing greenhouse gas emissions, the United States did not do so. President George W. Bush steadfastly refused to join other nations in signing the treaty, citing the damaging effects of the Protocol on the U.S. economy. In contrast, former Vice President Al Gore gained national attention as an advocate for awareness of climate change with the 2006 film *An Inconvenient Truth,* winning the Nobel Peace Prize in 2007 for his activism. Still, no comprehensive change in national policy took place. In the absence of major national activity to control global warming, state governments began taking the lead with climate change action plans, regional agreements, and legislation to reduce emissions, increase efficiency, and promote alternative fuel.

Domestic policy making in the United States has evolved over time, shifting responsibility and leadership back and forth between the states and the federal government. The role of government in domestic policy making at all levels has expanded, increasing the number and types of domestic policies. Within each policy area, the nature of an issue often changes as well. Ultimately, the domestic policy-making process reflects the country's historical experiences, values, and attitudes toward social and economic conditions.

☐ A Model of the Policy-Making Process

Political scientists and other social scientists have developed many theories and models to explain the formation of public policies. These theories include elite theory, bureaucratic theory, interest group theory, and pluralist theory. According to elite theory, all societies are divided into elites and masses. The elites have power to make and implement policy, while the masses simply respond to the desires of the elites. Elite theorists believe that an unequal distribution of power in society is normal and inevitable.[12] Elites, however, are not immune from public opinion, nor do they, by definition, oppress the masses.

Bureaucratic theory dictates that all institutions, governmental and nongovernmental, have fallen under the control of a large and ever-growing bureaucracy that carries out policy using standardized procedures. This growing complexity of modern organizations has empowered bureaucrats, who become dominant as a consequence of their expertise and competence. Eventually, the bureaucrats wrest power from others, especially elected officials.

In contrast, according to interest group theory, interest groups—not elites or bureaucrats—control the governmental process. Interest group theorists believe that so many potential pressure points are in the three branches of the national government, as well as at the state level, that interest groups can step in on any number of competing sides. The government then becomes the equilibrium point in the system as it mediates among competing interests.[13]

Finally, many political scientists subscribe to the pluralist perspective. This theory argues that political resources in the United States are scattered so widely that no single group could ever gain monopoly control over any substantial area of policy.[14] Participants in every political controversy gain something; thus, each has some impact on how political decisions are made. The downside is that, because governments in the United States rarely say no to any well-organized interest, what is good for the public at large often tends to lose out in the American system.[15]

Which theory applies depends, in part, on the type of policy. Some policies are procedural in nature, incrementally changing existing policy, while others are substantive, involving bold revisions or innovation to change a policy outcome. Policy types can also be categorized as distributive, regulatory, or redistributive.[16] Distributive policies provide benefits to individuals, groups, communities, or corporations. These policies are the most common and, typically, the least controversial form of federal action to solve public problems, providing tangible benefits to the recipient while costs are shared widely and not necessarily viewed as competitive. Examples include student loans, farm subsidies, and water projects. Regulatory policies limit choices in order to restrict unacceptable behavior. Land use regulations, for example, limit how property can be developed in order to protect the environment. These policies are typically more controversial because the costs are concentrated, in this case on developers, while the benefits are diffused, or shared by the larger community. Redistributive policy involves transferring resources from one group to assist another group. These policies such as health care reforms under the Obama administration have been perceived as redistributive in nature, fueling opposition to full implementation of the legislation.

Participants, both governmental and nongovernmental, enter and exit the policy-making process at different stages. Although the policy-making process is often described in terms of stages or functional activities, the process is not necessarily sequential. One illustration of such a model is shown in Figure 16.1. This model can be

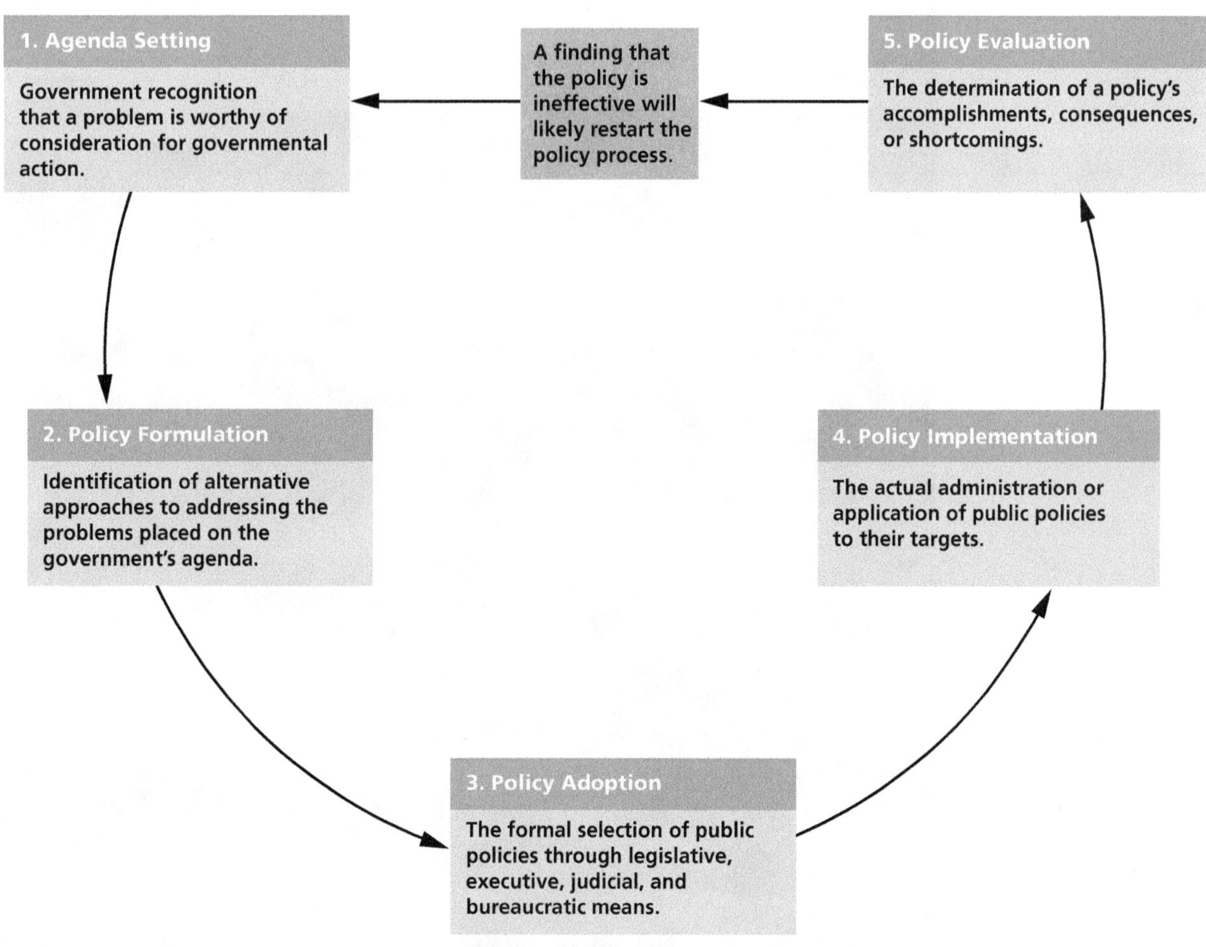

FIGURE 16.1 WHAT ARE THE STAGES OF THE PUBLIC POLICY PROCESS?

One of the best ways to understand public policy is to examine the process by which policies are made. Although there are many unique characteristics of policy making at the various levels of government, certain commonalities define the process from which public policies emerge. In the figure, the public policy process is broken down into five steps. Each step has distinguishing features, but it is important to remember that the steps often merge into one another in a less distinct manner.

16.1

16.2

16.3

16.4

16.5

agenda
A set of issues to be discussed or given attention.

systemic agenda
A discussion agenda; it consists of all public issues that are viewed as requiring governmental attention.

used to analyze any of the issues discussed in this book. Although models such as these can be useful, it is important to remember that they simplify the actual process. Moreover, models for analyzing the policy-making process do not always explain *why* public policies take the specific forms they do. Nor do models necessarily tell us *who* dominates or controls the formation of public policy.

Policy making typically can be regarded as a process of sequential steps:

1. *Agenda setting.* Government recognition that a problem is worthy of consideration for governmental intervention.
2. *Policy formulation.* Identification of alternative approaches to addressing the problems placed on the government's agenda.
3. *Policy adoption.* The formal selection of public policies through legislative, executive, judicial, and bureaucratic means.
4. *Policy implementation.* The actual funding and administration or application of public policies to their targets.
5. *Policy evaluation.* The determination of a policy's accomplishments, consequences, or shortcomings. With this overview in mind, we examine the various stages of the policy process or cycle.

AGENDA SETTING An **agenda** is a set of issues to be discussed or given attention. Every political community—national, state, and local—has a **systemic agenda.** The systemic agenda is essentially a discussion agenda; it consists of all issues viewed as

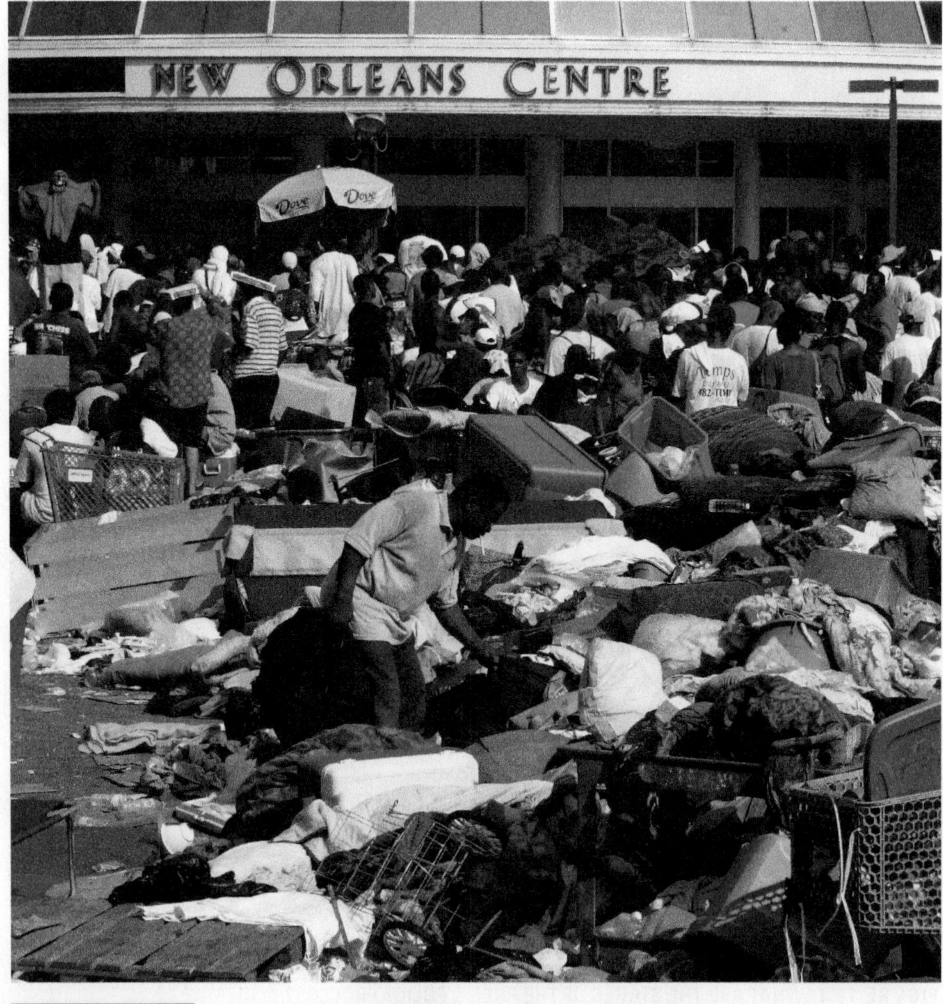

HOW DOES GOVERNMENT IDENTIFY PUBLIC POLICY PROBLEMS?

Public policy problems are circumstances that can be addressed by government action. One example is disaster relief. During and after Hurricane Katrina, the New Orleans Centre housed thousands of people displaced by the storm in appalling circumstances never before seen on such a massive basis in the United States.

requiring public attention and as involving matters within the legitimate jurisdiction of governments.[17] A **governmental or institutional agenda**, in contrast, is much narrower. It includes only problems to which public officials feel obliged to devote active and serious attention. The movement of an issue from the systemic to the institutional agenda is known as **agenda setting**. John Kingdon describes this process as three streams—problems, policies, and politics—that must converge to create a policy window, or opportunity, for government action.[18]

governmental (institutional) agenda
Problems to which public officials feel obliged to devote active and serious attention.

agenda setting
The process of forming the list of issues to be addressed by government.

policy formulation
The crafting of proposed courses of action to resolve public problems.

First, a consensus must be reached that a societal condition is actually a problem. For a condition to become a problem, some criterion, a standard or value, must lead people to believe that the condition does not have to be accepted and, further, that it is something with which government can deal effectively and appropriately. For example, natural disasters such as hurricanes are unlikely to be identified as a policy problem because government can do little about them directly. The consequences of hurricanes—the human distress and property destruction they bring—are another matter. Usually, no single, agreed-on definition of a problem exists. Indeed, political struggle often occurs at this stage because how the problem is defined helps determine what sort of action is appropriate. Note that public policies themselves are frequently viewed as problems or the causes of other problems. Thus, for some people, gun control legislation is a solution to gun violence. To the National Rifle Association (NRA), however, any law that restricts gun ownership is a problem because the NRA views such laws as inappropriately infringing on an individual's constitutional right to keep and bear arms. To social conservatives, legal access to abortion is a problem; for social liberals, laws restricting abortion access fall into the problem category.

Second, in the policies stream, possible solutions must be available to address the problem. Policy experts are prolific in measuring indicators of problems and debating the costs and benefits of various proposals. If the problem has no apparent solution, or no perceived "acceptable" solution, few will advocate moving the issue forward. Immigration policy has numerous possible reforms, for example, but no consensus on whether the solution is to build and secure more fencing, deport illegal immigrants, or provide pathways to citizenship. In part, the lack of consensus on policy solutions is related to debates over whether or not immigration represents an economic or security threat. This lack of consensus on both problem definition and policy solutions has effectively kept comprehensive immigration reform off the national government's agenda.

Third, in the politics stream, changes in the public mood, interest group campaigns, or electoral turnover can create opportunities for agenda setting. With each new presidential administration, for example, the president enjoys a brief honeymoon period when he is more effective at launching policy initiatives. In his first 100 days, for example, President Barack Obama issued nineteen executive orders, signed twelve bills into laws, and used his inaugural address to help focus the nation's attention on a broad agenda covering health care, education, energy, economic recovery, and foreign policy. Presidents, members of Congress, or interest group representatives can act as policy entrepreneurs, selling an issue to the point where the public demands a governmental response. Crises, or critical mobilizing events, can also create momentum for an issue. The attacks on the World Trade Center and the Pentagon on September 11, 2001, placed the issue of homeland security at the top of the policy agenda. The home mortgage crisis and continuing recession in 2010 received significant media attention and corresponding responses from Congress, remaining on the agenda through the 2012 election.

Very few problems ever reach the government's agenda, however, and typically they do not stay there for long. Anthony Downs describes an issue attention cycle in which the intensity of the public's concern over an issue fades with time, either because solutions are perceived as too costly, another issue has taken its place, or time has simply passed.[19] In this early stage of the policy-making process, if the problems, policies, and politics streams converge, then a policy window opens temporarily and the issue can reach the institutional agenda.

POLICY FORMULATION **Policy formulation** is the crafting of proposed courses of action to resolve public problems. It has both political and technical components.[20]

16.1

16.2

16.3

16.4

16.5

All legislative Powers herein granted shall be vested in a Congress of the United States, which shall consist of a Senate and House of Representatives. —ARTICLE I, SECTION 1

Article 1, section 1 of the Constitution vests the law-making power in the hands of the legislative branch of government because the Framers believed that Congress, with its large and diverse membership, was a much lesser threat to tyranny than the executive branch. The judicial branch, the Framers thought, was little more than a theoretical necessity and would be the "least dangerous branch."

Today, Congress retains its law-making power and does a great deal of public policy formulation and adoption. But, it is by no means the only source of public policy in the national government. The president, for example, has the power to make public policy by using executive orders. In such a way, President Barack Obama has made policy on subjects such as abortion, foreign policy, energy, and stem cell research.

The bureaucracy is also an important policy maker. Through a quasi-legislative process known as rule making, executive branch agencies formulate and implement policies in nearly every imaginable issue area. Rules, in fact, are the largest source of policy decisions made by the national government.

Even the judicial branch, which the Framers thought would be essentially powerless, has evolved into an important source of policy decisions. In recent years, the Supreme Court has made policy prescriptions in each of the domestic policy issue areas discussed in this chapter, as well as in criminal justice, civil liberties, and civil rights.

CRITICAL THINKING QUESTIONS

1. **Is the decentralized nature of the policy-making process an advantage or disadvantage in producing the best possible solutions to the country's problems?**
2. **Choose two areas of domestic policy. Who do you think should ultimately decide policy in each area? Are your answers for each policy area the same or different? Why or why not?**

The political aspect of policy formulation involves determining generally what should be done to address a problem. The technical facet involves correctly stating in specific language what one wants to authorize or accomplish, to adequately guide those who must implement policy and to prevent distortion of legislative intent.

Policy formulation may take many forms:

1. *Routine formulation* is the process of altering existing policy proposals or creating new proposals within an issue area the government has previously addressed. For instance, the formulation of policy for veterans' benefits is routine.
2. *Analogous formulation* handles new problems by drawing on experience with similar problems in the past or in other jurisdictions. What has been done in the past to cope with the activities of terrorists? How have other states dealt with child abuse or divorce law reform?
3. *Creative formulation* involves attempts to develop new or unprecedented proposals that represent a departure from existing practices and that will better resolve a problem. For example, plans to develop an anti-missile defense system to shoot down incoming missiles represent a departure from previous defense strategies of mutual destruction.

Various players in the policy process may undertake policy formulation: the president, presidential aides, agency officials, specially appointed task forces and commissions, interest groups, private research organizations (or "think tanks"), and legislators and their staffs. The people engaged in formulation are usually looking ahead toward policy adoption. These individuals may include or exclude particular provisions of a proposal in an attempt to enhance its likelihood of adoption. To the extent that formulators think in this strategic manner, the formulation and adoption stages of the policy process often overlap.

POLICY ADOPTION **Policy adoption** is the approval of a policy proposal by the people with requisite authority, such as a legislature or chief executive. This approval gives the policy legal force. Because most public policies in the United States result from legislation, policy adoption frequently requires building a series of majority coalitions necessary to secure the enactment of legislation in Congress. To secure the needed votes, a bill may be watered down or modified at any point in the legislative process. Or, the bill may fail to win a majority at one of them and die, at least for the time being.

policy adoption
The approval of a policy proposal by people with the requisite authority, such as a legislature.

policy implementation
The process of carrying out public policy.

The tortuous nature of congressional policy adoption has some important consequences. First, complex legislation may require substantial periods of time to pass. Second, the legislation passed is often incremental, making only limited or marginal changes in existing policy. Third, legislation is frequently written in general or ambiguous language, as in the Clean Air Act, which provided amorphous instructions to administrators in the Environmental Protection Agency to set air quality standards that would allow for an "adequate margin of safety" to protect the public health. Phrases such as "adequate margin" are highly subjective and open to a wide range of interpretations. Language such as this may provide considerable discretion to the people who implement the law and also leave them doubting its intended purposes.

Ideally, policies would be adopted on the basis of comprehensive rational decision making, in which policy makers would make decisions with complete information and expertise about the nature of the problem and the costs and benefits of proposed solutions. In the real world, however, policy making is not always rational. Decision makers often lack the time, information, or expertise to analyze accurately the likely effectiveness of various policies. They may be biased by their own personal values or experiences. The decentralization of the legislative process also encourages bargaining and compromise. Finally, once a course of action has been chosen and funds committed, "sunk costs" have been established, making it easier to continue in the same policy direction, adjusting policies incrementally rather than comprehensively.

POLICY IMPLEMENTATION **Policy implementation** is the process of carrying out public policies, most of which are implemented by administrative agencies. Some policies, however, are enforced in other ways. Voluntary compliance by businesses and individuals is one such technique. When grocers take out-of-date products off their shelves or when consumers choose not to buy food products after their expiration dates, voluntary compliance is at work. Implementation also involves the courts when they are called on to interpret the meaning of legislation, review the legality of agency rules and actions, and determine whether institutions such as prisons and mental hospitals conform to legal and constitutional standards.

Administrative agencies may be authorized to use a number of techniques to implement public policies within their jurisdictions. These techniques can be categorized as authoritative, incentive, capacity, or hortatory, depending on the behavioral assumptions on which they are based.[21]

1. *Authoritative techniques* for policy implementation rest on the notion that people's actions must be directed or restrained by government in order to prevent or eliminate activities or products that are unsafe, unfair, evil, or immoral. For example, consumer products must meet certain safety regulations, and radio stations can be fined heavily or have their broadcasting licenses revoked if they broadcast obscenities.
2. *Incentive techniques* for policy implementation encourage people to act in their own best interest by offering payoffs or financial inducements for compliance with public policies. Such policies may provide tax deductions to encourage charitable giving or the purchase of alternative fuel vehicles, such as hybrid automobiles. Farmers also receive subsidies to make their production (or nonproduction) of wheat, cotton, and other goods more profitable. Conversely, sanctions, such as

policy evaluation
The process of determining whether a course of action is achieving its intended goals.

high taxes, may discourage the purchase and use of products such as tobacco and liquor, and pollution fees may reduce the discharge of pollutants by making this action more costly to businesses.

3. *Capacity techniques* provide people with information, education, training, or resources that enable them to participate in desired activities. The assumption underlying these techniques is that people have incentive or desire to do what is right but lack the capacity to act accordingly. Job training may help able-bodied people find work, and accurate information on interest rates will enable people to protect themselves against interest-rate gouging.
4. *Hortatory techniques* encourage people to comply with policy by appealing to their "better instincts" and thereby directing them to act in desired ways. In this instance, policy implementers assume that people decide how to act according to their personal values and beliefs. During the Reagan administration, First Lady Nancy Reagan implored young people to "Just say no" to drugs. Hortatory techniques to discourage littering include the use of highway signs displaying slogans like "Don't Be a Litterbug" and "Don't Mess with Texas."

Often government will turn to a combination of authoritative, incentive, capacity, and hortatory approaches to reach its goals. For example, public health officials use all of these tools in their efforts to reduce tobacco use. These techniques include laws prohibiting smoking in public places, taxes on the sales of tobacco products, warning labels on packs of cigarettes, and anti-smoking commercials on TV. There is no easy formula that will guarantee successful policy implementation; in practice, many policies only partially achieve their goals.

Budgeting also influences policy implementation. When a policy is adopted, funding levels are recommended but must be finalized by another set of policy makers. Congress separates the authorizations of new policies from the appropriations of funds so that debates over new policies do not delay or derail the national budgetary process. Whether a policy is well funded, poorly funded, or funded at all has a significant effect on its scope, impact, and effectiveness. For example, as a result of limited funding, the Occupational Safety and Health Administration (OSHA) can inspect annually only a small fraction of the workplaces within its jurisdiction. Similarly, the Department of Housing and Urban Development has funds sufficient to provide rent subsidies only to approximately 20 percent of eligible low-income families.

POLICY EVALUATION Practitioners of **policy evaluation** seek to determine whether a course of action is achieving its intended goals. They may also try to determine whether a policy is being fairly or efficiently administered. Although policy evaluation has become more rigorous, systematic, and objective over the past few decades, policy makers still make judgments often on the basis of anecdotal and fragmentary evidence rather than on solid facts and thorough analyses. Sometimes a program is judged as a good program simply because it is politically popular or fits the ideological beliefs of an elected official.

Policy evaluation may be conducted by a variety of players, including congressional committees, presidential commissions, administrative agencies, the courts, university researchers, private research organizations, and the Government Accountability Office (GAO). The GAO, created in 1921, conducts hundreds of studies of government agencies and programs each year, either at the request of members of Congress or on its own initiative. The titles of two of its 2012 evaluations convey a notion of the breadth of its work: "Homelessness: Fragmentation and Overlap in Programs Highlight the Need to Identify, Assess, and Reduce Inefficiencies" and "Unconventional Oil and Gas Production: Opportunities and Challenges of Oil Shale Development."

Evaluation research and studies can stimulate attempts to modify or terminate policies and thus restart the policy process. Legislators and administrators may formulate and advocate for amendments designed to correct problems or shortcomings in a policy. In 2006, for example, national legislation establishing the Medicare program was amended to create a prescription drug benefit for senior citizens, known as Medicare Part D. The evaluation process may also result in the termination of policies; for example, in 2011, Congress terminated subsidies for ethanol, ending the tax credit established in 1986. Congress took this action in response to research suggesting that increased use of ethanol had a minimal positive impact on the environment. Policies may also be terminated automatically through sunset provisions, or "expiration dates" that Congress can add to legislation. Without reauthorization by Congress, a 1994 ban on civilian use of assault weapons, for example, expired in 2004 under a sunset provision. The 2001 USA PATRIOT Act initially was set to expire in 2005, but was evaluated, amended, and reauthorized. Most recently, in 2011, President Barack Obama signed a four-year extension of three components of the law: the government's ability to search records, use roving wiretaps, and conduct surveillance of terrorist suspects.

The budgetary process also gives the president and the Congress an opportunity to review the government's many policies and programs, to inquire into their administration, to appraise their value and effectiveness, and to exercise some influence on their conduct. In 2011, a national debate arose over government funding of Planned Parenthood. Critics unsuccessfully tried to end what they deemed public funding of abortion, while supporters advocated the need to protect women's health services, including cancer screening. Not all of the government's thousands of programs undergo full examination every year. But, over a period of several years, most programs come under scrutiny. The demise of programs is relatively rare; more often, a troubled program is modified or allowed to limp along because it provides a popular service. For example, the nation's passenger rail system, Amtrak, remains dependent on government funds. Although its northeastern lines are financially self-sufficient, many of Amtrak's longer-distance routes are not able to operate without significant government subsidies. Nevertheless, the more rural routes remain popular with legislators in western states; thus Amtrak continues to receive governmental support.[22]

Medicare
The federal program established during the Lyndon B. Johnson administration that provides medical care to elderly Social Security recipients.

Health Policy Today

16.2 Describe health policy in the United States.

The national government's involvement in health policy extends to a number of other policy areas. Many millions of people receive medical care through the medical branches of the armed forces, the hospitals and medical programs of the Department of Veterans Affairs, and the Indian Health Service. In the 1960s, the government began funding health programs for senior citizens and the poor and disabled, known as Medicare and Medicaid, respectively. And, in 2010, the Democratic Congress passed, and President Barack Obama signed into law, the Patient Protection and Affordable Care Act, which expanded the federal government's role in providing health insurance. The federal government estimated that it would spend $941 billion in the 2013 fiscal year for health and human services.[23]

Explore on MyPoliSciLab Simulation: You Are an OMB Staffer

☐ Medicare

Medicare, which was created by Congress and Democratic President Lyndon B. Johnson in 1965, covers persons who are disabled or over age 65. It is administered by the Centers for Medicare and Medicaid Services in the Department of Health and Human Services. Medicare is financed by a payroll tax of 1.45 percent paid by both employees and employers on the total amount of one's wages or salary In 2014, this tax will increase to 3.8 percent for Americans making more than $200,000 per year. Medicare coverage has four components: Parts A, B, C, and D. Benefits under Part A are

Explore on MyPoliSciLab

Is Health Care a Public Good?

A public good is a material item or service provided by the government to all members of society without competition or exclusion. Before Obama's presidency, most Americans believed the government should guarantee health care coverage to all citizens, but after 2009, the debate on health care reform divided public opinion. Since the signing of the Patient Protection and Affordable Care Act (PPACA), Americans remained dissatisfied with the cost of health care and the number of of people who disagree with government provided health care increased.

Should the Government Provide Americans with Health Care Coverage?

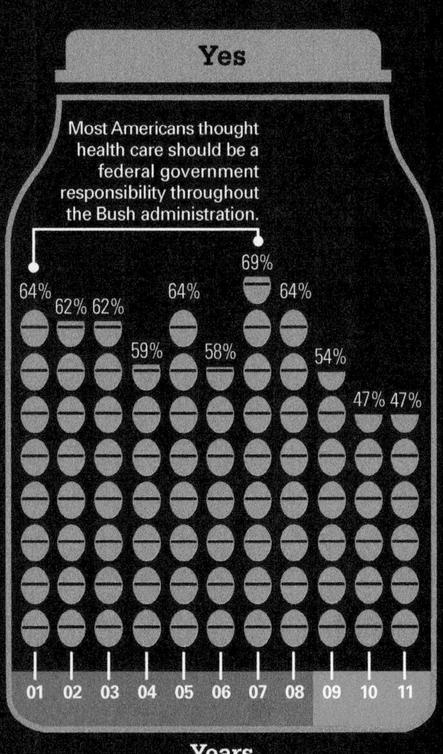

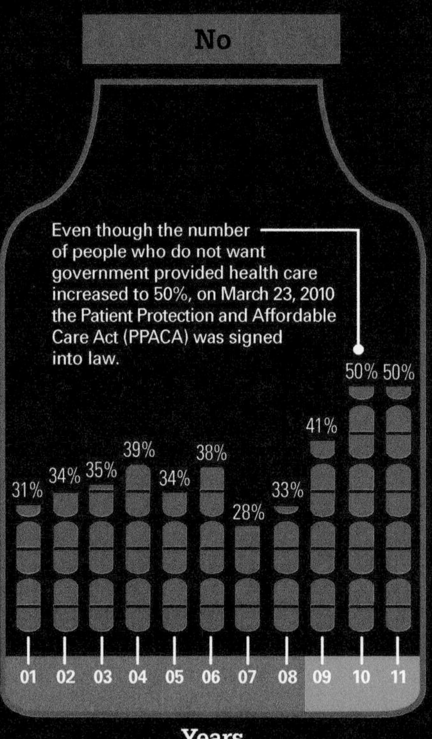

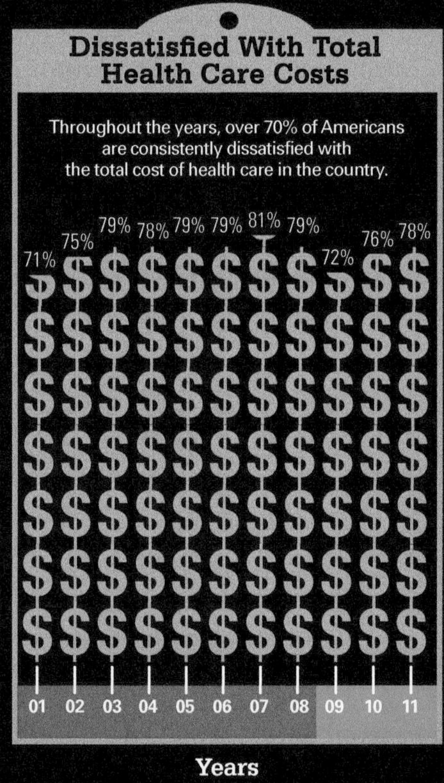

01–08 Bush Years 09–11 Obama Years

SOURCE: Data from Gallup

Investigate Further

Concept Do Americans think health care is a public good? During George W. Bush's presidency, most Americans wanted government provided health care. However, in recent years, support has declined and more people believe private insurers should provide health care.

Connection Is the public unhappy with their health care costs? Yes, most Americans are dissatisfied with health care costs. Concern about health care is driven more by the perception that health care costs are too high, than by personal dissatisfaction. People are upset with health care because of broad circumstances, rather than individual circumstances.

Cause Why did public support for guaranteed government health care decline? After Barack Obama took office, support and opposition for reform became a party issue. In a heavily polarized political environment, support for government-funded health care declined and the public split evenly on issue. After the Obama administration passed the Patient Protection and Affordable Care Act, a majority of the public remained dissatisfied with the costs of health care.

granted to all Americans automatically at age sixty-five, when they qualify for Social Security. It covers hospitalization, some skilled nursing care, and home health services.

Part B, which is optional, covers payment for physicians' services, outpatient and diagnostic services, x-rays, and some other items not covered by Part A. Excluded from coverage are eyeglasses, hearing aids, and dentures. This portion of the Medicare program is financed partly by monthly payments from beneficiaries and partly by general tax revenues.

Medicare Part C programs are also known as Medicare Advantage programs. Administered by private insurance companies, they provide coverage that meets or exceeds the coverage of traditional Medicare programs. Medicare Advantage programs may also include additional services for a fee, such as prescription drug coverage and dental and vision insurance.

Medicare Part D is the optional prescription drug benefit that went into effect in 2006. Participants pay a monthly premium that varies by plan: after an annual deductible, 75 percent of prescription costs are covered until the subscriber reaches a coverage gap, known as a "donut hole." Participants are then responsible for 100% of prescription costs until they reach their yearly maximum for out-of-pocket expenses, after which additional costs are covered at 90% to 95%. The 2010 Patient Protection and Affordable Care Act gradually phases out the coverage gap by 2020.

Today, Medicare provides health insurance coverage for more than 45 million Americans. Roughly 20 percent of these enrollees choose Medicare Advantage programs. More than half of Medicare enrollees also choose to take advantage of the Medicare prescription drug benefit. In 2010, the first wave of baby boomers reached retirement age. As the number of eligible beneficiaries continues to increase, the cost of Medicare is expected to grow at an annual rate of 6.3%, with projected budget shortfalls as soon as 2020. To address these budget issues, the Medicare tax will increase by 0.9 percent starting in 2013 for individuals with incomes over $200,000 or married couples with incomes over $250,000. An additional 3.8% tax increase will be applied to unearned investment income.

Medicaid

A government program that subsidizes medical care for the poor.

☐ Medicaid

Medicaid, a government program that subsidizes health insurance for the poor and disabled, was enacted in 1965, at the same time as Medicare. It provides health insurance coverage for low-income Americans who meet a set of eligibility requirements. To receive Medicaid benefits, citizens must meet minimum-income thresholds, be disabled, or be pregnant.

Unlike Medicare, which is financed and administered by the national government, Medicaid is a joint venture between the national and state governments. The national government provides between 50 and 75 percent of the funding necessary to administer Medicaid programs (depending on state per capita income). This money is given to the states in the form of block grants. States then supplement the national funds with money from their own treasuries. They also are given the latitude to establish eligibility thresholds and the level of benefits available to citizens.

As a result, Medicaid programs vary widely from state to state. Most states provide coverage for all pregnant women and all children younger than one year. In a majority of states, the income requirement is set to provide coverage to citizens with incomes up to 185 percent of the federal poverty line. This is equivalent to an income of about $18,000 for an individual or $37,000 for a family of four. In some states, all low-income residents receive Medicaid assistance, whereas in other states, only one-third of the needy are protected. And, in some states "medically indigent" people—those who do not meet traditional income requirements but have large medical expenses—receive coverage, whereas in other states, these citizens must find their own funding.

In 2010, Medicaid provided coverage for almost 50 million Americans, making it the largest government health insurance program in the United States. This program comes with a substantial price tag: more than $400 billion in national and state funds. Medicaid is also one of the largest and fastest growing portions of state budgets. In recent years, it has accounted for roughly 17 percent of state general expenditures. Starting in 2014, the Patient Protection and Affordable Care Act expands Medicaid eligibility to include low-wage workers and their families (up to 133% of the poverty line). The state health insurance exchanges are also expected to facilitate increased enrollment of those currently eligible for Medicaid. These two factors combined will increase Medicaid coverage to an estimated 95 million Americans by 2022 at a cost of more than $840 billion.

☐ Health Insurance

One of the most significant issues that policy makers must confront in the area of health policy is the rising cost of care. As medical technology advances, citizens live longer. But, this increased lifespan comes with a price tag. Often, it comes in the form of long-term care, prescription drugs, and costly medical procedures that would have been unimaginable forty years ago. These rising costs place a significant burden on individuals and insurance companies, as well as the national and state government commitments to Medicare and Medicaid.

A quick review of the increase in health care costs over the past forty years helps to demonstrate the magnitude of the problem. In 1970, Americans spent about $356 per capita on health care costs. By 2013, spending increased to an estimated $9,349 per person on health care costs—more than 26 times 1970 levels. These levels far exceed the rate of inflationary growth and are projected to continue to rise to more than $13,709 per capita by 2020.

In reality, of course, these expenditures are not evenly distributed across all Americans; 10 percent of citizens account for 63 percent of all health care costs. The majority of these expenditures pay for physician's office visits and hospital care. However, prescription drug costs and nursing home expenditures constitute rapidly rising proportions of American health care costs.[24] (To learn more about Americans' health care expenditures, see Figure 16.2.)

The Patient Protection and Affordable Care Act of 2010 marked the first major change in national health policy since the adoption of Medicare and Medicaid in 1965. Its primary purpose was to establish government-run health insurance exchanges to ensure that nearly all Americans would have access to health care coverage. These exchanges, which will not be fully implemented until 2014, are financed by a number

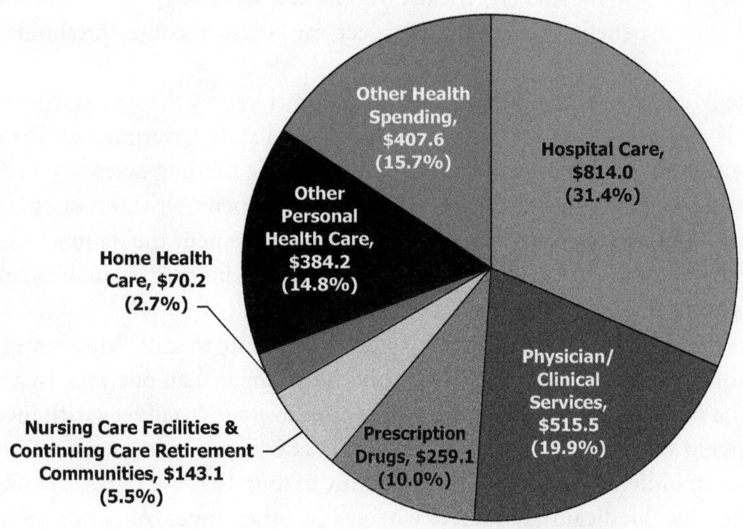

FIGURE 16.2 WHERE DO AMERICAN HEALTH CARE EXPENDITURES GO?

Physicians and hospital care constitute a majority of health care expenditures. However, prescription drug and nursing home costs are rapidly rising.

SOURCE: Kaiser Family Foundation, www.kff.org/insurance/upload/7692_02.pdf.

Take a Closer Look

The year 2013 marks the twentieth anniversary of three strikes laws, or habitual offender laws, requiring states to impose a life sentence when a criminal is convicted of a third serious felony. First passed in Washington State and popular through the mid-1990s, currently twenty-four states retain three strikes legislation. Over time, these longer sentences have produced an aging inmate population with escalating health care needs, which states are required to meet. The Supreme Court ruled in *Estelle* v. *Gamble* (1976) that to deny prisoners access to professional medical diagnosis and treatment violates the Eighth Amendment's protection against cruel and unusual punishment.

The inmates are shown to be advancing in years, a reference to the fact that the inmate population—perhaps as a result of habitual offender laws—is aging and in need of continued and sustained health care.

J.B. Handelsman/The New Yorker Collection/www.cartoonbank.com

"My third felony was a smart move. Folks on the outside are still waiting for health care."

The prisoner's comment is a reference to the fact that he will be guaranteed health care—unlike Americans who are not incarcerated—for the duration of his life sentence.

CRITICAL THINKING QUESTIONS

1. Why are inmates the only class of people constitutionally guaranteed the right to health care?
2. How will states fund the rising costs of prison health care?
3. Should the "three strikes, and you're out" policy have an age limit?

16.1

16.2

16.3

16.4

16.5

of taxes and fees, most notably an increase in the Medicare tax for Americans earning more than $200,000 per year. Americans do not have to buy in to these exchanges; they have the option of retaining their private health insurance if they so choose. The bill also provides incentives for businesses to offer health insurance—a very costly proposition for many employers. And, importantly, it prevents health insurance companies from denying Americans coverage on the basis of preexisting conditions.

Reaction to the bill has been mixed. Large majorities of Americans believe that the legislation will lead to significant changes in the American health care system. However, only 30 percent of taxpayers believe that these changes will improve the system. (To learn more about public opinion on health insurance reform, see Table 16.1.)

The legislation has been especially unpopular with state governments. More than half of the states have already sued or announced that they will sue the national government to block implementation of the policy. These states believe that the act is an infringement on states' reserved powers, which are granted to them under the Tenth Amendment of the U.S. Constitution. In July 2012, however, the Supreme Court upheld the constitutionality of the new law.

□ Public Health

Government also plays a major role in managing the spread of, and increase in, infectious and chronic disease, respectively. From AIDS to obesity, public policy makers have attempted to use government power to fight threats to the nation's health. Among the government's tools are immunizations, education, advertisements, and regulations. For many contagious diseases such as polio, measles, and chickenpox, the government requires immunization of young children if they are enrolled in day care, preschool, or elementary school. Public health officials also use vaccines in the adult population to manage the spread of diseases such as influenza (the flu). While not requiring citizens to receive flu shots, the government recommends that high-risk groups (infants, senior citizens) receive immunizations and also subsidizes vaccines for low-income populations.

In 2006, the Food and Drug Administration approved a vaccine to prevent human papillomavirus (HPV) infection, a sexually transmitted infection (STI) linked to cervical cancer. Although the national Advisory Committee on Immunization Practices (ACIP) recommended the vaccine, commonly known as Gardasil, for boys and girls starting at ages eleven and twelve, debate has raged over whether to *require* this vaccination.

TABLE 16.1 WHAT DO AMERICANS THINK ABOUT HEALTH INSURANCE REFORM?

"In general, would you say that the 2010 health care law recently upheld by the Supreme Court will make things better or worse for each of the following?"

	Make things better	Make things worse	Same/No difference (vol.)	No opinion
	%	%	%	%
People who currently do not have health insurance	59	32	2	6
People who get sick	55	34	2	8
Hospitals	45	45	2	8
You, personally	38	42	13	7
Doctors	37	51	3	9
People who currently have health insurance	36	46	10	8
Businesses	33	57	3	8
Taxpayers	30	60	3	8

(vol.) = Volunteered response

SOURCE: Data from Gallup, National adults, July 9–12, 2012.

Opponents argue that mandating Gardasil vaccination violates parents' rights, is too expensive, and could increase promiscuity by giving a false sense of security concerning their protection against STIs. Uncertainties about the long-term safety and immunity provided by the vaccine also complicate the debate. Since 2006, forty-one states have proposed legislation to require the vaccine, twenty states have enacted legislation, and in 2012, eight states were considering legislation.

The national government also finances medical research, primarily through the National Institutes of Health (NIH). The National Cancer Institute, the National Heart, Lung, and Blood Institute, the National Institute of Allergy and Infectious Diseases, and the other NIH institutes and centers spend more than $30 billion annually on biomedical research. NIH scientists and scientists at universities, medical schools, and other research facilities receiving NIH research grants conduct the research. Most Americans accept and support extensive government spending on medical research. Congress, in fact, often appropriates more money for medical research than the president recommends.

Evidence supported by medical research has moved obesity onto the agenda as a public health issue. The policy debate has evolved from emphasizing individual responsibility to a comprehensive solution, including the food industry, schools, marketing, the workplace, and communities. First Lady Michelle Obama launched the "Let's Move" campaign to fight childhood obesity in 2010. A year later, President Barack Obama proclaimed September as National Childhood Obesity Awareness

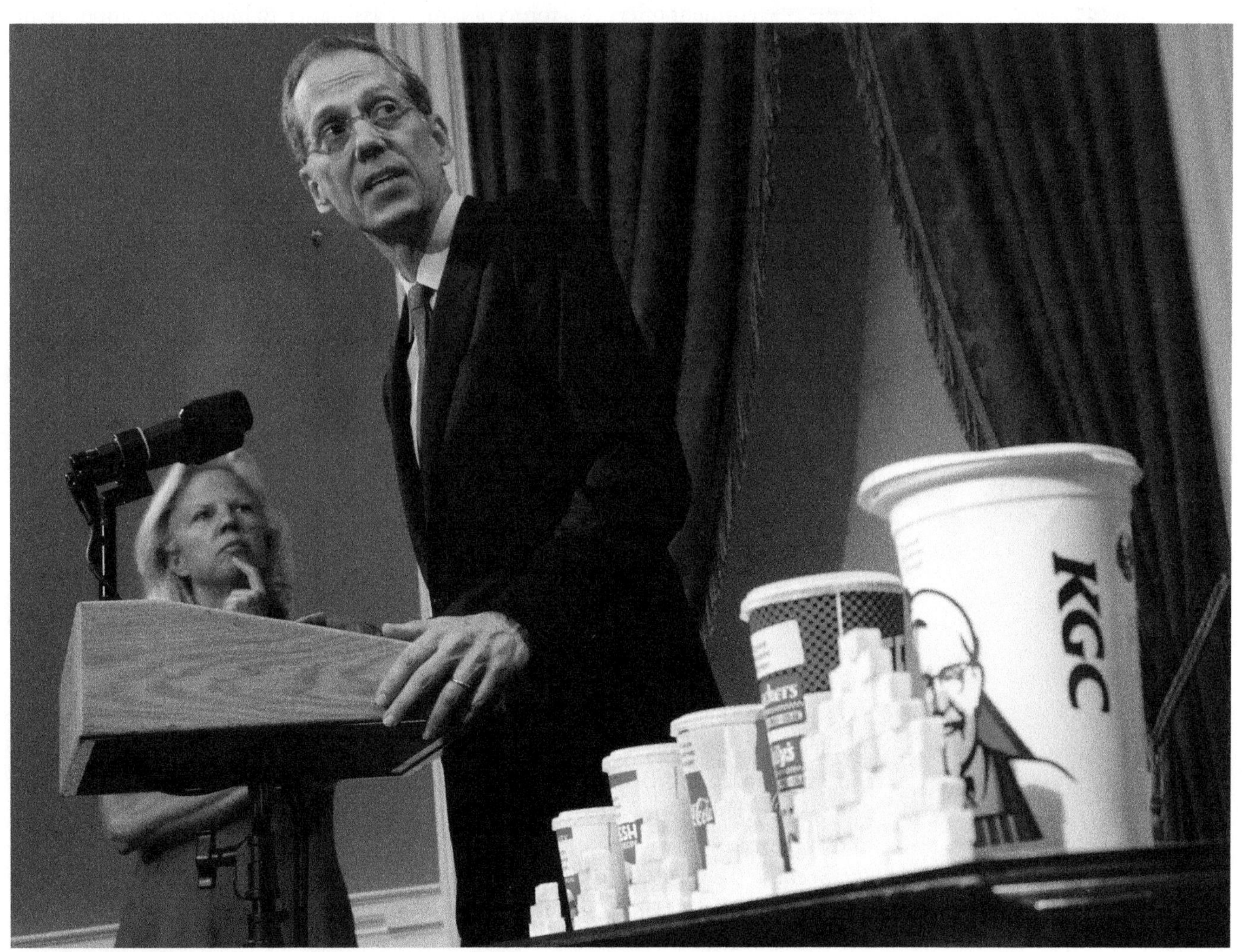

HOW DOES THE GOVERNMENT PROMOTE PUBLIC HEALTH?

A 2012 New York City proposal called for a ban on the sale of large sodas in city restaurants, theaters, and sporting venues. As part of Obama's health care reform, restaurants with twenty or more locations now have to provide nutritional information on menus, including calories and calories from fat.

No Child Left Behind Act (NCLB)
Education reform passed in 2002 that employs high standards and measurable goals as a method of improving American education.

Month. In 2012, the Institute of Medicine issued a report, "Accelerating Progress in Obesity Prevention: Solving the Weight of the Nation," further capturing national attention with startling statistics on the prevalence of obesity in America. Approximately two-thirds of adults and one-third of children are overweight or obese, an epidemic that costs $190.2 billion per year.[25] In 2012, as well, the U.S. Department of Agriculture issued new rules for federally subsidized school lunch programs, requiring that schools increase servings of fruits and vegetables while decreasing salt and fat. At the local level, in June 2012, New York City Mayor Michael Bloomberg proposed a ban on large sugary soft drinks in city restaurants; this was followed by a discussion of a similar ban in Cambridge, Massachusetts. All three streams of the agenda-setting process—problems, policies, and politics—are at work pushing the issue of obesity onto the government's agenda.

Education Policy Today

16.3 Outline education policy in the United States.

In 2012, more than $1.5 trillion was spent on education at all levels of government. The federal government paid approximately 10% of the bill. In addition to aiding states for K–12 and higher education, the federal government offers two forms of indirect assistance to higher education: grants for low-income students and guaranteed student loans. Ultimately, states and localities dominate education funding and policy making, although national policies provide monetary incentives for compliance with standardized goals. The largest shift toward the federal government in educational policy making came with the 2002 bipartisan education reform bill supported by the late Democratic Senator Edward M. Kennedy (D–MA) and Republican President George W. Bush, commonly referred to as the **No Child Left Behind Act (NCLB).** NCLB employs high standards and measurable goals as a method of improving American education across states, with states left to decide if the new requirements are worth complying with in exchange for limited federal funding. In the wake of this major reform, the policy debate has shifted from comprehensive solutions to perceived problems in education to incremental changes in the implementation of NCLB.

The No Child Left Behind Act

Signed into law in January 2002, NCLB has four main pillars. First, results-oriented accountability plays a central role in NCLB. The legislation is designed to monitor student achievement in schools, paying special attention to disadvantaged student populations. Each year, students take a battery of standardized tests designed to measure whether they have met a set of educational goals. Test results are then tabulated and broken down by race, ethnicity, and gender to better measure students' progress. Schools and school districts also use these data to issue annual report cards on their achievement. Schools that do not meet their goals are encouraged to offer ancillary education services, such as tutoring, to improve their students' educational achievement. If progress is still not made, schools or school districts may be forced to reorganize.

Second, the design of NCLB encourages state and local flexibility in the use of national funds. Flexibility in funding is an effort to build a cooperative education enterprise between national, state, and local government by reducing commitment to "one size fits all" policy reforms. Thus, depending on their local needs, schools can use resources to enhance school technology, develop experimental programs intended to improve education outcomes, or invest in programs to upgrade teacher training and quality. Outcomes are viewed as more important than uniformity in process.

Has the No Child Left Behind Act Influenced Education?

This map shows state education report cards across the United States as of January 2010, as reported in *Education Week.* The report provides a comprehensive measure of policy and performance across six areas that include K–12 achievement, teaching profession, and school finance. Each state is assigned a "grade" in each category using a complex grading rubric. The summary grades reported in the map below allow for comparisons across states and regions. Overall, the nation scores a C. For the third year in a row, Maryland has the highest score with a B+. States with a dotted fill are ones that do not allow collective bargaining rights for teachers. Some argue that collective bargaining rights prevent state flexibility in reforming education. Critics, however, point to the positive impact that collective bargaining rights have on recruiting and retaining teachers. They also note that some of the top performing states allow collective bargaining rights.

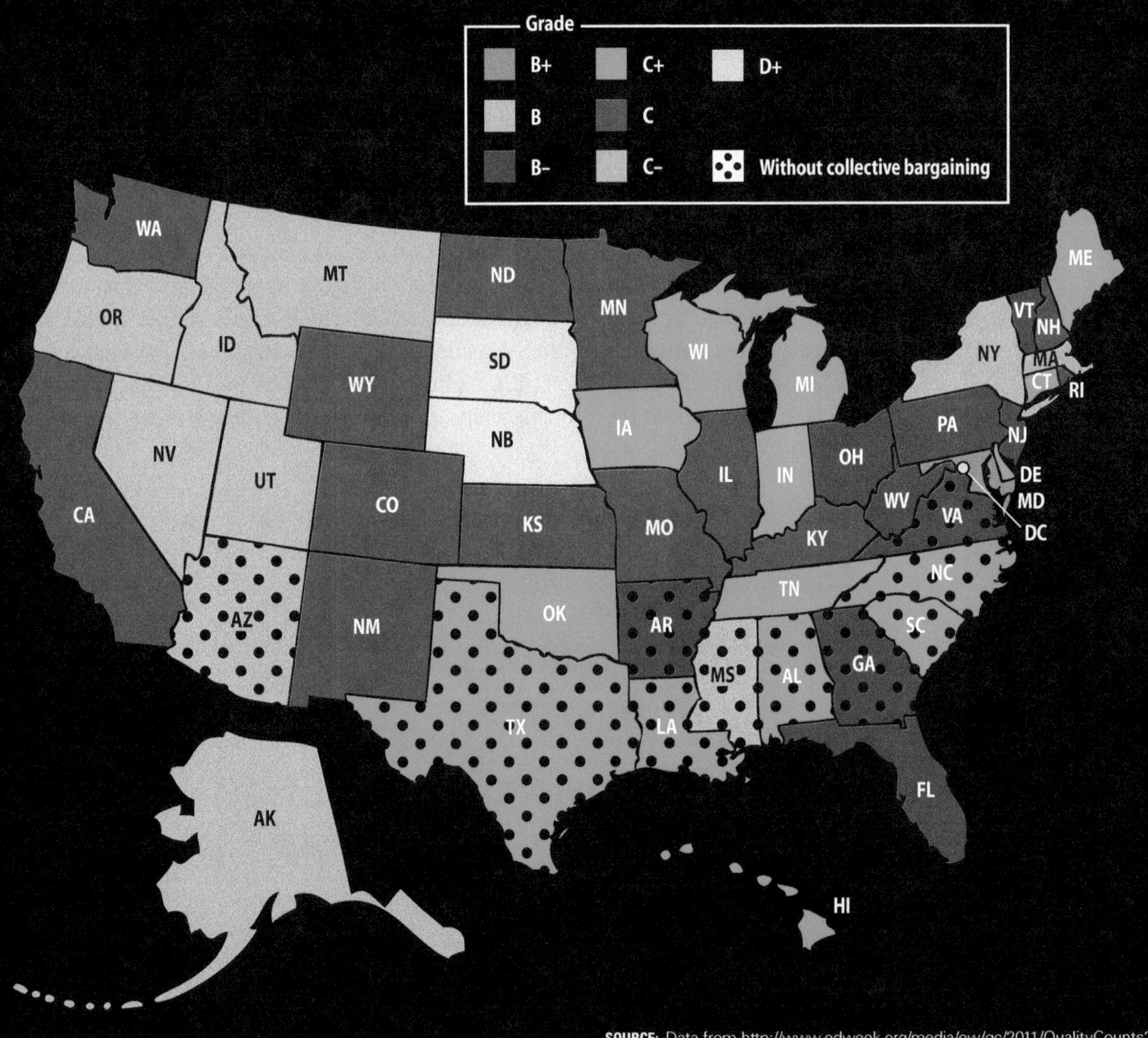

SOURCE: Data from http://www.edweek.org/media/ew/qc/2011/QualityCounts2011_PressRelease.pdf; http://voices.washingtonpost.com/answer-sheet/guest-bloggers/how-states-with-no-teacher-uni.html

CRITICAL THINKING QUESTIONS

1. Which states have the lowest ranking for overall quality of public schools?
2. Why do you think school quality rankings vary substantially from state to state?
3. How might policy makers use this data to improve educational equity in the United States?

16.1

16.2

16.3

16.4

16.5

vouchers
Certificates issued by the government that may be applied toward the cost of attending private or other public schools.

charter schools
Semipublic schools that have open admission but may also receive private donations to increase the quality of education.

The third pillar of NCLB envisions the national government as a purveyor of proven methods of achieving high-quality education outcomes. National policy analysts and curriculum experts create best practices in a range of subject areas ranging from reading to mathematics to science and share this information and curriculum with schools and school districts. For example, NCLB's "Reading First" and "Early Reading First" programs are designed to produce high-quality readers. The programs have established a track record for educational success.

At times, schools and districts are unable to meet educational goals despite all efforts. Thus, NCLB's fourth pillar involves school choice. If a child is attending a failing school, students and their parents may have the option to enroll at an institution that is successfully meeting its educational achievement goals. In some cases, this may mean sending a child to another public school at no cost in the district or to a private school.

One way to implement a school choice policy is through the use of **vouchers,** or certificates issued by the government that may be applied toward the cost of attending private or other public schools. The monetary value of these certificates usually correlates with the cost of educating a student in his or her local public school. Supporters of vouchers essentially argue that money talks. They believe that if parents remove their students from failing schools, these schools will quickly learn that they have to take steps to improve educational quality, or they will no longer have a reason to exist. Opponents, however, contend that allowing students to take money away from failing schools is counterintuitive and actually makes it harder for failing schools to improve.

Parents may also choose to send their children to **charter schools.** Charter schools are semipublic schools founded by universities, corporations, or concerned parents. They have open admission and receive some support from the government; they may also receive private donations to increase the quality of education. When the number of students interested in attending a school exceeds the openings available, students are usually selected by means of a random lottery. Charter schools are rapidly increasing in popularity in the United States. In some jurisdictions, such as New Orleans, charter schools are consistently among the highest performing institutions in the city. Critics, however, charge that it is difficult to ensure that charter schools are meeting educational

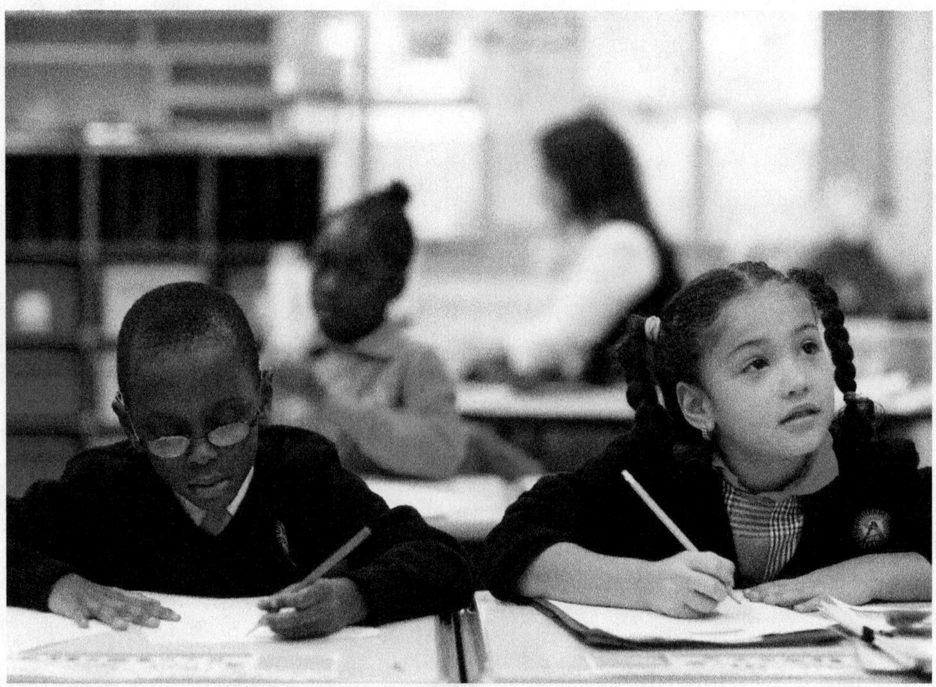

WHAT ARE CHARTER SCHOOLS?

Charter schools are semipublic institutions that are run by universities, nonprofits, or corporations. Many charter schools, such as Harlem Success Academy, seen here, have achieved outstanding results in traditionally underprivileged communities.

standards, and that a system that cannot accommodate all students interested in attending is inherently flawed. Because they are semi-private they do not have the same controls on curriculum—and the fact that there are not enough slots for all those who want to attend—creates inequality in access to good education.

Despite efforts to improve education quality and equality, implementation of the NCLB remains controversial across the political spectrum. Critics often claim that the reform places too much emphasis on standardized testing as a means of measuring student achievement. This, they argue, ignores many of the nonmeasurable but equally important aspects of student learning. It also encourages teachers to "teach to the test" rather than helping students learn analytical thinking skills. Finally, the requirements of NCLB may force schools and teachers to sacrifice education in subject areas that are untested, such as civics, art, or music. These sacrifices may produce less well-rounded students or fail to engage or prepare students for the professional world.

Other critics contend that the primary problem with NCLB is that it further nationalizes elementary and secondary education, which is best administered by state and local governments. These observers believe that state and local governments are better able to understand the unique social and economic challenges that face communities and may affect educational policies and achievements. What is worse, these critics argue, is that NCLB contains a host of national mandates for state and local governments, but it contains little funding to help with policy implementation.

As a result of these criticisms, the National Education Association and its affiliates filed a lawsuit charging that the act was unconstitutional because it required state and local governments to spend their own funds to comply with national legislation. The courts, however, disagreed. Legislative attempts to express opposition to the law have been more successful. The states of Utah, Vermont, and Hawaii, to name a few, have passed legislation or resolutions opting out of portions of the law they consider to be unfunded or underfunded.

Opponents of NCLB appeared to gain an ally in the White House with the election of President Barack Obama in 2008. Obama's Race to the Top initiative provided funding for education through competitive grant programs, rather than a formula based on student achievement on standardized tests.[26] In response, states have begun to adopt a common core curriculum, implement new systems for performance-based teacher evaluations, and convert low-performance schools to charter schools, among numerous other reforms.

The Obama administration also took a number of other steps outside NCLB to advance education policy. Within one month of taking office, President Obama signed the American Recovery and Reinvestment Act. The act, which became law in February 2009, awarded $94.7 billion to education programming. Under the law, Head Start programs for low-income preschoolers received over $2 billion in supplemental funding. State departments of education, which were struggling with budget shortfalls and teacher furloughs and layoffs, were given nearly $45 billion in aid. Additional monies also were allocated for childcare programs and the low-interest college loans known as Pell Grants. Grant recipients reported that over 275,000 jobs in education were saved as a result of the additional funding provided by the law.

☐ Federal Aid to Higher Education

Federal governmental policies toward higher education provide indirect support through funding of research grants and financial assistance to students, representing about 15% of total spending by all levels of government in higher education. The federal government also funds the U.S. Military Academy, U.S. Naval Academy, U.S. Air Force Academy, U.S. Coast Guard Academy, and the U.S. Merchant Marine Academy. Any school that receives federal funding (K–12 or higher education) must comply with Title IX of the Educational Amendment Acts of 1972, barring any discrimination on the basis of sex in admissions, student financial aid, or athletics.

Access to college, however, has been the most prominent higher education policy focus in recent years. Students graduate from college with an average debt of $23,000,

16.1

16.2

16.3

16.4

16.5

yet the federal government spends more than $140 billion each year in grants and loans. Grants, based on financial need, do not require repayment, including Federal Pell Grants, Federal Supplemental Educational Opportunity Grants (FSEOG), Teacher Education Assistance for College and Higher Education (TEACH) Grants, and Iraq and Afghanistan Service Grants. The Federal Direct Student Loan Program allows students and families to borrow money to pay for college, with repayment (with interest) deferred until a student graduates or leaves college. This program includes the Federal Perkins Loans, Federal Stafford Loan, PLUS Loan for Parents, PLUS Loan for Graduate and Professional Degree Students, and Consolidation Loans. College Work Study programs, providing part-time jobs to college students while enrolled in school, also rely on federal funding.

Changes to student aid that went into effect in the 2012–2013 school year under the College Cost Reduction and Access Act (2007) include requirements that a student graduate from high school or pass the GED in order to be eligible for federally funded college grants or loans. The federally subsidized Stafford loans have a fixed interest rate of 3.4%. Additional reforms take effect in 2013–2014 with the Health Care and Education Reconciliation Act, signed into law by President Barack Obama in 2010, increasing Pell Grants by more than $40 billion, allowing new borrowers of student loans to cap their repayments at 10% of their income with the entire balance forgiven after 20 years, and providing $2 billion to community colleges to implement career training programs.

Energy and Environmental Policy Today

16.4 Explain energy and environmental policy in the United States.

Energy and environmental policy are inextricably linked in today's global economy. Environmental pollution is the by-product or consequence of development that imposes unwanted costs, or externalities, on society at large. Balancing the demand for inexpensive and abundant sources of energy, the costs of regulation, and the need to address issues of climate change creates controversy within this policy area, preventing comprehensive policy reform.

□ Energy Policy

In 2013, President Barack Obama's budget included $27.2 billion for the Department of Energy to implement an "all-of-the-above" approach to energy policy. Highlights of the budget included increased funding for research and development of clean technologies, incentives to create clean energy jobs, and increased measures to provide nuclear safety while maintaining nuclear deterrence. Obama also pledged to further reduce dependence on foreign oil by a third; in 2011, for the first time in thirteen years, the United States imported less than half of the crude oil it consumed. Still, the U.S. contains only 2% of the world's oil reserves but consumes 20% of the world's oil (see Figure 16.3).

The budget reflects the energy priorities first established during the energy crisis of the 1970s and expanded incrementally through both Republican and Democratic administrations. The need for energy is constant, and just 6.8% of energy sources in the United States are renewable, or derived from natural resources that can be replenished, including solar, wind, biomass, rain, tide, and geothermal energy. Fossil fuels—oil, coal, and natural gas—are nonrenewable, and each has advantages and disadvantages in terms of efficiency, costs, and the environmental impact of production and consumption.

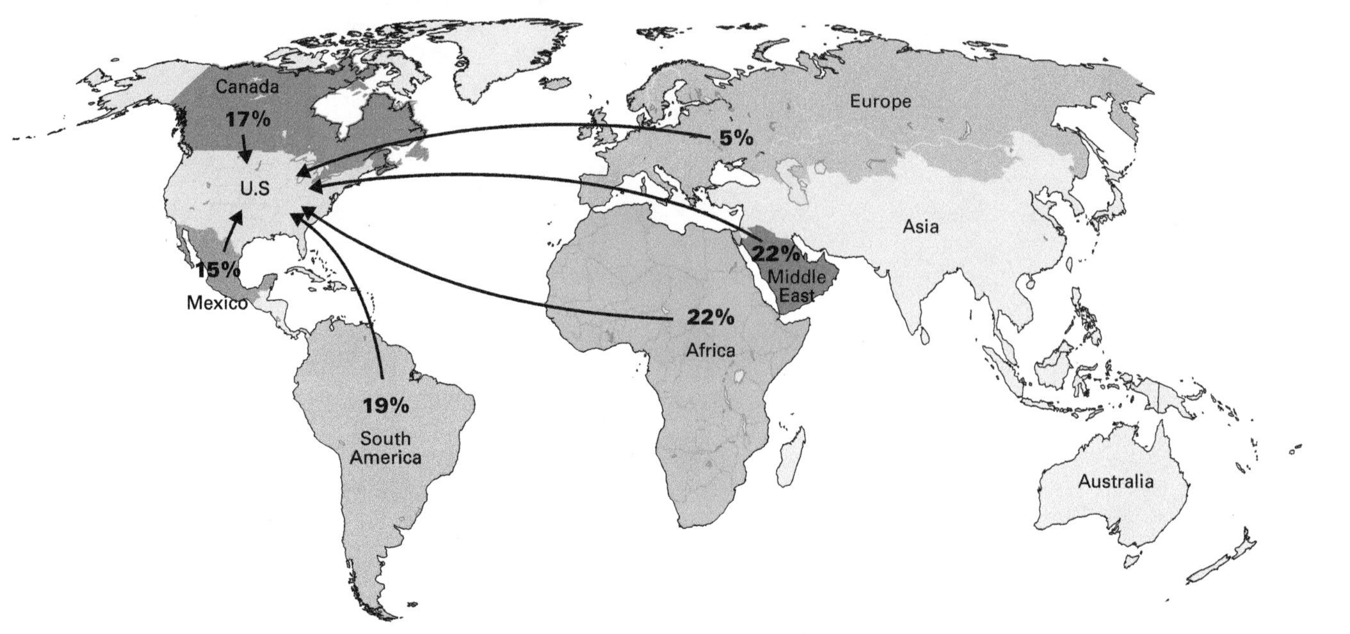

FIGURE 16.3 WHERE DO U.S. OIL IMPORTS COME FROM?

American oil imports come from sources around the globe. Although the largest percentages come from the Middle East and Africa, significant proportions also come from South America, Mexico, and Canada.

SOURCE: U.S. Energy Information Administration, Office of Senator Richard Lugar, lugar.senate.gov/energy/graphs/oilimport.html.

Extraction of natural gas, for example, has raised concerns about groundwater and drinking water contamination and about potential links to earthquakes induced by hydraulic fracturing, commonly known as fracking, in which fluids are pumped into a rock layer to create a wellbore to collect natural gas. In 2012, Vermont became the first state to ban fracking, and a growing number of states now require companies to disclose the chemicals used in the process. While nuclear power is the cleanest source of energy, it is perhaps the most controversial, including concerns about the safety of nuclear power's impact on health, the environment, and national security. Republicans and Democrats are also divided over plans to increase drilling for oil in the United States, including the Alaska National Wildlife Refuge (ANWR), and in offshore waters. In 2012, Obama initially rejected the Keystone XL Pipeline proposal to link oil refineries in Canada to the Gulf of Mexico, citing concerns regarding its environmental impact. In 2012, as well, Obama also announced support for exploration, but not actually drilling, offshore along the Atlantic Coast. A five-year environmental survey will assess where drilling might occur, but Obama offered no guarantee that new offshore drilling leases would be granted. While construction of the southern portion of the pipeline is now approved, the northern section is still on hold.

Energy policy addresses energy consumption in addition to energy production. The federal government has a long history of regulating the car manufacturing industry, for example, to produce automobiles that maintain fuel efficiency standards. Current policy requires an average standard of 54.5 MPG for passenger vehicles by 2025. The fuel efficiency and greenhouse gas emissions of trucks have also been limited for models manufactured from 2014 to 2018. In addition, investments are being made in the development and production of enough batteries to support a million plug-in, electric, and hybrid vehicles by 2015. Moreover, the Department of Energy and the Department of Housing and Urban Development have joined forces to upgrade the efficiency of buildings, factories, and homes across the United States.

Incrementally, energy policy reforms have focused on issues of supply and demand while balancing costs, safety, and the environment. Addressing the environmental impact of the production and consumption of energy, however, often requires regulations that increase costs for businesses and consumers, at the pump and in environmental degradation (see Figure 16.4).

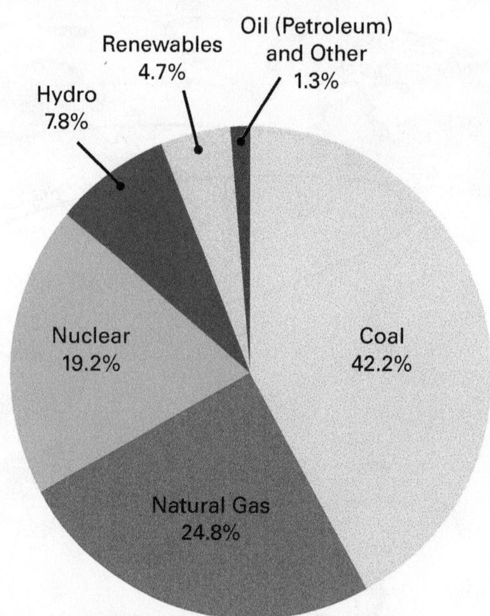

FIGURE 16.4 HOW DOES THE UNITED STATES GENERATE ELECTRICITY?

Although the percentage of American power coming from alternative fuel sources has increased in recent years, coal is still the largest source of electrical power.

SOURCE: U.S. Energy Information Administration, www.eia.doe.gov.

Clean Air Act of 1970
The law that established national primary and secondary standards for air quality in the United States. A revised version was passed in 1990.

Clean Water Act of 1972
The Act that created water quality standards to control pollution, including elimination of point source discharge of pollutants.

☐ Environmental Policy

In the United States in recent years, the need for economic recovery and the demand for reduced dependency on foreign oil have overshadowed the issue of environmental protection. The major federal government environmental policies in effect today were passed during the 1970s in efforts to address air and water pollution, endangered species, and hazardous waste disposal.

The National Environmental Policy Act (NEPA) of 1969 required the completion of environmental impact statements by bureaucratic agencies when the government proposed a project. These impact statements are available to the public, opening up the policy-making process to citizens, interest groups, and other levels of government. The intended result is to require agencies to consider the environmental consequences of their decision making. To help facilitate the oversight of NEPA and other environmental protection efforts, the Environmental Protection Agency (EPA) was created in 1970. The EPA consolidated many national environmental programs under one independent executive branch agency, with the agency administrator reporting directly to the president.

Congress followed up its efforts with NEPA by passing the most significant piece of environmental legislation in American history. Under the **Clean Air Act of 1970** (CAA), Congress established national primary and secondary air quality standards for six air pollutants. The primary standards were for the protection of human health, and the secondary standards were to protect nonhealth values, such as crops, buildings, lakes, and forests. The CAA also established emissions standards for vehicles and regulated fuels and toxic and hazardous sources of pollution.

In 1972, Congress followed up the Clean Air Act with the **Clean Water Act** (CWA). With nearly unanimous support among members of Congress, the law established the goal of making all American surface water "swimmable and fishable by 1985." The law gave states the authority to implement the policy within federal guidelines, including water quality standards and technological controls on discharges of pollutants. The law also provided funding for states to construct new wastewater treatment plants.

National policy initiatives grew throughout the 1970s, with the passage of legislation such as the Safe Drinking Water Act (1974), which established national standards for drinking water quality; the Resource Conservation and Recovery Act (1976), which eliminated the existence of unsanitary town dumps; and the Comprehensive Environmental

Explore Your World

Gas prices vary significantly both within the United States and around the globe, depending on the price of crude oil and levels of supply and demand. Within the United States, gas prices increase as distance from the source of crude oil increases. Regions that produce crude oil have lower gas prices than those that have to either transport crude oil across states or import oil internationally. However, these differences are minimal in comparison to gas prices in Europe, where governments have imposed high taxes on fuel to encourage conservation and fuel-efficient technologies.

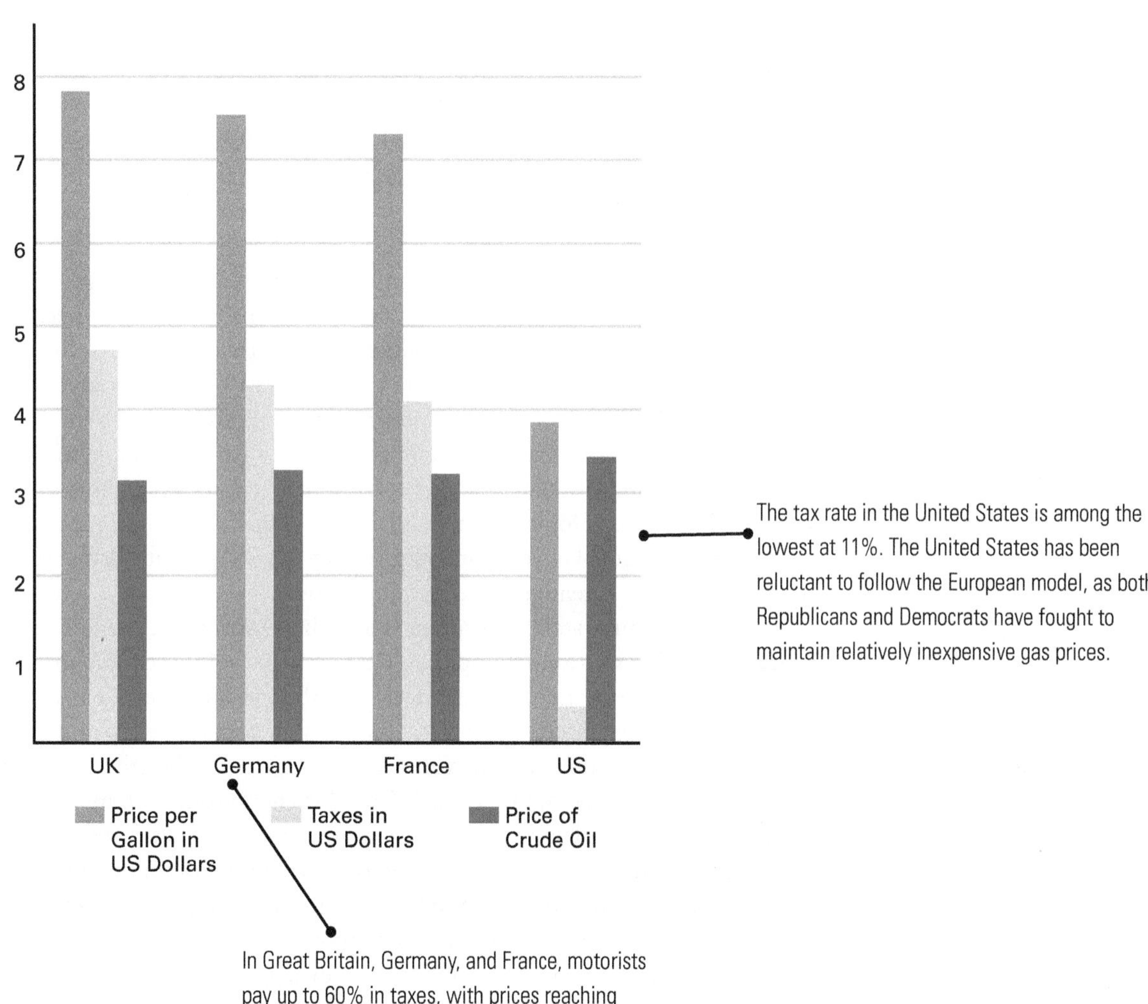
8
7
6
5
4
3
2
1
UK
Germany
France
US
Price per Gallon in US Dollars
Taxes in US Dollars
Price of Crude Oil
The tax rate in the United States is among the lowest at 11%. The United States has been reluctant to follow the European model, as both Republicans and Democrats have fought to maintain relatively inexpensive gas prices.
In Great Britain, Germany, and France, motorists pay up to 60% in taxes, with prices reaching nearly $10 per gallon in 2012.

SOURCE: http://www.eia.gov/countries/prices/gasolinewithtax.cfm, accessed June 6, 2012.

CRITICAL THINKING QUESTIONS

1. What would be the financial impact of a significant tax increase on gas in the United States? How would this tax influence low-income versus moderate- to high-income families?
2. What long-term changes in behavior might result from increased taxes on gas in the United States? How might these behavioral changes affect environmental, transportation, and housing issues in the United States?
3. Is it possible to reduce American consumption of gasoline if prices remain low? Aside from increasing taxes, what policy changes might encourage people to buy more fuel-efficient cars or to make better use of public transportation?

Response, Compensation, and Liability Act (Superfund), which was designed to clean up many of the nation's hazardous waste sites.

As the 1970s ended, so did the prominent role held by energy and environmental policy on the national government's agenda. With a few notable exceptions, such as the Clean Air Act of 1990 and a 2009 requirement for the EPA to regulate carbon dioxide, the national government has not aggressively tackled environmental issues with policy reforms as it had done in the 1970s.

☐ Climate Change

The need for comprehensive policy focusing on both energy and environmental issues became apparent as global climate change advanced to the forefront of environmental concerns. However, scientists cannot predict the absolute consequences of climate change, nor does the problem have an easy solution. President Barack Obama has been involved in international agreements on climate change, including the Copenhagen Accord in 2009 and the follow-up 2010 Cancun Agreement and 2011 Durban meeting, reaching agreements to limit greenhouse gas emissions. Obama's Climate Change Adaptation Task Force continues to make recommendations for policy changes at the national level.

Meanwhile, states have taken their own initiatives to address greenhouse gas emissions. In 2002, the state of California passed a law aimed at reducing greenhouse gas emissions from automobiles by 30 percent before 2016. This law went far beyond the national standards for greenhouse gas emissions established by the Environmental Protection Agency. By 2012, thirteen other states adopted enforceable emissions standards, while twenty-three states created emissions goals or targets. States are also cooperating with each other to address climate change. Currently, five regional climate initiatives are in operation, including, for example, the Regional Greenhouse Gas Initiative (RGGI), a cap and trade agreement between nine states to buy and sell permits for greenhouse emissions, creating financial incentives to reduce emissions.

By 2012, thirty state governments and the District of Columbia adopted mandatory Renewable Portfolio Standards (RPS), which require set amounts of electricity to be generated from alternative sources. Another seven states have adopted voluntary standards. For example, California has mandated that the percentage of renewable energy sales reach at least 33 percent by the end of 2020. Nearly half of states also have "public benefit funds" to provide subsidies for energy-efficient appliances, weatherization, and renewable technologies. Nearly all states have "net metering" and green pricing, allowing individuals to sell electricity back to the grid or to pay a higher premium for renewable sources of energy. States are also adopting policies to limit power plant emissions, encourage energy efficiency, provide incentives for low-carbon fuels and vehicles, and promote biomass initiatives. For example, Maine offers its residents up to a $7,000 tax rebate on residential photovoltaic system (solar power) installations and $1,250 on solar thermal water heaters. Texas also offers tax incentives for individuals and corporations who use solar or wind power to generate energy. By 2012, more than two-thirds of states adopted comprehensive climate action plans. For its part, the national government offers tax incentives for energy-efficient construction and has also taken steps to encourage the usage of compact fluorescent light bulbs, which are more energy efficient and last longer than their incandescent counterparts.

State and local governments have taken a number of additional steps to encourage citizens to become more environmentally friendly, or "green," in other areas of their lives. Many states and localities offer mandatory or optional recycling programs. The state of North Carolina, for example, recently passed legislation making it illegal to throw plastic bottles and aluminum cans in trash bins. Although the law has proved difficult to enforce, activists still argue that it is a step in the right direction and that it will have a significant environmental impact. And, in an attempt to reduce the waste generated from plastic bags, a number of cities, including San Francisco, have adopted legislation banning plastic bag use or charging consumers for plastic bags with their purchases. In Washington, D.C., shoppers who want a plastic bag must pay

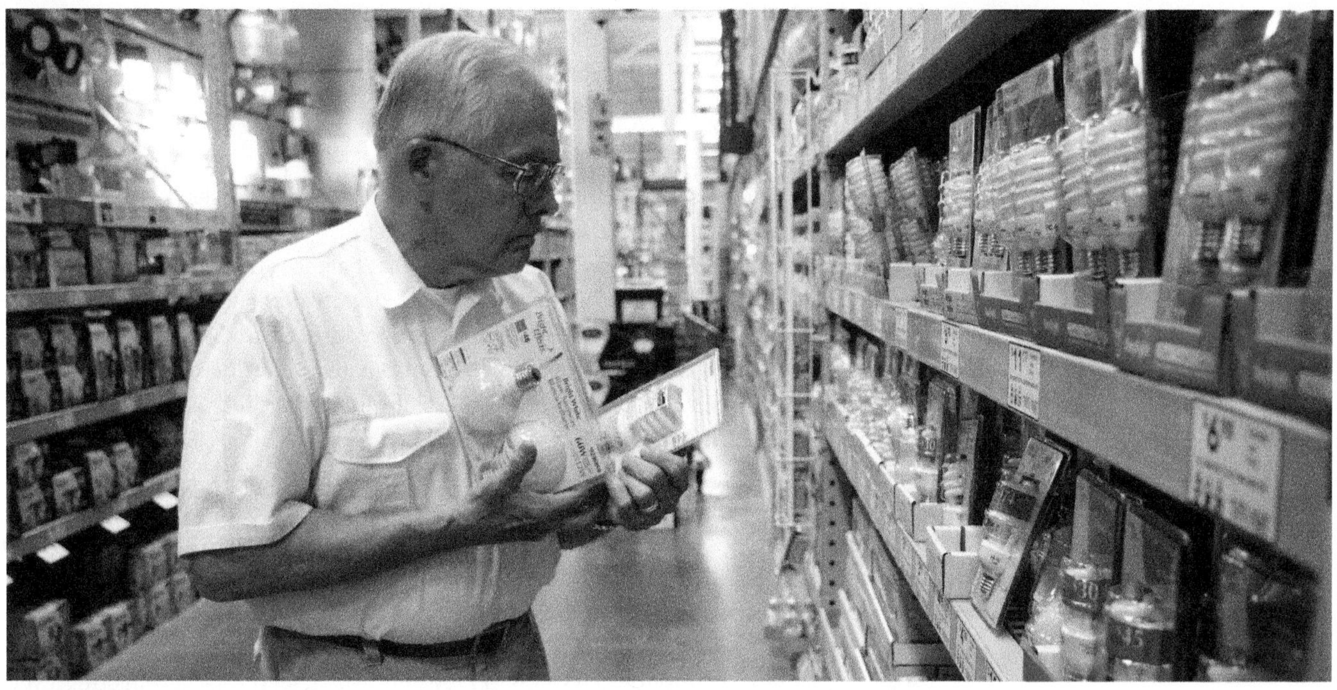

HOW CAN GOVERNMENTS ENCOURAGE AMERICANS TO GO GREEN?

One simple way governments have encouraged environmental consciousness is to provide citizens with incentives to purchase compact fluorescent light bulbs, shown here.

an additional five cents per bag. In the city of Seattle, the fee is twenty cents per bag for paper or plastic to encourage shoppers to bring their own reusable cloth bags.

These public policies represent only a small sampling of the legislation enacted in recent years. They also say little about citizens' and interest groups' actions to put Earth-friendliness on the systematic and governmental agendas. It is likely that these policy areas, along with the other domestic policy issues we have discussed in this chapter, will continue to have importance to Americans in years to come.

Toward Reform: Ongoing Challenges in Domestic Policy

16.5 Assess the ongoing challenges in U.S. domestic policy.

Domestic policy legislation has a rich history in the United States, as we have discussed in this chapter. However, in each of the issue areas considered, public policy challenges are yet to be solved. Health care costs continue to rise, implementation of the No Child Left Behind Act has not met goals for standards and performance, and the need for a comprehensive policy to address energy and climate change continues. Innovative, bold solutions to problems, however, are difficult to achieve in a decentralized policy-making process. Ultimately, which group dominates the process varies by issue. The elite theory, bureaucratic theory, interest group theory, and pluralist theory are useful models for understanding the politics of domestic policy making. The process also changes, depending on whether the proposed policy is routine or comprehensive in nature, and on how it is categorized—as distributive, redistributive, or regulatory policy. It is also important to understand that each stage of the policy-making process presents both opportunities and barriers to change.

16.1

16.2

16.3

16.4

16.5

At the agenda-setting stage, rarely do all three streams—problems, policies, and politics—converge to open a policy window. In addressing climate change, for example, disagreement exists over the exact cause and extent of the problem. Without a clear definition of the problem, it is even more difficult to gain consensus on a solution, or capture the attention of elected officials and the public.

Policy often is formulated in the context of uncertainty. The risks of offshore drilling were visibly apparent in the wake of the BP oil spill. How are these risks contained and prevented in a comprehensive energy policy that balances the need for energy with protection of the environment? Policy makers do not always have complete information on the long-term costs and benefits of proposed policy solutions. As a result, incrementalism often describes the policy adoption stage. President Obama's energy policy, for example, includes limited expansion of offshore drilling and exploration of additional sites, but no guarantee of future leases.

At the implementation stage, policies can change shape as they are carried out day to day by the bureaucracy. As teachers implemented No Child Left Behind, new standards and teaching to the test changed the content and delivery of information to K–12 students. Policies also are constantly subject to challenge, in routine evaluations and budget allocations, or in constitutional challenges in the courts. Challenges to the Patient Protection and Affordable Care Act jeopardized full implementation of Obama's health care initiative. As new policy concerns rise, the policy-making cycle starts over again. At the same time, this process has limits. Anthony Downs describes an issue attention cycle in which problems are easier to address when a crisis or critical mobilizing event captures the public's attention. As the problem is addressed, or the shocking nature of the crisis fades, the public loses interest. Sometimes realization dawns that no easy solution is possible, or that the costs outweigh benefits. Incremental steps toward solving the problem, or just the perception that something is going to be done, can also shift the public's attention to another issue. Once the intensity of public interest fades, comprehensive policy making is much more difficult to achieve.

On MyPoliSciLab

Review the Chapter

Listen to Chapter 16 on MyPoliSciLab

Roots of Domestic Policy in the United States

16.1 Trace the stages of the policy-making process, p. 483.

Public policy is an intentional course of action or inaction followed by government in dealing with some problem or matter of concern. A popular model used to describe the policy-making process views it as a sequence of stages that include agenda setting, policy formulation, policy adoption, policy implementation, and policy evaluation. Although this model can be useful, it is a simplification of the actual process, and it does not always explain why policies take the forms they do or who controls the formation of public policy.

Health Policy Today

16.2 Describe health policy in the United States, p. 495.

Governments in the United States have a long history of involvement in the health of Americans. Beginning in the 1960s, the government began to fund health programs for senior citizens and the poor, known as Medicare and Medicaid, respectively. And in 2010, after several failed attempts by prior administrations, the Democratic Congress passed and President Barack Obama signed the Patient Protection and Affordable Care Act, expanding the national government's role in providing health insurance. The U.S. government also plays a prominent role in public health through the use of immunizations, education, advertisements, research, and regulations.

Education Policy Today

16.3 Outline education policy in the United States, p. 502.

Education policy in the United States has been a work in progress for over two centuries, and reform has focused on social and political order, individual liberty, and social and political equity. In 2002, President George W. Bush signed into law a bipartisan bill commonly referred to as No Child Left Behind. It set high standards and measurable goals as a method of improving American education. One of the act's more controversial tenets involves the issue of school choice, whereby if a child is attending a failing school, parents have the option of sending the child to another public, private, or charter school that is subsidized through government vouchers. President Barack Obama's Race to the Top initiative encourages states to develop their own innovative education reforms to accelerate progress.

Energy and Environmental Policy Today

16.4 Explain energy and environmental policy in the United States, p. 506.

As energy sources have become more limited and environmental problems have magnified, government efforts in these policy fields have expanded. Before the 1970s, activity on the part of government to establish policies related to energy and environmental protection was very limited. Energy shortages and expanding pollution problems propelled these policy areas into the forefront of the government's agenda in the 1970s, but their prominence at the national level has fluctuated greatly. During recent years, skyrocketing energy prices and increasing concerns about global warming and other aspects of climate change have placed these issues once again at the center of American politics, with states currently taking the lead in policy development.

Toward Reform: Ongoing Challenges in Domestic Policy

16.5 Assess the ongoing challenges in U.S. domestic policy, p. 511.

Policy making in the United States is a decentralized process that makes it difficult to pass comprehensive reform. Each of the domestic policy areas highlighted in this chapter—health care, education, and energy and the environment—illustrate the forces that create opportunities for and constraints on change. Each of the five stages of policy making—agenda setting, policy formulation, policy adoption, implementation, and evaluation—presents an additional hurdle for policies to survive. Often it takes policy entrepreneurs or crises to elevate an issue to national attention and force governmental action. Still, most policy making takes place in a context of uncertainty, related to science and technology, costs and benefits, or politics. The nature of problems also constantly evolves, and the policy cycle repeats itself continuously. The issue attention cycle suggests, however, that the country's attention does not stay focused on any one problem for very long.

Key Terms

Study and **Review** the **Flashcards**

agenda, p. 490
agenda setting, p. 491
charter schools, p. 504
Clean Air Act of 1970, p. 508
Clean Water Act of 1972, p. 508
domestic policy, p. 483
global warming, p. 488
governmental (institutional) agenda, p. 491
greenhouse gases, p. 488
Medicaid, p. 497
Medicare, p. 495
No Child Left Behind Act, p. 502
Patient Protection and Affordable Care Act, p. 484
policy adoption, p. 493
policy evaluation, p. 494
policy formulation, p. 491
policy implementation, p. 493
public policy, p. 483
systemic agenda, p. 490
vouchers, p. 504

Test Yourself

Study and **Review** the **Practice Tests**

1. The intentional course of action followed by government in dealing with problems or matters of concern is called

a. policy formulation.
b. social welfare policy.
c. policy administration.
d. public administration.
e. public policy.

2. Domestic policy making in the United States is characterized by

a. a highly centralized process.
b. ideological consensus over policy goals.
c. incrementalism.
d. constant bold initiatives that transform policies.
e. a very large range of issues.

3. Medicaid was designed to provide health care

a. for the aged and ill.
b. for the poor.
c. for the working class.
d. for children.
e. for everyone.

4. Obama's health care reform focused on

a. decreasing physician costs by socializing the medical profession.
b. government ownership of the pharmaceutical industry.
c. community-based free clinics.
d. affordable health insurance.
e. privatization of all health care.

5. The earliest example of national government involvement in education policy is the

a. Northwest Ordinance.
b. creation of the League of Nations.
c. Civil Rights Act.
d. creation of the Department of Education.
e. passage of the No Child Left Behind Act.

6. The No Child Left Behind Act sought to improve education by

a. providing vouchers for parents to choose public or private school.
b. assessing performance on standardized tests.
c. improving enrichment programs in music and the arts.
d. eliminating charter schools
e. privatizing elementary education.

7. The federal government's response to global warming has been

a. ratification of the Kyoto Protocol.
b. generally absent.
c. extensive, particularly since the Clean Air Act of 1990.
d. mandating that all new homes built must be green.
e. banning the sale of incandescent light bulbs.

8. States have responded to global climate change by

a. decreasing emissions standards
b. increasing the use of coal.
c. exploring offshore drilling opportunities.
d. entering agreements with other states to "cap and trade" pollution.
e. increasing gasoline taxes.

9. Health care costs

a. are increasing at about the rate of inflation.
b. are lower in the United States than in other industrialized nations.
c. are affected by life expectancy.
d. have declined as a result of the Medicare program.
e. do not affect states' public policy decisions.

10. The issue attention cycle

a. refers to the never-ending national focus on education, health care, and the environment.

b. makes it difficult to sustain long-term policy progress as the visibility of an issue fades.

c. rotates predictably through major policy areas.

d. makes it easy to increase funding for policies once they are enacted.

e. makes it easy to create new government programs.

Explore Further

Bryce, Robert. *Power Hungry: The Myths of "Green" Energy and the Real Fuels of the Future.* New York: Public Affairs, 2010.

Dye, Thomas R. *Understanding Public Policy,* 13th ed. New York: Longman, 2010.

Feldstein, Paul. *Health Policy Issues: An Economic Perspective on Health Reform,* 4th ed. Chicago: Health Administration Press, 2007.

Gerston, Larry N. *Public Policy Making: Process and Principles.* Armonk, NY: M. E. Sharpe, 2010.

Kingdon, John W. *Agendas, Alternatives, and Public Policies,* 2nd ed. New York: Longman, 2010.

Kraft, Michael. *Environmental Policy and Politics,* 5th ed. New York: Longman, 2010.

Longest, Beaufort B. *Health Policymaking in the United States,* 4th ed. Chicago: Health Administration Press, 2005.

Oberlander, Jonathan. *The Political Life of Medicare.* Chicago: University of Chicago Press, 2003.

Olson, Laura Katz. *The Politics of Medicaid.* New York: Columbia University Press, 2010.

Rabe, Barry G. *Statehouse and Greenhouse: The Emerging Politics of American Climate Change Policy.* Washington, DC: Brookings Institution, 2004.

Ravitch, Diane. *The Death and Life of the Great American School System: How Testing and Choice Are Undermining Education.* New York: Basic Books, 2010.

Ristinen, Robert P., and Jack P. Kraushaar. *Energy and the Environment,* 2nd ed. Hoboken, NJ: Wiley, 2005.

Springer, Matthew G. *Performance Incentives: The Growing Impact on American K-12 Education.* Washington, DC: Brookings Institution, 2009.

Washington Post. Landmark: The Inside Story of America's New Health Care Law and What It Means for All of Us. New York: Public Affairs, 2010.

Wilson, Steven F. *Learning on the Job: When Business Takes on Public Schools.* Cambridge, MA: Cambridge University Press, 2006.

To learn more about how public policies are prioritized and analyzed, go to the Web site of the National Center for Policy Analysis at **www.ncpa.org**.

To learn more about public health initiatives and consumer health advisories, go to the Web site of the National Institutes of Health at **www.nih.gov**.

To learn more about education policy in the United States, go to the Web site of the U.S. Department of Education at **www.ed.gov**.

To learn more about major environmental policies, go to the Web site of the Environmental Protection Agency at **www.epa.gov**.

Listen to Chapter 17 on MyPoliSciLab

17

Economic Policy

In 2012, lawmakers faced what economists described as "the fiscal cliff." On its current trajectory, the economic policy of the United States government was deemed unsustainable. Revenues would continue to fall short of government spending, and the debt, increasingly owed to foreign countries, would grow exponentially. Projected increases in the cost of health care for an aging population would compound the trend. No easy solution was apparent, or necessarily recommended by policy experts. On the table for discussion were the tax cuts enacted by the Bush administration, set to expire in 2013. The temporary reduction in income and payroll tax rates would also expire. Combined with spending cuts that would automatically go into effect in January 2013 under the Budget Act of 2011, these policy changes were expected to increase federal government revenues by an estimated $607 billion, or 4 percent of the gross domestic product (GDP). While these increased revenues could reduce the deficit for 2012–2013 by $560 billion, the financial impact of higher taxes combined with spending cuts could devastate a weak economy still recovering from the worst recession since the Great Depression. The price tag for deficit reduction would be slower economic growth, higher unemployment, and lower wages in the short term. Alternatively, if lawmakers decided to postpone policy changes, the U.S. debt would continue to outpace the GDP, forcing more drastic austerity measures in the future.[1] The dismal outlook for reining in the debt has already prompted Standard & Poor to downgrade the U.S. credit rating from AAA to AA+.[2]

Republicans, fueled by the Tea Party movement, fought to prevent any new tax increases and to make permanent the tax cuts enacted during the Bush administration, preferring to decrease debt solely through spending cuts. Democrats argued in favor of greater government spending to stimulate the economy and increasing tax revenue by closing loopholes and ending the Bush administration's tax cuts favoring the wealthy. According to Gallup Poll data, 73 percent of the public attributes the deficit to too much spending, compared with 22 percent who blame insufficient taxes.[3] While spending cuts are consistently more palatable than tax increases to reduce the deficit, most Americans recognize the need for a combined approach.[4]

THE GOVERNMENT OFTEN TAKES A PROMINENT ROLE IN STIMULATING THE ECONOMY Above, John Maynard Keynes, the father of modern macroeconomic theory, which favors government spending to promote economic growth, speaks at a conference in the 1940s. Below, Congressional Budget Office Director Douglas Elmendorf testifies that projected tax hikes and spending cuts for 2013 could put the United States back into recession.

MyPoliSciLab Videos

Watch on MyPoliSciLab

The Big Picture Does the federal government need to have a balanced budget? Author Alixandra B. Yanus highlights some of the key debates surrounding economic policy today by analyzing the ways that the government can affect the economy.

The Basics Watch this video to learn why economic policy is so complicated in the United States. Find out how policies developed to solve new challenges that arose from industrialization. Then, consider whether you should be worried about the national debt.

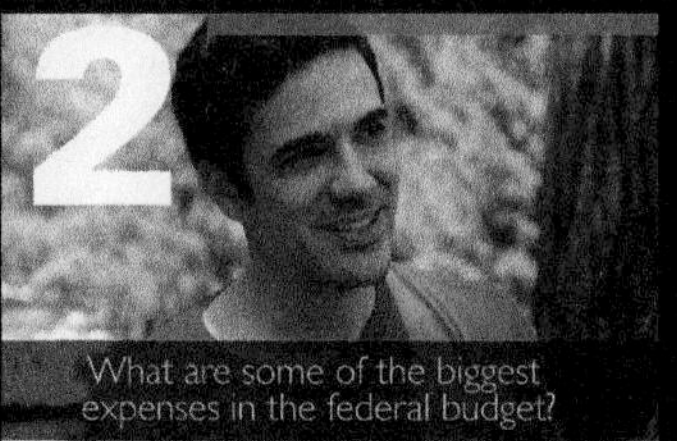

What are some of the biggest expenses in the federal budget?

In Context Is your personal budget like the federal budget? If not, how is it different? University of Oklahoma political scientist Alisa H. Fryar breaks down the complexities of the federal budget and explains how the study of economic policy is changing in a more globalized society.

Thinking Like a Political Scientist Was the federal government wise to provide tax cuts during the most recent economic recession? University of Oklahoma political scientist Alisa H. Fryar examines how researchers determine the answer to these and other economic policy questions. She also explores the challenges state and local governments face in achieving their economic goals

In the Real World Should the wealthy pay a larger percentage of their income in taxes than people with lower incomes? Real people tackle this central question, and they weigh in on what they believe is the fairest system of taxation and what tax reforms need to be made in the United States.

So What? The economy of the United States is incredibly complex—especially in the age of globalization—so why should you care? Author Alixandra B. Yanus explains why the economic policies of the government can have a direct impact on your job prospects and quality of life after graduation.

The fiscal policy cliff produced tough choices for economic policy makers. In the long run, debt reduction is an important goal in sustaining strong economic growth. Debt can be reduced by raising taxes, cutting spending, or both. In the short run, however, the need to stabilize the economy as it continues to emerge from recession warrants increased government spending, rather than cuts, but at the risk of running even larger deficits into the future. Ultimately, economic policy making reflects an ongoing debate over the role and size of government. The perfect combination of increased or decreased taxing and spending to guarantee economic stability does not exist; rather, ideological values dictate policy preferences.

•••

The U.S. economic system is a mixed free-enterprise system characterized by private ownership of property, private enterprise, and marketplace competition. But, the national government has long played an important role in fostering economic development through its tariffs (taxes on imported goods), tax policies, use of public lands, and creation of a national bank. Today the federal government actively uses economic policy making to promote economic stability, as well as to recognize and respond to economic crises. The government also uses built-in "automatic stabilizers," or income security policies—including welfare, unemployment insurance, and progressive income tax rates—to lessen the impact of economic crises, expanding the economy during recessions and contracting it during periods of expansion.

With this greater involvement comes debate over the proper role of government in the economic sector. Those favoring limited government participation are pitted against others who believe the government is responsible for managing the economy through policy. In this chapter, we will consider both viewpoints as we describe the policies of the government in achieving its economic goals.

economic regulation
Government regulation of business practices, industry rates, routes, or areas serviced by particular industries.

laissez-faire
A French term meaning "to allow to do, to leave alone." It holds that active governmental involvement in the economy is wrong.

business cycles
Fluctuations between periods of economic growth and recession, or periods of boom and bust.

Roots of Economic Policy

17.1 Trace the evolution of economic policy in the United States.

The government's role in regulating the economy has evolved over our nation's history. During the nineteenth century, the national government defined its economic role narrowly, although it did collect tariffs, fund public improvements, and encourage private development. The national government increased its involvement in **economic regulation** during the Progressive and New Deal eras. In more recent years, it has turned its attention to financial regulation and deregulation.

The Nineteenth Century

For much of the nineteenth century, the national government subscribed to a **laissez-faire** (literally "to allow to do" or "to leave alone") economic philosophy. The laissez-faire economic system holds that active governmental involvement in the economy is wrong, and that the role of government should be limited to the maintenance of order and justice, the conduct of foreign affairs, and the provision of necessary public works. As a result, most national intervention in the economy during this time amounted to setting and adjusting tariffs and maintaining the liberty necessary to fuel economic fires.

But, the Civil War and the growing industrialization of the postwar economy changed the political landscape. Industrialization, for example, led to industrial accidents and disease, labor–management conflicts, unemployment, and the emergence of huge corporations that could exploit workers and consumers. Industrialization also worsened the effects of natural **business cycles**, or fluctuations between periods of economic growth and recession (or periods of boom and bust).

The first major government effort to regulate business came about by growing concern over the power of the railroads. After nearly two decades of pressure from

17.1

17.2

17.3

17.4

17.5

trusts
Large-scale, monopolistic businesses that dominate an industry.

farmers, owners of small businesses, and reformers in the cities, Congress adopted the Interstate Commerce Act in 1887. Enforced by the new Interstate Commerce Commission (ICC), the act required railroad rates to be "just and reasonable."[5] The act also prohibited such practices as pooling (rate agreements), rate discrimination, and charging more for a short haul than for a long haul of goods.

Three years later, Congress dealt with the problem of **trusts**, the name given to large-scale, monopolistic businesses that dominated many industries, including oil, sugar, whiskey, salt, and meatpacking. The Sherman Anti-Trust Act of 1890 prohibited all restraints of trade, including price fixing, bid-rigging, and market allocation agreements. It also forbade all monopolization or attempts to monopolize, including domination of a market by one or a few companies.

☐ The Progressive Era

The Progressive movement drew much of its support from the middle class and sought to reform America's political, economic, and social systems. Many desired to bring corporate power under the control of government and make it more responsive to

The Congress shall have power to lay and collect taxes on incomes, from whatever source derived, without apportionment among the several States, and without regard to any census or enumeration.
—SIXTEENTH AMENDMENT

As the national government's role in economic regulation grew larger in the late eighteenth century, its administrative costs began to grow. Congress sought to rectify this situation by enacting a law that levied a national income tax. However, in *Pollock* v. *Farmers' Loan & Trust Co.* (1895), a divided Supreme Court held that levying such a tax by statute was unconstitutional.

Ratified on February 3, 1913, the Sixteenth Amendment addressed this shortcoming by modifying the Article I prohibition against levying a "direct tax" on individual property. The first income tax was levied concurrently with adoption of the amendment. At that time, the national government required all Americans to give 2 percent of their income as tax.

Although the U.S. government continues to levy an income tax today, much about the tax rate has changed. Today, national income taxes are progressive, meaning that the tax rate paid by citizens increases with income. If the Bush-era tax cuts are allowed to expire, the tax rate in 2013 for a single American making less than $8,750 in taxable income will be 15 percent. In contrast, those who make more than $390,050 will be required to pay 39.6 percent of their income in taxes.

The national income tax continues to be one of the most controversial federal policies. Few Americans truly enjoy paying taxes, and many citizens find the tax code to be complicated and full of loopholes. Reformers across the political spectrum have suggested ways to alter the tax code to make it fairer, or to ensure that it does not place too great a burden on low-income Americans. Proposals include simplifying the existing tax code to eliminate deductions. In 2011, Warren Buffet made national headlines by complaining that a wealthy man like himself paid a lower percentage of his income in taxes than his secretary paid. Obama proposed the "Buffet Rule," which would require a minimum 30% tax rate for individuals earning in excess of one million dollars. The income tax would remain progressive, and marginal tax rates for everyone would decrease. Opponents, however, perceive the elimination of tax loopholes as a tax increase on the wealthy. Conversely, a flat tax would create a single tax rate for all citizens regardless of income. While proponents of the flat tax perceive this proposal as "fair," the tax is regressive if wealthy taxpayers are still allowed to deduct large portions of their earnings. A more radical reform would create a consumption-based tax system, such as Europe's Value Added Tax. Critics contend that these taxes can be more regressive, but economists argue that they encourage more individual saving because taxes are paid only on the portion of income spent on goods and services.

CRITICAL THINKING QUESTIONS

1. What type of proposed reform to the U.S. tax code seems fairest to all citizens and why?
2. What types of government programs or services would you be willing to pay more taxes for? Which ones would you be willing to give up to lower your taxes?

democratic ends. Progressive administrations under Presidents Theodore Roosevelt and Woodrow Wilson established or strengthened regulatory programs to protect consumers and to control railroads, business, and banking.

The Pure Food and Drug Act and the Meat Inspection Act, both enacted in 1906, marked the beginning of consumer protection as a major responsibility of the national government. These laws prohibited adulteration and mislabeling of food and drugs and set sanitary standards for the food industry.

To control banking and regulate business, Congress passed three acts. The Federal Reserve Act (1913) created the Federal Reserve System to regulate the national banking system and to provide for flexibility in the money supply in order to better meet commercial needs and combat financial panics. Passage of the Federal Trade Commission (FTC) Act and Clayton Act of 1914 strengthened anti-trust policy. These statutes, like the Sherman Anti-Trust Act, sought to prevent businesses from forming monopolies or trusts.

As the national government's functions expanded in the late nineteenth and early twentieth centuries, fiscal constraints forced public officials to focus on new ways to raise federal revenue. Congress attempted to enact an income tax, but in 1895, the Supreme Court held that such a tax was unconstitutional.[6] Consequently, the Sixteenth Amendment to the Constitution was adopted in 1913. The Sixteenth Amendment authorized the national government "to lay and collect taxes on incomes, from whatever source derived" without being apportioned among the states. Personal and corporate income taxes have since become the national government's major source of general revenues.

HOW DID THE PROGRESSIVE ERA CHANGE GOVERNMENT REGULATION OF THE ECONOMY?

During this era, the national government began to pass workplace and product safety measures such as the Meat Inspection Act to prevent the public from eating tainted beef.

17.1

17.2

17.3

17.4

17.5

interventionist state
Alternative to the laissez-faire state; the government took an active role in guiding and regulating the private economy.

☐ The Great Depression and the New Deal

During the early 1920s, the economy grew at a rapid pace, and many Americans assumed that the resulting prosperity would last forever. But, "forever" came to an end in October 1929, when the stock market collapsed and the catastrophic worldwide economic decline known as the Great Depression set in. Although the Depression was worldwide in scope, it hit the United States especially hard. All sectors of the economy suffered, with no economic group or social class spared.

Initially, Herbert Hoover's administration declared the economy fundamentally sound, a claim few believed. Investors, businesspeople, and others lost confidence in the economy. Prices dropped, production declined, and unemployment rose to staggering levels. According to Bureau of Labor Statistics estimates, about one-fourth of the civilian workforce was unemployed in 1933.[7] Many other people worked only part-time or at jobs below their skill levels. The economic distress produced by the Great Depression, which lasted for a decade, was unparalleled before or since that time.

The Depression and President Franklin D. Roosevelt's New Deal marked a major turning point in U.S. economic history. During the 1930s, the laissez-faire state was replaced with an **interventionist state**, in which the government took an active role in guiding and regulating the private economy. The New Deal, for example, established reforms in almost every area, including finance, agriculture, labor, and industry.

FINANCIAL REFORMS The New Deal first directed attention at reviving and reforming the nation's financial system. Because of bad investments and poor management, many banks failed in the early 1930s. To restore confidence in banks, Roosevelt declared a bank holiday the day after his inauguration, closing all of the nation's banks. Emergency legislation passed by Congress permitted only financially sound banks to reopen. Many unsound banks were closed for good and their depositors paid off.

Major New Deal banking laws included the Glass-Steagall Act (1933). The Glass-Steagall Act required the separation of commercial and investment banking and set up the Federal Deposit Insurance Corporation (FDIC) to insure bank deposits, originally for $5,000 per account. The act aimed to prevent the bank failures of the Great Depression by removing the conflicts of interest and excessive risk-taking associated with securities dealing from savings and loans. Congress also passed legislation to control abuses in the stock markets. The Securities Act (1933) required that prospective investors be given full and accurate information about the stocks or securities being offered. The Securities Exchange Act (1934) created the Securities and Exchange Commission (SEC), an independent regulatory commission. This legislation authorized the SEC to regulate the stock exchanges, enforce the Securities Act, and reduce the number of stocks bought on margin (that is, with borrowed money).

AGRICULTURE American agriculture had struggled even during the prosperous 1920s. The Great Depression only worsened this state of affairs. To protect this important industry, Congress and FDR adopted a number of public policies. The most notable was the second Agricultural Adjustment Act (AAA), enacted in 1938, after the Supreme Court declared the first AAA unconstitutional.

The second AAA provided subsidies to farmers raising crops such as corn, cotton, and wheat who grew on no more than their allotted acreage. The government also made direct payments and commodity loans available to participating farmers. The Supreme Court upheld the constitutionality of the second AAA, finding it an appropriate exercise of Congress's power to regulate interstate commerce.[8]

LABOR The fortunes of labor unions, which strongly supported the New Deal, improved significantly in 1935, when Congress passed the National Labor Relations Act. Better known as the Wagner Act after its sponsor, Senator Robert Wagner

(D–NY), this statute guaranteed workers' rights to organize and bargain collectively through unions of their own choosing. The act prohibited a series of "unfair labor practices," such as discriminating against employees because of their union activities. The National Labor Relations Board (NLRB) was created to carry out the act and to conduct elections to determine which union, if any, employees wanted to represent them. Unions prospered under the protection provided by the Wagner Act.

Another important piece of New Deal legislation designed to protect the rights of laborers was the Fair Labor Standards Act (FLSA). The act set minimum wage and maximum hour requirements at 25¢ per hour and forty-four hours per week, respectively. The act also banned child labor. The FLSA did not cover all employees, however; it exempted farm workers, domestic workers, and fishermen.

deregulation
A reduction in market controls (such as price fixing, subsidies, or controls on who can enter the field) in favor of market-based competition.

INDUSTRY REGULATIONS During the New Deal, Congress established new or expanded regulatory programs for several industries. The Federal Communications Commission (FCC), created in 1934 to replace the old Federal Radio Commission, attained extensive jurisdiction over the radio, telephone, and telegraph industries. The Civil Aeronautics Board (CAB) was instituted in 1938 to regulate the commercial aviation industry. The Motor Carrier Act of 1935 placed the trucking industry under the jurisdiction of the Interstate Commerce Commission (ICC). Like railroad regulation, the regulation of industries such as trucking and commercial aviation extended to such matters as entry into the business, routes of service, and rates. To a substantial extent, government regulation, as a protector of the public interest, replaced competition in these industries. Supporters of these programs believed they were necessary to prevent destructive or excessive competition. Critics warned that limiting competition resulted in users' having to pay more for services.

THE LEGACY OF THE NEW DEAL ERA Just as World War I brought down the curtain on the Progressive era, the outbreak of World War II diverted Americans' attention from domestic reform and brought an end to the New Deal era. Many New Deal programs, however, became permanent parts of the American public policy landscape. Moreover, the New Deal established the legitimacy and viability of national governmental intervention in the economy. Activist government replaced passive government.

□ Deregulation

In the mid-1970s, President Gerald R. Ford, viewing regulation as one cause of the high inflation that existed at the time, decided to make **deregulation**, a reduction in market controls in favor of market-based competition, a major objective of his administration. Deregulation was also a high priority for Ford's successor, President Jimmy Carter, who supported deregulated commercial airlines, railroads, motor carriers, and financial institutions. All successive presidents have encouraged some degree of deregulation, though it has produced mixed effects, as illustrated by the airline and agricultural sectors.

The Airline Deregulation Act of 1978, for example, completely eliminated economic regulation of commercial airlines over several years. Although many new passenger carriers flocked into the industry when barriers to entry were first removed, they could not compete successfully with the existing major airlines. Consequently, now fewer major carriers exist than was the case under the regulatory regime. Competition has lowered some passenger rates, but disagreement has arisen over the extent to which passengers have benefited. For example, since enactment of the Airline Deregulation Act, small communities across the United States have lost service as airlines make major cuts in their routes, despite government subsidies to help maintain service.[9]

In spite of this mixed record, economic deregulation and reregulation have continued to receive a great deal of attention from citizens and politicians. In the 1980s and 1990s, agricultural price support programs came under increasing attack from conservatives, who claimed that such government price supports promoted inefficiency. In 1996, congressional Republicans passed a landmark agriculture bill with the aim of

HOW DO AGRICULTURE SUBSIDIES REGULATE THE ECONOMY?

Subsidies are government funds paid to farmers to grow—or not grow—particular crops. They have come under fire in recent years because they disproportionately benefit the wealthiest farmers.

phasing out crop subsidies and making prices more dependent upon the workings of the free market. But five years later, the 2002 farm bill actually increased agricultural subsidies by 70 percent as part of a ten-year, $180 billion package. The political pressure coming from large-scale farms and agribusinesses was obvious. According to one analyst, "Nearly three-quarters of these funds will go to the wealthiest 10 percent of farmers—most of whom earn more than $250,000 per year."[10]

In the banking industry, deregulation in the 1990s played a role in the subprime mortgage crisis that began in 2007, prompting new government policies to provide economic relief. The 1994 Riegle-Neal Interstate Banking and Branching Efficiency Act removed restrictions on interstate banking, resulting in a concentration of large banks at the national level and the crowding out of small, locally owned banks. This became an important policy consequence when large financial institutions, deemed "too big to fail," would later receive bailouts from the federal government to prevent serious ripple effects on the economy. In 1994, the Security Exchange Commission created the Consolidated Supervised Entities program, allowing international investment bank conglomerates to voluntarily comply with regulations on the amount of capital they must hold in reserve. In 1996, the Federal Reserve reinterpreted the Glass-Steagall Act to allow bank holding companies to increase their investment portfolios, and then Congress repealed the act entirely with the 1999 Gramm-Leach-Bliley Act. This act allowed banks to consolidate traditional banking services (savings and loans) with riskier securities and insurance business. When large securities investments and trading brokerage firms, including Goldman Sachs, Morgan Stanley, Merrill Lynch, Lehman Brothers, and Bear Stearns, suffered financially as the housing mortgage crises unfolded with the first wave of subprime mortgage defaults in 2007, their interconnectedness worsened the fallout. The government institutions created to guarantee mortgages, Fannie Mae and Freddie Mac, were also implicated; they had raised their risk by securitizing subprime mortgages in their efforts to increase bank liquidity. Congress passed the Emergency Economic Stabilization Act, creating the Troubled Asset Relief Program, authorizing the U.S. Treasury to purchase mortgage-backed securities to provide some relief to the troubled banking system. Finding the right balance between too much and too little regulation is a constant struggle in economic policy making.

Fiscal Policy

17.2 Assess the impact of the budget process on fiscal policy.

fiscal policy
The deliberate use of the national government's taxing and spending policies to maintain economic stability.

budget deficit
The economic condition that occurs when expenditures exceed revenues.

Fiscal policy is the deliberate use of the national government's taxing and spending policies to maintain economic growth and stability. Government spending and taxes are the tools used to expand or contract the economy as needed. Deficits or surpluses are the outcomes of these policy decisions. When government spending is not offset by tax revenue, the result is a deficit at the end of the fiscal year. If, however, tax revenue exceeds spending, the result is a government surplus. Economists argue that increased government spending stimulates economic growth, which can help the economy rebound from a recession. However, it also means that government is likely to run a deficit. The continuation of deficits long term, especially after the economy has recovered, can have adverse effects, including inflation and increased national debt. The national debt is the total amount owed by the federal government to its creditors, both domestic and international. Financing a large national debt reduces government savings and the amount of capital available for investment. As the debt grows, interest payments increase and must be offset by tax increases or spending cuts. If investor confidence in the government's ability to manage its finances weakens, lenders will charge the government higher interest rates. High debt also reduces the government's ability to use taxes and spending to address fiscal crises in the future. The right combination of government spending and taxes is a constant source of debate, influenced by economic theory, history, politics, and public opinion.

The Foundations of Fiscal Policy

In the 1930s, British economist John Maynard Keynes revolutionized economic policy theory by arguing that governments could prevent the worst impacts of recession or depression by stimulating aggregate demand, even at the risk of running government deficits. This view represented a departure from laissez-faire capitalism, which suggested that, if left alone, a free market would regulate itself. In contrast, Keynesian economists maintained that increasing demand would increase employment, stimulating a cycle of economic growth much faster than a free market would accomplish on its own. The benefits of more immediate economic growth, they believed, outweighed the costs of government deficits in the short run. Governments could increase demand through increased government spending, tax cuts, or a combination of the two. Economists argued, however, that government spending would increase consumption and demand more directly than tax cuts. This is the case because people do not always spend their tax cuts; they often save the money or use it to pay down existing debt. The precise mix of government spending and taxes, however, is often dictated more by politics than economics.

In the United States, the early 1960s saw the first significant contemporary application of fiscal policy. President John F. Kennedy, a Democrat committed to getting the country moving again, brought economists to Washington, D.C., who believed that greater government spending, even at the expense of an increase in the **budget deficit**, was needed to achieve full employment. This thinking is consistent with Keynesian economics; however, many conservatives opposed budget deficits as bad public policy. To appease these critics, the president's advisers decided that many Americans would find deficits less objectionable if they were achieved by cutting taxes rather than by increasing government spending.

This decision resulted in adoption of the Revenue Act of 1964, which President Lyndon B. Johnson signed into law. The act reduced personal and corporate income tax rates. The tax-cut stimulus contributed to the expansion of the economy throughout the remainder of the 1960s and reduced the unemployment rate to less

17.1

17.2

17.3

17.4

17.5

inflation
A rise in the general price levels of an economy.

than 4 percent, its lowest peacetime rate and what many people then considered to be full employment.[11]

In the short term, budget deficits may have positive economic benefits. However, in the long term, running deficits year after year can have negative consequences. A high national debt such as this can stifle economic growth and cause **inflation**, a rise in the general price levels of an economy. The national debt—as with personal debt in the form of credit cards and student loans—must also be paid back with interest. This repayment can be a costly proposition that diverts attention and money from other governmental programs for years to come.

While most states are required by constitution or by statute to have a balanced budget—revenues must meet or exceed expenditures—this is not the norm for the federal government. The Constitution does not limit debt at the national level and rarely does the federal budgetary process produce a balanced budget. During the 1980s, President Ronald Reagan cut taxes, in part to stimulate the economy but also to shrink the size of the federal government. The Democratic-controlled Congress, however, refused to make the deep cuts in domestic spending that Reagan proposed. At the same time, defense spending increased in response to the Cold War. Deficits continued, and public intolerance of the escalating national debt pressured Congress to respond with the 1985 Balanced Budget and Emergency Reduction Act. When the new law fell short of deficit reduction goals, Congress passed the Budget Enforcement Act of 1990, setting overall limits on federal government spending. A federal balanced budget amendment was also proposed and debated, and in 1994 the federal government shut down twice when Congress and President Clinton could not agree on budget priorities. Ultimately, the economy expanded during the late 1990s, and the government ran surpluses from 1998 to 2001. This expansion shifted the political focus away from spending cuts and deficit reduction and back to tax cuts. In the context of a budget surplus, the newly elected President Bush and his administration ushered in a series of tax cuts in 2001 and 2003, lowering marginal tax rates. Although politically favorable, tax cuts are difficult to repeal, and economists warn that they reduce the government's flexibility in handling future economic crises, as evident in the recession that started in 2007. Figure 17.1 illustrates the current budget priorities in terms of tax revenues and expenditures.

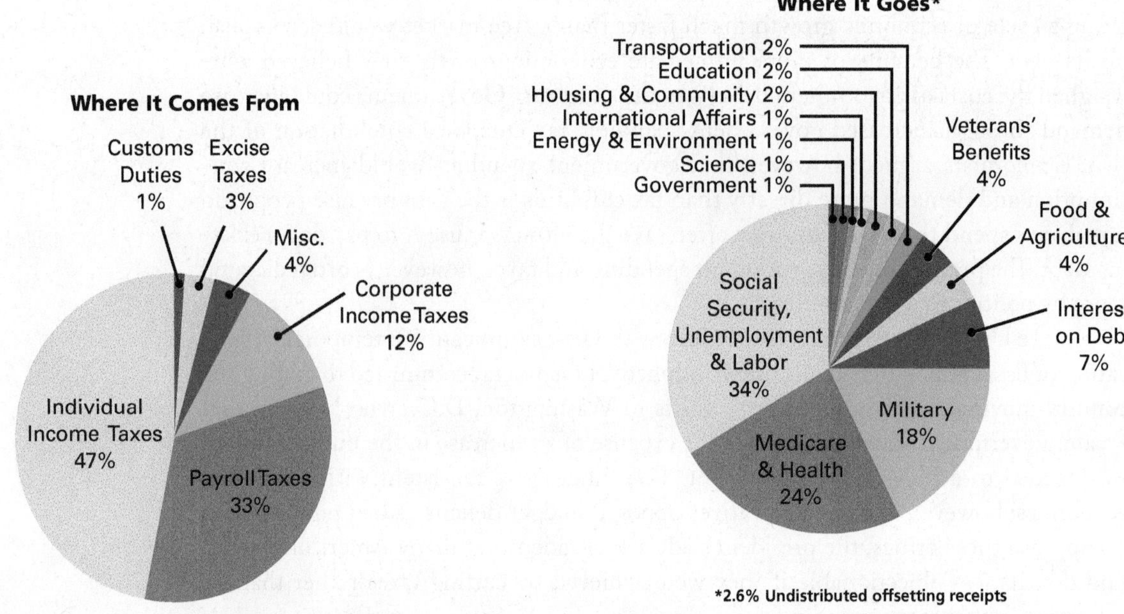

FIGURE 17.1 HOW DOES THE FEDERAL GOVERNMENT RAISE AND SPEND MONEY?

The federal government budget outlines how taxpayer revenues are raised and spent, summarizing the priorities of federal government policy making.

SOURCE: United States Budget, Fiscal Year 2011, www.gpoaccess.gov.

How Much Government Debt Is Too Much?

Around the globe countries have amassed large government debts. The U.S. government debt is neither the highest nor the lowest as a percentage of GDP. An individual country's debt level reflects the history, values, and political choices of its citizens. At what point, however, should the world financial markets worry about an individual country's debt? In 2012, for example, concerns over Greece's inability to pay its debts threatened the stability of the European Monetary Union. Within a country, the level of debt also takes on more significance as the portion that is held by foreigners increases. Paying interest on that portion of the debt transfers income from one country to another. The graphic below shows the distribution of U.S. debt.

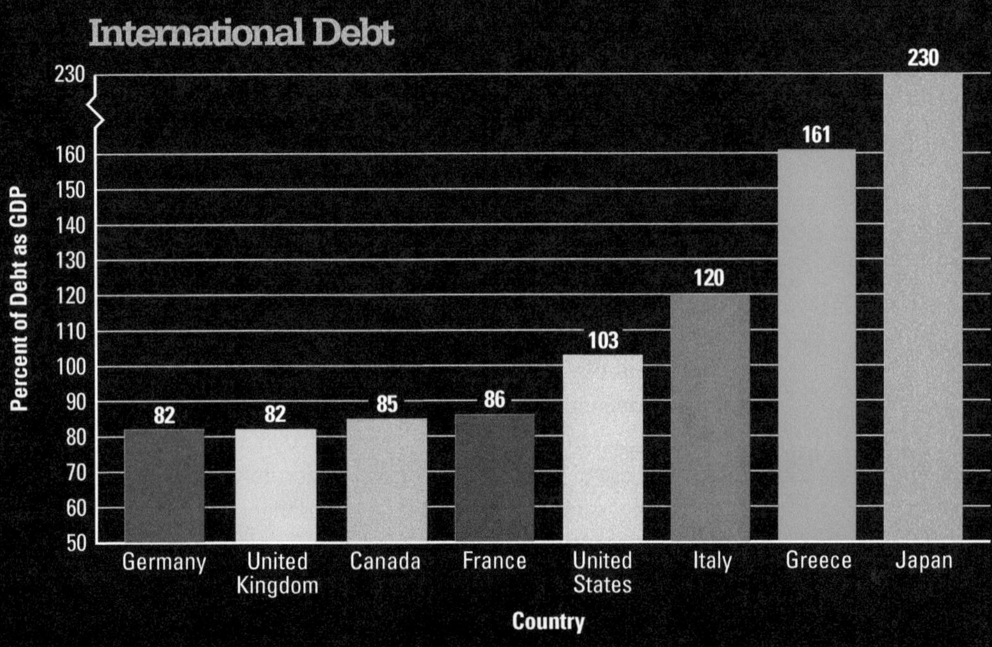

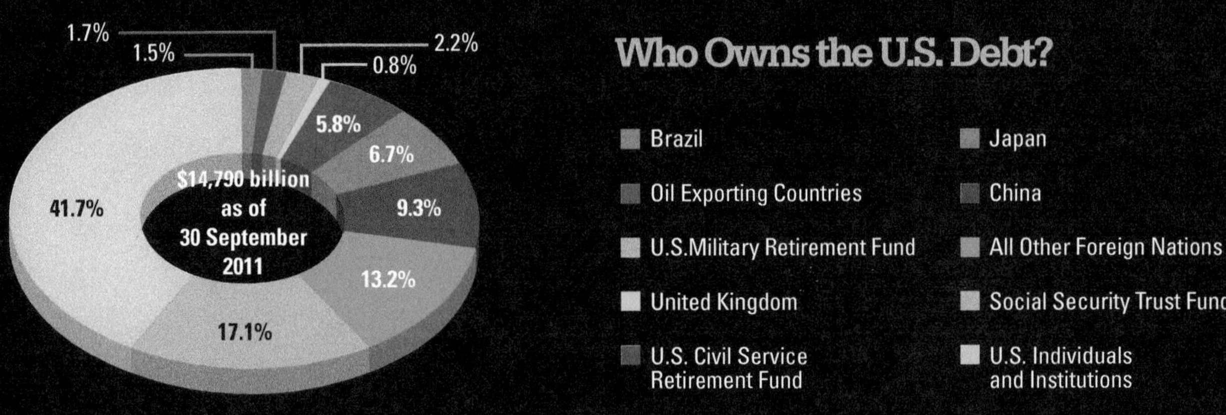

Source: U.S. Treasury Department, Revised March 2012

CRITICAL THINKING QUESTIONS

1. By borrowing money from the Social Security Trust Fund, the federal government has essentially loaned money to itself. Should the federal government have to pay back this loan?
2. How much of the debt is owed to U.S. citizens vs. foreign nations? Why do you think foreign nations want to own our debt?
3. What are some reasons that might justify having the government go into debt? How much debt is too much?

Responding to Recession

At the first signs of an economic slowdown in early 2008, the national government acted quickly to stimulate the economy and reinvigorate consumer spending through fiscal policy. The first government action was to fund a $168 billion stimulus package that included individual tax rebates for most people who had paid taxes for tax year 2007. These payments were designed to encourage lower- and middle-income people to spend money. Most citizens who received a check got $600 if they filed individually or $1,200 if they filed jointly. There were increasing incentives for dependent children, and decreasing incentives for wealthy Americans.

But, in late September 2008, it became clear that, despite the government's attempts to stimulate the economy through tax cuts, economic conditions had worsened. Approximately 2.6 million people had lost their jobs as large companies downsized and many smaller companies struggled to stay in business. Oil and other commodity prices began to rise rapidly—gasoline prices reached $4 and even $5 per gallon in some jurisdictions. Collapse of the subprime mortgage industry had escalated into a full-blown financial crisis necessitating government action. To address this situation, the Bush administration proposed a $700 billion federal bailout package.

The first version of the bailout plan failed to garner enough votes in the House of Representatives, forcing frenzied rounds of House and Senate negotiation. Supporters increased efforts to make the plan more palatable to politicians up for reelection who were facing constituents overwhelmingly opposed to using taxpayer funds for bailing out Wall Street. President George W. Bush, members of his administration, and congressional leaders sought to present the financial bailout plan as an economic rescue plan. They emphasized the extent to which financial collapse on Wall Street and virtually frozen credit markets would affect the ability of those on Main Street to do business, refinance their homes, or buy a car. As a result of these efforts, Congress passed a modified version of the administration's initial bailout plan known as the Emergency Economic Stabilization Act in October 2008. It provided enhanced oversight of the Department of the Treasury use of the $700 billion, an option to use the money to buy equity stakes in faltering banks, some protection to those in danger of losing their homes, and a variety of tax cuts and incentives. Congress intended the plan to reassure the financial markets by allowing the government to buy up the assets that had led to the crisis. This was known as the Troubled Assets Relief Program (TARP), and the monies were TARP funds (Figure 17.2 illustrates how the recovery funds were distributed).

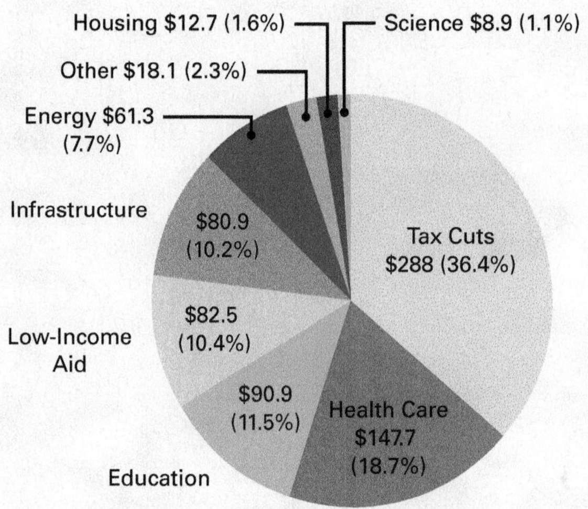

FIGURE 17.2 WHERE DID THE ECONOMIC STIMULUS FUNDS GO?

The American Recovery and Reinvestment Act allocated almost $800 billion to aid in the economic recovery. The largest proportion of these funds—more than one-third—went to tax cuts.

SOURCE: U.S. Government, www.recovery.gov.

 Explore on MyPoliSciLab

Who Broke the Economy?

When Americans ask who "broke" the economy in 2008, there is a practical answer and a political answer. The practical answer involves a chain of events that began with the collapse of the real estate market and resulted in millions of newly unemployed Americans. The political answer usually comes down to the presidents who responded to the events. President Barack Obama has spent more time coping with the recession and increasingly bears more responsibility for the economy, but as of late 2012, more Americans still blamed President George W. Bush—particularly Democrats.

Who Do Americans Blame?

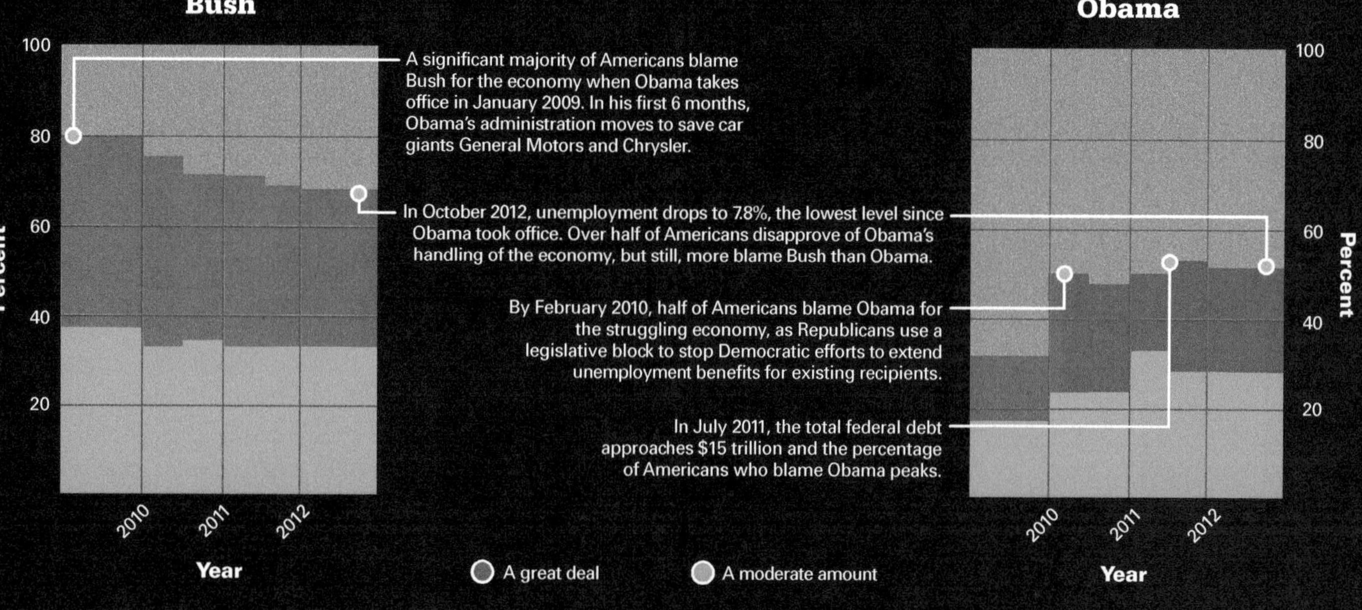

Bush
Obama
100
80
60
40
20
Percent
A significant majority of Americans blame Bush for the economy when Obama takes office in January 2009. In his first 6 months, Obama's administration moves to save car giants General Motors and Chrysler.
In October 2012, unemployment drops to 7.8%, the lowest level since Obama took office. Over half of Americans disapprove of Obama's handling of the economy, but still, more blame Bush than Obama.
By February 2010, half of Americans blame Obama for the struggling economy, as Republicans use a legislative block to stop Democratic efforts to extend unemployment benefits for existing recipients.
In July 2011, the total federal debt approaches $15 trillion and the percentage of Americans who blame Obama peaks.
2010
2011
2012
Year
A great deal
A moderate amount

Partisanship Influences the Answer

Republicans | Independents | Democrats

Obama Bears the Majority of the Blame for U.S. Economic Problems.

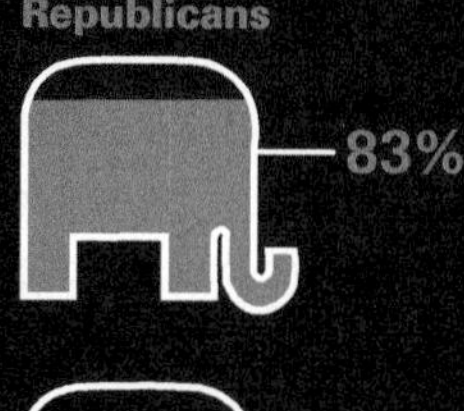

83%

51%

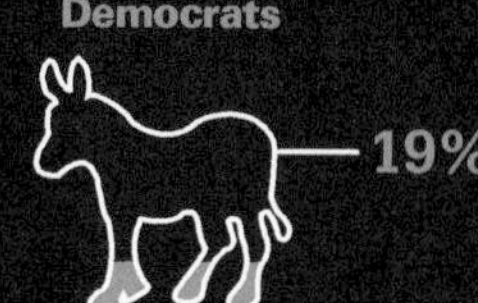

19%

Bush Bears the Majority of the Blame for U.S. Economic Problems.

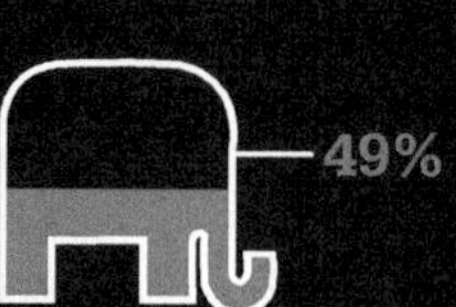

49%

67%

90%

SOURCE: Data from Gallup.

Investigate Further

Concept Who gets more blame for the broken economy—Bush or Obama? Four years later, Bush is still blamed by the majority of Americans. Obama avoided much of this spotlight until February 2010. The longer a president is in office, the more public attention shifts towards him and away from his predecessor.

Connection Does improvement in the economy shift the blame to or from Obama? Despite the drop in unemployment since Obama took office, half the public still blames him for the bad economy.

Cause Does partisanship influence "blame"? After four years, Democrats overwhelming hold Bush responsible for the economy, instead of Obama. More Republicans hold Obama responsible, but half of them still think Bush is to blame. Though the public has shifted responsibility for the economy to Obama, partisanship largely determines where people place the blame for the recession.

Although TARP funds helped to stabilize American banks, individuals were still struggling with the economic downturn. After he took office in early 2009, President Barack Obama made it one of his first priorities to address this situation by working with Congress to pass an economic stimulus and recovery bill, the American Recovery and Reinvestment Act. This legislation authorized the government to spend more than $787 billion on a variety of tax cuts and public works programs designed to stimulate the economy and to maintain and create jobs in transportation, education, health care, and other industries. Among the programs funded by the Recovery Act were road and bridge construction projects, scientific research, and the expansion of Internet access to underserved populations. The federal government also extended and expanded unemployment benefits.

The government's response to the economy—increased government spending plus tax cuts—fits the Keynesian model, and labor market indicators did begin to improve. GDP started to grow steadily by the third quarter of 2009 and employment increased. By 2012, unemployment decreased to 8.1 percent from a peak of 10 percent in October 2009. The Recovery Act, however, was designed to be temporary, and the direct impact of these measures was offset in part by state government cuts. Initially, stimulus money was transferred to the states to help fill state budget gaps, but as the money ended, states had to slash their budgets. The public began to doubt the effectiveness of government stimulus packages. Large deficits continued, increasing the national debt to unprecedented levels and ultimately sparking ideological warfare over the size and role of the federal government.

☐ The Debt Ceiling

The extraordinary annual deficits of the past decade resulting from Bush administration tax cuts, the wars in Iraq and Afghanistan, and spending on the bailout and recovery bills have increased the total amount of debt owed by the United States. The national government debt exceeded $10 trillion for the first time in 2008, and reached a limit in 2011 at $14.2 trillion. The soaring debt forced Congress to debate the debt ceiling, or the limit on how much the United States government can borrow. Congress first created a debt ceiling in 1917 with the Second Liberty Bond Act. The debt ceiling is like the credit limit on your credit card, except that Congress has to periodically raise the debt ceiling *after* it has committed to spending beyond the limit. The consequences of not raising a debt ceiling under such circumstances would be default, in which the government would be unable to pay all of its debt obligations. So far, Congress has increased the debt ceiling 72 times since 1962 (including 11 times since 2001), but not without contentious debate over government spending, taxes, and the longer term impact of high debt.

In 2011, President Barack Obama and congressional leaders struggled to reach a compromise that linked an increase in the debt ceiling to long-term spending cuts. The Budget Control Act of 2011 authorized a series of automatic debt ceiling increases ($16.39 trillion in 2012) and created the Joint Select Committee on Deficit Reduction, commonly referred to as the congressional "super committee," to propose budget cuts. The committee's failure to reach an agreement by their November 2011 deadline, however, triggered automatic across-the-board budget cuts, or sequestration, beginning in 2013 unless Congress takes action. Ending the Bush-era tax cuts in addition to spending cuts would further decrease the debt; however, the increased ideological polarization of Democrats and Republicans prevented easy compromise. By 2012, the national debt increased to $15.7 trillion, over 100 percent of GDP. The federal government budget included a projected $1.3 trillion deficit for fiscal year 2012.[12]

☐ Fiscal Policy in a Global Context

Advances in transportation, communication, and technology have strengthened the links between the United States and the rest of the world and expanded free trade. As a result, international affairs influence business decisions of American companies that wish to reduce labor costs as well as expand their markets. Globalization can be seen in the greater movement of goods, services, and capital across borders. Offshore outsourcing of production and services has increased. International trade as a percentage of the world GDP has also increased. While these trends have their critics, most economists agree that globalization increases the variety of goods available to consumers, lowers costs, and raises the standard of living in countries that have stable financial and political institutions and policies in place. It is argued that this consumer "surplus" outweighs the job losses—particularly among unskilled labor—accompanied by globalization. International trade also promotes national competitiveness as each country specializes and improves efficiency in order to maintain a global competitive advantage. Increased globalization, though, has risks for fiscal policy, both in the United States and internationally. When creditors are connected internationally, a financial collapse in one country has the potential to trigger an economic crisis in another country. In 2012, world growth was projected to slow down as several Euro area economies entered mild recessions.[13] Financial crises were more critical in Greece and Spain.

gross domestic product (GDP)
The total market value of all goods and services produced in an area during a year.

One way to measure this increasing interdependence is to examine regional shares of the world **gross domestic product (GDP)**, or the total market value of all goods and services produced in an area during a year. In 2012, the United States, the European Union, and Asia each represented between 25 and 27 percent of the world's GDP. Latin America and the Middle East each held another 3 to 7 percent of the world's GDP. This distribution represents much greater international equality than in other eras.[14]

Interdependence can also be measured by the transfer of financial capital across borders. This greater equity is at least in part attributable to emerging economies such as Brazil, Russia, India, and China, which are continuing to post robust growth rates, driven by strong domestic demand and fiscal solvency. Oil-rich countries are also posting large surpluses. The United States, on the other hand, has been running persistent deficits. Foreigners held almost $4.5 trillion in U.S. securities in 2011. The confidence of international creditors in the safety of the United States as a credit investment has kept interest rates low, holding down the costs of borrowing money. Still, concerns have arisen regarding the interconnectedness of the financial markets and the global ripple effect that can occur when one market experiences economic crisis. Concerns over this development have increased support for capital controls, or limits on the amount of capital that can flow across borders.

HOW HAS ECONOMIC INTERDEPENDENCE ALTERED THE AMERICAN ECONOMY?

The cheap cost of labor abroad has led many Americans to lose their jobs, particularly at manufacturing plants. Here, workers at a factory in Pakistan assemble soccer balls.

Monetary Policy

17.3 Analyze the effect of the Federal Reserve System on monetary policy.

monetary policy
A form of government regulation in which the nation's money supply and interest rates are controlled.

Board of Governors
In the Federal Reserve System, a seven-member board that makes most economic decisions regarding interest rates and the supply of money.

open market operations
The buying and selling of government securities by the Federal Reserve Bank.

Explore on **MyPoliSciLab** **Simulation:** You Are a Federal Reserve Chair

Economic stability is also promoted through **monetary policy**, by regulating the nation's supply of money and influencing interest rates. The Federal Reserve System (informally, "the Fed"), especially its Board of Governors, handles much of the day-to-day management of monetary policy. The Fed is given a number of tools to aid its efforts, including open market operations, manipulation of the discount rate, and the ability to set reserve requirements.

☐ The Federal Reserve System

Created in 1913 to adjust the money supply to the needs of agriculture, commerce, and industry, the Federal Reserve System comprises the Federal Reserve Board, the Federal Open Market Committee (FOMC), the twelve Federal Reserve Banks in regions throughout the country, and other member banks.[15] Today, the Federal Reserve operates under a dual mandate: to control inflation and limit unemployment. These two mandates can come into conflict, however, forcing the government to prioritize which goal is more important at any given time. Government stimulation to increase employment levels, for example, can lead to inflation and higher prices for goods and services. American economist and Nobel Prize winner Milton Friedman first argued in the 1960s that government should avoid inflation. Instead, Friedman promoted "monetarism," arguing that a constant gradual expansion of the money supply is the only government action needed to promote economic growth. The Federal Reserve has responded to economic crises, however, with active use of monetary policy tools to increase employment in the short run, only to have to deal with debt and inflation in the long run.

Typically, the **Board of Governors** of the Federal Reserve System, a seven-member board that makes most economic decisions regarding interest rates and the supply of money, dominates this process. The board is designed to be independent financially as well as politically.

The president appoints (subject to Senate confirmation) the seven members of the Board of Governors, who serve fourteen-year, overlapping terms. The president can remove a member for stated causes, but this has never occurred. The president designates one board member to serve as chair for a four-year term, which runs from the midpoint of one presidential term to the midpoint of the next to ensure economic stability during a change of administrations. It also prevents monetary policy from being influenced by political considerations. The current chair, Ben Bernanke, has served since 2006 and was initially appointed by President George W. Bush. He was reappointed by President Barack Obama for a second term beginning in 2010. Prior to this appointment, he served as chair of President George W. Bush's Council of Economic Advisors (see Figure 17.3 for the structural organization of the Federal Reserve).

☐ The Tools of Monetary Policy

The primary monetary policy tools used by the Fed are open market operations, control of the discount rate, and the setting of reserve requirements for member banks. **Open market operations** are the buying and selling of government securities, or debt, by the Federal Reserve Bank. The Federal Open Market Committee meets periodically to decide on purchases or sale of government securities to member banks. When member banks buy long-term government bonds, they make dollar payments to the Fed and reduce the amount of money available for loans. Fed purchases of securities from member banks in essence give the banks an added supply of money. This action increases the availability of loans and should decrease interest rates.

Explore Your World

In the United States, the Federal Reserve has two mandates: control inflation and limit unemployment. In Europe, the European Central Bank prioritizes the prevention of inflation. In Japan, the main objective of the Bank of Japan is also to maintain price stability. The common focus on inflation is related to each country's past negative experiences with inflation. Inflation occurs when the price of goods and services increases, reducing the purchasing power of consumers and the value of money. Economists advocate using monetary policy to regulate the supply of money to prevent severe inflation. The United States also prioritizes full employment, which is rooted in the idea of the American Dream. Promoting full employment, however, can increase inflation through increased government spending.

The European Central Bank was created in 1998 to promote stable prices and financial integration among member states of the European Union. Its currency, the euro, was introduced in eleven member states electronically in 1999 and in cash form in 2002. Today the bank has 27 member states.

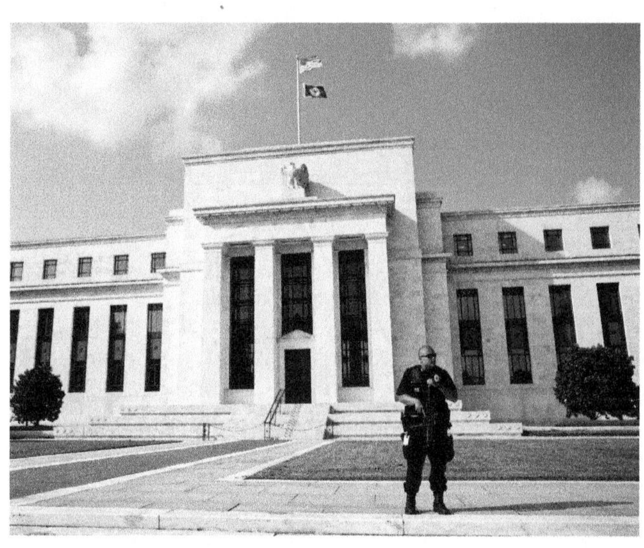

The Federal Reserve was created in 1913 to prevent and contain economic crises. It consists of the Federal Reserve Board and its Chair in Washington, D.C., and twelve regional Federal Reserve Banks.

The Bank of Japan was established in 1882 to regulate monetary policy, to control inflation, and to promote stable economic growth. Currently, the bank is controlled by a policy board, including a governor, deputy governor, and six executive directors.The bank has 32 branches plus an additional 14 local offices.

CRITICAL THINKING QUESTIONS

1. Is it the government's responsibility to minimize the economic impact of recessions, or to prevent depressions?
2. What should a government do when economic goals come into conflict? If, for example, combating inflation increases unemployment, which goal should be prioritized?
3. Should there be more global economic regulation?

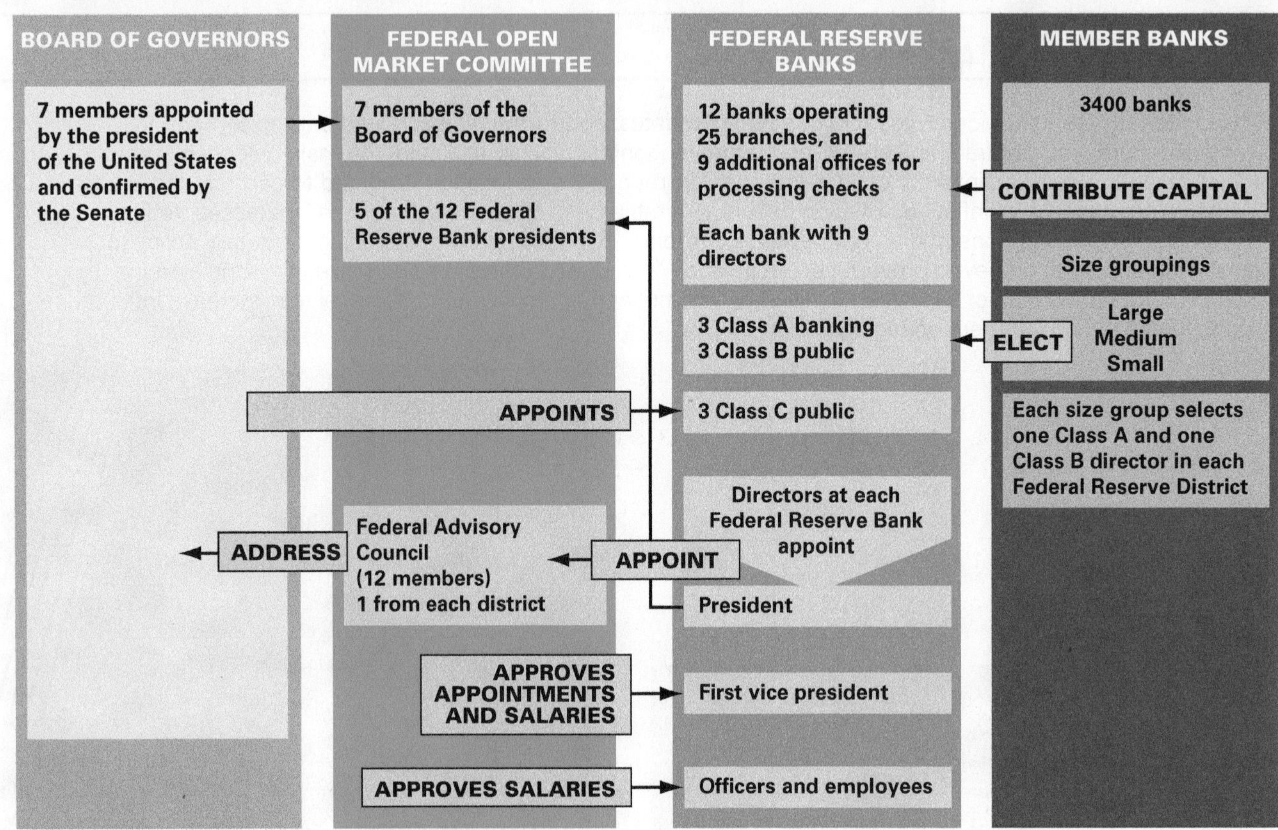

FIGURE 17.3 HOW DOES THE FEDERAL RESERVE SYSTEM WORK?

In making appointments to the Federal Reserve Board, the president is required by law to provide balanced representation of geographic, financial, agricultural, industrial, and commercial interests.

SOURCE: Board of Governors of the Federal Reserve System.

discount rate
The rate of interest at which the Federal Reserve Board lends money to member banks.

reserve requirements
Government requirements that a portion of member banks' deposits be retained as backing for their loans.

The Fed also influences interest rates through the **discount rate**, or the rate of interest at which it lends money to member banks. Lowering the discount rate encourages member banks to increase their borrowing from the Fed and extend more loans at lower rates. This practice expands economic activity, since more people should be able to qualify for car loans or mortgages if rates are lower. As a consequence of cheaper interest rates, more large durable goods (such as houses and cars) should be produced and sold.

Reserve requirements set by the Federal Reserve designate the portion of deposits that member banks must retain on hand. The reserves determine how much or how little banks can lend to businesses and consumers. For example, if the Fed changed the reserve requirements and allowed banks to keep $10 on hand rather than $15 for every $100 in deposits that it held, it would free up additional money for loans. This tool of monetary policy is rarely used, however. Increasing the percentage of deposits that a bank has to keep in reserve may force banks to call in loans. Decreasing reserve requirements, on the other hand, exposes banks to increased risk of failure.

In addition to these formal tools, the Fed can also use "moral suasion" to influence the actions of banks and other members of the financial community by suggestion, exhortation, and informal agreement. Because of its commanding position as a monetary policy maker, the media, economists, and market observers pay attention to verbal signals sent by the Fed and its chair with regard to economic trends and conditions.

In recent years, the Fed has resorted to nontraditional tools when traditional ones failed to stabilize the banking industry in the wake of the recession that started in 2007. The Fed decreased the discount rate, for example, to nearly zero, and yet banks did not substantially increase lending. Moving away from traditional government bonds and securities, the Fed started buying riskier mortgage-backed securities, in an effort to remove guaranteed debt from banks so that more capital was free to lend again. The Fed's purchase of private sector assets, or commercial paper, is referred to as "credit easing." The goal is to relieve banks of enough debt to help their credit flow again. Quantitative easing occurs when the purchase of such debt is funded by the government's creating new money. These policies are controversial because they can increase inflation dramatically if banks do not start to lend the additional reserves created by the Fed's purchases.

One lesson learned in the recent financial crisis is the danger of allowing banks to become "too big to fail." As the lender of last resort, the Fed was initially reluctant to bail out banks for their risky investment mistakes. In 2007, Bear Sterns went bankrupt; the government ultimately took over Fannie Mae and Freddie Mac as foreclosures escalated on the subprime mortgages they had bought and securitized. The Fed assisted JP Morgan Chase with $29 billion in 2008 to buy Bear Stearns. When Lehman Brothers failed next, the Fed chose instead to send a message that big banks would not be bailed out at taxpayer expense. The financial impact of the collapse of these mammoth institutions, however, threatened to damage the entire financial system. The Fed acted quickly to rescue American International Group (AIG), despite growing public opposition to bailing out Wall Street. The Chairman of the Federal Reserve Board, Ben Bernanke, called for new regulations to strengthen capital requirements for banks to provide better cushions to protect against potential losses and for investigation of the linkages among financial companies to better identify potential channels of financial contagion.

After 18 months of debate, Congress passed the Dodd-Frank Wall Street Reform and Consumer Protection Act in 2010, a 2,300-page reform of the financial industry. The new legislation created a ten-member Financial Stability Oversight Council to monitor individual financial institutions that pose a risk of economic crisis. Regulators then have authority, as a last resort, to dismantle troubled firms before damage is done. New rules about capital leverage, risk management, and liquidity make it more difficult for banks to grow excessively large. The legislation also created the Consumer Financial Protection Bureau to regulate mortgage lending, credit cards, and consumer loan practices, providing more information and protection for consumers.

HOW HAS THE GOVERNMENT RESPONDED TO THE RECESSION?
President Obama appointed Richard Cordray in 2012 to serve as Director of the new Consumer Finance Protection Bureau. The new agency is charged with assisting consumers in understanding financial products and services, including mortgages and credit cards.

Social Security Act
A 1935 law that established old age insurance; assistance for the needy, aged, blind, and families with dependent children; and unemployment insurance.

17.1

17.2

17.3

17.4

17.5

Income Security Policy

17.4 Describe the evolution of income security policy in the United States.

Income security programs protect people against loss of income because of retirement, disability, unemployment, or death or absence of the family breadwinner. In 1780, for example, national legislation was passed to provide a pension to the widows of sailors. These programs, however, like many of the other issues we have discussed in this chapter, were not a priority for the federal government during much of its first 150 years. Beginning with the passage of the Social Security Act as a part of the 1930s New Deal, the government began to pay greater attention to this policy area. Today, the federal government administers a range of income security programs. These policies fall into two major areas—non-means-tested programs (in which benefits are provided regardless of income) and means-tested programs (in which benefits are provided to those whose incomes fall below a designated level).

Economists refer to income security policies as "automatic stabilizers." If the economy enters a recession, income security policies have the effect of expanding the economy automatically, whether or not the federal government takes action to change fiscal or monetary policy. The money spent by the government to provide assistance to people in need is injected back into the economy through purchases of rent, food, health care, and other basic expenditures. When the economy recovers and fewer people need assistance, government spending automatically decreases, preventing the inflation that could occur with deficit spending in periods of expansion. Income security policies also provide a safety net for times when the government delays recognition or response to economic crises.

☐ The Foundations of Income Security Policy

With the election of President Franklin D. Roosevelt in 1932, the federal government began to play a more active role in addressing the hardships and turmoil that grew out of the Great Depression. An immediate challenge facing the Roosevelt administration was massive unemployment, viewed as having a corrosive effect on the economic well-being and moral character of American citizens. An array of programs to put people back to work would, in Roosevelt's words, "eliminate the threat that enforced idleness brings to spiritual and moral stability."[16]

To address unemployment, Roosevelt issued an executive order in November 1933 that created the Civil Works Administration (CWA). The intent of the CWA was to put people to work as quickly as possible for the stated goal of building public works projects. Within a month of its start, CWA had hired 2.6 million people; at its peak in January 1934, it employed more than 4 million workers. But, critics quickly claimed that it was too political and rife with corruption. The CWA was disbanded in 1934.

In 1935, the Works Progress Administration (WPA) revived the idea of a federal work program. The WPA paid a wage of about $55 a month, which was sizeable for the time, but below what would be available in the private sector. Such a wage was designed to reward work, but not discourage individuals from seeking market-based employment. The WPA attained a number of concrete accomplishments. This program absorbed about 30 percent of the unemployed; the WPA also constructed or improved more than 20,000 playgrounds, schools, hospitals, and airfields.[17] These jobs programs established the concept that, in extreme circumstances, the government might become the employer of last resort.

A more permanent legacy of the New Deal was the creation of the Social Security program. The intent of Social Security was to go beyond various "emergency" programs such as the WPA and provide at least a minimum of economic security for all Americans. Passage of the **Social Security Act** in 1935 thus represented the beginning of a permanent welfare state in America and a dedication to the ideal of greater equity. The act consisted of three major components: (1) old-age insurance (what we now call Social Security); (2) public assistance for the needy, aged, blind, and families with dependent children (known as SSI); and (3) unemployment insurance and compensation. Since that time, the program has expanded to include a much greater percentage of American workers. It has also become one of the most successful government programs. In the 1930s, poverty rates were highest among the elderly. Today, seniors age sixty-five or older have the lowest rate of poverty among any age group in the United States.

Income Security Programs Today

Modern income security programs help a wide variety of citizens to survive in cases of unintentional loss of income. They also help disabled, elderly, and low-income citizens to make ends meet and provide a minimally decent standard of living for themselves and their families. In 2012, the poverty threshold for a four-person family unit was $23,050. (To learn more about the number of Americans who benefit from income security programs, see Table 17.1.)

Many income security programs are **entitlement programs**, government benefits that all citizens meeting eligibility criteria—such as age, income level, or unemployment—are legally "entitled" to receive. Unlike programs such as public housing, military construction, and space exploration, spending for entitlement programs is mandatory and places a substantial ongoing financial burden on the national and state governments.

Income security programs fall into two general categories. Many social insurance programs are **non–means-tested programs** that provide cash assistance to qualified beneficiaries, regardless of income. These social insurance programs operate in a manner somewhat similar to that of private automobile or life insurance. Contributions are made by or on behalf of the prospective beneficiaries, their employers, or both. When a person becomes eligible for benefits, he or she is paid as a matter of right, regardless of wealth or unearned income. Among these programs are old age, survivors, and disability insurance (Social Security) and unemployment insurance.

In contrast, **means-tested programs** require people to have incomes below specified levels to be eligible for benefits. Benefits of means-tested programs may come either as cash or in-kind benefits, such as help with finding employment or child care. Included in the means-tested category are the Supplemental Security Income (SSI) program and the Supplemental Nutrition Assistance Program (SNAP, also known as food stamps). Temporary Assistance for Needy Families (TANF) is also means-tested, but the program is not an entitlement. States are given discretion to determine TANF eligibility and benefits.

OLD AGE, SURVIVORS, AND DISABILITY INSURANCE As mentioned earlier, the Social Security program is a non–means-tested program that began as old-age insurance,

entitlement programs
Government benefits that all citizens meeting eligibility criteria—such as age, income level, or unemployment—are legally "entitled" to receive.

non–means-tested programs
Programs that provide cash assistance to qualified beneficiaries, regardless of income. Among these are Social Security and unemployment insurance.

means-tested programs
Programs that require that beneficiaries have incomes below specified levels to be eligible for benefits. Among these are SSI, TANF, and SNAP.

TABLE 17.1 HOW MANY AMERICANS BENEFIT FROM INCOME SECURITY PROGRAMS?

Program Population	Number of Recipients (millions)	Percentage of U.S. Population
Non–means-tested		
Social Security (old-age, survivors, and disability insurance, or OASDI)	56.0	18
Unemployment insurance	4.6	1.5
Means-tested		
Supplemental Security Income	7.9	2.5
Temporary Assistance for Needy Families	4.4	1.4
Supplemental Nutrition Assistance Program	45.8	14.6

SOURCES: Social Security Administration, www.ssa.gov; Center on Budget and Policy Priorities, http://www.cbpp.org/; Department of Health and Human Services, www.acf.hhs.gov; Food Research Action Center, www.frac.org; Veterans' Affairs, Bureau of Labor Statistics, www.bls.gov/cps.

SHOULD SOCIAL SECURITY BE PRIVATIZED?

Social Security privatization has been a hot-button issue. Here, members of Congress speak at a rally opposing privatization.

providing benefits only to retired workers. Its coverage was extended to survivors of covered workers in 1939 and to the permanently disabled in 1956. Nearly all employees and most of the self-employed are now covered by Social Security. Americans born before 1938 are eligible to receive full retirement benefits at age sixty-five. The full retirement age gradually rises until it reaches sixty-seven for persons born in 1960 or later. In 2012, the average monthly Social Security benefit for retired workers was $1,230, with the maximum monthly benefit set at $2,513.

Social Security is not, as many people believe, a pension program that collects contributions from workers, invests them, and then returns them with interest to beneficiaries. Instead, current workers pay employment taxes that go directly toward providing benefits for retirees. In 2012, for example, a tax of 4.2 percent was levied on the first $110,100 of an employee's wages and placed into the Social Security Trust Fund. An additional 6.2 percent tax was levied on employers.

As a result of this system, in recent years, it has become increasingly apparent that the current Social Security system is on a collision course with itself. Americans are living longer and having fewer children. And, beginning in 2010, the Baby Boom generation (roughly speaking, those born in the two decades immediately following World War II) began to retire. These factors, taken together, skew the number of working Americans per retiree, and lead the Social Security system toward financial insolvency. The trustees of the Social Security Trust Fund have estimated that—barring major policy changes—by 2030, payments to beneficiaries will exceed revenues collected from employees.

A number of proposals have been made to address these shortcomings. Among them is raising the eligibility for beneficiaries, increasing the Social Security tax withheld from employees, or gradually privatizing the system for younger workers. Both of these proposals have received criticism from citizens—seniors and those who will soon retire do not wish to see their benefits cut or limited, and workers do not want to pay additional taxes.

One reform proposal that received a great deal of attention in the 2000 presidential election and the years that followed was Social Security privatization. Essentially, this would amount to the federal government's allowing citizens to work with private industry to administer and invest monies in the Social Security Trust Fund. Some Americans believe that such a system would increase the government's return on investment and prolong the life of the existing Social Security system with few other changes. Others believe that a privatized Social Security system is risky and will leave behind those who need it the most. The volatility of the stock market during the economic recession has, at least temporarily, reduced enthusiasm for privatization.

UNEMPLOYMENT INSURANCE Unemployment insurance is a non–means-tested program financed by a payroll tax paid by employers. The program benefits full-time employees of companies of four or more people who become unemployed through no fault of their own. Unemployed workers who have been fired for personal faults or who have quit their jobs, or those who are unwilling to accept suitable employment, do not receive benefits.

State governments administer unemployment insurance programs. As a result, unemployment programs differ a great deal in levels of benefits, length of benefit payment, and eligibility for benefits. For example, in 2012, average weekly benefit payments ranged from less than $200 in Mississippi to just over $400 in Hawaii. In general, less generous programs exist in southern states, where labor unions are less powerful. Nationwide, only about half of people who are counted as unemployed at any given time are receiving benefits.

In April 2012, the national unemployment rate stood at 8.1 percent. But, differences were considerable across the country (as illustrated in Figure 17.4). In North Dakota the unemployment rate was 3 percent, while levels of unemployment in many southern and western states such as Florida and California were over 9 percent. Rhode Island and Nevada both experienced unemployment rates over 11 percent. Unemployment rates also varied quite a bit across races and by age. For example, levels of unemployment for African American men were nearly twice that of whites, with unemployment rates exceeding 40 percent or greater common among young African American men.

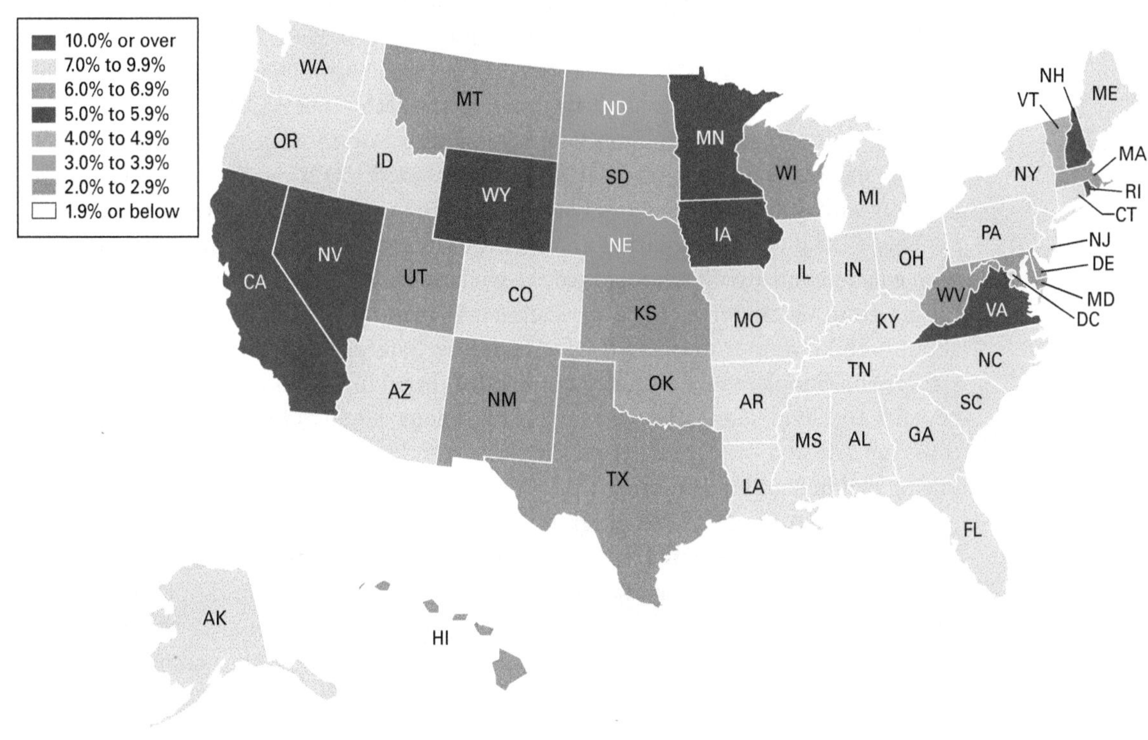

FIGURE 17.4 HOW DO STATE UNEMPLOYMENT RATES VARY?

In July 2012, the national unemployment rate was 8.2 percent. However, this rate varied tremendously across the country, with the highest levels in the South and West, and the lowest levels in the Midwest.

SOURCE: United States Department of Labor, www.dol.gov.

SUPPLEMENTAL SECURITY INCOME The Supplemental Security Income (SSI) program is a means-tested program that began under the Social Security Act as a government benefit for needy elderly or blind citizens. In 1950, Congress extended coverage to needy people who were permanently and totally disabled. The federal government, which provides primary funding for SSI, prescribes minimum national benefit levels. The states may also choose to supplement national benefits, and forty-eight states take advantage of this option.

To be eligible for SSI, beneficiaries can have only limited income; the lower an individual's income, the higher the SSI payment. SSI beneficiaries may also have only a limited number of possessions. The total of an individual's personal resources, including bank accounts, vehicles, and personal property, cannot exceed $2,000. In 2012, monthly payments to eligible beneficiaries were about $517 per person.

FAMILY AND CHILD SUPPORT The Aid to Dependent Children program is a means-tested program that was first established as part of the Social Security Act in 1935. In 1950, it was broadened to include not only dependent children without fathers but also mothers or other adults with whom dependent children were living. At this time, it was retitled the Aid to Families and Dependent Children (AFDC) program. As a result of this change and changes in the American family (including a rise in the birthrate to unwed mothers and a rise in the divorce rate), the family and child support rolls expanded significantly in the latter part of the twentieth century.

By the 1990s, the growth of this program began to attract widespread criticism from many conservatives and moderates, including Democratic President Bill Clinton. Critics pointed to the rising number of recipients and claimed that the AFDC program encouraged promiscuity, out-of-wedlock births, and dependency that resulted in a permanent class of welfare families. To restrict the availability of aid, to ferret out fraud and abuse, and to hold down cost, public officials sought to reform the program.

In what was hailed as the biggest shift in income security policy since the Great Depression, a new family and child support bill, the Personal Responsibility and Work Opportunity Reconciliation Act (PRWORA) of 1996, created the Temporary Assistance for Needy Families (TANF) program to replace AFDC. The most fundamental change enacted in the new law was the switch in funding welfare from an open-ended matching program to a block grant to the states. PRWORA also gave states more flexibility in reforming their welfare programs toward work-oriented goals.

Significant features of the TANF plan included: (1) a requirement that single mothers with a child over five years of age must find work within two years of receiving benefits; (2) a provision requiring unmarried mothers under the age of eighteen to live with an adult and attend school to receive welfare benefits; (3) a five-year lifetime limit for aid from block grants; (4) a requirement that mothers must provide information about a child's father in order to receive full welfare payments; (5) cutting off food stamps and Supplemental Security Income for illegal immigrants; (6) cutting off cash benefits and food stamps for convicted drug felons; and, (7) limiting food stamps to three months in a three-year period for persons eighteen to fifty years old who are not raising children and not working.[18]

The success of the TANF program has been widely debated. The total number of Americans receiving benefits has fallen. The program is not an entitlement, and states use diversion payments, for example, to minimize the number of TANF recipients. Little evidence supports the success of the program in job training or as a means of reducing economic and social inequality. Despite these potential shortcomings, the act was reauthorized several times during the Bush administration. In 2010, it became the subject of significant political wrangling, and the Emergency Contingency Fund, which provided additional federal revenues to states, was cut.

SUPPLEMENTAL NUTRITION ASSISTANCE PROGRAM The first attempt at this means-tested program (1939–1943), which is more commonly known as food stamps, was primarily an effort to expand domestic markets for farm commodities. Food stamps provided the poor with the ability to purchase more food, thus increasing the demand for American agricultural produce. Attempts to reestablish the program during the Eisenhower administration failed, but in 1961, a $381,000 pilot program began under the Kennedy administration. It became permanent in 1964 and extended nationwide in 1974.

The method of delivering the food stamp benefit has changed dramatically over time. For much of the program's history, the benefit was administered as actual paper coupons—quite literally, food "stamps"—given to citizens who were eligible for relief. Today, the program is administered entirely using an electronic debt program, much like an ATM card. This change in administration necessitated a formal name change for the program—from food stamps to the Supplemental Nutrition Assistance Program—in 2008. Still, this benefit continues to be an important means of ensuring income security. In 2012, more than 46 million Americans received SNAP aid. The average participant received $133.85 worth of assistance per month.

In addition to SNAP, the national government operates several other food programs for the needy. These programs include a special nutritional program for women, infants, and children, known as WIC; a school breakfast and lunch program; and an emergency food assistance program including cheese and cereal.

economic stability
A situation in which there is economic growth, rising national income, high employment, and steadiness in the general level of prices.

recession
A decline in the economy that occurs as investment sags, production falls off, and unemployment increases.

Toward Reform: Recession and Economic Recovery

17.5 Evaluate the role of fiscal, monetary, and income security policy in the economic recession and recovery.

By 2008, it became increasingly clear that the extended period of American **economic stability**—a situation characterized by economic growth, rising national income, high employment, and steadiness in the general level of prices—was quickly coming to an end. Growing unemployment and government expenditures, coupled with a collapsing mortgage industry, created a severe economic downturn. By the end of 2008, this downturn had become a full-blown **recession**, a decline in the economy that occurs as investment sags, production falls off, and unemployment increases.

The national government identified this crisis situation quickly and, using fiscal, monetary, and income security policies, took a number of actions in an attempt to restart economic growth and stimulate the economy. We consider the ways the government used each of these policies in turn.

Fiscal Policy

In February 2008, realizing the severity of the economic situation, the Bush administration, along with Congress, announced a $168 billion federal stimulus package to provide Americans with tax rebates and relief intended to help boost consumer demand and reduce economic hardship. But, these efforts were insufficient, and the financial meltdown worsened. The collapse of many financial institutions as a result of the subprime mortgage crisis in September 2008 led Congress to pass the Temporary Assets Relief Program (TARP), an approximately $700 billion bailout of the financial industry.

Although these efforts made great strides in preserving American savings and loan companies, they did little to help average citizens. To address these concerns, in February 2009, President Barack Obama signed the $787 billion American Recovery and Reinvestment Act, designed to cut taxes and create jobs through deficit spending.

These fiscal policy choices did improve economic recovery. By 2010, GDP and employment both increased. The long-term consequence of deficit spending, however, is a national debt that, economists argue, is unsustainable. Ending Bush tax cuts combined with budget cuts could reduce the deficit, but at the expense of slowing the rate of economic recovery. Policy makers face tough choices as they continue to balance ideological preferences regarding the role and size of government.

☐ Monetary Policy

Monetary policy is often the preferred way to address an economic crisis, in part because it can be easily implemented and has fewer long-term financial consequences than the deficit spending typified by fiscal policy and the Recovery Act. In early 2008, the Federal Reserve Board responded quickly to the economic slowdown, taking extraordinary action to lower interest rates and engaging in large open market operations and discount rate reductions to increase liquidity in the markets. In March 2008, the Fed also injected about $200 billion into the U.S. banking system by offering banks low-interest, one-month loans to ease the tightening credit conditions. It later took action to adjust mortgage lending rules and expand the commodities that U.S. markets could borrow against in order to increase the money supply in the market.

Despite signs of an economic recovery in early 2010, the Fed has continued to keep interest rates low in the hope of attracting borrowers who will inject money into the market. In addition to these traditional tools of monetary policy, the Fed has taken extraordinary measures designed to stimulate bank lending, including the purchase of mortgage-backed securities, credit easing, and quantitative easing. New regulations on capital leverage, risk management, and liquidity passed in the Dodd-Frank Wall Street Reform and Consumer Protection Act of 2011 attempt to reduce the risks associated with the international interconnectedness of large financial institutions. Critics argue that the new regulations unfairly restrict banks, reducing their global competitive advantage. Others suggest that recent reforms do not go far enough to prevent economic crises in the future. As business cycles increase in severity, finding the right balance of regulation and deregulation is a constant challenge.

☐ Income Security Policy

Income security policies automatically expand the economy during recessions by providing benefits to those affected by worsening economic conditions and rising unemployment. These programs, however, have put pressure on federal and state governments, with severe consequences for state budgets and the national deficit and debt. Recall that states must have balanced budgets—the amount of revenues must be equal to or greater than expenditure levels. Thus, as the rolls for programs such as unemployment insurance and food stamps rise, state costs to administer these programs—and therefore, projected expenditures—rise rapidly. At the same time, however, state revenues in the form of income and sales taxes decline as a result of fewer workers and lower consumer spending. This combination has placed great pressure on state governments. Many states have had to find creative ways to raise revenue or make large budget cuts in other areas in order to make ends meet.

For its part, the national government has engaged in deficit spending in order to fund these and other programs, as well as to help states balance their budgets. The costs of these expenditures will not be fully realized for years, as the nation faces a growing national debt and the threat of economic instability from owing large sums of money to creditors. As the economy recovers, the federal government will also have to deal with the financial insolvency of Social Security and other programs.

☐ Evaluating the Government's Response

Signs of the economic downturn—and the ultimate collapse of financial institutions—were severe enough that both Republicans and Democrats agreed on the need to act in forestalling long-term consequences, both for individuals and for the nation at large. It is, however, worth noting that both parties encouraged responses to the economic collapse that were consistent with their political and economic worldviews.

Take a Closer Look

In May 2012, the Group of Eight Summit was held at Camp David, Maryland, and included world leaders from the United States, Japan, Britain, Germany, France, Italy, Canada, and Russia. The main focus of the conference was how to prevent a growing fiscal crisis in the Euro area from harming the global economy.

U.S. President Barack Obama supports the European Central Bank's using monetary policy to rescue failing European banks from collapse.

French President François Hollande was elected in the spring of 2012 on a platform that rejected the austerity measures advocated by Merkel. Hollande supports increased government spending to stimulate economic growth.

German Chancellor Angela Merkel firmly supports austerity measures to improve economic growth. She argues that reducing deficits is the most important goal in stabilizing the debt crisis faced by many Euro area economies.

CRITICAL THINKING QUESTIONS

1. Should banks be rescued with government bailouts if their collapse threatens the economic stability of a country? Should they be rescued even if they have engaged in risky behavior?
2. Is government debt justified by the creation of jobs? What are the long-term consequences of increased government deficits? What are the long-term consequences of increased employment?
3. Should world leaders coordinate their economic policies to prevent global economic recessions? Who should decide what policies to pursue?

Seeing the signs of a downturn in early 2008, for example, President George W. Bush and the Republican Party urged the Fed to take action to increase the supply of money and lower interest rates. The Bush administration also worked with Congress to pass a tax rebate designed to put more money in citizens' pockets. After taking office in 2009, President Barack Obama, leading the Democrats, significantly increased government spending and provided additional tax relief in addition to the aggressive use of monetary policy tools by the Fed.

As the economy recovers, economists will debate which of these policy approaches was most effective. Not surprisingly, assessments generally break down along partisan lines. White House economists, for example, credit the Recovery Act for bringing about economic growth and increasing employment by late 2009. Conservative scholars and former Republican governmental officials do not dispute this growth, but they argue that it has resulted from monetary policy and decisive bailout actions through the TARP program.[19]

In all likelihood, however, both fiscal policy and monetary policy, as well as the safety net provided by national and state income security programs, have helped improve the American economy. The government shoulders the responsibility of taking decisive action in all three areas—fiscal, monetary, and income security policy—to prevent or reduce the impact of future downturns in the business cycle.

On MyPoliSciLab

Review the Chapter

Listen to **Chapter 17** on **MyPoliSciLab**

Roots of Economic Policy

17.1 Trace the evolution of economic policy in the United States, p. 519.

The government's role in regulating the economy has evolved over the nation's history. During the nineteenth century, the national government defined its economic role narrowly and subscribed to a laissez-faire economic philosophy. By the 1890s, however, it became clear that the national government needed to take greater steps to regulate the economy, which it did by creating the Interstate Commerce Commission and passing anti-monopoly legislation. Later, to help bring the nation out of the Great Depression, President Franklin D. Roosevelt's New Deal in the 1930s brought increased government intervention in a number of economic policy areas including financial markets, agriculture, labor, and industry. In the 1960s and 1970s, the government expanded its role to include social regulations dealing with health, safety, and environmental protection. Finally, at the end of the twentieth century, a backlash occurred against regulation, and deregulation, or the reduction in market controls in favor of market-based competition, gained prominence. In the wake of the recent global economic recession, debate continues over the proper role of government in responding to economic conditions.

Fiscal Policy

17.2 Assess the impact of the budget process on fiscal policy, p. 525.

Fiscal policy is the deliberate use of the national government's taxing and spending policies to maintain economic stability. Many factors influence fiscal policy, including the global economy through increased international interdependence. Government spending and taxes are the tools of fiscal policy; they can be manipulated to stabilize the economy and to counteract fluctuations in federal revenues. Except for a short period from 1998 to 2001, the federal government has generally run a budget deficit, which can have negative consequences for the economy over the long term. The government has responded to economic recession with different combinations of increased government spending and tax cuts. Congress raised the debt ceiling as the long-term continuation of annual deficits increased the national debt, prompting debates over the size and role of the federal government. In 2012, the United States faced what economists referred to as a fiscal cliff, as current policies were deemed unsustainable. Conflicting goals of stimulating a weak economy still recovering from recession and the necessity of reducing long-term debt and the risk of inflation created tough choices for policy makers.

Monetary Policy

17.3 Analyze the effect of the Federal Reserve System on monetary policy, p. 532.

Monetary policy is a form of government regulation in which the nation's money supply and interest rates are controlled. In 1913, the federal government created the Federal Reserve System ("the Fed") to adjust the money supply to the needs of agriculture, commerce, and industry. Today, it handles much of the day-to-day management of monetary policy. It has a number of tools to aid its efforts, including open market operations, which involve the buying and selling of government securities by the Federal Reserve Bank in the securities market; control of the discount rate, or the rate of interest at which the Federal Reserve Board lends money to member banks; and the ability to set reserve requirements, or government requirements that a portion of member banks' deposits be retained as backing for their loans. The Fed has also used nontraditional tools, including the purchase of mortgage-backed securities, credit easing, and quantitative easing, to encourage banks to increase lending.

Income Security Policy

17.4 Describe the evolution of income security policy in the United States, p. 536.

Income security programs protect people against loss of income. These programs also serve as automatic stabilizers, increasing government spending during economic crises. Income security policy was not a priority for the federal government until the 1930s, when it passed the Social Security Act. Today, the federal government administers a range of income security programs that fall into two major areas: non–means-tested and means-tested programs Non–means-tested programs provide cash assistance to qualified beneficiaries regardless of income; they include old age, survivors, and disability insurance, and unemployment insurance. Means-tested programs require that people have incomes below specified levels to be eligible for benefits; they include Supplemental Security Income (SSI), family and child support and the Supplemental Nutrition Assistance Program (food stamps).

Toward Reform: Recession and Economic Recovery

17.5 Evaluate the role of fiscal, monetary, and income security policy in the economic recession and recovery, p. 541.

By the end of 2008, the nation was in a full-blown recession, a decline in the economy that occurs as investment sags, production falls off, and unemployment increases. The national government identified the crisis situation quickly and took a number of actions to restart economic growth and stimulate the economy through the use of fiscal, monetary, and income security policy. In terms of fiscal policy, the Bush administration offered tax rebates and proposed a $700 billion federal bailout package for the banking industry, known as TARP. When President Barack Obama took office, he worked with Congress to pass the $787 billion American Recovery and Reinvestment Act to help stimulate the economy and to maintain and create new jobs. In terms of monetary policy, the Federal Reserve Board responded to the crisis by cutting interest rates and engaging in open market operations and discount rate reductions. The costs of income security programs during this economic downturn have put a strain on both national and state budgets. As the economy continues to move forward, policy makers will analyze the successes and failures of fiscal policy, monetary policy, and income security policies in responding to the worst economic crisis since the Great Depression.

Key Terms

 **Study** and **Review** the **Flashcards**

Board of Governors, p. 532
budget deficit, p. 525
business cycles, p. 519
deregulation, p. 523
discount rate, p. 534
economic regulation, p. 519
economic stability, p. 541
entitlement programs, p. 537
fiscal policy, p. 525
gross domestic product (GDP), p. 531
inflation, p. 526
interventionist state, p. 522
laissez-faire, p. 519
means-tested programs, p. 537
monetary policy, p. 532
non–means-tested programs, p. 537
open market operations, p. 532
recession, p. 541
reserve requirements, p. 534
Social Security Act, p. 536
trusts, p. 520

Test Yourself

 **Study** and **Review** the **Practice Tests**

1. During the Progressive era, the federal government supported ____ of the banking industry to help stabilize the money supply and prevent financial panics.

a. regulation
b. deregulation
c. socialization
d. monopolization
e. privatization

2. Congressional termination of the Glass-Steagall Act in 1999

a. meant that large multinational banks could no longer merge with other banks.
b. allowed banks to consolidate traditional savings and loans services with riskier securities investments.
c. prohibited banks from borrowing money from the Federal Reserve.
d. helped to prevent bank failures during the recession that began in 2007.
e. reduced the competitiveness of multinational financial institutions.

3. The government makes fiscal policy by increasing or decreasing

a. the supply of money.
b. the interest rate.
c. taxes and government spending.
d. the capital reserve that banks must hold.
e. the amount that banks are charged to borrow money.

4. Economist John Maynard Keynes argued that

a. increasing government spending can stimulate a weak economy.
b. increasing interest rates can decrease consumer spending.
c. decreasing government taxes reduces the national debt.
d. decreasing the supply of money can stimulate borrowing.
e. increasing consumer spending destabilizes the economy.

5. The portion of a bank's deposits that the bank must retain as backing for its loans is known as the

- **a.** loan requirement.
- **b.** reserve requirement.
- **c.** financial backing proportion.
- **d.** earnest money.
- **e.** fiduciary responsibility.

6. The goals of the Federal Reserve include

- **a.** limiting consumption.
- **b.** increasing inflation.
- **c.** decreasing unemployment.
- **d.** decreasing consumer savings.
- **e.** increasing consumer debt.

7. Income security programs intended to assist persons whose income falls below a designated level are called

- **a.** security assistance laws.
- **b.** social insurance statutes.
- **c.** means-tested programs.
- **d.** non–means-tested programs.
- **e.** Medicare and Medicaid.

8. Social Security, an example of an income security policy,

- **a.** provides temporary income to workers who have lost their jobs.
- **b.** is paid for entirely by contributions from employers.
- **c.** is a means-tested entitlement.
- **d.** may be underfunded by 2030 if the system is not reformed.
- **e.** provides jobs to low-income elderly workers.

9. Much of the current economic downturn is attributable to

- **a.** the cost of the war in Iraq.
- **b.** automobile loans.
- **c.** the cost of No Child Left Behind.
- **d.** the cost of presidential campaigns.
- **e.** the subprime mortgage crisis.

10. In response to economic recession, the U.S. federal government

- **a.** enacted austerity measures.
- **b.** increased interest rates.
- **c.** abandoned Keynesian economic policies.
- **d.** stimulated economic growth with increased government spending.
- **e.** decreased government debt.

Explore Further

Blank, Rebecca M. *Changing Inequality.* Los Angeles: University of California, 2011.

Cassidy, John. *How Markets Fall: The Logic of Economic Calamities.* New York: Farrar, Straus, and Giroux, 2010.

Chernow, Ron. *Alexander Hamilton.* New York: Penguin, 2004.

Fleckenstein, William, and Fred Sheehan. *Greenspan's Bubbles: The Age of Ignorance at the Federal Reserve.* New York: McGraw Hill, 2008.

Hacker, Jacob S. *The Great Risk Shift: The New Economic Insecurity and the Decline of the American Dream.* New York: Oxford University Press, 2008.

Keech, William. *Economic Politics: The Costs of Democracy.* Cambridge, MA: Cambridge University Press, 1995.

Kettl, Donald F. *Deficit Politics: Public Budgeting in Its Institutional and Historical Context,* 2nd ed. New York: Longman, 2010.

Lee, Robert D., Ronald W. Johnson, and Philip G. Joyce. *Public Budgeting Systems,* 9th ed. Boston: Jones and Bartlett, 2013.

Miller, Roger LeRoy, Daniel K. Benjamin, and Douglass C. North. *The Economics of Public Issues,* 17th ed. New York: Addison Wesley, 2011.

Page, Benjamin I., and Lawrence R. Jacobs. *Class War: What Americans Really Think About Economic Inequality.* Chicago: University of Chicago Press, 2009.

Phillips, Kevin. *Wealth and Democracy: A Political History of the American Rich.* New York: Broadway, 2002.

Reinhart, Carmen M., and Kenneth Rogoff. *This Time Is Different: Eight Centuries of Financial Folly.* Princeton: Princeton University Press, 2009.

Rubin, Irene S. *The Politics of Public Budgeting: Getting and Spending, Borrowing and Balancing,* 5th ed. Washington, DC: CQ Press, 2005.

Rubin, Robert E., with Jacob Weisberg. *In an Uncertain World: Tough Choices from Wall Street to Washington.* New York: Random House, 2003.

Schiff, Peter D. *How an Economy Grows and Why It Crashes.* New York: Wiley, 2010.

Schiller, Robert. *Irrational Exuberance.* Princeton, NJ: Princeton University Press, 2000.

Sheehan, Frederick. *Panderer to Power: The Untold Story of How Alan Greenspan Enriched Wall Street and Left a Legacy of Recession.* New York: McGraw Hill, 2009.

Stiglitz, Joseph, and Linda Bilmes. *The Three Trillion Dollar War: The True Cost of the Iraq Conflict.* New York: Norton, 2008.

Tietenberg, Tom, and Lynne Lewis. *Environmental Economics and Policy,* 6th ed. New York: Prentice Hall, 2009.

To learn more about the Bureau for Economic Analysis, go to its Web site at **www.bea.gov.**

To learn more about current fiscal policy, go to **www.gpoaccess.gov/usbudget/index.html.**

To learn more about regulation of financial markets, go to the Federal Reserve Board Web site at **www.federalreserve.gov.**

To learn more about Social Security, go to the Social Security Web site at **www.ssa.gov.**

Listen to Chapter 18 on MyPoliSciLab

18

Foreign and Defense Policy

The United States of America has a large foreign policy agenda on the world stage. It involves a broad range of issues, numerous actors, and all parts of the world. On any given day, U.S. foreign policy makers devote attention and resources to problems involving not only terrorism and the proliferation of weapons of mass destruction but also humanitarian intervention, democratization, trade, economic development, globalization, the environment, oil supplies, and the United Nations, to name but a few.

Since he became president in 2009, Barack Obama has sought a foreign policy that maintains continuity with the past but that also charts a path different from his predecessor, George W. Bush. Upon entering office, President Obama called for a "new era of engagement," pledging to rebuild America's image abroad and strengthen relations—especially in the Middle East—with countries that had become highly critical of U.S. foreign policy as a result of the war in Iraq. He also pledged to bring home American troops from Iraq and wind down the war in Afghanistan.

The president began this effort with a speech in Cairo, Egypt, in 2009, in which he called for a "new beginning" between the United States and Muslims around the world, while acknowledging that rebuilding trust would be a long-term effort. In Iraq, all American combat forces left the country by the end of 2011, and in Afghanistan, after deploying additional forces for a time to bolster the war effort, the president began withdrawing troops, announcing that "by the end of 2014 the Afghans will be fully responsible for the security of their country."[1] At the same time, the president continued to pursue the war against terrorism, targeting Osama bin Laden and al-Qaeda in Pakistan and Afghanistan, using pilotless drones to conduct attacks against terrorists and keeping the U.S. detainment center at Guantanamo Bay in Cuba open (after pledging to close it).

THE PRESIDENT PLAYS A DOMINANT ROLE IN THE DEVELOPMENT OF FOREIGN AND DEFENSE POLICY. Above President Ronald Reagan speaks at the Brandenburg Gate in Berlin, near the Berlin Wall, issuing a challenge to Soviet leader Mikhail Gorbachev to "tear down this wall." Below President Barack Obama in Cairo, Egypt, visiting a mosque after speaking at Cairo University, where he called for a new era of cooperation between the United States and Muslims around the world.

MyPoliSciLab Videos

The Big Picture It takes the whole world to solve some problems. Author Alixandra B. Yanus explains the difference between foreign policy and defense policy and shares some reasons why a network of international allies—like the United Nations—is necessary for addressing global issues.

The Basics Who develops America's foreign policy? How has America emerged as a world leader and what challenges does this present? In this video, you will learn about the actors in the foreign policy arena and consider the United States' role in international affairs.

2
Why is the United States considered a "superpower"?

3

In Context Explore the history of American foreign policy. In this video, Boston University political scientist Neta C. Crawford explains the international challenges the United States has faced during three stages of development. She also reveals who is chiefly responsible for deciding foreign policy.

Thinking Like a Political Scientist Learn what foreign policy scholars are researching. Boston University political scientist Neta C. Crawford reveals how scholars use levels of analysis and advances in cognitive psychology to assess decision-making.

In the Real World The United States has intervened in many countries in order to promote democracy, including Iraq, Germany, Japan, and most recently, Libya. Is this the right thing to do? Learn what real people have to say about this divisive issue, and about the consequences brought on by U.S. involvement abroad.

So What? Most American products used to be made in America. Today, they are made all around the world. Author Alixandra B. Yanus lays out what this shift means for the United States, and she proves that it is impossible to study American government anymore without also studying America's relationships with other countries.

Addressing these problems has been only part of Obama's foreign policy. In Asia, he has pursued a "strategic pivot," seeking to diminish the American focus on the Middle East while investing greater time and attention to the Asia-Pacific region, where economic and military power is rapidly growing, especially in China. This rebalancing of U.S. foreign policy has involved building on previous policy, such as strengthening ties with the Association of Southeast Asian Nations and securing congressional approval of a U.S.-South Korea free trade agreement, but it has also meant initiating new and expanded military deployments in Australia and Singapore.

The United States has also sought to reduce the number of nuclear weapons and limit their spread to other countries—long-standing American foreign policy goals—with particular focus on Iran and North Korea. While the United States has been unable to achieve its goals with these two countries, President Obama did sign the New Strategic Arms Reductions Treaty (New START) with Russia, which reduces the number of deployed nuclear weapons in both countries. He also broke with previous U.S. policy by calling for the elimination of all nuclear weapons around the world, though he has pointed out that this is unlikely to happen anytime soon, even in his lifetime.

One highly visible element of U.S. foreign policy in recent years has been the pursuit of women's rights and empowerment, a cause championed by former Secretary of State Hillary Clinton, as well as by two of her predecessors as Secretary of State, Condoleezza Rice and Madeleine Albright. Stating that "the rights of women and girls is the unfinished business of the 21st century," Secretary Clinton is continuing the work she has done for decades, combating the inequality by which "women are denied the right to go to school by their own fathers and brothers . . . forced into prostitution . . . barred from the bank lending offices and banned from the ballot box."[2]

•••

Although popular and governmental opinions on the role of the United States in the world have changed dramatically in the past 220 years, many fundamental challenges remain the same. Should the United States, for example, isolate itself from other nations or become engaged in international conflicts? When do diplomatic solutions fall short, necessitating warfare? And, how do economic policies at home and abroad affect these relationships?

Evaluating the potential strengths and weaknesses of U.S. foreign policy today starts with acquiring a broad understanding of past foreign and defense policies and the political forces that have shaped them. We must also look closely at the key issues confronting the United States as it attempts to address emerging issues in foreign and defense policy.

foreign policy
Area of policy making that encompasses how one country builds relationships with other countries in order to safeguard its national interest.

defense policy
Area of policy making that focuses on the strategies that a country uses to protect itself from its enemies.

Roots of U.S. Foreign and Defense Policy

18.1 Trace the evolution of U.S. foreign and defense policy.

oreign and defense policy are two separate areas of policy making. **Foreign policy** relates to how one country (referred to as a state by political scientists) builds relationships with other countries to safeguard its national interests. **Defense policy** comprises the strategies a country uses to protect itself from its enemies. However, foreign policy and defense policy are interrelated. Countries use defense policy for many problems that are better addressed by well-planned foreign policy, and a failure to make good foreign policy can require the use of defense policy.

Like domestic and economic policies, U.S. foreign and defense policies have evolved. Today, the United States is a powerful and influential presence on the world stage. It was not always this way. Upon its founding, the United States was a weak country on the margins of world affairs, with an uncertain future.

18.1

18.2

18.3

18.4

18.5

isolationism
The U.S. policy of avoiding entangling alliances with European powers.

Farewell Address
When President George Washington left office, he wrote a letter, addressed to the People of the United States, warning people of the dangers to avoid in order to preserve the republic.

Monroe Doctrine
President James Monroe's 1823 pledge that the United States would oppose attempts by European states to reestablish their political control in the Western Hemisphere.

tariffs
Taxes on imported goods.

The historical roots of American foreign and defense policy are found in the period from the founding of the republic to the period leading up to World War II (1941–1945). The importance of these early experiences comes into clearer focus when we consider three distinct periods: (1) isolation in the early republic; (2) the United States as an emerging power; (3) World War I (1917–1918), and the interwar years (between World Wars I and II).

☐ Isolationism in the Early Republic

Independence did not change the fundamental foreign policy problem faced by colonial America: steering a safe course between Great Britain and France, the two feuding giants of world politics in the late 1700s. For some Framers, the best course of action was to maintain a close relationship with one of these two powers. Alexander Hamilton, for example, became a champion of a pro-British foreign policy, whereas Thomas Jefferson was an early supporter of a pro-French foreign policy.

For other early political leaders, the best course of action was one of neutrality and relative **isolationism,** a national policy that did not mean avoiding participation in foreign affairs but, instead, sidestepping "entangling alliances" with the major European powers. President George Washington articulated this neutrality position most forcefully. In his **Farewell Address,** he called for a policy that would "steer clear of permanent alliances with any portion of the foreign world."

The dual goals of isolationism and neutrality, however, did not guarantee the ability of the United States to always stay out of international conflicts. The United States fought an undeclared naval war in the 1790s with France because France was seizing U.S. ships that were trading with its enemies. Shortly thereafter, the United States fought the Barbary Wars against North African Barbary States, which had captured ships and held sailors for ransom.

Nor was conflict with the British resolved after the American Revolution. In the early 1800s, the ongoing wars between France and Great Britain, British support for American Indian tribes opposing U.S. westward expansion, and the British naval practice of impressment (stopping U.S. ships to seize suspected deserters of the British Royal Navy, and sometimes seizing ships and cargo while forcing American sailors to serve on British ships) led to the War of 1812 between the U.S. and Great Britain.

After the 1815 defeat of French leader Napoleon Bonaparte at Waterloo, Europe was at peace for the first time in almost two decades. Europeans celebrated, but the United States feared that European powers would try to reestablish control in the Western Hemisphere. To prevent this, President James Monroe issued the **Monroe Doctrine** in 1823. It warned European states that the United States would view "any attempt on their part to extend their system to any portion of this hemisphere as dangerous to our peace and safety." It also promised to continue the American policy of noninterference in the internal concerns of European powers.

☐ The United States as an Emerging Power

Throughout most of the nineteenth century, the United States gained territory, developed economically, and emerged as a world power. This process centered on four areas: (1) trade policy and commerce, (2) continental expansion and manifest destiny, (3) dominance over the Western Hemisphere, and (4) interests in Asia.

TRADE POLICY AND COMMERCE The policy of neutrality articulated in Washington's Farewell Address made free trade a cornerstone of early American foreign policy. Reciprocity and most favored nation status were its guiding principles. Reciprocity meant that the U.S. government treated foreign traders in the same way that foreign countries treated American traders. Most favored nation status guaranteed that a country's imports into the United States would be given the lowest possible **tariffs,** or taxes on imported goods.

Increased global trade and competition following the end of the Napoleonic Wars led the United States to abandon the policies of reciprocity and most favored nation status. Beginning in 1816, Congress adopted the "American System" of trade protection by adding increasingly higher tariffs, sometimes as high as 100 percent of the value of the goods being imported.[3] High protectionist tariffs remained the American norm well into the twentieth century.

manifest destiny
Theory that the United States was divinely supported to expand across North America to the Pacific Ocean.

Roosevelt Corollary
Concept developed by President Theodore Roosevelt early in the twentieth century declaring that it was the responsibility of the United States to ensure stability in Latin America and the Caribbean.

CONTINENTAL EXPANSION AND MANIFEST DESTINY During the nineteenth century, the United States acquired immense quantities of land in various ways. It took land from American Indians in wars against the Creek, Seminole, Sioux, Comanche, Apache, and other tribes. It bought territory from the French (the Louisiana Territory), Spanish (Florida), and Russians (Alaska). It also fought the 1846 Mexican War, acquiring a large expanse of Mexican territory in the American Southwest and California.

Manifest destiny is the summary phrase used to capture the logic behind American continental expansionism. According to this idea, the United States had a divinely supported obligation to expand across North America to the Pacific and "overspread the continent allotted by Providence for the free development of our multiplying millions."[4] Manifest destiny was viewed as natural and inevitable, far different from the colonial expansion of European states.

DOMINANCE OVER THE WESTERN HEMISPHERE The twentieth century began with a revision of the Monroe Doctrine. In what came to be known as the **Roosevelt Corollary** to the Monroe Doctrine, President Theodore Roosevelt asserted in 1904 that it was the responsibility of the United States to ensure stability in Latin America and the Caribbean. In accordance with this role, the United States would intervene with military force to punish wrongdoing and establish order in these nations when their own governments were incapable of doing so.

Roosevelt was particularly concerned with the Dominican Republic. It was deeply in debt, plagued by growing domestic unrest, and faced the threat of hostile military action by France. Roosevelt blocked French action by taking over customs collection there in 1906. Later, the United States sent troops to other countries, including Cuba, Haiti, Nicaragua, Panama, and Mexico.

HOW DID THE ROOSEVELT COROLLARY AFFECT AMERICAN FOREIGN POLICY?

In this political cartoon, President Theodore Roosevelt is shown policing Panama, carrying the "big stick" of military intervention proposed by the Roosevelt Corollary.

collective security
The idea that an attack on one country is an attack on all countries.

Although these exercises of military power were significant in establishing regional dominance, the signature event of this period for American foreign policy was the acquisition of the Panama Canal Zone. The United States wished to build a canal through Panama, which was then part of Colombia, but when the Colombian government refused to approve the necessary treaty, the Roosevelt administration supported a Panamanian independence movement. When this movement achieved success, the U.S. government quickly recognized the independent state and signed an agreement granting the United States rights to a ten-mile strip of land connecting the Atlantic and Pacific Oceans. Construction of the Panama Canal began in 1904 and was completed in 1914, providing a way for ships to avoid the long and dangerous trip around South America in reaching western U.S. territories.

Supporting Panamanian independence was not the only way the United States established its influence in Central America and the Caribbean. Beginning with the William H. Taft administration, the United States also began to use its economic power through "dollar diplomacy." Dollar diplomacy was designed to make the United States the banker of the region, and to open up countries throughout all of Latin America to American investment.

INTERESTS IN ASIA The 1898 Spanish-American War, fought between the United States and Spain over Spanish policies and presence in Cuba, gave the United States control over Cuba, as well as other Spanish colonies such as Puerto Rico and the Philippines. As a result, the United States now had an overseas colony and a major stake in Asian affairs. The major problems confronting the United States in Asia were the disintegration of China and the rising power of Japan.

In 1898 and 1899, as European powers were extending their influence in China, the United States issued the Open Door Notes to Russia, Germany, France, and Great Britain, calling upon them not to discriminate against other investors in their spheres of influence. While the United States could not force other countries to agree, the logic behind this Open Door Policy was consistent with long-standing American support for opening up foreign markets to U.S. investment.

In sharp contrast to the unilateral action taken on China, President Theodore Roosevelt sought to contain Japan through a series of international agreements. The most notable of these was the Taft-Katsura Agreement of 1905. This act recognized Japanese preeminence over Korea in return for a Japanese agreement to respect American control over the Philippines and Hawaii.

☐ World War I and the Interwar Years

When World War I broke out in Europe in 1914, the United States remained neutral at first. It was a European war, and no U.S. interests were directly involved. In addition, the United States was largely a nation of European immigrants, and Americans were deeply divided about whom to support. As the war progressed, however, it became increasingly difficult to remain neutral. Under Germany's policy of unrestricted submarine warfare, German subs sank U.S. ships carrying cargo to Great Britain and France. Finally, declaring that the United States was fighting "to make the world safe for democracy," President Woodrow Wilson led the nation into the war in 1917. Wilson also put forward a statement of American aims, the Fourteen Points. The Fourteenth Point was the creation of a League of Nations at the conclusion of the war.

At the Paris Peace Conference following the war, Wilson succeeded in getting the League of Nations established. Its guiding principle was **collective security,** the idea that an attack on one country is an attack on all countries. Wilson failed, however, to build support for the League of Nations at home, and so the United States never joined.

The period between the two world wars saw U.S. foreign policy dominated by two issues: (1) disarmament, and (2) isolationism. In 1920, isolationist Senator William Borah (R–ID) offered a resolution inviting Great Britain and Japan to an arms limitation conference. The result was the 1921 Washington Conference, which left a mixed legacy. Although the conference did not produce lasting security in the Far East or end arms races, it did mark a shift in the global balance of power, because two of the main players represented—the United States and Japan—were from outside Europe.

Support for disarmament also led to the signing of the Kellogg-Briand Pact. In this pact, the United States, Japan, and the European powers (including Great Britain, France, and Germany) agreed to renounce war "as an instrument of national policy" and to resolve their disputes "by pacific means." This agreement, however, did not stop the United States from taking defensive actions, such as building new naval vessels.

Second, isolationist sentiment hardened within the United States. This sentiment led Congress to increase tariffs to protect U.S. industry from foreign competition. In 1930, Congress passed the Smoot-Hawley Tariff Act, and other countries responded by raising their tariffs. The higher tariffs, in conjunction with the Great Depression, had a dramatic impact on world trade. By 1932, trade dropped to about one-third its former level.[5]

Belief in isolationism also led to the passage of four neutrality acts in the 1930s. Among their core provisions were arms embargoes and a prohibition on loans to countries involved in international conflicts. After Great Britain and France declared war on Nazi Germany in the late 1930s, however, President Franklin D. Roosevelt was able to soften these bans to allow Great Britain to obtain American weapons in return for allowing the United States to lease British military bases (this was the beginning of what was called the "lend-lease" program during World War II).

UN Security Council
A principal part of the United Nations, charged with authorizing peacekeeping operations, international sanctions, and military action in order to maintain global peace and security.

The United States as a World Power

18.2 Explain U.S. foreign policy as the country rose to become a world power.

The status of the United States as a world power was cemented by its entry into and subsequent victory in World War II. Between World War II and the new millennium, American political leaders guided the nation through two distinct periods: the Cold War and the post–Cold War period. Today, the Obama administration is working to guide the country through a changing world defined by globalization and the rise of emerging powers such as China.

World War II and Its Aftermath

The United States entered World War II with the December 7, 1941, Japanese bombing of Pearl Harbor in Hawaii. The war was fought on two fronts—in Europe and in the Pacific. It concluded in Europe first, in May 1945. It did not end in the Pacific until August of that same year, following the U.S. decision to drop atomic bombs on Hiroshima and Nagasaki, Japan.

World War II was a watershed in U.S. foreign policy. Prior to the war, isolationist sentiment dominated American thinking on world politics, but after it, internationalism emerged triumphant. In contrast to its earlier rejection of the League of Nations, the United States enthusiastically led in the creation of the United Nations (UN), establishing itself as a permanent member of the **UN Security Council,** along with Great Britain, France, China, and the Soviet Union. It also entered into security alliances with countries around the globe, with an understanding that America's role was to be "the leader of the free world."

President Franklin D. Roosevelt took an activist role in World War II diplomacy, holding or attending several major conferences until he died in April 1945. These meetings began with British Prime Minister Winston Churchill in Newfoundland, Canada, in August 1941 and ended with the Potsdam Conference in Germany in July and August 1945 after his death. The best known of these conferences was the Yalta Conference, held in the Soviet Union in February 1945, to decide the future of Germany and Eastern Europe, and to discuss the development of the UN.

In the belief that protectionist trade policies had led to the rise of dictators and the beginning of World War II, the United States moved to create a set of international economic organizations to encourage and manage global trade and finance.

HOW DID WORLD WAR II CHANGE U.S. FOREIGN POLICY?

World War II cemented America's role as a world power. Here President Franklin D. Roosevelt meets with British Prime Minister Winston Churchill and Soviet Premier Josef Stalin at Yalta in 1945 to plan the postwar settlement.

Bretton Woods System
International financial system devised shortly before the end of World War II that created the World Bank and the International Monetary Fund.

International Monetary Fund (IMF)
International governmental organization designed to stabilize international currency transactions.

World Bank
International governmental organization created to provide loans for large economic development projects.

General Agreement on Tariffs and Trade (GATT)
Post–World War II economic development treaty designed to help facilitate international trade negotiations and promote free trade.

containment
U.S. policy of opposing Soviet expansion and communist revolutions around the world with military forces, economic assistance, and political influence.

Collectively, they came to be known as the **Bretton Woods System,** after Bretton Woods, New Hampshire, where negotiations were held in July 1944. The **International Monetary Fund (IMF)** was established to stabilize international currency transactions. In addition, the International Bank for Reconstruction and Development, also called the **World Bank,** was set up to help the world recover from the destruction of World War II and to help poorer countries prosper by providing loans for large economic development projects.

Created in 1947, the **General Agreement on Tariffs and Trade (GATT)** had as its mission the facilitation of international trade negotiations and promotion of free trade. This process occurred through negotiating "rounds" or multiyear international conferences.

☐ The Cold War and Containment

The Cold War was the defining feature of the international system from the end of World War II in 1945 until the collapse of communism in Eastern Europe and the Soviet Union in the late 1980s and early 1990s. It was a period of competition, hostility, tension, and occasional moments of cooperation between the Western powers (the United States, Great Britain, and Western Europe) and the communist bloc states (Eastern Europe and the Soviet Union). Although it was frequently intense, the Cold War never escalated into direct and open warfare.

American foreign policy during the Cold War was organized around two key concepts. The first was **containment,** which held that the "the main element of any United States policy toward the Soviet Union must be that of a long-term, patient but firm and vigilant containment of Russian expansionist tendencies."[6] This meant that the United

States would oppose Soviet expansion with military forces, economic assistance, and political influence. The second concept was deterrence. From the 1950s through the 1980s, the United States and the Soviet Union developed large nuclear arsenals. Having stockpiles of weapons of mass destruction on either side of the conflict ensured that both sides would prevent one another from actually using their nuclear weapons. This created a condition of mutually assured destruction (MAD).

Although the Cold War began in Europe, it quickly became a global conflict. In the 1940s, the conflict spread to Greece and Turkey, leading to the Marshall Plan. It also spread to Latin America, especially Cuba, and to Asia. In 1949, for example, Mao Zedong won the Chinese Civil War and aligned China with the Soviet Union, a move that the United States viewed as significantly increasing Soviet power. This action also precipitated the Korean War of the 1950s and the Vietnam War of the 1960s and 1970s.

THE COLD WAR IN EUROPE Among the first Cold War trouble spots were Greece and Turkey, both of which came under pressure from Communists. In February 1947, Great Britain informed the United States that it could no longer meet its traditional obligations to protect Greece and Turkey. Less than one month later, on March 12, 1947, President Harry S Truman addressed a joint session of Congress and requested economic and military aid for the two countries. The language Truman used as justification was as important as this request for aid. He argued that the United States "must support free peoples who are resisting attempted subjugation by armed minorities or by outside pressure."[7] Known as the **Truman Doctrine,** this policy led the United States to provide economic assistance and military aid to countries fighting against communist revolutions or political pressure, and remained the basis of U.S. policy throughout the Cold War.

Three months later, the United States took a major action consistent with this political worldview. Secretary of State George Marshall announced that the United States would help finance Europe's economic recovery. All European states were invited to participate in the drafting of a European collective recovery plan known as the **Marshall Plan.** Importantly, the Soviet Union chose not to participate in this program and prevented Eastern European states (Poland, Czechoslovakia, Hungary, Romania, and Bulgaria) from participating as well. This effectively served to divide postwar Europe into two parts.

In 1949, the economic division of Europe was reinforced by its military partition with the establishment of the **North Atlantic Treaty Organization (NATO).** This alliance, the first peacetime military treaty joined by the United States, was a collective security pact among the United States, Canada, and Western Europe. In retaliation, the Soviet Union organized its Eastern European allies into the Warsaw Pact. This division of Europe was further established by the **Berlin Wall,** built by East Germany in 1961 to cut off democratic West Berlin from communist East Berlin.

THE COLD WAR IN LATIN AMERICA Cold War competition between the United States and the Soviet Union moved to Latin America in the late 1950s and early 1960s. The most intense confrontation involved Cuba, where Fidel Castro came to power in 1959. Following this revolution, President Dwight D. Eisenhower approved a plan to send a small group of Cuban exiles back to Cuba to conduct a guerrilla warfare campaign against the new leader. This plan evolved into the Bay of Pigs invasion, authorized by President John F. Kennedy in April of 1961. The results were disastrous. Some 1,400 Cuban exiles landed at the Bay of Pigs and quickly were surrounded and defeated by well-equipped and loyal Cuban soldiers.

The following year, in October 1962, the United States and Soviet Union confronted one another over the deployment of nuclear missiles in Cuba. Perhaps at no time was the world closer to a nuclear war than it was during this event, known as the **Cuban Missile Crisis.** In response, President Kennedy established a "quarantine" on Cuba, a naval blockade that prevented Soviet ships from landing in Cuba. The crisis ended after two weeks, when Soviet Premier Nikita Khrushchev agreed to remove the Soviet missiles.

THE VIETNAM WAR America's involvement in Vietnam began in the 1950s. After the end of World War II, France unsuccessfully sought to reestablish its colonial rule

Truman Doctrine
U.S. anti-communist policy initiated in 1947 that became the basis of U.S. foreign policy throughout the Cold War.

Marshall Plan
European collective recovery program, named after Secretary of State George C. Marshall, that provided extensive American aid to Western Europe after World War II.

North Atlantic Treaty Organization (NATO)
The first peacetime military treaty joined by the United States; NATO is a collective security pact that includes the United States, Canada, and Western Europe.

Berlin Wall
A barrier built by East Germany in 1961 to cut off democratic West Berlin from communist East Berlin.

Cuban Missile Crisis
The 1962 confrontation over the deployment of ballistic missiles in Cuba that nearly escalated into nuclear war between the United States and the Soviet Union.

18.1

18.2

18.3

18.4

18.5

détente
The improvement in relations between the United States and the Soviet Union that occurred during the 1970s.

human rights
The protection of people's basic freedoms and needs.

in Southeast Asia. After being defeated on the battlefield in 1954, France negotiated a withdrawal from Vietnam. The resultant Geneva Peace Accords temporarily divided Vietnam at the 17th parallel, with communist forces in control of the North and a noncommunist government in control of the South. A unification election scheduled for 1956 was never held, as South Vietnam, with the support of the United States, refused to participate. As a result, North Vietnam began a military campaign to unify the country.

The war became increasingly Americanized in the 1960s under President Lyndon B. Johnson. American forces carried out sustained and massive bombing campaigns against the North, and U.S. ground troops began fighting in the South. The war was a difficult one, fought in unfamiliar terrain with little chance of success. Casualties escalated quickly, and the American public soon turned against the war. The peace movement that emerged at this time in response to the war and the military draft significantly influenced public opinion, helping to bring about America's withdrawal from Vietnam.

In the 1970s, President Richard M. Nixon set the stage for American withdrawal by implementing a policy of Vietnamization, under which the South Vietnamese army would do the bulk of the fighting. To prepare for this turnover, the United States invaded Cambodia to clean out North Vietnamese sanctuaries and increased bombing of North Vietnam. The American strategy failed, but in the absence of public support for the war effort, U.S. forces left South Vietnam in 1973 following the Paris Peace Agreement. South Vietnam fell to communism and was reunified with the North in April 1975.

DÉTENTE AND HUMAN RIGHTS When Richard M. Nixon became president in 1969, he declared it was time to move from "an era of confrontation" to "an era of negotiation" in relations with the Soviet Union.[8] The improvement in U.S.–Soviet relations was called **détente.** At its core was a series of negotiations that aimed to use linked rewards and punishments (rather than military power) to contain the Soviet Union.

Another key element of détente was improved relations with China. Politicians at the time believed that this achievement would give the United States a potential ally against the Soviet Union. A prerequisite for playing the "China card" was diplomatic recognition of China. President Nixon took the first steps in that direction when, in 1971, he announced to a stunned world that the United States would "seek the normalization of relations." He followed up with a visit to China in 1972.

The greatest success of détente was in the area of arms control, most notably with the signing of the Strategic Arms Limitation Treaties (SALT I and SALT II), which limited the deployment of nuclear weapons. The greatest failure of détente, however, was an inability to establish agreed-upon rules to govern competition in the developing world. In Africa, Asia, and Latin America, the United States and Soviet Union each armed and supported competing sides in many civil wars. In Chile, Nixon used covert action to undermine the government of President Salvador Allende and reestablish a strong pro-American regime.

When Jimmy Carter became president in 1977, he changed the emphasis of American foreign policy from the management of the Cold War to the promotion of **human rights,** the protection of people's basic freedoms and needs. Carter's policies targeted the dictators that the United States had relied upon to contain communism. Among these was the shah of Iran, who had committed many human rights abuses against his own people. Popular unrest forced the shah into exile in 1979, but after his ouster, radical Iranians, with the support of Iran's fundamentalist Islamic government, overran the U.S. Embassy in Tehran and held the embassy staff captive for 444 days. The nation watched and waited in dismay as negotiations and military efforts to free the hostages failed. They were not released until the day Carter left office in 1981, only minutes after Ronald Reagan was sworn in as president.

THE END OF THE COLD WAR Republican President Ronald Reagan replaced Carter in the White House in January 1981. Reagan promised to reestablish American credibility and restore American military strength. The Reagan administration's commitment to combating communism by providing military assistance to anti-communist groups became known as the **Reagan Doctrine.** Two prominent examples of the Reagan Doctrine include support for anti-communist forces in Nicaragua and Afghanistan.

In Nicaragua, forty years of pro-American dictatorial rule ended in July 1979. The new Sandinista government soon began assisting rebels in El Salvador who were trying to bring down another pro-U.S. right-wing government. To block this effort, Reagan authorized creation of the **Contras,** an armed guerilla organization that opposed the Sandinista government. A connection between the controversial creation and funding of this rebel group and the sale of unauthorized arms to Iranian militants later surfaced. This resulted in what is now known as the Iran-Contra Affair, which led to congressional oversight hearings, as well as the firing and conviction of several members of the Reagan administration.

American interest in Afghanistan resulted from the Soviet Union's 1979 invasion of that country, which supported a pro-Soviet government in power. The Soviet occupation army grew to 110,000 soldiers but could never defeat the guerrilla forces, known as the mujahedeen. American military aid to the mujahedeen rose from $120 million in 1984 to $630 million in 1987, contributing to the Soviet defeat and its eventual withdrawal.

The Soviet retreat from Afghanistan was part of a larger change in Soviet policy, which resulted from the ascent of Mikhail Gorbachev. Gorbachev entered into nuclear arms control agreements with the United States, and reduced foreign aid to Soviet allies. He also implemented a series of political and economic reforms that were meant to strengthen communism, but instead they undermined it throughout the Soviet Union and Eastern Europe, leading in 1989 to the collapse of communist governments in Poland, Hungary, Czechoslovakia, Romania, Bulgaria, and East Germany, where the Berlin Wall came down. Two years later the Soviet Union collapsed and broke apart into 15 separate countries. These surprising and long-sought developments ended the Cold War, and represented the most significant occurrence in U.S. foreign policy since World War II.

The Post–Cold War World

President George Bush, who became president in 1989, sought to navigate through this new, post–Cold War world. The defining moment of the first Bush administration's foreign policy was the Persian Gulf War that was brought on by Iraq's invasion of Kuwait in August 1990. Proclaiming that the end of the Cold War was ushering in a "new world order" unaffected by the superpower rivalry, Bush turned to the United Nations, whose members voted to impose economic sanctions and authorized the use of force. Congress did likewise. In January 1991, Operation Desert Storm began with an air campaign against Iraq. Ground forces arrived in February, and after six weeks, the US-led coalition forces were victorious in removing Iraqi forces from Kuwait.

The United States also sought to strengthen ties with China. However, on June 4, 1989, Chinese troops attacked pro-democracy demonstrators on Tiananmen Square, killing hundreds of people. As a result, President Bush suspended political contact and imposed economic sanctions, but he also secretly sent a delegation to China to make sure that broader U.S. security and economic interests were not permanently harmed.

Bush's successor in office, Bill Clinton, sought to define a clear role for the United States in world affairs now that a dismantled Soviet Union no longer posed a clear and present danger. The president chose to pursue a policy of **democratic enlargement,** or actively promoting the expansion of democracy and free markets throughout the world.

Economic enlargement centered primarily on the issue of trade and the expansion of globalization. Clinton secured Senate approval for the North American Free Trade Agreement (NAFTA), an agreement promoting free movement of goods and services among Canada, Mexico, and the United States. He followed up this success by obtaining Senate approval for permanent most favored nation status for China and completing negotiations that led to the establishment of the **World Trade Organization (WTO),** which replaced the GATT, expanding its scope and adding a new judicial body to resolve trade disputes. Democratic enlargement involved securing democratic change in Eastern Europe by bringing former Soviet allies into the NATO alliance, and supporting their admission into the **European Union.**

Reagan Doctrine
The Reagan administration's commitment to ending communism by providing military assistance to anti-communist groups.

Contras
An armed guerilla organization that opposed Nicaragua's Sandinista government and received funding and arms from the U.S.

democratic enlargement
Policy implemented during the Clinton administration in which the United States would actively promote the expansion of democracy and free markets throughout the world.

World Trade Organization (WTO)
An international organization that replaced the GATT in 1995 to supervise and expand international trade.

European Union
An organization that joins 27 countries in Europe into a union that includes free trade, a central bank, a common currency, ease of immigration, a European Parliament, and other political institutions to govern and administer the organization.

18.1
18.2
18.3
18.4
18.5

Explore Your World

All countries spend some proportion of their national budget on military and defense expenditures, but no country spends as much as the United States. In 2011, the United States spent $711 billion, accounting for 41 percent of the world's total military spending ($1.7 trillion). The next highest spender, China, accounts for only one-fifth of the U.S. total.

The United States spends far more on its military than any other country. This is reflected in U.S. bases around the world, military operations in places like Iraq and Afghanistan, and the significant foreign policy role that the United States plays involving issues and problems around the world.

Country	Dollars (billions)	% of World Total
United States	711.0	41.0%
China	143.0	8.2%
Russia	71.9	4.1%
United Kingdom	62.7	3.6%
France	62.5	3.6%
Japan	59.3	3.4%
Saudi Arabia	48.5	2.8%
India	48.9	2.8%
Germany	46.7	2.7%
Brazil	35.4	2.0%
Italy	34.5	2.0%
South Korea	30.8	1.8%
Australia	26.7	1.5%
Canada	24.7	1.4%
Turkey	17.9	1.0%
Rest of the World	312.6	18.0%

In spite of the close economic ties that the United States and China maintain, many in the United States believe that China represents a rising threat and is likely to become a significant strategic competitor to the United States in the coming decades.

Historically, countries with the strongest economies have enjoyed the greatest military power. The graph demonstrates that today, this is still the case, as countries that currently have large and/or rapidly growing economies top the list of military spending.

SOURCE: Stockholm International Peace Research Institute, "The 15 Countries with the Highest Military Expenditure in 2011," www.sipri.org/research/armaments/milex/resultoutput/milex_15.

CRITICAL THINKING QUESTIONS

1. Are these numbers surprising? Why or why not?
2. What do you think accounts for the high level of U.S. military spending?
3. In 2004, China spent $57.5 billion on defense, representing 4% of the world's total military spending. Now it spends far more. How might China's rapid increase in military spending impact its relations with the United States?

At the same time, the United States aimed to address the civil wars and ethnic conflict that had erupted in several failed states. In Somalia, clashes with rebels killed eighteen American soldiers in 1993, producing vivid media images and the withdrawal of U.S. forces. In Yugoslavia, which began to splinter in 1991, the government unleashed a campaign of "ethnic cleansing," which included: (1) the deliberate, forcible removal of particular ethnic groups from parts of the disintegrating country; (2) the killing of thousands of people; and, (3) the mass raping of women and girls. In 1995, international pressures and American involvement allowed for a political resolution to this conflict. In 1999, ethnic cleansing and fighting in Kosovo, a part of Yugoslavia, led to American intervention and the fall of the Yugoslav government, whose leader was later put on trial for human rights violations against his own people. And in Haiti, thousands took to the sea and headed to the United States in makeshift boats to flee the violence that followed the ouster of President Jean-Bertrand Aristide by the military. The United States threatened invasion to restore Aristide to power, but this was avoided when a delegation led by former President Jimmy Carter arranged for the return of Aristide to office peacefully.

☐ September 11, 2001, and the War on Terrorism

During the 2000 presidential campaign, George W. Bush greatly criticized President Bill Clinton's foreign policy. Bush's soon-to-be National Security Advisor, Condoleezza Rice, summarized his views on foreign policy when she wrote that their administration would "exercise power without arrogance" and forsake an overly broad definition of American national interests that led to frequent interventions into humanitarian crises.[9]

At first, the Bush administration largely adhered to this agenda and distanced itself from Clinton's foreign policy legacy. The administration rejected the international global warming treaty known as the Kyoto Protocol, withdrew from the Anti-Ballistic Missile Treaty, and refused to participate in the formation of the International Criminal Court. The terrorist attacks of September 11, 2001, however, ushered in a new era in American foreign policy.

SEPTEMBER 11 AND THE WAR IN AFGHANISTAN On September 11, 2001, nineteen members of the al-Qaeda terrorist organization headed by Osama bin Laden

HOW DID THE SEPTEMBER 11 TERRORIST ATTACKS AFFECT AMERICAN FOREIGN POLICY?

The twin towers of the World Trade Center collapsed September 11, 2001, after they were struck by hijacked airplanes. The attacks caused enormous loss of life and resulted in the beginning of an ongoing war on terrorism.

global war on terrorism
An international action, initiated by President George W. Bush after the 9/11 attacks, to weed out terrorist operatives throughout the world.

Taliban
A fundamentalist Islamic group that controlled Afghanistan from 1996 until U.S. military intervention in 2001. The Taliban provided refuge for al-Qaeda, allowing terrorist training camps to operate in the country.

hijacked four U.S. commercial airliners and crashed two of them into the World Trade Center in New York City and one into the Pentagon near Washington, D.C. The fourth plane crashed into an open field in Somerset County, Pennsylvania. More than 3,000 people lost their lives that day.

The United States responded by declaring a **global war on terrorism** to weed out terrorist operatives throughout the world. It demanded that the **Taliban**-led government of Afghanistan expel Osama bin Laden and al-Qaeda and sever its ties with international terrorist groups. When this did not occur, the United States began aerial strikes against terrorist facilities and Taliban military targets inside Afghanistan on October 7, 2001. On the ground, the United States sent troops, who relied heavily on support from troops provided by the Northern Alliance, a coalition in the country that opposed the Taliban. The Taliban proved no match for this combination of air and ground power, and its last stronghold fell on December 16. Osama bin Laden was not captured, and the Taliban and al-Qaeda began pursuing a guerrilla war against American troops and the new Afghan government. American forces have remained in Afghanistan since that time. President Barack Obama, who succeeded George W. Bush in office in 2009, increased the number of American troops there to better protect the government and defeat the Taliban, but the effort has not been entirely successful, nor has the war effort been popular with the American public. The president has promised to have most of the troops home by 2014.

THE WAR IN IRAQ A broader foreign policy agenda emerged in President Bush's 2002 State of the Union Address. In this speech, Bush identified Iraq, North Korea, and Iran as an "axis of evil" that threatened American security interests. The administration moved toward war with Iraq, a controversial decision that divided the United States. Following a series of authorization negotiations with Congress, Operation Iraqi Freedom began on March 19, 2003, with a decapitation strike aimed at targets in Baghdad, Iraq's capital city. On April 9, Baghdad fell, and one month later, Bush declared the "mission accomplished."

The Bush administration did not prepare for a long or contested occupation of Iraq, but the reality of ground warfare soon challenged this vision. Forces opposing the new government and the presence of American troops launched a guerrilla war. American casualties began to rise, and in September 2004, U.S. casualties reached 1,000. By mid-2008, more than 4,000 U.S. military personnel and Department of Defense civilians had died in Iraq, and 30,000 had been wounded, prompting increased calls for an end to the war. The Obama administration came into office pledging to end the war in Iraq. It announced an end to formal combat operations in 2010, and in December 2011, the last U.S. combat forces left Iraq, leaving nearly 50,000 troops in an advisory capacity. However, violence in the country continues.

Foreign and Defense Policy Decision Making

18.3 Outline the factors that shape foreign and defense policy decision making.

Explore on MyPoliSciLab Simulation: You Are a President During a Foreign Policy Crisis

The basic structure of foreign and defense policy decision making is laid out in the Constitution. The executive branch is the most powerful branch of government in the formulation and implementation of U.S. foreign and defense policy. Congress also influences and shapes policy through oversight, treaties, appointments, appropriations, and the War Powers Resolution. The judiciary has a more limited role in foreign and defense affairs, usually addressing questions of executive authority. In addition, interest groups such as the military-industrial complex also play an important role.

Explore on MyPoliSciLab

How Much Does America Spend on Defense?

The United States has the largest defense budget in the world, but many observers still ask "Do we spend enough?" At the end of the Vietnam War, Americans all agreed that defense spending should be increased. Since then, Democrats and Independents became more "dovish" (anti-defense spending), while Republicans became far more "hawkish" (pro-defense spending). These differences became most pronounced in the years following the Iraq War and after George W. Bush's reelection in 2004.

Partisan Differences over Defense Spending

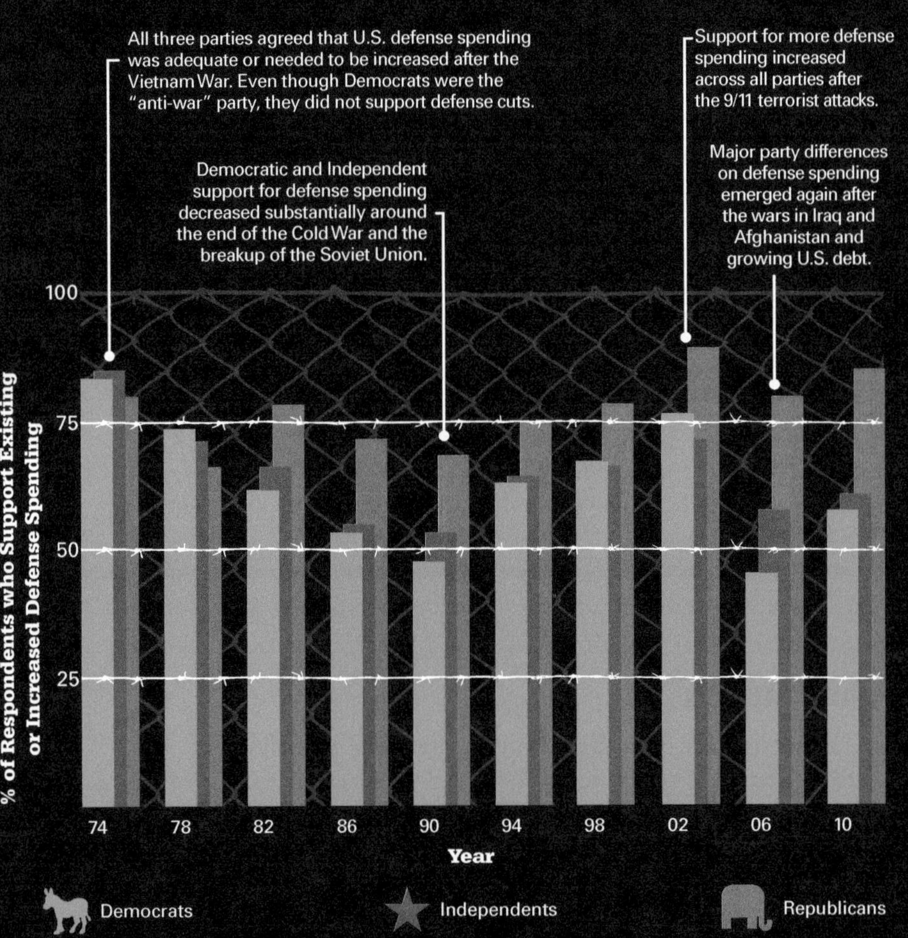

All three parties agreed that U.S. defense spending was adequate or needed to be increased after the Vietnam War. Even though Democrats were the "anti-war" party, they did not support defense cuts.
Democratic and Independent support for defense spending decreased substantially around the end of the Cold War and the breakup of the Soviet Union.
Support for more defense spending increased across all parties after the 9/11 terrorist attacks.
Major party differences on defense spending emerged again after the wars in Iraq and Afghanistan and growing U.S. debt.
100
75
50
25
% of Respondents who Support Existing or Increased Defense Spending
74
78
82
86
90
94
98
02
06
10
Year
Democrats
Independents
Republicans

The United States Spends the Most on Defense

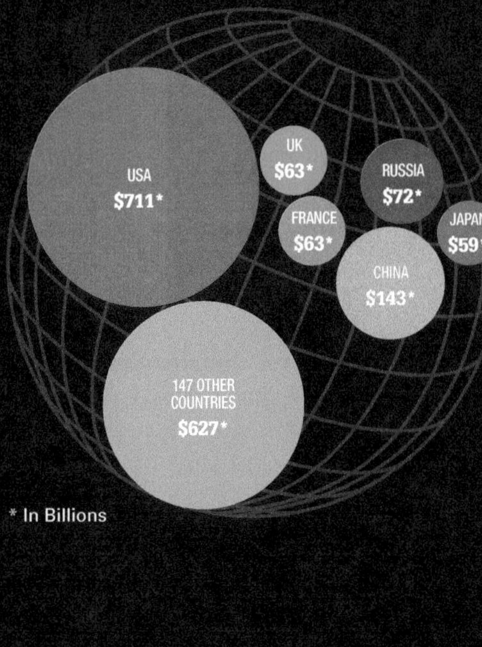

* In Billions

SOURCE: Data from Stockholm International Peace Research Institute (SIPRI) Yearbook, www.sipri.org; and the General Social Survey, 1982-2010.

Investigate Further

Concept Do Americans view defense spending as excessive? The United States currently has the largest defense budget in the world—twice the amount of China, the U.K., France, Japan, and Russia combined. But most Americans think the U.S. spends enough or should spend even more on defense.

Connection How do events relate to changes in support for defense spending? Wars, terrorist attacks, and recessions all influence public opinion of government spending. After the Cold War, both parties agreed not to maintain or increase the defense budget. After the 9/11 attacks, both parties supported increased spending.

Cause How does partisanship shape perceptions of defense spending? Democrats and Independents are more likely than Republicans to say that we spend too much on defense. These differences have become more pronounced in the last decade as the global war on terrorism became increasingly politicized.

18.1

18.2

18.3

18.4

18.5

> *To provide for calling forth the Militia to execute the Laws of the Union, suppress Insurrections and repel Invasions;*
>
> *To provide for organizing, arming, and disciplining, the Militia, and for governing such Part of them as may be employed in the Service of the United States . . .* —ARTICLE I, SECTION 8

A fundamental weakness of the Articles of Confederation was that it did not grant the national government adequate means for national defense. This defect hampered the Revolutionary War effort. These clauses of the Constitution consequently give the federal government the authority to call up the state militias in times of national emergency or distress. The clauses address the understanding that military training, proficiency, and organization should be uniform across state and national forces, to ensure effectiveness and efficiency in military operations.

Despite the fact that the militia clauses passed the convention, many Anti-Federalists were concerned that the federal government would call together the state militias for unjust ends. They believed that state governments should control their militias in order to prevent any deceit on the part of the federal government. To this end, the Constitution gives the states authority to name militia officers and train their forces. During the War of 1812—to the consternation of President James Madison—two state governments withheld their militias from the national government. The Supreme Court has since held that, except for constitutional prohibitions, the Congress has "unlimited" authority over the state militias. In addition, the National Defense Act of 1916 mandated the use of the term "National Guard" and gave the president authority to mobilize the National Guard during times of national emergency or war.

Throughout U.S. history, the National Guard has proven effective and essential in defending the United States. The National Guard, for example, plays a significant role in American efforts in Iraq and Afghanistan. The militia clauses ensure the unity, effectiveness, and strength of the U.S. military not only during wartime but also during other national emergencies.

CRITICAL THINKING QUESTIONS

1. **According to the Constitution, the president is the commander in chief of the armed forces. But, Congress has the power to organize the military, fund it, and call it to duty. How does this division of authority work in practice?**
2. **Should individual states retain the right to withhold National Guard troops if the state government does not approve of the way the president intends to use them?**

☐ The Constitution

When the Framers of the U.S. Constitution met in Philadelphia in 1789, they wanted a stronger national government to keep the United States out of European affairs and to keep Europe out of American affairs. As a result, they bequeathed the power to formulate and implement foreign policy to the national government rather than the states. In addition, many foreign and military powers not enumerated in the Constitution were accorded to the national government.

The Framers of the Constitution divided national authority for foreign and military policy functions between the president and Congress. The Framers named the president commander in chief of the armed forces but gave Congress power to fund the army and navy and to declare war. The president has authority to negotiate and sign treaties, but those agreements take effect only after the Senate ratifies them by a two-thirds majority. Similarly, the president appoints ambassadors and other key foreign and military affairs officials, but the Senate grants advice and a majority of senators must give their consent to nominees. Ultimately, all such actions are subject to judicial review.

The Constitution provides a starting point for understanding the way in which the president and Congress come together to make U.S. foreign policy. It does not, however, provide the final word on how they will interact. As we are often reminded, the Constitution is best seen as an "invitation to struggle." Consider, for example, the war powers. Congress has declared only five wars: (1) the War of 1812; (2) the Spanish-American War; (3) the Mexican-American War; (4) World War I; and, (5) World War II. However, presidents have deployed troops overseas without congressional approval more than 125 times.[10]

☐ The Executive Branch

The executive branch is the central place for creating and implementing U.S. foreign and defense policy, and within the executive branch, the president is the most important individual. Among executive departments, the Department of State is primarily responsible for diplomatic activity and the Department of Defense for military policy. Other parts of the executive branch, such as the National Security Council, the Joint Chiefs of Staff, and the Central Intelligence Agency, provide additional resources for the president. The Department of Homeland Security also functions in foreign and defense policy making.

THE PRESIDENT The president is preeminent in foreign and defense policy. As the Framers intended, presidents have greater access to and control over information than any other government official or agency, and the president alone can act with little fear that his actions will be countermanded. As such, we tend to discuss U.S. foreign policy in terms of presidential action. For example, Ronald Reagan ordered air strikes against Libya and the invasion of Grenada, and Barack Obama committed additional U.S. troops to Afghanistan.

Presidents have also come to rely increasingly on organizations and individuals located within the White House to help them make foreign policy. The most notable of these organizations is the National Security Council (NSC), led by the national security adviser. The NSC brings together key foreign policy actors, including the vice president, the secretaries of state and of defense, intelligence officials, military leaders, and other presidential advisers. The organization's primary goal is to advise and assist the president on foreign and defense policy, particularly in crisis situations when speed in decision making is essential. Originally, the national security adviser was a neutral voice in the decision-making process, but over time, this appointee has become a powerful

WHO ARE THE PRESIDENT'S FOREIGN AND DEFENSE POLICY ADVISERS?

The secretaries of state and defense, along with the Joint Chiefs of Staff and the intelligence community, are among the most important advisers to the president. Here, President Obama announces his national security team, including Secretary of Homeland Security Janet Napolitano, Secretary of Defense Robert Gates, Vice President Joe Biden, Secretary of State Hillary Clinton, National Security Advisor General James Jones, and Ambassador to the United Nations Susan Rice.

18.1

18.2

18.3

18.4

18.5

Department of State
Chief executive branch department responsible for formulation and implementation of U.S. foreign policy.

Department of Defense
Chief executive branch department responsible for formulation and implementation of U.S. defense and military policy.

Joint Chiefs of Staff
Military advisory body that includes the Army chief of staff, the Air Force chief of staff, the chief of naval operations, and the Marine commandant.

Department of Homeland Security
Cabinet department created after the 9/11 terrorist attacks to coordinate domestic security efforts.

voice, independent of the president, in policy making. Former national security advisers include Henry Kissinger, Colin Powell, and Condoleezza Rice.

THE DEPARTMENTS OF STATE, DEFENSE, AND HOMELAND SECURITY According to tradition, the **Department of State,** one of the first Cabinet agencies created by George Washington, is the chief executive branch department responsible for formulation and implementation of U.S. foreign policy. The Department of State serves as a link between foreign governments and U.S. policy makers and as a source of advice on how to deal with problems.

Today the Department of State's position of prominence has been challenged from many directions. Within the White House, the national security adviser may have competing views. In addition, the complexity of foreign policy problems has increased the importance of views held by the Departments of Defense, Treasury, and Commerce. Complexity has also made managing foreign policy more difficult. The ambassador is often described as head of the "country team" that operates inside a U.S. embassy. In the U.S. Embassy in Mexico, for example, this means not only coordinating Department of State officials but also individuals from the Departments of Defense, Agriculture, Commerce, Labor, and Homeland Security, as well as the Federal Bureau of Investigation, the Drug Enforcement Agency, and the U.S. Trade Representative.

The **Department of Defense** is the chief executive branch department responsible for formulation and implementation of U.S. military policy. It came into existence after World War II, when the War Department and the Navy Department were combined into a single agency for military affairs. Still, within the department numerous lines of disagreement exist. Among the most prominent are those between professional military officers and civilians working in the Office of the Secretary of Defense, and between the separate branches of the armed services (Army, Navy, Air Force, and Marines) over missions, weapons, and priorities. To overcome these differences in outlook, the president relies on the **Joint Chiefs of Staff,** the military advisory body that includes the Army chief of staff, the Air Force chief of staff, the chief of naval operations, and the Marine commandant.

The **Department of Homeland Security,** the Cabinet department created after the 9/11 terrorist attacks to coordinate domestic security efforts, straddles the line between foreign and domestic policy making. The department brought together twenty-two existing agencies, approximately thirty newly created agencies or offices, and 180,000 employees into a single agency. Among its key units are the Transportation Security Administration (TSA), the organization responsible for aviation security; the Federal Emergency Management Agency (FEMA), the primary federal disaster relief organization; Customs and Border Protection; the U.S. Coast Guard; the Secret Service; and immigration services and enforcement.

THE INTELLIGENCE COMMUNITY The intelligence community is a term used to describe the agencies of the U.S. government that are involved in the collection and analysis of information, counterintelligence (the protection of U.S. intelligence), and covert action. The head of the intelligence community is the Director of National Intelligence (DNI). Until this position was created after the 9/11 terrorist attacks, the head of the Central Intelligence Agency (CIA) held this position.

Beyond the CIA, other key members of the intelligence community include the Bureau of Intelligence and Research in the Department of State, the Defense Intelligence Agency, the military service intelligence agencies, the National Security Agency in the Department of Defense, the Federal Bureau of Investigation, and the Department of Homeland Security. Coordinating these units can be difficult. Each has control over its own budget, and they do not always share intelligence information with each other.

☐ Congress

While the U.S. Constitution specifies several responsibilities for Congress, in practice it has much less influence over foreign and defense policy than does the president.

Congress also tends to be deferential to the executive in times of war or threats to national security. For example, the attacks on September 11, 2001, prompted adoption of the USA PATRIOT Act, a law proposed by the Department of Justice and passed by Congress in October 2001. The law gave the government greater law enforcement authority to gather intelligence domestically, detain and deport immigrants, search business and personal records, and conduct wiretaps. Nevertheless, the legislative branch plays a significant role in the policy process. Congress influences foreign and defense policy through its congressional leadership, oversight, approval of treaties and appointments, appropriations, and the War Powers Resolution.

OVERSIGHT The most common method of congressional oversight is holding hearings that monitor agency activities, as well as the content and conduct of U.S. policy. Another method is the establishment of reporting requirements. The Department of State, for example, is required to submit annual evaluations of other nations' human rights practices, religious freedoms, anti-drug and narcotics efforts, stance on human trafficking, and nuclear proliferation activities. A particularly famous reporting requirement is the Hughes-Ryan Amendment, passed in 1974, which requires that "except under exceptional circumstances" the president notify Congress "in a timely fashion" of CIA covert actions. Members of Congress also engage in oversight of foreign and defense policy by visiting other countries, where they conduct "fact finding" missions and meet with political leaders, businesspeople, and even dissidents.

TREATIES AND EXECUTIVE AGREEMENTS The Constitution gives the Senate explicit power to approve treaties, but the Senate has rejected treaties only twenty

HOW DOES CONGRESS EXERCISE FOREIGN AFFAIRS OVERSIGHT?

One of the roles of Congress is to oversee U.S. foreign policy. This includes not only Congressional hearings and legislation, but also fact finding trips overseas and meetings with foreign leaders. Here, former Speaker of the House Nancy Pelosi meets with Prime Minister Nuri al-Maliki of Iraq.

War Powers Resolution
Passed by Congress in 1973; the president is limited in the deployment of troops overseas to a sixty-day period in peacetime (which can be extended for an extra thirty days to permit withdrawal) unless Congress explicitly gives its approval for a longer period.

times in U.S. history.[11] The most famous of these unapproved treaties is the Treaty of Versailles, which established the League of Nations, later to be replaced by the United Nations by Senate confirmation. More recently, in 1999, the Senate rejected the Comprehensive Test Ban Treaty, which prohibits testing of nuclear weapons among the 157 countries that have currently approved it.

Presidents can avoid the treaty process by using executive agreements, which, unlike treaties, do not require Senate approval. Prior to 1972, the president did not have to inform Congress of the text of these accords. Although many executive agreements deal with routine foreign policy matters, a great many also involve major military commitments on the part of the United States. Among them are agreements allowing for military bases in the Philippines (Truman) and defense in Saudi Arabia (George Bush).

APPOINTMENTS Although the Constitution gives the president the power to appoint ambassadors and others involved in foreign and defense policy, it bestows upon the Senate the responsibility to provide advice and consent on these appointments. The Senate has not exercised this power in any systematic fashion. It has approved nominees with little expertise largely on the basis of their party affiliation and contributions to presidential campaign funds. It has also rejected otherwise qualified nominees because of objections to the president's foreign policies.

Presidents have long circumvented congressional approval by using and creating new positions not subject to Senate confirmation. Most recent presidents have created policy "czars" to coordinate the administration's foreign policy in specific areas. President Obama, for example, has established czars for the Middle East peace process, border security with Mexico, and the war in Afghanistan.

APPROPRIATIONS Congress also shapes foreign and defense policy through its power to appropriate funds, and it influences when and where the United States fights through its control of the budget. Although the power to go to war is shared by the executive and legislative branches of government, the power to appropriate funds belongs to the legislature alone. One example of this appropriation power occurred in 2007, when Congress considered several bills introduced to end U.S. military involvement in Iraq. The proposals, which did not pass, called upon President George W. Bush to begin withdrawing troops from Iraq, and would have prohibited funding for U.S. combat operations beyond a fixed date.[12]

A significant problem faced by Congress in using budgetary powers to set the foreign policy agenda is that after the president publicly commits the United States to a high-profile course of action, it is hard for Congress to stop effort on that initiative. This is why trying to to stop the war in Iraq by cutting appropriations failed. Once U.S. troops were already involved in combat, any effort to cut funding was seen as a lack of support for American troops (see Figure 18.1).

THE WAR POWERS RESOLUTION Frustrated with its inability to influence policy on Vietnam, a war that deeply divided the nation, Congress passed the **War Powers Resolution** in 1973 to try preventing future interventions overseas without specific congressional approval. Under the resolution, the president is required to consult with Congress before deploying American troops into hostile situations. Under certain conditions, the president is required to report to Congress within forty-eight hours of the deployment. A presidential report can trigger a sixty-day clock that requires congressional approval for any continued military involvement past the sixty-day window. If Congress does not give explicit approval within sixty days, the president then has thirty days to withdraw the troops. Under the resolution, the president can respond to an emergency such as rescuing endangered Americans but cannot engage in a prolonged struggle without congressional approval.

The War Powers Resolution is controversial and has not been an effective restraint on presidential military authority. No president has recognized its constitutionality, nor has any president felt obligated to inform Congress of military action. President

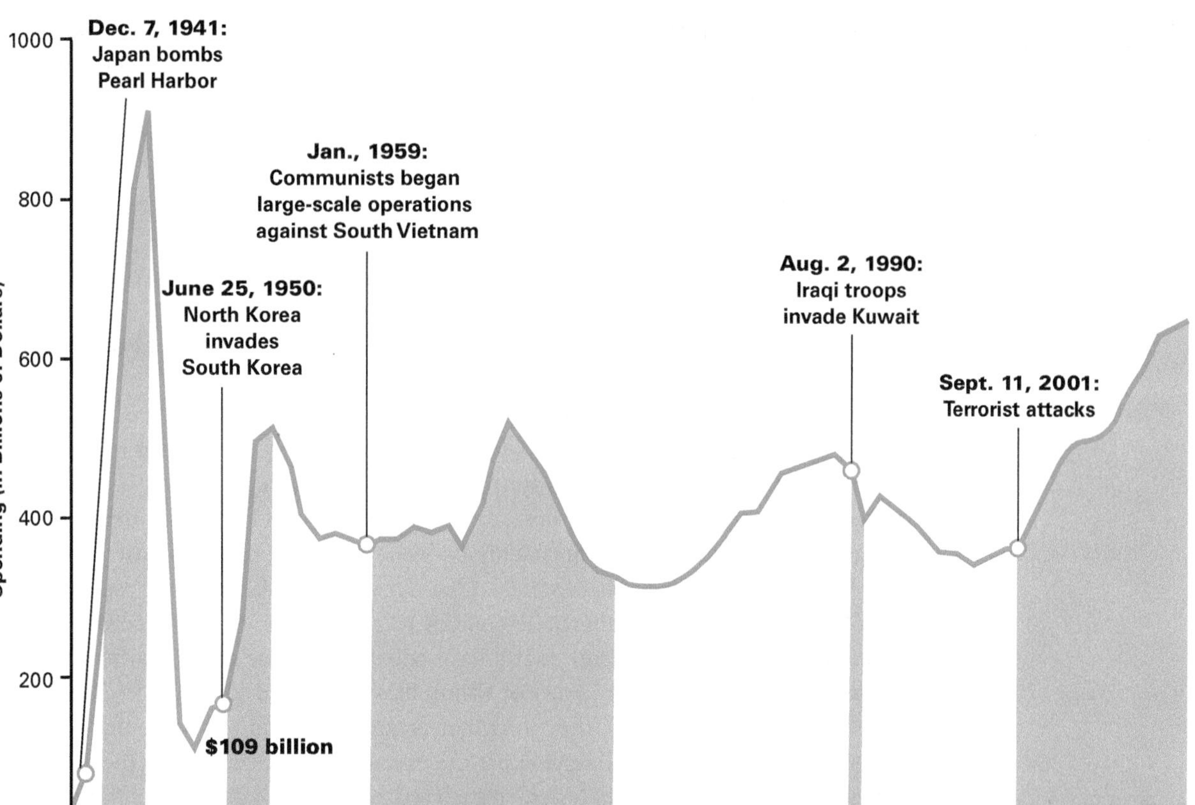

FIGURE 18.1 HOW HAS DEFENSE SPENDING CHANGED OVER TIME?

Defense spending was at its highest absolute levels during World War II. Today, as a result of the wars in Iraq and Afghanistan, it continues to stand at relatively high levels, about $644 billion constant dollars in 2010.

SOURCE: Mackenzie Eaglen, "U.S. Defense Spending: The Mismatch Between Plans and Resources," *The Heritage Foundation* (June 7, 2010): www.heritage.org.

Jimmy Carter argued that his unsuccessful Iranian hostage mission was a humanitarian effort that fell outside the scope of the War Powers Resolution. President Reagan stated that U.S. Marines were invited into Lebanon and therefore he did not have to tell Congress. And, President Clinton said he did not need to inform Congress when he sent troops to Haiti because he was implementing a UN resolution.

☐ The Judiciary

The judicial branch has a limited role in foreign policy, as the courts have usually avoided clearly demarcating executive and legislative functions in this area. The judiciary has generally regarded most disputes over foreign policy to be political in nature, and thus not subject to judicial rulings. For example, with regard to the War Powers Act, at times the president's authority to deploy troops has been challenged by members of Congress. In all instances, however, the courts have dismissed the cases. Most recently, a lawsuit filed by ten members of Congress against President Obama for sending U.S. forces to Libya was thrown out of court.

Sometimes, however, the courts do step in to determine the appropriate role for each branch when a dispute arises in the realm of foreign policy. Such cases most likely involve the extent of executive authority with respect to protecting the nation's security. And, just like Congress, the courts tend to be deferential to the president in times of war or threats to security.

military-industrial complex
The network of political and financial relations formed by defense industries, the U.S. armed forces, and Congress.

During the Civil War, the Supreme Court ruled in *The Prize Cases* on the powers of the president as sole commander in chief of the armed forces, authorizing President Abraham Lincoln's deployment of troops without a declaration of war from Congress.[13] In another case from this period, the Supreme Court held in *ex parte McCardle* that the suspension of habeas corpus initiated by the president in certain cases was constitutional, since the jurisdiction of the courts in such cases had been stripped by Congress.[14]

During World War II, President Franklin D. Roosevelt adopted the policy of forcing Japanese Americans from their homes and into internment camps, on the understanding that they represented a threat to national security. When this policy was challenged in *Korematsu* v. *United States* (1944), the Supreme Court upheld the policy as constitutional, saying that it was not a violation of the Fourteenth Amendment, nor a violation of the government's constitutional authority.[15] Korematsu's conviction was reversed by a federal district court in 1983, but the Supreme Court's decision was never overturned although Congress finally appropriated reparative funds.

More recently, the U.S. response to the attacks of 9/11 has resulted in several instances of judicial rulings on presidential powers, the most significant of which have involved the U.S. detainment center in Guantanamo Bay, Cuba. In these cases, the courts have not been consistently deferential to the executive—the record has been mixed. For example, the federal courts have ruled on habeas corpus with respect to detainees at Guantanamo Bay, some of whom have been held for years. In *Boumediene* v. *Bush* (2008), the Supreme Court held that detainees should not be denied access to petitions of habeas corpus, ruling against the executive and overturning the actions of lower courts, which had routinely denied such reviews.[16] In 2012, however, the Supreme Court seemed to ignore its earlier ruling, upholding the actions of lower courts by denying review of the petitions of several detainees. The Supreme Court also ruled against the executive in *Hamdan* v. *Rumsfeld* (2004).[17] The Court said that the military tribunals set up to try detainees at Guantanamo could not proceed, since they did not conform to U.S. law. Subsequent legislation, however, authorized the military tribunals, and the Court has upheld this authority.

☐ Interest Groups

Four types of interest groups are especially active in trying to influence foreign and defense policy decisions. Business groups are the first type that lobbies heavily on foreign policy issues. Particularly controversial is the lobbying carried out by defense industries, often in cooperation with the military. These groups are often identified as part of the **military-industrial complex,** a term coined by President Dwight D. Eisenhower.

Ethnic interest groups are a second type of group heavily involved in foreign policy decision making. The American-Israel Public Affairs Committee (AIPAC) and the Cuban-American National Foundation (CANF) are generally the two most influential groups. Periodically, Trans Africa has also emerged as an important foreign policy lobbying force for the African American community. Among the most significant new ethnic lobbying groups are ones centered on Indian Americans and Pakistani Americans.

Foreign governments and companies are a third type of organized lobbying interest. The most common concerns of foreign governments are acquiring foreign aid and preventing hostile legislation from being passed. Turkey, for example, has lobbied extensively to prevent Congress from passing resolutions cutting off foreign aid and labeling as genocide the deaths of Armenians at the hands of Turks around the time of World War I. Foreign companies also actively lobby to gain access to the American market and improve the terms under which their investments in the United States are made.

Ideological-public interest groups are the final type of group active in foreign policy lobbying. This broad category encompasses think tanks such as the Brookings Institution and the Heritage Foundation, nongovernmental organizations such as Amnesty International and Greenpeace, and religious organizations. Opinions on major foreign policy issues such as military interventionism, free trade, and environmental agreements often vary widely on the basis of the political ideology held by these organizations.

Contemporary Challenges in Foreign and Defense Policy

18.4 Identify contemporary foreign and defense policy challenges confronting the United States.

he United States faces a series of foreign and defense policy challenges. In this section we highlight three of the most pressing concerns: (1) trade; (2) terrorism; and, (3) the spread of nuclear weapons. For each, we present an overview of basic concepts, a survey of policy options, and a case study.

Trade

Countries adopt one of three basic approaches in constructing their international trade policy: (1) protectionism; (2) strategic trade; and, (3) free trade. In practice, most countries use some elements of each approach. First, countries may engage in **protectionism.** In this trade policy, a country takes steps to limit the import of foreign goods. It may also provide domestic producers with subsidies to help them compete against foreign imports. The early American system was rooted in protectionist thinking. So, too, was global trade policy in the 1930s, when, as a result of the Great Depression, the United States and other countries tried to "export unemployment" and protect jobs.

Second, countries may embrace a **strategic trade policy.** Under such a policy, governments identify key industries that they want to see grow. They then provide those industries with economic support through tax breaks, low-interest loans, and other benefits. In the United States, computers, aerospace, and biotechnology are sectors that have often been singled out for support. The driving force behind modern American strategic trade policy is China. It is now the second largest market for new cars. General Motors has sold millions of cars in China over the past several years, after going through a bankruptcy managed by the U.S. government. In 2011, the United States exported \$104 billion worth of goods to China while at the same time importing \$399 billion worth of goods from China, for a trade balance deficit of \$295 billion.[18]

Finally, countries may choose a **free trade system.** The hallmark of such a system is limited government interference in international trade. Instead, goods and services cross borders according to supply and demand, as well as the principle of comparative advantage, in which countries sell goods they can produce most efficiently and buy from countries what they cannot. Creating and supporting a free trade system has been a major goal of U.S. trade policy since World War II.

MAKING TRADE POLICY Three broad policy options exist for the United States under a free trade approach. The first is to emphasize bilateral trade, or that between two nations. Bilateral agreements have a rich history in the United States and continue to be used today. President George W. Bush was able to gain congressional approval for bilateral trade agreements with Australia, Chile, and Singapore. Under President Obama, Congress approved long-stalled trade agreements with South Korea, Colombia, and Panama.

In an attempt to adapt to globalization and incorporate a greater number of trading partners, presidents have increasingly turned to regional trade agreements. Such agreements involve more than two but as few as three states. This was the case with the 1994 **North American Free Trade Agreement (NAFTA),** which further unites the economies of Mexico, Canada, and the United States. NAFTA created the world's largest regional free trade area with a market of some 450 million people and \$17 trillion in goods and services produced annually. American exports to Canada and Mexico have increased greatly, and the U.S. economy has grown significantly since NAFTA was enacted, but criticism of the agreement is widespread. The major criticisms are that American manufacturing jobs have been lost to companies establishing operations in

protectionism
A trade policy wherein a country takes steps to limit the import of foreign goods through tariffs and subsidies to domestic firms.

strategic trade policy
A trade policy wherein governments identify key industries that they wish to see grow and enact policies to support their development and success.

free trade system
A system of international trade that has limited government interference on the sale of goods and services among countries.

North American Free Trade Agreement (NAFTA)
Agreement that promotes free movement of goods and services among Canada, Mexico, and the United States.

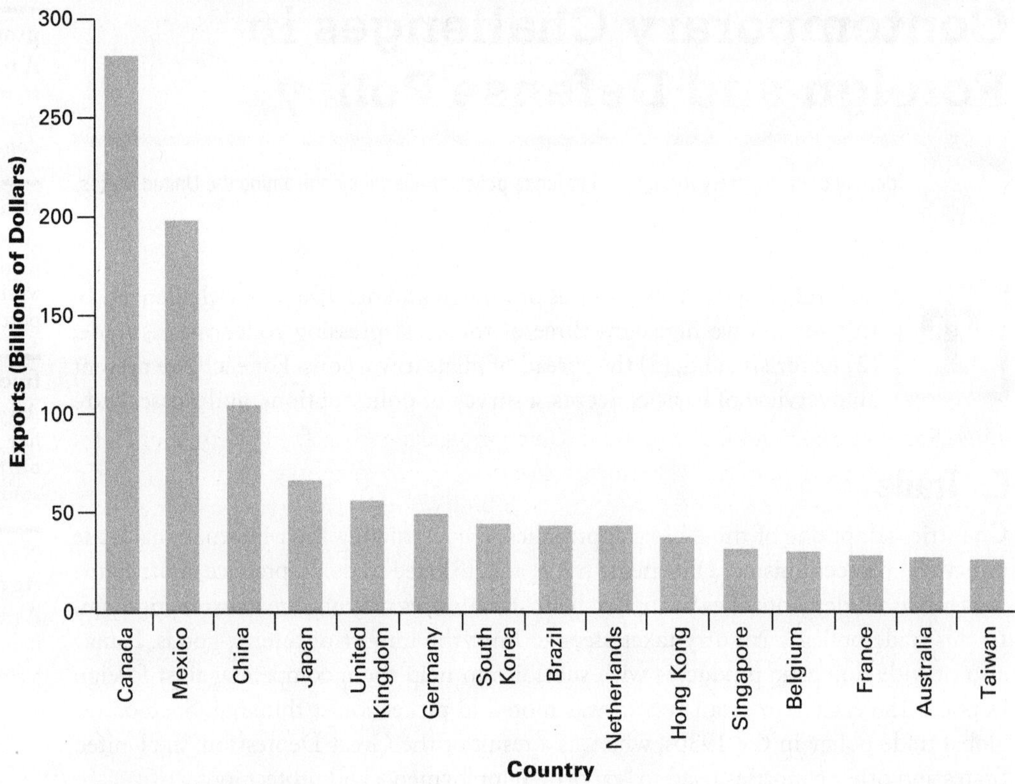

FIGURE 18.2 WHO ARE THE UNITED STATES' MAJOR TRADING PARTNERS?

The United States exports more goods to Canada than any other country. China, Mexico, and Japan also account for large shares of U.S. exports.

SOURCE: U.S. Census Bureau, Foreign Trade Statistics.

Mexico (where labor is cheaper) and that salaries have stagnated for jobs in the United States. (To learn more about the United States' major trading partners, see Figure 18.2.)

A wide variety of issues produce congressional opposition to bilateral and regional trade agreements. Among the most frequent are concerns for workers' rights, labor standards, and environmental protection policies. Presidents have sought to overcome congressional opposition and tried to stop legislators from inserting amendments to these agreements by obtaining what is known as fast track authority. Congress gives this power to the president for a specific period of time. It requires that Congress may vote on—but not amend—trade agreements concluded by the president.

Most modern trade agreements are concluded under a global free trade system. The best known (but not always the most successful) example of this system is the WTO, the international organization created in 1995 to replace the General Agreement on Tariffs and Trade (GATT) and to supervise and expand international trade. Like its predecessor, GATT, the WTO reaches agreements through negotiating rounds. The latest round of WTO talks began in 2001 and has involved more than 150 countries. It quickly stalled as rich and poor countries found themselves in deep disagreement over free trade in agricultural products and clothing, protecting the environment, and intellectual property rights. Negotiations have continued, but as of 2012 no agreement has been reached.

THE CASE OF CHINA From 1949 to 1979, China and the United States existed in virtual economic isolation from one another. The total value of U.S.-China trade during this time was about $1 billion. A far different picture exists today. China and the United States are major bilateral trading partners and powerful voices in the WTO. They also are competitors in global trade, competing for markets worldwide.

The bilateral trade relationship between the United States and China has grown dramatically over the past three decades. In 1980, the year after the first U.S.-China bilateral trade agreement was signed, total trade (the value of imports and exports) was valued at $5 billion. By 2011, it was $503 billion. This growth has made China the United States' second largest trading partner, the single largest source of imports in the United States, and its third largest export market.

Three issues have been of particular concern to American policy makers in judging the impact of Chinese imports on the U.S. economy. The first is the loss of jobs that appears to have resulted from the surge in Chinese imports. The AFL-CIO, for example, estimates that since 1998 approximately 1.3 million American jobs have been lost because of Chinese imports. In 2012, the Obama administration placed tariffs on solar panels made in China, stating that China was providing unfair subsidies to their firms and harming U.S. manufacturers. The second major issue involves the U.S. trade deficit with China, which in 2011 was $295 billion. Part of this issue concerns China's currency, which trades with the dollar at a low value, making Chinese exports to the United States cheaper and U.S. exports to China more expensive. The U.S. government has accused China of manipulating the value of its currency to boost exports. Congress has considered legislation to impose tariffs on Chinese imports in retaliation, but no such legislation has passed. The third issue involves health and safety problems associated with Chinese imports. In 2007, the Food and Drug Administration issued warnings on more than 150 brands of pet foods manufactured in China. This was followed in the same year by a high-profile recall of Chinese-produced toys. Similar recalls involved infant formula in 2008 and potential health and safety issues associated with Chinese-made drywall products in 2009.

Still, China joined the WTO in 2001 with American support. As a condition of its membership, China agreed to undertake a series of reforms. Among them were pledges to reduce tariffs on agricultural and industrial products, limit agricultural subsidies, open its banking system to foreign banks, permit full trading rights to foreign firms, and respect intellectual property rights. China's failure to fully meet these conditions has been a repeated source of conflict with the United States and others. The United States has filed dozens of WTO complaints against China in the past several years. For its part, China has also filed complaints against the United States. China, for example, has protested a September 2009 decision by the Obama administration to place additional tariffs on tires imported from China. The United States justified this action on the basis of provisions that were agreed upon when China joined the WTO. Under the terms of this agreement, the United States had permission to impose trade restrictions on Chinese products for twelve years when they harmed the bottom line of American industry. The Obama administration argued that Chinese tire imports had unfairly harmed the American tire industry, causing the loss of about 5,000 jobs from 2004 to 2008.

Regional trade issues with China are an emerging concern for the United States, as regional trading blocks within Asia have been slower to form than in Europe or the Western Hemisphere. A significant movement in the direction of an Asian regional trade block occurred in January 2010 when a Free Trade Area was created between China and the Association of South East Asian (ASEAN) states. Japan and India also have such agreements with ASEAN. The economic potential of an Asian trading block is great, with significant consequences for the American economy.

□ Terrorism

Terrorism is violence designed to achieve political intimidation and instill fear (terror) in a population. It is generally pursued for ideological, political, or religious goals, and deliberately targets or disregards the safety of noncombatants. Terrorism is usually regarded as a tactic pursued by nongovernmental organizations, but governments also engage in or support terrorism.

Terrorism is not a new phenomenon and may last for generations. The first wave of modern terrorism, for example, advanced an anti-government agenda and began in Russia in the early twentieth century. It was set in motion by the political and economic reforms of the czars. Disappointment with these policies led to a series of assassinations throughout Europe, including that of Archduke Ferdinand of Austria, which helped spark World War I.

The second wave of modern terrorism began in the 1920s and ended in the 1960s. Defining themselves as freedom fighters, colonial terrorists aimed to obtain independence from European powers. Prominent examples of countries with factions of freedom fighters include Ireland, Vietnam, and Algeria. Hit-and-run tactics in urban areas and guerrilla warfare in rural areas became defining features of this second wave of terrorism.

The third wave of modern terrorism, set in motion by the Vietnam War, contained elements of each of the two preceding waves. One part of this wave comprised Marxist groups such as the Weather Underground in the United States and the Red Army Faction in Germany, which directed their terrorism at capitalist institutions. The second part of this wave was made up of groups seeking self-determination for ethnic minority groups. Prominent examples have included the Palestine Liberation Organization and the Irish Republican Army. This wave lost much of its energy in the 1980s as anti-capitalist revolutions failed to occur and separatist groups met military defeat.

The defining features of the current wave of terrorism are twofold. First, it is based in religion, especially Islam. Its initial energy was drawn from three events in 1979: (1) the start of a new Muslim century; (2) the ouster of the shah in Iran; and, (3) the Soviet invasion of Afghanistan. The United States is a special target of this religious wave of terrorism. The common goal shared by Islamic terrorist groups has been to drive the United States out of the Middle East, and to return this region to Muslim rule.

Even before 9/11, this wave of terrorist activity had produced a steady flow of attacks on the United States marine barracks in Lebanon in 1983, the World Trade Center in 1993, American embassies in Kenya and Tanzania in 1998, and the *USS Cole* in 2000. Notably, while earlier waves of terrorism focused on assassinating key individuals or the symbolic killing of relatively small numbers of individuals, these more recent attacks resulted in large numbers of casualties.

MAKING COUNTERTERRORISM POLICY Terrorist activity is difficult to combat because it is planned and conducted with stealth and sometimes has a broad base of support. It can also be difficult to define victory against terrorist groups. The National Strategy for Combating Terrorism, which was first released in 2003 by the U.S. National Security Council, defined victory over terrorism in terms of a world in which terrorism does not define the daily lives of Americans. To that end, it put forward a "4D strategy." The United States will: (1) defeat terrorist organizations; (2) deny them support from rogue states; (3) work to diminish the conditions that give rise to terrorism; and, (4) defend the United States, its citizens, and foreign interests from attack.[19]

American policy makers have four policy instruments to choose from in designing a strategy to combat terrorism. The first policy tool is diplomacy. The essence of the diplomatic challenge in fighting terrorism is to persuade other states to assist the United States in combating terrorism. This requires cooperation not only in defeating terrorists beyond their borders but also in taking on terrorist groups and their sympathizers within their own countries.

A second policy tool is military power. The critical question is how does a country best fight a war against terrorism? Modern state warfare is essentially a series of discrete and separate steps that build on one another and culminate in destroying the opponent's "center of gravity." Terrorists, in contrast, fight cumulative wars. No single military action lays the foundation for the next, and military undertakings need not occur in a given sequence. Terrorism attacks the enemy through a series of largely independent and episodic strikes that, when added together, have an effect far greater than the sum of the individual military actions.

Policy makers may also use economic power to defeat terrorism. This may happen in two different ways. First, imposition of economic sanctions can coerce states to stop supporting terrorists. The goal of sanctions is to affect a hostile government's decision-making process by imposing economic hardship on the country. The second use of economic power in a war against terrorism is to provide foreign aid to alleviate the social, economic, and political conditions that may give rise to terrorism. As intuitively appealing as it is to use foreign aid to combat terrorism, much uncertainty exists about the link between poverty and terrorism.

Finally, policy makers may use covert or undercover action to combat terrorism. The United States employed this approach when American special forces killed Osama bin Laden in Pakistan in 2011. Skeptics question the cost effectiveness of covert action that is designed to neutralize specific individuals or groups. Former Director of Central Intelligence George Tenet noted that even if the United States had found and killed Osama bin Laden before September 11, 2001, it probably would not have stopped the attacks.

THE CASE OF AL-QAEDA Al-Qaeda is a militant Islamic terrorist group founded in Pakistan in the late 1980s. Its initial purpose was to conduct a *Jihad,* or holy war, in the name of the Islamic religion. The United States was not initially a major target of the group, which was formed in part to oppose Soviet occupation of Afghanistan. But, following the Persian Gulf War, its leader, Osama bin Laden, returned to his homeland, Saudi Arabia. When Iraqi President Saddam Hussein threatened that country, bin Laden offered his forces to Saudi King Fahd. The king turned down his offer and instead allowed U.S. troops into Saudi Arabia. Bin Laden vehemently objected to this intrusion of foreign troops. His outspoken opposition to the American presence led to U.S. hostility and bin Laden's exile to Sudan. From there, he fled back to Afghanistan, where he directed the September 11, 2001, terrorist attacks.

Combating terrorism demands more than understanding al-Qaeda's history. It also requires an understanding of its organization. Most observers believe that today's al-Qaeda is not the same as it was on September 11, 2001. Rather than being tightly centralized and run from a single headquarters, the current al-Qaeda is a series of concentric circles. Located in the innermost circle is al-Qaeda Central, which is believed to be operating out of Afghanistan and parts of Pakistan. In the next ring are al-Qaeda affiliates and associates. These are established terrorist groups found largely in the Middle East, Asia, and Africa. In the third ring are al-Qaeda locals. This ring comprises individuals with active or dominant ties to al-Qaeda that engage in terrorist activities supporting its overarching goals. Finally, in the outermost ring is the al-Qaeda Network, made up of homegrown radicals who have no direct connection to al-Qaeda but who are drawn to its ideology.

Prior to declaring war on terrorism after 9/11, the United States responded with military force against terrorists three times and made several efforts to capture Osama bin Laden. The earliest reported covert action program to capture bin Laden involved the recruitment of a team of Afghan tribal members in the mid-1990s. The last effort before 9/11 involved the recruitment of a guerrilla commander in 1999. Between these two episodes, the Central Intelligence Agency contacted and recruited at least three proxy forces from Pakistan, Uzbekistan, and Afghanistan to try to capture or kill bin Laden.

Following 9/11, the United States moved from covert action and limited strikes to large-scale military action in the war on terrorism. On September 20, 2001, President George W. Bush issued an ultimatum to the Taliban government of Afghanistan to turn over Osama bin Laden and close all terrorist camps operating in that country. The Taliban rejected this demand, and on October 7, the United States and Great Britain began Operation Enduring Freedom, which resulted in the fall of the Taliban, the end of a safe haven for al-Qaeda, and the capture and killing of many al-Qaeda operatives, which severely weakened the organizations. After searching for bin Laden for many years, U.S. intelligence found him in Pakistan, where U.S. Navy SEALs launched a surprise attack on his compound in the city of Abbotabad in May 2011 (the United States did not even inform the Pakistani government of the raid) and killed him.

The United States also targeted Iraq in the war against terrorism. The Bush administration asserted that Saddam Hussein possessed weapons of mass destruction and was a supporter of al-Qaeda, though the evidence of these claims, along with the wisdom of targeting Iraq in the war on terror, were significantly criticized both in the United States and abroad. The United States launched Operation Iraqi Freedom on March 19, 2003, and American combat troops remained in Iraq until the end of 2011.

The conflicts in these countries illustrate an ongoing dilemma in U.S. anti-terrorism policy. What does victory look like in a war against terrorism? Does victory lie in destroying al-Qaeda's leadership? Defeating its sponsors and protectors? Stopping it from obtaining nuclear weapons? Or, does it require that no one take up the terrorists' cause and act against the United States?

☐ Nuclear Weapons

Starting to think about how to control nuclear weapons raises two questions. The first is, why do countries "go nuclear"? No single reason exists, but three motivations are particularly common. The first involves defense. Countries want to have nuclear weapons so that they do not have to depend on other nations for assistance. Israel's and Pakistan's pursuit of nuclear weapons fits this logic. Remembering the Holocaust, Jewish leaders were determined to protect Israel from all threats without relying on others for help. Pakistan sought the bomb after its neighbor and frequent opponent, India, became a nuclear power.

The second reason for going nuclear involves the pursuit of international influence and prestige. Nuclear weapons carry such qualities because of the central role military power plays in world politics. Possession of nuclear weapons elevates a country into a small, select group of states whose power dwarfs all others. Attaining influence and prestige is seen as an important factor in India's pursuit of nuclear weapons; being a nuclear power established India as an important state in its own right.

Domestic politics are a third motivating factor behind countries' efforts to acquire nuclear weapons. Pressure to go nuclear may come from the military looking to add to its power, scientists seeking to demonstrate their knowledge and qualifications, political parties striving for electoral victory and running on a strong defense platform, or individual leaders attempting to realize political power for themselves or their country.

A second major question is, how inevitable is the proliferation, or spread, of nuclear weapons? The historical record suggests that extreme fear of these weapons is unnecessary. As evidenced by Germany, Japan, and other industrialized countries, having access to technologies associated with weapons of mass destruction does not compel countries to seek or use these weapons. Recently, Libya, South Africa, Ukraine, Belarus, and Kazakhstan have all turned away from the possession or pursuit of nuclear weapons. More recently yet, however, the examples of North Korea and Iran suggest that the impetus toward proliferation may be increasing.

MAKING ARMS PROLIFERATION POLICY Efforts to deal with nuclear weapons and the means of delivering them have taken numerous forms. Several strategies traditionally are in place to limit arms proliferation: disarmament, arms control, defense, and counterproliferation.

Disarmament takes the very existence of weapons as the cause for conflict and hopes to secure peace through eliminating the means of conflict. The first nuclear disarmament proposal to command global attention was the Baruch Plan. Presented by the United States at the United Nations in 1946, it aimed to place all aspects of nuclear energy production and use under international control. The Soviet Union, as a permanent member of the UN Security Council, rejected the Baruch Plan, and it was not implemented.

The vision of a world without weapons, however, remains alive today. President Barack Obama endorsed disarmament in a July 2009 speech in Moscow. In pledging the United States to this goal, Obama acknowledged that its achievement would not likely happen in his lifetime.

A second strategy is arms control. It takes the existence of conflict between countries as a given in world politics and attempts to find ways of reducing the chances that those conflicts will become deadly. Decreasing the numbers and types of weapons at the disposal of policy makers is one approach. All but one of the world's major nuclear arms control agreements have been made between the United States and Russia, as

How Big Is the World's Stockpile of Nuclear Weapons?

The United States and Russia possess by far more nuclear weapons than any of the other seven countries that have them. The Nuclear Nonproliferation Treaty (NPT), which came into force in 1970, seeks to limit the spread of nuclear weapons around the world. It is based on the idea that countries without nuclear weapons will agree not to acquire them, and in exchange the countries with nuclear weapons will agree to provide economic and technical support for the peaceful development of nuclear power. The nuclear weapons states also promised to reduce their stockpiles and ultimately eliminate their nuclear arsenals. Only the U.S., Russia, the U.K., France and China are permitted to possess nuclear weapons under the NPT. India, Pakistan and Israel have not entered the treaty, North Korea withdrew in 2003, and Iran continues to pursue nuclear capabilities but has not developed a weapon. The nuclear programs of North Korea and Iran in particular have prompted concern that the spread of nuclear weapons could increase rapidly over the next decade.

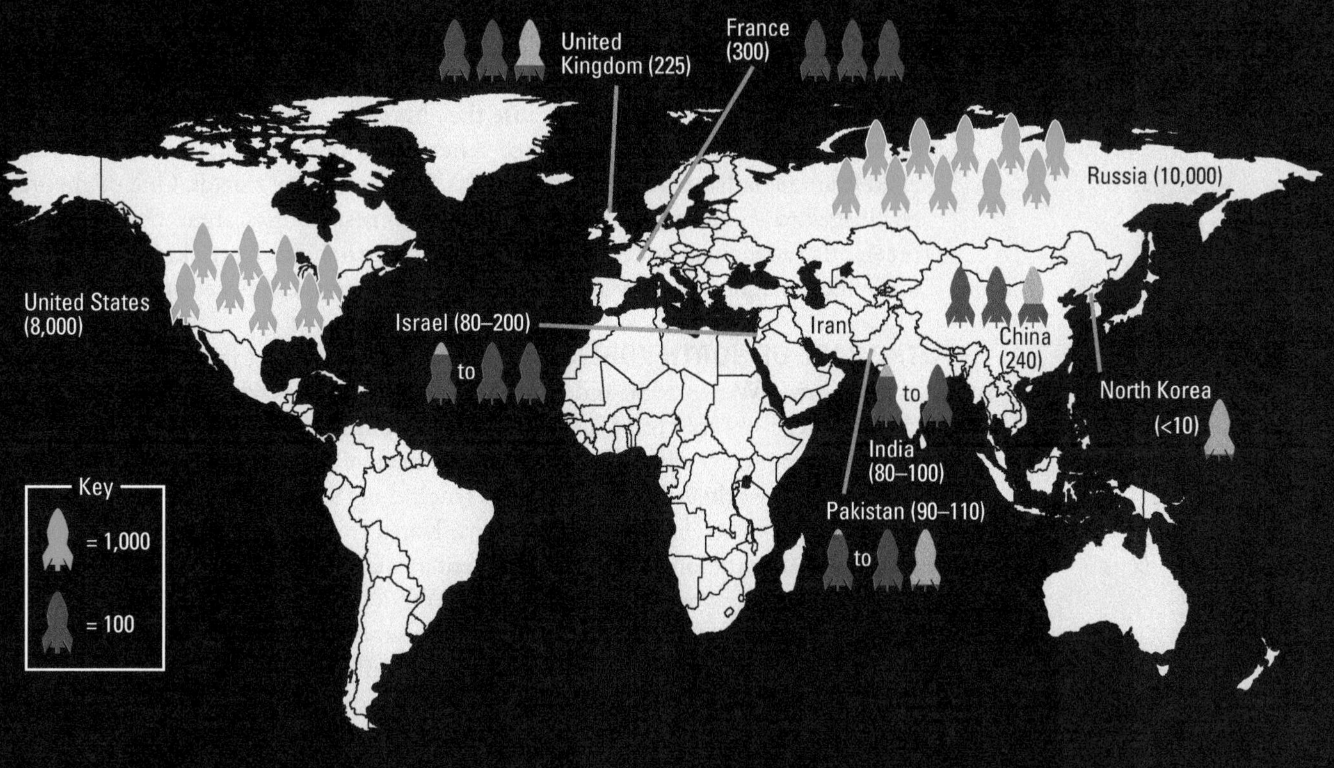

SOURCE: Data from Federation of American Scientists: State of World Nuclear Forces.

CRITICAL THINKING QUESTIONS

1. Why do countries develop nuclear weapons?
2. Has the NPT been effective in preventing the spread of nuclear weapons?
3. What are the possible consequences of the spread of nuclear weapons to Iran?

they have possessed the largest numbers of these weapons. These include the 1963 Limited Test Ban Treaty, the 1972 Anti-Ballistic Missile (ABM), the 1970s Strategic Arms Limitation Treaties (SALT I and II), the Strategic Arms Reduction Treaties of the 1990s (START I and II), and the New START Treaty of 2010. The only significant nuclear arms agreement including other countries is the Nuclear Nonproliferation Treaty of 1968, which focuses on limiting the spread of nuclear weapons.

A third strategy is denial. The goal of denial is to prevent would-be nuclear states from gaining access to the technology they need to make or deliver nuclear weapons. Denial has become more difficult in a globalized world, though many nations continue to pursue this goal. Key international groups working on arms denial are the Nuclear Suppliers Group and the Missile Technology Control Regime.

A fourth strategy is defense; this strategy is gaining popularity today. Essentially, this goal encourages the creation of a system to block or intercept attacks from other countries. Surprise missile tests by Iran and North Korea in 1998 provided new political backing for the creation of a missile defense system. In December 2002, President George W. Bush acted on this plan, ordering the initial deployment of long-range missile interceptors in Alaska and California.

A final strategy embraced by many countries today is counterproliferation. It involves the use of preemptive military action against a country or terrorist group. Counterproliferation begins with the assumption that certain terrorist groups and some states cannot be deterred because they have shown evidence of responding irrationally to threats of military force or other forms of coercion. The most frequently cited example is Israel's 1981 raid on Iraq's Osiraq nuclear reactor. One of the major challenges to counterproliferation is its effectiveness. Critics argue that attempts at preemptive action will not forestall the driving force behind an attack, and may actually make the situation worse by altering public opinion in the attacked state.

THE CASE OF NORTH KOREA Except for periods of direct military conflict—such as the Korean War in 1950 and crises that have arisen—as when North Korea seized the American spy ship the *USS Pueblo* in 1968 and held its crew captive—direct U.S. diplomatic contacts with North Korea have been all but absent. The United States, however, has worked through its allies (including South Korea) and international organizations to attempt to prevent North Korea from developing and using nuclear technology. Limitations on the development of such weaponry were a condition of the peace agreement signed to end the Korean War.

The United States also maintains an active surveillance program that monitors the activities of the North Korean government. In 1993, for example, the Central Intelligence Agency believed there was a 50–50 chance that North Korea had developed nuclear technology. The Defense Intelligence Agency declared it already had a working nuclear weapon. The United States demonstrated its disapproval of this arms program in two ways. It asked the United Nations to impose sanctions on North Korea, and it sent Patriot missiles to South Korea as a defense mechanism.

Ultimately, this conflict was resolved a year later, when North and South Korea reached a new agreement on denuclearizing the Korean peninsula, the Agreed Framework. The Agreed Framework included an agreement by North Korea to freeze its existing nuclear program and allow external monitoring by the International Atomic Energy Association (IAEA), a promise by the United States to supply it with oil and other fuels, and an agreement by both sides to move to full normalization of political and economic relations.

From the start, troubles plagued the implementation of the agreement. Oil was slow to be delivered, U.S. economic sanctions were not effectively removed, and, most importantly, full diplomatic relations were never established, largely because the United States objected to continued North Korean nuclear activity. In 1998, for example, the United States identified an underground site suspected of involvement in nuclear activities and North Korea tested a ballistic missile.

By the end of 2002, relations between the United States and North Korea had deteriorated sharply. Fuel imports to North Korea were suspended, and North Korea terminated its freeze on the plutonium-based nuclear facility. In early 2003, it expelled IAEA inspectors and withdrew from the international Nuclear Nonproliferation Treaty. The Agreed Framework was now held to be null and void by both sides.

Movement beyond this point has been slow and halting. In 2003, the United States proposed multilateral talks with North Korea on its nuclear program. North Korea initially refused, asserting this was a bilateral matter. But, under pressure from China, North Korea agreed to multilateral talks between those three states. Later, the talks were expanded and became known as the Six Party Talks when South Korea, Japan, and Russia joined the United States, North Korea, and China. As these negotiations dragged on, North Korea continued with its nuclear program. In 2006 and 2009, North Korea tested nuclear weapons, prompting tougher economic sanctions by the United States and new ones by the United Nations.

In 2007, the Six Party Talks finally led to a bilateral agreement between North Korea and the United States. The agreement mirrored closely the terms of the 1994 Agreed Framework, and initially, it appeared that both sides were making progress. But relations again turned sour when North Korea tested a rocket and a nuclear weapon in 2009, leading to tighter economic sanctions that North Korea called "a declaration of war." In March of 2010, North Korea sank a South Korean naval warship, and later that year it fired shells at a South Korean island, killing two people and wounding several others. The United States joined other nations in condemning these attacks, and has called for an end to North Korea's nuclear weapons and missile programs. Continued confrontation between the United States and North Korea appears likely for the foreseeable future.

HOW HAS THE UNITED STATES HANDLED NUCLEAR PROLIFERATION IN NORTH KOREA?

Relations between the United States and North Korea have been tense since the Korean War. A military parade in 2012, shown here, showcases the country's missile technology.

Toward Reform: New Challenges in American Foreign Policy

18.5 Understand emerging challenges to American foreign policy that have arisen in recent years.

In addition to addressing issues related to trade, terrorism, and nuclear weapons, the United States faces a number of other challenges that have emerged in recent years—both threats and opportunities. The United States remains a dominant power in world politics, with the world's largest economy and its largest military. It also provides economic and military aid to many countries around the globe. At the same time, however, the lengthy wars in Iraq and Afghanistan, along with the financial crisis in 2008, rapidly increasing U.S. debt, and a struggling economy, have demonstrated some of the limits to American power.

In recent years a number of developments around the world have posed challenges to the United States. The most notable change has been the tremendous economic growth and global influence of countries such as China and India (Brazil and Russia are often included in this group, leading to the group's identification as the "BRIC" countries).

China has become an economic powerhouse and a major global power. After opening up to global trade and investment in the 1980s, it has achieved the world's

Source To Come

WHAT ARE THE BRIC COUNTRIES?

Former Brazilian President Luiz Inacio Lula da Silva, former Russian President Dmitry Medvedev, Chinese President Hu Jintao, and Indian Prime Minister Manmohan Singh at the BRIC Summit in Brazil in 2010. The BRIC countries are among the fastest growing emerging economies in the world, with 40% of the world's population and more than 15% of the global economy.

Take a Closer Look

In 2011, Secretary of State Hillary Clinton addressed members of the African Women's Entrepreneurship Program in Zambia. Initiated by the U.S. Department of State in 2010, the program helps to build networks of small-business owners so they can transform their communities through leadership in economic development. "No country can thrive when half of its people are left behind," she stated. "If you don't see all citizens get the rights and freedoms they deserve, you are on the wrong side of history." This kind of political leadership is an example of America's soft power. In contrast to coercion, threats, and financial rewards, soft power is the ability to attract and co-opt, to set the agenda and get others to support the same goals the United States wants. Secretary Clinton's visit to Africa and others like it are at least as effective as military or economic aid in serving the cause of securing friendly relations and support for the United States among peoples and countries around the world.

When the secretary of state attends an event, it indicates that the issue at hand is a high priority for the United States. Support from such a high level in the American government helps to build strong relations and goodwill for the United States.

At this event, whenever former Secretary of State Clinton started to speak, the crowd broke into song. The singing, along with the enthusiasm evident on people's faces, demonstrates agreement with the message that the secretary is delivering about America's policy of supporting women's rights and entrepreneurship.

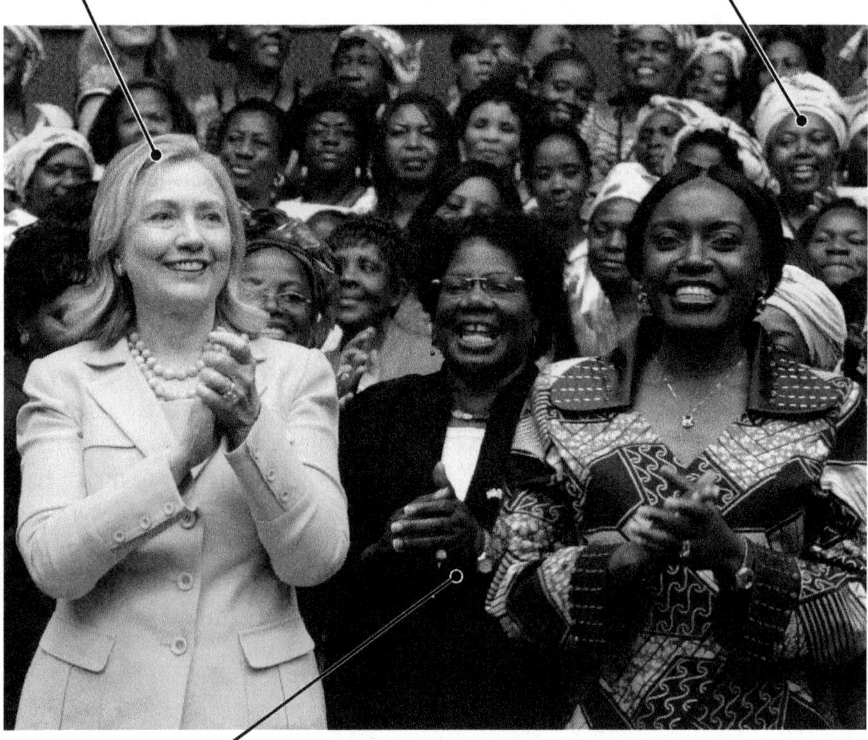

Soft power is developed over time through policies and values. This photo reflects shared values and goals among the U.S. government and women in Africa who are entrepreneurs benefiting from American aid. The impact of U.S. policy and the values that led to it is likely to spread well beyond the people shown in the photo.

CRITICAL THINKING QUESTIONS

1. What are the ways in which the United States exercises soft power?
2. How might the promotion of women's rights and economic opportunities strengthen a country?
3. What U.S. policies and values contribute to its soft power? What does it mean to "set the agenda"?

fastest growing economy and become the world's largest exporter. This growth also means that China enjoys greater power and influence throughout the world, along with a complicated relationship with the United States. Complexity characterizes the interplay between these two nations because China appears to be both the primary challenger to the United States and its most logical partner. Both countries benefit from trade and globalization; both want to limit the spread of nuclear weapons; and both are served by reining in countries, such as Iran and North Korea, that threaten peace and stability. But, tensions and mistrust are in the mix, too. China depends on the U.S. market to sell exports and grow economically, while the United States borrows heavily from China, which finances growing U.S. budget deficits by purchasing American Treasury bonds. This type of interaction creates an unhealthy mutual dependency for economic prosperity. At the same time, China is modernizing its navy, missiles, aircraft, cyber warfare, and anti-satellite weapons, while the United States has begun deploying more military forces in the Pacific, including a new deployment of 2,500 Marines in Australia. The relationship between these two countries will increasingly determine how peaceful or dangerous the world becomes.

India has also experienced rapid economic growth since opening up its economy, becoming a global leader in information technology and software development. It is also one of the world's largest exporters and a major trading partner of the United States. As both a democracy and a nuclear power, India shares many interests with the United States, with the two countries pursuing what they call a "strategic partnership" that includes increased military ties and arms sales, cooperation on nonmilitary nuclear power, growing bilateral trade and investment, and the admission of more than 100,000 Indian students in American universities. The relationship is also seen as a counterweight to the growing clout of China.

In Europe, an economic crisis regarding the euro, the common currency of seventeen nations, poses a challenge for the United States, whose economic fortunes are tied to those of Europe. Like the United States, many countries in Europe have acquired large national debts; unlike the United States, however, countries such as Greece, Spain, Portugal, Italy, and Ireland may not be able to pay back the money they owe, which is creating a growing fear. These countries are being told by lenders, and by fellow EU member Germany, to cut their spending and borrowing; but in fact, they continue to borrow even more money in an attempt to revive economic growth, which has declined in the past few years. Germany is key in this crisis, as it has the strongest economy in Europe and is not heavily indebted. With Germany's, at times, reluctant support, the European Central Bank and others have continued to lend money to prevent a default on the loans. At the same time, the countries in trouble try to find a balance between cutting spending to reduce debt and not cutting too much, which will make their recessions and unemployment rates even worse. Since it is unclear how much the United States and other countries could suffer if Europe has a severe economic downturn, or if Greece and other countries abandon the euro and return to their own national currencies, the United States is working with European countries to keep the crisis from deepening. President Obama has recommended that the EU create a banking union that shares financial risk across the region, and that lending be eased to spur economic growth. The EU, however, does not enjoy a great deal of leverage in this situation.

Complicating the conduct of American foreign policy is public opinion. The bipartisan consensus on the need to contain communism during the Cold War has long vanished, and no new consensus has emerged. Instead, the American public is often deeply divided over how to proceed on different issues. It can also be difficult to get citizens to devote attention to foreign policy. This is known as the "guns" and "butter" theory. Generally speaking, most citizens are more interested in domestic policy issues ("butter") because they have a greater impact on their everyday lives. Only in case of emergency or times of crisis do citizens express significant concern over foreign policy issues ("guns"). This tendency complicates foreign policy making, and can make it difficult for foreign policy issues to occupy space on the policy agenda.

Review the Chapter

Listen to Chapter 18 on MyPoliSciLab

Roots of U.S. Foreign and Defense Policy

18.1 Trace the evolution of U.S. foreign and defense policy, p. 551.

U.S. foreign policy and defense policy have evolved. Foreign and defense policy largely involved trade and commerce, isolationism with regard to Europe, and expansion across North America for most of the nation's first century. As U.S. economic interests expanded, the United States intervened more and more overseas, especially in Latin America and Asia. After a delayed entry into World War I, America retreated into isolation.

The United States as a World Power

18.2 Explain U.S. foreign policy as the country rose to become a world power, p. 555.

The United States' status as a world power was cemented by its entry into, and subsequent victory in, World War II. After the war, foreign and defense policy often dominated the American political agenda, with a focus on internationalism rather than isolationism. American foreign policy during the Cold War was organized around containment and deterrence, and led to U.S. confrontation with the Soviet Union around the world. The post–Cold War period was ushered in by the fall of communism in the Soviet Union and Eastern Europe, and featured policies of democratic enlargement to promote the expansion of democracy and free markets throughout the world. The September 11, 2001, terrorist attacks marked a new direction in American foreign policy, as the United States pursued a war on terrorism both at home and overseas in Iraq and Afghanistan.

Foreign and Defense Policy Decision Making

18.3 Outline the factors that shape foreign and defense policy decision making, p. 562.

The basic structure of foreign and defense policy decision making is laid out in the Constitution. The executive branch of government dominates foreign and defense policy. The president is preeminent, with the Departments of State, Defense, and Homeland Security also playing important roles, along with the intelligence community. Congress also influences and shapes policy through oversight, treaties, appointments, appropriations, and the War Powers Act. Four types of interest groups are also especially active in trying to influence foreign and defense policy decisions; these groups include the military-industrial complex, ethnic interest groups, foreign governments and companies, and ideological-public interest groups.

Contemporary Challenges in Foreign and Defense Policy

18.4 Identify contemporary foreign and defense policy challenges confronting the United States, p. 571.

The United States faces major challenges in foreign and defense policy during the twenty-first century. These include trade, terrorism, and controlling the spread of nuclear weapons. In terms of trade, China presents the United States with the biggest challenge because of the loss of jobs associated with a surge in Chinese imports, as well as the health and safety problems associated with Chinese imports. The biggest challenge related to terrorism comes from al-Qaeda, the perpetrators of the September 11, 2001, terrorist attacks. Al-Qaeda's highly decentralized network of terrorist cells makes it difficult to achieve victory in the traditional sense. Finally, one significant challenge related to nuclear weapons comes from North Korea. This country has tested nuclear weapons and missiles, and has responded to economic sanctions with violence against South Korea.

Toward Reform: New Challenges in American Foreign Policy

18.5 Understand emerging challenges to American foreign policy that have arisen in recent years, p 580.

The United States remains a dominant power in world politics, with vast economic and military power. However, war and economic difficulties present limits to American power, and in recent years a number of new developments have posed challenges to the United States. The rise of China and India is having an impact on American influence around the world. China has become both a partner and a competitor of the United States, while India has enjoyed a more cooperative relationship with the United States in recent years. In Europe, the financial crisis over the euro threatens American economic prosperity.

Learn the Terms

Berlin Wall, p. 557
Bretton Woods System, p. 556
collective security, p. 554
containment, p. 556
Contras, p. 559
Cuban Missile Crisis, p. 557
defense policy, p. 551
Department of Defense, p. 566
Department of Homeland Security, p. 566
Department of State, p. 566
détente, p. 558
democratic enlargement, p. 559
European Union, p. 559
Farewell Address, p. 552
foreign policy, p. 551
free trade system, p. 571
General Agreement on Tariffs and Trade (GATT), p. 556
global war on terrorism, p. 562
human rights, p. 558
International Monetary Fund (IMF), p. 556
isolationism, p. 552
Joint Chiefs of Staff, p. 566
manifest destiny, p. 553
Marshall Plan, p. 557
military-industrial complex, p. 570
Monroe Doctrine, p. 552
North American Free Trade Agreement (NAFTA), p. 571
North Atlantic Treaty Organization (NATO), p. 557
protectionism, p. 571
Reagan Doctrine, p. 559
Roosevelt Corollary, p. 553
strategic trade policy, p. 571
Taliban, p. 562
tariffs, p. 552
Truman Doctrine, p. 557
UN Security Council, p. 555
War Powers Resolution, p. 568
World Bank, p. 556
World Trade Organization (WTO), p 559

Test Yourself

Study and **Review** the **Practice Tests**

1. In his 1796 Farewell Address, George Washington suggested that the United States

a. make peace treaties with France.
b. avoid international trade.
c. avoid permanent alliances.
d. depend heavily on Europe for trade.
e. make peace treaties with England.

2. The Roosevelt Corollary

a. was an extension of the Monroe Doctrine.
b. justified U.S. intervention in Latin America and the Caribbean.
c. resulted in the creation of the Panama Canal.
d. was proclaimed by Theodore Roosevelt.
e. all of the above.

3. The strategy of opposing Soviet expansion with military forces, economic assistance, and political influence was known as

a. containment.
b. alliance theory.
c. balance of power.
d. preventionism.
e. isolationism.

4. The policy of democratic enlargement involved all but which of the following?

a. Promotion of democracy and free markets
b. Creation of the World Trade Organization
c. Cutting off all relations with China after the killing of demonstrators at Tiananmen Square
d. Signing the North American Free Trade Agreement
e. Expanding the NATO alliance

5. The Framers intended to

a. endow the states with foreign policy powers.
b. divide foreign policy powers between the Congress and the president.
c. give all foreign policy powers to the president.
d. give the states and federal government equal foreign policy powers.
e. give the Supreme Court the power to declare war.

6. Congress conducts oversight of foreign and defense policy through

a. cutting funding for presidential initiatives it opposes.
b. periodic questioning of the president in Congressional hearings.
c. removing Cabinet members from their positions.
d. maintaining the "Office of Presidential Oversight" in the White House.
e. establishing reporting requirements.

7. Which of the following is NOT a major foreign policy challenge facing the United States?

- **a.** The spread of nuclear weapons
- **b.** The U.S. trade deficit with China
- **c.** Maintaining peaceful relations with Canada and Mexico
- **d.** Defeating al-Qaeda
- **e.** Terrorism

8. The most common methods by which the United States tries to stop the spread of nuclear weapons are

- **a.** disarmament, arms control, and, as a last resort, invasion.
- **b.** disarmament, defense, denial, counterproliferation, and arms control.
- **c.** deterrence and defense.
- **d.** shock, denial, anger, and acceptance.
- **e.** arms control treaties with China.

9. Which of the following is NOT a major issue between the United States and China?

- **a.** China's increasing military modernization
- **b.** The U.S. deployment of Marines to Australia
- **c.** American indebtedness to China
- **d.** China's dependence on the United States to purchase its exports
- **e.** The periodic change of political parties in control of the White House

10. Limitations to American power and influence are demonstrated by

- **a.** the lengthy wars in Iraq and Afghanistan.
- **b.** growing U.S. debt.
- **c.** the rise of the BRIC countries.
- **d.** the euro crisis.
- **e.** all of the above.

Explore Further

Allison, Graham F., and Philip Zelikow. *Essence of Decision: Explaining the Cuban Missile Crisis*, 2nd ed. New York: Pearson, 1999.

Axelrod, Alan. *American Treaties and Alliances.* Washington, DC: CQ Press, 2000.

Bacevich, Andrew. *Washington Rules: America's Path to Permanent War.* New York: Metropolitan Books, 2010.

Barnett, Thomas P. M., *The Pentagon's New Map: War and Peace in the Twenty-First Century*. New York: Putnam, 2004.

Byman, Daniel, and Matthew C. Waxman. *The Dynamics of Coercion: American Foreign Policy and the Limits of Military Might.* New York: Cambridge University Press, 2002.

Ervin, Clark Kent. *Open Target: Where America Is Vulnerable to Attack.* New York: Palgrave Macmillan, 2006.

Goldstein, Joshua S., and Jon C. Pevehouse. *International Relations*, 10th ed. New York: Longman, 2012.

Hook, Steven W. *U.S. Foreign Policy: The Paradox of World Power*, 3rd ed. Washington, DC: CQ Press, 2010.

Howard, Russell D., James J. F. Forest, and Joanne Moore. *Homeland Security and Terrorism: Readings and Interpretations.* New York: McGraw-Hill, 2006.

Hunt, Michael H. *Ideology and U.S. Foreign Policy.* New Haven, CT: Yale University Press, 2009.

Kagan, Robert. *Dangerous Nation: America's Foreign Policy from Its Earliest Days to the Dawn of the Twentieth Century.* New York: Vintage, 2007.

Kaufman, Joyce P. *A Concise History of U.S. Foreign Policy*, 2nd ed. Lanham, MD: Rowman and Littlefield, 2010.

Kennan, George F. *American Diplomacy, 1900–1950.* Chicago: University of Chicago Press, 1951.

LaFeber, Walter. *The American Age: United States Foreign Policy at Home and Abroad*, 2nd ed. New York: W.W. Norton and Company, 1994.

Lowenthal, Mark M. *Intelligence: From Secrets to Policy*, 5th ed. Washington, DC: CQ Press, 2011.

McCormick, James M. *American Foreign Policy and Process*, 5th ed. New York: Wadsworth, 2009.

Mead, Walter Russell. *Special Providence: American Foreign Policy and How It Changed the World.* New York: Alfred A. Knopf, 2001.

Nye, Joseph S., Jr. *The Paradox of American Power: Why the World's Only Superpower Can't Go It Alone.* New York: Oxford University Press, 2002.

To learn more about the reach and worldwide involvement of the United Nations, go to **www.unsystem.org.**

To learn more about the Department of Defense and U.S. military operations around the globe, go to **www.defenselink.mil.**

To learn more about the Department of State, go to **www.state.gov**.

To learn more about the CIA and the larger intelligence community, go to **www.cia.gov**.

GLOSSARY

A

administrative adjudication A quasi-judicial process in which a bureaucratic agency settles disputes between two parties in a manner similar to the way courts resolve disputes.

administrative discretion The ability of bureaucrats to make choices concerning the best way to implement congressional or executive intentions.

affirmative action Policies designed to give special attention or compensatory treatment to members of a previously disadvantaged group.

agenda A set of issues to be discussed or given attention.

agenda setting The process of forming the list of issues to be addressed by government.

American dream An American ideal of a happy, successful life, which often includes wealth, a house, a better life for one's children, and, for some, the opportunity to grow up to be president.

amicus curiae "Friend of the court"; *amici* may file briefs or even appear to argue their interests orally before the court.

Anti-Federalists Those who favored strong state governments and a weak national government; opposed ratification of the U.S. Constitution.

appellate court Court that generally reviews only findings of law made by lower courts.

appellate jurisdiction The power vested in particular courts to review and/or revise the decision of a lower court.

apportionment The process of allotting congressional seats to each state according to its proportion of the population, following the decennial census.

Articles of Confederation The compact between the thirteen original colonies that created a loose league of friendship, with the national government drawing its powers from the states.

B

***Barron* v. *Baltimore* (1833)** The Supreme Court ruled that the due process clause of the Fifth Amendment did not apply to the actions of states. This decision limited the Bill of Rights to the actions of Congress alone.

Berlin Wall A barrier built by East Germany in 1961 to cut off democratic West Berlin from communist East Berlin.

bicameral legislature A two-house legislature.

bill A proposed law.

bill of attainder A law declaring an act illegal without a judicial trial.

Bill of Rights The first ten amendments to the U.S. Constitution, which largely guarantee specific rights and liberties.

Black Codes Laws denying most legal rights to newly freed slaves; passed by southern states following the Civil War.

block grant A large grant given to a state by the federal government with only general spending guidelines.

Board of Governors In the Federal Reserve System, a seven-member board that makes most economic decisions regarding interest rates and the supply of money.

Bretton Woods System International financial system devised shortly before the end of World War II that created the World Bank and the International Monetary Fund.

brief A document containing the legal written arguments in a case filed with a court by a party prior to a hearing or trial.

***Brown* v. *Board of Education* (1954)** U.S. Supreme Court decision holding that school segregation is inherently unconstitutional because it violates the Fourteenth Amendment's guarantee of equal protection.

budget deficit The economic condition that occurs when expenditures exceed revenues.

business cycles Fluctuations between periods of economic growth and recession, or periods of boom and bust.

C

Cabinet The formal body of presidential advisers who head the fifteen executive departments. Presidents often add others to this body of formal advisers.

campaign consultant A private-sector professional who sells to a candidate the technologies, services, and strategies required to get that candidate elected.

campaign manager The individual who travels with the candidate and coordinates the campaign.

candidate-centered politics Politics that focus on the candidates, their particular issues, and character rather than party affiliation.

categorical grant Grant that appropriates federal funds to states for a specific purpose.

charter A document that, like a constitution, specifies the basic policies, procedures, and institutions of local government. Charters for local governments must be approved by state legislatures.

charter schools Semipublic schools that have open admission but may also receive private donations to increase the quality of education.

checks and balances A constitutionally mandated structure that gives each of the three branches of government some degree of oversight and control over the actions of the others.

citizen journalists Ordinary individuals who collect, report, and analyze news content.

civic virtue The tendency to form small-scale associations for the public good.

civil liberties The personal guarantees and freedoms that the government cannot abridge by law, constitution, or judicial interpretation.

civil rights The government-protected rights of individuals against arbitrary or discriminatory treatment by governments or individuals.

Civil Rights Act of 1964 Wide-ranging legislation passed by Congress to outlaw segregation in public facilities and discrimination in employment, education, and voting; created the Equal Employment Opportunity Commission.

***Civil Rights Cases* (1883)** Name attached to five cases brought under the Civil Rights Act of 1875. In 1883, the Supreme Court decided that discrimination in a variety of public accommodations, including theaters, hotels, and railroads, could not be prohibited by the act because such discrimination was private, not state, discrimination.

civil service system The merit system by which many federal bureaucrats are selected.

Clean Air Act of 1970 The law that established national primary and secondary standards for air quality in the United States. A revised version was passed in 1990.

Clean Water Act of 1972 The Act that created water quality standards to control pollution, including elimination of point source discharge of pollutants.

clear and present danger test Test articulated by the Supreme Court in *Schenck* v. *U.S.* (1919) to draw the line between protected and unprotected speech; the Court looks to see "whether the words used" could "create a clear and present danger that they will bring about substantive evils" that Congress seeks "to prevent."

closed primary A primary election in which only a party's registered voters are eligible to cast a ballot.

cloture Mechanism requiring the vote of sixty senators to cut off debate.

collective good Something of value that cannot be withheld from a nonmember of a group, for example, a tax write-off or a better environment.

collective security The idea that an attack on one country is an attack on all countries.

Committees of Correspondence Organizations in each of the American colonies created to keep colonists abreast of developments with the British; served as powerful molders of public opinion against the British.

communications director The person who develops the overall media strategy for the candidate.

concurrent powers Powers shared by the national and state governments.

confederation Type of government in which the national government derives its powers from the states; a league of independent states.

conference committee Special joint committee created to reconcile differences in bills passed by the House and Senate.

Congressional Budget Act of 1974 Act that established the congressional budgetary process by laying out a plan for congressional action on the annual budget resolution, appropriations, reconciliation, and any other revenue bills.

congressional review A process whereby Congress can nullify agency regulations by a joint resolution of legislative disapproval.

conservative One who favors limited government intervention, particularly in economic affairs.

constitution A document establishing the structure, functions, and limitations of a government.

constitutional courts Federal courts specifically created by the U.S. Constitution or by Congress pursuant to its authority in Article III.

Containment U.S. policy of opposing Soviet expansion and communist revolutions around the world with military forces, economic assistance, and political influence.

content regulations Limitations on the substance of the mass media.

contrast ad Ad that compares the records and proposals of the candidates, with a bias toward the candidate sponsoring the ad.

conventional political participation Activism that attempts to influence the political process through commonly accepted forms of persuasion such as voting or letter writing.

cooperative federalism The intertwined relationship between the national, state, and local governments that began with the New Deal, often referred to as marble-cake federalism.

county The basic administrative unit of local government.

critical election An election that signals a party realignment through voter polarization around new issues and personalities.

crossover voting Participation in the primary election of a party with which the voter is not affiliated.

Cuban Missile Crisis The 1962 confrontation over the deployment of ballistic missiles in Cuba that nearly escalated into nuclear war between the United States and the Soviet Union.

D

Declaration of Independence Document drafted largely by Thomas Jefferson in 1776 that proclaimed the right of the American colonies to separate from Great Britain.

deep background Information provided to a journalist that will not be attributed to any source.

***de facto* discrimination** Racial discrimination that results from practice (such as housing patterns or other social or institutional, nongovernmental factors) rather than the law.

defense policy Area of policy making that focuses on the strategies that a country uses to protect itself from its enemies.

***de jure* discrimination** Racial segregation that is a direct result of law or official policy.

delegate Representative to the party convention.

delegate Role played by an elected representative who votes the way his or her constituents would want, regardless of personal opinions.

democracy A system of government that gives power to the people, whether directly or through elected representatives.

democratic enlargement Policy implemented during the Clinton administration in which the United States would actively promote the expansion of democracy and free markets throughout the world.

Department of Defense Chief executive branch department responsible for formulation and implementation of U.S. defense and military policy.

Department of Homeland Security Cabinet department created after the 9/11 terrorist attacks to coordinate domestic security efforts.

Department of State Chief executive branch department responsible for formulation and implementation of U.S. foreign policy.

departments Major administrative units with responsibility for a broad area of government operations. Departmental status usually indicates a permanent national interest in a particular governmental function, such as defense, commerce, or agriculture.

deregulation A reduction in market controls (such as price fixing, subsidies, or controls on who can enter the field) in favor of market-based competition.

détente The improvement in relations between the United States and the Soviet Union that occurred during the 1970s.

Dillon's Rule A premise articulated by Judge John F. Dillon in 1868 which states that local governments do not have any inherent sovereignty and instead must be authorized by state governments that can create or abolish them.

direct democracy A system of government in which members of the polity meet to discuss all policy decisions and then agree to abide by majority rule.

direct incitement test Test articulated by the Supreme Court in *Brandenburg* v. *Ohio* (1969) holding that the First Amendment protects advocacy of illegal action unless imminent lawless action is intended and likely to occur.

discharge petition Petition that gives a majority of the House of Representatives the authority to bring an issue to the floor in the face of committee inaction.

discount rate The rate of interest at which the Federal Reserve Board lends money to member banks.

disturbance theory The theory that interest groups form as a result of changes in the political system.

divided government The political condition in which different political parties control the presidency and Congress.

domestic policy A category of public policy that includes a broad and varied range of government programs affecting the lives of citizens within a country.

double jeopardy clause Part of the Fifth Amendment that protects individuals from being tried twice for the same offense in the same jurisdiction.

***Dred Scott* v. *Sandford* (1857)** The Supreme Court concluded that the U.S. Congress lacked the constitutional authority to bar slavery in the territories. This decision narrowed the scope of national power, while it enhanced that of the states.

dual federalism The belief that having separate and equally powerful levels of government is the best arrangement, often referred to as layer-cake federalism.

due process clause Clause contained in the Fifth and Fourteenth Amendments; over the years, it has been construed to guarantee a variety of rights to individuals.

E

economic interest group A group with the primary purpose of promoting the financial interests of its members.

economic regulation Government regulation of business practices, industry rates, routes, or areas serviced by particular industries.

economic stability A situation in which there is economic growth, rising national income, high employment, and steadiness in the general level of prices.

Eighth Amendment Part of the Bill of Rights that states: "Excessive bail shall not be required, nor excessive fines imposed, nor cruel and unusual punishments inflicted."

elector Member of the Electoral College.

Electoral College Representatives of each state who cast the final ballots that actually elect a president.

electorate The citizens eligible to vote.

entitlement programs Government benefits that all citizens meeting eligibility criteria—such as age, income level, or unemployment—are legally "entitled" to receive.

enumerated powers The powers of the national government specifically granted to Congress in Article I, section 8 of the Constitution.

Equal Pay Act of 1963 Legislation that requires employers to pay men and women equal pay for equal work.

equal protection clause Section of the Fourteenth Amendment that guarantees all citizens receive "equal protection of the laws."

Equal Rights Amendment Proposed amendment to the Constitution that states "Equality of rights under the law shall not be denied or abridged by the United States or any state on account of sex."

equal time rule The rule that requires broadcast stations to sell air time equally to all candidates in a political campaign if they choose to sell it to any.

establishment clause The first clause of the First Amendment; it directs the national government not to sanction an official religion.

European Union An organization that joins 27 countries in Europe into a union that includes free trade, a central bank, a common currency, ease of immigration, a European Parliament, and other political institutions to govern and administer the organization.

exclusionary rule Judicially created rule that prohibits police from using illegally seized evidence at trial.

executive agreements Formal international agreements entered into by the president that do not require the advice and consent of the U.S. Senate.

Executive Office of the President (EOP) A mini-bureaucracy created in 1939 to help the president oversee the executive branch bureaucracy.

executive order Rule or regulation issued by the president that has the effect of law. All executive orders must be published in the *Federal Register*.

executive privilege An implied presidential power that allows the president to refuse to disclose information regarding confidential conversations or national security to Congress or the judiciary.

exit polls Polls conducted as voters leave selected polling places on Election Day.

***ex post facto* law** Law that makes an act punishable as a crime even if the action was legal at the time it was committed.

extradition clause Part of Article IV of the Constitution that requires states to extradite, or return, criminals to states where they have been convicted or are to stand trial.

F

Farewell Address When President George Washington left office, he wrote a letter, addressed to the People of the United States, warning people of the dangers to avoid in order to preserve the republic.

federal bureaucracy The thousands of federal government agencies and institutions that implement and administer federal laws and programs.

federal system System of government in which the national government and state governments share power and derive all authority from the people.

Federalists Those who favored a stronger national government and supported the proposed U.S. Constitution; later became the first U.S. political party.

Fifteenth Amendment One of the three Civil War Amend-ments; specifically enfranchised newly freed male slaves.

Fifth Amendment Part of the Bill of Rights that imposes a number of restrictions on the federal government with respect to the rights of persons suspected of committing a crime. It provides for indictment by a grand jury and protection against self-incrimination, and prevents the national government from denying a person life, liberty, or property without the due process of law. It also prevents the national government from taking property without just compensation.

fighting words Words that "by their very utterance inflict injury or tend to incite an immediate breach of peace." Fighting words are not subject to the restrictions of the First Amendment.

filibuster A formal way of halting Senate action on a bill by means of long speeches or unlimited debate.

finance chair The individual who coordinates the financial business of the campaign.

First Amendment Part of the Bill of Rights that imposes a number of restrictions on the federal government with respect to civil liberties, including freedom of religion, speech, press, assembly, and petition.

First Continental Congress Meeting held in Philadelphia from September 5 to October 26, 1774, in which fifty-six delegates (from every colony except Georgia) adopted a resolution in opposition to the Coercive Acts.

fiscal policy The deliberate use of the national government's taxing and spending policies to maintain economic stability.

501(c) group Interest groups whose primary purpose is not electoral politics.

527 political committee Organizations created with the primary purpose of influencing electoral outcomes; the term is typically applied only to freestanding interest groups that do not explicitly advocate for the election of a candidate.

foreign policy Area of policy making that encompasses how one country builds relationships with other countries in order to safeguard its national interest.

Fourteenth Amendment One of the three Civil War Amend-ments; guarantees equal protection and due process of the law to all U.S. citizens.

Fourth Amendment Part of the Bill of Rights that reads: "The right of the people to be secure in their persons, houses, papers, and effects, against unreasonable searches and seizures, shall not be violated, and no Warrants shall issue, but upon probable cause, supported by Oath or affirmation, and particularly describing the place to be searched, and the persons or things to be seized."

framing The process by which a news organization defines a political issue and consequently affects opinion about the issue.

free exercise clause The second clause of the First Amendment; it prohibits the U.S. government from interfering with a citizen's right to practice his or her religion.

free rider problem Potential members fail to join a group because they can get the benefit, or collective good, sought by the group without contributing the effort.

free trade system A system of international trade that has limited government interference on the sale of goods and services among countries.

front-loading The tendency of states to choose an early date on the nomination calendar.

full faith and credit clause Section of Article IV of the Constitution that ensures judicial decrees and contracts made in one state will be binding and enforceable in any other state.

fundamental freedoms Those rights defined by the Court as essential to order, liberty, and justice and therefore entitled to the highest standard of review.

G

General Agreement on Tariffs and Trade (GATT) Post–World War II economic development treaty designed to help facilitate international trade negotiations and promote free trade.

general election Election in which voters decide which candidates will actually fill elective public offices.

general election campaign Phase of a political campaign aimed at winning election to office.

gerrymandering The drawing of congressional districts to produce a particular electoral outcome without regard to the shape of the district.

get-out-the-vote (GOTV) A push at the end of a political campaign to encourage supporters to go to the polls.

***Gibbons* v. *Ogden* (1824)** The Supreme Court upheld broad congressional power to regulate interstate commerce. The Court's broad interpretation of the Constitution's commerce clause paved the way for later rulings upholding expansive federal powers.

global war on terrorism An international action, initiated by President George W. Bush after the 9/11 attacks, to weed out terrorist operatives throughout the world.

global warming The increase in global temperatures due to carbon emissions from burning fossil fuels such as coal and oil.

government The formal vehicle through which policies are made and affairs of state are conducted.

government corporations Businesses established by Congress to perform functions that private businesses could provide.

governmental (institutional) agenda Problems to which public officials feel obliged to devote active and serious attention.

grandfather clause Voter qualification provision in many southern states that allowed only those citizens whose grandfathers had voted before Reconstruction to vote unless they passed a wealth or literacy test.

Great Compromise The final decision of the Constitutional Convention to create a two-house legislature, with the lower house elected by the people and with powers divided between the two houses. It also made national law supreme.

greenhouse gases Gases in the atmosphere that lead to higher global temperatures.

gross domestic product (GDP) The total market value of all goods and services produced in an area during a year.

H

Hatch Act The 1939 act to prohibit civil servants from taking activist roles in partisan campaigns. This act prohibited federal employees from making political contributions, working for a particular party, or campaigning for a particular candidate.

hate speech Any communication that belittles a person or group on the basis of characteristics.

hold A procedure by which a senator asks to be informed before a particular bill or nomination is brought to the floor. This request signals leadership that a member may have objections to the bill (or nomination) and should be consulted before further action is taken.

Honest Leadership and Open Government Act of 2007 Lobbying reform banning gifts to members of Congress and their staffs, toughening disclosure requirements, and increasing time limits on moving from the federal government to the private sector.

human rights The protection of people's basic freedoms and needs.

I

impeachment The power delegated to the House of Representatives in the Constitution to charge the president, vice president, or other "civil officers," including federal judges, with "Treason, Bribery, or other high Crimes and Misdemeanors." This is the first step in the constitutional process of removing government officials from office.

implementation The process by which a law or policy is put into operation.

implied powers The powers of the national government derived from the enumerated powers and the necessary and proper clause.

incorporation doctrine An interpretation of the Constitution holding that the due process clause of the Fourteenth Amendment requires state and local governments to guarantee the rights stated in the Bill of Rights.

incumbency Already holding an office.

independent executive agencies Governmental units that closely resemble a Cabinet department but have narrower areas of responsibility and perform services rather than regulatory functions.

independent expenditures Spending for campaign activity that is not coordinated with a candidate's campaign.

independent regulatory commission An entity created by Congress outside a major executive department.

indirect democracy A system of government that gives citizens the opportunity to vote for representatives who work on their behalf.

inflation A rise in the general price levels of an economy.

inherent powers Powers that belong to the president because they can be inferred from the Constitution.

initiative An election that allows citizens to propose legislation or state constitutional amendments by submitting them to the electorate for popular vote.

inoculation ad Advertising that attempts to counteract an anticipated attack from the opposition before the attack is launched.

interagency councils Working groups created to facilitate coordination of policy making and implementation across a host of governmental agencies.

interest group A collection of people or organizations that tries to influence public policy.

International Monetary Fund (IMF) International governmental organization designed to stabilize international currency transactions.

interstate compacts Contracts between states that carry the force of law; generally now used as a tool to address multistate policy concerns.

interventionist state Alternative to the laissez-faire state; the government took an active role in guiding and regulating the private economy.

iron triangles The relatively ironclad relationships and patterns of interaction that occur among agencies, interest groups, and congressional committees or subcommittees.

isolationism The U.S. policy of avoiding entangling alliances with European powers.

issue networks The loose and informal relationships that exist among a large number of actors who work in broad policy areas.

J

Jim Crow laws Laws enacted by southern states that required segregation in public schools, theaters, hotels, and other public accommodations.

Joint Chiefs of Staff Military advisory body that includes the Army chief of staff, the Air Force chief of staff, the chief of naval operations, and the Marine commandant.

joint committee Standing committee that includes members from both houses of Congress set up to conduct investigations or special studies.

judicial activism A philosophy of judicial decision making that posits judges should use their power broadly to further justice.

judicial implementation How and whether judicial decisions are translated into actual public policies affecting more than the immediate parties to a lawsuit.

judicial restraint A philosophy of judicial decision making that posits courts should allow the decisions of other branches of government to stand, even when they offend a judge's own principles.

judicial review Power of the courts to review acts of other branches of government and the states.

Judiciary Act of 1789 Legislative act that established the basic three-tiered structure of the federal court system.

jurisdiction Authority vested in a particular court to hear and decide the issues in a particular case.

L

laissez-faire A French term meaning "to allow to do, to leave alone." It holds that active governmental involvement in the economy is wrong.

legislative courts Courts established by Congress for specialized purposes, such as the Court of Appeals for Veterans Claims.

***Lemon* test** Three-part test created by the Supreme Court for examining the constitutionality of religious establishment issues.

libel False written statement that defames a person's character.

liberal One who favors greater government intervention, particularly in economic affairs and in the provision of social services.

libertarian One who believes in limited government interference in personal and economic liberties.

line-item veto The authority of a chief executive to delete part of a bill passed by the legislature that involves taxing or spending. Ruled unconstitutional by the U.S. Supreme Court.

lobbying The activities of a group or organization that seek to persuade political leaders to support the group's position.

lobbyist Interest group representative who seeks to influence legislation that will benefit his or her organization or client through political and/or financial persuasion.

logrolling Vote trading; voting to support a colleague's bill in return for a promise of future support.

M

majority leader The head of the party controlling the most seats in the House of Representatives or the Senate; is second in authority to the Speaker of the House and in the Senate is regarded as its most powerful member.

majority party The political party in each house of Congress with the most members.

majority rule The central premise of direct democracy in which only policies that collectively garner the support of a majority of voters will be made into law.

mandate A command, indicated by an electorate's votes, for the elected officials to carry out a party platform or policy agenda.

manifest destiny Theory that the United States was divinely supported to expand across North America to the Pacific Ocean.

***Marbury* v. *Madison* (1803)** Case in which the Supreme Court first asserted the power of judicial review by finding that the congressional statute extending the Court's original jurisdiction was unconstitutional.

margin of error A measure of the accuracy of a public opinion poll.

markup A session in which committee members offer changes to a bill before it goes to the floor.

Marshall Plan European collective recovery program, named after Secretary of State George C. Marshall, that provided extensive American aid to Western Europe after World War II.

mass media The entire array of organizations through which information is collected and disseminated to the general public.

matching funds Donations to presidential campaigns whereby every dollar raised from individuals in amounts less than $251 is matched by the federal treasury.

***McCulloch* v. *Maryland* (1819)** The Supreme Court upheld the power of the national government and denied the right of a state to tax the federal bank, using the Constitution's supremacy clause. The Court's broad interpretation of the necessary and proper clause paved the way for later rulings upholding expansive federal powers.

means-tested programs Programs that require that beneficia-ries have incomes below specified levels to be eligible for benefits. Among these are SSI, TANF, and SNAP.

media effects The influence of news sources on public opinion.

Medicaid A government program that subsidizes medical care for the poor.

Medicare The federal program established during the Lyndon B. Johnson administration that provides medical care to elderly Social Security recipients.

mercantilism An economic theory designed to increase a nation's wealth through the development of commercial industry and a favorable balance of trade.

merit system A system of employment based on qualifications, test scores, and ability, rather than party loyalty.

mid-term election An election that takes place in the middle of a presidential term.

military-industrial complex The network of political and financial relations formed by defense industries, the U.S. armed forces, and Congress.

minority leader The head of the party with the second highest number of elected representatives in the House of Representatives or the Senate.

minority party The political party in each house of Congress with the second most members.

***Miranda* rights** Statements required of police that inform a suspect of his or her constitutional rights protected by the Fifth Amendment, including the right to an attorney provided by the court if the suspect cannot afford one.

***Miranda* v. *Arizona* (1966)** A landmark Supreme Court ruling holding that the Fifth Amendment requires individuals arrested for a crime to be advised of their right to remain silent and to have counsel present.

moderate A person who takes a relatively centrist or middle-of-the-road view on most political issues.

monarchy A form of government in which power is vested in hereditary kings and queens who govern in the interest of all.

monetary policy A form of government regulation in which the nation's money supply and interest rates are controlled.

Monroe Doctrine President James Monroe's 1823 pledge that the United States would oppose attempts by European states to reestablish their political control in the Western Hemisphere.

muckraking A form of journalism, in vogue in the early twentieth century, devoted to exposing misconduct by government, business, and individual politicians.

municipality City governments created in response to the emergence of relatively densely populated areas.

N

narrowcasting Targeting media programming at specific populations within society.

national convention A party meeting held in the presidential election year for the purposes of nominating a presidential and vice presidential ticket and adopting a platform.

national party platform A statement of the general and specific philosophy and policy goals of a political party, usually promulgated at the national convention.

natural law A doctrine that society should be governed by certain ethical principles that are part of nature and, as such, can be understood by reason.

necessary and proper clause The final paragraph of Article I, section 8, of the Constitution, which gives Congress the authority to pass all laws "necessary and proper" to carry out the enumerated powers specified in the Constitution; also called the elastic clause.

negative ad Advertising on behalf of a candidate that attacks the opponent's character or platform.

New Deal The name given to the program of "Relief, Recovery, Reform" begun by President Franklin D. Roosevelt in 1933 to bring the United States out of the Great Depression.

New Federalism Federal–state relationship proposed by Reagan administration during the 1980s; hallmark is returning administrative powers to the state governments.

New Jersey Plan A framework for the Constitution proposed by a group of small states. Its key points were a one-house legislature with one vote for each state, a Congress with the ability to raise revenue, and a Supreme Court with members appointed for life.

news media Media providing the public with new information about subjects of public interest.

***New York Times Co.* v. *Sullivan* (1964)** Case in which the Supreme Court concluded that "actual malice" must be proven to support a finding of libel against a public figure.

Nineteenth Amendment Amendment to the Constitution that guaranteed women the right to vote.

Ninth Amendment Part of the Bill of Rights that makes it clear that enumerating rights in the Constitution or Bill of Rights does not mean that others do not exist.

No Child Left Behind Act (NCLB) Education reform passed in 2002 that employs high standards and measurable goals as a method of improving American education.

nomination campaign Phase of a political campaign aimed at winning a primary election.

non–means-tested programs Programs that provide cash assistance to qualified beneficiaries, regardless of income. Among these are Social Security and unemployment insurance.

North American Free Trade Agreement (NAFTA) Agreement that promotes free movement of goods and services among Canada, Mexico, and the United States.

North Atlantic Treaty Organization (NATO) The first peacetime military treaty joined by the United States; NATO is a collective security pact that includes the United States, Canada, and Western Europe.

nullification The right of a state to declare void a federal law.

O

off the record Information provided to a journalist that will not be released to the public.

Office of Management and Budget (OMB) The office that prepares the president's annual budget proposal, reviews the budget and programs of the executive departments, supplies economic forecasts, and conducts detailed analyses of proposed bills and agency rules.

oligarchy A form of government in which the right to participate depends on the possession of wealth, social status, military position, or achievement.

on background Information provided to a journalist that will not be attributed to a named source.

on the record Information provided to a journalist that can be released and attributed by name to the source.

open market operations The buying and selling of government securities by the Federal Reserve Bank.

open primary A primary election in which party members, independents, and sometimes members of the other party are allowed to participate.

original jurisdiction The jurisdiction of courts that hear a case first, usually in a trial. These courts determine the facts of a case.

P

pardon An executive grant providing restoration of all rights and privileges of citizenship to a specific individual charged or convicted of a crime.

party caucus or conference A formal gathering of all party members.

party identification A citizen's personal affinity for a political party, usually expressed by a tendency to vote for the candidates of that party.

party realignment Dramatic shifts in partisan preferences that drastically alter the political landscape.

Patient Protection and Affordable Care Act 2010 legislation aimed at reducing the number of uninsured individuals and decreasing health care costs.

patron A person who finances a group or individual activity.

patronage Jobs, grants, or other special favors that are given as rewards to friends and political allies for their support.

Pendleton Act Reform measure that established the principle of federal employment on the basis of open, competitive exams and created the Civil Service Commission.

personal liberty A key characteristic of U.S. democracy. Initially meaning freedom *from* governmental interference, today it includes demands for freedom *to* engage in a variety of practices without governmental interference or discrimination.

***Plessy* v. *Ferguson* (1896)** Supreme Court case that challenged a Louisiana statute requiring that railroads provide separate accommodations for blacks and whites. The Court found that separate-but-equal accommodations did not violate the equal protection clause of the Fourteenth Amendment.

pluralist theory The theory that political power is distributed among a wide array of diverse and competing interest groups.

pocket veto If Congress adjourns during the ten days the president has to consider a bill passed by both houses of Congress, the bill is considered vetoed without the president's signature.

polarization The presence of increasingly conflicting and divided viewpoints between the Democratic and Republican Parties.

policy adoption The approval of a policy proposal by people with the requisite authority, such as a legislature.

policy coordinating committees Subcabinet-level committees created to facilitate interactions between agencies and departments to handle complex policy problems.

policy evaluation The process of determining whether a course of action is achieving its intended goals.

policy formulation The crafting of proposed courses of action to resolve public problems.

policy implementation The process of carrying out public policy.

political action committees (PACs) Officially recognized fund-raising organizations that represent interest groups and are allowed by federal law to make contributions directly to candidates' campaigns.

political culture Commonly shared attitudes, beliefs, and core values about how government should operate.

political equality The principle that all citizens are the same in the eyes of the law.

political ideology The coherent set of values and beliefs about the purpose and scope of government held by groups and individuals.

political machine A party organization that recruits voter loyalty with tangible incentives and is characterized by a high degree of control over member activity.

political party An organized group with shared goals and ideals that joins together to run candidates for office and exercise political and electoral power.

political socialization The process through which individuals acquire their political beliefs and values.

politico An elected representative who acts as a trustee or as a delegate, depending on the issue.

politics The study of who gets what, when, and how—or how policy decisions are made.

pollster A campaign consultant who conducts public opinion surveys.

poll tax A tax levied in many southern states and localities that had to be paid before an eligible voter could cast a ballot.

popular consent The principle that governments must draw their powers from the consent of the governed.

popular sovereignty The notion that the ultimate authority in society rests with the people.

population The entire group of people whose attitudes a researcher wishes to measure.

pork Legislation that allows representatives to bring money and jobs to their districts in the form of public works programs, military bases, or other programs.

positive ad Advertising on behalf of a candidate that stresses the candidate's qualifications, family, and issue positions, with no direct reference to the opponent.

precedent A prior judicial decision that serves as a rule for settling subsequent cases of a similar nature.

preemption A concept that allows the national government to override state or local actions in certain policy areas.

president pro tempore The official chair of the Senate; usually the most senior member of the majority party.

press briefing A relatively restricted session between a press secretary or aide and the press.

press conference An unrestricted session between an elected official and the press.

press release A document offering an official comment or position.

press secretary The individual charged with interacting and communicating with journalists on a daily basis.

primary election Election in which voters decide which of the candidates within a party will represent the party in the general election.

prior restraint Constitutional doctrine that prevents the government from prohibiting speech or publication before the fact; generally held to be in violation of the First Amendment.

privileges and immunities clause Part of Article IV of the Constitution guaranteeing that the citizens of each state are afforded the same rights as citizens of all other states.

programmatic request Federal funds designated for special projects within a state or congressional district.

progressive federalism A pragmatic approach to federalism that views relations between national and state governments as both coercive and cooperative.

proportional representation A voting system that apportions legislative seats according to the percentage of the vote won by a particular political party.

prospective judgment A voter's evaluation of a candidate based on what he or she pledges to do about an issue if elected.

protectionism A trade policy wherein a country takes steps to limit the import of foreign goods through tariffs and subsidies to domestic firms.

public funds Donations from general tax revenues to the campaigns of qualifying presidential candidates.

public interest group An organization that seeks a collective good that will not selectively and materially benefit group members.

public opinion What the public thinks about a particular issue or set of issues at any point in time.

public opinion polls Interviews or surveys with samples of citizens that are used to estimate the feelings and beliefs of the entire population.

public policy An intentional course of action or inaction followed by government in dealing with some problem or matter of concern.

push polls Polls taken for the purpose of providing information on an opponent that would lead respondents to vote against that candidate.

R

random sampling A method of poll selection that gives each person in a group the same chance of being selected.

Reagan Doctrine The Reagan administration's commitment to ending communism by providing military assistance to anti-communist groups.

reapportionment The reallocation of the number of seats in the House of Representatives after each decennial census.

recall An election in which voters can remove an incumbent from office prior to the next scheduled election.

recession A decline in the economy that occurs as investment sags, production falls off, and unemployment increases.

reconciliation A procedure that allows consideration of controversial issues affecting the budget by limiting debate to twenty hours, thereby ending threat of a filibuster.

redistricting The process of redrawing congressional districts to reflect increases or decreases in seats allotted to the states, as well as population shifts within a state.

referendum An election whereby the state legislature submits proposed legislation or state constitutional amendments to the voters for approval.

regulations Rules governing the operation of all government programs that have the force of law.

republic A government rooted in the consent of the governed; a representative or indirect democracy.

reserve requirements Government requirements that a portion of member banks' deposits be retained as backing for their loans.

reserved powers Powers reserved to the states by the Tenth Amendment that lie at the foundation of a state's right to legislate for the public health and welfare of its citizens.

retrospective judgment A voter's evaluation of a candidate based on past performance on a particular issue.

right to privacy The right to be left alone; a judicially created principle encompassing a variety of individual actions protected by the penumbras cast by several constitutional amendments, including the First, Third, Fourth, Ninth, and Fourteenth Amendments.

***Roe* v. *Wade* (1973)** The Supreme Court found that a woman's right to an abortion was protected by the right to privacy that could be implied from specific guarantees found in the Bill of Rights applied to the states through the Fourteenth Amendment.

Roosevelt Corollary Concept developed by President Theodore Roosevelt early in the twentieth century declaring that it was the responsibility of the United States to ensure stability in Latin America and the Caribbean.

rule making A quasi-legislative process resulting in regulations that have the characteristics of a legislative act.

Rule of Four At least four justices of the Supreme Court must vote to consider a case before it can be heard.

runoff primary A second primary election between the two candidates receiving the greatest number of votes in the first primary.

S

sample A subset of the whole population selected to be questioned for the purposes of prediction or gauging opinion.

Second Continental Congress Meeting that convened in Philadelphia on May 10, 1775, at which it was decided that an army should be raised and George Washington of Virginia was named commander in chief.

secular realignment The gradual rearrangement of party coalitions, based more on demographic shifts than on shocks to the political system.

select (or special) committee Temporary committee appointed for a specific purpose.

selective incorporation A judicial doctrine whereby most, but not all, protections found in the Bill of Rights are made applicable to the states via the Fourteenth Amendment.

senatorial courtesy A process by which presidents generally allow senators from the state in which a judicial vacancy occurs to block a nomination by simply registering their objection.

seniority Time of continuous service on a committee.

separation of powers A way of dividing the power of government among the legislative, executive, and judicial branches, each staffed separately, with equality and independence of each branch ensured by the Constitution.

Seventeenth Amendment Amendment to the U.S. Constitution that made senators directly elected by the people, removing their selection from state legislatures.

Shays's Rebellion A rebellion in which an army of 1,500 disgruntled and angry farmers led by Daniel Shays marched to Springfield, Massachusetts, and forcibly restrained the state court from foreclosing mortgages on their farms.

signing statements Occasional written comments attached to a bill signed by the president.

Sixteenth Amendment Amendment to the U.S. Constitution that authorized Congress to enact a national income tax.

Sixth Amendment Part of the Bill of Rights that sets out the basic requirements of procedural due process for federal courts to follow in criminal trials. These include speedy and public trials, impartial juries, trials in the state where the crime was committed, notice of the charges, the right to confront and obtain favorable witnesses, and the right to counsel.

slander Untrue spoken statements that defame the character of a person.

social capital Cooperative relationships that facilitate the resolution of collective problems.

social conservative One who believes that the government should support and further traditional moral teachings.

Social Security Act A 1935 law that established old age insurance; assistance for the needy, aged, blind, and families with dependent children; and unemployment insurance.

solicitor general The fourth-ranking member of the Department of Justice; responsible for handling nearly all appeals on behalf of the U.S. government to the Supreme Court.

Speaker of the House The only officer of the House of Representatives specifically mentioned in the Constitution; the chamber's most powerful position; traditionally a member of the majority party.

special district A local government that is restricted to a particular function.

spoils system The firing of public-office holders of a defeated political party to replace them with loyalists of the newly elected party.

Stamp Act Congress Meeting of representatives of nine of the thirteen colonies held in New York City in 1765, during which representatives drafted a document to send to the king that listed how their rights had been violated.

standing committee Committee to which proposed bills are referred; continues from one Congress to the next.

stare decisis In court rulings, a reliance on past decisions or precedents to formulate decisions in new cases.

statist One who believes in extensive government control of personal and economic liberties.

strategic trade policy A trade policy wherein governments identify key industries that they wish to see grow and enact policies to support their development and success.

stratified sampling A variation of random sampling; the population is divided into subgroups and weighted based on demographic characteristics of the national population.

straw poll Unscientific survey used to gauge public opinion on a variety of issues and policies.

strict constructionist An approach to constitutional interpretation that emphasizes interpreting the Constitution as it was originally written and intended by the Framers.

strict scrutiny A heightened standard of review used by the Supreme Court to determine the constitutional validity of a challenged practice.

substantive due process Judicial interpretation of the Fifth and Fourteenth Amendments' due process clauses that protects citizens from arbitrary or unjust state or federal laws.

suffrage movement The drive for voting rights for women that took place in the United States from 1890 to 1920.

Super PACs Political action committees established to make independent expenditures.

superdelegate Delegate to the Democratic Party's national convention that is reserved for a party official and whose vote at the convention is unpledged to a candidate.

supremacy clause Portion of Article VI of the Constitution mandating that national law is supreme to (that is, supersedes) all other laws passed by the states or by any other subdivision of government.

suspect classification Category or class, such as race, that triggers the highest standard of scrutiny from the Supreme Court.

symbolic speech Symbols, signs, and other methods of expression generally considered to be protected by the First Amendment.

systemic agenda A discussion agenda; it consists of all public issues that are viewed as requiring governmental attention.

T

Taliban A fundamentalist Islamic group that controlled Afghanistan from 1996 until U.S. military intervention in 2001. The Taliban provided refuge for al-Qaeda, allowing terrorist training camps to operate in the country.

tariffs Taxes on imported goods.

Tenth Amendment The final part of the Bill of Rights that defines the basic principle of American federalism in stating that the powers not delegated to the national government are reserved to the states or to the people.

The Federalist Papers A series of eighty-five political essays written by Alexander Hamilton, James Madison, and John Jay in support of ratification of the U.S. Constitution.

think tank Institutional collection of policy-oriented researchers and academics who are sources of policy ideas.

Thirteenth Amendment One of the three Civil War Amendments; specifically bans slavery in the United States.

Three-Fifths Compromise Agreement reached at the Constitutional Convention stipulating that each slave was to be counted as three-fifths of a person for purposes of determining population for representation in the U.S. House of Representatives.

ticket-splitting Voting for candidates of different parties for various offices in the same election.

Title IX Provision of the Education Amendments of 1972 that bars educational institutions that receive federal funds from discriminating against female students.

totalitarianism A form of government in which power resides in a leader who rules according to self-interest and without regard for individual rights and liberties.

tracking polls Continuous surveys that enable a campaign or news organization to chart a candidate's daily rise or fall in support.

trade association A group that represents a specific industry.

transactions theory The theory that public policies are the result of narrowly defined exchanges or transactions among political actors.

trial court Court of original jurisdiction where cases begin.

Truman Doctrine U.S. anti-communist policy initiated in 1947 that became the basis of U.S. foreign policy throughout the Cold War.

trustee Role played by an elected representative who listens to constituents' opinions and then uses his or her best judgment to make a final decision.

trusts Large-scale, monopolistic businesses that dominate an industry.

turnout The proportion of the voting-age public that casts a ballot.

Twenty-Fifth Amendment Adopted in 1967 to establish procedures for filling vacancies in the office of president and vice president as well as providing for procedures to deal with the disability of a president.

Twenty-Second Amendment Adopted in 1951; prevents a president from serving more than two terms, or more than ten years if he came to office via the death, resignation, or impeachment of his predecessor.

U

UN Security Council A principal part of the United Nations, charged with authorizing peacekeeping operations, international sanctions, and military action in order to maintain global peace and security.

unconventional political participation Activism that attempts to influence the political process through unusual or extreme measures, such as protests, boycotts, and picketing.

unified government The political condition in which the same political party controls the presidency and Congress.

unitary system System of government in which the local and regional governments derive all authority from a strong national government

***U.S. v. Nixon* (1974)** Supreme Court ruling on power of the president, holding that no absolute constitutional executive privilege allows a president to refuse to comply with a court order to produce information needed in a criminal trial.

veto The formal, constitutional authority of the president to reject bills passed by both houses of Congress, thus preventing them from becoming law without further congressional action.

Virginia Plan The first general plan for the Constitution offered in Philadelphia. Its key points were a bicameral legislature, as well as an executive and a judiciary chosen by the national legislature.

voter canvass The process by which a campaign reaches individual voters, either by door-to-door solicitation or by telephone.

vouchers Certificates issued by the government that may be applied toward the cost of attending private or other public schools.

W

War Powers Resolution Passed by Congress in 1973; the president is limited in the deployment of troops overseas to a sixty-day period in peacetime (which can be extended for an extra thirty days to permit withdrawal) unless Congress explicitly gives its approval for a longer period.

whip Party leader who keeps close contact with all members of his or her party, takes vote counts on key legislation, prepares summaries of bills, and acts as a communications link within a party.

winner-take-all system An electoral system in which the party that receives at least one more vote than any other party wins the election.

World Bank International governmental organization created to provide loans for large economic development projects.

World Trade Organization (WTO) An international organization that replaced the GATT in 1995 to supervise and expand international trade.

writ of *certiorari* A request for the Supreme Court to order up the records from a lower court to review the case.

writs of *habeas corpus* Petition requesting that a judge order authorities to prove that a prisoner is being held lawfully and that allows the prisoner to be freed if the government's case does not persuade the judge. *Habeas corpus* rights imply that prisoners have a right to know what charges are being made against them.

yellow journalism A form of newspaper publishing in vogue in the late nineteenth century that featured pictures, comics, color, and sensationalized news coverage.

NOTES

1

1. John Hammond, *Leah and Rachael, or the Two Fruitful Sisters, Virginia and Maryland; their Present Condition Impartially Stated and Related* (London: Force Tracts, 1656).
2. Pew Forum on Religion and Public Life, "Growing Number of Americans Say Islam Encourages Violence" (July 24, 2003), www.pewforum.org.
3. Susan A. MacManus, *Young v. Old. Generational Combat in the 21st Century* (Boulder, CO: Westview, 1995), 3.
4. Dennis Cauchon, "Who Will Take Care of an Older Population?" *USA Today* (October 25, 2005): 1–2B.
5. James B. Gimpel and Kimberly A. Karnes, "The Rural Side of the Urban-Rural Gap," *PS: Political Science and Politics* (July 2006): 467–72.
6. CNN Exit Polls, http://www.cnn.com/election/2012/results/race/president#exit-polls.
7. "Americans' Preference for Smaller Families Edges Higher," Gallup Poll (June 30, 2011): http://www.gallup.com/poll/148355/Americans-Preferences-Smaller-Families-Edges-Higher.aspx.
8. U.S. Census Bureau, *2012 Statistical Abstract of the United States.*
9. This discussion draws heavily from Terence Ball and Richard Dagger, *Political Ideologies and the Democratic Ideal*, 5th ed. (New York: Longman, 2004).
10. Ball and Dagger, *Political Ideologies and the Democratic Ideal*, 2.
11. Isaiah Berlin, *The Crooked Timber of Humanity: Chapters in the History of Ideas* (New York: Vintage, 1992), 1.
12. William Safire, *Safire's New Political Dictionary* (New York: Random House, 1993), 144–5.
13. Jack C. Plano and Milton Greenberg, *The American Political Dictionary*, 9th ed. (Fort Worth, TX: Harcourt Brace, 1993), 16.
14. Philip E. Converse, "The Nature of Belief Systems in Mass Publics," in David E. Apter, ed., *Ideology and Discontent* (New York: Free Press, 1964), 206–21.
15. Allstate/National Journal Poll (November 30-December 4, 2011): syndication.nationaljournal.com/communications/Allstate%20National%20Journal%20Heartland%20Monitor%20XI%20TOPLINE.pdf.
16. Rasmussen Reports, "Right Direction or Wrong Track," (June 27, 2012): http://www.rasmussenreports.com/public_content/politics/mood_of_amercian/right_direction_or_wrong_track/.

2

1. See Richard B. Bernstein with Jerome Agel, *Amending America* (New York: New York Times Books, 1993), 138–40.
2. *Oregon* v. *Mitchell,* 400 U.S. 112 (1970).
3. Bernstein with Agel, *Amending America,* 139.
4. For an account of the early development of the colonies, see D. W. Meining, *The Shaping of America,* vol. 1: *Atlantic America, 1492–1800* (New Haven, CT: Yale University Press, 1986).
5. For an excellent chronology of the events leading up to the writing of the Declaration of Independence and the colonists' break with Great Britain, see Calvin D. Lonton, ed., *The Bicentennial Almanac* (Nashville, TN: Thomas Nelson, 1975).
6. See Garry Wills, *Inventing America: Jefferson's Declaration of Independence* (New York: Random House, 1978). Wills argues that the Declaration was signed solely to secure foreign aid for the ongoing war effort.
7. See Gordon S. Wood, *The Creation of the American Republic, 1776–1787,* reissue ed. (New York: Norton, 1993).
8. For more about the Articles of Confederation, see Merrill Jensen, *The Articles of Confederation* (Madison: University of Wisconsin Press, 1940).
9. Charles A. Beard, *An Economic Interpretation of the Constitution of the United States,* reissue ed. (Mineola, NY: Dover, 2004).
10. Quoted in Richard N. Current, et al., *American History: A Survey,* 6th ed. (New York: Knopf, 1983), 170.
11. John Patrick Diggins, "Power and Authority in American History: The Case of Charles A. Beard and His Critics," *American Historical Review* 86 (October 1981): 701–30; and Robert Brown, *Charles Beard and the Constitution: A Critical Analysis of "An Economic Interpretation of the Constitution"* (Princeton, NJ: Princeton University Press, 1956).
12. Jackson Turner Main, *The Anti-Federalists: Critics of the Constitution, 1781–1788* (Chapel Hill: University of North Carolina, 2004).
13. Wood, *Creation of the American Republic.*
14. For more on the political nature of compromise at the convention, see Calvin C. Jillson. *Constitution Making: Conflict and Consensus in the Federal Constitution of 1787* (New York: Agathon, 1988).
15. Quoted in Doris Faber and Harold Faber, *We the People* (New York: Scribner's, 1987), 31.
16. Quoted in Current, et al., *American History,* 168.
17. Bernard Bailyn, *The Ideological Origins of the American Revolution* (Cambridge, MA: Belknap Press, 1967).
18. Richard E. Neustadt, *Presidential Power: The Politics of Leadership from FDR to Carter* (New York: Macmillan, 1980), 26.
19. Quoted in Faber and Faber, *We the People,* 51–52.
20. Federal Republicans favored a republican or representative form of government (do not confuse this term with the modern Republican Party, which came into being in 1854. Ultimately, the word *federal* referred to the form of government embodied in the new Constitution, and *confederation* referred to a "league of states," as under the Articles, and later was applied in the "Confederacy" of 1861–1865 that governed the southern states.
21. See Ralph Ketcham, ed., *The Anti-Federalist Papers and the Constitutional Debates* (New York: New American Library, 1986).
22. See Herbert J. Storing, *What the Anti-Federalists Were For* (Chicago: University of Chicago Press, 1981), for a fuller discussion of Anti-Federalist views.
23. David E. Kyvig, *Repealing National Prohibition* (Chicago: University of Chicago Press, 1978).
24. See Jane J. Mansbridge, *Why We Lost the ERA* (Chicago: University of Chicago Press, 1986).
25. *Marbury* v. *Madison,* 5 U.S. 137 (1803).
26. See, for example, the speech by Attorney General Edwin Meese III before the American Bar Association, July 9, 1985, Washington, DC. See also Antonin Scalia and Amy Gutman, eds., *A Matter of Interpretation: Federal Courts and the Law* (Princeton, NJ: Princeton University Press, 1998).

27. See, for example, the speech by Associate Justice William J. Brennan Jr. at Georgetown University Text and Teaching Symposium, October 10, 1985, Washington, DC.
28. Bruce Ackerman, *We the People: Foundations* (Cambridge, MA: Belknap Press, 1991).
29. Social Security Administration Office of Retirement and Disability Policy, "Old Age, Survivors, and Disability Insurance." Accessed online at http://www.ssa.gov/policy/docs/statcomps/supplement/2010/5a.html#table5.a4.

3

1. Randal C. Archibold, "Arizona Enacts Stringent Law on Immigration," *New York Times* (April 23, 2010): A1.
2. *Arizona* v. *United States,* 567 U.S.____(2012).
3. *Missouri* v. *Holland,* 252 U.S. 416 (1920).
4. John Mountjoy, "Interstate Cooperation: Interstate Compacts Make a Comeback," Council of State Governments, www.csg.org.
5. *McCulloch* v. *Maryland,* 17 U.S. 316 (1819).
6. For more on *McCulloch,* see Richard E. Ellis, *Aggressive Nationalism:* McCulloch *v.* Maryland *and the Foundation of Federal Authority in the Young Republic* (New York: Oxford University Press, 2008).
7. *Gibbons* v. *Ogden,* 22 U.S. 1 (1824).
8. For more on *Gibbons,* see Thomas H. Cox, Gibbons *v.* Ogden: *Law and Society in the Early Republic* (Athens, OH: Ohio University Press, 2010).
9. *Barron* v. *Baltimore,* 32 U.S. 243 (1833).
10. For more on *Barron,* see Brendan J. Doherty, "Interpreting the Bill of Rights and the Nature of Federalism: *Barron* v. *City of Baltimore*." *Journal of Supreme Court History* 32 (2007): 211–28.
11. *Abelman* v. *Booth,* 62 U.S. 506 (1859).
12. *Dred Scott* v. *Sandford,* 60 U.S. 393 (1857).
13. *Pensacola Telegraph* v. *Western Union,* 96 U.S. 1 (1877).
14. U.S. v. *E. C. Knight,* 156 U.S. 1 (1895).
15. *Pollock* v. *Farmers Loan and Trust,* 157 U.S. 429 (1895); and *Springer* v. *U.S.,* 102 U.S. 586 (1881).
16. John O. McGinnis, "The State of Federalism," Testimony before the Senate Government Affairs Committee, May 5, 1999.
17. Morton Grodzins, "Centralization and Decentralization in the American Federal System," in Robert A. Goldwin, ed., *A Nation of States* (Chicago: Rand McNally, 1963), 3–4.
18. Jeff Shesol, *Supreme Power: Franklin Roosevelt vs. the Supreme Court* (New York: W.W. Norton, 2010).
19. *NLRB* v. *Jones and Laughlin Steel Co.,* 301 U.S. 1 (1937).
20. *Wickard* v. *Filburn,* 317 U.S. 111 (1942).
21. Richard P. Nathan, Fred C. Doolittle, and Associates, *Reagan and the States* (Princeton, NJ: Princeton University Press, 1987), 4.
22. Gene Healy and Timothy Lynch, "Power Surge: The Constitutional Record of George W. Bush" (Washington, DC: Cato Institute, 2006), 20.
23. Conn Carroll, "A Brief History of Earmarks," The Heritage Foundation, blog.heritage.org/2010/12/23/a-brief-history-of-earmarks/.
24. Linda Greenhouse, "The Rehnquist Court and Its Imperiled States' Rights Legacy," *New York Times* (June 12, 2005): A3.
25. *U.S.* v. *Lopez,* 514 U.S. 549 (1995).
26. *Arizona* v. *United States,* 567 U.S. ____(2012) and *National Federation of Independent Business* v. *Sebelius,* 567 U.S.____ (2012).
27. Paul E. Peterson, *The Price of Federalism* (Washington, DC: Brookings Institution, 1995).
28. Peter Harkness, "What Brand of Federalism Is Next?" *Governing* (January 2012): http://www.governing.com/columns/potomac-chronicle/gov-col-what-brand-of-federalism-is-next.html.
29. William J. Kovacs, quoted in John Schwartz, "Obama Seems to Be Open to a Broader Role for States," *New York Times* (January 30, 2009): A16.

4

1. *U.S.* v. *Jones,* 564 U.S. ____ (2012); Robert Barnes, "Supreme Court: Warrants Needed in GPS Tracking," *Washington Post* (January 23, 2012).
2. *Florence* v. *Board of Chosen Freeholders of the County of Burlington,* 566 U.S. ____ (2012).
3. The absence of a bill of rights led Mason to refuse to sign the proposed Constitution, noting that he "would sooner chop off his right hand than put it to the Constitution as it now stands." Quoted in Eric Black, *Our Constitution: The Myth That Binds Us* (Boulder, CO: Westview, 1988), 75.
4. Quoted in Jack N. Rakove, "Madison Won Passage of the Bill of Rights but Remained a Skeptic," *Public Affairs Report* (March 1991): 6.
5. *Barron* v. *Baltimore,* 32 U.S. 243 (1833).
6. *Allgeyer* v. *Louisiana,* 165 U.S. 578 (1897).
7. *Gitlow* v. *New York,* 268 U.S. 652 (1925).
8. *Near* v. *Minnesota,* 283 U.S. 697 (1931). For more about *Near,* see Fred W. Friendly, *Minnesota Rag: The Dramatic Story of the Landmark Case That Gave New Meaning to Freedom of the Press* (New York: Random House, 1981).
9. *Palko* v. *Connecticut,* 302 U.S. 319 (1937).
10. *Benton v. Maryland,* 395 U.S. 784 (1969).
11. *Reynolds* v. *U.S.,* 98 U.S. 145 (1879).
12. *Cantwell* v. *Connecticut,* 310 U.S. 296 (1940).
13. *Zobrest* v. *Catalina Foothills School District,* 506 U.S. 813 (1992).
14. *Engel* v. *Vitale,* 370 U.S. 421 (1962).
15. *Abington School District* v. *Schempp,* 374 U.S. 203 (1963).
16. *Lemon* v. *Kurtzman,* 403 U.S. 602 (1971).
17. *Widmar* v. *Vincent,* 454 U.S. 263 (1981).
18. *Rosenberger* v. *University of Virginia,* 515 U.S. 819 (1995).
19. *Mitchell* v. *Helms,* 530 U.S. 793 (2000).
20. *Zelman* v. *Simmons-Harris,* 536 U.S. 639 (2002).
21. *Lee* v. *Weisman,* 505 U.S. 577 (1992).
22. *McCreary County* v. *ACLU of Kentucky,* 545 U.S. 844 (2005).
23. *Salazar* v. *Buono,* 559 U.S. ____ (2010).
24. *U.S.* v. *Seeger,* 380 U.S. 163 (1965).
25. *Cruz* v. *Beto,* 405 U.S. 319 (1972).
26. *O'Lone* v. *Shabazz,* 482 U.S. 342 (1987).
27. *Employment Division, Dept. of Human Resources of Oregon* v. *Smith,* 494 U.S. 872 (1990).
28. *Boerne* v. *Flores,* 521 U.S. 507 (1997).
29. *Gonzales* v. *O Centro Espirita Beneficente União do Vegetal,* 546 U.S. 418 (2006).
30. David M. O'Brien, *Constitutional Law and Politics,* vol. 2: *Civil Rights and Civil Liberties* (New York: Norton, 1991), 345.
31. *Schenck* v. *U.S.,* 249 U.S. 47 (1919).
32. *Brandenburg* v. *Ohio,* 395 U.S. 444 (1969).
33. *New York Times Co.* v. *U.S.,* 403 U.S. 713 (1971).
34. *Nebraska Press Association* v. *Stuart,* 427 U.S. 539 (1976).
35. *Abrams* v. *U.S.,* 250 U.S. 616 (1919).
36. *Stromberg* v. *California,* 283 U.S. 359 (1931).

37. *Tinker* v. *Des Moines Independent Community School District,* 393 U.S. 503 (1969).
38. *Morse* v. *Frederick,* 551 U.S. 393 (2007).
39. Harry Kalven Jr., *Negro and the First Amendment* (Chicago: University of Chicago Press, 1966).
40. Henry Louis Gates Jr., "Let Them Talk: Why Civil Liberties Pose No Threat to Civil Rights," *New Republic* (September 20, 1993): 12-13.
41. *R.A.V.* v. *City of St. Paul,* 505 U.S. 377 (1992).
42. *Virginia* v. *Black,* 538 U.S. 343 (2003).
43. *Chaplinsky* v. *New Hampshire,* 315 U.S. 568 (1942).
44. *New York Times Co.* v. *Sullivan,* 376 U.S. 254 (1964).
45. *Hustler Magazine* v. *Falwell,* 485 U.S. 46 (1988).
46. *Chaplinsky* v. *New Hampshire,* 315 U.S. 568 (1942).
47. *Regina* v. *Hicklin,* L.R. 2 Q.B. 360 (1868).
48. *Roth* v. *U.S.,* 354 U.S. 476 (1957).
49. *Miller* v. *California,* 413 U.S. 15 (1973).
50. *Barnes* v. *Glen Theater,* 501 U.S. 560 (1991).
51. *Reno* v. *American Civil Liberties Union,* 521 U.S. 844 (1997); David G. Savage, "Ban on 'Virtual' Child Porn Is Upset by Court," *Los Angeles Times* (April 17, 2002): A1; and *Ashcroft* v. *American Civil Liberties Union,* 542 U.S. 656 (2004).
52. *U.S.* v. *Williams,* 553 U.S. 285 (2008).
53. *DeJonge* v. *Oregon,* 229 U.S. 353 (1937).
54. *John Doe #1* v. *Reed,* 561 U.S. ____ (2010).
55. *Barron* v. *Baltimore,* 32 U.S. 243 (1833).
56. *Dred Scott* v. *Sandford,* 60 U.S. 393 (1857).
57. *U.S.* v. *Miller,* 307 U.S. 174 (1939).
58. *D.C.* v. *Heller,* 554 U.S. 290 (2008).
59. *Heller* v. *District of Columbia,* civil action 08-1289 (2010).
60. *McDonald* v. *City of Chicago,* 561 U.S. ____ (2010).
61. *U.S.* v. *Sokolov,* 490 U.S. 1 (1989).
62. *Georgia* v. *Randolph,* 547 U.S. 103 (2006).
63. *Hester* v. *U.S.,* 265 U.S. 57 (1924).
64. *Johnson* v. *U.S.,* 333 U.S. 10 (1948).
65. *Michigan* v. *Tyler,* 436 U.S. 499 (1978).
66. *Carroll* v. *U.S.,* 267 U.S. 132 (1925).
67. *U.S.* v. *Arvizu,* 534 U.S. 266 (2002).
68. *South Dakota* v. *Neville,* 459 U.S. 553 (1983).
69. *Arizona* v. *Gant,* 556 U.S. 332 (2009).
70. *United States* v. *Jones,* 564 U.S. ____ (2012).
71. *Skinner* v. *Railway Labor Executives' Association,* 489 U.S. 602 (1989).
72. *Vernonia School District* v. *Acton,* 515 U.S. 646 (1995).
73. *Board of Education of Independent School District No. 92 of Pottawatomie County* v. *Earls,* 536 U.S. 822 (2002).
74. *Counselman* v. *Hitchcock,* 142 U.S. 547 (1892).
75. *Brown* v. *Mississippi,* 297 U.S. 278 (1936).
76. *Lynum* v. *Illinois,* 372 U.S. 528 (1963).
77. *Miranda* v. *Arizona,* 384 U.S. 436 (1966).
78. *Rhode Island* v. *Innis,* 446 U.S. 291 (1980).
79. *Arizona* v. *Fulminante,* 499 U.S. 279 (1991).
80. *Weeks* v. *U.S.,* 232 U.S. 383 (1914).
81. *Mapp* v. *Ohio,* 367 U.S. 643 (1961).
82. *Stone* v. *Powell,* 428 U.S. 465 (1976).
83. *U.S.* v. *Grubbs,* 547 U.S. 90 (2006).
84. *Powell* v. *Alabama,* 287 U.S. 45 (1932).
85. *Johnson* v. *Zerbst,* 304 U.S. 458 (1938).
86. *Gideon* v. *Wainwright,* 372 U.S. 335 (1963).
87. *Argersinger* v. *Hamlin,* 407 U.S. 25 (1972).
88. *Rothgery* v. *Gillespie County,* 554 U.S. 191 (2008).
89. *Rompilla* v. *Beard,* 545 U.S. 374 (2005).
90. *Hernandez* v. *Texas,* 347 U.S. 475 (1954).
91. *Batson* v. *Kentucky,* 476 U.S. 79 (1986).
92. *J.E.B.* v. *Alabama,* 511 U.S. 127 (1994).
93. *Maryland* v. *Craig,* 497 U.S. 836 (1990).
94. *Hallinger* v. *Davis,* 146 U.S. 314 (1892).
95. *O'Neil* v. *Vermont,* 144 U.S. 323 (1892).
96. See Michael Meltsner, *Cruel and Unusual: The Supreme Court and Capital Punishment* (New York: Random House, 1973).
97. *Furman* v. *Georgia,* 408 U.S. 238 (1972).
98. *Gregg* v. *Georgia,* 428 U.S. 153 (1976).
99. *McCleskey* v. *Kemp,* 481 U.S. 279 (1987).
100. *McCleskey* v. *Zant,* 499 U.S. 467 (1991).
101. *Baze* v. *Rees,* 553 U.S. 35 (2008).
102. *Atkins* v. *Virginia,* 536 U.S. 304 (2002); and *Roper* v. *Simmons,* 543 U.S. 551 (2005).
103. *House* v. *Bell,* 547 U.S. 518 (2006).
104. *Skinner* v. *Switzer,* 562 U.S. ____ (2011).
105. *Olmstead* v. *U.S.,* 277 U.S. 438 (1928).
106. *Griswold* v. *Connecticut,* 381 U.S. 481 (1965).
107. *Eisenstadt* v. *Baird,* 410 U.S. 113 (1972).
108. *Roe* v. *Wade,* 410 U.S. 113 (1973).
109. *Beal* v. *Doe,* 432 U.S. 438 (1977); and *Harris* v. *McRae,* 448 U.S. 297 (1980).
110. *Webster* v. *Reproductive Health Services,* 492 U.S. 490 (1989).
111. *Planned Parenthood of Southeastern Pennsylvania* v. *Casey,* 505 U.S. 833 (1992).
112. *Stenberg* v. *Carhart,* 530 U.S. 914 (2000).
113. Alison Young, "States Seek New Ways to Restrict New Abortions," *USA Today* (April 26, 2010): 1A.
114. *Bowers* v. *Hardwick,* 478 U.S. 186 (1986); and *Lawrence* v. *Texas,* 539 U.S. 558 (2003).
115. Jennifer Levin, "Alternative Reality About Public, War," *Associated Press* (May 29, 2007).
116. "Surveillance Under the USA Patriot Act," American Civil Liberties Union, April 3, 2003.
117. *Rasul* v. *Bush,* 542 U.S. 466 (2004).
118. *Boumediene* v. *Bush,* 553 U.S. 723 (2008).
119. *Hamdan* v. *Rumsfeld,* 548 U.S. 557 (2006).
120. Shane Scott, David Johnston, and James Risen, "Secret U.S. Endorsement of Severe Interrogations," *New York Times* (October 7, 2007): A1.
121. Jennifer Loven and Devlin Barrett, "CIA Officials Won't Be Prosecuted for Waterboarding, Obama Admin Says," *Huffington Post* (April 16, 2009), www.huffingtonpost.com.

5

1. This vignette draws on Abigail Lofberg, "Pay Equity: Calling Out Walmart's Two Wealthiest Women," *Huffington Post* (June 4, 2012): www.huffingtonpost.com; Roberta Guise, "Women's Pay Equity Still a Sore Point," *San Francisco Gate* (April 10, 2011): www.sfgate.com; and *Walmart* v. *Dukes,* 564 U.S. ____ (2011).
2. *Civil Rights Cases,* 109 U.S. 3 (1883).
3. *Plessy* v. *Ferguson,* 163 U.S. 537 (1896).
4. Jack Greenberg, *Judicial Process and Social Change: Constitutional Litigation* (St. Paul, MN: West, 1976), 583–86.
5. Juan Williams, *Eyes on the Prize: America's Civil Rights Years, 1954–1965* (New York: Penguin, 1987), 10.
6. *Williams* v. *Mississippi,* 170 U.S. 213 (1898); and *Cummins* v. *Richmond County Board of Education,* 175 U.S. 528 (1899).
7. *Bailey* v. *Alabama,* 211 U.S. 452 (1908).
8. *Muller* v. *Oregon,* 208 U.S. 412 (1908).
9. *Missouri* ex rel. *Gaines* v. *Canada,* 305 U.S. 337 (1938).
10. Richard Kluger, *Simple Justice* (New York: Vintage, 1975), 268.

11. *Sweatt* v. *Painter,* 339 U.S. 629 (1950); and *McLaurin* v. *Oklahoma,* 339 U.S. 637 (1950).
12. *Sweatt* v. *Painter,* 339 U.S. 629 (1950).
13. *Brown* v. *Board of Education,* 347 U.S. 483 (1954).
14. But see Gerald Rosenberg, *The Hollow Hope: Can Courts Bring About Social Change?* (Chicago: University of Chicago Press, 1991).
15. Quoted in Williams, *Eyes on the Prize,* 10.
16. Michael McCann, "Reform Litigation on Trial." *Law and Social Inquiry* 17(1992): 715–43.
17. *Brown* v. *Board of Education II,* 349 U.S. 294 (1955).
18. Quoted in Williams, *Eyes on the Prize,* 37.
19. *Cooper* v. *Aaron,* 358 U.S. 1 (1958).
20. *Heart of Atlanta Motel* v. *U.S.,* 379 U.S. 241 (1964).
21. *Swann* v. *Charlotte-Mecklenburg School District,* 402 U.S. 1 (1971).
22. *Parents Involved in Community Schools* v. *Seattle School District,* 551 U.S. 101 (2007).
23. *Griggs* v. *Duke Power Co.,* 401 U.S. 424 (1971).
24. Jo Freeman, *The Politics of Women's Liberation* (New York: Longman, 1975), 57.
25. Betty Friedan, *The Feminine Mystique* (New York: Dell, 1963).
26. *Korematsu* v. *U.S.,* 323 U.S. 214 (1944). This is the only case involving race-based distinctions applying the strict scrutiny standard where the Court has upheld the restrictive law.
27. *Reed* v. *Reed,* 404 U.S. 71 (1971).
28. *Craig* v. *Boren,* 429 U.S. 190 (1976).
29. *Mississippi University for Women* v. *Hogan,* 458 U.S. 718 (1982).
30. *Craig* v. *Boren,* 429 U.S. 190 (1976).
31. *Orr* v. *Orr,* 440 U.S. 268 (1979).
32. *J.E.B.* v. *Alabama* ex rel. *TB,* 440 U.S. 268 (1979).
33. *U.S.* v. *Virginia,* 518 U.S. 515 (1996).
34. *Rostker* v. *Goldberg,* 453 U.S. 57 (1981).
35. *Michael M.* v. *Superior Court of Sonoma County,* 450 U.S. 464 (1981).
36. *Nguyen* v. *INS,* 533 U.S. 53 (2001).
37. *Rostker* v. *Goldberg,* 453 U.S. 57 (1981).
38. *U.S.* v. *Virginia,* 518 U.S. 515 (1996).
39. *Ledbetter* v. *Goodyear Tire and Rubber Co.,* 550 U.S. 618 (2007).
40. *Meritor Savings Bank* v. *Vinson,* 477 U.S. 57 (1986).
41. *Oncale* v. *Sundowner Offshore Services, Inc.,* 523 U.S. 75 (1998).
42. *Hishon* v. *King & Spalding,* 467 U.S. 69 (1984).
43. *Johnson* v. *Transportation Agency,* 480 U.S. 616 (1987).
44. Joyce Gelb and Marian Lief Palley, *Women and Public Policies* (Charlottesville: University of Virginia Press, 1996).
45. *Davis* v. *Monroe County Board of Education,* 526 U.S. 629 (1999).
46. *Jackson* v. *Birmingham Board of Education,* 544 U.S. 167 (2005).
47. *Hernandez* v. *Texas,* 347 U.S. 475 (1954).
48. *White* v. *Register,* 412 U.S. 755 (1973).
49. *San Antonio Independent School District* v. *Rodriguez,* 411 U.S. 1 (1973).
50. *Edgewood Independent School District* v. *Kirby,* 777 S.W.2d 391 Texas 1989.
51. "MALDEF Pleased with Settlement of California Public Schools Inequity Case, *Williams* v. *California,*" August 13, 2004: www.maldef.org.
52. *LULAC* v. *Perry,* 548 U.S. 399 (2006); and "Redistricting in Texas," *New York Times* (January 20, 2012): online.
53. *Cobell* v. *Salazar,* 573 F3d 808 (2009). For more on the Indian trust, see www.indiantrust.com.
54. *Employment Division of the Oregon Department of Human Resources* v. *Smith,* 494 U.S. 872 (1990).
55. *Boerne* v. *Flores,* 521 U.S. 507 (1997).
56. Dee Brown, *Bury My Heart at Wounded Knee* (New York: Holt, Rinehart and Winston, 1971).
57. Roger Daniels, *Asian America: Chinese and Japanese in the United States Since 1850* (Seattle: University of Washington Press, 1988).
58. *Yick Wo* v. *Hopkins,* 118 U.S. 356 (1886).
59. *Ozawa* v. *U.S.,* 260 U.S. 178 (1922).
60. *Korematsu* v. *U.S.,* 323 U.S. 214 (1944).
61. Diane Helene Miller, *Freedom to Differ: The Shaping of the Gay and Lesbian Struggle for Civil Rights* (New York: New York University Press, 1998).
62. Sarah Brewer et al., "Sex and the Supreme Court: Gays, Lesbians, and Justice," in Craig A. Rimmerman, Kenneth D. Wald, and Clyde Wilcox, eds., *The Politics of Gay Rights* (Chicago: University of Chicago Press, 2000): 377-408.
63. Evan Gerstmann, *The Constitutional Underclass: Gays, Lesbians, and the Failure of Class-Based Equal Protection* (Chicago: University of Chicago Press, 1999).
64. *Romer* v. *Evans,* 517 U.S. 620 (1996).
65. *Lawrence* v. *Texas,* 539 U.S. 558 (2003).
66. Joan Biskupic, "Court's Opinion on Gay Rights Reflects Trends," *USA Today* (July 18, 2003): 2A.
67. Maura Dolan, "Prop. 8 Backers Seek Full Review by Appeals Court," *Los Angeles Times* (February 22, 2012): www.latimes.com.
68. *Perry* v. *Brown,* 671 F.3d 1052 (9th Circuit, February 7, 2012)
69. David Pfeiffer, "Overview of the Disability Movement: History, Legislative Record and Political Implications," *Policy Studies Journal* (Winter 1993): 724–42; and "Understanding Disability Policy," *Policy Studies Journal* (Spring 1996): 157–74.
70. Joan Biskupic, "Supreme Court Limits Meaning of Disability," *Washington Post* (June 23, 1999): A1.
71. *Sutton* v. *United Air Lines, Inc.,* 527 U.S. 471 (1999).
72. *Tennessee* v. *Lane,* 541 U.S. 509 (2004).
73. American Association of People with Disabilities, www.aapd.com.
74. *Regents of the University of California* v. *Bakke,* 438 U.S. 265 (1978).
75. *United Steelworkers of America* v. *Weber,* 443 U.S. 193 (1979).
76. *Johnson* v. *Santa Clara County,* 480 U.S. 616 (1987).
77. Ruth Marcus, "Hill Coalition Aims to Counter Court in Job Bias," *Washington Post* (February 8, 1990): A10.
78. *Adarand Constructors* v. *Pena,* 515 U.S. 200 (1995).
79. Cert. denied, *Texas* v. *Hopwood,* 518 U.S. 1033 (1996). See also Terrance Scurz, "UT Minority Enrollment Tested by Suit: Fate of Affirmative Action in Education Is at Issue," *Dallas Morning News* (October 14, 1995).
80. *Grutter* v. *Bollinger,* 539 U.S. 306 (2003).
81. *Gratz* v. *Bollinger,* 539 U.S. 244 (2003).
82. *Fisher* v. *Texas,* _____ U.S. _____ (2013).

6

1. Charles S. Bullock III, "House Careerists: Changing Patterns of Longevity and Attrition," *American Political Science Review* 66 (December 1972): 1295–1300.
2. Richard F. Fenno Jr., "U.S. House Members in Their Constituencies: An Exploration," *American Political Science Review* 71 (September 1977): 883–917.
3. Richard F. Fenno Jr., *Home Style: House Members in Their Districts* (New York: Longman, 2009), 32; and Judy Schneider and Michael L. Koempel, *Congressional Deskbook 2005–2007: 109th Congress* (Alexandria, VA: Capital Net, 2005).
4. Hedrick Smith, *The Power Game* (New York: Ballantine Books, 1989), 108.

5. Jennifer E. Manning, "Membership of the 111th Congress: A Profile," *Congressional Research Service Report for Congress* (July 19, 2010): http://opencrs.com.
6. Gary W. Cox and Jonathan N. Katz, "Why Did the Incumbency Advantage in U.S. House Elections Grow?" *American Journal of Political Science* 40 (May 1996): 478–97; Kenneth N. Bickers and Robert M. Stein, "The Electoral Dynamics of the Federal Pork Barrel," *American Journal of Political Science* 40 (November 1996): 1300–26; "2010 Overview: Incumbent Advantage," www.opensecrets.org; and Scott Ashworth and Ethan Bueno de Mesquita, "Electoral Selection, Strategic Challenger Entry, and the Incumbency Advantage," *Journal of Politics* 70 (October 2008): 1006–25.
7. Marjorie Randon Hershey, "Congressional Elections," in Gerald M. Pomper, et al., *The Election of 1992: Reports and Interpretations* (Chatham, NJ: Chatham House, 1993), 159.
8. Jennifer Steinhauer, "Republicans Retain House by Shoring Up Incumbents," *New York Times* (November 7, 2012): http://www.nytimes.com/2012/11/07/us/politics/republicans-stand-firm-in-controlling-the-house.html?pagewanted=all.
9. "How to Rig an Election," *Economist* (April 25, 2002) 51-54.
10. In *Davis* v. *Bandemer,* 478 U.S. 109 (1986), the Court found that gerrymandering was not a political question but was unable to determine a standard by which to judge constitutionality.
11. *Wesberry* v. *Sanders,* 376 U.S. 1 (1964).
12. *Reynolds* v. *Sims,* 377 U.S. 533 (1964).
13. *Thornburg* v. *Gingles,* 478 U.S. 30 (1986).
14. *Shaw* v. *Reno,* 509 U.S. 630 (1993).
15. *LULAC* v. *Perry,* 548 U.S. 399 (2006).
16. "What is the Democratic Caucus?": www.dcaucusweb.house.gov.
17. Barbara Hinckley, *Stability and Change in Congress,* 3rd ed. (New York: Harper and Row, 1983), 166.
18. David R. Mayhew, "Supermajority Rule in the U.S. Senate," *PS: Political Science and Politics* 36 (January 2003): 31–36.
19. Barbara Sinclair, "The Struggle over Representation and Law-making in Congress: Leadership Reforms in the 1990s," in James A. Thurber and Roger H. Davidson, eds., *Remaking Congress: Change and Stability in the 1990s* (Washington, DC: CQ Press, 1995), 105.
20. Woodrow Wilson, *Congressional Government: A Study in American Politics* (Cambridge, MA: Riverside Press, 1885).
21. Roger H. Davidson, "Congressional Committees in the New Reform Era: From Combat to the Contract," in Thurber and Davidson, eds. *Remaking Congress,* 28.
22. Christopher Deering and Steven S. Smith, *Committees in Congress,* 3rd ed. (Washington, DC: CQ Press, 1997).
23. Wilson, *Congressional Government.*
24. Kenneth A. Shepsle, *The Giant Jigsaw Puzzle: Democratic Committee Assignments in the Modern House* (Chicago: University of Chicago Press, 1978).
25. *Wall Street Journal* (April 13, 1973): 10.
26. "The Mysteries of the Congressional Review Act," *Harvard Law Review* 122 (June 2009): 2163–83.
27. Cindy Skrzycki, "Reform's Knockout Act, Kept Out of the Ring," *Washington Post* (April 18, 2006): D1.
28. Gregory Korte, " 'Legislative Veto' Little Used Tool," *USA Today* (September 18, 2011): 7A.
29. Quoted in Stewart M. Powell, "Lee Fight Signals Tougher Battles Ahead on Nomination," *Commercial Appeal* (December 21, 1997): A15.
30. Warren E. Miller and Donald Stokes, "Constituency Influence in Congress," *American Political Science Review* 57 (March 1963): 45–57.
31. John W. Kingdon, *Congressmen's Voting Decisions,* 3rd ed. (Ann Arbor: University of Michigan Press, 1989). See also Lee Sigelman, Paul J. Wahlbeck, and Emmett H. Buell Jr., "Vote Choice and the Preference for Divided Government: Lessons of 1992," *American Journal of Political Science* 41 (July 1997): 879–94.
32. Barbara S. Romzek and Jennifer A. Utter, "Congressional Legislative Staff: Political Professionals or Clerks?" *American Journal of Political Science* 41 (October 1997): 1251–79; and Michael T. Heaney, "Brokering Health Policy: Coalitions, Parties, and Interest Group Influence," *Journal of Health Politics, Policy, and Law* 31 (October 2006): 887–944.
33. Russell A. Miller, "Lords of Democracy: The Judicialization of 'Pure Politics' in the United States and Germany," *Washington and Lee Law Review* 61 (2004): 587; Adam Liptak, "Court Under Roberts is Most Conservative in Decades," *New York Times* (July 28, 2010): www.nytimes.com.

7

1. "Two Hundred Years of Presidential Funerals," *Washington Post* (June 10, 2004): C14.
2. Gail Russell Chaddock, "The Rise of Mourning in America," *Christian Science Monitor* (June 11, 2004): 1.
3. Richard E. Neustadt, *Presidential Power and the Modern Presidency* (New York: Free Press, 1991).
4. Edward S. Corwin, *The President: Office and Powers, 1787–1957,* 4th ed. (New York: New York University Press, 1957), 5.
5. Quoted in Corwin, *The President,* 11.
6. Winston Solberg, *The Federal Convention and the Formation of the Union of the American States* (Indianapolis, IN: Bobbs-Merrill, 1958), 235.
7. Reynolds Holding, "Executive Privilege Showdown," *Time* (March 21, 2007): 21-24.
8. Craig Whitlock, "Gates Says Pentagon Faces Spending 'Crisis' over Congressional Inaction," *Washington Post* (January 28, 2011): Al.
9. Benjamin I. Page and Mark P. Petracca, *The American Presidency* (New York: McGraw-Hill, 1983), 262.
10. "Treaties," United States Senate Web site, www.senate.gov.
11. Jim Lobe, "Bush 'Unsigns' War Crimes Treaty," AlterNet, (May 6, 2002), www.alternet.org. See also Lincoln P. Bloomfield Jr., "The U.S. Government and the International Criminal Court," Remarks to the Parliamentarians for Global Action, Consultative Assembly of Parliamentarians for the International Criminal Court and the Rule of Laws, Address delivered at the United Nations, New York, September 12, 2003.
12. Quoted in Solberg, *The Federal Convention,* 91.
13. *Clinton* v. *City of New York,* 524 U.S. 417 (1998).
14. Quoted in Neustadt, *Presidential Power,* 9.
15. Quoted in Paul F. Boller Jr., *Presidential Anecdotes* (New York: Penguin Books, 1981), 78.
16. Lyn Ragsdale and John Theis III, "The Institutionalization of the American Presidency, 1924–1992," *American Journal of Political Science* 41 (October 1997): 1280–1318.
17. Quoted in Page and Petracca, *The American Presidency,* 57.
18. Alfred Steinberg, *The First Ten: The Founding Presidents and Their Administrations* (New York: Doubleday, 1967), 59.
19. George Reedy, *The Twilight of the Presidency* (New York: New American Library, 1971), 38–39.
20. Neustadt, *Presidential Power,* 1–10.
21. Nassir Ghaemi, *A First Rate Madness: Uncovering the Links Between Leadership and Mental Illness* (New York: Penguin, 2011).
22. Kernell, *Going Public.*
23. Tom Rosenstiel, *Strange Bedfellows: How Television and Presidential Candidates Changed American Politics* (New York: Hyperion Books, 1992).

24. Associated Press, "Twitter's Role in 2012 Presidential Campaign Extends Beyond 140 Characters." *Washington Post* (May 7, 2012): B7.
25. See Louis Fisher, *Constitutional Conflicts Between Congress and the President,* 7th ed. (Lawrence: University Press of Kansas, 2007).
26. Franklin D. Roosevelt, Press Conference, July 23, 1937.
27. Lyndon B. Johnson, *The Vantage Point* (New York: Holt, Rinehart and Winston, 1971), 448.
28. See Cary Covington, J. Mark Wrighton, and Rhonda Kinney, "A 'Presidency-Augmented' Model of Presidential Success on House Roll Call Votes," *American Journal of Political Science* 39 (November 1995): 1001–24; and Wayne P. Steger, "Presidential Policy Initiation and the Politics of Agenda Control," *Congress & the Presidency* 24 (Spring 1997): 102–14.
29. Quoted in Thomas E. Cronin, *The State of the Presidency,* 2nd ed. (Boston: Little, Brown, 1980), 169.
30. *Youngstown Sheet and Tube* v. *Sawyer,* 343 U.S. 579 (1952).
31. Charlie Savage, "Are Signing Statements Constitutional?" *Boston Globe* (April 30, 2006): A4.
32. Josh Gerstein, "Obama: Ignore Signing Statements," *Politico* (March 9, 2009): www.politico.com.
33. Charlie Savage, "Obama Takes New Route to Opposing Parts of Laws," *New York Times* (January 9, 2010): A1.

8

1. Federal Bureau of Investigation, "Most Wanted Terrorist Dead," (May 2, 2011): http://www.fbi.gov/news/stories/2011/may/binladen_050211/binladen_050211; Central Intelligence Agency, "Message from the Director: Justice Done," (May 5, 2011): https://www.cia.gov/news-information/press-releases-statements/press-release-2011/justice-done.html; and CBS News, "SEAL's First Hand Account of Bin Laden Killing," (September 9, 2012): http://www.cbsnews.com/8301-18560_162-57508646/seals-first-hand-account-of-bin-laden-killing/?tag=currentVideoInfo;videoMetaInfo.
2. Gallup Poll, July 10–12, 2009.
3. Harold D. Lasswell, *Politics: Who Gets What, When and How* (New York: McGraw-Hill, 1938).
4. Quoted in Robert C. Caldwell, *James A. Garfield* (Hamden, CT: Archon Books, 1965).
5. David Osborne and Ted Gaebler, *Reinventing Government* (Reading, MA: Addison-Wesley, 1992), 20–21.
6. Al Kamen, "Feingold, McCain Try to Trim Appointees," *Washington Post* (March 9, 2010): B3.
7. Office of Personnel Management, *The Fact Book* (September 27, 2010), www.opm.gov/feddata/factbook/2007/factbook2007.pdf.
8. Barbara Slavin, "State Department Having Staffing Trouble," *USA Today* (November 30, 2005): 10A.
9. USASpending.Gov (May 12, 2012), www.usaspending.gov.
10. Patricia Niehaus, "Statement on State of the Civil Service" (April 22, 2009), www.fedmanagers.org.
11. Niehaus, "Statement on the State of the Civil Service."
12. "A Century of Government Growth," *Washington Post* (January 3, 2000): A17. On the difficulty of counting the exact number of government agencies, see David Nachmias and David H. Rosenbloom, *Bureaucratic Government: U.S.A.* (New York: St. Martin's Press, 1980).
13. The classic work on regulatory commissions is Marver Bernstein, *Regulating Business by Independent Commission* (Princeton, NJ: Princeton University Press, 1955).
14. *Humphrey's Executor* v. *U.S.,* 295 U.S. 602 (1935).
15. John F. Duffy, "The Death of the Independent Regulatory Commission and the Birth of a New Independence," www.law.georgetown.edu/faculty/documents/duffy_paper.pdf.
16. Joe Davidson, "Details of Hatch Act Difficult to Enforce." *Washington Post* (June 28, 2011): B4.
17. H. H. Gerth and C. Wright Mills, *From Max Weber* (New York: Oxford University Press, 1958).
18. Michael Lipsky, *Street-Level Bureaucracy: Dilemmas of the Individual in Public Services* (New York: Russell Sage Foundation, 1980).
19. Cornelius M. Kerwin, *Rulemaking: How Government Agencies Write Law and Make Policy,* 2nd ed. (Washington, DC: CQ Press, 1999), xv.
20. Quoted in Arthur Schlesinger Jr., *A Thousand Days* (Greenwich, CT: Fawcett Books, 1967), 377.
21. Spencer S. Hsu, "Job Vacancies at DHS Said to Hurt U.S. Preparedness." *Washington Post* (July 9, 2007): A1.
22. Thomas V. DiBacco, "Veep Gore Reinventing Government—Again!" *USA Today* (September 9, 1993): 13A.
23. George A. Krause, "Presidential Use of Executive Orders, 1953–1994," *American Politics Quarterly* 25 (October 1997): 458–81.
24. Irene Murphy, *Public Policy on the Status of Women* (Lexington, MA: Lexington Books, 1974).
25. Mathew McCubbins and Thomas Schwartz, "Congressional Oversight Overlooked: Police Patrols Versus Fire Alarms," *American Journal of Political Science* 28 (1987): 165–79.
26. Rosemary O'Leary, *Environmental Change: Federal Courts and the EPA* (Philadelphia: Temple University Press, 1995).
27. Wendy Hansen, Renee Johnson, and Isaac Unah, "Specialized Courts, Bureaucratic Agencies, and the Politics of U.S. Trade Policy," *American Journal of Political Science* 39 (August 1995): 529–57.

9

1. Bernard Schwartz, *The Law in America* (New York: American Heritage, 1974), 48.
2. Julius Goebel Jr., *History of the Supreme Court of the United States, vol. 1: Antecedents and Beginnings to 1801* (New York: Macmillan, 1971), 206.
3. Quoted in Goebel, *History of the Supreme Court,* 280.
4. *Chisholm* v. *Georgia,* 2 U.S. 419 (1793).
5. *Fletcher* v. *Peck,* 10 U.S. 87 (1810); *Martin* v. *Hunter's Lessee,* 14 U.S. 304 (1816); and *Cohens* v. *Virginia,* 19 U.S. 264 (1821).
6. *McCulloch* v. *Maryland,* 17 U.S. 316 (1819).
7. *Marbury* v. *Madison,* 5 U.S. 137 (1803).
8. *Marbury* v. *Madison,* 5 U.S. 137 (1803).
9. David W. Neubauer, *Judicial Process: Law, Courts, and Politics* (Pacific Grove, CA: Brooks/Cole, 1991), 57.
10. Cases involving citizens from different states can be filed in state or federal court.
11. Sheldon Goldman and Elliot E. Slotnick, "Clinton's First Term Judiciary: Many Bridges to Cross," *Judicature* (May/June 1997): 254–5.
12. Betsy Palmer, "Evolution of the Senate's Role in the Nomination and Confirmation Process." CRS Report RL 31498 (March 29, 2005).
13. Quoted in Nina Totenberg, "Will Judges Be Chosen Rationally?" *Judicature* (August/September 1976): 93.
14. Quoted in Lawrence Baum, *The Supreme Court,* 3rd ed. (Washington, DC: CQ Press, 1989), 108.
15. See Barbara A. Perry, *A Representative Supreme Court? The Impact of Race, Religion, and Gender on Appointments* (New

York: Greenwood, 1991). Clarence Thomas was raised a Catholic but attended an Episcopalian church at the time of his appointment, having been barred from Catholic sacraments because of his remarriage. He again, however, is attending Roman Catholic services.
16. Karen O'Connor and Alixandra B. Yanus, "Judging Alone: Reflections on the Importance of Women on the Court," *Politics & Gender* 6 (2010): 441–52.
17. Amy Goldstein, "Bush Set to Curb ABA's Role in Court Appointments," *Washington Post* (March 18, 2001): A2.
18. Quoted in Judge Irving R. Kaufman, "Charting a Judicial Pedigree," *New York Times* (January 24, 1981): A23.
19. John Brigham, *The Cult of the Court* (Philadelphia: Temple University Press, 1987).
20. Stephen L. Wasby, *The Supreme Court in the Federal Judicial System,* 4th ed. (Chicago: Nelson-Hall, 1988), 194.
21. Wasby, *The Supreme Court in the Federal Judicial System,* 199. Much of this change occurred as the result of an increase in state criminal cases, of which nearly 100 percent concerned constitutional questions.
22. *Indian River School District* v. *Doe,* No. 11-569 (Cert. denied).
23. Paul Wahlbeck, et al., "Ghostwriters on the Court? A Stylistic Analysis of U.S. Supreme Court Opinion Drafts," *American Politics Research* 30 (March 2002): 166–92. Wahlbeck et al. note that "between 1969 and 1972—the period during which the justices each became entitled to a third law clerk . . . the number of opinions increased by about 50 percent and the number of words tripled."
24. Richard A. Posner, *The Federal Courts: Crisis and Reform* (Cambridge, MA: Harvard University Press, 1985), 114.
25. "Retired Chief Justice Warren Attacks Freund Study Group's Composition and Proposal," *American Bar Association Journal* 59 (July 1973): 728.
26. Kathleen Werdegar, "The Solicitor General and Administrative Due Process," *George Washington Law Review* (1967–1968): 482.
27. Rebecca Mae Salokar, *The Solicitor General: The Politics of Law* (Philadelphia: Temple University Press, 1992), 3.
28. Elder Witt, *A Different Justice: Reagan and the Supreme Court* (Washington, DC: CQ Press, 1986), 133.
29. See, for example, Lawrence Baum, *The Supreme Court,* 4th ed. (Washington, DC: CQ Press, 1992), 106.
30. Richard C. Cortner, *The Supreme Court and Civil Liberties* (Palo Alto, CA: Mayfield, 1975), vi.
31. *Brown* v. *Board of Education,* 347 U.S. 483 (1954); *Planned Parenthood of Southeastern Pennsylvania* v. *Casey,* 585 U.S. 833 (1992); and *Grutter* v. *Bollinger,* 539 U.S. 306 (2003).
32. Gregory A. Caldeira and John R. Wright, "*Amicus Curiae* Before the Supreme Court: Who Participates, When and How Much?" *Journal of Politics* 52 (August 1990): 803.
33. *U.S.* v. *Nixon,* 418 U.S. 683 (1974).
34. Linda Greenhouse, "With O'Connor Retirement and a New Chief Justice Comes an Awareness of Change," *New York Times* (January 28, 2006): A10.
35. Donald L. Horowitz, *The Courts and Social Policy* (Washington, DC: Brookings Institution, 1977), 538.
36. Timothy R. Johnson and Andrew D. Martin, "The Public's Conditional Response to Supreme Court Decisions," *American Political Science Review* 92 (June 1998): 299–309.
37. *Korematsu* v. *U.S.,* 323 U.S. 214 (1944).
38. *Youngstown Sheet & Tube Co.* v. *Sawyer,* 343 U.S. 579 (1952). The Supreme Court ruled that President Truman's seizure and operation of U.S. steel mills in the face of a strike threat were unconstitutional, because the Constitution implied no such broad executive power. See Alan Westin, *Anatomy of a Constitutional Law Case* (New York: Macmillan, 1958); and Maeva Marcus, *Truman and the Steel Seizure Case* (New York: Columbia University Press, 1977).
39. *U.S.* v. *Nixon,* 418 U.S. 683 (1974).
40. Pew Research Center for People and the Press, "Supreme Court Favorability Reaches New Low" (May 1, 2012).
41. Alixandra B. Yanus, "Neither Force Nor Will: A Theory of Judicial Power," doctoral dissertation, University of North Carolina, 2010.
42. *Boumediene* v. *Bush,* 553 U.S. 723 (2008).
43. *Arizona v. United States,* 567 U.S. ___ (2012).
44. "Supreme Court Cases Overruled by Subsequent Decision," www.gpoaccess.gov/constitution/pdf/con041.pdf.
45. See, for example, *Colegrove* v. *Green,* 328 U.S. 549 (1946).
46. *Baker* v. *Carr,* 369 U.S. 186 (1962).
47. Kevin T. McGuire, "Public Schools, Religious Establishments, and the U.S. Supreme Court: An Examination of Policy Compliance," *American Politics Research,* 37 (2009): 50–74.
48. Charles Johnson and Bradley C. Canon, *Judicial Policies: Implementation and Impact,* 2nd ed. (Washington, DC: CQ Press, 1998), ch. 1.
49. *Reynolds* v. *Sims,* 377 U.S. 533 (1964).
50. *Mississippi University for Women* v. *Hogan,* 458 U.S. 718 (1982).

10

1. Alan M. Winkler, "Public Opinion," in Jack Greene, ed., *The Encyclopedia of American Political History* (New York: Charles Scribner's Sons, 1988).
2. *Literary Digest* 125 (November 14, 1936): 1.
3. Robert S. Erikson, Norman R. Luttbeg, and Kent L. Tedin, *American Public Opinion: Its Origin, Contents, and Impact* (New York: Wiley, 1980), 28.
4. Diane J. Heith, "Staffing the White House Public Opinion Apparatus 1969–1988," *Public Opinion Quarterly* 62 (Summer 1998): 165.
5. Francis J. Connolly and Charley Manning, "What 'Push Polling' Is and What It Isn't," *Boston Globe* (August 16, 2001): A21.
6. Richard Dawson and Kenneth Prewitt, *Political Socialization,* 2nd ed. (Boston: Little, Brown, 1977), 33.
7. Nicholas J. G. Winter, *Dangerous Frames: How Ideas About Race and Gender Shape Public Opinion* (Chicago: University of Chicago Press, 2008).
8. Edward S. Greenberg, "The Political Socialization of Black Children," in Edward S. Greenberg, ed., *Political Socialization* (New York: Atherton, 1970), 131.
9. Pew Research Center, 2012 American Values Survey, www.people-press.org/values-questions/.
10. Susan A. MacManus, *Young v. Old: Generational Combat in the 21st Century* (Boulder, CO: Westview, 1995).
11. Jan W. van Deth, Simone Abendschon, and Meike Vollmar, "Children and Politics: An Empirical Reassessment of Early Political Socialization," *Political Psychology* 32 (2011): 147–74.
12. James Simon and Bruce D. Merrill, "Political Socialization in the Classroom Revisited: The Kids Voting Program," *Social Science Journal* 35 (1998): 29–42.
13. Kaiser Family Foundation, "Daily Media Use Among Children and Teens up Dramatically from Five Years Ago," (January 21, 2010): www.kff.org/entmedia/entmedia012010nr.cfm.
14. Fairleigh Dickinson University Public Mind Poll, May 3, 2012, http://publicmind.fdu.edu/2012/confirmed/.
15. Roderick P. Hart, *The Sound of Leadership: Presidential Communication in the Modern Age* (Chicago: University of Chicago Press, 1989).

16. National Geographic-Roper Public Affairs Poll, December 17, 2005–January 20, 2006, www.nationalgeographic.com.
17. Kathleen Dolan, "Do Women and Men Know Different Things? Measuring Gender Differences in Political Knowledge," *Journal of Politics* 73 (2011): 97–107.
18. Joy K. Dow, "Gender Differences in Political Knowledge: Distinguishing Characteristics-Based and Returns-Based Differences," *Political Behavior* 31 (2009): 117–36.
19. Andrew Kohut, "But What Do the Polls Show? How Public Opinion Surveys Came to Play a Major Role in Policymaking and Politics," PewResearchCenter Publications, (October 14, 2009): http://pewresearch.org/pubs/.
20. Quoted in Kohut, "But What Do the Polls Show?"

11

1. This conception of a political party was originally put forth by V. O. Key Jr. in *Politics, Parties, and Pressure Groups* (New York: Crowell, 1958).
2. John H. Aldrich, *Why Parties? The Origin and Transformation of Party Politics in America* (Chicago: University of Chicago Press, 1995).
3. By contrast, Great Britain did not develop truly national, broad-based parties until the 1870s.
4. See *Historical Statistics of the United States: Colonial Times to 1970,* part 2, series Y-27-28 (Washington, DC: Government Printing Office, 1975), based on unpublished data prepared by Walter Dean Burnham. See also Harold W. Stanley and Richard G. Niemi, *Vital Statistics on American Politics 2009–2010* (Washington, DC: CQ Press, 2009), for contemporary turnout figures.
5. On the subject of party realignment, see Walter Dean Burnham, *Critical Elections and the Mainsprings of American Politics* (New York: Norton, 1970); Kristi Andersen, *The Creation of a Democratic Majority* (Chicago: University of Chicago Press, 1979); and John R. Petrocik, "Realignment: New Party Coalitions and the Nationalization of the South," *Journal of Politics* 49 (May 1987): 347–75.
6. See, for example, V. O. Key Jr., "A Theory of Critical Elections," *Journal of Politics* 17 (February 1955): 3–18.
7. For a discussion of secular realignment in the South, see Jeffrey M. Stonecash, "Class and Party: Secular Realignment and the Survival of Democrats Outside the South," *Political Research Quarterly* 53:4 (2000): 731–52.
8. John Green and Paul S. Herrnson, eds., *Responsible Partisanship: The Evolution of American Political Parties Since the 1950s* (Lawrence: University Press of Kansas, 2003).
9. Cornelius P. Cotter, et al., *Party Organizations in American Politics* (Pittsburgh: University of Pittsburgh Press, 1989).
10. See David E. Price, *Bringing Back the Parties* (Washington, DC: CQ Press, 1984), 284–88.
11. Congressional Quarterly Vote Studies, http://media.cq.com/media/2011/votestudy_2011/graphics/.
12. Sidney M. Milkis, *The President and the Parties: The Transformation of the American Party System Since the New Deal* (New York: Oxford University Press, 1993).
13. Jeffrey M. Jones, "D.C., Hawaii, Most Democratic, Utah Most Republican State in '11." *Gallup* (August 11, 2011): http://www.gallup.com/poll/148949/hawaii-democratic-utah-republican-state.aspx.
14. Karen M. Kaufmann and John R. Petrocik, "The Changing Politics of American Men: Understanding the Sources of the Gender Gap," *American Journal of Political Science* 43 (July 1999): 864–87.
15. William H. Flanigan and Nancy H. Zingale, *Political Behavior of the American Electorate,* 12th ed. (Washington, DC: CQ Press, 2010).
16. Flanigan and Zingale, *Political Behavior of the American Electorate.*
17. The Pew Forum on Religion and Public Life, "Trends in Party Identification of Religious Groups," (February 2, 2012): http://www.pewforum.org/Politics-and-Elections/Trends-in-Party-Identification-of-Religious-Groups.aspx.
18. Flanigan and Zingale, *Political Behavior of the American Electorate.*
19. This section draws on Morris Fiorina, *Culture War? The Myth of a Polarized America* (New York: Longman, 2011); Morris P. Fiorina and Samuel J. Abrams, "Political Polarization in the American Public," *Annual Review of Political Science* 11 (2008): 563–88; and Alan I. Abramowitz and Kyle L. Saunders, "Is Polarization a Myth?" *Journal of Politics* 70 (2008): 542–55.

12

1. Jennifer Steinhauer, "Senate Races Expose Extent of Republicans Gender Gap," New York Times (November 7, 2012): http://www.nytimes.com/2012/11/08/us/politics/womens-issues-were-a-problem-for-gop.html?pagewanted=all&_r=0.
2. Paul Allen Beck, *Party Politics in America,* 8th ed. (New York: Longman, 1998); David Adamany, "Cross-Over Voting and the Democratic Party's Reform Rules," *American Political Science Review* 70 (1976): 536–41; Ronald Hedlund and Meredith W. Watts, "The Wisconsin Open Primary: 1968 to 1984," *American Politics Quarterly* 14 (1986): 55–74; and Gary D. Wekkin, "The Conceptualization and Measurement of Crossover Voting," *Western Political Quarterly* 41 (1988): 105–14.
3. Gary D. Wekken, "Why Crossover Voters Are Not 'Mischievous' Voters," *American Politics Quarterly* 19 (1991): 229–47; and Todd L. Cherry and Stephan Kroll, "Crashing the Party: An Experimental Investigation of Strategic Voting in Primary Elections," *Public Choice* 114 (2003): 387–420.
4. Of these ten states, South Dakota is the only state outside the South to hold a runoff primary. A runoff is held only if no candidate receives at least 35 percent of the vote, however. See "Statutory Election Information of the Several States," *The Green Papers,* www.thegreenpapers.com/slg/sei.phtml?format=sta.
5. Shaun Bowler, et al., eds., *Citizens as Legislators: Direct Democracy in the United States* (Columbus: Ohio State University Press, 1998).
6. For a more in-depth discussion of initiative, referendum, and recall voting, see Larry J. Sabato, Howard R. Ernst, and Bruce Larson, *Dangerous Democracy? The Battle over Ballot Initiatives in America* (Lanham, MD: Rowman and Littlefield, 2001); and David S. Broder, *Democracy Derailed: Initiative Campaigns and the Power of Money* (New York: Harcourt, 2000).
7. Howard R. Ernst, "The Historical Role of Narrow-Material Interests in Initiative Politics," in Larry J. Sabato, Howard R. Ernst, and Bruce Larson, eds., *Dangerous Democracy?*
8. Joshua Spivak, "The 21st Century Recall—Cheaper, Faster, Easier," *Politico* (March 18, 2011): 19.
9. Elaine Ciulla Kamarck and Kenneth M. Goldstein, "The Rules Matter: Post-Reform Presidential Nominating Politics," in L. Sandy Maisel, ed., *The Parties Respond: Changes in American Parties and Campaigns* (Boulder, CO: Westview, 1994), 174.
10. Nancy Scola, "At Campaign Fundraisers, Obama's Tech Staffers Are the Stars," *The Atlantic* (May 8, 2012): www.theatlantic.com/politics/archive/2012/05/at-campaign-fundraisers-obamas-tech-staffers-are-the-stars/256882/#.
11. George Serra, "What's in It for Me?: The Impact of Congressional Casework on Incumbent Evaluation," *American Politics Quarterly* 22 (1994): 403–20.

12. Glenn R. Parker and Suzanne L. Parker, "Correlates and Effects of Attention to District by U.S. House Members," *Legislative Studies Quarterly* 10 (May 1985): 223–42.
13. Jamie L. Carson, "Strategy, Selection, and Candidate Competition in U.S. House and Senate Elections," *Journal of Politics* 67 (2005): 1–28.
14. Gary W. Cox and Jonathan N. Katz, "Why Did the Incumbency Advantage in U.S. House Elections Grow?" *American Journal of Political Science* 40 (May 1996): 478–97.
15. Sunhil Ahuja, et al., "Modern Congressional Election Theory Meets the 1992 House Elections," *Political Research Quarterly* 47 (1994): 909–21; and Paul S. Herrnson, *Congressional Elections: Campaigning at Home and in Washington,* 2nd ed. (Washington, DC: CQ Press, 1998).
16. Gary C. Jacobson and Michael A. Dimock, "Checking Out: The Effects of Bank Overdrafts on the 1992 House Elections," *American Journal of Political Science* 38 (1994): 601–24; and Herrnson, *Congressional Elections.*
17. Mark Mellman, "Splitting the Ticket Not So Rare," *The Hill* (February 7, 2012): http://thehill.com/opinion/columnists/mark-mellman/209315-splitting-the-ticket-not-so-rare.
18. Morris P. Fiorina, *Divided Government* (Boston: Allyn and Bacon, 1996); rereleased as a Longman Classic in 2002, New York: Longman, 2002. Kyle E. Saunders, Alan I. Abramowitz, and Jonathan Williamson, "A New Kind of Balancing Act: Electoral Uncertainty and Ticket-Splitting in the 1996 and 2000 Elections," *Political Research Quarterly* 58 (March 2005): 69–78.
19. Martin P. Wattenberg, *The Decline of American Political Parties, 1952–1996* (Cambridge, MA: Harvard University Press, 1998).
20. CNN, 2008 election results, www.cnn.com/ELECTION/2008/.
21. Warren E. Miller and J. Merrill Shanks, *The New American Voter* (Cambridge, MA: Harvard University Press, 1996), 270.
22. CNN, 2008 election results, www.cnn.com/ELECTION/2008/.
23. Paula McClain and James Stewart, *"Can We All Get Along?": Racial and Ethnic Minorities in American Politics,* 4th ed. (Boulder, CO: Westview, 2005); and Pei-te Lien, *The Politics of Asian Americans: Diversity and Community* (New York: Routledge, 2004).
24. Allison Kopicki, "Santorum Trails Among Women in Poll," *New York Times* (February 22, 2012): thecaucus.blogs.nytimes.com/2012/02/22/santorum-trails-among-women-in-new-poll/.
25. See www.cnn.com/ELECTION/2008/.
26. John C. Green, *The Faith Factor: How Religion Influences American Elections* (Westport, CT: Praeger, 2007).
27. Michael S. Lewis-Beck and Mary Stegmaier, "Economic Determinants of Electoral Outcomes," *Annual Review of Political Science* 3 (2000): 183–219.
28. Steven J. Rosenstone and John Mark Hanson, *Mobilization, Participation, and Democracy in America* (New York: Macmillan, 1993).
29. William A. Galston, "Civic Education and Political Participation," *PS: Political Science and Politics* 37 (2004): 263–66.
30. Thomas M. Guterbock and Bruce London, "Race, Political Orientation, and Participation: An Empirical Test of Four Competing Theories," *American Sociological Review* 48 (1983): 439–53.
31. Karlo Bakkios Marcelo, et al., "Young Voter Registration and Turnout Trends," www.civicyouth.org. Estimates of young voter registration vary widely, in large part because they are often based on polling numbers, and these numbers are subject to overreporting as well as difficulties in reaching and surveying this demographic group.
32. See, for example, Laura Stoker and M. Kent Jennings, "Life-Cycle Transitions and Political Participation: The Case of Marriage," *American Political Science Review* 89 (1995): 421–36; and Paul R. Abramson, John H. Aldrich, and David W. Rohde, *Change and Continuity in the 1996 Elections* (Washington, DC: CQ Press, 1998).
33. Sidney Verba, Kay Lehman Schlozman, and Henry Brady, *Voice and Equality: Civic Voluntarism in American Politics* (New York: Belknap, 1996). Data on relationship between religious service attendance and voting were calculated by the authors with data obtained from the Pew Research Center's study *Political Landscape More Favorable to Democrats: Trends in Political Values and Core Attitudes, 1987–2007,* March 22, 2007.
34. National Conference of State Legislatures, "Electronic (or Online) Voter Registration," *The Forum* (February 9, 2012): http://www.ncsl.org/legislatures-elections/elections/electronic-or-online-voter-registration.aspx.
35. Ashley Lopez, "Blocking the Vote," *Ms. Magazine* (Winter 2012): 36–38.
36. J. Eric Oliver, "The Effects of Eligibility Restrictions and Party Activity on Absentee Voting and Overall Turnout," *American Journal of Political Science* 40 (May 1996): 498–513.
37. International Institute for Democracy and Electoral Assistance, "Global Database," www.idea.int/vt/survey/voter_turnout_pop2.cfm.
38. Rosenstone and Hansen, *Mobilization, Participation, and Democracy in America.*
39. Ian Urbina, "States Move to Allow Overseas and Military Voters to Cast Ballots by Internet," *New York Times* (May 7, 2010): http://www.nytimes.com/2010/05/09/us/politics/09voting.html.
40. Christopher Keating, "Senate Approves Election Day Registration by 19 to 16 on Saturday," *Hartford Courant* (May 5, 2012): http://courantblogs.com/capitol-watch/election-da/.
41. Stacy C. Ulbig and Tamara Waggener, "Getting Registered and Getting to the Polls: The Impact of Voter Registration Strategy and Information Provision on Turnout of College Students," *PS: Political Science and Politics* (July 2011): 544-50.
42. Verified Voting, www.verifiedvoting.org.
43. Mackenzie Weiner, "New Voting Tech Innovations for 2012," *Politico* (November 30, 2011): http://www.politico.com/news/stories/1111/69402.html.
44. MIT News Office, " MIT, Caltech Join Forces to Develop Reliable, Uniform US Voting Machine," December 14, 2000.

13

1. See "Candidates and Nominations," in Paul S. Herrnson, *Congressional Elections: Campaigning at Home and in Washington,* 4th ed. (Washington, DC: CQ Press, 2004), 35–68.
2. Dennis W. Johnson, *No Place for Amateurs: How Political Consultants Are Reshaping American Democracy* (New York: Routledge, 2001).
3. See www.opensecrets.org.
4. *McConnell* v. *FEC,* 540 U.S. 93 (2003).
5. *FEC* v. *Wisconsin Right to Life, Inc.,* 551 U.S. 449 (2007).
6. *Davis* v. *FEC,* 554 U.S. 729 (2008).
7. *Citizens United* v. *FEC,* 558 U.S. 50 (2010).
8. Herrnson, *Congressional Elections,* 133.
9. Center for Responsive Politics, http://www.opensecrets.org/pres12/index.php.
10. *Buckley* v. *Valeo,* 424 U.S. 1 (1976).
11. Center for Responsive Politics, www.opensecrets.org/.
12. Steven T. Engel and David J. Jackson, "Wielding the Stick Instead of Its Carrot: Labor PAC Punishment of Pro-NAFTA

Democrats," *Political Research Quarterly* 51 (September 1998): 813–28.

13. Janet M. Box-Steffensmeier and J. Tobin Grant, "All in a Day's Work: The Financial Rewards of Legislative Effectiveness," *Legislative Studies Quarterly* 24 (November 1999): 511–23.
14. Campaign Finance Institute, "501(c) Groups Emerge as Big Players Alongside 527s," www.cfinst.org. Information also drawn from www.opensecrets.org/527s/types.php.
15. Campaign Finance Institute, "501(c) Groups Emerge."
16. Diana C. Mutz, "Effects of Horse-Race Coverage on Campaign Coffers: Strategic Contributing in Presidential Primaries," *Journal of Politics* 57 (November 1995): 1015–42.
17. See "Media, Old and New," in Johnson, *No Place for Amateurs,* 115–47.
18. Jody C. Baumgartner and Jonathan S. Morris, "MyFaceTube Politics: Social Networking Sites and Political Engagement of Young Adults," *Social Science Computer Review* 28 (2010): 24–44.
19. Emily Schultheis, "Campaigns Picking Up on Mobile Ads," *Politico* (November 29, 2011): 21–22.
20. Five liberal Democratic U.S. senators, including George McGovern of South Dakota, were defeated in this way in 1980, for example.

14

1. Pew Research Center, "State of the News Media 2012," http://www.stateofthemedia.org/2012/mobile-devices-and-news-consumption-some-good-signs-for-journalism/infographic/.
2. See Mitchell Stephens, *A History of News: From the Drum to the Satellite* (New York: Viking, 1989).
3. See Shelley Ross, *Fall from Grace* (New York: Ballantine, 1988), chapter 12.
4. Richard L. Rubin, *Press, Party, and Presidency* (New York: Norton, 1981), 38–39.
5. Stephen Bates, *If No News, Send Rumors* (New York: St. Martin's, 1989), 185.
6. See Doris A. Graber, *Mass Media and American Politics,* 3rd ed. (Washington, DC: CQ Press, 1989), 12; and Thomas C. Leonard, *The Power of the Press: The Birth of American Political Reporting* (New York: Oxford University Press, 1986), chapter 7.
7. Darrell M. West, *The Rise and Fall of the Media Establishment* (Boston: Bedford/St. Martin's, 2001).
8. Fairness and Accuracy in Reporting, "How Public Is Public Radio?" www.fair.org.
9. Pew Research Center, "Internet Gains on Television as Public's Main News Source," (January 4, 2011): www.people-press.org/2011/01/04/internet-gains-on-television-as-publics-main-news-source/.
10. Pew Research Center, "The State of the News Media 2012: CNN Ends Its Ratings Slide, Fox Falls Again," (March 19, 2012): http://stateofthemedia.org/2012/cable-cnn-ends-its-ratings-slide-fox-falls-again/.
11. Pew Research Center, "Internet Gains on Television as Public's Main News Source," (January 4, 2011): www.people-press.org/2011/01/04/internet-gains-on-television-as-publics-main-news-source/.
12. Nielsen Media Research, "Buzz in the Blogosphere: Millions More Bloggers and Blog Readers," (March 8, 2012): http://blog.nielsen.com/nielsenwire/online_mobile/buzz-in-the-blogosphere-millions-more-bloggers-and-blog-readers/.
13. Henry Farrell and Daniel W. Drezner, "The Power and Politics of Blogs," *Public Choice* 134 (2008): 15–30.
14. Cecilia Kang, "Obama First to Hold Twitter Town Hall," *Washington Post* (June 1, 2011): A4.
15. Donna Tam, "Chirpify: Tweet if You Want to Give Money to Obama or Romney," CNET.com (June 19, 2012): http://news.cnet.com/8301-1023_3-57455585-93/chirpify-tweet-if-you-want-to-give-money-to-obama-or-romney/.
16. Wesley Donehue, "The Danger of Twitter, Facebook Politics," CNN.com (April 24, 2012): www.cnn.com/2012/04/24/opinion/donehue-social-media-politics/index.html.
17. "Dan Rather: Corporate Media Is 'in Bed' with Washington," *Huffington Post* (May 20, 2012): www.huffingtonpost.com/2012/05/20/dan-rather-cbs-news-corporate-media_n_1531121.html?ref=fb&src=sp&comm_ref=false.
18. Pew Research Center for the People and the Press, "Partisanship and Cable News Audiences," (October 30, 2009): www.pewresearch.org/.
19. Shanto Iyengar and Kyu S. Hahn, "Red Media, Blue Media: Evidence of Ideological Selectivity in Media Bias," *Journal of Communication* 59 (2009): 19–39.
20. Cass R. Sunstein, *Republic.com 2.0* (Princeton, NJ: Princeton University Press, 2009).
21. David Brock and Ari Rabin-Havit, *The Fox Effect: How Roger Ailes Turned a Network into a Propaganda Machine* (New York: Anchor Books, 2012).
22. "Sunday Hosts Slam Narrowcasting," *Politico* (November 12, 2010): www.politico.com/blogs/onmedia/1110/Sunday_hosts_slam_narrowcasting.html.
23. Rachel Smolkin, "What the Mainstream Media Can Learn from Jon Stewart," *American Journalism Review* (June/July 2007): http://www.ajr.org/article.asp?id=4329.
24. Matthew A. Baum and Angela Jamison, "The Oprah Effect: How Soft News Helps Inattentive Citizens Vote Consistently," *Journal of Politics* 68 (2008): 946–59.
25. Donald L. Jorand and Benjamin I. Page, "Shaping Foreign Policy Opinions: The Role of TV News," *Journal of Conflict Resolution* 36 (June 1992): 227–41.
26. Philip E. Tetlock, *Expert Political Judgment: How Good Is It? How Can We Know?* (Princeton, NJ: Princeton University Press, 2006).
27. Kelly Kaufhold, Sebastian Valenzuela, and Homero Gil de Zuniga, "Citizen Journalism and Democracy: How User-Generated News Use Relates to Political Knowledge and Participation," *Journalism and Mass Communication Quarterly* 87 (2010): 515–29.
28. *New York Times Co.* v. *U.S.,* 403 U.S. 713 (1971).
29. Vivek Wadhwa, "Social Media's Role in Politics," *Washington Post* (January 25, 2012): www.washingtonpost.com/national/on-innovations/social-medias-role-in-politics/2012/01/25/gIQAQvZgdQ_story.html; Google, "Take Action," https://www.google.com/takeaction/.
30. "Current Membership by Name," United States House of Representatives Radio-Television Correspondents' Gallery, http://radiotv.house.gov/membership/list-name.shtml.
31. John R. Hibbing and Elizabeth Theiss-Morse, *Congress as Public Enemy: Political Attitudes Toward American Political Institutions* (New York: Cambridge University Press, 1995).
32. Karen Aho, "Broadcasters Want Access, but Will They Deliver Serious Coverage?" *Columbia Journalism Review* 5 (September/October 2003): www.cjr.org.
33. Tony Mauro, "A Gun Case in Need of Some Explaining: But Because of Our Reclusive Court, Today's Argument Is All We'll Get," *USA Today* (March 2, 2010): www.usatoday.com.
34. Benjamin I. Page, et al., "What Moves Public Opinion?" *American Political Science Review* 81 (March 1987): 23–44.
35. Thomas E. Nelson, et al., "Media Framing of a Civil Liberties Conflict and Its Effect on Tolerance," *American Political Science Review* 92 (September 1997): 567–83.

36. Shanto Iyengar and Donald R. Kinder, *News That Matters,* reprint ed. (Chicago: University of Chicago Press, 1989).
37. American Society of Newspaper Editors, *The Changing Face of the Newsroom* (Washington, DC: ASNE, 1989), 33; William Schneider and I. A. Lewis, "Views on the News," *Public Opinion* 8 (August/September 1985): 6–11, 58–59; and S. Robert Lichter, et al., *The Media Elite* (Bethesda, MD: Adler and Adler, 1986).
38. Eric Alterman, *What Liberal Media? The Truth About Bias and the News* (New York: Basic Books, 2003).
39. The Fourth Estate, "Silenced: Gender Gap in the 2012 Election Coverage," www.4thestate.net/female-voices-in-media/infographic.
40. Girish Gulati, et al., "News Coverage of Political Campaigns," in Lynda Kaid, ed., *The Handbook of Political Communication Research* (New York: Lawrence Erlbaum, 2004).
41. Pew Research Center Project for Excellence in Journalism, "How the Media Covered the 2012 Primary Campaign," (April 23, 2012): http://pewresearch.org/pubs/2249/mitt-romney-rick-santorum-newt-gingrich-ron-paul-media-coverage-republican-presidential-nomination-primary-campaign-horse-race.
42. Pew Research Center for the People and the Press, "Press Widely Criticized, But Trusted More Than Other Information Sources," (September 22, 2011): www.people-press.org/2011/09/22/press-widely-criticized-but-trusted-more-than-other-institutions/.
43. Pew Research Center for the People and the Press, "Press Widely Criticized, But Trusted More Than Other Information Sources."

15

1. Robert D. Putnam, "Bowling Alone: America's Declining Social Capital," *Journal of Democracy* 6 (1995): 650–65; and Putnam, *Bowling Alone: The Collapse and Revival of American Community* (New York: Simon and Schuster, 2000).
2. Everett Carll Ladd, quoted in Richard Morin, "Who Says We're Not Joiners," *Washington Post* (May 2, 1999): B5.
3. John Brehm and Wendy Rahn, "Individual-Level Evidence for the Causes and Consequences of Social Capital," *American Journal of Political Science* 41 (July 1997): 999.
4. Mark Schneider, et al., "Institutional Arrangements and the Creation of Social Capital: The Effects of Public School Choice," *American Political Science Review* 91 (March 1997): 82–93.
5. Nicholas Lemann, "Kicking in Groups," *Atlantic Monthly* (April 1996), NEXIS.
6. David B. Truman, *The Governmental Process: Political Interests and Public Opinion* (New York: Knopf, 1951), ch. 16.
7. Mancur Olson, *The Logic of Collective Action* (Cambridge, MA: Harvard University Press, 1965).
8. E. E. Schattschneider, *The Semisovereign People* (New York: Holt, Rinehart and Winston, 1960), 35.
9. Jeffrey M. Berry, *Lobbying for the People: The Political Behavior of Public Interest Groups* (Princeton, NJ: Princeton University Press, 1977), 7.
10. Berry, *Lobbying for the People,* 7.
11. Quoted in Grant McConnell, "Lobbies and Pressure Groups," in Jack Greene, ed., *Encyclopedia of American Political History,* vol. 2 (New York: Macmillan, 1984), 768.
12. Lee Epstein, *Conservatives in Court* (Knoxville: University of Tennessee Press, 1985).
13. Jack L. Walker, "The Origins and Maintenance of Interest Groups in America," *American Political Science Review* 77 (June 1983): 390–406.
14. Peter Steinfels, "Moral Majority to Dissolve: Says Mission Accomplished," *New York Times* (June 12, 1989): A14.
15. David Mahood, *Interest Group Participation in America: A New Intensity* (Englewood Cliffs, NJ: Prentice Hall, 1990), 23.
16. Chris Kutalik, "What Does the AFL-CIO Split Mean?" *Labor Notes* (September 2005): www.labornotes.org.
17. Michael Wines, "For New Lobbyists, It's What They Know," *New York Times* (November 3, 1993): B14.
18. Quoted in Kay Lehman Schlozman and John T. Tierney, *Organized Interests and American Democracy* (New York: Harper and Row, 1986), 85.
19. Ken Kollman, "Inviting Friends to Lobby: Interest Groups, Ideological Bias, and Congressional Committees," *American Journal of Political Science* 41 (April 1997): 519–44.
20. Quoted in Norman J. Ornstein and Shirley Elder, *Interest Groups, Lobbying and Policy Making* (Washington, DC: CQ Press, 1978), 77.
21. Some political scientists speak of "iron rectangles," reflecting the growing importance of a fourth party, the courts, in the lobbying process.
22. Clement E. Vose, "Litigation as a Form of Pressure Group Activity," *Annals* 319 (September 1958): 20–31.
23. Paul M. Collins Jr., *Friends of the Supreme Court* (New York: Oxford University Press, 2008).
24. Karen O'Connor, "Lobbying the Justices or Lobbying for Justice?" in Paul Herrnson, Ronald G. Shaiko, and Clyde Wilcox, eds., *The Interest Group Connection,* 2nd ed. (Washington, DC: CQ Press, 2005), 267–88.
25. Amy Harder and Charlie Szymanski, "Sotomayor in Context: Unprecedented Input from Interest Groups," *National Review* (August 5, 2009): www.nationaljournal.com.
26. Brian Ross, "Supreme Court Ethics Problem?" *Nightline,* ABC News, January 23, 2006.
27. Robert A. Goldberg, *Grassroots Resistance: Social Movements in Twentieth Century America* (Belmont, CA: Wadsworth, 1991).
28. Michelle Garcia, "Animal Rights Activists Step Up Attacks in N.Y.," *Washington Post* (May 9, 2005): A3.
29. North American Animal Liberation Press Office, May 2010.
30. Ken Kollman, *Outside Lobbyists: Public Opinion and Interest Group Strategies* (Princeton, NJ: Princeton University Press, 1998); and Karen O'Connor, *Women's Organizations' Use of the Courts* (Lexington, MA: 1980).
31. Marie Hojnacki, "Interest Groups' Decisions to Join Alliances or Work Alone," *American Journal of Political Science* 41 (January 1997): 61–87.
32. Lee Ann Banaszak, *Why Movements Succeed or Fail: Opportunity, Culture, and the Struggle for Woman Suffrage* (Princeton, NJ: Princeton University Press, 1996); Frank R. Baumgartner and Beth L. Leech, *Basic Interests: The Importance of Groups in Politics and in Political Science* (Princeton, NJ: Princeton University Press, 1990); Nancy E. McGlen, et al., *Women, Politics, and American Society,* 5th ed. (New York: Longman, 2010); Robert H. Salisbury, "An Exchange Theory of Interest Groups," *Midwest Journal of Political Science* 13 (1969): 1–32; and Jack Walker, *Mobilizing Interest Groups in America: Patrons, Professions, and Social Movements* (Ann Arbor: University of Michigan Press, 1991).
33. Walker, *Mobilizing Interest Groups in America.*
34. Schattschneider, *The Semisovereign People,* 35.
35. Olson, *The Logic of Collective Action.*
36. William Browne, "Organized Interests and Their Issue Niches: A Search for Pluralism in a Policy Domain," *Journal of Politics* 52 (May 1990): 477.
37. Donald P. Haider-Markel, "Interest Group Survival: Shared Interests Versus Competition for Resources," *Journal of Politics* 59 (August 1997): 903–12.

38. Leslie Wayne, "And for His Next Feat, Billionaire Sets Sights on Bush," *New York Times* (May 31, 2004): A14.
39. Walker, "The Origins and Maintenance of Interest Groups," 390–406.
40. Center for Responsive Politics, www.opensecrets.org.
41. Richard Simons, "Bush Signs Bill to Tighten Lobbying Rules," *Los Angeles Times* (September 15, 2007): A13.

16

1. Jake Tapper and Bradley Blackburn, "BP Oil Spill: Jindal Asks for Permission to Build Barrier Islands," *ABC News* (May 26, 2010): www.abcnews.go.com.
2. Helene Cooper and Jackie Calmes, "In Oval Office Speech, Obama Calls for New Focus on Energy Policy," *New York Times* (June 15, 2010): www.nytimes.com.
3. This discussion draws on James E. Anderson, *Public Policy-making: An Introduction*, 2nd ed. (Boston: Houghton Mifflin, 1994), 5.
4. *Hammer* v. *Dagenhart*, 247 U.S. 251 (1918).
5. Susan Aud, et al., *The Condition of Education 2012* (NCES 2012-045), U.S. Department of Education, National Center for Education Statistics, Washington, DC, 2012, retrieved June 6, 2012, from http://nces.ed.gov/pubsearch.
6. Richard H. K. Vistor, *Energy Policy in America Since 1945: A Study of Business-Government Relations* (Cambridge: Cambridge University Press, 1987).
7. Vito Stagliano, *A Policy of Discontent: The Making of a National Energy Strategy* (Tulsa, OK: Pennwell, 2001).
8. Energy Information Administration, Department of Energy, "25th Anniversary of the 1973 Oil Embargo," 1998, www.eia.doe.gov/emeu/25opec/anniversary.html.
9. Energy Information Administration, Department of Energy, www.eia.doe.gov/oil_gas/petroleum/data_publications/wrgp/mogas_history.html.
10. Department of Energy, Energy Timeline 1971–1980, www.energy.gov/about/timeline1971-1980.htm.
11. Charles O. Jones and Randall Strahan, "The Effect of Energy Politics on Congressional and Executive Organizations in the 1970s," *Legislative Studies Quarterly* 10 (May 1985): 151–79.
12. Thomas R. Dye, *Who's Running America?* (Englewood Cliffs, NJ: Prentice Hall, 1976).
13. David B. Truman, *The Governmental Process* (New York: Knopf, 1951).
14. Robert Dahl, *Who Governs?* (New Haven, CT: Yale University Press, 1961).
15. Theodore J. Lowi, *The End of Liberalism* (New York: Norton, 1979).
16. Theodore J. Lowi, "American Business, Public Policy Case Studies, and Political Theory," *World Politics*, XVI (July 1964): 677–715.
17. Roger W. Cobb and Charles D. Elder, *Participation in American Politics: The Dynamics of Agenda-Building*, 2nd ed. (Baltimore, MD: Johns Hopkins University Press, 1983), 85.
18. John W. Kingdon, *Agendas, Alternatives, and Public Policies*, 2nd ed. (New York: Harper Collins, 1995).
19. Anthony Downs, "Up and Down with Ecology: The Issue-Attention Cycle," *Public Interest*, XXXII (Summer 1972): 38–50.
20. Charles O. Jones, *An Introduction to the Study of Public Policy*, 3rd ed. (Monterey, CA: Brooks/Cole, 1984), 87–89.
21. This discussion draws on Anne Schneider and Helen Ingram, "Behavioral Assumptions of Policy Tools," *Journal of Politics* 52 (May 1990): 510–29.
22. Government Accountability Office, "Amtrak Management: Systematic Problems Require Actions to Improve Efficiency, Effectiveness, and Accountability," GAO-06-145, April 2005, www.gao.gov.
23. U.S. Department of Health and Human Services, "Fiscal Year 2013 Budget in Brief: Strengthening Health and Opportunity for All Americans," 2012, http://www.hhs.gov/budget/budget-brief-fy2013.pdf.
24. Kaiser Family Foundation, www.kff.org/insurance/upload/7692_02.pdf.
25. Dan Glickman, Lynn Parker, Leslie J. Sim, Heather Del Valle Cook, and Emily Ann Miller, eds., "Accelerating Progress in Obesity Prevention: Solving the Weight of the Nation," 2012, Committee on Accelerating Progress in Obesity Prevention; Food and Nutrition Board; Institute of Medicine, http://www.iom.edu/Reports/2012/Accelerating-Progress-in-Obesity-Prevention.aspx.
26. Amanda Paulson, "Education Reform: Obama Budget Reboots No Child Left Behind," *Christian Science Monitor* (February 1, 2010).

17

1. Benjamin Page, "Economic Effects of Reducing the Fiscal Restraint That Is Scheduled to Occur in 2013," Congressional Budget Office, May 2012, www.cbo.gov/publication/43262.
2. Marcia Clemmitt, "National Debt," *CQ Researcher* (March 18, 2011): 241–64.
3. Frank Newport, "Americans Blame Wasteful Government Spending for Deficit," Gallup, April 29, 2011, www.gallup.com/poll/147338/Americans-Blame-Wasteful-Government-Spending-Deficit.aspx.
4. Jeffrey M. Jones, "On Deficit, Americans Prefer Spending Cuts; Open to Tax Hikes," Gallup, July 13, 2011, www.gallup.com/poll/148472/Deficit-Americans-Prefer-Spending-Cuts-Open-Tax-Hikes.aspx.
5. After 108 years of operation, the ICC expired at the end of 1995 as part of the effort by congressional Republicans to reduce federal regulations and allow market forces more freedom in which to operate.
6. *Pollack* v. *Farmers' Loan and Trust Co.*, 158 U.S. 429 (1895).
7. Department of Labor, http://www.bls.gov/opub/cwc/cm20030124ar03p1.htm.
8. *Wickard* v. *Filburn*, 317 U.S. 111 (1942).
9. Micheline Maynard, "Airlines' Cuts Making Cities No-Fly Zones," *New York Times* (May 21, 2008): www.nytimes.com.
10. Sara Fitzgerald, "Liberalizing Agriculture: Why the U.S. Should Look to New Zealand and Australia," www.heritage.org.
11. James D. Savage, *Balanced Budgets and American Politics* (Ithaca, NY: Cornell University Press, 1988), 176–79.
12. Budget of the United States Government, Fiscal Year 2013 Historical Tables, www.whitehouse.gov/sites/default/files/omb/budget/fy2013/assets/hist.pdf.
13. International Monetary Fund, "World Economic Outlook Update: Global Recover Stalls, Downside Risks Intensify," January 24, 2012, www.imf.org/external/pubs/ft/weo/2012/update/01/pdf/0112.pdf.
14. United States Department of Agriculture Economic Research Service, "International Macroeconomic Data Set," www.ers.usda.gov/Data/Macroeconomics/.
15. About 38 percent of the nation's commercial banks are members of the Federal Reserve System. See www.richmondfed.org.
16. Ronald Edsforth, *The New Deal: America's Response to the Great Depression* (Boston: Blackwell, 2000), 137.

17. Robert McElvaine, *The Great Depression: America 1929–1941* (New York: Times Books, 1984), 265.
18. Steven G. Koven, et al., *American Public Policy: The Contemporary Agenda* (Boston: Houghton Mifflin, 1998), 271.
19. Edmund L. Andrews, "Economists See Limited Boost from Stimulus," *New York Times* (August 6, 2009): www.nytimes.com.

18

1. Barack Obama, "President Barack Obama's Remarks on the War in Afghanistan," The White House, May 2, 2012.
2. "The Hillary Doctrine," *Newsweek,* March 6, 2011; and Hillary Rodham Clinton, "Remarks to the U.N. 4th World Conference on Women," September 1995.
3. Alfred E. Eckes Jr., *Opening America's Market: U.S. Foreign Trade Policy Since 1776* (Chapel Hill: University of North Carolina Press, 1995).
4. John L. O'Sullivan, writing in 1845, quoted in Julius W. Pratt, "The Ideology of American Expansion," in Avery Craven, ed., *Essays in Honor of William E. Dodd* (Chicago: University of Chicago Press, 1935), 343–44.
5. Charles P. Kindleberger, *The World in Depression, 1929–1939* (Berkeley: University of California Press, 1986).
6. Mr. X., "The Sources of Soviet Conduct," *Foreign Affairs* (July 1947): 566–82. Mr. X. was later revealed to be U.S. ambassador and diplomat George Kennan.
7. Harry S Truman, Speech to Congress, April 12, 1947.
8. Richard M. Nixon, Inaugural Address, January 20, 1969, Public Papers of the Presidents of the United States (Washington, DC: Government Printing Office).
9. Condoleezza Rice, "Campaign 2000: Promoting the National Interest," *Foreign Affairs* (January/February 2000): www.foreignaffairs.com/articles/55630/condoleezza-rice/campaign-2000-promoting-the-national-interest.
10. "The President's Constitutional Authority to Conduct Military Operations Against Terrorists and Nations Supporting Them," Department of Justice, September 25, 2001, http://justice.gov/olc/warpowers925/htm.
11. *Congress A to Z,* 4th ed. (Washington, DC: CQ Press, 2003).
12. David M. Herszenhorn and Carl Hulse, "Bid to Cut Off Iraq War Funding Fails," *New York Times* (September 20, 2007).
13. *The Prize Cases,* 67 U.S. 2 Black 635 (1862).
14. *Ex parte McCardle,* 74 U.S. 7 Wall. 506 506 (1868).
15. *Korematsu* v. *United States,* 323 U.S. 214 (1944).
16. *Boumediene* v. *Bush,* 553 U.S. 723 (2008).
17. *Hamdan* v. *Rumsfeld,* 548 U.S. 557 (2006).
18. U.S. Census Bureau, Trade in Goods with China, http://www.census.gov/foreign-trade/balance/c5700.html.
19. National Strategy for Combating Terrorism, www.globalsecurity.org/security/library/policy/national/nsct_sep2006.htm.

PHOTO CREDITS

Page xv: *The News & Observer,* Chuck Liddy/AP Images

CHAPTER 1 Page 3T: MPI/Getty Images; 3B: Michael S. Yamashita/National Geographic/Getty Images; 7: Bettmann/CORBIS; 8: Jeff J. Mitchell/AP Images; 13: Chang W. Lee/AP Images; 15TR: Paul J. Richards/AFP/Getty Images; 15L: Dan Peled/AP Images; 15BR: Riccardo De Luca/AP Images; 17: ABC/Photofest; 24: Pablo Martinez Monsivais/AP Images

CHAPTER 2 Page 29T: Bettmann/CORBIS; 29B: The Hawk Eye, John Lovretta/AP Images; 32: John Singleton Copley (1738-1815), "Samuel Adams," ca. 1772. Oil on canvas, 49 1/2 x 39 1/2 in. (125.7 cm x 100.3 cm). Deposited by the City of Boston, 30.76c. Courtesy, Museum of Fine Arts, Boston. Reproduced with permission. ©2000 Museum of Fine Arts, Boston. All Rights Reserved.; 33: Collection of The New-York Historical Society; 36: The Granger Collection, NYC—All rights reserved; 39: North Wind Picture Archives/Alamy; 47TL: Rob Hill/Fotolia; 47TR: Vacclav/Fotolia; 47B: Trekandshoot /Fotolia; 50: Virginia Mayo/AP Images; 56: National Park Service, Edison National Historic Site

CHAPTER 3 Page 63T: Lewis W Hine/Getty Images; 63B: Paula Bronstein/Getty Images; 67: Charles Dharapak/AP Images; 75: Southern Pacific News Bureau/AP Images; 77: February 10, 1937, *Columbus (Ohio) Dispatch,* "Trying to Change the Umpiring"; 82: John Duricka/AP Images; 83: Rich Pedroncelli/AP Images; 86: David Sipress/The New Yorker Collection/www.cartoonbank.com

CHAPTER 4 Page 91T: SZ Photo/Scherl/The Image Works; 91B: Gilles Mingasson/Getty Images; 95: AP Images; 98: Bettmann/CORBIS; 102L: Buyenlarge/Getty Images; 102R: Ng Han Guan/AP Images; 103: Clay Good/ZUMA Press; 105: Adam Lau/AP Images; 110: AP Images; 112: Comstock/Getty Images; 114: Nick Anderson. Cartoonist Group. Reprinted with permission. All rights reserved.; 117: Bettmann/CORBIS; 119: David J. Phillip/AP Images; 122: Reuters/Shane T. McCoy/Department of Defense

CHAPTER 5 Page 127T: Lewis W. Hine/Buyenlarge/Getty Images; 127B: William Thomas Cain/Getty Images; 131: Bettmann/Corbis; 134: The New York Public Library Photographic Services/Art Resource, NY; 136: Schomburg Center, NYPL/Art Resource, NY; 137: Library of Congress; 142: AP Images; 144TL: The Granger Collection, NYC—All rights reserved.; 144TR: The Granger Collection, NYC—All rights reserved.; 144B: The Granger Collection, NYC—All rights reserved.; 145: Charles Moore/Stock Photo/Black Star; 149TR: Carsten Koall/Getty Images; 149L: Huang Xin/Getty Images; 149BR: David McNew/Getty Images; 150: Office of Congresswoman Carolyn Maloney.; 152: Clay Bennett/*Christian Science Monitor;* 155: Eric Gay/AP Images; 156: Photo courtesy of Arts & Culture/Eastern Washington State Historical Society, Spokane Washington. ER. 4.20.5.; 158: Russell Lee/Corbis; 160: Marcio Jose Sanchez/AP Images; 162: Jason R. Davis/AP Images

CHAPTER 6 Page 169T: Bettmann/Corbis; 169B: Scott J. Ferrell/Congressional Quarterly/Getty Images; 172: Paul Beaty/AP Images; 176: Lois Raimondo/*The Washington Post*/Getty Images; 179: Bettmann/Corbis; 182: Photo courtesy: Official White House Photo by Pete Souza; 183T: Khin Maung Win/AP Images; 183BL: Rob Hill/Fotolia; 183BR: Vladimir Rys/Getty Images; 188: REUTERS/Reuters TV; 190: J. Scott Applewhite/AP Images; 193: Jonathan Ernst/Getty Images; 197: Photo courtesy: Office of Senator Kay Hagan

CHAPTER 7 Page 205T: George Eastman House/Getty Images; 205B: Dennis Brack Photography; 208: Tim Sloan/AFP/Getty Images; 212: Tim Sloan/AFP/Getty Images; 214TL: John Bryson/Time Life Pictures/Getty Images; 214TM: Bettmann/Corbis; 214TR: Charles Dharapak/AP Images; 214BL: MPI/Getty Images; 214BM: Ruth Fremson/AP Images; 214BR: Bettmann/Corbis; 219: The Granger Collection, NYC—All rights reserved.; 222: Alex Brandon/AP Images; 226: *The News & Observer,* Chuck Liddy/AP Images; 228L: GL Archive/Alamy; 228R: Bob Daemmrich/Alamy; 230TR: JPF/Shutterstock; 230L: Visions of America/UIG/Getty Images; 230BR: Itsuo Inouye/AP Images; 231: J. Scott Applewhite/AP Images

CHAPTER 8 Page 237T: Popperfoto/Getty Images; 237B: Rex Features/AP Images; 241: Bettmann/Corbis; 243: AP Images; 249: Gerald Herbert/AP Images; 253: Drew Dernavich; 257TR: Jacques Demarthon/AFP/GettyImages); 257L: Fethi Belaid/AFP/GettyImages; 257BR: Jay Price/*Raleigh News & Observer*/MCT/Getty Images; 258: John Moore/Getty Images

CHAPTER 9 Page 265T: Supreme Court of the United States; 265B: Larry Downing/Reuters/Landov Media; 270: Boston Athenaeum; 275TR: AP Images; 275L: APTN/AP Images; 275BR: REUTERS/Alex Domanski; 281: John Duricka/AP Images; 285: Chip Somodevilla/Getty Images; 289: Dana Verkouteren/AP Images; 294: Bettmann/Corbis

CHAPTER 10 Page 301T: Grey Villet//Time Life Pictures/Getty Images; 301B: Zhang Jun/Xinhua/Photoshot/Newscom; 305: Bettmann/Corbis; 309: Melanie Stetson Freeman/*The Christian Science Monitor*/Getty Images); 310: Used with the permissions of Mike Luckovich and Creators Syndicate. All rights reserved.; 314: Chip Somodevilla/Getty Images; 317: Allen Brisson-Smith/*The New York Times*/Redux

CHAPTER 11 Page 327T: H. Armstrong Roberts/ ClassicStock/The Image Works; 327B: Brendan Smialowski/AFP/GettyImages; 329: The Granger Collection, NYC—All rights reserved.; 337: Chris Maddaloni/CQ Roll Call/Getty Images; 342: Bettmann/Corbis; 346: Joe Raedle/Getty Images; 348: Liz Martin/*The Gazette*/AP Images

CHAPTER 12 Page 357T: Cornell Capa/Time Life Pictures/Getty Images; 357B: Steven Senne/AP Images 361: Winston-Salem Journal, Walt Unks/AP Images; 366: The Granger Collection, NYC—All rights reserved.; 369: *Middletown Journal,* Nick Daggy/AP Images; 374: Jason Reed/REUTERS; 378: Hans Deryk/Reuters/Corbis; 382: Justin Sullivan/Getty Images; 384TR: Paula Bronstein/Getty Images; 384L: *The Daily Times*/Tom Sherlin/AP Images; 384BR: Harold Cunningham/Getty Images

CHAPTER 13 Page 391T: Bettmann/Corbis; 391B: Carolyn Kaster/AP Images; 394: ; 397: REUTERS/Brian Snyder; 407L: Bettmann/Corbis; 407R: Pablo Martinez Monsivais/AP Images; 409L: Lyndon Baines Johnson Library Collection; 409R: U.S. Air Force/AP Images; 413: Charles Dharapak/AP Images; 417: Mark Hirsch/Getty Images

CHAPTER 14 Page 425T: Bettmann/Corbis; 425B: John Raoux/AP Images; 428: Stock Montage, Inc./Historical Pictures Collection; 438: William B. Plowman/NBC/NBCU Photo Bank/Getty Images; 440: CBS Photo Archive/Getty Images; 443: Jewel Samad/AFP/Getty Images; 444: Chris Maddaloni/CQ Roll Call/Getty Images; 446TR: Seyllou/AFP/Getty Images; 446L: Jin Lee/Bloomberg/Getty Images; 446BR: Arif Ali/AFP/Getty Images

CHAPTER 15 Page 453: Mondadori Portfolio/Getty Images; 453B: Bill Clark/Roll Call/Getty Images; 457: Tom Toles/Universal Uclick. Reprinted with permission. All rights reserved.; 459: The Granger Collection, NYC—All rights reserved.; 462: Michal Czerwonka/Getty Images; 466: Used with the permissions of Mike Luckovich and Creators Syndicate. All rights reserved.; 471T: Alexander Joe/AFP/Getty

Images; 471B: REUTERS/Rafiquar Rahman; 472: Charley Gallay/ Getty Images; 474: Jim West/Alamy

CHAPTER 16 Page 481T: Keystone/Hulton Archive/Getty Images; 481B: A.J. SISCO/Landov Media; 485: Bettmann/Corbis; 486: Meghan O'Connor McDonogh/The Catholic University of America; 490: Bill Haber/AP Images; 499: J.B. Handelsman/The New Yorker Collection/www.cartoonbank.com; 501: Richard Drew/AP Images; 504: Harlem Success Academy; 511: *The Greenville News,* Patrick Collard/AP Images

CHAPTER 17 Page 517T: Bettman/Corbis; 517B: Kevin Dietsch/ UPI/Newscom; 521: Library Of Congress [LC-USZ62-51782]; 524: Used with the permissions of Dwane Powell and Creators Syndicate. All rights reserved.; 531: EPA/RAHAT DAR/Landov LLC; 533TR: Jens Kuhfs/Getty Images; 533L: Brendan Hoffman/Getty Images; 533BR: Toshifumi Kitamura/AFP/Getty Images; 535: Saul Loeb/ AFP/Getty Images; 538: Michael Kleinfeld/UPI/Landov LLC; 543: Charles Dharapak/AP Images

CHAPTER 18 Page 549T: Mike Sargent/AFP/Getty Images; 549B: Pete Souza/The White House via Getty Images; 553: Bettman/Corbis; 556: Keystone/Getty Images; 561: Thomas Nilsson/ Getty Images; 565: Pablo Martinez Monsivais/AP Images; 567: Iraqi Government/ AP Images; 579: David Guttenfelder/AP Images; 580: REUTERS/ Sergei Karpukhin: 581: Susan Walsh/AP Images

INDEX

A

B

C

D

E

F

G

H

I

J

K

L

M

N

O

P

S

T

U

V

W

Y

Z

ANSWER KEY

1	2	3	4	5	6	7	8	9
1. c	1. b	1. c	1. d	1. c	1. d	1. a	1. a	1. c
2. c	2. d	2. a	2. e	2. e	2. d	2. a	2. b	2. d
3. d	3. a	3. e	3. e	3. b	3. a	3. e	3. e	3. c
4. b	4. d	4. b	4. b	4. b	4. b	4. b	4. d	4. a
5. b	5. a	5. a	5. a	5. c	5. c	5. c	5. d	5. c
6. a	6. b	6. c	6. c	6. c	6. b	6. a	6. c	6. d
7. d	7. c	7. a	7. e	7. c	7. c	7. e	7. e	7. e
8. e	8. e	8. b	8. d	8. e	8. b	8. b	8. e	8. a
9. d	9. b	9. d	9. c	9. b	9. d	9. b	9. b	9. e
10. d	10. d	10. c	10. e	10. c	10. d	10. e	10. b	10. d

10	11	12	13	14	15	16	17	18
1. c	1. b	1. d	1. e	1. c	1. a	1. e	1. a	1. c
2. c	2. d	2. a	2. d	2. e	2. d	2. c	2. b	2. e
3. d	3. d	3. b	3. c	3. a	3. b	3. b	3. c	3. a
4. c	4. c	4. c	4. b	4. b	4. a	4. d	4. a	4. c
5. a	5. b	5. b	5. a	5. c	5. c	5. a	5. b	5. b
6. b	6. d	6. b	6. c	6. e	6. e	6. b	6. c	6. e
7. a	7. a	7. d	7. b	7. a	7. d	7. b	7. c	7. c
8. c	8. d	8. a	8. d	8. c	8. b	8. d	8. d	8. b
9. b	9. d	9. c	9. d	9. a	9. b	9. c	9. e	9. e
10. d	10. e	10. e	10. e	10. d	10. c	10. b	10. d	10. e